MICHIE ON BANKS AND BANKING

By The Editorial Staff of the Publishers

Under the Supervision of
Paul Ernest

VOLUME 8

2019 REPLACEMENT VOLUME

LexisNexis®

Library of Congress Catalog Card No. 31-16694
ISBN 978-0-3270-0931-3 (print)

LexisNexis

Matthew Bender & Company, Inc.
Editorial Offices
9443 Springboro Pike, Miamisburg, OH 45342 (937) 865-6800
701 East Water Street, Charlottesville, VA 22902-7587 (434) 972-7600
www.lexisnexis.com

Editorial Office
230 Park Ave., 7th Floor, New York, NY 10169 (800) 543-6862
www.lexisnexis.com

MATTHEW BENDER

(2019–Pub.74600)

Publisher's Note

This replacement has been necessitated by the numerous decisions concerning its subject matter. The publisher is indebted to the West Publishing Company for permission to use copyrighted material appearing in the Current and General Digests and to Shepard's Citations, Inc., for the use of their Citations in tracing citations to the selected cases.

CHAPTER XVI.

Savings Banks.

Synopsis

I. GENERAL CONSIDERATION.

§ 1. Nature, Status and Control.

§ 2. Incorporation, Organization, Reorganization and Dissolution.

II. CORPORATORS AND STOCKHOLDERS.

§ 3. General Considerations.

§ 4. Liability of Stockholders.

III. OFFICERS AND AGENTS.

§ 5. General Considerations.

§ 6. Duties and Liabilities.

§ 7. Representation of Bank by Officers and Agents.

IV. POWERS IN GENERAL.

§ 8. Power to Choose Officers and Admit New Members.

§ 9. Power to Contract in General.

§ 10. Power to Acquire and Sell Property.

§ 11. Power to Make Loans and Borrow Money.

§ 11.1. Power to Operate Checking Account Service.

V. DEPOSITS.

a. General Considerations.

§ 12. In General.

§ 13. Bylaws, Rules, Passbooks and Charter as Part of Contract.

b. Title to and Disposition of Deposits.

§ 14. To Whom Payments to Be Made.
§ 15. Negligence in Paying Wrong Person.
§ 16. Payment on Death of Depositor.
§ 17. Contributory Negligence of Depositor.
§ 18. Assignment of Deposits.
§ 19. Interest and Dividends on Deposits.
§ 20. Repayment of Deposits.
§ 21. Losses.

VI. INVESTMENTS, LOANS AND DISCOUNTS.

§ 22. In General.
§ 23. Investments.
§ 24. Loans and Discounts.

VII. INSOLVENCY AND RECEIVERS.

§ 25. General Consideration.
§ 26. Order of Payment—Preference.
§ 27. Setoffs Against Debt Due Bank.
§ 28. Parties to Actions.

VIII. ACTIONS.

§ 29. General Considerations.
§ 30. Parties.
§ 31. Pleading—In Actions Against Bank.
§ 32. Pleading—In Actions Against Directors, Officers or Stockholders of Bank.
§ 33. Evidence.
§ 34. Trial.
§ 35. Appeal and Error.

I. GENERAL CONSIDERATION.

§ 1. Nature, Status and Control.

In General.—Savings banks are what their name indicates, banks of deposit for the accumulation of small savings belonging to the industrious and thrifty,[1] whose trustees sometimes give their services gratuitously, and for which the state prescribes the required investment.[2] A "savings bank" is not a bank in the commercial sense of that word,[3] nor is it for all purposes, a charitable society,[4] but in certain instances, it has been held to be a business corporation.[5] On the other hand, a statute providing for conducting

---

[1] **In general.—**

Mercantile Bank v. New York, 121 U.S. 138, 7 S. Ct. 826, 30 L. Ed. 895. See also Society for Sav. v. Coite, 78 U.S. (6 Wall.) 594, 18 L. Ed. 897; Provident Institution v. Massachusetts, 78 U.S. (6 Wall.) 611, 18 L. Ed. 907; In re Wilkins' Will, 131 Misc. 188, 226 N.Y.S. 415; Bulakowski v. Philadelphia Sav. Fund Soc., 270 Pa. 538, 113 A. 553; Greenfield Sav. Bank v. Abercrombie, 211 Mass. 252, 97 N.E. 807, 39 L.R.A. (n.s.) 173, 1913B Ann. Cas. 420.

Institutions held not savings banks.—

Institutions called savings and building associations are stock associations of a novel and peculiar character, organized under a general law, and are quite distinct from savings banks and societies for savings, which are merely banks of deposit and loan. Society for Sav. v. Coite, 73 U.S. (6 Wall.) 594, 18 L. Ed. 897; Provident Institution v. Massachusetts, 78 U.S. (6 Wall.) 611, 18 L. Ed. 907.

The power given to *femes covert* and minors to make deposits, and when their deposit reach $100, at their option to be converted into stock, if valid, does not denote savings bank. State v. Lincoln Sav. Bank, 82 Tenn. 42 (1884); State v. Nashville Sav. Bank, 84 Tenn. 111 (1885).

A corporation is not a mere savings bank where it was organized for the following named purposes to do a general savings and commercial banking business; to buy and sell real and personal property; to discount bills, notes, and other commercial and negotiable paper and instruments; to buy and sell exchange; to receive money on deposit; to borrow and loan money and to do any and all acts incident to or necessary to the transaction of any and all the matters above stated. Such corporation has all the attributes of an ordinary commercial bank. Mitchell v. Beckman, 64 Cal. 117, 28 P. 110.

[2] In re Wilkins' Will, 131 Misc. 188, 226 N.Y.S. 415.

[3] Andrew v. American Sav. Bank, 217 Iowa 447, 252 N.W. 245.

The term "banking corporation or institution" was held not to include a savings bank. Andrew v. American Sav. Bank, 217 Iowa 447, 252 N.W. 245.

The purpose of a mutual savings bank is encouragement of thrift by mutuality of ownership. It is a different type of financial institution from a commercial bank. Application of Howard Sav. Institution, 32 N.J. 29, 159 A.2d 113 (1960).

[4] Sheren v. Mendenhall, 23 Minn. 92.

A savings bank, formed for the pecuniary benefit of its members, is not a "benevolent" or a "charitable" society, within the meaning of those words in a statute authorizing the incorporation of benevolent and charitable societies. Sheren v. Mendenball, 23 Minn. 92; Bulakowski v. Philadelphia Sav. Fund Soc., 270 Pa. 538, 113 A. 553.

[5] Bulakowski v. Philadelphia Sav. Fund Soc., 270 Pa. 538, 113 A. 553.

banking and other business with separate capital and separate accounts, has been held to refer only to mercantile corporations, and does not provide authority for a corporation securing its charter under the general incorporation laws to carry on as a part of its business the operation of a savings bank.[6] All of a savings bank's funds and investments are held exclusively for the benefit of its depositors, and the bank is a mere agency for managing the moneys.[7] A savings bank is a private undertaking, and not an agency of government; it performs no public function.[8] Whether a bank is a savings bank is determined not by a designation in its charter, but by its organization, powers, and mode of doing business, as provided in its act of incorporation.[9] Frequently savings banks and societies for savings have no capital stock or stockholders,[10] and are without authority to make discounts or issue any

---

[6] First Thrift & Loan Ass'n v. State, 62 N.M. 61, 304 P.2d 582.

Statute authorizing mercantile corporations to carry on as one phase of their business, a savings bank, in towns of less than 1,500 population denies such corporations the authority to do so in towns of more than 1,500 population. First Thrift & Loan Ass'n v. State, 62 N.M. 61, 304 P.2d 582.

[7] Petitions of Allen, 241 Mass. 346, 136 N.E. 269; Williams v. Johnson, 50 Mont. 7, 144 P. 768, 1916D Ann. Cas. 595.

Until recently, the primary idea of a savings bank has been, that it is an institution in the hands of disinterested persons, the profits of which, after deducting the necessary expenses of conducting the business, enure wholly to the benefit of the depositors, in dividends, or in reserved surplus for their greater security. Huntington v. National Sav. Bank, 96 U.S. 388, 24 L. Ed. 777.

The profits of a national savings bank of the District of Columbia, after deducting the necessary expenses of conducting it, enure wholly to the benefit of the depositors, in dividends, or in a reserved surplus for their greater security. Huntington v. National Sav. Bank, 96 U.S. 388, 24 L Ed. 777.

[8] Second Nat'l Bank v. Old Guar. Sav. Bank, 84 N.H. 342, 150 A. 737, 69 A.L.R. 1250.

[9] State v. Lincoln Sav. Bank, 82 Tenn. 42; State v. Nashville Sav. Bank, 84 Tenn. 111; Williams v Johnson, 50 Mont. 7, 144 P. 768, 1916D Ann. Cas. 595.

[10] Society for Sav. v. Coite, 73 U.S. (6 Wall.) 594, 18 L. Ed. 897; Provident Inst. v. Massachusetts, 73 U.S. (6 Wall.) 611, 18 L. Ed. 907; Bank v. Collector, 70 U.S. (3 Wall.) 495, 18 L Ed. 207; Bulakowski v. Philadelphia Sav. Fund Soc., 270 Pa. 538, 113 A. 553; Jefferson v. Cox, 246 Mass. 495, 141 N.E. 493; Williams v Johnson, 50 Mont. 7, 144 P. 768, 1916D Ann. Cas. 595. See also § 3 of this chapter.

Savings banks and savings and loan associations are incorporated agencies without capital stock organized to accumulate savings of members and invest same in mortgages, loans and such other securities as are allowed by law. State v. Vars, 154 Conn. 255, 224 A.2d 744 (1966).

In New York at least, "savings banks" are mutual institutions, having no stockholders but earning money for depositors, the fundamental purpose of their existence being protection of

circulating medium.[11] In the absence of rules assented to by its customers, a savings bank is to be governed by the same legal principles which apply to other moneyed institutions.[12]

A savings account is not a negotiable instrument transferable by endorsement or delivery. Nevertheless, state statute provides for other transfers evidenced by certificates or documents as long as the requirements applicable to that type of transfer have been met. For all practical purposes, a party divests himself of his control over an account when he names a joint co-owner who has identical rights to the funds.[13]

As used in the Act establishing the Federal Deposit Insurance Corporation,[14] the term "depository institution" means any bank or savings association. An "insured depository institution" under the Act is any bank or savings association the deposits of which are insured by the Corporation.[15] The term "insured depository institution" includes any uninsured branch or agency of a foreign bank or a commercial lending company owned or controlled by a foreign bank for purposes of the Act.[16]

A "savings association" is defined under the Home Owners' Loan Act (HOLA)[17] and the Federal Deposit Insurance Act as any federal or state savings association, the deposits of which are insured by the Federal Deposit Insurance Corporation ("Corporation").[18] A "federal savings association" means any federal savings association or federal savings bank which is

---

small deposits, and their principal method of accomplishing that purpose being cautious and conservative in investments. People v. Franklin Nat'l Bank, 305 N.Y. 453, 113 N.E.2d 796, rev'd on other grounds sub nom. Franklin Nat'l Bank v. New York, 347 U.S. 373, 74 S. Ct. 550, 98 L. Ed. 767. And see People v. Franklin Nat. Bank, 105 N.Y.S.2d 81, rev'd on other grounds, 281 App. Div. 757, 118 N.Y.S.2d 210.

[11] Society v. Coite, 73 U.S. (6 Wall.) 594, 18 L Ed. 897; Provident Inst. v. Massachusetts, 73 U.S. (6 Wall.) 611, 18 L. Ed. 907; Bank v. Collector, 70 U.S. (3 Wall.) 495, 18 L. Ed. 207.

[12] Mills v. Albany Exch. Sav. Bank, 28 Misc. 251, 59 N.Y.S. 149; Siegel v. State Bank (App. Div.), 123 N.Y.S. 220.

[13] Succession of Gassiott, 159 So. 3d 521 (La. 2015). See La. C.C. Art. 1550.

[14] 12 U.S.C.S. § 1811 et seq.

[15] 12 U.S.C.S. § 1813.

[16] 12 U.S.C.S. § 1813. As to foreign banks, see 12 U.S.C.S. § 1818 et seq.

[17] 12 U.S.C.S. §§ 1461–1470.

[18] See 12 U.S.C.S. § 1462(2); 12 U.S.C.S. § 1813(b)(1).

See also 12 U.S.C.S. § 1462(1) (the term "Corporation" means the Federal Deposit Insurance Corporation).

chartered under HOLA[19] and a "state savings association" is defined as: (1) Any building and loan association, savings and loan association, or homestead association or (2) any cooperative bank (other than a cooperative bank which is a "state bank" under the statute), which is organized and operating according to the laws of the state in which it is chartered or organized.[20] The term "savings association" in this context includes any corporation (other than a bank) that the Board of Directors and the Comptroller of the Currency jointly determine to be operating in substantially the same manner as a savings association.[21]

Savings-and-loan institutions are also called "thrifts." Thrifts collect customer deposits, which are maintained in interest-bearing savings accounts, and they originate and service mortgage loans funded by those deposits. Historically, thrifts were profitable because the interest they collected on outstanding loans exceeded the interest they paid out to customers.[22] That changed, however, in the late 1970s. First, interest rates rose to unprecedented levels, and thrifts, which were locked into long-term, fixed-rate mortgages, were unable to compensate for this increase by raising the interest rate on their mortgage loans. To maintain their customers, moreover, thrifts were forced to raise the interest rates they paid on deposit accounts, causing the thrifts to operate at a loss. Second, the industry suffered from "disintermediation," whereby customers withdrew their deposits in favor of alternative investments paying higher interest rates. This one-two punch had a devastating effect on the industry, causing many thrifts to become insolvent.[23] Lacking the funds to liquidate the failing thrifts during the Savings-and-Loan Crisis, the Federal Savings and Loan Insurance Corporation (FSLIC), as thrift regulator and insurer of deposits, responded to the crisis by encouraging healthy thrifts to take over failing ones in what were called "supervisory mergers." These transactions relieved the FSLIC of its deposit insurance liability for the insolvent thrifts, and, in exchange, provided a package of non-cash incentives to acquiring thrifts.[24] Two of

---

[19] 12 U.S.C.S. § 1462(3); 12 U.S.C.S. § 1813(b)(2).

[20] 12 U.S.C.S. § 1813(b)(3).

[21] 12 U.S.C.S. § 1813(b)(1)(C).

[22] WMI Holdings Corp. v. United States, 891 F.3d 1016 (2018).

[23] WMI Holdings Corp. v. United States, 891 F.3d 1016 (2018). Between 1981 and 1983 alone, some 435 thrifts failed. WMI Holdings Corp. v. United States, 891 F.3d 1016 (2018).

[24] WMI Holdings Corp. v. United States, 891 F.3d 1016 (2018).

those incentives are: (1) "Branching" rights and (2) "RAP"—or "regulatory accounting purposes"—rights.[25]

Legislative Control and Regulation Generally.—A mutual savings bank is a creature of the legislature, and all powers which it can lawfully exercise are prescribed by its charter and by statute.[26] An activity necessary to carry on a bank's business within the meaning of a statute granting to banks such incidental powers as shall be necessary to carry on the business of savings banks is one which is convenient or useful in connection with the performance of the bank's established activities pursuant to express powers, or such powers as are necessary or usual and convenient for the attainment of the purposes of the creation of a bank.[27] Savings banks are subject to legislative control and regulation.[28] For example, in some jurisdictions,

---

[25] WMI Holdings Corp. v. United States, 891 F.3d 1016 (2018).

[26] Androscoggin County Sav. Bank v. Campbell, 282 A.2d 858 (Me. 1971).

The Home Owners' Loan Act of 1933 authorizes the federal government to issue charters to mutual savings associations, pursuant to 12 U.S.C.S. § 1464(a). Under the federal charter, those associations are owned and governed by their members, who have the right to vote on all questions requiring action by the members and the right to receive an equal distribution of assets, pro rata to the value of their accounts in the event the association is liquidated, dissolved, or wound up. This ownership structure differs from that of a stock bank, shares of which are bought and sold by members of the public at large. Stilwell v. Office of Thrift Supervision, 569 F.3d 514, 2009 U.S. App. LEXIS 14945 (D.C. Cir. 2009). See former 12 C.F.R. § 544.1 regarding federal mutual charter, removed, effective Oct. 11, 2018. See 82 FR 47083, 47084, Oct. 11, 2017.

See also 82 F.R. 47083 providing that the OTS, a Bureau of the Department of the Treasury, was abolished by the Dodd-Frank Wall Street Reform and Consumer Protection Act (Dodd-Frank Act or Act) n1 on October 19, 2011. Titles III and X of the Act transferred the powers, authorities, rights, and duties of the OTS to the Office of the Comptroller of the Currency, the Federal Deposit Insurance Corporation, the Board of Governors of the Federal Reserve System, and the Consumer Financial Protection Bureau (collectively, the Agencies), effective July 21, 2011.

The Department of the Treasury removed chapter V of title 12, Code of Federal Regulations (CFR), which contains regulations of the former Office of Thrift Supervision (OTS). The OTS, a Bureau of the Department of the Treasury, was abolished effective October 19, 2011, and its rulemaking authority and operative rules were transferred to other agencies pursuant to the Dodd-Frank Wall Street Reform and Consumer Protection Act. Because those agencies have issued regulations that supersede chapter V, chapter V is no longer necessary. 82 F.R. 47083, 47084.

[27] Washington Bankers Ass'n v. Washington Mut. Sav. Bank, 92 Wash. 2d 453, 598 P.2d 719 (1979).

[28] Andrew v. American Sav. Bank, 217 Iowa 447, 252 N.W. 245; West v. Topeka Sav. Bank, 66 Ken. 524, 72 P. 252, 97 Am. St. R. 385, 63 L.R.A. 137; State v. Field, 49 Mo. 270.

savings banks are defined by statute, or their purposes, functions and powers are prescribed by the act under which they are incorporated.[29] The purposes of the savings bank statute, governing permissible uses of a bank's funds, and the excise tax statute which exempts pass-through certificates, are not identical, and the purposes have never been explicitly connected by the legislature despite numerous amendments.[30] And a statute may provide for a periodic examination of the management and affairs of savings banks.[31] A statute creating a mutual savings guaranty fund to protect deposits in savings banks has been held valid under the police power.[32]

A state banking board, organized by legislative act, should require savings banks to remove objectionable security on which loans have been made, where the safety of their depositors requires it.[33] And the order of a state bank commissioner directing a mutual savings bank to discontinue its policy

---

As to statutes regulating joint deposits and dormant deposits, see Chapter IX.

State has broad latitude in exercise of police powers to regulate savings banks, with principal objective of securing safety of depositors. Peterborough Sav. Bank v. King, 103 N.H. 206, 168 A.2d 116.

Regulations made by the legislature regarding investments to be made by business corporations, such as savings banks, are in the exercise of the broad powers of the legislature to secure the safety of the depositors. Opinion of Justices, 306 A.2d 55 (N.H. 1973).

Where a national association acquires the loan of a federal savings bank, it is proper to apply preemption under the Home Owners' Loan Act of 1933, 12 U.S.C.S. § 1461 et seq. Copeland-Turner v. Wells Fargo Bank, N.A., 800 F. Supp. 2d 1132 (D. Or. 2011).

[29] Dottenheim v. Union Sav. Bank & Trust Co., Co., 114 Ga. 788, 40 S.E. 825; Mercantile Bank v. New York, 121 U.S. 138, 7 S. Ct. 826, 30 L Ed. 895; Bank of Redemption v. Boston, 125 U.S. 60, 8 S. Ct. 772, 31 L. Ed. 689; Huntington v. National Sav. Bank, 96 U.S. 388, 24 L. Ed. 777.

Michigan's Savings Bank Act, Mich. Comp. Laws § 487.3101 et seq., provides for the incorporation of savings banks within the state. This act grants a savings bank, incorporated under the statute, the power to engage in the business of banking and exercise all powers incidental to the business of banking or which further or facilitate the purposes of a savings bank. The Savings Bank Act further allows a bank to collect interest and charges on loans as permitted by the credit reform act. Dressel v. Ameribank, 247 Mich. App. 133, 635 N.W.2d 328 (2001), rev'd on other grounds, 468 Mich. 557, 664 N.W.2d 151 (2003). See Mich. Comp. Laws §§ 487.3401(1), 487.3430(1)(a).

[30] South Boston Sav. Bank v. Commissioner of Revenue, 418 Mass. 695, 640 N.E.2d 462 (1994).

[31] State v. Henderson, 135 Iowa 499, 113 N.W. 328.

[32] In re Opinion of the Justices, 278 Mass. 607, 181 N.E. 833, 82 A.L.R. 1021.

[33] Youmans v. Hanna, 35 N.D. 479, 160 N.W. 705, 1917E Ann. Cas. 263, rehearing denied, 43 ND. 536, 171 N.W. 835, holding that it justified by the facts in so doing, the motives of the board members are immaterial.

of offering checking accounts to depositors was not in excess of his statutory authority.[34] However, a superintendent of banks had no statutory authority to promulgate regulations pertaining to savings banks' offering checking accounts.[35] And a banker aggrieved by an order of such a board should apply to the courts for relief and, if he does not do so, the order will remain in force.[36] The New York Banking Law provisions governing the powers of savings banks are not free from ambiguity and must be read in light of their legislative history.[37]

---

[34] Androscoggin County Sav. Bank v Campbell, 282 A.2d 858 (Me. 1971).

[35] N.Y. State Bankers Ass'n v. Albright, 46 App. Div. 2d 269, 361 N.Y.S.2d 949 (1974); New York State Bankers Ass'n v. Albright, 38 N.Y.2d 430, 381 N.Y.S.2d 17, 343 N.E.2d 735 (1975), aff'd, 38 N.Y.2d 953, 383 N.Y.S.2d 597, 347 N.E.2d 923 (1976).

A Banking Law provision that a savings bank may accept a deposit without issuance of the passbook and issue such other evidence of its obligation to repay as may be appropriate to safeguard the interests of the depositors and of the savings bank was not intended to authorize savings banks to offer checking accounts, including "NOW" accounts, that is, negotiable order of withdrawal accounts. New York State Bankers Ass'n v. Albright, 38 N.Y.2d 430, 381 N.Y.S.2d 17, 343 N.E.2d 735 (1975), aff'd, 38 N.Y.2d 953, 383 N.Y.S.2d 597, 347 N.E.2d 923 (1976).

Savings banks had no authority to offer checking accounts but since the accounts had presumably been used widely by many customers of the savings bank, it would be unduly deceptive to terminate those services abruptly and thus there would be a stay of enforcement of determination that the Banking Law provisions did not authorize savings banks to offer checking accounts. New York State Bankers Ass'n. v. Albright, 38 N.Y.2d 430, 381 N.Y.S.2d 17, 343 N.E.2d 735 (1975), aff'd, 38 N.Y.2d 953, 383 N.Y.S.2d 597, 347 N.E.2d 923 (1976).

[36] Youmans v. Hanna 35 N.D. 479, 160 N.W. 705, 1917E Ann. Cas. 263, rehearing denied 48 N.D. 536, 171 N.W. 835.

[37] New York State Bankers Ass'n v. Albright, 38 N.Y.2d 430, 381 N.Y.S.2d 17, 343 N.E.2d 735 (1975), aff'd, 38 N.Y.2d 953, 383 N.Y.S.2d 597, 347 N.E.2d 923 (1976).

The purpose of the statute providing that a savings bank may accept deposits without issuance of a passbook and issue such other evidence of its obligation to repay as may be appropriate to safeguard the interests of the depositors and of the savings bank was to authorize the use of nonpassbook savings accounts, but true savings accounts for accumulation of reserves, thus permitting savings banks to take advantage of technological innovations in record keeping and to maintain competitive position with commercial bank savings accounts. New York State Bankers Ass'n v. Albright, 38 N.Y.2d 430, 381 N.Y.S.2d 17, 343 N.E.2d 735 (1975), aff'd, 38 N.Y.2d 953, 383 N.Y.S.2d 597, 347 N.E.2d 923 (1976). See N.Y. C.L.S. Bank § 238.

Rules promulgated by the banking board which differentiated among banking organizations insofar as "branching out" was concerned and which did not make any provisions for protecting a savings and loan association against unsound and destructive competition from another banking organization if such organization was a savings bank violated the direct,

The Board of Trust Company Incorporation may encourage conversions of mutual banks by adopting regulations, but a regulatory scheme cannot supplant depositors' charter rights.[38]

Federal Regulation.—Congress has created an extensive federal statutory and regulatory scheme in the field of banking. As part of this extensive federal scheme, Congress enacted the Home Owners' Loan Act (HOLA)[39] to charter savings associations under federal law as a means of restoring public confidence through a nationwide system of savings and loan associations that are centrally regulated according to nationwide "best practices."[40] HOLA initially created the Federal Home Loan Bank Board and granted its

---

unequivocally stated purpose of the statute to eliminate unsound and destructive competition among banking organizations. Cross County Sav. & Loan Ass'n v. Siebert, 93 Misc. 2d 609, 403 N.Y.S.2d 864 (1978).

Rules promulgated by the banking board pursuant to which only another "savings bank" may raise objections to the establishment of a new savings bank branch were beyond the statutory power granted to the banking board and were, therefore, invalid. Cross County Sav. & Loan Ass'n v. Siebert, 93 Misc. 2d 609, 403 N.Y.S.2d 864 (1978).

The rights of both savings banks and savings and loan associations are definitively identical and similar as pertains to branches being allowed or considered and, therefore, rules promulgated by banking board which deprive savings and loan associations of an opportunity to object to the establishment of a savings bank branch are not only invalidly discriminatory but fail to afford equal protection to those seeking protection against unsound, destructive competition. Cross County Sav. & Loan Ass'n v. Siebert, 93 Misc. 2d 609, 403 N.Y.S.2d 864 (1978).

[38] In re Corporators of Portsmouth Sav. Bank, 525 A.2d 671 (N.H. 1987).

[39] 12 U.S.C.S. §§ 1461–1470.

[40] Odinma v. Aurora Loan Servs., 2010 U.S. Dist. LEXIS 28347 (N.D. Cal. 2010).

Congress enacted the Home Owners' Loan Act of 1933 (HOLA), 12 U.S.C.S. §§ 1461–1468, in order to charter savings associations under federal law, at a time when record numbers of home loans were in default and a staggering number of state-chartered savings associations were insolvent. HOLA was designed to restore public confidence by creating a nationwide system of federal savings and loan associations to be centrally regulated according to nationwide best practices. The Ninth Circuit has explained that HOLA and its implementing regulations are a radical and comprehensive response to the inadequacies of the existing state system, and so pervasive as to leave no room for state regulatory control. Because there has been a history of significant federal presence in national banking, the presumption against preemption of state law is inapplicable. Copeland-Turner v. Wells Fargo Bank, N.A., 800 F. Supp. 2d 1132 (2011).

As a response to the Great Depression, when nearly half of all home loans were in default and credit was scarce, Congress enacted the Home Owners' Loan Act (HOLA) as a radical and comprehensive response to the inadequacies of the existing state systems of mortgage regulation. Henning v. Wachovia Mortgage, FSB, 969 F. Supp. 2d 135, 2013 U.S. Dist. LEXIS 133394 (2013).

director broad authority to regulate the powers and operations of every federal savings and loan association from its cradle to its corporate grave. When Congress amended HOLA in 1989, it transferred this power to the Office of Thrift Supervision (OTS). It would have been difficult for Congress to give the OTS a broader mandate pertaining to loan regulation authority under HOLA.[41] Under the broad grant of authority in HOLA, OTS issued regulations which purport to preempt state law in the areas of federal savings regulation. Such laws included contract, tort, criminal, and homestead laws but the area of exception ought be interpreted narrowly with any doubt resolved in favor of preemption.[42]

The Dodd-Frank Wall Street Reform and Consumer Protection Act significantly diminished the extent to which the Home Owners' Loan Act and its implementing regulations may preempt state law.[43] Courts have uniformly held, however, that the provisions of Dodd-Frank are not retroactive, and HOLA preemption applies to mortgages originated before either July 21, 2010 or July 21, 2011.[44] Following the enactment of Dodd-Frank, the OTS was abolished effective October 19, 2011, and its rulemaking authority and operative rules were transferred to other agencies.[45]

Regulation of Use of Word "Savings".—In some jurisdictions it is a penal offense for a non-savings bank to fraudulently advertise or put forth a sign as a savings bank, or in any way solicit or receive deposits under a claim or pretense of being a savings bank.[46] But a New York statute which forbids the use of the word "savings" or a variant thereof, by any banks other than savings banks and savings and loan associations chartered by the state, was held in conflict with provisions of the Federal Reserve Act and the National

---

[41] Henning v. Wachovia Mortgage, FSB, 969 F. Supp. 2d 135, 2013 U.S. Dist. LEXIS 133394 (2013).

[42] Henning v. Wachovia Mortgage, FSB, 969 F. Supp. 2d 135, 2013 U.S. Dist. LEXIS 133394 (2013).

[43] See 12 U.S.C.S. § 25b.

[44] Because borrower's claims against lender's assignee arose out of loans that were originated in 2006, Dodd-Frank preemption in 12 U.S.C.S. § 25b did not apply, and appropriate preemption standard to apply was that under the Home Owners' Loan Act. Henning v. Wachovia Mortgage, FSB, 969 F. Supp. 2d 135, 2013 U.S. Dist. LEXIS 133394 (2013).

Henning v. Wachovia Mortgage, FSB, 969 F. Supp. 2d 135, 2013 U.S. Dist. LEXIS 133394 (2013).

[45] 82 FR 47083, 47084.

[46] People v. Binghamton Trust Co., 20 N.Y.S. 179, 65 Hun 384, aff'd, 139 N.Y. 185, 34 N.E. 898; State v. People's Nat. Bank, 75 N.H. 27, 70 A. 542.

Bank Act authorizing national banks to receive savings deposits and permitting them to advertise for business, and thus was held invalid because of the doctrine of supremacy of federal over state legislation in the event of a conflict.[47]

Internal Rules and Bylaws.—Reasonable rules or bylaws, made by a savings bank pursuant to statute for the regulation of its business, should not be interfered with by the courts without substantial reason therefor.[48] However, a bank's bylaws are not refractory and must yield to regulatory authority, legislation and judicial orders.[49] And where new bylaws are adopted by a savings bank which supersede its old bylaws, a provision that is contained in the old bylaws but not in the new, is no longer in force.[50] But where the duties of the president of a savings bank are defined by its bylaws, which also provide that such bylaws can only be amended after notice, a resolution enlarging the powers and duties of the president is void if no notice is given.[51] It has also been held that a savings bank may enact bylaws under a power, conferred by statute on all corporations, of making bylaws for the management of their property and regulation of their affairs.[52]

§ 2. Incorporation, Organization, Reorganization and Dissolution.

Incorporation and Organization.—The incorporation and organization of a savings bank or savings society must be in conformity with constitutional and statutory provisions authorizing and prescribing the method for such

---

[47] Franklin Nat'l Bank v. New York, 347 U.S. 373, 74 S. Ct. 550, 98 L. Ed. 767, rev'g People v. Franklin Nat'l Bank, 305 N.Y. 453, 113 N.E.2d 796. See also People v. Franklin Nat'l Bank, 281 App. Div. 757, 118 N.Y.S.2d 210, rev'g 105 N.Y.S.2d 81.

[48] Rosenthal v. Dollar Sav. Bank, 61 Misc. 244, 113 N.Y.S. 787.

A savings bank has power to adopt reasonable regulations, if they are in conformity with statute, and these regulations, if asserted to by the depositor, constitute the contract between bank and depositor. R.H. Macy & Co. v. Tyler, 21 Misc. 2d 998, 193 N.Y.S.2d 243. See also § 13 of this chapter. A savings bank may adopt reasonable bylaws providing for payment. R. H. Macy & Co. v. Tyler, 21 Misc. 24 998, 193 N.Y.S.2d 243.

[49] Lewis v. Franklin Sav. Bank, 98 Misc. 2d 1098, 415 N.Y.S.2d 362 (1979).

[50] Murphy v. Pacific Bank, 130 Cal. 542, 62 P. 1059.

[51] French v. O'Brien (N.Y.), 52 How. Pr. 394; Savings Bank v. Hunt, 72 Mo. 597, 37 Am. R. 449.

[52] Under the power, conferred by statute on all corporations, of making bylaws for the management of their property and the regulation of their affairs, a savings bank may enact a bylaw requiring its cashier to give bond for the faithful performance of the duties of his office. Savings Bank v. Hunt, 72 Mo. 597, 87 Am. H. 449.

incorporation and organization.[53] Statutes may regulate the authority and duties of state banking officials in regard to such incorporation,[54] and may

---

[53] Reed v. People, 125 Ill. 592, 18 N.E. 295, 1 L.R.A. 324; Murphy v. Pacific Bank, 119 Cal. 334, 51 P. 317; Richards v. Minnesota Sav. Bank, 75 Minn. 196, 77 N.W. 822.

[54] **In general.—**

State v. Kingston, 214 Wis. 362, 253 N.W. 401.

Approval of articles of incorporation.—

Commissioner of banking had duty within reasonable time to approve mutual savings bank articles of incorporation if sufficient under law, under statute providing that true copy of articles of incorporation verified by affidavits, with certificate showing when articles were flied and approved by commissioner of banking should be recorded. And the commissioner had no authority to refer approval to banking board of review. State ex rel. Wember v. Kingston, 214 Wis. 862, 253 N.W. 401.

The state banking board may be vested with a discretionary power to refuse a charter for a savings bank, where it appears that the bank is to be conducted in the same room, or in a room immediately adjacent to one occupied by a national bank, and the officers and directors of the two are substantially the same. State v. Morehead, 99 Neb. 146, 155 N.W. 879.

Scope of review.—

Decision of commissioner of banking to permit establishment of branch office of savings bank in township, based on finding that general economy of the area and reasonable potential were such that there was room for the branch bank without causing excessive competition to any existing institution, was not arbitrary, capricious or unreasonable. Application of Montclair Sav. Bank, 114 N.J. Super. 196, 275 A.2d 746 (1971).

Although it would have been better practice for department of banking to add to statistics set forth in record in proceeding on application for branch savings bank the source of the statistics as to deposit potential, grant of application would not be set aside on ground the decision was based partly on evidence outside the record where there was ample other proof to support fact findings, accuracy of figures was not challenged and there was no showing of prejudice. Application of Montclair Sav. Bank, 114 N.J. Super. 196, 275 A.2d 746 (1971).

Finding held unlawful.—

Finding by the Board of Trust Company incorporation that a proposed guaranty savings bank would not serve a useful purpose in the community based on the factor that it would be owned by a bank holding company which also owned a commercial bank could not be reasonably supported and was thus unlawful. In re Incorporators of Manchester Sav. Bank, 412 A.2d 421 (N.H. 1980).

In considering an application for a proposed guaranty savings bank, the finding of the Board of the Trust Company Incorporation with respect to statutory undue injury criterion based upon the effects that the operation of the proposed bank might have had on structure of banking in New Hampshire was not justified and therefore was unlawful. In re Incorporators of Manchester Sav. Bank, 412 A.2d 421 (N.H. 1980).

prohibit the payment of compensation for organizing a savings bank.[55] For cases dealing with depositorship as a requirement for membership in a savings bank, see the footnote.[56]

Findings held lawful.—

Record, including bank examiner's report stating that 31 percent of savings deposits of residents of community were placed outside community and that there was need for new capital in market area of proposed guaranty savings bank permitted Board of Trust Company Incorporation to find that proposed bank would serve useful purpose. In re Kingswood Trust & Sav. Bank, 455 A.2d 1027 (N.H. 1983).

Though Board of Trust Company Incorporation required increase in capitalization from amount stated in original application to establish guaranty savings bank, record as a whole permitted Board to find that proposed bank had reasonable expectation of financial success. In re Kingswood Trust & Sav. Bank, 455 A.2d 1027 (N.H. 1983).

Notwithstanding evidence provided by opponent of application to establish guaranty savings bank, record which did not suggest that new bank would jeopardize ultimate security of funds deposited by customers of existing banks did not preclude Board of Trust Company Incorporation from finding that no undue injury would be caused to existing savings institutions. In re Kingswood Trust & Sav. Bank, 455 A.2d 1027 (N.H. 1983).

Mere speculation by opponent of application to establish guaranty savings bank that Federal Reserve Board would not approve exchange of capital for stock between applicant and another financial institution did not preclude Board of Trust Company Incorporation from finding that applicant had reasonable prospect of raising necessary amount of capital funds. In re Kingswood Trust & Sav. Bank, 455 A.2d 1027 (N.H. 1983).

[55] Guardian Agency v. Guardian Mut. Sav. Bank, 227 Wis. 550, 279 N.W. 79, 115 ALR. 1366.

A statute prohibiting commission, compensation, bonus, right, or privilege for organizing any "banking corporation" in the state or securing subscriptions to stock thereof, applies to savings banks as well as to state banks, notwithstanding that it is, by statutory revision, contained in chapter entitled "State Banks." Guardian Agency v. Guardian Mut. Sav. Bank, 227 Wis. 550, 279 N.W. 79, 115 A.L.R. 1356.

Hence, contract whereby promoter agreed to act as manager of sale of savings contracts for savings bank and bank agreed to employ promoter for specified term in consideration for service charges paid by depositors, subject to distribution of portions thereof to members of sales organization, and in consideration for certain acts of promoter in promoting organization of bank, was void. Guardian Agency v. Guardian Mut. Sav. Bank, 227 Wis. 550, 279 N.W. 79, 115 A.L.R. 1356.

[56] Where the successful operation of a savings and loan incorporated society, the bylaws of which indicated that deposits were restricted to members, depended upon the members' use of it, depositorship was a requirement for membership, entrance fee of two dollars required of members was a nonrefundable payment for the privilege of membership and was not a deposit and, in view of the withdrawal of deposits by two members before the board of trustees elected to incorporate the society as a savings bank, which did not limit depositors to members, the successors in interest to such members had no interest in the bank. Spencer v. Hibernia Bank, 186 Cal. App. 2d 702, 9 Cal. Rptr. 867.

Consolidation and Merger.—The "purchase and liquidation" of a savings bank constitutes an undertaking by the purchaser to pay the obligations of the bank and wind up its affairs.[57] Thus, the assets of a guaranty savings bank which is sold to, or merged with, another bank are a trust fund for the payment of the savings bank's debts and the claims of its general depositors.[58] But a trust company which took over the assets of a savings bank, and assumed an obligation to deal with deposits coming into its possession only, would not be liable to a depositor of the bank where the bank had paid his deposit to a person having possession of his passbook, since the trust company could not be held liable as trustee of a fund which never came into its possession.[59] Where stock of a savings bank is surrendered and cancelled, so as to increase its assets, a merger agreement, approved by the superintendent of banks, who understood how the assets were increased, is not invalid as the result of fraud or conspiracy.[60]

During the Savings-and-Loan Crisis, the Federal Savings and Loan Insurance Corporation (FSLIC), as insurer of deposits and regulator of "thrifts" or savings-and-loan institutions, responded to the crisis by encouraging healthy thrifts to take over failing ones in what were called "supervisory mergers." These transactions relieved the FSLIC of its deposit insurance liability for the insolvent thrifts, and, in exchange, provided a package of non-cash incentives to acquiring thrifts.[61] These transactions relieved the FSLIC of its deposit insurance liability for the insolvent thrifts, and, in exchange, provided a package of non-cash incentives to acquiring thrifts.[62] Two of those incentives are: (1) "Branching" rights and (2) "RAP"—or "regulatory accounting purposes"—rights.[63]

---

[57] Wasmann v. City Nat. Bank, 52 F.2d 705.

[58] Second Nat'l Bank v. Old Guar. Sav. Bank, 84 N.H. 342, 150 A. 737, 69 A.L.R. 1250.

Where savings bank A took over all the assets of savings bank B under a merger agreement, creditors of bank B held entitled after failure of bank A to have any assets of bank B which still remain in hands of receiver of bank A applied to payment of their claims, and had equitable lien on such assets. Andrew v. American Sav. Bank, etc., Co., 219 Iowa 1059, 258 N.W. 921.

[59] Myers v. Washington Trust Co., 42 RI. 91, 105 A. 565.

[60] Gibbs v. Knickerbocker Sav., etc., Co., 166 App. Div. 517, 152 N.Y.S. 4, appeal denied, 168 App. Div. 954, 153 N.Y.S. 1116.

[61] WMI Holdings Corp. v. United States, 891 F.3d 1016 (2018).

[62] WMI Holdings Corp. v. United States, 891 F.3d 1016 (2018).

[63] WMI Holdings Corp. v. United States, 891 F.3d 1016 (2018).

For other cases relating to consolidation and merger agreements,[64] and the rescission of such agreements, see the footnotes.[65]

---

[64] **Merger agreement held not to provide for new financial institution** and therefore one of banks receiving cash and liquidating dividend on stock of the other bank from stockholder of such other bank under subscription for stock in bank receiving money did not hold such funds in trust for special purpose of investment in stock of new financial institution. Andrew,. American Sav. Bank, etc., Co., 219 Iowa 921, 258 N.W. 911.

Assumption of deposit liabilities.—Savings account shown on books of state bank when national bank assumed all deposit liabilities of state bank as shown by its books constituted deposit for which national bank was liable, notwithstanding that cashier of state bank had possession of ledger sheet showing account when examination was made, where national bank issued new passbook, computed interest on passbook and permitted withdrawals from account to be made for considerable time after deposit liabilities of state bank were taken over. Blakeley v. First Nat'l Bank, 151 Ore. 655, 51 P.2d 1034, overruled on another point, Godell v. Johnson, 244 Ore. 587, 418 P.2d 505.

Where depositor's commercial account contained sufficient funds to cover check accepted by officer of bank for deposit in savings account, savings account was established as a depositor's liability, as respects consolidation, when bank issued savings account passbook to depositors. Blakeley v. First Nat'l Bank, 151 Ore. 655, 51 P.2d 1034, overruled on another point, Godell v. Johnson, 244 Ore. 587, 418 P.2d 505.

Claim against receiver.—See § 27 of this chapter.

Depositor had standing to sue.—

Depositor of state chartered mutual savings bank had legal standing to question legality of proposed union or merger of savings bank and state chartered trust company and of savings bank's acquisition of stock of trust company which was essential part of plan. Manchester Sav. Bank v. New Hampshire Ass'n of Sav. Banks, 266 A.2d 838 (N.H. 1970).

Acquisition of commercial banking powers by merger.—Finding that primary purpose of state chartered mutual savings bank, which sought to merge with state chartered trust company, in acquiring outstanding stock of trust company was not investment but acquisition of stock control of such commercial banking powers as were contained in charter of trust company was not erroneous. Manchester Sav. Bank v. New Hampshire Ass'n of Sav. Banks, 266 A.2d 838 (N.H. 1970).

Curing defects of previous vote on merger agreement.—

Action of trustees of charitable foundation, which purchased three-fourths of stock of state chartered trust company held by state chartered mutual savings bank under agreement providing that savings bank should have irrevocable option to reacquire stock if proposed merger between bank and. trust company should be approved, in voting to ratify and confirm action of trust company's stockholders in voting to consolidate with savings bank and to ratify and confirm action of directors and officers of trust company taken pursuant to plan of reorganization cured any defects in previous vote by savings bank as sole stockholder to consolidate with trust company and rendered merger properly and legally authorized. Manchester Sav. Bank v. New Hampshire Ass'n of Sav. Banks, 266 A.2d 838 (N.H. 1970).

(Text continued on page 19)

Determination held arbitrary.—

Determination that approval of merger of two thrift institutions might be precedent encouraging statewide concentration of thrift institution resources was arbitrary where institution to be acquired had a serious management succession problem and would have to merge in order to survive and possibility of acquiring institution branching de novo into the latter's service area was remote due to economic condition of area and present population per institution. Washington Mut. Sav. Bank v. Federal Deposit Ins. Corp., 347 F. Supp. 790 (W.D. Wash. 1972).

Where Federal Deposit Insurance Corporation failed to apply relevant factors based on established principles under antitrust laws in denying request for consolidation of two thrift institutions, reviewing court was required to remand notwithstanding that it might have been of the opinion that only proper decision on basis of files and records was approval of consolidation. Washington Mut. Sav. Bank v. Federal Deposit Ins. Corp., 347 F. Supp. 790 (W.D. Wash. 1972).

Cash options.—Unlike some other states, New Hampshire has no statute requiring that depositors be given a cash option in the event of a merger. In re City Sav. Bank, 309 A.2d 31 (N.H. 1973).

Objecting depositors of a mutual savings bank, which is consolidated into a resulting commercial bank with capital stock, may be required to accept payment for the value of their equity in the surplus of the savings bank in shares of the capital stock of the resulting commercial bank, without the option of having their interest appraised and paid for in cash. In re City Sav. Bank, 309 A.2d 31 (N.H. 1973).

Value of dissenting minority shareholders' stock.—

Factors to be considered in determining value of dissenting minority shareholders' stock in savings bank at time of merger included earning capacity, investment value, history and nature of business, economic outlook, book value, dividend paying capacity, and market price of stock of similar businesses, with weight given to factors being matter for trial judge to determine. Stanton,. Republic Bank, 144 Ill. 2d 472, 581 N.L2d 678, 163 Ill. Dec. 524 (1991).

Trial court determining value of dissenting minority shareholders' stock in savings bank at time of merger received adequate evidence from experts, in accordance with relevant factors to be considered, and correctly determined respective weight to be given to each valuation factor under circumstances of case. Stanton v. Republic Bank of S. Chicago, 144 Ill. 2d 472, 581 N.E.2d 678, 163 Ill. Dec. 524 (1991).

Trial court acted within its discretion, in determining value of dissenting minority shareholders' stock in savings bank at time of merger, in applying minority discount and discount for lack of marketability, though it was not required to do so. Stanton v. Republic Bank, 144 Ill. 2d 472, 163 Ill. Dec. 524, 581 N.E.2d 678 (1991).

Aggregate discount of 10 percent given by district court for minority and lack of marketability, in determining value of dissenting minority shareholders' stock in savings bank at time of merger, fell within range proposed by experts for both bank and shareholders, and thus was supported by evidence. Stanton v. Republic Bank, 144 Ill. 2d 472, 163 Ill. Dec. 524, 581 N.E.2d 678 (1991).

(Text continued on page 19)

Conversion from mutual savings bank to stock financial institution.—

Under Maine law, certificate of conversion issued to bank by Superintendent of Banking authorizing conversion from mutual savings bank to stock financial institution and expiration of time limit for obtaining judicial review of final agency action barred account holders' action against bank for breach of contract, breach of fiduciary duty, fraudulent and negligent misrepresentation, conversion, and unjust enrichment arising from bank's failure to make distribution of net worth to account holders upon conversion. Lovell v. Peoples Heritage Sav. Bank, 818 F. Supp. 427 (D. Me. 1993).

Certificate of conversion issued to bank by Maine Superintendent of Banking authorizing conversion from mutual savings bank to stock financial institution and expiration of time limit for obtaining judicial review of final agency action barred account holders' action, based on alleged violations of Maine statutory law, for declaratory and equitable relief or, in the alternative, damages for alleged defects in conversion process; certificate constitutes conclusive evidence of correctness of all proceedings. Lovell v. Peoples Heritage Sav. Bank, 818 F. Supp. 427 (D. Me. 1993).

Notice to account holders of conversion of bank from mutual savings bank to stock financial institution did not deny account holders due process; they had no property interest in connection with conversion meriting constitutional protection, and they received adequate notice via publication in newspapers and mailed notices prior to conversion. Lovell v. Peoples Heritage Sav. Bank, 818 F. Supp. 427 (D. Me. 1993).

Account holders received sufficient notice of conversion of bank from mutual savings bank to stock corporation; account holders received published notice of plan conversion early on in process and individual notice of conversion before alleged deprivation occurred. Lovell v. One Bancorp, 818 F. Supp. 412 (D. Me. 1993).

Maine statute governing conversion of bank from mutual savings to stock form and superintendent of banking's approving conversion plan did not impair obligation of contract of account holders; there was no evidence in record of any express contract between account holders and bank providing that account holders had interest in net worth of bank and they had no reasonable expectations based on their relationship with bank concerning bank's surplus. Lovell v. One Bancorp, 818 F. Supp. 412 (D. Me. 1993).

Maine statute governing conversion of mutual savings banks to stock form is rationally related to state concern with raising of capital for banks while maintaining safety and capital adequacy of converting institutions and, thus, did not violate equal protection. Lovell v. One Bancorp, 818 F. Supp. 412 (B. Me. 1993).

Statutory and administrative scheme governing conversion of mutual savings bank to stock form effectively displaced private rights of action relating to conversion process; issuance of certificate of conversion and failure to seek judicial review under Administrative Procedure Act barred common-law causes of action such as breach of fiduciary duty, intentional and negligent misrepresentation, tortious conversion of property, unjust enrichment, and breach of contract. Lovell v. One Bancorp, 818 F. Supp. 412 (D. Me. 1993).

Procedure.—

Trial court's order remanding case for contested case hearing before state Savings Institution Division was not immediately appealable, where members of savings bank had

Reorganization.—The Comptroller of the Currency was held justified in refusing to approve a reorganization plan for a savings bank where depositors, by waiving a percentage of deposits, would contribute toward the capital structure of the reorganized bank beyond the amount necessary to restore its solvency.[66] Under the bylaws of a savings society which stated that, until otherwise provided, depositors should be entitled to the same share of profits and dividends as members, depositors who were not members were not entitled to share in the reserve fund on the reincorporation of the society as a capital stock corporation.[67] The fact that a holder of certificates of participation under the reorganization agreement of a savings bank was an administrator did not change his status as a member of the class before the court in a proceeding by the trustee for construction of the agreement.[68] For other cases relating to the reorganization of savings banks, see the footnote.[69]

---

challenged Division's decision approving conversion of savings bank into stock-owned bank and simultaneous merger of stock-owned bank into second bank, Division denied members' petition for contested case hearing, and, on judicial review, trial court found that denial of that petition violated Administrative Procedures Act. Byers v. North Carolina Sav. Insts. Div., 474 S.E.2d 404 (N.C. App. 1996).

[65] **On failure of one bank to perform substantial part of merger agreement** with another bank, option of waiving partial nonperformance seeking rescission was in the other bank and could not be exercised by one of such bank's stockholders. Andrew v. American Sav. Bank, etc., Co., 219 Iowa 921, 258 N.W. 911.

Any rescission of merger agreement must be in toto, and one of banks cannot be required to suffer all detriments of such contract and at the same time be deprived of its benefits. Andrew v. American Sav. Bank, Co., 219 Iowa 921, 258 N.W. 911.

Bank attempting rescission must put other bank in position it occupied before performance of merger agreement was attempted. Andrew v. American Sav. Bank, etc., Co., 219 Iowa 921, 258 N.W. 911.

Where nothing was done to accomplish rescission before assets of bank passed into hands of receiver, title to property which such bank had received from the other bank under merger agreement held in bank when receiver took charge, even though merger contract had been so substantially nonperformed by such bank as to give the other a right to rescind. Andrew v. American Sav. Bank, Co., 219 Iowa 921, 258 N.W. 911.

[66] Cooper v. Woodin, 72 F.2d 179.

[67] Maguire v. Hibernia Sav., etc., Soc. (Cal. App.), 128 P.2d 149, rev'd on other grounds, 23 Cal. 2d 719, 146 P.2d 673.

[68] American State Sav. Bank v. American State Sav. Bank, 288 Mich. 78, 284 N.W. 652.

[69] **In general.—**

Attempts to reorganize or liquidate bank in village of Penacook, closed by order of court, with minimum loss to depositors, indicate existence of a specific local need which would justify enactment of special local legislation, and hence amended bill authorizing Board of

(*Text continued on page 22*)

Incorporation of Trust Companies to authorize any trust company or mutual or guaranty savings bank, authorized to engage in banking business in Concord, to establish and operate a branch bank in Penacook, would not violate any provision of state constitution, particularly in view of legislative practice of chartering or authorizing banks on a local territorial basis. Opinion of the Justices (N.H.), 154 A.2d 184.

Reorganization plan not rendered illegal.—

Regardless of whether or not original purchase of stock of state chartered trust company by state chartered mutual savings bank for purpose of union or merger between bank and trust company was ultra vires under state law regarding investments by mutual savings banks, transfer of 75 percent of trust company's stock held by savings bank to charitable foundation under agreement providing that bank should have irrevocable option to reacquire stock if merger should be approved operated to bring bank's investment in trust company stock into compliance with state law, complied with order of bank commissioner to bank to bring itself in compliance with state law by divesting itself of its investment and did not render plan of reorganization illegal. Manchester Sav. Bank v. New Hampshire Ass'n of Sav. Banks, 266 A.2d 838 (N.H. 1970).

What constitutes investment under reorganization plan.—

Where, so far as depositors were affected, their interest in surplus of savings bank was preserved by converting it to interest in equity or trust company which would own banking assets formerly held by savings bank, reacquisition of trust company stock by mutual savings bank, after bank had ceased to do business as savings bank and solely for purpose of exchanging stock for shares of stock of holding company under plan of reorganization providing for merger of savings bank and trust company and providing for distribution of beneficial interest of shares of stock of holding company to depositors would be in no realistic sense an "investment" by savings bank controlled by statute. Manchester Sav. Bank v. New Hampshire Ass'n of Sav. Banks, 266 A.2d 838 (N.H. 1970).

Effect of illegal investment under reorganization plan.—

Where it did not appear that state chartered mutual savings bank paid anything for option to repurchase three-fourths of state chartered trust company stock owned by bank and sold to charitable foundation, savings bank did not continue to have any investment in such shares after sale to foundation and, from standpoint of depositors of savings bank, assuming original investment of bank funds in such shares of trust company under reorganization plan proposing merger of savings bank and trust company was illegal under statute, such stock was no longer held by bank after sale to foundation. Manchester Sav. Bank v. New Hampshire Ass'n of Sav. Banks, 266 A.2d 838 (N.H. 1970).

Conversion of Savings Bank.—

Corporators of savings bank who were also depositors of bank had standing to appeal from decision of Board of Trust Company Incorporation granting bank's application for conversion from mutual savings bank to guaranty form of organization and for simultaneous acquisition of bank by bank holding company. In re Corporators of Portsmouth Sav. Bank, 525 A.2d 671 (N.H. 1987).

Statute permitting Board of Trust Company Incorporation to adopt rules permitting mutual savings banks to convert to stock form, with comparable limitations as applied to federal savings and loan associations under federal law, allowed board to evaluate conversion-

(Text continued on page 22)

---

acquisitions, rather than only stand-alone conversions, even though board regulation was not exactly identical to federal rule governing conversions involving acquisitions by existing bank holding companies. In re Corporators of Portsmouth Sav. Bank, 525 A.2d 671 (N.H. 1987).

Lack of depositor approval for proposed plan for conversion-acquisition of mutual savings bank did not violate federal law requiring approval of plan of conversion by members of converting bank, where bank's charter contemplated that members of bank were corporators, rather than depositors. In re Corporators of Portsmouth Sav. Bank, 525 A.2d 671 (N.H. 1987).

Conversion-acquisition plan pursuant to which converting savings bank would remain in existence as, essentially, a wholly owned subsidiary of bank holding company was governed by statute governing conversions and regulations promulgated thereunder, rather than statute governing consolidation or union of banks. In re Corporators of Portsmouth Sav. Bank, 525 A.2d 671 (N.H 1987).

Fact that savings bank's proposed conversion-acquisition plan corresponded to technical and legal requirements of conversion regulations did not insure that plan was fair to depositors. In re Corporators of Portsmouth Sav. Bank, 525 A.2d 671 (N.H. 1987).

Statute defining depositors' proprietary interests as proportionate inchoate interests in net worth of mutual savings bank, such interest maturing and being realized upon bank's liquidation, did not apply to reorganization of mutual savings banks and to mutual holding companies. In re Corporators of Portsmouth Sav. Bank, 525 A.2d 671 (N.H. 1987).

Fact that depositors had no voice in management of mutual savings bank was irrelevant in determining whether depositors' ownership of mutual savings bank had diminished to technical fiction, for purposes of determining right of appraisal. In re Corporators of Portsmouth Sav. Bank, 525 A.2d 671 (N.H. 1987).

Proposed plan of conversion and acquisition of savings bank, pursuant to which surplus of savings bank would be transferred to bank holding company and put into liquidation account, to be distributed only upon liquidation, failed to preserve depositors' charter rights to surplus, even though proposed plan granted depositors subscription rights to purchase stock of holding company prior to public offering. In re Corporators of Portsmouth Sav. Bank, 525 A.2d 671 (N.H. 1987).

Proposed plan of conversion and acquisition of mutual savings bank, which failed to preserve depositors' charter rights to direct distribution of bank's surplus, was unfair to depositors, even though federal regulation preempted depositors' contractual right to direct distribution of surplus at time bank applied for approval of plan, where federal regulation expired on date Board of Trust Company Incorporation approved proposed plan. In re Corporators of Portsmouth Sav. Bank, 525 A.2d 671 (NA 1987).

Determination of fairness of proposed conversion and acquisition of mutual savings bank depends on relationship between parties. In re Corporators of Portsmouth Sav. Bank, 525 A.2d 671 (N.H. 1987).

Fiduciary duty of trustee of mutual savings bank to protect depositors' rights to dividends, pursuant to bank charter and statute, superseded regulation authorizing conversion-acquisition which failed to preserve depositors' rights to direct distribution of surplus. In re Corporators of Portsmouth Sav. Bank, 525 A.2d 671 (N.H. 1987).

Branch Banks.—In determining whether the public interest would be served by the establishment of a branch banking office, the existence of

---

Action by depositor challenging conversion of bank from a mutual association to a stock corporation was not barred by Maine statute providing that a "conversion certificate" of the Maine Superintendent of Banking is "conclusive evidence" of the correctness of a conversion proceeding, in view of fact that the Maine conversion statutes expressly subject the Superintendent's decisions to state court review, by incorporating Maine's Administrative Procedure Act. Lovell v. One Bancorp, 690 F. Supp. 1090 (D. Me. 1988).

Depositor who challenged bank's conversion from a mutual association to a stock corporation stated a claim for relief based on allegation that he "owned" a portion of the association proportionate to his deposits there, and thus had a protected property interest for which he was entitled to be compensated. Lovell v. One Bancorp, 690 F. Supp. 1090 (D. Me. 1988).

Depositors of mutual savings bank were essentially creditors of institution, and did not have "ownership" rights entitling them to share of bank's assets or to guaranteed profit upon conversion of bank to stock form. In re East New York Sav. Bank Depositors Litigation, 547 N.Y.S.2d 497 (N.Y. Sup. Ct. 1989).

Mutual savings bank's depositors' claim that trustees breached their duty to act as depositors' fiduciaries with respect to plan for conversion of bank to stock corporation and subsequent merger with another corporation, alleging that plan was improperly not structured to maximize depositors' profit and that plan should have been renegotiated after stock market crash to provide for benefit to depositors, constituted challenge to legal sufficiency of conversion plan duly approved by state banking department, rather than separate challenge to financial sufficiency of plan that might warrant rescission. In re East New York Sav. Bank Depositors Litigation, 547 N.Y.S.2d 497 (N.Y. Sup. Ct. 1989).

Statutory and administrative scheme governing conversion of mutual savings bank to stock corporation effectively displaced private rights of action relating to conversion process; issuance of certificate of conversion and failure to seek judicial review under Administrative Procedure Act barred common-law causes of action such as breach of fiduciary duty, intentional and negligent misrepresentation, tortuous conversion, unjust enrichment, and breach of contract. Lovell v. One Bancorp, 614 A.2d 56 (Me. 1992).

Depositors or account holders in mutual savings bank had no statutory right to vote by mail or by proxy on bank's conversion to stock ownership; governing statute expressly provided that any eligible account holders not present at meeting were to be regarded as having affirmatively voted for conversion and were to be counted toward two-thirds majority required for approval. Lovell v. One Bancorp, 614 A.2d 56 (Me. 1992).

Account holders' beneficial interest in mutual savings bank and statutory requirement of "equitable" treatment of account holders did not require distribution to them of surplus as part of plan for conversion of bank to stock corporation. Lovell v. One Bancorp, 614 A.2d 56 (Me. 1992).

Mutual savings bank's charter did not give account holders any right that did not exist under statutes governing conversion to stock corporation to receive distribution of any surplus; statutes controlled if charter conflicted in any way. Lovell v. One Bancorp, 614 A.2d 56 (Me. 1992).

established institutions in the area, and the effect of the proposed branch on them is generally required to be considered by the state's administrative authority.[70] Interpretations of the statutes of several jurisdictions relating to savings bank branches, and the power to establish them, are discussed in the footnote.[71]

---

[70] **In general.—**

Application of Howard Sav. Institution, 32 N.J. 29, 159 A.2d 113 (1960).

Effect of customer convenience.—

In a hearing on the petition of a mutual savings bank to establish a branch in a specified community, the convenience of customers is not determinative of the inadequacy of local banking facilities, but does have some bearing on such inadequacy. Philadelphia Sav. Fund Soc. v. Myers, 383 Pa. 253, 118 A.2d 561.

Main office of bank in same county as proposed branch.—

In a proceeding on the application of a mutual savings bank for approval of the establishment of a branch office in a municipality within the same county as its main office, the burden is on the bank to establish that the statutory requisites are met. Application of Howard Sav. Institution, 32 N.J. 29, 159 A.2d 113 (1960).

Grounds for appeal.—

Although objecting savings and loan associations had not appealed from determination of Commissioner of Banking and Insurance approving application of mutual savings bank to establish branch in municipality which was in same county as main office located in another municipality, banks which had appealed could present point that commissioner cannot legally ignore, in determining advantage to public interest, effect of proposed branch on established savings and loan associations in area and that commissioner did not in fact consider such effect. Application of Howard Sav. Institution, 32 N.J. 29, 159 A.2d 113 (1960).

[71] *Maryland.*—It has been held that the charter power of a mutual savings bank to establish branch banks cannot be abrogated or reduced by the legislature's enactment of a general law relating to branch banks without some mention thereof in both the title and body of the statute. Kirkwood v. Provident Sav. Bank, 205 Md. 48, 106 A.2d 103.

Act, giving mutual savings banks the right to establish branch banks in same city, town or village with approval of bank commissioner, did not impliedly abrogate charter power of such a bank to establish branch banks in counties. Kirkwood v. Provident Sav. Bank, 205 Md. 48, 106 A.2d 103.

And a mutual savings bank, which is authorized by its charter to carry on its operations in a state has the power to establish branch banks in the counties of such state without the state bank commissioner's approval, and would be entitled to a prohibitory injunction restraining the state bank commissioner and attorney general from prohibiting it from establishing any such branch offices. St. James Sav. Bank v. Kirkwood, 206 Md. 186, 111 A.2d 212.

Minnesota.—A mutual savings bank organized under law of 1879 providing for the organization of savings banks did not have power to establish a branch office in the city in which it was chartered to act. Farmers & Mechanics Sav. Bank v. Department of Commerce,

(Text continued on page 25)

Securities Division, 258 Minn. 99, 102 N.W.2d 827.

New Hampshire.—Where Board of Trust Company Incorporation permitted banks who were challenging applications of savings bank and trust company to establish branch banks to see bank examiner's report but also held second hearing, permitted cross-examination of bank examiner who prepared reports and allowed additional witnesses to testify and record to be supplemented after hearing, procedures by which applications were granted complied with due process. In re Portsmouth Sav. Bank, 455 A.2d 1023 (N.H. 1983).

After applications of savings bank and trust company to establish branch banks were remanded to Board of Trust Company Incorporation in order for protesting banks to obtain access to bank examiner's report, Board did not err in limiting scope of remand to events and conditions existing at time examiner's report was prepared. In re Portsmouth Sav. Bank, 455 A.2d 1023 (N.H. 1983).

New Jersey.—Where savings bank branch bank application was deemed to have been approved ninety days after effective filing of application and charter application for state bank could have been granted on the same date if statute had been complied with, neither state bank nor branch bank approval had Priority and state bank was not entitled to "home office protection" so as to preclude approval of savings bank branch application. Application of Montclair Sav. Bank, 114 N.J. Super. 196, 275 A.2d 746 (1971).

The hearing on an application by a savings bank for approval to open a full service branch office was to be conducted as in a "contested case" in accordance with the applicable provisions of the Administrative Procedure Act, as amended and supplemented by the legislation establishing the Office of Administrative Law, where the commissioner of banking had decided that a formal hearing was to be held on the application. In re Orange Sav. Bank, 172 N.J. Super. 275, 411 A.2d 1150 (1980).

New York.—Postal and telephone district boundaries were not evidence of an unincorporated village's boundaries for the purpose of applying the Banking Law provision which prohibits opening a savings bank branch in certain unincorporated villages, where the postal and telephone district boundaries spilled over into areas which were beyond any reasonable boundaries for the unincorporated village. Putnam County Nat'l Bank v. Albright, 384 N.Y.S.2d 669 (1976).

The term "unincorporated village" in a provision of the Banking Law which prohibits a savings bank branch from opening in any "unincorporated village" with a population of 50,000 or less wherein is located the principal office of a bank or trust company means the combination of the minimum requirements necessary for incorporation as a village plus other appropriate attributes of a cohesive community containing contiguous clusterings of population and business enterprises. Putnam County Nat'l Bank v. Albright, 384 N.Y.S.2d 669 (1976).

In view of the Banking Law section which provides that the term "population" means population as determined by the latest federal census except when the term is used in connection with the population of an unincorporated village, it is not required that an unincorporated village be determined by boundaries established by the United States Bureau of the Census, for the purpose of applying in connection with an unincorporated village provision of the Banking Law which prohibits opening of a savings bank branch in certain cities or villages, but must be determined by the superintendent of banks from the best

A superintendent of banks may permit a change in location of any place where the business of a savings bank is conducted, and this includes branch offices acquired by merger.[72] For cases involving the question of parties,[73] see the footnote. For cases involving the questions of burden of proof,[74] sufficiency of evidence[75] and findings of fact[76] with respect to applications for branch banks, see the footnotes.

---

available sources. Putnam County Nat'l Bank v. Albright, 384 N.Y.S.2d 669 (1976).

Pennsylvania.—Commercial banks, bank and trust companies, trust companies and savings banks are all included within term "institution" as used in code providing for establishment of branches. Philadelphia Sav. Fund Soc. v. Myers, 406 Pa. 438, 179 A.2d 209.

Vermont.—Proceeding wherein the banking commissioner approved the application of a savings bank to establish a branch operation was not a proceeding in which the legal rights, duties or privileges of a party were required by law to be determined by an agency after an opportunity for hearing and, hence, was not a "contested case" from which the national bank opposing the application could appeal under the statute permitting any party entitled by law to appeal from a decision of any governmental agency in a contested case. In re Marble Sav. Bank, 137 Vt. 123, 400 A.2d 1022 (1979).

Washington.—Mutual savings bank in State of Washington is not "state bank" within meaning of Washington state statute allowing national banking association, with approval of comptroller of currency, to establish and operate new branches at any point within the state in which the association is situated if such establishment and operation are at the time authorized to "state banks" by statute law of state in question, etc. Mutschler v. Peoples Nat'l Bank, 607 F.2d 274 (9th Cir. 1979).

[72] Lincoln Sav. Bank v. Broderick, 140 Misc. 380, 251 N.Y.S. 762.

[73] A savings and loan association did not have standing to contest the issuance of a certificate authorizing a savings bank to open a branch. Canajoharie Bldg., Sav. & Loan Ass'n v. Albright, 72 Misc. 2d 557, 339 N.Y.S.2d 737 (1972).

[74] **Proponent has burden of proving need for branch.—**

Notwithstanding differences between mutual savings banks, of which there were only seven in state, and commercial banks, it was incumbent upon mutual bank, seeking approval of establishment of branch bank, to prove need for contemplated services or facilities of proposed branch. Philadelphia Sav. Fund Soc. v. Myers, 406 Pa. 438, 179 A.2d 209.

Opponents of branch have burden on appeal.—

Opponents had burden to show that decision of board of trust company incorporation on application to establish branch mutual savings bank was clearly unreasonable or unlawful. First Fed. Sav. & Loan Ass'n v. State Bd. of Trust Co., 254 A.2d 835 (N.H. 1969).

[75] **Evidence supporting findings.—**

In proceedings on application of mutual savings bank for approval of establishment of branch office in municipality in same county as main office located in another municipality, evidence supported findings of Commissioner of Banking and Insurance that establishment of branch would be to advantage of public, that branch would not provide unfair competition for existing facilities, and that geographical and economic situation indicated probable

(Text continued on page 27)

---

success of the branch. Application of Howard Sav. Institution, 32 N.J. 29, 159 A.2d 113 (1960).

Evidence sustained finding of banking board that services and facilities, which were then in existence and which could be continued to be furnished by then banking institutions, were adequate both in quantity and quality to meet all requirements of area in which mutual bank sought to establish branch and that there was no present need for services and facilities which mutual bank proposed to furnish. Philadelphia Sav. Fund Soc. v. Myers, 406 Pa. 438, 179 A.2d 209.

That mutual bank was one of only seven in commonwealth and particularly encouraged and promoted thrift and paid on savings deposits a slightly higher interest than commercial banks did not entitle it to have branch in community that did not have mutual savings bank. Philadelphia Sav. Fund Soc. v. Myers, 406 Pa. 438, 179 A.2d 209.

Decision of board of trust company incorporation granting application to establish branch mutual savings bank was not unlawful because losses were projected for the first three years of operation. First Fed. Sav. & Loan Ass'n v. State Bd. of Trust Co., 254 A.2d 835 (N.H. 1969).

Evidence that, inter alia, the site of a savings bank branch was not within an unincorporated village's fire, sewer or water districts, that the branch would not pay taxes to the village and that the site of the branch was separated from the village's business section by a residential area, a cemetery and a wide expanse of undeveloped and sparsely settled farm acreage established that the branch was not within the unincorporated village and, therefore, not in violation of the Banking Law section which prohibits, inter alia, opening a savings bank branch in village wherein is located the home office of a national bank. Putnam County Nat'l Bank v. Albright, 384 N.Y.S.2d 669 (Sup. Ct. 1976).

In view of the fact that "enumeration districts" and "unincorporated places" are drawn by the United States Bureau of the Census solely for the purpose of efficiently counting people, evidence as to the boundaries of "enumeration districts" and "unincorporated places" as defined by the bureau lacks probative value as evidence of the boundaries of an unincorporated village for purposes of applying the Banking Law provision which prohibits, inter alia, opening a savings bank branch in any unincorporated village with a population of 50,000 or less wherein is located the principal office of a bank or trust company. Putnam County Nat'l Bank v. Albright, 384 N.Y.S.2d 669 (Sup. Ct. 1976).

Evidence supported conclusion of Board of Trust Company Incorporation that branches proposed by savings bank and trust company were consistent with sound banking, with public interest and with preservation of competition in field of banking. Appeal of Portsmouth Sav. Bank, 455 A.2d 1023 (N.H. 1983).

Evidence supported conclusion of Board of Trust Company Incorporation that savings banks who sought to establish branch banks had excellent management. In re Portsmouth Sav. Bank, 455 A.2d 1023 (N.H. 1983).

Evidence supported conclusion of Board of Trust Company Incorporation that savings banks who sought to establish branch banks had prospects for overall earnings that were healthy and that specific prospects of proposed branches pointed to success in marketplace. In re Portsmouth Sav. Bank, 455 A.2d 1023 (N.H. 1983).

Evidence supported conclusion of Board of Trust Company Incorporation that banks who

"Branching" Rights and "RAP" Rights.—When the Federal Savings and Loan Insurance Corporation (FSLIC) lacked the funds to liquidate failing savings and loan associations, also called "thrifts," during the Savings-and-Loan Crisis, the FSLIC responded to the crisis by encouraging healthy thrifts to take over failing ones in what were called "supervisory mergers." These transactions relieved the FSLIC of its deposit insurance liability for the insolvent thrifts, and, in exchange, provided a package of non-cash incentives to acquiring thrifts, including "branching" rights.[77] Branching rights

---

sought to establish branch banks were in strong capital position and that no unreasonable risk would be posed to existing depositors through expansion of operations into area in which savings bank and trust company sought to establish branch banks. In re Portsmouth Sav. Bank, 455 A.2d 1023 (N.H. 1983).

Evidence offered by savings bank and trust company who sought to establish branch banks showing that communities in area to be served by branches was active and growing and offered good business opportunities in years to come supported conclusion of Board of Trust Company Incorporation that there was present and continuing need for extensive involvement of banks to provide capital and services to individuals and business customers and that proposed branches would not only supplement services currently being provided by existing banks but would add new services to meet needs of community and area. In re Portsmouth Sav. Bank, 455 A.2d 1023 (N.H. 1983).

Even if savings bank was required to disclose specifically its mortgages and deposits within primary trade area in which it sought to establish branch, other evidence on savings bank and trust company's needs for branch banks in that area was sufficient and justified granting applications to establish branch banks. In re Portsmouth Sav. Bank, 455 A.2d 1023 (N.H. 1983).

Evidence not supporting finding.—

Conclusion of banking board that community had adequate banking facilities was without support in the evidence, and board's disapproval of proposed branch was unwarranted. Philadelphia Sav. Fund Soc. v. Myers, 383 Pa. 253, 118 A.2d 561.

[76] **Case not remanded for fuller finding.—**

Where there was really no basic fact issue in proceeding on application of mutual savings bank for approval of establishment of branch once in municipality in same county as main office located in another municipality, but legal questions were main bones of contention, and factual dispute as to probable success of proposed branch resulted from differing legal theories of the parties, and controlling considerations, parties' positions thereon, and commissioner's views, although somewhat vaguely and negatively expressed, were not left in doubt, case would not be remanded for fuller and clearer findings. Application of Howard Sav. Institution, 32 N.J. 29, 159 A.2d 113 (1960).

Approval held not arbitrary.—

Superintendent of banks' approval of application by savings bank, which was located in city with population of less than 80,000 to open brunch office in same county was not arbitrary, capricious or unlawful. Tooker v. Albright, 336 N.Y.S.2d 278 (Sup. Ct. 1972).

[77] WMI Holdings Corp. v. United States, 891 F.3d 1016 (2018).

permitted acquiring thrifts to open and operate branches in states other than their home states, which, prior to 1981, was generally prohibited. This prohibition was eliminated for thrifts entering into supervisory mergers across state lines.[78]

Regulatory accounting purposes or "RAP" rights, by contrast, affected regulatory accounting treatment for business combinations. Formerly, regulations mandated, in part, that each thrift maintain a minimum capital of at least three percent of its liabilities, which presented an obstacle for healthy thrifts seeking to acquire failing ones because, by definition, failing thrifts' liabilities exceeded their assets. Regulators eliminated this obstacle by permitting acquiring thrifts to use generally accepted accounting principles (GAAP). In essence, GAAP allowed acquiring thrifts to treat failing thrifts' excess liabilities as an asset called "supervisory goodwill," which, in turn, could be counted toward the acquiring thrifts' minimum regulatory capital requirement and amortized over a 40-year period (later reduced to 25 years). The RAP rights provided by FSLIC guaranteed such treatment, regardless of future regulatory changes.[79]

Dissolution and Forfeiture.—The right of a savings bank to cease business is not dependent on its right to cease existence, and it may voluntarily liquidate under a valid plan of liquidation.[80] Thus, dissolution of

---

Thrifts collect customer deposits, which are maintained in interest-bearing savings accounts, and they originate and service mortgage loans funded by those deposits. Historically, thrifts were profitable because the interest they collected on outstanding loans exceeded the interest they paid out to customers. WMI Holdings Corp. v. United States, 891 F.3d 1016 (2018).

[78] WMI Holdings Corp. v. United States, 891 F.3d 1016 (2018).

[79] WMI Holdings Corp. v. United States, 891 F.3d 1016 (2018).

[80] **In general.—**

Second Nat. Bank v. Old Guaranty Sav. Bank, 84 N.H. 342, 150 A. 737, 69 A.L.R. 1250.

The mere grant of a perpetual charter create, no obligation for such a savings bank to act, in the absence of other evidence. Second Nat. Bank v. Old Guaranty Sav. Bank, 84 N.H. 342, 150 A. 737, 69 A.L.R. 1250.

Statutory provision.—

The New Jersey statute authorizes the managers of a savings institution to dissolve it, if at a meeting of the managers, "a resolution declaring the dissolution to be advisable be passed by a two-thirds vote of the whole board." Barrett v. Bloomfield Sav. Inst., 66 N.J. Eq. 431, 57 A. 1131, aff'g 64 N.J. Eq. 425, 54 A. 543.

In determining whether dissolution is "advisable," the managers must not be guided by their own personal pecuniary interests. They are to consider whether further continuance of the institution would be of "public benefit," and "expedient and desirable," as tested by the

a mutual savings bank under a plan by which its assets and liabilities are transferred to a national bank which purchased such assets and assumed such liabilities is not an illegal merger.[81] However, the attorney general of a state is not the only person entitled to maintain an action to prevent the managers

---

need, of a considerable number of depositors, by the density of the population, and by the reasonable promise of adequate support. Barrett v. Bloomfield Sav. Inst., 66 N.J. Eq. 431, 57 A. 1131, aff'g 64 N.J. Eq. 425, 54 A. 543.

The mere fact that a trust company has been organized in the same community with a savings institution does not show that the dissolution of the latter is "advisable." Barrett v. Bloomfield Sav. Inst., 66 N.J. Eq. 431, 57 A. 1131, aff'g 64 N.J. Eq. 425, 54 A. 543, holding that the unwillingness of the managers to continue in office is no ground for dissolving the institution.

Invalid plan.—

A plan to accomplish stock acquisition and to attempt the liquidation of plaintiff state savings bank was invalid where the plan required the voting of two thirds of the stock of plaintiff bank for dissolution and was an attempt to circumvent the application of the Financial Institutions Act with respect to voluntary liquidation and sale of assets. Peoples Sav. Bank v. Stoddard, 359 Mich. 297, 102 N.W.2d 777, 83 A.L.R.2d 344.

Where competitor bank sought to accomplish the dissolution of a solvent state savings bank by the purchase of two thirds of its capital stock for the purpose of having that stock voted for dissolution, the purchase was violative of both state and federal law. Peoples Sav. Bank v. Stoddard, 359 Mich. 297, 102 N.W.2d 777, 83 A.L.R.2d 344.

Such plan was also invalid where it required defendant to execute a false oath as a member of the board of directors of plaintiff bank when he was not the owner in good faith and in his own right of a single share of plaintiff bank stock, and required defendant to violate his oath of office requiring that he honestly perform his duties by perpetrating a false masquerade as plaintiff bank's president upon the bank and directors and stockholders thereof as to whom he stood in a fiduciary relationship while he was actually serving as agent of a competitor bank and was seeking to destroy the institution he purported to serve. Peoples Sav. Bank v. Stoddard, 359 Mich. 297, 102 N.W.2d 777, 83 A.L.R.2d 344.

[81] In re Cleveland Sav. Soc'y (Ohio Ct. Com. Pleas), 25 Ohio Op. 2d 402, 192 N.E.2d 518 (1961), appeal dismissed, 183 N.E.2d 234.

Evidence failed to disclose that either members, trustees or officers of mutual savings bank or directors, stockholders or officers of national bank realized any unjust enrichment or committed a breach of any fiduciary duty in connection with dissolution of mutual savings bank under a plan by which its asset. and liabilities were transferred to national bank which purchased such assets and assumed such liabilities. In re Cleveland Sav. Soc'y (Ohio Ct Com. Pleas), 25 Ohio Op. 2d 402, 192 N.E.2d 518 (1961), appeal dismissed, 183 N.E.2d 234.

Evidence established that mutual savings bank and national bank had taken all proper procedural steps requisite to a dissolution of the savings bank through transfer of its assets and liabilities to the national bank which purchased such assets and assumed such liabilities. In re Cleveland Sav. tugs In re Cleveland Sav. Soc'y (Ohio Ct Com. Pleas), 25 Ohio Op. 2d 402, 192 N.E.2d 518 (1961), appeal dismissed, 183 N.E.2d 234.

of a savings institution from dissolving it, but a depositor may, as a depositor, and also as a citizen of the community, maintain such an action.[82]

The intangible ownership interest of a depositor in a mutual savings bank at any given time is in the proportion which his deposit balance bears to the aggregate of the deposit balances of all depositors, so that the distribution of the bank's remaining assets upon its dissolution must be in the same ratio as each depositor's intangible ownership interest therein.[83] Upon dissolution of such a bank, only those depositors having savings deposits in the bank as of the close of business on the final day of business are entitled to share in the distribution of the bank's remaining assets, as against the contention that former depositors, persons owning Christmas club accounts, escrow accounts, bond deposits, public funds on account, and savings accounts from corporations for profit should also share therein.[84] And upon such dissolution, unclaimed deposits should be held in a special trust created therefor with periodic publication from time to time of the names and last known addresses of such depositors, and the eventual final approval by a court of the distribution thereof.[85]

---

[82] Barrett v. Bloomfield Sav. Inst., 66 N.J. Eq. 431, 57 A. 1131, erg 64 N.J. Eq. 425, 54 A. 543.

[83] In re Cleveland Sav. Soc'y (Ohio Ct Com. Pleas), 25 Ohio Op. 2d 402, 192 N.E.2d 518 (1961), appeal dismissed, 183 N.E.2d 234.

Upon dissolution of mutual savings banks the intangible ownership interest of each depositor would be represented by scrip issued to represent a depositor's fractional interest in voting trust certificates, except that the school savings department depositors, because of their large number and relatively small amount of deposits, would be paid in cash. In re Cleveland Sav. Soc'y (Ohio Ct Com. Pleas), 25 Ohio Op. 2d 402, 192 N.E.2d 518 (1961), appeal dismissed, 183 N.E.2d 234.

[84] **In general.—**

In re Cleveland Sav. Soc'y (Ohio Ct Com. Pleas), 25 Ohio Op. 2d 402, 192 N.E.2d 518 (1961), appeal dismissed, 183 N.E.2d 234.

Governmental bodies as depositors.—

Where plan adopted by trustees for voluntary dissolution of savings society empowered court to determine what depositors were beneficial owners of surplus and court determined that holders of certificates of deposit, other than governmental agencies, were beneficial owners of surplus, it was improper to deny city right to share its surplus arising out of its ownership of certificates of deposit in society solely on ground that such deposits had been secured in manner required by Uniform Depository Act. In re Springfield Sav. Soc., 12 Ohio App. 2d 120, 231 N.E.2d 314, 41 Ohio Op. 191 (1968).

[85] In re Cleveland Sav. Soc'y (Ohio Ct Com. Pleas), 25 Ohio Op. 2d 402, 192 N.E.2d 518 (1961), appeal dismissed, 183 N.E.2d 234.

It has been held in Louisiana that the temporary suspension of a savings company for seven days will not operate as an absolute forfeiture of its charter if no creditor complains.[86]

II. CORPORATORS AND STOCKHOLDERS.

§ 3. General Considerations.

As previously mentioned, in some jurisdictions, there can be no shares of stock in a savings bank.[87] Money paid for membership in an institution of this type, for which no charter has been granted, may be recovered, such a bank being a purely mutual institution without stock.[88] In other jurisdictions, where stock in savings banks is permitted by law, such stock is sometimes, by statute, made security for depositors who are not stockholders.[89] And a purchase of the controlling stock in a savings bank closed by state banking officials, procured without fraud or duress under a contract ratified by the seller, is a valid transaction.[90]

Under the bylaws of a savings society providing that those who signed the bylaws and paid entrance fees should be considered members, and otherwise referring to "members and stockholders," it was held all "stockholders" were necessarily "members," but all "members" were not necessarily "stockholders."[91]

And where the bylaws of a savings bank had been amended to provide that membership therein ceased when a member closed his or her account, the membership of one who became a member after the bylaws had been amended terminated upon the closing of his account.[92] For other cases

---

[86] State v. Louisiana Sav. Co., 12 La. Ann. 568.

A fraudulent suspension of payment, or gross negligence in loaning money without sufficient guaranty, by which temporary suspension of payment might ensue, would be different. State v. Louisiana Sav. Co., 12 La. Ann. 568.

[87] Jefferson v. Cox, 246 Mass. 495, 141 N.E. 493. See also § 1 of this chapter.

A mutual savings bank has no stockholders. Application of Howard Sav. Institution, 32 N.J. 29, 159 A.2d 113 (1960).

[88] Jefferson v. Cox, 246 Mass. 495, 141 N.E. 493.

[89] Murphy v. Pacific Bank, 130 Cal. 542, 62 P. 1059.

[90] Youmans v. Hanna, 35 N.D. 479, 160 N.W. 705, 1917E Ann. Cas. 263, rehearing denied, 43 N.D. 536, 171 N.W. 835.

[91] Maguire v. Hibernia Sav., etc., Soc. (Cal. App.), 128 P.2d 149, rev'd on other grounds, 23 Cal. 2d 719, 146 P.2d 673.

[92] **In general.—**

Jacob v. Hibernia Bank, 186 Cal. App. 2d 756 9 Cal. Rptr. 901.

dealing with a savings bank's bylaws as affecting a member's status, see the footnote.[93]

One who subscribes for stock in a savings and loan company is not a creditor of the company, but a shareholder or member.[94] With respect to such a company, provisions in the articles of association and stock certificate for withdrawals, do not apply to withdrawals made before the maturity of shares, nor to the rights of certificate holders after maturity.[95] Thus, a provision to the effect that, whenever incomes shares of such a company are not withdrawable until after the expiration of a fixed period, a statement thereof must be printed on the face of the share certificate, limits not merely the certificate holder's right to withdraw, but the company's power to prevent withdrawal after the stated period. But such a provision does not require that the truth or falsity of such statement be determined by the holder at his peril after an examination of the articles of association.[96] On the other

---

Rights of membership did not descend.—Where a savings bank was structured upon the concept of member-depositor and its bylaws as amended provided that no one should be a member whose account was once closed, membership terminated upon the dosing of the account prior to amendment and rights did not descend. Jacob v. Hibernia Bank, 186 Cal. App. 2d 756, 9 Cal. Rptr. 901.

[93] Amendment, in 1868, to bylaw of bank, incorporated in 1864, providing that no one should be a member whose account was once closed was not unreasonable in severance of narrow right, if any, of parties who paid entrance fee to preceding savings and loan society incorporated in 1859 to redeposit in 1864 corporation. Spencer v. Hibernia Bank, 186 Cal. App. 2d 702, 9 Cal. Rptr. 867.

Under 1882 statute permitting savings and loan associations to incorporate as savings banks and including among corporate powers authority to make bylaws with respect to time and manner in which any person may become, or cease to be, a member of the corporation, legislature validly empowered board of directors of savings bank to sever right of descendibility of membership in bank. Spencer v. Hibernia Bank, 186 Cal. App. 2d 702, 9 Cal. Rptr. 867.

Where bylaws provided that all persons, who were members of savings and loan society, incorporated in 1859, on stated day in 1864, would be deemed members of new bank corporation and that other persons might be allowed to become members by vote of board of directors, it was not intended to create two classes of membership or to permit descendibility of membership and successors in interest of members of society could not claim interest in bank on basis that interest descended to them. Spencer v. Hibernia Bank, 186 Cal. App. 2d 702, 9 Cal. Rptr. 867.

[94] Wallis v. Eagle Sav., etc., Co., 163 N.Y.S. 470.

[95] Wallis v. Eagle Sav., etc., Co., 180 App. Div. 719, 168 N.Y.S. 513.

[96] Figueira v. Eagle Sav., etc., Co., 107 Misc. 101, 176 N.Y.S. 845.

hand, certificates of shares in such company are subject to its articles of association, though the articles differ from recitals in the certificates.[97]

The fact that a statute which attempts to relieve stockholders from personal liability for the debts of savings banks is invalid, leaving in existence such personal liability, does not alter a stockholder's rights as a depositor.[98] And the holder of a savings and loan company's certificate of deposit may sue in equity to recover his deposit and to cancel the certificate on the ground of a misrepresentation on its face as to the terms of withdrawal and notice required, by reason of which he became a member of the company subject to any liabilities of membership.[99] Shareholders of a savings bank had standing to bring derivative claims on behalf of the corporation.[100] Also, a savings bank cannot apply stock belonging to a decedent's estate in payment of his indebtedness to the bank; the decedent's administrator is entitled to the amount of such stock for distribution among creditors generally.[101]

§ 4. Liability of Stockholders.

In General.—Savings banks are creatures of the legislature which may impose any liability it pleases on their stockholders.[102] But a constitutional provision relating to the liability of stockholders in a "banking corporation or institution" was held applicable only to banks of issue and not to savings banks.[103]

Additional Liability of Stockholders.—In some states an additional liability for the benefit of creditors is imposed by statute on the stockholders of a savings bank if it becomes insolvent.[104] This additional liability depends

---

[97] Wallis v. Eagle Sav., etc., Co., 163 N.Y.S. 470.

[98] Murphy v. Pacific Bank, 119 Cal. 334, 51 P. 317.

[99] Figueira v. Eagle Sav., etc., Co., 107 Misc. 101, 176 N.Y.S. 845.

[100] Slattery v. United States, 35 Fed. Cl. 180 (1996).

[101] Merchants' Bank of Easton v. Shouse, 102 Pa. 488.

The lien given by the general banking act of Pennsylvania applies to banks of issue only. Merchant's Bank of Easton v. Shouse, 102 Pa. 488.

[102] Andrew v. American Sav. Bank, 217 Iowa 447, 252 N.W. 245. See also § 3 of this chapter.

[103] Andrew v. American Sav. Bank, 217 Iowa 447, 252 N.W. 245.

[104] **In general.—**

State v. Savings Bank, 87 Minn. 473, 92 N.W. 403; Conway v. Owensboro Sav., etc., Trust Co., 165 F. 822.

The statutory added liability of savings banks' stockholders is not for benefit of bank,

upon the terms of the statute creating it, and the statute cannot be extended beyond the words used.[105] Such liability is not a penal liability;[106] it establishes a trust fund, so that the creditors of the insolvent bank may sue to have the trust administered in equity without first obtaining a judgment at law on their demands.[107]

Depositors in a savings bank, whose deposits are payable within a certain time after demand and bear such interest as the bank's directors may determine, where the bank's profits, less such interest payments, belong to its stockholders, are creditors to whom the stockholders are liable.[108] And a statute relating to liabilities "accruing" while stockholders remain such means liabilities incurred during such period; thus, a savings bank stockholder was liable to assessment for the benefit of unpaid holders of certificates of deposit issued while he was a stockholder, although he later sold his stock.[109]

Effect of Limited Liability Clause.—A provision in the constitution of a savings-fund society that only the joint fund shall be liable for the debts of

---

which have no interest in nor right to enforce it, but exists for banks' creditors only, and is not available unless bank becomes insolvent. Andrew v. Bronson Sav. Bank, 221 Iowa 98, 265 N.W. 113.

Renewal of charter.—

Where savings bank charter providing that stockholders should be individually liable for debts of company in proportion to amount of stock held by each was renewed with provision that it was renewed as to all parts not in conflict with constitution and laws, stockholder of bank on liquidation held not liable for assessment greater than 100 per centum of his stockholdings in bank. Gormley v. Hart, 54 Ga. App. 373, 188 S.E. 66.

Stockholders have no right to set off against their statutory added liability their deposits in a closed savings bank when it closed or collections made and retained by bank on securities owned by them. Andrew v. Bronson Sav. Bank, 221 Iowa 98, 265 N.W. 113.

Sums paid into savings bank by its shareholders in nature of stock assessments on banking superintendent's demand to restore bank's impaired capital while it was going concern cannot be credited on or set off against their statutory added liability after bank closed, whether payments were coercive or purely voluntary, though money was used by bank to pay depositors. Andrew v. Bronson Sav. Bank, 221 Iowa 98, 265 N.W. 113.

[105] Jones v. Rankin, 19 N.M. 56, 140 P. 1120.

Statute construed to impose no individual liability on stockholders in a savings bank, for the debts of such a bank, where the original subscribers have paid the full par value for the stock. Jones v. Rankin, 19 N.M. 56, 140 P. 1120.

[106] Queenan v. Palmer, 117 Ill. 619, 7 N.E. 613.

[107] Conway v. Owensboro Sav., etc., Trust Co., 165 F. 822. See vol. 2, ch.5, § 53.

[108] Wells v. Black, 117 Cal. 157, 48 P. 1090, 59 Am. St. R. 162, 37 L.R.A. 619.

[109] Andrew v. American Sav. Bank, 217 Iowa 447, 252 N.W. 245.

the society, and no creditor shall have recourse to the separate property of any member, will not relieve the society members from personal liability for money received upon special deposit where the certificates of deposit are without limitation as to personal liability. This is so notwithstanding the fact that such depositor was formerly a member of the society.[110]

Defenses.—In a suit by a depositor against a stockholder of a savings bank on his individual liability, it is a good defense that prior to the commencement of the suit, the stockholder has discharged his obligation by paying other depositors an amount equal to the full proportion his stock bears to the total amount due all depositors. But if such payment is not made until after the suit is begun, it is no defense.[111] Where a state's general incorporation statute contains no provision for capital stock, and the stockholders of a banking corporation organized under the law have no voice in the management of its affairs, they cannot be held to a double liability.[112] And it has been held that where the stock of a savings bank greatly exceeds its debts and remains wholly unpaid, the double liability of the bank's stockholders cannot be enforced.[113] Where a petition is filed by a savings bank's assignee for the benefit of creditors against its stockholders for unpaid assessments, and the court, in accordance with the petition, orders an assessment, it is error to hold that when the stockholders deny liability on grounds other than want of notice, they are not entitled to notice.[114] On the other hand, a creditor proceeding to enforce the secondary liability of a savings bank's stockholders is not chargeable with knowledge that the bank has not complied with the law and paid up half its capital stock because he was informed that certain stockholders gave notes for their subscription, where it did not appear that such creditor knew that the notes represented the entire stock subscription.[115]

III. OFFICERS AND AGENTS.

§ 5. General Considerations.

Eligibility for Office.—Where the charter of a savings institution provides that no director or officer of a bank of circulation or deposit shall be eligible

[110] Beaver v. McGrath, 50 Pa. 479.

[111] Jones v. Wiltberger, 42 Ga. 575.

[112] State v. Savings Bank, 87 Minn. 473, 92 N.W. 403.

[113] Herron v. Vance, 17 Ind. 595.

[114] Franklin Sav. Bank v. Fatzinger (Pa.), 4 A. 912, 8 Sadler 21.

[115] Dickason v. Grafton Sav. Bank Co., 17 Ohio Cir. Dec. 357.

to act as trustee or officer of the institution, a director of a bank of circulation and deposit who has allowed himself to be voted an officer of the institution, will be presumed to have thereby resigned as director of the bank, and therefore is eligible for the office.[116]

The grandfather clause contained in the banking law section prohibiting a person from serving as trustee of a savings bank if that person's child is one of the five highest paid salaried officers of the bank applied to an individual who was a trustee on the date specified, even though his son's employment as one of the five highest paid salaried officers of the savings bank did not commence until some time thereafter.[117]

Elections.—Savings banks and societies may choose their own officers like other corporations.[118] Where the charter of a savings institution requires the vote of a majority of the trustees present to elect an officer, and at a meeting of twelve trustees, six votes are cast for one person, four for another and one for another, with one trustee refusing to vote, no officer is elected.[119]

Term of Office.—Under a statute providing that the trustees of a savings bank shall be chosen annually, and shall appoint a treasurer who shall hold office during their pleasure, the office of treasure is not an annual one.[120] And where a savings bank's bylaw provides that "the attorney shall hold office at the pleasure of the trustees," the appointment of an attorney for one year is insufficient to constitute a contract of employment for that term.[121]

An employee's wrongful discharge claim against a federal mutual savings bank was preempted by federal banking law; the regulation stating that the exercise of authority by the Office of Thrift Supervision preempted state law incorporated a second regulation authorizing the termination of employees via third a regulation which stated that a federal savings association could enter into contracts with employees in accordance with the second regulation.[122]

Compensation.—The compensation of an attorney for a savings bank, consisting of various sums paid from time to time for the examination of the

---

[116] People v. Conklin (N.Y.), 7 Hun 188.

[117] Oneida Sav. Bank v. Tese, 485 N.Y.S.2d 614 (N.Y.A.D. 3 Dep't 1985).

[118] Society for Sav. v. Coite, 73 U.S. (6 Wall.) 594, 18 L. Ed. 897; Provident Inst. v. Massachusetts, 73 U.S. (6 Wall.) 611, 18 L. Ed. 907. See vol. 1, ch. 3, § 88.

[119] People v. Conklin (N.Y.), 7 Hun 188.

[120] Rebadow v. Buffalo Sav. Bank, 63 Misc. 407, 117 N.Y.S. 282.

[121] Rebadow v. Buffalo Sav. Bank, 63 Misc. 407, 117 N.Y.S. 282.

[122] Weber v. First Fed. Bank, 523 N.W.2d 720 (S.D. 1994).

title to securities of applicants for loans from the bank, is in no sense a "salary," as that word means "a fixed sum to be paid by the year or periodically for services."[123] And an attorney for a savings bank, having rendered valuable services, is entitled to recover the difference between his actual expenses and the statutory limit placed on such expenses, where the amount he was to receive brought the total beyond such limit.[124] Where the compensation of an officer of a savings bank is made contingent upon its net profits, and the bank holds government bonds which rise in value, but which the bank does not propose to sell, such increase in value is not a "profit."[125]

Right to Participate in Assets Upon Dissolution.—The trustees, directors or officers of a mutual savings bank are not precluded from having an account in the bank or from participating in the same manner and to the same extent as its other members in its assets remaining upon dissolution of the bank.[126]

§ 6. Duties and Liabilities.

In General.—The officers and agents of a savings bank are required to exercise reasonable care in the performance of their duties, and a depositor has the right to expect that they will, in the management of his property, exercise the same degree of care that men prompted by self interest generally exercise in their own affairs.[127] But such officers and agents are not liable for honest errors of judgment made while acting with ordinary skill and prudence, measured according to the demands of the duties or business which they have taken upon themselves.[128]

---

[123] Rebadow v. Buffalo Sav. Bank, 63 Misc. 407, 117 N.Y.S. 282.

As to compensation of attorney generally, see vol. 1, ch. 3, § 88

[124] Gibbs v. Knickerbocker Sav., etc., Co., 166 App. Div. 517, 152 N.Y.S. 4, appeal denied, 168 App. Div. 954, 153 N.Y.S. 1116.

[125] Jennery v. Olmstead (N.Y.), 36 Hun 536, aff'd, 105 N.Y. 654, 13 N.E. 926.

[126] In re Cleveland Savings Soc'y (Ohio Ct. Com. Pleas), 25 Ohio Op. 2d 402, 192 N.E.2d 518 (1961), appeal dismissed, 183 N.E.2d 234.

[127] **In general.—**

Liffiton v. National Sav. Bank, 267 App. Div. 32, 44 N.Y.S.2d 770, aff'g, 38 N.Y.S.2d 822, aff'd, 293 N.Y. 799, 59 N.E.2d 35.

Officers were chargeable with knowledge which proper inquiry would have disclosed where they had facts before them which should have aroused their suspicion and put them on their guard if they had exercised ordinary care. Liffiton v. National Sav. Bank, 267 App. Div. 32, 44 N.Y.S.2d 770, aff'g 38 N.Y.S.2d 822, aff'd, 293 N.Y. 799, 59 N.E.2d 35.

[128] Liffiton v. National Sav. Bank, 267 App. Div. 32, 44 N.Y.S.2d 770, aff'g 38 N.Y.S.2d 822, aff'd, 293 N.Y. 799, 59 N.E.2d 35. See Greenfield Sav. Bank v. Abercrombie,

The failure of a savings bank was not a "change of control event" under the bank employee's employment contract and, thus, the bank employee had no claim against the Federal Deposit Insurance Corporation as receiver for payment of additional benefits under the employment contract.[129]

Trustees, Directors or Managers in General.—Trustees of a savings association occupy a fiduciary relation toward its depositors,[130] and like trustees of specific trust property they must exercise good faith and sound discretion as understood by reasonable men of wise judgment.[131] While trustees are not personally liable for honest mistakes of judgment,[132] they will be held liable on a showing that a loss resulted from their failure to exercise ordinary skill, care, and vigilance.[133] And the trustees of a savings bank are also responsible for the acts of the officers whom they place and retain in positions.[134] Under the provisions of certain statutes, a savings bank is exclusively under the management and control of its board of trustees,[135] and the trustees are prohibited from becoming sureties for money loaned by their bank.[136]

---

211 Mass. 252, 97 N.E. 897, 39 L.R.A. (n.s.) 173, 1913B Ann. Cas. 420.

129 Winters v. FDIC, 812 F. Supp. 1 (D. Me. 1992).

130 Dickson v. Baker, 75 Minn. 168, 77 N.W. 820, 74 Am. St. R. 447; Cosmopolitan Trust Co. v. Mitchell, 242 Mass. 95, 136 N.E. 403.

Trustees and officers of mutual savings bank owed fiduciary duty to depositors. In re Corporators of Portsmouth Sav. Bank, 525 A.2d 671 (N.H. 1987).

131 Cosmopolitan Trust Co. v. Mitchell, 242 Mass. 95, 136 N.E. 403; Greenfield Sav. Bank v. Abercrombie, 211 Mass. 252, 97 N.E. 897, 39 L.R.A. (n.s.) 173, 1913B Ann. Cas. 420.

132 Greenfield Sav. Bank v. Abercrombie, 211 Mass. 252, 97 N.E. 897, 39 L.R.A. (n.s.)173, 1913B Ann. Cas. 420. See Liffiton v. National Sav. Bank, 267 App. Div. 32, 44 N.Y.S.2d 770, aff'g 38 N.Y.S.2d 822, aff'd, 293 N.Y. 799, 59 N.E.2d 35.

133 Greenfield Sav. Bank v. Abercrombie, 211 Mass. 252, 97 N.E. 897, 39 L.R.A. (n.s.) 173, 1913B Ann. Cas. 420.

134 Paine v. Irwin (N.Y.), 59 How. Pr. 316.

A transaction entered upon the books of a savings bank, although made by the bank officers, is presumed to have been done with the knowledge and assent of the trustees.

Paine v. Irwin (N.Y.), 59 How. Pr. 316.

135 Congregation & Talmud Torah Sons of Israel v. Harlem Sav. Bank, 48 N.Y.S.2d 882 (1944) (applying New York Banking Law).

136 Best v. Thiel, 79 N.Y. 15.

A trustee of a savings bank, who, to make up a deficiency in its assets, caused by a loss on a loan made by it, executes a mortgage to a party that assigns the same to the bank, does not thereby become a surety or obligor for money loaned by the bank within the statute

It is said that directors of savings banks also stand in the position of trustees to their depositors,[137] and must use due care in the management of the banks' affairs.[138] Thus, the directors of a savings bank are personally liable to its depositors for maladministration of their office,[139] and for improper care of deposits, even though they are ignorant of a fraud in the bank's organization.[140] And where the directors of a savings bank for nearly forty years did not require its treasurer to furnish any trial balance or its auditors to take one, their negligence will be deemed the proximate cause of the defalcations of the treasurer.[141]

The managers of a savings institution are similarly trustees of a public franchise, granted to and held by them for the benefit of the public, especially for that part of the public in the immediate neighborhood of the institution, as well as for its depositors.[142] Such managers are liable for the want of ordinary care and diligence in the management of their bank, and the fact that they are unpaid will not relieve them from this liability.[143] Thus, such managers are liable if they participate in or promote prohibited acts which lead to loss, or if they fail to give their bank's affairs that measure of care which the law requires, in consequence of which their associates are enabled to do acts causing loss.[144]

---

prohibiting a trustee from becoming such surety. Best v. Thiel, 79 N.Y. 15.

[137] **In general.—**

Peterborough Sav. Bank v. King, 103 N.H. 206, 168 A.2d 116.

A bank which allows a stated interest on deposits is not a savings bank, in the sense that the directors are trustees, and hold to the depositors a relation of confidence and trust. Colorado Sav. Bank v. Evans, 12 Colo. App. 334, 56 P. 981.

[138] Peterborough Sav. Bank v. King, 103 N.H. 206, 168 A.2d 116 (including loan policies).

The high degree of care required of bank directors should not be relaxed in the case of directors of a savings bank. Lippitt v. Ashley, 89 Conn. 451, 94 A. 995.

[139] Maisch v. Saving Fund, 5 Phila. (Pa.) 30.

But the directors of such a society, who never took their seats on the board, and against whom the depositors do not allege any knowledge of frauds, are not personally liable for maladministration. Maisch v. Saving Fund, 5 Phila. (Pa.) 30.

[140] Leffman v. Flanigan, 5 Phila. (Pa.) 155.

[141] Lippitt v. Ashley, 89 Conn. 451, 94 A. 995.

[142] Barrett v. Bloomfield Sav. Inst., 64 N.J. Eq. 425, 54 A. 543, aff'd, 66 N.J. Eq. 431, 57 A. 1131.

[143] Williams v. McKay, 40 N.J. Eq. 189, 53 Am. R. 775.

[144] Wilkinson v. Dodd, 40 N.J. Eq. 123, 3 A. 360, aff'd, 41 N.J. Eq. 566, 7 A. 337;

Losses on Loans and Investments.—The trustees, directors, managers or other responsible officers of a savings bank who make loans or invest the funds of the bank in a manner contrary to law, or in a manner prohibited by the charter of the bank or the act under which it is incorporated, are personally liable for losses resulting from such loans or investments.[145] As regards those bank managers not individually concerned in unlawful loans, the primary liability is on the members of the bank's executive committee; for money taken by the bank's president from the bank without security on a check signed by himself and its treasurer, the order of liability is: (1) The president; (2) the treasurer; (3) the executive committee and (4) all

---

Wilkinson v. Dodd, 42 N.J. Eq. 234, 7 A. 327, aff'd, 42 N.J. Eq. 647, 9 A. 685; Williams v. McDonald, 42 N.J. Eq. 892, 7 A. 866; Williams v. McKay, 46 N.J. Eq. 25, 18 A. 824.

While the managers could appoint officers and committees to conduct the affairs of the bank, they were bound to such circumspection of the actions of such officers and committees as a reasonably prudent man would exercise in his own business, and were liable for losses occasioned by the omission of such circumspection. Williams v. McKay, 46 N.J. Eq. 25, 18 A. 824.

[145] **In general.—**

Knapp v. Roche, 44 N.Y. Super. Ct 247, rev'd on other grounds, 94 N.Y. 329.

Loans not permitted by act of incorporation.—

Knapp v. Roche, 44 N.Y. Super. Ct 247, rev'd on other grounds, 94 N.Y. 329.

Loan to president on insufficient security.—

Williams v. McKay, 46 N.J. Eq. 25, 18 A. 824.

Loan to one person of sum greater than that allowed by statute.—

Thompson v. Greeley, 107 Mo. 577, 17 S.W. 962 (1891); Thompson v. Swain, 107 Mo. 594, 17 S.W. 967; Greenfield Sav. Bank v. Abercrombie, 211 Mass. 252, 97 N.E. 897, 39 L.R.A. (n.s.) 173, 1913B Ann. Cas. 420.

Loans upon insufficient security to corporation in which trustee is stockholder.—

Paine v. Irwin (N.Y.), 59 How. Pr. 316.

Ultra vires loan for which all trustees are personally liable.—

Paine v. Barnum (N.Y.), 59 How. Pr. 303.

Investments in contravention of charter and bylaws.—

Williams v. McKay, 46 N.J. Eq. 25, 18 A. 824.

Investment in mortgage on real estate prohibited by charter.—

Williams v. McDonald, 42 N.J. Eq. 392, 7 A. 866; Williams v. Riley, 34 N.J. Eq. 398.

Investments by means of checks signed in blank—secondary liability.—

Williams v. McKay, 46 N.J. Eq. 25, 18 A. 824.

Purchase of valueless paper of another bank.—

Rice v. Howard, 136 Cal. 432, 69 P. 77, 89 Am. St. R. 153.

managers.[146] Where a savings bank's manager or responsible officer knows of an irregular or unlawful loan and acquiesces in it, he will be liable for the losses occasioned thereby.[147] And such managers cannot avoid responsibility for losses occasioned by prohibited investments upon the grounds that they did not have the time or ability to perform their duties and did not know of such investments, or upon the ground that they believed the investments to be legal, even if it appears that their belief arose from misconstruing the bank's charter.[148] But for losses sustained by reason of a savings bank president's releasing securities for a loan to one of its managers, so as to reduce the security below the lawful limit without authority from the bank's board of managers, the president and manager only are liable, it not appearing that any of the other managers knew of such release.[149]

Even though a savings bank's directors are ignorant of the affairs of the bank, and are not guilty of bad faith, they are liable to its depositors for losses resulting from their gross negligence.[150] But such a director will not be held liable to indemnify his bank against a loss resulting from a mortgage investment where he acted in good faith for the benefit of the bank with ordinary care and prudence.[151]

---

[146] Williams v. McKay, 46 N.J. Eq. 25, 18 A. 824.

[147] **In general.—**

Paine v. Barnum (N.Y.), 59 How. Pr. 303.

For losses occasioned by loans made by the president, habitually and continually, in disregard of the charter and bylaws, and not interfered with by the managers, all managers in office at the time of the making of the loan are liable. Paine v. Barnum (N.Y.), 59 How. Pr. 303.

But they are not liable for the loss of the first of such loans, made a year or more before the others, as it could not reasonably have been anticipated. Paine v. Barnum (N.Y.), 59 How. Pr. 303.

Loans by bookkeeper without knowledge of trustee.—

A trustee is not personally liable for prohibited loans made by the bookkeeper where he had no knowledge thereof. Knapp v. Roche, 44 N.Y. Super. Ct 247, rev'd on other grounds, 94 N.Y. 329.

[148] Williams v. McKay, 46 N.J. Eq. 25, 18 A. 824.

[149] Williams v. McKay, 46 N.J. Eq. 25, 18 A. 824.

[150] Marshall v. Farmers' & Mechanics Sav. Bank, 85 Va. 676, 8 S.E. 586, 17 Am. St R. 84, 2 L.R.A. 534, overruled on another point, Williams v. Fidelity Loan & Sav. Co., 142 Va. 43, 128 S.E. 615, 45 A.L.R. 664.

[151] Williams v. McDonald, 37 N.J. Eq. 409, rev'd on other grounds, 42 N.J. Eq. 392, 7 A. 866.

A savings bank trustee may be released from liability for an illegal investment on payment of the resulting loss by a subsequent trustee.[152]

A senior savings bank officer who was allegedly discharged for violating bank's code of conduct with respect to family loans was not similarly situated to employee who was involved in processing offending loans but was not disciplined, for purposes of establishing ERISA discrimination claim based on disparate treatment; employee had only been working at bank for less than one year and was unable to approve loans, while officer had been working for bank for 16 years and had authority to approve loans.[153]

Paying Unearned Dividends or Interest.—The question has arisen whether the trustees of a savings bank are jointly and severally liable for payment of unearned dividends or interest under a resolution declaring dividends which is passed with their concurrence or subsequent approval.[154] But in any case, where the directors of a bank who are not negligent assent to the payment of illegal dividends in ignorance of the bank's true condition, they are not liable for any loss resulting therefrom.[155]

Improvidence and Reckless Extravagance.—The trustees of a savings bank are personally liable for losses resulting from their improvidence and reckless extravagance.[156] And the unauthorized withdrawal of a bank's property by its treasurer by the negotiation of its own binding check based

---

[152] Hun v. Van Dyck (N.Y.), 26 Hun 567, aff'd, 92 N.Y. 660.

[153] Employee Retirement Income Security Act of 1974, § 510, 29 U.S.C.S. § 1140. Benham v. Lenox Sav. Bank, 118 F. Supp. 2d 132 (D. Mass. 2000).

Senior savings bank officer who was allegedly discharged for violating bank's code of conduct with respect to family loans was similarly situated with other bank officers who were involved in processing offending loans, did not follow bank policy, but were not disciplined for their actions, for purposes of establishing ERISA discrimination claim based on disparate treatment; officers held similar positions of seniority and authority and had similar powers to accept or reject loan applications. Employee Retirement Income Security Act of 1974, § 510, 29 U.S.C.S. § 1140. Benham v. Lenox Sav. Bank, 118 F. Supp. 2d 132 (D. Mass. 2000)

[154] Van Dyck v. McQuade, 57 How. Pr. 62, aff'd, 45 N.Y. Super. Ct. 620, rev'd, 86 N.Y. 38 (1881).

If a trustee votes for a dividend less than the whole amount of interest or profits earned, without any deduction therefrom for expenses, although the earnings have not been actually received, he does not, in the absence of fraud or bad faith, overstep his statutory duty, and he is not liable to the penalty. Van Dyck v. McQuade, 57 How. Pr. 62, aff'd, 45 N.Y. Super. Ct. 620, rev'd on other grounds, 86 N.Y. 38 (1881).

[155] Lippitt v. Ashley, 89 Conn. 451, 94 A. 995.

[156] Hun v. Cary, 82 N.Y. 65, 59 How. Pr. 439, 37 Am. H. 546.

on the receipt of a check known not to be good, is a misapplication of property; in such a case, it is immaterial that there was no intent to defraud and that no loss resulted.[157]

Liability for Another's Misapplication of Funds.—Where the directors of a savings bank act with ordinary diligence in the employment of a cashier, but are deceived by a systematic and ingenious statement of false accounts, they are not liable to the bank's stockholders for his misapplication of the bank's funds; to render such directors liable, fraud or willful neglect of duty must be shown.[158] But the fact that a bank's directors fully discharge their duty in all other respects does not excuse them from the duty of exercising reasonable oversight and supervision over the bank treasurer's conduct of his office.[159]

Liability for Doing Nothing in Execution of Corporate Power.—Trustees who qualify under a statute for the establishment of savings banks, and do nothing in the execution of the corporate power, but under a corporate name do a general banking business, loan money at interest and give certificates of deposit signed by a cashier, are personally liable on such certificates, and are not shielded from liability by the mere existence of the corporate agency.[160] The failure of directors of a bank to require trial balances for a period of forty years is negligence, and reports by private auditors and the bank commissioners as to the condition of the bank made up by the bank's treasurer, which on their face showed that no trial balances had been taken, do not justify the directors in failing to require trial balances.[161]

Receiving Commission or Benefit from Loan.—A savings bank trustee was not subject to automatic removal under a statute prohibiting a bank trustee from receiving directly or indirectly and retaining any commission or benefit from any loan made by the bank where, even though he received a benefit when he inadvertently voted on a mortgage application for the purchasers of property on which his wife would receive a commission, he did not retain the benefit in that he gave prompt notice of the conflict before the closing and had the commission placed in escrow.[162]

---

[157] Commonwealth v. Nichols, 257 Mass. 289, 153 N.E. 787.

[158] Dunn v. Kyle, 77 Ky. (14 Bush) 134.

[159] Lippitt v. Ashley, 89 Conn. 451, 94 A. 995.

[160] Ridenour v. Mayo, 40 Ohio St. 9.

[161] Lippitt v. Ashley, 89 Conn. 451, 94 A. 995.

[162] Devane v. Troy Sav. Bank, 475 N.Y.S.2d 540 (N.Y.A.D. 3 Dep't 1984).

Method of Determining Liability.—The liability of individual members of a board of directors charged with mismanagement of the affairs of a savings fund society will be determined by the aid of a master appointed to inquire as to whose default occasioned the loss.[163] And whether a bank director is guilty of negligence is not, as in the case of an ordinary individual, a question of fact, but depends upon whether the director has exercised the care required of those holding such position.[164]

Method of Enforcing Liability.—The mode of enforcing the liability of trustees and officers of savings banks is prescribed by statute in some states.[165] A bill brought by a bank commissioner in possession of a savings bank against the officers and trustees of the bank is sufficient to charge them with personal liability if it alleges the making of loans in contravention of statute, acceptance of insufficient security and negligence of the officers in so doing; in such a case, it is not necessary to allege the amount of the officers' compensation or to negative any excuse than the defendants might be able to set up for their illegal acts.[166] But, a declaration in an action against savings bank directors to recover a deposit on the ground that such directors willfully and negligently failed to perform their duties, resulting in the insolvency of the bank and the appointment of a receiver, is demurrable where it does not allege that the bank's receiver had been requested to bring the action and refused to do so.[167]

Prosecutions.[168]—An indictment under a statute which fixes punishment for any officer or employee of a bank who knowingly subscribes or makes any false statement with the intent to deceive any person authorized to examine the bank's condition, charging generally that a false statement was made to the directors of a bank, is demurrable if the directors were not among the persons authorized by the statute to examine the bank's condition.[169] In the prosecution of an officer of a savings bank, it is not error to give an instruction as to the interpretation to be given to the words

---

[163] Leffman v. Flanigan, 5 Phila. (Pa.) 155.

[164] Lippitt v. Ashley, 89 Conn. 451, 94 A. 995.

[165] Ryan v. Ray, 105 Ind. 101, 4 N.E. 214.

[166] Greenfield Sav. Bank v. Abercrombie, 211 Mass. 252, 97 N.E. 897, 39 L.R.A. (n.s.) 173, 1913B Ann. Cas. 420. See also § 34 of this chapter.

[167] Hardin v. McKnight, 107 Miss. 73, 64 So. 965. See also § 34 of this chapter.

[168] See also § 258 at seq. of ch. 3.

[169] State v. Henderson, 135 Iowa 499, 113 N.W. 328.

"willfully misapply."[170] And whether in the exchange of a savings bank's checks there was a misapplication of the bank's property is a question for the jury.[171]

§ 7. Representation of Bank by Officers and Agents.

In General.—The powers which the executive officers of savings banks and like institutions have, merely by virtue of their office, unenlarged by vote of the trustees or bank bylaws, are very limited.[172] However, in some jurisdictions, statutes grant them special powers such as the power to pledge assets to secure a savings bank's obligations without authorization from its board of directors.[173]

President.—The president of a savings bank has authority to receive deposits, issue certificates of deposit,[174] and negotiate commercial paper with other banks.[175] Where the directors of a bank which holds shares of stock in another corporation as collateral security for a debt, authorize the bank's president to sell such shares for the best interests of the bank, the president has authority to employ a broker to sell the shares on a stock exchange.[176] But a savings bank president has no authority, merely by virtue of his office, to borrow money on behalf of the bank,[177] agree to convey its

---

170 Commonwealth v. Nichols, 257 Mass. 289, 153 N.E. 787. See also § 36 of this chapter.

171 Commonwealth v. Nichols, 257 Mass. 289, 153 N.E. 787. See also § 36 of this chapter

172 Slattery v. North End Sav. Bank, 175 Mass. 380, 56 N.E. 606.

173 Bates v. First Sav. Bank, 219 Iowa 1358, 261 N.W. 797.

174 Scow v. Farmers', etc., Sav. Bank, 136 Iowa 1, 111 N.W. 32.

Where a bank authorize, the establishment of a savings department, paying interest to depositors, and no particular official is charged with the management thereof, if the president holds himself out to others.

In control thereof, and such others deposit their money with him as in charge of such savings department, the bank is liable therefor. Bickley v. Commercial Bank, 43 S.C. 528, 21 S.E. 886.

175 Carroll v. Corning State Sav. Bank, 139 Iowa 338, 115 N.W. 937 (1908).

Where a savings bank clothes its president, who is its chief executive officer, with apparent authority to represent it in transacting business appropriate to the proper discharge of its corporate functions, it is bound by his dealings in negotiating commercial paper with another bank, though he appropriated the proceeds to his own use, where the other bank was acting in good faith and without notice of his want of fidelity in the discharge of his duties. State ex rel. Carroll v. Corning State Sav. Bank, 139 Iowa 338 (1908), 115 N.W. 937.

176 Sistare v. Best, 88 N.Y. 527, aff'g 24 Hun. 384.

177 Fifth Ward Sav. Bank v. First Nat. Bank, 47 N.J.L. 357, 1 A. 478.

real property,[178] or represent the bank in such matters as may arise in connection with building loans.[179]

Vice-President.—A savings bank's customer who is induced by the bank's vice-president to leave his deposit in the bank by an offer to pay increased interest, is not guilty of fraud, although the vice-president's action is not authorized by the bank's directors, since a bank customer has the right to believe that a transaction of the managing officer at the bank's counter is proper.[180]

Treasurer.—The treasurer of a savings bank has authority to extend a note from time to time by receiving interest in advance.[181] Such treasurer also has power to collect the debts of his bank, and under orders of the bank's board of investment, execute a power of sale of a mortgage to the bank by conveying to the purchaser, and the bank's acceptance of the purchaser's deed of release ratifies the treasurer's act.[182] There is a presumption that treasurer has authority, on behalf of his bank, to take possession of land on which the bank holds a mortgage for the purpose of gathering growing crops.[183] He also has the authority to pay off a mortgage indebtedness assumed by his bank.[184]*And* if a bank's trustees vote to authorize its

---

[178] Institution for Sav. v. Brookline, 220 Mass. 300, 107 N.E. 939.

The president has no authority to offer to convey to a town the fee in a private way over property owned by the bank. Institution for Sav. v. Brookline, 220 Mass. 300, 107 N.E. 939.

Under provisions of the Banking Law, a savings bank is exclusively under the management and control of its board of trustees, and the president of such bank, unless authorized so to do by the trustees, cannot bind the bank to sell any real property owned by it. Congregation & Talmud Torah Sons of Israel v. Harlem Sav. Bank, 48 N.Y.S.2d 882 (1944).

[179] Slattery v. North End Sav. Bank, 175 Mass. 380, 56 N.E. 606.

[180] Murray v. First Trust, etc., Bank, 201 Iowa 1325, 207 N.W. 781 (1926).

[181] New Hampshire Sav. Bank v. Ela, 11 N.H. 335.

In such case the effect of the extension in releasing the surety on the note cannot be avoided by the bank, notwithstanding the treasurer had no authority to discharge the surety. New Hampshire Sav. Bank v. Ela, 11 N.H. 335.

[182] North Brookfield Sav. Bank v. Flanders, 161 Mass. 335, 37 N.E. 307.

[183] Bangor Sav. Bank v. Wallace, 87 Me. 28, 32 A. 716.

[184] Sherry v. Wakefield Inst., 21 R.I. 162, 42 A. 268.

Complainant was to pay an incumbrance on property conveyed to him. He subsequently executed to the grantor a mortgage of the property, with a verbal agreement that the amount paid by him on the prior incumbrance was to be deducted from the amount due on the mortgage. He arranged with a bank for a loan on the property, whereby it was agreed that the bank should pay off all prior incumbrances, making its mortgage a first lien. The bank, through its treasurer, paid the grantor's mortgage, without making any deduction for the prior

treasurer to assign mortgages held by the bank, such vote is not ultra vires as to a person who, in good faith and for a valuable consideration, takes an assignment of a mortgage from the treasurer.[185] But the fact that treasurer, by verbal consent and under the direction of his bank's investment committee, has assigned mortgages relating to estates, does not give him a general authority to assign mortgages, nor does it entitle an assignee to infer that he has such authority.[186] And if an assignment by a bank's treasurer is defectively executed, a court of equity may correct it.[187]

Where the treasurer of a savings bank who is also trustee and a member of its financial committee, is entrusted by the bank with the duty of selling its property, he acts as agent of the bank, and is bound to the degree of diligence and good faith which should govern the conduct of agents generally. He cannot, by claiming to act as trustee and a member of the finance committee, escape liability to the bank if he sells the property for less than the best price that might have been obtained.[188]

The treasurer of a savings bank is not, by virtue of his office, invested with the power of borrowing money for the bank and pledging its securities as collateral.[189] Nor has he, by virtue of his office only, implied authority to transfer to a purchaser a promissory note belonging to the bank,[190] or bind the bank by indorsing its name on a promissory note.[191] But a treasurer's authority to indorse a note for his bank may be inferred from the conduct of the bank's trustees without any express direction or vote.[192] However, such

incumbrance. The treasurer, subsequently learning that a mistake had been made, continued to receive payments from complainant without giving him notice, and leaving him to suppose that he was paying the full interest on all mortgage debts on his property, until the grantor became insolvent, whereby he lost his chance for recovery against him. Held that, as the treasurer was acting in the line of his employment, complainant was entitled to an allowance, on an accounting between him and the bank, for the amount so lost through the treasurer's neglect. Sherry v. Wakefield Inst., 21 R.I. 162, 42 A. 268.

[185] Commonwealth v. Reading Sav. Bank, 137 Mass. 431; Whiting v. Wellington, 10 F. 810.

[186] Holden v. Phelps, 135 Mass. 61.

[187] Commonwealth v. Reading Sav. Bank, 137 Mass. 431.

[188] Greenfield Sav. Bank v. Simons, 133 Mass. 415.

[189] Fifth Ward Sav. Bank v. First Nat'l Bank, 48 N.J.L. 513, 7 A. 318; Commonwealth v. Reading Sav. Bank, 133 Mass. 16, 43 Am. R. 495; Fishkill Sav. Institute v. Bostwick, 19 Hun 354, 80 N.Y. 162, 36 Am. R. 595.

[190] Holden v. Upton, 134 Mass. 177.

[191] Bradlee v. Warren, etc., Sav. Bank, 127 Mass. 107, 34 Am. R. 351.

[192] Chase v. Hathorn, 61 Me. 505.

authority is not conferred by a vote of a savings bank to sell notes held by it; nor is it conferred by a provision in the bank's bylaws that the treasurer "shall draw all necessary papers and discharge all obligations of the corporation, and his signature shall be binding upon the corporation."[193]

In the absence of authority other than that which may be inferred from his office, a treasurer cannot bind his bank by a contract incidental to a building loan made by the bank,[194] by executing a release in the name of the bank,[195] or by the acceptance of an order drawn on the bank.[196] And a savings bank's treasurer may be liable to a third party for misrepresentation of his authority as treasurer to accept an order on his bank for the payment of money; he cannot escape such liability on the ground that he made no direct representation as to his authority to accept the order.[197]

---

[193] Bradlee v. Warren Five Cents Sav. Bank, 127 Mass. 107, 34 Am. R. 351.

[194] Slattery v. North End Sav. Bank, 175 Mass. 380, 56 N.E. 606.

[195] Dedham Inst. v. Slack, 60 Mass. (6 Cush.) 408.

Where the treasurer of an institution for savings became a party to an assignment for the benefit of creditors, and thereby undertook to release one of the promisors on a joint and several note belonging to the institution, but without any authority, either "general or special, for that purpose, and payments of dividends were subsequently made to the treasurer's successor in office, and indorsed on the note, and entered in the books of the institution as so much received of the assignees of such promisor, and the treasurer's accounts and cash, including the sum so received, and the notes of the institution, including the note in question, were subsequently examined by a committee and certified as correct, it was held that these acts did not amount to a ratification of the release. Dedham Inst. v. Slack, 60 Mass. (6 Cush.) 408.

[196] Jewett v. West Somerville Co-Op., 173 Mass. 54, 52 N.E. 1085, 73 Am. St. R. 259.

Such power is not conferred by a statute providing that "all payments made by the corporation for any purpose whatsoever, shall be by order, check or draft upon the treasurer, signed by the treasurer and secretary," and that the "treasurer shall dispose of and secure the safekeeping of all moneys, securities and property of the corporation in the manner designated by the bylaws," where there is no authority therefor in the bylaws. Jewett v. West Somerville Co-Op., 173 Mass. 54, 52 N.E. 1085, 73 Am. St. R. 259.

[197] United States Gypsum Co. v. Carney, 293 Mass. 581, 200 N.E. 283.

The assignee of a bank's order, accepted by its treasurer, to pay money to assignor, was not precluded from relying on treasurer's implied representation of his authority to accept order for bank, though his lack of authority might have been discovered by inspecting bank's records or inquiring of board of investment. United States Gypsum Co. v. Carney, 293 Mass. 581, 200 N.E. 283.

Judge's finding in actions for misrepresentation of defendant's authority as bank treasurer to accept order on bank for payment of money to order of plaintiff's assignor that defendant's acceptance of order was unauthorized, as he knew, held reasonable inference from his official position and acceptance of order for bank; plaintiff having right to assume that bank board of

Cashier.—The cashier of a savings bank has authority to receive a bond on deposit.[198] But he has no authority to draw checks in the name of his bank in favor of persons with whom he has a speculative account, and deposit same with them as margin;[199] in such a case, the bank is entitled to recover back the amount of the checks notwithstanding the payees had no actual knowledge of the cashier's fraud or want of authority.[200] Where the charter of a savings bank provides what shall be requisite to authorize a transfer of securities, a transfer by the bank's cashier without the required authority is not binding on the bank.[201] A savings bank is not a holder of a note without notice of its infirmity, where its cashier knew that the note was obtained from the maker by false representations for shares of stock in an insolvent bank.[202] But a bank cashier, in arranging the transfer of a saving deposit to an estate of which he is administrator in payment of an indebtedness to the estate, is considered to be acting solely in his capacity as administrator.[203]

Clerk.—A savings bank clerk, to whom authority is not given to make agreements outside of the usual course of business of his bank, cannot bind the bank by an agreement that a deposit shall be withdrawn only when the depositor and two particular persons are present.[204]

Estoppel of Bank to Deny Authority.—A savings bank may, upon the principal of estoppel, be precluded from denying the authority of an officer or agent to act for it.[205]

---

investment authorized defendant to sign acceptance in bank's behalf. United States Gypsum Co. v. Carney, 293 Mass. 581, 200 N.E. 283.

[198] Zugner v. Best, 44 N.Y. Super. Ct. 393.

[199] St. Charles Sav. Bank v. Edwards, 243 Mo. 553, 147 S.W. 978.

[200] St. Charles Sav. Bank v. Edwards, 243 Mo. 553, 147 S.W. 978, holding that the burden is on the defendants, in an action by the bank to recover the amount, to show that the checks were authorized, or that the bank had received value therefor.

[201] Zimmerman v. Miller, 2 Pa. 226.

[202] Atchison Sav. Bank v. Potter, 104 Kan. 373, 179 P. 319.

[203] Leach v. Treynor Sav. Bank, 203 Iowa 988, 213 N.W. 601.

[204] Riley v. Albany Sav. Bank (N.Y.), 36 Hun. 513, aff'd, 103 N.Y. 669.

[205] **In general.—**

Commonwealth v. Reading Sav. Bank, 137 Mass. 431.

Estoppel to deny authority of treasurer to assign mortgage.—

A bylaw of a savings bank provided that the record, which it was the duty of the secretary and treasurer to keep, should be held in proof of the votes and transactions of the corporation. The treasurer was authorized by vote to discharge and release mortgages, and he fraudulently altered the record so that it purported to give him authority to assign them also.

Engaging in the Unauthorized Practice of Law.—Where borrowers obtained a mortgage from the lender, the charging of a separate fee for the preparation of the standard mortgage form by the lender for the borrowers did not constitute the unauthorized practice of law under Michigan law. As the lender did not counsel or assist the borrowers in matters requiring legal discretion or profound legal knowledge, the lender did not engage in the practice of law and did not violate the statute.[206]

IV. POWERS IN GENERAL.

§ 8. Power to Choose Officers and Admit New Members.

Like other corporations, savings banks and societies may choose their own officers and admit new members.[207]

§ 9. Power to Contract in General.

It may be stated as a general rule that a savings bank is a corporation with limited powers. Its authority to contract is generally limited by its charter or by statute,[208] and it cannot be held liable upon a contract that is ultra

---

Held, that the bank was liable for his act in assigning a mortgage, the assignee taking for value in good faith, and in reliance on the record. Commonwealth v. Reading Sav. Bank, 137 Mass. 431.

Transfer of stock by treasurer.—

A savings bank treasurer caused certificates of stock belonging to the bank to be transferred to A. and new certificates issued. On the strength of these, he borrowed, In the name of the bank, money from A., which he converted. Held, that the bank could not deny the validity of the transfer and at the same time claim the stock. Holden v. Metropolitan Nat. Bank, 138 Mass. 48.

No estoppel to deny liability for materials purchased.—

Where the president and treasurer of a savings bank made a building loan, took a mortgage on the premises, and retained the proceeds to pay for the materials which it was agreed the bank should purchase at the mortgagor's direction for the completion of the building, it was held that the bank was not estopped to deny its liability for materials so purchased and used, as the building in which the material was used was not one owned by the bank, and the transaction was so far out of the ordinary business of the bank that plaintiff was put on inquiry. Slattery v. North End Sav. Bank, 175 Mass. 380, 56 N.E. 606.

[206] Dressel v. Ameribank, 468 Mich. 557, 664 N.W.2d 151 (2003). See Mich. Comp. Laws § 450.681.

[207] Society for Sav. v. Coite, 73 U.S. (6 Wall.) 594, 18 L. Ed. 897; Provident Institution v. Massachusetts, 73 U.S. (6 Wall.) 611, 18 L. Ed. 907.

[208] **In general.—**

Laidlaw v. Pacific Bank, 87 P. 897, rev'd on rehearing on other grounds, 137 Cal. 392, 70

vires.[209] A savings bank may, however, be precluded upon the principle of estoppel from pleading that a contract into which it has entered is ultra

---

P. 277; Batchelder, etc., Co. v. Saco Sav. Bank, 108 Me. 89, 79 A. 13; Henderson v. Farmers' Sav. Bank, 199 Iowa 496, 202 N.W. 259.

Even if statutory and administrative scheme governing conversion of mutual savings bank to stock corporation had not displaced private rights of action relating to conversion process, account holders were barred from recovering damages on common-law causes of action for breach of fiduciary duty, intentional and negligent misrepresentation, tortious conversion of property, unjust enrichment, and breach of contract in the absence of showing of injury. Lovell v. One Bancorp, 818 F. Supp. 412 (D. Me. 1993).

California statute making it unlawful for a savings bank corporation to contract any debt or liability against the corporation for any purpose whatsoever is to be construed in connection with the statutes which authorize such corporation to purchase a lot and building for its business, and to employ and compensate help, and to incur other expenses, and to do a commercial banking business, buying bonds, securities, etc., and hence the first-mentioned statute does not prevent the bank from incurring any liabilities whatsoever, but only those not authorized by the other legislation mentioned. Laidlaw v. Pacific Bank, 67 P. 897, rev'd on rehearing on other grounds, 137 Cal. 392, 70 P. 277.

Illinois act making it unlawful for savings banks to guarantee bonds of another held not repealed by subsequently enacted sections of general banking act, authorizing formation of savings banks and granting them corporate powers and making limitations on their loans. Hoffman v. Sears Community State Bank, 356 Ill. 598, 191 N.E. 280.

[209] Jemison v. Citizens' Sav. Bank, 122 N.Y. 135, 25 N.E. 264, 19 Am. St. R. 482, 9 L.R.A. 708, aff'g 44 Hun 412; In re Mutual Bldg. Fund Soc., 17 F. Cas. 1075 (No. 9976), 2 Hughes 374.

A savings bank contracted with plaintiff to act as plaintiff's agent at a public sale to take notes of purchasers with approved security, and retain and collect such notes.

Held, that since the contract was ultra vires the bank, and beyond its apparent authority, it was not liable to plaintiff for loss resulting from the negligence of its agent in taking a note on which the indorsement was forged. Willett v. Farmer's Sav. Bank, 107 Iowa 69, 77 N.W. 519.

Contract whereby savings bank agreed to repurchase real estate bonds it sold held unenforceable. Hoffman v. Sears Community State Bank, 356 Ill. 598, 191 N.E. 280.

Agreement between a bank and a member of its Board of Directors to the effect that a loan to the director of a savings bank would not be called for payment until the redemption of debentures which had been issued by the bank to the director and which were pledged as collateral security for the loan had the unlawful object of prepayment of the debentures; thus the agreement was void ab initio and neither the president of the bank nor the Board of Directors had the authority to approve or ratify it. Dominguez v. FDIC, 90 F.R.D. 595 (D.P.R. 1981).

vires.[210] It has been held that the action of certain saving societies in taking over the assets of a savings bank and liquidating it as a matter of self-preservation during a financial crisis without guaranteeing anything was not "ultra vires."[211]

§ 10. Power to Acquire and Sell Property.

A savings bank may acquire title to shares of stock of another corporation, where such stock is taken in compromise or discharge of a debt of an insolvent debtor and no circumstances casting suspicion on the transaction are shown.[212] A savings bank may also be permitted by statute to purchase

---

[210] **In general.—**

Laidlaw v. Pacific Bank, 67 P. 897, rev'd on rehearing on other grounds, 137 Cal. 392, 70 P. 277.

Bank held estopped.—

Where the debt of a creditor of a bank is for money expended for its benefit and at its request, it will not be heard, in an action by the creditor to recover the money, to deny liability on the ground that it could not legally be bound by a contract to pay. Laidlaw v. Pacific Bank, 67 P. 897, rev'd on rehearing on other grounds, 137 Cal. 392, 70 P. 277.

Even if a savings bank has no authority to pay an attorney for examination of titles to securities offered for loans, where the attorney employed for that purpose has performed the services, it cannot plead the invalidity of his employment to avoid paying him. Rebadow v. Buffalo Sav. Bank, 63 Misc. 407, 117 N.Y.S. 282.

The fact that the amount a savings bank agreed to loan on a real estate mortgage was in excess of the amount allowed by statute is a matter to be adjusted between the bank and the state authorities, and does not affect the validity of the agreement as between the parties. Machado v. Bank of Italy, 67 Cal. App. 769, 228 P. 369.

Bank held not estopped.—

In an action by a commission merchant against a savings bank to recover commissions and for money expended for speculating purposes at the bank's direction, the defendant is not estopped from pleading the transaction ultra vires, since it was not only immoral, and in violation of the rights of stockholders and depositors, but the bank received nothing thereby. Jemison v. Citizens' Sav. Bank, 122 N.Y. 135, 25 N.E. 264, 19 Am. St. R. 482, 9 L.R.A. 708, aff'g 44 Hun 412.

[211] Commonwealth v. Philadelphia Sav. Fund Soc., 335 Pa. 406, 6 A.2d 840; Commonwealth v. Western Sav. Fund Soc., 335 Pa. 414, 6 A.2d 843.

[212] Hill v. Shilling, 69 Neb. 152, 95 N.W. 24.

After the bank has acquired stock in another corporation in settlement of a debt, the bank becomes subject to any liability thereon, the same as other stockholders. Hill v. Shilling, 69 Neb. 152, 95 N.W. 24.

bonds if they are properly secured.[213] And a savings bank may invest in securities of manufacturing companies on a basis other than their corporate earnings.[214] Under some statutes a savings bank is not authorized to hold real estate beyond that sufficient for its offices, except within limits, real estate may be acquired by foreclosure of mortgages or upon judgments to secure debts.[215] And where such a bank acquires land within the terms prescribed by statute, provisions declaring forfeiture must be pointed out before forfeiture can be decreed.[216]

A savings bank generally has the power to sell property owned by it, and this includes such incidental powers as are essential to make the sale advantageous.[217] For example, a trust and savings bank may sell mortgage securities held by it, and pursuant to such sale may render itself liable as an indorser by indorsement.[218] And a savings bank owning stock in another corporation may sell, or employ a broker to sell, such stock on the stock exchange, with an option in the seller to deliver the stock at any time within sixty days if the contract is not ultra vires as a speculative enterprise.[219] But under certain statutes, a sale, lease, or exchange of the assets of a state savings bank can be made only to another corporation authorized to do business under the laws of the state, not to a national bank.[220]

---

[213] **In general.—**

Quinn v. Guaranty Trust Co., 82 N.H. 392, 134 A. 45 (1926).

Statute applicable.—

An obligation that is made a first mortgage lien on real estate is "directly secured by a first mortgage" within the meaning of the statute. Quinn v. Guaranty Trust Co., 82 N.H. 392, 134 A. 45 (1926).

Statute inapplicable.—

Bank's officers held not required to affix to purchased bond certificate provided for by statute which is applicable only to notes. Quinn v. Guaranty Trust Co., 82 N.H. 392, 134 A. 45 (1926).

[214] Quinn v. Guaranty Trust Co., 82 N.H. 392, 134 A. 45 (1926).

[215] Maine Unemployment Compensation Com. v. Maine Sav. Bank, 136 Me. 136, 3 A.2d 897.

[216] Patterson v. Southern Trust Co., 80 Cal. App. 411, 251 P. 938.

[217] Batchelder, etc., Co. v. Sam Sav. Bank, 108 Me. 89, 79 A. 13.

[218] Grant v. City Trust & Sav. Bank, 11 Ohio Op. 3, 46 N.E.2d 453 (Ohio App. 1937).

[219] Sistare v. Best, 88 N.Y. 527, aff'g 24 Hun 384.

[220] In re Watkins' Estate, 113 Vt. 126, A.2d 305.

§ 11. Power to Make Loans and Borrow Money.

A savings bank incorporated by special charter has the implied, and sometimes express, power of borrowing money required In the course of its business, and of making negotiable paper or pledging its securities as a means of borrowing;[221] such a bank may also issue shares.[222] And bonds, though secured by first mortgages on property in different states, may properly be combined in one issue.[223] However, the right of other savings banks to borrow for certain purposes is inhibited.[224] And where savings banks are prohibited by statute from borrowing money, but a loan is made to a savings bank and the indebtedness represented by a certificate of deposit, no recovery can be had upon the certificate.[225] On the other hand, upon the principle of estoppel, a savings bank's depositors may be precluded from pleading that loans made to the bank were void as beyond the power of the bank.[226]

---

[221] **In general.—**

Perry v. Commercial Bank, etc., Co., 119 Conn. 115, 174 A. 326.

Savings bank or savings department of commercial bank has right, auxiliary to legitimate purpose of paying depositors' withdrawal demands without endangering security of other deposits, to borrow money and pledge its assets as security. And it is not deprived of this power by the mere fact that it used borrowed money to pay withdrawals before insolvency, thereby producing inequality in amounts received by depositors making withdrawals and other depositors. Perry v. Commercial Bank & Trust Co., Co., 119 Conn. 115, 174 A. 326.

Implied power to borrow money and give security.—

Fifth Ward Sav. Bank v. First Nat. Bank, 48 N.J.L. 513, 7 A. 318.

Statute expressly authorizing banks to borrow money.—

Under the Ohio statute providing that a corporation may borrow money and issue its notes or registered bonds therefor, a savings bank is authorized to borrow money. Dickason v. Grafton Sav. Bank Co., 17 Ohio C.C. (n.s.) 357.

[222] Wallis v. Eagle Sav., etc., Co., 180 App. Div. 719, 168 N.Y.S. 513.

[223] Quinn v. Guaranty Trust Co., 82 N.H. 392, 134 A. 45 (1926).

[224] Laidlaw v. Pacific Bank, 137 Cal. 392, 70 P. 277.

[225] Carroll v. Corning State Sav. Bank, 136 Iowa 79, 113 N.W. 500.

[226] Heironimus v. Sweeney, 83 Md. 146, 34 A. 823, 55 Am. St R. 333, 33 L.R.A. 99.

Savings bank provided by its bylaws for three classes of depositors—weekly depositors, who were stockholders on the deposit of a minimum sum, special depositors, and irregular depositors. Plaintiff made a special deposit, receiving a certificate acknowledging receipt of the money on special deposit, at a specific rate of interest, if not drawn out within one year. Held, that the special deposit was, in effect, a loan, creating an indebtedness on the part of the bank; and the weekly depositors having, as stockholders, received benefits from the loans, in the way of increased dividends, they are estopped from pleading that such loans

A savings bank which is authorized by its charter to give security for public funds deposited with it is not thereby empowered to become a surety for a school treasurer on his official bond.[227] And in some states statutes limit the authority of savings banks to guarantee obligations of others.[228]

§ 11.1. Power to Operate Checking Account Service.

A checking account service is not incidental to the operation of a mutual savings bank.[229] Such a service is foreign to the mutual savings bank's purpose of encouraging thrift by mutuality of ownership and mutuality of investment, to be accomplished by long-term investments, and there is no statutory authority for a checking account service.[230] Whether savings banks should be allowed to offer checking accounts is more properly a matter of statutory regulation than common law.[231] A banking law provision that a

---

were void, as being beyond the power of the corporation. Heironimus v. Sweeney, 83 Md. 146, 34 A. 823, 55 Am. St. R. 333, 38 L.R.A. 99.

[227] In re Miners' Bank (Pa.), 18 Wkly. Notes Cu 370. As to power to make loans, see also § 25 of this chapter.

[228] Perkins v. Farmers, etc., Sav. Bank, 12 Cal. App. 2d 495, 55 Am. P.2d 524.

Savings bank could be compelled to return what it received through fraudulent representation inducing purchase of mortgage, notwithstanding statutory limitation on authority to guarantee obligation of another. Perkins v. Farmers & Merchants Sav. Bank, 12 Cal. App. 2d 495, 56 P.2d 524.

[229] Androscoggin County Sav. Bank v. Campbell, 282 A.2d 858 (Me. 1971).

[230] Androscoggin County Sav. Bank v. Campbell, 282 A.2d 858 (Me. 1971).

Neither statute that savings banks may accept sums of money for Christmas clubs or special purpose accounts on terms to be agreed upon, with provision for repayment of same without interest, nor statute that savings banks may provide acceptance of nonpassbook accounts on terms deemed appropriate, authorizes savings banks to offer and maintain checking accounts. Androscoggin County Sav. Bank v. Campbell, 282 A.2d 858 (Me. 1971).

Statute authorizing savings banks to receive and repay deposits, to lend and invest same, to declare dividends, and to exercise by its board of trustees or duly authorized officers or agents all such powers as are "reasonably incidental to the business of mutual savings bank" does not authorize savings banks to offer and maintain checking accounts. Androscoggin County Sav. Bank v. Campbell, 282 A.2d 858 (Me. 1971).

[231] Terre Haute Sav. Bank v. Indiana State Bank, 380 N.E.2d 1288 (Ind. App. 1978).

Where a mutual savings bank organized and existing under the Savings Bank Act of 1869 had, for more than 80 years, maintained practice of offering and maintaining checking accounts, and where the bank was and had been at all relevant times in sound financial condition, the state Department of Financial Institutions could properly approve such practice. Terre Haute Sav. Bank v. Indiana State Bank, 380 N.E.2d 1288 (Ind. App 1978).

Department of banking did not exceed its rule-making authority in promulgating regulations which allowed mutual savings banks to offer depositors noninterest bearing

savings bank may accept deposits without issuance of a passbook and issue such other evidence of its obligation to repay as may be appropriate to safeguard the interests of depositors and the savings bank did not authorize savings banks to in effect offer checking accounts.[232] While commercial banks are given broad powers to invest in and otherwise deal with a virtual gamut of debt obligations, including time sales contracts, savings banks do not have such powers but are limited to investment in "installment loans" in narrowest sense of those terms.[233]

V. DEPOSITS.

a. General Considerations.

§ 12. In General.

Making of a Deposit.—In limited amounts money may be deposited in savings banks for safekeeping and investment, and may be withdrawn at the pleasure of the owner under such regulations as the bank's charter and bylaws may prescribe.[234] And such banks have the authority to issue certificates of time deposit in return.[235] And a bank customer has the right to deposit money in the name of another without informing the bank that such name is not her own.[236]

What Constitutes a Deposit.—All moneys received by savings banks for safekeeping or investment are deposits within the meaning of their bylaws

---

accounts from which money could be withdrawn by means of a negotiable order of withdrawal payable to a named third party and which would permit savings banks to exercise an option to require 14 days' notice before making payment. Pennsylvania Banker. Asso. v. Secretary of Banking, 481 Pa. 332, 392 A.2d 1319 (1978).

[232] N.Y. State Bankers Ass'n v. Albright, 46 App. Div. 2d 269, 361 N.Y.S.2d 949 (1974).

[233] Tri-County Sav. & Loan Asso. v. Commissioner of Banking, 170 N.J. Super. 576, 407 A.2d 844 (1979).

[234] Society for Sav. v. Coite, 73 U.S. (6 Wall.) 594, 18 L. Ed. 897; Provident Inst. v. Massachusetts, 73 U.S. (6 Wall.) 611, 18 L. Ed. 907; State v. People's Nat. Bank, 75 N.H. 27, 70 A. 542, 21 Ann. Cas. 1204.

[235] Murray v. First Trust, etc., Bank, 201 Iowa 1325, 207 N.W. 781 (1926).

Issuance by savings bank of certificate of time deposit, bearing interest at 7½ percent held not illegal or contrary to public policy. Murray v. First Trust, etc., Bank, 201 Iowa 1325, 207 N.W. 781 (1926).

[236] Roughan v. Chenango Valley Sav. Bank, 158 App. Div. 786, 144 N.Y.S. 508, aff'd, 216 N.Y. 696, 110 N.E. 1049.

and the words of their charters.[237] But whether a transaction is a loan or deposit must be decided on the facts of each individual case.[238] Thus, money left in a savings bank by a depositor on agreement that increased interest should be paid for three years was held a deposit.[239] Similarly, where one places money in a bank and receives a written instrument by which the bank promises to pay him the sum deposited plus interest on return of the properly indorsed certificate, the transaction is a deposit and not a loan.[240] And the sending of a draft by a customer to a savings bank, with a request for a time certificate of deposit payable to him, and the receiving of it from the bank constitute a deposit.[241] But a deposit in a savings account was held to be a loan of money by the deposit to the bank on the express contract by the bank, as printed on the passbook, to pay the depositor the amount of the deposit with interest on presentation of the passbook.[242]

Relation between Bank and Depositor.—The contractual relation between a savings bank and its depositors is subject to the proper exercise of the police power of the state.[243] The facts of each case determine the relationship,[244] and the rights and liabilities of the depositor and the bank are determined by the provisions, express or implied, of the contract between them.[245] According to the weight of authority, if there is no bylaw or

---

[237] Bank for Sav. v. Collector, 70 U.S. (3 Wall.) 495, 18 L. Ed. 207.

A "deposit account," within the provision of the Uniform Commercial Code specifically exempting transfer of an interest in a deposit account from its coverage, includes a passbook savings account. Iser Elec. Co. v. Ingran Constr. Co., 48 Ill. App. 3d 110, 6 Ill. Dec. 136, 362 N.E.2d 771 (1977).

[238] **In general.**—

Murray v. First Trust, etc., Bank, 201 Iowa 1325, 207 N.W. 781 (1926); Mercantile Sav. Bank v. Appler, 151 Md. 571, 135 A. 373.

The issuance of a certificate of deposit by a savings bank is not conclusive proof that the transaction represents a deposit rather than a loan. Partch v. Krogman, 202 Iowa 524, 210 N.W. 612.

[239] Murray v. First Trust, etc., Bank, 201 Iowa 1325, 207 N.W. 781 (1926).

[240] Partch v. Krogman, 202 Iowa 524, 210 N.W. 612.

[241] State ex rel. Carrol v. Corning State Sav. Bank, 136 Iowa 79, 113 N.W. 500.

[242] Perdue v. State Nat. Bank, 254 Ala. 80, 47 So. 2d 261.

[243] In re Opinion of Justices, 278 Mass. 607, 181 N.E. 833, 82 A.L.R. 1021.

[244] Mercantile Sav. Bank v. Appler, 151 Md. 571, 135 A. 373.

[245] Forbes v. First Camden Nat'l Bank, etc., Co., 21 N.J. Super. 133, 90 A.2d 547, rev'd on other grounds, 25 N.J. Super. 17, 95 A.2d 416.

It is the contract or understanding, express or implied, between the parties which

regulation limiting the liability of such a bank,[246] and no agreement to the contrary,[247] a deposit of money in the bank creates the relation of debtor and creditor between the depositor and the bank.[248] But it also has been held that

---

determines the nature and character of the undertaking in connection with a savings account as well as the liability of the parties; it is the contract which controls the rights and liabilities, not the recording of activities which reflects its execution. Gregory v. Harper, 48 Ohio App. 2d 184, 356 N.E.2d 500, 2 Ohio Op. 3d 152 (1975).

Once depositor's knowledge of and voluntary acceptance of terms and conditions of joint and survivorship account are placed into question, statute binding depositor to bank's regulations upon opening of savings account and acceptance of passbook does not relieve bank of responsibility to show that it provided depositor with reasonable means of understanding consequences of deposit contract. Rives v. Krupzsield, 60 Ohio App. 3d 97, 573 N.E.2d 1199 (1989).

[246] Ladd v. Androscoggin County Sav. Bank, 96 Me. 520, 52 A. 1016; Pursiful v. First State Bank, 251 Ky. 498, 65 S.W.2d 462.

[247] Ide v. Pierce, 134 Mass. 260; Pope v. Burlington Sav. Bank, 56 Vt. 284, 48 Am. R. 781; Zinn v. Mendel, 9 W. Va. 580; Pursiful v. First State Bank, 251 Ky. 498, 65 S.W.2d 462.

[248] *United States.*—Blakey v. Brinson, 286 U.S. 254, 52 S. Ct. 516, 76 L. Ed. 1089, 82 A.L.R. 1288, rev'g Schumacher v. Brinson, 52 F.2d 821.

California.—State v. San Francisco Sav. & Loan Soc., Soc., 66 Cal. App. 53, 225 P. 309; Beery v. County of Los Angeles, 116 Cal. App. 2d 290, 253 P.2d 1005.

Connecticut.—Wood v. Connecticut Sav. Bank, 87 Conn. 341, 87 A. 983; Lippitt v. Thames Loan, etc., Co., 88 Conn. 185, 90 A. 369; Wawrzynowicz v. Wawrzynowicz, 164 Conn. 200, 319 A.2d 407 (1972).

Illinois.—Ward v. Johnson, 5 Ill. App. 30, aff'd, 95 Ill. 215 (1880).

Kentucky.—Pursiful v. First State Bank, 251 Ky. 498, 65 S.W.2d 462.

Louisiana.—Smith v. Richland State Bank (La. App.), 9 So. 2d 327.

Maine.—Ladd v. Androscoggin County Sav. Bank, 96 Me. 520, 52 A. 1016.

Maryland.—Mercantile Sav. Bank v. Appler, 151 Md. 571, 135 A. 373; Hileman v. Hulver, 243 Md. 527, 221 A.2d 693 (1966).

Massachusetts.—Ide v. Pierce, 134 Mass. 260.

Missouri.—Entry of deposit in passbook is admission of indebtedness and, when not explained, it creates relationship of debtor and creditor. Fischer v. Morris Plan Co., 275 S.W.2d 393 (Mo. App. 1955).

New Hampshire.—Economic changes of twentieth century, including Federal Deposit Insurance Corporation and statutory guaranty funds, do not affect fundamental nature of depositary relationship and mutual savings bank. In re Corporators of Portsmouth Sav. Bank, 525 A.2d 671 (N.H. 1987).

New Jersey.—Schippers v. Kempkes (N.J. Ch.) 67 A. 1042, aff'd, 72 N.J. Eq. 948, 78 A. 1118; Redzina v. Provident Inst. for Savings, 121 A. 519, aff'd, 96 N.J. Eq. 346, 125 A. 133; Fiocchi v. Smith (N.J. Ch.), 97 A. 283; Forbes v. First Camden Nat'l Bank, etc., Co., 21 N.J.

the depositor is not a mere creditor, and is more like a stockholder in a bank of discount or even in a business corporation.[249] However, depositors are not, as such, stockholders of a savings bank.[250] Courts have said a savings bank is the agent of its depositors.[251]

Money deposited in a savings bank becomes the property of the bank,[252] which is under an obligation to pay, on demand, not the identical money

---

Super. 133, 90 A.2d 547, rev'd on other grounds, 25 N.J. Super. 17, 95 A.2d 416.

New York.—Kantor Bros. v. Wile, 93 Misc. 438, 158 N.Y.S. 115; Crosby v. Bowery Sav. Bank, 67 How. Pr. 329, 50 N.Y. Super. Ct 453; People v. Mechanics', etc., Sav. Inst., 92 N.Y. 7; In re Wilkins' Will, 131 Misc. 188, 226 N.Y.S. 415; Hartford Acci. & Indem. Co. v. First Nat'l Bank & Trust Co., 281 N.Y. 162, 22 N.E.2d 324, 123 A.L.R. 1149, rev'd, 256 App. Div. 30, 9 N.Y.S.2d 590, rev'g 162 Misc. 348, 294 N.Y.S. 522; In re Gross, 62 N.Y.S.2d 392; Myers v. Albany Sav. Bank, 270 App. Div. 466, 60 N.Y.S.2d 477, aff'd, 296 N.Y. 562, 68 N.E.2d 866; Abate v. Bushwick Sav. Bank, 207 Misc. 372, 138 N.Y.S.2d 140; Romero v. Sjoberg, 5 N.Y.2d 518, 186 N.Y.S.2d 246, 158 N.E.2d 828; R. H. Macy & Co. v. Tyler, 21 Misc. 2d 998, 193 N.Y.S.2d 243; Novak v. Greater New York Sav. Bank, 331 N.Y.S.2d 377, 30 N.Y.2d 136, 282 N.E.2d 285 (Ct App. 1972).

The depositor is a creditor of the bank and the passbook issued to a depositor is evidence of the debt and the contract between them, but passbook is not in itself negotiable. People v. Jenkins, 61 App. Div. 2d 705, 403 N.Y.S.2d 751 (1978).

Relationship between a bank and customers who had a joint savings account in the bank is that of creditor and debtor to the extent of monies on deposit in the savings account. The passbook issued by the bank is not negotiable, but is assignable. Lewis v. Franklin Sav. Bank, 98 Misc. 2d 1098, 415 N.Y.S.2d 362 (1979).

South Carolina.—Leaphart v. Commercial Bank, 45 S.C. 563, 23 S.E. 939, 55 Am. St. R. 800, 33 L.R.A. 700.

Vermont.—Pope v. Burlington Sav. Bank, 56 Vt. 284, 48 Am. R. 781.

Virginia.—Deal's Adm'r v. Merchants' & Mechanics' Sav. Bank, 120 Va. 297, 91 S.E. 135, 1917C L.R.A. 548.

West Virginia.—Zinn v. Mendel, 9 W. Va. 580.

249 Mann v. State Treasurer, 74 N.H. 345, 68 A. 130, 15 L.R.A. (n.s.) 150.

In New Jersey it has been held that depositors are in the nature of partners or stockholders. Barrett v. Bloomfield Sav. Inst., 64 N.J. Eq. 425, 54 A. 543, aff'd, 68 N.J. Eq. 431, 57 A. 1131.

250 Savings Bank v. New London, 20 Conn. 111.

251 Alexiou v. Bridgeport-People's Sav. Bank, 110 Conn. 397, 148 A. 374.

The relationship between a savings society and a depositor therein is that of agent and principal. Surso v. Lucak (Ohio App.), 113 N.E.2d 388.

252 **In general.—**

Massachusetts.—Ide v. Pierce, 134 Mass. 260.

New Jersey.—Fiocchi v. Smith (N.J. Ch.) 97 A. 283.

received but a sum equal in legal value,[253] and a depositor has only the peculiar interest created by statute in the bank's assets.[254]

In some jurisdictions, it has been held that a trust relation exists between a savings bank and its depositors.[255] And it has been said that a deposit is in some respects an interest in a trust fund rather than an absolute debt.[256] However, the better opinion seems to be that there is nothing like a private

---

New York.—Crosby v. Bowery Sav. Bank, 67 How. Pr. 329, 50 N.Y. Super. Ct. 453; People v. Mechanics', etc., Sav. Inst., 92 N.Y. 7.

South Carolina.—Leaphart v. Comm. Bank, 45 S.C. 563, 23 S.E. 939, 55 Am. St. R. 800, 33 LRA. 700.

Vermont.—Pope v. Burlington Sav. Bank, 56 Vt. 284, 48 Am. R. 781.

West Virginia.—Zinn v. Mendel, 9 W. Va. 580.

Where administrator deposited draft in usual savings department of a bank, bank became absolute owner of draft and debtor of administrator. Such draft became a general asset only. Cuttell v. Fluent, 51 F.2d 974.

Therefore, the bank has full power to negotiate or pledge any of its securities obtained by loaning said funds. Ward v. Johnson, 5 Ill. App. 30, aff'd, 95 Ill. 215 (1880).

253 **In general.—**

Zinn v. Mendel, 9 W. Va. 580; Kantor Bros. v. Wile, 93 Misc. 438, 158 N.Y.S. 115.

Bank becomes sole owner of moneys deposited with a promise on bank's part to repay. Abate v. Bushwick Sav. Bank, 207 Misc. 372, 138 N.Y.S.2d 140.

Rule inapplicable to commodity.—

This rule does not apply where the thing deposited is not money but a commodity. Zinn v. Mendel, 9 W. Va. 580; Kantor Bros. v. Wile, 93 Misc. 438, 158 N.Y.S. 115.

254 Perry v. Commercial Bank, etc., Co., 119 Conn. 115, 174 A. 326.

Depositors in commercial bank's savings department have no lien, strictly speaking, on assets thereof, and are not strictly equitable owners of such assets, nor beneficial rise of trust therein, but have only peculiar interest, created by statute, in them. Perry v. Commercial Bank & Trust Co., 119 Conn. 115, 174 A. 326.

255 In re Newark Sav. Inst., 28 N.J. Eq. 552; State v. People's Nat. Bank, 75 N.H. 27, 70 A. 542; Bachrach v. Commissioner of Banks, 239 Mass. 272, 131 N.E. 857.

The relation of a savings bank to its depositors is a trust defined by its act of incorporation, and a court of chancery has not the power, by virtue of its general jurisdiction over trusts, to make orders changing the constitution and terms of such trusts as established by the legislature. Dodd v. Una, 40 N.J. Eq. 672, 5 A. 155.

The depositors in a savings institution occupy a double relation to the corporation as such. In case of insolvency, they are its creditors, whereas in other cases, they are in the nature of partners or stockholders; but in all cases they are the cestuis que trustent of the managers. Barrett v. Bloomfield Sav. Inst., 64 N.J. Eq. 425, 54 A. 543, aff'd, 66 N.J. Eq. 431, 57 A. 1131.

256 Forastiere v. Springfield Inst. for Savings, 303 Mass. 101, 20 N.E.2d 950 (1939).

trust between a savings bank or its trustees and the depositors in respect to their deposits,[257] and that a bank is not rendered a trustee by one person's making a deposit in another's name, or by making a deposit payable to another's order.[258] Thus, where a corporation is by its charter only a trustee for its stockholders in its management, the fact that it bears the name of a savings bank will not, in the absence of proof that its depositors were thereby deceived, render its deposits in trust.[259] Similarly, a bank's bylaw which does not declare that investments of savings deposits are made for the benefit of the depositors does not render the same trust property,[260] and a bylaw authorizing the withdrawal of a savings deposit after certain notice, without regard to how it is invested at the time, indicates that a depositor has no trust interest in the investment; otherwise, he would have to await the maturity of the investment before withdrawal.[261] And a trust is not created by a promise of a bank's officers to its savings depositors to keep and use the securities held for loans by investment for their benefit.[262]

There is no distinction between accounts in savings and loan associations and accounts in savings banks as far as the rights of depositors as between themselves are concerned.[263]

As their names suggest, savings-and-loan institutions, also called "thrifts," provide two main services: (1) They collect customer deposits, which are maintained in interest-bearing savings accounts and (2) they originate and

---

[257] People v. Mechanics', etc., Sav. Inst., 92 N.Y. 7; Pope v. Burlington Sav. Bank, 56 Vt. 284, 48 Am. B. 781; Johnson v. Ward, 2 Ill. App. 261; Leaphart v. Commercial Bank, 45 S.C. 563, 23 S.E. 939, 55 Am. St. R. 800, 33 L.R.A. 700.

[258] Pope v. Burlington Sav. Bank, 56 Vt. 284, 48 Am. B. 781. Contra, Blasdel v. Locke, 52 N.H. 238.

[259] Ward v. Johnson, 95 Ill. 215 (1880).

[260] Ward v. Johnson, 95 Ill. 215 (1880).

Savings bank bylaw provided that "All savings deposited in this bank, over and above such sums as it may be expedient to reserve for immediate use, shall be invested in the stocks and obligations of the United States or the state of Illinois," etc.—not declaring the investments to be made for the benefit of the depositors—does not render the same trust property. The bank could sell, assign, pledge, or mortgage them, in good faith, to secure other loans or deposits Ward v. Johnson, 95 Ill. 215 (1880).

[261] Ward v. Johnson, 95 Ill. 215 (1880).

[262] Ward v. Johnson, 95 Ill. 215 (1880).

[263] Jones v. Hamilton, 211 Md. 371, 127 A.2d 519; Wolf v. Crystal, 239 Md. 22, 209 A.2d 920 (1965).

service mortgage loans funded by those deposits.[264] Historically, thrifts were profitable because the interest they collected on outstanding loans exceeded the interest they paid out to customers.[265]

Special Deposits.—Special deposits in a savings bank which are not made as savings-bank deposits nor to draw interest or dividends, and which go into the general funds of the bank, are in the nature of loans, the true relation between these depositors and the bank being that of debtor and creditor; special deposits are not subject to losses, as are general deposits, so long as the bank's assets are sufficient to pay its debts.[266] Under a statute providing that savings banks may receive on deposit the savings and funds of persons, preserve and invest the same, and transact the usual business of such institutions, a savings bank has the power to receive a special deposit of securities for safekeeping.[267] An amendment to a savings account to require the signatures of the depositor and the administrator of the depositor's estate did not transform a general account into a special account and create a fiduciary relationship between the bank and the depositor.[268] For other cases involving special deposits, see the footnote.[269]

---

[264] WMI Holdings Corp. v. United States, 891 F.3d 1016 (2018).

[265] WMI Holdings Corp. v. United States, 891 F.3d 1016 (2018).

[266] Abbott v. Wolfeborough Sav. Bank, 68 N.H. 290, 38 A. 1050; Lund v. Seaman's Bank (N.Y.), 20 Bow. Pr. 461.

[267] Sherwood v. Home Sav. Bank, 131 Iowa 528, 109 N.W. 9.

[268] Rush v. South Carolina Nat'l Bank, 343 S.E.2d 667 (S.C. App. 1986).

Conversation between administrator of depositor's estate and bank in which administrator communicated depositor's desire to preserve funds for major contingencies such as purchase of refrigerator, medical expenses, or burial expenses and which was made in presence of depositor prior to amendment of savings account to require signatures of depositor and administrator for withdrawal of funds was insufficient to evidence intent to transform general account into special account creating fiduciary relationship between bank and depositor. Rush v. South Carolina Nat'l Bank, 343 S.E.2d 667 (S.C. App. 1986).

[269] A bank having accepted a deposit of checks and credited the same to the depositor's general account as cash, against which it charged the depositor's notes payable at the bank, and canceled the same, is not entitled, on the checks being subsequently lost and unpaid because of the drawer's insolvency, to charge the notes again against the depositor's savings account. Heinrich v. First Nat'l Bank, 83 Misc. 566, 145 N.Y.S. 342, aff'd, 164 App. Div. 960, 149 N.Y.S. 1086, aff'd, 219 N.Y. 1, 113 N.E. 531, 1917A L.R.L 655.

Where passbook provided that checks were credited subject to withdrawal only on actual payment of them, and the deposit of a check was designated therein as a check deposit and not treated as money, the deposit was for collection, and title to the check did not pass to the bank. Hefling v. Public Nat. Bank, 128 Misc. 762, 219 N.Y.S. 479.

Demand Accounts.—In some jurisdictions, savings banks have been held entitled to maintain demand accounts because of statutory provisions,[270] administrative practice,[271] or long-established custom.[272] For examples of issues arising when savings banks maintain demand accounts, see the footnote.[273]

---

[270] Hudson County Nat'l Bank v. Provident Inst. for Savings in Jersey City, 80 N.J. Super. 339, 193 A.2d 697, aff'd, 44 N.J. 282, 208 A.2d 409.

Under statute granting power to receive money on deposit according to usual custom, savings banks could accept deposits which were subject to withdrawal by check. Hudson County Nat'l Bank v. Provident Institution for Sav., 44 N.J. 282, 208 A.2d 409 (1965).

[271] Hudson County Nat'l Bank v. Provident Institution for Sav., 80 N.J. Super. 339, 193 A.2d 697, aff'd, 44 N.J. 282, 208 A.2d 409.

Whether practice of mutual savings banks in maintaining demand accounts was ultra vires powers of savings banks was a question which Banking Act did not, on its face, expressly answer, and the practical construction accorded practice under the act which was substantially contemporaneous with the adoption thereof would be accorded great weight. Hudson County Nat'l Bank v. Provident Institution for Sav., 80 N.J. Super. 339, 198 A.2d 697, aff'd, 44 N.J. 282, 208 A.2d 409.

[272] Savings Bank v. Bank Comm'r, 248 Md. 461, 237 A.2d 45 (1968).

A savings bank which had been issuing treasurer's checks and selling money orders for many years without objection from the authorities and which was established under a legislative charter prohibiting the issuance by it of any bills or notes in the nature of bank notes was allowed to provide checking accounts to its customers provided all of the funds received were invested by the bank. Savings Bank v. Bank Comm'r, 248 Md. 461, 237 A.2d 45 (1968).

Evidence that savings bank issued 73,000 treasurer's checks to depositors making withdrawals and sold 247,000 money orders sustained bank's contention that there was demand for bank to make checking accounts a service available to its customers. Savings Bank v. Bank Comm'r, 248 Md. 461, 237 A.2d 45 (1968).

[273] **Failure to charge checking account.—**

A husband, entering into property settlement agreement, providing that wife should retain spouses' money then in her possession, after her withdrawal from spouses' joint bank checking account of amount previously transferred therefrom by husband to savings account in his separate name, cannot recover such amount from bank because of its mistake in falling to charge amount transferred against checking account at close of business on day of transfer, in which case wife's subsequent check thereon would have been dishonored as overdraft. Cowen v. Valley Nat'l Bank, 67 Ariz. 210, 193 P.2d 918.

Attempted recapture of deposit invalid.—

Where bank accepted a check on a joint account for $900, and credited such sum to a savings account in the name of a minor with the drawer as trustee, and later cashed a check on the joint account drawn by the codrawer, and on bank's second business day sought to charge $900 against the trust account after ascertainment of an insufficiency of funds in the joint account to cover both checks drawn upon it, such charge to recapture the deposit was

Special Statutory Provisions with Respect to Deposits.—A statute authorizing a corporation to establish a savings department, requiring it to pledge its entire capital stock and property for the payment of its depositors, and providing that deposits may be received after such pledge, does not itself create a lien on such capital stock and property, since it authorizes and requires the corporation to do so, and contemplates the securing of deposits before their receipt.[274] Statute defining depositors' proprietary interests as proportionate inchoate interests in net worth of mutual savings bank did not extinguish the depositors' charter rights.[275] The word "person" within the meaning of a statutory provision that no savings bank shall accept any deposit if, by acceptance thereof, liability of the bank to any person will be in excess of a specified amount, includes entities other than individuals.[276] A statutory provision that no savings bank shall accept any deposit for credit to any organization for profit did not preclude such a bank from accepting a savings account in trust for a foster home service operated by the Salvation Army.[277] Savings deposits made by a father in 1956 in his own name as custodian for his minor children were not affected by a 1959 statute making the Uniform Gifts to Minors Act applicable to gifts of money to minors.[278] As to statutes providing time limits for a bank's dishonor of demand items, see the footnote.[279]

Depositor's Claim against Bank and Recovery Thereon.—The claim of a depositor against a savings bank for his deposit is a chose in action,[280] not

---

untimely and invalid. Vatakis v. Asbury Park Nat. Bank & Trust Co., 43 N.J. Super. 193, 128 A.2d 9 (1956).

[274] Newton v. Eagle, etc., Mfg. Co., 101 F. 149.

[275] In re Corporators of Portsmouth Sav. Bank, 525 A.2d 671 (N.H. 1987).

[276] In re Coughlan's Estate, 29 Misc. 2d 516, 218 N.Y.S.2d 168.

[277] In re Coughian's Estate, 29 Misc. 2d 516, 218 N.Y.S.2d 168.

[278] Application of Muller, 235 N.Y.S.2d 125.

[279] New Jersey statute provides that in any case in which a bank receives, other than for immediate payment over the counter, a demand item payable by, at or through such bank and gives credit therefor before midnight of the day of receipt, the bank may have until midnight of its next business day after receipt within which to dishonor or refuse payment of such item. Vatakis v. Asbury Park Nat'l Bank & Trust Co., 43 N.J. Super. 193, 128 A.2d 9 (1956). See former N.J. Stat. Ann. § 17:9A-235 (now N.J. Stat. Ann. § 12A:4-301).

[280] Ornbaun v. First Nat'l Bank, 215 Cal. 72, 8 P.2d 470, 81 A.L.R. 1146; Ornbaun v. Savings Bank of Mendocino County, 215 Cal. 770, 8 P.2d 473; Watson v. Stockton Morris Plan Co., 34 Cal. App. 2d 393, 93 P.2d 855, aff'g 88 P.2d 927; Lund v. Seaman's Bank (N.Y.), 37 Barb. 129.

a bailment.[281] And a certificate of deposit issued without authority therefor is illegal and void, and no action can be maintained thereon for any purpose.[282] Where savings banks are prohibited by statute from borrowing money, but a loan is made to such a bank and the indebtedness represented by a certificate of deposit, no recovery can be had upon the certificate itself.[283] But where a savings bank delivered to a depositor a check drawn on another bank, which cashed it upon forged indorsements and charged such amount against the drawer bank, it was held not to be a payment which prevents the depositor from suing the savings bank on the original deposit.[284]

Taxation.—For purposes of taxation under Delaware law, a savings institution is "located" in the state in which the amount of aggregate deposits of all its offices in that state is greatest.[285]

§ 13. Bylaws, Rules, Passbooks and Charter as Part of Contract.

In General.—The reasonable bylaws of a savings bank are part of the contract between the bank and a depositor when they have been brought to the latter's notice,[286] unless they are contrary to law or public policy.[287]

---

[281] Alexiou v. Bridgeport-People's Sav. Bank, 110 Conn. 397, 148 A. 374; Lund v. Seaman's Bank (N.Y.), 37 Barb. 129.

[282] Sweet v. Security Sav. Bank, 200 Iowa 895, 205 N.W. 470.

[283] State v. Corning State Sav. Bank, 136 Iowa 79, 113 N.W. 500.

[284] Szwento Juozupo Let Draugystes v. Manhattan Sav. Inst., 178 App. Div. 57, 164 N.Y.S. 498.

[285] Lehman Bros. Bank, FSB v. State Bank Comm'r, 937 A.2d 95, 2007 Del. LEXIS 496 (Del. 2007).

See 5 Del. C. § 831(8).

[286] **In general.—**

Hough Ave., etc., Bkg. Co. v. Anderson, 78 Ohio St. 341, 85 N.E. 498, 125 Am. St. R. 707, 18 L.R.A. (n.s.) 431; Mercantile Sav. Bank v. Appler, 151 Md. 571, 135 A. 373; Fourth, etc., Trust Co. v. Rowe, 122 Ohio St. 1, 170 N.E. 439; State v. San Francisco Sav. & Loan Soc., 66 Cal. App. 53, 225 P. 309; Société de Bienfaisance St. Jean Baptiste de Millbury v. People's Sav. Bank, 228 Mass. 556, 117 N.E. 921; Highfield v. First Nat. Bank, 45 Ga. App. 431, 165 S.E. 135.

Bylaw requiring depositor to notify bank of loss or theft of passbook constituted a part of contract between depositor and bank. Connolly v. Manchester Sav. Bank, 92 N.H. 89, 25 A.2d 412 (N.H. 1942).

Bylaw requiring entry of deposits in deposit book is part of contract between depositor and bank. Mutual Assurance Co. v. Norwich Sav. Soc., 128 Conn. 510, 24 A.2d 477, 139 A.L.R. 829.

A savings bank's charter is also part of such contract.[288] A savings bank depositor is also bound by the reasonable rules of his bank to which he

---

Bylaw requiring presentation of deposit book for withdrawals is part of contract between depositor and bank. Mutual Assur. Co. v. Norwich Sav. Soc., 128 Conn. 510, 24 A.2d 477, 139 A.L.R. 829.

Such bylaw held reasonable. Walde v. Walde, 45 N.Y.S.2d 791.

A bylaw provided that payments to persons presenting passbook should discharge the bank, though the bank would endeavor to prevent fraudulent payments. It was held that this constituted a contract by the bank to take ordinary care not to pay others than the depositor, but saving itself harmless on payments of the deposit to one other than the person rightfully entitled thereto on presentation of the passbook. Kenney v. Harlem Sav. Bank, 61 Misc. 144, 114 N.Y.S. 749 (1908). But this judgment was subsequently reversed in Kenny v. Harlem Sav. Bank, 65 Misc. 466, 120 N.Y.S. 82 (1909).

Provision of statute permitting adoption of bylaws concerning lost passbooks was not limited by another provision of same statute to effect that bylaws contained in passbook and posted at bank's premises should be evidence of terms on which deposits were made. Krupp v. Franklin Sav. Bank, 255 App. Div. 15, 5 N.Y.S.2d 365.

A statement in deposit certificate, payable on demand, that, if demand were made within six months, there would be no interest due on the certificate is a limitation on the payment of interest. Partch v. Krogman, 202 Iowa 524, 210 N.W. 612.

Bank's obligation implicit in bylaws.—Implicit in a bank's agreement, in its bylaws, to maintain the records of all savings account was the bank's obligation to keep its accounts correctly and to see that the transactions were credited properly to the depositor's accounts. Menicocci v. Archer Nat'l Bank, 67 Ill. App. 3d 388, 24 Ill. Dec. 296, 385 N.E.2d 63 (1978).

Savings banks have power to make regulations governing receipts and disbursement of deposits which are binding on depositors and their personal representatives when they have actual or constructive notice. Layman v. Western Sav. Bank, 302 Pa. Super. 433, 448 A.2d 1119 (1982).

Contract deemed unconscionable.—Contract between bank and passbook savings account depositor in which depositor agreed to "abide by rules and regulations of bank" was unconscionable at time it was made to extent that it allowed bank to confiscate money in depositor's account without adequately notifying him of reasons therefor, though bank has power generally to receive money on deposit subject to terms and conditions prescribed by it. Levy v. Chemical Bank, 475 N.Y.S.2d 771 (N.Y. Dist. Ct. 1984).

[287] Fourth, etc., Trust Co. v. Rowe, 122 Ohio St. 1, 170 N.E. 439.

Amendments to savings bank's charter, which expanded power of bank to own real property and enabled bank to pay officers and employees, did not alter charter provisions relating to depositors' rights, and thus, provisions relating to depositors' rights were not superseded by general banking laws. In re Corporators of Portsmouth Sav. Bank, 525 A.2d 671 (N.H. 1987).

[288] **In general.—**

Wharton v. Poughkeepsie Sav. Bank, 262 App. Div. 598, 31 N.Y.S.2d 311, aff'd, 288 N.Y. 610, 42 N.E.2d 611.

assents by an agreement in writing,[289] and by rules of the bank adopted

---

The terms of contract between savings bank and depositor were charter and bylaws in bankbook which was issued on opening of bank account and which remained in custody of bank. Wharton v. Poughkeepsie Sav. Bank, 262 App. Div. 598, 31 N.Y.S.2d 311, aff'd, 288 N.Y. 610, 42 N.E.2d 611.

A depositor deposited all money in savings bank subject to charter of bank and bylaws contained in bankbook. Wharton v. Poughkeepsie Sav. Bank, 262 App. Div. 598, 31 N.Y.S.2d 311, aff'd, 288 N.Y. 610, 42 N.E.2d 611.

Bylaw superseding charter provision.—

Where savings bank adopted in 1857 a bylaw providing that deposit, should not draw interest after expiration of 20 years from time of last deposit or draft, charter provision protecting existing depositors against changes in regulations until personal notice did not apply to person who became depositor in 1864. Wharton v. Poughkeepsie Sav. Bank, 262 App. Div. 598, 31 N.Y.S.2d 311, aff'd, 288 N.Y. 610, 42 N.E.2d 611.

[289] **In general.—**

Langdale v. Citizens' Bank, 121 Ga. 105, 48 S.E. 708, 104 Am. St. R. 94, 69 L.R.A. 341.

Signature card as agreement.—

A provision of signature card signed by depositor at time of opening savings account stating that he agreed to bylaws and any amendments or additions that might thereafter be made was a part of contract between depositor and savings bank. Krupp v. Franklin Sav. Bank, 255 App. Div. 15, 5 N.Y.S.2d 365.

Where depositors had signature cards required to be signed prior to opening of savings account at home overnight and had opportunity to read statement over place for signatures to effect that depositor agreed that funds in account should be governed by bylaws, regulations and rules and practices of the bank and depositors returned the signed cards, depositors were bound by rules of bank, notwithstanding that depositors were not advised of contents of bylaws, rules and regulations. Larrus v. First Nat. Bank, 122 Cal. App. 2d 884, 266 P.2d 143.

The rights and liabilities of depositor and bank depend upon contract between them, of which the signature card contains the primary terms, and into which the rules printed in the passbook, as well as other statements therein which reasonable parsons would consider binding, enter. Forbes v. First Camden Nat. Bank, etc., Co., 25 N.J. Super. 17, 95 A.2d 416.

Provision on bank's joint savings account signature card stating "We jointly and severally agree to the rules and regulations as set forth in the savings passbook issued to us" incorporated rules and regulations of the bank into the contract between depositor and bank and joint tenant. Welch v. North Hills Bank, 442 S.W.2d 98 (Mo. App. 1969).

Presentation requirement.—

Where passbook recited that all deposits were made subject to bylaws as therein printed and made a part of "this deposit contract" and contained statement that no payments were to be made or money withdrawn without presentation of the book, the presentation requirement became a part of the deposit contract, express or implied, governing the duty of the bank to depositor's wife, whose name appeared on passbook, and neither the bank alone nor the bank and the husband had power to waive the presentation requirement, and when the bank paid money out of account to husband without the book it breached the deposit contract. Stillings

under statutory authority of which he has knowledge.[290] Moreover, the signature of a depositor is not the only way to show his agreement to be bound by the regulations of a savings bank; the agreement may be evidenced by his conduct.[291] A "bank signature card" is a contract which creates a savings account when signed by the creator or creators.[292] On the other hand, a bank will be held strictly responsible for the language in the rules and regulations promulgated by it.[293] And the adoption of rules and regulations which affect the contractual relations between a savings bank

---

v. Citizens Bank, 637 S.W.2d 401 (Mo. App. 1982).

290 Campbell v. Schenectady Sav. Bank, 114 App. Div. 337, 99 N.Y.S. 927.

Statute requiring bank to post its regulations held not to make posting necessary to bind depositor having actual knowledge of regulations. Andrew v. Union Sav. Bank, etc., Co., 222 Iowa 881, 270 N.W. 465 (1936).

A savings bank has power to adopt reasonable regulations if they are in conformity with statute, and such regulations, if assented to by a depositor, constituted a contract between bank and depositor, although the exercise of ordinary care is required by the bank in making payments, even when one making demand therefor presents a passbook. R.H. Macy & Co. v. Tyler, 21 Misc. 2d 998, 193 N.Y.S.2d 243.

Bank was required to refund to depositor monthly service charges which were deducted from depositor's passbook savings account because it contained less than $200, where bank declared monthly service charge on such accounts after depositor opened his account and bank did not offer proof to show that depositor received form letter which informed him of rules regarding monthly service charges. Levy v. Chemical Bank, 475 N.Y.S.2d 771 (N.Y. Dint. Ct. 1984).

Payee's indorsement of check at time copayees' signatures had been forged did not trigger transfer warranties of section providing that person who transfers instrument and receives consideration warrants that he has good title to instrument and all signatures are genuine or authorized. Hayner v. Fox, 182 Ill. App. 3d 989, 134 Ill. Dec. 627, 542 N.E.2d 1134 (1989).

291 Estate of Cilvik, 439 Pa. 522, 267 A.2d 836 (1970).

292 **In general.—**

Ladd v. Augusta Sav. Bank, 96 Me. 510, 52 A. 1012, 58 L.R.A. 288.

Illustrative case.—

Though the bylaw of a savings bank require that depositors shall subscribe their names in a book, and thereby be considered as assenting to all the bylaws, such assent may be implied, and will be, where a depositor living at a distance, and receiving a deposit book by mail with the bylaws printed in it, leaves the deposit, and keeps the book for several years, without going to the bank, and leaving his signature. Gifford v. Rutland Sav. Bank, 63 Vt. 108, 21 A. 340, 25 Am. St. R. 744, 11 L.R.A. 794 (1890).

293 **In general.—**

Kalb v. Chemical Bank N.Y. Trust Co., 62 Misc. 2d 458, 309 N.Y.S.2d 502 (1969), rev'd on other grounds, 64 Misc. 2d 824, 316 N.Y.S.2d 381 (1970).

Any ambiguity in the construction of rules printed in a bank passbook is to be resolved

and its depositors may be shown by their long use, with the knowledge and approval of the bank's trustees, as well as by the record of a formal vote.[294]

Waiver of Regulations.—While regulations of banks are normally to be complied with, especially where compliance places no undue burden on the depositor, they are not so obligatory that they cannot be dispensed with when the occasion demands.[295] Thus, a provision of a bank's bylaw for the entry of deposits in a deposit book is for the protection of both the bank and the depositor, but they may waive compliance therewith by joint agreement or action.[296] But rules and regulations incorporated into a contract of deposit cannot be dispensed with by a bank at will on the ground that they are purely for the bank's protection and convenience.[297]

Change in Bylaws as Affecting Rights of Depositor.—Where no notice is given to a depositor in a savings bank of a change in its bylaws, and the

---

against bank. Badders v. Peoples Trust Co., 236 Ind. 357, 140 N.E.2d 235, 62 A.L.R.2d 1103.

[294] Ladd v. Augusta Sav. Bank, 96 Me. 510, 52 A. 1012, 58 L.R.A. 288.

[295] D'Agostino v. Home Federal Sav. & Loan Asso., 237 N.Y.S.2d 413 (1963).

Bank rules may be waived by bank itself since they were made for convenience and protection of bank. Layman v. Western Sav. Bank, 302 Pa. Super. 433, 448 A.2d 1119 (1982).

[296] Mutual Assurance Co. v. Norwich Sav. Soc., 128 Conn. 510, 24 A.2d 477, 139 A.L.R. 829.

[297] **In general.**—

Welch v. North Hills Bank, 442 S.W.2d 98 (Mo. App. 1969).

Where contract of deposit for joint tenancy account between bank and codepositors included rules and regulations of bank, each one of three parties had right to rely on such rules and regulations and to hold other parties to compliance therewith. Welch v. North Hills Bank, 442 S.W.2d 98 (Mo. App. 1969).

Provision in contract between bank and depositor prohibiting withdrawal. unless passbook was presented did not inure to benefit of bank alone and could not be waived by the unilateral action of the bank. Forbes v. First Camden Nat. Bank, etc., Co., 25 N.J. Super. 17, 95 A.2d 416.

Presentation requirement.—

Where passbook recited that all deposits were made subject to bylaw as therein printed and made a part of "this deposit contract" and contained statement that no payments were to be made or money withdrawn without presentation of the book, the presentation requirement became a part of the deposit contract, express or implied, governing the duty of the bank to depositor's wife, whose name appeared on passbook, and neither the bank alone nor the bank and the husband had power to waive the presentation requirement, and when the bank paid money out of account to husband without the book, it breached the deposit contract. Stillings v. Citizens Bank, 637 S.W.2d 401 (Mo. App. 1982).

depositor has no actual knowledge of such change, all deposits made after the change will be regarded as made under the original contract.[298] And a provision in a bank's bylaws that depositors shall be bound by any change therein, regardless of notice, is of no effect.[299] Similarly, the depositor's written assent at the time of deposit to all bank regulations does not include in the contract of deposit subsequently enacted bylaws of which the depositor has no knowledge.[300] But a savings bank may, on notice to its depositors, amend its bylaws so as to reduce the rate of interest on deposits or to refuse to continue deposits.[301] A bank's authority to make changes in its bylaws, however, does not empower it to change, without the consent of a depositor, a contract made with such depositor, nor to discharge its debt to a depositor by payment to a stranger.[302] The bank acted entirely within the bounds of its authority when it amended its rules and, thus, unilaterally modified a contract made with two joint depositors by eliminating the presentation of the savings passbook requirement as a condition precedent to the withdrawal of funds.[303]

Passbook Containing Contract.—A bank's bylaws, rules and regulations printed in a passbook given to a depositor and accepted by him, become part

---

[298] Kimins v. Boston Five-Cent Sav. Bank, 141 Mass. 33, 6 N.E. 242, 55 Am. B. 441; State v. San Francisco Sav. etc., Soc., 66 Cal. App. 53, 225 P. 309; Société de Bienfaisance St. Jean Baptiste de Millbury v. People's Sav. Bank,. 228 Mass. 556, 117 N.E. 921.

Bylaws printed in a passbook are upheld as necessary for protection of banks, but the bylaws, constituting as they do terms of contract of deposit between depositor and the bank, inure also to benefit of depositor, and a bank which undertakes to alter the terms of the contract does so at its own risk.

Hileman v. Hulver, 243 Md. 527, 221 A.2d 693 (1966).

[299] Hudson v. Roxbury Inst., 176 Mass. 522, 57 N.E. 1021 (1900).

A rule of a savings bank forbidding any gift of a deposit, except by an assignment in writing, duly acknowledged, does not bind one who became a depositor before the rule was made, though he had agreed that notices as to deposits should be deemed and taken as personal notices, and though the rule had been posted in the bank for many years before his death. Ranney v. Bowery Sav. Bank, 39 Misc. 301, 79 N.Y.S. 487.

[300] Société de Bienfaisance St. Jean Baptiste de Millbury v. People's Sav. Bank, 228 Mass. 556, 117 N.E. 921.

[301] State v. San Francisco Sav., etc., Soc., 66 Cal. App. 53, 225 P. 309.

[302] Kimins v. Boston Five-Cent Sav. Bank, 141 Mass. 33, 6 N.E. 242, 55 Am. B. 441; State v. San Francisco Sav. & Loan Soc., 66 Cal. App. 53, 225 P. 309.

[303] Kuehl v. Terre Haute First Nat'l Bank, 436 N.E.2d 1160 (Ind. App. 1982).

of the contract between him and the bank,[304] and they are also binding on

---

[304] **In general.—**

Arkansas.—Generally, a depositor by accepting a passbook is bound by the rules it contains, and he need not read or understand the terms to be bound by them. Haseman v. Union Bank, 597 S.W.2d 67 (Ark. 1980).

Connecticut.—Chase v. Waterbury Sav. Bank, 77 Conn. 295, 59 A. 37, 69 L.R.A. 329.

Indiana.—Rules of bank voluntarily adopted by it become valid agreement between bank and its depositors when account is opened and passbook is issued pursuant thereto with rules set forth therein. Badders v. Peoples Trust Co., 236 Ind. 357, 140 N.E.2d 235, 62 A.L.R.2d 1103.

Iowa.—Rules appearing in a savings account passbook are part of deposit contract. Keokuk Sav. Bank & Trust Co. v. Desvaux, 143 N.W.2d 296 (Iowa 1966).

Maryland.—Mercantile Sav. Bank v. Appler, 151 Md. 571, 135 A. 373; Gillen v. Maryland Nat'l Bank, 274 Md. 96, 333 A.2d 329 (1975).

Massachusetts.—Wall v. Provident Institution for Sav., 85 Mass. (3 Allen) 96; Wall v. Provident Inst., 88 Mass. (6 Allen) 320; Wasilauskas v. Brookline Sav. Bank, 259 Mass. 215, 156 N.E. 34, 52 A.L.R. 758.

New Hampshire.—Heath v. Portsmouth Sav. Bank, 46 N.H. 78, 88 Am. Dec. 194;

Brown v. Merrimack River Sav. Bank, 67 N.H. 549, 39 A. 336, 68 Am. St. R. 700.

New Jersey.—Cosgrove v. Provident Inst., 64 N.J.L. 653, 46 A. 617, rev'g 64 N.J.L. 39, 44 A. 936.

New York.—Warhus v. Bowery Sav. Bank, 12 N.Y. Super. Ct. 67, aff'd, 21 N.Y. 543; Kelly v. Chenango Valley Sav. Bank, 22 App. Div. 202, 47 N.Y.S. 1041, rev'g 21 Misc. 240, 45 N.Y.S. 651; Ferguson v. Harlem Sav. Bank, 43 Misc. 10, 86 N.Y.S. 825; Mitchell v. Home Sav. Bank, 38 Hun 255.

Ohio.—Royon v. Greenstein, 122 Ohio St. 340, 171 N.E. 595.

Rhode Island.—When savings bank issues passbook to each depositor and set, out therein rules, regulations, and bylaws for conduct of business, such rules, regulations and bylaws, when assented to by depositor, constitute his contract with bank. Griffin v. Centreville Sav. Bank, 93 R.I. 47, 171 A.2d 204.

Vermont.—If depositor accepts and retains a savings account passbook wherein are printed rules of bank respecting repayment of the deposit, he is deemed to acquiesce therein, and such rules become a part of the contract between bank and depositor. Davis v. Chittenden County Trust Co., 115 Vt. 349, 61 A.2d 553.

Requirement that passbook accompany withdrawal.—

Notice, printed in passbook, that no payments would be made unless check or order is accompanied by passbook of withdrawing depositor, was a part of the contract between bank and depositor and would be construed to mean that bank would pay upon presentation of passbook and would not pay if book were not presented. Forbes v. First Camden Nat. Bank, etc., Co., 25 N.J. Super. 17, 95 A.2d 416.

Bylaws printed in passbook, including rule that book must be presented before

subsequent holders of the passbook.[305] But a savings bank regulation with reference to withdrawals, printed in the depositor's bankbook, applies only to the deposits made in that bank.[306] And savings bank depositors have been held not bound by attempted limitations on their bank's liability for wrongful payment as contained in their passbook, under certain extenuating circumstances.[307]

Passbook as Evidence or Representation of Bank's Liability.—A depositor's passbook is not only part of the contract between his savings bank and himself as discussed above, but also is evidence of, and represents, the bank's debt to him.[308] Thus, a savings bankbook, like a bill of exchange or

---

withdrawals may be made, become part of a contract between them. Hileman v. Hulver, 243 Md. 527, 221 A2d 693 (1966).

305 Royon v. Greenstein, 122 Ohio St. 340, 171 N.E. 595.

The passbook charges the parties and their assignees with full knowledge of the terms of the deposit Hopkins Place Sav. Bank v. Holzer, 175 Md. 481, 2 A.2d 639.

306 Commonwealth Bank v. Goodman, 128 Md. 452, 97 A. 1005.

307 **In general.—**

Siegel v. State Bank, 123 N.Y.S. 220.

Contra.—

Bulakowski v. Philadelphia Sav. Fund Soc., 270 Pa. 538, 113 A. 553; Dinni v. Mechanics' Sav. Bank, 85 Conn. 225, 82 A. 580.

A depositor, not sufficiently familiar with English to understand what was printed on the fly leaf of his passbook, cannot be charged with the knowledge of a limitation of the bank's liability, when it was not called to his attention by the bank officials, and there was nothing in the circumstances to indicate to him the necessity for knowing what this printed matter meant; and hence it is solely responsible for payments made on his forged signature, notwithstanding the limitation. Siegel v. State Bank, 123 N.Y.S. 220.

For case of depositor being unable to read, see Koutsis v. Zion's Sav. Bank & Trust Co., 63 Utah 254, 225 P. 339.

Limitation not contained in proper title.—

Depositor held not presumed to know of provision exempting bank from liability for wrongful payments where reasonable discretion was exercised, where it was not in the title relating to withdrawals of deposits. Wood v. Connecticut Sav. Bank, 87 Conn. 341, 87 A. 983.

308 Myers v. Albany Sav. Bank, 270 App. Div. 466, 60 N.Y.S.2d 477, aff'd, 296 N.Y. 562, 68 N.E.2d 866.

A passbook of a savings bank evidences both the bank's liability to the depositor and the contract between the debtor and creditor as to the time and manner in which payment shall be made to the creditor. R.H. Macy & Co. v. Tyler, 21 Misc. 2d 998, 193 N.Y.S.2d 243.

note, is a chattel for many purposes such as giving of collateral.[309] It is said that a credit entry in a depositor's savings bank passbook is "prima facie evidence," the "best evidence," or "intrinsic evidence" that a deposit was made; however, it is also said such an entry is not conclusive, but is merely "presumptive evidence," and may be controverted.[310] But possession of a commercial bank deposit book or a broker's statement of credit has no such intrinsic quality.[311] And under a statute permitting a bank to make payment

---

[309] **In general.—**

Grant v. Colonial Bank & Trust Co., 356 Mass. 392, 252 N.E.2d 339 (1969); Stebbins v. North Adams Trust Co., 243 Mass 69, 136 N.E. 880; Forastiere v. Springfield Inst. for Savings, 303 Mass. 101, 20 N.E.2d 950 (1939).

Bankbook used as collateral.—

Where debtor told bank president that he had two savings account books held by escrow agent as security for debts, and bank asked that account be transferred to bank and bank issued bankbook which was substituted as collateral with escrow agent for account transferred, bank had knowledge of escrow agent's security interest in bankbook it issued and intended to continue that interest. Grant v. Colonial Bank & Trust Co., 356 Mass. 392, 252 N.E.2d 339 (1969).

Where no explicit terms of contract between bank and debtor tended to restrict debtor's power to transfer security interest in account by pledge of bankbook and delivery of executed withdrawal order, and bank, through its president, knew of security interest of escrow agent in passbook and directly participated in substituting its account for account in another bank in which security agent had escrow interest, bank could not appropriate, by setoff, funds in account as wholly property of debtor for payment of debt not shown to have matured and to be due to bank on date that account was opened if particular indebtedness was in existence at all on that date. Grant v. Colonial Bank & Trust Co., 356 Mass. 392, 252 N.E.2d 339 (1969).

[310] **In general.—**

Smith v. Richland State Bank, 9 So. 2d 327 (La. App. 1942).

Prima facie evidence.—

Entry of deposit in passbook is admission of indebtedness to depositor and is prima facie evidence as to amount thereof; and when not explained, it becomes conclusive and created relationship of debtor and creditor. Fischer v. Morris Plan Co., 276 8.W.2d 898 (Mo. App. 1955).

Illustrative case.—

In suit to recover amount of credit entry in savings account book with defense that entry was made through error and was not the basis of any deposit, testimonial proof to contradict verity of entry was admissible. Smith v. Richland State Bank, 9 So. 2d 327 (La. App. 1942).

The depositor is a creditor of the bank and the passbook issued to a depositor is evidence of the debt and the contract between them, but passbook is not in itself negotiable. People v. Jenkins, 61 App. Div. 2d 705, 403 N.Y.S.2d 751 (1978).

[311] In re Cassola's Estate, 47 N.Y.S.2d 90.

from a deposit upon an order of court without presentation of a passbook, it was held that an assignee of a passbook is not entitled to believe that a deposit is safely his although he has possession of the passbook.[312]

b. Title to and Disposition of Deposits.

§ 14. To Whom Payments to Be Made.

In General.—In the absence of a modifying agreement between a savings bank and a depositor, the bank may pay deposits only to the depositor or his legal representatives.[313] And a bank, having received a deposit from a

---

[312] **In general.**—

United States v. Emigrant Industrial Sav. Bank, 122 F. Supp. 547.

The New York banking statute permitting board of trustees of a savings bank to provide in the bylaws for making payments in case of loss of passbook and precluding any reliance on possession of the passbook as assurance that the deposit was intact is not limited to the situation only when the superintendent has determined that the right to make exceptional payments is being improperly exercised. United States v. Bowery Sav. Bank, 185 F. Supp. 30 (S.D.N.Y. 1960), aff'd, 297 F.2d 380 (2d Cir. 1961).

[313] Highfield v. First Nat. Bank, 45 Ga. App. 431, 165 S.E. 135.

Where money was deposited in savings bank account by and in the name of depositor, and words indicating that deposit was made for a third person were added in a handwriting not that of the depositor, and there was no proof that depositor approved of such addition, or that the person named therein owned the money deposited, upon application made after death of depositor by person entitled to deposit if it was the property of depositor, state comptroller was directed to pay to such applicant the proceeds of such deposit and the accrued interest thereon which had been received by state comptroller under statute with respect to abandoned bank accounts. Application of Bakerman, 262 App. Div. 341, 29 N.Y.S.2d 567.

A bank may not permit withdrawal of funds from a savings account absent an order of its depositor. Maddox v. First Westroads Bank, 199 Neb. 81, 256 N.W.2d 647 (1977).

Where a savings bank grants withdrawal payments to a person not representing himself to be the depositor and who obtains payment on the strength of an order purported to be signed by the depositor, the rule which is applicable with respect to forged checks applies; that is, that a bank paying a forged check may not charge the amount of the check against the account of the person whose name is forged. Therefore, a bank cannot properly charge its depositor's account on the basis of a forged withdrawal slip. Maddox v. First Westroads Bank, 199 Neb. 81, 256 N.W.2d 647 (1977).

Where a bank charged and closed customers' savings accounts on the receipt of withdrawal slips bearing the forged signature of the customers' guardian, the fact that the bank made cashier's checks issued in the transaction payable to the customer's guardian did not permit the bank to escape liability to customers for charging their accounts on the basis of forged withdrawal slips. Maddox v. First Westroads Bank, 199 Neb. 81, 256 N.W.2d 647 (1977).

Savings bank was not precluded by case law nor contract between parties from releasing

depositor and given him credit therefor on its books, cannot question his right to the deposit or plead title in another, unless the title has been transferred upon the depositor's authority or he is estopped to claim otherwise.[314] But the names in which bank deposits are entered on the records of the bank, or the names of those authorized by contract with the bank to withdraw funds from bank accounts of others, may or may not be conclusive as to the true ownership of such deposits and accounts.[315] For example, where a depositor permits another person to withdraw from his savings account, such person acquires no interest in the account and upon the death of the depositor, the entire balance in the account is a "probate asset" of his estate unless the question of a valid gift is presented.[316] Payment to a depositor's receiver of the depositor's property relieves a bank of its

---

funds to attorney for estate who presented passbook and a withdrawal slip properly signed by administrator; bank's measure of care in demanding two documents and checking the signature on one of them was at least "ordinary" and was not "negligent," and therefore bank was not liable to administrator for disbursing the funds. Layman v. Western Sav. Bank, 302 Pa. Super. 433, 448 A2d 1119 (1982).

The District of Columbia's Uniform Nonprobate Transfers on Death Act, among other things, identifies different types of multiple-party bank accounts, recognizes the various purposes for which they might be held, and clarifies the rights and relationships among joint account holders, including survivorship rights. D.C. Code § 19-602.03 requires that all accounts, including those established before the Act went into effect, be categorized as one of several types of accounts—namely, as a single-party account or multiple-party account, with or without right of survivorship. D.C. Code § 19-602.04 provides forms for the types of accounts listed in D.C. Code § 19-602.03. If an account's documents are not substantially similar to one of the provided forms, then the account is categorized as the type of account that most nearly conforms to the depositor's intent. D.C. Code § 19-602.12 addresses the disposition of multiple-party account funds upon a party's death. Estate of Walker v. Stefan, 160 A.3d 1165 (D.C. App. 2017).

[314] Fischer v. Morris Plan Co., 275 S.W.2d 393 (Mo. App. 1955).

Under New York law, general rule is that legal title to money deposited in bank account is vested in bank, while depositor holds chose in action against bank; such rule applies for most part to savings accounts also. Silverman v. Johnson Controls, Inc., 139 Bankr. 765 (Bankr. E.D.N.Y. 1992).

[315] Jones v. Neu, 106 Ohio App. 161, 6 Ohio Op. 2d 428, 150 N.E.2d 858 (not conclusive).

The way an account is opened and maintained by the depositor is the controlling factor in determining ownership of a savings account carried without any deposit contract or express provision for survivorship. In re Schroeder's Estate (Ohio Prob.), 144 N.E.2d 512.

[316] In re Schroeder's Estate (Ohio Prob.), 144 N.E.2d 512.

Intention of grantor, as evidenced by terms of contract between grantor and bank in relation to savings account, is the crucial factor. In re Estate of Smith, 199 Kan. 89, 427 P.2d 443 (1967).

obligation pro tanto to the depositor whose rights vested in the receiver.[317] A treasurer of a committee who deposits in his own name a fund appropriated for a particular purpose, and which the bank pays to a new treasurer appointed by the committee to receive it, cannot recover the fund from the bank.[318] And in some states, provision is made by statute for the disposition of deposits where the depositor cannot be found, or the claimant is unknown.[319] When a bank's agents learned that a depositor had withdrawn money on a nonexistent account number, it became incumbent upon the bank to inform the depositor, who had two savings accounts with the bank, and learn her wishes. The bank had no authority to charge one of the accounts without first making inquiry of the plaintiff and it breached its contractual duties by doing so.[320]

Passbook.—A "passbook" issued by a savings bank is the record of the customers' account, and its production authorizes control of the deposit.[321]

Bank's passbook rules which required recognition by the bank of assignments or transfers of the "Bank Book" referred to money represented by the passbook as the subject of transfer or assignability, and not to the passbook itself.[322] But it also has been said that the possession of a passbook does not constitute proof of the right to withdraw moneys thereon, but only imports a liability of the bank to the depositor, and an agreement to repay at such time and in such manner as the depositor shall direct.[323] A passbook is

---

[317] McCabe v. Union Dime Sav. Bank, 150 Misc. 157, 268 N.Y.S. 449.

[318] Tay v. Concord Sav. Bank, 60 N.H. 277.

[319] Commonwealth v. Dollar Sav. Bank, 259 Pa. 138, 102 A. 569, 1 A.L.R. 1048.

A statute, providing that deposits which have remained inactive and unclaimed for a great many years, where the claimant is unknown or the depositor cannot be found, shall be paid to the treasurer and receiver general, to be held by him as trustee for the true owner or his legal representative, is not unconstitutional. Provident Inst. v. Malone, 221 U.S. 660, 31 S. Ct. 661, 55 L Ed. 899, aff'g Malone v. Provident Inst. for Sav., 201 Mass. 23, 86 N.E. 912; Commonwealth v. Dollar Sav. Bank, 259 Pa. 138, 102 A. 569, 1 A.L.R. 1048.

[320] Menicocci v. Archer Nat'l Bank, 67 Ill. App. 3d 388, 24 Ill. Dec. 296, 385 N.E.2d 63 (1978).

[321] Wade v. Edwards, 23 Ga. App. 677, 99 S.E. 160.

[322] Rosenstein v. Mechanics & Farmers Bank, 51 N.C. App. 437, 276 S.E.2d 710 (1081).

[323] Myers v. Albany Sav. Bank, 57 N.Y.S.2d 448; Geller v. Levitt, 25 Misc. 2d 564, 202 N.Y.S.2d 59.

Savings book imports a liability of bank to depositor for moneys deposited, and an agreement to repay them at such time and in such manner as depositor shall direct. Rivera v. Central Bank & Trust Co., 155 Colo. 383, 395 P.2d 11 (1964).

not a negotiable instrument,[324] although it has been said a savings bankbook is not a mere passbook or statement of an account, but is the depositor's voucher as evidence of his debt, in the nature of security for the payment of money and analogous to a stock certificate in many respects.[325]

Generally, a savings account can only be withdrawn upon presentation of a deposit book, and if the book gets into unauthorized hands, the rights and liabilities of the bank and depositor are subject to the contract between them pertaining to the deposit.[326] And a bank, in making payment, cannot rely solely upon the possession and presentation of a bankbook or passbook, but must exercise ordinary care and diligence, to ascertain that the person receiving the money is entitled to it.[327] The wrongful conversion of a

---

[324] Royon v. Greenstein, 122 Ohio St. 340, 171 N.E. 595; Brogna v. Commissioner of Banks, 248 Mass. 241, 142 N.E. 746; Bryson v. Security Trust, etc., Bank, 29 Cal. App. 596, 156 P. 987; Forastiere v. Springfield Inst. for Savings,. 303 Mass. 101, 20 N.E.2d 950 (1939); Hopkins Place Sav. Bank v. Holzer, 175 Md. 481, 2 A.2d 639; Myers v. Albany Sav. Bank, 57 N.Y.S.2d 448; Myers v. Albany Sav. Bank, 270 App. Div. 466, 60 N.Y.S.2d 477, aff'd, 296 N.Y. 562, 68 N.E.2d 866. See 19 of this chapter.

Public policy that creates a special rule respecting payments to an innocent creditor with cash or negotiable paper has no application to an assignment of a bank passbook since it is not negotiable. In re Givis' Estate, 109 N.Y.S.2d 456.

A "bank savings account book" is a book evidencing deposits of money or credit which if left on deposit for stated periods of time draw interest, and such book does not pass as money or by endorsement only as a "check." In re Hartzell's Estate, 26 Ohio Op. 466, 12 Ohio Supp. 62.

[325] Old Colony Trust Co. v. Hale, 302 Mass. 68, 18 N.E.2d 432, 120 A.L.R. 1207.

[326] Miller v. First Granite City Nat. Bank, 349 Ill. App. 347, 110 N.E.2d 651.

Where wife acquiesced in husband's withdrawal of funds from savings account without presenting passbook, contrary to terms of contract of deposit, the wife was not entitled to any recovery against the bank for those funds. Stilling. v. Citizens Bank of Ava, 637 S.W.2d 401 (Mo. App. 1982).

Where passbook recited that all deposits were made subject to bylaws as therein printed and made a part of "this deposit contract" and contained statement that no payments were to be made or money withdrawn without presentation of the book, the presentation requirement became a part of the deposit contract, express or implied, governing the duty of the bank to depositor's wife, whose name appeared on passbook, and neither the bank alone nor the bank and the husband had power to waive the presentation requirement, and when the bank paid money out of account to husband without the book it breached the deposit contract. Stilling. v. Citizens Bank, 687 8.W.2d 401 (Mo. App. 1982).

[327] Bloom v. Bank for Savings, 14 Misc. 2d 693, 180 N.Y.S.2d 934; R. H. Macy & Co. v. Tyler, 21 Misc. 2d 998, 193 N.Y.S.2d 243. See § 18 of this chapter.

Savings banks and commercial banks with savings accounts must exercise ordinary care for protection of depositor in paying money out of depositor's account. Kalb v. Chemical

passbook carries with it no title to the account represented thereby, and the real owner of a passbook may maintain an action, independently of his possession of the passbook, to establish his title to the account.[328]

But in the absence of a showing that a decedent's delivery of a passbook and execution of a power of attorney to an individual who used them for the withdrawal of the decedent's funds had been involuntary, there could be no recovery against the depository bank by the decedent's administrator on account of such withdrawal of the decedent's funds.[329]

Under certain state statutes, a savings bank may pay the amount of a judgment against its depositor without presentation of his bankbook.[330] But even though a statute permits a savings bank to waive presentation of a passbook in certain situations, a bank must be extraordinarily careful in using this exception.[331] And there is ample justification for a savings bank requiring either an indemnity bond or save-harmless agreement whenever a

---

Bank New York Trust Co., 62 Misc. 2d 458, 309 N.Y.S.2d 502 (1969), rev'd on other grounds, 64 Misc. 2d 824, 316 N.Y.S.2d 381.

[328] Watson v. Stockton Morris Plan Co., 34 Cal. App. 2d 393, 93 P.2d 855, aff'g 86 P.2d 927.

A depositor in a savings bank may maintain an action to recover the amount of his deposit, although, upon production of the deposit book, the bank has paid the amount due to one who has been appointed as his administrator under the erroneous belief that he was dead, after he had been absent for more than seven year, without being heard from. Jochumsen v. Suffolk Sav. Bank, 85 Mass. (3 Allen) 87.

[329] Romero v. Sjoberg, 6 App. Div. 2d 674, 173 N.Y.S.2d 690, aff'd, 5 N.Y.S.2d 518, 186 N.Y.S.2d 246.

[330] Swytak v. Duda, 44 N.Y.S.2d 498.

In light of a statute governing payment to one of two or more depositors, the first codepositor could not recover against the bank for the payment of the $5,145.48 savings account balance to the second codepositor even though the bank issued a passbook to the codepositors which provided that the presentation of such passbook was required for the depositor to make a withdrawal and the first codepositor possessed such passbook at all times. Gray v. Landmark Union Trust Bank, N.A., 864 So. 2d 1256 (Fla. App. 1978).

A court had inherent power to direct a depositor bank to pay over funds on deposit in a judgment debtors' bank account without the judgment creditor producing a passbook and, also, under the statute the bank would be discharged from liability to the depositors to the extent of their funds paid to the sheriff on levy of execution. Brezenoff v. Franklin Sav. Bank etc., 108 Misc. 2d 626, 438 N.Y.S.2d 171 (1981).

[331] Central Nat'l Bank v. Gallagher, 13 Ohio App. 2d 115, 42 Ohio Op. 2d 226, 234 N.E.2d 524 (1968).

Passbook presentation clauses are for the purpose of preventing payment to one who is not a depositor and may be waived by the bank, and such clauses are not meant to protect a

depositor without a passbook requests his money.[332] And if a third person has the passbook, with or without an assignment, the bank is protected in paying the depositor the amount of the account until the third person presents the passbook with an assignment bearing the signature of the depositor.[333]

Adverse Claimants.—The purpose of the New York statute providing that notice to a savings bank of an adverse claim to a deposit shall not be effectual to cause the bank to recognize the adverse claimant unless he shall either procure a restraining order or execute a bond indemnifying the bank from any liability, is to protect banks against the hazards of double liability in cases where there are adverse claimants.[334] The fact that a bank is unwilling to avail itself of the remedy given by statute of interpleading adverse claimants, or is unable to do so because no adverse claimant is found, so that it pays at its peril, does not relieve it from liability to pay a claimant if his claim is established.[335] For other cases dealing with the determination of ownership of property deposited in savings banks, see the footnote.[336]

---

depositor against withdrawals by a codepositor. Gray v. Landmark Union Trust Bank, 364 So. 2d 1256 (Fla. App. 1978).

332 Central Nat'l Bank v. Gallagher, 13 Ohio App. 2d 115, 42 Ohio Op. 2d 226, 234 N.E.2d 524 (1968).

333 Myers v. Albany Sav. Bank, 57 N.Y.S.2d 448; Geller v. Levitt, 25 Misc. 2d 564, 202 N.Y.S.2d 59.

334 Ciriello v. Eastchester Sav. Bank, 343 N.Y.S.2d 526 (Sup. Ct. 1973).

335 Scheffer v. Erie County Sav. Bank, 229 N.Y. 50, 127 N.E. 474.

336 Where three books of savings bank accounts were found in decedent's safety deposit box, and the books were in the name of decedent's brother alone, and the brother had originally supplied the funds in the accounts, and the accounts had originally been in brother's name, and he had transferred them to decedent's name, and they had remained in her name for 16 months until a date from four and one-half months alter her marriage, when she had transferred all three accounts back to brother, and ever since, for a period of over 16 years, the accounts had remained in his name, the brother was the owner of the books and the funds represented by them. Geller v. Levitt, 25 Misc. 2d 564, 202 N.Y.S.2d 59.

Where there was no transcript or record of proceedings had in trial court and the trial court made no specific finding about which parent supported minor children who, after divorce, were in custody of their mother, the supreme court could not as a matter of law hold that the trial court erred in finding that funds in savings accounts established by the father for minor children prior to the divorce belonged to the children and not to the father who signed bank signature cards, who, from time to time, deposited certain moneys into the accounts and who never relinquished control of passbooks. Beaudoin v. Beaudoin, 386 A.2d 1261 (N.H. 1978).

New York statute providing that withdrawal of moneys from bank savings account or time

Bylaws and Rules of Bank Regulating Payments.—The person or persons to whom money deposited in a savings bank will be paid, and the methods of its withdrawal are matters that are generally regulated by the bylaws and rules of the bank; the validity of some of these bylaws and rules has been sustained by the courts.[337] Bylaws of a bank which provide that it shall be

---

deposit account which is made by means of unauthorized signature is wholly inoperative as to the person whose name is signed unless such person has authorized or ratified such withdrawal did not apply to depositor who placed funds in bank's checking account. Tevdorachvili v. Chase Manhattan Bank, 103 F. Supp. 2d 632 (E.D.N.Y. 2000).

[337] **In general.—**

R. H. Macy & Co. v. Tyler, 21 Misc. 2d 998, 193 N.Y.S.2d 243.

Drawer of check had right to rely on rules and insist on observance thereof by bank. Keller v. Davis, 123 Pa. Super. 240, 187 A. 267.

A regulation requiring the production of passbooks before payment by a savings bank of moneys on deposit therein is reasonable. Walde v. Walde, 45 N.Y.S.2d 791.

Bylaw requiring production of passbook or indemnity bond not applicable to city.—

Bylaw of bank providing that payment to depositor or anyone claiming through depositor will not be made unless there is production of passbook or double indemnity bond furnished should not be applied to the city of New York to compel it to furnish security by way of cash or surety. Dumpson v. Taylor, 38 Misc. 2d 118, 237 N.Y.S.2d 871.

Rule authorizing savings bank to pay person presenting passbook unless notified of loss of book is reasonable and binding upon depositors assenting. But the mere printing in passbook of provision authorizing savings bank to pay person presenting passbook binds depositor only when required to sign it or actually notified thereof. Highfield v. First Nat. Bank, 45 Ga. App. 431, 165 S.E. 135.

A rule providing that payment to a person presenting a passbook shall be good on account of the owner unless the passbook has been lost and notice in writing given the bank before payment is made is binding on depositors in savings banks. Langdale v. Citizens' Bank of Savannah, 121 Ga. 105, 48 S.E. 708, 104 Am. St. R. 94, 69 L.R.A. 341, 2 Ann. Cas. 257; Commonwealth Bank v. Goodman, 128 Md. 452, 97 A. 1005.

A rule of a savings bank, stipulating that a payment to a party presenting a passbook shall be a valid payment of the deposit, adopted under a statute, providing that sums deposited with a savings bank shall be repaid to the depositor in such manner and at such times and under such regulations as the trustees shall prescribe, etc., and known to a depositor, is a part of the contract between the bank and the depositor. Campbell v. Schenectady Sav. Bank, 114 App. Div. 337, 99 N.Y.S. 927.

Bylaw excluding all other methods of withdrawing deposit.—

A bylaw of a savings bank, to the effect that money might be drawn personally, or on the written order of the depositor or his attorney, when accompanied by the "passbook," excludes by implication all other methods of withdrawing the deposit. Smith v. Brooklyn Sav. Bank, 101 N.Y. 58, 4 N.E. 123, 54 Am. K 653.

Rules in passbook prohibiting assignment without bank's consent held not

open for business during certain hours only do not render illegal the payment of a draft outside such hours.[338] Where a bank deposit is received and payable only in accordance with specified rules, one of which requires payments to be made by draft, the bank has no authority to deplete the deposit by charging against it notes of the depositor received by the bank for collection.[339] And in a suit against a bank for its refusal to pay a deposit, the bank's right to set up the defense that the plaintiff had not complied with its bylaws may be lost by waiver.[340]

Joint Deposits Generally.[341]—A savings account to the joint credit of the depositor and another creates a present joint interest, and the bank may make payment to either of them.[342] However, to justify a bank in paying out moneys deposited in a joint account, a passbook must be produced, and there

---

unreasonable nor against public policy. Royon v. Greenstein, 122 Ohio St. 340, 171 N.E. 595.

Bank's obligation implicit in bylaw.—

Implicit in a bank's agreement, in its bylaws, to maintain the records of all savings accounts was the bank's obligation to keep its accounts correctly and to see that the transactions were credited properly to the depositor's accounts. Menicocci v. Archer Nat'l Bank, 67 Ill. App. 3d 388, 24 Ill. Dec. 296, 385 N.E.2d 63 (1978).

[338] Butler v. Broadway Sav. Institution, 171 App. Div. 682, 157 N.Y.S. 532.

[339] Heinrich v. First Nat'l Bank, 83 Misc. 566, 145 N.Y.S. 342, aff'd, 164 App. Div. 960, 149 N.Y.S. 1086, aff'd, 219 N.Y. 1, 113 N.E. 531, 1917A L.R.A. 655.

[340] **In general.—**

Christensen v. Ogden State Bank, 75 Utah 478, 286 P. 638; Brooks v. Erie County Sav. Bank, 169 App. Div. 73, 154 N.Y.S. 692, aff'd, 224 N.Y. 639, 121 N.E. 857.

Illustrative case.—

Where a depositor in a savings bank is a nonresident and places the collection of her accounts in the hands of an attorney, who presents the passbook and demands of the bank's officers the payment of the balance shown therein, the rules of the bank allowing it to pay out deposits to any one holding the passbook, and the officers inform the attorney that they will not pay the interest claimed but will look into the question of paying the principal, in a suit against the bank it cannot set up as a defense that the attorney had not complied with the bylaws by showing written authority from his client to collect what was due her, this objection not having been made at the time of the demand was waived. See Fenn v. Ware, 100 Ga. 563, 28 S.E. 238; Atlanta, etc., Banking Co. v. Close, 115 Ga. 939, 42 S.E. 265.

[341] See § 17 of this chapter. See also vol. 5A, ch. 9, § 46.

[342] **In general.—**

Cleveland Trust Co. v. Scobie, 114 Ohio St. 241, 151 N.E. 373, 48 A.L.R. 182.

The entry of a savings deposit to credit of two persons or survivor rendered deposit subject to withdrawal to either who presented passbook, but left separate interests of each in deposit undetermined. Peoples Bank v. Turner, 169 Md. 430, 182 A. 314, 103 A.L.R. 490.

must not be any notice of a hostile claim by one of the depositors.[343] Thus, one joint depositor could not recover the amount of a deposit from a bank on

---

Payment made in capacity of joint owner.—

Though a banking institution may, under proper conditions, make payment of a joint account to one of the joint owners in complete discharge of its obligations, payment in such a case is made to the joint owner in the capacity of joint owner. La Valley v. Pere Marquette Employees' Credit Union, 342 Mich. 639, 70 N.W.2d 798.

No right of survivorship.—

It has been held that the writing on the face of a certificate of deposit is the controlling factor in determining the ownership of a deposit in names of two or more persons evidenced by such certificate, and unless the certificate contains express words of survivorship, the deposit is not payable to the survivor upon the death of one of the depositors. In re Schroeder's Estate, 144 N.E.2d 512 (Ohio Prob. 1957).

Statutory provision.—

Under statute providing that in certain circumstances payments may be made by banking institution from a joint and survivor account to any one of the depositors, individual obligations of banking institution may run to any one of the depositors and may be enforced by any one of the depositors in his own name and right. La Valley v. Pere Marquette Employees' Credit Union, 842 Mich. 839, 70 N.W.2d 798.

Statutory construction.—

Statute insulating savings bank from liability to one joint tenant when the other withdrew money from joint bank account confers immunity from liability and therefore must be strictly construed. Brown v. Bowery Sav. Bank, 51 N.Y.2d 411, 434 N.Y.S.2d 916, 415 N.E.2d 906 (1980).

[343] **In general.—**

Caruso v. Dry Dock Sav. Institution, 170 Misc. 867, 11 N.Y.S.2d 411.

Requirement of production cannot be waived.—

Bank could not waive provisions of contract with joint depositors requiring passbook to be presented when withdrawals were made and thereby escape liability to one joint depositor when it allowed withdrawal by other without passbook. Badders v. Peoples Trust Co., 236 Ind. 357, 140 N.E.2d 235 (1957).

Allowance of withdrawal without passbook.—

When bank failed to comply with provision of its rules and regulations, incorporated into contract of deposit by reference, requiring presentation of passbook in order for depositor to be entitled to make withdrawal from savings deposits, such action constituted breach of contract of deposit rendering bank liable to plaintiff codepositor in amount of withdrawal permitted in violation of contract. Welch v. North Hills Bank, 442 S.W.2d 98 (Mo. App. 1969).

Where bank rules and regulations provided that passbook "must accompany any withdrawal check or receipt" and that payments to persons presenting passbook should relieve bank from liability, and conditioned right of depositor to make withdrawal on presentation of passbook in addition to order or receipt, neither party to joint tenancy

the ground that he was the sole owner thereof, where it appeared that the other depositor who had possession of the bankbook had no intention of relinquishing it or his claim to the deposit.[344] The statute insulating a savings bank from liability to one joint tenant when the other tenant withdraws money from the joint savings account did not confer immunity on the bank from liability to a tenant whose name was removed from the account, without her consent, at the request of the other tenant and the tenant whose name was removed was entitled to recover half of the money which was in the account when all of it was withdrawn by the person whose name had been substituted as joint tenant.[345] And a savings bank that issued a new passbook and paid a deposit to a joint depositor without inquiry was held liable to the other joint depositor to whom the original passbook was issued.[346] However, where a savings bank has paid a deposit to a joint tenant without a passbook in an emergency situation, it may establish an equitable defense to an action against it for the amount of such deposit.[347]

---

account had right to withdraw until passbook was presented. Welch v. North Hills Bank, 442 S.W.2d 98 (Mo. App. 1969).

Where decedent and one other person opened joint savings account and accepted passbook stating that depositors must present passbook in person or send it with written order for payment of money, and signed signature card stating that funds could be withdrawn by or upon order of either, transfer by bank of funds in account to new joint account, with decedent and second person as depositors, upon latter's presentation of letter from decedent authorizing withdrawal, without presentation of passbook, was ineffectual, and first depositor with decedent was entitled to funds under survivorship provisions of joint tenancy agreement. Keokuk Sav. Bank & Trust Co. v. Desvaux, 143 N.W.2d 296 (Iowa 1966).

Where wife acquiesced in husband's withdrawal of funds from savings account without presenting passbook, contrary to terms of contract of deposit, the wife was not entitled to any recovery against the bank for those funds. Stillings v. Citizens Bank, 637 8.W.2d 401 (Mo. App. 1982).

Fact that wife did not sign "joint account" signature card in connection with savings account opened by husband did not mean that the bank had no duty or obligation to wife in respect to the deposited funds, as whether bank had a duty was dependent on whether wife had an interest in the account especially as passbook stated that account was with husband or wife or minor daughter. Stillings v. Citizens Bank, 637 S.W.2d 401 (Mo. App. 1982).

[344] Caruso v. Dry Dock Sav. Inst., 170 Misc. 867, 11 N.Y.S.2d 411.

[345] Brown v. Bowery Sav. Bank, 51 N.Y.2d 411, 434 N.Y.S.2d 916, 415 N.E.2d 906 (1980).

[346] Mercantile Sav. Bank v. Appler, 151 Md. 571, 135 A. 373.

[347] Kramer v. First Nat'l Bank, 163 So. 2d 341 (Fla. App. 1964).

Where bank, being sued for funds deposited in names of plaintiff and minor daughter as joint tenants with right of survivorship, established without genuine issue of fact its affirmative defense in nature of equitable defense that funds had been paid out to daughter

As between a bank and the joint owners of a savings account therein, the owners are joint obligees, and their right against the bank is joint and not several.[348] A statute relating to bank savings deposits by more than one depositor, and permitting payment to any such depositor, is intended to protect banks, but it also establishes property rights in such depositors.[349] And a statute governing joint accounts and the discharge from liability of a bank by payment to, and receipt of, one of the joint tenants of a bank account, does not purport to govern contracts which the bank can make with its depositors, and does not prohibit a bank from making a contract with provisions different from the statute's, and thus the liability of a bank for allowing withdrawal of funds without presentation of a passbook will be decided on the basis of the contract entered into by the parties and is not governed by the statute.[350] The bank acted entirely within the bounds of its

---

and her aunt upon demand by daughter and certification that passbook was lost and representation that funds were necessary for emergency care of daughter during serious illness of plaintiff, such payment operated as release to bank, notwithstanding bank rule requiring presentation of passbook for all withdrawals, and bank was entitled to judgment. Kramer v. First Nat'l Bank, 163 So. 2d 341 (Fla. App. 1964).

[348] Forbes v. First Camden Nat. Bank, etc., Co., 25 N.J. Super. 17, 95 A.2d 416.

[349] DeLong v. Farmers Bldg. & Loan Ass'n, 148W. Va. 625, 137 S.E.2d 11 (1964).

Whether a savings account designated as a joint account of a mother, daughter and daughter's husband with right of survivorship was opened by the mother or the daughter, opening of the account vested interest in the daughter and husband under the statute authorizing the bank to pay proceeds to any of the parties named in the deposit, in that the signature card itself constituted a designation "in writing to the banking institution that the account be held in joint tenancy with right of survivorship." Coristo v. Twin City Bank, 520 S.W.2d 218 (Ark. 1975).

[350] Welch v. North Hills Bank, 442 S.W.2d 98 (Mo. App. 1969).

Statutes relating to savings banks and safe deposit institutions did not prohibit contractual provisions requiring presentation of passbook for withdrawal and did not relieve bank from liability for permitting withdrawal without passbook, even if statutes were complied with. Welch v. North Hills Bank, 442 S.W.2d 98 (Mo. App. 1969).

Where rules and regulations of bank were incorporated by reference as part of contract of deposit, court of appeals would determine liability of bank for allowing withdrawal of funds from such joint tenancy account without presentation of passbook by ascertaining intention of parties as set out in contract as a whole, including such rules and regulations. Welch v. North Hills Bank, 442 S.W.2d 98 (Mo. App. 1969).

The bank, against which two joint tenants, one of whom had deposited the funds, brought an action after the third joint tenant had withdrawn the funds from the joint savings account without presenting the passbook, was not estopped, by a notation on the first page of the passbook to the effect that funds could be withdrawn only upon presentation of the passbook, to deny that funds could be withdrawn without the passbook, since the notation was for the

authority when it amended its rules and, thus, unilaterally modified a contract made with two joint depositors by eliminating the presentation of the savings passbook requirement as a condition precedent to the withdrawal of funds.[351]

By statute in Tennessee, a bank is required to utilize account documents that enable a depositor to designate ownership interest when establishing an account in the names of two or more people. The statute expressly provides that such account documents may include any of the following: (1) The signature card; (2) the deposit agreement; (3) a certificate of deposit; (4) a document confirming purchase of a certificate of deposit or (5) other documents provided by the bank or deposit institution that indicate the intent of the depositor. Conspicuous by its absence in the section is a requirement that any documents referred to therein be signed by anyone.[352]

A non-debtor depositor is allowed under the statute to prove his or her rights in the funds held in a joint account.[353] The plain language of the statute does not contain a requirement that the non-debtor account holder prove that the funds held in a joint non-marital account are in any way exclusive to the non-debtor; rather, it merely requires that the non-debtor establish his or her rights in the disputed funds.[354] A non-debtor meets his

---

bank's protection and not for the benefit of the depositor and the bank never represented to the depositor that it was for her protection or that it afforded her any protection. Coristo v. Twin City Bank, 522 S.W.2d 417 (Ark. 1975).

Statute insulating a savings bank from liability to one joint tenant when the other withdrew money from the joint bank account confers immunity from liability and therefore must be strictly construed. Brown v. Bowery Sav. Bank, 51 N.Y.2d 411, 434 N.Y.S.2d 916, 415 N.E.2d 906 (1980).

351 Kuehl v. Terre Haute First Nat'l Bank, 436 N.E.2d 1160 (Ind. App. 1982).

352 In re Estate of Bingham, 2017 Tenn. App. LEXIS 396 (2017) (decedent's intent that the certificate of deposit carries with it a right of survivorship is conclusively established by the documents utilized by the bank). See T.C.A., § 45-2-703(d).

353 Trustmark Nat'l Bank v. Sunshine Carwash No. 5 Partners, 558 S.W.3d 157, 2018 Tenn. App. LEXIS 179 (Tenn. Ct. App. 2018). See T.C.A., § 45-2-703(a).

354 Trustmark Nat'l Bank v. Sunshine Carwash No. 5 Partners, 558 S.W.3d 157, 2018 Tenn. App. LEXIS 179 (Tenn. Ct. App. 2018).

Non-debtor depositor met his burden to establish the rights that he had in the funds in the joint bank account because there was no dispute that he was the sole source of the funds at issue—as he was the party who placed the funds into the account for the purpose of furthering a business partnership endeavor—and that the judgment debtor had no right in or to the funds outside of business involving the construction of a building for the partnership. Accordingly, the non-debtor depositor was entitled to dismissal of the garnishment of execution and a release of the funds in the joint bank account. Trustmark Nat'l Bank v.

or her burden to establish rights in disputed funds in a joint account by showing that the non-debtor is the source of the funds to the exclusion of the debtor, i.e. that the funds were solely deposited in the account by the non-debtor. The fact that both the debtor and non-debtor have access to the funds in a joint account will not defeat a claim by the non-debtor to establish rights in the funds under the statute.[355]

For cases involving the changing of a savings account from an individual to a joint and survivorship account,[356] and vice versa,[357] see the footnotes.

Sunshine Carwash No. 5 Partners, 558 S.W.3d 157, 2018 Tenn. App. LEXIS 179 (Tenn. Ct. App. 2018).

[355] Trustmark Nat'l Bank v. Sunshine Carwash No. 5 Partners, 558 S.W.3d 157, 2018 Tenn. App. LEXIS 179 (Tenn. Ct. App. 2018). T.C.A., § 45-2-703(a).

Non-debtor depositor met his burden to establish the rights that he had in the funds in the joint bank account because there was no dispute that he was the sole source of the funds at issue—as he was the party who placed the funds into the account for the purpose of furthering a business partnership endeavor—and that the judgment debtor had no right in or to the funds outside of business involving the construction of a building for the partnership. Accordingly, the non-debtor depositor was entitled to dismissal of the garnishment of execution and a release of the funds in the joint bank account. Trustmark Nat'l Bank v. Sunshine Carwash No. 5 Partners, 558 S.W.3d 157, 2018 Tenn. App. LEXIS 179 (Tenn. Ct. App. 2018).

[356] **Where depositor and donee signed signature card** on which was indicated that both checking account and savings account in bank were to be transferred to their joint ownership with right of survivorship, though normal bank practice required that separate signature card be signed for each account, and depositor died, and his administrator claimed accounts on ground of mental incompetency and undue influence, bank was justified in refusing to pay over savings account to donee. Saylor v. Southern Ariz. Bank & Trust Co., 8 Ariz. App. 368, 446 P.2d 474 (1968).

Where bank depositor and donee signed signature card indicating that checking and savings accounts were to be transferred to joint ownership with right of survivorship, though normal bank practice required separate signature cards for each account, and depositor died, and donee brought action against bank, and bank asked that donee and depositor's administrator, who claimed undue influence and mental incapacity of depositor, to interplead claims, and donee settled with administrator for half of savings account, bank was not liable to donee for entire amount of savings account. Saylor v. Southern Ariz. Bank & Trust Co., 8 Ariz. App. 368, 446 P.2d 474 (1968).

Savings accounts originally in individual name of deceased depositor had not been converted to joint and survivorship savings accounts by action of original depositor in signing a signature card with another person for a joint and survivorship account where original depositor failed to return to the institutions his passbooks and the new signature card in accordance with rules and regulations of the institutions for changing of an account from an individual to a joint survivorship account. Daramus v. Hategan, 2 Ohio App. 2d 347, 208 N.E.2d 542, 31 Ohio Op. 2d 521 (1965).

Deposits to Credit of Husband and Wife.—Joint tenancies of savings bank deposits may be created, if the parties so intend, regardless of whether the tenants are husband and wife, and if a joint tenancy is created, the right of survivorship exists.[358] And a husband and wife who sign an agreement that deposits in their joint bank account may be paid to either are bound thereby

---

[357] **In general.**—

Joint account card, which deceased and his sister signed, and which provided that deceased and his sister as joint depositors owned sums and account jointly with rights of survivorship, and that agreement was not to be changed except by written notice to bank signed by both deceased and his sister, as it existed prior to added typing providing that it was an individual checking account and that deceased sister was authorized to sign, was sufficient to satisfy requirements of statute authorizing establishment of joint savings account and was enforceable as such absent allegation or evidence of fraud, undue influence, mental incapacity or fiduciary duty. First Nat'l Bank v. Waller, 442 S.W.2d 171 (Mo. App. 1969).

Transfer from one joint account to another.—

The fact that a mother and son's joint savings account, into which the mother placed money after she had withdrawn it from the mother's, daughter's and daughter's husband's joint account and placed it into the mother's own savings account, was assigned the same account number by the bank as had been assigned to the mother's joint account with daughter and the husband did not establish that there had been a redeposit into such original account. Coristo v. Twin City Bank, 520 S.W.2d 218 (Ark. 1975).

[358] **In general.**—

West v. McCullough, 123 App. Div. 846, 108 N.Y.S. 493, aff'd, 194 N.Y. 518, 87 N.E. 1130; Wisner v. Wisner, 82 W. Va. 9, 95 S.E. 802. As to rights of survivor, see § 17 of this chapter.

Where a bank account is established to the joint credit of depositor and another, payable to either, with right of survivorship, a joint interest is created and upon death of depositor without having revoked authority to draw, survivor is entitled to balance of account. In re Schroeder's Estate, 144 N.E.2d 512 (Ohio Prob. 1957).

Where deposits were made in name of husband "or" wife, "or" should be given disjunctive meaning and either could withdraw without other's assent Marble v. Treasurer & Receiver Gen., 245 Mass. 504, 139 N.E. 442.

The mere fact that a savings bankbook is made out in the name of "J. or wife, B.," does not prove ownership of J. in the deposit, but simply evidences a purpose that the money may be drawn out by either of the persons named. Clary v. Fitzgerald, 155 App. Div. 659, 140 N.Y.S. 536, aff'd, 213 N.Y. 696, 107 N.E. 1075; Burke v. Slattery, 10 Misc. 754, 31 N.Y.S. 825, 64 N.Y. St. R. 631.

No intent to create joint tenancy.—

That savings bank deposit was in husband's name, and that book was always in his possession, held evidence that the deposit was his property and not that of his wife. Gower v. Keene, 113 Me. 249, 93 A. 546.

as between themselves and the bank.[359] Husbands and wives may also arrange their joint deposits so as to be withdrawable in whole or in part by either, and by the survivor in case of death,[360] or so that nothing can be withdrawn except on the order or receipt of both spouses during their joint lives.[361] But in the absence of any such arrangement, money deposited in an account to the joint credit of a man and his wife is presumed to belong one-half to each of them.[362] And in such a case, one spouse cannot recover from a bank any amount drawn by the other spouse from their joint savings account.[363] And a bank is authorized to pay a wife money from her husband's account if the husband actually authorized her to present his bankbook and draw the money, or if the bank had the right to assume that

---

[359] **In general.—**

Landretto v. First Trust & Sav. Bank, 333 Ill. 442, 164 N.E. 836; Milan v. Boucher, 285 Mass. 590, 189 N.E. 576; In re Schroeder's Estate, 144 N.E.2d 512 (Ohio Prob. 1957).

Breach of contract by bank.—

Where contract printed on the passbook issued by a bank on the joint savings account of husband and wife provided that the signature of either one would be sufficient for withdrawal of all or part of the funds deposited, failure of the bank to pay the amount of the deposit to wife upon her demand and presentation of the passbook was a breach of its contract. Perdue v. State Nat. Bank, 254 Ala. 80, 47 So. 2d 261.

Under such a contract the bank had no right to inquire into ownership of money deposited upon presentation of passbook and demand by wife of payment of entire amount of deposit Perdue v. State Nat. Bank, 254 Ala. 80, 47 So. 2d 261.

The money, under such circumstances, in hands of bank was not property of depositors but property of the bank which it was under duty to use in discharge of its obligation upon demand of wife who had passbook in her possession and made demand on bank to pay. Perdue v. State Nat. Bank, 254 Ala. 80, 47 So. 2d 261.

Either the plaintiff or her husband had a right to withdraw funds from a savings account opened by the husband as a joint account in both of their names. Copeland v. Peachtree Bank & Trust Co., 150 Ga. App. 262, 257 S.E.2d 353 (1979).

[360] First Nat. Bank v. Lawrence, 212 Ala. 45, 101 So. 663.

[361] Splaine v. Morrissey, 282 Mass. 217, 184 N.E. 670.

[362] In re Brooks, 5 Dem. 326, 5 N.Y. St. R. 381.

Where certificates of deposit carried in the names of husband or wife contained no provision for right of survivorship, such accounts were owned by named husband and wife as tenants in common with each owning an undivided one-half interest therein, and upon death of either, only one-half of such accounts went into estate for probate purposes and thus became taxable, and the other one-half belonged to survivor and was not taxable as a succession. In re Schroeder, 144 N.E.2d 512 (Ohio Prob. 1957).

[363] Landretto v. First Trust & Sav. Bank, 333 Ill. 442, 164 N.E. 836; Barstow v. Tetlow, 115 Me. 96, 97 A. 829.

he had authorized her to do so from their course of business and other circumstances.[364] Similarly, a husband, as codepositor with his wife in a joint savings account, has the power to waive a contractual provision that no withdrawal shall be made unless the passbook is presented.[365] As to the liability of savings banks for payments made to one spouse from a joint account during marital difficulties, see the footnote.[366]

Deposit in Name of Another.—It is possible for one to deposit his funds in another's bank account, and by affirmative proof thereafter establish his proportionate share or interest therein. When a provision granting such a depositor the power to withdraw his funds in the other account has been contracted for with the bank, he may withdraw such funds at will.[367] For another case relating to a deposit in the name of another, see the footnote.[368]

---

[364] Moline State Sav. Bank v. Liggett, 106 Ill. App. 223.

Therefore, on an action by a husband against a bank for money paid to his wife from his account, an instruction to the jury that, unless they found that defendant had shown, by a preponderance of the evidence, that plaintiff intended to authorize his wife to present his bankbook and draw his money, they should find the issues for the plaintiff, is erroneous. The question is, not what plaintiff intended to authorize his wife to do, but what he either actually authorized her to do, or what defendant had the right to assume be had authorized her to do. Moline State Sav. Bank v. Liggett, 106 Ill. App. 223.

[365] Forbes v. First Camden Nat. Bank, etc., Co., 25 N.J. Super. 17, 95 A. 2d 416, rev'g 21 N.J. Super. 133, 90 A.2d 547.

[366] A savings bank could not charge a wife's separate account for the amount of an overdraft in a joint savings account which husband and wife had opened in the bank under a contract providing that either or both depositors had the right to withdraw all deposits in the joint account, where the wife, after disclosing a marital rift to the bank, withdrew a major portion of the account, and the bank thereafter permitted the husband to make from a joint account a withdrawal which resulted in the overdraft.

Nielson v. Suburban Trust & Savings Bank, 37 Ill. App. 2d 224, 185 N.E.2d 404.

Where husband and wife had joint bank account and passbook was issued to them containing bank's rule requiring depositor to present passbook or proof of its loss or destruction in order to be entitled to withdraw deposit, bank's permitting husband to make withdrawal without passbook after marital difficulties had developed between the parties and without wife's consent rendered bank liable to wife for amount withdrawn by husband. Davis v. Chittenden County Trust Co., 115 Vt. 349, 61 A.2d 553.

[367] Jones v. Neu, 106 Ohio App. 161, 6 Ohio Op. 2d 428, 150 N.E.2d 858.

[368] Where decedent had opened savings account in name of his nephew "by" decedent, deposit book was issued to decedent, signature card showed that withdrawals could he made only by decedent and decedent made the only deposit to account, funds were owned by decedent rather than nephew. Basco v. Central Bank & Trust Co., 231 So. 2d 425 (La. App. 1970).

Deposit in Name of Minor or Insane Person.—A minor in whose name a relative makes a savings bank deposit has only presumptive title thereto, and the real purpose of such a deposit may be proven.[369] Thus, a son in whose name a savings account was opened by his parents, but in which they deposited their own funds, acquired no title to such deposits when he withdrew portions thereof on the presentation of passbooks given him by his parents for the purpose of making specific withdrawals, in the absence of voluntary delivery of the passbooks to him for the purpose of making gifts to him, and no title to the funds passed to the son's estate on his death.[370] And a statute which provides that money deposited in a savings bank in the name of a minor may be paid to the person making the deposit does not validate a payment by a bank to a father of deposits standing in the name of his minor child, which were made partly by the minor and partly by the father, except as to the amount deposited by the father.[371] Nor does it validate a payment to minor's stepfather who presents a passbook, unless the stepfather has authority in writing from the depositor to withdraw the funds.[372]

Where a bank pays a deposit without knowledge of the insanity of the depositor, and without notice of any facts which would charge it with such knowledge, it is protected in making payment.[373]

Embezzlement by Trustee.—Where a savings bank fails to assure itself of a trustee's authority to deal with trust funds, and disregards information contained in its own records and notices to its officers that he is dishonest, thereby permitting him to embezzle an entire trust fund by means of orders payable to cash, the bank became a guilty participant in the embezzlement and privy to the trustee's fraud, and is liable to the beneficiary.[374]

§ 15. Negligence in Paying Wrong Person.

In General.—Officers of savings banks making payments of deposits are required to act in good faith,[375] and to exercise reasonable care and diligence

---

[369] Carroll v. Smith, 229 App. Div. 286, 241 N.Y.S. 546.

[370] Ruffalo v. Savage, 252 Wis. 175, 31 N.W.2d 175, 1 A.L.R.2d 534.

[371] Dickinson v. Leominster Sav. Bank, 152 Mass. 49, 25 N.E. 12.

[372] Gibson v. First Nat. Bank, 213 Mo. App. 63, 245 S.W. 1072.

[373] Riley v. Albany Sav. Bank (N.Y.), 36 Hun 513, aff'd, 103 N.Y. 669.

[374] Liffiton v. National Sav. Bank, 267 App. Div. 32, 44 N.Y.S.2d 770, aff'd, 293 N.Y. 799, 59 N.E.2d 35.

[375] Hough Ave. Sav. & Banking Co. v. Anderson, 78 Ohio St. 341, 85 N.E. 498, 125 Am. St. 707, L.R.A. (n.s.) 431.

to avoid payment to a person not lawfully entitled thereto;[376] if they fail to

---

[376] **In general.—**

California.—Evans v. Bank of Italy, 96 Cal. App. 259, 274 P. 74.

Maine.—Sullivan v. Lewiston Inst., 56 Me. 507, 96 Am. Dec. 500.

Maryland.—Gillen v. Maryland Nat'l Bank, 274 Md. 96, 333 A.2d 329 (1975).

Minnesota.—Daivish v. Farmers', etc., Sav. Bank, 177 Minn. 243, 225 N.W. 100.

New York.—Kelly v. Buffalo Sav. Bank, 180 N.Y. 171, 72 N.E. 995, 105 Am. St. H. 720, 69 L.R.A. 317; Rosen v. State Bank, 32 Misc. 231, 65 N.Y.S. 666; Siegel v. State Bank, 123 N.Y.S. 220; Noah v. Bowery Sav. Bank, 225 N.Y. 284, 122 N.E. 235; Myerowich v. Emigrant Industrial Sav. Bank, 184 App. Div. 668, 172 N.Y.S. 540.

Ohio.—Hough Ave. Sav. & Banking Co. v. Anderson, 78 Ohio St. 341, 85 N.E. 498, 125 Am. St. H. 707, L.R.A. (n.s.) 431.

Pennsylvania.—Responsibility of savings bank is one of "ordinary care." Layman v. Western Sav. Bank, 302 Pa. Super. 433, 448 A.2d 1119 (1982).

Savings bank was not precluded by case law nor contract between parties from releasing funds to attorney for estate who presented passbook and a withdrawal slip properly signed by administrator; bank's measure of care in demanding two documents and checking the signature on one of them was at least "ordinary" and was not "negligent," and therefore bank was not liable to administrator for disbursing the funds. Layman v. Western Sav. Bank, 302 Pa. Super. 433, 448 A.2d 1119 (1982).

Utah.—Koutsis v. Zion's Sav. Bank Co., Co., 63 Utah 254, 225 P. 339.

Whether bank has exercised reasonable care depends on circumstances of each case; and ordinary or reasonable care does not mean utmost care and diligence, or great or extraordinary care, but care of man of ordinary foresight and prudence under similar circumstances. Fiero v. Franklin Sav. Bank, 124 Misc. 38, 207 N.Y.S. 235.

A savings bank is not held to the high degree of care required of a commercial bank respecting its depositors or creditors, and is liable to its depositors for want of ordinary care, but it does not insure a fund on deposit, nor is its work purely gratuitous. Bulakowski v. Philadelphia Sav. Fund Soc., 270 Pa. 538, 113 A. 553.

It is not required to close all possible avenues to fraud. And ordinary care did not require savings bank, in accepting account opened for a depositor by another, to require the depositor's signature card be witnessed by party other than person acting for depositor, or that depositor come and have his mark witnessed by an officer. Commonwealth Bank v. Goodman, 128 Md. 452, 97 A. 1005.

Comparison of signatures.—

Where depositor left deposit book with savings fund society and society paid out sum to third person on depositor's purported withdrawal order, society was required to exercise only ordinary care in comparing signatures, and it need not prove signature was genuine to be relieved of liability. Saji v. Philadelphia Sav. Fund Soc., 112 Pa. Super. 149, 170 A. 334.

Payment to guardian of one joint tenant.—

In absence of notice of any adverse claim on the jointly held savings account, the bank could not be held liable to one party to a joint account for permitting the appointed guardian

do so, the bank will be liable to repay the deposit to its rightful owner.[377] This rule does not deprive a bank of the protection of its contract with a depositor but simply imposes on it the consequences of its negligence.[378] As

---

of the other party to make a withdrawal of funds, especially considering that the bank had eliminated the requirement that the savings passbook be presented as a condition precedent to a withdrawal. Kuehl v. Terre Haute First Nat'l Bank, 436 N.E.2d 1160 (Ind. App. 1982).

[377] **In general.—**

Hough Aye. Sav., etc., Co. v. Anderson, 78 Ohio St. 341, 85 N.E. 498, 125 Am. St. H. 707, L.R.A. (n.s.) 431; Sullivan v. Lewiston Inst., 56 Me. 507, 96 Am. Dec. 500.

In absence of facts showing mistake, fraud, duress or estoppel, plaintiff, who had deposited money in bank in his own name, was entitled to recover amount of deposit from such bank, which had paid amount in question without plaintiff's consent to representative of one from whom plaintiff had received money and who was named as joint depositor with plaintiff of other funds deposited with bank at same time. Fischer v. Morris Plan Co., 275 S.W.2d 393 (Mo. App. 1955).

Illustrative case.—

If tenant withdrew money from landlord's savings account without necessary passbook or power of attorney and without landlord's knowledge or authorization, bank would be liable to landlord, even though tenant sent money withdrawn to landlord in payment of rent. Rivera v. Central Bank & Trust Co., 155 Colo. 383, 395 P.2d 11 (1964).

Bank liable where one joint tenant removed other's name without consent.—

The statute insulating a savings bank from liability to one joint tenant when the other tenant withdraws money from the joint savings account did not confer immunity on the bank from liability to a tenant whose name was removed from the account, without her consent, at the request of the other tenant, and the tenant whose name was removed was entitled to recover half of the money which was in the account when all of it was withdrawn by a person whose name had been substituted as joint tenant. Brown v. Bowery Sav. Bank, 51 N.Y.2d 411, 434 N.Y.S.2d 916, 415 N.E.2d 906 (1980).

Negligence inapplicable to drawer.—

Savings bank, as drawer on check made out to estate, given to attorney of estate and representing estate fends, was not liable to administrator for payment of the check, which was indorsed with attorney's signature, on its face inadequate, on basis that collecting bank was negligent in honoring the check, because such negligence under statute does not apply to drawer. Layman v. Western Sav. Bank, 302 Pa. Super. 433, 448 A.2d 1119 (1982).

[378] Commonwealth Bank v. Goodman, 128 Md. 452, 97 A. 1005.

As to the weight and sufficiency of evidence necessary to find negligence, see § 85 of this chapter.

Savings bank, as drawer on check made out to estate, given to attorney of estate and representing estate funds, was not liable to administrator for payment of the check, which was indorsed with attorney's signature, on its face inadequate, either under savings bank's "contract" with a holder or indorser, since the draft was not dishonored but was paid by both collecting bank and drawee bank, or as "admitting" existence of payee and his then capacity to indorse, because defalcating attorney signed only his own name, neglecting to put any

long as a bank acts in accordance with the contract existing between itself and its depositor, the bank is not liable if it makes payments from the depositor's account in conformity with the depositor's orders.[379] If, using such care and diligence, but lacking a present means of identifying a claimant to a deposit, such officers make payment upon presentation of a passbook to one apparently in the lawful possession of it as owner, the true depositor is bound by the payment,[380] especially where the depositor has subscribed to a rule that payment to one presenting a passbook is valid, unless it has been lost and written notice thereof given to the bank before payment.[381] But payment of a deposit to a person not entitled to it who presents a passbook will not discharge a bank from liability to the owner, if at the time of payment, a fact or circumstance is brought to the knowledge of the bank officers which would be reasonably calculated to excite suspicion and inquiry by an ordinarily careful person, and the officers fail to make inquiry or exercise proper care;[382] a bank cannot avoid such liability

---

indication of his agency on the indorsement. Layman v. Western Sav. Bank, 302 Pa. Super. 433, 448 A.2d 1119 (1982).

[379] Menicocci v. Archer Nat'l Bank, 67 Ill. App. 3d 388, 24 Ill. Dec. 296, 385 N.E.2d 63 (1978).

[380] Sullivan v. Lewiston Inst., 56 Me. 507, 96 Am. Dec. 500; Hayden v. Brooklyn Sav. Bank (N.Y.), 15 Abb. Pr. (n.s.) 290; Campbell v. Schenectady Sav. Bank, 114 App. Div. 337, 99 N.Y.S. 927.

[381] Wilson v. Citizens & Southern Ban, 23 Ga. App. 654, 99 S.E. 239; Smith v. Republic Nat. Bank, etc., Co., 73 S.W.2d 552 (Tex. Civ. App. 1984).

A rule of a savings bank provided that payments made to persons presenting a passbook should be deemed valid payments of the deposit. A depositor had knowledge of the rule. She went to the bank, accompanied by her niece, and drew out two sums. Her checks were signed by her making a mark, witnessed by her niece. Subsequently she gave her passbook to her attorney, who delivered the same to the niece, who presented the passbook to the bank, and checks purporting to have been signed by the depositor, and obtained money on them. When the first check was presented by the niece, reference was made to the signature book and to the former checks, and she was then asked if she saw plaintiff sign the check, and she replied that she did. The first money drawn by the depositor was about 14 months after her first deposit, and the second check was drawn about 14 months thereafter. The checks drawn by the niece were drawn in six months. Held insufficient to show negligence on the part of the bank, so as to make it liable to the depositor for the money paid. Campbell v. Schenectady Sav. Bank, 114 App. Div. 337, 99 N.Y.S. 927.

[382] **In general.—**

Noah v. Bowery Sav. Bank, 225 N.Y. 284, 122 N.E. 235.

Lack of suspicion, cannot always be the determinative factor, as reasonable care might in certain instances, demand suspicion. Noah v. Bowery Sav. Bank, 225 N.Y. 284, 122 N.E. 235.

by the adoption of arbitrary rules and causing them to be printed in its passbooks.[383]

Payment to Impostor or Forger.—Payment by a bank in the form of a check on a commercial or national bank payable to a real depositor's order which is made to an impostor does not protect the bank from liability to the true depositor.[384] Under a bank's bylaw providing that money may be withdrawn by a depositor or any other person duly authorized to receive it, the bank's officers must decide upon the genuineness of authority presented to them at their peril.[385] A savings bank is not negligent as a matter of law in paying a depositor's money on a forged order accompanied by the

---

Privilege of withholding payment.—

Where auspicious circumstances exist, connected with the withdrawal of a savings bank account, reasonable care for the protection of the depositor requires the bank to avail itself of its privilege of withholding payment for 60 days, in order to make inquiry as to whether the withdrawal is by the depositor's authority. Myerowich v. Emigrant Industrial Sav. Bank, 170 N.Y.S. 38, modified, 184 App. Div. 668, 172 N.Y.S. 540.

Absence of suspicious circumstances.—

Where there was no discrepancy between the signature on a written order and that of a depositor with a savings bank, and inquiry would have revealed that the woman presenting the order was the depositor's wife, held, there were no suspicious circumstances requiring the bank to make inquiries. McKenna v. Bowery Sav. Bank, 93 Misc. 135, 157 N.Y.S. 16, aff'd, 180 App. Div. 933, 167 N.Y.S. 1111.

The fact that the person presenting a passbook demands the entire amount on deposit, where only small sums had been drawn out theretofore, is not a suspicious circumstance, which should put the bank on inquiry as to the identity of the person presenting the book. Geitelsohn v. Citizens' Sav. Bank, 17 Misc. 574, 40 N.Y.S. 662, 75 N.Y. St. R. 84 (1896).

383 Gerardi v. New York Sav. Bank, 58 Misc. 183, 109 N.Y.S. 22; People's Sav. Bank v. Cupps, 91 Pa. 315; Ferguson v. Harlem Sav. Bank, 43 Misc. 10, 86 N.Y.S. 825.

384 Ladd v. Augusta Sav. Bank, 98 Me. 510, 52 A. 1012, 58 L.R.A. 288.

If a comparison by the officers of a savings bank of the signature of the person falsely presenting a deposit book with the genuine one on file would prevent a fraudulent imposition, then payment to an impostor without such comparison, and without requiring any proof of the identity of the person demanding payment, other than the possession of the bankbook, is no defense to an action by the depositor against the bank to recover the deposit. Ladd v. Augusta Sav. Bank, 98 Me. 510, 52 A. 1012, 58 L.R.A. 288.

385 **In general.—**

Ladd v. Augusta Sav. Bank, 98 Me. 510, 52 A. 1012, 58 L.R.A. 288.

Duly authenticated power of attorney.—

A savings bank's duty of care to a depositor was performed when it acted on a duly authenticated power of attorney in proper form and on production of the passbook. Romero v. Sjoberg, 5 N.Y.2d 518, 186 N.Y.S.2d 246, 158 N.E.2d 828.

depositor's passbook.[386] However, unless there exists some modifying agreement, bylaw, rule, regulation or statute, a savings bank is governed by the same rule of liability for payments based on forgeries as governs commercial banks, and the exercise of ordinary care by a savings bank does not relieve it from liability for such payments.[387] Where a bank allowed a

---

Illustrative case.—

Where an employee of the assignee of savings account fraudulently secured possession of passbook and sent it to bank requesting payment, transmission of check to assignee by bank which was cashed by employee after affixing unauthorized indorsement held not to constitute "payment upon presentation of deposit book," such as would discharge liability of bank to depositor upon termination of assignment for amount so paid. Tapper v. Boston Penny Sav. Bank, 294 Mass. 335, 2 N.E.2d 198.

[386] **In general.—**

Daivish v. Farmers', etc., Sav. Bank, 177 Minn. 243, 225 N.W. 100.

In cases of withdrawal from a savings account one forged withdrawal slip accompanied by a passbook providing that possession of book of deposits shall be sufficient evidence of ownership of deposit to authorize payment of money, the bank is bound to exercise ordinary care in paying out the deposit, and that which constitutes ordinary care or due diligence depends on the circumstances and is for the trier of the facts. Watt. v. American Sec., etc., Co., 47 A.2d 100 (D.C. Mun. App. 1946).

Discrepancy between signatures.—

Bank is not liable for payment of forged withdrawal orders unless discrepancy between signatures is so marked that ordinarily competent clerk exercising reasonable care could detect the forgery. Bellantese v. Bronx Sav. Bank, 152 Misc. 325, 273 N.Y.S. 885.

Savings bank is liable for cashing forged draft only where negligent in failing to discover forgery, where discrepancy between signatures on draft and deposit book is so marked and plain that ordinarily competent clerk with reasonable care should detect forgery Noah v. Bank for Sav., 171 App. Div. 191, 157 N.Y.S. 324.

In order that negligence can be imputed, there must be evidence that the dissimilarity is so marked and apparent that it would be readily discovered by a person competent to hold the position of teller. Appleby v. Erie County Sav. Bank, 62 N.Y. 12.

Discrepancy between signatures on withdrawal orders drawn on savings bank and signatures appearing on resolution and identification card held insufficient to put savings bank on inquiry so as to render it liable to depositor for payment of forged orders. Bellantese v. Bronx Sav. Bank, 152 Misc. 325, 273 N.Y.S. 885.

In view of similarity between alleged forged signature on withdrawal slip and genuine signature of depositor on file with bank, bank was not negligent in making payment on forged withdrawal order on depositor's account presented with bankbook. Novak v. Greater New York Sav. Bank, 37 App. Div. 2d 571, 322 N.Y.S.2d 587 (1971).

[387] **In general.—**

Ogborn v. Bank of America National Trust & Savings Assn., 28 Cal. App. 565, 83 P.2d 44.

savings account withdrawal without presentation of the passbook as required in the withdrawal order, the bank became liable to the depositor as a matter of law for the withdrawal under forged and unauthorized signatures.[388]

Payment to One Wrongfully in Possession of Passbook.—A savings bank passbook is not a negotiable instrument,[389] and a bank is not liable for money paid from a deposit to one wrongfully in possession of a passbook if it has exercised reasonable care to protect the depositor.[390] But if a savings

---

Bank is liable on its contract.—

Where payments are made by the officers of a bank on orders purporting to be signed by a depositor, but in fact forgeries, accompanied by the deposit book, of the loss of which the bank has not been notified, no question of the negligence of the bank is involved in a suit by the depositor to recover his money, in the absence of any regulation requiring notice of the loss of the book. However, the contract of debtor and creditor between the bank and the depositor still continues, and the bank is liable thereon. Ladd v. Androscoggin County Sav. Bank, 96 Me. 520, 52 A. 1016.

Illustrative case.—

Where depositor's savings bank deposit books were stolen and the thief without depositor's knowledge or consent obtained depositor's signature on blank papers and forged withdrawal orders, the savings bank which paid the deposits on the forged withdrawal orders was liable to the depositor for the amount of the withdrawals, in absence of any bylaw of the bank or agreement between the bank and depositor covering such a case, notwithstanding fact that bank used ordinary care and diligence in satisfying itself of the propriety of making the payments. Ogborn v. Bank of America National Trust & Savings Assn., 28 Cal. App. 565, 83 P.2d 44.

388 Colagiovanni v. City & County Sav. Bank, 48 App. Div. 2d 966, 369 N.Y.S.2d 554 (1975).

The bank must be found to have been negligent in regard to examining the forged signature of a depositor before liability can be imposed for unauthorized withdrawals of deposits. Colagiovanni v. City & County Sav. Bank, 48 App. Div. 2d 966, 369 N.Y.S.2d 554 (1975).

389 Brogna v. Commissioner of Banks, 248 Mass. 241, 142 N.E. 746; Royon v. Greenstein, 122 Ohio St. 340, 171 N.E. 595.

See also §§ 15, 19 of this chapter.

A passbook showing deposits in a savings bank is not negotiable, but the bank is always under the duty of ascertaining if the book when presented is in the hands of the legal holder. Bryson v. Security Trust & Sav. Bank, 29 Cal. App. 596, 156 P. 987.

390 **In general.—**

Ferguson v. Harlem Sav. Bank, 92 N.Y.S 261; Kenney v. Harlem Sav. Bank, 61 Misc. 144, 114 N.Y.S. 749 (1908), rev'd on other grounds, 65 Misc. 466, 120 N.Y.S. 82 (1909); Wall v. Emigrant Industrial Sav. Bank, 64 Hun 249, 19 N.Y.S. 194, 46 N.Y. St. R. 601; Commonwealth Bank v. Goodman, 128 Md. 452, 97 A. 1005; Geitelsohn v. Citizens' Sav. Bank, 17 Misc. 574, 40 N.Y.S. 662, 75 N.Y. St. R. 64 (1896); Brooks v. Erie County Sav.

bank fails to exercise such reasonable care,[391] or acts in direct contravention

---

Bank, 169 App. Div. 73, 154 N.Y.S. 692, aff'd, 224 N.Y. 639, 121 N.E. 857.

The one test of bank's liability for negligence in paying on savings account withdrawal slips and presentation of savings account book is reasonable care of given teller. Clyman v. Glasse, 39 Misc. 2d 198, 240 N.Y.S.2d 532.

A bank must exercise reasonable care and not be negligent when it makes payment to a person presenting a savings account passbook. Flatow v. Amalgamated Trust & Sav. Bank, 97 Ill. App. 2d 357, 240 N.E.2d 161 (1968).

Possession of a passbook is an important factor in determining whether a savings bank exercised ordinary care in disbursing a depositor's funds. Gillen v. Maryland Nat'l Bank, 274 Md. 96, 333 A.2d 329 (1975).

Bank not negligent.—

Where, because of depositor's illiteracy, savings deposit was made in brother's name, and such name, at depositor's request, was signed on signature card and ledger sheet by a person whom bank employee believed to be the brother, bank, in view of bank's rule, held not liable for subsequently paying the deposit to such person who unlawfully obtained possession of passbook and withdrew the money by signing name of depositor's brother on withdrawal receipt, there being nothing to show that bank was negligent. Smith v. Republic Nat. Bank, etc., Co., 73 S.W.2d 552 (Tex. Civ. App. 1934).

A depositary bank's issuance of its cashier's check to a person who presented the depositor's passbook and a forged withdrawal slip did not alter the bank's obligation to use ordinary care in permitting the withdrawal from the account, especially where the depositary bank made final payment of its cashier's check before receiving notification of the forgery. Gillen v. Maryland Nat'l Bank, 274 Md. 96, 333 A.2d 329 (1975).

In making payments, a bank cannot rely solely upon the possession and presentation of the bankbook; the passbook must be accompanied by a withdrawal slip or order containing the depositor's signature. Gillen v. Maryland Nat'l Bank, 274 Md. 96, 333 A.2d 329 (1975).

[391] **In general.—**

Anderson v. Hough Ave. Sav. & Banking Co., 4 Ohio N.P. (n.s.) 22, 16 Ohio Dec. 490, aff'd, 78 Ohio St. 341, 85 N.E. 498; First Nat. Bank v. Karas, 14 Ohio App. 147; Tobin v. Manhattan Sav. Inst., 6 Misc. 110, 26 N.Y.S. 14, 57 N.Y. St. R. 856; Tobin v. Manhattan Sav. Inst., 7 Misc. 744, 27 N.Y.S. 1124; Kummel v. Germania Sav. Bank, 127 N.Y. 488, 28 N.E. 398, 13 L.R.A. 786; Weigel v. First Nat. Bank, 20 So. 2d 21 (La. App. 1944).

Where payment is made to a person wrongfully in possession of passbook, bank is liable if under all circumstances of case, it was negligent in making payment without further inquiry or precaution. Kalb v. Chemical Bank New York Trust Co., 62 Misc. 2d 458, 309 N.Y.S.2d 502 (1969), rev'd on other grounds, 64 Misc. 2d 824, 316 N.Y.S.2d 381 (1970).

In making payments, a bank cannot rely solely upon the possession and presentation of the bankbook, but must exercise ordinary care and diligence to ascertain that the person receiving money is entitled to its savings account. Laurent v. Williamsburgh Sav. Bank, 137 N.Y.S.2d 750 (1954); Kalb v. Chemical Bank New York Trust Co., 62 Misc. 2d 458, 309 N.Y.S.2d 502 (1969), rev'd on other grounds, 64 Misc. 2d 824, 316 N.Y.S.2d 381 (1970).

of instructions given by the depositor as to the disposition of his funds, it will be liable to him for the amount so paid.[392]

Perfunctory ministerial act of permitting withdrawal of funds upon presentation of a passbook and a signed withdrawal slip without any other related act of vigilance or caution on part of bank is a deficiency in due care in safeguarding funds of its depositor and standing alone unexplained is a failure to use ordinary care and constitutes negligence on part of the bank. Kalb v. Chemical Bank New York Trust Co., 62 Misc. 2d 458, 309 N.Y.S.2d 502 (1969), rev'd on other grounds, 64 Misc. 2d 824, 316 N.Y.S.2d 381 (1970).

Bank must make signature comparisons.—

That savings account book was presented to bank with forged withdrawal slips did not immunize bank from liability for negligence, and bank was negligent in failing to make signature comparisons. Clyman v. Glasser, 39 Misc. 24 198, 240 N.Y.S.2d 532.

Where the signature on an order presented to the savings bank by one having a depositor's passbook would reveal to one experienced in comparing handwriting that it was not the same signature as that of the depositor on file, the bank is liable to the depositor for making payment. Schneider v. Union Dime Sav. Bank, 93 Misc. 166, 156 N.Y.S. 753.

Public policy will not allow bank so to strip itself of responsibility by contract as to enable it safely to pay, intentionally or heedlessly, to one who has come into possession of passbook fraudulently or criminally. Kalb v. Chemical Bank N.Y. Trust Co., 62 Misc. 2d 458, 309 N.Y.S.2d 502 (1969), rev'd on other grounds, 64 Misc. 2d 824, 316 N.Y.S.2d 381 (1970).

Where a bank permitted the payee of check to have access to drawer's safe deposit box and take therefrom drawer's savings account passbook, and paid amount of check on presentation of savings account passbook thus improperly obtained, bank and payee would be required to repay such money to drawer's estate. Keller v. Davis, 123 Pa. Super. 240, 187 A. 267.

Bank held negligent.—

Where plaintiff deposited money under the name of Antonina H., and could not write, but always signed her checks by mark, with a notary's certificate attached, the bank, in paying a check signed by mark of "Antuia" H., with the certificate of a notary known by the teller, and to a person to whom the teller had paid money before, although the passbook was presented (having been stolen), did not exercise ordinary care and diligence, and was not discharged. Hankowska v. Buffalo Sav. Bank, 155 App. Div. 694, 140 N.Y.S. 891, appeal denied, 156 App. Div. 926, 141 N.Y.S. 1122.

Savings bank, paying money from guardian's trust deposit to one wrongfully in possession of passbook, upon an order not approved by the guardian's surety, although knowing such approval was required, was negligent. Myerowich v. Emigrant Industrial Sav. Bank, 184 App. Div. 668, 172 N.Y.S. 540.

A bank, with knowledge of requirement of surety's approval of order for withdrawing guardian's deposit of trust funds, is not freed from inference of negligence in paying to wrong person, by showing that the guardian withdrew a sum from another guardianship account without surety's approval. Myerowich v. Emigrant Industrial Sav. Bank, 184 App. Div. 668, 172 N.Y.S. 540.

[392] Gruszka v. Mitchell St. State Bank, 185 Wis. 620, 200 N.W. 680.

Agreement Rendering Bank Liable Notwithstanding Good Faith and Ordinary Care.—A bank may by agreement make itself liable for a payment to one wrongfully in possession of a deposit book, although the payment is made in good faith, in the exercise of ordinary care, and in accordance with the general practice among savings banks.[393]

Bylaws and Rules Intended to Protect Bank from Liability.—The bylaws or rules of savings banks usually contain a provision intended to protect the bank from liability for payments made to one who has wrongfully obtained possession of, and who presents at the bank, a passbook belonging to a

---

Where depositor of savings account had made another person a joint tenant only so she might make withdrawals for him in case he was sick or disabled, and joint tenant took bankbook from depositor, and bank paid amount of account to her, although depositor had warned bank not to make such payment, depositor could recover amount of withdrawals from account from bank. Laurent v. Williamsburgh Sav. Bank, 137 N.Y.S.2d 750 (1954).

Where deposit made by a wife in a savings bank is marked "Special," and she testifies that she told the officer to pay it to no one but herself the fact that the bank subsequently paid the money to her husband, who was without authority from her, merely upon his presenting her passbook with the assurance that he was her authorized agent, is sufficient to warrant the jury in finding that proper diligence was not used by the bank in protecting her interests. Clark v. Saugerties Sav. Bank, 17 N.Y.S. 215, 62 Hun 346, 42 N.Y. St. R. 285.

[393] Chase v. Waterbury Sav. Bank, 77 Conn. 295, 59 A. 37, 69 L.R.A. 329, 1 Ann. Cas. 96.

Such is the effect of an agreement that deposits and dividends withdrawn shall be paid only to the depositor, or his order or legal representatives, and then only on the depositor's book being presented, in the absence of any modifying agreement, where the bank makes a payment on a forged order of one who had fraudulently obtained possession of the deposit book. Chase v. Waterbury Sav. Bank, 77 Conn. 295, 59 A. 37, 69 L.R.A. 329, 1 Ann. Cas. 96.

But in Georgia it has been held that a rule of a savings bank that depositors must always present their passbooks when depositing or withdrawing money, and that "if not present personally" an order signed and witnessed must accompany the presentation of the book, does not affect the principle that where a bank pays in good faith a forged check to a person presenting the bankbook, and whom it believe, to be the depositor, it is not liable to the depositor therefor. Langdale v. Citizens' Bank of Savannah, 121 Ga. 105, 48 S.E. 708, 104 Am. St. R. 94, 69 L.R.A. 341, 2 Ann. Cas. 257.

Where a husband executed a collateral assignment of a joint savings account pursuant to the statute in favor of a pledgee, neither the husband nor the wife, who were bound by statute, by joint savings account contract with the bank, and by collateral assignment of the account, had any right to withdraw funds from the account unless a release was first obtained from the pledges, and thus the bank, which due to an admitted mistake allowed the funds to be withdrawn by the wife, was liable to the pledges by virtue of the collateral assignment and by statute. National Bank of Commerce v. Hart Cotton Co., 273 Ark. 78, 617 S.W.2d 343 (1981).

depositor, and it is customary to print such rules in the bank's passbooks. While these bylaws and rules vary somewhat in phraseology, there is, in substance and legal effect, much similarity between them. One of the common bylaws or rules provides that all payments to persons producing the passbook shall be valid payments to discharge the bank. It has been held that such a bylaw or rule, or one of similar import, will not prevent a recovery by a depositor whose passbook has been stolen or obtained from him by fraud, unless the bank uses ordinary care in making payment.[394] But where

---

[394] **In general.—**

Connecticut.—Dinini v. Mechanics' Sav. Bank, 85 Conn. 225, 82 A. 580.

Georgia.—Wilson v. Citizens & Southern Bank, 23 Ga. App. 864, 90 S.E. 239.

Louisiana.—Rule in bank passbook that bank is not liable for withdrawals made by person presenting book is valid, but bank is required to exercise reasonable care in making payment to a person other than depositor and it is liable for failure to exercise such care. Weigel v. First Nat. Bank, 20 So. 2d 21 (La. App. 1944).

Maryland.—Gillen v. Maryland Nat'l Bank, 274 Md. 96, 333 A.2d 329 (1975).

Michigan.—Ackenhausen v. People's Sav. Bank, 110 Mich. 175, 68 N.W. 118, 64 Am. St. R. 338, 33 L.R.A. 408.

New Hampshire.—Kimball v. Norton, 59 N.H. 1, 47 Am. R. 171; Connolly v. Manchester Sav. Bank, 92 N.H. 89, 25 A.2d 412 (1942).

New York.—Kelly v. Emigrant, etc., Sav. Bank (N.Y.), 2 Daly 227; Appleby v. Erie County Sav. Bank, 62 N.Y. 12; Allen v. Williamsburgh Sav. Bank, 69 N.Y. 314; Cornell v. Emigrant Industrial Sav. Bank, 44 Hun 630, 9 N.Y. St. R. 72; Saling v. German Sav. Bank, 7 N.Y.S. 642, 15 Daly 386, 27 N.Y. St. R. 975, appeal denied, 8 N.Y.S. 469, 15 Daly 527; Clark v. Saugerties Sav. Bank, 17 N.Y.S. 215, 62 Hun 346, 42 N.Y. St. R. 285; Kummel v. Germania Sav. Bank, 127 N.Y. 488, 28 N.E. 398, 13 L.R.A. 786; Wall v. Emigrant Industrial Sav. Bank, 64 Hun 249, 19 N.Y.S. 194, 48 N.Y. St. R. 601; Kress v. East Side Sav. Bank, 66 Hun 635, 21 N.Y.S. 652, 50 N.Y. St. R. 278, appeal denied, 22 N.Y.S. 1124, 68 Hun 608; Tobin v. Manhattan Sav. Inst., 6 Misc. 110, 26 N.Y.S. 14, 57 N.Y. St. R. 856, appeal denied, 7 Misc. 744, 27 N.Y.S. 1124; Abramowitz v. Citizens' Sav. Bank, 17 Misc. 297, 40 N.Y.S. 385; Israel v. Bowery Sav. Bank (N.Y.), 9 Daly 507; Fiero v. Franklin Sav. Bank, 124 Misc. 38, 207 N.Y.S. 235; Schneider v. Union Dime Sav. Bank, 93 Misc. 166, 156 N.Y.S. 753; McKenna v. Bowery Sav. Bank, 93 Misc. 135, 157 N.YS. 16, aff'd, 180 App. Div. 933, 167 N.Y.S. 1111.

Despite incorporation of a rule that bank is not liable for withdrawals made by persons presenting bankbook, the bank is required to exercise reasonable care in making payment to a person other than the depositor himself and is liable for the failure to exercise such care. Kalb v. Chemical Bank N.Y. Trust Co., 62 Misc. 2d 458, 309 N.Y.S.2d 502 (1969), rev'd on other grounds, 86 Misc. 2d 824, 316 N.Y.S.2d 381.

Bank is bound at its own peril to determine identity of payee, even though bank has a regulation that possession of passbook is sufficient evidence of ownership to authorize bank to make payment and that any payment made to a person producing the passbook is valid as

a bank is not chargeable with any want of diligence or omission of duty in making such a payment, it is valid and binding upon the depositor,[395] and in

---

against the depositor and operates to release the bank to the amount of the payment made. Kalb v. Chemical Bank New York Trust Co., 62 Misc. 24 458, 309 N.Y.S.2d 502 (1969), rev'd on other grounds, 64 Misc. 2d 824, 316 N.Y.S.2d 381.

Fact that a bank has printed in passbook issued to depositor a rule to effect that payment shall be made to person presenting book does not relieve bank of duty to exercise care in making payments. Kalb v. Chemical Bank New York Trust Co., 62 Misc. 2d 458, 309 N.Y.S.2d 502 (1969), rev'd on other grounds, 64 Misc. 2d 824, 316 N.Y.S.2d 381.

Bank's rule to effect that payment made to a person producing passbook is valid as against depositor and operates to release bank to amount of payment made does not permit bank officers to carelessly shut their eyes and pay to any person presenting the passbook, but on the contrary, they owe the depositor active vigilance in order to detect fraud and forgery. Kalb v. Chemical Bank New York Trust Co., 62 Misc. 2d 458, 309 N.Y.S.2d 502 (1969), rev'd on other grounds, 64 Misc. 2d 824, 316 N.Y.S.2d 381.

Ohio.—Fourth, etc., Trust Co. v. Rowe, 122 Ohio St. 1, 170 N.E. 439.

Pennsylvania.—Bulakowski v. Philadelphia Sav. Fund Soc., 270 Pa. 538, 113 A. 553.

West Virginia.—Zuplkoff v. Charleston Nat'l Bank, 77 W. Va. 621, 88 S.E. 116.

Payment without passbook.—

If a bank under a bylaw makes payment to one not presenting the passbook, it will be held to a standard of ordinary care in identifying the person demanding payment. R. H. Macy & Co. v. Tyler, 21 Misc. 2d 998, 193 N.Y.S.2d 243.

[395] **In general.—**

Schoenwald v. Metropolitan Sav. Bank, 57 N.Y. 418; Ninoff v. Hazel Green State Bank, 174 Wis. 560, 183 N.W. 673; Wasilauskas v. Brookline Sav. Bank, 259 Mass. 215, 156 N.E. 34, 52 A L.R. 758; Krishkan v. New York Sav. Bank, 93 Misc. 52, 156 N.Y.S. 298.

Construction of bylaw.—

Check given by bank to person presenting passbook after payment held "money paid out," within meaning of bylaw exempting bank from liability. Wasilauskas v. Brookline Sav. Bank, 259 Mass. 215, 156 N.E. 34, 52 A.L.R. 768.

Jury Instruction.—

Where, in an action by a depositor against a savings bank to recover the amount paid out on a stolen passbook, it appears that the bank's rules provide that presentation of the book shall be sufficient authority to pay the deposit to the bearer, it is error to charge that possession by a stranger of the book constitutes no right to draw the money thereon. Geitelsohn v. Citizens' Sav. Bank, 17 Misc. 574, 40 N.Y.S. 662, 75 N.Y. St. R. 64 (1896).

Illustrative case.—

Where evidence established that bank reasonably believed, when owner's sister presenting owner's passbook made withdrawals from owner's savings account, that she was authorized by owner to make such withdrawals, and passbook authorized withdrawals by possessor of passbook, bank was not liable to owner who denied that he authorized sister to make withdrawals, notwithstanding it knew that at time of such withdrawals owner was an inmate

such a case, it is immaterial that a passbook when presented was accompanied by a forged order purporting to have been signed by the depositor.[396] However, the requisite degree of care is not shown where payment is made to a person producing a deposit book under circumstances raising a reasonable suspicion as to his ownership thereof,[397] or where any fact or circumstance existed to put the bank on inquiry.[398]

It has been held that a bank cannot avail itself of the protection of such a bylaw or rule unless it was brought to the knowledge of the depositor at the time he made the deposit.[399] And where there is a statute providing that regulations of banks shall be put in a conspicuous place where business is transacted, and shall be printed in the passbooks, a bank will not be protected by such a bylaw from liability for money paid to a person presenting a stolen passbook, unless it shows affirmatively that it has complied with the statute.[400] Bank bylaws or rules frequently contain, in addition to the provision that payments to persons producing the passbook shall be valid payments to discharge the bank, the provision that the bank will endeavor to protect depositors, or that it will endeavor to prevent fraud and imposition.

---

of a penitentiary. Weigel v. First Nat'l Bank, 20 So. 2d 21 (La. App. 1944).

[396] Schoenwald v. Metropolitan Sav. Bank, 65 N.Y. 418; Winter v. Williamsburgh Sav. Bank, 68 App. Div. 193, 74 N.Y.S. 140.

[397] Allen v. Williamsburgh Sav. Bank, 69 N.Y. 314. As to weight and sufficiency of evidence, see § 35 of this chapter.

[398] Geitelsohn v. Citizens' Sav. Bank, 17 Misc. 574, 40 N.Y.S. 662, 75 N.Y. St. R. 64 (1896).

Where a person gives to another a power of attorney to draw money from a savings bank, and describes himself in the body of the instrument as executor of the estate owning the deposit, and gives the number of the bankbook, and signs the document merely as an individual, it confers no authority on the bank to pay the money to the attorney, and such payment on presentation of the passbook does not show the ordinary care that will relieve the bank from liability, when the passbook and power of attorney were obtained by fraud, although the bylaws of the bank authorized it to pay to the person presenting the passbook. Gearns v. Bowery Sav. Bank, 135 N.Y. 557, 32 N.E. 249.

A bank which paid a savings account withdrawal without presentation of the passbook as required in the withdrawal order was liable to the depositor for a withdrawal under forged, unauthorized signatures. Colagiovanni v. City & County Sav. Bank, 48 App. Div. 2d 966, 369 N.Y.S.2d 554 (1975).

[399] Eaves v. People's Sav. Bank, 27 Corn. 229, 71 Am. Dec. 59; Ackenhausen v. People's Sav. Bank, 110 Mich. 175, 68 N.W. 118, 64 Am. St. R. 338, 33 L.R.A. 408. See also § 13 of this chapter.

[400] Kress v. East Side Sav. Bank, 66 Hun 635, 21 N.Y.S. 652, 50 N.Y. St. R. 278, appeal denied, 22 N.Y.S. 1124, 68 Hun 608.

Under such provisions, a bank is required to exercise ordinary care and diligence to identify persons presenting passbooks, or to ascertain whether they are authorized to receive payment.[401]

Bank bylaws or rules also sometimes provide that a depositor must notify the bank if his passbook is lost or stolen, or that the bank will not be responsible for loss sustained when a depositor has not given notice of his passbook being lost or stolen; this notice is sometimes required to be in writing. Such a requirement is reasonable and binding upon depositors,[402] even in the case of a depositor who is illiterate and cannot read the rules of his bank.[403] But such a bylaw or rule does not relieve a bank from the duty of acting in good faith with reasonable care in making payment on presentation of a passbook.[404] And the binding effect of such a rule is not

---

[401] Kummel v. Germania Sav. Bank, 127 N.Y. 488, 28 N.E. 398, 13 L.R.A. 786; Clark v. Saugerties Sav. Bank, 17 N.Y.S. 215, 62 Hun 346, 42 N.Y. St. R. 285; Wall v. Emigrant, etc., Sav. Bank, 19 N.Y.S. 194, 64 Hun 249, 46 N.Y. St. B. 601: Tobin v. Manhattan Sav. Inst., 6 Misc. 110, 26 N.Y.S. 14, 57 N.Y. St. R. 856, appeal denied, 7 Misc. 744, 27 N.Y.S. 1124; Kenney v. Harlem Sav. Bank, 61 Misc. 144, 114 N.Y.S. 749 (1908), rev'd on other grounds, 65 Misc. 466, 120 N.Y.S. 82 (1909); Ficken v. Emigrants', etc., Sav. Bank, 33 Misc. 92, 67 N.Y.S. 143, rev'd on other grounds, 65 Misc. 466, 120 N.Y.S. 82; Ferguson v. Harlem Sav. Bank, 43 Misc. 10, 86 N.Y.S. 825; Appleby v. Erie County Sav. Bank, 62 N.Y. 12; Cornell v. Emigrant Industrial Sav. Bank, 44 Hun 630, 9 N.Y. St. R. 72; Langdale v. Citizens' Bank of Savannah, 121 Ga. 105, 48 S.E. 708, 104 Am. St. R. 94, 69 L.R.A. 341, 2 Ann. Cas. 257.

If a bank under a bylaw makes payment to one not presenting the passbook, it will be held to a standard of ordinary care in identifying the person demanding payment. R.H. Macy & Co. v. Tyler, 21 Misc. 2d 998, 193 N.Y.S.2d 243.

[402] Langdale v. Citizens' Bank of Savannah, 121 Ga. 105, 48 S.E. 708, 104 Am. St. R. 94, 69 L.R.A. 341, 2 Ann. Cas. 257; Wilson v. Citizens & Southern Bank, 23 Ga. App. 654, 99 S.E. 239.

[403] Wilson v. Citizens & Southern Bank, 23 Ga. App. 654, 99 S.E. 239; Burrill v. Dollar Sav. Bank, 92 Pa. 134, 37 Am. R. 669. See also § 18 of this chapter.

[404] *Maine.*—Ladd v. Augusta Sav. Bank, 96 Me. 510, 52 A. 1012, 58 L.R.A. 288.

Massachusetts.—Goldrick v. Bristol County Sav. Bank, 123 Mass. 320; Kimins v. Boston, etc., Sav. Bank, 141 Mass. 33, 6 N.E. 242, 55 Am. H. 441; Kingsley v. Whitman Sav. Bank, 182 Mass. 252, 65 N.E. 161, 94 Am. St. H. 650; Donlan v. Provident Inst., 127 Mass 183, 34 Am. R. 358. See also Jochumsen v. Suffolk Sav. Bank, 85 Mass. (3 Allen) 87; Levy v. Franklin Sav. Bank, 117 Mass. 448; McCarthy v. Provident Inst., 159 Mass. 527, 34 N.E. 1073.

New Hampshire.—Brown v. Merrimack River Sav. Bank, 67 N.H. 549, 39 A. 336, 68 Am. St. R. 700.

Ohio.—Anderson v. Hough Ave. Sav. & Banking Co., 4 Ohio N.P. (n.s.) 22, 16 Ohio Dec. 490, aff'd, 78 Ohio St. 341, 85 N.E. 498.

affected by another rule of the bank requiring depositors to present their passbooks when depositing or withdrawing money, and providing that "if not present personally, an order properly signed and witnessed must accompany the presentation of the book, in case of withdrawal."[405] Where the bylaws of a savings bank, printed in the passbooks of depositors, provide that deposits withdrawn shall be paid only to the depositor or his order, and only on the depositor's book being presented, but that the bank will not be responsible to any depositor for any fraud practiced on it by forged signatures, or by presenting a depositor's book and drawing money without the knowledge or consent of the depositor, the bank is not relieved of its duty of exercising ordinary care in preventing the payment of a deposit to the wrong person even if he presents a depositor's book,[406] but it is not liable to a depositor for payments made in the exercise of ordinary care to a person wrongfully in possession of a passbook.[407]

§ 16. Payment on Death of Depositor.

In General.—On a depositor's death, a bank becomes indebted to the depositor's estate, and a payment of the deposit to any person other than his executor or administrator is at the bank's peril.[408] Thus, a savings bank must

---

Vermont.—Gifford v. Rutland Sav. Bank, 63 Vt. 108, 21 A. 340, 25 Am. St. R. 744, 11 L.R.A. 794 (1890).

[405] Langdale v. Citizens' Bank of Savannah, 121 Ga. 105, 48 S.E. 708, 104 Am. St. R. 94, 69 L.R.A. 341, 2 Ann. Cas. 257.

[406] Chase v. Waterbury Sav. Bank, 77 Corn. 295, 59 A. 37, 69 L.R.A. 329, 1 Ann. Cas. 96; Kummel v. Germania Sav. Bank, 127 N.Y. 488, 28 N.E. 398, 13 L.R.A. 786, criticizing Schoenwald v. Metropolitan Sav. Bank, 57 N.Y. 418; Szwento Juozupo Let Draugystes v. Manhattan Sav. Inst., 178 App. Div. 57, 164 N.Y.S. 498.

[407] Chase v. Waterbury Sav. Bank, 77 Corn. 295, 59 A. 37, 69 L.R.A. 329, 1 Ann. Cas. 96; Cosgrove v. Provident Inst., 64 N.J.L. 653, 46 A. 617.

[408] **In general.—**

Grill v. Manhattan Sav. Inst., 148 Misc. 181, 265 N.Y.S. 610.

In order for savings account in bank or savings and loan association to be payable on depositor's death to third person, the depositor must designate in writing that the account is so payable; requirement of written designation means that the depositor must affix his signature to instrument stating his intention. McDonald v. Treat, 593 S.W.2d 462 (Ark. 1980).

Authorization to pay in case of emergency.—

A depositor's written memorandum on record of savings account in savings and loan association that "in case of emergency I hereby authorize you to honor the signature of my sister as attached hereto" imported only an agency effective in case of emergency which terminated on death of depositor and did not operate to transfer funds, so that on death of

exercise diligence to ascertain whether one who presents a decedent's passbook is entitled to receive payment, and if it negligently makes payment

---

depositor without an emergency having arisen the administratrix of depositor was entitled to sums on deposit in account. Smith v. Benj. Franklin Sav. & Loan Ass'n, 156 Ore. 541, 68 P.2d 1045.

Intestate depositor.—

Where decedent died before making will and before he could precisely and specifically delineate his intention with respect to disposition of five savings accounts established by him, and exact nature of his dispositional intention, if in fact he had formed such an intention, therefore remained suppositional speculation, general rules of law controlled, and ownership of savings accounts would be determined by titles in which they stood at time of decedent's death. In re Estate of Friedman, 20 Cal. App. 3d 399, 97 Cal. Rptr. 653 (1971).

Where decedent died before making a will and before he could precisely and specifically delineate his intention with respect to disposition, after his death, office savings accounts established by him, proceeds of savings account opened in decedent's name, with power of attorney to his wife, belonged to his estate. In re Estate of Friedman, 20 Cal. App. 3d 399, 97 Cal. Rptr. 653 (1971).

Deposit in names of two persons.—

Bank, in which decedent had established two savings accounts in his name "payable on death" to his nephews, properly paid money from those accounts to nephews or pursuant to their directions, under the statute governing deposits made in names of two persons payable to either of such persons or payable to survivor of them, notwithstanding the claim that the statute requires a joint account with right of survivorship. Macon v. First Nat'l Bank, 378 So. 2d 1128 (Ala. App. 1979), cert. denied, ex parte Macon, 378 So. 2d 1131 (Ala. 1980).

Construction of statutes.—

In view of legislative rule of statutory construction that singular includes plural and that plural includes singular, statute allowing natural persons to enter into written contract with bank, etc., whereby proceeds of certificate, account or deposit may be made payable on death of owner to another person authorizes owner of POD savings account to designate more than one person as beneficiary of account. Wingate v. Hordge, 60 Ohio St. 2d 55, 14 Ohio Op. 3d 212, 396 N.B.2d 770 (1979).

Law governing.—

Where bank account was in Ohio at the time of the death of the testatrix-depositor, who bequeathed to three named legates "All the rest of my property . . . which includes my savings account . . . at the . . . [Ohio bank] which I may own or have the right to dispose of at the time of my death," but who also added name of one legatee to depositor card at the bank, disposition of funds in the account was governed by the law of Ohio. Herbin v. Farrish, 47 N.C. App. 193, 266 S.E.2d 698 (1980).

See also In re Estate of Blake, 856 A.2d 1151 (D.C. 2004) (remand required in probate proceeding to consider effect the District of Columbia Nonprobate Transfers on Death Act, D.C. Code § 19-601.01, had on determination of ownership of Maryland joint bank accounts).

to a person not so entitled, it will be liable for the amount so paid.[409] But a bank will not be liable if a deposit paid to the wrong person ultimately comes into the control of the depositor's executor or administrator.[410] And a bank may transfer a testator's account to his executor individually, on his producing the necessary papers, and is not liable if he thereafter uses the funds for his individual purpose.[411] A bank need only exercise ordinary care to determine whether a depositor is alive before paying an order on the depositor's savings account, and a bank paying an order without notice of the depositor's death is not liable to the depositor's estate.[412] Certain savings bank bylaws and rules intended to protect banks from liability for payment of deposits, in whole or in part, to persons not entitled thereto, have been construed by the courts in relation to their effect on a bank's liability where payment is made after the death of a depositor.[413] And a statute providing that the public administrator upon court order may withdraw, without notice,

---

[409] Podmore v. South Brooklyn Sav. Inst., 48 App. Div. 218, 62 N.Y.S. 961; Kelley v. Buffalo Sav. Bank, 180 N.Y. 171, 72 N.E. 995, 105 Am. St. R. 720, 69 L.R.A. 317.

[410] Dolbashian v. Rhode Island Hosp. Trust Co., 53 R.I. 462, 167 A. 262.

Depository bank paying deceased's deposit to bank forwarding deceased's passbook and withdrawal slip containing deceased's purported signature, and from which money was subsequently withdrawn by person presenting passbook, held not liable for deposit where money came into control of deceased's executor, though deceased's death was unknown to depository bank when making payment. Dolbashian v. Rhode Island Hospital Trust Co., 53 R.I. 462, 167 A. 262.

[411] Wickenheiser v. Colonial Bank, 168 App. Div. 329, 153 N.Y.S. 1035, aff'd, 224 N.Y. 651, 121 N.E. 898.

[412] Paddock v. Anglo-California Trust Co., 107 Cal. App. 430, 290 P. 550 (1930).

Question whether certain facts are sufficient to constitute constructive notice to savings bank of depositor's death is to be determined in light of all circumstances. Paddock v. Anglo-California Trust Co., 107 Cal. App. 430, 290 P. 550 (1930).

[413] Hoffman v. Union Dime Sav. Inst., 41 Misc. 517, 85 N.Y.S. 16, rev'd on other grounds, 95 App. Div. 329, 88 N.Y.S. 686: O'Brien v. Elmira Sav. Bank, 99 App. Div. 76, 91 N.Y.S. 364; Boone v. Citizens' Sav. Bank, 84 N.Y. 83, 9 Abb. N. Cas. 146, 38 Am. R. 498; Donlan v. Provident Inst., 127 Mass. 183, 34 Am. R. 358.

As to construction of bylaws and rules intended to protect banks from liability for unauthorized payments in relation to their effect on a bank's liability for payments made during the life of a depositor, see § 16 of this chapter.

A recital on bankbooks that no gift, assignment or transfer of any or all parts of any account need be recognized by the bank unless the bank has written notice thereof in a form satisfactory to it, would be complied with by the service of a certified copy of a judgment establishing a gift of bankbooks from a decedent to the plaintiff. Shumsky v. Dime Sav. Bank of Brooklyn, 190 N.Y.S.2d 274.

Tennessee Code Annotated § 45-2-704 permits the creation of payable-on-death accounts

money of a decedent, authorizes the administrator to withdraw a decedent's deposit from a savings bank without his passbook, where it has been lost, the bank knows of the loss and has not paid the deposit to another.[414] For other cases construing statutes authorizing payment of a decedent's savings account, see the footnote.[415]

Authority to Appoint Person to Whom Deposit Shall Be Paid.—An act incorporating a savings fund society, and providing that a book shall be kept at its office, in which every depositor may appoint someone to whom his money shall be paid at his death, if not otherwise disposed of by will, is constitutional,[416] and under such act, the appointee of a depositor, not his administrator, is entitled to his deposit upon the depositor's death.[417] But where a bylaw of a savings bank provides that the deposit of a deceased depositor shall be paid to his representative, and the bank has on file a power of attorney executed by the depositor to a third person to draw the deposit, the power is revoked by the death of the depositor, and the bank will be liable to his administrator if it pays the deposit to the power holder.[418] Where decedent opened two savings accounts at the bank, it was plainly typed on the signature cards that accounts were payable-on-death accounts, individuals were named to receive the accounts if they survived decedent, and the cards were signed, the decedent properly designated in writing that such accounts were to be paid upon her death, notwithstanding the fact that the typing was below the signatures.[419]

---

and shields banks from liability when disbursing funds to designated beneficiaries. If a third party challenges a bank's ability to disburse funds to a designated beneficiary, Tenn. Code Ann. § 45-2-706 provides that a bank does not have to recognize the adverse claimant until the claimant can procure a restraining order, injunction or other appropriate process against the bank from a court of competent jurisdiction. T.C.A., § 45-2-710 places a statute of limitations on when third parties may bring such actions. If the bank so chooses, it may file an interpleader action and ask a court to determine the rights of the relevant parties. Jarnigan v. Moyers, 2018 Tenn. App. LEXIS 118.

414 Bryson v. Security Trust, etc., Bank, 29 Cal. App. 596, 156 P. 987.

415 The Massachusetts statute authorizing the payment of checks and savings bank orders upon presentation for payment within a specified time after the date of the check or order, notwithstanding the death of the drawer, protects a bank making such payment according to the provisions of the statute and does not affect the rights of the parties inter se. Smith v. Merchants Nat. Bank, 330 Mass. 481, 115 N.E.2d 143 (1953).

416 Knorr's Appeal, 89 Pa. 93.

417 Fidelity Ins. Co. v. Wright (Pa.), 16 Wkly. Notes Cas. 177.

418 Hoffman v. Union Dime Sav. Inst., 41 Misc. 517, 85 N.Y.S. 16, rev'd on other grounds, 95 App. Div. 329, 88 N.Y.S. 686.

419 Morton v. McComb, 281 Ark. 125, 662 S.W.2d 471 (1983).

Joint Deposits.—Where a savings bank deposit is in joint names, and the intent appears to be to create a joint tenancy, the survivor takes title to the entire fund, whether or not he ever had possession of the passbook,[420] and

[420] **In general.**—

Farrelly v. Emigrant, etc., Sav. Bank, 179 N.Y. 594, 72 N.E. 1141. Compare Schippers v. Kempkes, 67 A 1042 (N.J. 1907), aff'd, 72 N.J. Eq. 948, 73 A. 1118; McCarthy v. Holland, 80 Cal. App. 495, 158 P. 1045; Williams v. Sav. Bank, 33 Cal. App. 655, 166 P. 366; Dunn v. Houghton, 51 A. 71 (N.J. 1902); Bonnette v. Molloy, 153 App. Div. 73, 138 N.Y.S. 67; Clary v. Fitzgerald, 155 App. Div. 659, 140 N.Y.S. 536, aff'd, 213 N.Y. 696, 107 N.E. 1075; In re Schroeder's Estate, 144 N.E.2d 512 (Ohio Prob. 1957).

Joint savings account, which provides that "either is authorized, under any circumstances, to sign checks for the withdrawal of funds, in whole or part," held joint tenancy with right of survivorship, so that bank could pay to survivor. First Nat. Bank v. Lawrence, 212 Ala. 45, 101 So. 663.

See also § 15 of this chapter, and vol. 5A, ch. 9, § 46.

Upon death of one depositor in savings account payable to either of two depositors or survivor, bank was obligated to pay proceeds of account to surviving depositor. Hollman v. Exeter Banking Co., 266 A.2d 209 (N.H. 1970).

Interests of husband and wife in joint savings account, payable to either, or to survivor of them were to be determined as of time of husband's death, and where, on that date, no action had been taken by bank or by depositors to either secure husband's alleged indebtedness by account or to indicate any intention to create anything other than a joint tenancy, and no proof was offered to overcome statutory presumption of ownership of funds in wife, funds became property of wife and were not subject to indebtedness of deceased husband nor claim of bank to a lien or setoff by reason of alleged indebtedness. Guilds v. Monroe County Bank, 41 Mich. App. 616, 200 N.W.2d 769 (1972).

Issuing duplicate passbook for savings account in name of father and son after father's death, where father owned account, held not to render savings association liable to son. Daly v. Pacific Sav., etc., Ass'n, 154 Wash. 249, 282 P. 60.

Deposit with creditor.—

A bank deposit, originally made in the deceased's name, and later credited to the deceased and a creditor, does not become the property of the survivor. In re Mt. Vernon Trust Co., 175 App. Div. 353, 161 N.Y.S. 1060, aff'd, 223 N.Y. 563, 119 N.E. 1061.

Deposit to credit of "A or B".—

A and B deposited money in a savings bank, the credit being given to "A or B" at their request. They afterwards deposited frequently in the same way, stating to the bank officers that either or both could draw the money. B died. A notified the bank that B's widow and administratrix had the book, and directed the bank not to pay her. The bank did pay her the deposit however, on her producing the book and her letters. Held, a joint tenancy was not created, but that A could maintain an action for her actual share of the deposits. Mulcahey v. Emigrant, etc., Sav. Bank, 89 N.Y. 435.

Where a deposit in a savings bank was made by A out of his own funds, but in the name of "A or B," a joint tenancy was not created, and the savings bank was protected, on

whether or not the money deposited belonged to the decedent.[421] But the presumption that a deposit in a bank in the form of a joint survivorship account was intended to vest title in the survivor must yield to proof of the actual agreement of the parties.[422] Where a joint deposit is made, the law of

---

payment of the funds to A's executrix on presentation by her of the passbook and testamentary letters, where: (1) B had never made any claim to the deposit up to that time; (2) B had never deposited or withdrawn any money, and had never had the passbook and (3) A's intention in making the deposit in the form recited was immaterial. Grafing v. Irving Sav. Inst., 69 App. Div. 566, 75 N.Y.S. 48 (1902).

[421] Bonnette v. Molloy, 153 App. Div. 73, 138 N.Y.S. 67, rev'd on other grounds, 209 N.Y. 167, 102 N.E. 559; Osterland v. Schroeder, 22 Ohio App. 213, 153 N.E. 758; Barstow v. Tetlow, 115 Me. 96, 97 A. 829; In re Delmore's Estate, 174 App. Div. 99, 160 N.Y.S. 62; Deal's Adm'r v. Merchants' & Mechanics' Sav. Bank, 120 Va. 297, 91 S.E. 135, 1917C L.R.A. 548; Daly v. Pacific Sav. etc., Ass'n 154 Wash. 249, 282 P. 60.

Where deceased deposited money in savings bank to joint account of himself and another payable to their survivor, further provision in deposit agreement that "the parties agree to become partners" therein did not affect the right of survivorship, when the contract was construed as a whole. Halsted v. Central Sav. Bank, 36 Cal. App. 500, 172 P. 613; Halsted v. Oakland Bank, 36 Cal. App. 816, 172 P. 614.

[422] **In general.—**

In re Buchanan's Estate, 100 Misc. 628, 166 N.Y.S. 947, aff'd 184 App. Div. 237, 171 N.Y.S. 708.

Statutory provision.—The Ohio statute with regard to deposits in the name of two or more persons was enacted for protection of banks and the right of any of those named in a bank account to the account, unless the contract or surrounding circumstances can be interpreted otherwise, must be established by evidence beyond or outside the terms of the contract with the bank. Jones v. Neu, 106 Ohio App. 161, 150 N.E.2d 858, 6 Ohio Op. 428.

Evidence sufficient to override presumption of survivorship.—Even assuming that a savings account, which was opened in 1963 when decedent was 11-years-old and which was payable to decedent or his mother, gave rise to a presumption of survivorship, there was sufficient evidence to override that presumption and to support the conclusion that decedent did not intend to create in his mother any beneficial interest in the account, either during his lifetime or upon his death; accordingly, decedent's widow was entitled to the money in the account upon decedent's death. Shields v. United States Nat'l Bank, 97 Ore. Adv. 1658, 266 Ore. 562, 514 P.2d 348 (1978).

Although the passbook for a savings account, which was opened in 1953 when decedent was 11-years-old, was made out to decedent or his mother, evidence that nearly all the funds in the account came from decedent and that, during his life, the funds were used for his purposes was sufficient to establish that his mother was not intended to have a beneficial interest in the account during his lifetime. Shields v. United States Nat'l Bank, 97 Ore. Adv. 1658, 266 Ore. 562, 514 P.2d 348 (1978).

In Tennessee, the contract approach to questions of joint ownership has supplanted the common law approach of joint tenancy with its requirement of four unities. Under the contract theory, the formal requirements of an inter vivos gift are likewise irrelevant, and the

the state where the transactions occurred governs in the determination of a claim of title as the surviving joint tenant of the deposit.[423] Joint tenancies of savings bank deposits may be created, if the parties so intend, regardless of whether the tenants are husband and wife, and if a joint tenancy is created, the right of survivorship exists.[424] And in the absence of proof of an agreement or the ownership of funds deposited in the names of husband and wife, such a deposit belongs to the surviving spouse and is not a part of the decedent's estate.[425] And a deposit made payable by a decedent to himself

---

issue is whether the parties intended to create a right of survivorship. To establish a testator's intent, a court may consider, for example, signed bank signature cards which express the contractual right of survivorship, or the parties may present extrinsic evidence to demonstrate intent as to the type of ownership. In re Estate of Kirkman, 2017 Tenn. App. LEXIS 104.

[423] Barstow v. Tetlow, 115 Me. 96, 97 A. 829.

[424] **In general.—**

West v. McCullough, 194 N.Y. 518, 87 N.E 1130; First Nat. Bank v. Lawrence, 212 Ala. 45, 101 So. 663, citing Michie on Banks and Banking; Augsbury v. Shurtliff, 180 N.Y 138, 72 N.E. 927; Crowley v. Savings Union Bank, etc., Co., 30 Cal. App. 144, 157 P. 516.

Facts not creating a joint tenancy in husband and wife.—

A husband deposited money belonging to himself in a savings bank, saying that he wanted it so that either he or his wife could draw the money, and both he and his wife entered their names on the signature book opposite which the clerk of the bank wrote the words "to be drawn by either." A passbook was given to the husband as a voucher for the deposit. The wife, after the death of her husband, presented the passbook at the bank, and drew out the money, giving a receipt therefor, signed by her in behalf of her husband. Held, she was bound to refund the money in an action brought by her husband's administrator. Brown v. Brown (N.Y.), 23 Barb. 565.

[425] **In general.—**

In re Missionary Soc., 95 Misc. 76, 160 N.Y.S. 512.

Agreement.—

Where a husband and wife, by an agreement signed by them and the bank as provided by statute, make a joint savings deposit, the survivor's rights are created by the agreement and are not determined by the rules controlling joint tenancy or tenancy in common, nor by those governing gifts inter vivos. In re McIlrath's Estate, 276 Ill. App. 408 (1934).

Where residuary legatees contest widow's title to money in savings account and she claims title thereto by virtue of a deposit contract which provided for joint ownership by the husband and wife with the right of survivorship and the contract is provided for by statute, and is regular on its face, the contract made a prima facie case for the widow, and the burden was then on the petitioners to prove that the contract had been entered into under such circumstances as to vitiate it. In re McIlrath's Estate, 276 Ill. App. 408 (1934).

Proof inadmissible.—

In an action by a bank to determine the ownership of a deposit claimed by the personal

or daughter, but with instructions that no withdrawals are to be made by others during his lifetime, does not authorize payment to the survivor.[426] Where depositor did not inform bank that she desired to open joint account with right of survivorship, and where bank did not engage in any prohibited practices, depositor's daughter, subsequent to depositor's death, could not recover from bank on theory that it was negligent in not establishing joint account with right of survivorship in savings account opened in both their names.[427]

Executor was properly awarded decedent's certificate of deposit where: (1) Account was a joint account with right of survivorship in the executor, conclusively establishing the decedent's intent; (2) her signature on a signature card was not statutorily required and (3) no fraud, duress, or undue influence was alleged or shown.[428]

In probate proceeding in where brother of decedent and decedent's estate both claimed ownership of joint bank accounts in Maryland, remand was required to consider effect the District of Columbia Nonprobate Transfers on Death Act had on determination of ownership of Maryland joint bank

---

representatives of a husband and wife, nothing can be predicated by either party on what was said or done after the wife's death, where no new contract was thereafter made by the bank. Wayne County & Home Sav. Bank v. Smith, 194 Mich. 151, 160 N.W. 472.

[426] In re Gokey, 140 Misc. 779, 252 N.Y.S. 434.

[427] Tucker v. Colburn 140 Vt. 186, 436 A.2d 1095 (1981).

[428] In re Estate of Bingham, 2017 Tenn. App. LEXIS 396 (2017). See T.C.A., § 45-2-703(e).

Although neither party disputed that the certificate of deposit should be analyzed under the Tennessee statute pertaining to multiple-party deposit accounts, T.C.A., § 45-2-703, the Tennessee Court of Appeals acknowledged that the court had reached differing conclusions on the applicability of the statute to certificates of deposit. For instance, in Roberts v. Roberts, 827 S.W.2d 788 (Tenn. Ct. App. 1991), the court of appeals held that the statute does not apply to certificates of deposit which require no signature card and provide no withdrawal until maturity. Several years later, the court in Guess v. Finlay, 2012 Tenn. App. LEXIS 241 (Tenn. Ct. App. 2012), found that Roberts was wrongly decided because the plain language of the statute extending its application to multiple-party deposit accounts expressly includes a certificate of deposit, established in the names of, payable to, or in form subject to withdrawal by two or more natural persons. However, a recent decision of the court in In re Estate of Kirkman, 2017 Tenn. App. LEXIS 104 (Tenn. Ct. App. 2017), cited to its holding in Roberts and held that an appellant's reliance on T.C.A., § 45-2-703 for determining ownership of a certificate of deposit was misplaced. The Tennessee Court of Appeals, like the court in Guess v. Finlay, declined to ignore the plain language of the statute extending its application to "a certificate of deposit, established in the names of, payable to, or in form subject to withdrawal by two or more natural persons," In re Estate of Bingham, 2017 Tenn. App. LEXIS 396 (Tenn. Ct. App. 2017).

accounts, as: (1) The Act took effect three days before the trial court rendered its decision; (2) the Act applied to accounts that existed before its effective date; (3) neither party addressed the applicability of the Act and (4) the Act provided that transfers of funds through right of survivorship provisions of joint bank accounts were non testamentary and not subject to estate administration.[429]

Deposits in Names of Others.—Where, after a depositor's death, savings bankbooks are found showing deposits in the names of different persons, in the absence of evidence of the sources from which the moneys were derived, the claims of those intended must be determined by the names on the books.[430]

Deposit in Trust for Another.—A "Totten trust" is a deposit by a person of his own money in his own name as trustee for another. It does not establish an irrevocable trust during the lifetime of the depositor, but is a tentative trust revocable at will until the depositor dies or completes the gift in his lifetime by some unequivocal act or declaration, such as the delivery of the passbook or notice to the beneficiary.[431] But if the depositor dies before the beneficiary without revocation or some decisive act of declaration or disaffirmance, the presumption arises that an absolute trust was created as to the balance on hand at the death of the depositor.[432] Thus, upon the death of the depositor, the beneficiary is entitled to the amount so deposited.[433]

---

[429] In re Estate of Blake, 856 A.2d 1151 (D.C. 2004). See D.C. Code § 19-601.01.

[430] In re Smith (N.Y.), 17 Abb. N. Cas. 78; Gaffney v. Public Administrator (N.Y.), 4 Dam. 223.

[431] **In general.—**

In re Estate of Jeruzal, 269 Minn. 183, 130 N.W.2d 473 (1964); Cunningham v. Davenport, 147 N.Y. 43, 41 N.E. 412, 49 Am. St. R. 641, 32 L.R.A. 873; Gerrish v. New Bedford Institution for Sav., 128 Mass. 159, 35 Am. R.365.

See In re Totten. 179 N.Y. 112, 71 N.E. 748, 70 L.R.A. 711 (1904).

Subject to creditors' claims.—

Accounts deposited in bank by depositor in trust for another are tentative trusts only, revocable at will until depositor dies or completes the gift by some unequivocal act or declaration, and may be subject to claims of creditors. United States v. State Nat'l Bank, 421 F.2d 519 (2d Cir. 1970).

A Totten trust is created when a deposit is made by a person (the holder) of his or her own money in his or her own name as trustee for another. Baurhyte v. Smith (In re Estate ofWeiland), 338 Ill. App. 3d 585, 788 N.E.2d 811 (2003).

[432] In re Estate of Jeruzal, 269 Minn. 183, 130 N.W.2d 473 (1964).

A woman deposited money in a savings bank in her name, as trustee for her husband, and

Such trusts are called "Totten trusts" after the leading case of In re Totten,[434] which established the validity of such savings account trusts in New York; the New York rule has now been adopted by statute or common law in several other states.[435]

---

drew the interest thereon during her life. She survived her husband, and at her death the passbook was found among her assets, but was presented to the bank, and the deposit drawn out, by the administrator of her husband, before any demand was made therefor by the administrator of the wife. Held in the absence of proof rebutting the presumption of trust, that the bank was protected in its payment. Bishop v. Seamen's Bank for Sav., 33 App. Div. 181, 53 N.Y.S. 488.

[433] **In general.—**

Martin v. Funk, 75 N.Y. 134, 31 Am. R. 446; Harrison v. Totten, 53 App. Div. 178, 65 N.Y.S. 725; Williams v. Brooklyn Sav. Bank, 51 App. Div. 332, 64 N.Y.S. 1021; Scott v. Harbeck, 1 N.Y.S. 788, 49 Hun 292; Robertson v. McCarthy, 54 App. Div. 103, 66 N.Y.S. 327; In re Finn, 44 Misc. 622, 90 N.Y.S. 159; Weaver v. Emigrant, etc., Sav. Bank (N.Y.), 17 Abb. N. Cas. 82; Fowler v. Bowery Sav. Bank, 47 Hun 399, 14 N.Y. St. R. 515, rev'd on other grounds, 113 N.Y. 450, 21 N.E. 172; Walso v. Latterner, 140 Minn. 455, 168 N.W. 353.

In absence of written notice of express trust, moneys on deposit in "Totten" bank account trusts are payable to beneficiary named, upon death of trustee. D'Agostino v. Home Federal Sav. & Loan Asso., 237 N.Y.S.2d 413 (1963).

Multiple-party bank accounts, including joint accounts and Totten trusts, are governed by the probate code. A Totten trust is a tentative trust, created when a depositor opens a bank account in trust for another person, but reserves the power to withdraw funds during the depositor's lifetime. If the trust is not revoked before the depositor's death, any balance in the account is payable to the beneficiary. Higgins v. Higgins, 11 Cal. App. 5th 648, 217 Cal. Rptr. 3d 691 (2017). See Cal. Prob. Code, §§ 5100, 5132.

Possession of passbook.—

Professed belief of wife that as long as she held bank passbook, however account may have been denominated, title to proceeds remained in her afforded no basis for maintenance of lawsuit to recover savings bank deposit maintained in name of deceased husband in trust for one of his sons by prior marriage. Kwoczka v. Dry Dock Sav. Bank, 52 Misc. 2d 67, 275 N.Y.S.2d 156 (1966).

This is so though the cestui que trust was not notified of such deposit, and the depositor kept the passbook. Martin v. Funk, 75 N.Y 134, 81 Am. R. 446; Robertson v. McCarthy, 54 App. Div. 103, 66 N.Y.S. 327; Cunningham v. Davenport, 147 N.Y. 43, 41 N.E. 412, 49 Am. St. R. 641, 32 L.R.A. 373; Weaver v. Emigrant, etc., Sav. Bank (N.Y.), 17 Abb. N. Cas. 82.

In re Estate of Wright, 17 Ill. App. 3d 894, 308 N.E.2d 319 (1974).

[434] 179 N.Y. 112, 71 N.E. 748, 70 L.R.A. 711 (1904).

[435] *Illinois.*—Under Illinois statute, the guardian of a disabled person's estate may revoke a Totten trust only with court authorization. Moreover, such funds may only be used as necessary for the comfort and suitable support and education of the ward or for any other

Since the rule only establishes a presumption, evidence of contemporaneous facts and circumstances may be admitted to show that the real motive of a depositor was not to create a trust, but to accomplish some independent and different purpose inconsistent with an intention to divest himself of the beneficial ownership of the fund in question.[436] But the fact that a depositor dies leaving a will which can operate on nothing if not on the fund deposited,

---

purpose that the court deems to be for the best interests of the ward. Baurhyte v. Smith (In re Estate of Weiland), 338 Ill. App. 3d 585, 788 N.E.2d 811 (2003). See 755 Ill. Comp. Stat. Ann. 5/11a-18(a), (d).

Massachusetts.—The rule in Massachusetts, however, is to the effect that if the trust fund was established merely to evade a bylaw of the bank, it will be void as a trust fund. Clark v. Clark, 108 Mass. 522; Brabrook v. Boston Five Cents Sav. Bank, 104 Mass. 228, 6 Am. R. 222 (1870).

Pursuant to former Mass. Gen. Laws ch. 167D, § 6 (see now Mass. Gen. Laws ch. 167D, §§ 3, 5), deposits made by one person in trust for another shall be credited to the depositors as trustees for such person, and upon the death of the trustee of such an account, the amount then on deposit together with the interest thereon may be paid to the person for whom the deposit was made. Bongaards v. Millen, 55 Mass. App. Ct. 51, 768 N.E.2d 1107 (2002).

Former Mass. Gen. Laws ch. 167D, § 6 (see now Mass. Gen. Laws ch. 167D, §§ 3, 5) essentially shields a bank from liability for payment of an account to a trust beneficiary following the death of the trustee but also may be read as permitting withdrawal of part or all of the account by the trustee. Bongaards v. Millen, 55 Mass. App. Ct. 51, 768 N.E.2d 1107 (2002).

Minnesota.—In re Estate of Jeruzal, 269 Minn. 183, 130 N.W.2d 473 (1964).

The Minnesota Totten descent statute was adopted to protect banks. In case of payment to a beneficiary before receiving notice of the claim of the representative of the estate. But because of the special nature of this type of gift, court decisions have extended the scope of the statute to give broad protection to the interests of beneficiaries. In re Estate of Jeruzal, 269 Minn. 183, 130 N.W.2d 473 (1964).

New Jersey.—A beneficiary named in a trust savings account, in which a deposit was made in 1961, was entitled to the proceeds upon the death of the depositor trustee. In re Kloppenberg's Estate, 82 N.J. Super. 117, 196 A.2d 800.

And it has been held that an administrator, without obtaining judicial advice, was not justified in withdrawing all of a deposit in a trust savings account and distributing it to persons other than the named beneficiary on the basis of old court decisions or decisions not rendered by the highest court in the state, in view of the conclusive statutory presumption in favor of the named beneficiary, especially where the administrator was one of the distributees. In re Kloppenberg's Estate, 82 N.J. Super. 117, 196 A.2d 800, reviewing and discussing Bendix v. Hudson County Nat'l Bank, 142 N.J. Eq. 487, 59 A.2d 253, Howard Savings Inst. v. Quatra, 38 N.J. Super. 174, 118 A.2d 121, Howard Sav. Institution v. Kielb, 66 N.J. Super. 98, 168 A.2d 452, and Howard Savings Inst. v. Kielb, 38 N.J. 186, 183 A.2d 401.

[436] Mabie v. Bailey, 95 N.Y. 206; Cunningham v. Davenport, 147 N.Y. 43, 41 N.E. 412, 49 Am. St. R. 641, 32 L.R.A. 373.

will not negate the existence of a trust.[437] And even though a trust is created, the depositor may withdraw the funds on the death of the beneficiary of the trust.[438]

The ordinary consequence of a withdrawal and transfer of a trust account would be to revoke the trust. A savings bank trust is revocable by the depositor at any time during his life if the depositor changes the form of the account, withdraws the money on deposit, or makes a will leaving the account to someone other than the trust beneficiary.[439]

Gifts of Deposits and Rights of Donees after Depositor's Death.—The delivery by a depositor of his bankbook with an order for payment of his deposit constitutes a valid gift inter vivos, and when the bank is notified of this gift, there is a complete assignment of the right to the fund deposited; therefore, upon the subsequent death of the depositor, the assignee, not the administrator of the depositor, is the person to whom the deposit should be paid.[440] Even though a donee does not present such bankbook and order to

---

A trust is not created where the depositor survives the beneficiary, and the evidence clearly shows that there was no intention to create a trust. Cunningham v. Davenport, 147 N.Y. 43, 41 N.E. 412, 49 Am. St. R. 641, 32 L.R.A. 373; In re Barefield, 177 N.Y. 387, 69 N.E. 732, 101 Am. St. R. 814.

In a real sense, a tentative or Totten trust is not a trust at all but is a recognized exception to the law of testamentary disposition and, as such, obviates the necessity for compliance with the requisite statutory elements of executing a will. While all parties are living, an account belongs to the parties who have a present right to payment, in proportion to their contributions, unless there is clear and convincing evidence of a different intent. In the case of a Totten trust account, the beneficiary has no rights to the sums on deposit during the lifetime of any party, unless there is clear and convincing evidence of a different intent. If there is an irrevocable trust, the account belongs beneficially to the beneficiary. A finding under the clear and convincing evidence test requires evidence clear enough to leave no substantial doubt and strong enough that every reasonable person would agree. Higgins v. Higgins, 11 Cal. App. 5th 648, 217 Cal. Rptr. 3d 691 (2017).

[437] Weaver v. Emigrant, etc., Sav. Bank (N.Y.), 17 Abb. N. Cas. 82.

[438] Roughan v. Chenango Valley Sav. Bank, 158 App. Div. 786, 144 N.Y.S. 508, aff'd, 216 N.Y. 696, 110 N.E. 1049.

Bylaws of savings bank as to payment of trust accounts on death of trustee and beneficiary held not to require that fund deposited in tentative trust be paid estate of beneficiary who predeceased depositor. In re Vaughan's Estate, 145 Misc. 332, 260 N.Y.S. 197.

[439] Bongaards v. Millen, 55 Mass. App. Ct. 51, 768 N.E.2d 1107 (2002).

[440] **In general.—**

Foss v. Lowell Five Cents Sav. Bank, 111 Mass. 285; Brannan v. Eliot Five Cents Sav. Bank, 211 Mass. 532, 98 N.E. 572; Augsbury v. Shurtliff, 190 N.Y. 507, 83 N.E. 1122. As to assignment of deposits, see § 19 of this chapter.

a bank until after a depositor's death, his title is good as against the next of kin of the depositor.[441] But a card signed by a savings depositor instructing his bank to add another's name to his account does not require the bank to pay the third party on the depositor's death, where the passbook is not produced as required by the contract of deposit.[442] And where one has an active savings bank account which, because of incapacity resulting from age, she changes to the name of herself and son, the son thereby acquires the right to draw money from the account with the right of survivorship, but he acquires no title by gift which he can enforce after her death.[443] The fact that a savings deposit is designated on a passbook as belonging to one of two heirs so that such heir had apparent right to draw out the funds, does not as a matter of law, put such funds in her possession, and undrawn funds remain in the bank as trustee for the equitable owners thereof.[444]

The possession of a depositor's passbook under a parol gift made a day before the depositor's death, entitles the donee to draw the deposit as the "legal representative" of the donor under a bylaw of the bank which provides that on death of a depositor, payment shall be made to his "legal representative."[445] But it also has been held that where the rules of a bank

---

Where there is a gift causa mortis of money on deposit in a bank and a delivery to the donee of the bankbook, and the bank pays the money to the donor's administrator after receiving notice of the donee's claim, the donee is not compelled to look to the administrator, but may recover from the bank. Walsh v. Bowery Sav. Bank, 7 N.Y.S. 669, 15 Daly 403, 28 N.Y. St. R. 402 (1899), appeal denied, 8 N.Y.S. 344.

No notice until after death.—

But where savings bank depositor gave away his deposit and delivered passbook to donee, and donee did not give bank notice of the transaction until after depositor had died and bank had paid deposit to depositor's administratrix, bank was not liable to donee notwithstanding bank rule that deposit could not be withdrawn except on production of the passbook. Wade v. Security Sav., etc., Bank, 99 F.2d 995.

Compliance with forms necessary.—

A bank account or deposit is an incorporeal and can only be donated by a natural instrument, and the forms for donations, inter vivos or causa mortis, must be complied with to effect either a present donation or one in contemplation of death. Washington v. Sabine State Bank & Trust Co., 328 So. 2d 809 (La. App. 1976).

[441] Kimball v. Leland, 110 Mass. 325; Stacks v. Buten, 141 Wis. 235, 124 N.W. 403, 135 Am. St. R. 39; Brannan v. Eliot Five Cents Sav. Bank, 211 Mass. 532, 98 N.E. 572.

[442] Christensen v. Ogden State Bank, 75 Utah 478, 286 P. 638.

[443] Schippers v. Kempkes (N.J.), 67 A. 1042, aff'd, 72 N.J. Eq. 948, 73 A. 1118.

[444] Bishop v. Groton Sav. Bank, 96 Conn. 325, 114 A. 88.

[445] Cosgriff v. Hudson City Sav. Inst., 24 Misc. 4, 52 N.Y.S. 189 (1898).

provide that on the death of a depositor the fund shall be paid only to his personal representative, payment to one presenting the book and claiming the deposit by gift causa mortis is unwarranted,[446] and this is so notwithstanding another rule of the bank providing that possession of a passbook is authority to the bank to pay, as such rule ceases to be effective upon the death of a depositor.[447] But if a deposit is a gift of a chose in action, the bank cannot refuse payment after the donor's death under a bylaw requiring payment to a depositor's legal representative.[448]

A notarial act is required for the valid donation inter vivos of an incorporeal movable; however, the manual gift of a corporeal movable, accompanied by real delivery, is not subject to any formality. It is therefore evident that a savings account (an incorporeal movable) is not subject to manual gift, but the cash withdrawn from the account (a corporeal movable) may be subject to manual gift. The critical inquiry is whether the record establishes that the donor maintained an intention to donate the funds to the donee at a time when the donee possessed the funds in a form susceptible of manual gift.[449]

Payment to Administrator Appointed in Another State.—Where a savings bank in good faith pays a decedent's deposit to the administrator appointed in the state of his domicile, such payment is good as against an administrator appointed in the state where the bank is located, if the latter administrator has improvidently delayed collection of the account and the bank has had no notice of his appointment, where there are no creditors in the latter state.[450]

---

[446] Farmer v. Manhattan Sav. Inst., 15 N.Y.S. 235, 60 Hun 462; Mahon v. South Brooklyn Sav. Inst., 175 N.Y. 69, 67 N.E. 118, 96 Am. St. H. 603.

[447] Farmer v. Manhattan Sav. Institution, 15 N.Y.S. 235, 60 Hun 462; Mahon v. South Brooklyn Sav. Inst., 175 N.Y. 69, 67 N.E. 118, 96 Am. St. H. 603.

[448] Scheffer v. Erie County Sav. Bank, 229 N.Y. 50, 127 N.E. 474.

[449] Succession of Gassiott, 159 So. 3d 521 (La. 2015). See La. C.C. Art. 1550.

Joint savings account of a decedent and his wife was validly created, and once the decedent negotiated a settlement check from a lawsuit and deposited the funds into the joint account, when coupled with his donative intent, the donation was effectively complete and either could withdraw funds from the account at any time under statute. Succession of Gassiott, 159 So. 3d 521 (La. 2015).

[450] Mass v. German Sav. Bank, 176 N.Y. 377, 68 N.E. 658, 98 Am. St. R. 689 (appointment of in-state administrator was recorded in surrogate's office).

Waiver of Claim.—One having a valid claim against a bank with respect to money deposited by another in his own name, may after the death of the depositor, lose such claim by waiver.[451]

§ 17. Contributory Negligence of Depositor.

Where a bank, in good faith, pays money deposited with it to one who is not authorized to receive it, the depositor cannot recover the amount so paid from the bank, if his contributory negligence has been the proximate cause of the loss.[452] But no amount of negligence on a depositor's part can relieve

---

[451] McDermott v. Miners' Sav. Bank, 100 Pa. 285 (1882).

A first learned, after his wife's death, that she had deposited his money in a savings bank in her own name. He learned the fact from the cashier of the bank, who informed him of it upon his ordering the cashier not to pay out any of his money, as he could not find the bankbook. The cashier advised him to procure the appointment of someone as administrator, which A did, and the person so appointed demanded and received, as administrator, the amount paid out by itand therefore A had no claim against the bank; that, if his notification to the cashier would have given him any claim, it must be deemed to have been waived. McDermott v. Miners' Sav. Bank, 100 Pa. 285 (1882).

[452] **In general.—**

Arkofsky v. State Sav. Bank, 91 Minn. 440, 98 N.W. 326, 103 Am. St. R. 519; Wall v. Emigrant, etc., Sav. Bank, 19 N.Y.S. 194, 64 Hun 249, 46 N.Y. St. R. 601; Campbell v. Schenectady Sav. Bank, 114 App. Div. 337, 99 N.Y.S. 927.

In an action on behalf of a mutual aid society against savings bank for payment of forged withdrawal orders, officers of society who took treasurer's word for amount on deposit without inquiry at bank or examination of passbook held guilty of culpable negligence. Bellantese v. Bronx Sav. Bank, 152 Misc. 325, 273 N.Y.S. 885.

Failure to give notice of loss or theft of passbook as contributory negligence.—

Where bylaw provided that the bank would not be responsible for payment on the presentation of a stolen passbook if the depositor had not notified the bank of the loss or theft of the book, the bylaw required depositor to attempt in good faith to prevent wrongful payment through loss of the passbook by informing the bank of its loss. Connolly v. Manchester Sav. Bank, 92 N.H. 89, 25 A.2d 412 (N.H. 1942). See also § 16 of this chapter.

Carelessness as to passbook.—

Under a rule printed in a savings bank deposit book providing that bank should not be liable for payment to improper person presenting the book, if it exercised proper care, unless depositor gave notice of theft or loss, it was immaterial that depositor did not know that book was stolen, and hence could not give notice of its loss, since a depositor, carelessly leaving the book lying around, does so at his peril. Bulakowski v. Philadelphia Sav. Fund Soc., 270 Pa. 538, 113 A. 553.

Estoppel.—

Depositor failing for more than 70 days after notification of attachment to inform bank

a bank of its duty to use ordinary care in making payments.[453] And so where the bylaws of a bank printed in a depositor's passbook provide that money deposited will be paid only to the depositor, to his order or to his legal representative upon presentation of the passbook, and the bank negligently pays a deposit on forged orders to one who has fraudulently obtained the passbook from the owner, it will not be relieved from liability by showing that the owner was negligent.[454] Similarly, where the bylaws of a bank provide that in order to draw out money, a passbook must be presented at the bank, and absent depositors can withdraw their deposits on their order or check properly witnessed, the bank is liable to a depositor for money paid on forged checks which are not witnessed as required by the bylaws to one who has possession of the depositor's passbook, whether or not the depositor was guilty of contributory negligence in parting with the custody of the book, as

---

that he was not person named therein was estopped to question court's jurisdiction. Evans v. Bank of Italy, 96 Cal. App. 259, 274 P. 74.

Facts held not to constitute contributory negligence.—

Where plaintiff was shot by the man who stole the passbook, and remained helpless until the next day, when he endeavored to look after his valuables, but the bank had paid the money the same day, before plaintiff discovered the theft of the book, his failure to notify the bank of such theft was not negligence. Wegner v. Second Ward Sav. Bank, 76 Wis. 242, 44 N.W. 1096.

Failure to inspect statements as to withdrawal slip.—

A savings account withdrawal slip is an instrument and an "item" within the meaning of the section which precludes a customer's recovery from a bank on any "item" paid in good faith by the bank after the first "item" and the statement were available to the customer for a reasonable period not exceeding 14 days and before the bank is notified by the customer of any unauthorized signature. Burnette v. First Citizens Bank & Trust Co., 48 N.C. App. 585, 269 S.E.2d 317 (1980).

[453] **In general.—**

Commonwealth Bank of Baltimore v. Goodman, 128 Md. 452, 97 A. 1005; Fiero v. Franklin Sav. Bank, 124 Misc. 38, 207 N.Y.S. 235.

Remissness of auditor, of depositor in examining treasurer's accounts held to furnish no justification to banks to honor treasurer's forged orders. Société de Bienfaisance St. Jean Baptiste do Millbury v. People's Sav. Bank, 228 Mass. 556, 117 N.E. 921.

An instruction requiring a verdict for bank if money was lost as result of negligence of depositor alone, or on account of negligence of both bank and depositor, was error, since depositor's negligence did not preclude recovery of sum which bank negligently paid. Connolly v. Manchester Sav. Bank, 92 N.H. 89, 25 A.2d 412 (N.H. 1942).

[454] Chase v. Waterbury Sav. Bank, 77 Conn. 295, 59 A. 37, 69 L.R.A. 329, 1 Ann. Cas. 96. See also Ladd v. Androscoggin County Sav. Bank, 96 Me. 520, 52 A. 1016.

it is a case of mispayment in violation of the bank's published regulations.[455] However, a depositor must exercise care in protecting his own rights, and if his negligence enables an impostor to deceive his bank and obtain his deposits, the loss falls on the depositor.[456]

§ 18. Assignment of Deposits.

A savings bank deposit can be transferred by its owner only by an assignment, and the assignee must notify the bank of the assignment to perfect his right against the bank.[457] A savings bank passbook is not a negotiable instrument,[458] and its possession, in itself, constitutes no evidence of a right to draw money.[459] And a passbook is not rendered negotiable by an order signed by a depositor directing payment to a third person,[460] nor by a bank bylaw assented to by its depositors, providing that the passbook of each depositor shall be transferable to order.[461] Thus, a depositor may assign or transfer his interest in his deposit for a valuable consideration without the delivery of his passbook.[462]

---

[455] People's Sav. Bank v. Cupps, 91 Pa. 315.

[456] Fiero v. Franklin Sav. Bank, 124 Misc. 38, 207 N.Y.S. 235.

[457] Ornbaun v. First Nat. Bank, 215 Cal 72, 8 P.2d 470, 81 A.L.R. 1148; Ornbaun v. Savings Bank of Mendocino County, 215 Cal. 770, 8 P.2d 473.

The rule that an assignee of a nonnegotiable chose in action must notify debtor of assignment in order to protect assignee against payment by debtor to original creditor is applicable to passbook of a savings bank. Myers v. Albany Sav. Bank, 270 App. Div. 466, 60 N.Y.S.2d 477, aff'd, 296 N.Y. 562, 68 N.E.2d 866.

[458] Witte v. Vincenot, 43 Cal. 325; McCaskill v. Connecticut Sav. Bank, 60 Conn. 300, 22 A. 568, 25 Am. St. R. 323, 13 L.R.A. 737; Smith v. Brooklyn Sav. Bank, 101 N.Y. 58, 4 N.E. 123, 54 Am. R. 653; Mills v. Albany Exch. Sav. Bank, 28 Misc. 251, 59 N.Y.S. 149; McCabe v. Union Dime Sav. Bank, 150 Misc. 157, 268 N.Y.S. 449; Forastiere v. Springfield Inst. for Savings, 303 Mass. 101, 20 N.E.2d 950 (1939); Hopkins Place Sav. Bank v. Holzer, 175 Md. 481, 2 A.2d 639.

Passbook issued by savings bank to depositor was a nonnegotiable chose in action, but it could be assigned. Myers v. Albany Sav. Bank, 270 App. Div. 466, 60 N.Y.S.2d 477, aff'd, 296 N.Y. 562, 68 N.E.2d 866.

[459] Smith v. Brooklyn Sav. Bank, 101 N.Y. 58, 4 N.E. 123, 54 Am. R. 653; McCabe v. Union Dime Sav. Bank, 150 Misc. 157, 268 N.Y.S. 449; Hopkins Place Sav. Bank v. Holzer, 175 Md. 481, 2 A.2d 639.

[460] McCaskill v. Connecticut Sav. Bank, 60 Conn. 300, 22 A. 568, 25 Am. St. R. 323, 13 L.R.A. 737.

[461] Witte v. Vincenot, 43 Cal. 325.

[462] Augsbury v. Shurtliff, 190 N.Y 507, 83 N.E. 1122; Stacks v. Buten, 141 Wis. 235,

However, the transfer of a passbook and the giving of an order for a bank to pay the amount of a deposit on production of the book are a valid assignment,[463] and import a consideration.[464] Moreover a parol transfer of a savings account of which the bank has notice, accompanied by delivery of the passbook for a valuable consideration, is sufficient to pass title to the transferee.[465] But where a savings bank depositor delivers his passbook, with a letter directing the disposition of his account, to a bank which forwards them to the bank which issued the book, there is no irrevocable assignment.[466]

A delivery to a donee of a deposit book issued by a bank containing entries of deposits to the credit of the donor, with the intention to give the donee the deposits represented by the book and accompanied with appropriate words of gift, is sufficient to constitute a valid gift of such deposits, without an assignment in writing.[467] And such a gift is an assignment and subject to the general rules governing assignments, including the necessity

---

124 N.W. 403, 135 Am. St. R. 89; Watson v. Stockton Morris Plan Co., 34 Cal. App. 2d 393, 93 P.2d 855.

And if the assignment is valid, the bank must recognize it McCabe v. Union Dime Sav. Bank, 150 Misc. 157, 268 N.Y.S. 449.

[463] Brannan v. Eliot Five Cents Sav. Bank, 211 Mass. 532, 98 N.E. 572.

A delivery of the passbook together with formal written assignment of account represented by passbook is the best evidence of assignment. Watson v. Stockton Morris Plan Co., 34 Cal. App. 2d 393, 93 P.2d 855.

[464] McGuire v. Murphy, 107 App. Div. 104, 94 N.Y.S. 1005.

[465] Rimkus v. Olszewski, 193 Ill. App. 49.

[466] Gruska v. Mitchell St. State Bank, 185 Wis. 620, 200 N.W. 680.

[467] **In general.—**

Polley v. Hicks, 58 Ohio St. 218, 50 N.E. 809, 41 L.R.A. 858.

Bank rules not precluding depositor from making gift inter vivos.—

Rules of a savings bank that "drafts sent by mail or otherwise will not be entitled to payment unless the deposit book is produced, and the depositor sends, by letter accompanying the draft, correct answers to the questions asked when the first deposit was made in the bank," that "on the decease of the depositor the amount standing to the credit of the deceased shall be paid to his or her legal representative," and that "drafts may be made personally, or by the order in writing of the depositor, if the bank has the signature of the party on their signature book, or by letters of attorney duly authenticated"—do not prevent the depositor, as a creditor of the bank, from passing the demand by gift inter vivos. Gammond v. Bowery Sav. Bank, 15 Daly 483, 8 N.Y S. 856, 26 N.Y. St. R. 136.

of notice to protect the assignee against payment to the assignor or one standing in his right.[468]

The assignee of a passbook for a bank deposit cannot avail himself of part of the contract and escape the effect of the balance by disregarding same,[469] and an assignee who receives a passbook is charged with full knowledge of the conditions printed therein.[470] No depositor can convey to another any greater right in the funds of a bank than he himself has, and any defense by a bank which is good against an original depositor is equally good against his assignee, unless there are facts creating an estoppel.[471] But where a passbook is obtained from a bank by depositing a forged check, and is assigned as security for a loan, the assignee, if he is guilty of negligence, and not a bona fide holder of the passbook, cannot recover the amount standing to the credit of his assignor in such book from the bank.[472]

The delivery of a savings bankbook, although unaccompanied by a written assignment, and transferred with the intention that it shall only be held as collateral security for the payment of a debt, transfers an equitable title to the deposit represented by the book, which will prevail against a subsequent attachment of it by trustee process.[473] And an order on a savings bank made by a depositor in favor of a third person for a good consideration, in the amount due him in his bankbook, although accepted by the bank "except the amount trusteed," is a valid assignment, taking effect when delivered, as to all the depositor's funds then held by the bank, and will prevail against trustee process.[474] Once a joint savings account in the names of the plaintiff and her husband had been assigned to the defendant bank, the plaintiff could not withdraw the funds from the account without the permission of the bank unless it waived or released its assignment.[475]

---

[468] Wade v. Security Sav., etc., Bank, 99 F.2d 995. As to rights of assignee of deposit after death of depositor, see § 17 of this chapter.

[469] Royon v. Greenstein, 122 Ohio St. 340, 171 N.E. 595. As to passbooks as part of contract between bank and depositor, see § 18 of this chapter.

[470] Royon v. Greenstein, 122 Ohio St. 340, 171 N.E. 595; Hopkins Place Sav. Bank v. Holzer, 175 Md. 481, 2 A.2d 639.

[471] McCaskill v. Connecticut Sav. Bank, 60 Conn. 300, 22 A. 568, 25 Am. St. R. 323, 13 L.R.A. 737; Wilcox v. Onondaga County Sav. Bank (N.Y.), 40 Hun 297.

[472] McCaskill v. Connecticut Sav. Bank, 60 Conn. 300, 22 A. 568, 25 Am. St. R. 323, 18 L.R.A. 737.

[473] Taft v. Bowker, 132 Mass. 277.

[474] Kingman v. Perkins, 105 Mass. 111.

[475] Copeland v. Peachtree Bank & Trust Co., 150 Ga. App. 262, 257 S.E.2d 353 (1979).

An assignment of a bank account which has been completed between the parties by the execution and delivery of a writing as required by a statute is valid though not delivered to the bank as the statute requires until after the assignor's death.[476] After an assignment of a deposit, if a bank with knowledge thereof pays it to one other than the assignee,[477] or if, after the revocation of an assignment, a bank with knowledge pays funds to the former assignee, it is liable for the amount so paid.[478]

§ 19. Interest and Dividends on Deposits.

In General.—Where depositors in a savings bank do not receive a fixed rate of interest independently of what the bank itself makes or loses in lending their money, but receive a share of such profits as the bank by lending their money makes, after deducting expenses and the like, such shares of profits is a dividend, not interest.[479] Ordinarily, depositors of a savings society, including holders of certificates of deposit, own a beneficial interest in its surplus.[480] And interest on loans and investments of a savings bank accrued but not paid, though secured by mortgages and drawing interest, cannot figure in the dividends which such banks are authorized to

---

[476] Stacks v. Buten, 141 Wis. 235, 124 N.W. 403. As to rights of assignee of deposit after death of depositor, see § 17 of this chapter.

[477] McCarthy v. Provident Inst., 159 Mass. 527, 34 N.E. 1073.

Even if notice of assignment of the assignor's joint passbook savings account to the bank in which the account was held was completely adequate and even if the assignee bank could stop payment of the withdrawal order of another joint holder of the account, the stop payment order would not have been in effect at the time the joint holder made withdrawals from the account well after six months subsequent to date of the alleged notice, and thus defendant bank could not be held liable to assignee bank for the amount of the account allegedly paid in violation of the assignment. First Wyo. Bank v. First Nat'l Bank, 612 P.2d 469 (Wyo. 1980).

[478] Gruska v. Mitchell St. State Bank, 185 Wis. 620, 200 N.W. 680.

[479] Cary v. Savings Union, 89 U.S. (22 Wall.) 38, 22 L Ed. 779.

To the extent that the status of a member of a federal savings and loan association is determinative of the question of whether a periodic payment to him is a payment of interest or of a dividend, in determining whether such payments constitute operating expenses which are deductible in computing the excise imposed on such association, the weight of the circumstances supports the conclusion that any payment is more analogous to a dividend to an owner than to a payment of interest to a creditor. First Fed. Sav. & Loan Ass'n v. State Tax Comm'n, 363 N.E.2d 474 (Mass. 1977).

[480] In re Dissolution of Springfield Sav. Soc., 12 Ohio App. 2d 120, 231 N.E.2d 314, 41 Ohio Op. 2d 191 (1966).

pay out of their "surplus profits," since profits must consist of earnings actually received.[481]

An entry in a depositor's passbook crediting accrued interest on his bank account was held to constitute a "deposit," and render the account active within a bylaw provision for the closing of accounts without further payment of interest where no deposit is made for twenty years in succession.[482] But it was held otherwise where a bank retained a passbook in its possession.[483]

Agreements as to Interest.—A savings bank, if it pays interest to its depositors, can agree at what time and in what amounts it will pay interest.[484] Thus, an agreement between a bank and a special depositor that he will not draw out the interest due on his deposits, but will allow it to remain and draw more interest, is not illegal or void.[485] And where a bank contracts to pay four percent upon a deposit, and the deposit is made the subject of a gift causa mortis, and the donee sues the bank, interest at the rate of four percent is to be computed to the date of judgment.[486]

Statutory and Internal Regulations and Restrictions.—In some states, there are statutory regulations and restrictions as to the interest and dividends to be paid by savings bank on deposits, and some of these statutes have been interpreted by the courts.[487] A savings bank incorporated under a

---

[481] People ex rel. Farnum v. San Francisco Sav. Union, 72 Cal. 199, 13 P. 498.

[482] May v. Union Dime Sav. Bank, 243 App. Div. 815, 278 N.Y.S. 458.

Where a savings bank in 1897 pursuant to statute then in force passed a bylaw providing that no interest or dividends should be declared or paid on any account in which no entry of deposit or withdrawal was made for 20 successive years, there was no infringement of constitutional rights in procedure adopted by bank, nor was bylaw unreasonable. And a depositor was bound by the regulation. Vennard v. Albany Sav.Bank, 257 App. Div. 789, 15 N.Y.S.2d 503, aff'd, 282 N.Y. 718, 26 N.E.2d 826.

[483] Wharton v. Poughkeepsie Sav. Bank, 262 App. Div. 598, 31 N.Y.S.2d 311, aff'd, 288 N.Y. 610, 42 N.E.2d 611.

[484] Dottenheim v. Union Sav. Bank & Trust Co., 114 Ga. 788, 40 S.E. 825.

Payment of interest in advance by savings bank on certificate of time deposit held legal. Murray v. First Trust, etc., Bank, 201 Iowa 1325, 207 N.W. 781 (1926).

[485] Heironimus v. Sweeney, 83 Md. 146, 34 A. 823, 55 Am. St. R. 333, 33 L.R.A. 99; Edwards v. Sweeney, 83 Md. 146, 34 A. 823, 55 Am. St. R. 833, 33 L.R.A. 99.

[486] Pierce v. Boston Five Cents Sav. Bank, 129 Mass. 425, 37 Am. R. 371. As to rights of assignee after death of assignor of deposit, see § 17 of this chapter.

[487] In re Provident Inst., 30 N.J. Eq. 5; Bank Comm'rs v. Watertown Sav. Bank, 81 Conn. 261, 70 A. 1038; Taylor v. Empire State Sav. Bank, 66 Hun 538, 21 N.Y.S. 643, 50 N.Y. St. R. 269; Medford Trust Co. v. McKnight, 292 Mass. 1, 197 N.E. 649.

special act is not bound by the provisions of a statute enacted prior thereto regulating the amount of interest to be paid on deposits, if such provisions are incompatible with the provisions of the special act.[488] And a savings bank's depositors are not bound by an amendment to a bank bylaw which is retrospective in effect and an impairment of their pre-existing right to interest.[489] Under a statute which makes the depositors of an insolvent savings bank, when their deposits are scaled, the equitable owners in common of the property of the bank, a depositor's withdrawal of the reduced amount is not a gift of his share of the property to the other depositors; however, the latter may claim interest on the winding up.[490] The fact that deposits in mutual savings bank were federally insured did not change trustees' charter obligations to pay out profits on deposits.[491]

Right to Surplus after Payment of Depositors.—Where a savings institution's charter provides that its depositors shall receive as interest their ratable proportions of the profits, after deducting expenses and retaining a reasonable surplus or contingent fund, and that neither the bank nor its managers shall receive any benefit from any deposit or the produce thereof, and it goes into voluntary liquidation and after paying all of its depositors, has a surplus on hand, such surplus belongs only to those depositors who had deposits when the winding-up proceedings were commenced, to the exclusion of all those who withdrew their deposits prior to that time, and is to be distributed among them ratably according to the amount of their respective deposits.[492] A determination of whether the savings bank's depositors owned the bank's surplus depended only on the text of the charter, which defined depositary relationship.[493] The charter of a savings bank, providing that net income and profits of all deposits of money received by a corporation shall be paid out and distributed in just proportions among the several persons by or for whom

---

Where intent under former New York statute was that no savings bank may pay interest to depositor on deposit in excess of $7,500 with certain specified exceptions, even if bank knew that various accounts belonged to plaintiff's testator at time it accepted and retained deposits, plaintiff would not be entitled to recover interest on deposits in excess of $7,500. Hoeffler v. American Sav. Bank, 47 N.Y.S.2d 327 (1944).

[488] Werner v. German Sav. Bank (N.Y.), 2 Daly 406.

[489] State v. San Francisco Sav., etc., Soc., 66 Cal. App. 53, 225 P. 309.

[490] In re Francestown Sav. Bank, 63 N.H. 138. As to power of court to scale down deposits, see § 26 of this chapter.

[491] In re Corporators of Portsmouth Sav. Bank, 525 A.2d 671 (N.H. 1987).

[492] Morristown Inst. v. Roberts, 42 N.J. Eq. 496, 8 A. 315.

[493] In re Corporators of Portsmouth Sav. Bank, 525 A.2d 671 (N.H. 1987).

said deposits shall have been made, was mandatory.[494] "Income and profits," as used in the charter of the savings bank, providing that net income and profits of all deposits of money received by said corporation shall be paid out and distributed in just proportions among the several persons by or for whom said deposit shall have been made, included surplus.[495] "Persons by or for whom the said deposits shall have been made," as used in the charter of the savings bank, providing that the net income and profits of all deposits of money received by said corporation shall be paid out and distributed in just proportions among the several persons by or for whom said deposits shall have been made, meant depositors as a group of record at any given time, absent industry practice allowing withdrawing depositor to claim his or her share of surplus on an individual basis.[496] Absent any contractual specification of when payments were to be made, the payments of surplus to depositors pursuant to the charter of savings bank had to be made in reasonable amounts at reasonable intervals.[497]

Effect of Depositor's Death.—The death of a depositor does not stop the running of interest.[498]

§ 20. Repayment of Deposits.

In General.—Sums deposited with a savings bank and a savings deposit taken by any bank, together with interest credited thereto, must be repaid to depositors, or their legal representatives, after demand in such manner at such time and after such previous notice and under such regulations as the bank shall prescribe, interest being credited at such times and at such rate as may be prescribed by the bank's regulations.[499] But a savings bank does not become liable for repayment of money until after demand for it in accordance with its rules and regulations.[500] Withdrawals from a bank savings account may generally be made only on presentation of a passbook and the depositor's written order.[501] Mere possession of a passbook is not alone sufficient to establish the right to withdraw funds shown deposited in

---

494 In re Corporators of Portsmouth Sav. Bank, 525 A.2d 671 (N.H. 1987).

495 In re Corporators of Portsmouth Sav. Bank, 525 A.2d 671 (N.H. 1987).

496 In re Corporators of Portsmouth Sav. Bank, 525 A.2d 671 (N.H. 1987).

497 In to Corporators of Portsmouth Sav. Bank, 525 A.2d 671 (N.H. 1987).

498 In re Ott, 103 Pa. Super. 55, 158 A. 286.

499 Langford v. First Nat'l Bank, 122 Ga. App. 210, 176 S.E.2d 484 (1970).

500 Langford v. First Nat'l Bank, 122 Ga. App. 210, 176 S.E.2d 484 (1970).

501 **In general.—**

Ruffalo v. Savage, 252 Wis. 175, 31 N.W.2d 175, 1 A.L.R.2d 534.

the book.[502] Whether a contract exists which requires use of a passbook for withdrawal of funds from bank savings account depends on facts of case.[503] Account book is prima facie evidence of financial institution's liability to pay the amount indicated therein.[504] Under section of Uniform Commercial Code governing bank's liability to customer for wrongful dishonor, savings withdrawal order is an "item," wrongful dishonor of which may subject bank to consequential and punitive damages.[505] Under the statute which provides that when a bank pays out funds from a savings or time deposit account based on an unauthorized signature, it is the bank, rather than the depositor, that must bear the burden of any loss resulting therefrom, it is no defense that the bank exercised due care and diligence in ascertaining the identity of the person to whom it has paid the money.[506] But if a depositor shows a reasonable excuse for failure to present his passbook to a savings bank which has no rule governing such withdrawals, the failure to produce the book will not prevent a recovery of the deposit.[507] And money deposited with a savings institution to be repaid at certain times prescribed by the institution may, on demand, in pursuance of its bylaws, be sued for, and it is no defense that the institution, having in accordance with its bylaws,

---

Negligence.—

Bank which paid out depositor's savings account money to unauthorized third party was not liable for exemplary damages where evidence showed at most that bank's employees acted carelessly or negligently in paying funds to third party. Corpus Christi Nat'l Bank v. Lowry, 662 S.W.2d 402 (Tex. App. 13 Dist. 1984).

Improper order.—

"Savings withdrawal request" printed with word "nonnegotiable," and which omitted account number, did not constitute order or power of attorney acceptable to bank's attorneys, and was thus not "authorization" allowing bank to release money to any third party who presented document. Corpus Christi Nat'l Bank v. Lowry, 662 S.W.2d 402 (Tex. App. 13 Dust. 1984).

502 American Union Financial Corp. v. University Nat'l Bank, 44 Ill. App. 3d 566, 3 Ill. Dec. 248, 358 N.E.2d 646 (1976).

503 Haseman v. Union Bank, 562 S.W.2d 45 (Ark. 1978).

504 Liberty Sav. Ass'n v. Sun Bank, 572 F.2d 591 (7th Cir. 1978).

505 Shaw v. Union Bank & Trust Co., 640 P.2d 953 (Okla. 1981).

See 12A Okl. St. § 4-402.

506 American Lodge Ass'n v. East New York Sav. Bank, 474 N.Y.S.2d 332 (N.Y. App. Div. 2 Dep't 1984).

See N.Y. C.L.S. Bank § 676.

507 Meighan v. Emigrant Industrial Sav. Bank, 168 App. Div. 542, 153 N.Y.S. 312, aff'd, 222 N.Y. 578, 118 N.E. 1067.

invested its funds in stocks which have depreciated, is unable to pay the whole amount received.[508] A savings society is not justified in refusing to honor a depositor's withdrawal order on hearsay information that he is mentally incompetent.[509] Similarly, a bank unjustifiably refused to pay a deposit if, although the name of the depositor was an assumed one, his identity is shown by possession of the passbook and an affidavit.[510] And a savings bank which collects checks drawn in its favor for the account of a customer, but credits his account only to the extent of part of the amount, is liable to him for the amount not credited, in absence of evidence explaining the failure to credit.[511] A statutory provision authorizing a suspension of payments for a certain length of time for the purpose of protecting savings banks during panics cannot justify a delay in payment so that a bank may investigate a depositor's signature.[512] And a statute making it unlawful for a savings bank to receive from any person a deposit in excess of a certain amount does not prevent such a person from recovering money deposited by him in excess of that amount.[513] And a statute authorizing savings banks to receive and repay deposits, to lend and invest same, to declare dividends, and to exercise by its board of trustees or duly authorized officers or agents all such powers as are "reasonably incidental to the business of mutual savings bank" does not authorize savings banks to offer and maintain checking accounts.[514]

A savings bank's delivery of a check to a depositor does not constitute payment, since if the drawee bank refused payment, the depositor's only remedy would be against the savings bank.[515] But it is not necessary that a

---

[508] Makin v. Institution for Savings, 19 Me. 128, 36 Am. Dec. 740. See also Makin v. Savings Inst., 23 Me. 350, 41 Am. Dec. 349.

[509] Otto v. Western Sav. Fund Soc., 343 Pa. 615, 23 A.2d 462.

[510] Davenport v. Bank for Sav. (N.Y.), 36 Hun 303.

[511] Commonwealth Bank v. Goodman, 128 Md. 452, 97 A. 1005.

[512] Myerowich v. Emigrant Industrial Sav. Bank, 184 App. Div. 668, 172 N.Y.S. 540.

[513] Taylor v. Empire State Bank, 66 Hun 538, 21 N.Y.S. 643, 50 N.Y. St. R. 269.

[514] Androscoggin County Sav. Bank v. Campbell, 282 A.2d 858 (Me. 1971).

Actions of mutual savings bank in amending its bylaws to permit a classification of deposit accounts subject to withdrawal by check and in permitting its depositors and customers to open such accounts were not authorized by statute. Androscoggin County Sav. Bank v. Campbell, 282 A.2d 858 (Me. 1971).

[515] **In general.—**

Szwento Juozupo Let Draugystes v. Manhattan Sav. Inst., 178 App. Div. 57, 164 N.Y.S. 498.

depositor receive coin or currency in order to constitute a withdrawal.[516] And a written instrument whereby a bank depositor acknowledged the receipt from the bank of a specified sum of money, "which amount charge to my account," was, in effect, a draft, notwithstanding its receipt or withdrawal order form.[517]

Although a bank rule requires a depositor to appear in person to withdraw his account, where a depositor assigns his account, the rule will not justify the bank's refusal to pay the assignee.[518] But a party who converts a bankbook obtains no title to the deposits represented thereby, and the true owner may sue to recover the money deposited.[519] A bank has a duty to exercise due care and diligence in making payments from a savings account and may be held liable for failure to comply with that duty.[520] A bank's release of savings account funds on only one signature, rather than two as required by the agreement, was a breach of the contract between the depositor and the bank and, as such, the depositor would have had a valid cause of action against the bank were he still alive, and thus the executor of

---

Bylaw of bank which provided that issuance by bank of check drawn upon any other bank to order of depositor constituted final payment and discharge of the bank would not discharge bank unless shown that money represented by check was actually paid to depositor or one properly authorized to receive it in his behalf. Volpe v. Emigrant Industrial Sav. Bank, 99 N.Y.S.2d 6.

The receipt of a check issued by bank upon another bank to order of depositor would constitute payment to depositor only when check was paid in due course, notwithstanding bank's bylaw providing that issuance of such check constituted final payment. Volpe v. Emigrant Industrial Sav. Bank, 99 N.Y.S.2d 6.

516 People's Sav. Bank v. Rynn, 57 R.I. 411, 190 A. 440.

Where father who had at all times exercised complete dominion over a savings account in the name of himself and his son, and payable to either or the survivor, received a check for the balance in the account or a new bank book as evidence of a new account in the names of himself and a third person, there was a withdrawal of the money on deposit and not a mere bookkeeping transaction. People's Sav. Bank v. Rynn, 57 R.I. 411, 190 A. 440.

517 Dalmatinsko Dobrotvorno Drustvo Sveti Frano Imotski v. First Union Trust, etc., Bank, 268 Ill. App. 314.

518 Bank of the United States v. Public Bank, 88 Misc. 568, 151 N.Y.S. 26, aff'd, 168 App. Div. 915, 152 N.Y.S. 1098.

519 Newman v. Munk, 86 Misc. 639, 74 N.Y.S 467, rev'd on other grounds, 38 Misc. 733, 78 N.YS. 1128.

520 First Nat'l Bank v. Stephens, 124 Ga. App. 530, 184 S.E.2d 484 (1971).

Evidence authorized finding that defendant bank had negligently paid out plaintiff depositor's money to an unauthorized person. First Nat'l Bank v. Stephens, 124 Ga. App. 530, 184 S.E.2d 484 (1971).

the depositor's estate could bring a cause of action against the bank for the payment of the funds on less than the required number of signatures.[521] And a bank rule does not operate to discharge a bank for its negligence in allowing an unauthorized person to withdraw a depositor's savings.[522] An order by a depositor on the treasurer of a certain bank to allow the depositor's wife to sign the bank's books, and to draw any and all money standing in his name as a depositor, is upon its face no more than an authority to the wife to receive money for the depositor.[523] But where a savings account depositor orally authorized her bank to charge against her account checks drawn by her brother-in-law, and the bank did so, the depositor was estopped from recovering the amount so charged in obedience to her verbal order from the bank.[524] A savings bank may be authorized by statute to arrange for transfer of funds from savings accounts by withdrawal orders in negotiable form without requiring the depositor or his representative to appear at the bank's offices.[525] Where the original savings account

---

[521] Menerey v. Citizens First Nat'l Bank, 122 Ill. Dec. 139, 160 Ill. App. 3d 223, 513 N.E.2d 553 (1987).

[522] First Nat'l Bank v. Stephens, 124 Ga. App. 530, 184 S.E.2d 484 (1971).

[523] Wayne County Sav. Bank v. Airey, 95 Mich. 520, 55 N.W. 355.

[524] Mathey v. Central Nat'l Bank, 179 Ken. 291, 293 P.2d 1012.

[525] Consumers Sav. Bank v. Commissioner of Banks, 282 N.E.2d 416 (Mass. 1972).

A passbook is not required for withdrawal from savings bank savings accounts; a negotiable withdrawal order qualifies as "other instrument" evidencing deposit within statute which defines deposit book as the book or other instrument issued to the depositor's evidence of his deposit. Consumers Sav. Bank v. Commissioner of Banks, 282 N.E.2d 416 (Mass. 1912).

Savings banks in Pennsylvania could offer depositors noninterest bearing accounts from which money might be withdrawn by means of negotiable order of withdrawal payable to named third party; banks could require 14 days' notice before making payment on such negotiable order of withdrawal. Pennsylvania Bankers Ass'n v. Commonwealth, Secretary of Banking, 379 A.2d 1062 (Pa. Commw. Ct. 1977).

State-chartered mutual savings banks in Washington are authorized to allow depositors to withdraw funds from savings accounts by the use of negotiable orders of withdrawal. Use of negotiable orders of withdrawal as a method of withdrawal from mutual savings banks is convenient or useful in connection with a mutual bank's express power to repay depositors and within its implied powers. Washington Bankers Asso. v. Washington Mut. Sav. Bank, 92 Wash. 2d 453, 598 P.2d 719 (1979).

Negotiable order of withdrawal (NOW) accounts are interest-bearing checking accounts held by individuals, nonprofit organizations, or public entities, in which the depository institution reserves the right to require at least seven days' written notice prior to withdrawal or transfer of funds. 12 C.F.R. § 204.2(b)(3)(ii). Title companies are not obligated to open up

was opened by the decedent in his own name and the plaintiff was merely a signatory to the account and, at the point of the deletion of the plaintiff's name at the decedent's direction, the account only had $821.45, the plaintiffs' claim for fraud, even if it were a valid claim, could only be for such funds.[526]

Agreements as to Time and Manner of Payment.—An agreement as to the time of payment of a savings deposit can be made by parol, and in the absence of a contrary agreement, a deposit is payable on demand where the passbook contains no provision as to when it is payable.[527] And to authorize the payment of an ordinary check from a savings account, the depositor and the bank must both agree thereto, since the giving of a check drawn on a checking account does not amount to a direction or agreement that the check shall be paid from a savings account.[528] By voluntarily opening a checking account with a savings bank, the plaintiffs implicitly agreed to the terms of the "Collection Agreement," which imposed time restrictions on checking account withdrawals, and this agreement was further ratified each time the plaintiffs voluntarily deposited checks into their account. Therefore the six/fifteen-day time restrictions imposed by the bank satisfied the requirements of an agreement and effectively preempted the more ambiguous language of the Uniform Commercial Code provision stating, in part, that credit given by a bank on an item in an account with its customer becomes available for withdrawal as of right when ". . . the bank has had a reasonable time to learn that the settlement is final."[529]

NOW accounts. Hirsch v. Bank of America, 107 Cal. App. 4th 708, 132 Cal. Rptr. 2d 220 (2003).

[526] Turner v. Delta Bank & Trust Co., 462 So. 2d 678, writ denied, 468 So. 2d 602 (La. App. 4 Cir. 1984).

[527] Sol Popofsky Co. v. Wearmouth, 216 Iowa 114, 248 N.W. 358.

[528] Keller v. Davis, 123 Pa. Super. 240, 187 A. 267.

[529] **In general.—**

Rapp v. Dime Sav. Bank, 64 App. Div. 2d 964, 408 N.Y.S.2d 540 (1978).

Record demonstrated that the time restrictions imposed by a savings bank "thrift" institution on checking account withdrawals, viz., six business days from the deposit of local checks and 15 business days from the deposit of other checks, were reasonable and substantially related to the actual time period in which the bank might expect to be notified that a check is uncollectible. Rapp v. Dime Sav. Bank, 64 App. Div. 2d 964, 408 N.Y.S.2d 540 (1978).

Exercised ordinary care.—

"Thrift" savings bank, which was not directly associated with either the Federal Reserve Bank or the New York Clearing House Association, exercised ordinary care in imposing

Notice of Intention to Withdraw.—A statute providing that savings banks may require sixty days notice of intention to withdraw savings deposits merely authorizes such banks to adopt regulations providing for such requirement, and does not of itself authorize the demand of such notice before paying deposits.[530] Therefore, a bank may demand such notice where it has adopted a regulation providing therefor which became part of the contract between the bank and its depositor.[531] The provision of a bank's passbook with respect to notice of intention to withdraw is for the benefit of the bank, and is waived by the bank's paying money on the depositor's order without exacting compliance with such provision.[532]

Setoff—Overdrafts on a depositor's commercial account with a bank may generally be set off by the bank against a credit balance in the same depositor's savings account.[533] But the entry of a savings deposit to the credit of two persons or the survivor was held not to give a bank a lien or right to setoff against a debt due from one of the depositors, in the absence of evidence showing the debtor's separate interest in the deposit.[534]

The right of set-off is given by law, apart from agreement. Nothing in a statute declaring a negotiable instrument payable at a bank equivalent to an order to the bank to pay it for the principal debtor's account, or in the general law of set-off, gives a bank such a right against a borrower from it, who makes a savings deposit with the bank in which the bank knows a third

---

time restrictions on when the proceeds of a deposit consisting of checks are available to the depositor for withdrawal, namely six business days from the deposit of local checks and 15 business days from the deposit of other checks. Rapp v. Dime Sav. Bank, 64 App. Div. 2d 964, 408 N.Y.S.2d 540 (1978).

Engaged in neither false advertisement nor fraudulent concealment.—

"Thrift" savings bank, which imposed certain time restrictions on when the proceeds of a deposit consisting of checks are available to the depositor for withdrawal, engaged in neither false advertising nor fraudulent concealment by advertising "free checking accounts" without also advertising its aforesaid policy restricting withdrawals for a period of time on check deposits, as the record clearly showed that no charge is imposed for maintaining a checking account at the bank, nor was any minimum balance required to keep the checking account active, and that was all the advertising could fairly be claimed as representing. Rapp v. Dime Sav. Bank, 64 App. Div. 2d 964, 408 N.Y.S.2d 540 (1978).

[530] Brooke v. White, 219 Iowa 624, 258 N.W. 766.

[531] Andrew v. Iowa Sav. Bank, 214 Iowa 105, 241 N.W. 412, cited in Brooke v. White, 219 Iowa 624, 258 N.W. 766.

[532] Pruett v. First Nat. Bank (Tex. Civ. App.), 175 S.W.2d 658.

[533] Cowen v. Valley Nat. Bank, 67 Ariz. 210, 193 P.2d 918.

[534] Peoples Bank of Denton v. Turner, 169 Md. 430, 182 A. 314, 103 A.L.R. 490.

person has an equitable interest for which he has given value. Thus, savings bank was not authorized to pay a note the maker's account by means of a setoff made in violation of the doctrine that a bank may set off a deposit against a depositor's secured debt to a bank only in the amount of the debt beyond the value of the security.[535] For other cases dealing with a bank's right of setoff, see the footnote.[536]

---

[535] Forastiere v. Springfield Inst. for Savings, 303 Mass. 101, 20 N.E.2d 950 (1939).

In action to recover amount of savings bank deposit assigned to plaintiff, to whom bank refused payment thereof before depositor defaulted in payment of interest on his secured debt to bank, demand for payment thereof was made, or anything was done toward setting off deposit against note for such debt, the bank had no right to set off balance due on note against deposit, in absence of evidence that security was inadequate. Forastiere v. Springfield Inst. for Savings, 303 Mass. 101, 20 N.E.2d 950 (1939).

[536] Nothing in statute governing right of action of assignee of chose in action, or in general law of setoff, gives bank such right against borrower from it, who makes savings deposit with bank in which bank knows that third party has equitable interest for which he has given value, and there is no violation of public policy behind such statute in enforcing that equitable interest and denying any right of setoff. Grant v. Colonial Bank & Trust Co., 356 Mass. 392, 252 N.E.2d 339 (1969).

Act of mother of promissor-husband in giving passbook of investment thrift account to promissor-wife with instruction to insert name of wife as payee of account constituted a "gift inter vivos" under law of Arkansas, absent evidence of a lack of donative intent on part of donor, thus, where wife kept passbook in her personal possession, with proper notice of change of ownership given to promisee, assignee of note could not prevent funds in account from being set off against mortgage indebtedness underlying note on ground that husband, as donor's only heir, owned account and that husband, as officer and director of promisee, was bound by court order that directors could receive no payments on thrift accounts owned by them until all other creditors were paid in full. Bryan v. Humphrey, 443 F.2d 243 (8th Cir. 1971).

Where depositor opened savings account in names of himself and another individual by deposit of funds he had just borrowed from bank, bank had statutory right to set off funds in accounts against debt owed it by borrower; bank had such right even if borrower and other had been depositors with equal ownership and rights to fund deposited. Burgess v. First Nat'l Bank, 497 P.2d 1035 (Colo. App. 1972).

Unless a depositor and the bank agree to the contrary, the fact that the bank secures collateral for its loan in no way affects its right to set off the debt owed it by the depositor against the depositor's savings account. Nietzel v. Farmers & Merchants State Bank, 238 N.W.2d 437 (Minn. 1976), citing Michie on Banks and Banking.

Where a depositor had executed an assignment of his savings account to the bank which stated that the assignment would operate as security for the payment of any debts or liabilities of the depositor to the bank "now in existence or hereafter contracted," bank had both equitable and contractual rights to set off a debt owed it by the depositor which had been in existence at time of the assignment against the depositor's passbook savings account, and that the right was not affected by the fact that the bank had secured collateral for its loan. Nietzel

Pledge of Deposit as Security for Loan.—Ordinarily, when a person borrows money from a savings institution in which that person is a party to account, and pledges deposits in that account as security for the loan, the pledge is effective as payment of that account and the financial institution is discharged from all claims for amounts so paid so long as the loan remains unpaid.[537]

Statutes, Bylaws and Rules Requiring Production of Passbook.—The bylaws or rules of savings banks generally contain a provision which, in substance, declares that deposits will not be paid except on production of a passbook. Such a requirement is for the benefit of the bank,[538] as well as for the protection of depositors,[539] and is reasonable.[540] When printed in a passbook, such a requirement is part of the contract between a bank and its depositor,[541] and the latter cannot recover his deposit without producing either the book or evidence of its loss.[542] But such a bylaw is not an arbitrary condition which must be complied with at all costs,[543] and where circumstances render the production of a bank passbook impossible, or a reasonable excuse for failure to present it is shown, a depositor is entitled to receive his

---

v. Farmers & Merchants State Bank, 238 N.W.2d 437 (Minn. 1976), citing Michie on Banks and Banking.

[537] Smith v. Idaho State Univ. Fed. Credit Union, 646 P.2d 1016 (Idaho 1982).

[538] Mills v. Albany Exch. Sav. Bank, 28 Misc. 251, 59 N.Y.S. 149; Mutual Assur. Co. v. Norwich Sav. Soc., 128 Conn. 510, 24 A.2d 477, 139 A.L.R. 829; Davis v. Chittenden County Trust Co., 115 Vt. 349, 61 A.2d 553.

[539] Mutual Assur. Co. v. Norwich Sav. Soc., 128 Conn. 510, 24 A.2d 477, 139 A.L.R. 829.

[540] Rosenthal v. Dollar Sav. Bank, 61 Misc. 244, 113 N.Y.S. 787; Warhus v. Bowery Sav. Bank, 12 N.Y. Super. 67, aff'd, 21 N.Y. 543; Davis v. Chittenden County Trust Co., 115 Vt. 349, 61 A.2d 553.

[541] Wall v. Provident Inst., 85 Mass. (3 Allen) 96; Warhus v. Bowery Sav. Bank, 12 N.Y. Super. 67, aff'd, 21 N.Y. 543; Heath v. Portsmouth Sav. Bank, 46 N.H. 78, 88 Am. Dec. 194; Davis v. Chittenden County Trust Co., 115 Vt. 349, 61 A.2d 553. See also § 13 of this chapter.

Provisions of bylaw, printed in deposit book, that no payment should be made to depositor except on presentation of deposit book, and that payment to person producing such book should be valid payment to discharge bank, became part of contract between depositor and bank, which could not properly pay out any part of deposit except in accordance with such provisions, in absence of further agreement or waiver. Mutual Assurance Co. v. Norwich Sav. Soc., 128 Conn. 510, 24 A.2d 477, 139 A.L.R. 829.

[542] Werhus v. Bowery Sav. Bank, 12 N.Y. Super. 67, aff'd, 21 N.Y. 543; Mercantile Sav. Bank v. Appler, 151 Md. 571, 135 A. 373; Held v. Fitzwald, 144 Misc. 35, 257 N.Y.S. 69.

[543] Dunn v. Seamen's Bank for Savings, 118 Misc. 434, 194 N.Y.S. 416.

money.[544] For example, such a bylaw will not be applied to a depositor who is unable to produce his book by reason of its loss, destruction or wrongful retention by another.[545] And the test of whether a passbook has been lost is not the arbitrary decision of the bank's trustees or treasurer, but the mind of a reasonable man.[546] Compliance with such bylaw or rule may also be waived by the joint agreement or action of a bank and its depositor.[547] The framing and hanging of such bylaws or rules in several conspicuous places in a banking room, as required by the bank's charter is constructive notice to all depositors of their contents.[548]

The provisions of a statute and rules of a bank made pursuant thereto, that deposits shall not be paid to any person unless the depositor's passbook is produced, are binding on an assignee of a deposit made in the name of the assignor and his wife and payable to either of them, and the assignee's failure to produce the passbook, though caused by the wife's refusal to surrender it, justifies the bank in refusing payment to him.[549] And where

---

[544] Dunn v. Seamen's Bank for Sav., 118 Misc. 434, 194 N.Y.S. 416; Grill v. Manhattan Sav. Inst., 148 Misc. 181, 265 N.Y.S. 610.

Reasonableness of savings bank depositor's excuse for not producing book held to be determined in light of the purpose of the rule requiring the book's production. Meighan v. Emigrant Industrial Savings Bank, 168 App. Div. 542, 153 N.Y.S. 312, aff'd, 222 N.Y. 578, 118 N.E. 1067.

Savings bank depositor held to have sufficient excuse for failure to produce book shown to be in the possession of his wife, whose whereabouts he had been unable to ascertain. Meighan v. Emigrant Industrial Savings Bank, 168 App. Div. 542, 153 N.Y.S. 312, aff'd, 222 N.Y. 578, 118 N.E. 1067.

[545] Palmer v. Providence Inst., 14 R.I. 68, 51 Am. H. 341; Hudson v. Roxbury Inst. for Sav., 176 Mass. 522, 57 N.E. 1021 (1900); Kenney v. Harlem Sav. Bank, 61 Misc. 144, 114 N.Y.S. 749 (1908), rev'd on other grounds, 65 Misc. 466, 120 N.Y.S. 82 (1909); Webber v. Cambridgeport Sav. Bank, 186 Mass. 314, 71 N.E. 567; Wagner v. Howard Sav. Inst., 52 N.J.L. 225, 19 A. 212.

[546] Webber v. Cambridgeport Sav. Bank, 186 Mass. 314, 71 N.E. 567.

[547] Davis v. Chittenden County Trust Co., 115 Vt. 349, 61 A.2d 553.

Compliance with such bylaw may be waived by joint action or agreement of bank and depositor. Mutual Assurance Co. v. Norwich Sav. Soc., 128 Conn. 510, 24 A.2d 477, 139 A.L.R. 829.

A depositor and a banking institution may expressly or impliedly waive a provision requiring production of passbook by depositor before withdrawal by depositor. La Valley v. Pere Marquette Employees' Credit Union, 342 Mich. 639, 70 N.W.2d 798.

[548] Warhus v. Bowery Sav. Bank, 12 N.Y. Super. 67, aff'd, 21 N.Y. 543.

[549] Rosenthal v. Dollar Sav. Bank, 61 Misc. 244, 113 N.Y.S. 787.

bank rules require the production of a passbook, payment without it to either of two joint depositors is not authorized by statute.[550]

Adverse Claim Statutes.—A statute regulating the procedure in case of an adverse claim to a bank deposit is remedial, and therefore will be liberally construed and applied to contracts existing prior to its passage.[551] The term "adverse claimant" as used in such a statute means one who is not shown on the books of the bank as a depositor.[552] Under the New York statute, a bank is justified in not making payment where a claim is made upon it which is apparently meritorious, and under such conditions the bank may call upon parties making adverse claims to litigate the issue of ownership or title to a bank account, and in that manner may place itself in the position of a stakeholder.[553]

---

[550] **In general.—**

Mercantile Sav. Bank v. Appler, 151 Md. 571, 135 A. 373.

The provisions of statute that deposit in joint account maybe paid by bank to either of the joint depositors and that receipt by person so paid is valid release as against other joint depositor do not prevent bank from enlarging its liabilities in such respect by contract, and where bank adopted contract with joint depositors that withdrawals could not be made without presentation of passbook, but it paid balance to one of them without presentation of passbook, it was liable to other for that amount. Badders v. Peoples Trust Co., 236 Ind. 357, 140 N.E.2d 235, 82 A.L.R.2d 1103.

Bank could not waive provisions of contract with joint depositors requiring passbook to be presented when withdrawals were made and thereby escape liability to one joint depositor when it allowed withdrawal by other without passbook. Badders v. Peoples Trust Co., 236 Ind. 357, 140 N.E.2d 235, 82 A.L.R.2d 1103.

Notice of change of bank rule.—

Bank could give adequate notice of change of its rule requiring use of passbook for a withdrawal from joint savings account by merely giving notice referred to in passbook's provision stating that any change in rules would be binding on depositors after having been conspicuously posted in lobby of bank for five consecutive business days; fact that a depositor was not given actual notice of the change did not cause the notice to fail to satisfy any requirement of due process. Haseman v. Union Bank, 597 S.W.2d 67 (Ark. 1980).

[551] Perdue v. State Nat. Bank, 254 Ala. 80, 47 So. 2d 261.

[552] Perdue v. State Nat. Bank, 254 Ala. 80, 47 So. 2d 261.

Where contract printed on passbook issued by bank on joint savings account of husband and wife provided that signature of either one would be sufficient for withdrawal of all or part of funds deposited, husband's guardian was not an "adverse claimant" to deposit under statute regulating procedure in case of adverse claim to bank deposit, and bank had no right to exact a bond from him. Perdue v. State Nat. Bank, 254 Ala. 80, 47 So. 2d 261.

[553] Abate v. Bushwick Sav. Bank, 207 Misc. 372, 138 N.Y.S.2d 140.

When Bank May Require Indemnity as a Condition of Payment.—Though the duty devolves upon a bank's officers to exercise care to protect depositors from fraud, and they are not absolved from liability for disregarding constructive notice thereof, when paying a person in possession of a passbook, they cannot by their own authority require a bond of indemnity nor absolute security as a condition of payment.[554] Thus, where a depositor is personally known to the officers of a bank, his refusal to give a bond of indemnity is not an excuse for the bank's refusal to pay his deposit, even though the passbook is lost, if there is no bank bylaw requiring such a bond as a condition of payment.[555]

But where a depositor's bankbook contains a bylaw provision that no withdrawal will be allowed without the book, a depositor who has lost his book cannot recover his deposit from the bank upon evidence of such loss, without offering indemnity.[556] Such a bylaw is reasonable, where it is within

---

[554] **In general.—**

Cosgriff v. Hudson City Sav. Inst., 24 Misc. 4, 52 N.Y.S. 189 (1898); Wallace v. Lowell Inst., 73 Mass. (7 Gray) 134; First Nat'l Bank v. Karas, 14 Ohio App. 147, 32 Ohio C.C. (n.s.) 33. See also 15 of this chapter.

Administration.—

Where the identity of the depositor with the intestate is admitted by the bank, and the deposit book is shown to have been lost or destroyed, the administrator cannot be required to furnish a bond of indemnity as a condition of payment. Hudson v. Roxbury Inst., 176 Mass. 522, 57 N.E. 1021 (1900); Mierke v. Jefferson County Sav. Bank, 134 N.Y.S. 44, aff'd, 151 App. Div. 899, 135 N.Y.S. 1127.

[555] Mierke v. Jefferson County Sav. Bank, 208 N.Y. 347, 101 N.E. 889, 46 L.R.A. (n.s.) 194, 1914D Ann. Cas. 21; Dunn v. Seamen's Bank for Savings, 118 Misc. 434, 194 N.Y.S. 416; Bayer v. Commonwealth Trust Co., 144 Mo. App. 676, 129 SW. 268.

It has been held that where there was no question about the identity of a depositor, and the officers of the bank were satisfied that he was the right party, and that his passbook had been lost or stolen, the bank was not entitled to require him to give bond to protect the bank against payment to the wrong person. Bayer v. Commonwealth Trust Co., 144 Mo. App. 676, 129 S.W. 268.

A bank may not refuse to pay savings account to one unable to present passbook because of loss thereof, on ground that it is entitled to an indemnity bond, where bylaws contain nothing entitling it to insist upon such condition. Krupp v. Franklin Sav. Bank, 255 App. Div. 15, 5 N.Y.S.2d 365.

[556] Wall v. Provident Inst., 85 Mass. (3 Allen) 96; Wall v. Provident Inst., 88 Mass. (6 Allen) 320; Mitchell v. Home Sav. Bank (N.Y.), 38 Hun. 255; Heath v. Portsmouth Sav. Bank, 46 N.H. 78, 88 Am. Dec. 194.

Generally, a savings account can only be withdrawn upon presentation of the deposit book, and if the book gets into unauthorized hands, the rights and liabilities of the bank and

the power of a depositor to indemnify the bank.[557] And when adopted by a bank,[558] it is binding on the administrator of a depositor, as well as on a depositor,[559] and is also binding on the committee of an incompetent person.[560] And where the receiver of a depositor did not have possession of passbooks, in view of bank rule requiring production of passbooks, it was held an order directing banks to turn over the deposits to the receiver would be made only if the receiver was prepared to give indemnity bonds.[561] Similarly, even though a bank's bylaw requiring a depositor's judgment creditor to post a bond for double the proposed withdrawal from the debtor's account may be unreasonable in certain cases, the reasonableness rule should be applied in aid of enforcement of a court's mandate where this can be done without danger of double liability.[562] But indemnification cannot be required

---

depositor are subject to the contract between the parties pertaining to the deposit, and before paying out without presentment of the book, the bank may require an indemnifying bond. Miller v. First Granite City Nat. Bank, 349 Ill. App. 347, 110 N.E.2d 651.

[557] Myers v. Albany Sav. Bank, 270 App. Div. 466, 60 N.Y.S.2d 477, aff'd, 296 N.Y. 562, 68 N.E.2d 866; Mitchell v. Home Sav. Bank (N.Y.), 38 Hun. 255.

[558] Krupp v. Franklin Sav. Bank, 255 App. Div. 15, 5 N.Y.S.2d 365.

Savings bank held entitled to adopt bylaw providing that no new passbook would be issued upon loss of old book, where balance exceeded $10, except after expiration of 30 days from insertions of daily advertisement in newspapers and filing of bond for 100 percent in excess of amount of deposit. Krupp v. Franklin Bay. Bank, 255 App. Div. 15, 5 N.Y.S.2d 365.

[559] Wall v. Provident Inst., 85 Mass. (8 Allen) 96.

[560] Krupp v. Franklin Sav. Bank, 255 App. Div. 15, 5 N.Y.S.2d 365.

Where signature card signed by war veteran at time of opening savings account stated that he agreed to bylaws of bank and any subsequent additions thereto, and bylaw subsequently enacted pursuant to statute made issuance of new passbook after loss of original passbook conditional upon furnishing of indemnify bond, committee of incompetent veteran could not recover amount of deposit without furnishing indemnity bond. Krupp v. Franklin Sav. Bank, 255 App. Div. 15, 5 N.Y.S.2d 365.

[561] Walde v. Walde, 45 N.Y.S.2d 791.

[562] Moran v. Toth, 195 Misc. 570, 92 N.Y.S.2d 162.

A savings bank was not entitled to a provision in the decree that payment by bank of a deposit of an estate in compliance with a prior determination of the court be conditioned upon either presentation of a passbook or the furnishing by the executor of an indemnity bond on the ground that the direction of the court might subject bank to payment a second time to an assignee of the depositor, since the assignee would stand in no better position than his assignor. In re Givis' Estate, 109 N.Y.S.2d 456.

where a bank cannot possibly be injured by reason of payment.[563] And it has been held that a statute which declares that no payment or check against any savings account shall be made unless accompanied by and entered in the passbook, except for good cause shown and on assurances satisfactory to the officers of the bank, does not authorize a refusal to pay unless the book is presented or indemnity given, where the passbook is not negotiable, the

---

[563] **In general.—**

Ornbaun v. First Nat. Bank, 215 Cal. 72, 8 P.2d 470, 81 A.L.R. 1146.

Where it appeared that the loss of a passbook was so long ago that there was no reasonable possibility of liability by the bank to any third person, the bank's insistence upon depositor furnishing a bond of indemnity in accordance with the bank's bylaws before receiving the deposit was unwarranted. Myers v. Albany Sav. Bank, 57 N.Y.S.2d 448.

Where a depositor has been dead so long that there is no reasonable possibility of the liability of the bank to any third person for the deposit, the bank's insistence on the furnishing of a bond of indemnity, in accordance with a bylaw providing that the bank may require such a bond whenever a passbook is lost, is unwarranted. Payment of deposit by bank under decree of court to public administrator representing deceased depositor would be adequate protection to bank against any subsequent claim to the deposit. In re Newsome's Estate, 179 Misc. 862, 38 N.Y.S.2d 702.

Where deposit, made a year before depositor's death, had remained unclaimed in bank 11 years after such death and passbook had been lost, public administrator, as decedent's legal representative, could recover amount of deposit without furnishing indemnity bond, notwithstanding bylaw of bank, providing that whenever passbook was lost bank's board of trustees might require bond of indemnity therefor before paying the deposit evidenced by the passbook. In re Newsome's Estate, 179 Misc. 862, 38 N.Y.S.2d 702.

A bylaw of a bank, providing that "in case of lost books, the bank will decide as to the persons to whom payment shall be made," does not authorize a refusal to pay unless the book is presented or adequate indemnity given, where notice of the loss of the book was given more than seven years before the commencement of action, and no claim had been made for the deposit, except by the depositor and her executor. Mills v. Albany Exch. Sav. Bank, 28 Misc. 251, 59 N.Y.S. 149.

Administrator's receipt in lieu of indemnity.—

Where deceased's savings bank passbook could not be found, but bank had received no notification of assignment, administrator is entitled to withdraw deposit without giving indemnification, notwithstanding depositor's agreement therefor. A receipt given by the administrator will completely release the bank from liability. Ornbaun v. First Nat. Bank, 215 Cal. 72, 8 P.2d 470, 81 A.L.R. 1148.

Depositor unable to furnish bond.—

But where depositor's passbook had been lost more than eight years and depositor was unable to furnish a bond to indemnify bank against any possible loss, enforcement of bank's bylaw requiring indemnification bond in case of lost passbook, to enable depositor to obtain a new passbook and to make withdrawals, was unreasonable and arbitrary. Myers v. Albany Sav. Bank, 57 N.Y.S.2d 448.

demand is made by the duly qualified administrator of the depositor's estate, and no other demand has been made though several months have intervened between the death and the demand.[564]

A provision of banking laws authorizing savings banks to require the presentation of bankbooks or indemnity bonds before paying an account is to be reasonably applied.[565] Such a provision applies to judgment creditors, and where there is small chance of the account having been assigned, or great difficulty in procuring the book or bond, a court is warranted in directing payment to a judgment creditor of the owner of the account without compliance with the statutory conditions.[566]

Payment Pursuant to Order of Attachment or Court Order.—A bank's payment to a sheriff of a savings account levied upon pursuant to an order of attachment would protect the bank even though a passbook is not presented as required by the bank's rules and regulations.[567] And a bank will be required to pay an account to the sheriff notwithstanding its rules requiring presentation of passbooks and giving the bank the option of requiring posting of a surety bond before paying without a passbook.[568]

A savings bank in which the proceeds of settlement of an infant's personal injury action were deposited will not be compelled to make payments to his physicians, pursuant to a court order procured by his guardian ad litem, without the presentation of the passbook and withdrawal slip by such guardian in compliance with the bank's bylaws, but the guardian ad litem will be directed to present such book and slip to the bank on the physician's application for enforcement of the order.[569] But, an order of court directing a bank to pay the amount of an account to a depositor who had lost her passbook nearly eight years before would protect the bank from any subsequent claim on the account.[570]

---

[564] Vincent v. Port Huron Sav. Bank, 147 Mich. 437, 111 N.W. 90.

Under such statute the question of "good cause" and "satisfactory assurance" is for judicial triers, not the officers of the bank. Vincent v. Port Huron Sav. Bank, 147 Mich. 437, 111 N.W. 90.

[565] Reese v. Chappelle, 206 Misc. 887, 135 N.Y.S.2d 200.

[566] Reese v. Chappelle, 206 Misc. 887, 135 N.Y.S.2d 200.

[567] Dumpson v. Empire City Sav. Bank, 44 Misc. 2d 8, 252 N.Y.S.2d 811 (Sup. Ct. 1964).

[568] Dumpson v. Empire City Sav. Bank, 44 Misc. 2d 8, 252 N.Y.S.2d 811 (Sup. Ct. 1964).

[569] Kohl v. A.W.A. Realty Corp., 49 N.Y.S.2d 804.

[570] Myers v. Albany Sav. Bank, 57 N.Y.S.2d 448.

Payment to Beneficiaries of Deposit without Depositor's Consent.[571]

Notification to Bank of Adverse Claim of Joint Holder of Certificate.—Where a husband and wife deposited $10,000 jointly on a savings certificate but, before the husband presented the certificate which was in his possession for payment of $10,000 plus interest, the wife wrote a letter to the bank requesting that no withdrawals be permitted without both signatures, the bank was within its legal rights in refusing to honor the husband's demand for payment as there existed the possibility of double liability and was properly discharged from all further liability after filing an interpleader action and paying the principal and interest into court.[572]

Estoppel of Bank.—Where a savings bank takes a depositor's money as a special deposit, and converts it to its use, and enjoys gratuitous benefits therefrom, it is estopped from denying its liability to repay the money, whether the receiving of the money as such deposit was ultra vires or not.[573] But a bank is not estopped to claim that it was not authorized by its charter to receive for safekeeping bonds delivered to a clerk of its treasurer, when neither the bonds nor their avails have come in to its possession.[574]

Waiver by Bank.—A requirement of notice for the withdrawal of savings funds[575] or the presentation of a passbook upon such withdrawal may be waived by the conduct of a bank's officers.[576] Similarly, a bank bylaw

---

[571] **Payment of employee funds without union consent required.—**

Agreement executed by labor organization and bank for deposit of certain percentages of wages earned by employees in savings accounts for respective benefits of the employees upon remittance by employers which purported to require union's consent to employees' withdrawal of funds did not limit employees' right to money credited to account and bank would be compelled to permit withdrawal even without union's consent. Newark Roofing Contractors Ass'n v. Composition Roofers Damp & Waterproof Workers, Local 4, 270 F. Supp. 326 (D.N.J. 1967).

[572] DeLuca v. Fidelity Bank, 422 A.2d 1159 (Pa. Super. Ct. 1980).

[573] Abbott v. Wolfeborough Sav. Bank, 68 N.H. 290, 38 A. 1050; Cogswell v. Rockingham Ten Cents Savings-Bank, 59 N.H. 43.

[574] Greeley v. Nashua Sav. Bank, 63 N.H. 145.

[575] McNair v. Davis, 68 F.2d 935, cert. denied, 292 U.S. 647, 54 S. Ct. 780, 78 L. Ed. 1497; Pruett v. First Nat. Bank, 175 S.W.2d 658 (Tex. Civ. App.).

A bank assenting to a depositor's request to use savings deposits in buying bonds waived its rule requiring notice of intention to withdraw savings deposits. McNair v. Davis, 68 F.2d 935, cert. denied, 292 U.S. 647, 54 S. Ct. 780, 78 L. Ed. 1497.

[576] **In general.—**

Watson v. Stockton Morris Plan Co., 34 Cal. App. 2d 393, 93 P.2d 855.

requiring immediate notice in writing in case of loss of a passbook, is waived where no written notice is requested and a refusal to pay the deposit is based on the ground that the depositor must give an indemnity bond.[577] And provisions of a passbook with respect to payment to a depositor in person, or to a person holding a written order duly witnessed, are for a bank's benefit and are waived by a bank paying money on a depositor's order without exacting compliance therewith.[578] In a suit against a savings bank for its refusal to pay a deposit, the bank cannot set up as a defense that the plaintiff had not complied with the bylaws of the bank by showing a written authority from the depositor to collect the deposit, as the bank, by not making this objection at the time of plaintiff's demand, waives it.[579]

Recovery by Bank of Payment of Deposit.—See the footnote.[580]

In an action in which issue was raised whether a bank savings passbook account designated as a joint account with the right of survivorship could be withdrawn by one of the depositors, evidence did not warrant a finding that the bank and executor of the estate of a deceased depositor, who had withdrawn the account, were estopped by their contract to deny that the funds could not be withdrawn unless a passbook was presented. Coristo v. Twin City Bank, 520 S.W.2d 218 (Ark. 1975).

A savings bank, which does not base its refusal to pay a deposit on the failure to present passbook, waives its right to insist on the presentation of the book. Wood v. Connecticut Sav. Bank, 87 Conn. 341, 87 A. 983; Mallet v. Tunnicliffe, 102 Fla. 809, 136 So. 346, 80 A.L.R. 785.

Interpretation of contract provisions.—

Even if the passbook for a joint savings account constituted a contract between depositors, such a contract did not prevent a depositor, who had agreed to be bound by terms of the passbook rules and regulations, from withdrawing the account without presenting the passbook, in that, though it was stated on the first page of the passbook that the passbook had to be presented when money was deposited or withdrawn, location of such requirement and its separation from the "Terms and Conditions", which were in back of the passbook and which did not mention such requirement, indicated that the requirement of presentation was for the bank's benefit only and subject to waiver by the bank. Coristo v. Twin City Bank, 520 S.W.2d 218 (Ark. 1975).

[577] Mierke v. Jefferson County Sav. Bank, 208 N.Y. 347, 101 N.E. 889, 46 L.R.A. (n.s.) 194, 1914D Ann. Cas. 21; Wood v. Connecticut Sav. Bank, 87 Conn. 341, 87 A. 983.

[578] Pruett v. First Nat'l Bank (Tex. Civ. App.), 175 S.W.2d 658.

[579] Atlanta Trust & Bkg. Co. v. Close, 115 Ga. 939, 42 S.E. 265.

[580] **Overpayment.—**

Bank which credited $4,184.96 to customer's savings account through bookkeeping error was entitled to recover money in suit for money had and received where customer went to bank, withdrew entire amount and closed account. Phillips v. Citizens & S. Nat'l Bank, 117 Ga. App. 108, 159 S.E.2d 742 (1968).

§ 21. Losses.

Where a savings bank is incorporated for the purpose of receiving deposits to be used to best advantage, the income to be divided among the depositors, and the bank officers receiving no compensation, there is no absolute promise to repay any depositor the full amount of his deposit, and in case of loss from an investment carefully and lawfully made, it must be borne pro rata by the depositors.[581] But where a bank bylaw provides that a specified rate of interest shall be paid on deposits and depositors are permitted to withdraw deposits without reference to the condition of the investment at the time, the bank is obligated for the payment of interest and is compelled to repay deposits irrespective of losses and bona fide investments.[582] A court cannot order the sums to which the deposits of a savings bank are reduced under statute to be paid by installments.[583] And where, by vote of the officers of a savings bank, five percent was deducted from the accounts of all depositors on account of a loss by the bank, and three days later a

---

Payment of pledged funds.—

If amount paid out of depositors' savings account subsequent to an assignment thereof as collateral for a loan was paid out by virtue of failure of officers making the loan to notify savings tellers of the assignment, such failure and subsequent payment by the bank might have been a mistake warranting recovery by bank from depositors of amount paid out. Mungo v. Bank of Broadway, 104 Ill. App. 2d 97, 243 N.E.2d 853 (1988).

Knowledge of prior withdrawal.—

A bank, which permitted a wife to withdraw all but $10 from two joint savings accounts though she did not have the passbooks with her and which, due to fact that the information as to the balance in an account was temporarily unavailable, subsequently permitted the husband to withdraw $3,020.52 from the account, could recover the amount of the overdrawal from the husband, in light of fact that the wife had apprised the husband of her withdrawal before he withdrew funds and that the requirement that the wife present passbooks at the time of withdrawal could be and was waived. Miranda v. Fidelity Nat'l Bank, 334 So. 2d 74 (Fla. App. 1978).

581 Lewis v. Lynn Inst. for Sav., 148 Mass. 235, 19 NE. 365, 12 Am. St. R. 535, 1 L.R.A. 785; State v. People's Nat'l Bank, 75 N.H. 27, 70 A. 542, 21 Ann. Cas. 1204. As to losses where there are insolvency proceedings, see § 26 of this chapter.

Where, under the bylaws of a bank, the depositors stand on an equality, though only profits are spoken of in them and in statements on the books given to depositors, by intendment of law, losses are to be shared equally. Johnson v. Ward, 2 Ill. App. 261.

Where a savings bank is only an incorporated agency for receiving and investing the money of the depositor, if a loss of deposits is incurred, one depositor cannot recover from the bank his share of the loss. Bunnell v. Collinsville Sav. Soc., 38 Conn. 203, 9 Am. R. 380.

582 Johnson v. Ward, 2 Ill. App. 261.

583 In re Newport Sav. Bank, 68 Me. 396.

depositor withdrew her deposit from which the discount was made, and the account was balanced on the books of the bank, in a suit by the depositor's administrator fifty years later to recover the amount of the discount, it will be assumed that the apportionment was just, notice was given to the depositors, and it was known the depositor or her attorney to whom the money was paid.[584]

VI. INVESTMENTS, LOANS AND DISCOUNTS.

§ 22. In General.

One of the basic functions of banking is dealing in notes, bills of exchange and credits.[585] Ordinarily, incidental banking powers essential to the execution of those expressly conferred by statute will be implied, and hence, in the absence of limitation, the authority to "discount, purchase, sell, and make loans upon commercial paper, notes," and the like, carries with it the power to employ the means and assume the obligations customary in such transactions, and savings banks dealing with such paper may incur such liability in transferring it as is customary under the law merchant.[586] A mutual savings bank does not invest funds for the bank's own profit, but for the depositor's benefit.[587]

Where a check was made out to two indorsers, an individual indorser had no statutory duty to contact the maker or make inquiry of the maker about why he placed individual indorsee's name on the check.[588]

§ 23. Investments.

Under the power conferred by statute on savings and loan corporations to "invest" the funds of their members, stockholders and depositors, they may

---

[584] Lewis v. Lynn Inst. for Sav., 148 Mass. 235, 19 N.E. 365, 12 Am. St. R. 535, 1 L.R.A. 785.

[585] Carroll v. Corning State Sav. Bank, 139 Iowa 338, 115 N.W. 937 (1908).

[586] Carroll v. Corning State Sav. Bank, 139 Iowa 338, 115 N.W. 937 (1908).

California-based federal savings bank could charge annual fees, overlimit fees, late fees, and returned check fees to its Pennsylvania credit card holders, even if such charges where prohibited by Pennsylvania law; bank could charge out-of-state customers in accordance with California law under Home Owners' Loan Act (HOLA). Ament v. PNC Nat'l Bank, 849 F. Supp. 1015 (W.D. Pa. 1994).

[587] In re Corporators of Portsmouth Sav. Bank, 525 A.2d 671 (N.H. 1987).

[588] Knopf v. Dallas-Fort Worth Roofing Supply Co., 786 S.W.2d 37 (Kan. App. 1990).

use their funds to buy interest-bearing notes and mortgages.[589] And under authority to purchase notes, a savings bank can make a contract for the purchase of notes, notwithstanding a statutory provision prohibiting such banks from contracting any debt except for deposits and necessary expenses of management.[590] Similarly, a statute prohibiting savings banks from loaning money on notes, drafts or other personal security, does not necessarily render void the purchase of notes by such a bank.[591] But a subscription by the trustees of a savings institution to the capital stock of another corporation, at a time when they have no funds to pay therefor, is ultra vires.[592] The receiver of a bank having a savings department which carried as an investment a note of a depositor therein could upon the note's maturity realize upon a bankbook deposited as collateral and apply so much as was necessary to discharge the debt.[593] For cases relating to particular statutory provisions on the investments of savings banks, see the footnote.[594]

---

[589] *California.*—The exception by the statute of mortgages on real estate from personal property which it prohibited savings and loan corporations from purchasing implies that they are authorized to purchase such mortgages; and the authority to do so necessarily carries with it the right to purchase obligations secured thereby. Savings Bank v. Barrett, 126 Cal. 413, 58 P. 914.

Whether the purchase of a mortgage is required by the purposes of the corporation, within the California statute, is to be determined by its board of directors, and it is not open to investigation at the instance of the mortgagor. Savings Bank v. Barrett, 126 Cal. 413, 58 P. 914.

Iowa.—Savings bank, having sufficient funds available, could legally issue certificate of deposit for negotiable notes. Andrew v. Peterson, 214 Iowa 582, 243 N.W. 340.

New York.—The statute relating to investment of funds by savings banks limits investments in mortgagee to whole mortgages only and does not authorize investment in mortgage participations, unless bank holds all participations under one mortgage. In re Hoyt's Estate, 47 N.Y.S.2d 929.

The statutes authorizing investments of trust funds in guaranteed mortgage certificates did not enlarge authority of savings banks with respect to investment in mortgages, but savings banks were restricted to bonds and mortgages on unencumbered realty situated within state to extent of 60 percent of appraised value thereof. In re Farina, 253 App. Div. 510, 2 N.Y.S.2d 987, rev'd on other grounds sub nom. In re Hewson, 279 N.Y. 780, 18 N.E.2d 865.

[590] Ubbinga v. Farmers' Sav. Bank, 108 Iowa 221, 78 N.W. 840.

[591] Citizens' Sav. Bank v. Couse, 68 Misc. 153, 124 N.Y.S. 79.

[592] Franklin Co. v. Lewiston Inst., 68 Me. 43, 28 Am. R. 9.

[593] Bassett v. Merchants' Trust Co., 115 Conn. 364, 161 A. 785.

[594] *Massachusetts.*—A national banking association, organized by a conversion from a state trust company, retained its former corporate identity to the extent that the dividend record of the trust company might be considered that of the national bank for the purpose of

§ 24. Loans and Discounts.

Power to Lend and Discount.—A charter conferring on a savings institution the power to invest deposits made with it in public stocks or "other securities" authorizes lending upon bills, bonds, notes and mortgages, as well as on stocks, and also gives the power of making loans by way of discount.[595] And authority to "invest in personal security" empowers a bank to lend money on paper, discount bills of exchange, notes drafts and the like, but not to lend on chattel mortgages.[596] Under the authority given to a bank to keep its available funds "on deposit, on interest or otherwise, or in such available form as the trustees may direct," a loan on a borrower's promissory

---

qualifying stock of the national bank as a legal investment for Massachusetts savings banks. Worcester County Nat. Bank v. Commissioner of Banks, 340 Mass. 695, 166 N.E.2d 551.

Even though charter of trust company became void upon date of conversion of company to a national banking association, such fact would not be decisive as to whether the continuing banking institution was the same entity for purpose of having a record of dividend payments for at least five years such as would be necessary to qualify the stock of such continuing institution as a legal investment for Massachusetts savings banks. Worcester County Nat. Bank v. Commissioner of Banks, 340 Mass. 695, 166 N.E.2d 551.

New Jersey.—The court of chancery is, by statute, given guardianship over savings banks, and such banks can invest in mortgages only under authority from that court. In re Newark Sav. Inst., 32 N.J. Eq. 644.

New York.—Under the statute savings banks are authorized to keep ten percent of their deposits on deposit in any incorporated bank. Erie Co. Sav. Bank v. Coit, 104 N.Y. 532, 11 N.E. 54.

A contract of deposit by a savings bank with a national bank, calling for interest, does not effect an unauthorized loan, and such a contract is not a violation of the statute prescribing the securities in which investments by savings banks may be made. Erie County Sav. Bank v. Coit, 104 N.Y. 532, 11 N.E. 54.

The purpose of the amendment to the New York Banking Law relating to investments in railroad securities was to make eligible for investment by savings banks obligations of railroad corporations provided corporations had not defaulted in payment of matured principal or interest of any of their funded debts, notwithstanding that railroads failed in years set forth in original statute and in amendatory ones to have income equal to one and one-half times their fixed charges.

In re Wade's Will, 270 App. Div. 712, 61 N.Y.S.2d 16, aff'd, 296 N.Y. 244, 72 N.E.2d 306.

595 Duncan v. Maryland Sav. Inst. (Md.), 10 Gill & J. 299.

Whether or not a particular use of the term "investment" in the banking laws is narrow and excludes loans or is generic and includes them depends on its specific context and particularly the explicit or implicit legislative intent. Suburban Sav. Loan Asso. v. Commissioner of Banking, 150 N.J. Super. 339, 375 A.2d 1185 (1977).

596 Colorado Sav. Bank v. Evans, 12 Colo. App. 334, 56 P. 981.

note is authorized.[597] Similarly, under its charter power to invest its capital in "bonds, notes and other evidences of debt," and to "hold any real estate necessary to carry on its business," a savings bank has power to lend money and to secure loans by a trust deed.[598]

A savings bank, empowered to discount notes, may purchase such notes,[599] and may purchase and hold city warrants.[600] And a duly incorporated savings bank whose charter does not restrict its power to lend money upon security in or out of state, may take and hold a mortgage upon lands in another state, and enforce such mortgage in the courts of that state.[601] A savings bank making loans on the credit of two-name paper satisfying legal requirements, could also take as additional security nonlegal collateral without invalidating the loans.[602] The rules and bylaws of a savings bank may limit the powers of its investment committee and other officers with respect to making loans.[603] Persons dealing with savings banks must take notice of their limited powers, and no recovery can be had against a bank for breach of contract in failing to make a loan, where a statutory condition precedent to making the loan has not been complied with.[604]

Statutory Requirements as to Security.—A statute prohibiting savings banks from lending money on personal security is directory to bank trustees,

---

[597] Rome Sav. Bank v. Kramer, 82 Hun. 270, aff'd, 102 N.Y. 331, 6 N.E. 682.

A charter authorizing the trustees to keep one-third of the deposits to meet payments, "and which may by them be kept on deposit on interest or otherwise, in such available form as the trustees may direct," does not authorize the trustees to loan funds on note and mortgages. Paine v. Barnum, 59 How. Pac. 803 (N.Y.).

[598] Tishimingo Sav. Institution v. Buchanan, 60 Miss. 496.

Savings bank had authority to enter into an agreement for a "permanent" mortgage loan on a shopping center, and could therefore require borrowers to give consideration for their exposure in the transaction; banks were entitled to retain fees charged for the mortgage commitment, even though the permanent mortgage loan was never made, where their agreement provided for such retention. Weiner v. Salem Five Cents Sav. Bank, 360 N.E.2d 306 (Mass. 1977).

[599] Pape v. Capitol Bank of Topeka, 20 Kan. 440, 27 Am. R. 183.

[600] Aull Sav. Bank v. Lexington, 74 Mo. 104.

[601] Lebanon Sav. Bank v. Hallenbeck, 29 Minn. 322, 13 N.W. 145.

[602] Peterborough Sav. Bank v. King, 103 N.H. 206, 168 A.2d 116.

[603] Greenfield Sav. Bank v. Abercrombie, 211 Mass. 252, 97 N.E. 897, 39 L.R.A. (n.s.) 173, 1913B Ann. Cas. 420.

[604] Gilson v. Cambridge Sav. Bank, 180 Mass. 444, 62 N.E. 728.

and designed for the protection of bank depositors,[605] and if a bank receives corporate stock as a pledge for a loan, its title thereto is merely voidable, not void.[606] Such a statute will not prevent a bank from enforcing the payment of a promissory note,[607] nor will it affect a bank's liability for damages where a bank directs a broker to sell at a specific price certain stock which it has taken to secure a loan, and after the broker's sale, informs him that it has already sold the stock, and refuses to deliver it.[608] Nor does a bank lend on a "note" in violation of statutes prohibiting loans on notes, bills of exchange or other personal securities, if it lends on the security of a bond and mortgage as well as a note.[609] Similarly, where the charter of a savings bank provides that its funds shall be invested in or loaned on public stocks or private mortgages, and that when loaned on—not invested in—such stocks or mortgages, "a sufficient bond or other satisfactory personal security in addition shall be required of the borrower," the promissory note of a borrower is perfectly lawful even though secured merely by a pledge of bank stock.[610] A Maine statute which limits the amount of a loan a savings bank may make to eighty percent of the appraised market value of the real estate taken as security, can be disregarded by the trustees of a savings bank, if, in their discretion, the loan is nonetheless prudent.[611]

---

[605] Farmington Sav. Bank v. Fall, 71 Me. 49.

[606] Sistare v. Best, 88 N.Y. 527.

[607] Farmington Sav. Bank v. Fall, 71 Me. 49; United German Bank v. Katz, 57 Md. 128.

But in a case in a federal court, it was held that where the charter of a safe-deposit and savings institution provides in what it shall invest its funds, but gives it no power to loan money on personal security, and the constitution and statutes expressly prohibit such corporations from doing a banking business, if the corporation loans money by discounting notes of the borrower, the loan itself, as well as the notes, is void, and the corporation cannot recover for money had and received. In re Jaycox, 13 F. Cas. 390 (No. 7237) (C.C.N.D.N.Y. 1874).

[608] Sistare v. Best (N.Y.), 16 Hun. 611.

[609] Auburn Sav. Bank v. Brinkerhoff, 44 Hun 142, 8 N.Y. St. R. 275; United States Trust Co. v. Brady, 20 Barb. 119(N.Y.); Pratt v. Eaton, 79 N.Y. 449.

[610] Mott v. United States Trust Co. (N.Y.), 19 Barb. 568.

[611] Auburn Sav. Bank v. Campbell, 273 A.2d 846 (Me. 1971).

Loan by savings bank in amount of $14,400 secured by first mortgage of real estate having market value of $16,000 and further protected by contract of mortgage guarantee insurance providing reimbursement up to 20 percent of outstanding balance in event of default was legal loan under "prudent man" statute giving savings bank authority to make discretionary loans not otherwise legal but in their judgment sound and prudent. Auburn Sav. Bank v. Campbell, 273 A.2d 846 (Me. 1971).

But a statute which prohibits savings banks from taking second mortgages, or lending except upon report by members of their board of investment, is mandatory,[612] and is designed to secure the interest of depositors.[613] And while a loan taken without observing such requirements may be valid, as between a bank and the borrower, or as to third persons,[614] as between bank officers on the one hand and a bank and its depositors on the other, such irregular loans are ultra vires.[615] And under statutes or charter provisions in some states, savings banks are not permitted to accept real estate as security for a loan unless it is worth double the amount of the loan.[616] But where a statute requires that real estate on which savings banks

---

[612] Greenfield Sav. Bank v. Abercrombie, 211 Mass. 252, 97 N.E. 897, 39 L.R.A. (U.S.) 173, 1913B Ann. Cas. 420.

Where a bank makes a loan secured by second mortgage on property on which bank holds first mortgage, no merger of mortgages results, so as to give second mortgage standing of first mortgage, and thus avoid prohibition of statute forbidding investment of deposits in savings departments of trust companies in loan on security of pledge of second mortgage. Medford Trust Co. v. McKnight, 292 Mass. 1, 197 N.E. 649.

[613] Greenfield Sav. Bank v. Abercrombie, 211 Mass. 252, 97 N.E. 897, 39 L.R.A. (U.S.) 173, 1913B Ann. Cas. 420.

[614] **In general.—**

York County Sav. Bank v. Wentworth, 136 Me. 330, 9 A.2d 265, 125 A.L.R. 1509; Greenfield Sav. Bank v. Abercrombie, 211 Mass. 252, 97 N.E. 897, 39 L.R.A. (U.S.) 173, 1913B Ann. Cas. 420.

Noncompliance held no defense against bank.—

Legislature did not intend that nonconformance by bank officials with statutory enactments with reference to making of loans, although mandatory, but enacted solely for proper government of bank, should inure to benefit of and constitute a defense for a borrower of the bank's money. York County Sav. Bank v. Wentworth, 136 Me. 330, 9 A.2d 265, 125 A.L.R. 1509.

Failure of trustees of savings bank to comply with statutory enactments with reference to making of loans and foreclosure of mortgagee securing loans was not a defense to proceeding by bank to recover possession of mortgaged realty. York County Sav. Bank v. Wentworth, 136 Me. 330, 9 A.2d 265, 125 A.L.R. 1509.

Evidence admissible.—

In action by savings bank to recover possession of realty, evidence consisting of five mortgages covering realty and notes secured by mortgages was admissible, even though trustees of bank did not comply with statutory enactments with reference to the making of the loans. York County Sav. Bank v. Wentworth, 136 Me. 330, 9 A.2d 265; 125 A.L.R. 1509.

[615] Greenfield Sav. Bank v. Abercrombie, 211 Mass. 252, 97 N.E. 897, 39 L.R.A. (U.S.) 173, 1913B Ann. Cas. 420.

[616] Duncan v. Maryland Sav. Inst. (Md.), 10 Gill & J. 299.

make loans shall be unencumbered, and provides that no loan shall be made except on the report of a bank's committee, if an action is brought against the maker of a mortgage bond on which a bank has made a loan, the defendant cannot defend by showing that the realty was encumbered by liens prior to the mortgage or that no committee reported on the loan.[617]

Statutory Provisions as to Loan Purposes and Prohibited Transactions.—A savings bank which has no funds with which to purchase notes, and which exchanges certificates of deposit therefor, is held to have made a loan for a purpose not authorized by statute, so that the certificates are void.[618] And the issuance of a certificate of deposit by a savings bank in exchange for notes, the make of which the bank knew to be financially irresponsible, creates an indebtedness not within the purview of a statute providing the purposes for which a bank may contract indebtedness.[619]

A bank which is prohibited by statute from discounting commercial paper has no right to discount such paper, and notes discounted by it are illegal and void, but such an act is simply malum prohibitum, and is no defense to an action for money had and received against parties receiving the benefits of the illegal loans.[620] But a savings bank does not "discount" a bond in violation of a statute, if it pays its full face value, not reserving interest.[621] An assignment of a mortgage to a savings bank made in good faith to protect it, cannot be assailed because the bank is, by statute, prohibited from taking the assignment, and under its charter powers cannot bind itself by an accompanying agreement.[622] And a violation of a statute prohibiting directors and officers of savings and loan corporations from borrowing therefrom, and declaring that their offices shall immediately become vacant therefor, is available only to the sovereign power, and a loan made to a director is valid and may be recovered, and a pledge securing same may be

---

Such a statute, however, does not require the bonds or other security, except the realty, to be worth double the loan. Colorado Sav. Bank v. Evans, 12 Colo. App. 334, 56 P. 981.

It should mean, though, that the real estate shall be worth at least double the investment and double the encumbrances. Williams v. McKay, 46 N.J. Eq. 25, 18 A. 824.

617 Auburn Sav. Bank v. Brinkerhoff, 44 Hun. 142, 8 N.Y. St. R. 275.

618 Henderson v. Farmers' Sav. Bank, 199 Iowa 496, 202 N.W. 259.

619 Sweet v. Security Sav. Bank, 200 Iowa 895, 205 N.W. 470.

620 Pratt v. Short, 79 N.Y. 437, 35 Am. R. 531.

621 Auburn Sav. Bank v. Brinkerhoff 44 Hun. 142, 8 N.Y. St. R. 275.

622 Gerrity v. Wareham Sav. Bank, 202 Mass. 214, 88 N.E. 1084.

held until the loan is paid.[623] Statutes which require written applications for loans to be approved by a board of investment shield a savings bank against contractual obligations not incurred in accordance with such statutes, but in the absence of appropriate language, a court may not extend their operation so as to exempt savings banks from liability for deceit or other torts under general law.[624] And a statute relating to the appraisal of property to be mortgaged to a savings bank, and requiring that such appraisal together with a certificate of title issued by some person approved by the bank shall be lodged with and kept by the bank, is "remedial" in character and must be liberally construed; its purpose is to protect depositors from improvident loans.[625]

Statutory Requirements as to Loan Amount.—A statute which provides that the total liabilities to any savings bank association of any person, firm or corporation for money borrowed shall at no time exceed a certain prescribed percent of the paid in capital stock of the association, does not apply to a bond intended to indemnify an obligee association from a principal's failure to pay present and future indebtedness; such a statute also does not make a loan in excess of the percent named void.[626]

Statutory Requirements as to Duration of Loans.—A statute providing that a savings bank shall not make a contract or agreement to lend or extend the time of payment of a loan on personal security for longer than one year, is not violated by an agreement extending the time of payment of a note until the payee shall be dissatisfied with the security, or until payment is demanded or offered.[627]

Usury.—A savings bank, unless authorized to do so by its charter or by statute, cannot charge a higher rate of interest on loans than that allowed by

---

[623] Brittan v. Oakland Bank of Sav., 124 Cal. 282, 57 P. 84, 71 Am. St R. 58.

[624] Schleifer v. Worcester North Sav. Inst., 306 Mass. 226, 27 N.E.2d 992; Schleifer v. Worcester North Sav. Inst., 310 Mass. 110, 37 N.E.2d 255.

[625] Grievance Committee v. Payne, 128 Conn. 325, 22 A.2d 623.

Under the statute, the certificate of title must be made by an attorney at law, and conduct of town clerk who was not an attorney and who engaged in preparing such certificates was not excepted, by the passage of such statute, from the operation of statute relating to unlawful practice of law. Grievance Committee v. Payne, 128 Conn. 325, 22 A.2d 623.

[626] Benton County Sav. Bank v. Boddicker, 105 Iowa 548, 75 N.W. 632, 67 Am. St. R. 310, 45 L.R.A. 321.

[627] Lyndon Sav. Bank v. International Co., 78 Vt. 169, 62 A. 50, 112 Am. St. R. 900.

general law.[628] In some states where a bank discounts a note at a usurious rate of interest, the transaction is not entirely void, but void only as to the excess of interest over the legal rate.[629] Notes for money borrowed from a savings institution, and in payment of the principal and interest thereon, even though calculated at eight percent, if in accordance with the plan permitted by statute and payable in monthly installments, are not subject to the defense of usury.[630]

---

[628] **In general.—**

Candler v. Corra, 54 Ga. 190.

Unless expressly excepted therefrom, usury laws apply as fully to corporate as to natural persons, and general usury laws apply to loans made by savings banks. Feldman v. Kings Highway Sav. Bank, 102 N.Y.S.2d 600, rev'd on other grounds, 278 App. Div. 589, 102 N.Y.S.2d 306, aff'd, 303 N.Y. 675, 102 N.E.2d 835.

Provision of New York banking law prescribing maximum rate of interest and authorizing recovery of penalty of twice amount of interest paid for charging usurious rate applies to savings banks as well as commercial banks. Lyons v. National Sav. Bank, 200 Misc. 652, 110 N.Y.S.2d 564, rev'd on other grounds, 280 App. Div. 339, 113 N.Y.S.2d 695.

Constitutionality of statute or charter.—

A statute authorizing theretofore usurious loans is a general law and not repugnant to the constitutional prohibition against special or local laws. Union Sav., etc., Trust Co. v. Dottenheim, 107 Ga. 606, 34 S.E. 217 (1899).

There is a dictum, however, in the case of Union Sav. Bank & Trust Co. v. Dottenheim, 107 Ga. 606, 34 S.E. 217, to the effect that such a special provision in a particular bank charter would be unconstitutional.—Editor's Note.

What constitutes usury.—

Bank's increased expenses as to retirement of certain notes under circumstances of bank's own choice, and bank's added bookkeeping expense incident to loans were not expenses which could be added to lawful interest rate on notes without constituting usury, particularly where principal accounting was done by a warehouse company at which goods forming security for notes were stored, rather than by bank. Independent Foods v. Lucas County Sav. Bank, 70 N.E.2d 139 (Ohio App. 1946).

Georgia Supreme Court adheres to the actual declining-principal balance method originally set out in Union Sav. Bank & Trust Co. v. Dottenheim, 107 Ga. 606, 34 S.E. 217 (1899), because the court believes that usury on a particular loan can only be determined by proper reference to the actual outstanding principal balance on that loan. Southern Federal Sav. & Loan Asso. v. Lyle, 249 Ga. 284, 290 S.E.2d 455 (1982).

[629] Chafin v. Lincoln Sav. Bank, 54 Tenn. 499. For a fuller discussion of usury, see § 80 et seq. of chapter 11, vol. 6.

[630] Ficken v. Bank of Cerro Gordo, 25 Ge. App. 644, 104 S.E. 14.

VII. INSOLVENCY AND RECEIVERS.

§ 25. General Consideration.

Right of Depositor When Bank Receives Deposit with Knowledge of its Insolvency.—Where a bank has knowledge of its insolvency when it receives a deposit, the depositor is entitled to have such deposit returned.[631]

Transfer of Property or Payment of Debts Prior to Appointment of Receiver.—When a savings bank is insolvent and has ceased to be a going concern, and its officers know or ought to know that suspension is impending, such officers are trustees so that they may not transfer corporate property to themselves in payment of debts due them, and if such a transfer is made, it constitutes a fraud in law.[632]

But the mere fact of insolvency will not preclude savings bank, prior to its going into the hands of a receiver, from drawing a check in favor of a commercial bank for the amount of its deposit in such bank to be credited on a larger debt which it owes to such bank.[633]

A savings bank or the savings department of a commercial bank must pay savings deposits to depositors demanding them so long as the bank is a going concern, and a depositor withdrawing money in good faith, without knowledge of the bank's insolvency, is legally entitled to retain it.[634] And that a savings bank was insolvent when it paid a stockholder for his stock does not authorize recovery of the payment as an illegal and preferential payment, where the payment was not made in contemplation of insolvency and the bank had committed no act of insolvency at the time.[635] It has been held that a bank organized for savings without power to issue notes, may

---

[631] Chicago Title, etc., Co. v. Household Guest Co., 88 Ill. App. 126.

Where a savings bank, within an hour after a deposit was made, closed its doors, and its officers concluded within 24 hours that it was impossible to realize on the assets an amount sufficient to meet liabilities and enable the bank to continue in business, the bank was presumed to have had knowledge of its insolvency when the deposit was received. Chicago Title, etc., Co. v. Household Guest Co., 88 Ill. App. 126.

[632] Slack v. Northwestern Nat. Bank, 103 Wis. 57, 79 N.W. 51, 74 Am. St. H. 841.

And the same rule applies, where the persons making the transfer, while not officers de jure, are in fact acting as officers and managing the business of the bank. Slack v. Northwestern Nat. Bank, 103 Wis. 57, 79 N.W. 51, 74 Am. St. H. 841.

[633] Slack v. Northwestern Nat. Bank, 103 Wis. 57, 79 N.W. 51, 74 Am. St. H. 841.

[634] Perry v. Commercial Bank, etc., Co., 119 Conn. 115, 174 A. 326.

[635] Moran v. Schlosberg, 90 F.2d 408, holding receiver's bill against stockholder was properly dismissed for failure to state cause of action.

make an assignment for the benefit of its creditors by its board of directors, without the consent of a majority of its stockholders having first been obtained as is required by statute for banks of issue.[636] But where the officers of a bank, just before its insolvency, offer a depositor a note and mortgage for his deposit, and he accepts the offer but there is no delivery, he obtains no title thereto.[637]

A statute requiring a bank to maintain a reserve fund and forbidding it to increase loans and discounts or make any investments of funds or pay any dividends while its reserve is below the required amount has been held to prohibit the removal of assets from the savings department at a bank and the substitution therefor of assets belonging to another department after the bank's insolvency.[638]

Appointment of Receiver.—When a savings bank becomes insolvent, a receiver may be appointed to make distribution of its assets and wind up its affairs.[639] But where a bank's officers and depositors can agree on a settlement among themselves, it is not necessary that a receiver be appointed.[640]

Duties and Powers of Trustees and Receivers.—It is the duty of a trustee appointed to settle the affairs of an insolvent savings company to protect the trust property in every reasonable way, get possession of the company's assets, reduce them to money, and under court direction, apply the funds to the satisfaction of creditors' claims.[641] Such a trustee does not have, in the absence of a proper court order, power to lend the trust funds, and a general deposit by such a trustee of trust funds in a bank is a loan to the bank, constituting, unless authorized by court, a violation of duty.[642] But where

---

636 In re Miners' Bank (Pa.), 13 Wkly. Notes Cas. 370.

637 Shattler v. Taft, 7 Ohio Dec. R. 631, 4 Wkly. Law Bul. 419.

638 Wilde v. Richards, 49 Wyo. 408, 55 P.2d 476.

639 Finney v. Bennett, 68 Va. (27 Gratt.) 365; Savings Inst. v. Makin, 23 Me. 360.

But a petition by a stockholder alleging that a savings bank is insolvent, that the directors are inefficient and are about to make assessments for their own gain, and praying for a receiver, etc., but not charging fraud or breach of trust, is no present ground for interference by a court of equity. Gorman v. Guardian Sav. Bank, 4 Mo. App. 180.

640 Lewis v. Lynn Inst., 0, 19 N.E. 365, 12 Am. St. R. 535, 1 L.R.A. 785.

641 Smith v. Fuller, 86 Ohio St. 57, 99 N.E. 214, L.R.A. 1916C, 6, Ann. Cas. 1913D, 387.

Invalidity of certificates for deposits, issued in exchange for notes, held available to receiver of defunct savings banks, though notes had not been turned over to holders of certificates. Henderson v. Farmers' Sav. Bank, 199 Iowa 496, 202 N.W. 259.

642 Smith v. Fuller, 86 Ohio St. 57, 99 N.E. 214, L.RA. 1916C6, Ann. Cas. 1913D387.

such a trustee deposits trust money in a bank, taking as evidence thereof a certificate of deposit certifying that he as trustee has deposited the fund payable to himself on return of the certificate properly endorsed, the same not being subject to check with no stipulation for interest, there is a presumption in the absence of proof to the contrary, that the trustee intended to perform his duty, and that the deposit was intended as a special, not a general, deposit.[643]

The individual liability of a trustee of a savings bank for willfully cooperating with other bank trustees in declaring and paying dividends when there were no surplus profits may be enforced by the bank's receiver.[644] And by accepting securities for a loan improperly made by managers of a savings bank, the bank's receiver is not barred from recourse against the managers.[645] Where a bond payable to a savings bank, the capital of which has become impaired, is given for the purpose of being exhibited to banking officials as an asset so that the bank can continue business, and afterwards the bank becomes insolvent, the bank's receiver may recover on the bond even though the transaction was ultra vires.[646] And an action may be maintained by the receiver of a savings bank whose treasurer made an unauthorized assignment of a mortgage owned by the bank, to restrain the assignee who was a bank depositor from enforcing a power of sale in the mortgage, and to compel him to surrender and cancel the assignment, although upon receiving the assignment, he had released the bank's debt to him as such depositor.[647] But an assignee of mortgages may obtain a title by estoppel against a bank which will be a good defense in an action by the bank's receiver to obtain a conveyance of the mortgages.[648]

Receiver's Sales.—It is not proper for a receiver of an insolvent savings bank to sell the bank's charter.[649] And a savings bank, by consenting to an

---

643 Smith v. Fuller, 86 Ohio St. 57, 99 N.E. 214, L.RA. 1916C6, Ann. Cas. 1913D387.

644 Van Dyck v. McQuade, 57 How. Pr. 62, 45 N.Y. Super. 620, rev'd on other grounds, 86 N.Y. 38.

645 Dodd v. Wilkinson, 41 N.J. Eq. 566, 7 A. 337.

646 Hurd v. Kelly, 78 N.Y. 588, 34 Am. R. 567.

647 Holden v. Phelps, 135 Mass. 61.

648 Holden v. Whiting, 29 F. 881. See also Commonwealth v. Reading Sav. Bank, 137 Mass. 431; Holden v. Phelps, 141 Mass. 456, 5 N.E. 815; Whiting v. Wellington, 10 F. 810.

649 Douglas v. Savings Bank, 102 Minn. 199, 113 N.W. 268; State v. Sav. Bank, 102 Minn. 199, 113 N.W. 268.

A creditor of an insolvent savings bank sought to procure an order directing the receiver to sell the bank's charter, which provided for the distribution of net proceeds after the

order appointing a receiver which does not fix the terms, conditions or time of a sale of its property to pay debts, is not estopped from resisting a subsequent order of sale by the receiver.[650]

Liability of Stockholders.[651]—Where an assessment is levied on stockholders of an insolvent savings bank, the claim therefor becomes liquidated by the assessment, and draws interest from that time until paid.[652]

Power of Court in Case of Insolvency.—Under a statute declaring that when suit is brought against a savings institution, alleging its insolvency and demanding its dissolution, the court may grant such relief and render such judgment as the interest of the parties seems to require, the court may scale down deposits and authorize the resumption of business, where the effect of such an order will be to allow the institution to continue on a solvent basis.[653] Under a statute providing for the reduction of a savings and loan association's liability to its members, the court upon petition therefor approved by the superintendent of banks, without determining its authority therein, would experimentally order such reduction.[654] And in a proceeding to wind up a savings bank, a court can reappoint commissioners to receive and pass upon claims and extend the time within which claims may be presented and determined.[655]

Presentation of Claims.—Under a statute requiring creditors of insolvents to exhibit their claims, the filing of insolvent savings bank passbooks with a bank's receiver showing nonpayment of accrued interest, constitutes a sufficient presentation of a claim.[656] The allowance of a claim against a savings bank in dissolution proceedings is not improper if such claim is

---

payment of interest to depositors to the holders of the stock. Subsequent legislation returned all the net profits to the stockholders and prohibited trustees from having any interest in deposits. It was held that such an order would have sanctioned the bank's continued existence after the discharge of the receiver and have adjudicated that such existence should not be terminated by the judgment to be entered, and that such extension of special privilege was against public policy. State v. Savings Bank, 102 Minn. 199, 113 N.W. 268.

650 State v. Fawcett, 58 Neb. 371, 78 N.W. 636.

651 See §§ 8 and 4 of this chapter.

652 May v. Ullrich, 132 Mich. 6, 92 N.W. 493.

653 People v. Ulster County Sav. Inst., 133 N.Y. 689, 31 N.E. 738.

654 In re Eagle Sav., etc., Co., 164 App. Div. 867, 150 N.Y.S. 442.

655 In re Nutter, 109 Me. 124, 82 A. 1012.

656 Bank Comm'n v. Watertown Sav. Bank, 81 Conn. 261, 70 A. 1038.

presented after the time originally fixed, but within an extension of time for the presentation of claims.[657]

Renunciation of Claims.—See the footnote.[658]

Distribution and Application of Assets.—Managers of an insolvent savings bank who have applied to a court to protect the interests of its depositors, are under the duty of converting the bank's assets into cash as rapidly as possible without sacrifice, and making distribution among the bank's depositors without unnecessary delay.[659] Money recovered by a receiver of an insolvent savings bank from the sureties and property of a defaulting treasurer of the bank partakes of all the characteristics of the money which it replaced, and should be distributed in accordance with the bank's charter. Such money should be applied to the payment of unpaid interest on deposits, the principal of which has been paid in full, and is not returnable to the treasurer's sureties.[660] But an insolvent bank's surety is entitled to restrain the bank's receiver from enforcing payment of the surety's debt to the bank out of the surety's property, until the extent of the surety's liability on the bank's obligations is ascertained.[661]

Advance interest paid on a deposit which had not been earned by accrual when a savings bank was taken over by receivers, should be charged as partial payment of the depositor's claim.[662] A state statute providing that whenever any savings bank shall be found to be insolvent, the account of each depositor shall be reduced so as to divide the losses equitably among

---

[657] In re Nutter, 109 Me. 124, 82 A. 1012.

[658] Letter by senior vice-president and treasurer of bank to liquidator for receiver for savings bank stating that bank desired to relinquish claim against certificate of deposit issued by savings bank and requesting that liquidator surrender instrument to named party using certificate as collateral for loan from bank renounced bank's right to certificate of deposit, and renunciation was not conditioned upon delivery of certificate to named party. First & Citizens Nat'l Bank v. Federal Deposit Ins. Corp., 210 Va. 434, 171 S.E.2d 856 (1970).

Term "desire" in letter from bank vice-president and treasurer to liquidator for receiver of savings bank stating that it was bank's desire to relinquish claim against savings certificate in hands of liquidator clearly showed an expression of present purpose and intent to renounce bank's rights rather than an indication of some possible contemplated action at a future time. First & Citizens Nat'l Bank v. Federal Deposit Ins. Corp., 210 Va. 434, 171 S.E.2d 856 (1970).

[659] In re Dime Sav. Inst., 29 N.J. Eq. 109.

[660] Bank Comm'rs v. Watertown Sav. Bank, 81 Conn. 261, 70 A. 1038.

[661] Cockrill v. Peoples Sav. Bank, 155 Tenn. 342, 293 S.W. 996.

[662] Murray v. First Trust, etc., Bank, 201 Iowa 1325, 207 N.W. 781 (1926).

them, is not unconstitutional as impairing the obligation of contracts, as being contrary to the bankruptcy law, or as being retrospective in its operation.[663] But the previously accrued liability of a savings bank to its members cannot be reduced thereafter on account of the bank's insolvency.[664] Under a statute providing that the assets of the savings department of a bank shall be held solely for the repayment of the savings depositors, such savings assets are chargeable with a just and equitable part of the expenses of liquidating the insolvent bank.[665] And where a surplus remained after payment of claims in the commercial department of a bank in liquidation, it was held the liquidating agent should transfer the money or assets remaining in such department to the savings department where some claims had not been paid.[666]

State Deposit Insurance Fund Corporation properly determined the amount of insurance payable to the depositors of a closed bank when it subtracted the difference between the maximum insured amount and the amount in the account from the "gross loss" as determined by subtracting pro rata dividend received on sale of net assets from amount in account.[667] The express reservation to state Deposit Insurance Fund Corporation of sovereign immunity and statutory immunity conferred on director did not excuse the Corporation from an obligation to consider reformation claim brought by trustee of pension and retirement funds which maintained accounts in closed bank seeking correction of number of accounts.[668]

---

[663] Simpson v. City Sav. Bank, 56 N.H. 466, 22 Am. R. 491.

[664] Wallis v. Eagle Sav., etc., Co. 180 App. Div. 719, 168 N.Y.S. 513.

[665] Upham v. Bramwell, 105 Ore. 597, 210 P. 706, 25 A.L.R. 919.

But it is held that the expenses of administration of receivership of insolvent state bank, which conducted both commercial and savings departments, are primarily chargeable against general assets in hands of receiver. Reichert v. Farmers', etc., Sav. Bank, 257 Mich. 500, 242 N.W. 239, 81 A.L.R. 1461.

[666] Greva v. Rainey (Cal. App.), 33 P.2d 697, modified, 2 Cal. 2d 338, 41 P.2d 328.

[667] Silverman v. Maryland Deposit Ins. Fund Corp., 317 Md. 306, 563 A.2d 402 (1989).

State Deposit Insurance Fund Corporation properly established $100,000 per account maximum insurance liability for welfare payments; assumption of greater insurance responsibility would have resulted in exceeding statutory insurance limitation imposed on Corporation's predecessor by statute. Silverman v. Maryland Deposit Ins. Fund Corp., 317 Md. 306, 563 A.2d 402 (1989).

[668] Silverman v. Maryland Deposit Ins. Fund Corp., 317 Md. 306, 563 A.2d 402 (1989).

§ 26. Order of Payment—Preference.

As between Depositors in General.—Depositors in savings institutions are similar to partners, and on the insolvency of such an institution, become owners in common of its assets and entitled to share in them after the payment of privileged debts, in the proportion which their respective deposits bears to the net amount available.[669] Where there is no proof that a deposit was accepted by a bank as a special trust, or a deposit differing materially from the other deposits of the bank, it is not entitled to preference in payment.[670] And a depositor is not entitled to preference in the amount of a check given for a deposit, which was refused payment by the drawee bank for insufficient funds.[671]

General or Special Depositors.—Whether there shall be any preference as between general or ordinary depositors and so-called "special" depositors in the distribution of assets of an insolvent savings bank, is generally determined by the provisions of the bank's charter or bylaws providing for and defining different classes of deposits.[672] A savings bank's receiver is in

---

[669] Kennedy v. New Orleans Sav. Inst., 36 La. Ann. 1.

Savings depositors are merely general creditors of insolvent financial institution and thus must share those funds with other general creditors after secured claims have been satisfied. Minnesota Trust Co. v. Hatch, 368 N.W.2d 372 (Minn. App. 1985).

[670] **In general.—**

Vail v. Newark Sav. Institution, 32 N.J. Eq. 627.

Although depositor served notice on savings bank in accordance with statutes and thereafter made various demands on bank for payment, including demand by sight draft through another bank, and receiver was not appointed for bank until several days after the last demand and after expiration of the 60 days, depositor was merely a general creditor of the bank and not entitled to preference. People v. First Italian State Bank, 281 Ill. App. 1.

Pension funds constituting loans, not deposits.—

Provision in savings account passbooks prohibiting withdrawal of deposits except on 60 days' notice if bank desired, made trustees' savings account deposits of policemen's and firemen's pension funds "investments" or loans" which trustees had no authority to make, and not "deposits"; hence trustees were entitled to preferred claim against assets of closed bank, notwithstanding that bank did not adopt regulation requiring notice of withdrawal as required by statute. Andrew v. Union Sav. Bank, etc., Co., 222 Iowa 881, 270 N.W. 465 (1936).

[671] Stockton v. Mechanics', etc., Sav. Bank, 32 N.J. Eq. 163.

[672] **In general.—**

Stockton v. Mechanics', etc., Sav. Bank, 32 N.J. Eq. 163, holding that the institution in question was a mere trustee for the benefit of depositors, and the so-called "special" depositors were not entitled to priority in payment over the other class of depositors. And see

no better position to resist a depositor's preference claim than the bank itself.[673] Where a bank in which a trustee of an insolvent savings company has made a special deposit of trust funds fails, and the bank has mingled the trust money with its own funds, but it had at all times an amount equal to the deposit, a court of equity will ingraft a trust on such money, and the trustee will become a preferred creditor; a deposit by such trustee will be presumed to have been intended as a special, not a general, deposit.[674] The amount of assets of an insolvent savings bank in which a preferred claimant can participate is the lowest amount of cash in the bank at any time between the claimant's deposit and the bank's receivership.[675]

Stockholding or Nonstockholding Depositors.—Bank depositors who are not stockholders are to be preferred to depositors who are stockholders, and this preference is sometimes given by statute.[676] Therefore, where a bank's

---

Bank Comm'rs v. New Hampshire Banking Co., 74 N.H. 292, 67 A. 583, holding that general depositors were entitled to interest on deferred dividends as against "depositors for the guaranty fund who were shareholders."

Where closed bank advertised that it would resume business by receiving deposits in trust to new account to be used only in paying checks against such account, such deposits were not special, though termed special separate deposits in the advertisement, but such new depositors became creditors on an equality with the old depositors. In re Mutual Bldg. Fund Soc., F. Cas. (No. 9976), 2 Hughes C.C. 374.

Where a claim was filed for money paid to carry out subscription for stock under merger agreement between a savings bank and another, preference in payment being asked on theory that such fund was held in trust by bank because merger was incomplete and ineffective, subscription contract and merger contract held fully performed, so that what bank received became its property notwithstanding failure to carry out provisions of merger agreement respecting readjustments between bank and its affiliate company. Andrew v. American Sav. Bank, etc., Co., 219 Iowa 921, 258 N.W. 911.

673 Leach v. Treynor Sav. Bank, 203 Iowa 988, 213 N.W. 601.

674 Smith v. Fuller, 86 Ohio St. 57, 99 N.E. 214, L.R.A. 1916C, 6, Ann. Cas. 1913D, 387.

675 Leach v. Farmers' Sav. Bank, 205 Iowa 114, 217 N.W. 437, 56 A.L.R. 801.

676 **In general.**—

Dallemand v. Odd Fellows' Sav. Bank, 74 Cal. 598, 16 P. 497, writ of error dismissed, 154 U.S. 499, 14 S. Ct. 1144, 38 L. Ed. 1076; Murphy v. Pacific Bank, 130 Cal. 542, 62 P. 1059.

Subscriber for stock in savings and loan company, held not creditor but shareholder or member, whose rights were to be determined by relations existing between company and member, and, as such, amenable to rules of company respecting withdrawal and payment of shares, and bound by provision of banking law as to manner in which such claims shall be paid. Wallis v. Eagle Sav., etc., Co., 163 N.Y.S. 470.

ordinary depositors are stockholders and its special depositors are not, the latter will be preferred.[677]

Depositors in Corporation Doing Both Savings and Commercial Bank Business.—In the absence of a special provision giving them a preference, savings depositors of a corporation doing both a savings bank and a commercial bank business are not given any preference over commercial depositors,[678] and an agreement for such a preference between a corporation

---

Holders of certificates in savings and loan association, who were merely to receive dividends at 6 percent, and principal at end of 12 years, have prior equities to payment over holders of certificates who shared in excess profits. Wallis v. Eagle Sav., etc., Co., 180 App. Div. 719, 168 N.Y.S. 513.

Illustrative case.—

A corporation incorporated as the "F. Building & Loan Association" changed its name to that of the "F. Savings Association," and deposits were made with it by persons who were led to believe that they were making deposits in a savings bank. The depositors received passbooks styled "Savings Deposit Account," and on the last page of each book appeared a certificate entitled "Savings Certificate," and certifying that the depositor, as a member, had paid into the company's treasury the sums represented in the passbook as per balance, "for nonassessable deposit shares of a face value equal to the credit balance which shall be in lieu of further participation in the earnings of the association and bear a dividend, payable out of the gross earnings not exceeding" a certain per centum per annum, and provisions were made for withdrawals. The statute authorized the association to sell its shares fully or partially paid up in periodical or other installments with or without full participation in the earnings or partially in limited dividend-bearing stock, and provided that stockholders might withdraw. Held, that the depositors became members and were not within the statute preferring savings depositors in case of the insolvency of any bank. Askey v. Fidelity Sav. Ass'n, 37 Colo. 432, 86 P. 1025.

677 Hieronymus v. Sweeney, 83 Md. 146, 34 A. 823, 55 Am. St. R. 333, 33 L.R.A. 99; Maryland Sav. Inst. v. Schroeder (Md.), 8 Gill & J. 93, 29 Am. Dec. 528.

678 **In general.—**

People v. California, etc., Trust Co., 160 Cal. 374, 117 P. 321.

Both the savings depositors and the commercial depositors are entitled to share in the funds collected from stockholders. Hodgell v. Wilde, 52 Wyo. 310, 74 P.2d 336, 114 A.L.R. 671.

Procedure for allocation.—

The proceeds from stockholders' liability allotted to the banking branch of insolvent trust company should be apportioned between commercial and savings departments in proportion to claims filed and allowed in each department. Reichert v. Fidelity Bank, etc., Co., 261 Mich. 107, 245 N.W. 808.

The preferred claims chargeable against the savings department and against the commercial department of an insolvent bank which maintains both should be subtracted from the total claims chargeable against each in determining the distribution of funds

and its savings depositors, not known and consented to by its commercial depositors, is ineffective.[679] But a preference may be given to savings depositors over commercial depositors by special statute.[680] And a statute may require savings deposits and their increment to be held solely for the payment of savings depositors.[681] And under a statute providing that in case of a bank's insolvency or liquidation, its savings depositors shall have a prior lien upon the bank's savings assets, the savings depositors have the right where such savings assets are insufficient to pay the savings depositors in fall, to share ratably with the other depositors in the bank's general assets; the basis for such sharing is the depositors' unpaid balances after distribution of the savings assets.[682] The receiver of such a bank is justified, within certain limitations, in paying liquidating dividends to other than savings

---

obtained from stockholders in payment of their statutory liability between the creditors of the two departments. Hodgell v. Wilde, 52 Wyo. 310, 74 P.2d 336, 114 A.L.R. 671.

[679] People v. California, etc., Trust Co., 160 Cal. 374, 117 P. 321.

[680] Tabor v. Mullen, 37 Colo. 399, 86 P. 1007.

Holders of time certificates of deposit, as well as holders of savings account passbooks, are "savings depositors," within the Colorado statute giving preference in case of insolvency of a bank to the savings depositors. Tabor v. Muffin, 37 Colo. 399, 86 P. 1007.

[681] Peters v. Union Trust Co., 131 Mich. 322, 91 N.W. 273; Reichert v. Farmers' & Workingmen's Sav. Bank, 257 Mich. 500, 242 N.W. 239, 81 A.L.R. 1461.

Under such statute depositors in savings department are entitled to preference relative to investments made with their deposits upon insolvency of bank. Wilde v. Richards, 49 Wyo. 408, 55 P.2d 476.

But general assets of insolvent state bank, carried as combined account assets and not relating specifically to either savings investments or commercial investments, are general assets distributable ratably to all creditors. Reichert v. Farmers', etc., Sav. Bank, 257 Mich. 500, 242 N.W. 239, 81 A.L.R. 1461.

[682] Upham v. Bramwell, 105 Ore. 597, 209 P. 100, 210 P. 706, 25 A.L.R. 919; Bassett v. Merchants' Trust Co., 115 Conn. 364, 161 A. 785; Reichert v. Farmers', etc., Sav. Bank, 257 Mich. 500, 242 N.W. 239, 81 A.L.R. 1461; Hodgell v. Wilde, 52 Wyo. 310, 74 P.2d 336, 114 A.L.R. 671.

Where an insolvent state bank conducted both savings and commercial departments and the proceeds from liquidation of savings department investments are insufficient to pay savings depositors in full, the savings depositors are entitled, subject to limitations, to share in the balance of assets of the bank with other claimants. In such case, the ratio of division should be determined on the basis of claims filed and accepted or proven. Reichert v. Farmers', etc., Sav. Bank, 257 Mich. 500, 242 N.W. 239, 81 A.L.R. 1461.

Savings bank depositors had right to look for payment in common with the creditors of the commercial department to the stockholders' liability fund, on the basis of the unpaid portion of the claims in each department remaining after all the assets of each department had been collected and applied. Hodgell v. Wilde, 52 Wyo. 310, 74 P.2d 336, 114 A.L.R. 671.

depositors before a final determination is made as to what assets are available.[683] The rights of one depositor in a savings department cannot be discriminated against by giving a particular deposit preference over others.[684]

As between Creditors.—When a savings bank becomes insolvent, creditors whose loans are prohibited by statute should not be allowed to share with lawful creditors.[685] And if the funds of an insolvent savings bank are insufficient to pay all preferred claims, preferred creditors must share therein pro rata.[686]

As between Depositors and Creditors.—A statute providing that the assets and stock of a savings bank shall be security for depositors who are not stockholders does not give priority to the claim of a depositor who is not a stockholder over the claim of a bank creditor who is a stockholder.[687] Though the charter of a bank provides that for the security of depositors, a certain capital shall be raised prior to incorporation, "which shall at all times be liable to the depositors for the amount of their deposits," such capital cannot be claimed exclusively by its depositors.[688] Similarly, the mere promise of a bank to use certain securities for the benefit of its savings depositors cannot be held to create a trust or lien in favor of such depositors.[689] For rules in particular states with respect to the distribution of an insolvent savings bank's assets as between its depositors and creditors, see the footnote.[690]

---

683 Reichert v. Farmers', etc., Sav. Bank, 257 Mich. 500, 242 N.W. 239, 81 A.L.R. 1461.

684 Bassett v. City Bank, etc., Co., 115 Conn. 1, 160 A. 60, 81 A.L.R. 1488 (1932); In re Astoria Sav. Bank, 139 Ore. 573, 11 P.2d 1062.

685 State v. Corning State Sav. Bank, 136 Iowa 79, 113 N.W. 500.

686 Leach v. Farmers' Sav. Bank, 205 Iowa 114, 217 N.W. 437, 56 A.L.R. 801.

687 Laidlaw v. Pacific Bank, 67 P. 897, 6 Cal. Unrep. 849, rev'd on other grounds on rehearing, 137 Cal. 392, 70 P. 277.

688 Fox's Appeal, 93 Pa. 406.

689 Ward v. Johnson, 95 Ill. 215 (1880).

690 *Iowa.*—In ordinary savings banks, the general depositors are not stockholders and their claims in case of insolvency are not postponed to creditor's claims. Henderson v. Farmers' Sav. Bank, 199 Iowa 496, 202 N.W. 259.

Where a savings bank without funds with which to purchase promissory notes, issued certificates of deposit in exchange for notes, the certificates represented loans, and not deposits, and were not entitled to preference on the insolvency of the savings bank.

Henderson v. Farmers' Sav. Bank, 199 Iowa 496, 202 N.W. 259.

New Hampshire.—In ordinary savings banks, the general depositors in some respects are stockholders, and their claims in case of insolvency are postponed to the claims of creditors.

§ 27. Setoffs Against Debt Due Bank.

In General.—A conflict, if any, between the right of setoff as regards an insolvent bank and a customer, and statutory preferences of savings depositors must be resolved to conserve both the setoff and the preferences, if possible.[691]

Of Deposit.—In the absence of statute it is generally held that an ordinary depositor in an insolvent savings bank cannot set off his deposit against a debt he owes to the bank,[692] this is so even though the debt is for borrowed money and the deposit consists of such borrowed money.[693] But evidence is

---

Bank Comm'rs v. New Hampshire Banking Co., 74 N.H. 292, 67 A. 583; Cogswell v. Rockingham, etc., Sav. Bank, 59 N.H. 43.

New Jersey.—Upon winding up the affairs of an insolvent savings bank, the debts and expenses contracted by the bank in carrying on its ordinary business will be preferred. Stockton v. Mechanics', etc., Sav. Bank, 32 N.J. Eq. 183.

New York.—The general creditors of a savings bank have no superior equity to the depositors to payment in case of deficiency of assets. People v. Mechanics', etc., Sav. Inst., 92 N.Y. 7.

691 Reichert v. Fidelity Bank, etc., Co., 257 Mich. 535, 242 N.W. 236.

692 **In general.**—

Osborn v. Byrne, 43 Conn. 155, 21 Am. R. 641; Cogswell v. Rockingham, etc., Sav. Bank, 59 N.H. 43; Hannon v. Williams, 34 N.J. Eq. 255, 38 Am. R. 378; Stockton v. Mechanics', etc., Sav. Bank, 32 N.J. Eq. 163; Bachrach v. Commissioner of Banks, 239 Mass. 272, 131 N.E. 857.

But in New York, where one who had given his bond and mortgage to a savings bank was also a depositor therein, and the bank became insolvent, and a receiver was appointed, it was held, that the mortgagor was entitled to a credit on his bond to the amount of his deposit at the time of the failure of the bank. New Amsterdam Sav. Bank v. Tartter (N.Y.), 4 Abb. N. Cas. 215, 54 How. Pr. 385, criticized In Hannon v. Williams, 34 N.J. Eq. 255, 38 Am. R. 378.

And in Florida it has been held that where a party owes the bank a note, and also has a credit to his deposit account for deposits made while the bank is solvent, and not in contemplation of its insolvency, and the bank officials and such party, after the bank becomes insolvent, enter the amount of the balance due such party on his deposit account as a credit on the note, such credit may be pleaded as a payment on the note in an action brought to recover on such note by a receiver subsequently appointed.

Robinson v. Aird, 43 Fla. 30, 29 So. 633.

But where a party indebted to a bank after it becomes insolvent purchases from certain depositors their deposits in the bank, and the amounts of such deposits so purchased are by the bank officials entered as credits on the debt owing by such party, such payments are invalid, and will not be binding on a receiver subsequently appointed, who sues to recover the debt owing by said party. Robinson v. Aird, 43 Fla. 30, 29 So. 633.

693 Hannon v. Williams, 34 N.J. Eq. 255, 38 Am. R. 378.

admissible to show the true nature of such a transaction.[694] And neither a depositor's pledge of his deposit book to a bank as collateral security, nor a bank's expectation at the time a debt is created that a depositor will apply his deposit in payment thereof, entitles the depositor to set off his deposit in payment of the debt.[695] But where a person indebted to a savings bank as a borrower deposits an amount less than the debt, intending to use such deposit as a payment upon the debt, the deposit can be set off against the debt.[696] And where there is an executed agreement by a depositor that his deposit shall be applied in payment of his debt, or where a deposit is a special deposit made to be withdrawn upon demand, a depositor may set off the deposit against his debt.[697] An agreement by a savings bank to hold the deposit of one party as security for the overdrafts of another, is not enforceable by the debtor after the bank's insolvency.[698] But where a savings bank procures a bank debtor to assume a liability to a depositor, agreeing to credit the bank debt with the amount paid by the debtor to the depositor, and the debtor legally assumes such liability with the consent of the depositor and the bank, the fact that before the payment to such depositor becomes due, the bank becomes insolvent and a receiver is appointed, will not affect the debtor's right to claim as a payment on his debt to the bank the amount paid by him to such depositor in pursuance of the arrangement in an action on the debt by the bank's receiver.[699]

In some states there are statutes authorizing the setoff of a deposit in a savings bank against a debt due the bank by the depositor.[700] But even under such a statute in an action by a savings bank against two persons on a joint

---

[694] Henderson v. Farmers' Sav. Bank, 199 Iowa 496, 202 N.W. 259.

[695] Hall v. Paris, 59 N.H. 71.

[696] Osborn v. Byrne, 43 Conn. 155, 21 Am. R. 641.

Borrowers receiving loans from bank's commercial department, whose notes were transferred before maturity and before bank's insolvency to savings department, to compensate for depreciation in market value of that department's investments, could, on bank's insolvency, set off deposits in both savings and commercial departments. Bassett v. City Bank, etc., Co., 115 Conn. 1, 160 A. 60, 81 A.L.R. 1488 (1932).

[697] Hall v. Paris, 59 N.H. 71.

[698] Van Dyck v. McQuade, 20 Hun 262, aff'd, 85 N.Y. 616.

[699] Robinson v. Aird, 43 Fla. 30, 29 So. 633.

[700] Van Wagoner v. Paterson Gaslight Co., 23 N.J.L. 283; North Bridgewater Sav. Bank v. Soule, 129 Mass. 528 (1880).

and several note, the defendants cannot set off the amounts severally due them from the bank.[701]

It has been held that depositors in the savings department of an insolvent bank may offset their deposits against their indebtedness to the bank where such depositors have no interest in the profits of the bank and are not liable for its losses.[702] But a depositor in the savings department of an insolvent trust company cannot set off his deposit in the commercial department or savings department against his debt to the company as a borrower from the savings department.[703] And under a statute providing that all assets of the savings department of a bank shall be held solely for repayment of the savings depositors, and not be used to pay any other obligation or liability of the bank until after such depositors are paid, a commercial depositor cannot set off his deposit against his debt to the savings department, but a savings deposit may be offset by a debt to the savings department or the commercial department, and a commercial deposit may be offset by a debt to the commercial department.[704]

Of Amount Appropriable to Stockholder's Stock.—An insolvent savings bank which has declared a pro rata distribution of its assets to its stockholders cannot set off an indebtedness due it by a deceased stockholder who was insolvent against the amount appropriable to such stockholder's stock; the right to such setoff is not given by a statute which does not apply to savings and deposit banks, but only to banks of issue.[705]

---

[701] Barnstable Sav. Bank v. Snow, 128 Mass. 512; Upham v. Bramwell, 105 Ore. 597, 209 P. 100, 210 P. 706, 25 A.L.R. 919.

[702] Upham v. Bramwell, 105 Ore. 597, 209 P. 100, 210 P. 706, 25 A.L.R. 919.

[703] Lippitt v. Thames Loan, etc., Co., 88 Conn. 185, 90 A. 369; Bassett v. City Bank, etc., Co., 115 Conn. 1, 160 A. 60, 81 A.L.R. 1488 (1932).

[704] Upham v. Bramwell, 105 Ore. 597, 209 P. 100, 210 P. 706, 25 A.L.R. 919; Kelly v. Allen, 239 Mass. 298, 131 N.E. 855; Reichert v. Farmers', etc., Sav. Bank, 257 Mich. 500, 242 N.W. 239, 81 A.L.R. 1461.

Depositor, whose unsecured note was transferred from commercial to savings department without knowledge of depositor after insolvency of bank and after depositor had been dissuaded from paying note, held entitled to require retransfer of note to commercial department and restoration of securities exchanged therefor to savings department and to set off liability on note against liability of bank on deposit in commercial department. Wilde v. Richards, 49 Wyo. 408, 55 P.2d 476.

[705] Merchants' Bank v. Shouse, 102 Pa. 488. See Appeal of Parrish, 133 Pa. 560, 19 A. 569.

§ 28. Parties to Actions.

Actions by Assignee.—An assignee of an insolvent savings bank may sue in his own name on a treasurer's bond.[706]

Actions by Receivers.—Receivers of savings banks may maintain suits in their own name or the bank's, and may purchase at an execution sale in favor of the bank.[707] Where a bank has become insolvent, a court may properly order that all its stockholders be joined in an action to determine their liabilities on their stock and for a general settlement of the affairs of the bank.[708] And although it is the general rule in equity that all persons interested in the subject matter of a litigation must be made parties, there are exceptions to this rule when it is impossible to give personal notice to all interested, and the notice given is the only one that can be given; such exceptions are applicable in a suit by a receiver of an insolvent savings bank to determine preferences claimed by depositors.[709] In an action by a receiver of a savings bank charging its managers with liability for loss resulting from an improper loan of bank funds to third parties, such third parties are not necessary parties to the suit.[710]

A receiver of a bank stands in the shoes of his bank for the purpose of paying taxes owed by it, and is the only person against whom proceedings may be instituted by a state to collect such taxes.[711]

Actions by Depositors.—A suit against the officers of a savings bank which has been placed in the hands of a receiver for mismanagement of its corporate affairs may be brought by its depositors on the refusal of the bank to do so, but since the damages recovered would be assets of the bank, the receiver is a necessary party.[712]

Actions by Creditors.—Under a statute authorizing courts to appoint assignees for insolvent savings banks, with power to collect and distribute among creditors the funds thereof, and empowering the courts to restrain

---

[706] Hall v. Brackett, 60 N.H. 215.

[707] Hobart v. Bennett, 77 Me. 401.

But it has been held that one styling himself a receiver of a savings bank could not, without showing special authority, sue in his own name the stockholders to enforce their individual liability. Herron v. Vance, 17 Ind. 595.

[708] Herron v. Vance, 17 Ind. 595.

[709] Dewey v. St. Albans Trust Co., 60 Vt. 1, 12 A. 224, 6 Am. St. R. 84.

[710] Dodd v. Wilkinson, 41 N.J. Eq. 566, 7 A. 337.

[711] People ex rel. Nelson v. Bank of Rushville, 271 Ill. App. 130 (1933).

[712] Chester v. Halliard, 34 N.J. Eq. 341, aff'd, 36 N.J. Eq. 313.

proceedings at law against such banks, the creditors of a bank in the hands of such an assignee cannot maintain a creditor's bill against a debtor of the bank.[713]

Actions by Commissioner of Banking.—A statute providing for the regulation and supervision of the banking business within a state may stipulate against authorization of the commissioner of banking to maintain an action to administer the affairs of an insolvent savings bank as against the creditors of the bank.[714]

Class or Representative Actions.—One person may file a creditor's suit, on behalf of himself and all other stockholders, creditors and depositors, against a savings bank that has ceased to do business and its president, for the settlement of its affairs and distribution of its assets.[715]

VIII. ACTIONS.

§ 29. General Considerations.

Right of Action.—The right to collect a chose in action is not less available against savings banks than against other debtors.[716] And an action by a depositor against a savings bank for failing to repay money deposited is predicated on the relationship of debtor and creditor.[717] In an action to recover the amount of a savings deposit credited to the plaintiff and a debtor of the bank wherein the bank asserted a right of set-off against the debtor, the

---

[713] Brown v. Folsom, 62 N.H. 527.

[714] Bergh v. Security Sav. Bank, 122 Wisc. 514, 100 N.W. 831.

[715] Finney v. Bennett, 68 Va. (27 Gratt.) 365.

[716] McCabe v. Union Dime Sav. Bank, 150 Misc. 157, 268 N.Y.S. 449.

Texas statute requiring foreign bank to obtain certificate of authority before it could maintain suit in Texas would infringe upon national bank's power as granted by federal banking statute that gave national banks the power to sue in any court of law and equity, as fully as natural persons; thus, federal statute preempted application of the state statute. In re Hibernia Nat'l Bank, 21 S.W.3d 908 (Tex. App. Corpus Christi 2000).

Although foreign corporation is generally required by Texas law to procure certificate of authority to have the right to transact business in Texas, national bank's suit to collect debt was the type of action that was exempted by statute from that requirement, and thus, bank had standing to bring the collection without first obtaining certificate of authority. In re Hibernia Nat'l Bank, 21 S.W.3d 908 (Tex. App. Corpus Christi 2000).

[717] Abate v. Bushwick Sav. Bank, 207 Misc. 372, 138 N.Y.S.2d 140.

bank's knowledge of plaintiff's interest in the deposit was not essential for a recovery.[718]

Conditions Precedent to Action.—The claim of a creditor of a savings bank need not be reduced to judgment before bringing an action against the directors of the bank for misappropriation of its funds.[719] And an action by a creditor of a savings bank against the directors thereof for misappropriation of its funds is not primarily an action to enforce an accounting, and a specific demand for an accounting need not be made.[720] Compliance with a bylaw of a savings bank requiring immediate written notice of the loss of a depositor's passbook is not a condition precedent to recovery of a deposit.[721]

Under the Financial Institutions Reform, Recovery and Enforcement Act, a former savings bank employee asserting a wrongful discharge action that was never suspended or stayed did not have to take affirmative action to continue the pending case within sixty days of expiration of the administrative review period; the requirement that the action be restored to active status could not apply to an action that was not inactive.[722]

Whether Remedy at Law or in Equity.—Under a statute making the trustees of a savings bank liable to creditors for any excess of indebtedness contracted over a certain amount, it has been held that the remedy is in equity alone for the benefit of all creditors.[723] It also has been held that a wife may not sue a savings bank at law to recover a deposit of her money made by her husband in his name in trust for her.[724]

---

[718] Peoples Bank v. Turner, 169 Md. 430, 182 A. 314, 103 A.L.R. 490.

[719] Winchester v. Howard, 136 Cal. 432, 64 P. 692, 69 P. 77, 89 Am. St. R. 153.

[720] Winchester v. Howard, 136 Cal. 432, 64 P. 692, 69 P. 77, 89 Am. St. R. 153.

[721] Mierke v. Jefferson County Sav. Bank, 134 N.Y.S. 44, aff'd, 135 N.Y.S. 1127.

[722] Rey v. Oak Tree Sav. Bank, 817 F. Supp. 634 (E.D. La. 1998).

See 12 U.S.C.S. § 1821(d)(6).

[723] **In general.—**

Hornor v. Henning, 93 U.S. 228, 23 L. Ed. 879.

Contra.—

But in Missouri it has been held that the liability of the directors of a savings bank, who have loaned to one person a sum greater than one-fourth of the bank's capital stock, contrary to statute, may be enforced by an action at law, where no accounting is necessary in order to determine the extent of the loss. Thompson v. Greeley, 107 Mo. 577, 17 S.W. 962 (1891).

[724] **In general.—**

Herpe v. Herpe, 89 Misc. 142, 151 N.Y.S. 503.

Whether Joint Action or Separate Actions Proper.—It has been held that if a person makes deposits in two separate accounts at a savings bank in trust for two of his children, the claims of the children against the bank after his death are several, not joint, and cannot be united in one action, and the fact that the bank at trial makes no objection to the joint action does not enable an appellate court to enter a judgment which the law does not warrant.[725] A joint action merely for the purpose of collecting the amount due on subscriptions to the capital stock of a savings bank cannot be maintained against all subscribers.[726] But the issue of title to money in a joint savings account in the name of a husband and wife, who had filed an action for separate maintenance, will not be confined to the dispute as between the husband and the bank; the court will also determine ownership of the money as between husband and wife.[727]

Accrual of Cause of Action.—Where a savings bank refuses payment to a depositor who has failed to comply with the bylaws and rules of the bank without requesting such compliance, the depositor's cause of action against the bank accrues immediately upon such refusal.[728] An action for recovery of a deposit brought against a savings bank within ninety days after a demand therefor has been made, is not premature, where the bank refused to pay, not on the ground that it was entitled to ninety days' notice, but on the ground that it had paid the money to another;[729] or where the notice provision was intended to apply to occasions of public distress, and there was no such occasion at the time of the bank's refusal to pay.[730]

Statute of Limitations and Laches.—Managers of a savings bank are trustees; therefore, if they commit a breach of trust, they cannot plead the statute of limitations.[731] For other cases dealing with statute of limitations[732] and laches[733] in actions involving savings banks, see the footnotes.

Action ex contractu.—

A savings bank depositor may sue in an action for breach of contract to enforce the bank's contractual obligation to use ordinary care in disbursing the depositor's funds. Offlen v. Maryland Nat'l Bank, 274 Md. 96, 333 A.2d 329 (1975).

[725] Ellison v. New Bedford, etc., Sav. Bank, 130 Mass. 48.

[726] Herron v. Vance, 17 Ind. 595.

[727] McGuire v. Benton State Bank, 232 Ark. 1008, 342 S.W.2d 77.

[728] Kenny v. Harlem Sav. Bank, 65 Misc. 466, 120 N.Y.S. 82.

[729] Abramowitz v. Citizens' Sav. Bank, 17 Misc. 297, 40 N.Y.S. 385.

[730] Mierke v. Jefferson County Sav. Bank, 134 N.Y.S. 44, aff'd, 135 N.Y.S. 1127.

[731] Williams v. McKay, 40 N.J. Eq. 189, 53 Am. R. 775.

Summons and Process.—See the footnote.[734]

Custody of Deposits Pending Suit.—Provision is sometimes made by statute for the custody of a fund in controversy in a suit against a savings bank for moneys on deposit, where persons claiming the fund who are plaintiffs in the action are made defendants thereto.[735] But it has been held that in an action against a savings bank for a deposit claimed by a third person added as a party defendant, the money need not be paid into court to await the final determination of the action, but should remain with the bank until such final determination, so as to be entitled to the same dividends as other deposits of the same class.[736]

---

[732] The New York banking law providing that actions against savings banks to recover deposits must be brought within 20 years, serves merely to fix the time limit within which action for unauthorized payments of funds may be prosecuted by a depositor against the savings bank but has no effect upon the rights of drawee and payee under a guarantee of genuineness. Teepell v. Jefferson County Sav. Bank, 3 Misc. 2d 508, 148 N.Y.S.2d 347.

Employees' claim for surplus money from company's preferred stock association was not an action for deposits therein, and thus action was not subject to statute exempting actions "against savings banks for deposits therein" from statute of limitations; all depositors received all money they had deposited plus agreed-upon interest on their deposits, and action pertained only to surplus that association had accumulated. Davies v. West Publ'g Co., 622 N.W.2d 836 (2001).

See also former Minn. St. § 50.17, which required the board of every savings bank with a surplus of 15 percent of its deposits to, at least once every three years, divide proportionately the excess among its depositors as an extra dividend. This requirement to pay the excess to depositors pro rata was eliminated following a 1995 amendment. The new language of § 50.17 does not discuss the distribution of surplus. Hauschildt v. Beckingham, 686 N.W.2d 829 (2004).

[733] Where depositor brought actions against banks to recover alleged balance due on savings accounts, which money had been collected by guardian of depositor's estate appointed in North Carolina, with reasonable promptness after his incarceration for two years in North Carolina mental hospital and his release from another hospital where he had been confined for injuries received in automobile accident depositor was not barred by laches from bringing present actions. Volpe v. Emigrant Industrial Sav. Bank, 99 N.Y.S.2d 6.

[734] Where plaintiff's writ in tort action against defendant issued as both an attachment and a capias, and trustee process, which was issued summoning savings bank as defendant's trustee to appear and make disclosure, was served on assistant treasurer of trustee on whom process could not be legally served, bank, which did not enter appearance and which did not waive service, was not before the court. Ackerman v. Kogut, 117 Vt. 40, 84 A.2d 131.

[735] Faivre v. Union Dime Sav. Inst., 59 N.Y. Super. 558, 13 N.Y.S. 423. See also McKeown v. Bank for Savings, 26 Misc. 824, 56 N.Y.S. 1080.

[736] Waterman v. Albany City Sav. Inst., 86 Misc. 274, 149 N.Y.S. 174.

Setoff—A bank sued by a depositor for the amount it withdrew from his savings account to cover his overdrafts on checking accounts could set off its claim for the overdrafts against the depositor's claim, where a debtor-creditor relationship existed between the parties as regards both accounts.[737]

Damages.—Under the rule that all damages for delay in the payment of money owing on a contract are provided for in the allowance of interest, a plaintiff recovering a judgment awarding moneys on deposit in a bank together with interest, could not also recover consequential damages allegedly sustained by the bank's failure to pay over the moneys on deposit.[738]

Damages were not presumed in an action by depositors to recover from the bank for negligent impoundment of their savings account deposit under a garnishment writ; the depositors were required to prove the elements of their damages without the aid of any presumption of injury to their credit.[739]

Review of the record established that the trial court did not err when it refused to direct a verdict in favor of a bank on its claim that exercising set off against plaintiff's savings account did not warrant award of punitive damages.[740]

Garnishment.—By statute, a creditor is provided with nearly an absolute right to garnish the funds held in an account by two or more parties when one of those parties is its debtor.[741] In the case of unmarried joint account holders, the non-debtor depositor is required to prove that all, or part of, the

---

[737] Pursiful v. First State Bank, 251 Ky. 498, 65 S.W.2d 462.

In depositor's suit for savings account which bank used to cover overdrafts on his checking accounts, bank's right to set-off overdrafts against withdrawals held not affected by fact checking account was used by depositor's wife in business he transferred to her where such transfer was unknown to bank. Pursiful v. First State Bank, 251 Ky. 498, 65 S.W.2d 462.

[738] Abate v. Bushwick Sav. Bank, 207 Misc. 372, 138 N.Y.S.2d 140.

[739] **In general.—**

Valley Nat'l Bank v. Brown, 110 Aria. 280, 517 P.2d 1256 (1974).

As proven damages, depositors were entitled to recover $1,010 from the bank, which had negligently impounded funds pursuant to a writ of garnishment despite knowledge that the depositors were innocent parties, for attorney's fees and costs to secure a court order releasing the funds, cost of wife's return trip from New York to Phoenix to attend to the matter, and interest on the impounded funds. Valley Nat'l Bank v. Brown, 110 Ariz. 260, 517 P.2d 1256 (1974).

[740] Young v. Mercantile Trust Co. Nat'l Ass'n, 598 8.W.2d 482 (Mo. App. 1980).

[741] Trustmark Nat'l Bank v. Sunshine Carwash No. 5 Partners, 558 S.W.3d 157 (Tenn. Ct. App. 2018). See T.C.A., § 45-2-703.

garnished-upon funds are directly attributable to him or her to the exclusion of the debtor depositor, for that portion of funds to be returned to the non-debtor depositor.[742] The Tennessee statute merely emphasizes that a creditor has, and still has, the right to garnish upon the funds in jointly-held bank accounts; it does not mean that the creditor ultimately will be entitled to keep the funds garnished upon. The creditor's right to keep the funds will depend upon the proof adduced at the hearing in the subsequently-filed separate action by the non-debtor depositor. In other words, the statute simply instructs banks to: (1) Pay the funds into court; (2) get out of the way and (3) let the non-debtor depositor fight it out with the creditor by showing such rights as that depositor may have with the funds.[743]

Even when the funds in the joint account is payable to either, i.e. accessible by all parties on the account, the second part of the statute still allows the non-debtor depositor to establish his or her right in the funds and request that those funds be returned by the creditor. Nothing in the section indicates that this mechanism is limited to the unusual situation wherein only one party currently has the right to access the funds, but the debtor maintains a survivorship interest in the account. To hold that a judgment creditor may garnish and keep the garnished funds from a joint account simply because the debtor has access to the account would essentially negate the non-debtor's right in all cases where the account is payable to either. Tennessee declines to interpret the statute in such a limited fashion that is inconsistent with the statute's plain language and intent.[744]

Costs.—A savings bank unjustifiably refuses to pay a deposit so that costs are properly chargeable against it, if although the name of a depositor is an assumed one, his identity is shown by the possession of a passbook and an affidavit of the fact.[745] A statute relating to costs in actions against savings

---

[742] Trustmark Nat'l Bank v. Sunshine Carwash No. 5 Partners, 558 S.W.3d 157, 2018 Tenn. App. LEXIS 179 (Tenn. Ct. App. 2018).

Non-debtor depositor was entitled to dismissal of a garnishment of execution and a release of the funds in a joint bank account because the depositor was the sole source of the funds at issue and the judgment debtor had no right in or to the funds outside of a business partnership with the depositor. Trustmark Nat'l Bank v. Sunshine Carwash No. 5 Partners, 558 S.W.3d 157, 2018 Tenn. App. LEXIS 179 (Tenn. Ct. App. 2018).

[743] Trustmark Nat'l Bank v. Sunshine Carwash No. 5 Partners, 558 S.W.3d 157, 2018 Tenn. App. LEXIS 179 (Tenn. Ct. App. 2018).

[744] Trustmark Nat'l Bank v. Sunshine Carwash No. 5 Partners, 558 S.W.3d 157 (Tenn. Ct. App. 2018).

[745] Davenport v. Bank of Sav. (N.Y.), 36 Hun 303.

banks does not empower a court to tax costs against a bank which acts solely as a stakeholder and does not make claim to a fund or dispute the plaintiff's title thereto.[746]

Counsel Fees.—Where savings banks make no claim to funds on deposit to which adverse claims have been made, and desire only that final adjudication be had with respect to ownership of the deposits, a claimant who is awarded the deposits cannot recover from the banks counsel fees expended in the litigation.[747]

§ 30. Parties.

To Actions against Bank.—The assignee of a deposit book issued by a savings bank cannot maintain an action on it in his own name against the bank.[748] But one to whom a depositor in a savings bank has given a bankbook and an order for payment of a deposit may, after due notice to the bank on the death of the depositor, and payment by the bank to the administrator, recover the amount in an action against the bank brought in the name of the administrator without his assent.[749] In some states there are statutes prescribing who may be made a defendant in an action against a savings bank to recover a deposit.[750] For other cases involving parties to actions against a savings bank, see the footnote.[751]

To Actions against Directors, Officers and Trustees of Bank.—A creditor of a savings bank may sue the directors thereof for misappropriation of its funds, although he becomes a creditor after the misappropriation.[752]

---

[746] Friedman v. North Side Sav. Bank, 27 N.Y.S.2d 608 (New York statute).

[747] Abate v. Bushwick Sav. Bank, 207 Misc. 372, 138 N.Y.S.2d 140.

[748] Howard v. Windham County Sav. Bank, 40 Vt. 597. As to parties to actions after bank has been placed in hands of receiver, see § 28 of this chapter.

[749] Foes v. Lowell, etc., Sav. Bank, 111 Mass. 285.

[750] Pierce v. Boston, etc., Sav. Bank, 125 Mass. 593.

[751] **County claiming by escheat not necessary party.—**

In suit by alleged donee of moneys in savings accounts against banking institutions, public administrator of county, and unknown heirs of deceased donor to recover the moneys in the savings accounts, on ground that donor gave donee savings account books and stated that he wanted donee to have all his money, county, which claimed the moneys in the savings accounts by escheat, was not a necessary party to the suit, and failure to join the county as a party did not render the judgment in favor of the donee void. Boghosian v. Mid-City Nat'l Bank, 25 Ill. App. 2d 455, 167 N.E.2d 442.

[752] Winchester v. Howard, 136 Cal. 432, 64 P. 692, 69 P. 77, 89 Am. St. R. 153, also holding that this action may be brought by any one creditor, independent of the others, especially where it does not appear that there are other creditors.

Similarly, the assignee of a savings bank depositor can maintain an action against the directors of such bank for misappropriation of funds.[753] But the authorities differ as to whether a creditor of a savings bank can maintain an action at law against its directors for damages resulting from their negligence in the management and disposition of the bank's moneys and property.[754] Directors of a savings bank may also be liable to an action at law for damages resulting from false representations made or caused to be made by them, and perhaps from acts done or caused to be done by them, with intent to deceive and defraud.[755] Under at least one state statute, the auditor of the state is the only person authorized to maintain an action against the officers and trustees of savings banks for violation of their statutory duties.[756] The trustees of a savings bank may be sued for exceeding their authority in making an unsafe loan, without joining the borrowers who had no knowledge of the breach of trust by the trustees as parties defendant.[757] And in an action against the trustees of a savings bank, the legal personal representatives of a deceased trustee are properly joined.[758]

Allegations of fraud and breach of fiduciary duty in preparation of proxy materials regarding the conversion of a mutual savings bank to a stock corporation and subsequent merger could only be asserted against the individual trustees in their individual capacities, and only damages could be sought.[759]

Substitution of Parties.—Where, in an action against a savings bank to recover a deposit by an alleged donee thereof, an order is made substituting the depositor's administrator as a defendant, it is proper for the court, in its discretion, to direct that the passbook be surrendered to the bank.[760]

Interpleader.—A savings bank cannot interplead an adverse claimant of a deposit who claims by a title superior to that of the depositor, where such

---

[753] Winchester v. Howard, 136 Cal. 432, 64 P. 692, 69 P. 77, 89 Am. St. R. 153.

[754] Marshall v. Farmers', etc., Sav. Bank, 85 Va. 676, 8 S.E. 586, 17 Am. St. R. 84, 2 L.R.A. 534, holding such action may be maintained.

In West Virginia, the contrary has been held. Zinn v. Mendel, 9 W. Va. 580.

[755] Zinn v. Mendel, 9 W. Va. 580.

[756] Ryan v. Ray, 105 Ind. 101, 4 N.E. 214.

[757] Paine v. Barnum, 59 How. Pr. 303.

[758] Paine v. Irwin (N.Y.), 59 How. Pr. 316.

[759] In re East New York Sav. Bank Depositors Litigation, 547 N.Y.S.2d 497 (N.Y. Sup. Ct. 1989).

[760] Quinn v. Bank, 86 N.Y.S. 285.

adverse claimant does not proceed by process of law to enforce his rights.[761] It may be prescribed by statute that before interpleader will be permitted in an action against a bank to recover a deposit, the affidavits and papers on which the motion is founded must set out facts showing that there is some foundation or plausibility for the claim asserted to the fund, or there is justification for a reasonable doubt in the mind of the movant as to the claim's validity.[762] Under the New York statute, if an action is brought against a savings bank to recover moneys on deposit, and any persons not parties to the action claim the same fund, the court may, on petition of the bank, make such claimants parties defendant.[763] And assuming that a

---

[761] German Sav. Bank v. Friend, 20 N.Y.S. 434, 48 N.Y. St. R. 400, 61 N.Y. Super. 400; Edwards v. Greenwich Sav. Bank, 109 N.Y.S. 721.

[762] Mars v. Albany Sav. Bank, 19 N.Y.S. 791, 64 Hun 424, 46 N.Y. St. R. 464, aff'd, 69 Hun 398, 23 N.Y.S. 658, 53 N.Y. St. R. 144.

[763] **In general.—**

Mahro v. Greenwich Sav. Bank, 16 Misc. 537, 40 N.Y.S. 29, 74 N.Y. St. R. 639; McKeown v. Bank, 26 Misc. 824, 56 N.Y.S. 1080; Quinn v. Bank, 86 N.Y.S. 285; McGuire v. Auburn Sav. Bank, 78 App. Div. 22, 79 N.Y.S. 91; Booke v. Dime Sav. Bank, 204 Misc. 840, 127 N.Y.S.2d 59.

An application under this statute is not an application for an interpleader. Mahro v. Greenwich Sav. Bank, 16 Misc. 537, 40 N.Y.S. 29, 74 N.Y. St. R. 639.

It is only essential that such application make it appear that the person sought to be made defendant claims the fund in suit, and it need not state facts showing the nature of his claim. Mahro v. Greenwich Sav. Bank, 16 Misc. 537, 40 N.Y.S. 29, 74 N.Y. St. R. 639.

The purpose of the statute was to relieve bank from two or more litigations over same deposits and danger of having to pay deposits to two or more different persons. Back v. Bowery Sav. Bank, 162 Misc. 403, 294 N.Y.S. 818.

The statute has no application where persons claiming the fund in suit have only a future interest, and not a present right to the fund. Gifford v. Oneida Sav. Bank, 99 App. Div. 25, 90 N.Y.S. 693.

Where an administrator sued for savings deposits made by his intestate in defendant's bank in her name "in trust for T.H.," plaintiff having alleged that the name "T.H." was fictitious, that the deposits were really made by decedent for her own benefit, and that the defendant knew this to be true, plaintiff's case depends on her proving such allegations, and defendant is not, therefore, entitled under the statute, to an order making T.H. and other parties defendants. Washington v. Seamen's Bank, 29 Misc. 492, 61 N.Y.S. 971, aff'd, 47 App. Div. 625, 62 N.Y.S. 1150.

Where depositor had $4,000 on deposit, bankbook was lost or stolen and came into possession of depositor's husband, bank was notified, thereafter bank paid $4,000 to depositor's husband as result of alleged forgery by husband, and husband deposited the $4,000 in bank in his own name in trust for daughter, and depositor brought action against bank, on ground of negligence, bank was not entitled to implead husband under the statute.

defendant in an action to recover money on deposit in a savings bank is entitled to notice of a proceeding to make other claimants of the fund parties defendant, an ex parte order so doing must stand until vacated upon application, the court having jurisdiction of the parties and the subject matter.[764]

§ 31. Pleading—In Actions Against Bank.

Complaint.—In order to institute an action for an asserted breach of contract by the bank in refusing to make the payment of money in a savings account, the passbook holder was required to file a formal complaint and permit the bank to interpose a formal answer.[765] A complaint in an action to recover money from a savings bank, alleging that certain money, the property of plaintiff, was deposited with the bank by a third party, and that the bank refuses to pay over the money on demand, is defective in failing to allege that the bank knew that the money was the plaintiff's, or that it was left for his benefit or in trust for him.[766] A complaint in an action against a savings bank for a refusal to pay on demand is sufficient without anticipating the defense of nonproduction and presentation of a passbook, and alleging its loss or facts excusing the nonproduction.[767] In an action to recover a savings deposit, a complaint alleging that a bank purchased notes on which it had applied the deposit after maturity and with knowledge that plaintiff's execution thereof was induced by fraud and that plaintiff denied liability

---

Booke v. Dime Sav. Bank, 204 Misc. 840, 127 N.Y.S.2d 59.

Applied in Gottschall v. German Sav. Bank, 45 Misc. 27, 90 N.Y.S. 896.

Where the fund in controversy is deposited in the name of plaintiff and another, defendant is entitled, under the statute, to have the latter made a party. McKeown v. Bank, 26 Misc. 824, 56 N.Y.S. 1080.

Failure to secure restraining order or execute bond.—

In husband's action to recover savings deposit to which wife assorted adverse claim, bank held entitled to amend proceedings by making wife party defendant, notwithstanding wife's failure to procure restraining order, injunction, or other appropriate process or to execute bonds to savings bank as provided by interpleader statute, in view of court's discretion under statute to grant or refuse interpleader on showing that claim was baseless, as against contention that statutory provision that claimant secure order or execute bond imposed mandatory requirement. Back v. Bowery Sav. Bank, 162 Misc. 403, 294 N.Y.S. 818.

[764] Szirtes v. Bly, 185 App. Div. 274, 172 N.Y.S. 802.

[765] Stern v. Chemical Bank, 372 N.Y.S.2d 913 (Civ. Ct. 1975).

[766] Crosby v. Bowery Sav. Bank, 67 How. Pr. 329, 50 N.Y. Super. 453.

[767] Mierke v. Jefferson County Sav. Bank, 208 N.Y. 347, 101 N.E. 889, 46 L.R.A. (n.s.) 194, 1914D Ann. Cas. 21; Grill v. Manhattan Sav. Inst., 148 Misc. 181, 265 N.Y.S. 610.

thereon because of such fraud, was held to state a cause of action.[768] And a complaint alleging that a depositor's tenant withdrew funds from the depositor's savings account without the necessary passbook or power of attorney and without the depositor's knowledge or authorization, and paid the money withdrawn to the depositor for rent, states a claim against a bank.[769] Where both plaintiff wife and defendant bank, which allegedly wrongfully refused to pay the wife money deposited in a savings account opened by her husband, presented their case on the basis that the husband's daughter by a prior marriage had no interest in the account, although her name appeared on the passbook, the case would be considered on that basis.[770]

In a proceeding by quo warranto against a savings bank prosecuted for usury, an allegation that the bank purchased negotiable bills at amounts exceeding the current rates of exchange, with a view to evading its charter restrictions as to interest, is insufficient to charge usury, where the charter merely restricted the interest to be charged on notes, and did not affect purchases of bills of exchange at whatever rates might be agreed upon between the bank and those dealing with it.[771]

Sufficiency of Pleadings.—Where counts of a complaint against the depositary bank which disbursed a depositor's funds to a person who presented the depositor's passbook and a forged withdrawal slip were in contract, and the case was tried predominantly on the issue of whether the depositary bank breached its contractual duty to exercise ordinary care in honoring the withdrawal slip, the depositary bank's alleged conversion of a cashier's check which had been issued to the person making the withdrawal was not a matter cognizable under the pleadings.[772]

Defenses; Answer and Reply.—Where, in an action to recover a savings bank deposit, to escape a default and before moving to have an adverse claimant of the deposit made a party defendant, a bank answers, denying the possession of the amount claimed, the answer does not affect the bank's right to such relief.[773] Where, in an action by a creditor against a bank, the defense of ultra vires of the contract incurring the indebtedness is pleaded to the

---

[768] Stelling v. Wachovia Bank & Trust Co., 208 N.C. 838, 181 S.E. 560.

[769] Rivera v. Central Bank & Trust Co., 155 Cole. 383, 395 P.2d 11 (1964).

[770] Stillings v. Citizens Bank of Ava, 637 S.W.2d 401 (Mo. App. 1982).

[771] State v. Boatmen's Sav. Inst., 48 Mo. 189.

[772] Gillen v. Maryland Nat'l Bank, 274 Md. 96, 333 L.2d 329 (1975).

[773] Quinn v. Bank, 88 N.Y.S. 285.

plaintiff's complaint only, and the answer to the pleading of an intervener claiming as an attaching creditor of the plaintiff's assignor, merely denies any indebtedness to the assignee, a finding of ultra vires required by the evidence should be against the intervenor as well as the plaintiff, it appearing that such intervener was not harmed by the omission to again plead ultra vires and that the court treated it as properly pleaded against him.[774] For other cases dealing with defenses and answers and replies in actions against savings banks, see the footnote.[775]

§ 32. Pleading—In Actions Against Directors, Officers or Stockholders of Bank.

Complaint or Bill.—Where the directors of a savings bank are sued for damages resulting from false representations made or caused to be made, or acts done or caused to be done by them, and relied on by the plaintiff the false representations or acts, and the intent thereby to deceive and defraud the plaintiff, must be averred in positive terms.[776] Where a bill filed by a

---

[774] Laidlaw v. Pacific Bank, 137 Cal. 392, 70 P. 277.

[775] **Specificity of answer.—**

Allegations that the depositor's son, when receiving the money, gave correct answers and that defendant exercised due diligence in examining a signature of the depositor, are too specific. In such a case, the bank should plead that it did all that a reasonably prudent person would have done. Noah v. Bowery Sav. Bank, 225 N.Y. 284, 122 N.E. 235.

Setoff.—

In action to recover amount of savings deposit entered in name of two persons or survivor, plea alleging entry of deposit as described and taking over one of depositor's notes in reliance upon right of setoff against deposit held demurrable as insufficient to show right to setoff. Peoples Bank v. Turner, 169 Md. 430, 182 A. 314, 103 A.L.R. 490.

Waiver.—

In corporation's action against savings bank for balance due on plaintiff's deposits with defendant, defendant's pleading alleging that deposit book was not presented, as required by defendant's bylaw, when plaintiff's executive officer fraudulently withdrew moneys from deposit, but that defendant accepted receipt, signed by such officer as defendant's treasurer, asserted in effect a claim of "waiver" of such requirement. Mutual Assurance Co. v. Norwich Sav. Soc., 128 Conn. 510, 24 A.2d 477, 139 A.L.R. 829.

Reply attempting to set up waiver of presentation of passbook by placing refusal to pay on another ground was held insufficient because it did not allege defendant's knowledge of loss or destruction of passbook. Wood v. Connecticut Sav. Bank, 87 Conn. 341, 87 A. 983.

[776] Zinn v. Mendel, 9 W. Va. 580.

Chapter 11 trustee was entitled to amend complaint to state breach of fiduciary duty claim against investment banker, which was hired to advise debtor in connection with acquisition

receiver charges that defendants, as managers of a savings bank, improperly loaned bank funds without adequate security, and that the receiver was compelled to accept in settlement securities worth considerably less than the loan, a loss is sufficiently averred although the securities have not been converted into cash.[777] Where a statute requires persons seeking to organize a bank to file with the secretary of state a certificate specifying, among other things, the name, residence and amount of shares of each stockholder, a suit to enforce the liability of stockholders on their subscriptions and settle the affairs of a savings bank which has become insolvent, should be based on such certificate flied with the complaint.[778]

Demurrer.—Where a bill in equity avers a long and systematic violation of a savings bank charter by the bank's president and committeemen, the bank's managers cannot demur on the ground that the misconduct was not traced to them.[779]

§ 33. Evidence.

Presumptions and Inferences.—In an action against a savings bank to recover a deposit, plaintiff need not show that, by the rules of his bank a depositor was entitled to his money without prior notice, as there is no legal presumption that a bank has a rule entitling it to prior notice.[780] In an action by a guardian of a minor against a bank for an amount deposited to the minor's credit and paid out by the bank to the minor's stepfather without written authority, the fact that the money was deposited to the credit of the minor is prima facie evidence that it belonged to him, though such presumption can be overcome by evidence.[781] In an action by the administratrix of a savings bank depositor against another depositor in such bank to

---

of another company in which the investment banker may have owed duty to debtor, as: (1) Investment banker was hired to advise debtor in type of transaction with which debtor had no experience; (2) investment banker suspended efforts to secure financing for debtor's merger even though banker may have had duty to continue its financing efforts and (3) banker failed to provide debtor with reliable information regarding transaction. In re Daisy Sys. Corp., 97 F.3d 1171 (9th Cir. 1996).

[777] Dodd v. Wilkinson, 41 N.J. Eq. 566, 7 A. 337.

[778] Herron v. Vance, 17 Ind. 595.

[779] Williams v. McKay, 40 N.J. Eq. 189, 53 Am. R. 775.

Prima facie, in such case, the managers must be presumed to have known of the conduct of the president and committeemen, and they are liable for injury from want of ordinary care. Williams v. McKay, 40 N.J. Eq. 189, 53 Am. R. 775.

[780] Weld v. Eliot Five Cents Sav. Bank, 158 Mass. 389, 33 N.E. 519.

[781] Gibson v. First Nat'l Bank, 213 Mo. App. 63, 245 S.W. 1072.

recover an amount which had stood in the decedent's name, but had been changed to stand in the name of both depositors as a joint account payable to either or the survivor, the court must assume that the accounts were merged by consent, indicating an intention to declare property rights.[782] Savings deposits made fifty years before a depositor's death, on which no demand for payment had been made, nor books presented for entries at times required by bank rules, are presumed paid.[783] And where a depositor had made a series of withdrawals on orders executed by her mark which was witnessed and acknowledged, and only the last order was questioned, the inference is that the other orders were regular and proper.[784]

Burden of Proof.—One who seeks to charge as a partner, a person who has purchased stock in an organized bank doing business as a savings bank, has the burden of proving that the bank was a partnership.[785] A savings bank has the burden of showing good faith and reasonable care in paying a depositor's funds on presentation of a passbook and an order for payment,[786] regardless

---

[782] McNett v. Crandall, 172 App. Div. 375, 158 N.Y.S. 1020.

[783] Morse v. National Central Bank, 150 Md. 142, 132 A. 598.

[784] **In general.—**

Otto v. Western Sav. Fund Soc., 343 Pa. 615, 23 A.2d 462.

Inference as to bank's liability.—

Whose bank employee testified that resolution was altered after it was in bank's custody and testimony was uncontroverted and no reason appeared for doubting accuracy of observation of credibility of witness, statement should be accepted as true and was sufficient to create an inference as to bank's liability to plaintiff corporation which charged bank was wrongfully paying out savings account to individual defendants without authority to do so and with dishonoring check. Indianapolis Saenger Chor, Inc. v. American Fletcher Nat'l Bank & Trust Co., 274 N.E.2d 728 (Ind. App. 1971).

[785] In re Gibbs' Estate, 157 Pa. 59, 27 A. 383, 22 L.RA. 276; Pease's Appeal, 157 Pa. 75, 27 A. 386.

[786] Fourth, etc., Trust Co. v. Rowe, 122 Ohio St. 1, 170 N.E. 439; Noah v. Bowery Sav. Bank, 225 N.Y. 284, 122 N.E. 235; Daivish v. Farmers', etc., Sav. Bank, 177 Minn. 243, 225 N.W. 100; Bulakowski v. Philadelphia Sav. Fund Soc., 270 Pa. 538, 113 A. 553.

Bank had burden of showing due care in permitting withdrawals by depositor's husband, who allegedly forged withdrawal slips. Tribulas v. Continental Equitable Title, etc., Co., 331 Pa. 283, 200 A. 659.

Where savings bank defends action by its depositor for recovery of amount paid from depositor's account on ground that the debt has been paid to a person presenting a passbook, it bears the burden of proving such defense and must establish by preponderance of the evidence that, under the circumstances, it exercised due care and diligence in ascertaining the identity of the person to whom it has given the money. Novak v. Greater New York Sav. Bank, 30 N.Y.2d 136, 331 N.Y.S.2d 377, 282 N.E.2d 285 (N.Y. Ct. App. 1972).

of provisions in the bylaws of the bank.[787] Where a bank has complied with its own regulations, the burden is on the depositor to prove that the bank was negligent.[788] And the defense that a deposit sued for was withdrawn on the depositor's order alleged to be a forgery is affirmative, and must therefore be proven by a bank.[789] But a depositor, after establishing that a withdrawal order was a forgery, has the burden of proving that defendant bank's employees failed to exercise ordinary care in comparing signatures before paying out money.[790] And where a depositor's passbook shows payment, and the depositor testifies that the money was not paid, the burden of proving payment is on the bank.[791] In an action against a savings bank to recover money deposited by the plaintiff, which the bank refused to pay on the ground that it had been paid to a third person presenting a passbook, plaintiff does not have the burden of showing negligence by the bank.[792]

But the burden of proving that a holder of certificates in a savings and loan association is not entitled to payment under provisions applicable to withdrawals by such holders is on the association.[793] For other cases relating to burden of proof in actions by or against savings banks, see the footnote.[794]

Where bank knew that owner of passbook was in penitentiary at time withdrawals were made from his savings account by his sister, burden was upon bank to establish that it was free from negligence in permitting withdrawals in order to be relieved from liability to owner. Weigel v. First Nat. Bank (La. App.), 20 So.2d 21.

[787] Berndt v. Hoboken Bank for Sav., 103 N.J.L. 478, 185 A. 818.

[788] Layman v. Western Sav. Bank, 302 Pa. Super. 433, 448 A.2d 1119 (1982).

[789] Fourth & Cent. Trust Co. v. Rowe, 122 Ohio St. 1, 170 N.E. 439.

[790] Saji v. Philadelphia Sav. Fund Soc., 112 Pa. Super. 149, 170 A. 334.

[791] Berndt v. Hoboken Bank for Sav., 103 N.J.L. 478, 135 A. 818; Robison v. Upton, 12 Ohio C.C. (n.s.) 314, 21 Ohio Cir. Dec. 330.

[792] Abramowitz v. Citizens' Sav. Bank, 17 Misc. 297, 40 N.Y.S. 385. But see Israel v. Bowery Sav. Bank (N.Y.), 9 Daly 507.

[793] Wallis v. Eagle Sav. & Loan Co., 180 App. Div. 719, 168 N.Y.S. 513; Rimkus v. Tananevics, 207 Ill. App. 96; Bulakowski v. Philadelphia Sav. Fund Soc., 270 Pa. 538, 113 A. 553.

[794] **Burden of proving incompetency of depositor,** in relation to contract relating to savings account, rested with bank which sought to invalidate the instrument. Simmons First Nat'l Bank v. Luzader, 438 S.W.2d 25 (Ark. 1969).

Burden of proving inaccuracy of bankbook.—

Where defense, in suit by spouses to recover $465 allegedly owing to them from defendant bank by virtue of a savings account, was based on proposition that deposit book balance did not represent true state of the account, bank was required to come forth with

Admissibility.—Where one deposits money in a savings bank to the credit of another, retains the deposit book himself, and notes upon it that the money could be paid to him, evidence is admissible upon his death to show his intent in making the deposit.[795] Similarly, where one deposits money in his own name as trustee for another, evidence of his acts and declarations is admissible upon his death to show whether he intended to create a trust.[796] In an action on a loan which plaintiff alleges is usurious, evidence of the nature of the lending institution is admissible.[797] And the admission of evidence tending to raise the presumption of payment of a savings deposit made fifty years before a depositor's death, is not reversible error.[798] In an action against a savings bank on an account annexed, to recover the amount of a deposit, a deposit book is admissible to show the amount received by the bank, although such book contains printed conditions of deposit and payment.[799] In an action against a bank by a husband for money paid to his wife from his account, evidence that his wife frequently made deposits on his account, presenting his bankbook and drawing money from the bank for her husband, and that the bank had no notice of any change in the relationship between the husband and wife, is admissible to show whether the wife had actual or implied authority from her husband to draw on his

---

some evidence to that effect. Tate v. Sears Bank & Trust Co., 90 Ill. App. 2d 382, 234 N.E.2d 126 (1967).

Burden of proving discharge of debt.—

In a suit by a widow, as individual and as administratrix of her husband's estate, to recover money deposited in the defendant bank in an alleged joint savings account of husband and wife, wherein son claimed ownership of the deposit on the theory that the account was in husband's name and son's name, admission by the bank that the husband was owner of the moneys deposited established relation of debtor and creditor between the bank and the husband, and the bank assumed the burden of showing it had discharged its debt to the husband or his representative. Sides v. Citizens Nat. Bank, 246 N.C. 672, 100 S.E.2d 67.

Burden to show that payments reached surviving joint tenant.—

In action brought by administrator of estate of deceased who had been the surviving joint tenant of a savings account against bank to recover proceeds of account which allegedly had been paid to administrator of predeceased joint tenant, burden was upon bank to establish not only that its payments reached surviving joint tenant, but that they were received by him on account of bank's indebtedness. Hollman v. Exeter Banking Co., 266 A.2d 209 (N.H. 1970).

[795] Northrop v. Hale, 72 Me. 275.

[796] Gerrish v. New Bedford Institution for Sav., 128 Mass. 159, 35 Am. R. 365; Brabrook v. Boston Five Cents Sav. Bank, 104 Mass. 228, 8 Am. R. 222 (1870).

[797] Ficken v. Bank of Cerro Gordo, 25 Ga. App. 644, 104 S.E. 14.

[798] Morse v. National Cent. Bank, 150 Md. 142, 132 A. 598.

[799] Brown v. Abington Sav. Bank, 119 Mass. 69.

account.[800] And in an action against a savings bank to recover a deposit, evidence that the depositor whose bankbook had been stolen and the balance therein paid to the thief, was at the time of his death about two and a half months after such money was drawn, possessed of only a small amount of money, was properly admitted as tending to negative the bank's position that such depositor, or someone with whom he was in collusion to defraud the bank, drew such money.[801]

In an action against a savings bank by a depositor to recover money paid to a third party from his account, evidence of the third party as to whether another bank refused to pay a check which she took to it with the depositor's name signed thereto, is inadmissible.[802] And, in such a case, statements of the plaintiff's counsel to such third party, not reflecting upon either of the issues, are improperly admitted.[803]

For other instances of evidence held admissible[804] or inadmissible,[805] see the footnotes.

---

[800] Moline State Sav. Bank v. Liggett, 106 Ill. App. 223.

[801] Brown v. Merrimack River Sav. Bank, 67 N.H. 549, 39 A. 336, 68 Am. St. R. 700.

[802] Commonwealth Bank v. Goodman, 128 Md. 452, 97 A. 1005.

[803] Commonwealth Bank v. Goodman, 128 Md. 452, 97 A. 1005.

[804] In action to recover amount of savings deposit entered in name of two persons or survivor, wherein bank claimed right to setoff against debt of one of depositors, evidence that money originally deposited in bank belonged to plaintiff, and that she held possession of passbook and all withdrawals were made by her or for her, and that other depositor never added to deposit, held admissible to establish right of plaintiff in opposition to right of setoff. Peoples Bank v. Turner, 169 Md. 430, 182 A. 314, 103 A.L.R. 490.

[805] In action on savings deposit liability assumed by national bank purchasing assets and assuming liabilities of state bank, lists of savings depositors, commercial accounts, and time deposits of state bank held properly excluded, since lists would not have been binding on plaintiffs. Blakeley v. First Nat'l Bank, 151 Ore. 655, 51 P.2d 1034.

In action on savings deposit liability assumed by national bank purchasing assets and assuming liabilities of state bank, refusal to permit state superintendent of banks to testify as to whether he ever approved assumption by purchasing bank of embezzlement liability or liability for nonexistent deposit or liability in selling bank by purchasing bank held not error. Blakeley v. First Nat'l Bank, 151 Ore. 655, 51 P.2d 1034.

In action to recover amount of savings deposit entered in name of plaintiff and debtor of bank wherein defendant claimed right of setoff against debtor, evidence offered by defendant that it had no knowledge of facts tending to prove plaintiff's separate interest in deposit held inadmissible. Peoples Bank of Denton v. Turner, 169 Md. 430, 182 A. 314, 103 A.L.R. 490.

Where the counts of a complaint against a depositary bank which disbursed the depositor's funds to a person who presented the depositor's passbook and a forged withdrawal slip were in contract, and the case was tried predominantly on the issue whether the depositary bank

Weight and Sufficiency.—For cases relating to the weight of the evidence and its sufficiency to prove particular facts, in actions by or against savings banks, against the officers or stockholders of such banks, or between persons claiming money deposited in such banks, see the footnote.[806]

---

breached its contractual duty to exercise ordinary care in honoring the withdrawal slip, the depositary bank's alleged conversion of a cashier's check which had been issued to the person making the withdrawal was not a matter cognizable under the pleadings. Gillen v. Maryland Nat'l Bank, 274 Md. 96, 333 A.2d 329 (1975).

[806] **Evidence held to show bank's negligence.—**

A finding that a savings bank was negligent in paying plaintiff's deposit to a person who presented the passbook and answered correctly as to all information given by plaintiff when he opened the account is supported by evidence that the paying teller knew plaintiff by sight. Geitelsohn v. Citizens' Sav. Bank, 19 Misc. 422, 44 N.Y.S. 89, aff'd, 20 Misc. 84, 45 N.Y.S. 90.

In depositor's action to recover payment from his savings deposit to one who had stolen his passbook and presented a withdrawal receipt, evidence that when the receipt was first presented to the bank the depositor's signature had been misspelled, but was corrected by the thief upon his attention being called to it by the teller, held to sustain finding that the bank did not exercise due care in making the payment. Boguslawski v. Mitchell Street State Bank, 180 Wis. 295, 192 N.W. 1001.

In action to recover money allegedly wrongfully paid from plaintiff's savings account, evidence that plaintiff's daughter withdrew certain sums from account on forged withdrawal slips, that plaintiff told bank not to give money out from the account to anyone except herself and another daughter, and thereafter 16 withdrawals were made by daughter on forged slips over a two-month period, conclusively established bank's negligence. Connolly v. Manchester Sav. Bank, 92 N.H. 89, 25 A.2d 412 (N.H. 1942).

Bank held negligent in paying on forged orders.—

Robesteien v. Franklin Sav. Bank, 152 N.Y.S. 227.

Evidence supported finding that savings and loan which purchased participation in loan was negligent in failing to detect fraud of savings bank which sold participation in loan where: (1) Loan agreement referred to option to extend loan, so careful review of documents would have notified buyer that loan term was or could be more than one year; (2) savings and loan's president was given access to selling lender's files and (3) president should have been alerted to some irregularity by fact that only 9 of 29 planned buildings were under construction when he inspected site. First Federal Sav. & Loan Asso. v. Twin City Sav. Bank, FSB, 868 F.2d 725 (5th Cir. 1989).

Evidence held to show want of good faith in permitting embezzlement.—

In action by trustee against savings bank for amount of trust deposit which bank permitted trustee to embezzle, evidence showed that bank did not act in good faith and without knowledge of trustee's sinister conduct. Liffiton v. National Sav. Bank, 267 App. Div. 32, 44 N.Y.S.2d 770, aff'd, 293 N.Y. 799, 59 N.E.2d 35.

Evidence held to show bank not negligent in making payment.—

Kelly v. Buffalo Sav. Bank, 88 App. Div. 374, 84 N.Y.S. 642, 14 N.Y. Ann. Cas. 81,

(Text continued on page 193)

---

rev'd, 180 N.Y. 171, 72 N.E. 995, 105 Am. St. R. 720, 69 L.R.A. 317; Myerowich v. Emigrant Industrial Sav. Bank, 184 App. Div. 668, 172 N.Y.S. 540; Bulakowski v. Philadelphia Sav. Fund Soc., 270 Pa. 538, 113 A. 553; Paddock v. Anglo-California Trust Co., 107 Cal. App. 430, 290 P. 550 (1930); Felman v. Schiff, 186 Ill. App. 67; Krishkan v. New York Sav. Bank, 93 Misc. 52, 156 N.Y.S. 298.

Negligence in paying out deposit on forged withdrawal order held not shown by the evidence.—

Johnbaptist v. East Side Sav. Bank, 246 A.D. 569, 282 N.Y.S. 838 (1935).

Where a savings society paid out money on an order signed by the mark of the depositor, duly witnessed and acknowledged, accompanied by the passbook and otherwise in strict accordance with the rules, and there was no proof by the depositor's administratrix that the order was forged, or that the depositor was of unsound mind, or that the society failed to exercise ordinary care in making the payment, the action of the administratrix to recover the money failed for want of proof. Otto v. Western Sav. Fund Soc., 343 Pa. 615, 23 A.2d 462.

Rule of savings bank's liability for negligence in failing to discover forged draft is that, if the discrepancy between signature on draft and that of depositor on passbook or in signature book was not marked or apparent, or would require a critical examination to detect failure to discover, it is not negligent. Noah v. Bank for Savings, 171 App. Div. 191, 157 N.Y.S. 324.

That signature on draft does not precisely resemble that of depositor written in signature book does not impute culpable negligence to the savings bank for failing to detect forgery. Noah v. Bank for Sav., 171 App. Div. 191, 157 N.Y.S. 324.

Evidence of bank's negligence held insufficient to warrant submission to jury.—

Bulakowski v. Philadelphia Sav. Fund Soc., 270 Pa. 538, 113 A. 553.

Evidence that savings society was negligent in comparing signatures held insufficient for jury. Saji v. Philadelphia Sav. Fund Soc., 112 Pa. Super. 149, 170 A. 334.

When the bank's assistant teller who paid the money to an imposter testifies that he compared the signature to the receipt with that of plaintiff upon the books, and was satisfied of the genuineness of the former, but the evidence adduced by a plaintiff tends to show that the signatures were alike, it is proper to refuse to submit to the jury the question whether the failure to discover the discrepancy was not negligence. Appleby v. Erie County Sav. Bank, 62 N.Y. 12.

In an action against a savings bank by the administratrix of a deceased depositor to recover an alleged unpaid balance, it was established that the deposits made by the decedent were subject to a bylaw requiring, in case of withdrawals, production of the bankbook, and that during her lifetime practically the entire deposit had been so withdrawn. The bankbook was not produced or accounted for at the trial. Held, that a verdict for defendant was properly directed. Hales v. Seamen's Bank, 28 App. Div. 407, 51 N.Y.S. 140.

Evidence held insufficient to show trustee liable for mismanagement.—

In an action against trustees of a savings bank for damages caused by their misconduct in the management of the bank, as to one defendant there was no evidence other than the minutes of his attendance at the meeting which authorized the purchase of certain realty, which purchase was alleged to be reckless and unreasonable extravagance. He denied such attendance, and asserted his ignorance of the transaction until it was closed. Held, that

(Text continued on page 193)

defendant was entitled to a dismissal of the complaint. Hun v. Cary (N.Y.), 59 How. Pr. 426, aff'd, 82 N.Y. 65, 37 Am. R. 546.

Ownership of deposits.—

In a contest involving the ownership of deposits in a savings bank, as between the estates of deceased husband and wife, facts establishing ownership by husband included: (1) Husband's ability and the wife's inability to earn and accumulate; (2) that the wife had never personally deposited or withdrawn a single sum and (3) that wife was unknown to the officers of the bank. Kennebec Sav. Bank v. Fogg, 83 Me. 374, 22 A. 251 (1891).

The entries upon the books of a savings bank, and upon the passbooks issued by such bank to a depositor, are not conclusive evidence of the ownership of a deposit in the bank. Kennebec Sav. Bank v. Fogg, 83 Me. 374, 22 A. 251 (1891).

Evidence, in an action to recover bank deposits made in the name of plaintiff's nephew and mother, who died without having learned of the deposits, held to show that plaintiff when she made a deposit did not intend to then pass title to her mother and nephew. Roughan v. Chenango Valley Sav. Bank, 158 App. Div. 786, 144 N.Y.S. 508, aff'd, 216 N.Y. 696, 110 N.E. 1049.

A savings bank depositor, suing the bank for payments made another person from his account, was entitled to recover amounts deposited and not placed to his credit in his bankbook, except insofar as checks for the same were paid to him or upon his authority. Commonwealth Bank v. Goodman, 128 Md. 452, 97 A. 1005.

Control of deposit.—

Evidence that a passbook showing a deposit of a savings fund in the name of both father and daughter was kept by the daughter in the common receptacle of the household in her mother's room where the daughter could and did get it whenever she wished, does not warrant a holding that the book was not in the daughter's possession sufficiently to indicate a control of the fund as claimed by her. Carlin v. Carlin (N.J.), 64 A. 1018.

Interest in joint deposits.—

In action to recover amount of savings deposit entered in name of plaintiff and debtor of bank, or survivor, evidence held to support judgment based on finding that debtor of bank against whom setoff was claimed had no separate interest in deposit which could be made subject of setoff. Peoples Bank of Denton v. Turner, 169 Md. 430, 182 A. 314, 103 A.L.R. 490.

Evidence, in an action to determine title to a savings bank account by plaintiff's testatrix with defendant, in the name of "Frederick or Karolina Beier," held to show that testatrix intended to make Frederick, who was her only child and an incompetent, joint owner of the account. Schwickert v. South Brooklyn Sav. Institution, 83 Misc. 377, 145 N.Y.S. 1003.

Administrator's right to deposits.—

The administrator of the intestate is entitled to bank deposits made by the intestate, it being shown that deposit books were lost, notification and indemnity were given the bank and no claim by another person having been put in. Powers v. Provident Institution for Sav., 124 Mass. 377.

But a mere statement of an administrator of a savings bank depositor that the passbook was lost is not such proof as would require the bank to pay over the deposit. Mierke v.

(Text continued on page 193)

Jefferson County Sav. Bank, 134 N.Y.S. 44, aff'd, 151 App. Div. 899, 135 N.Y.S. 1127.

Whether beneficiary of deposit received benefit of its money.—

Where money was deposited in a savings bank for an infant, and the bank negligently paid the same to the child's father, in a suit by the beneficiary to recover from the bank, testimony of the father that the money was expended for personal expenses resulting in the child's remaining at a certain college a year longer than she otherwise would have done, did not justify a conclusion that she received the benefit of the money in such sense as to defeat her recovery. Ficken v. Emigrants', etc., Sav. Bank, 33 Misc. 92, 67 N.Y.S. 143.

Contract to assign funds in account held not shown by evidence. Smith v. Benj. Franklin Sav., etc., Ass'n, 156 Ore. 541, 68 P.2d 1045.

Consideration for assignment of bank account.—

Evidence held sufficient to warrant a finding that a decedent's assignment of a savings bank account was supported by a sufficient consideration. Stacks v. Buten, 141 Wisc. 235, 124 N.W. 403.

Order authorizing transfer of passbook.—

In an action to recover possession of a savings bank passbook issued to plaintiff's testatrix, the evidence held to show that an order executed by testatrix, authorizing the bank to transfer her passbook and her interest therein to defendant, was presented to the bank and acted upon prior to testatrix's death. Augsbury v. Shurtliff, 114 App. Div. 626, 99 N.YS. 989, aff'd, 190 N.Y. 507, 83 N.E. 1122.

Oral authorization.—

In action by savings account depositor to recover money paid by bank from her account without authority, evidence sustained finding that depositor had orally authorized bank to charge against her savings account checks drawn by her brother-in-law, thus precluding recovery. Mathey v. Central Nat'l Bank, 179 Ken. 291, 293 P.2d 1012.

Notice of loss of bankbook.—

That bank was informed of loss held not shown so as to render bank liable for sums wrongfully paid on forged withdrawal slips. Connolly v. Manchester Sav. Bank, 92 N.H. 89, 25 A.2d 412 (N.H. 1942).

In an action by an administrator to recover from bank the balance due on a deposit by the intestate, a finding that the book was destroyed by the fire was sustained where: (1) There was evidence of a fire in the house occupied by the intestate, in which many of his papers were destroyed; (2) the treasurer of the bank testified that he had been connected with the bank for 25 years, and that no one had demanded payment of the account, or had presented the deposit book and (3) there was also evidence that notice was given that the book was lost. In an action by administrator to recover from bank the balance due on a deposit by the intestate, a finding that deposit book was destroyed by fire was sustained, where: (1) There was evidence of a fire in the house occupied by the intestate, in which many of his papers were destroyed; (2) the treasurer of the bank testified that he had been connected with the bank for 25 years, and that no one had demanded payment of the account or had presented the deposit book and (3) there was also evidence that notice was given that the book was lost. Hudson v. Roxbury Inst., 176 Mass. 522, 57 N.E. 1021 (1900).

(Text continued on page 193)

Constructive notice of depositor's death.—

Order for payment of depositor's account, form thereof, and presentment six days after date, held insufficient to constitute constructive notice to savings bank, as matter of law, of depositor's death. Paddock v. Anglo-California Trust Co., 107 Cal. App. 430, 290 P. 550 (1930).

Waiver of right to notice of withdrawal.—

There was evidence tending to show that the plaintiff, no notice in writing having been given by her, went to the bank, and asked for the funds standing in her name, and that the treasurer replied that she had no funds in the bank, and the treasurer testified that he declined to pay the money to the plaintiff because the funds claimed were held by trustee process, and that, if they had not been so held, he would have paid her. The plaintiff testified, without contradiction, that the money was her own; and her husband, who was summoned in as claimant, disclaimed said funds. Held, that the evidence warranted a finding that the right to notice had been waived. Townsend v. Webster, etc., Sav. Bank, 143 Mass. 147, 9 N.E. 521.

Time of demand on bank.—

In action for deposits against bank who paid deposits to depositor's stepfather on his presentation of passbook, evidence as to time of demand on bank for deposits held to warrant allowance of interest from such time. Gibson v. First Nat. Bank, 213 Mo. App. 63, 245 S.W. 1072.

Forged signatures.—

Evidence in action by depositors to recover balance in their savings account with bank was insufficient to sustain finding that depositors' signatures on an assignment of the savings account as collateral for a loan made to depositors' son-in-law were forged. Mungo v. Bank of Broadway, 104 Ill. App. 2d 97, 243 N.E.2d 853 (1968).

Want of authority and fraud in drawing money.—

In an action by a bank to recover money drawn from a third person's deposit by defendant's intestate, the depositor denied intestate's authority. Depositor could not read English, but could read certain numerals. He deposited money after the withdrawals by intestate, but denied having seen the charges against him on the passbook. Held sufficient to show want of authority and fraud on intestate's part in drawing the money. City Sav. Bank v. Enos, 135 Cal. 167, 67 P. 52.

Identity of judgment debtor and defendant's depositor held established by evidence in action against bank by receiver of property of alleged depositor. McCabe v. Union Dime Sav. Bank, 150 Misc. 157, 268 N.Y.S. 449.

Accuracy of bankbook balance.—

Spouses, joint owners of savings account suing bank to recover $465 allegedly owed them by bank by virtue of the account, established prima facie case by introducing evidence that: (1) Deposit book indicated balance of $465 in the account; (2) husband presented the deposit book, demanded payment, and was refused and (3) deposit book provided that no withdrawal should be made unless deposit book was produced and withdrawal entered therein. Tate v. Sears Bank & Trust Co., 90 Ill. App. 2d 382, 234 N.E.2d 126 (1967).

General practice to honor checks on savings accounts standing in drawers' names held

(Text continued on page 193)

---

not shown by evidence. Keller v. Davis, 123 Pa. Super. 240, 187 A. 267.

Whether bank a partnership.—

Not even a prima facie case that the bank is a partnership is made by evidence that the bank was organized under a certain name, that it has officers, that its organization was under the laws of the state, and that its profits were distributed in the shape of dividends on stock. In re Gibbs' Estate, 157 Pa. 59, 27 A. 383, 22 L.R.A. 276; Pease's Appeal, 157 Pa. 75, 27 A. 386.

Purpose of payment of money.—

In an action to recover money as paid for membership in savings bank, evidence held to sustain a general finding in favor of plaintiffs as against contention of defendants that the money was intended for, and was used to defray, expenses in petitioning for a charter, no charter ever being granted. Jefferson v. Cox, 246 Mass. 495, 141 N.E. 493.

Estoppel of depositor.—

Evidence held insufficient to establish that depositor had said or done anything to encourage bank to transfer account such as would preclude his recovery from beak, on basis of estoppel. Fischer v. Morris Plan Co., 275 S.W.2d 393 (Mo. App. 1955).

Number of witnesses.—

In an action to recover a savings deposit, evidence held to support a verdict for plaintiff, though he was the only witness in his own behalf while six witnesses testified for defendant. Rimkus v. Tananevicz, 207 Ill. App. 96.

Evidence held to show bank wrongly paid administrator of estate.—

Under evidence, payments which surviving joint tenant of savings account received from administrator of estate of predeceased joint tenant were not received with an intention to accept them in payment of surviving joint tenant's interest in the savings account and bank was liable to estate of surviving joint tenant for amounts which it paid from the joint savings account to the administrator of the estate of the predeceased joint tenant plus interest. Hollman v. Exeter Banking Co., 266 A.2d 209 (N.H. 1970).

Evidence would support finding that bank voluntarily paid proceeds of account payable to either of two depositors or survivor to a stranger to account upon death of one depositor without authorization from surviving depositor. Hollman v. Exeter Banking Co., 266 A.2d 209 (N.H. 1970).

In action brought by administrator of deceased who had been surviving joint tenant of a savings account against bank to recover proceeds of account, where final account of administrator of estate of predeceased joint tenant was received in evidence for the limited purpose of showing that the account contained an entry of $2,000 advanced to surviving joint tenant from savings account and for impeaching testimony of surviving joint tenant, final account of administrator of estate of predeceased joint tenant could not be relied upon to establish error in finding of trial court that surviving joint tenant had an interest in real and personal property of predeceased joint tenant's estate. Hollman v. Exeter Banking Co., 266 A.2d 209 (N.H. 1970).

Evidence was sufficient to support a judgment in favor of estate of an alleged depositor for proceeds of a savings account held by defendant in name of decedent as against claim that he was not in fact during his lifetime owner of account First Nat'l Bank v.

(Text continued on page 193)

Langford, 126 Ga. App. 325, 190 S.E.2d 803 (1972).

Bank ledger sheet showing that savings account was closed, together with facts that plaintiff, as alleged owner of account, made no withdrawals from account for over 36 years, made no inquiry about status of account, and permitted his brother to keep passbook for account for such period of time, constituted substantial evidence in support of judgment in favor of bank alleged by plaintiff to be indebted to him in amount of alleged account plus interest. Hicks v. Exchange Bank & Trust Co., 478 S.W.2d 54 (Ark. 1972).

Evidence generated a jury question as to the negligence of the bank, which was on notice by its own records that, although the names appeared to be the same, the individuals named in a garnishment writ and individuals named on savings account records were not the same, and which impounded depositors' funds for 15 days despite acknowledgment by the creditor's attorney of a mistake in identity. Valley Nat'l Bank v. Brown, 110 Ark. 260, 517 P.2d 1256 (1974).

In an action by a depositor against a bank to recover unauthorized withdrawals of funds from a savings account, evidence that the depositor had not authorized another person to make withdrawals from his account and that the depositor's statement that that other individual would be handling his business affairs was not sufficient for the bank to rely upon so as to insulate bank from liability under the Uniform Fiduciaries Act was sufficient for the jury. Boutros v. Riggs Nat'l Bank, 655 F.2d 1257 (D.C. Cir. 1981).

Evidence held to show bank exercised ordinary care in making a payment to a person who presented a passbook and a withdrawal slip on which the depositor's forged signature compared favorably with that on the bank signature card. The fact that a depositary bank in making a disbursement did not contact either the depositor or his nieces who had made prior withdrawals before disbursing the funds and that the withdrawal was for $7,200 did not mandate a finding, as a matter of law, that depositary bank did not exercise ordinary care. Gillen v. Maryland Nat'l Bank, 274 Md. 96, 838 L.2d 829 (1975).

Evidence held to show bank's negligence.—

There was substantial evidence, in suit to recover proceeds of passbook savings account, to support finding that the passbook belonged to plaintiff and had been in her possession, that plaintiff had made no withdrawals, that plaintiff had not authorized anyone else to make the withdrawals from her account, that plaintiff did not make an affidavit of lost passbook and that bank's record of withdrawals and deposits was not a record of the savings account of plaintiff. Central Nat'l Bank v. Booher, 557 8.W.2d 563 (Tex. Civ. App. 1977).

Evidence that plaintiff had been told by president of bank when joint savings account with her now deceased father was opened that both she and her father had to be present to withdraw funds from account supported jury's conclusion that bank had acted without proper authorization when it transferred funds from joint account on the signature (an X) of the father alone. Washington Loan & Banking Co. v. Mitchell, 292 S.E.2d 424 (Ga. App. 1982).

Evidence that bank teller released money from depositor's savings account to third party rather than to depositor, that teller did not properly identify man to whom she released money, and that bank was not authorized to release money was sufficient to sustain jury's award to depositor of amount of money released plus interest. Corpus Christi Nat'l Bank v. Lowry, 662 S.W.2d 402 (Tex. App. 18 Dist. 1984).

Evidence that bank teller released money to third party rather than to depositor, that teller

(Text continued on page 193)

did not properly identify third party, and that withdrawal request had savings account number omitted, was sufficient to support jury's verdict that bank teller did not have proper authorization from depositor to deliver funds from depositor's account to third party. Corpus Christi Nat'l Bank v. Lowry, 662 S.W.2d 402 (Tex. App. 13 Dist. 1984).

Evidence held to show bank not negligent in making payment.—

In a suit wherein a mother with a life estate in certain land sought to recover against the remainderman son and to recover against the bank on the theory that it wrongfully permitted the son to withdraw over $12,000 which had been in a joint savings account and which largely consisted of proceeds of the sale of timber on such land, verdict in favor of the bank was supported by substantial evidence. Haseman v. Union Bank, 597 S.W.2d 67 (Ark. 1980).

Evidence failed to support theory of emotional disturbance.—

In a suit against a bank to recover some $13,500 that had been withdrawn from plaintiff's savings account without plaintiff's authorization, plaintiff's evidence was insufficient to support a verdict on the theory of emotional disturbance. Burnette v. First Citizens Bank & Trust Co., 48 N.C. App. 585, 269 S.E.2d 317 (1980).

Testimony of bank officers sufficient as to bank rules.—

At the trial of an action by the assignees of a savings account against the bank, the bank did not have to produce the original books of the board of directors in which the rules and regulations governing the savings account were adopted to establish that such rules were adopted, where the testimony of bank officers on the rules was produced. Rosenstein v. Mechanics & Farmers Bank, 51 N.C. App. 437, 276 S.E.2d 710 (1981).

Addition of name to signature card sufficient as to ownership of account.—

Evidence that the plaintiff and her cotenant went to a savings bank and added her signature to the signature card of the savings account previously standing in the cotenant's name alone, and that the bankbook and bank's records were revised to show joint ownership, was sufficient to warrant the finding that the ownership of the account was intended to be as indicated in the bank's records. Doran v. Nally, 409 N.E.2d 1321 (Mass. App. 1980).

Bank's misrepresentation not proximate cause of injury.—

Even if bank's agent had misrepresented to depositor that savings account held jointly with his wife was "frozen" so as to prevent wife from withdrawing the funds, depositor failed to prove that costs he incurred when wife subsequently withdrew all of the proceeds were proximately caused by the misrepresentation. Gulesian v. Northeast Bank, 447 A.2d 814 (Me. 1982).

Right to decedent's funds.—

In action involving dispute among three children of decedent concerning savings accounts or certificates of deposit which at time of father's death were in name of father and names of one of defendants or in father's name as trustee for each defendant and involving alleged taking of certain personal property items of plaintiff daughter by defendant son, evidence was sufficient to support findings that: (1) Anything taken from plaintiff daughter by defendant son was returned without damage to plaintiff; (2) funds in certain account came solely from plaintiff daughter and were to be hers or to be used only for her benefit and (3) remaining accounts came from funds of father who had right to place them so that upon his

§ 34. Trial.

Province of Court and Jury.—Where a savings bank pays a deposit to one other than the depositor, who without authority presents a deposit book, the question of whether the bank exercised reasonable care in making the payment, if there is evidence that it did not exercise such care, is for the jury, notwithstanding a bank bylaw providing that all payments made by the bank on presentation of a deposit book shall be binding on depositors.[807] But it has been held that where the officer of a bank who made such payment

---

death defendants were owners. Le Grand v. Le Grand, 663 S.W.2d 339 (Mo. App. 1983).

Omissions not material.—

Alleged omissions from proxy statement regarding conversion of mutual savings bank to stock corporation and subsequent merger were not material, so claims of fraud and breach of fiduciary duty by individual trustees with respect to bank's depositors had no basis, although depositors asserted trustees were obligated to describe nature of depositors' equitable interest as owners of savings bank and fiduciary duty owed to them by trustees and state that plan had originally called for depositors to make profit which was lost because of stock market crash, that corporation with which converted bank was merging would realize "windfall" as result, and that depositors in other mutual savings banks had received benefit upon conversion of those institutions. In re East New York Sav. Bank Depositors Litigation, 547 N.Y.S.2d 497 (N.Y. Sup. Ct. 1989).

[807] **In general.—**

New Hampshire.—Brown v. Merrimack River Sav. Bank, 67 N.H. 549, 39 A. 336, 68 Am. St. R. 700.

New Jersey.—Berndt v. Hoboken Bank for Sav., 103 N.J.L. 478, 135 A. 818.

New York.—Smith v. Brooklyn Sav. Bank, 101 N.Y. 58, 4 N.E. 123, 54 Am. R. 653; Allen v. Williamsburgh Sav. Bank, 69 N.Y. 314; Fricke v. German Sav. Bank, 56 N.Y. Super. 468, 4 N.Y.S. 627, 23 N.Y. St. R. 121; Kenny v. Harlem Sav. Bank, 65 Misc. 466, 120 N.Y.S. 82; Szwento Juozupo Let Draugystes v. Manhattan Sav. Inst., 178 App. Div. 57, 164 N.Y.S. 498; Saling v. German Sav. Bank, 7 N.Y.S. 642, 15 Daly 386, 27 N.Y. St. R. 975; Fiero v. Franklin Sav. Bank, 124 Misc. 38, 207 N.Y.S. 235; Fox v. Onondaga County Sav. Bank, 7 N.Y.S. 17, 53 Hun 638, 25 N.Y. St. R. 672, 3 Silvernall 397; Podmore v. South Brooklyn Sav. Inst., 48 App. Div. 218, 62 N.Y.S. 961; Farmer v. Manhattan Sav. Inst., 15 N.Y.S. 235, 60 Hun 462.

Whether the discrepancy between signature on file and signature on withdrawal orders presented to savings bank was so marked that ordinarily competent clerk exercising reasonable care could have noticed difference and withheld payment held question of fact. Bellantese v. Bronx Sav. Bank, 152 Misc. 325, 273 N.Y.S. 885.

Ohio.—First Nat'l Bank v. Karas, 14 Ohio App. 147, 32 Ohio C.C. (n.s.) 83.

Utah.—Koutsis v. Zion's Sav. Bank & Trust Co., Co., 68 Utah 254, 225 P. 339.

West Virginia.—Zuplkoff v. Charleston Nat. Bank, 77 W. Va. 621, 88 S.E. 116.

Wisconsin.—Wegner v. Second Ward Sav. Bank, 76 Wis. 242, 44 N.W. 1096; Ninoff v. Hazel Green State Bank, 174 Wis. 560, 183 N.W. 673.

testifies that he applied the usual tests for identification, according to the custom and rules of the bank, and his testimony is not contradicted nor his credibility impeached, it is error to submit to the jury the question of whether reasonable care was used by the bank.[808] In a suit against a bank for breach of contract and negligence for permitting plaintiff's adopted son to withdraw about $12,000 from a joint savings account, whether the passbook was required to be used at the time of withdrawal was for the jury in light of evidence that the bank rule requiring passbooks had been changed.[809] In a suit to recover a balance allegedly due in a savings account, the depositor's positive testimony that she never saw a check payable to her husband purporting to be signed by her by mark, and did not receive the proceeds, made a jury question of the issue of payment.[810] And where a husband and wife, having individual accounts at a savings bank, execute an order on the bank to merge same, in an action on the death of the wife to recover possession of the bankbook, it was held reversible error to nonsuit the plaintiff without submitting to the jury the question of whether such order was delivered by the husband to the bank during the life of the wife.[811]

Whether after a savings bank has been notified by one claiming the right of control over money deposited in the bank, not to pay the money to a person who is in possession of the deposit book, the assent of the notifier to the payment of the money to the person having possession of the book can be inferred from facts in evidence, is a question of fact for the jury, and not one of law for determination by the court.[812] And in an action by a savings bank receiver to recover from a national bank the proceeds of drafts drawn in the savings bank's name at the direction of its president, which proceeds were received and applied on a claim against the president individually, the question whether the national bank's officers were charged with knowledge that such president had not arranged to take up the drafts and that his acts in

---

Authorization of business associate to make withdrawal a jury question.—

In an action by a depositor against a bank to recover unauthorized withdrawals of funds from a savings account, evidence that the depositor was not negligent in arranging for bank statements to be mailed to an associate, who made the allegedly unauthorized withdrawals, was sufficient for the jury. Boutros v. Riggs Nat'l Bank, 655 F.2d 1257 (D.C. Cir. 1981).

808 Geitelsohn v. Citizens' Sav. Bank, 17 Misc. 574, 40 N.Y.S. 662, 5 N.Y. St. R. 64 (1896); Ferguson v. Harlem Sav. Bank, 43 Misc. 10, 86 N.Y.S. 825.

809 Haseman v. Union Bank, 562 S.W.2d 45 (Ark. 1978).

810 Tribulas v. Continental Equitable Title, etc., Co., 331 Pa. 283, 200 A. 659.

811 Augsbury v. Shurtliff 180 N.Y. 138, 72 N.E. 927.

812 Eagle, etc., Mfg. Co. v. Beicher, 89 Ga. 218, 15 S.E. 482.

regard thereto were unauthorized, is for the jury.[813] In a suit by a bank against joint savings account depositors, the existence of an overdraft was for the jury; the depositors' contention was that they had made a $4,000 deposit which the bank had erroneously treated as a $1,000 deposit.[814] In a suit for breach of contract and negligence for permitting plaintiff's adopted son to withdraw about $12,000 from a joint savings account, the question whether the son or plaintiff owed the money was for the jury in light of plaintiff's argument that she, her husband and her son had agreed that proceeds from sale of timber on land deeded to son in which the parents had reserved a life estate belonged to the parents until their death, and the facts that she paid income taxes on the interest on the proceeds for two years, and that the plaintiff and husband had deposited over $1,000 to the account before the timber proceeds were added.[815]

The following questions have also been held to be questions of fact for the determination of the jury: (1) Whether a particular bank is under the evidence a savings institution which pays interest on its deposits not subject to check;[816] (2) whether the purchase of land by the trustees of a savings bank is, considering the financial condition of the bank, a reasonable exercise of the discretion vested in them;[817] (3) whether, where one deposits money in a savings bank in his own name as "trustee," without naming any beneficiary, the money so deposited belongs to the depositor absolutely or is held in trust;[818] (4) whether a savings depositor gave a written order authorizing payment to his son;[819] (5) whether there was negligence in signing an order or cashing it[820] and (6) whether a plaintiff suing as the niece and administratrix of an original depositor is actually his niece.[821] The question of whether funds received by the surviving joint tenant from the administration of the estate of the predeceased joint tenant were received by

813 Harwood v. Fort Worth Nat. Bank (Tex. Civ. App.), 205 S.W. 484, aff'd (Tex. Com. App.), 229 S.W. 487.

814 Brooks v. National City Bank, 142 Ga. App. 492, 236 S.E.2d 132 (1977).

815 Haseman v. Union Bank, 562 S.W.2d 45 (Ark. 1978).

816 Dottenheim v. Union Sav. Bank, etc., Co., 114 Ga. 788, 40 S.E. 825.

817 French v. Redman (N.Y.), 13 Hun 502.

818 Powers v. Provident Inst., 124 Mass. 377.

819 Barnes v. First Nat'l Bank, 256 Mich. 600, 240 N.W. 42.

820 Dalmatinsko Dobrotvorno Drustvo Sveti Frano Imotski v. First Union Trust, etc., Bank, 268 Ill. App. 314.

821 Vennard v. Albany Sav. Bank, 257 App. Div. 789, 15 N.Y.S.2d 503, aff'd, 282 N.Y. 718, 26 N.E.2d 826.

him as payment of the joint savings account was for the jury.[822] The question of whether the depositor exercised reasonable care and promptness to examine bank statements was one for the jury.[823]

Instructions.—Where a deposit book has been destroyed by fire, a depositor's administrator is thereby excused from producing it,[824] and therefore requests for instructions based on the necessity of presenting a book in order to obtain payment are properly refused.[825] An instruction denying a joint depositor recovery if a savings bank used reasonable care in disbursing his deposit on presentation of a duplicate passbook is properly refused, the real issue being the bank's compliance with its contract.[826] In an action by a guardian of a minor against a bank to recover an amount deposited to the credit of the minor's savings account, which was paid by the bank to the minor's stepfather on his presentation of a passbook, an instruction authorizing a verdict for the guardian in the event the jury should find certain facts, is not erroneous because it ignores an amount subsequently deposited by the stepfather to the minor's credit, where the amount so deposited did not constitute part of the sum previously withdrawn for which the action was brought, but was the minor's share of the proceeds of sale of property of his deceased mother.[827] But in an action by a depositor against a savings bank for paying a forged draft, an instruction that if the discrepancy between the signature on the draft and the depositor's signature was not marked and apparent, such fact might be considered by the jury in determining whether the bank exercised ordinary care, is erroneous.[828] As to

---

[822] Hollman v. Exeter Banking Co., 266 A.2d 209 (N.H. 1970).

[823] In suit against bank to recover $13,500 that was withdrawn from depositor's savings account without depositor's authorization, evidence that, when depositor received her bank statements during the relevant period, she examined them to see if they showed the right amounts, that depositor did not detect that any numbers had been erased or substituted and that when depositor noticed white tape on a statement, she thought the bank was responsible for the tape was sufficient to present a jury question as to whether depositor exercised reasonable care and promptness to examine the statements and items to discover that money had been withdrawn from her account by a boarder who forged the depositor's signature on withdrawal slips. Burnette v. First Citizens Bank & Trust Co., 48 N.C. App. 585, 269 S.E.2d 317 (1980).

[824] See § 21 of this chapter.

[825] Hudson v. Roxbury Inst. for Sav., 176 Mass. 522, 57 N.E. 1021 (1900).

[826] Mercantile Sav. Bank v. Appler, 151 Md. 571, 135 A. 373.

[827] Gibson v. First Nat. Bank, 213 Mo. App. 63, 245 S.W. 1072.

[828] Noah v. Bank for Sav., 171 App. Div. 191, 157 N.Y.S. 324.

the doctrine of harmless error in the giving of an instruction, see the footnote.[829]

§ 35. Appeal and Error.

Where there is a finding in an action against a savings bank by a creditor that the debt in question is for money expended by the creditor for the use and benefit of the bank and at its request, it will be presumed on appeal that the money was expended for purposes for which the bank could incur a liability.[830] And where in an action against a savings bank for money deposited by the plaintiff in the name of another, judgment is entered for the bank, the affirmance of which might embarrass the plaintiff in enforcing an equitable right he may have to the deposit, the appellate court should of its own motion reverse the judgment pro forma and remand the case, so that the person in whose name the money was deposited may be brought in, where there is a statute under which such person may be made a party defendant.[831] And in a suit against a bank for wrongful payment and conversion, it was held that the trial court erred in granting judgment in favor of the bank at the close of the plaintiff's evidence.[832] A state bank commissioner's informal letter, sent in response to a banker's association's complaint and stating that the issuance by savings banks of negotiable orders of withdrawal did not violate the banking statutes has been held to constitute a judicially reviewable decision.[833]

---

[829] In a suit where in a mother wlth a life estate in land sought to recover against the remainderman son and against the bank for wrongfully permitting the son to withdraw over $12,000, which had been in a joint savings account and which largely consisted of proceeds of sale of timber on such land, instruction that if it were found that the son was owner of the land and that the mother had life estate, the jury would have to find in favor of the son unless there was a contract establishing a different ownership of the account was erroneous, but the giving of the instruction did not prejudice the mother, in that the jury's determination that she was only entitled to $6, 500 indicated that the instruction was disregarded. Haseman v. Union Bank, 597 S.W.2d 67 (Ark. 1980).

[830] Laidlaw v. Pacific Bank, 67 P. 897, 6 Cal. Unrep. 849, rev'd on rehearing, 137 Cal. 392, 70 P. 277, on ground evidence showed contract was ultra vires.

[831] Kavanagh v. Vermont Sav. Bank, 68 Vt. 494, 35 A. 461.

[832] Indianapolis Saenger Chor, Inc. v. American Fletcher Nat'l Bank & Trust Co., 274 N.E.2d 728 (Ind. App. 1971).

[833] **In general.—**

New Hampshire Bankers Ass'n v. Nelson, 302 A.2d 810 (N.H. 1973).

Parties and standing to appeal.—

A banker's association, which had filed a protest with the bank commissioner complaining that the issuance of negotiable order, of withdrawal by savings banks was beyond the scope of the banking statutes, would suffer "injury in fact" by the commissioner's determination that such account did not violate the statutes, in that the determination would allow savings banks to compete with checking accounts of commercial banks; thus, the association had standing to appeal the commissioner's action. New Hampshire Bankers Ass'n v. Nelson, 302 A.2d 810 (N.H. 1973).

A depositor in a savings bank would not be made an additional party to an appeal from the state bank commissioner's denial of a hearing on a banker's association's protest to the issuance of negotiable orders of withdrawal by savings bank, where the depositor failed to allege any injury in fact. New Hampshire Bankers Mdn v. Nelson, 302 A.2d 810 (N.H. 1973).

CHAPTER XVII.

LOAN, TRUST AND INVESTMENT COMPANIES.

Synopsis

I. GENERAL CONSIDERATIONS.

a. Control and Regulation.

§ 1. In General.

§ 2. Statutory Provisions.

§ 3. Incorporation, Organization, Name, Location, Merger and Reorganization.

§ 4. Forfeiture of Franchise and Dissolution.

b. Stock and Stockholders.

§ 5. General Considerations.

§ 6. Stock Increase.

§ 7. Liability of Stockholders.

§ 8. Actions to Enforce Liability of Stockholders.

II. OFFICERS AND AGENTS.

§ 9. In General.

§ 10. Directors.

§ 11. Management Services Generally.

§ 11.1. Investment Advisers.

§ 11.2. Principal Underwriters.

§ 12. Liability.

III. FUNCTIONS AND DEALINGS.

a. General Considerations.

§ 13. Nature of Trust Company.
§ 14. Dealings in General.
§ 15. Dealings with Trust Property.
§ 16. Powers.
§ 17. Ultra Vires Acts.
§ 18. Actions.

b. Representation by Officers and Agents.

§ 19. In General.
§ 20. President.
§ 21. Vice-President.
§ 22. Treasurer.
§ 23. Other Officers.
§ 24. Notice to or Knowledge of Officer or Agent.
§ 25. Dealings Through Mutual Agent.

c. Deposits.

§ 26. General Considerations.
§ 27. Incidental Powers and Rights.
§ 28. Particular Statutory Provisions.
§ 29. Interest.
§ 30. Payment.
§ 31. Segregated Assets.
§ 32. Particular Deposits.
§ 33. Liability.
§ 34. Waiver and Estoppel.
§ 35. Actions.
§ 36. Depositor's Right of Setoff.

d. Loans, Discounts and Participation Certificates.

§ 37. In General.

IV. INSOLVENCY AND RECEIVERS

§ 38. General Considerations.
§ 39. Rights, Powers, Duties and Liabilities of State Banking Officials.

§ 40. **Collection and Sale of Assets.**

§ 41. **Distribution and Application of Assets, In General.**

§ 42. **Filing, Presentment and Proof of Claims.**

§ 43. **Allowable Claims.**

§ 44. **Payment or Disallowance of Claims.**

§ 45. **Preferences and Secured Claims.**

§ 46. **Property Held in Trust or Fiduciary Capacity.**

§ 47. **Money Received by Company Whose Insolvency Is Known to Its Officers.**

§ 48. **Interest and Dividends**

§ 49. **Setoff.**

§ 50. **Expenses of Administration and Compensation of Receivers and Their Attorneys.**

§ 51. **Actions.**

I. CONTROL AND REGULATION.

a. General Considerations.

§ 1. Control and Regulation In General.

Definitions.—The distinction between a bank and a trust company has been well defined.[834] The primary and ordinary concept of a trust company is as a corporation to take and administer trusts.[835] Under certain state statutes a trust company is defined as any corporation organized under the laws of the state engaged in a trust business.[836] And while a section of a banking statute which is devoted to definitions declares that the term "bank" means any moneyed corporation, and thus would include trust companies, in view of specific provisions applicable to banks and other equally specific

---

[834] Dietrich v. Rothenberger (Ky.), 75 S.W. 271. See § 13 of this chapter.

[835] People v. National Security Co., 189 App. Div. 38, 177 N.Y.S. 838, aff'd, 232 N.Y. 586, 134 N.E. 582; Loudoun Nat. Bank v. Continental Trust Co., 164 Va. 536, 180 S.E. 548, appeal dismissed, 297 U.S. 698, 56 S. Ct. 597, 80 L. Ed. 988.

[836] Union Trust Co. v. Moore, 104 Wash. 50, 60, 175 P. 565 (1918).

See e.g., Massachusetts' statute, ALM GL ch. 172, § 1(b) providing that a "trust company" or "corporation" means a trust company incorporated as such in the commonwealth of Massachusetts.

provisions applicable to trust companies, provisions as to banks cannot be extended to cover trust companies by reason of the inclusive definition.[837]

Under the Internal Revenue Code, the term "bank" means a bank or trust company incorporated and doing business under the laws of the United States (including laws relating to the District of Columbia) or of any state.[838] The statute is not a model of statutory clarity. Its construction and circular use of the term bank are inherently ambiguous.[839] However, the most consistent and harmonious reading supports the conclusion that being a bank within the commonly understood meaning of that term is an independent requirement.[840]

The National Bank Act[841] defines a banking "branch" as any branch bank, branch office, branch agency, additional office, or any branch place of business located in any state or territory of the United States or in the District of Columbia at which deposits are received, or checks paid, or money lent.[842] And, as used in the section of the Act regulating branch banks, the words "state bank," "state banks," "bank," or "banks," include trust

---

[837] Richards v. Carpenter, 261 F. 724.

"Trust company" is state-chartered commercial bank that may, but need not, provide fiduciary services. First Fiduciary Corp. v. Office of Comm'r of Banks, 43 Mass. App. Ct. 457, 684 N.E.2d 1 (1997).

[838] Moneygram Int'l v. Comm'r, 664 Fed. Appx. 386 (5th Cir. 2016). See 26 U.S.C.S. § 581 as to the full definition of "bank"; 26 U.S.C.S. § 582 as to bad debts, losses, and gains with respect to securities held by financial institutions; and 26 U.S.C.S. § 584 regarding common trust funds.

Section 581 of the Tax Code defines "bank" as follows: "For purposes of sections 582 and 584 [26 U.S.C.S. §§ 582 and 584], the term "bank" means a bank or trust company incorporated and doing business under the laws of the United States (including laws relating to the District of Columbia) or of any State, a substantial part of the business of which consists of receiving deposits and making loans and discounts, or of exercising fiduciary powers similar to those permitted to national banks under authority of the Comptroller of the Currency, and which is subject by law to supervision and examination by State, or Federal authority having supervision over banking institutions. Such term also means a domestic building and loan association."

[839] Moneygram Int'l v. Comm'r, 664 Fed. Appx. 386 (5th Cir. 2016). See 26 U.S.C.S. § 581.

[840] Moneygram Int'l v. Comm'r, 664 Fed. Appx. 386 (5th Cir. 2016).

[841] 12 U.S.C.S. § 21 et seq.

[842] Jose v. Wells Fargo Bank, N.A., 89 Mass. App. Ct. 772, 54 N.E.3d 1130 (2016). See 12 U.S.C.S. § 36(j).

companies, savings banks, or other such corporations or institutions carrying on the banking business under the authority of state laws.[843]

Under the Dodd-Frank amendments to the National Banking Act which clarify state law preemption standards for national banks and subsidiaries, the term "national bank" includes any bank organized under the laws of the United States and any federal branch established in accordance with the International Banking Act of 1978.[844] The term "state consumer financial law" means a state law that does not directly or indirectly discriminate against national banks and that directly and specifically regulates the manner, content, or terms and conditions of any financial transaction (as may be authorized for national banks to engage in), or any account related thereto, with respect to a consumer.[845] And, for these purposes, the terms "affiliate", "subsidiary", "includes", and "including" have the same meanings as in the Federal Deposit Insurance Act.[846]

The California Revenue and Taxation Code does not furnish a statutory definition of "financial corporations." The classification was adopted to avoid preferential tax treatment in favor of corporations in substantial competition with national banks. Under the governing test, the classification includes savings and loans as well as other kinds of moneyed corporations performing some of the functions of a national bank or dealing in money or financing in competition with activities of national banks.[847]

An industrial loan company has been defined as a corporation which, in the regular course of its business, loans money and issues choses in action.[848] For example, a corporation organized under the California Industrial Loan Act is a special type of corporation intentionally surrounded with safeguards not provided for general corporations which are intended to

---

843 12 U.S.C.S. § 36(l).

844 12 U.S.C.S. § 25b(a)(1).

845 12 U.S.C.S. § 25b(a)(2).

846 12 U.S.C.S. § 25b(a)(3). See 12 U.S.C.S. § 1813.

847 California Fed. Savings & Loan Assn. v. City of Los Angeles, 54 Cal. 3d 1, 812 P.2d 916 (1991).

848 State v. Hinkle, 134 Wash. 140, 235 P. 359.

A bond and mortgage corporation, proposing to loan money on personal or other security, and to sell and negotiate written evidences of debt for the payment of money, either fixed or uncertain, and to receive payment therefor in installments or otherwise, is required to comply with the statutory provisions relating to industrial loan companies. State ex rel. Northwestern Bond & Mortg. Corp. v. Hinkle, 134 Wash. 140, 235 P. 359.

protect the interests not only of creditors, but also of shareholders and all others interested in or affected by, the business of such a corporation.[849]

An "investment company" is essentially a liquid aggregation of capital consisting of public savings turned over to the company for investment and productive enterprise; it normally invests for yield as distinguished from control of productive enterprise, and it is to be distinguished from a "holding company" in this way.[850] Normally the question of whether a person is acting as an investment counsellor or a broker is a question of fact for the jury.[851]

Although the Financial Institutions Reform, Recovery, and Enforcement Act of 1989 (FIRREA) does not include a definition of the term "asset," it may be generally defined as an item that is owned and has value. In contrast, a "liability" is a financial or pecuniary obligation.[852] Authorities in some jurisdictions have concluded that a performance bond is similar to a standby letter of credit, which is a liability.[853] A performance bond creates a tripartite relationship between the surety, the principal, and the oblige; in other words, the performance bond protects the oblige from the principal's default.[854]

A covered security is one issued by an investment company registered under the Investment Company Act of 1940.[855]

---

[849] In re Peoples Finance & Thrift Co., 61 Cal. App. 2d 11, 141 P.2d 742.

[850] Aldred Inv. Trust v. Securities, etc., Comm., 151 F.2d 254, 260, aff'g 58 F. Supp. 724, cert. denied, 326 U.S. 796, 66 S. Ct. 486, 90 L. Ed. 483.

Corporation organized under New York banking laws was not "investment company" within meaning of the New Jersey Investment Company Act applicable New York law precluded corporation from making, issuing, or guaranteeing investment contacts. In re Topcroft, Inc., 136 Bankr. 99 (D.N.J. 1991).

[851] James De Nicholas Associates, Inc. v. Heritage Constr. Corp., 5 Cal. App. 3d 421, 85 Cal. Rptr. 288 (1970).

Letter indicating that plaintiff's company had considered purchasing an investment firm and that, under oral agreement with defendant, plaintiff was merely accepting consideration from defendant for waiving its own rights to purchase controlling stock of firm and for furnishing to defendant information plaintiff had acquired about firm did not establish, as a matter of law, that plaintiff was acting as investment counsellor which, without a license, would have precluded suit on agreement. James De Nicholas Associates, Inc. v. Heritage Constr. Corp., 5 Cal. App. 3d 421, 85 Cal Rptr. 233 (1970).

[852] Douglas County v. Hamilton State Bank, 340 Ga. App. 801, 798 S.E.2d 509 (2017).

[853] Douglas County v. Hamilton State Bank, 340 Ga. App. 801, 798 S.E.2d 509 (2017).

[854] Douglas County v. Hamilton State Bank, 340 Ga. App. 801, 798 S.E.2d 509 (2017).

[855] Freeman Invs., L.P. v. Pac. Life Ins. Co., 704 F.3d 1110 (9th Cir. 2013). See 15 U.S.C.S. § 77r(b)(2).

A "debt cancellation contract" is defined as a loan term or contractual arrangement modifying loan terms under which a bank agrees to cancel all or part of a customer's obligation to repay an extension of credit from that bank upon the occurrence of a specified event.[856]

"Foreclosure" is a legal proceeding to terminate a mortgagor's interest in property, instituted by the lender (the mortgagee) either to gain title or to force a sale in order to satisfy the unpaid debt secured by the property.[857] "Foreclosure" is not included in the term "servicing."[858] The United States Supreme Court has noted (in a different context) that "servicing" is essentially the administrative tasks associated with collecting mortgage payments.[859] Thus, "servicing" concerns the collection of mortgage payments; "foreclosure" concerns the termination of a borrower's interest in property. Under these definitions, "servicing" is not an umbrella term that includes "foreclosure."[860]

Courts that have considered the meaning of "loans," as that term is used in the Internal Revenue Code provision defining "bank,"[861] and its statutory predecessor,[862] have defined this term as an agreement, either expressed or implied, whereby one person advances money to the other and the other agrees to repay it upon such terms as to time and rate of interest, or without interest, as the parties may agree. In another context, a loan of money is a contract by which one delivers a sum of money to another and the latter agrees to return at a future time a sum equivalent to that which he borrows. Notably, courts have repeatedly stated that interest is not required.[863]

Under New York banking law, a "premium finance agreement" is a promissory note or other written agreement by which an insured promises or

---

[856] Gordon v. Kohl's Dep't Stores, Inc., 172 F. Supp. 3d 840 (E.D. Pa. 2016). See 12 C.F.R. 37.2(f).

[857] Higley v. Flagstar Bank, FSB, 910 F. Supp. 2d 1249 (D. Or. 2012).

[858] Higley v. Flagstar Bank, FSB, 910 F. Supp. 2d 1249 (D. Or. 2012).

[859] Morrison v. Nat'l Australia Bank Ltd., 561 U.S. 247, 130 S. Ct. 2869, 177 L. Ed. 2d 535 (2010).

[860] Higley v. Flagstar Bank, FSB, 910 F. Supp. 2d 1249 (D. Or. 2012).

[861] 26 U.S.C.S. § 581.

[862] Former 26 U.S.C.S. § 104.

[863] Moneygram Int'l v. Comm'r, 664 Fed. Appx. 386 (5th Cir. 2016).

agrees to pay the amount advanced under the agreement to an authorized insurer.[864]

A refund anticipation loan (or "RAL") is a loan that is made to a taxpayer at or about the time of filing his or her income tax return and that is expected to be repaid to the lender directly from the proceeds of the borrower's anticipated tax refund. Generally, the borrower receives cash or a check in the amount of the refund, minus the bank's loan fees and a fee charged by an independent entity that prepares the loan application.[865]

Financial institutions commonly sell mortgages on a secondary market; the term "sale" applies to the sale of mortgage instruments in this market, rather than to the sale of the property securing the mortgage at a foreclosure.[866]

A standby letter of credit means any letter of credit, or similar arrangement however named or described, which represents an obligation to the beneficiary on the part of the issuer: (1) To repay money borrowed by or advanced to or for the account of the account party; or (2) to make payment on account of any indebtedness undertaken by the account party or (3) to make payment on account of any default (including any statement of default) by the account party in the performance of an obligation.[867]

Savings-and-loan institutions are also called "thrifts," and, as their names suggest, they provide two main services: (1) Collect customer deposits, which are maintained in interest-bearing savings accounts and (2) originate and service mortgage loans funded by those deposits.[868]

Scope of Legislative Power.[869]—A trust company, like other corporations, is a creature of statute, and a legislature may prescribe what it can do and what it cannot do.[870] For example a legislature has power to authorize the

---

[864] All Is. Credit Corp. v. Country-Wide Ins., Co., 35 Misc. 3d 318, 936 N.Y.S.2d 882 (2012).

See N.Y C.L.S. Bank § 554(8).

[865] Pac. Capital Bank, N.A. v. Connecticut, 542 F.3d 341 (2nd Cir. 2008) (superseded by statute as stated in Gordon v. Kohl's Dep't Stores, Inc., 172 F. Supp. 3d 840 (E.D. Pa. 2016).).

[866] Higley v. Flagstar Bank, FSB, 910 F. Supp. 2d 1249 (D. Or. 2012).

[867] Douglas County v. Hamilton State Bank, 340 Ga. App. 801, 798 S.E.2d 509 (2017). See 12 C.F.R. 337.2(a).

[868] WMI Holdings Corp. v. United States, 891 F.3d 1016 (2018).

[869] See § 2 of this chapter.

[870] People v. Knapp, 147 App. Div. 436, 132 N.Y.S. 747, 26 N.Y. Crim. 448, aff'd, 206 N.Y. 373, 99 N.E. 841, 1914B Ann. Cas. 243; Shaw v. Brisbine, 68 S.D. 470, 260 N.W. 710

commingling of trust funds, provided it does not authorize the taking of property without due process of law.[871] A legislature, in the exercise of its power to create banks under general laws and regulate the business of banking, may classify trust companies which frequently do a general banking business, as banks for purposes of regulation.[872] And it is within the power of a legislature, in enacting a general law for the creation, government and control of all trust companies, to impose under given conditions certain limitations on the powers granted, or to reserve to existing trust companies brought under the act, certain powers already possessed by them under existing laws.[873] For cases dealing with foreign trust companies, see the footnote.[874]

(trust companies are subject to legislative control under police power); American Trust Co. v. South Carolina State Board of Bank Control, 381 F. Supp. 313 (D.S.C. 1974).

South Carolina has a legitimate interest in assuring that corporate fiduciaries serve the public faithfully, and laws prescribing fiduciaries' financial resources, governing their conduct and defining their responsibilities are an appropriate means of controlling trust companies. American Trust Co. v. South Carolina State Board of Bank Control, 381 F. Supp. 318 (D.S.C. 1974).

Massachusetts statutes prohibiting alteration of payment amount more than once yearly and alteration of interest rate more than every six months applied only to Massachusetts-chartered banks, and did not apply to federally chartered bank or its non-bank subsidiary incorporated under New York law. Salois v. Dime Sav. Bank, 128 F.3d 20 (1st Cir. 1997).

[871] In re Lincoln Rochester Trust Co., 111 N.Y.S.2d 45.

[872] In re Wellings, 192 Cal. 506, 221 P. 628.

[873] State v. Twining, 78 N.J.L. 3, 62 A. 402, aff'd, 73 N.J.L. 683, 64 A. 1073, 1185, aff'd, 211 U.S. 78, 29 S. Ct. 14, 53 L. Ed. 97.

[874] Where California trust company, either as executor or testamentary trustee under testator's will, collected rents from testator's Chicago real estate until receiver was appointed by Illinois court, trust company submitted itself to the jurisdiction of the Illinois courts in an action for an accounting of the rents collected during that period. Keats v. Cates, 100 Ill. App. 2d 177, 241 N.E.2d 645 (1968).

A foreign trust company which had not qualified to do business in Florida was not thereby precluded from acquiring property in the state as trustee or from defending title to the property. Pierson v. Bill, 138 Fla. 104, 189 So. 679.

Under the Oregon statute, a syndicate organized under the laws of another state, seeking permit to sell its capital shares or certificates, receiving funds therefor to invest in property which the association shall hold in trust for its shareholders, is a "foreign trust company," and is not under the supervision of the corporation commissioner, provided for in the "Blue Sky Law." Superior Oil & Refining Syndicate, Ltd. v. Handley, 99 Ore. 146, 195 P. 159.

Legislation must impact evenhandedly on in-state and out-of-state firms.—

A state may act by legislation to control or prevent undue concentrations of economic power in the banking, investment and trust businesses. However, in order not to run afoul of

A statute providing for publicity as to the conditions and business methods of installment investment companies, and providing for reasonable classification of companies for that purpose, is within the power of a legislature.[875] But in order for a state banking official to refuse a mutual investment association, mortgage company, mortgage discount company, or any company of like kind or character, a certificate of authority to do business, it must appear that the provisions of the company's charter, constitution and bylaws are impracticable, unjust, inequitable, oppressive, or lacking in security to any class of shareholders or stockholders; he cannot refuse a certificate simply because such company is authorized by its charter to issue no par stock if such right is accorded by law.[876] And where a voluntary burial association is an "investment company" and not a "life insurance company," a bank commissioner should consider the association's application for a permit to sell membership certificates without regard to insurance laws.[877] A foreign investment company may be required to obtain a license to do business in a state.[878] And a statute may fix the general standard to

---

the commerce clause such legislation must impact evenhandedly on in-state and out-of-state firms alike. BT Inv. Managers, Inc. v. Lewis, 461 F. Supp. 1187 (N.D. Fla. 1978).

[875] **In general.—**

State v. Northwestern Trust Co., 72 Neb. 497, 101 N.W. 14.

Act held unconstitutional.—

Act providing for the regulation and supervision of investment companies held unconstitutional. Alabama & N. O. Transp. Co. v. Doyle, 210 F. 173.

[876] State v. Jackson, 95 W. Va. 365, 121 S.E. 162.

[877] Herndon v. Wasson, 188 Ark. 329, 66 S.W.2d 633.

[878] **In general.—**

Kaufman v. Investors' Syndicate, 148 Misc. 624, 266 N.Y.S. 386 (1933).

Statute constitutional.—

A statute requiring a foreign investment company to obtain a license to do business is not unconstitutional as taking its property without due process or denying it equal protection of law. Kaufman v. Investors' Syndicate, 148 Misc. 624, 266 N.Y.S. 386 (1933).

Failure to obtain license.—

Reliance on advice of the superintendent of banks and qualification under stock corporation law to do business in state did not excuse a foreign investment company's violation of banking laws by failure to obtain license from superintendent of banks. Kaufman v. Investors' Syndicate, 148 Misc. 624, 266 N.Y.S. 386 (1933).

Contract of foreign investment company without license from superintendent of banks to do business in state is void, where parties' minds met therein, though instrument is dated and signed in another state. Kaufman v. Investors' Syndicate, 148 Misc. 624, 266 N.Y.S. 386 (1933).

which all foreign installment investment companies must conform to entitle them to a license to transact business in a state;[879] and may vest in a state department or official, quasi judicial power to determine whether a company applying for a certificate of approval to transact business in the state conforms to the prescribed standard.[880]

By statute in some states, trust or investment companies are required to deposit with a designated officer of the state, security for the benefit or protection of creditors or investors.[881] A trust company doing no business except to administer a trust for a stockholder is not entitled to the return of

---

Thus, a foreign corporation conducting investment company business in New York without complying with statutory requirements cannot sue on contract made in New York in conducting such business. Phillips v. Investors' Syndicate, 145 Misc. 361, 259 N.Y.S. 462.

Purchaser of investment certificates from foreign corporation not authorized to do investment or banking business within state, though authorized to do business in state as business corporation, could not recover money paid. Benwitt v. Investors' Syndicate, 149 Misc. 635, 288 N.Y.S. 163.

The rule applies to moneys paid according to terms of accumulative installment certificates. Fosdick v. Investors' Syndicate, 266 N.Y. 130, 194 N.E. 58 (1934).

[879] Investors' Syndicate v. Bryan, 113 Neb. 816, 205 N.W. 294, aff'd sub nom., Investors Syndicate v. McMullen, 274 U.S. 717, 47 S. Ct. 588, 71 L. Ed. 1822; Phillips v. Investors' Syndicate, 145 Misc. 361, 259 N.Y.S. 462.

A state may limit competition in the trust business if the public interest will be served. American Trust Co. v. South Carolina State Board of Bank Control, 381 F. Supp. 313 (D.8.C. 1974).

Foreign investment company which had failed to register as "foreign corporation" in accordance with New Jersey law would be denied access to courts to enforce mortgage agreement with debtor. In re Topcroft, Inc., 122 Bankr. 235 (Bankr. D.N.J. 1990).

[880] **In general.—**

Investors' Syndicate v. Bryan, 118 Neb. 816, 205 N.W. 294, aff'd sub nom., Investors Syndicate v. McMullen, 274 U.S. 717, 47 S. Ct. 588, 71 L. Ed. 1822.

Such a power, however, is not an unrestrained, arbitrary power to grant to, or withhold from, the applicant company a certificate of approval to transact business in the state. And such a statute cannot authorize the taking of property without due process of law or deny any person or corporation the equal protection of law. Investors' Syndicate v. Bryan, 113 Neb. 816, 205 N.W. 294, aff'd sub nom., Investors Syndicate v. McMullen, 274 U.S. 717, 47 S. Ct. 588, 71 L. Ed. 1322.

An aggrieved party may prosecute error from the determination denying a foreign installment investment company a permit to transact business in the state. Investors' Syndicate v. Bryan, 113 Neb. 816, 205 N.W. 294, aff'd sub nom., Investors Syndicate v. McMullen, 274 U.S. 717, 478 Ct. 588, 71 L. Ed. 1822.

[881] **In general.—**

Farmers' Loan & Trust Co. v. Lake S. E. R. R. Co., 68 Ill. App. 666, aff'd, 173 Ill. 439,

(*Text continued on page 212*)

---

51 N.E. 55, rev'd on other grounds, 177 U.S. 51, 20 S. Ct. 564, 44 L. Ed. 667; Stevenson v. Stephens, 136 Mo. 537, 37 S.W. 506; State v. Tontine Surety Co., 62 Ohio St. 428, 57 N.E. 60.

Construction of statutes.—

A statute regulating certificate bond and investment companies need not require that the security to be deposited with the treasurer of state by a company doing the business of placing or selling securities, etc., shall be derived wholly from its capital stock. State ex rel. Interstate Sav. Inv. Co. v. Matthews, 62 Ohio St. 146, 56 N.E. 658.

Tax certificate is included in term "evidences of indebtedness," and a corporation which sells bonds secured by deposit with trustee of such certificates is subject to supervision of superintendent of banks. Petters & Co. v. Viegel, 167 Minn. 286, 209 N.W. 9.

Rights of beneficiaries.—

Beneficiaries under trust agreement with national bank held entitled, on proof of bank's conversion of proceeds of trust res, to obtain payment of their claims from bonds deposited by bank with state auditor. And new bank organized to take over assets of defunct bank could not, by purchase of bonds deposited by defunct bank with state auditor, acquire right therein superior to such beneficiaries. Marvin v. First Nat. Bank, 10 F. Supp. 275.

Assets of trust company deposited with state treasurer held intended as security only for payment of trust obligations as distinguished from obligations incurred in general banking business. Erion Packing Co. v. Strain, 62 S.D. 589, 255 N.W. 794 (1934).

Where corporation, issuing investment certificates, had been required as a condition to engaging in business in Alabama to deposit securities with trustee for protection of Alabama investors, the relation of investor, who was not a party to trust agreement, was that of a secured creditor to full extent of corporation's liability under certificate held by investor and in case of default by corporation in respect to its liability to investor he would become one of the cestui que trustents. In absence of allegations showing fraud or breach of contract, obligations or duties, a resident certificate holder was not in a position to invoke aid of equity court to seize and administer the trust property. Allen v. Investors Syndicate, 247 Ala. 386, 24 So.2d 909 (1946).

Where corporation issuing investment certificate had been required by state securities commissioner as condition to its engaging in business in Alabama to deposit securities with trustee for protection of Alabama investors, the acting commissioner was neither a necessary nor proper party to bill by resident holder of investment certificate seeking aid of equity court to seize and administer the trust property, since in requiring the trust to be set up the commissioner acted as an agency under statutory power. Allen v. Investors Syndicate, 247 Ala. 386, 24 So.2d 909 (1946).

In such case the acting state securities commissioner had no pecuniary interest in trust property, and in absence of breach of trust or a violation of rights of investment certificate holders, no duty rested on the commissioner to take over and administer the trust property. Allen v. Investors Syndicate, 247 Ala. 386, 24 So.2d 909 (1946).

Insufficiency of fund.—

Where fund held by state superintendent of banks of New York as trustee for beneficiaries of trust funds is insufficient to satisfy all entitled to share therein, claimants may receive only

(Text continued on page 212)

---

their proportionate part of fund. Fesenmeyer v. Salt Springs Nat. Bank, 92 F.2d 599.

But where bank, as trustee, accepted money for deposit at interest and for distribution of fund on depositor's death, and became insolvent, and it did not appear that fund held by state superintendent would be insufficient to pay all claims, beneficiaries of such trust could assert lien against fund held by superintendent for full amount due from bank. Fesenmeyer v. Salt Springs Nat. Bank, 92 F.2d 599.

The Florida statute contemplates that securities deposited by trust company shall be held by state treasurer subject to all judgments against trust company while going concern, regardless of nature of judgment claims. Florida Bank & Trust Co. v. Nichols, 100 Fla. 203, 135 So. 906.

Securities required to be deposited by trust company with state treasurer are required as prerequisite to doing trust business, though nothing more than substitutes for indemnity bonds. Knott v. Morris, 101 Fla. 1299, 134 So. 615; Florida Bank & Trust Co. v. Nichols, 100 Fla. 208, 135 So. 906; Carcaba v. McNair, 68 F.2d 795, cert. denied, 292 U.S. 646, 54 S. Ct. 780, 78 L. Ed. 1497; Leyvraz v. Johnson, 114 Fla. 396, 154 So. 159.

Where banking corporation has qualified to do trust company business by making deposit of securities with state treasurer, proceeds of such securities, upon performance of all trust obligations, become assets of banking corporation. Leyvraz v. Johnson, 114 Fla. 396, 154 So. 159.

When all specific or other trust funds held by trust company are satisfied and there are no judgments or decrees against it, state treasurer is under duty to return securities to trust company or its receiver or liquidators. Knott v. Morris, 101 Fla. 1299, 134 So. 615.

Where securities held by trust company as security for trust are worth face value, judgment in full against them should be affirmed. Florida Bank, etc., Co. v. Nichols, 102 Fla. 203, 135 So. 906.

Illinois statute held applicable to banking corporations, and not to require that securities be held for benefit of all creditors. Barrett v. Reuter, 289 Ill. App. 221, 7 N.E.2d 74.

Such securities are for benefit of trust creditors only and not for general creditors. People v. Canton Nat. Bank, 288 Ill. App. 418, 6 N.E.2d 220; People v. Cody Trust Co., 294 Ill. App. 342, 13 N.E.2d 829.

And state official has no other interest than as pledged to secure trust creditors. In re Schmitt's Estate, 288 Ill. App. 250, 6 N.E.2d 444.

Trustee bank's liability for loss caused by failure to dispose of bank stock belonging to trust estate before insolvency of bank held properly satisfied out of deposited securities along with other trust claims. People v. Canton Nat. Bank, 288 Ill. App. 418, 6 N.E.2d 220.

Statute refers to trusteeship. which are made either by deed or its equivalent, or made by the court and accepted voluntarily in each instance by the trust company, and does not extend to "resulting" or "constructive" trust. People ex rel. Barrett v. Cody Trust Co., 294 Ill. App. 342, 13 N.E.2d 829.

Trust company's failure to make remittance in accordance with contract under which it had agreed to act as an insurance company's agent in the collection and remittance of principal and interest on notes which were forwarded to it by insurance company for bonds deposited to secure creditors.[882] In some jurisdictions, loan and trust companies are required to make statements or reports to a designated officer or department of the state,[883] or such officer or department may generally

---

collection created a "resulting" or "constructive" trust. People ex rel. Barrett v. Cody Trust Co., 294 Ill. App. 342, 13 N.E.2d 829.

But securities deposited with the auditor of public accounts were applicable to payment of insurance company's claim against liquidating receiver of trust company in the amount which trust company had collected under trust deed wherein it was named as trustee but which it had failed to remit in accordance with contract under which it had agreed to act as insurance company's agent in the collection and remittance of principal and interest of notes forwarded to it by the insurance company for collection. People ex rel. Barrett v. Cody Trust Co., 294 Ill. App. 342, 13 N.E.2d 829.

Indiana statute.—Under statutes relating to receivership of securities pledged by a foreign investment corporation with the auditor of the state, the auditor was not intended to administer liquidation of assets pledged by West Virginia investment corporation to secure authorization to do business in Indiana, where such corporation was in West Virginia receivership. State v. Marion Superior Court, 222 Ind. 26, 51 N.E.2d 844.

The auditor was not the only person authorized to maintain an action for receiver of assets pledged by a West Virginia investment corporation to secure authorization to do business in Indiana, but an Indiana certificate holder was entitled to maintain such action, where such corporation was in West Virginia receivership. State ex rel. James v. Marion Superior Court, 222 Ind. 26, 51 N.E.2d 844.

Nevada statute.—Mortgage company was required to obtain bond in order to provide minimum source of funds for those suffering compensable losses. New Hampshire Ins. Co. v. Gruhn, 670 P.2d 941 (Nev. 1983).

Purpose of statute requiring mortgage company to obtain bond as requisite for obtaining license to transact business is to protect public and not to protect mortgage company. New Hampshire Ins. Co. v. Gruhn, 670 P.2d 941 (Nev. 1988).

Texas statute requiring return of securities upon company's ceasing to do business in the state would not be construed as authorizing the retaining of the deposit for the benefit of resident shareholders of a company having no liabilities in the state and ceasing to do business therein, in absence of an intention expressed in the statute warranting such construction. Bankers Union Life Co. v. Sheppard, 131 Tex. 587, 117 S.W.2d 770, 116 A.L.R. 961.

Hence, solvent company which had shareholders in the state but which had no liabilities in the state and had ceased to do business therein was entitled to return of its deposit, as against contention that the deposit should be retained for the protection of the resident shareholders. Bankers Union Life Co. v. Sheppard, 131 Tex. 587, 117 S.W.2d 770, 118 A.L.R. 961.

[882] Spalding Co. v. Roberts, 170 Cal. 175, 149 P. 41.

[883] **In general.**—

Farmers' Loan, etc., Co. v. Lake St., etc., R. Co., 68 Ill. App. 666, aff'd, 173 Ill. 439, 51 N.E. 55, rev'd on other grounds, 177 U.S. 51, 20 S. Ct. 564, 44 L. Ed. 667; Anderson v.

supervise such companies.[884] Remedy of an investment company, seeking to challenge a declaratory ruling of the banking commissioner made without a hearing, was exclusively an action for declaratory judgment under the statute, not an administrative appeal.[885]

Corn. (Ky.), 117 S.W. 364; People v. Mutual Trust Co., 96 N.Y. 10; In re McKinley-Lanning Loan, etc., Co., 12 Pa. County Ct. 40; , Com. of Pa. v. Rousch, 113 P. Super. 182, 172 A. 484.

State banking regulation requiring that minutes be kept for common trust fund investment committee meetings did not prescribe contents of minutes and, thus, failure of trustee to maintain minutes detailing deliberative processes of trust committee could not be basis for surcharge. In re Bankers Trust Co., 636 N.Y.S.2d 741 (N.Y. App. Div. 1 Dep't 1995).

District of Columbia statute requiring that trust companies file reports in like form as national banks, etc., was intended to subject them to authority of comptroller, whose decision with respect to debts and engagements alleged to have been unlawfully incurred is not final beyond all re-examination. Dunn v. O'Connor, 89 F.2d 820.

[884] **In general.—**

Leary v. Capitol Trust Co., 238 App. Div. 661, 265 N.Y.S. 856, aff'd, 263 N.Y. 640, 189 N.E. 735.

Holder of subsequent mortgage had no standing to raise the issue of whether the taking of a third mortgage by a trust company was ultra vires under the statute, since such claims are reserved for assertion by the public authority, in this case the commissioner of banks. Financial Acceptance Corp. v. Garvey, 380 N.E.2d 1332 (Mass. App. 1978).

The California Industrial Loan Act subjected corporation organized thereunder to commissioner's supervision not only while exercising special powers enumerated therein, but also while exercising general powers under provision stating that such corporations should have general powers conferred upon corporations by the civil code. Daugherty v. Superior Court of Imperial County, 56 Cal. App. 2d 851, 133 P.2d 827.

Limitation act that corporations organized thereunder should have general powers conferred upon corporations by civil code, "except as herein otherwise provided," relates to powers which may be exercised by corporation organized under act, and not to matter of control or supervision over manner in which powers are to be exercised. Daugherty v. Superior Court of Imperial County, 56 Cal. App. 2d 851, 133 P.2d 827.

The refusal of the superintendent of banks to permit a newly organized trust company to invest nearly one-third of its total assets in a lease, fixtures and furniture was held not an arbitrary exercise of power. Leary v. Capitol Trust Co., 238 App. Div. 661, 265 N.Y.S. 856, aff'd, 263 N.Y. 640, 189 N.E. 735.

[885] Shearson American Express, Inc. v. Banking Com. of State, 466 A.2d 800, 39 Conn. Supp. 462 (1983).

Although investment company's original petition before banking commissioner, seeking a declaratory ruling that its brokers were not, by the mere act of making referrals, acting as investment adviser agents and thus were not obligated to register as such, was filed prior to the effective date of statutory amendment providing that the remedy for a person aggrieved by a declaratory ruling of the commissioner "shall be an action for declaratory judgment,"

Administrative Hearings.—As to cases related to administrative hearings and procedures, see the footnote.[886]

---

the commissioner's ruling and the investment company's appeal therefrom were filed after that date and, therefore, the statute, as amended, applied to bar investment company's administrative appeal. Shearson American Express, Inc. v. Banking Com. of State, 466 A.2d 800, 39 Conn. Supp. 462 (1983).

[886] **Standing.—**

Bank that intervened in administrative proceedings concerning another financial institution's application for trust powers to do business in bank's vicinity was person aggrieved under statute and, thus, bank had standing to challenge decision of commissioner of commerce granting application. In re Application by Black, 522 N.W.2d 352 (Minn. App. 1994).

Grant of hearing.—

Commissioner of commerce must grant hearing on proposed trust application only if written submissions would be inadequate or hearing would be beneficial to decision-making process. In re Application by Black, 522 N.W.2d 352 (Minn. App. 1994).

Bank was not entitled to hearing on another financial institution's application for trust powers where bank's objections to application were not unusual or complex, bank did not indicate that it intended to provide expert witness, there was lack of public concern or interest in application, and bank was able to explain issues involved in application in written statements. In re Application by Black, 522 N.W.2d 352 (Minn. App. 1994).

Finality of decision.—

Commissioner of commerce's denials of bank's requests for administrative hearings on another financial institution's application for trust powers were not final decisions for purposes of judicial review; final determination of bank's rights was not made until commissioner approved application, and denials could be reviewed on timely appeal from order granting application. In re Black, 522 N.W.2d 352 (Minn. App. 1994).

Evidence sufficient.—

Substantial evidence supported findings of commissioner of commerce in granting financial institution's application of trust powers, that financial institution had good moral character, that reasonable public demand for trust company existed, and that proposed market was large enough to absorb another trust institution without jeopardizing solvency of existing trust companies. In re Black, 522 N.W.2d 352 (Minn. App. 1994).

Conditional grant of powers.—

Commissioner of commerce did not exceed his authority by imposing conditions on application for trust powers that applicant deposit required capital in bank, complete sublease agreement, finish administrative agreements, notify commissioner of any change in ownership, establish guaranty fund, and provide proof of fidelity bond coverage and workers' compensation coverage. In re Application by Black, 522 N.W.2d 352 (Minn. App. 1994).

Memorandum deemed part of record.—

Memorandum attached to commissioner of commerce's order would not be stricken from record on judicial review, though memorandum was unsigned and undated, where it was

Regulations of the Small Business Administration governing the operation of small business investment companies have the force of law.[887] Under the provisions of the Small Business Investment Act of 1958 for participation by other lenders in loans by small business investment companies, such participants, although not licensed under the Act, are equally bound with the licensed lender by regulations of the Small Business Administration, at least insofar as the terms of their loan agreement are concerned.[888] For cases involving violations of the Small Business Administration regulations, see the footnote.[889]

---

attached to and served upon parties with commissioner's dated order and was part of agency record. In re Application by Black, 522 N.W.2d 352 (Minn. App. 1994).

Applicant letter not grounds for reversal.—

Letter from trust power applicant to commissioner of commerce requesting commissioner to act on application, stating that process was long and tedious, and requesting prompt resolution of issues, was highly unlikely to have unduly influenced commissioner, and therefore letter was not grounds for reversal of order granting application. In re Black, 522 N.W.2d 352 (Minn. App. 1994).

[887] Hernstadt v. Programs for Television, Inc., 36 Misc. 2d 628, 232 N.Y.S.2d 683. See also § 38 of this chapter.

As to provisions of Small Business Investment Act, see § 2 of this chapter. As to loans made in violation of regulations, see § 37 of this Chapter. The Small Business Administration was entitled to a judgment against the officers, directors and principal shareholders of a licensee under the Small Business Investment Act for losses sustained by an investment company as a result of loans made in violation of the Small Business Investment Act and regulations and for the interest on the amount of unpaid loans. Small Business Administration v. Segal, 383 F. Supp. 198 (D. Conn. 1974).

[888] Hernstadt v. Programs for Television, Inc., 36 Misc. 2d 628, 282 N.Y.S.2d 683.

The fact that a corporation to which a licensee under the Small Business Investment Act had made a loan in violation of the regulation prohibiting the making of a loan to any company in which an officer or director of the investment company had a ten or more percent interest had filed a Chapter XI proceeding under the Federal Bankruptcy Act, and an arrangement approved therein provided for repayment to the investment company of $80,000 of the $60,000 without interest did not release the officers of the investment company from liability for the remaining $30,000 plus interest on the full $60,000 of the illegal loan. Small Business Administration v. Segal, 383 F. Supp. 198 (D. Conn. 1974).

[889] **In general.—**

Small business investment company's license could be revoked for violating Small Business Administration (SBA) regulations pertaining to capital impairment, financial reporting and interest obligations. United States v. Vanguard Inv. Co., 907 F.2d 439 (4th Cir. 1990).

Local officials have no authority to interpret act.—

Small Business Administration properly determined that small business investment

(Text continued on page 218)

company violated section of statute relating to functions of investment companies and section of regulations with respect to company's purchase of shares of stock of two corporations, and informal approvals of such purchases by officials of Small Business Administration, however broadly construed, did not have standing as binding administrative constructions of the act and regulations, since the local officials had no authority to issue regulations or formally interpret the act. ANA Small Business Invs., Inc. v. Small Business Administration of United States, 391 F.2d 739 (9th Cir. 1968).

Retroactivity of regulation.—

Charge by Small Business Administration against small business investment company of violating certain regulation could not be sustained on basis of any conduct on part of the investment company occurring before effective date of the regulation, since to do so would be to give the regulation impermissible retroactive effect, notwithstanding fact that the regulation was designed to carry out the original objectives of the act. ANA Small Business Invest., Inc. v. Small Business Administration, 391 F.2d 739 (9th Cir. 1968).

Small Business Administration's order requiring small business investment company to comply with certain section of regulation promulgated under Small Business Investment Act could properly take cognizance of investment company's failure to comply with that regulation since it had become effective, and so viewed the agency order did not represent punishment for conduct occurring before effective date of the regulation, but was only an insistence that, beginning with that date, the regulation be honored, so that no impermissible retroactive application of the regulation was involved. ANA Small Business Ass'n, Inc. v. Small Business Administration of United States, 391 F.2d 739 (9th Cir. 1968).

Small Business Administration acted properly in notifying small business investment company that it should submit a plan for divesting itself of control over two corporations whose stock it had purchased, even though regulation providing that licensee could not acquire equity securities of small business concern primarily for purpose of exercising indefinite control over it was not in effect when such shares were acquired, where the small business investment company had maintained control of the two corporations for more than one year after the regulation became effective. ANA Small Business Invest., Inc. v. Small Business Administration, 391 F.2d 739 (9th Cir. 1968).

Licensee acquires no vested rights.—

Small business investment company licensed by Small Business Administration was subject to the principle that a licensee under a scheme of federal regulation acquires no vested rights which immunize it from reasonable regulation by an administrative agency. ANA Small Business Invest., Inc. v. Small Business Administration, 391 F.2d 739 (9th Cir. 1968).

Prosecution for past violations.—

Violations of the Small Business Investment Act are not cured because they are not detected and prosecuted before the violation ceases. United States v. Coleman Capital Corp., 295 F. Supp. 1016 (N.D. Ill. 1969).

Fact that alleged violations of Small Business Investment Act were corrected before action was brought against licensed investment company did not preclude suit. United State. v. Coleman Capital Corp., 295 F. Supp. 1016 (N.D. Ill. 1969).

(Text continued on page 218)

While an adjudication by a court is required to determine whether in fact a violation or noncompliance took place, the Small Business Investment Act does not restrict the court's consideration to question whether a violation or noncompliance is presently occurring. United States v. Coleman Capital Corp., 295 F. Supp. 1016 (N.D. Ill. 1969).

Violator may maintain action.—

Alleged violations of Small Business Investment Act by plaintiff in changing its name and principal place of business without approval of administrator did not preclude plaintiff from maintaining its present action arising out of note executed by individual defendant, in absence of showing that any procedures against plaintiff for its alleged violations had been instituted. Olympic Capital Corp. v. Newman, 276 F. Supp. 646 (C.D. Cal. 1967).

Suspension of license.—

In view of investment company's violation of regulations of Small Business Administration and statute by lending more than 20 percent of its paid-in capital and surplus to single business concern and by financing another company having a common director with investment company, directive of Small Business Administration requiring that investment company cease and desist from farther violation of act and regulations and divest itself of the illegal financing, and suspending its license pending obedience to order was not contrary to law. Electronic Systems Inv. Corp. v. Small Business Administration, 405 F.2d 188 (4th Cir. 1968), cert. denied, 394 U.S. 1014, 89 S. Ct. 1633, 23 L. Ed. 2d 41 (1969).

Revocation of license.—

Revocation of a small business investment corporation's license forces the corporation to cease all business operations. United States v. Norwood Capital Corp., 273 F. Supp. 236 (D.S.C. 1967).

Violations warranting the drastic remedy of revocation of a small business investment corporation's license are generally conduct which jeopardize program funds of the corporation whether through misuse or mismanagement of the funds. United States v. Norwood Capital Corp., 273 F. Supp. 236 (D.S.C. 1967).

The final act of adjudication after there has been adjudication of violations of the Small Business Investment Act or regulations thereunder is revocation, and a federal receivership to administer the assets during the proceedings is a receivership to liquidate. United States v. Norwood Capital Corp., 273 F. Supp. 236 (D.S.C. 1967).

Failure of small business investment company to maintain at all times unimpaired capital or to adequately establish reserves for losses and uncollectible, its extension of financing in excess of 20 percent of its paid-in capital and surplus, its control of debtor companies through interlocking directorates, and its sale of stock held by it as investment in portfolio concern to its stockholder without Small Business Administration consent, constituted violations of Small Business Administration regulations sufficient to warrant issuance of injunction, appointment of receiver, entry of money judgment, and award for costs to plaintiff, the United States. United States v. Boca Raton Capital Corp., 285 F. Supp. 504 (S.D. Fla. 1968).

The Small Business Administration has neither power nor right to forfeit any license of a small business investment company licensed pursuant to Small Business investment Act, but rather that power is reserved specifically to a court of the United States of competent

Federal Regulation and Preemption.—The Home Owners' Loan Act (HOLA)[890] was enacted by Congress as a response to the Great Depression, when nearly half of all home loans were in default and credit was scarce, as a radical and comprehensive response to the inadequacies of the existing state systems of mortgage regulation. HOLA initially created the Federal Home Loan Bank Board and granted its director broad authority to regulate the powers and operations of every federal savings and loan association from its cradle to its corporate grave. When Congress amended HOLA in 1989, it transferred this power to the Office of Thrift Supervision (OTS). It would have been difficult for Congress to give the OTS a broader mandate pertaining to loan regulation authority under HOLA.[891] OTS signaled its

---

jurisdiction. Olympic Capital Corp. v. Newman, 276 F. Supp. 646 (CD. Cal. 1967).

Evidence supported finding that small business investment company had maintained control of two corporations beyond a reasonable period, and thus was in violation of section of regulations promulgated by Small Business Administration providing, inter alia, that a license could not acquire equity securities of a small business concern primarily for purpose of exercising indefinite control over its corporations. ANA Small Business Invest., Inc. v. Small Business Administration, 391 F.2d 739 (9th Cir. 1968).

There was substantial evidence to sustain determination of Small Business Administration that investment company had violated Administration's regulations and statute by lending more than 20 percent of its paid-in capital and surplus to a single business concern and by financing another company which had a common director with investment company. Electronic Systems Inv. Corp. v. Small Business Administration, 405 F.2d 188 (4th Cir. 1968), cert. denied, 394 U.S. 1014, 89 S. Ct. 1633, 23 L. Ed. 2d 41 (1969).

Ultra vires.—

Any loans authorized by defendant officers, directors and principal shareholders of a licensee under the Small Business Investment Act to be made in violation of the act and the regulations issued thereunder were ultra vires, subjecting the defendants to liability for losses resulting from the illegal loans. Small Business Administration v. Segal v. Segal, 383 F. Supp. 198 (D. Conn. 1974).

Aggregation of amounts of loans to two corporations where both owned by same individual.—

Loans made by a licensee under the Small Business Investment Act to two corporations which were controlled by one individual could be aggregated in considering whether defendants, officers, directors and principal shareholders of the licensee, violated the statute and regulation prohibiting the lending of amounts in excess of 20 percent of the combined paid-in capital and paid-in surplus of any licensee to any single enterprise, even if neither borrower corporation was a sham or fictitious corporation. Small Business Administration v. Segal v. Segal, 383 F. Supp. 198 (D. Conn. 1974).

[890] 12 U.S.C.S. §§ 1461–1470.

[891] Henning v. Wachovia Mortgage, FSB, 969 F. Supp. 2d 135 (2013).

In the field of banking, Congress has created an extensive federal statutory and regulatory

authority to occupy the entire field of lending regulation, in order to facilitate the safe and sound operation of federal savings associations, and with the intent to give them maximum flexibility to exercise their lending powers in accordance with a uniform federal scheme.[892]

The Dodd-Frank Wall Street Reform and Consumer Protection Act[893] significantly diminished the extent to which the Home Owners' Loan Act (HOLA) and its implementing regulations may preempt state law.[894] Courts have uniformly held, however, that the provisions of Dodd-Frank are not retroactive, and HOLA preemption applies to mortgages originated before either July 21, 2010 or July 21, 2011.[895] Thus, in an evaluation of the issue of preemption, a court must consider the federal regulations in effect when the parties entered into the transaction.[896]

As a result of Congress's sweeping reform of federal financial regulatory oversight in Dodd-Frank, the legal analysis governing preemption by the National Bank Act (NBA) changed radically.[897] The Dodd-Frank Act directs courts to determine preemption by analyzing whether a state law is "irreconcilably in conflict" with the NBA.[898] The reservation of states'

---

scheme. As part of this extensive federal scheme, Congress enacted the Home Owners' Loan Act (HOLA), 12 U.S.C.S. § 1461 et seq., to charter savings associations under federal law as a means of restoring public confidence through a nationwide system of savings and loan associations that are centrally regulated according to nationwide best practices. Odinma v. Aurora Loan Servs., 2010 U.S. Dist. LEXIS 28347 (N.D. Cal. 2010).

[892] Henning v. Wachovia Mortgage, FSB, 969 F. Supp. 2d 135 (2013).

Former 12 C.F.R. § 560.2.

[893] 12 U.S.C.S. § 25b.

[894] Henning v. Wachovia Mortgage, FSB, 969 F. Supp. 2d 135 (2013).

[895] Henning v. Wachovia Mortgage, FSB, 969 F. Supp. 2d 135 (2013). See 12 U.S.C.S. § 25b.

Because borrower's claims against lender's assignee arose out of loans that were originated in 2006, Dodd-Frank preemption in 12 U.S.C.S. § 25b did not apply, and appropriate preemption standard to apply was that under the Home Owners' Loan Act. Henning v. Wachovia Mortgage, FSB, 969 F. Supp. 2d 135 (2013).

[896] Molosky v. Wash. Mut., Inc., 664 F.3d 109 (6th Cir. 2011); Deutsche Bank Nat'l Trust Co. v. Bliss, 159 Conn. App. 483, 124 A.3d 890 (2015).

[897] Cline v. Bank of Am., N.A., 823 F. Supp. 2d 387 (S.D. W. Va. 2011).

[898] Meluzio v. Capital One Bank (USA), N.A., 469 B.R. 250 (N.D. W. Va. 2012); Pryor v. Bank of Am., N.A. (In re Pryor), 479 B.R. 694 (Bankr. E.D. NC 2012).

Conflict preemption analysis is focused on whether the targeted state statute is irreconcilably in conflict with the NBA. Stated another way, the inquiry distills to whether the state measure either: (1) Imposes an obligation on a national bank that is in direct conflict

power to apply their laws of general applicability to national banks is reaffirmed by the NBA's preemption provisions which specify that laws governing the manner, content, or terms and conditions of any financial transaction or any account related thereto are not preempted as applied to national banks unless: (1) The state law would have a discriminatory effect on national banks, in comparison with the effect of the law on a bank chartered by that state; (2) the state law would be preempted under the standard set forth in *Barnett Bank* or (3) the state law is preempted by a federal law other than the NBA.[899] Dodd-Frank further clarified that the NBA does not occupy any field in any area of state law.[900]

The Office of Thrift Supervision (OTS) was abolished effective October 19, 2011, following the enactment of the Dodd-Frank Act, and its rulemaking authority and operative rules were transferred to other agencies.[901] The

---

with federal law or (2) stands as an obstacle to the accomplishment and execution of the full purposes and objectives of Congress. Under the Dodd-Frank Act, the proper preemption test asks whether there is a significant conflict between the state and federal statutes—that is, the test for conflict preemption. Cline v. Bank of Am., N.A., 823 F. Supp. 2d 387 (S.D. W. Va. 2011).

[899] Gordon v. Kohl's Dep't Stores, Inc., 172 F. Supp. 3d 840 (E.D. Pa. 2016). See 12 U.S.C.S. § 25b.

By codifying Barnett Bank, N.A. v. Nelson, 517 U.S. 25, 116 S. Ct. 1103, 134 L. Ed. 2d 237 (1996), the Dodd-Frank Act, 12 U.S.C.S. § 25b, directs courts to determine national bank preemption by analyzing whether a state statute is irreconcilably in conflict with the National Bank Act. Thus, courts must now determine whether the state measure either: (1) Imposes an obligation on a national bank that is in direct conflict with federal law or (2) stands as an obstacle to the accomplishment and execution of the full purposes and objectives of the United States Congress. Meluzio v. Capital One Bank (USA), N.A., 469 B.R. 250 (N.D. W. Va. 2012).

Because the Barnett Bank analysis is subsumed within Dodd-Frank, even assuming that Dodd-Frank's provisions did not apply, the preemption analysis essentially remained the same; in determining whether a statute is preempted by federal law, it is necessary to look first at Congress's intent in drafting the federal law. The congressional intent in enacting the NBA was to establish a national banking system that was free from intrusive state regulation. Sacco v. Bank of Am., N.A., 2012 U.S. Dist. LEXIS 178030 (D. N.C. 2012). See Barnett Bank, N.A. v. Nelson, 517 U.S. 25, 116 S. Ct. 1103, 134 L. Ed. 2d 237 (1996).

[900] Gordon v. Kohl's Dep't Stores, Inc., 172 F. Supp. 3d 840 (E.D. Pa. 2016). See 12 U.S.C.S. § 25b.

[901] 82 FR 47083, 47084.

Department of the Treasury is removing chapter V of title 12, Code of Federal Regulations (CFR), which contains regulations of the former Office of Thrift Supervision (OTS). The OTS, a Bureau of the Department of the Treasury, was abolished effective October 19, 2011, and its rulemaking authority and operative rules were transferred to other

Office of the Comptroller of the Currency (OCC) revised its own regulations to mirror the preemption framework present in the Dodd-Frank Act.[902]

For other cases involving preemption, see the footnote.[903]

The Dodd-Frank Wall Street Reform and Consumer Protection Act[904] was the first comprehensive effort to address the problems in the system that led—in sequence—to the subprime crisis, the housing crisis, and the

---

agencies pursuant to the Dodd-Frank Wall Street Reform and Consumer Protection Act. Because those agencies have issued regulations that supersede chapter V, chapter V is no longer necessary. 82 FR 47083, 47084.

[902] Pryor v. Bank of Am., N.A. (In re Pryor), 479 B.R. 694 (E.D. Bankr. NC 2012). See 12 U.S.C.S. § 25b (effective July 21, 2011).

[903] The ability to audit and tax under Mississippi's Finance Company Privilege Tax law was not preempted by the National Bank Act. Federal law did not preempt state law as to state taxation of national banks. Congress had not explicitly preempted state law in this area, Congress had not occupied the entire field, and there was no conflict between federal and state law in this area. The National Bank Act did not preempt state taxation; in fact, it explicitly exempted it, leaving taxation to the states. Furthermore, the Mississippi Department of Revenue had the authority to enforce state tax laws against the loan company, which could not claim an exemption under the statute because, although it was an operating subsidiary of a national bank, it was not a state or national bank. Miss. Dep't of Revenue v. Pikco Fin., Inc., 97 So. 3d 1203 (Miss. 2012). See Miss. Code Ann. § 27-21-1 et seq.

State law claims arising from debt cancellation contracts are preempted under Part 37 of the federal regulations. Gordon v. Kohl's Dep't Stores, Inc., 172 F. Supp. 3d 840 (E.D. Pa. 2016). See 12 C.F.R. 37.2(f).

State Debt Collection Act was not preempted by the National Bank Act (NBA) or any regulation promulgated by the Office of the Comptroller of the Currency (OCC), where the bank continued to call plaintiff's cellular phone in an attempt to collect an alleged debt, even after it had knowledge or reason to know that plaintiff had filed bankruptcy, that the debt was discharged, and that plaintiff was represented by counsel, who sent letters to defendant, warning that its attempts to collect plaintiff's debt were in violation of the law. Dixon v. Wells Fargo Bank, N.A., 798 F. Supp. 2d 336 (D. Mass. 2011). See also Sacco v. Bank of Am., N.A., 2012 U.S. Dist. LEXIS 178030 (D. N.C. 2012).

Bank was not entitled to dismissal of plaintiff homeowners' promissory estoppel complaint based on the bank's alleged failure to engage in negotiation of a loan modification prior to proceeding with foreclosure because the facts alleged in the complaint were sufficient to invoke the doctrine of promissory estoppel, and this common-law claim, as applied, was not preempted by federal law under the Home Owners' Loan Act and its implementing regulations. Dixon v. Wells Fargo Bank, N.A., 798 F. Supp. 2d 336 (D. Mass. 2011).

[904] 12 U.S.C.S. § 25b.

financial crisisis.[905] Nonetheless, according to one legal commentator, the extensive legislation contained in Dodd-Frank "deliberately did not deal with the biggest elephant (or perhaps elephants) in the room: Fannie Mae and Freddie Mac."

With the enactment of the Housing and Economic Recovery Act of 2008 (Recovery Act), Congress established the Federal Housing Finance Agency (FHFA) and authorized it to undertake extraordinary economic measures to resuscitate the Federal National Mortgage Association (Fannie Mae) and the Federal Home Loan Mortgage Corporation (Freddie Mac), including authorizing the director of the FHFA to appoint the FHFA as either conservator or receiver for Fannie and Freddie for the purpose of reorganizing, rehabilitating, or winding up their affairs.[906]

Power of Banking Board.—The banking board has the discretion to deny the issuance of a certificate of authority to engage in the banking and trust business once an applicant has satisfied the statutory requirements.[907] Thus, the banking board has the "sole discretion" with respect to the grant of the certificate of authority to engage in the banking and trust business only after the procedural safeguards of the Banking Code have been followed and within the constitutional limits which prohibit the exercise of discretion which is arbitrary or capricious.[908] Furthermore, the banking board did not abuse its discretion in denying the certificate of authority to engage in the savings and trust business because of the existence of the pending appeal by the State Banking Association of an earlier order of the federal reserve board approving the acquisition of the trust company by the applicant or denying the application without prejudice to resubmit it at the conclusion of the federal appeal since if the court of appeals reversed the federal reserve

---

905 **Law Review.—**

"Financial Reform Too Big To Fail? Emerging from the Financial Crisis with the Help of Increased Consumer Protection and Corporate Responsibility: Article: Laudable Goals and Unintended Consequences: The Role and Control of Fannie Mae and Freddie Mac," see 60 Am. U.L. Rev. 1489 (June 2011).

See also "Government Regulator Sues Wall Street Banks For Fraud in Subprime Mortgage Deals," https://www.huffingtonpost.com/2011/09/02/banks-sued-subprime-mortgage-deals_n_947349.html.

906 Perry Capital LLC ex rel. Inv. Funds v. Mnuchin, 864 F.3d 591 (D.C. Cir. 2017).

907 Citicorp Sav. & Thast Co. v. Banking Bd., 704 P.2d 490 (Okla. 1985).

908 Citicorp Sav. & Thast Co. v. Banking Bd., 704 P.2d 490 (Okla. 1985).

board's decision, then the applicant by its own admission would most likely have to divest itself resulting in new ownership with unknown consequences.[909]

Immunity from Liability Under Annunzio-Wylie Act.—Pursuant to the safe harbor provision of Annunzio-Wylie Act, a trust company was immune from all liability, not merely from liability arising from statements made in good faith, in employee's defamation action arising from employer's alleged filing of a Suspicious Activity Report (SAR) with the United States Attorney's Office.[910]

§ 2. Statutory Provisions.

In General.—Laws governing trust companies must be rigidly enforced,[911] but if penal, must be strictly construed.[912] A statute declaring the powers and duties of trust companies, if unambiguous, does not require construction by the courts.[913] And words will not be interpolated or inserted in a statute relating to trust companies unless clearly required to carry out the legislative intent.[914] Trust companies doing a general banking business may

---

[909] Citicorp Sav. & Thast Co. v. Banking Bd., 704 P.2d 490 (Okla. 1985).

[910] Lee v. Bankers Trust Co., 166 F.3d 540 (2nd Cir. 1999).

The immunity afforded banks under the Annunzio-Wylie Anti-Money Laundering Act, 31 U.S.C.S. § 5318 et seq., is absolute, and applies: (1) Whether the financial institution makes a required or volunteered report; (2) whether the report is made to federal, state, or local authorities; (3) whether the reported activity eventually turns out to be legal or illegal and (4) whether the report is made with or without a good faith investigation. Ventura v. Central Bank, 515 S.W.3d 680 (Ky. App. 2017).

The Court of Appeals of Kentucky has found case law from the United States Courts of Appeals for the First and Second Circuit to be instructive and persuasive authorities for a finding that the Annunzio-Wylie Anti-Money Laundering Act, 31 U.S.C.S. § 5318 et seq., does not impose a good faith requirement. The plain language of the Act provides immunity for the disclosure of any possible violation of law or regulation. The word "any" is broad and unambiguous. The Court of Appeals of Kentucky has concluded that the safe harbor provision of the Act is unambiguous, unqualified, and does not limit immunity to disclosures made in good faith. Ventura v. Central Bank, 515 S.W.3d 680 (Ky. App. 2017).

[911] In re Security Bank, etc., Co., 178 Minn. 209, 224 N.W. 235.

[912] Pacific Title, etc., Co. v. Sargent, 73 Ore. 485, 144 P. 452.

Statute prohibiting officer, director, employee, or attorney of a trust company from receiving any fee, commission, gift or other consideration in connection with any business of such corporation, subject to certain exceptions, is a penal statute and must be strictly construed. Commonwealth v. Bias, 337 Mass. 565, 150 N.E.2d 527.

[913] Union Trust Co. v. Moore, 104 Wash. 50, 175 P. 565.

[914] **In general.**—

Detroit Trust Co. v. Granger, 278 Mich. 152, 270 N.W. 239.

be classified by a legislature as banks for purposes of regulation,[915] or may be subject to a special legislative enactment.[916] The statutory requirement that the trust company be FDIC-insured effectively revoked the trust company's right under the corporate charter to underwrite surety bonds, for the Federal Deposit Insurance Corporation (FDIC) will not insure the trust company unless it ceases underwriting.[917] Thus, the FDIC insurance provides protection to depositors beyond that provided by the sections which require trust companies to keep on hand authorized securities in excess of deposits and empowers the commissioner to monitor compliance and which require the trust company to deposit additional securities with the state as a guaranty fund for depositors and creditors and for the faithful discharge of its duties; thus, the statute requiring the trust company to obtain the FDIC insurance on its savings deposit does not violate the contract clauses of the

---

Supreme court would not interpolate or insert word in statute providing that transfer of trust company stock with intent to defraud creditors, if made within four months of receivership, should be void, so that all transfers made within four months of receivership would be void, in absence of showing beyond haphazard guess that legislature intended statute to differ from its plain and unambiguous meaning. Detroit Trust Co. v. Granger, 278 Mich. 152, 270 N.W. 239; Detroit Trust Co. v. Hartwick, 278 Mich. 139, 270 N.W. 249.

Illustrative case.—

Under a statute requiring that bank acting as trustee be "authorized" to do business in the state, it was held that "authorized" meant that which the laws of the state had laid down as requirements to obtain authoritative permission to do business. Pennsylvania Co. for Ins. on Lives, etc. v. Gillmore, 142 N.J. Eq. 27, 59 A.2d 24.

915 In re Wellings, 192 Cal. 506, 221 P. 628.

916 **In general.—**

Kelly v. Guild, 42 Ill. App. 2d 143, 191 N.E.2d 377.

The Illinois Trust Companies Act was intended to apply to commercial for profit trust companies which are engaged as a regular business in the general administration of trusts for profit. Kelly v. Guild, 42 Ill. App. 2d 143, 191 N.E.2d 377.

Purpose of act.—

One of the objects and purposes of the act is to afford trust creditors a measure of protection that is not afforded general creditors of a bank or trust company operating thereunder. Kelly v. Guild, 42 Ill. App. 2d 143, 191 N.E.24 377.

A nonprofit corporation was not a "trust company" within the meaning of the statute where it was organized for charitable, benevolent or eleemosynary purposes. Kelly v. Guild, 42 Ill. App. 2d 143, 191 N.E.2d 377.

The provisions of the Surrogate's Court Act prevail over the provisions of the Banking Law which limit right of a trust company to act as a fiduciary. In re Sorensen's Estate, 195 Misc. 742, 91 N.Y.S.2d 220.

917 Minnesota Trust Co. v. Hatch, 368 N.W.2d 372 (Minn. App. 1985).

state or federal constitutions.[918] The discretion allowed by the state statute regarding the granting of certificates of authority to engage in the banking or trust business is not an unlawful delegation of legislative authority without proper standards or guidelines.[919]

A "bank," for purposes of the Internal Revenue Code, must be given its common meaning, which is in essence the receipt of deposits and making of loans. This is not purely duplicative of the statute's requirement that a substantial part of the taxpayer's business consists of receiving deposits and making loans and discounts because this later requirement adds an important modifier: "substantial part of the business." The statute thus qualifies these factors, requiring that a taxpayer seeking to take advantage of a tax benefit not only engage in the touchstone activities of a bank, but that these activities amount to a substantial part of its business.[920] While it is true that the common meaning of "bank" is similar to the Code's requirement that a substantial part of the taxpayer's business consists of receiving deposits and making loans and discounts, these components are not completely duplicative. For instance, an entity could be a bank within the common meaning of the term but still fail to satisfy the statute's requirement that receiving deposits and making loans amount to a substantial part of its business.[921]

---

[918] Minnesota Trust Co. v. Hatch, 368 N.W.2d 372 (Minn. App. 1985).

Goal of statute, which requires that all banks and trust companies, savings and loan associations, credit unions, and industrial loan and thrift companies obtain insurance with FDIC, is to protect depositors of institutions from loss through bank failure, and is undisputedly vital social concern. Minnesota Trust Co. v. Hatch, 368 N.W.2d 372 (Minn. App. 1985).

[919] Citicorp Sav. & Trust Co. v. Banking Bd., 704 P.2d 490 (Okla. 1985).

The legislature purposefully gave the Banking Commission a great deal of discretion in deciding factual questions regarding an application to organize and operate a trust company in South Dakota, because the Commissioners are individuals with specialized knowledge of the banking and trust industries whose judgment and insight in these specialized fields facilitate the admittance and overall regulation of these industries. In re Application of Dorsey, 2001 SD 35, 623 N.W.2d 468, (2001).

The legislature, in the statute regarding applications to organize and operate trust companies in South Dakota, intended to protect the participants in the trust industry by ensuring the creation and maintenance of adequate and sound trust facilities and services. In re Application of Dorsey, 2001 SD 35, 623 N.W.2d 468 (2001).

As to other statutes illustrating scope of power of legislature in matters of control and regulation, see § 1 of this chapter.

[920] Moneygram Int'l v. Comm'r, 664 Fed. Appx. 386 (5th Cir. 2016).

[921] Moneygram Int'l v. Comm'r, 664 Fed. Appx. 386 (5th Cir. 2016).

The section in the Internal Revenue Code defining "bank" provides that a substantial part of the taxpayer's business must consist of making "loans and discounts."[922] The statute's use of the conjunctive "and" rather than the disjunctive "or" in this phrase indicates that discounts is a required element. The conjunctive use of the word "and" indicates that each aspect must be satisfied.[923]

Applicability.—A constitutional provision reserving the right to amend, alter or repeal corporate laws enacted thereunder was held a part of the charter of a trust company organized under such a law, and the charter of such trust company was subject to the constitutional reservation of the power to amend, alter or repeal.[924] And where such law was repealed and a new law enacted, it was held the trust company could either quit doing business and settle its affairs, or reincorporate or amend its charter under the new law.[925] Similarly, if a state, in the law providing for a company's incorporation, reserves the right to alter, amend or repeal such law and to regulate, limit and restrain the business of the company, a subsequent regulatory statute is in no sense a taking of the company's property without due process of law.[926]

---

922 26 U.S.C.S. § 581.

923 Moneygram Int'l v. Comm'r, 664 Fed. Appx. 386 (5th Cir. 2016).

924 **In general.—**

Detroit Trust Co. v. Allinger, 271 Mich. 600, 261 N.W. 90, appeal dismissed, 297 U.S. 695, 56 S. Ct. 572, 80 L. Ed. 986.

Limitation of stockholders' liability under statute under which trust company was incorporated was a mere incident of corporate being, which existed only at pleasure of state, and such liability could be changed or increased by the legislature. Detroit Trust Co. v. Allinger, 271 Mich. 600, 261 N.W. 90, appeal dismissed, 297 U.S. 695, 56 S. Ct. 572, 80 L. Ed. 986.

925 **In general.—**

Detroit Trust Co. v. Allinger, 271 Mich. 600, 261 N.W. 90, appeal dismissed, 297 U.S. 695, 56 S. Ct. 572, 80 L. Ed. 986.

Acts of user under subsequent statute were evidence of acceptance thereof as rule of action by which trust was governed. Detroit Trust Co. v. Allinger, 271 Mich. 600, 261 N.W. 90, appeal dismissed, 297 U.S. 695, 56 S. Ct. 572, 80 L. Ed. 986.

It would not be presumed trust company intentionally forfeited its charter, or continued to do business illegally after repeal of statute under which it was incorporated. Detroit Trust Co. v. Allinger, 271 Mich. 600, 261 N.W. 90, appeal dismissed, 297 U.S. 695, 56 S. Ct. 572, 80 L. Ed. 986.

926 **In general.—**

Union Trust Co. v. Moore, 104 Wash. 50, 175 P. 565.

Insolvency.—Statutes limiting the time allowed for filing claims and bringing suits against insolvent trust companies have been held a valid exercise of the police power.[927] And a statute authorizing a state mortgage commission to receive the assets of insolvent trust companies held in the course of administration by the superintendent of banks was held constitutional.[928] A statute providing a remedy for winding up the affairs of trust companies to the exclusion of proceedings by stockholders for the appointment of a receiver,[929] and a provision for the transfer of trustee-ships on the transfer of the business of banking corporations are valid.[930]

Courts lack jurisdiction as to claim or action for payment from assets of any depository institution for which the Federal Deposit Insurance Corporation (FDIC) is receiver.[931]

The Housing and Economic Recovery Act of 2008 (Recovery Act) established the Federal Housing Finance Agency (FHFA) and authorized it to undertake extraordinary economic measures to resuscitate the Federal National Mortgage Association (Fannie Mae) and the Federal Home Loan Mortgage Corporation (Freddie Mac), including authorizing the director of the FHFA to appoint the FHFA as either conservator or receiver for Fannie and Freddie for the purpose of reorganizing, rehabilitating, or winding up their affairs.[932] The Recovery Act outlines what the FHFA (or Agency) as conservator "may" do and what actions it "may" take. The statute is thus framed in terms of expansive grants of permissive, discretionary authority

---

By statute restricting exercise of trust companies' powers as such to their principal places of business, legislature exercised its power, expressly reserved in charter granted trust company, to alter or modify it by imposing limitations on place of exercising trust company functions. Hudson-Harlem Valley Title & Mortg. Co. v. White, 164 Misc. 47, 298 N.Y.S. 652, modified, 251 App. Div. 1, 296 N.Y.S. 424, appeal dismissed, 276 N.Y. 603, 12 N.E.24 597.

Statute governing merger of banks and trust companies is constitutionally imposed on existing corporations under state's reserved power (Corporation Act, § 4 Comp. St. 1910, p. 16003; Trust Company and Bank Merger Act 1925). Bingham v. Savings Investment, etc., Co., 101 N.J. Eq. 413, 138 A. 659, aff'd, 102 N.J. Eq. 302, 140 A. 321; Colby v. Equitable Trust Co., 124 App. Div. 262, 108 N.Y.S. 978, aff'd, 192 N.Y. 535, 84 N.E. 1111. As to merger, see § 3 of this chapter.

927 Bowersock Mills, etc., Co. v. Citizens' Trust Co. (Mo. App.), 298 S.W. 1049.

928 Hutchinson v. Nassau County Trust Co., 283 N.Y.S. 257.

929 Koch v. Missouri-Lincoln Trust Co. (Mo.), 181 S.W. 44.

930 In re Barnett, 97 Cal. App. 138, 275 P. 453.

931 Douglas County v. Hamilton State Bank, 340 Ga. App. 801, 798 S.E.2d 509 (2017).

932 Perry Capital LLC ex rel. Inv. Funds v. Mnuchin, 864 F.3d 591 (D.C. Cir. 2017).

for FHFA to exercise as the Agency determines is in the best interests of the regulated entity or the Agency. It should go without saying that may means may. And "may" is, of course, permissive rather than obligatory.[933]

Congress did not say in the Recovery Act that the FHFA "should"—let alone, "should first"—preserve and conserve assets or "should" first put the Federal National Mortgage Association and the Federal Home Loan Mortgage Corporation ("Companies") in a sound and solvent condition. Nor did it articulate FHFA's power directly in terms of asset preservation or sound and solvent company operations. What the statute says is that FHFA may take such action as may be necessary to put the Companies in a sound and solvent condition and may be appropriate to preserve or conserve the Companies' assets. So at most, the Recovery Act empowers FHFA to "take such action" as may be necessary or appropriate to fulfill several goals.[934]

Constitutionality.—The following statutes as interpreted by the courts have been held not to contravene the constitution: a statute making trust companies subject to the regulation of a superintendent of banks;[935] a statute giving a commissioner of banking the power, when a company violates its charter, to take possession of its property and business,[936] and authorizing him to close trust companies under certain conditions;[937] a statute authorizing a commissioner to maintain an action for the full amount of the liability of stockholders in trust companies on his own determination of necessity;[938] a statute permitting the establishment of common trust funds;[939] and a statute authorizing a state official to permit a trust company to extend payment of time deposits where a notice of withdrawal has been given or

---

933 Perry Capital LLC ex rel. Inv. Funds v. Mnuchin, 864 F.3d 591 (D.C. Cir. 2017).

934 Perry Capital LLC ex rel. Inv. Funds v. Mnuchin, 864 F.3d 591 (D.C. Cir. 2017).

935 Hayden Plan Co. v. Wood, 97 Cal. App. 1, 275 P. 248.

936 Roseville Trust Co. v. Mott, 85 N.J. Eq. 297, 96 A. 402.

937 Cosmopolitan Trust Co. v. Mitchell, 242 Mass. 95, 136 N.E. 403.

938 Allen v. Prudential Trust Co., 242 Mass. 78, 136 N.E. 410.

939 **In general.—**

In re Lincoln Rochester Trust Co., 111 N.Y.S.2d 45.

As to common trust funds generally, see § 15 of this chapter.

Notice provisions as to settlement of trustee's accounts constitutional as to unknown or future beneficiaries but not as to present known beneficiaries.—

See Mullane v. Central Hanover Bank & Trust Co., 339 U.S. 306, 70 S. Ct. 652, 94 L. Ed. 865.

might be given, and to postpone payment of demand deposits.[940] A statute which prohibits unauthorized corporations from doing business under a name embracing the words "trust company" is also valid.[941] A statute prohibiting trust companies or similar corporations or national banks from advertising or circularizing the fact that they are authorized to act as executors is not unconstitutional.[942] But a statute, retroactive in its nature, which provides that a corporation cannot use the word "trust" in its name unless it complies with certain requirements, is an unreasonable exercise of the police power and a violation of the state's contract with companies theretofore incorporated.[943] A statute which called for a residency period for holders of stock of a secondary loan mortgage company license applicant was held to be unconstitutional as violative of the equal protection clause.[944] A statute requiring, with certain exceptions, that every corporation engaged in trust business before January 1, 1972, receive the approval of the state board of bank control before commencing operations, and authorizing the board to determine whether the conduct of business would serve the public

---

[940] Statler v. United States Sav. & Trust Co., 326 Pa. 247, 192 A. 250.

[941] McKee v. American Trust Co., 166 Ark. 480, 266 S.W. 293.

[942] New Hampshire Bankers Ass'n v. Nelson, 336 F. Supp. 1330 (D.N.H.), aff'd, 460 F.2d 307 (1st Cir.), cert. denied, 409 U.S. 1001, 93 S. Ct. 320, 34 L. Ed. 2d 262 (1972).

Advertising prohibition contained in New Hampshire statute prohibiting trust companies or similar corporations or national banks from advertising or circularizing fact that they are authorized to act as executors did not deny equal protection and due process guaranteed under the United States Constitution nor violate provisions of the New Hampshire Constitution. New Hampshire Bankers Asso. v. Nelson, 336 F. Supp. 1330 (D.N.H.), aff'd, 460 F.2d 307 (1st Cir.), cert. denied, 409 U.S. 1001, 93 S. Ct. 320, 34 L. Ed. 2d 262 (1972).

Fact that New Hampshire was only state in the nation with type of advertising prohibition contained in statute prohibiting trust companies or similar corporations or national banks from advertising or circularizing fact that they are authorized to act as executors would not make the statute vulnerable to constitutional attack. New Hampshire Bankers Asso. v. Nelson, 336 F. Supp. 1330 (D.N.H), aff'd, 460 F.2d 307 (1st Cir.), cert. denied, 409 U.S. 1001, 93 S. Ct. 320, 34 L Ed. 2d 262 (1972).

Even if it were conceded that purpose and effect of New Hampshire statute, prohibiting trust companies or similar corporations or national banks from advertising or circularizing fact that they are authorized to act as executors, was to prevent lawyers from losing executor appointments to banks because of bank advertising and that, as a result, lawyers received favored treatment, that would not make the statute constitutionally defective. New Hampshire Bankers Asso. v. Nelson, 336 F. Supp. 1330 (D.N.H.), aff'd, 460 F.2d 307(1st Cir.), cert. denied, 409 U.S. 1001, 93 S. Ct. 320, 34 L. Ed. 2d 262 (1972).

[943] Pacific Title & Trust Co. v. Sargent, 73 Ore. 485, 144 P. 462.

[944] Green v. Mid-Penn Nat'l Mtg. Co., 268 A.2d 876 (Del. 1970).

interest, taking into consideration local circumstances, etc., did not violate the due process clause, nor did it, on its face, violate the equal protection clause.[945]

Investments.—Trust companies that are expressly prohibited from making stock dividends cannot be exempted from such a provision by a law applicable to other corporations.[946] The reenactment of a statute relating to the investment of trust fluids does not repeal a statute authorizing a corporate trustee to purchase securities from itself.[947] And statutes regulating the sale of corporate bonds secured by a pledge or deposit with a trustee of mortgages or other evidences of indebtedness, and making such corporations subject to the supervision of the superintendent of banks, are not repealed by a Blue Sky Law.[948] But a statute limiting real estate loans of a savings department of a trust company to sixty percent of the property's value has no application to a commercial department of a trust company.[949]

Miscellaneous Matters.—An act prohibiting the transaction of a trust company's usual business at a place other than its principal place of business is inapplicable to a title insurance business, "usual business" relating to the trust company's ordinary business.[950] Industrial banks[951] and industrial loan

---

[945] American Trust Co. v. South Carolina State Board of Bank Control, 381 F. Supp. 313 (D.S.C. 1974).

Absent evidence, to show a fair and reasonable relationship of statute, to South Carolina's legitimate objective of assuring that corporate fiduciaries serve the public faithfully, those portions of South Carolina statutes which had the effect of barring a South Carolina Trust Company from serving as executor or administrator because it was controlled by a corporation domiciled in another state and those portions barring such trust company from serving as testamentary trustee because it was controlled by a corporation domiciled or licensed in a contiguous state were violative of the equal protection clause of the Fourteenth Amendment. American Trust Co. v. South Carolina State Board of Bank Control, 381 F. Supp. 313 (D.S.C. 1974).

[946] Smith v. Cotting, 231 Mass. 42, 120 N.E. 177.

[947] In re Thomson's Estate, 135 Misc. 32, 237 N.Y.S. 622.

[948] Petters & Co. v. Veigel, 167 Minn. 286, 209 N.W. 9.

[949] Commonwealth v. McKnight, 283 Mass. 35, 186 N.E. 42.

[950] Hudson-Harlem Valley Title & Mortg. Co. v. White, 164 Misc. 47, 298 N.Y.S. 652, modified, 251 App. Div. 1, 296 N.Y.S. 424, appeal dismissed, 276 N.Y. 603, 12 N.E.2d 597.

[951] Columbus Industrial Bank v. Miller, 125 Conn. 313, 6 A.2d 42 (1939).

Statute which permits industrial banks in effect to receive more than 12 percent interest notwithstanding other lenders of money are not permitted to do so was not unconstitutional as discriminatory legislation. Columbus Industrial Bank v. Miller, 125 Conn. 313, 6 A.2d 42 (1939).

and thrift companies[952] may be permitted to receive more interest than other lenders of money. The purpose of the provision of an Industrial Loan Act that every corporation organized thereunder is subject to the supervision of the state corporation commissioner is to protect the interests of shareholders, creditors and others interested in or affected by the business of such corporations.[953] And a statute requiring bank officers and employees to furnish a surety company bond was held not repealed by a subsequent act requiring bank officers and employees to furnish a fidelity bond, so as to authorize concerns which were not surety companies or authorized to do business in the state as insurance companies, to write fidelity bonds on officers or employees of trust companies.[954] If a safety deposit or a trust company is engaging in a practice prohibited by the Securities Act, the securities commissioner may apply to the district court for an injunction restraining the violator, or he may transfer the evidence to the attorney general.[955]

Investment Companies—An act perfecting or regulating the right of investment companies to do business in a state is valid.[956]

Investment Company Act.—The regulatory provisions of the Federal Investment Company Act of 1940[957] are of particular relevance to situations where an investor is committing his funds to the hands of others on an equity

---

[952] Mesaba Loan Co. v. Sher, 203 Minn. 589, 282 N.W. 823.

The Morris Plan Act, permitting industrial loan and thrift companies organized thereunder to charge 8 percent interest in advance on loans not to exceed one year, does not deny equal protection of the law to other money lenders similarly situated. Mesaba Loan Co. v. Seer, 203 Minn. 589, 282 N.W. 823.

[953] Daugherty v. Superior Court of Imperial County, 58 Cal. App. 2d 851, 133 P.2d 827 (California statute).

[954] Shaw v. Brisbine, 63 S.D. 470, 260 N.W. 710.

[955] State ex rel. Holloway v. First Am. Bank & Trust Co., 186 N.W.2d 573 (ND. 1971).

[956] **In general.—**

Ex parte Taylor, 68 Fla. 61, 66 So. 292, 1916A Ann. Cas. 701.

The Texas statute governing creation of corporations to deal in securities without banking or insurance privilege encompasses all corporations having or which may "hereafter" have as their purpose the powers found in certain designated statutes, regardless of repeal of such statutes; when a statute incorporated another, and that one was thereafter repealed, the incorporating statute's scope remained intact. Thus, article applied to corporations organized after repeal of such statutes. Falkner v. Allied Finance Co., 394 S.W.2d 208 (Tex. Civ. App.), writs of error dismissed and refused, 397 S.W.2d 846 (Tex. 1965).

[957] 15 U.S.C.S. § 80a-1 et seq.

basis, with the view that the funds will be invested in securities and his fortunes will depend on the success of the investment.[958] The history of the Act shows that Congress intentionally drafted statutory definitions in the Act in general terms in order to control such situations regardless of the legal form or structure of the investment enterprise.[959]

---

[958] **In general.—**

Prudential Ins. Co. v. Securities & Exchange Com., 326 F.2d 383, cert. denied, 377 U.S. 953, 84 S. Ct. 1629, 12 L. Ed. 2d 497.

See also § 16 of this chapter.

Purpose of Investment Company Act is to prevent abuses which may grow out of the unregulated power of management to use large pools of cash. Securities & Exch. Comm'n v. Fifth Ave. Coach Lines, Inc., 289 F. Supp. 3 (S.D.N.Y. 1968).

Investment Company Act was primarily aimed at protection of individuals who purchased securities issued by investment company. Greater Iowa Corp. v. McLendon, 378 F.2d 783 (8th Cir. 1967).

Investment Company Act of 1940 is intended as a comprehensive regulatory act with a purpose of curbing those practices which are inherent in investment company and may result to detriment of investors if not controlled. McMenomy v. Ryden, 276 Minn. 55, 148 N.W.2d 804 (1967).

One of the purposes of the Investment Company Act is to protect investors in investment companies against the managing of those companies in the interests of persons other than the investors. Breswick & Co. v. United States, 134 F. Supp. 132.

The Investment Company Act of 1940 was primarily designed to protect existing investors in an investment company's securities. Independent Investor Protective League v. Securities & Exch. Comm'n, 495 F.2d 311 (2d Cir. 1974).

Sale of mutual fund shares.—Under the Investment Company Act of 1940, sales of mutual fund shares to the public must be made at a current offering price as described in the prospectus. Baum v. Investors Diversified Services, Inc., 286 F. Supp. 914 (N.D. Ill. 1968), aff'd, 409 F.2d 872 (7th Cir. 1969).

[959] **In general.—**

Prudential Ins. Co. v. Securities & Exchange Com., 326 F.2d 383, cert. denied, 377 U.S. 953, 84 S. Ct. 1629, 12 L. Ed. 2d 497.

Meaning of "investment company".—

The Investment Company Act of 1940 is cast in broad terms. The critical term is "company," which is defined in part as a trust, a fund, or any organized group of persons whether incorporated or not. Prudential Ins. Co. v. Securities & Exchange Com., 326 F.2d 383 (3rd Cir. 1964), cert. denied, 377 U.S. 953, 84 S. Ct. 1629, 12 L. Ed. 2d 497. See 15 U.S.C.S. § 80a-2(a)(8).

Corporation formed for purpose of investing in domestic securities was an "investment company" within meaning of Investment Company Act of 1940 and subject to registration requirements in order to make use of mails in making sales, offers of sale, or delivery after

The Investment Company Act was intended to provide a comprehensive regulatory scheme to correct and prevent certain abusive practices in the management of investment companies for protection of persons who put up money to be invested by such companies on their behalf.[960] By reason of their liquidity, investment companies are peculiarly subject to abuse, and the

---

sales, of its securities. Securities & Exch. Comm'n v. Midland Basic, Inc., 283 F. Supp. 609 (D.S.D. 1968).

Under Investment Company Act definition relating to investment company as one who is engaged primarily in business of investing or holds itself out as being primarily engaged in that business or proposes to engage primarily in that business, "holding out" and "proposing" imply intent but word "is" does not necessarily imply intent, and to determine whether company is engaged primarily in business of investing its total activities of all sorts must be considered. SEC v. Fifth Ave. Coach Lines, Inc., 289 F. Supp. 3 (S.D N.Y. 1968).

Statements in annual report and by corporate officers concerning proposed investments by corporation as soon as it received substantial condemnation award for its properties were predictions as to corporation's plans in future and were too general in nature to justify finding that they amounted to a "holding out" or "proposing" that corporation would engage primarily in business of investing and require conclusion that corporation had become an investment company within meaning of Investment Company Act immediately when funds were received. SEC v. Fifth Ave. Coach Lines, Inc., 289 F. Supp. 3 (S.D.N.Y. 1968).

Meaning of "invest".—

In construing Investment Company Act, the undefined word "invest" must be given its normal meaning which is to put out money at risk in hope of gain, and Act should not be read to mean that buying stock for dividends or for capital gain is investing and that buying it for control is not. Securities & Exch. Comm'n v. Fifth Ave. Coach Lines, Inc., 289 F. Supp. 3 (S.D.N.Y. 1968).

Claim of corporation against individual for return of a duplicate payment made did not constitute an "investment" within meaning of Investment Company Act. SEC v. Fifth Ave. Coach Lines, Inc., 289 F. Supp. 3 (S.D.N.Y. 1968).

Mere putting of condemnation award into bank accounts whereby corporation received interest did not in and of itself constitute "investing," reinvesting or trading in securities within meaning of Investment Company Act. SEC v. Fifth Ave. Coach Lines, Inc., 289 F. Supp. 3 (SD.N.Y. 1968).

Word "business" as used in Investment Company Act section defining investment company as one engaged primarily in business of investing implies continued activity, and it is unreasonable to construe Act to mean that one's company which had no previous business begins to buy comparatively few blocks of stock, it automatically becomes engaged in business of investing in and holding securities, as company is entitled to reasonable time within which to turn around. SEC v. Fifth Ave. Coach Lines, Inc., 289 F. Supp. 3 (S.D.N.Y. 1968).

[960] Herpich v. Wallace, 430 F.2d 792 (5th Cir. 1970).

Investment Company Act was intended to deter mismanagement of investment companies, for protection of investment company's security holders, not to regulate

Investment Company Act meets the problems recognized therein by subjecting such companies to regulation by the Securities and Exchange Commission.[961] There can be no doubt that the act supports a private right

---

management of companies in which investment companies put their funds. Herpich v. Wallace, 430 F.2d 792 (5th Cir. 1970).

The Investment Company Act of 1940 was designed to establish broad standards which more easily enable the government to convict affiliated persons for self-dealing in the management of investment companies. United States v. Deutsch, 451 F.2d 98 (2d Cir. 1971), cert. denied, 404 U.S. 1019, 92 S Ct. 682, 30 L. Ed. 2d 667 (1972).

[961] **In general.—**

Aldred Inv. Trust v. Securities, etc., Comm., 151 F.2d 254, aff'g 58 F. Supp. 724. For other cases relating to the Act and the Securities Exchange Commission, see Breswick & Co. v. Briggs, 135 F. Supp. 397; Breswick & Co. v. United States, 138 F. Supp. 123, rev'd sub nom. Alleghany Corp. v. Breswick & Co., 353 U.S. 151, 77 S. Ct. 763, 1 L. Ed. 2d 726; Schwartz v. Bowman, 156 F. Supp. 361, appeal dismissed sub nom. Schwartz v. Eaton, 264 F.2d 195.

Investment Company Act of 1940 authorizes Securities and Exchange Commission to regulate a pricing system for mutual funds and contemplates a price-fixing scheme which would constitute a parse violation of Sherman Act if it occurred in a context free from other federal regulations. Baum v. Investors Diversified Servs. Inc., 286 F. Supp. 914 (N.D. Ill. 1968), aff'd, 409 F.2d 872 (7th Cir. 1969).

Determining violation of Investment Company Act.—

Securities and Exchange Commission, as specialized body with investigative powers, was competent body which could assist court in making determination of whether Investment Company Act was violated by defendant corporation in its efforts to acquire control of plaintiff corporation and court would accordingly, in issuing pendente lite order, require defendant corporation to make application to the Securities and Exchange Commission to determine whether it was required to register as investment company or was exempt from registration, and would order matters held in status quo until receipt of Commission report and further order of court. Natco Corp. v. Great Lakes Industries, Inc., 214 F. Supp. 185.

The Securities and Exchange Commission, as party plaintiff in action seeking to restrain corporations in operation of their businesses as investment companies based on violation of the Investment Company Act, had the right to submit recommendations as to allowances for attorneys' and trustee's fees. Securities & Exch. Comm'n v. S & P Nat'l Corp., 267 F. Supp. 562 (S.D.N.Y. 1967).

SEC did not exceed its authority.—

Securities and Exchange Commission in seeking to implement statute making it unlawful for affiliated person and registered investment company to effect any transaction in which registered company is a joint participant in contravention of rules and regulations of Commission by a general requirement of an advanced application and approval of transaction did not exceed authority granted by Congress. SEC v. Talley Industries, Inc., 399 F.2d 396 (2d Cir. 1968), cert. denied, 393 U.S. 1015, 89 S. Ct. 615, 21 L. Ed. 2d 560 (1969).

Prior determination by Securities Exchange Commission as to whether corporation

of action for damages.[962] One section of the Investment Company Act authorizes the Securities and Exchange Commission to bring actions against certain individuals or companies for breaches of fiduciary duty involving personal misconduct. The act, however, authorizes an action by the SEC, not by private individuals. Although this should not be read to prohibit suits by individuals when other sections of the act are violated, when only a general breach of fiduciary duty is alleged, a private suit should more properly be brought in a state court.[963] The courts should give the Investment Company Act a hospitable reception, but ought not to expand its words beyond their natural meaning to bring within its sweep a transaction which is not a "mischief and defect" aimed at by the Act, and which it is doubtful that Congress would have wished to include if it had considered the problem.[964]

---

which allegedly violated Investment Company Act of 1940 had been controlled by individual was not necessary to court's making such determination. SEC v. S & P Nat'l Corp., 360 F.2d 741 (2d Cir. 1966).

In absence of any affirmative action by Securities and Exchange Commission mere filing of contracts between principal underwriter and fund with Commission did not constitute administrative approval. Saminsky v. Abbott, 40 Del. Ch. 528, 185 A.2d 765.

Review of Securities and Exchange Commission Order.—

Review may be had pursuant to Investment Company Act of any portion of order of Securities and Exchange Commission that has been challenged effectively and meaningfully by any party to or participant in administrative proceedings so long as contentions raised are consistent with interest of person or participant seeking review as a person aggrieved. Hennesey v. Securities & Exchange Comm., 285 F.2d 511.

Although stockholder of corporation made objection to exempting corporation from Investment Company Act on only one of 27 days of hearings before Securities and Exchange Commission, stockholder, as a person aggrieved, was entitled to obtain review on objections raised by other objectors. Hennesey v. Securities & Exchange Comm., 285 F.2d 511.

[962] Goodall v. Columbia Ventures, 374 F. Supp. 1324 (S.D.N.Y. 1974).

A person showing the type of injury the Investment Company Act is meant to prevent may be afforded a civil remedy. Herpich v. Wallace, 430 F.2d 792(5th Cir. 1970).

[963] **In general.—**

Monheit v. Carter, 376 F. Supp. 334 (S.D.N.Y. 1974).

Pendent jurisdiction over state claim taken by federal district court.—

See Monheit v. Carter, 376 F. Supp. 334 (S.D.N.Y. 1974).

[964] Willheim v. Murchison, 342 F.2d 33 (2d Cir.), cert. denied, 382 U.S. 840, 86 S. Ct. 38, 15 L. Ed. 2d 82 (1965).

Even though fundamental purpose of Investment Company Act is to prevent unsupervised dealing between an investment company and its controlled affiliate, it does not necessarily follow that Congress intended to prevent every possible type of such dealing. Securities &

Thus, the courts are not overall supervisory agents of all the morals, equities or standards in the field regulated by the Investment Company Act.[965]

The sections of the Investment Company Act prohibiting certain transactions between a person affiliated with a registered investment company and such company were designed to protect investors.[966] Such sections create a private right of action for the benefit of persons injured by actions of the type the Act is designed to prevent.[967] But a foreign corporation which was an unregistered investment company within the meaning of the Investment

---

Exch. Comm'n v. Sterling Precision Corp., 276 F. Supp. 772 (S.D.N.Y. 1967), aff'd, 393 F.2d 214 (2d Cir. 1968).

The unsupervised self-dealing which Congress intended to prevent by the Investment Company Act would seem to be dealing of the sort which involved negotiations or bargaining between the two companies a redemption of securities does not involve such dealing. Securities & Rich. Comm'n v. Sterling Precision Corp., 276 F. Supp. 772 (S.D.N.Y. 1967), aff'd, 393 F.2d 214 (2d Cir. 1968).

965 Securities & Exchange Comm'n v. Insurance Securities Inc., 146 F. Supp. 778, aff'd, 254 F.2d 642, cert. denied, 358 U.S. 823, 79 S. Ct. 88, 3 L. Ed. 2d 64.

966 Entel v. Guilden, 223 F. Supp. 129.

Objective of statute prohibiting transactions by affiliated person and registered investment company by which company becomes a joint participant with affiliated person in violation of rules and regulations of Commission is to prevent affiliated persons from injuring interests of stockholders of registered investment companies by causing company to participate on a basis different from or less advantageous than that of such other participant. Securities & Exch. Comm'n v. Talley Indus., 399 F.2d 396 (2d Cir. 1968), cert. denied, 393 U.S. 1015, 89 S. Ct. 615, 21 L. Ed. 2d 560(1969).

Acceptance of compensation for purchase of property.—

Objective of statute making it unlawful for any affiliated person of a registered investment company, acting as agent, to accept from any source any compensation for purchase of any property for such registered company is to prevent affiliated persons from having their judgment and fidelity impaired by conflicts of interest. United States v. Deutsch, 451 F.2d 98 (2d Cir. 1971), cert. denied, 404 U.S. 1019, 92 S. Ct. 682, 30 L Ed. 2d 661 (1972).

967 **In general.—**

Entel v. Guilden, 223 F. Supp. 129.

Although the Investment Company Act makes no specific provision for private civil liability arising from violations of the Act such liability may be implied. Esplin v. Hirschi, 402 F.2d 94 (10th Cir. 1968), cert. denied, 394 U.S. 928, 89 S. Ct 1194, 22 L. Ed. 2d 459 (1969).

Private enforcement of Investment Company Act of 1940 provides necessary supplement to Securities Exchange Commission action to effect compliance with the Act, but private suit may be brought only by one showing an injury of the sort the Act is designed to prevent. Securities & Exch. Comm'n v. General Time Corp., 407 F.2d 65 (2d Cir. 1968), cert. denied, 393 U.S. 1026, 89 S. Ct. 637, 21 L. Ed. 2d 570 (1969).

Company Act of 1940 could not found a cause of action upon any believed right to sell stock under an illegal prospectus, and was not a proper party plaintiff in an action brought by it and a domestic corporation of which it owned all stock, wherein it alleged that because of a conspiracy against the domestic corporation the value of its stock had suffered.[968] However, where the corporation was exempt from the registration provisions of the Act because it dealt primarily through a wholly owned subsidiary engaged in businesses other than trading in securities, it was not barred from enforcing rights created by the Civil Rights Act because of its alleged misrepresentations in registration statements and prospectuses filed with the Securities and Exchange Commission.[969]

The purpose of the section of the Investment Company Act exempting therefrom any company subject to regulation under the Interstate Commerce Act is to avoid conflicting and overlapping regulation by two federal agencies.[970] But sections of the Act excluding investment companies

---

Standing to sue.—

Corporation whose stock had been purchased by registered investment company and affiliated person lacked standing to sue investment company and affiliated person under statute prohibiting transactions by affiliated person and registered investment company by which investment company becomes joint participant with affiliated person in violation of rules and regulations of Securities Exchange Commission to prevent affiliated persons from injuring interest of stockholder, of registered investment company by causing company to participate on basis different from or less advantageous than that of such other participant. Securities & Rich. Comm'n v. General Time Corp., 407 F.2d 65 (2d Cir. 1968), cert. denied, 393 U.S. 1026, 89 S. Ct. 637, 21 L. Ed. 2d 570 (1969).

Corporate issuer of stock is not entitled under Investment Company Act of 1940 to oversee the trading of its securities or object to acquisitions of its shares that may violate that Act. Securities & Exch. Comm'n v. General Time Corp., 407 F.2d 65 (2d Cir. 1968), cert. denied, 393 U.S. 1026, 89 S. Ct. 637, 21 L. Ed. 2d 570 (1969).

Even if corporation should be held to have standing to seek injunction against dealings in its securities that violate provisions of the securities laws designed to protect its own security holders, corporation would not have standing to espouse the cause of stockholders of a stockholder endangered by the violation of statute framed to meet their special needs. SEC v. General Time Corp., 407 F.2d 65 (2d Cir. 1968), cert. denied, 393 U.S. 1026, 89 S. Ct 637, 21 L. Ed. 2d 570 (1969).

968 Progress Development Corp. v. Mitchell, 182 F. Supp. 681, aff'd in part and rev'd in part, 286 F.2d 222.

969 Progress Development Corp. v. Mitchell, 286 F.2d 222.

970 **In general.—**

Hoover v. Allen, 241 F. Supp. 213 (S.D.N.Y. 1965).

(Text continued on page 239)

It is immaterial that carrier subject to regulation is not actively operating.—

If carrier is subject to regulation by Interstate Commerce Commission under sections of Interstate Commerce Act pertaining to keeping records and accounts, issuing securities and unifications, mergers and acquisitions or comparable sections, it is of no significance that it is not operating carrier, but, if there is no such regulation, actively operating carrier is not exempt under section of Investment Company Act of 1940 exempting from Act carriers subject to regulation under Interstate Commerce Act. Hoover v. Allen, 241 F. Supp. 213 (S.D.N.Y. 1965).

Effect of holding of certificate of public convenience and necessity.—

Dormant water carrier's mere holding of certificate of public convenience and necessity, without more, did not subject carrier to interstate commerce regulation within section of Investment Company Act of 1940 exempting from operation of Act any company subject to regulation under Interstate Commerce Act. Hoover v. Allen, 241 F. Supp. 213 (S.D.N.Y. 1965).

Water carriers are not subject to regulation under the Interstate Commerce Act within section of Investment Company Act of 1940 providing that company subject to regulation under Interstate Commerce Act is not an investment company within meaning of Act and therefore water carriers are not exempt from coverage of the Act. Hoover v. Allen, 241 F. Supp. 213 (S.D.N.Y. 1965).

Corporation which ceased its water carrier activities in 1953 was subject to registration and other provisions of Investment Company Act of 1940 during 1955 to 1959 when it engaged in business as investment company. Hoover v. Allen, 241 F. Supp. 218 (S.D.N.Y. 1965).

Notice to carrier that it may no longer be exempt.—

Water carrier who ceased its water carrier activities must be deemed to have been on notice that, as a dormant water carrier, it might no longer fall within literal purview of section of Investment Company Act of 1940 exempting from provisions of that Act corporations subject to regulation under Interstate Commerce Act. Hoover v. Allen, 241 F. Supp. 213 (S.D.N.Y. 1965).

Carrier not estopped from claiming exemption.—

Inasmuch as water carrier's certificate of public convenience and necessity was irrevocable, nothing it did or did not do would have presented the Interstate Commerce Commission with a situation in which it would have been called upon to terminate its jurisdiction and carrier was not estopped from claiming exemption from Investment Company Act of 1940. Hoover v. Allen, 241 F. Supp. 213 (S.D.NY. 1965).

Corporation held exempt.—

In stockholder's derivative action to set aside corporation's sale of owned railroad stock on theory that purchasing corporation was at time of sale an investment company which had failed to register with the Securities and Exchange Commission, evidence established that outstanding orders and decisions of Interstate Commerce Commission determined that at all relevant times the purchasing corporation was subject to regulation under Interstate Commerce Act as a carrier and was therefore, under Investment Company Act, not an investment company which was required to register with Securities and Exchange

therefrom must be narrowly construed.[971] Thus, an "organized group of persons," within the meaning of the Investment Company Act of 1940, does not refer only to recognizable business entities.[972] And purchasers of an insurance company's variable annuity contracts constituted purchasers and an "organized group of persons," and company's separate investment fund resulting from the sale of contracts was a "fund" within the Act, rendering the Act applicable to the fund, despite the Act's exclusion of insurance companies from the definition of investment company.[973] The provisions of an agreement and declaration of trust which purport to grant unlimited investment discretion to the trustees do not relieve them from the obligations

---

Commission. Schwartz v. Bowman, 244 F. Supp. 51 (S.D.N.Y. 1965), aff'd sub nom. Annenberg v. Alleghany Corp., 360 F.2d 211 (2d Cir.), cert. denied, 385 U.S. 921, 87 S. Ct. 230, 17 L. Ed. 2d 145 (1986).

Stockholder who brought derivative suit under the Urgent Deficiencies Act seeking holding that certain corporation was subject to registration requirements of the Investment Company Act once it disposed of railroad stock but not attacking basis of Interstate Commerce Commission ruling that corporation was still subject to ICC control stated no claim on which relief could be granted. Schwartz v. Alleghany Corp., 282 F. Supp. 161 (S.D.N.Y. 1968).

Question of standing to challenge propriety of SEC's grant of exemptions to various applicant companies under the Investment Company Act of 1940 went to jurisdiction of court of appeals, and thus all defenses in nature of waiver or estoppel were precluded. Independent Investor Protective League v. SEC, 495 F.2d 311 (2d Cir. 1974).

An investor protective league, which did not even allege that its members had suffered or would suffer actual injury or discrimination, and which merely alleged that it was quite conceivable that, in the future, its members would be investors, lacked standing to challenge propriety of the SEC's grant of exemptions to various applicant companies under the Investment Company Act of 1940. Independent Investor Protective League v. Securities & Exch. Comm'n, 495 F.2d 311 (2d Cir. 1974).

[971] Hoover v. Allen, 241 F. Supp. 213 (S.D.N.Y. 1965).

[972] Prudential Ins. Co. v. Securities & Exchange Com., 326 F.2d 383, cert. denied, 377 U.S. 953, 84 S. Ct. 1629, 12 L. Ed. 2d 497.

[973] Prudential Ins. Co. v. Securities & Exchange Com., 326 F.2d 383, cert. denied, 377 U.S. 953, 84 S. Ct 1629, 12 L. Ed. 2d 497.

Exclusion of insurance companies.—

Since Securities Act of 1938 specifically exempts annuity contracts, and since insurance companies are not investment companies under the Investment Company Act of 1940, neither Securities Act of 1933 nor Investment Company Act of 1940 were applicable to 1955 annuity contract between plaintiff hospital authority and defendant retirement association. Chatham County Hosp. Authority v. John Hancock Mut. Life Ins. Co., 325 F. Supp. 614 (S.D. Ga. 1971).

and standards imposed upon them by the Act[974] And trustees guilty of gross abuse of trust may be enjoined from acting as officers of a trust.[975] But the proscription of the Act that no investment company unless registered shall directly or indirectly control any company which is engaged in any business in interstate commerce, is limited to control, not an attempt to gain control.[976] And a parent corporation which owned all the shares of a residential developer was exempt from the registration provisions of the Investment Company Act.[977] For other cases dealing with exemptions from the Act, see the footnote.[978]

---

[974] Securities, etc., Comm. v. Aldred Inv. Trust, 58 F. Supp. 724, aff'd, 151 F.2d 254, cert. denied, 326 U.S. 795, 66 S. Ct 486, 90 L. Ed. 483.

[975] Aldred Inv. Trust v. Securities, etc., Comm., 151 F.2d 254, aff'g 58 F. Supp. 724.

Where purchaser of investment trust's common stock, which had no equity, acquired control which was exercised to change trust investment policy from concentration in utilities into concentration in horse racing industry for purpose of purchaser gaining control of race track, evidence established that purchaser who had himself elected president of investment trust and certain trustees whom purchaser had elected were guilty of gross abuse of trust within Investment Company Act, and warranted an injunction restraining them from acting as officers of the trust. Aldred Inv. Trust v. SEC, 151 F.2d 254, aff'g 58 F. Supp. 724.

Where one purchased common stock in an investment trust, which had no equity because debentures issued by trust exceeded value of its assets, for sole purpose of acquiring control of the trust, purchaser, as owner of voting control, did not have sole power to elect new trustees to supersede trustees who were enjoined from continuing to act in such capacities because of gross abuse of the trust. Aldred Inv. Trust v. SEC, 151 F.2d 254, aff'g 58 F. Supp. 724.

[976] Nationwide Corp. v. Northwestern Nat. Life Ins. Co., 251 Minn. 255, 87 N.W.2d 671, 73 A.L.R.2d 884.

Statute providing that no investment company unless registered, shall directly or indirectly control any company which is engaged in any business in interstate commerce, does not prohibit solicitation of proxies by unregistered investment company for purpose of attempting to gain control of company engaged in interstate commerce. Nationwide Corp. v. Northwestern Nat'l Life Ins. Co., 251 Minn. 255, 87 N.W.2d 671, 78 A.L.R.2d 884.

There is no recognized exception in Investment Company Act for the business of acquiring control of other companies. SEC v. Fifth Ave. Coach Lines, Inc., 289 F. Supp. 3 (S.D.N.Y. 1968).

[977] Progress Development Corp. v. Mitchell, 286 F.2d 222.

[978] **Retroactive exemption.—**

Securities and Exchange Commission was, under extraordinary circumstances of case, authorized to grant applicant retroactive exemption from the provisions of the Investment Company Act of 1940, from and after effective date of the act. Hennesey v. Securities & Exchange Com., 293 F.2d 48.

Evidence supported Securities and Exchange Commission's findings that applicant for

As to other matters arising under the Act, see the footnote.[979]

---

exemption had been primarily engaged in insurance business through controlled companies and was of type intended to be exempt from operation of Investment Company Act of 1940. Hennesey v. Securities & Exchange Com., 293 F.2d 48.

Company not engaged in business.—

A corporation which had ceased its long time business of manufacturing airplanes and had thereafter been used as a holding company by its president and which for more than three years had engaged in no business operations was excluded from operation of Investment Company Act as a company engaged, directly or through a wholly owned subsidiary, in business, and consequently the Investment Company Act did not void corporation's acquisition of all of the stock of seven California corporations. Orzeck v. Englehart, 41 Del. Ch. 361, 195 A.2d 375.

Shifting to less than majority ownership.—

Where corporation which existed primarily to hold stock of operating company continued to have absolute corporate control of operating company despite the shift from majority to less than direct majority ownership in operating company, such shift would not automatically require Securities and Exchange Commission to deprive corporation of its exempt status under Federal Investment Company Act of 1940. Manacher v. Reynolds, 39 Del. Ch. 401, 165 A.2d 741.

Determination of exemption's applicability.—

For purpose of determining whether stock held by investment company in loan company had value equal to at least 90 percent of value of company's investment, thereby making applicable exception to registration requirements, where no market quotations were shown on the stock, and "cost" was represented by arbitrary figure, computation of value of the stock would be on "book value" basis. SEC v. Midland Basic, Inc., 283 F. Supp. 609 (D.S.D. 1968).

Where largest proportion of investment securities held by investment company had value of approximately only 81 percent of total value of investment, company was required to be registered under Investment Company Act of 1940. Securities & Exch. Comm'n v. Midland Basic, Inc., 283 F. Supp. 609 (D.S.D. 1968).

Burden of proving exception from registration requirements of Investment Company Act of 1940 was upon investment company and its officers and directors charged with violation of Act. SEC v. Midland Basic, Inc., 283 F. Supp. 609 (D.S.D. 1968).

Company held subject to registration.—

Even if from time corporation received proceeds of condemnation award for its transportation system, it endeavored to gain operating control of companies with intent of becoming a conglomerate, where it actually traded securities and was unsuccessful in obtaining control of other companies, its activities came within ambit of investment company within Investment Company Act and it was subject to registration under the Act. Securities & Exch. Comm'n v. Fifth Ave. Coach Lines, 435 F.2d 510 (2d Cir. 1970).

[979] **Act permits funds organized as business trusts.—**

The Investment Company Act of 1940 recognizes and permits existence of funds organized as business trusts. Saminsky v. Abbott, 41 Del. Ch. 320, 194 A.2d 549, aff'd sub

(Text continued on page 246)

---

nom. Kleinman v. Saminsky, 41 Del. Ch. 572, 200 A.2d 572.

Annuity contracts subject to regulation under Securities Act and Investment Company Act.—

That challenged annuity policy allows annuitant some direct participation in investment experience of insurance company does not, standing alone, render contract amenable to federal regulation under Securities Act and Investment Company Act. Securities & Exchange Com. v. United Benefit Life Ins. Co., 359 F.2d 619 (W.C. Cir. 1966), rev'd on other grounds, 387 U.S. 202, 87 S. Ct. 1557, 18 L. Ed. 2d 673 (1987).

Application of 40 percent test as used in Investment Company Act to determine whether company is an investment company involved determination of value of company's total assets as defined in statute and the vain, of its investment securities. SEC v. Fifth Ave. Coach Lines, Inc., 289 F. Supp. 3 (S.D.N.Y. 1968).

A corporation's certificates of deposit should be excluded as cash items from the total assets of a corporation for the purpose of determining under the Investment Company Act whether such corporation's investments and securities had a value exceeding 40 percent of the corporation's total assets exclusive of government securities and cash items. Securities & Exch. Comm'n v. Fifth Ave. Coach Lines, Inc., 289 F. Supp. 3 (S.D.N.Y. 1968).

Certificates of deposit for 90 days or less and a six-month time deposit in bank should be considered as cash items excludable from total assets of corporation in determining whether corporation's investment securities exceeded 40 percent of its assets under investment Company Act, but time deposit in bank which was not available within one year to corporation was properly included in the total assets of corporation and not considered a cash item. SEC v. Fifth Ave. Coach Lines, Inc., 289 F. Supp. 3 (S.D.N.Y. 1968).

Where investment securities of corporation on particular date constituted only approximately 20 percent of total assets of corporation on the particular date, corporation was not an investment company on that date within meaning of 40 percent statutory test. Securities & Exch. Comm'n v. Fifth Ave. Coach Lines, Inc., 289 F. Supp. 3 (S.D.N.Y. 1968).

Although section of Investment Company Act relating to definition of value of securities literally applied only to registered investment companies, such literal application made no sense since definition must be employed in determining whether alleged investment company should be required to register. SEC v. Fifth Ave. Coach Lines, Inc., 289 F. Supp. 3 (S.D.N.Y. 1968).

For purpose of computing assets of corporation to determine if investment securities equalled 40 percent of assets within meaning of Investment Company Act, condemnation awards to corporation and its wholly-owned subsidiaries for intangibles of appropriated bus line properties as determined by New York courts would be accepted even though board of directors had determined a much higher figure to be the fair value and an appeal was pending in New York court of appeals concerning award. SEC v. Fifth Ave. Coach Lines, Inc., 289 F. Supp. 3 (S.D.N.Y. 1968).

Municipal bonds held by state Public Service Commission for tort and workmen's compensation claim arising out of corporation's former bus line operation could not be considered as investments for purpose of Investment Company Act in determining whether

(Text continued on page 246)

corporation was now an investment company. SEC v. Fifth Ave. Coach Lines, Inc., 289 F. Supp. 3 (S.D.N.Y. 1968).

Where time deposit was in a bank which had closed, it was no longer treatable as a cash item for purpose of ascertaining total assets of company to determine if it had become an investment company under the Investment Company Act of 1940. SEC v. Fifth Ave. Coach Lines, Inc., 289 F. Supp. 3 (S.D.N.Y. 1968).

Claims of corporation against individuals arising out of various financial transactions could not be considered as investment securities held by corporation for purpose of determining whether corporation was an investment company under the 40 percent test. Securities & Exch. Comm'n v. Fifth Ave. Coach Lines, Inc., 289 F. Supp. 3 (S.D.N.Y. 1968).

Corporation's judgment on award for intangibles for property of corporation taken by eminent domain proceedings was not an "evidence of indebtedness" for purpose of determining whether corporation was an investment company within the 40 percent test provided in Investment Company Act. SEC v. Fifth Ave. Coach Lines, Inc., 289 F. Supp. 3 (S.D.N.Y. 1968).

Corporation's advances to another corporation on open account would not be treated as "evidence of indebtedness" within meaning of Investment Company Act for purpose of determining whether corporation was an investment company. SEC v. Fifth Ave. Coach Lines, Inc., 289 F. Supp. 3 (S.D.N.Y. 1968).

Government bonds which corporation had to place on deposit with state Public Service Commission to meet claims for tort and workmen's compensation as a result of company's former operation of bus line, were frozen in hands of Commission and were not "government's securities" within moaning of statute excluding such securities from computation of total assets to determine whether company was an investment company under the 40% rule of statute. Securities & Exch. Comm'n v. Fifth Ave. Coach Lines, Inc., 289 F. Supp. 3 (S.D.N.Y. 1968).

Where corporation was required to register as "investment company" for five years and for two succeeding years the value of its securities did not meet 40 percent requirement of statute defining investment company to mean company owning investment securities having value exceeding 40 percent of value of total assets, but corporation went well over that requirement in succeeding year with rise in value of one stock held, 40 percent formula of statute was satisfied and company was investment company within Investment Company Act. SEC v. S & P Nat'l Corp., 360 F.2d 741 (2d Cir. 1966).

Transfer of control of corporation controlling investment company's principal underwriter and investment adviser was not an assignment of investment advisory and distribution agreements between investment company and underwriter-adviser and, therefore, did not thereby terminate the agreement, where transfer of control was due to successful proxy fight, not transfer of controlling block of stock by a security holder. Willheim v. Murchison, 231 F. Supp. 142 (S.D.N.Y. 1964), aff'd, 342 F.2d 33 (2d Cir.), cert. denied, 382 U.S. 840, 86 S. Ct. 36, 15 L. Ed. 2d 82 (1965).

De-registration of registered investment company.—

Once registered, an investment company can de-register only upon finding of Securities and Exchange Commission that it has ceased to be an investment company and order of

(Text continued on page 246)

Commission for protection of investors may be made upon appropriate conditions. Securities & Exch. Comm'n v. S & P Nat'l Corp., 360 F.2d 741 (2d Cir. 1966).

Suspension of right of redemption.—

The Federal Investment Company Act provides that no registered investment company shall suspend the right of redemption or postpone the date of payment or satisfaction upon redemption of any redeemable security in accordance with its terms for more than seven days after the tender of such security to the company or its agent designated for that purpose for redemption. SEC v. Fiscal Fund, 48 F. Supp. 712 (1943). See 15 U.S.C.S. § 80a–22(e).

Where management investment company issued beneficial shares which were redeemable at shareholder's option by making request of custodian but custodian had been compelled to dishonor all requests because it had no cash and had been unable to obtain any because investment company had no management to make sales or officers to sign required authorization certificate, investment company had in effect indefinitely suspended right of redemption and had postponed date of payment upon redemption of its redeemable securities for more than seven days after tender in violation of Act. SEC v. Fiscal Fund, 48 F. Supp. 712 (1943).

Where management investment company of open and diversified type had in effect indefinitely suspended right of redemption of its beneficial shares and had postponed date of payment upon redemption of its redeemable securities for more than seven days after tender in violation of Investment Company Act, a permanent injunction, mandatory and prohibitive, was granted against violation of statute regarding right of redemption. SEC v. Fiscal Fund, 48 F. Supp. 712 (1943).

Failure of diversified management investment company to file annual report with Securities and Exchange Commission as required by Investment Company Act could not be regarded as mere technical oversight. Tanzer v. Huffines, 287 F. Supp. 273 (D. Del. 1968), aff'd, 408 F.2d 42 (3d Cir. 1969).

Evidence warranting finding of filing of false reports.—

On application for preliminary injunction restraining corporations from operating their business as investment companies, evidence warranted finding that parent corporation over period of years had violated Securities Exchange Act of 1984 by filing with Securities Exchange Commission reports which were false and misleading in that they failed to list certain defendant as director and listed persons as directors who were not directors. SEC v. S & P Nat'l Corp., 360 F.2d 741 (3d Cir. 1966).

Converting assets of registered investment company.—

Term "converts" as used in statute making it a crime to convert assets of registered investment company is to be given its traditional meaning, and is technical term which has same connotation in criminal statute as in law of torts. Brown v. Bullock, 194 F. Supp. 207 (S.D.N.Y. 1961), aff'd, 294 F.2d 415.

Section of investment Company Act of 1940 making it a crime to convert assets of any registered investment company gives implied private right of action. Brown v. Bullock, 194 F. Supp. 207 (S.D.N.Y. 1961), aff'd, 294 F.2d 415.

No cause of action for violation of Investment Company Act stated.—

In absence of allegation of connection between corporation's functioning as unregistered

(Text continued on page 246)

---

investment company in interstate commerce and alleged waste, no cause of action for violation of Investment Company Act of 1940 was stated. Hoover v. Allen, 241 F. Supp. 213 (S.D.N.Y. 1965).

Evidence sustaining finding that corporation was investment company.—

Evidence sustained finding that defendant corporation had been investment company for many years, in proceeding to enjoin operation of business as investment company. SEC v. S & P Nat'l Corp., 360 F.2d 741 (2d Cir. 1966).

Evidence supported determination that defendant corporations not registered as investment companies had engaged in transactions improper under Investment Company Act for unregistered investment companies and were in fact investment companies, in proceeding for injunctive relief and appointment of receiver on basis of violation of Investment Company Act. SEC v. S & P Nat'l Corp., 360 F.2d 741 (2d Cir. 1966).

Evidence established that on particular date investing in securities had become corporation's primary business after condemnation of its bus line properties and that security investments met the 40 percent test of total assets as prescribed by Investment Company Act. Securities & Exch. Comm'n v. Fifth Ave. Coach Lines, Inc., 289 F. Supp. 3 (S.D.N.Y. 1968).

Evidence established that on particular date corporation met the 40 percent test under Investment Company Act in that investment securities were approximately 55 percent of total assets. SEC v. Fifth Ave. Coach Lines, Inc., 289 F. Supp. 3 (S.D.N.Y. 1968).

Corporation, which had practically no business while awaiting payment of condemnation award for its bus line properties except for operating a bus line through a subsidiary of a subsidiary but began purchasing stocks shortly after receiving eleven and a half million dollar award until it reached the point where its immediately available cash and time deposits totalled $1,818,000, as compared to a sum in excess of four and a half million dollars for these items six months earlier, had become primarily engaged in business of investing in securities within Investment Company Act. SEC v. Fifth Ave. Coach Lines, Inc., 289 F. Supp. 3 (S.D.N.Y. 1968).

Stock transactions not merely incidental to dissolution.—

Evidence sustained implied finding that stock transactions conducted by corporations for several years had not been merely incidental to dissolution as contended by corporations sued for violation of Investment Company Act. SEC v. S & P Nat'l Corp., 360 F.2d 741 (3d Cir. 1966).

Where it appeared that there might be substantial tax savings if stock held by alleged investment company were disposed of in one way rather than another, orders of Securities Exchange Commission would be modified to permit corporations to take necessary steps to propose but not adopt all appropriate plans to obtain such savings. Securities & Exch. Comm'n v. S & P Nat'l Corp., 360 F.2d 741 (3d Cir. 1966).

Terms of injunction not too broad.—

Where only real business of corporations in past few years had been ownership of securities, terms of injunction were not too broad, where they had no practical effect except to prevent corporations from disposing or dealing with securities or, for the time being, taking any steps to dissolve. SEC v. S & P Nat'l Corp., 360 F.2d 741 (2d Cir. 1966).

Small Business Investment Act.—The purpose of the federal Small Business Investment Act of 1958 is to produce financing for small businesses for long term loans.[980] The Small Business Investment Act does not support a private right of action, inasmuch as Congress has placed enforcement of the act solely within the discretion of jurisdiction of the Small Business Administration.[981]

Investment Advisers.—For cases decided under the federal Investment Advisers' Act, see the footnote.[982] As to state investigations of investment advisers, see the footnote.[983]

Act imposes more pervasive requirement where self-dealing is order of the day.—

Investment Company Act imposes a more fundamental and pervasive requirement where, because of structure of investment trusts, self-dealing is not the exception but, so far as management is concerned, the order of the day. Moses v. Burgin, 445 F.2d 369 (1st Cir.), rev'g 316 F. Supp. 31 (D. Mass.), cert. denied, 404 U.S. 994, 92 S. Ct. 582, 30 L. Ed. 3d 547 (1971).

Standing to sue.—

Plaintiffs who did not allege that they or their corporation held any ownership in alleged investment company, but only that company was unregistered and dominated their corporation to its detriment, did not have standing to sue under Investment Company Act. Herpich v. Wallace, 430 F.2d 792 (5th Cir. 1970).

Nonregistration of stock allegation insufficient.—

Allegation that lenders had not registered stock was insufficient to state cause of action against lender under Investment Company Act of 1940, which applied only to investment companies, absent showing that lenders were investment companies. Kicken v. Valentine Prod. Credit Ass'n, 628 F. Supp. 1008 (D. Neb.), aff'd, 754 F.2d 378 (8th Cir. 1984).

[980] Hernstadt v. Programs for Television, Inc., 86 Misc. 2d 628, 232 N.Y.S.2d 683.

As to regulations under Act, see § 1 of this chapter. See also § 18 of this chapter.

Small Business Investment Act was passed for purpose of making loans available to those engaging in comparatively small enterprises who cannot obtain adequate borrowed funds through customary financial institutions. First La. Inv. Corp. v. United States, 351 F.2d 495(5th Cir. 1965).

[981] Goodall v. Columbia Ventures, 374 F. Supp. 1324 (S.D.N.Y. 1974).

A shareholder did not have a private right of action against corporate defendants for alleged violations of regulations of the Small Business Administration. Goodall v. Columbia Ventures, 374 F. Supp. 1324 (S.D.N.Y. 1974).

[982] **In general.—**

See § 11.1 of this chapter for a discussion of investment advisers of investment companies.

An investment adviser is an occupation which can cause havoc unless engaged in by those with appropriate backgrounds and standards. Marketlines, Inc. v. SEC, 384 F.2d 264, 5

(Text continued on page 249)

A.L.R. Fed. 240 (2d Cir. 1967), cert. denied, 390 U.S. 947, 88 S. Ct. 1033, 19 L. Ed. 2d 1136 (1968).

General purpose of Investment Advisors Act is to protect the United States investing public from investment advisers who engage in fraudulent and deceitful practices. SEC v. Myers, 285 F. Supp. 743 (D. Md. 1968).

The registration and disclosure provisions are crucial to the operation of the Investment Advisers Act and the United States court of appeals cannot condone their blatant abuse. Marketlines, Inc. v. Securities & Exch. Comm'n, 384 F.2d 264, 5 A.L.R. Fed. 240 (2d Cir. 1967), cert. denied, 390 U.S. 947, 88 S. Ct. 1033, 19 L. Ed. 2d 1136 (1968).

Fee for services.—

Even if New York Stock Exchange's declaration that fee for investment advisory service may not be based upon profits realized amounted to a full-fledged rule, and even if such rule could operate with force of federal law, declaration was in conflict with Investment Company Act and Investment Advisers Act, and thus defendant's alleged violation of so-called rule was not actionable. De Renzis v. Levy, 297 F. Supp. 998 (S.D.N.Y. 1969).

Relation to freedom of press.—

Investment Advisers Act does not on its face abridge freedom of press simply because it may be applied to publications which are classified formally as part of the "press" for some purposes but are not bona fide newspapers, news magazines or business or financial publications of general and regular circulation excluded under Act; no constitutional conflict is inherent in fact that an investment advisory newspaper, which is not a bona fide or other specified publication, might be required to register. Securities & Exch. Comm'n v. Wall St. Transcript Corp., 422 F.2d 1371 (2d Cir.), cert. denied, 398 U.S. 958, 90 S. Ct. 2170, 26 L. Ed. 2d 542 (1970).

Fact that investigation of and demand on publisher of bona fide newspaper, news magazine or business or financial publication of general and regular circulation for disclosure under Investment Advisers Act may have some deterrent effect on speech does not automatically invalidate demand under chilling effect doctrine. SEC v. Wall Street Transcript Corp., 422 F.2d 1371 (2d Cir.), cert. denied, 398 U.S. 958, 90 S. Ct. 2170, 26 L. Ed. 2d 542 (1970).

Application of act to foreign persons or transactions.—

The necessary element which subjects a nondomiciliary to regulation under the Investment Advisers Act is the carrying on a business in the United States. Securities & Exch. Comm'n v. Myers, 285 F. Supp. 743 (D. Md. 1968).

Ample evidence existed to support contention of Securities and Exchange Commission that defendant, a Canadian citizen, had engaged in the business of investment advising the United States and that he would continue to carry on his business without complying with provisions of the Investment Advisers Act. Securities & Exch. Comm'n v. Myers, 285 F. Supp. 743 (D. Md. 1968).

While Investment Advisers Act is presumed to apply generally only to activities within the territorial United States, in its broad context it has, like all regulatory acts, application to those activities which have a substantial effect on commerce between the states or between

(Text continued on page 249)

---

the United States and foreign countries. Securities & Exch. Comm'n v. Myers, 285 F. Supp. 743 (D. Md. 1968).

SEC has broad discretion.—

In charging the Securities and Exchange Commission with the enforcement of the Investment Advisers Act in the public interest, Congress necessarily gave the Commission a broad discretion. Marketlines, Inc. v. Securities & Exch. Comm'n, 384 F.2d 264, 5 A.L.R. Fed. 240 (2d Cir. 1967), cert. denied, 390 U.S. 947, 88 S. Ct. 1033, 19 L. Ed. 2d 1136 (1968).

Burden of proof that investigation brought by Securities and Exchange Commission was unlawful was upon party against whom Commission had moved for order, pursuant to Investment Advisers Act, requiring respondent to appear, testify and produce documents. Securities & Exch. Comm'n v. Wall St. Transcript Corp., 294 F. Supp. 298 (S.D.N.Y. 1968), rev'd on other grounds, 422 F.2d 1371 (2d Cir.), cert. denied 398 U.S. 958, 90 S. Ct. 2170, 26 L. Ed. 2d 542.

Admissibility of evidence.—

Fact that president, treasurer and sole stockholder of corporate investment adviser failed to pass an examination to qualify as an investment adviser in Illinois and in 1950 was found guilty of various serious crimes and was disbarred in New York was relevant to a determination as to whether it was in the public interest for him to continue as an investment adviser, and the Securities Exchange Commission properly considered such evidence in proceedings that resulted in the revocation of corporate investment adviser's registration as an investment advisor under the Investment Advisers Act. Marketlines, Inc. v. Securities & Exch. Comm'n, 384 F.2d 264, 5 A.L.R. Fed. 240 (2d Cir. 1967), cert. denied, 390 U.S. 947, 88 S. Ct. 1033, 19 L. Ed. 3d 1136 (1968).

Sufficiency of evidence.—

Evidence supported findings of Securities and Exchange Commission that corporate investment adviser violated antifraud provisions of the Investment Advisers Act by publishing misleading advertisements soliciting subscriptions to its market letters and also violated registration and disclosure provisions of the Act by failing promptly to amend its registration application to disclose that its vice-president and secretary was associated with the firm and by not disclosing that vice-president had been found to have violated various provisions of the securities laws in another proceeding. Marketlines, Inc. v. Securities & Exch. Comm'n, 384 F.2d 264, 5 A.L.R. Fed. 240 (3d Cir. 1967), cert. denied, 390 U.S. 947, 88 S. Ct. 1033, 19 L. Ed. 2d 1136 (1968).

983 **Inquiry into publication of investment advice book.—**

Attorney general in Martin Act proceeding made sufficient showing for issuance of order directing petitioners to appear and produce certain books and records so as to allow him to inquire into publication of investment advice book. In re Attorney-General, 10 N.Y.2d 108, 217 N.Y.S.2d 603, 176 N.E.2d 402 (1961). See former N.Y. Gen. Bus. Law § 23-A.

§ 3. Incorporation, Organization, Name, Location, Merger and Reorganization.

Incorporation and Organization in General.—A trust company, like other corporations, is a creature of statute,[984] and some of the unique provisions of acts providing for the incorporation of trust companies have been interpreted by the courts.[985]

---

[984] People v. Knapp, 147 App. Div. 436, 132 N.Y.S. 747, 26 N.Y. Crim. 448, aff'd, 206 N.Y. 373, 99 N.E. 841, 1914B Ann. Cas. 243; Shaw v. Brisbine, 63 S.D. 470, 260 N.W. 710.

[985] **In general.—**

In re Turley, 20 D.C. (9 Mackey) 815.

Act applicable to companies incorporated under previous laws.—

Act providing for the incorporation of trust corporations within the District of Columbia was held applicable to trust companies incorporated under previous laws and which have complied with the provisions of the act. In re Turley, 20 D.C. (9 Mackey) 315.

Statutes held constitutional.—

Georgia Acts 1898, p. 78, authorizing secretary of state to grant charters to trust companies with banking privileges, held valid; the companies provided for in that act being embraced within the description "banking companies," as used in the constitution. Mulherin v. Kennedy, 120 Ga. 1080, 48 S.E. 437.

Minnesota Laws 1883, c. 107, p. 133, providing for the incorporation of annuity, safe deposit, and trust companies, was not unconstitutional because of a defective title. State v. Barnes, 108 Minn. 230, 122 N.W. 11.

Registration of company's charter.—

Where charter of bank and trust company with application therefor were registered in county registrar's office, but secretary of state's certificate and facsimile of seal did not immediately follow such record, but notation appeared at end of indexed charter reciting that certificate and facsimile of seal were registered on certain page, contention that there was no legal registration because of absence of index of secretary of state's certificate could not be sustained. Citizens' Bank, etc., Co. v. Scott, 18 Tenn. App. 89, 72 S.W.2d 1064.

Where a trust company's articles do not comply with the Kentucky statute, the state official may refuse to file them, but where the articles are filed, their failure to comply with the statute can be taken advantage of only by the state in a direct proceeding. Dornian v. Bankers' Trust Co.'s Receiver, 259 Ky. 430, 82 S.W.2d 494.

Secretary of state did not have discretionary power to deny applications for corporate charters or amendments to such charters authorizing applicants to engage in business as industrial banks, but under statutes governing such applications at the time they were filed, the secretary of state was required to issue the charters or amendments where all requirements of such statutes were met. Commonwealth Inv. Co. v. Thornton, 244 S.C. 146, 185 S.E.2d 762 (1964).

Sufficiency of capital.—

Where doubt exists regarding the profitability of a proposed trust company, the Board of

Where the charter of a corporation having all the powers of a trust company incorporated by a special act, provides that the corporation shall be subject to and entitled to the benefits of all general laws relating to corporations and "applicable to such corporations," it is subject to all general laws applicable to trust companies.[986] And a charter provision that the business of a corporation shall be "a general banking and trust business," is a sufficient compliance with a statute requiring a statement of the nature of a company's business, and prescribing the nature of the business of trust companies.[987] When bylaws are adopted by a trust company, they are the law of the company as if they were part of its charter.[988] A provision of a state constitution prohibiting the creation by special charter of corporations for banking purposes, does not apply to a trust company, the provision contemplating the business of banking in a popular sense.[989] And where there is in a state, in addition to a general corporation law, an act which provides for the incorporation of trust companies, and declares that thereafter no corporation shall be organized to carry on a trust company business in the state except under such act, a proposed corporation whose powers, as defined by its articles, are almost, if not wholly, confined to an agency or trust business, is not entitled to incorporate under the general law, though its articles do not include all items or powers named in the act providing for the incorporation of trust companies.[990] And the Maine bank commissioner lacks power and jurisdiction to apply "public convenience and

---

the Trust Company Incorporation may reasonably require greater capital. Hanaway v. State, 352 A.2d 715 (N.H. 1976), citing Michie on Banks and Banking.

Under the evidence that approximately 14,000 persons resided in a trade area of the proposed trust company, that there had been little recent economic growth in the area, and that several financial institutions already served the area, the Board of Trust Company Incorporation was justified in finding that the capital of a proposed trust company was inadequate and that the economic conditions would limit its profitability. Hanaway v. State, 352 A.2d 715 (N.H. 1976), citing Michie on Banks and Banking.

In New Jersey, trust company is incorporated under Banking Laws and as a practical matter is actually a bank which has specially qualified itself to exercise fiduciary powers. National State Bank v. Smith, 591 F.2d 223 (3d Cir. 1979).

[986] Skinner v. Schwab, 188 App. Div. 457, 177 N.Y.S. 143, aff'd, 229 N.Y. 549, 129 N.E. 910.

[987] Brown v. Threlkeld, 154 Ky. 833, 159 S.W. 595.

[988] Kavanaugh v. Gould, 223 N.Y. 103, 119 N.E. 237.

[989] United States Trust Co. v. Brady (N.Y.), 20 Barb. 119.

[990] State ex rel. Gorman v. Nichols, 40 Wash. 437, 82 P. 741.

advantage" criteria to new trust company applications;[991] but in Delaware[992] and Oklahoma such considerations may be dispositive.[993] A mutual fund is an open-end investment company.[994] Under Colorado law, an investment fund on whose behalf a receiver brought suit was an unincorporated association having the capacity to sue in the light of the facts that the original investment agreement recognized the fund as a common investment fund, the investors agreed to band together for a common intent and purpose, using a common name, the investors signed identical documents governing the fund, and the fund had an identifiable managing agent and a specific set of operating procedures.[995]

The Banking Commission's discretion regarding an application to organize and operate a trust company in South Dakota is not absolute; it must

---

[991] Nealley v. Brown, 284 A.2d 480 (Me. 1971).

Under impact of constitutionally governing federal law, bank commissioner lacked power and jurisdiction to render decision, purportedly final, in which he predicated lack of public convenience and advantage on essential relationships of bank holding company to new trust companies being established, and to be operated, under bank holding company control. Nealley v. Brown, 284 A.2d 480 (Me. 1971).

[992] American Guar. & Trust Co. v. Green, 282 A.2d 16 (Del. Super. 1971).

Showing of "public convenience," necessary to statutory formation of new corporations intended to be formed with trust powers under the general corporation law after 1988, was inapplicable to trust company which had been incorporated in 1914 "to transact a general trust company business" and which had been actively engaged in nontrust business within state prior to 1988, and bank commissioner's denial of an unlimited certificate of authority to transact trust business, on ground that the company had made "no demonstration of public convenience and advantage," was an abuse of discretion. American Guar. & Trust Co. v. Green, 282 A.2d 16 (Del. Super. 1971).

[993] Hazen v. Banking Bd., 476 P.2d 323 (Okla. 1970).

Evidence sustained ruling of Court of Bank Review approving ruling of state banking board denying application for permission to organize a trust company, on ground that there was not sufficient business to make it economically feasible. Hazen v. Banking Bd., 476 P.2d 323 (Okla. 1970).

[994] Investment Co. Inst. v. Camp, 401 U.S. 617, 91 S. Ct. 1091, 28 L. Ed. 2d 367 (1971).

[995] Johnson v. Chilcott, 599 F. Supp. 224 (D.C. Colo. 1984).

Under Colorado law, investment fund operated under agreement between fund's manager and investors to combine investors' money with manager's investment skill and services in a business where profits and losses would be proportionately shared was not a partnership, even though it was an association of two or more persons to carry on a business for profit, since investors had no intention of forming an organization which could expose them to liability for claims against fund or manager, and manager unilaterally exercised power to determine who entered fund as an investor. Johnson v. Chilcott, 599 F. Supp. 224 (D.C. Colo. 1984).

base its actions on factual determinations limited to the factors enumerated in the statute.[996]

The feature that distinguishes an "open-end investment company" is the company's standing offer to redeem capital stock issued by it.[997] Recovery against an investment company and its president, who owned all of its stock, was not barred because of their separate existence, where the president so confused his identity with the company that there was no separate individuality and the observance of separate existence would allow both defendants to escape liability.[998] A statute providing for the deposit of securities by investment corporations is not complied with by the execution by a corporation of a deed to real estate in which it has invested its entire capital stock, as the deposit must be either of cash or of securities enumerated in the statute.[999] The provisions of the Small Business Investment Act do not contemplate the creation and maintenance of a corporate entity but only the licensing of a corporate entity created under state law, as a small business investment company, and it is state law that governs the creation and existence of a corporate entity with capacity to sue and be sued.[1000] Certificates issued by a state banking commission and a state industrial commission have been held to be sufficient evidence that a former loan association was an industrial bank.[1001]

---

[996] In re Application of Dorsey, 2001 SD 35, 623 N.W.2d 468 (2001).

Banking Commission's determination that granting of law firm's application to organize and operate a trust company in South Dakota would serve a "public need" was not clearly erroneous; the proposed trust company would serve a specialized market, namely current trust clients of the law firm who wished to enjoy the benefits of South Dakota law and to continue their long-term relationship with the law firm. In re Application of Dorsey, 2001 SD 35, 623 N.W.2d 468 (2001).

A specialized market, consisting of current trust clients of law firm who wished to enjoy the benefits of South Dakota law and to continue their long-term relationship with the law firm, was a "community" for purposes of law firm's application to organize and operate a trust company in South Dakota, within meaning of the statutory factor of public need for the proposed trust company in the community. In re Application of Dorsey, 2001 SD 35, 623 N.W.2d 468, (2001).

[997] New York Stocks v. Commissioner of Internal Revenue, 164 F.2d 75.

[998] Pearsall v. Townsend, 7 Cal. App. 2d 162, 45 P.2d 824.

[999] Goodpaster v. United States Mortg. Bond Co., 174 Ky. 284, 192 S.W. 35.

[1000] Olympic Capital Corp. v. Newman, 276 F. Supp. 646 (C.D. Cal. 1967).

[1001] Atlantic Industrial Bank v. Centonze 130 Conn. 18, 81 A.2d 392.

Certificate of banking commission authorizing loan association to transact business as industrial bank, and copy of certificate of industrial commission authorizing the association

Name Generally.—A statute defining "trust company" and stating which companies may use the word "trust" in their business names, may prohibit any corporation whose charter gives it trust powers from using such a name unless it exercises those powers.[1002] It may also authorize a state bank commissioner to bring suit to restrain a corporation from doing business under a name so prohibited.[1003] Under a statute providing for the incorporation of trust companies and declaring that no trust company thereafter organized under any other act shall use the word "trust" as part of its name, a change in name of a preexisting corporation so as to use the word "trust" as a part thereof is the creation of a new corporation and prohibited.[1004] Similarly, a corporation filing amended articles but omitting the word "trust" from its name cannot resume its original name and trust business without

---

to change its name to plaintiff industrial bank, properly authenticated, were sufficient evidence in absence of countervailing evidence, to justify finding that plaintiff was an industrial bank, in action involving issue whether note payable to plaintiff bank was usurious. Atlantic Industrial Bank v. Centonze, 130 Conn. 18, 81 A.2d 392.

1002 **In general.**—

Union Trust Co. v. Moore, 104 Wash. 50, 175 P. 565.

Purpose of statute.—

The Delaware act permitting only a corporation which reports to insurance commissioner to use word "Trust" as part of corporate name was in aid of public welfare, and its design was to differentiate certain businesses which by reason of their intimate relations with the public, were more likely to cause harm through incapacity, maladministration, or fraud than were other businesses of a more general nature in which corporations might engage. State ex rel. Lucey v. Terry, 39 Del. 32, 196 A. 163.

Such statute permits use of word "Trust" as part of corporate names only by corporations engaged in certain businesses which were by prior statute placed under supervision of insurance commissioner. State v. Terry, 39 Del. 32, 196 A. 163.

Violation of statute.—

A corporation, doing business as "A. Trust Company," and whose charter did not confer powers of trust companies, was guilty of violating statute. McKee v. American Trust Co., 166 Ark. 480, 266 SW. 293.

Phrase "trust company" read as limited in meaning.—

In a statute providing that a national bank association to which a certificate is issued is not illegally constituted solely because its operations are required to be limited to those of a trust company and activities related thereto, the phrase "trust company" must be read as limited in meaning to trust or fiduciary operations of such company. National State Bank v. Smith, 591 F.2d 223 (3d Cir. 1979).

1003 Union Trust Co. v. Moore, 104 Wash. 50, 175 P. 565.

1004 State v. Nichols, 38 Wash. 309, 80 P. 462.

complying with the statutory requirements applicable to such a company.[1005] As to the right to a company name[1006] and deceptive or misleading names,[1007] see the footnote.

[1005] Clark Bros. v. Hinkle, 157 Wash. 484, 289 P. 59.

[1006] **Unfair competition.—**

In a suit by one trust company against another to restrain the use of a name adopted by the latter, on the ground that its use will result in unfair competition, while the approval of the superintendent of banks, of the name adopted, is not a final determination of the matter, and is subject to review by the courts, his wide experience and apparent opinion that no confusion or injury can result are entitled to weight; and an injunction, in such a case, will be denied, where an issue has arisen whether the president of the plaintiff company has not acquiesced in the use thereof by the defendant, and irreparable damage may be worked defendant if an injunction issues. New York Trust Co. v. New York County Trust Co., 125 Misc. 735, 211 N.Y.S. 785, aff'd, 215 App. Div. 699, 212 N.Y.S. 882.

Company's right to name.—

Shares of open-end investment company were not product of company's investment advisor or of the distributor of its shares; and company, rather than distributor or advisor, had right to company name under which shares were sold. Tausig v. Wellington Fund, Inc., 187 F. Supp. 179, aff'd, 313 F.2d 472, cert. denied, 374 U.S. 806, 83 S. Ct. 1693, 1695, 10 L. Ed. 2d 1031.

In minority shareholders' action for judgment declaring their corporation to have exclusive rights to name "Wellington" in the investment company field, actions of individual who had chosen to align himself with defendant corporations, which were, in effect, his alter ego, could not be indorsed by virtue of industry-wide practice forming basis of his decision to proceed as he did; nor was fact that he acted on respected opinion of experienced counsel a factor entitling him to complete exoneration. Taussig v. Wellington Fund, Inc., 187 F. Supp. 179, aff'd, 313 F.2d 472, cert. denied, 374 U.S. 806, 83 S. Ct. 1693, 1695, 10 L. Ed. 2d 1031.

Evidence sustained finding that a mutual fund which used the word "Wellington" in its name was not benefited by action of directors in giving an open-end, diversified, common stock investment company the right to use such word in its name and that permission for use of word constituted the disposition of a valuable asset which was not in the best interest of the mutual fund. Taussig v. Wellington Fund, Inc., 313 F.2d 472, cert. denied, 374 US. 806, 88 S. Ct. 1688, 1695, 10 L. Ed. 2d 1031.

To hold that investment company must cease using its name if advisory contract were terminated or that investment adviser could exploit name of investment company for its own selfish ends would frustrate clearly defined legislative purpose in requiring yearly approval of investment management contracts by interjecting into deliberations subtle pressures tending to undermine objectivity required of directors and shareholders. Taussig v. Wellington Fund, Inc., 187 F. Supp. 179, aff'd, 313 F.2d 472, cert. denied, 374 U.S. 806, 88 S. Ct. 1693, 1695, 10 L. Ed. 2d 1081.

As to expenses in action to declare exclusive right to name, see § 5 of this chapter.

[1007] The Securities and Exchange Commission in determining whether a corporate name

Change of Name and Location.—For cases related to the changing of name and location, see the footnote.[1008]

---

is deceptive or misleading in violation of the Investment Company Act is entitled to insist that the public failed to look to the essential merits of an investment offered to it rather than matters extraneous to those merits. Civil & Military Investors Mut. Fund, Inc. v. Securities & Exchange Com., 288 F.2d 156.

Determination of Securities and Exchange Commission, that the name "Civil and Military Investors Mutual Fund, Inc.," was inherently deceptive or misleading in violation of the Investment Company Act, through implication in the name that the fund was particularly suited to meet investment needs of such personnel was sustained by the evidence. Civil & Military Investors Mut. Fund, Inc. v. Securities & Exchange Com., 288 F.2d 156.

A finding that there is a harmful tendency inherent in name of a corporation is enough basis for a declaration that name of a corporation is deceptive and misleading in violation of the Investment Company Act. Civil & Military Investors Mut. Fund, Inc. v. Securities & Exchange Com., 288 F.2d 156.

Greater degree of similarity permitted.—

Sophistication of depositors, who have learned to distinguish between savings banks and federal savings and loan associations, permits greater degree of similarity in names. Metropolitan Federal Sav. & Loan Assoc. v. East Brooklyn Sav. Bank, 319 F. Supp. 393 (E.D.N.Y. 1970).

[1008] Where trust company which sought to change its name and location initiated proceedings with commissioner of banks, but determination of question was taken over by Department of Commerce in accordance with long-established agency pattern and order granting application directed commissioner of banks to issue authorization, trust company had complied with statutory requirements insofar as same related to its change of name and location. Plunkett v. First Nat'l Bank, 262 Minn. 231, 115 N.W.2d 235.

While acceptance of petition far rehearing by Department of Commerce was discretionary, its denial did not enlarge time for certiorari to review order authorizing trust company to change its name. Plunkett v. First Nat'l Bank, 262 Minn. 231, 115 N.W.2d 235.

Because there was no statutory provision for judicial review by appeal from order authorizing trust company to change its name and location and because writ of certiorari was issued long after 60 days from time relator had received notice of order, proceeding to review order was barred by limitations and court had no jurisdiction to determine validity of Department of Commerce order. Plunkett v. First Nat'l Bank, 262 Minn. 231, 115 N.W.2d 235.

Determination that limitations barred review of Department of Commerce order authorizing trust company to change its name and location was not determinative of company's right to engage in what was claimed to be banking. Plunkett v. First Nat'l Bank, 262 Minn. 231, 115 N.W.2d 235.

Where a case presented substantial questions, and there was no showing of prejudice to result from considering the case in due course, the motion to quash a writ of certiorari to review a Commerce Commission order authorizing a trust company to move its place of business was denied without prejudice. Plunkett v. First Nat. Bank, 259 Minn. 562, 107 N.W.2d 220.

Branch Offices.—Under a statute vesting a superintendent of banks and state banking board with discretion in regard to the opening of branch offices by banks and trust companies, only where it clearly appears that they have exceeded their statutory authority or their actions have been "erroneous, arbitrary, capricious, discriminatory or palpably illegal," will the courts interfere.[1009] Miscellaneous matters pertaining to the establishment of branches in particular states are treated in the footnote.[1010]

[1009] **In general.—**

State Bank of Kenmore v. Bell, 197 Misc. 97, 96 N.Y.S.2d 851, aff'd, 277 App. Div. 924, 98 N.Y.S.2d 493.

But in Manufacturers, etc., Trust Co. v. Bell, 270 App. Div. 796, 59 N.Y.S.2d 615, aff'd, 296 N.Y. 844, 72 N.E.2d 28, it was held that a trust company was not authorized under banking law to open additional branch office, and state superintendent of banks was not authorized to approve company's application to open such office.

Where former commissioner of banking and insurance denied trust company's application based on informal letter to change location of its branch office in city but acting commissioner subsequently granted second application after notice and hearing, application would be considered as application for reconsideration addressed to commissioner's discretion, and decision was within discretion of commissioner. Central Home Trust Co. v. Gough, 5 N.J. Super. 295, 68 A.2d 848.

In absence of any express statutory authorization, trust company was not permitted to open branch office within state. Wyoming Trust & Mgt. v. Bonham, 694 P.2d 106 (Wyo. 1985).

No abuse of discretion.—Evidence failed to show that superintendent of banks and state banking board abused their discretion in approving application of trust company which had its principal place of business in city of Buffalo, to open a branch office in town of Tonawanda, an unincorporated village, on ground that public convenience and advantage were not thereby promoted. State Bank of Kenmore v. Bell, 277 App. Div. 924, 98 N.Y.S.2d 493, aff'g 197 Misc. 97, 96 N.Y.S.2d 851.

[1010] *Massachusetts.*—Under statute providing that trust company with approval of board of bank incorporation may establish and operate branch office in any town within same county having bank facilities which, in opinion of board, are inadequate for public convenience, board is sole arbiter of existence of such inadequacy, no hearing on application of trust company to establish branch office was required, bank and trust company which objected to establishment of branch were not entitled to a hearing, and question whether application should have been granted was a political one. Natick Trust Co. v. Board of Bank Incorporation, 337 Mass. 615, 151 N.E.2d 70.

The word "may" is used in its normal sense in statute providing that, after such notice and hearing as board of bank incorporation may prescribe, a trust company may, with approval of board, establish branch offices; a hearing is not mandatory. City Bank & Trust Co. v. Board of Bank Incorporation, 346 Mass. 29, 190 N.E.2d 107.

Hearing which board of bank incorporation held on application of trust company to establish branch office was not an "adjudicatory proceeding" within statute providing that

"Branching" Rights and "RAP" Rights.—During the savings and loan crisis, the Federal Savings and Loan Insurance Corporation (FSLIC) lacked the funds to liquidate failing savings and loan associations, also called "thrifts." As thrift regulator and insurer of deposits, the FSLIC responded to the crisis by encouraging healthy thrifts to take over failing ones in what

---

any person aggrieved by final decision of any agency in an adjudicatory proceeding shall be entitled to judicial review thereof, and appeal by bank and trust company, which objected to establishment of branch, from board's decision granting application could not be maintained. Natick Trust Co. v. Board of Bank Incorporation, 337 Mass. 615, 151 N.E.2d 70.

Decision by board on application of trust company for leave to move branch office was not subject to judicial review as to merits by certiorari, and demurrers to petition for writ of certiorari was properly surmised. South Shore Nat'l Bank v. Board of Bank Incorporation, 351 Mass. 363, 220 N.E.2d 899 (1966).

Existence of small number of branches, established by special act outside of county of main office of trust company, was not so repugnant to general act requiring branches to be established in seine county as main office that special acts could be deemed repealed by subsequent enactment of general act. South Shore Nat'l Bank v. Board of Bank Incorporation, 351 Mass. 363, 220 N.E.2d 899 (1966).

Missouri.—The statute providing that no bank or trust company shall maintain in the state a branch bank or trust company, or receive deposits or pay checks except in its own banking house or as provided by another section was intended to apply, as an antimonopolistic measure, to all banks, banks exercising trust powers, and trust companies not exercising banking powers.

St. Louis Union Trust Co. v. Pemberton, 494 S.W.2d 408 (Mo. App. 1973).

A second office wherein a trust company desired to interview and consult with persona and prospective customers, to carry on recordkeeping, real estate business, etc., was a "branch" prohibited by statute, despite a contention that none of the true fiduciary activities or decisions of the trust company, which was assertedly a "pure" trust company without banking functions, would occur in the second office but only at its downtown office. St Louis Union Trust Co. v. Pemberton, 494 S.W.2d 408 (Mo. App. 1973).

New Jersey.—Banks opposing application of trust company for permission to establish branch bank in a township were not entitled to public hearing as matter of constitutional right. First Nat. Bank of Whippany v. Trust Co. of Morris County, 76 N.J. Super. 1, 183 A.2d 706.

New York.—Where certificate of organization of a trust company specifically stated that its business was to be transacted in a certain city in compliance with statutes then existing at time of the company's organization, the company was not required to have its certificate amended before it could make application to open a branch office outside the designated city pursuant to statute subsequently enacted. State Bank of Kenmore v. Bell, 197 Misc. 97, 96 N.Y.S.2d 851, aff'd, 277 App. Div. 924, 98 N.Y.S.2d 493.

Pennsylvania.—Commercial banks, bank and trust companies, trust companies and savings banks are all included within term "institution" as used in Code providing for establishment of branches. Philadelphia Sav. Fund Soc. v. Myers, 406 Pa. 438, 179 A.2d 209.

were called "supervisory mergers." These transactions relieved the FSLIC of its deposit insurance liability for the insolvent thrifts, and, in exchange, provided a package of non-cash incentives to acquiring thrifts, including "branching" rights.[1011] Branching rights permitted acquiring thrifts to open and operate branches in states other than their home states, which, prior to 1981, was generally prohibited. This prohibition was eliminated for thrifts entering into supervisory mergers across state lines.[1012]

"Regulatory accounting purposes" or "RAP" rights, by contrast, affected regulatory accounting treatment for business combinations. Formerly, regulations mandated, in part, that each thrift maintain a minimum capital of at least three percent of its liabilities, which presented an obstacle for healthy thrifts seeking to acquire failing ones because, by definition, failing thrifts' liabilities exceeded their assets. Regulators eliminated this obstacle by permitting acquiring thrifts to use generally accepted accounting principles (GAAP). In essence, GAAP allowed acquiring thrifts to treat failing thrifts' excess liabilities as an asset called "supervisory goodwill," which, in turn, could be counted toward the acquiring thrifts' minimum regulatory capital requirement and amortized over a forty-year period (later reduced to twenty-five years). The RAP rights provided by FSLIC guaranteed such treatment, regardless of future regulatory changes.[1013]

Merger and Consolidation.—Under the reserved power of a state to alter or repeal corporate charters, the enactment of a statute authorizing the merger of trust companies is a valid exercise of legislative power as applied to specially chartered trust companies existing at the time of its enactment.[1014] But domestic corporations organized as trust companies may not merge in the absence of statutory authority,[1015] and where a statute authorizes such a

---

[1011] WMI Holdings Corp. v. United States, 891 F.3d 1016 (2018).

Thrifts collect customer deposits, which are maintained in interest-bearing savings accounts, and they originate and service mortgage loans funded by those deposits. Historically, thrifts were profitable because the interest they collected on outstanding loans exceeded the interest they paid out to customers. WMI Holdings Corp. v. United States, 891 F.3d 1016 (2018).

[1012] WMI Holdings Corp. v. United States, 891 F.3d 1016 (2018).

[1013] WMI Holdings Corp. v. United States, 891 F.3d 1016 (2018).

[1014] Colby v. Mt. Morris, 191 N.Y. 510, 84 N.E. 1111; Bingham v. Savings Investment, etc., Co., 101 N.J. Eq. 413, 138 A. 659, aff'd, 102 N.J. Eq. 302, 140 A. 321; Colby v. Equitable Trust Co., 192 N.Y. 535, 84 N.E. 1111.

[1015] Bresnick v. Franklin Capital Corp., 6 N.J. Super. 579, 70 A.2d 524, rev'd on other

merger, its effect is exclusively what it is declared to be by the statute.[1016] A statute relating to the merger of banks and trust companies, may require

---

grounds, 10 N.J. Super. 234, 77 A.2d 53, aff'd, 7 N.J. 184, 81 A.2d 6 (trust company and title company).

Merger of trust company and mortgage guaranty company was authorized by statute. Pink v. Alden, 174 Misc. 69, 18 N.Y.S.2d 604.

Despite a statute authorizing the creation of a trust company to be endowed with certain privileges, the board of directors and majority stockholders held without power to trade trust company's property and good will for stock of title guaranty company, thus in effect dissolving trust company, and not being within the provisions of the above mentioned statute. Luehrmann v. Lincoln Trust, etc., Co. (Mo.), 192 S.W. 1026.

[1016] **In general.—**

In re Bergdorf 206 N.Y. 309, 99 N.E. 714.

Applicability of statute.—

Trust company, by amending articles to include rights conferred by statute, effected practical reorganization so as to come within statute respecting mergers. Bingham v. Savings Inv. & Trust Co., 102 N.J. Eq. 302, 140 A. 321.

Statutes authorizing merger of trust companies construed.—

Statute held to permit a trust company to merge itself into another, and a trust company which merges into another company, without surrendering its corporate existence, retains only its corporate entity, but otherwise it is nonexistent, and its property rights and interests vest in the company into which it is merged. In re Bergdorf, 206 N.Y. 309, 99 N.E. 714.

Under Illinois law upon consolidation of banking corporations and trust companies, the merging corporations, though they cease to exist as individual entities, are merged into and become integral parts of the new corporation, and though they therefore lack formal legal existence for the purpose of performance of their trust duties and obligations they remain alive by permission of the legislative body in a new corporate entity. De Korwin v. First Nat'l Bank, 179 F.2d 347, cert. denied, 339 U.S. 982, 70 S. Ct. 1025, 1026, 1028, 94 L. Ed. 1386.

Under the New York statute, companies created by special acts and empowered by subsequent special acts to execute trusts, are subject to the provision., of the banking law, and a merger of such specially chartered companies is authorized though such merger was unlawful when such specially chartered companies were formed. Colby v. Mt Morris, 191 N.Y. 510, 84 N.E. 1111.

Statute governing merger of banks and trust companies includes all trust companies, however "organized." Bingham v. Savings Investment, etc., Co., 101 N.J. Eq. 413, 138 A. 659, aff'd, 102 N.J. Eq. 302, 140 A. 321.

Under statute, on consolidation of two trust company banks the new corporation takes the place of the old companies, and, succeeding to their assets and assuming their liabilities, succeeds to the ownership of the securities deposited by them with the state treasurer, and need not deposit additional securities, but may withdraw that part of those deposited by them exceeding the maximum of $100,000 required of such a company, however large its capital. First Wisconsin Trust Co. v. Johnson, 173 Wis. 564, 181 N.W. 828.

that dissenting stockholders take compensation for their shares.[1017] However, a merger plan must be fair and equitable before dissenting stockholders can be required to join therein or take compensation for their shares.[1018] Thus, in a merger of a trust company with another institution, the directors of the trust company occupy a position of trust towards its stockholders, and cannot lawfully obtain undue advantage or enrich themselves at the expense of the company or stockholders in assenting to the merger.[1019]

A new corporation into which trust companies have been merged cannot, by prematurely filing a duplicate of the merger agreement, foreclose the right of dissenting stockholders to object to the merger and demand payment for their stock within the allowable twenty-day period.[1020] Where a trustee company merges with another, its liabilities with respect to the trust become

---

1017 Bingham v. Savings Inv. & Trust Co., 101 N.J. Eq. 413, 138 A. 659, aff'd, 102 N.J. Eq. 302, 140 A. 321.

Trust company's minority stockholder, who objected to majority's selling property and good will of company to title guaranty company for stock in latter, may recover against guaranty company interest in property and good will of trust company represented by his stock at time of transfer, though cause of action was not lien on property, and prayer for enforcement did not authorize court to follow specific property. Luehrmann v. Lincoln Trust & Title Co., 192 S.W. 1026.

1018 **In general.—**

Bingham v. Savings Inv. & Trust Co., 101 N.J. Eq. 413, 138 A. 659, aff'd, 102 N.J. Eq. 302, 140 A. 321.

Plan held fair.—

Merging bank and trust company, by giving one share in new corporation for each share in merged corporations, held not unfair or inequitable to stockholders under circumstances. Bingham v. Savings Inv. & Trust Co., 101 N.J. Eq. 413, 138 A. 659, aff'd, 102 N.J. Eq. 302, 140 A. 321.

Where 83/85 of stock of trust company present is voted for merger, court will not enjoin merger as inequitable unless merger is without legal authority. Bingham v. Savings Inv. & Trust Co., 101 N.J. Eq. 413, 138 A. 659, aff'd, 102 N.J. Eq. 302, 140 A. 321.

In suit by stockholder of trust company to enjoin its merger they are not necessary parties against whom no relief is sought Bonner v. Chapin Nat. Bank, 251 Mass. 401, 146 N.E. 666 (1925).

1019 Bonner v. Chapin Nat. Bank, 251 Mass. 401, 146 N.E. 666 (1925).

Directors' segregation and setting apart of assets of trust company, to be divided among stockholders assenting to merger plan, was fraudulent and illegal, and breach of trust by directors, for which corporation was entitled to equitable relief. Bonner v. Chapin Nat. Bank, 251 Mass. 401, 146 N.E. 666 (1925).

1020 Application of Wynegar, 144 Misc. 805, 259 N.Y.S. 328.

liabilities of the merged company.[1021] And the merger of a trust company with other banking corporations does not change the contract of its corporators or destroy the vested rights of its stockholders,[1022] and is not invalid because it deprives stockholders of a right to participate in an increase of stock.[1023] But a bank taking over all the assets of a trust company for liquidation was held not liable for taxes on its property where the bank had agreed to pay only the amount due depositors, loans and incidental expenses, and nothing had been said about taxes assessed on real estate.[1024]

A trust company may not consolidate with another entity if there is no statute plainly permitting such consolidation.[1025] A national bank which is

---

[1021] Jongers v. First Trust & Deposit Co., 147 Misc. 260, 263 N.Y.S. 619.

Merger of trustee in another trust company which in turn was absorbed continued corporate personality, as regards accounting. In re Blake's Will, 146 Misc. 780, 263 N.Y.S. 310.

The merger of trust companies placed new company in same position as that occupied by old company and made new company liable for breach of duty with respect to testamentary trust to the same extent as if the debts, liabilities or duties had been incurred or controlled by it. Thruston v. Nashville & American Trust Co., 32 F. Supp. 929.

[1022] Bingham v. Savings Investment, etc., Co., 102 N.J. Eq. 302, 140 A. 321.

Where a trust company, which had been appointed the committee of the property of a deceased employee's incompetent dependent, merged with another trust company, under Banking Law, § 494, in view of Code Civ. Proc. §§ 2321, 2340, and Workmen's Compensation Law, § 11, and § 16, subd. 2, the latter company was entitled to receive the compensation due to dependent. O'Rourke v. Standard Wood Turning Co., 204 App. Div. 658, 198 N.Y.S. 632.

Stockholder of trust company upon a merger with another trust company is entitled to conversion of his shares into shares of resulting trust company and he cannot be compelled to take stock in a third company or cash as a dissenting stockholder. Marcou v. Federal Trust Co., 268 A.2d 629 (Me. 1970).

[1023] Bingham v. Savings Investment, etc., Co., 102 N.J. Eq. 302, 140 A. 321.

[1024] Metropolitan Life Ins. Co. v. Commercial Nat. Bank, 115 Pa. Super. 224, 175 A. 295.

[1025] **In general.—**

Bresnick v. Franklin Capital Corp., 6 N.J. Super. 579, 70 A.2d 524, rev'd on other grounds, 10 N.J. Super. 234, 77 A.2d 53, aff'd, 7 N.J. 184, 81 A.2d 6.

Consolidation authorized by federal law.—

In absence of any statute prohibiting consolidation of a state trust company and a national bank, such a consolidation in 1981 authorized by federal law was not in contravention of law and public policy of Vermont, although not then specifically authorized by statute. In re Watkins' Estate, 113 Vt. 126, 30 A.2d 305.

Vermont statute forbidding a savings bank or trust company from making sale, lease, or

consolidated with a trust company organized under state laws remains under the supervision of state banking authorities so far as trust functions are concerned.[1026] For other matters relating to consolidation, see the footnote.[1027]

---

exchange of all of its asset. without consent of bank commissioner, given on petition and after hearing, did not apply to consolidation of a state trust company and a national bank. In re Watkins' Estate, 113 Vt. 126, 30 A.2d 305.

[1026] **In general.—**

Adams v. Atlantic Nat'l Bank, 115 Fla. 399, 155 So. 648.

In absence of any statute, permitting transfer of state trust company's right to be a corporation, that right remained subject to Vermont law although trust company was consolidated with a national bank under federal law. In re Watkins' Estate, 113 Vt. 126, 80 A.2d 805.

Federal legislation could not authorize state trust company in Pennsylvania to consolidate with national bank, hence consolidation did not dissolve trust company, whose franchise to be corporation remained subject to state law, though company transferred its property to bank. Commonwealth v. Merchants Nat. Bank, 323 Pa. 145, 185 A. 823.

And state retained power to terminate corporate existence of trust company upon its failure to pay franchise tax. In re Watkins' Estate, 113 Vt. 126, 80 A.2d 305.

New corporation does not become executor in trust company's place.—

Where state trust company acting as executor was consolidated with national bank under federal law, the new banking corporation did not thereby become legal executor in place of the trust company, since whether the new banking corporation automatically succeeded to the executorship depended upon law of Vermont. In re Watkins' Estate, 113 Vt. 126, 30 A.2d 305.

Corporate identity of trust company not dissolved.—

In absence of any statute providing that charter of state trust company shall become void when company is consolidated with a national bank, corporate identity of trust company is not destroyed and its charter is not dissolved by the consolidation. In re Watkins' Estate, 113 Vt. 126, 30 A.2d 305.

[1027] **Consolidation forms new corporate entity.—**

A trust company born of the consolidation of two existing trust companies was a new corporate entity, distinct from the constituent corporations, and in absence of express contract by new company assuming liabilities of existing trust or acquiring any of the assets thereof with knowledge of an existing claim against that trust or substitution of the new company for either of defendants in action to enforce alleged claim, new company was not before the court for determination of its rights and liabilities. Thruston v. Nashville, etc., Trust Co., 32 F. Supp. 929.

The validity of an accomplished consolidation of trust companies can only be questioned by the state and is not subject to collateral attack in action on guaranty held by the consolidated company. Albers v. McNichols, 301 Ill. App. 551, 23 N.E.2d 220.

Rights under guaranty.—

Where consolidated trust company received, as part of its assets, a guaranty from merged

Reorganization and Reopening.—A statute providing that a closed trust company might be reorganized with the consent of three-fourths of its creditors and two-thirds of its stockholders, and that creditors not consenting thereto are bound and must accept the stock and securities provided for in the reorganization, was held unconstitutional.[1028] But other statutes authorizing the reorganization of banks and trust companies have been held constitutional.[1029] And a reorganization plan is not unconstitutional because no provision is made for immediate payment of all debts, as against an

---

trust company, and where it was not made to appear that not all of the assets of the merged company were turned over to the consolidated company, the consolidated company succeeded to the rights and powers of the merged company and could institute proceedings to recover the amount due and unpaid from the guarantor, notwithstanding the guaranty was a nonnegotiable instrument and had not been endorsed. Albers v. McNichols, 301 Ill. App. 551, 23 N.E.2d 220.

Unrevoked guaranty held by trust company at time of its consolidation with national bank passed without impairment to the bank and inured to its benefit in connection with loans subsequently made, notwithstanding that at date of consolidation there was no outstanding indebtedness covered by the guaranty. Chase Nat'l Bank v. Burg, 32 F. Supp. 230.

Suretyship liability-not avoided by consolidation.—

Though bank resulting from consolidation of national bank and state trust company was lawfully existing national bank, in view of federal consent thereto, trust company, having become surety on guardian's bond, could not avoid performance thereof even by lawful consolidation. Commonwealth v. Merchants Nat. Bank, 323 Pa. 145, 185 A. 823.

De facto consolidation of state trust company directly with national bank with comptrollers approval held to impose on consolidated national bank liability previously assumed by trust company as surety on guardian's bond. Commonwealth use of Grammes v. Merchants Nat'l Bank, 323 Pa. 145, 185 A. 823.

1028 Basen v. Clinton Trust Co., 13 N.J. Misc. 252, 177 A. 675, rev'd on other grounds, 115 N.J.L. 546, 181 A. 67.

Whether statute providing method of reorganizing closed trust companies could be sustained as an exercise of the police power under guise of emergency legislation could not be raised where statute did not contain emergency provision. Basen v. Clinton Trust Co., 13 N.J. Misc. 252, 177 A. 675, rev'd on other grounds, 115 N.J.L. 546, 181 A. 67.

1029 In general.—

Reilly v. Hamilton Trust Co., 133 N.J. Eq. 232, 31 A.2d 784.

Statute authorizing reorganization of banks and trust companies by issuance to depositors of shares of par value of $10 for each $100 of deposit, redeemable at $80 a share, with consent of 75 percent of depositors, is constitutional, and all depositors are bound, including those not assenting, where plan was approved by requisite percentage of depositors. Reilly v. Hamilton Trust Co., 133 N.J. Eq. 232, 31 A.2d 784.

Emergency legislation.—

Statutory provision for reorganization of trust companies by banking commissioner, as

objection that a creditor is deprived of property without due process.[1030] The extinguishment of an obligation of an insolvent trust company or its directors or stockholders is sufficient consideration for the execution of a reorganization agreement providing for the issuance of new securities.[1031] And the result of a receivership of a Massachusetts invest trust must be fair and equitable, regardless of whether it be deemed a partial liquidation or a reorganization;[1032] the words "fair and equitable" are words of art with a fixed meaning as applied to receiverships, and the rationale thereof is the recognition of contractual rights.[1033]

---

emergency legislation, held valid. Attorney Gen. v. Union Guardian Trust Co., 273 Mich. 554, 263 N.W. 866.

[1030] **In general.—**

Jennings v. Fidelity, etc., Trust Co., 240 Ky. 24, 41 S.W.2d 537.

Provision that deposits of which trust company was trustee should be paid in full, held not to require payment in full of funds deposited by executrices of an estate, since relationship between trust company and executrices was that of debtor and creditor and not trustee and beneficiary. Basen v. Clinton Trust Co., 13 N.J. Misc. 252, 177 A. 675, rev'd on other grounds, 115 N.J.L. 546, 181 A. 67.

Plan binding on dissenting creditor.—

See Statler v. United States Sav., etc., Co., 122 Pa. Super. 189, 186 A. 290, aff'd, 326 Pa. 247, 192 A. 250.

[1031] **In general.—**

Jennings v. Fidelity, etc., Trust Co., 240 Ky. 24, 41 S.W.2d 537.

That stockholders paying statutory liability received one-half thereof in new capital stock of reorganized trust company did not render reorganization plan objectionable. State v. Title Guarantee, etc., Co., 168 Md. 376, 177 A. 617, 99 A.L.R. 1204 (1935).

Though plan exempted directors from financial liability for wrongful acts and stockholders from restitution of dividends improperly declared, and payment of statutory liability, bank commissioner was required to receive and file the proposed plan for the reorganization and reopening of the banking institution, and then to make such study and investigation of the plan as the bank commissioner should deem necessary. State v. Title Guarantee & Trust Co., 168 Md. 376, 177 A. 617, 99 A.L.R. 1204 (1935).

[1032] Bailey v. Minsch, 168 F.2d 635, cert. denied, 335 U.S. 854, 69 S. Ct. 83, 98 L. Ed. 402.

[1033] **In general.—**

Bailey v. Minsch, 168 F.2d 635, cert. denied, 335 U.S. 854, 69 S. Ct. 83, 93 L. Ed. 402.

Plans not "fair and feasible".—

Where Securities and Exchange Commission opposed all reorganization plans for investment trust in receivership and each proponent opposed all plans but his own plan, and possibility of mutually acceptable plans which could be approved by Commission seemed remote, finding that plans of reorganization were not "fair and feasible" was not an abuse of

The questions of depositors' preferences and rights of depositors holding collateral security were held not properly before a court in a proceeding for the approval of a general plan of reorganization of a closed trust company.[1034] And where a trust company and a bank commissioner refused to furnish depositors with certain information respecting the company to enable the depositors intelligently to elect whether to dissent from a reorganization plan, the depositors, by dissenting, were held without grounds for a demand in a court action to enforce the plan.[1035] Trustees are held to a high standard of conduct in their dealing with a trust, and where an examination into the operations of reorganization trustees discloses a number of irregularities and actions beyond the limits of their powers, the trustees may be surcharged for

---

discretion. Bailey v. Proctor, 160 F.2d 78, cert. denied, 331 U.S. 834, 67 S. Ct. 1515, 91 L. Ed. 1847.

Payment of debentures issued by Massachusetts investment trust as result of court order in receivership proceeding against the trust, secured a behest of bondholders' committee, and against desire of controlling shareholders, was not within terms of agreement that debentures were subject to redemption at "option of the trust" at principal amount thereof; accrued interest, and premium, so as to require payment of the premium in order to make the reorganization "fair and equitable" though majority stockholders decided to continue the trust. Bailey v. Minsch, 168 F.2d 635, cert. denied, 335 U.S. 854, 69 S. Ct. 83, 93 L. Ed. 402.

1034 In re Application Mt. Vernon Trust Co., 241 App. Div. 835, 271 N.Y.S. 288.

1035 Nagel v. Ghingher, 166 Md. 231, 171 A. 65, 92 A.L.R. 1315.

losses sustained by the trust estate.[1036] For miscellaneous matters relating to reopening and reorganization plans, see the footnote.[1037]

[1036] **In general.—**

Behrman v. Egan, 25 N.J. Super. 109, 95 A.2d 599, modified, 16 N.J. 97, 106 A.2d 284.

Unwarranted assumption of liability.—

Reorganization trustees would be surcharged with loss to trust estate resulting from their unwarranted assumption of liability of debtor-bank for making illegal investment in bank role as guardian. Behrman v. Egan, 25 N.J. Super. 109, 95 A.2d 599, modified, 16 N.J. 97, 106 A.2d 284.

Failure to insist upon contract rights.—

Reorganization trustees would be surcharged for loss to trust estate resulting from their failure to stand upon their rights under contract for sale of realty, where they submitted to purchasers' demand for reduction in price instead of insisting upon performance of contract according to its terms. Behrman v. Egan, 25 N.J. Super. 109, 95 A.2d 599, modified, 16 N.J. 97, 106 A.2d 284.

Failure to diligently collect claims.—

Reorganization trustees would be surcharged for loss to trust estate occasioned by their failure to proceed diligently with collection of claims, in absence of some satisfactory explanation for course of action taken. Behrman v. Egan, 25 N.J. Super. 109, 95 A.2d 599, modified, 16 N.J. 97, 106 A.2d 284.

Discounted certificates used as face-value setoffs.—

It was improper for reorganization trustees, who had issued beneficiary certificates to depositors of debtor-bank, to permit face value of certificate. to be set off against sums owed bank, when certificates had been acquired for a small part of their face value and result of practice was that debtors so favored, among whom were employees of bank, were able to settle their obligations for fractional part of their debts. Behrman v. Egan, 25 N.J. Super. 109, 95 A.2d 599, modified, 16 N.J. 97, 106 A.2d 284.

Where reorganization trustees used cash payments made on account of obligations to debtor-bank to purchase at discount beneficiaries-certificates previously issued by trustees to bank's depositors and then credited such certificates at face value against obligations owed to bank, trustees would be surcharged for entire amount of certificates so used, in absence of proof as to amount of cash paid by bank's debtor. and in absence of proof that transactions were proper. Behrman v. Egan, 25 N.J. Super. 109, 95 A.2d 599, modified, 16 N.J. 97, 106 A.2d 284.

Burden was upon reorganization trustees seeking approval of their account to justify their acceptance of beneficiary certificates, acquired at discount, as face-value setoffs against sums owed to debtor-bank; such setoffs being items of discharge. Behrman v. Egan, 26 N.J. Super. 109, 95 A.2d 599, modified, 16 N.J. 97, 106 A.2d 284.

Purchasing certificates through "dummies".—

Where reorganization trustees, knowing that liquidating dividends would be much higher then amounts paid for beneficiary-certificates, nevertheless concealed such fact by purchasing certificates through "dummies," their conduct, though resulting in no loss to

(Text continued on page 271)

estate, was a violation of duty owed by trustees to beneficiaries and deserved court's severe condemnation. Behrman v. Egan, 25 N.J. Super. 109, 95 A.2d 599, modified, 16 N.J. 97, 106 A.2d 284.

Fraud not shown.—

Evidence would not sustain contention that decree, approving reorganization trustees' transfer of building to debtor-bank and sanctioning increase in capital of debtor-bank, had been procured by fraud. Behrman v. Egan, 25 N.J. Super. 109, 95 A.2d 599, modified, 16 N.J. 97, 106 A.2d 284.

1037 **Bank commissioner can permit reopening upon such conditions as he approves.** So reorganization plan was not objectionable because company, while retaining right to function as bank of deposit, was reopened with business limited to general trust and safe deposit business, etc., since such condition was well within authority of commissioner. State v. Title Guarantee & Trust Co., 168 Md. 376, 177 A. 617, 99 A.L.R. 1204 (1935).

Reorganization statute held applicable to all trust companies, including those not formally permitted to engage in general banking business. Attorney Gen. v. Union Guardian Trust Co., 273 Mich. 554, 263 N.W. 866.

Reorganization held not to change corporate entity of trust company so as to preclude action against reorganized company for debt owed by trust company to depositors who did not consent to reorganization. Basen v. Clinton Trust Co., 13 N.J. Misc. 252, 177 A. 675, rev'd on other grounds, 115 N.J.L. 546, 181 A. 67.

Reorganization of trust company for which conservator had been appointed did not interrupt or change corporate entity. Union Guardian Trust Co. v. Stillman, 300 Mich. 27, 1 N.W.2d 439.

Trust company held not to cease functioning as trustee in trust mortgage because a conservator was appointed and it was subsequently reorganized. Union Guardian Trust Co. v. Stillman, 300 Mich. 27, 1 N.W.2d 439.

Cause of action against stockholder, officer or director held inchoate asset to be appropriately enforced as respects validity of reorganization plan. State v. Title Guarantee, etc., Co., 168 Md. 376, 177 A. 617, 99 A.L.R. 1204 (1935).

In ascertaining present cash value of claim of any depositor or creditor not approving reorganization plan, court should take into consideration, investigate, and value every asset, including rights of action ex delicto or ex contractu, or by force of statute against any officer, director, or stockholder. State v. Title Guarantee & Trust Co., 168 Md. 376, 177 A. 617, 99 A.L.R. 1204 (1935).

Necessity for shareholders' meeting prior to approval of plans.—

Prior to court approval of plans of reorganization of investment trust and receivership, there was no necessity for calling a shareholders' meeting to consider such plans, and hence denial of shareholders' motion for permission to call a meeting of the shareholders of the trust at time liquidation of trust was ordered was proper. Bailey v. Proctor, 160 F.2d 78, cert. denied, 331 U.S. 834, 67 S. Ct. 1515, 91 L. Ed. 1847.

Recovery of assessment from nonassenting stockholders.—

Nyen Holding Corp. v. Kahle, 177 Misc. 216, 29 N.Y.S.2d 793.

(Text continued on page 271)

Shares issued to depositors under reorganization plan constituted preferred stock.—

Shares of preferred stock of par value of $10 for each $100 of deposit and redeemable at $80 a share, issued under authorized reorganization plan for a trust company, constituted "preferred stock" and depositors to whom they were issued were not "creditors" to extend of 80 percent of deposits so as to allow participation with new depositors in trust company's assets upon subsequent liquidation, where it was clear from statute and certificate of incorporation under which stock was issued that stock was not a certificate of indebtedness in the nature of a "debenture," and there was intent to subordinate right. of preferred stockholders to general creditors. Reilly v. Hamilton Trust Co., 133 N.J. Eq. 232, 31 A.2d 784.

Mere fact that evidences of transaction were called preferred stock would not bar participation in assets of liquidation of trust company as full creditors, since equity would consider substance and not form, but where purpose of transaction was to enable company to resume operations and ultimately allow original depositors to receive the 80 percent balance of their deposits, substance of plan was not to continue depositors as full creditors with postponed payment, but as preferred stockholders subordinated to general creditors. Reilly v. Hamilton Trust Co., 133 N.J. Eq. 232, 31 A.2d 784.

And where subscription agreements for certificates showed nature of obligation issued to be preferred stock, certificates could not be construed as evidences of deferred deposits despite statements to effect that 30 percent of deposit proposed to be applied to preferred stock would be safe in a good interest-bearing security, and that the 30 percent was really a temporarily deferred deposit; the statements meaning only that there was hope for ultimate return of the 30 percent with interest. Reilly v. Hamilton Trust Co., 133 N.J. Eq. 232, 31 A.2d 784.

Preference only against common stockholders.—

Where statute authorized a reorganization plan whereby depositors of trust company accepted, in place of portion of deposits, shares of preferred stock, and referred to the obligations, specifically, as preferred stock by providing that subscription for preferred stock should be paid for by offset against deposit balance, and instrument incorporating reorganization plan provided no payment could be made to holders of common stock until preferred stockholders were paid, intention was that preference should be only as against common stockholders and that preferred stockholders should have no right to share with general creditors. Reilly v. Hamilton Trust Co., 133 N.J. Eq. 232, 31 A.2d 784.

Even if certificates issued under reorganization plan were considered as debentures evidencing a debt, rights of holders of certificates must be postponed to those of general creditors where it was purpose of both statute under which plan was authorized and plan itself to scale down the debt of the company so as to enable it to survive. Reilly v. Hamilton Trust Co., 133 N.J. Eq. 232, 31 A.2d 784.

And where depositors accepted one share of preferred stock of par value of $10 for each $100 of deposit redeemable at $80 a share to stand in place of 80 percent of indebtedness, and the 30 percent was applied to the trust company's capital structure, new obligations to later depositors were undertaken, insurance thereon entered into based on reduction in debt, and dividends over a period of years accepted by original depositors as preferred stockholders, original depositors were "estopped" from claiming status of general creditors

(Text continued on page 271)

so as to permit equal participation with new depositors and other creditors in assets of trust company in subsequent liquidation. Reilly v. Hamilton Trust Co., 133 N.J. Eq. 232, 31 A.2d 784.

Participation certificate holders' rights as to assets retransferred to reorganized company under substitution agreement.—

Where plan of reorganization reserved to insolvent trust company the right for five years to substitute any of the assets retained by it for any of the assets transferred to mortgage company which issued participation certificates to trust company depositors, certificate holders had no equitable lien on assets retransferred to reorganized trust company pursuant to power of substitution enforceable against surplus remaining after liquidation of reorganized company as against common stockholders of reorganized company. Temple v. Clinton Trust Co., 1 N.J. 219, 62 A.2d 690.

Where, upon reorganization of insolvent trust company, unacceptable assets were transferred to a holding company for benefit of depositors to whom were issued participation certificates, the trust company retaining the right during a five-year period to substitute other assets in place of those transferred to holding company, substitution of worthless assets during the five-year period violated no right of the certificate holders. Temple v. Clinton Trust Co., 142 N.J. Eq. 285, 59 A.2d 590, aff'd, 1 N.J. 219, 62 A.2d 690.

Where holding company settled its accounts in chancery and obtained a decree that its account and substitution of assets be approved and representative certificate holders were defendants, decree was conclusive in favor of the holding company and others into whose hands the assets or proceeds of the assets were transmitted and constituted a bar against the assertion by the certificate holders that such substitutions were a violation of the duty owed to such holders. Temple v. Clinton Trust Co., 142 N.J. Eq. 285, 59 A.2d 590, aff'd, 1 N.J. 219, 62 A.2d 690.

Depositor's suit to enjoin payment to reorganized trust company's stockholders of proceeds of sale of assets.—

A mortgage company, organized to effectuate part of insolvent trust company's reorganization plan, pursuant to which mortgage company issued participation certificates to trust company's depositors, or mortgage company's trustees in dissolution, were necessary parties to depositors' suit to enjoin payment to reorganized trust company's stockholders of proceeds of sale of such company's assets. Temple v. Clinton Trust Co., 141 N.J. Eq. 372, 57 A.2d 514.

An insolvent trust company's depositors were not entitled to injunction against payment to reorganized trust company's stockholders of proceeds of sale of such company's assets on ground of its substitution of worthless assets for good assets previously transferred by it to mortgage company, thus enhancing value of reorganized company's common stock at expense of holders of mortgage company's participation certificates, in absence of statement of terms of certificates or allegation that depositors held certificates in their bill for injunction. Temple v. Clinton Trust Co., 141 N.J. Eq. 372, 57 A.2d 514.

An insolvent trust company's depositors, accepting cash or demand deposits in reorganized trust company, preferred stock thereof, and mortgage company's participation certificates in full satisfaction of amounts due them, had no interest in reorganized company's assets or proceeds of subsequent sale thereof, and hence were not entitled to

(*Text continued on page 271*)

---

injunction against payment of such proceeds to reorganized company's stockholders. Temple v. Clinton Trust Co., 141 N.J. Eq. 372, 57 A.2d 514.

Collateral securing bonds.—

The obligation of a trust company as the maker of bonds issued by it was primary and direct, and company was not entitled to share pro rata in liquidation of collateral securing bonds, but was only entitled to receive surplus after other bondholders were paid in full, notwithstanding plan of reorganization adopted under statute dealing with issuance of preferred and depositors' common stock by state banks, trust companies, and savings banks. Howell v. Bartlett, 126 N.J. Eq. 315, 8 A.2d 690.

Delay in objecting to reorganization.—

A request by trust company's creditor, objecting to its reorganization, for revaluation of his claim and allocation of assets to meet it, after reorganization plan had been in operation for four years, came too late, but should have been made in reorganization proceedings. O'Brien v. Hirschfield, 285 Mich. 308, 281 N.W. 9.

Where three years and two months elapsed between date of approval by banking commissioner of plan for reorganization of trust company and institution of action by depositor to recover checking account and savings account during which time the plan to authorize bank to resume business on an unrestricted basis was perfected and put into operation, the depositor was "estopped" from maintaining action attacking validity of the reorganization plan. McSweeney v. Equitable Trust Co., 127 N.J.L. 299, 22 A.2d 282, 139 A.L.R 653, appeal dismissed, 315 U.S. 785, 62 S. Ct. 805, 86 L. Ed. 1191.

Stockholders of trust company could not delay for five years after court approval of plans for reorganization filed in liquidation proceedings and then attack validity of proceedings and the order, where innocent persons had acquired rights and positions had been changed, the rescission of which would result in almost inextricable confusion. Holmes v. Union Bank, 79 Ohio App. 272, 35 Ohio Op. 22, 73 N.E.2d 100.

Plan not set aside.—

Objecting creditor who did not request court to determine value of his claim or to provide for its payment held not entitled to order setting aside plan for trust company's reorganization, by which all assets were allocated to pay all of claims, where plan appeared fair and had been accepted by interested parties and approved by trial court and had been in operation over one year. Attorney Gen. v. Union Guardian Trust Co., 273 Mich. 554, 263 N.W. 866.

Service by publication and posting in reorganization proceedings held sufficient as against holders of bonds secured by trust mortgage in which trust company prior to reorganization was designated as trustee. Union Guardian Trust Co. v. Stillman, 300 Mich. 27, 1 N.W.2d 439.

Order of court approving plan for reorganization of trust company in liquidation proceedings is binding upon all those who failed to challenge the order within five days and also upon those who did challenge within that time. Holmes v. Union Bank of Commerce, 79 Ohio App. 272, 78 N.E.2d 100, 35 Ohio Op. 22.

Review of approval or disapproval of plan.—

State v. Title Guarantee & Trust Co., 168 Md. 376, 177 A. 617, 99 A.L.R. 1204 (1935).

Contractual Liquidation.—A contract whereby a trust company conveyed its assets to a bank, which assumed its obligations and agreed to liquidate its assets and return any net balance, was held a valid contract for a loan with a conveyance of assets as security or collateral, creating the relation of debtor and creditor and pledgor and pledgee.[1038]

§ 4. Forfeiture of Franchise and Dissolution.

A statute authorizing a state banking board to revoke a certificate of an installment investment company if the grounds provided by statute for such revocation exist, is not unconstitutional as giving the state banking board arbitrary powers.[1039] And if a trust company has disqualified itself from the lawful pursuit of its trust business by reducing its nominal capital stock below the minimum prescribed by statute, the statute may authorize a state superintendent of banks to proceed in chancery for the liquidation of the

---

Chancellor's approval will prevail in absence of abuse of judicial discretion. State v. Title Guarantee, etc., Co., 168 Md. 376, 177 A. 617, 99 A.L.R. 1204 (1935), wherein discretion was held not abused.

Considering the factual nature of the inquiry made by the Banking Commission and the factual nature of the arguments in the appellate briefs, the Banking Commission's grant of law firm's application to organize and operate a trust company in South Dakota involved "mixed questions of law and fact," to which reviewing court would apply the clearly erroneous standard of review. In re Application of Dorsey, 2001 SD 35, 623 N.W.2d 468, (2001).

Disapproval of plan held an abuse of discretion.—

Where liquidation of trust by receivers had been ordered, and all debenture holders had been paid, trial court's disapproval of a plan, which was submitted by shareholders and which had approval of Securities and Exchange Commission, for continuation of trust but permitting shareholders who desired to withdraw to do so and to receive their full pro rata share, was an abuse of discretion, though shareholders would obtain certain tax advantages by continuation of the trust and debenture holders who had been paid off did not receive call premium provided in trust instrument. Bailey v. Proctor, 166 F.2d 392 (1948).

1038 Citizens, etc., Nat. Bank v. King, 184 Ga. 238, 190 S.E. 857, holding that such contract was not a voluntary liquidation of the trust company where its corporate existence was maintained.

Where in such case the trustees of the trust company accepted a clarifying contract declaring the bank's right to profits from the trust business of the trust company, a minority stockholder of the trust company suing on its behalf was not entitled to an accounting with reference to such profits, though clarifying contract was made after suit was brought. Citizens, etc., Nat. Bank v. King, 184 Ga. 238, 190 S.E. 857.

1039 State v. Northwestern Trust Co., 72 Neb. 497, 101 N.W. 14. See also §§ 7 and 8 of this chapter.

company.[1040] But a statute authorizing the winding up of "any corporation" when insolvent or in danger thereof, or on mismanagement of its affairs, does not apply to trust companies over which a bank examiner is vested with sole authority.[1041]

Commissioners of a trust company appointed in pursuance of statute to close up the company's business, and vested with legal title to all of the company's property therefor, may maintain a suit in their own names to foreclose a mortgage to the company.[1042] And where a trust company, in the process of dissolution, has ceased business, but left on deposit with a superintendent of insurance certain securities, and has complied with a statute as to dissolution, inspection, and request for the return of such securities, it is entitled to a return of the securities from the insurance superintendent.[1043] A plan to transfer the property of a trust company in liquidation to a new company is approved if two thirds of the stockholders of the liquidating company sanction the enterprise, although a small minority objects; however, a court, in approving such plan, must have a view toward safeguarding creditors' interest.[1044] But an insolvent trust company's liability as surety on a bond terminates on the sale of its assets to a bank which assumes its liabilities.[1045] Although the charter of a trust company provides that, in case of the dissolution of the company, deposits of minors, insane persons, or married women shall be preferred claims, and the company becomes insolvent in one sense, a receiver is appointed, and an injunction is issued restraining the company and its officers from transacting further business or interfering with its property, if the company is not insolvent in fact, and does not lose its power to resume business, there is not such a dissolution as entitles the deposits of minors, insane persons, and married women to be preferred.[1046]

Ordinarily, liquidation of an investment trust being a drastic remedy, it will only be decreed in an extraordinary case or where peculiar circum-

---

[1040] Montgomery Bank, etc., Co. v. State, 201 Ala. 447, 78 So. 825.

[1041] Craughwell v. Mousam River Trust Co., 113 Me. 531, 95 A. 221.

[1042] Creswell v. Williams, 9 D.C. (2 Arthur) 246.

[1043] State v. Chorn, 269 Mo. 172, 190 S.W. 17.

[1044] In re City Trust Co., 133 Misc. 856, 234 N.Y.S. 363; In re City Trust Co., 133 Misc. 869, 234 N.Y.S. 550.

[1045] State v. Huxtable, 178 Ark. 361, 12 S.W.2d 1.

[1046] Dewey v. St. Albans Trust Co., 56 Vt. 476, 48 Am. R. 803.

stances exist.[1047] And a weekly paper in which legal notices are published has been held a "newspaper of general circulation" within a statute requiring publication of notice calling a meeting of shareholders to determine the dissolution of a loan association.[1048] As to miscellaneous matters relating to forfeiture of franchise and dissolution, see the footnote.[1049]

[1047] Bailey v. Proctor, 160 F.2d 78, cert. denied, 331 U.S. 834, 67 S. Ct. 1515, 91 L. Ed. 1847.

Where investment trust assets had had a value substantially less than principal amount of outstanding debentures, trust earnings in one year were insufficient to meet interest charges on debentures, and recurrence of receivership was possible, ordering liquidation of the trust was not an abuse of discretion. Bailey v. Proctor, 160 F.2d 78, cert. denied, 331 U.S. 834, 67 S. Ct. 1515, 91 L. Ed. 1847.

[1048] Beutelspacher v. Spokane Sav. Bank, 164 Wash. 227, 2 P.2d 729.

[1049] **Legal remedies after expiration of charter.—**

A trust company had right to sue out writ of error to review judgment against it for money had and received on rescission of contract to purchase from it mortgage notes issued by livestock company, though trust company's corporate charter expired before entry of judgment in view of statutory provision that corporation's dissolution shall not impair any remedy against it for liability incurred before its dissolution. Bankers Trust Co. v. Hall, 116 Colo. 566, 183 P.2d 986.

Minority shareholders objecting to dissolution are entitled to be paid the full value of their shares, including proportionate value of a reserve fund. Beutelspacher v. Spokane Sav. Bank, 164 Wash. 227, 2 P.2d 729.

Sale of assets.—

Evidence justified conclusion that trust company's trustees in dissolution were justified in accepting a bank's proposal to purchase company's assets for price amounting to $80.49 per share of company's stock and pay $32 per share for all stock tendered for cancellation. Milberg v. Seaboard Trust Co., 7 N.J. 236, 81 A.2d 142.

Sale and conveyance of real estate.—

Where title to land was vested in trust company and not in company's officers as trustees, deed from sole surviving director or trust company conveyed no title to land. Flader v. Campbell, 120 Colo. 66, 207 P.2d 1188.

A liquidation agreement between a trust company and a bank constituting an officer and another cotrustee with power to sell real estate owned by the trust company and held in its own name or in trust for its use and benefit did not authorize officer to dispose of real estate held by trust company as trustee for plaintiff by an alleged oral agreement conferring upon plaintiff a right of redemption to the property which trust company had acquired at an execution sale. Alter v. Logan Trust Co., 360 Pa. 491, 62 A.2d 25, 11 A.L.R.2d 1302.

Modification of order for liquidation.—

Public interest requires that receiverships be terminated as soon as may reasonably be done and that previous orders not be reopened continually, but where no one would be prejudiced by modification of order for liquidation of trust, modification plan could not

(Text continued on page 277)

properly be rejected merely because of delay due to an earlier appeal by shareholders on questions of law which were fairly litigable. Bailey v. Proctor, 166 F.2d 392 (1948).

Compensation of trustees.—

Trustees in dissolution of trust company were entitled to no compensation until their account had been allowed, and fact that payment of $2, 400 to themselves without court approval was prompted by desire to deduct payments from income of trust estate for certain tax year did not justify such action. Gardner v. Baldi, 24 N.J. Super. 228, 93 A.2d 644.

Trustees in dissolution of trust company would be entitled to aggregate allowance of $7, 500 where, with exception of one trustee, the services performed consisted of signing various documents by which transfer of corporate assets was effected. Gardner v. Baldi, 24 N.J. Super. 228, 93 A.2d 644.

Profit from purchase prior to service as trustees.—

Action of bank directors in contributing to account out of which fractional preferred stock in bank was purchased was proper, and directors, who subsequently served as trustees in dissolution of trust company which held stock of the bank, would not be surcharged for any profit made because of such purchases. Gardner v. Baldi, 24 N.J. Super. 228, 93 A.2d 644.

Payment for services of attorney as tax expert.—

Trustees in dissolution of trust company acted at their peril in paying for services rendered by attorney as tax expert without court's consent and exposed themselves to a surcharge to the extent that the court should find the payment to be excessive. The burden of sustaining the propriety of the payment was on the trustees. Gardner v. Baldi, 24 N.J. Super. 228, 93 A.2d 644.

Burden of sustaining charge of self-dealing on part of trustees in dissolution of trust company was upon exceptants to intermediate account of trustees. Gardner v. Baldi, 24 N.J. Super. 228, 93 A.2d 644.

Disposition of unclaimed distributions.—

Where intent of plan of settlement and reorganization of investment companies was that amounts to be paid to public stockholders were to be made available to them in two ways, by offer to purchase and by making same amounts available to stockholders not accepting purchase offer, with time limitation placed on acceptance of purchase offer but no time limitation placed on availability of distribution after dissolution, part of fund remaining for public stockholders not paid out within five years would be paid to clerk of court to be held and disposed of pursuant to statutes governing deposits and withdrawal of money paid into court. Securities & Exch. Comm'n v. S & P Nat'l Corp., 285 F. Supp. 415 (S.D.N.Y. 1968).

Management investment company.—

In seeking source of power to order liquidation of management investment company, federal district court was not required to look to the statutory or decisional law of state in which the company was organized and transacted business. Securities, etc., Comm. v. Fiscal Fund, 48 F. Supp. 712.

And under Federal Investment Company Act authorizing securities and exchange commission to bring action to enforce compliance with act, court had right to exercise general equity power to order liquidation of company on application of the commission

(Text continued on page 277)

where liquidation was sole practical method of enforcing the act. Securities, etc., Comm. v. Fiscal Fund, 48 F. Supp. 712.

So, where failure of corporate purpose of company was permanent and irremediable, and there was no functioning management, court would order liquidation of company. Securities, etc., Comm. v. Fiscal Fund, 48 F. Supp. 712

Under Small Business Investment Act which provides for forfeiture of rights, privileges, and franchises of small business investment company for violation of act or "regulations" thereunder, fact that word "regulations" is not mentioned in part of act relating to adjudication by court does not preclude adjudication as to violations of regulations. United States v. Cape Fear Capital Corp., 286 F. Supp. 135 (M.D. Pa. 1968).

The Small Business Investment Act prohibited dissolution of or forfeiture of franchise or benefits of small business investment company pending district court's adjudication of action by the United States for decision that federal courts have exclusive jurisdiction over small business investment companies and for incidental relief including injunction to prevent disbursement of any of company's funds, the incumbrance of its assets, or further violations of the act or its regulations, and district court had jurisdiction over the company and its assets, wherever located, pending the adjudication. United States v. Norwood Capital Corp., 273 F. Supp. 236 (D.S.C. 1967).

The final act of adjudication after there has been adjudication of violations of the Small Business Investment Act or regulations thereunder is revocation of franchise, and a federal receivership to administer the asset. during the proceeding. is a receivership to liquidate. United States v. Norwood Capital Corp., 273 F. Supp. 236 (D.S.C. 1987).

Under California Industrial Loan Act, providing that corporation organized thereunder should have power, subject to supervision of corporation commissioner, to do certain specified things, and that in addition such corporation should have general powers conferred upon corporations by civil code, "except as herein otherwise provided," the reference to civil code authorized superior court's supervision of loan company's voluntary dissolution, and corporation commissioner, although having right of supervision in connection with such dissolution, was not given exclusive control thereof. Daugherty v. Superior Court of Imperial County, 56 Cal. App. 2d 851, 133 P.2d 827.

Under Illinois law, where investment company which had executed guaranties was dissolved more than two years before commencement of equitable action against company and its stockholders to recover upon guaranties, plaintiff could not recover against company's property in hands of its stockholders on theory that in equity, assets of a dissolved corporation pass to its stockholders and constitute a "trust fund" which can be reached in their hands by corporation's creditors, regardless of whether allegations of bill were termed a common creditors' bill or a creditors' suit. The company was an "indispensable party defendant" to the action. Reconstruction Finance Corp. v. Teter, 117 F.2d 716, cert. denied, 314 U.S. 620, 62 S. Ct. 62, 86 L. Ed. 498.

Venue.—

Application seeking prohibition to bar administrative proceeding, to revoke mortgage company's license until motion to suppress allegedly illegally seized evidence could be heard, was not required to be brought in county in which grand jury had been convened where it was unclear whether any indictment relating to company's operation would be

(Text continued on page 277)

---

handed down. Gouiran Holdings, inc. v. Miller, 531 N.Y.S. 2d 441 (N.Y. Sup. 1988).

Failure to meet reporting requirements.—

Record established that small business investment company had failed to meet financial reporting requirements for particular fiscal year; witness testified company had not submitted form required by regulation for particular fiscal year, and company offered no evidence disputing witness' testimony and affidavit. United States v. Vanguard Inv. Co., 694 F. Supp. 1219 (M.D.N.C. 1988).

Failure to make interest payments.—

Evidence established that small business investment company had failed to make interest payment. when due in violation of federal regulation, where company had admittedly failed to meet interest and principal obligations when due on particular debenture, although that debenture had subsequently been paid off. United States v. Vanguard Inv. Co., 694 F. Supp. 1219 (M.D.N.C. 1988).

Correction of violation.—

After the fact correction of regulatory violation by small business investment company does not "cure" the violation. United States v. Vanguard Inv. Co., 694 F. Supp. 1219 (M.D.N.C. 1988).

Violation of regulations as to notion.—

Small Business Administration was justified in accelerating small business investment company's obligations under its outstanding debentures and preferred stock by company's default in principal and interest payments on particular debenture and company's capital impairment without written notice, in violation of federal regulations. United States v. Vanguard Inv. Co., 694 F. Supp. 1219 (M.D.N.C. 1988).

Violations of federal regulations as to reporting, capital impairment, and in-threat obligations.—

Company's license as small business investment company should be forfeited and company dissolved, based on totality of circumstances surrounding the company's operation, including established violations of federal regulations pertaining to capital impairment, financial reporting and interest obligations; company had long history of difficulty in meeting its obligations despite Small Business Administration's attempts to work with company, and company's operation had declined, so that it more closely resembled real estate holding company than small business investment company and no longer served purpose for which it had been licensed. United States v. Vanguard Inv. Co., 694 F. Supp. 1219 (M.D.N.C. 1988).

Discretionary functions of State Department of Banking and Finance not actionable.—

Allegations of negligence on part of State Department of Banking and Finance, regarding its handling of industrial loan and investment company, which allegedly led to collapse of corporation formed under State Depository Institution Guaranty Corporation Act, were within purview of discretionary function exception of State Tort Claims Act and therefore were not actionable; while Department was statutorily empowered to perform tasks mentioned in allegations, none of statutes which were basis for allegations of negligence

b. Stock and Stockholders.

§ 5. General Considerations.

In General.—The words "capital stock" as used in a statute relating to trust companies may designate the money paid by the original stockholders for subscriptions to shares, and the word "capital," although often used interchangeably with "capital stock," may be used to indicate a company's general assets, including investments and surplus.[1050] And the shares of

---

required Department to execute any of its authorized power. Security Inv. Co. v. State, 231 Neb. 536, 437 N.W.2d 439(1989).

State Department of Banking and Finance was not liable for its alleged concealment of unsound financial condition of industrial loan and investment company in light of section of State Tort Claims Act providing that State was not liable for misrepresentation or deceit. Security Inv. Co. v. State, 231 Neb. 536, 437 N.W.2d 439 (1989).

Capital impairment.—

Undisputed evidence offered by Small Business Administration established that small business investment company was capitally impaired for purposes of federal regulation, based on undistributed net realized earnings deficit as percentage of private capital investment. United States v. Vanguard Inv. Co., 694 F. Supp. 1219 (M.D.N.C. 1988).

Funds invested by the Department of Transportation could not be considered as private capital, for purposes of determining whether small business investment company was capitally impaired under federal regulation based on undistributed net realized earnings deficit as percentage of private capital investment. United States v. Vanguard Inv. Co., 694 F. Supp. 1219 (M.D.N.C. 1988).

Small business investment company did not qualify for grandfather provision so as to make company capitally impaired only when undistributed net realized earnings deficit exceeded 100 percent of private capital investment for purposes of federal regulation; to qualify for grandfather provision, licensee's earnings deficit could not have exceeded 100 percent of private capital during five-year period after September 30, 1988, but the company's ratio had exceeded 100 percent during that five-year period. United States v. Vanguard Inv. Co., 694 F. Supp. 1219 (M.D.N.C. 1988).

Small business investment company's failure to give prompt written notice of its capital impairment and failure to cure its capital impairment by time set by Small Business Administration constituted events of default with respect to SBA. United States v. Vanguard Inv. Co., 694 F. Supp. 1219 (M.D.N.C. 1988).

Self-dealing by officers.—

Undisputed facts establishing that president and treasurer of small business investment company violated federal regulation by engaging in self-dealing transaction were relevant to determination of whether company should continue to operate, although record did not demonstrate beyond any issue of fact that company itself violated the federal regulation. United States v. Vanguard Inv. Co., 694 F. Supp. 1219 (M.D.N.C. 1988).

[1050] In re Prudential Trust Co., 244 Mass. 64, 138 N.E. 702.

The quoted words were so used in a statute providing that capital stock of trust companies

stock in a trust company are distinct from the capital stock or property and assets of the company.[1051] The purpose of paid-up capital of a trust company is to create a fund in the nature of collateral security for the benefit of all the company's creditors, including depositors in its savings department.[1052] A trust company's surplus, not segregated as capital, may be appropriated to the payment of dividends, and premiums paid for stock may be dealt with as a fund derived from the company's business.[1053]

The statement of a trust company president to the board of directors of his intention to sell all his stock does not give the company notice that he owns stock in the name of another on the company books.[1054] A commissioner of banks has the right to treat a deceased stockholder of a trust company as the owner of stock, where no transfer appears on the company books, and it is immaterial that a demand for payment of liability on the stock was made in notices addressed to him at his last-known residence.[1055]

Under a provision of the federal Investment Company Act defining "control," the existence of "control" is an issue of fact, but a person who controls directly or indirectly more than 25 percent of the voting securities of an investment company is presumed to control it.[1056]

---

shall be security for payment of savings deposits, and that such depositors shall have equal claim with other creditors on the capital and other property. In re Prudential Trust Co., 244 Mass. 64, 138 N.E. 702.

[1051] Peters Trust Co. v. Douglas County, 106 Neb. 877, 184 N.W. 812, aff'd, 260 U.S. 709, 43 S. Ct. 250, 67 L. Ed. 475.

Stock which trust company held in fiduciary capacity did not constitute any part of its corporate estate. Graves v. Security Trust Co., (Ky.), 369 S.W.2d 114.

[1052] Parent v. Rand, 88 N.H. 169, 185 A. 163.

[1053] Smith v. Cotting, 231 Mass. 42, 120 N.E 177.

[1054] Meramec Trust Co. v. Johnson, 220 Mo. App. 686, 293 S.W. 517.

[1055] Allen v. Hanover Trust Co., 247 Mass. 347, 142 N.E. 105.

[1056] **In general.—**

Willheim v. Murchison, 231 F. Supp. 142 (S.D.N.Y. 1964), aff'd, 342 F.2d 33 (2d Cir.), cert. denied, 382 U.S. 840, 86 S. Ct. 36, 15 L. Ed. 2d 82. See 15 U.S.C.S. § 80a-2(a)(9).

In assessing an individual's potential influence for purpose of determining whether be is presumably in "control" of corporation within statute providing that any person who owns beneficially more than 25 percent of company's voting securities shall be presumed to control the company and that any person who does not shall be presumed not to control it, the Securities and Exchange Commission must consider not merely legal power but the special circumstances of each case. Phillips v. Securities & Exch. Comm'n, 388 F.2d 964 (9th Cir. 1968).

Statutory provision that person beneficially owning more than 25 percent of voting

(Text continued on page 280)

securities of a company shall be presumed to control it and that person not owning more than 25 percent thereof shall be presumed not to control it does not direct Securities and Exchange Commission to consider every piece of evidence with a bias in favor of the presumption. Phillips v. Securities & Exch. Comm'n, 388 F.2d 964 (9th Cir. 1968).

Issue of whether defendant corporation dominated or controlled corporate owner of over 27 percent of voting stock in investment company, the stockholders of which brought derivative action under Investment Company Act, was not concluded by defendant's sworn disclaimer of domination or control Fogel v. Chestnutt, 296 F. Supp. 530 (S.D.N.Y. 1969).

Review of SEC order.—

On petition to review order of Securities and Exchange Commission determining who controlled a corporation five years earlier, court of appeals was required to consider initially whether a decision so seemingly academic was reviewable under statute concerning court review of orders, although no one had contested jurisdiction. Phillips v. Securities & Exch. Comm'n, 388 F.2d 964 (9th Cir. 1968).

In deciding whether court of appeals had jurisdiction under court review statute to review determination of Securities and Exchange Commission as to who controlled corporation some five years earlier, the fact that the determination had the form of an order was not decisive, but the question was whether the determination was the kind of an order that Congress had instructed or could constitutionally instruct the court to review. Phillips v. SEC, 388 F.2d 964 (9th Cir. 1968).

Court of appeals had jurisdiction under court review statute to review determination of Securities and Exchange Commission as to who controlled corporate parent five years earlier, in view of fact that if stockholder in four mutual funds with which subsidiary had investment advisory and principal underwriting contracts were to sue derivatively to recover fees paid subsidiary on theory that they were excess, he would be met with Commission's order in the determination proceeding, which he had initiated. Phillips v. Securities & Exch. Comm'n, 388 F.2d 964 (9th Cir. 1968).

That corporate buyer of 1,500,000 shares constituting about 15 percent of voting shares of corporate parent controlling subsidiary that possessed investment advisory and principal underwriting contracts with mutual funds had put-call agreement whereby buyer could obtain an additional 1, 600,000 shares, was insufficient to warrant setting aside of conclusion of Securities and Exchange Commission, in proceeding instituted by shareholder in the funds, that statutory presumption that person having beneficial ownership of more than 25 percent of a company's voting securities controls the company, had not become applicable. Phillips v. Securities & Exch. Comm'n, 388 F.2d 964 (9th Cir. 1968).

Evidence warranted finding of Securities and Exchange Commission that corporate buyer which purchased 1,500,000 shares and thus acquired about 16 percent of the shares of parent controlling subsidiary that had investment advisory and principal underwriting contracts with mutual funds and which could acquire additional 1,600,000 shares under put-call arrangement had not been able to exercise controlling influence over parent, within statute defining "control" as beneficial ownership of more than 25 percent of company's voting securities, in proceeding on application by stockholder in the mutual funds for determination of control. Phillips v. SEC, 388 F.2d 964 (9th Cir. 1968).

Evidence supported finding of Securities and Exchange Commission that stock sellers

Subscriptions to and Purchase of Stock.—The liability of an original subscriber for the stock of a trust company arises either by express contract or by implication of law from his acceptance of a certificate from the company, and the company's cause of action for an unpaid balance due on a subscription is on a simple contract liability.[1057] Generally, a transferor of trust company stock is not relieved from liability for an unpaid subscription until such transfer is duly registered on the company books.[1058] And a transferee of stock upon which a portion of the original subscription price is unpaid is liable therefor to the same extent as the original subscriber upon the company's recognition of the transfer.[1059] Alleged misrepresentations by an official inducing a subscription to the capital stock of a trust company do

---

who had selected eight of the ten directors and all but one major officer of parent controlling subsidiary that had investment advisory and principal underwriting contracts with mutual funds and who sold about 16 percent of parent's stock, had retained a controlling influence in parent despite making put-call arrangement for possible transfer of additional 15 percent of parent's stock to same buyer. Phillips v. SEC, 388 F.2d 964 (9th Cir. 1968).

Illustrative cases.—

Individual who together with associates held approximately 30 percent of shares of corporate parent controlling subsidiary that had investment advisory and principal underwriting contracts with mutual funds presumably had "controlling influence" over parent, within statutory prevision that one who beneficially owns more than 25 percent of voting securities of a company shall be presumed to control it. Phillips v. Securities & Exch. Comm'n, 388 F.2d 964 (9th Cir. 1968).

Defendant corporation which owned 166 out of 350 shares of voting stock of corporate owner of over 27 percent of voting stock of investment corporation, stockholders of which brought derivative action, had presumptive control of owner of investment company stock under Investment Company Act. Fogel v. Chestnutt, 296 F. Supp. 530 (S.D.N.Y. 1969). See 15 U.S.C.S. § 80a-1 et seq.

[1057] Harr v. Wright, 164 Misc. 395, 298 N.Y.S. 270, aff'd, 250 App. Div. 830, 296 N.Y.S. 463.

[1058] Meramec Trust Co. v. Johnson, 220 Mo. App. 686, 293 S.W. 517.

[1059] Harr v. Wright, 164 Misc. 395, 298 N.Y.S. 270, aff'd, 250 App. Div. 830, 296 N.Y.S. 463.

And such transferee must allege any circumstances excusing him from implied liability to pay such unpaid portion. Harr v. Wright, 164 Misc. 395, 298 N.Y.S. 270, aff'd, 250 App. Div. 830, 296 N.Y.S. 463.

Complaint against transferee of stock of trust company whose records showed transferee to be owner of stock, for unpaid portion of original subscription price, stated a contract obligation at common law, and reference to statute relating to liability of transferee was not necessary except to negative possible defense or to show extent of contract liability and time when installments were due. Harr v. Wright, 164 Misc. 395, 298 N.Y.S. 270, aff'd, 250 App. Div. 830, 296 N.Y.S. 463.

not make the stock void, but only give the stockholder the right to rescind such subscription before the liquidation of the company begins.[1060]

In an action by a buyer of a trust company's stock to recover the price paid on the ground of fraud, the burden rests on the buyer to show reliance on the statements of the seller, for if the buyer did not act on such representations but on his own judgment or on information gained in an investigation, he cannot recover.[1061] Thus, a note and mortgage given for stock in a trust company were not subject to the defense of want or failure of consideration, though the company's assets were no more than sufficient to cover its liability and pay two or three per cent to stockholders, in a case where the purchaser had been vice-president of the company for one month, had every opportunity to learn the company's condition and no representations regarding the value of the stock had been made.[1062] Nor could a stockholder set up lack of consideration as a defense to a suit by a receiver of a trust company to recover on notes given for the purchase price of the company's stock, on the ground that corporations are forbidden by state constitution and statutes to issue stocks or bonds except for money, labor done, or property actually received, for one who lends himself to acts, the effect of which is to lessen the stability of a bank or trust company, must abide the consequences of what he has done.[1063]

A contract for the sale of trust company stock on credit, the purchaser giving his note covering the price of the stock borrowed from the trust company, is ultra vires and void, where there was an actual delivery of the stock with the intention to have title vest in the purchaser who redelivered it to the trust company as collateral security for his note.[1064] And where a contract to purchase stock in a trust company was entered into between the plaintiff, an officer of a bank, and the defendant, the principal stockholder of a trust company, by which the plaintiff was to purchase a large number of shares of the trust company's stock and his bank was to take over the assets of the trust company, and a few days later on discovery of the trust company's bookkeeper's defalcation materially reducing the trust company's assets, and the bank's refusal to take over the trust company, a new contract was entered into between the trust company and the bank, the

---

[1060] Bittenbender v. Cosmopolitan Trust Co., 253 Mass. 230, 148 N.E. 619.

[1061] Farrell v. Hunt, 189 Ind. 45, 124 N.E. 745, holding that plaintiff's decision to purchase stock was based on statements made by defendant.

[1062] American Sav. Bank, etc., Co. v. Peterson, 112 Wash. 101, 191 P. 837.

[1063] Bell v. Aubel, 151 Pa. Super. 569, 30 A.2d 617.

[1064] Rousseau v. Everett (Tex. Civ. App.), 209 S.W. 460.

second contract is separate and distinct from the contract between the plaintiff and defendant, and there having been a mistake as to the trust company's assets, the plaintiff may rescind the first contract.[1065] And the buyer of a loan company's stock under the representation that a loan would be made to qualify an insurance company whose directors were the loan company's directors as a legal reserve company, could rescind for voluntary abandonment of the plan to make the loan.[1066] Where an applicant for stock in a trust company executes a bond and mortgage to the company for the stock at its par value, though its market value is lower, and the bond and mortgage is dated at the time his application is accepted by the company's committee, but the stock is not issued nor delivered for thirty days thereafter, such a contract is not usurious since it is a sale of stock, not a loan.[1067]

Determining Genuineness of Stock Power.—An investment company had the duty of determining whether a stock power was genuine when certificates were presented for transfer by a broker acting under the power, particularly if, as alleged, the investment company had the true signature of the purported grantor of the power on file because such signature appeared on the original application made to the investment company for the purchase of stock.[1068]

Lien on or Restriction on Transfer on Stock Certificate.—Under a New York statute a trust company's directors may refuse to consent to a transfer of stock until the stockholder's indebtedness to the company is paid, provided a copy of the statute or substance thereof is written or printed upon the stock certificate.[1069] This statute gives a company a lien, in the nature of an attorney's lien, against the stock of a debtor stockholder, and the company may forbid a transfer of the stock until the lien is discharged.[1070] The lien granted a trust company by such a statute on its own stock for indebtedness

---

[1065] Lindeberg v. Murray, 117 Wash. 483, 201 P. 759.

[1066] Wann v. Mt. Diablo Finance Corp., 132 Cal. App. 621, 23 P.2d 303.

[1067] Leavitt v. Pell, 27 Barb. 322.

[1068] Frye v. Commonwealth Inv. Co., 107 Ga. App. 739, 131 S.E.2d 569, aff'd, 219 Ga. 498, 134 S.E.2d 39.

[1069] Lacy v. First Trust, etc., Co., 140 Misc. 877, 252 N.Y.S. 213.

[1070] **In general.—**

Lacy v. First Trust & Deposit Co., 140 Misc. 877, 252 N.Y.S. 213.

Not a preferred lien.—

Trust company, though holding lien on stock of stockholder indebted to it, has no preferred claim or lien, but must share pro rata with creditors of stockholder's estate. Lacy v. First Trust, etc., Co., 140 Misc. 877, 252 N.Y.S. 213.

owned by the stockholder extends only to transactions between the company and its stockholders, and does not cover obligations given by the stockholder to a third person and assigned to the company.[1071]

Other state statutes, providing that there shall be no restriction upon the transfer of shares represented by a certificate unless the right of the corporation to such restriction is stated upon the certificate, have been held applicable to shares of stock of a trust company. And where a stockholder, when purchasing stock from a trust company, enters into a contract with the company that neither he nor his executors will transfer the shares without first offering them for sale to the company, such restrictions are binding during the stockholder's life and after his death.[1072]

Lost Certificate.—A trust company must issue the executors of a stockholder a certificate to replace a lost certificate on receiving a suitable indemnity bond.[1073] And a purchaser of stock from the estate of a trust company stockholder knowing that the certificate was lost, was held not barred from suing the company to compel the issuance of a new certificate.[1074]

Dividends.—A trust company's surplus, consisting of profit and loss, undivided profits, and the like, which has not been segregated as capital, may be appropriated to the payment of dividends.[1075] A statutory prohibition against the payment of dividends by a trust company in an amount greater than its net profits on hand is held to apply to the payment of dividends on shares of stock of a trust company out of its general funds, but not to the

---

Where a trust company takes over a national bank, an indebtedness of a stockholder to the bank becomes an indebtedness to the trust company, giving it a lien on stock. Lacy v. First Trust & Deposit Co., 140 Misc. 877, 252 N.Y.S. 213.

[1071] First Bank, etc., Co. v. Whipp, 230 Iowa 911, 299 N.W. 424.

[1072] New England Trust Co. v. Spaulding, 310 Mass. 424, 38 N.E.2d 672.

The executors could not deprive company of its right to enforce such restrictions by transferring stock to trustees under stockholder's will or to anyone else. And upon failure of executors to comply with contract the company could bring an action at law for damages or a bill in equity for specific performance where stock was not readily procurable in open market, but its cause of action accrued only after a demand by company and a refusal by executors to transfer stock in compliance with restrictions. New England Trust Co. v. Spaulding, 310 Mass. 424, 38 N.E.2d 672.

[1073] Lacy v. First Trust & Deposit Co., 140 Misc. 877, 252 N.Y.S. 213, holding that the company had the right to print on new certificate provisions of law giving it lien thereon for indebtedness of stockholder.

[1074] Lacy v. First Trust & Deposit Co., 140 Misc. 877, 252 N.Y.S. 213.

[1075] Smith v. Cotting, 231 Mass. 42, 120 N.E. 177.

declaration or payment of dividends on deposits in its savings department.[1076] A dividend declared from a company's surplus ordinarily and legally imports its distribution among its stockholders.[1077] But the right of an individual stockholder to receive dividends is justifiable only on the theory that he is a stockholder.[1078] Trust companies may be expressly prohibited from making stock dividends.[1079]

Where small business investment companies have not paid out the earnings they accrue on any regular basis, either as dividends or in any other form, and their shares are not cumulative, their shareholders' claims for dividends or distributions of earnings expire.[1080] And a corporate charter article providing that the purpose of the corporation was to own and hold investment securities of other corporations, receive dividends, interest, and income, and distribute the same to its stockholders does not require the corporation to channel corporate earnings directly to its stockholders after payment of operating expenses.[1081]

Right to Examine Corporate Books.—A stockholder in a trust company is entitled to examine its books and list of stockholders, in the absence of a showing of bad faith and ulterior motive in seeking the examination.[1082]

[1076] Medford Trust Co. v. McKnight, 292 Mass. 1, 197 N.E. 649.

[1077] Smith v. Cotting, 231 Mass. 42, 120 N.E. 177.

[1078] Commissioner of Banks v. Cosmopolitan Trust Co., 253 Mass. 205, 148 N.E. 609, 41 A.L.R. 658.

[1079] Smith v. Cotting, 231 Mass. 42, 120 N.E. 177.

[1080] Calvert v. Capital Southwest Corp., 441 S.W.2d 247 (Tex. Civ. App. 1969), appeal dismissed, 397 U.S. 321, 90 S. Ct. 1120, 25 L. Ed. 2d 336 (1970).

[1081] Leibert v. Grinnell Corp., 41 Del. Ch. 340, 194 A.2d 846.

[1082] Brown v. Central Home Trust Co., 129 N.J.L. 213, 28 A.2d 773.

Stockholders of banks and trust companies have a right to inspect their books and records at proper times and for proper purpose. State v. Crookston Trust Co., 222 Minn. 17, 22 N.W.2d 911.

A stockholder of trust company, which paid large sum in securities as result of proceeding by persons in charge of liquidation of mortgage company to surcharge trust company for dereliction in its duty as trustee for holders of mortgage bonds under agreements with mortgage company, held entitled to inspect list of trust company's stockholders in order to invite them to join in proposed stockholders' suit against trust company's officers and directors and inform such stockholders of mismanagement and misappropriation of trust company's funds and assets. Brown v. Central Home Trust Co., 129 N.J.L. 213, 28 A.2d 773.

In determining whether stockholder sought an inspection of trust company's books and records for a proper purpose, stockholder's refusal to consent to a renewal of trust company's corporate life and refusal to transact banking business with trust company, did not show

Right of Trust Company to Vote Stock Held in Fiduciary Capacity.—A bank and trust company at a stockholders' meeting to vote on a proposed consolidation with another bank and trust company, properly voted shares of its own stock which were legally held by it in a fiduciary capacity in absence of a showing of fraud or special circumstances.[1083] And in Ohio the prior rule prohibiting such voting has been changed so that in the absence of a complaint by anyone interested in, or authorized to represent those interested in a trust, a trust company which holds its own shares as trustee in such trust may vote those shares in an election for its directors, if the trust company is authorized by the instrument creating the trust to hold and vote such shares.[1084]

Proxies, Proxy Statements and Contracts.—The right of an individual stockholder of a trust company to execute proxies for use at stockholders' meetings is justifiable only on the theory that he is a stockholder.[1085] A federal statute providing that no officer, clerk, teller or bookkeeper of a national bank shall act as a proxy in voting shares of stock does not prohibit officers of a state bank and trust company from voting stock, as proxies, at a stockholders' meeting at which a vote is taken on a proposed consolidation with a national bank and trust company.[1086] Proxy statements are covered by a section of the Investment Company Act of 1940 making it unlawful for any

---

anything improper. Stats v. Crookston Trust Co., 222 Minn. 17, 22 N.W.2d 911.

[1083] Security Trust Co. v. Dabney (Ky.), 372 S.W.2d 401.

[1084] Cleveland Trust Co. v. Eaton, 50 Ohio Op. 2d 354, 21 Ohio St. 2d 129, 256 N.E.2d 198 (1970).

As to any fiduciary relationship created on and after January 1, 1968, section of Banking Act dealing with voting rights of trust company specifies whether and how trust company may vote on its own shares held by it in fiduciary capacity. Cleveland Trust Co. v. Eaton, 50 Ohio Op. 2d 354, 21 Ohio St. 2d 129, 256 N.E.2d 198 (1970).

In determining present right of trust company in election for its directors to vote its own shares held by it in fiduciary capacity created prior to January 1, 1968, effect should be given to statutory sections enacted by Banking Act of 1967, and effect should also be given to part of that act which repealed statutory sections previously existing. Cleveland Trust Co. v. Eaton, 50 Ohio Op. 2d 354, 21 Ohio St. 24 129, 256 N.E.2d 198(1970).

Section of General Corporation Act providing that no corporation shall directly or indirectly vote any shares issued by it does not now apply to trust company. Cleveland Trust Co. v. Eaton, 50 Ohio Op. 2d 354, 21 Ohio St. 2d 129, 256 N.E.2d 198(1970).

[1085] Commissioner of Banks v. Cosmopolitan Trust Co., 253 Mass. 205, 148 N.E. 609, 41 A.L.R. 658.

[1086] Security Trust Co. v. Dabney (Ky.), 372 S.W.2d 401.

person to state any material untruth in a document filed or transmitted pursuant to the Act.[1087]

And a proxy contract procured in violation of the Investment Company Act of 1940 is void, and civil relief by damages must be granted.[1088]

Stockholder's Actions.—The alleged fraud and violations of the Investment Company Act of 1940 by a corporation do not establish a basis for

---

[1087] Brown v. Bullock, 194 F. Supp. 207 (S.D.N.Y. 1961), aff'd, 294 F.2d 415.

[1088] **In general.—**

Brown v. Bullock, 194 F. Supp. 207 (S.D.N.Y. 1961), aff'd, 294 F.2d 415.

Right to accurate and fair proxy statement is that of stockholders of mutual fund, and whether in representative or derivative capacity stockholders may secure appropriate relief against investment advisory contract allegedly renewed by means of false or misleading proxy statements. Brown v. Bullock, 194 F. Supp. 207 (S.D.N.Y. 1961), aff'd, 294 F.2d 415.

Stockholders of mutual fund were entitled to protection of those portions of Investment Company Act making it unlawful to solicit a proxy in contravention of SEC rules or to state any material untruth therein and had private right of action against alleged wrongdoers. Brown v. Bullock, 194 F. Supp. 207 (S.D.N.Y. 1961), aff'd, 294 F.2d 415.

Privity of contract between shareholders of a mutual fund and the officers of the mutual fund was not a condition precedent to a private remedy for violation of the Investment Company Act of 1940. Brown v. Bullock, 194 F. Supp. 207 (S.D.N.Y. 1961), aff'd, 294 F.2d 415.

Funds in hands of wrongdoers.—

Mutual fund was member of class for whose protection that section of Investment Company Act of 1940 making it a crime to convert assets of registered investment company was enacted, and had implied remedy for alleged conversion of its money, but because fund was in hands of alleged wrong-doers, stockholders could enforce right on behalf of fund. Brown v. Bullock, 194 F. Supp. 207 (S.D.N.Y. 1961), aff'd, 294 F.2d 415.

If information on investment advisory contract for mutual fund is falsely stated, stockholders are denied their statutory right to terminate such services. Brown v. Bullock, 194 F. Supp. 207 (S.D.N.Y. 1961), aff'd, 294 F.2d 415.

Under statute prohibiting use of malls to solicit proxy or consent in contravention of rules and regulations protecting investors, where stockholders of investment company were not asked to approve allegedly improper sale of company's interest in airline in proxy statements mailed to them, there was no violation of statute. Entel v. Allen, 270 F. Supp. 60 (S.D.N.Y. 1967).

Violation of statute as proximate cause of damaging charter amendment.—

Although facts meeting the "but for" test with respect to violation of section of investment Company Act of 1940 prohibiting solicitation on of proxy in respect to security of which registered investment company is the issuer in contravention of rules and regulations of Commission would not necessarily establish proximate cause of alleged damaging charter amendment, failure to satisfy that test would necessarily negate possibility of proximate cause. Hoover v. Allen, 241 F. Supp. 213 (S.D.N.Y. 1965).

maintenance of a representative or class action on behalf of all stockholders who might have sold shares to the corporation pursuant to its invitation for a tender of shares.[1089] As to expenses in actions to declare an exclusive right to a corporate name, see the footnote.[1090] For another case dealing with stockholders' actions, see the footnote.[1091]

Where action complained of could have been accomplished regardless of proxy solicitation.—

In as much as charter amendment authorizing company to conduct business as investment company could have been accomplished by defendants regardless of certain proxy solicitation, stockholders were not entitled to relief on basis of violation of Investment Company Act of 1940 in connection with the proxy solicitation. Hoover v. Allen, 241 F. Supp. 213 (S.D.N.Y. 1966).

[1089] Koos v. Ludwig, 22 App. Div. 2d 666, 253 N.Y.S.2d 880 (1964).

[1090] in minority shareholders' action against corporations for a judgment declaring their corporation to have the exclusive rights to the name "Wellington" in the investment company field, counsel for plaintiffs were entitled to compensation for their efforts and successful conduct of the suit. in such case, it would be unconscionable for plaintiffs' corporation to be saddled with their attorney's fees in view of the conduct of its president and directors in acquiescing in use of the company's name by others. Taussig v. Wellington Fund, Inc., 187 F. Supp. 179, aff'd, 313 F.2d 472, cert. denied, 374 U.S. 806, 83 S. Ct. 1693, 1695, 10 L. Ed. 2d 1031.

In such case, to assess part of plaintiffs' expenses against innocent shareholders of defendant Wellington Equity Fund would not be in keeping with equitable principles, and corporate investment managers and share distributors which had stood to gain most by conferring on Wellington Equity

Fund the purported right to use the "Wellington" name were proper defendants to bear those costs. Taussig v. Wellington Fund, Inc., 187 F. Supp. 179, aff'd, 313 F.2d 472, cert. denied, 374 U.S. 806, 83 S. Ct. 1693, 1695, 10 L. Ed. 2d 1031.

[1091] **In general.—**

Investment corporation stockholder who had right to transfer her investment in corporation to any of three other investment corporations did not have an interest, beneficial or otherwise, in other corporations and hence could not institute derivative actions on behalf of latter corporations, where corporations were separate, each possessing its own body of stockholders, a separate board of directors and different investment policies. Verrey v. Ellsworth, 303 F. Supp. 497 (S.D.N.Y. 1969).

Standing to sue.—

Mutual fund shareholder who brought derivative action against fund's manager. under Investment Company Act, Securities Act, and Securities Exchange Act did not have standing to maintain derivative action on behalf of his fund's sister funds, in which he held no shares, as well. Weiner v. Winters, 50 F.R.D. 306 (S.D.N.Y. 1970).

That worth of shares of plaintiff's stock in mutual fund was directly proportionate to value of mutual fund's net assets was insufficient to alter basic shareholder-corporation relationship, and shareholder did not have primary or personal cause of action to recover

(Text continued on page 289)

---

damages allegedly sustained by corporation by reason of violations of antitrust and securities laws. Kauffman v. Dreyfus Fund, Inc., 434 F.2d 727 (3d Cir. 1970), cert. denied, 401 U.S. 974, 91 S. Ct. 1190, 28 L. Ed. 2d 323 (1971).

The shareholder of a mutual fund does not attain a primary right to sue because the value of his shares reflects the net asset value of the fund; rather, it is the nature of the right sought to be enforced that determines the proper way to bring suit. Marcus v. Putnam, 60 F.R.D. 441 (D. Mass. 1978).

The sale of an advisory contract claim arose out of the contract and the duty existing between the open-end mutual funds and adviser. The right to sue for a breach of that duty was with the mutual funds. Marcus v. Putnam, 60 F.R.D. 441 (D. Mass. 1973).

An action did not lie in favor of a participant in an open-end mutual fund established by a bank for a violation by the bank of federal law regulating bank investments.

Russell v. Continental Illinois Nat'l Bank & Trust Co., 479 F.2d 131 (7th Cir. 1973).

Demand.—

Shareholder of investment company was not required to make a demand on director, prior to commencing suit under the Investment Company Act to challenge the company's contracts with its investment advisors. Weiss v. Temporary Inv. Fund, Inc., 730 F.2d 939 (3d Cir. Del. 1984).

Second demand on trustees of money market mutual fund was not required prior to shareholder's derivative suit under the Investment Company Act even though first demand contained allegations concerning only investment adviser's initial fees, and not fees as subsequently revised, where trustees were on clear notice that shareholder intended to attack the fees in general and met with shareholder's counsel to discuss his demand, and revised fees were approved 10 days after trustees rejected shareholder's demand. Evangelist v. Fidelity Mgt. & Research Co., 554 F. Supp. 87 (D. Mass. 1982).

Even the most reasonable decision by trustees of money market mutual fund not to bring suit against investment adviser for breach of fiduciary duties in collection of allegedly excessive fees, following shareholder's demand, could not cut shareholder off at the threshold, before trial, from pressing claim under the Investment Company Act ass derivative suit. Evangelist v. Fidelity Management & Research Co., 554 F. Supp. 87 (D. Mass. 1982).

Jurisdiction of federal district court.—

Federal district court had jurisdiction insofar as plaintiff stockholder of mutual fund alleged that she had been injured by violations of statute authorizing Securities Exchange Commission to enjoin registered mutual fund's officers who have been guilty of gross misconduct or abuse of trust, statute making unlawful conversion of assets of registered investment company a crime and statute prohibiting investment adviser from advising registered mutual fund except pursuant to contract precisely describing all compensation to be paid thereunder and for principal underwriter to sell shares of registered mutual fund except pursuant to written contract. Moses v. Burgin, 316 F. Supp. 31 (D. Mass.), rev'd on other grounds, 446 F.2d 369, cert. denied, 404 U.S. 994, 92 S. Ct. 532, 30 L. Ed. 2d 547 (1971).

"Open End" Investment Fund Plans.—See the footnote.[1092]

Determining value of securities.—

The failure of the directors of a mutual fund to recapture part of the brokerage commissions paid by the fund on portfolio transactions did not result in such a dilution of the per share net asset value as to constitute a breach of a provision of the certificate of incorporation of the fund that the consideration per share to be received by the fund after the deduction of any load or commission paid for the distribution of shares of the fund not be less than the net asset value. Fogel v. Chestnutt, 533 F.2d 731 (2d Cir. 1975), rev'g 383 F. Supp. 914 (S.D.N.Y. 1974), cert. denied, 429 U.S. 824, 97 S. Ct. 77, 50 L. Ed. 2d 86 (1976).

Duty of bank.—

Bank that managed stockholder's investment in mutual fund owed stockholder a fiduciary duty of loyalty and care, although stockholder's account with bank was nondiscretionary and stockholder had a long history of making his own investment decisions, where bank failed to sell stockholder's shares as originally instructed, and bank contacted stockholder on its own initiative and allegedly advised stockholder not to sell his shares. Ward v. Atlantic Sec. Bank, 777 So. 2d 1144, (Fla. Dist. Ct. App. 3d Dist. 2001).

[1092] **In general.—**

"Open end" investment fund plan, with provision for issuance of stock in fund in return for investor's deposit of other securities, stock issue being in proportion that securities deposited bore to all deposited securities, was apparently designed to preserve for each fund shareholder a proportional indirect interest in total assets despite redemptions or changes in fund's assets, and to entitle shareholders to advantage of Internal Revenue ruling limiting recognition of gain on such exchanges. Saphier v. Devonshire St. Fund, Inc., 352 Mass. 683, 227 N.E.2d 714(1967).

Determining value of securities.—

Under arrangement whereby persons wishing to invest in fund, exchanging other securities for stock in fund, securities to be deposited with bank which was to determine their value in accordance with provisions of fund's prospectus, bank faced with problems of evaluating unlisted securities had a limited judgment in view of range of "over-the-counter" quotations at various amounts, although its determination could be reviewed to see whether bank had misconceived its lawful function. Saphier v. Devonshire Street Fund, Inc., 352 Mass. 683, 227 N.E.2d 714 (1967).

Precision cannot be expected in fixing value or bid price for unlisted securities where several bid prices are reported at same time, since such bids do not reflect actual transactions and are, at best, indication of interest by broker-dealer in buying or selling securities at time of submission at given price. Saphier v. Devonshire St. Fund, Inc., 352 Mass. 683, 227 N.E.2d 714 (1987).

Even if reviewing court were to take judicial notice, in dispute over valuation of securities deposited with bank as custodian of exchange fund, of New York Stock Exchange rules to effect that the highest bid and the lowest offer shall have precedence in all cases, such rules could not be given controlling weight with reference to the "over-the-counter" market upon which deposited shares were traded, since such market differs from organized exchange markets, and bank was not required to give them such weight. Saphier v. Devonshire Street Fund, Inc., 352 Mass. 683, 227 N.E.2d 714 (1967).

Agreement to Purchase Assets.—The stockholders of a trust company, in order to keep it going, may sign an agreement to pay its trustees certain sums to be used to purchase the assets of the company.[1093]

§ 6. Stock Increase.

Where, in a meeting of a trust company to increase its capital stock, enough shares are represented, either in person or by proxy, to vote an increase, which is unanimously voted and approved by the commissioner of banks, stockholders receiving certificates of stock and participating in the ordinary way in the management of the company are estopped to assert the invalidity of the shares of increased capital stock issued to them.[1094]

Bank which was custodian of investment fund did not err, as a matter of law, in viewing five quotations as reported in national quotation sheet for "over-the-counter" stock deposited with the fund, as a group as constituting the last quoted bid price, and bank did not act improperly in selecting median bid as representative of the group for purposes of valuing the stock deposited for exchange for fund shares. Saphier v. Devonshire St. Fund, Inc., 352 Mass. 683, 227 N.E.2d 714 (1967).

Conduct of bank, which was custodian of investment fund, in interpreting valuation provisions of fund's prospectus as calling for the high "pink sheet" quotation on each valuation date for "over-the-counter" stock, was not a binding interpretation of the prospectus by the bank, so as to require bank to have taken high quotation as median value of plaintiffs' stock when such stock was placed in the fund in exchange for fund shares. aphier v. Devonshire Street Fund, Inc., 352 Mass. 683, 227 N.E.2d 714(1967).

Statute Inapplicable.—

Statute providing that when a price left to be fixed otherwise than by agreement of the parties falls to be fixed through fault of one party, the other may himself fix a reasonable price, was inapplicable to dispute between bank, which was custodian of investment fund, and plaintiff stockholders who deposited stock with the bank for exchange for fund shares and later sought recovery because of alleged under-valuations of deposited securities, since fund's prospectus provided that the price for deposited stock would be the last quoted bid price known to person making such determination, which in this case was the bank, and it was not shown that failure to fix price resulted from fund's fault or because of bank's fault. Saphier v. Devonshire Street Fund, Inc., 352 Mass. 683, 227 N.E.2d 714 (1967).

[1093] Ferguson & Co. v. Ricketts, 82 F.2d 14.

In such a case, a subscribing stockholder who delivered securities to company to be applied to subscription, withdrew securities, and redelivered part thereof for another purpose, could not recover redelivered securities from company's trustee in bankruptcy as against contentions that subscription agreement did not obligate stockholder to company, but only to trustees named therein, that withdrawal of securities divested company rights therein, and that trustees refused to allow stockholder to participate in property purchased. Ferguson & Co. v. Ricketts, 82 F.2d 14.

[1094] Commissioner of Banks v. Cosmopolitan Trust Co., 253 Mass. 205, 148 NL 609, 41 A.L.R. 658.

"Approved," as used in a statute requiring approval by a bank commissioner of stock increases by trust companies, has been held to imply the exercise of sound judgment, practical sagacity, wise discretion and final direct affirmative action.[1095] An oral approval of an increase of capital stock of a trust company by a commissioner of banks cannot make that legal which is otherwise defective.[1096] But increased stock issued by a trust company is not invalid because no alteration in the company's agreement of association or articles of organization was filed in the office of the secretary of the commonwealth as required by statute, all other essential prerequisites to the issuance of such stock having been observed.[1097]

§ 7. Liability of Stockholders.

Statutory Liability in General.—In many states there are statutes making stockholders of loan and trust companies individually liable for corporate debts to the amount of the stock owned by them.[1098] Such liability is

---

[1095] **In general.**—

Cunningham v. Commissioner of Banks, 249 Mass. 401, 144 N.E. 447.

Illustrative case.—Commissioner of finance properly refused to approve transaction whereby bank and trust company proposed to retire 28 of the outstanding 600 shares of $100 par value common stock at bank's expense to be charged to undivided profits and to Increase authorized capital to $300,000 represented by 8,000 shares of stock by declaring a stock dividend to the holders of 572 shares of original stock, since the 28 shares of common stock did not receive the same treatment as the 572 shares. State ex rel. Pine Lawn Bank & Trust Co. v. Culley, 399 S.W.2d 49 (Mo. 1966).

[1096] Commissioner of Banks v. Cosmopolitan Trust Co., 253 Mass. 205, 148 N.E. 609, 41 A.L.R. 658.

[1097] Cunningham v. Commissioner of Banks, 249 Mass. 401, 144 N.E. 447.

[1098] **In general.**—

Indiana.—Rowley v. Pogue, 203 Ind. 655, 181 N.E. 589, 185 N.E. 273; Klotz v. First Nat. Bank, 78 Ind. App. 679, 134 N.E. 220.

Maine.—Johnson v. Libby, 111 Me. 204, 88 A. 647, 1916C Ann. Cas. 681.

Maryland.—Miners', etc., Bank v. Snyder, 100 Md. 57, 59 A. 707, 108 Am. St. R. 390, 68 L.R.A. 312, error dismissed, 200 U.S. 624, 26 S. Ct. 756, 50 L. Ed. 626; Murphy v. Wheatley, 102 Md. 501, 63 A. 62; Mister v. Thomas, 122 Md. 445, 89 A. 844; Sterling v. Reecher, 176 Md. 567, 6 A.2d 237.

Massachusetts.—Nichols v. Taunton Safe Deposit, etc., Co., 203 Mass. 551, 89 N.E. 1035.

Minnesota.—International Trust Co. v. American Loan & Trust Co., 62 Minn. 501, 65 N.W. 78, vacated on rehearing, 65 N.W. 632.

New York.—Skinner v. Schwab, 188 App. Div. 457, 177 N.Y.S. 143, aff'd, 229 N.Y. 549, 129 N.E. 910.

(Text continued on page 293)

Oklahoma.—Lankford v. Menefee, 45 Okla. 228, 145 P. 375.

Pennsylvania.—De Haven v. Pratt, 223 Pa. 633, 72 A. 1068.

Wisconsin.—It may be provided by statute that stockholders are individually liable to creditors to the amount of their stock at par value, in addition to the amount invested therein, for six months after any transfer of stock, as to affairs of the company before such transfer. Cousins v. Flertzheim, 182 Wis. 275, 196 N.W. 250.

Such liability must be determined from words of statute creating it, without application of general principles or precedents not dealing with particular statute or substantially similar statutes, though ordinary canons of statutory construction may be invoked in interpreting ambiguous language thereof. Robinson v. Hospelhorn, 169 Md. 117, 179 A. 515, 184 A. 903, 108 A.L.R. 740.

The statute is in derogation of common law and its meaning cannot be extended beyond words used. Robinson v. Hospelhorn, 169 Md. 117, 179 A. 515, 184 A. 903, 103 A.L.R. 740.

When liability conditional or fixed.

—Stockholders' statutory double liability for trust company's debts is conditional and contingent and dormant and unenforceable until needed to pay such debts, and hence is primary only in sense that it is an original undertaking and arises under statute out of their original subscription, and secondary in that it cannot be enforced until company's inability to pay debts from its other assets sufficiently appears and then only to extent of deficit. Robinson v. Hospelhorn, 169 Md. 117, 179 A. 515, 184 A. 908, 103 A.L.R. 740.

Such liability becomes fixed when necessity therefor appear., and does not depend on whether appreciation on in value of assets by date to which creditor, agreed to postpone collection of debts will reduce amount of assessment or obviate necessity therefor. Robinson v. Hospelhorn, 169 Md. 117, 179 A. 515, 184 A. 903, 108 A.L.R. 740.

Such liability depends on judicial establishment of fact that enforcement of such liability is needed to pay company's debts after exhaustion of its tangible assets by application thereof to creditors' claims. Robinson v. Hospelhorn, 169 Md. 117, 179 A. 515, 184 A. 903, 103 A.L.R. 740.

Stockholder is subject to additional liability when company becomes insolvent, where statute does not restrict liability merely to restore impaired capital. State v. Martin, 177 Okla. 490, 60 P.2d 783.

Where company was organized before enactment of statute creating additional liability, stockholder held subject thereto. State ex rel. State Bank Comm'r v. Martin, 177 Okla. 490, 60 P.2d 783.

Where company was formed through merger of a title insurance and mortgage guarantee corporation with a trust company, and thereafter company performed both functions until 1988, when it terminated business as a trust company but continued as a title insurance and mortgage guaranty corporation, and company was empowered to and did engage in business of banking, constitutional and statutory liability of company's stockholders extended to obligations arising out of company's guarantees to holders of mortgages and mortgage certificates, since company was a "corporation for banking purposes," notwithstanding that it possessed and exercised nonbanking powers. That mortgage creditors would be in a better

sometimes imposed by a company's charter, and one who voluntarily becomes a stockholder thereof assumes the liability.[1099] The question of the application to loan and trust companies of statutes imposing "double" liability on bank stockholders has been considered by the courts of various states.[1100] And a stockholder in a trust company who retains his stock after

---

position than similar creditors of other mortgage companies not engaged in banking business was not ground for denying liability of stockholders to mortgage creditors. Pink v. Alden, 260 App. Div. 564, 23 N.YS.2d 365, aff'd, 285 N.Y. 800, 35 N.E.2d 193.

Liability accruing before repeal of statute is not affected by repeal of "double liability" statute. Pink v. Alden, 174 Misc. 69, 18 N.Y.S.2d 604, rev'd on other grounds, 260 App. Div. 564, 23 N.Y.S.2d 365, aff'd, 285 N.Y. 800, 35 N.E.2d 193.

Trust company which functioned after repeal of statute under which it was Incorporated held de facto corporation so as to impose statutory liability on stockholders on its insolvency. Detroit Trust Co. v. Allinger, 271 Mich. 600, 261 N.W. 90, appeal dismissed, 297 U.S. 695, 56 S. Ct. 572, 80 L. Ed. 986.

Whether trust company acted under such statute or under repealing statute held immaterial whose it was statutory duty of receiver to enforce stockholders' liability if necessary to pay trust company's debts. Detroit Trust Co. v. Allinger, 271 Mich. 600, 261 N.W. 90, appeal dismissed, 297 U.S. 695, 56 S. Ct. 572, 80 L. Ed. 986.

Statute relating to termination of liability of stockholders on shares originally issued after fixed date, did not relieve stockholders whose liability had been previously established. Sterling v. Reecher, 176 Md. 567, 6 A.2d 237.

1099 **In general.—**

Johnson v. Libby, 111 Me. 204, 88 A. 647, 1916C Ann. Cas. 681.

The special charter of savings and loan company making "stockholders" individually liable for debts of corporation to par value of their stock, in addition to liability therefor to extent of unpaid stock subscriptions, applied only to original subscribers and did not impose double liability on their transferees. Rowland v. Wilson, 180 Ga. 242, 178 S.E. 432.

The liability under the charter of a loan and trust company, providing that the shareholders shall be individually responsible, equally and ratably, for all contracts, debts, and engagements of the corporation, to a sum equal to the amount of the par value of the shares owned by each, in addition to the amount invested in the shares, is separate and distinct from that created by the general statutes pertaining to corporations, so that such stockholders are not exempt from additional liability, even though the debt of the corporation is a mortgage debt. Maine Trust, etc., Co. v. Southern Loan, etc., Co., 92 Me. 444, 43 A. 24.

1100 *Indiana.*—Constitutional "double" liability of bank stockholder, held applicable to a trust company carrying on a banking business. Rowley v. Pogue, 203 Ind. 655, 181 N.E. 589, 185 N.E. 278.

Iowa.—Statute imposing liability on bank stockholders held not apply to an investment company, the charter of which provided it might receive deposits of money, and hence the stockholders in such company were not individually liable. Williams v. Lewis Inv. Co., 110 Iowa 635, 82 N.W. 332.

Kansas.—Trust company held not "banking corporation" within statute regarding double

the enactment of a statute imposing a double liability on shareholders in such a company is deemed to have accepted the effect of the statute.[1101]

---

liability of stockholders of banking corporations. International Mortg. Trust Co. v. Henry, 139 Kan. 154, 30 P.2d 311.

Statute making provisions of banking law, relating to double liability of bank stockholders, applicable to trust companies, held without retrospective force. International Mortg. Trust Co. v. Henry, 139 Kan. 154, 30 P.2d 311.

New York.—Constitution making the stockholders of every banking corporation individually responsible to the amount of their stock for its debts and liabilities, applies to all corporations and associations engaged in banking activities, whether such activities are the sole object of organization, or merely incidental, and hence applies to a corporation having the powers of a trust company. Skinner v. Schwab, 188 App. Div. 457, 177 N.Y.S. 143, aff'd, 229 N.Y. 549, 129 N.E. 910.

Where the charter of a corporation having the powers of a trust company, incorporated under a special act, provided that as to matters not expressly covered by the charter act it should be subject to all general laws relating to trust companies, and there was no express provision as to stockholders' liability, such liability is regulated by the banking law of the state. Skinner v. Schwab, 188 App. Div. 457, 177 N.Y.S. 143, aff'd, 229 N.Y. 549, 129 N.E. 910.

Oklahoma.—Where a trust company does a "banking business," and fails, a stockholder in the trust company is not chargeable as a stockholder of a bank and made liable to the amount of his stock. Lankford v. Menefee, 45 Okla. 228, 145 P. 375.

Texas.—The constitutional and statutory provisions for stock assessments against bank stockholders do not apply to a corporation taking advantage of the provisions of the act concerning loan and investment companies. The act enumerates the provisions of the statute relating to banks and banking which shall apply to such corporations, and omits to mention the section concerning such assessment. The act does not confer banking and discounting privileges on a corporation taking advantage of its provisions so as to make it subject to the constitutional provision as to assessment against stockholders of banks. Kaliski v. Gossett (Tex. Civ. App.), 109 S.W.2d 340.

The power of a corporation under the statute relating to loan and investment companies to deduct 6 per cent on loans in advance does not in itself constitute it a banking corporation subject to the constitutional provision for stock assessments. Kaliski v. Gossett (Tex. Civ. App.), 109 S.W.2d 340.

West Virginia.—In order that the stockholders of a trust company organized under the laws of this state shall become liable for its debts, accruing while they own the shares, to an amount equal to their respective shares, the trust company must have contracted such debts in the conduct of the business of banking. Hogg v. Armstrong, 112 W. Va. 142, 164 S.E. 496.

Where such trust company exercises statutory powers, although some of them may be incidental to banking, it will not be deemed, ipso facto, a banking institution and thereby subjecting its stockholders to the "double" liability imposed by the constitution and statute upon stockholders of a bank. Hogg v. Armstrong, 112 W. Va. 142, 164 S.E. 496.

[1101] Johnson v. Libby, 111 Me. 204, 88 A. 647, 1916C Ann. Cas. 681.

Moreover, stockholders who appear to be such on the books of a company at the time it goes into liquidation cannot, because they have been defrauded, repudiate their liability to creditors.[1102] The liability of stockholders of a trust company is established by the determination of the public official in charge of banks that it ought to be enforced.[1103] And where such official gives notice on a certain date that stockholders' liability will be enforced, the amount due from the stockholders bears interest from that date.[1104]

Liability Contractual in Nature.—The liability of a stockholder in a trust company for the company's debts is part of the contract by which the company comes into existence, and though created by statute, is contractual in nature, and any rational method of determining the extent of the liability is part of the contract.[1105] As such liability is contractual in nature, it does not abate on a stockholder's death, and his estate is liable therefor.[1106]

Liability as Security and Asset of Creditors.—The object of constitutional and statutory provisions for individual liability of stockholders of a trust company is to furnish additional security to all creditors of the company.[1107] And such liability may be presumed to be part of the basis on which deposits are made in both commercial and savings departments.[1108] Thus, where a trust company was authorized by its charter to conduct a savings department, losses in either its commercial or savings department were its stockholders' losses.[1109] But by the express terms of a statute, the stockholders' liability may be made a special security for the benefit of savings depositors.[1110] The

---

[1102] Bittenbender v. Cosmopolitan Trust Co., 253 Mass. 230, 148 N.E. 619.

[1103] Allen v. Cosmopolitan Trust Co., 247 Mass. 334, 142 N.E. 100.

A decision of the comptroller as to insolvency and necessity of assessment of stockholders' liability is not subject to review except for fraud or such abuse of authority as amounts to fraud. Dunn v. O'Connor, 89 F.2d 820.

[1104] Commissioner of Banks v. Cosmopolitan Trust Co., 253 Mass. 205, 148 N.E. 609, 41 A.L.R. 658.

[1105] Allen v. Prudential Trust Co., 242 Mass. 78, 136 N.E. 410. See Johnson v. Libby, 111 Me. 204, 88 A. 647, 1916C Ann. Cas. 681.

[1106] Johnson v. Libby, 111 Me. 204, 88 A. 647, 1916C Ann. Cas. 681.

[1107] Pink v. Alden, 260 App. Div. 564, 23 N.Y.S.2d 365, aff'd, 285 N.Y. 800, 35 N.E.2d 193.

[1108] Bittenbender v. Cosmopolitan Trust Co., 253 Mass. 230, 148 N.E. 619. See Commissioner of Banks v. McKnight, 281 Mass. 467, 183 N.E. 720.

[1109] Parent v. Rand, 88 N.H 169, 185 A. 163.

[1110] Commissioner of Banks v. Cosmopolitan Trust Co., 253 Mass. 205, 148 N.E. 609, 41 A.L.R. 658.

liability of stockholders is an asset of a corporation's creditors, not of the corporation.[1111] And the right of creditors to enforce such liability is vested, and cannot be discharged without their consent where the tangible assets of a trust company are insufficient to pay its debts.[1112] A fund collected from a company's stockholders is in the nature of a trust fund for the benefit of all its creditors.[1113]

Persons Liable.—Statutes imposing additional liability on the stockholders of trust companies subject owners of such stock to such liability,[1114] whether or not the stock stands in their names.[1115] Thus, a purchaser of stock indorsed to him in blank is an "owner" subject to stockholders' liability, though no new certificate is issued in his name.[1116] in the absence of further findings, the fact that a decedent was the record owner of a trust company's stock at the time of his death makes his estate subject to stockholders' liability.[1117] Stockholders of a trust company in liquidation by a state official in charge of banks are liable in a suit by the official to enforce stockholders'

[1111] Dunn v. O'Connor, 89 F.2d 820.

[1112] Robinson v. Hospelhorn, 169 Md. 117, 179 A. 515, 184 A. 908, 103 A.L.R. 740.

[1113] Klotz v. First Nat. Bank, 78 Ind. App. 679, 134 N.E. 220.

[1114] **In general.—**

Commissioner of Banks v. Waltham Trust Co., 293 Mass. 62, 199 N.E. 303.

Stock not delivered.—

Stockholders accepting stock and giving note for accommodation of trust company held subject to stockholders' liability, though certificates were not delivered or were cancelled on closing day. Commissioner of Banks v. Tremont Trust Co., 259 Mass. 162, 156 N.E. 7.

Beneficial owner of all stock in trust company held liable for full amount of statutory stockholders' double liability thereon, notwithstanding statute prohibiting any person from owning more than one-half of capital stock of any corporation, where stock was originally legally issued by trust company, since purpose of statute was to protect creditors of trust company and not to enable it to defeat liability. Banco Kentucky's Receiver v. Louisville Trust Co.'s Receiver, 263 Ky. 155, 92 S.W.2d 19.

Corporation, holding trust deed participation certificate issued in exchange for stock in trust company and national bank pursuant to trust agreement, whereunder trustees were subject to control of holders of participation certificate. who were declared to be liable as holders of stock in corporations, held liable as beneficial owner of stock for statutory stockholders' double liability as to stock of trust company. Banco Kentucky's Receiver v. Louisville Trust Co.'s Receiver, 263 Ky. 155, 92 S.W.2d 19.

[1115] Commissioner of Banks v. Waltham Trust Co., 293 Mass. 62, 199 N.E. 303; Director of Liquidations v. Wood, 306 Mass. 1, 26 N.E.2d 979.

[1116] Commissioner of Banks v. McKnight, 281 Mass. 467, 183 N.E. 720.

[1117] Commissioner of Banks v. McKnight, 281 Mass. 467, 183 N.E 720.

liability, if they held stock when he took possession of the company's property and business.[1118]

An individual who was once an owner of a trust company's stock registered as such on its books cannot escape liability without showing that before the significant date he transferred his ownership to someone else, and secured the transfer on the company's books or at least did all he could to divest himself of the indicia of title.[1119] But if such a stockholder has done everything which a reasonably prudent business man would do to divest himself of the indicia of title, and his name remains upon a company's books through no fault of his own, he is not chargeable as a "stockholder"; he need not personally see that the transfer is made.[1120] As to other decisions relating to such liability where stock has been transferred, see the footnote.[1121]

[1118] Allen v. Hanover Trust Co., 247 Mass. 347, 142 N.E. 105.

[1119] Friede v. Mackey, 298 Mass. 193, 10 N.E.2d 102; Director of Liquidations v. Wood, 306 Mass. 1, 26 N.E.2d 979; Commissioner of Banks v. Waltham Trust Co., 293 Mass. 62, 199 N.E 303.

[1120] **In general.—**

Director of Liquidations v. Wood, 306 Mass. 1, 26 N.E.2d 979.

In such case, where stockholder had not attempted to evade liability and had no reason to doubt that stock would be transferred, his estate was not subject to liability, although stock was not actually transferred on books. Director of Liquidations v. Wood, 306 Mass. 1, 26 N.E.2d 979.

Illustrative cases.—

Where stockholder in trust company, which had authority to act as a trustee, irrevocably assigned trust company stock certificates in trust to company and delivered certificates to company's officers with instrument authorizing their transfer on its books, he did all that was necessary to transfer title to stock to company, as respects statutory liability of his estate. Director of Liquidations v. Wood, 306 Mass. 1, 26 N.E.2d 979.

One offering to sell, and indorsing in blank a written assignment of, and power of attorney to sell, his stock in a trust company on the stock certificate and leaving it with a bank, which sold and delivered it to the president of the company more than six months before the commissioner of banking took it over as insolvent, is not liable to creditors, though the stock was never transferred on the company's books, as required by statute and he made no demand to that effect; he being entitled to presume that the president of the company would see that the stock was properly transferred, in the absence of knowledge which should reasonably raise a doubt. Cousins v. Flertzheim, 182 Wis. 275, 196 N.W. 250.

[1121] **Insolvent transferee.—**

Transfer of stock by trustees of estate for low price within four months of receivership held not to relieve trustees of liability where transferee was insolvent. Detroit Trust Co. v. Hartwick, 278 Web. 189, 270 N.W. 249.

Statute voiding transfer of stock with intent to defraud creditors, if made within four

Stockholders receiving certificates of stock as gifts are subject to a statutory liability.[1122] And where a purchaser of trust company stock caused another's name to be entered upon the company's books without his knowledge or consent, but afterwards told him of it, such other, having the right either to repudiate or ratify, by consenting to such purchase and transfer, becomes liable as a stockholder.[1123] But where a stockholder of record never purchased or subscribed for the stock, and never knew of the existence of a certificate in his name or received dividends, he is exonerated from liability as a stockholder.[1124]

Infant stockholders of a trust company are not subject to such liability,[1125] but holders of stock as trustees for their minor children are subject thereto.[1126] A bankrupt has been held liable as a stockholder in an insolvent trust company, even though the shares were not transferred to him on the company books as required by law, and some of the stock was new stock and a statute requiring an amended article to be filed in the office of the secretary of the commonwealth was not complied with, where the increase was voted,

---

months of receivership, does not provide that such transfer does not relieve transferor of liability for assessment. Detroit Trust Co. v. Hartwick, 278 Mich. 139, 270 N.W. 249.

But stockholder who transferred stock within four months of receivership under such circumstances as to leave sole inference that stockholder was intending to evade statutory liability, and who offered no reasonable explanation of transfer, held not relieved of such liability. Detroit Trust Co. v. Hockett, 278 Mich. 124, 270 N.W. 243.

Assumption that seller of stock for very low price knew of statutory liability would not prevent holder from making bona fide sale of stock to someone who cared to purchase stock in belief that value would increase. Detroit Trust Co. v. Granger, 278 Mich. 152, 270 N.W. 239.

Attempted alienation of stock without compliance with bylaws of company does not save stockholder from statutory liability. Commissioner of Banks v. Tremont Trust Co., 259 Mass. 162, 156 N.E. 7.

Under Illinois law, one who was a stockholder of Illinois trust company at time of its organization was liable to unpaid creditors of such company whose claims accrued while she remained the owner, but not to creditors whose claims accrued after she ceased to be a stockholder. United States v. Earling, 39 F. Supp. 864.

[1122] Commissioner of Banks v. Cosmopolitan Trust Co., 253 Mass. 205, 148 N.E. 609, 41 A.L.R. 658.

[1123] Richards v. Ackerman, 175 App. Div. 746, 162 N.Y.S. 657, aff'd, 223 N.Y. 721, 120 N.E. 874.

[1124] Commissioner of Banks v. Cosmopolitan Trust Co., 253 Mass. 205, 148 N.E. 609, 41 A.L.R. 658.

[1125] Commissioner of Banks v. Tremont Trust Co., 259 Mass. 162, 156 N.E. 7.

[1126] Commissioner of Banks v. Tremont Trust Co., 259 Mass. 162, 156 N.E. 7.

approved by the bank commissioner and paid for.[1127] Where a trust company had no power to buy its shares, the delivery of a stock certificate to it and receipt of a check therefor by the holder, not being for the purpose of transfer, does not relieve him of liability where his name appears as owner on the corporate books.[1128] But as respects stockholder's liability, that a trust company by virtue of statute cannot be a purchaser or holder of its own capital stock, does not prevent it from receiving such shares as part of the assets of a trust created for a stockholder's benefit.[1129]

Extent of Liability.—The charter liability of stockholders of a loan and trust company for "all contracts, debts, and engagements" of the company is not limited to the banking features of the company,[1130] since a statutory liability cannot be construed to exclude part of the obligations of a company.[1131] Such statutory liability is not restricted by the words of a section whereby the state official in possession of a trust company is empowered to enforce the stockholders' liability "if necessary to pay the debts of any such trust company," the word "debts" as used being a generic word including every liability of stockholders established under general law.[1132] And in a constitutional provision imposing individual responsibility for all a company's "debts and liabilities of every kind," the quoted language must be given its natural meaning, without inquiring whether private interest may be prejudiced by such a sweeping mandate.[1133] A stockholder of a trust company who sells his shares to the company at a time when it has no surplus, is liable to the extent of the amount received therefor which was paid out of the company's capital stock.[1134] Stockholders of an insolvent trust company which issued certificates of deposit pursuant to the attorney general's opinion that it had authority to do so, were held liable to the

---

[1127] Cunningham v. Commissioner of Banks, 249 Mass. 401, 144 N.E. 447. See Commissioner of Banks v. McKnight, 281 Mass. 467, 183 N.E 720.

[1128] Commissioner of Banks v. Cosmopolitan Trust Co., 253 Mass. 205, 148 N.E. 609, 41 A.L.R. 658.

[1129] Director of Liquidations v. Wood, 306 Mass. 1, 26 N.E.2d 979.

[1130] Maire Trust, etc., Co. v. Southern Loan, etc., Co., 92 Me. 444, 43 A. 24.

[1131] Pink v. Alden, 260 App. Div. 564, 23 N.Y.S.2d 865, aff'd, 285 N.Y. 800, 35 N.E.2d 193.

[1132] Allen v. Cosmopolitan Trust Co., 247 Mass. 334, 142 N.E. 100.

[1133] Pink v. Alden, 260 App. Div. 564, 23 N.Y.S.2d 365, aff'd, 285 N.Y. 800, 35 N.E.2d 193.

[1134] Lefker v. Harner, 123 Ark. 575, 186 S.W. 75, 1916F L.R.A. 281.

certificate holders.[1135] And under at least one state statute stockholders are not liable for debts due creditors who became such prior to the time stockholders acquired their stock.[1136]

Payments Not Allowed as Credits.—That the stockholders of a trust company have paid it an amount in excess of the par value of their stock does not entitle them to credit for such excess as against the double liability imposed on stockholders by statute.[1137] Nor can such a credit be allowed for amounts paid on an assessment to restore impaired capital,[1138] or payments made to keep a company's credit good.[1139]

Release and Settlement of Liability.—The liability of stockholders of a trust company to third persons is that of "partners," and the release of one releases the others in spite of any attempted reservations of right. against the others.[1140] But such liability is not discharged by a plan for liquidation of a company's assets by a liquidating corporation instead of a receiver, the liquidating corporation being the mere creature of such company which owned its entire stock.[1141] And where a court authorized the acceptance in settlement of stockholders' liability of fifty percent of the assessments imposed, conditioned upon payment without litigation and in cash within a specified time, a stockholder who because of financial disability did not timely avail himself of the settlement was held liable for the entire assessment.[1142]

[1135] Lamb v. Abendroth, 268 Mich. 73, 255 N.W. 447.

[1136] Murphy v. Wheatley, 102 Md. 501, 63 A. 62 (Maryland statute).

[1137] Skinner v. Schwab, 188 App. Div. 457, 177 N.Y.S. 143, aff'd, 229 N.Y. 549, 129 N.E. 910; Richards v. Schwab, 101 Misc. 128, 167 N.Y.S. 535.

[1138] **In general.—**

Commissioner of Banks v. McKnight, 281 Mass. 467, 183 N.E. 720.

Purpose of assessments.—Assessments to restore Impaired capital are provided for by statute. Their main purpose is to enable stockholders to avoid liquidation. Commissioner of Banks v. McKnight, 281 Mass. 467, 183 N.E. 720.

Statute is permissive.—Statute providing that trust company "shall" restore impaired capital by assessing stockholders imports permissive choice. Commissioner of Banks v. McKnight, 281 Mass. 467, 183 N.E. 720.

[1139] Detroit Trust Co. v. Allinger, 271 Mich. 600, 261 N.W. 90, appeal dismissed, 297 U.S. 695, 56 S. Ct. 572, 80 L. Ed. 986.

[1140] Reconstruction Finance Corp. v. Central Republic Trust Co., 128 F.2d 242, cert. denied, 317 U.S. 660, 63 S. Ct. 60, 87 L. Ed. 531.

[1141] Robinson v. Hospelhorn, 169 Md. 117, 179 A. 515, 184 A. 903, 103 A.L.R. 740.

[1142] Hospelhorn v. Poe, 174 Md. 242, 198 A. 582, 118 A.L.R. 682.

§ 8. Actions to Enforce Liability of Stockholders.

In General.—The remedy provided by statute is the exclusive method of enforcing individual liability of stockholders in banks and trust companies.[1143] And a stockholder cannot complain because the legislature changes the remedy by which a previously imposed liability may be enforced.[1144] It is sometimes provided by statute that stockholders' liability may be enforced in a suit at law or in equity.[1145] And it has been held that where a trust company has been taken over by a state banking official, and it is essential to enforce the stockholders' liability to pay debts, an action at law will not lie against a single stockholder to enforce his liability, but can be enforced only by a suit in equity where the liabilities of all stockholders may be equally and ratably ascertained and apportioned.[1146] But it also has been held that the convenience of avoiding a multiplicity of law actions alone does not justify

---

[1143] **In general.**—

Pink v. Alden, 260 App. Div. 564, 23 N.Y.S.2d 365, aff'd, 285 N.Y. 800, 35 N.E.2d 193.

Under the Maine statute the individual liability of stockholders in trust companies can only be enforced under proper orders of the court. Cooper v. Fidelity Trust Co., 132 Me. 260, 170 A. 726. As to actions generally, see § 18 of this chapter. As to actions to enforce liability of directors and officers, see § 12 of this chapter.

To enforce the liability of stockholders of a trust company in Massachusetts, the commissioner of banks, insofar as forms of remedy are concerned, must follow the general law. Allen v. Hanover Trust Co., 247 Mass. 347, 142 N.E. 105.

Intervening statutory amendments pending appeal.—

Even though the court of appeal had originally held that plaintiff had no right to petition for executory process because it had not complied with the legal requirements to be recognized as a real estate investment trust, where the state supreme court reversed that determination in view of intervening statutory amendments the plaintiff could maintain its action. Tri-South Mortg. Investors v. Rozands, 354 So. 2d 669 (La. App. 1977).

[1144] Johnson v. Libby, 111 Me. 204, 88 A. 647, 1916C Ann. Cas. 681.

[1145] Detroit Trust Co. v. Hockett, 278 Mich. 124, 270 N.W. 243.

[1146] **In general.**—

Cheney v. Scharmann, 145 App. Div. 456, 129 N.Y.S. 993.

The commissioner of banks enforcing the liability of stockholders has been held required to sue in equity, and then only after judgment and the return of execution unsatisfied. Cosmopolitan Trust Co. v. Cohen, 244 Mass. 128, 138 N.E. 711.

The federal court in Wisconsin would entertain representative suit to enforce liability of stockholders in Illinois trust company, in lieu of individual actions at law against stockholders. United States v. Earling, 39 F. Supp. 864.

an equity court in taking jurisdiction of a suit to enforce such liability.[1147] In a representative suit to enforce the liability of stockholders in a trust company, a court should determine who the creditors are, the amounts of their claims and when they accrued, who the stockholders are, the amount of their liability and when it accrued; collect the amount of such liability and make some arrangement for its equitable proportionate distribution.[1148] In proceedings for liquidation of a trust company, a court may make an assessment against the shareholders of the company upon their liability without personal service upon them, the proceeding being against the corporation which is presumed to represent them; where a shareholder in a trust company dies during the liquidation, an assessment against the shareholders is valid against such shareholder's estate without personal service on his representatives, the shareholder being represented in the proceeding by the corporation.[1149] And where a statute providing for stockholders' liability makes no provision for its enforcement, a court must recognize such procedure as will be appropriate for the accomplishment of the statute.[1150]

Conditions Precedent to Action.—It is sometimes required by statute that the holder of a claim against a trust company reduce it to judgment before

---

[1147] **In general.—**

United States v. Freeman, 21 F. Supp. 593.

Suit to enforce constitutional liability of trust company's stockholders was not a "creditors' bill," presenting a case cognizable in equity, where trust company was not a party to suit. United States v. Freeman, 21 F. Supp. 593.

No adequate remedy at law.—

The Reconstruction Finance Corporation on behalf of itself and other creditors of a trust company could maintain a suit in equity to enforce stockholders' constitutional liability, since there was not an adequate remedy at law. United State. v. Arthur, 23 F. Supp. 537; United States v. Freeman, 21 F. Supp. 593.

[1148] United State. v. Earling, 39 F. Supp. 864.

[1149] Johnson v. Libby, 111 Me. 204, 88 A. 647, 1916C Ann. Cas. 881.

[1150] **In general.—**

Klotz v. First Nat'l Bank, 78 Ind. App. 679, 134 N.E. 220.

The court may consider not only facts proved but also any reasonable inferences that might be drawn therefrom. Klotz v. First Nat. Bank, 78 Ind. App. 679, 134 N.E. 220.

Burden of proof and pleading.—

In an action to enforce stockholders' liability under Indiana statute, creditors have the burden of proving that the assets of the trust company have been exhausted. And, in such a case, the issue is properly presented by a general denial, instead of by plea in abatement. Klotz v. First Nat. Bank, 78 Ind. App. 679, 134 N.E. 220.

suing the company's stockholders to enforce any liability on account thereof.[1151] But it has been held that the determination of a commissioner of banks in possession of a trust company for purposes of liquidation, to enforce stockholders' liability, is valid though made before the recovery of a judgment by creditors and before the occurrence of other conditions precedent to the maintenance of proceedings to enforce such liability.[1152] And a commissioner need not delay bringing suit to enforce the individual liability of stockholders until the return day of execution against a trust company; nor is court approval a prerequisite to bringing suit.[1153] Where an insolvent trust company was in liquidation for nearly two years, a demand upon its assistant secretary on an execution issued on a judgment against the company was held sufficient, although its bylaws made no provisions for such an officer.[1154] And the fact that a company's charter has not been dissolved by a judgment does not prevent the maintenance of a suit against the stockholders of the company.[1155]

Statute of Limitations.—An action to enforce the liabilities of stockholders of a trust company must be brought within the time prescribed by the applicable statute of limitations.[1156] Thus, where a stockholder is alive at the time the property of a trust company is taken over by a commissioner of

---

[1151] Gause v. Boldt, 188 N.Y. 546, 80 N.E. 566; Allen v. Cosmopolitan Trust Co., 247 Mass. 334, 142 N.E. 100; Cosmopolitan Trust Co. v. Cohen, 244 Mass. 128, 138 N.E. 711.

A judgment obtained against a trust company, when its property and business were in the possession of the commissioner of banks, was such judgment as is intended by the statute, and the commissioner could rely upon it as basis for a suit to enforce individual liability of stockholders. Allen v. Cosmopolitan Trust Co., 247 Mass. 334, 142 N.E. 100.

[1152] Cunningham v. Commissioner of Banks, 249 Mass. 401, 144 N.E. 447; Commissioner of Banks v. McKnight, 281 Mass. 467, 183 N.E. 720.

Neither by statute, nor on reason, is there any requirement that a determination of the necessity for enforcing individual liability of stockholders of a trust company cannot be made until after the occurrence of other conditions precedent to the actual enforcement of the liability, it being the execution of the determination, and not the determination itself which must wait upon the arising of the prerequisites established, and such determination may be made prior to the return unsatisfied of execution issued on a judgment against the trust company. Allen v. Cosmopolitan Trust Co., 247 Mass. 334, 142 N.E. 100.

[1153] Allen v. Cosmopolitan Trust Co., 247 Mass. 334, 142 N.E. 100.

[1154] Commissioner of Banks v. Cosmopolitan Trust Co., 253 Mass. 205, 148 N.E. 609, 41 A.L.R. 658.

[1155] Van Tuyl v. Scharmann, 208 N.Y. 53, 101 N.E. 779.

[1156] **In general.—**

Hobbs v. National Bank, 101 F. 75, cert. denied, 178 U.S. 613, 20 S. Ct. 1030, 44 L. Ed. 1216.

banks, and the claim of stockholders' liability is primarily against him, not his estate, the liability claim against his personal representative may be barred by a short statute of limitations.[1157] But such statute is not a bar to a suit against the personal representative of a stockholder of a trust company to enforce the individual liability of stockholders, where the liability has not accrued at the death of the stockholder because a commissioner has not yet taken possession, not yet determined to enforce the stockholders' liability, and the judgment against the trust company required by statute as a prerequisite has not yet been entered, the personal representative being the holder of legal title at the time the liability accrues and in that capacity being liable to assessment.[1158] And under a general law which declares that prescribed limitations do not affect an action against a director or stockholder of a banking association to enforce a liability created by the commonwealth or statute, but that such action must be brought within three years after its accrual, the liability imposed on stockholders in trust companies by a banking law must be enforced by an action brought within three years after accrual, the three-year period being a condition, not a limitation.[1159]

Accrual of Action.—An action lies for the full amount of stockholders' liability on a determination to that effect by commissioners appointed for that purpose; a court determination in such a case is unnecessary.[1160] But the

---

Three-year limitation.—

A trust company empowered to receive deposits and to loan money on real estate and personal property security is a "moneyed corporation" within the meaning of the New York statute prescribing a three-year limitation for actions to enforce stockholders' liabilities. Platt v. Wilmot, 193 U.S. 602, 24 S. Ct. 542, 48 L. Ed. 809.

Application to out-of-state company.—

The term "moneyed corporation," as used in the New York statute, which prescribe. the limitations governing actions against stockholders of moneyed corporations, held to include a mortgage trust company of another state, authorized to issue and sell its debenture bonds secured by mortgagee, if it does business within the state of New York.

Hobbs v. National Bank, 101 F. 75, cert. denied, 178 U.S. 613, 20 S. Ct. 1030, 44 L. Ed. 1216.

[1157] Commissioner of Banks v. Cosmopolitan Trust Co., 253 Mass. 205, 148 N.E. 609, 41 A.L.R. 658.

[1158] Allen v. Hanover Trust Co., 247 Mass. 347, 142 N.E 105.

[1159] Richards v. Carpenter, 261 F. 724.

[1160] Allen v. Prudential Trust Co., 242 Mass. 78, 136 N.E. 410.

The question of the necessity of enforcing the liability of stockholders of a trust company and the extent to which that liability shall be enforced are not open further to judicial inquiry

liability of a shareholder in a trust or banking company does not accrue as a claim against the shareholder's estate until assessed by a court decree if that is the method provided by statute for determination of the liability.[1161] And the enforcement of such liability need not wait until all other available assets of a company have been converted into cash and paid out, but such liability may be enforced whenever the necessity therefor to pay the company's debts is judicially established.[1162]

Parties to Suit.—The persons entitled to enforce the statutory liability of stockholders of a trust company, and the proper parties to the enforcement proceedings, generally depend upon statute.[1163] For example, a state official in charge of banks may sue in his own name to enforce such liability,[1164] or the liability may be enforceable for the benefit of creditors by a receiver or

---

in a proceeding to enforce that liability. Allen v. Cosmopolitan Trust Co., 247 Mass. 334, 142 N.E. 100.

[1161] Johnson v. Libby, 111 Ma. 204, 88 A. 647, 1916C Ann. Cas. 681; Cooper v. Fidelity Trust Co., 132 Me. 260, 170 A. 726.

[1162] Robinson v. Hospelhorn, 169 Md. 117, 179 A. 515, 184 A. 908, 103 A.L.R. 740.

[1163] Pink v. Alden, 260 App. Div. 564, 23 N.Y.S.2d 365, aff'd, 285 N.Y. 800, 35 N.E.2d 193.

Superintendent of insurance taking over a trust company in liquidation proceedings was a "proper party" to action by creditors to enforce statutory liability of stockholders. Pink v. Alden, 260 App. Div. 564, 23 N.Y.S.2d 365, aff'd, 285 N.Y. 800, 35 N.E.2d 193.

[1164] **In general.—**

Skinner v. Schwab, 188 App. Div. 457, 177 N.Y.S. 143, aff'd, 229 N.Y. 549, 129 N.E. 910; Allen v. Cosmopolitan Trust Co., 247 Mass. 334, 142 N.E. 100.

When circumstances are such that joint suit against all stockholders cannot be brought by the commissioner of banks, in possession of a trust company for purposes of liquidation, he may sue them separately to enforce their individual liability. Cunningham v. Commissioner of Banks, 249 Mass. 401, 144 N.E. 447.

In action by secretary of banking on stock subscriptions against shareholder, of insolvent trust company, it is better, so far as reasonably possible, to let all shareholders be included in proceedings unless they are unknown, insolvent, or beyond the jurisdiction of the court, but the failure to do so is not a vital defect, since each shareholder is liable in any event for the full amount of the assessment on his shares. Beckman v. Brownback, 341 Pa. 565, 20 A.2d 200.

The New York statute providing that, where a permanent receiver has been appointed and the corporation has been dissolved, actions or proceedings to enforce the liability of stockholder. are to be prosecuted only in the name and on behalf of the receiver, unless the receiver refuses to take such action, applies only to banks and not to trust companies. Cheney v. Scharmann, 145 App. Div. 456, 129 N.Y.S. 993.

conservator having the powers of a receiver.[1165] Also, some statutes provide a remedy for creditors.[1166]

While a trust company is a proper party, it is not, however, a necessary party to suit to enforce the individual liability of its stockholders for its debts.[1167] And error, if any, in bringing an action to enforce the liability of stockholders of a trust company in the name of a superintendent of banks,

---

[1165] **In general.—**

Cooper v. Fidelity Trust Co., 132 Me. 260, 170 A. 726.

Under District of Columbia statute stockholders' liability is enforceable only by comptroller's receiver. Dunn v. O'Connor, 89 F.2d 820.

Under the Maryland statute the double liability of trust company's stockholders is enforceable by a receiver representing the interests of the corporation as well as all its creditors, and not by individual creditors. Sterling v. Reecher, 176 Md. 567, 6 A.2d 237.

[1166] **In general.—**

Pink v. Alden, 260 App. Div. 564, 23 N.Y.S.2d 365, aff'd, 285 N.Y. 800, 35 N.E.2d 193.

Under the New York statute, primarily, the right of action is vested in the superintendent of banks, but a remedy is granted to creditors upon the occurrence of certain conditions precedent And creditors can maintain an action without performing conditions precedent where performance is impossible. Pink v. Alden, 260 App. Div. 564, 23 N.Y.S.2d 365, aff'd, 285 N.Y. 800, 35 N.E.2d 193.

A secured creditor may enforce the liability of stockholders in an Illinois trust company. United States v. Freeman, 37 F. Supp. 720.

Real interest in enforcing liability.—

The United States and Reconstruction Finance Corporation, which had made loan to Illinois trust company, had a real interest in enforcing liability of one who was a stockholder before the loan was made, if there were other creditor, whose claims antedated claim of Reconstruction Finance Corporation. United States v. Earling, 39 F. Supp. 864

[1167] **In general.—**

Van Tuyl v. Scharmann, 208 N.Y. 53, 101 N.E. 779.

Several and individual actions by an insolvent trust company to recover stock assessments are proper, where, under statute, stockholders are individually liable. Detroit Trust Co. v. Hockett, 278 Mich. 124, 270 N.W. 243.

Nominal plaintiff.—

In New York, it is held that it is proper to make the trust company nominal plaintiff. Skinner v. Schwab, 188 App. Div. 457, 177 N.Y.S. 143, aff'd, 229 N.Y. 549, 129 N.E 910.

Defendant.—

But in Massachusetts it is held that the joining of the trust company should be, if at all, as defendant. Allen v. Cosmopolitan Trust Co., 247 Mass. 334, 142 N.E. 100.

instead of the company, is waived by failing to raise the question by special demurrer for incapacity to sue.[1168]

Sufficiency of Complaint or Petition.—It is not essential that a bill to enforce the individual liability of stockholders of a trust company state with excessive accuracy of detail every preliminary step taken, or conclusion reached, by a commissioner of banks before deciding to bring suit to enforce such liability.[1169] A bill sets forth sufficient facts where it alleges that it is necessary to enforce the individual liability of the stockholders, as described by statute, to the full amount, "in order to pay the liabilities of said trust company," the express reference to the statute showing that the word "liabilities" is used as including only "contracts, debts and engagements."[1170] And a petition by a bank examiner to collect stockholders' liability, alleging that one defendant was a dominant factor in the control of certain trust and investment companies, is sufficient to state a cause of action against all defendants for an accounting.[1171] And a complaint of a trust company depositor shows that a defendant stockholder's sale of his shares to the company reduced its capital stock and rendered it insolvent, when it state. that the defendant sold his shares, aggregating almost half of the company's

---

[1168] Skinner v. Schwab, 188 App. Div. 457, 177 N.Y.S. 143, aff'd, 229 N.Y. 549, 129 N.E. 910.

[1169] **In general.—**

Allen v. Cosmopolitan Trust Co., 247 Mass. 334, 142 N.E. 100.

And while an allegation that a curtain trust company was insolvent and that its assets were insufficient to pay its obligations would not be out of place, in such a case, it is not essential and it is sufficient to simply allege that the commissioner determined that it was necessary to enforce the individual liability of the stockholders, such an allegation importing inevitably a previous ascertainment of the fact that other assets were insufficient to meet the obligations. Allen v. Cosmopolitan Trust Co., 247 Mass. 334, 142 N.E 100.

Allegation as to recovery of judgment.—

In a suit by the commissioner of banks to enforce the individual liability of stockholder, it is not necessary to aver that the judgment in an action against the trust company was recovered upon a cause of action for which a stockholder would be liable; the only requirement being that a judgment should be recovered. Allen v. Cosmopolitan Trust Co., 247 Mass. 334, 142 N.E. 100.

An allegation as to demand on execution to the effect that demand was made on the corporation and on a person named as its assistant treasurer is sufficient. Allen v. Cosmopolitan Trust Co., 247 Mass. 334, 142 N.E 100.

[1170] Allen v. Cosmopolitan Trust Co., 247 Mass. 334, 142 N.E. 100.

[1171] Allen v. Cosmopolitan Trust Co., 247 Mass. 334, 142 N.E. 100.

total shares, to the company at a time when there was no surplus in its treasury.[1172]

In a suit by a commissioner of banks to enforce the individual liability of stockholders of a trust company, it is not necessary that he allege that suit is brought "in behalf of himself and all other creditors," the commissioner himself not being a creditor; nor is it necessary that he allege that it is brought against all persons who were stockholders at the time of the commencement of a suit in which judgment against the company was recovered, as suit need not be brought against stockholders who have already paid.[1173] And in a suit by a trust company's creditor on behalf of himself and other creditors to enforce stockholders' constitutional liability, the fact that one stockholder was not a registered stockholder on the dates when the company's liability to the creditor was incurred, is no ground for dismissal in view of allegations that there are other creditors to whom the stockholder might be liable.[1174]

Defenses, Counterclaim or Setoff.—The following have been held not to constitute adequate defenses in an action to enforce stockholders' liability: (1) That before the date of the writ all of a company's property had been put into receivership;[1175] (2) that the fraud of the president of a company had induced certain defendants to become subscribers;[1176] (3) that payment for stock was made by note, not cash as required by statute;[1177] (4) that the conduct of officers of a company prevented sale of defendant's stock[1178] or (5) that stock was irregularly issued, where those subscribing for an increase within the company's power had received certificates issued to them, had their names entered on the books, collected and kept dividends, and generally acted as stockholders.[1179] And where shares of stock stand in the

---

[1172] Lefker v. Harner, 123 Ark. 575, 576, 186 S.W. 75, 1916F L.R.A. 281.

[1173] Allen v. Cosmopolitan Trust Co., 247 Mass. 334, 142 N.E. 100.

[1174] United States v. Arthur, 23 F. Supp. 537.

[1175] Coyle v. Taunton Safe Deposit, etc., Co., 207 Mass. 441, 93 N.E. 791.

[1176] Commissioner of Banks v. Cosmopolitan Trust Co., 253 Mass. 205, 148 N.E. 609, 41 A.L.R. 658.

Stockholders cannot, because they have been defrauded, repudiate liability to creditors. Bittenbender v. Cosmopolitan Trust Co., 253 Mass. 230, 148 N.E. 619.

[1177] Commissioner of Banks v. Cosmopolitan Trust Co., 253 Mass. 205, 148 N.E. 609, 41 A.L.R. 658.

[1178] Commissioner of Banks v. Waltham Trust Co., 293 Mass. 62, 199 N.E. 303.

[1179] Commissioner of Banks v. Cosmopolitan Trust Co., 253 Mass. 205, 148 N.E. 609, 41 ALR. 658.

names of defendants on the corporate books, they cannot be relieved from liability merely because they held the stock as collateral security.[1180] Nor will stockholders be released from liability because of the promise of the secretary of a company to transfer stock when it is delivered to him, where the stock in question is delivered to another.[1181] And that a defendant was not an original stockholder, and had paid more for his stock than the original stockholders, does not place him on a different footing from them in an action to enforce stockholders' liability.[1182] As to other defenses in such actions, see the footnote.[1183]

In an action to enforce the liability of stockholders of a trust company in liquidation, the stockholders cannot set up as a counterclaim debts owed by

---

[1180] Richards v. Schwab, 101 Misc. 128, 167 N.Y.S. 535.

[1181] Richards v. Schwab, 101 Misc. 128, 167 N.Y.S. 535.

[1182] Commissioner of Banks v. Cosmopolitan Trust Co., 253 Mass. 205, 148 N.E. 609, 41 A.L.R. 858.

[1183] Agreement of creditors to defer enforcement of their claims against trust company until later date held not to bar enforcement of stockholder's statutory double liability before such date on ground that company's inability to pay debts was not shown moratorium plan having been adopted because of insufficiency of company's assets to pay debts. Robinson v. Hospelhorn, 169 Md. 117, 179 A. 515, 184 A. 903, 103 A.L.R. 740.

Trust company's creditors' postponement of collection of debts until date stated in certificates of indebtedness accepted by them held not to bar enforcement of stockholders' statutory double liability on ground that debts would not become due until such date. Robinson v. Hospelhorn, 169 Md. 117, 179 A. 515, 184 A. 903, 103 A.L.R. 740.

Note to creditors.—

Evidence held to prove that note executed to creditors who had loaned sufficient sum to pay debtors was executed merely to secure creditors against loss requiring them to avail themselves of remedy against stockholders before it could be ascertained whether they had sustained loss and did not constitute a bar to an action to enforce stockholders' individual liability. Klotz v. First Nat. Bank, 78 Ind. App. 679, 134 N.E. 220.

Miscellaneous defenses.—

The United States and Reconstruction Finance Corporation could maintain action in Massachusetts federal district court against some stockholders of Illinois trust companyto which corporation had made a loan, regardless of the trust company's solvency, as against contentions that plaintiffs could seek relief only in Illinois courts and had "adequate remedy at law," that receiver had not been asked to enforce stockholders' liability, and that other stockholders were not joined. Nor were plaintiffs barred from maintaining action on ground that such loan violated Illinois laws, and was "ultra vires" the bank, and that statute under which corporation proceeded was unconstitutional. And the fact that corporation accepted collateral, allegedly adequate to satisfy loan, did not show that plaintiff "waived" right to recover from stockholders. United States v. Freeman, 37 F. Supp. 720.

the trust company to them,[1184] nor can a stockholder set off against his statutory liability payments made by him to keep the credit of the company good.[1185]

Estoppel.—Stockholders were held estopped to assert that assessments against them were invalid on the ground that their trust company was without authority to engage in banking, where it had so engaged for more than twenty years without challenge by the state or the stockholders.[1186] And stockholders may be estopped to deny the legal existence of a company.[1187]

Burden of Proof.—The fact that stock stands on the books of a trust company in the name of a person is prima facie evidence that such person is the owner thereof, and the burden of proving that he is not in order to avoid statutory liability, rests upon him.[1188] And it has been held that in a proceeding against trust company stockholders to enforce liability allegedly

---

[1184] Van Tuyl v. Lewis, 165 App. Div. 412, 150 N.Y.S. 786; Richards v. Schwab, 101 Misc. 128, 167 N.Y.S. 535.

[1185] Detroit Trust Co. v. Allinger, 271 Mich. 600, 261 N.W. 90, appeal dismissed, 297 U.S. 695, 56 S. Ct. 572, 80 L. Ed. 986.

[1186] Independence Trust Co. v. Keesler, 206 N.C. 12, 173 S.E. 53.

[1187] Detroit Trust Co. v. Allinger, 271 Mich. 600, 261 N.W. 90, appeal dismissed, 297 U.S. 695, 56 S. Ct. 572, 80 L. Ed. 986.

Stockholders who treated trust company after statute under which it was incorporated was repealed as validly organized trust company legally functioning under statute purporting to enable trust companies organized under repealed statute to continue to function held estopped from questioning legal existence of trust company in suit to enforce stockholders' statutory liability after insolvency of trust company. Detroit Trust Co. v. Allinger, 271 Mich. 600, 261 N.W. 90, appeal dismissed, 297 U.S. 695, 56 S. Ct. 572, 80 L. Ed. 986.

Stockholder who did not question validity of corporate acts of trust company after statute under which trust company was incorporated was repealed, but who permitted and directed company to continue to exercise its functions as a corporation by advancing money to enable it to pay its creditors and who pleaded equitable set-off to extent of money so advanced in suit to enforce stockholders' statutory liability after insolvency of trust company, held estopped to deny legal existence of trust company in such suit. Detroit Trust Co. v. Allinger, 271 Mich. 600, 261 N.W. 90, appeal dismissed, 297 U.S. 695, 56 S. Ct. 572, 80 L. Ed. 986.

[1188] Commissioner of Banks v. Waltham Trust Co., 293 Mass. 62, 199 N.E. 303; Friede v. Mackey, 298 Mass. 193, 10 N.E.2d 102; Director of Liquidations v. Wood, 306 Mass. 1, 26 N.E.2d 979.

Evidence that person in whose name stock stands on books of trust company did all that he could to secure transfer of stock on books, and that his name remained thereon as stockholder wholly through fault of trust company or its officers, tends to rebut prima facie evidence of books that he is owner of stock, as respects imposition of stockholders' statutory liability. Commissioner of Banks v. Waltham Trust Co., 293 Mass. 62, 199 N.E. 303.

imposed by law, a claimant is required to prove himself to be a creditor of the company.[1189]

Presumptions and Inferences.—In a suit to charge a former stockholder with statutory liability on the ground that he sold his stock with the fraudulent intent of avoiding such liability, intent is not required to be separately proven by direct evidence, but may be found as an inference from all the facts.[1190]

Evidence.—Cases dealing with sufficiency and weight of evidence will be found in the footnote.[1191]

Decree.—It appearing that certain defendants against whom a default decree was taken were not real owners of any stock, and that a bank commissioner, suing to enforce stockholders' liability, had elected to hold the real owners, no decree would be entered against such defendants.[1192]

II. OFFICERS AND AGENTS.

§ 9. In General.

Eligibility for Office.—A court which removes the trustees of a trust company has no power to declare that they shall never at any time in the future, be eligible for election or appointment as trustees or officers of the

---

[1189] Reconstruction Finance Corp. v. Central Republic Trust Co., 128 F.2d 242, cert. denied, 317 U.S. 660, 63 S. Ct. 60, 87 L. Ed. 531 (Illinois law).

[1190] Detroit Trust Co. v. Drummond, 284 Mich. 399, 279 N.W. 877.

[1191] Evidence held sufficient to establish prima facie case of default in payment of debts or liabilities contracted exceeding the capital stock. Richards v. Schwab, 101 Misc. 128, 167 N.Y.S. 535.

Evidence held to establish that trust company did not conduct banking business, so as to subject stockholders to double liability. Hogg v. Armstrong, 112 W. Va. 142, 164 S.E. 496.

Evidence held to show insolvency of trust company and transfer of stock to evade statutory liability, thus shifting burden upon stockholder. Detroit Trust Co. v. Hockett, 278 Mich. 124, 270 N.W. 243.

Evidence held Insufficient.—

Evidence held not to prove negligence alleged. Chambers v. Land Credit Trust Co., 92 Kan. 30, 139 P. 1178.

Evidence held insufficient to show fraudulent intent of stockholder to escape statutory liability. Detroit Trust Co. v. Granger, 278 Mich. 152, 270 N.W. 239; Detroit Trust Co. v. Drummond, 284 Mich. 399, 279 N.W. 877.

[1192] Commissioner of Banks v. McKnight, 281 Mass. 467, 183 N.E. 720.

company.[1193] One who has wide business commitments and whose interests are so divided that he has no time to attend to the details of management of a banking institution, is nevertheless eligible for the directorate of such an institution, the detailed management being in the hands of an executive committee.[1194]

Compensation.—Where, in an action by the president of a mortgage and trust company for a percentage of its profits claimed to be due him as compensation, the evidence permits the drawing of different inferences and it presents a question for the jury, but where a verdict for the president is against the weight of the evidence, it will be set aside.[1195]

As to decisions relating to compensation of officers and agents, see the footnote.[1196]

Miscellaneous Matters.—See the footnotes for decisions relating to the conduct of officers,[1197] and their powers and authority.[1198] See the footnote for matters relating to the removal or resignation of officers or director.[1199]

[1193] Kibby v. Leon (Tex. Civ. App.), 241 S.W. 1064. As to representation of company by officers and agents, see § 19 et seq. of this chapter.

[1194] Kavanaugh v. Gould, 147 App. Div. 281, 131 N.Y.S. 1059.

[1195] Young v. United States Mtg., etc., Co., 181 N.Y.S. 38.

[1196] Contract promising to pay vice president of investment banking firm "total compensation for 1987" in the range of $500,000 to $600,000 obliged firm to pay vice president at least $500,000 for 1987 and did not allow pro rata reduction either because he did not begin his employment until March 2, 1987, or because he was notified of termination on October 31, 1987, where it was contemplated in the letter agreement, dated January 29, 1987, that he would not start work at the beginning of the year, and where his "official date of resignation" was specified as December 31, 1987. Mayer v. Morgan Stanley & Co., 703 F. Supp. 249 (S.D.N.Y. 1988).

[1197] **Purchase of beneficial interest in trust.—**

If corporate trustee cannot profit from purchase of beneficial interests in trust, neither can its officers or affiliates. Dick & Reuteman Co. v. Doherty Realty Co., 16 Wis. 2d 342, 114 N.W.2d 475.

Right to buy shares in closed-end investment company.—

Chief executive officer had right to buy shares in closed-end investment company registered to do business under Investment Company Act of 1940, absent showing of inequity in the purchase. Equity Corp. v. Milton, 42 Del. Ch. 425, 213 A.2d 439 (1965).

Chief executive officer causing his wholly owned subsidiary to acquire options for purchase of 1, 773, 665 shares in closed-end investment company did not violate officer's fiduciary duty where company had not established policy to acquire investment property in exchange for its own shares and had never purchased more than 18, 605 thereof in one year and where the shares in question were to all intents and purposes the same as those officers

(Text continued on page 314)

had held interest in from 1933 through 1962. Equity Corp. v. Milton, 42 Del. Ch. 425, 213 A.2d 439 (1965).

President chargeable with knowledge of law.—

President of small business investment corporation was chargeable with the responsibility of being acquainted with the laws and regulations governing his family-owned small business investment company. United States v. Norwood Capital Corp., 273 F. Supp. 236 (D.S.C. 1967).

Duty of full disclosure of facts.—

Where bank held stock of corporation as testamentary trustee, and bank president was also president of the corporation, and bank director was vice-president thereof, bank and officers owed duty to trust beneficiary to make full disclosure of condition of corporation at time sale of stock to officers was contemplated by the bank even though beneficiary had only a beneficial interest and legal title was in bank as trustee, and officers of corporation owed duty to trust beneficiary to deal with him in utmost fairness and to communicate actual conditions to enable him to determine the proper price. Dalton v. Lawrence Nat. Bank, 169 Kan. 401, 219 P.2d 719.

Duty to manage without self-dealing.—

Officers of mutual fund have fiduciary duty to manage companies with single eye to their best interest, free from any self-dealing. Brown v. Bullock, 194 F. Supp. 207 (S.D.N.Y. 1961), aff'd, 294 F.2d 415.

When rule against self-dealing inapplicable.—

Usual rule prohibiting trustees from self-dealing had no application to relationship between trustee of open-end investment funds and funds constituting arrangement set up by contract and of which investors knew when they acquired interests in funds. Kleinman v. Saminsky, 41 Del. Ch. 572, 200 A.2d 572, cert. denied, 379 U.S. 900, 85 S. Ct. 186, 13 L. Ed. 2d 174 (1964).

Improper conduct not shown.—

In a stockholder's suit against a loan company and its officers the evidence was held not to show that a member of the executive committee was guilty of improper conduct in securing loans to others far compensation. Williams v. Fidelity Loan, etc., Co., 142 Va. 43, 128 S.E. 615, 45 A.L.R. 664.

Wrongful use of trustee influence.—

Executive officer of corporate trustee, though not personally a trustee of the trust, was subject to same disabilities as to wrongful use of his trustee influence as the trustee for whom he acted in administration of trust Kenny v. Citizens Nat. Trust, etc., Bank (Cal. App.), 269 P.2d 641.

1198 President of trust company held not vested by virtue of his officer with power of withdrawing and substituting securities underlying participation certificates issued by company under provisions of which such power was confided and reposed in company. Seaboard Trust Co. v. Shea, 118 N.J. Eq. 433, 180 A. 206.

Treasurer's execution of note and transfer of collateral by trust company to national bank to cover an overdraft of trust company's commercial account with national bank held within

§ 10. Directors.

Relation of Directors to Company and Stockholders.—The directors of a trust company have the general supervision and active management of all its concerns; each director sustains a distinct relation not only to it, but to its

---

scope of authority conferred by trust company's directors who authorized treasurer to "borrow" from the national bank from time to time as needs of trust company might require, since transaction was in essence, though not in form, a borrowing. Salem Trust Co. v. Federal Nat. Bank, 11 F. Supp. 105, aff'd, 78 F.2d 407.

In determining whether trust company's treasurer, when executing note and delivering collateral far a debt owing by trust company to a national beak, acted within scope of authority, earlier course of dealing between trust company and national bank in which the treasurer had always acted on behalf of trust company held sufficient basis for bona fide belief on part of national bank that treasurer was duly authorized to sign the note and indorse and assign security. Salem Trust Co. v. Federal Nat. Bank, 11 F. Supp. 105, aff'd, 78 F.2d 407.

Statute prohibiting officers of industrial bank from purchasing its evidences of debt for less than face value held not applicable to certificate of interest which yielded 8 percent interest if, as, and when earned, did not represent a fixed liability, and was subject and subordinate to investment certificates and claims of all other creditors. Newman v. Scheer, 170 Misc. 1027, 11 N.Y.S.2d 649, aff'd, 257 App. Div. 1036. 14 N.Y.S.2d 493.

[1199] **Letter of resignation.—**

On the issue whether a defendant was a director of a trust company when he overdrew his account, a letter of resignation addressed to the board of directors and sent to its secretary is insufficient withdrawal unless the letter was received by the board. State v. Scarlett, 91 N.J.L. 200, 102 A. 160, 2 A.L.R. 88.

On review of banking board proceeding looking to removal of director of trust company pursuant to statute providing that decision of banking board shall be conclusive and not subject to any review, the only question for supreme court related to jurisdiction and regularity of proceeding. Swank v. Myers, 386 Pa. 331, 126 A.2d 267.

Where banking board made determination requiring trust company to remove director from office and director's term thereafter expired and director did not receive sufficient votes to be reelected, on subsequent review of proceedings, matter of jurisdiction and regularity of proceeding before banking board was moot. Swank v. Myers, 386 Pa. 331, 126 A.2d 267.

Under statute providing that any director who is removed from his office or position shall be disqualified from acting as an attorney, officer, employee, director, or trustee of any institution for such period as banking board shall proscribe, determination of period of disqualification of director of trust company rested within the sound discretion of banking board and could not be inquired into by supreme court on certiorari. Swank v. Myers, 386 Pa. 331, 126 A.2d 267.

Actions of secretary of banking in demanding ouster of president of trust company and removal of president by board of directors did not entail exercise of any judicial or quasi-judicial function, but were purely administrative in character, and hence not cognizable on certiorari. Swank v. Myers, 386 Pa. 331, 126 A.2d 267.

stockholders.[1200] It has been held that the directors of a loan or trust company act in a fiduciary capacity,[1201] and are under a legal responsibility akin to that of trustees.[1202] But it also has been held that a director of a bank or loan institution is an agent, not a trustee.[1203] And it has been said that a trust company director is to some extent a trustee for its stockholders as a group, but not for the stockholders individually.[1204] However, a trust company director owes no duty to disclose to a prospective purchaser of stock what he may know affecting the stock's value.[1205]

Duties Incidental to Office of Director.—Directors of a trust company, required by law to know the condition of their company, cannot say that they did not know what a fair and intelligent discharge of their duties must have disclosed.[1206] And they must use ordinary diligence in ascertaining the condition of their company's business.[1207] Thus, under a statute imposing

---

[1200] Kavanaugh v. Gould, 147 App. Div. 281, 131 N.Y.S. 1059.

[1201] **Loan society.—**

Directors of loan society act in trust capacity. Beutelspacher v. Spokane Sav. Bank, 164 Wash. 227, 2 P.2d 729.

Trust company.—

Directors of trust company occupy a fiduciary relation to the company and its stockholders. In re Prudential Trust Co., 244 Mass. 64, 138 N.E. 702; Bonner v. Chapin Nat. Bank, 251 Mass. 401, 146 N.E. 666 (1925); Brown v. Bullock, 194 F. Supp. 207 (S.D.N.Y. 1961), aff'd, 294 F.2d 415.

Directors of trust company are fiduciaries in the same sense as trustees of savings banks. Commissioner of Banks v. Harrigan, 291 Mass 353, 197 N.E. 92.

Mutual fund.—

The directors of a mutual fund held a position of trust and confidence with respect to the fund's shareholders, and owed them the obligations commonly associated with fiduciaries. Galfand v. Chestnutt, 402 F. Supp. 1318 (S.D.N.Y. 1975).

[1202] Prudential Trust Co. v. Moore, 245 Mass. 311, 139 N.E. 645.

[1203] Williams v. Fidelity Loan, etc., Co., 142 Va. 43, 128 S.E. 615, 45 A.L.R. 664.

[1204] Connolly v. Shannon, 105 N.J. Eq. 155, 147 A. 234, aff'd, 107 N.J. Eq. 180, 151 A. 905 (president has similar status).

[1205] Connolly v. Shannon, 105 N.J. Eq. 155, 147 A. 234, aff'd, 107 N.J. Eq. 180, 151 A. 905 (similar rule as to president).

[1206] Gregory v. Binghamton Trust Co., 168 App. Div. 805, 154 N.Y.S. 376, aff'd, 220 N.Y. 626, 115 N.E. 1040.

[1207] Medford Trust Co. v. McKnight, 292 Mass. 1, 197 N.E. 649.

Fund's director, on the request of the adviser and portfolio manager for indemnification for counsel fees, had no duty to explore independently their legal liability where there was nothing to "sharpen his attention" so as to indicate to him that he should not rely upon the

duties on directors of trust companies, the performance of which forces them to know the exact status of their company, the law presumes that they perform their duties and possess the knowledge which would come from such performance, and this would be especially true in the case of a director-president who has stated that he has inside knowledge; hence, in such a case, it is not error to charge in an action for fraud that the law presumes a director is familiar with his company's surplus and profits, the intrinsic value of its assets, and the amount of its liabilities.[1208]

Directors must live up to the bylaws of a corporation, and where in violation of a banking law, officers speculate in a company's stock, the directors should not permit it to continue, even though profitable.[1209] And where the bylaws of a trust company provide for an executive committee to exercise all the powers of the board of directors when not in session, it has been held proper for the directors to divide their duties and responsibilities, and the directors who are not members of the executive committee are not chargeable with knowledge reported only to the executive committee, nor are they liable for the negligence of the members of that committee.[1210]

The directors of a loan society are not qualified to authorize a transfer of the society's assets to a bank of which the directors are stockholders and directors.[1211] The position of nonaffiliated directors of a mutual fund company in relation to its investment adviser is adversary in character, and to properly fulfill their mission, the directors are obligated to scrutinize the acts and doings of the adviser with great care.[1212] The directors of a registered mutual fund owe a duty to the fund, whose charter requires that upon sale of its shares it receive their full asset value, to see that all charter requirements are met;[1213] but they have no duty to change from an independent brokerage to an affiliated broker.[1214]

---

counsel to the fund to adequately inform him as to the legal considerations relating to the indemnification, and where such director did fully explore those issues that were meaningfully brought to his attention, no liability would be imposed. Cambridge Fund, Inc. v. Abella, 501 F. Supp. 598 (S.D.N.Y. 1980).

[1208] Morrow v. Franklin, 289 Mo. 549, 233 S.W. 224.

[1209] State v. Barnes, 108 Minn. 230, 122 N.W. 11; State v. Barnes, 108 Minn. 527, 122 N.W. 12; Kavanaugh v. Gould, 223 N.Y. 103, 119 N.E. 237.

[1210] Kavanaugh v. Gould, 147 App. Div. 281, 181 N.Y.S. 1059.

[1211] Beutelspacher v. Spokane Sav. Bank, 164 Wash. 227, 2 P.2d 729.

[1212] Acampora v. Birkland, 220 F. Supp. 527.

[1213] Moses v. Burgin, 445 F.2d 369 (1st Cir.), rev'g 316 F. Supp. 31 (D. Mass.), cert. denied, 404 U.S. 994, 92 S. Ct. 532, 30 L. Ed. 2d 547 (1971).

The business judgment rule, permitting disinterested directors who were the minority of the board to determine the decision to be taken in the stockholders' derivative suit against, inter alia, an investment advisor was not inapplicable merely because each minority director had received remuneration for service on boards of other mutual funds advised by the investment advisor.[1215] Application of the business judgment rule permitting disinterested directors who were the minority of the board to determine what position the company should take in a stockholders' derivative suit was not rendered inapplicable on the theory that a minority director of a mutual fund can never act independently given the relationship between mutual funds and their advisors.[1216] Federal courts should apply state law governing the authority of petitioners to discontinue derivative suits to the extent such law is consistent with the Investment Company Act and the Investment Advisors Act.[1217]

A voluntary assessment by directors of a trust company so that the company might operate on a more sound financial basis was held supported by a sufficient consideration.[1218]

§ 11. Management Services Generally.

In determining whether there is compliance with the terms and conditions of a management service agreement between a mutual fund company and a management company, it is necessary to construe the contract in light of the

---

If, by directing give-ups to broker, who sold registered mutual fund's shares and choosing not to recapture the give-ups, fund's directors violated any duty owed the fund whose charter required that upon sale of its shares it receive their full asset value, directors could not be absolved on basis that directing give-ups to brokers benefited fund by stimulating sales of its shares. Moses v. Burgin, 445 F.2d 369 (1st Cir.), *rev'd*, 316 F. Supp. 31 (D. Mass.), cert. denied. 404 U.S. 994, 92 S. Ct. 532, 30 L. Ed. 2d 547 (1971).

[1214] Moses v. Burgin, 445 F.2d 369 (1st Cir.), rev'g 316 F. Supp. 31 (D. Mass.), cert. denied, 404 U.S. 994, 92 S. Ct. 532, 30 L. Ed. 2d 547 (1971).

[1215] Lasker v. Burks, 426 F. Supp. 844 (S.D.N.Y. 1977).

[1216] Lasker v. Burks, 426 F. Supp. 844 (S.D.N.Y. 1977).

The presence of several defendant directors during initial presentations at a meeting of disinterested quorum did not demonstrate the minority directors' lack of independence thus precluding a determination of the position the company should take in a stockholders' derivative suit on behalf of an investment company, since the minority directors had invited such defendants to join the meeting and such defendant. and their counsel were excused before the disinterested quorum made its determination. Lasker v. Burks, 426 F. Supp. 844 (S.D.N.Y. 1977).

[1217] Burks v. Lasker, 441 U.S. 471, 99 S. Ct. 1831, 60 L. Ed. 2d 404 (U.S. 1979).

[1218] Thomson v. Holt, 345 Mo. 296, 132 S.W.2d 974.

relationship of the parties where they did not conduct arm's length negotiations.[1219] Where such an agreement is drafted by counsel for a management company and the construction given it by the parties is not the result of arm's length negotiations, the management company is required to observe its terms strictly and refrain from resolving ambiguous issues in a manner unfairly beneficial to it, and it cannot justifiably interpret the agreement's unambiguous terms in its favor.[1220] Any ambiguity in such a management agreement as to the obligation of a management company to render clerical services is not within the mandate of the Investment Company Act that such an agreement must precisely describe all compensation to be paid an adviser.[1221] The Investment Company Act also provides that it is unlawful for any affiliated person of a registered investment company, acting as an agent, to accept from any source any compensation for the purchase of property for the company.[1222] The offense is complete

---

[1219] Acampora v. Birkland, 220 F. Supp. 527.

[1220] Acampora v. Birkland, 220 F. Supp. 527.

[1221] Acampora v. Birkland, 220 F. Supp. 527.

[1222] **In general.—**

15 U.S.C.S. § 80a-17(e) (1).

Phrase "acting as agent" in statute making it unlawful for any affiliated person of a registered investment company, acting as agent, to accept from any source any compensation for purchase of any property for such registered company, is a descriptive phrase and does not require showing that the recipient of the compensation took any action as a result thereof. United States v. Deutsch, 451 F.2d 98 (2d Cir. 1971), cert. denied, 404 U.S. 1019, 92 S. Ct. 682, 30 L. Ed. 2d 667 (1972).

Phrase "acting as agent," in statute making it unlawful for any affiliated person of a registered investment company, acting as agent, to accept from any source any compensation for purchase of any property for such registered company, does not define a more limited subclass of affiliated persons those who have capacity to influence investment decisions, but rather the phrase "acting as agent" is a descriptive phrase distinguishing affiliated persona acting as brokers from those who are not acting as brokers in connection with a sale or purchase of securities for investment company. United States v. Deutsch, 451 F.2d 98 (2d Cir. 1971), cert. denied, 404 U.S. 1019, 92 S. Ct. 682, 30 L. Ed. 2d 667 (1972).

Phrase "acting as agent," in statute making it unlawful for any affiliated person of a registered investment company, acting as agent, to accept from any source any compensation for purchase of any property for such registered company, was not intended to mean acting as agent for an outsider dealing with the investment company and not as agent for the investment company itself. United States v. Deutsch, 451 F.2d 98 (2d Cir. 1971), cert. denied, 404 U.S. 1019, 92 S. Ct. 682, 30 L. Ed. 2d 667 (1972).

Trial court's interpretation of phrase "acting as agent," in statute making it unlawful for any affiliated person of a registered investment company, acting as agent, to accept from any source any compensation for purchase of any property for such registered company, as being

when the compensation is delivered and received with the forbidden intent.[1223] The forbidden intent is intent to give and accept a gratuity in appreciation of past or future conduct.[1224] As to various matters arising under management service agreements, see the footnote.[1225]

---

merely descriptive of a subclass of affiliated persons was incorrect, but defendant was not prejudiced, in that such interpretation, if anything, imposed a greater burden on government in proving its case than was necessary. United States v. Deutsch, 451 F.2d 98 (2d Cir. 1971), cert. denied, 404 U.S. 1019, 92 S. Ct. 682, 30 L. Ed. 2d 667 (1972).

An affiliated person is acting as agent within meaning of statute making it unlawful for any affiliated person of a registered investment company, acting as agent, to accept from any source any compensation for purchase of any property for such registered company in all cases when he is not acting as broker for the investment company. United States v. Deutsch, 451 F.2d 98 (3d Cir. 1971), cert. denied, 404 U.S. 1019, 92 S. Ct. 682, 30 L. Ed. 2d 667 (1972).

Evidence established that defendant's codefendant, who was an affiliated person and was not acting as broker, was acting as agent for investment companies within meaning of statute making it unlawful for any affiliated person of registered investment company, acting as agent, to accept from any source any compensation for purchase of any property for such registered company; accordingly, it was improper to submit such issue to jury, but error was harmless, where defendant suffered no prejudice. United States v. Deutsch, 451 F.2d 98 (2d Cir. 1971), cert. denied, 404 U.S. 1019, 92 S. Ct. 682, 30 L. Ed. 2d 667 (1972).

[1223] United States v. Deutsch, 451 F.2d 98 (2d Cir. 1971), cert. denied, 404 U.S. 1019, 92 S. Ct. 682, 30 L. Ed. 2d 667 (1972).

[1224] **In general.—**

United States v. Deutsch, 451 F.2d 98 (2d Cir. 1971), cert. denied, 404 U.S. 1019, 92 S. Ct. 682, 30 L. Ed. 2d 667 (1972).

In prosecution for violating statute making it unlawful for any affiliated person of a registered investment company, acting as agent, to accept from any source any compensation for the purchase of any property for such registered company, defendant, who admittedly sold an affiliated person registered company's note at a substantial discount, and who claimed that when he made commitment to sell note he had no idea that the note and attached warrant would be so valuable eight or nine months later, was entitled to an instruction merely that the jury could not convict without being persuaded beyond a reasonable doubt that agreement to buy the note was made with knowledge that it constituted something of value. United States v. Deutsch, 451 F.2d 98 (2d Cir. 1971), cert. denied, 404 U.S. 1019, 92 S. Ct. 682, 30 L. Ed. 2d 667 (1972).

Intent to influence.—

Intent to influence is not element of statute making it unlawful for any affiliated person of a registered investment company, acting as agent, to accept from any source any compensation for the purchase of any property for such registered company. United States v. Deutsch, 451 F.2d 98 (3d Cir. 1971), cert. denied, 404 U.S. 1019, 92 S. Ct. 682, 30 L. Ed. 2d 667 (1972).

(Text continued on page 321)

Aiding and abetting an affiliated person.—

In prosecution for aiding and abetting an affiliated person of registered investment companies in receiving compensation for purchase of securities for such investment companies, comment on defendant's sophistication in financial matters was relevant to show knowledge on his part of what he was doing; his insistence on use of nominee names evinced a desire to conceal transaction, from which jury could infer consciousness of guilt. United States v. Deutsch, 451 F.2d 98 (2d Cir. 1971), cert. denied, 404 U.S. 1019, 92 S. Ct. 682, 30 L. Ed. 2d 667 (1972).

Evidence, in prosecution for aiding and abetting affiliated person of registered investment companies in receiving compensation for purchase of securities for such investment companies in violation of the Investment Company Act of 1940 and of the aider and abettor statute, was sufficient to prove compensation. United States v. Deutsch, 451 F.2d 98 (2d Cir. 1971), cert. denied, 404 US. 1019, 92 S. Ct. 682, 30 L. Ed. 2d 667 (1972).

1225 **Expense of twice-daily computation of net asset value.—**

Management service agreement between mutual fund company and management company did not impose upon management company expense of twice-daily computation of net asset value. Acampora v. Birkland, 220 F. Supp. 527.

Expenses incident to routine functions of funds.—

Management service agreement between mutual fund company and management company did not impose upon management company expense of making necessary entries with respect to sale of fund shares, recording receipts of sales, correspondence with shareholders and planholders, mailing reports, and computing and paying dividends, but such items were rather incident to routine substantive functions of funds. Acampora v. Birkland, 220 F. Supp. 527.

Bookkeeping and clerical expenses.—

Management service agreement between mutual fund company and management company stating that management would perform all necessary administrative functions and listing as examples preparation of reports, prospectuses, registration statements, purchase agreements and statistical data did not impose upon management company obligation to pay all offend company's bookkeeping and clerical expenses. Acampora v. Birkland, 220 F. Supp. 527.

Expenses of data-processing equipment.—

The fact that new and substantially more expensive office equipment was developed subsequent to consummation of 1940 management service agreement requiring management company to furnish at its own expense for use of mutual fund such office equipment as reasonably necessary to carry on business offend did not constitute alteration or condition which would relieve management of its obligation and it was thereunder required to assume expense of data-processing equipment used mainly to facilitate twice-daily computation of fund shares. Acampora v. Birkland, 220 F. Supp. 527.

Expenses regarding sale of shares under installment investment plan.—

Under agreement between mutual fund company and management company, management company was required to assume extent of difference between maintenance expense on shares sold under installment investment plan and total servicing and processing costs where management as underwriter derived commissions on continuing sale of shares and benefited

"Control," as used in the context of the provisions of the Investment Company Act defining an "affiliated person" as any person controlling, controlled by, or under common control with other persons, means the act or fact of control, power or authority to guide or manage, or directing or restraining domination, and proof of control demands the presentation of evidence establishing actual domination in operation.[1226] The presumption

---

by growth buildup in amount of its fee as adviser and its failure to assume obligations constituted breach of distribution agreement, entitling mutual fund company to restitution. Acampora v. Birkland, 220 F. Supp. 527.

Compensation to be paid management for advisory service.—

Agreement between mutual fund company and management company was entirely clear as to compensation to be paid management company for advisory service so as to conform to Investment Company Act provision that it precisely describe all compensation to be paid thereunder. Acampora v. Birkland, 220 F. Supp. 527.

Reasonableness of salaries of officers.—

Provision of management service agreement between mutual fund company and management company requiring deduction from advisory fee payable by fund to management of such sum, if any, paid by fund as salaries to its officers to extent that they should, in opinion of management company, be reasonable gave management company no carte blanche to determine whether officers were functioning as such but rather only right to question reasonableness of salaries, and its failure to pay reasonable salaries was a breach of the agreement. Acampora v. Birkland, 220 F. Supp. 527.

Amendment not requiring submission of agreements to shareholders.—

Amendment, adopted after passage of Investment Company Act, to administrative and service agreement between mutual fund company and management company, striking the term "administrative" wherever it appeared, including title, and substituting term "management," and permitting shareholders to terminate agreement to conform to act did not change contract substantially so that submission to shareholders would be required under act but could be properly promulgated by board. Acampora v. Birkland, 220 F. Supp. 527.

[1226] **In general.—**

Acampora v. Birkland, 220 F. Supp. 527.

No one fact would automatically call for finding that any director of investment company was controlled within Investment Company Act and was thus an affiliated director. Coran v. Thorpe, 42 Del. Ch. 67, 203 A.2d 620 (1984).

Proof of economic relationship between investment company director and its advisers, underwriters or brokers does not, ipso facto, overcome burden and compel conclusion that he is controlled or affiliated director within meaning of Investment Company Act. Coran v. Thorpe, 42 Del. Ch. 67, 203 A.2d 620 (1964).

Directors benefited or interested.—

Even if each of five of directors of investment company had been benefited or interested by virtue of relationship of company to firm with which each was associated such did not compel conclusion that those directors were in fact controlled and affiliated directors under

that a natural person is not controlled within the meaning of the section of the Act defining control of management or policy of a company is a heavy one, and not easily overturned.[1227] Where the number of an investment company's directors affiliated with an investment adviser and principal underwriter does not reach the quantum prohibited by the Investment Company Act, a shareholder alleging that the board is dominated by the adviser and underwriter must show that additional directors are dominated.[1228]

In the context of the section of the Investment Company Act making it unlawful for a company to act as investment adviser or principal underwriter after assignment of a contract, and defining assignment as including any direct transfer of a controlling block of the assignor's outstanding voting securities by a security holder of the assignor, the "assignor" is the person rendering the investment advisory or underwriting services, and there can be no direct transfer within the section in the absence of a transfer of stock of the company rendering the advisory or underwriting services.[1229] in construing the term "controlling block" in the Investment Company Act

---

Investment Company Act, and advisory services and underwriting agreements approved by majority of board of directors, including those five directors, were not void on that basis. Coran v. Thorpe, 42 Del. Ch. 67, 203 A.2d 620(1964).

Jurisdiction of state court to resolve issue of control.—

State court, in proceeding to determine whether underwriting and management contracts of investment company were void on ground that they had been approved by board of directors when a majority of its members were affiliated directors within Investment Company Act, had jurisdiction to resolve issue of whether certain directors of investment company were controlled within section of Investment Company Act defining affiliated person as a person directly or indirectly controlled by such other person. Coran v. Thorpe, 42 Del. Ch. 67, 203 A.2d 620 (1964).

[1227] Rome v. Archer, 41 Del. Ch. 404, 197 A.2d 49.

A determination that a charge of domination of a board of directors of an investment company by the investment adviser and principal underwriter was sufficiently doubtful to warrant a settlement of a stockholder's derivative action involving alleged excessive advertisement fees was not an abuse of discretion. Rome v. Archer, 41 Del. Ch. 404, 197 A.2d 49.

[1228] Rome v. Archer, 41 Del. Ch. 404, 197 A.2d 49.

Evidence adduced by plaintiff claiming that unlawful percentage of directors of mutual fund consisted of affiliated persons within meaning of Investment Company Act fell short of establishing that individuals involved were dominated and managed by a controlling company, notwithstanding showing that companies with which some directors were affiliated performed services for fund management company. Acampora v. Birkland, 220 F. Supp. 527.

[1229] Willheim v. Murchison, 342 F.2d 33 (2d Cir.), cert. denied, 382 U.S. 840, 86 S. Ct. 36, 15 L. Ed. 2d 82 (1965).

provision that an assignment terminating an investment company's contract with an adviser or underwriter shall include any transfer of a "controlling block" of the assignor's outstanding voting securities, emphasis must be on transferable elements of power, and where the amount of stock transferred is less than 25 percent and there are no indicia of control, it is not a "controlling block" unless such ownership fairly presages victory in a fight for control.[1230] And the term "indirect transfer of a contract" in the Investment Company Act provision defining an assignment as including any such indirect transfer does not extend to every change of "control or management" of an investment adviser.[1231]

§ 11.1. Investment Advisers.

Status, Duties and Liabilities Generally.—Investment advisers of an investment company or a mutual fund are fiduciaries,[1232] and they have a

---

[1230] Willheim v. Murchison, 342 F.2d 33 (2d Cir.), cert. denied, 382 U.S. 840, 86 S. Ct. 36, 15 L. Ed. 2d 82 (1965).

Coordinated transfer by several associates sharing controlling interest among them may meet Investment Company Act definition of assignment terminating investment company's contract with investment adviser or principal underwriter, but statutory provision contemplates that "controlling block" of stock exist and be transferred and not merely that purchases of large and small amounts of stock eventually bring controlling interest into one pair of hands. Willheim v. Murchison, 342 F.2d 33 (2d Cir.), cert. denied, 382 U.S. 840, 86 S. Ct. 36, 15 L. Ed. 2d 82 (1965).

[1231] Willheim v. Murchison, 342 F.2d 33 (2d Cir.), cert. denied, 382 U.S. 840, 86 S. Ct. 36, 15 L. Ed. 2d 82 (1965).

It was not congressional intent that mere change in management or control of investment adviser or underwriter should constitute an "assignment" terminating its contract with investment company. Willheim v. Murchison, 342 F.2d 33 (2d Cir.), cert. denied, 382 U.S. 840, 86 S. Ct. 36, 15 L. Ed. 2d 82 (1965).

It was not congressional intent that change in management or control of investment adviser or underwriter as result of proxy contest in parent corporation but without transfer of controlling block of parent's stock should constitute an "indirect transfer . . . of a controlling block of the assignor's securities," terminating contract with investment company. Willheim v. Murchison, 342 F.2d 33 (2d Cir.), cert. denied, 382 US. 840, 86 S. Ct. 36, 15 L. Ed. 2d 82 (1965).

[1232] **In general.**—

Brown v. Bullock, 194 F. Supp. 207 (S.D.N.Y. 1961), aff'd, 294 F.2d 415.

See § 2 of this chapter for discussion of investment advisers generally.

Who is "investment adviser".—

Trustee of funds constituting common-law trusts and open-end investment companies was not "investment adviser" of funds and was accordingly excluded from statutory definition of investment adviser. Kleinman v. Saminsky, 41 Del. Ch. 572, 200 A.2d 572, cert. denied, 379

fiduciary duty to manage companies with a single eye to their best interests, free from any self-dealing.[1233] And if the stockholders of a corporate investment adviser and the directors of an investment company use the power of their fiduciary positions for personal gain, they are legally responsible regardless of the form and sequence of their undertakings.[1234]

When a registered representative is giving more than the normal amount of incidental investment advice and has instilled in his customer such a degree of confidence in himself and reliance upon his advice that the customer clearly feels, and the registered representative knows that the

---

U.S. 900, 85 S. Ct. 186, 13 L. Ed. 2d 174 (1964).

A contract between an investment advisory company engaged by a mutual fund company and another whereby he was empowered to determine what securities should be purchased or sold by the mutual fund company rendered him an "investment adviser" within the Investment Company Act. Lutz v. Boas, 39 Del. Ch. 585, 171 A.2d 381.

[1233] Brown v. Bullock, 194 F. Supp. 207 (S.D.N.Y. 1961), aff'd, 294 F.2d 415.

Where the decision of a fund's director-officer who was employed by the adviser to serve as the portfolio manager of the fund to purchase securities was the result of his access to information developed by, and for the benefit of, the fund, and there was use of information developed by the fund for his own personal benefit, he was liable under common law to account to his principal, the fund, for profits derived. Cambridge Fund, Inc. v. Abella, 501 F. Supp. 598 (S.D.N.Y. 1980).

[1234] Krieger v. Anderson, 40 Del. Ch. 61, 173 A.2d 626.

If stockholders of corporate adviser of investment company breached fiduciary duty by dominating and causing board of directors of company to not really discharge its duty, to do what was best for company, by deciding to reinstate service contracts between adviser and company, company would be entitled to excess, if any, that adviser's stockholders received from purchaser of their stock in adviser over its fair value. Krieger v. Anderson, 40 Del. Ch. 61, 173 A.2d 626.

Question whether action of directors of investment company in voting to approve reinstatement of advisory contract between company and its corporate adviser was ineffective because director necessary to make quorum was interested through stock ownership in adviser was moot where stockholder approval of reinstatement of the advisory contract was required under Investment Company Act of 1940. Krieger v. Anderson, 40 Del. Ch. 61, 173 A.2d 626.

Investment adviser to mutual fund, which realized profits in connection with appointment of new adviser upon its recommendation, violated fiduciary duty. Rosenfeld v. Black, 445 F.2d 1337 (2d Cir. 1971).

Where investment adviser contracts were between investor, and investment adviser, officers, directors and major shareholders of adviser were not parties to contract, and no basis for piercing corporate veil was alleged, breach of contract claims against individual officers, directors and shareholders failed to state claim. Margaret Hall Found., Inc. v. Atlantic Fin. Mgt., Inc., 572 F. Supp. 1475 (D.C. Mass. 1983).

customer feels, that the registered representative is acting in the customer's interest, a fiduciary relationship may arise, notwithstanding the fact that a "blue card" giving the registered representative a power of attorney to trade the account has never been signed and filed.[1235] Generally, investment advisors are responsible only for making recommendations based upon their own business judgment and are not responsible for learning, let alone transmitting, all information which could influence market prices.[1236] Under certain circumstances, a duty to communicate information may exist from the time of the signing of a margin agreement, as in the case of an actual investment adviser as opposed to a mere broker.[1237] Mere decline in value from one day to another is insufficient to impose liability against an investment adviser for purchases of securities made for its customer or to measure damages therefor upon a wholesale basis.[1238] An investment adviser is not under a fiduciary duty to disclose to its client the mechanical research procedures it utilizes on the client's behalf.[1239]

Shareholders of an investment company have the right to insist that their directors engage investment advisory services to keep the company's portfolio attuned to the times.[1240]

Conflict of Interest.—A conflict of interest necessarily arises where a single investment adviser manages the portfolios of two investment companies bearing the same, or substantially similar, names.[1241] And by undertaking to manage two separate investment funds, an investment adviser's managers expose themselves to conflicting obligations and pressures, and if any duty owing either fund is breached, a suitable remedy is available to innocent injured persons.[1242] And it has been held that a registered mutual fund's investment adviser and its underwriter are under a duty of full

---

[1235] Courtland v. Walston & Co., 340 F. Supp. 1076 (S.D.N.Y. 1972).

[1236] Robinson v. Merrill Lynch, Pierce, Fenner & Smith, Inc., 337 F. Supp. 107 (ND. Ala. 1971), aff'd, 453 F.2d 417 (5th Cir. 1972).

[1237] Robinson v. Merrill Lynch, Pierce, Fenner & Smith, Inc., 337 F. Supp. 107 (ND. Ala. 1971), aff'd, 453 F.2d 417 (5th Cir. 1972).

[1238] Jones Mem. Trust v. Tsai Inv. Servs., Inc., 367 F. Supp. 491 (S.D.N.Y. 1973).

[1239] Jones Mem. Trust v. Tsai Inv. Servs., Inc., 367 F. Supp. 491 (S.D.N.Y. 1973).

[1240] Taussig v. Wellington Fund, Inc., 187 F. Supp. 179, aff'd, 318 F.2d 472, cert. denied, 374 U.S. 806, 83 S. Ct. 1693, 1695, 10 L. Ed. 2d 1031.

[1241] Taussig v. Wellington Fund, Inc., 187 F. Supp. 179, aff'd, 313 F.2d 472, cert. denied, 374 U.S. 806, 83 S. Ct. 1693, 1695, 10 L. Ed. 2d 1031.

[1242] Taussig v. Wellington Fund, Inc., 187 F. Supp. 179, aff'd, 313 F.2d 472, cert. denied, 374 U.S. 806, 83 S. Ct. 1693, 1695, 10 L. Ed. 2d 1031.

disclosure of information to those unaffiliated directors of the fund in every area where there was even a possible conflict of interest between their interests and the interests of the fund.[1243] But an improper conflict-of-interest situation was held not present in the organization of an investment fund although the trustee and the adviser were one and the same, where such arrangement was patently apparent to any prospective investor.[1244]

Approval of Investment Adviser's Contract.—Provisions of the Investment Company Act requiring approval of an investment adviser's contract cannot be frustrated by making a contract terminable at the will of either party, or by the mere absence of a formal written contract if a contract can be implied in fact between the parties.[1245] The statutory provision requiring stockholder approval of a new investment adviser to a mutual fund is not intended to withdraw safeguards already afforded by equity, but impliedly incorporates them.[1246] In requiring yearly approval of investment management contracts, Congress attempted to create an atmosphere of objectivity for the directors and shareholders of investment companies so they could specifically appraise and evaluate the performance of an investment adviser at relatively short periodic intervals, and if an investment adviser was not performing satisfactorily, Congress intended that an investment company should have complete freedom to terminate an advisory contract.[1247] But the requirement

---

[1243] Moses v. Burgin, 445 F.2d 369 (1st Cir.), rev'g 316 F. Supp. 31 (D. Mass.), cert. denied, 404 U.S. 994, 92 S. Ct. 532, 30 L. Ed. 2d 547 (1971).

A management investment company's (fund's) director-officer who had been employed by the adviser to serve as portfolio manager for the fund had a fiduciary duty of disclosure, there being sufficient "simultaneous" trading so that potential conflicts of interest arose in that his personal purchases might have resulted from his access to information developed by and/or for the benefit of the fund and in that the fund's purchase of some securities might have been influenced by his personal investment in those securities, but failure to make a disclosure was not a knowing breach where he understood that conflicts of interest did not arise when transactions involved small purchases such as his of only a few hundred shares. Cambridge Fund, Inc. v. Abella, 501 F. Supp. 598 (S.D.N.Y. 1980).

[1244] Saminsky v. Abbott, 41 Del. Ch. 320, 194 A.2d 549 (1968), aff'd sub nom. Kleinman v. Saminsky, 41 Del. Ch. 572, 200 A.2d 572, cert. denied, 379 U.S. 900, 85 S. Ct. 186, 13 L. Ed. 2d 174 (1964).

The structural arrangement of the fund, whereby the trustee and the adviser were one and same, did not violate the Investment Company Act. Saminsky v. Abbott, 41 Del. Ch. 320, 194 A.2d 549(1963), aff'd sub nom. Kleinman v. Saminsky, 41 Del. Ch. 572, 200 A.2d 572, cert. denied, 379 U.S. 900, 85 S. Ct. 186, 13 L. Ed. 2d 174 (1964).

[1245] Lutz v. Boas, 39 Del. Ch. 585, 171 A.2d 381.

[1246] Rosenfeld v. Black, 445 F.2d 1337 (2d Cir. 1971).

[1247] Taussig v. Wellington Fund, Inc., 187 F. Supp. 179, aff'd, 313 F.2d 472, cert. denied,

of approval of investment advisory agreements does not require shareholder approval of an accounting service agreement made with an investment adviser.[1248] The provision of the Investment Company Act relating to affiliations of directors, officers and employees, and the provision requiring, for renewal of a contract with an adviser, approval of a majority of the directors who are not parties to the contract or affiliated persons, must be read and considered separately.[1249] Thus, although an officer of a mutual fund company is within the classification of "affiliated persons of an investment adviser" for the purpose of the Investment Company Act provision precluding a company from having more than 60 percent directors who are investment advisers or affiliated persons, he is not an "affiliated person" within the meaning of the provision requiring, for the renewal of an advisory service agreement, approval by a majority of the directors who are not affiliated persons of the investment adviser.[1250]

Compensation Generally.—An investment advisory company under contract to provide investment advice to an investment company is entitled to make a profit aside from the salaries paid its executive personnel.[1251] The expectation of profits, however, is not an asset which the adviser can assign outright.[1252] And shareholders of an investment company who claim that compensation paid under an investment advisory contract is legally excessive have the risk of nonpersuasion.[1253] A federal statute makes it unlawful for any affiliated person of a registered investment company, acting as agent, to accept from any source any compensation for the purchase of any property for such registered company.[1254]

---

374 U.S 806, 83 S. Ct. 1693, 1695, 10 L. Ed. 2d 1031.

[1248] Acampora v. Birkland, 220 F. Supp. 527.

[1249] Acampora v. Birkland, 220 F. Supp. 527.

[1250] Acampora v. Birkland, 220 F. Supp. 527.

Where open-end investment funds had no investment adviser within meaning of Investment Company Act, there was none with whom directors offends could be affiliated within prohibitory limits of the Act. Kleinman v. Saminsky, 41 Del Ch. 572, 200 A.2d 572, cert. denied, 379 U.S. 900, 85 S. Ct. 186, 13 L. Ed. 2d 174.

[1251] Saxe v. Brady, 40 Del. Ch. 474, 184 A.2d 602.

[1252] Rosenfeld v. Black, 445 F.2d 1337 (2d Cir. 1971).

[1253] Saxe v. Brady, 40 Del. Ch. 474, 184 A.2d 602.

[1254] **In general.—**

15 U.S.C.S. § 80a-17(e) (1).

Elements of offense.—

Requisite intent, under statute making it unlawful for any affiliated person of a registered

(Text continued on page 329)

---

investment company, acting as agent, to accept from any source any compensation for the purchase of any property for such registered company, is intent to give and accept a gratuity in appreciation of past or future conduct. United States v. Deutsch, 451 F.2d 98 (2d Cir. 1971), cert. denied, 404 U.S. 1019, 92 S. Ct. 682, 30 L. Ed. 2d 667 (1972).

Intent to influence is not element of statute making it unlawful for any affiliated person of a registered investment company, acting as agent, to accept from any source any compensation for the purchase of any property for such registered company. United States v. Deutsch, 451 F.2d 98 (2d Cir. 1971), cert. denied, 404 U.S. 1019, 92 S. Ct. 682, 30 L. Ed. 2d 667 (1972).

Under statute making it unlawful for any affiliated person of a registered investment company, acting as agent, to accept from any source any compensation for purchase of any property for such registered company, offense is complete when the compensation is delivered and received with the forbidden intent. United States v. Deutsch, 451 F.2d 98 (2d Cir. 1971), cert. denied, 404 U.S. 1019, 92 S. Ct. 682, 30 L. Ed. 2d 667 (1972).

Phrase "acting as agent," in statute making it unlawful for any affiliated person of a registered investment company, acting as agent, to accept from any source any compensation for purchase of any property for such registered company, does not define a more limited subclass of affiliated persons: those who have capacity to influence investment decisions, but rather the phrase "acting as agent" is a descriptive phrase distinguishing affiliated persons acting as brokers from those who are not acting as brokers in connection with a sale or purchase of securities for investment company. United States v. Deutsch, 451 F.2d 98 (2d Cir. 1971), cert. denied, 404 U.S. 1019, 92 S. Ct. 682, 30 L. Ed. 2d 667 (1972).

Phrase "acting as agent," in statute making it unlawful for any affiliated person of a registered investment company, acting as agent, to accept from any source any compensation for purchase of any property for such registered company, was not intended to mean acting as agent for an outsider dealing with the investment company and not as agent for the investment company itself. United States v. Deutsch, 451 F.2d 98 (2d Cir. 1971), cert. denied, 404 U.S. 1019, 92 S. Ct. 682, 30 L. Ed. 2d 667 (1972).

Trial court's interpretation of phrase "acting as agent," in statute making it unlawful for any affiliated person of a registered investment company, acting as agent, to accept from any source any compensation for purchase of any property for such registered company, as being merely descriptive of a subclass of affiliated persons was incorrect, but defendant was not prejudiced, in that such interpretation, if anything, posed a greater burden on government in proving its case than was necessary. United States v. Deutsch, 451 F.2d 98 (2d Cir. 1971), cert. denied, 404 U.S. 1019, 92 S. Ct. 682, 30 L. Ed. 2d 667 (1972).

Phrase "acting as agent," in statute making it unlawful for any affiliated person of a registered investment company, acting as agent, to accept from any source any compensation for purchase of any property for such registered company, is a descriptive phrase and does not require showing that the recipient of the compensation took any action as a result thereof. United States v. Deutsch, 451 F.2d 98 (2d Cir. 1971), cert. denied, 404 U.S. 1019, 92 S. Ct. 682, 30 L. Ed. 2d 667 (1972).

An affiliated person is acting as agent within meaning of statute making it unlawful for any affiliated person of a registered investment company, acting as agent, to accept from any source any compensation for purchase of any property for such registered company in all

Illustrative cases with regard to compensation paid to investment advisers are treated in the footnote.[1255]

---

cases when he is not acting as broker for the investment company. United States v. Deutsch, 451 F.2d 98 (2d Cir. 1971), cert. denied, 404 U.S. 1019, 92 S. Ct. 682, 30 L. Ed. 2d 667 (1972).

Admissibility of evidence.—

In prosecution for aiding and abetting an affiliated person of registered investment companies in receiving compensation for purchase of securities for such investment companies, comment on defendant's sophistication in financial matters was relevant to show knowledge on his part of what he was doing; his insistence on use of nominee names evinced a desire to conceal transaction, from which jury could infer consciousness of guilt. United States v. Deutsch, 451 F.2d 98 (2d Cir. 1971), cert. denied, 404 U.S. 1019, 92 S. Ct. 682, 30 L. Ed. 2d 667 (1972).

Sufficiency of evidence.—

Evidence, in prosecution for aiding and abetting affiliated person of registered investment companies in receiving compensation for purchase of securities for such investment companies in violation of the investment Company Act of 1940 and of the aider and abettor statute, was sufficient to prove compensation. United States v. Deutsch, 451 F.2d 98 (2d Cir. 1971), cert. denied, 404 U.S. 1019, 92 S. Ct. 682, 30 L. Ed. 2d 667 (1972).

Instructions to jury.—

In prosecution for violating statute making it unlawful for any affiliated person of a registered investment company, acting as agent, to accept from any source any compensation for the purchase of any property for such registered company, defendant, who admittedly sold an affiliated person registered company's note at a substantial discount, and who claimed that when he made commitment to sell note he had no idea that the note and attached warrant would be so valuable eight or nine months later, was entitled to an instruction merely that the jury could not convict without being persuaded beyond a reasonable doubt that agreement to buy the note was made with knowledge that it constituted something of value. United States v. Deutsch, 451 F.2d 98 (2d Cir. 1971), cert. denied, 404 U.S. 1019, 92 S. Ct. 682, 30 L. Ed. 2d 667 (1972).

[1255] **Comparison of compensation with other fees.—**

Comparison of services rendered other mutual funds by investment advisers for fees of one half of one per cent of net asset value charged by management company to mutual fund company could be no more than evidentiary on question of whether such a fee, in instant case, was excessive. Acampora v. Birkland, 220 F. Supp. 527.

Compensation held not excessive.—

Payment by open-end investment company, pursuant to contract with its investment adviser of an amount equal to one half of one per cent of average daily net assets of fund was not unreasonable percentage under all circumstances, and the dollar amount, being $2,780,000, was not by itself excessive. Saxe v. Brady, 40 Del. Ch. 474, 184 A.2d 602.

In stockholder's derivative action for an accounting by officers of an investment company providing investment advisory service, on ground that affiliated directors had through management company devices as fiduciaries paid themselves excessive contributions to

(*Text continued on page 331*)

---

detriment of fund and its stockholders, evidence failed to establish that compensation paid for investment advisory service was legally excessive as to the years 1956 to 1960 inclusive. Meiselman v. Eberstadt, 39 Del. Ch. 563, 170 A.2d 720.

In view of impossibility of evaluating services rendered mutual company by management company which acted as investment adviser, it could not be said that one-half of one percent of net asset value paid management company was excessive. Acampora v. Birkland, 220 F. Supp. 527.

Fee based on average of quarter.—

Under the advisory fee paragraph of an agreement between a mutual fund and its investment adviser, the first payment to the adviser was not to be computed on the basis of average net asset value of the fund for the month of September only, but on the basis of a figure representing an average of the net asset values for each of the three months in the quarter, July 1 through September 30. Galfand v. Chestnutt, 402 F. Supp. 1318 (S.D.N.Y. 1975).

Attorneys fees.—

Equity required that counsel fees paid or accrued by a mutual fund as expenses for outside attorneys solely for the purpose of a stockholder's derivative action brought to void a new investment advisory agreement increasing the expense ratio limitation to one and one half should not be considered as expenses in applying the one percent limitation in the original agreement. Galfand v. Chestnutt, 402 F. Supp. 1318 (S.D.N.Y. 1975).

Reimbursement for attorney fees and costs not abuse of discretion.—

District court did not abuse its discretion in requiring real estate investment trust to reimburse manager for attorney fees and costs under section of declaration of trust which allowed court to direct trust to indemnify even officers who had been held liable to trust if in view of all circumstances, officer was fairly and reasonably entitled to indemnity for such expense, which court deemed proper even though officer of manager had been required to reimburse trust in his role as trustee for excess compensation paid to managers and even though trust prevailed on one aspect of prior interlocutory appeal. Wisconsin Real Estate Inv. Trust v. Weinstein, 781 F.2d 589 (7th Cir. 1986).

Fee credits used to reduce advisory compensation.—

District court was entitled to use fee credits manager returned to real estate investment trust to reduce amount of advisory compensation in determining amount officer of manager who had been appointed trustee was required to reimburse trust for commissions paid to manager which exceeded adjusted compensation in those years in which manager had positive adjusted advisory compensation under provision which required that advisory compensation be reduced by $1 per dollar of commissions paid to manager on particularly advantageous purchases or sales of property. Wisconsin Real Estate Inv. Trust v. Weinstein, 781 F.2d 589 (7th Cir. 1986).

Full contract commission after advisory compensation reduced to zero.—

Once real estate investment trust manager's advisory compensation was reduced to zero by offsets for commissions paid to manager on particularly advantageous purchases or sales of property and by credits paid by manager to trust, manager was entitled to full

Commissions Where Investment Company Act Violated.—The Investment Company Act provision limiting commissions to the usual amounts does not automatically permit a broker to keep the usual commissions where he has violated other provisions of the Act.[1256] Thus, a brokerage firm which entered into an unratified and void implied contract to act as an investment adviser to a mutual fund company could not profit from such violation of the Investment Company Act, and was liable to the company for the commissions received when it so acted, less its properly allocated expenses.[1257] And where an investment advisory company owned by the founders of a mutual fund entered into a void contract retaining another as an investment adviser for the fund, the founders were held liable to the fund for the full commissions paid the broker for which such investment adviser worked, but the fund was held required to elect whether to recover such commissions or management fees for which the founders were also liable to the fund.[1258] A registered mutual fund's investment adviser and its underwriter were guilty of gross misconduct within the meaning of the Investment Company Act in failing to disclose to the unaffiliated directors of the fund the possibility of recapture of the portion of brokerage commissions the fund was obligated to

---

commissions for which it contracted. Wisconsin Real Estate Inv. Trust v. Weinstein, 781 F.2d 589 (7th Cir. 1986).

Real estate investment trust was not entitled to return of shares of stock accepted by manager in lieu of amount trustees agreed to pay manager in connection with property trust acquired, in addition to return of excess advisory compensation paid to manager so as to permit trust to recoup appreciated value of stock and avoid paying dividends accrued thereon. Wisconsin Real Estate Inv. Trust v. Weinstein, 781 F.2d 589 (7th Cir. 1986).

Calendar year as accounting period.—

District court could choose calendar year as accounting period in determining amount of compensation to be received by manager of real estate investment trust where contract, which required manager's compensation as advisor to be reduced by $1 per dollar of commissions paid to manager on particularly advantageous purchases or sales of property, failed to specify period over which offsets should occur. Wisconsin Real Estate Inv. Trust v. Weinstein, 781 F.2d 589 (7th Cir. 1986).

1256 Lutz v. Boas, 39 Del. Ch. 585, 171 A.2d 381.

1257 Lutz v. Boas, 39 Del. Ch. 585, 171 A.2d 381.

Brokerage firm which entered into illegal and void contract, with investment advisory company owned by organizers of mutual fund, to act as investment adviser for mutual fund would, under general principles of equity, be held liable for management fees paid by fund company to advisory company only to extent that such payments exceeded amount which brokerage firm was to be required to repay fund company from commissions received. Lutz v. Boas, 89 Del. Ch. 585, 171 A.2d 381.

1258 Lutz v. Boss, 39 Del. Ch. 585, 171 A.2d 381.

pay on purchases and sales of securities in which it invested its assets through the fund's use of its underwriter as a recipient of a give-up on the understanding that the underwriter's parent, the fund's investment adviser, would give the fund a credit against charges for investment advisory services, and were liable for damages under the Investment Company Act.[1259]

Sale of Stock of Corporate Adviser.—Stockholders of a corporate adviser of an investment company have the right to approach representatives of a prospective buyer about the possibility of selling their stock, and absent any breach of duty, to obtain what they can for such shares, including as an element of value the good will arising from an expectancy of renewal of the service contracts between the adviser and the investment company.[1260] However, such stockholders do owe the investment company's board of directors the duty of disclosing what they intend to do as to selling their stock, and of not interfering with the exercise of the board's judgment in deciding what is best for the investment company in light of the proposed sale; that is, whether to reinstate the service contracts between the adviser and the company.[1261] And an investment company stockholder cannot object to a failure to give the company's stockholders an opportunity to vote upon whether to approve the sale of stock of the company's adviser, where the condition of such approval was not imposed by law, but by the parties to the sale of stock.[1262] But alleged breaches by stockholders of a corporate adviser of an investment company of their duty not to dominate and cause the board of directors of the company to decide to reinstate the service contracts

---

[1259] Moses v. Burgin, 445 F.2d 369 (1st Cir.), rev'g 316 F. Supp. 31 (D. Mass.), cert. denied, 404 U.S. 994, 92 S. Ct. 532, 30 L. Ed. 2d 547 (1971).

[1260] Krieger v. Anderson, 40 Del. Ch. 61, 173 A.2d 626.

Stockholders of a corporate adviser of an investment company were held not to have breached their fiduciary duty owed to the investment company, where the stockholders sold their stock in the corporate adviser and received only the fair value for their shares. Krieger v. Anderson, 40 Del. Ch. 151, 177 A.2d 203 (1962).

[1261] Krieger v. Anderson, 40 Del. Ch. 61, 173 A.2d 626.

Claims of investment company's stockholder against stockholders of corporate adviser of company for allegedly controlling company's board and making it decide, against best interests of company, to reinstate service contracts between corporations were not barred by estoppel or acquiescence, although company stockholder did not vote against renewal of advisory contract or bring derivative action until day of meeting of company's stockholders to decide whether to approve sale of adviser's stock and reinstatement of advisory contract. Krieger v. Anderson, 40 Del. Ch. 61, 173 A2d 626.

[1262] Krieger v. Anderson, 40 Del. Ch. 61, 173 A.2d 626.

between the adviser and the company, regardless of what was best for the company in view of a proposed sale of the adviser's stock, cannot be ratified by the company's stockholders without unanimous approval, and a majority approval by the company's stockholders of the proposed sale does not constitute approval of such breaches.[1263] And various matters and circumstances have been held relevant and material in determining whether stockholders of a corporate adviser have breached their fiduciary duty to an investment company in a sale of the adviser's stock.[1264]

As to miscellaneous matters arising with respect to investment advisers, see the footnote.[1265]

[1263] Krieger v. Anderson, 40 Del. Ch. 61, 173 A.2d 626.

[1264] **In general.—**

Krieger v. Anderson, 40 Del. Ch. 151, 177 A.2d 203 (1962).

It was relevant and material, though not dispositive of breach of duty issues, that stock sold by stockholders of a corporate adviser had relatively similar value in the hands of stockholders and buyers because consummation of purchase of stock was conditioned on renewal of service contracts. Krieger v. Anderson, 40 Del. Ch. 151, 177 A.2d 203 (1962).

Goodwill factor.—

In determining whether sellers of the stock received more than "fair value" of stock for violating their fiduciary duty to the company, "goodwill" or "expectancy" value arising from the possibility of renewal of the service contracts between the adviser and the company would be a relevant value factor. Krieger v. Anderson, 40 Del. Ch. 61, 173 A.2d 626.

[1265] Implied contract.—Contract by which brokerage firm would act as investment adviser for mutual funds within Investment Company Act provisions requiring approval of such agreements was to be implied where brokerage firm was told initially that fund company was its employee's new customer, it knew that investment advisory company which engaged it was paid large fee as investment adviser for fund and that its own department was providing most of such advice to mutual funds, fund company's chief executive officer caused substantial business to be diverted to firm in return for nominal employment of certain persons and arrangements were made directly with chief executive officer of fund company who owned majority interest in advisory company. Lutz v. Boas, 39 Del. Ch. 585, 171 A.2d 381.

Vote for advisory agreement did not preclude shareholder's action.—

Action of shareholder in mutual fund company in voting for investment advisory agreement was not in opposition to recovery in his derivative action on behalf of fund against investment adviser and others for contract violations. Acampora v. Birkland, 220 F. Supp. 527.

Liability for losses.—

Broker providing principal advice concerning purchase and sale of securities for mutual fund company, as investment adviser under void contract, and executing such orders was liable to fund company for losses sustained from costs and losses incurred on excessive

(Text continued on page 335)

---

trading but only to extent that such losses and costs could be specifically identified and sale-reacquisition prima facie liability period would be limited to 30 days and costs would not include profit made by brokerage firm which it was required to return on other grounds. Lutz v. Boas, 39 Del. Ch. 585, 171 A.2d 381.

Liability for unearned advisory fees.—

Nonaffiliated directors of mutual fund company who were grossly negligent in failing to discover illegal transactions between brokerage firm and its employee and investment advisory company which was receiving management fees from fund company and which was owned by fund company organizers were jointly and severally liable with advisory company and brokerage firm for unearned advisory fees paid to advisory company and for losses resulting from sale and repurchase of same securities. Lutz v. Boas, 39 Del. Ch. 585, 171 A.2d 381.

Liability for management fees paid to advisory company by fund company.—

Founders of mutual fund company who owned investment advisory company rendered themselves jointly and severally liable to fund company for management fees paid advisory company by fund company where they breached their fiduciary duty and exceeded their authorized powers by permitting advisory company purportedly to commit fund company's brokerage business to another far a period beyond that provided in agreement with fund company and took management fees for services substantially all of which were performed by such other party in return for brokerage fees. Lutz v. Boas, 39 Del. Ch. 585, 171 A.2d 381.

Denial of injunction held proper exercise of discretion.—

Denial of plaintiff's motion to enjoin investment adviser of defendant corporation from acting as broker for corporation was proper exercise of discretion in stockholder's derivative suit, where plaintiff failed to show that irreparable injury would result if injunction were denied. Leighton v. One William St. Fund, Inc., 343 F.2d 565 (2d Cir. 1965).

Transfer of fiduciary office.—

Fact that there was no change in either the managing personnel or policies followed by corporate investment advisor to mutual funds as a result of 1969 and 1971 transfers of the advisor's controlling stock by officer-shareholders did not mean that there was not an effective transfer of the fiduciary office. Kukman v. Baum, 346 F. Supp. 55 (N.D. Ill. 1972).

Claim for theft.—

Where president of investment company in dealing with investor's account believed he was acting as agent of the company and sent investor spurious monthly dividend statements and spurious inventories on letterheads and forms of the company, claim for thefts from investor's account against company in equitable receivership should have been allowed even though investor, more than 25 years before the thefts were committed, had executed power of attorney in favor of person who, after becoming president of the investment company committed the thefts. SEC v. First Sec. Co., 466 F.2d 1035 (7th Cir. 1972).

Shareholders' suit for breach of fiduciary duty in connection with merger.—

Where gain realized by shareholders and officers of corporate advisor of mutual funds in merger of advisor and another corporation would be measure of recovery for breach of fiduciary duty to funds and their shareholders, who allegedly approved merger as result of

§ 11.2. Principal Underwriters.

The purpose of the part of the Investment Company Act of 1940 which provides that if a principal underwriter's contract with a fund continues for more than two years, there must be annual approval thereof by the fund's board of directors or a majority of its shareholders, is to afford the shareholders (or nonaffiliated directors) an opportunity to pass upon the continuation of the relationship, and maintain some control over the conduct of the principal underwriter in its sale of securities.[1266] And such statutory provision cannot be subverted by an agreement limiting the term of a principal underwriter's contract to some particular period.[1267] Thus, a series of contracts between a principal underwriter and a common-law trust fund providing for no specified termination and differing only in regard to the amount of compensation allotted to the underwriter for its services, even though entered into at two-year intervals, was held void for failure to secure annual approval as required by the statute.[1268] An underwriter to a mutual fund does not owe any common-law fiduciary obligation with respect to a sale or change of control of a fund's investment advisor.[1269]

§ 12. Liability.

In General.—Directors of loan, trust and investment companies are under a legal responsibility akin to that of trustees and are liable for misconduct, ignorance or negligence;[1270] even mere honorary directors are not excused

---

misleading proxy statements, all pending cases involved same merger transaction, parties, facts and legal issues, and it was not clear whether current shareholders or shareholder, at time of statement should participate in recovery, one direct action by funds against defendants, with shareholders allowed to intervene, rather than class action or stockholders' derivative suits would be proper way to proceed. King v. Kansas City Southern Industries, Inc., 56 F.R.D. 96 (N.D. Ill. 1972).

Allocation of commissions.—

The action of an investment adviser in allocating the commissions to compensate dealers for sales promotion and research did not violate the provision of an open-end mutual fund's certificate of incorporation which required it to receive not less than the net asset value for each share sold. Tannenbaum v. Zeller, 552 F.2d 402 (2d Cir. 1977), rev'g 399 F. Supp. 945 (S.D.N.Y. 1975).

[1266] Saminsky v. Abbott, 40 Del. Ch. 528, 186 A.2d 765.

[1267] Saminsky v. Abbott, 40 Del. Ch. 528, 185 A.2d 765.

[1268] Saminsky v. Abbott, 40 Del. Ch. 528, 185 A.2d 765.

[1269] Schlusselberg v. Colonial Management Associates, Inc., 389 F. Supp. 733 (D. Mass. 1974).

[1270] Prudential Trust Co. v. Moore, 245 Mass. 311, 139 N.E. 645.

from this liability.[1271] And private parties can resort to the federal courts for relief from gross abuses of trust and gross misconduct on the part of directors of registered investment companies.[1272] Thus, the officers and directors of a bank or loan company must exercise ordinary care and prudence in the administration of its affairs, and the degree of care required depends on the facts and circumstances of each particular case.[1273]

Directors sued for malfeasance have no interest in and cannot complain of a settlement between a commissioner of banks and other directors, and they cannot compel such others to remain parties merely in order to contribute to the expenses of the litigation.[1274] And a settlement in such a case does not operate as a release of the other directors, the commissioner having reserved the right to sue them.[1275] Where a deceased director's signing of a certain contract between the vice-president of a trust company and its directors and officers was conditioned on all directors and officers signing the agreement,

---

[1271] **In general.—**

Kavanaugh v. Gould, 223 N.Y. 103, 199 N.E. 237.

But under the Iowa statute the estate of deceased trust company director held not liable for loss of funds of an estate, deposited with trust company as executor which had become commingled with other funds, on ground that director failed to object to company's illegal practice of commingling such funds, where director was not in active management of company affairs, was not large stockholder, and received no salary, since director was guilty of "nonfeasance," as distinguished from "misfeasance" and "malfeasance." Proksch v. Bettendorf, 218 Iowa 1376, 257 N.W. 383.

[1272] Tanzer v. Huffines, 314 F. Supp. 189 (D. Del. 1970).

[1273] **In general.—**

Williams v. Fidelity Loan, etc., Co., 142 Va. 43, 128 S.E. 615, 45 A.L.R. 664; Kavanaugh v. Gould, 223 N.Y. 103, 119 N.E. 237; Finley v. Exchange Trust Co., 183 Okla. 167, 80 P.2d 296, 117 A.L.R. 162.

Fiduciary obligations of officers of corporation engaged in handling and investment of money of others were not different from fiduciary obligations of officers of banking institution, and extended beyond good faith and freedom from evil intent, and included duty to exercise that degree of care, attention, and good judgment which competent businessman would exercise with reference to his own affairs. Goodwin v. Simpson, 292 Mass. 148, 197 N.E. 628 (1935).

Standard of duty of directors of trust company in declaring and paying dividend whose prescribed method is followed is the standard of integrity, skill, and prudence fixed by common law for performance of functions of such directors generally. Medford Trust Co. v. McKnight, 292 Mass. 1, 197 N.E. 649.

[1274] In re Commissioner of Banks, 249 Mass. 144, 144 N.E 73.

[1275] Roseville Trust Co. v. Mott, 93 N.J. Eq. 229, 107 A. 462, aff'd sub nom. La Monte v. Mott, 93 N.J. Eq. 229, 116 A. 269.

the agreement was held not binding on the deceased director's estate where two directors had not signed it.[1276]

For other cases illustrating the liability of officers and directors of such companies, see the footnote.[1277]

[1276] In re Riday's Estate, 317 Pa. 529, 177 A. 812.

[1277] Executive officers are responsible for truth of report voluntarily signed, verified, and attested by them with knowledge that it was report of condition of company in response to an official call notwithstanding that such report was prepared by another, in absence of showing that they were deceived without undue fault on their part. State v. Steneck, 118 N.J.L. 268, 192 A. 381, aff'd, 120 N.J.L. 188, 198 A. 848, cert. denied, 305 U.S. 627, 59 S. Ct. 89, 83 L. Ed. 401.

Liability for payments.—Treasurer of corporation which solicited handling and investment of money of others held not liable for payment to corporate officer of personal expenses or advance salary in absence of showing that officer was not entitled thereto or that treasurer knew or should have known that payment was improper. Goodwin v. Simpson, 292 Mass. 148, 197 N.E. 628 (1935).

Treasurer held not liable for payment to acting general manager on day treasurer assumed office, where managing director, whose statement there was no reason to doubt, informed treasurer that corporation was indebted to acting general manager in greater amount than sum paid and books of corporation so indicated, notwithstanding that director, had not voted to employ organizer and acting general manager. Goodwin v. Simpson, 292 Mass 148, 197 N.E 628.

Treasurer held not liable for payment to purchaser. on installment plan of collateral trustee shares which had not been covered by underlying securities of amount representing dividends to which purchaser would have been entitled had securities been bought, notwithstanding that treasurer knew about installment sales, and that sales had been made without approval by state public utilities department, where purchasers had not repudiated contracts of purchase. Goodwin v. Simpson, 292 Mass. 148, 197 N.E. 628 (1935).

Liability for dividends.—

Director of corporation which solicited handling and investment of money of others held liable for dividends with interest from date of payment declared with aid of his vote from corporation's assets on preferred stock of another corporation. Goodwin v. Simpson, 292 Mass. 148, 197 N.E. 628 (1935).

Directors of trust company having followed statutory method prescribed for ascertainment of earnings available for dividends on deposits in savings department, and having acted with integrity, skill and prudence, held not liable for dividends paid in excess of earnings available therefor, where they had been mistaken as to amount of earnings so available. Medford Trust Co. v. McKnight, 292 Mass. 1, 197 N.E. 649.

President of loan company, who persuaded directors to declare dividend which president paid to the stockholders, while representing to directors that the company had net earnings out of which dividends could be declared, was guilty of misapplication of corporation's moneys, within statute imposing double liability on officers for declaring dividends. or distributing corporation's moneys to its members otherwise than from actual legitimate net

(*Text continued on page 341*)

---

earnings, which in any manner increases corporation's debt. Franklin Say., etc., Co. v. American Employers Ins. Co., 99 F.2d 494.

Liability for profits in individual transactions.—Where trust company's subsidiary underwrote sale to public of 500,000 corporate shares, but responsible officers of subsidiary did not consider it expedient to take a larger amount, after subsidiary's interest in such stock had been fixed, directors of trust company and subsidiary war. not liable to stockholders for profits mad. by purchasing and reselling similar stock in such manner as not to compete with subsidiary's marketing operations, for breach of fiduciary duty in not buying for their corporation, on theory of "corporate opportunity" or "business opportunity." The stockholders were required to establish that circumstances imposed upon directors a mandate to buy for the subsidiary. Litwin v. Allen, 25 N.Y.S.2d 667.

Where directors of trust company comprised practically all directors of trust company's subsidiary which had accepted block of stock for underwriting sale thereof to public, it must be assumed that they knew that subsidiary's interest in the offering of such stock was limited to the block already taken, and directors' vote recording such fact, although desirable, would have been a mere formality, and its absence could not affect rights of such directors to purchase similar stock for their own individual profit. Litwin v. Allen, 25 N.Y.S.2d 667.

Investment of savings deposits in loan on security of pledge of second mortgage on property on which trust company already had first mortgage hold ultra vires, rendering members of investment committee approving loan prima facie responsible for losses resulting therefrom, notwithstanding absence of express finding of negligence on their part. And this is true although the loan had been made by finance committee before it was approved by investment committee. Medford Trust Co. v. McKnight, 292 Mass. 1, 197 N.E. 649.

Where investment committee of trust company would have been negligent in approving particular loan by savings department as a new loan, they were equally responsible for loss resulting therefrom, notwithstanding, though money was transferred from savings department to commercial department, no money was paid out on loan, and trust company as a whole was benefited, since deposits in savings department are required to be kept separate from general assets of company, and are specially protected. Medford Trust Co. v. McKnight, 292 Mass. 1, 197 N.E. 649.

Where clients sought trust company's participation in loan, disclosures showing clients' need of assistance and probable disastrous effect on business generally if loan were not made, would not justify making of bad loan for the purpose, but justified trust company's directors in making careful investigation and giving close consideration to clients' immediate needs, as affecting directors' personal liability to stockholders for resulting loss. Litwin v. Allen, 25 N.Y.S.2d 667.

President fraudulently placing defaulted mortgage in mortgage department of trust company for sale of participations to public held liable to purchasers of participations for amounts paid therefor on tender of certificates duly indorsed. He was under duty to warn purchaser. and guilty of fraud where no such warning was given. And nonjoinder of trust company in suit against him did not preclude recovery where no objection was raised until final argument. Pridmore v. Steneck, 120 NJ. Eq. 567, 186 A. 513, modified, 122 N.J. Eq. 35, 191 A. 861.

(Text continued on page 341)

Improvident purchase of bonds.—

Where trust company purchased block of railroad bonds at par, which was 5½ points below the market, giving an option to seller to repurchase for the same price within six months, at which time if option was not exercised the trust company's wholly-owned subsidiary would take over the bonds at the price paid, trust company's directors and officers were liable to stockholders for resulting loss, on ground that the transaction was ultra vires and improvident. Litwin v. Allen, 25 N.Y.S.2d 667.

Liability extended to all directors who were present and voted at meetings of executive committee and board of directors approving the transaction, and to one who did not actually vote on the transaction as director but actively participated and acquiesced, and to officers not director, who actively participated. Litwin v. Allen, 25 N.Y.S.2d 667.

The liability should be restricted to that portion of the loss which accrued within the option period, making allowance for a period thereafter during which directors could make reasonable efforts to sell the bonds, and should not extend to total loss suffered when bonds were ultimately sold. Litwin v. Allen, 25 N.Y.S.2d 667.

Officers of trustee corporation were liable to bondholders, to whom corporation had sold bonds, based upon a leasehold but purporting to be based upon mortgage upon the fee if they knew of fraudulent representations or had such knowledge of facts as would have led them to full knowledge of all the facts, had they acted in exercise of their duty as directors. Wells v. Carlsen, 130 Neb. 773, 266 N.W. 618 (1936).

Sale of collateral.—Where sale of collateral held by trust company for loan was fair, open, and competitive, price fixed at such sale determined value of the collateral sold, for purposes of suit by stockholders against trust company's directors to recover loss resulting from the sale on ground of breach of fiduciary duty. Litwin v. Allen, 25 N.Y.S.2d 667.

Making accommodation note.—

Where an officer of a trust company makes a note for a large amount, payable to the company, as an accommodation for the president of the company, on his assurance that he will never be asked to pay it, he is liable on the note, unless the company itself agreed that he should not be held upon it. Chestnut St. Trust, etc., Co. v. Hart, 217 Pa. 506, 66 A. 870 (1907).

Federal sanctions against gross misconduct and abuse of trust.—

Sections of Investment Company Act providing federal sanctions against gross misconduct and abuse of trust on part of directors, officers, investment advisers and principal underwriters of registered investment company, were enacted to enforce duties imposed by investment. Company Act. Brown v. Bullock, 194 F. Supp. 207 (S.D.N.Y. 1961), aff'd, 294 F.2d 415.

Annual approval of management contract.—

Complaint by stockholders of diversified open-end management investment company that directors' annual approval of management contracts occurred without any real consideration of merits was sufficient to allege violation of federal statute requiring annual approval of management contract. Brown v. Bullock, 294 F.2d 415.

(Text continued on page 341)

Excessive management fees.—

Complaint of shareholders of mutual fund against officers and directors of fund, alleging, among other things, excessive management fees, stated claim for conversion of funds, assets in violation of Investment Company Act of 1940. Brown v. Bullock, 194 F. Supp. 207 (S.D.N.Y. 1961), aff'd, 294 F.2d 415.

Mutual fund was entitled to recover from broker and nonaffiliated directors management fees paid advisory investment company and brokerage profits realized by broker under void contract but total recovery could not exceed management fees which were greater than brokerage profits. Lutz v. Boas, 40 Del. Ch. 130, 178 A.2d 853.

Effect of exculpatory clause.—

Corporate trustee responsible for management of mutual investment fund, except for purchase and sale of portfolio securities, was "director" within statute prohibiting indenture of trust of investment company from containing provision protecting or purporting to protect any director against liability, to which he would otherwise be subject for misfeasance, gross negligence or reckless disregard of duties, and clause of trust agreement to effect that no shareholder should have right to accounting except upon furnishing indemnity satisfactory to trustee, violated act. Chabot v. Empire Trust Co., 301 F.2d 453.

Brokerage practices held not violative of management contracts.—

Evidence in a derivative open-end mutual fund shareholder's suit complaining of brokerage practices, including testimony as to industry usage of the brokerage showed that the adviser by allocating brokerage commissions and give-ups to reward dealers for selling shares and providing the fund with research and statistical information did not violate the management and distribution contracts with the fund which were silent on the subject of allocation of excess portfolio commissions. Tannenbaum v. Zeller, 552 F.2d 402 (2d Cir. 1977), rev'g 399 F. Supp. 945 (S.D.N.Y. 1975).

Usability for acts of employee.—

Acts of investment banker's employee in disclosing information obtained through employment pertaining to tender offerer's plan to acquire target corporation's stock were not of same general nature or similar to authorized conduct so as to impose derivative liability on investment banker even though acts were unauthorized where only link between tip and employment duties was that latter constituted source of tip, illegal trading did not take place on or use facilities of employer, and employee's usual responsibilities did not relate to purchase and sale of securities for his own or for anyone else's account. Moss v. Morgan Stanley, Inc., 553 F. Supp. 1347 (S.D.N.Y. 1083).

Mere fact that business of investment banker related to securities generally was not sufficient to convert acts of investment banker's employee, who disclosed information obtained through employment pertaining to tender offerer's plan to acquire target corporation's stock, into acts within scope of employment or acts similar in nature to authorized conduct. Moss v. Morgan Stanley, Inc., 553 F. Supp. 1847 (S.D.N.Y. 1983).

Insider loans.—

"Insider" loan from an industrial loan and investment company which is in excess of $60,000, even with approval of board of directors, is unlawful. State v. Bargen, 219 Neb. 416, 363 N.W.2d 393 (1985).

Breach of Fiduciary Duty.—Directors of trust and investment companies occupy a fiduciary relationship to their company.[1278] Persons purporting to

---

Information charging that defendant was an active officer or director of an industrial loan and investment company and that he directly or indirectly borrowed funds of the company in an amount exceeding $160,000 on one note and approximately $8,700 on another note alleged a criminal offense. State v. Bargen, 219 Neb. 416, 363 N.W.2d 393 (1985).

Prosecution presented sufficient factual basis to convict defendant of obtaining loans from industrial loan and investment company for which he worked as an active officer or director in an amount which exceeded statutory limits. State v. Bargen, 219 Neb. 416, 363 N.W.2d 393 (1985).

Trial court did not abuse its discretion in imposing six months' county jail term following defendant's conviction for obtaining loans from industrial loan and investment company for which he worked as an active officer or director in an amount exceeding statutory limits. State v. Bargen, 219 Neb. 416, 363 N.W.2d 393 (1985).

Information charging that defendant was an active officer or director of an industrial loan and investment company and that he directly or indirectly borrowed funds of the company in an amount exceeding $160,000 or one note and approximately $8, 700 on another note alleged a criminal offense. State v. Bargen, 219 Neb. 416, 363 N.W.2d 393 (1985).

[1278] **In general.—**

In re Prudential Trust Co., 244 Mass. 64, 138 N.E. 702; Commissioner of Banks v. Harrigan, 291 Mass. 353, 197 N.E. 92 (trust companies).

investment company.—

Directors of mutual fund have fiduciary duty to manage companies with single eye to their best interest, free from any self-dealing. Brown v. Bullock, 194 F. Supp. 207 (S.D.N.Y. 1961), aff'd, 294 F.2d 415.

Power to extend or terminate advisory contracts.—

Directors of registered investment companies have fiduciary duty to use power to extend or terminate advisory contracts intelligently and for sole interest of company and its stockholders, and violation of these fiduciary duties created by investment Company Act subjects directors to liability which can be enforced in federal courts. Brown v. Bullock, 194 F. Supp. 207 (S.D.N.Y. 1961), aff'd, 294 F.2d 415.

Working for reinstatement of management contract.—

Directors of investment trust did not breach any fiduciary duty toward their stockholders when they worked for stockholders' approval of reinstatement of management contract following sale of a controlling block of management company stock to others for fair value. Krieger v. Anderson, 40 Del. Ch. 363, 182 A.2d 907.

Wrongful removal of assets.—

Director of trust company which was trustee for revocable inter vivos trust, whose actions included failure to keep correct account. regarding administration of trust and statements regarding receipts and disbursements, failure to give full disclosure statement and accounting to successor trustee, and transfer of trust assets out of trust to entities owned or controlled by director had breached fiduciary duty to trust and was personally liable for value of assets

act as directors of a loan corporation and making loans in bad faith are liable for resulting losses, whether they are de jure or de facto directors.[1279] And where directors of a trust company know the company is going to issue a prospectus encouraging the purchase of securities in a venture which is an ultra vires act, they are liable for losses occasioned thereby, whether or not the parties borrowing money from the company can defend an action on their notes because of the false statements in the prospectus.[1280] The liability

---

which he administered and which he wrongfully removed from trust. Detroit Bank & Trust Co. v. Trust Co. of V.I., Ltd., 644 F. Supp. 444 (D.P.R. 1985).

[1279] General Mortg. & Loan Corp. v. Guaranty Mortg. & Sec. Corp., 264 Mass. 253, 162 N.E. 819.

Master's finding that directors of loan corporation collected certain inspection fees for obtaining loans warranted finding that such sums should have been turned over to corporation. General Mortg. & Loan Corp. v. Guaranty Mortg. & Sec. Corp., 264 Mass. 253, 162 N.E. 319.

Loans by directors, pursuant to a scheme to get control of a loan corporation for personal gain only, constitute a breach of fiduciary duty. General Mortg. & Loan Corp. v. Guaranty Mortg. & Sec. Corp., 264 Mass. 253, 162 N.E. 319.

Director aiding coconspirators, for his own benefit, to obtain control of loan corporation unlawfully, and not properly investigating loans, held liable, apart from participation in conspiracy, for resulting losses and payments for services of no benefit to corporation. General Mortg. & Loan Corp. v. Guaranty Mortg. & Sec. Corp., 264 Mass. 253, 162 N.E. 319.

Duty to disclose information to other directors.—

A fund's investment adviser and an individual defendant who was a director-officer of the fund and was employed by the adviser to serve as portfolio manager for the fund breached the fiduciary duty with respect to the fund's indemnification of them for counsel fees incurred in an investigation by the Securities Exchange Commission, the breach consisting of presenting information with respect to indemnification in such a one-sided and incomplete manner that it discouraged any meaningful, independent evaluation of the indemnification request by the unaffiliated directors. Cambridge Fund, Inc. v. Abella, 501 F. Supp. 598 (S.D.N.Y. 1980).

A fund's officer-director who was employed by the adviser to serve as portfolio manager for the fund breached his fiduciary duty by failing to disclose to the unaffiliated directors of the fund that, in connection with bills submitted for counsel fees, there were charges for the representation of such director before the Securities Exchange Commission in connection with its investigation and that counsel had stated twice to the commission investigator on first appearance that he was representing the director personally, and in view of the want of indication as to a discussion of such bills, the adviser and portfolio manager were liable for compensatory damages and interest. Cambridge Fund, Inc. v. Abella, 501 F. Supp. 598 (S.D.N.Y. 1980).

[1280] State v. Barnes, 108 Minn. 230, 122 N.W. 11; State v. Barnes, 108 Minn. 527, 122 N.W. 12.

of directors of a trust company acting as a testamentary trustee based on a breach of trust, whether the breach is willful, fraudulent or negligent may ordinarily be enforced by a suit in equity.[1281] Matters not constituting defenses to such a suit are set out in the footnote.[1282] Where the defendant, a managing partner of an underwriter of a securities and merger broker, was a director of the defendant corporation and was also acting as a merger broker for an individual defendant with respect to merger negotiations with the plaintiff, and his firm was to receive a fee if the merger was completed, but his firm had also performed investment banking services for the plaintiff and the plaintiff's officials had confidence in him, the plaintiff could properly rely on its preexisting and contemporaneous banker-client relationship for fair disclosure, and in this posture as a quasi-fiduciary with respect to the plaintiff, the merger broker had an affirmative common-law duty to disclose material facts relating to the proposed merger.[1283]

The Investment Company Act provision authorizing suit if officers or directors of an investment adviser are guilty of gross misconduct or gross abuse of trust in respect of any registered investment company for which such person serves or acts was held not applicable to a transfer of control of an investment adviser and principal underwriter at a price in excess of its net asset value; there is no provision in the Act regulating the price paid for transfer of control of a service company.[1284]

[1281] Strauss v. United States Fidelity & G. Co., 63 F.2d 174, cert. denied, 289 U.S. 747, 53 S. Ct. 690, 77 L. Ed. 1492.

[1282] **Surety accepting dividends.—**

Fact that surety on bond of trust company, acting as testamentary trustee, accepted receivership dividends from funds collected from shareholders on account of their extra stockholders' liability, held not to estop surety from subsequently bringing suit against directors, also shareholders, for losses resulting to trust estate. Strauss v. United States Fidelity & G. Co., 63 F.2d 174, cert. denied, 289 U.S. 747, 53 S. Ct. 690, 77 L. Ed. 1492.

Annual reports of corporate trustee to probate court held not notice to trustee's surety of method in which trustee was handling trust funds so as to preclude recovery by surety from trustee's directors for resulting loss. Strauss v. United States Fidelity & G. Co., 63 F.2d 174, cert. denied, 289 U.S. 747, 53 S. Ct. 690, 77 L. Ed. 1492.

[1283] Sundstrand Corp. v. Sun Chemical Corp., 553 F.2d 1033(7th Cir.), cert. denied, 434 U.S. 875, 98 S. Ct. 224, 54 L. Ed. 2d 155 (1977).

[1284] Securities, etc., Comm. v. Insurance Securities, Inc., 254 F.2d 642.

Whose a fiduciary relationship which service company, including directors and stockholders, occupied with regard to a trust fund arose by virtue of service contracts, transfer of control of the service company did not effect a transfer or sale of the service contracts, and hence price received by directors for the sale of their stock in the service

The purpose of the provision includes protection of shareholders against self-dealing by the managers.[1285] But a violation of the Investment Company Act provision prohibiting securities transactions between investment companies and affiliated persons thereof unless such transactions are fair and do not involve overreaching may give rise to civil liability.[1286] The Investment

---

company did not represent compensation for sale or transfer of a fiduciary office involving a trust fund within the Investment Company Act authorizing suit if directors of investment adviser are guilty of gross misconduct or gross abuse of trust in respect of any registered investment company for which they act. Securities, etc., Comm. v. Insurance Securities, Inc., 254 F.2d 642.

[1285] **In general.—**

Moses v. Burgin, 445 F.2d 369 (1st Cir.), rev'g 316 F. Supp. 31 (D. Mass.), cert. denied, 404 US. 994, 92 S. Ct. 532, 30 L. Ed. 2d 547 (1971).

Fiduciary duty to minority shareholders.—

An investment banking firm which rendered a fairness opinion as to the terms of a merger did not owe the same fiduciary duty to minority shareholders as did the majority shareholder who initiated the merger, and in the absence of evidence of any understanding or overt combination between the majority shareholder and the controlled subsidiary, the investment banking firm was not liable to the minority shareholders who were forcibly removed by the merger transaction for inadequate compensation or breach of fiduciary duty. Weinberger v. UOP, Inc., 426 A.2d 1333 (Del. Ch. 1981).

[1286] **In general.—**

Entel v. Allen, 270 F. Supp. 60 (S.D.N.Y. 1967).

Definitions.—

A redemption of securities pursuant to terms upon which they were originally issued is not a "purchase" within the meaning of Investment Company Act making it unlawful for an affiliated person of a registered investment company "knowingly to purchase from such registered company . . . any security or other property" without approval of the Securities and Exchange Commission. Securities & Exch. Comm'n v. Sterling Precision Corp., 276 F. Supp. 772 (S.D.N.Y. 1967), aff'd, 393 F.2d 214 (2d Cir. 1968).

Under statute prohibiting securities transactions between investment companies and affiliated persons thereof unless transactions are fair and do not involve overreaching, beneficial owner of 10 percent of outstanding stock of investment company through voting trust and sole stockholder of purchaser of common stock and promissory notes of airline held by investment company appeared to be "affiliated person" of investment company and purchasing corporation as defined by statute. Entel v. Allen, 270 F. Supp. 60 (S.D.N.Y. 1967).

Illustrative cases.—

Under statute prohibiting securities transactions between in vestment companies and affiliated persons thereof unless transactions are fair and do not involve overreaching, where order of Securities Exchange Commission exempting sale by investment company of its common stock and notes of airlines from provisions of statute was allegedly obtained by fraud, fact that acts of officers and directors of investment company in conformity with order

Company Act of 1940 prohibits the willful conversion or embezzlement of property or assets of a registered investment company.[1287]

Conversion of Funds.—Where the managing agents of a trust company mingle money collected for another with the current funds of the company for use in its business in violation of the express directions of the owner, or knowingly permit their subordinates to do so, and the money is thereby lost, such agents are personally liable to the owner, even though such agents intended to account for and return the money to the owner on demand.[1288]

---

of commission were done in good faith was not ground for avoiding liability. Entel v. Allen, 270 F. Supp. 60 (S.D.NY. 1967).

Fact that registered investment company subsequent to entering into agreement for sale of its common stock and promissory notes of airline to another corporation obtained deregistration prior to consummating sale in substantial compliance with terms of original agreement would not relieve holding company of liability for violation of statute prohibiting securities transactions between investment companies and affiliated persons thereof unless transactions are fair and do not involve overreaching. Entel v. Allen, 270 F. Supp. 60 (S.D.N.Y. 1967).

[1287] **In general.—**

15 U.S.C.S. § 80a-36.

Sufficiency of complaint.—

Complaint containing allegations by plaintiff stockholder that defendants, who had gained control of nondiversified closed-end management investment corporation, used assets of corporation to buy and maintain control of portfolio companies and that such control was used to cause excessive salaries, bonuses, and other emoluments to be granted to individual defendants stated claim on which relief could be granted under statute prohibiting willful conversion or embezzlement of property or assets of registered investment company. Tanzer v. Huffines, 314 F. Supp. 189 (D. Del. 1970).

Where complaint alleging violation of statute prohibiting conversion or embezzlement of property or assets of registered investment companies made only one claim for relief; and suit was based on theory that all transactions identified in allegations were part of a scheme, complaint would not be divided into causes of action for purpose of dealing separately with each transaction. Tanzer v. Huffines, 314 F. Supp. 189 (D. Del. 1970).

Where complaint alleging violation of statute prohibiting willful conversion or embezzlement of property or assets of registered investment company made only one claim for relief, and it was based on theory that all transactions identified in allegations were part of a scheme, potential liability of defendant corporation would not, in proceeding on motion to dismiss, be segregated from that of other defendants. Tanzer v. Huffines, 314 F. Supp. 189 (D. Del. 1970).

[1288] **In general.—**

Sweet v. Montpelier Sav. Bank & Trust Co., 78 Kan. 47, 84 P. 542.

Good faith held no defense.—

Managing officers of corporation were liable for conversion by corporation of fund

And an officer of a company to which a customer entrusted money to invest is liable to such customer for the loss thereof through the intentional wrongful acts of the other company officers in which he actively participated.[1289] A trust company's officers and directors who convert the proceeds of sales of realty and bonds, and collections of mortgages held in trust, to the company's use, are liable to a substituted trustee for such proceeds.[1290] And as respects the liability of such officers, that a fund entrusted to their company for investment was handled like all other investment funds is no defense to an action for conversion if other funds were also mishandled;[1291] in such case whether the company, which failed to keep the fund invested and deposited it in its general checking account, was guilty of conversion for which the officers were personally liable was held a question for the jury.[1292] But the action of a trust company, as guardian of an insane veteran, in depositing his compensation payments in its own bank, was held not a tort so as to render its directors liable in damages for the failure to turn over the full deposit to the trust company's successor in guardianship, when the bank subsequently failed.[1293] For other decisions relating to conversion of funds, see the footnote.[1294]

---

entrusted to corporation for investment, regardless of their good faith, provided failure of corporation to keep fund invested and depositing of fund in corporation's general checking account amounted to conversion. Duncan v. Williamson, 18 Tenn. App. 153, 74 S.W.2d 215.

[1289] Goodnow v. Leeper (Mo.), 239 S.W. 135; Strauss v. United States Fidelity & G. Co., 63 F.2d 174, cert. denied, 289 U.S. 747, 53 S. Ct. 690, 77 L. Ed. 1492.

[1290] Winn v. Harby, 171 S.C. 301, 172 S.E. 135.

[1291] Duncan v. Williamson, 18 Tenn. App. 153, 74 S.W.2d 215.

[1292] Duncan v. Williamson, 18 Tenn. App. 153, 74 S.W.2d 215.

[1293] Bowen v. Strauss, 175 S.C. 23, 178 S.E. 252.

[1294] **Conversion of assets of investment company.—**

Complaint by stockholders of diversified open-end management investment company charging fund directors, who were also officers and directors of management company, with being tools of management company in whose interest they were acting rather then that of fund, was sufficient to state a claim under federal statute respecting willful conversion of assets of any registered investment company. Brown v. Bullock, 294 F.2d 415.

Officer stealing trust fund.—

Where trust company held money for investment and reinvestment for depositor's account, and an officer of company steals trust fund and uses it for his own account and profit, charging losses against account and taking profits as his own, officer is liable not only to company but to depositor as a "trustee en maleficio," and the depositor may demand from him as well as from the company an accounting in equity. Frier v. Sales Corp., 261 App. Div. 388, 25 N.Y.S.2d 576.

Negligence.—Directors of a trust or loan company are liable only for losses caused by, or attributable to, their own negligence.[1295] And directors cannot escape this liability by reason of the fact that their election was irregular,[1296] or they were merely honorary directors.[1297] But a director who is necessarily absent[1298] is not liable for losses occasioned by the negligent

---

Acceptance of mortgage.—

The officers and directors of trust company from which plaintiff purchased undivided shares in mortgages could not avoid liability for conversion, based upon company's acceptance of an additional mortgage on same property and entry into agreement consolidating the three mortgages, on ground that transaction was a mere bookkeeping transaction, where mortgages were all in default and original mortgagors would have a defense to any action against them. Mendelson v. Boettger, 257 App. Div. 167, 12 N.Y.S.2d 671, aff'd, 281 N.Y. 747, 23 N.E.2d 554.

No conversion in absence of trust relation.—

Contract whereby trust company established account for customer and agreed to pay interest on daily balance and to pay customer's premiums on insurance policies held not to create trust relation between trust company and customer so as to entitle customer to recover from officers of company which became bankrupt for alleged conversion of trust funds. Crancer v. Reichenbach, 130 Neb. 645, 266 N.W. 57.

[1295] Kavanaugh v. Gould, 147 App. Div. 281, 181 N.Y.S. 1059; Cosmopolitan Trust Co. v. Mitchell, 242 Mass. 95, 136 N.E. 403.

[1296] Cunningham v. Commissioner of Banks, 249 Mass. 401, 144 N.E. 447.

[1297] Kavanaugh v. Gould, 223 N.Y. 103, 119 N.E. 237.

Whether honorary director was negligent in not attending meetings resulting in loss, held question of fact. Kavanaugh v. Gould, 223 N.Y. 103, 119 N.E. 287.

A director of a trust company consented to serve as such on an understanding with the company's president that he should not be called upon to attend any of the meetings of the board, but would simply allow the use of his name in the directorate, the making of which agreement was beyond the authority of the president. In an action by a stockholder seeking to recover for loses alleged to be due to the negligence of the directors, such director's liability was to be determined as if no such agreement had been made, and, as a director, he was not charged, either actually or constructively, with knowledge of the making of loans or of the collateral upon which they were made by the executive committee and might rely upon the acknowledged financial responsibility of the parties to whom the loans were made, and for any loss not attributable to his own negligence he was not liable. Kavanaugh v. Gould, 147 App. Div. 281, 131 N.Y.S. 1059.

[1298] State v. Barnes, 108 Minn. 230, 122 N.W. 11; State v. Barnes, 108 Minn. 527, 122 N.W. 12.

The bylaws of a trust company provided that with the president two of the five members of the executive committee should constitute a quorum. A member of the executive committee, prior to going abroad, in July, suggested a mode of filling the vacancy upon that committee in his absence, and members of the executive committee sufficient in number to constitute a quorum were at all times during his absence within reach of the president. On his

acts of other directors during his absence, nor is a director who is inexperienced[1299] or has resigned[1300] liable for such losses caused by others during his period of inexperience or just prior to his resignation. Directors are also liable for losses resulting from the misconduct or mismanagement of other directors or subordinate officers if, had such directors been diligent in the discharge of their duties, they could have prevented or lessened such losses.[1301] However, a director may trust other corporate officers and rely

---

return in October he learned that in his absence the president of the company had made unauthorized loans of money, taking as collateral the bonds of a shipbuilding company of which the trust company was fiscal agent, and thereupon he organized a syndicate which took over such bonds and canceled the liability of the trust company. It was held that without fault in taking his vacation, he could not be held to have been guilty of any negligence making him liable for loss upon loans to responsible parties made upon the same security during his absence. Kavanaugh v. Gould, 147 App. Div. 281, 131 N.Y.S. 1059.

[1299] Roseville Trust Co. v. Mott, 85 N.J. Eq. 297, 96 A. 402, aff'd sub nom. La Monte v. Mott, 93 N.J. Eq. 229, 116 A. 269.

An inexperienced director, who was not a member of a trust company when it began business though a member of the examining committee, held not to be charged constructively with the negligence of the committee's chairman, in not requiring from correspondent banks a statement as to outstanding checks and drafts; such new director having taken part in only one examination. Roseville Trust Co. v. Mott, 85 N.J. Eq. 297, 96 A. 402, aff'd sub nom. La Monte v. Mott, 93 N.J. Eq. 229, 116 A. 269.

[1300] Kavanaugh v. Gould, 147 App. Div. 281, 131 N.Y.S. 1059.

The president of a trust company engaged in receiving subscriptions for bonds of a shipbuilding company, to be issued according to underwriting agreements, withdrew from the company the sum of $35,000 without security or authority and without the knowledge either of the executive committee or the board of directors, and during a two months' absence the misappropriation was discovered, and after his return defendant, a member of the executive committee, both advised suit against the president and sought to compel his resignation. Held, that such director, and another director who had resigned before the president's return and before suit could be brought, were not liable to a stockholder of the company for any negligence respecting the president's misappropriation. Kavanaugh v. Gould, 147 App. Div. 281, 131 N.Y.S. 1059.

[1301] Kavanaugh v. Commonwealth Trust Co., 64 Misc. 303, 118 N.Y.S. 758, rev'd on other grounds sub nom. Kavanaugh v. Gould, 147 App. Div. 281, 131 N.Y.S. 1059; STATE v. BARNES, 108 Minn. 230, 122 N.W. 11.

All directors of investors' corporation held liable to stockholders for losses due to mismanagement and misappropriation by one, where such directors never examined securities held, had no audits made, and after stock market crash authorized offending director to sell and deliver securities of corporation. O'Connor v. First Nat. Investors' Corp., 163 Va. 908, 177 S.E. 852.

Bill which alleged that directors of trust corporation abdicated control by turning entire management over to president, permitted large, open, unsecured loans to companies which

upon information given him, in the absence of suspicious circumstances.[1302] But directors of a trust company who knowingly retain a dishonest cashier and permit the lending of money, contrary to statute and bylaws, are liable to the same extent, irrespective of the relative degree of their negligence.[1303] Directors must exercise the same degree of care and prudence in conducting their company's business as is generally exercised by men in their own affairs.[1304] Thus, directors are generally liable for ordinary negligence in the management of the affairs of their corporation, not merely for gross negligence.[1305] On the other hand, the required standard for imposition of personal liability upon nonaffiliated directors of a mutual fund company for a failure to interpret a contract with a management company, and to insist upon the assumption by the management company of items of expense

---

were dominated, controlled and owned by such president and which were not financially sound, and failed to examine financial reports which would have disclosed illegal diversion was sufficient to state cause of action against such directors. Neese v. Brown, 218 Tenn. 686, 405 S.W.2d 577 (1964).

[1302] **In general.—**

Finley v. Exchange Trust Co., 183 Okla. 167, 80 P.2d 296, 117 A.L.R. 162.

Directors of a trust company may rely upon executive officers and subordinates for information. Finley v. Exchange Trust Co., 183 Okla. 167, 80 P.2d 296, 117 A.L.R. 162.

Vice-president and director of corporation which solicited handling and investment of money of others was not bound to be continuously present or to keep himself at all times familiar with everything which books would have shown, and he had right to trust others to reasonable extent and to rely upon information given him until something occurred to arouse his suspicion, and he was not bound to exhibit greater wisdom and foresight than could be fairly expected of ordinary man in similar conditions. Goodwin v. Simpson, 292 Mass. 148, 197 N.E. 628 (1935).

Directors of such corporation held not liable for dividend on preferred stock where president, whose veracity they had no reason to question, stated quarterly earnings were sufficient to pay dividend. Goodwin v. Simpson, 292 Mass. 148, 197 N.E. 628 (1935).

[1303] Roseville Trust Co. v. Mott, 85 N.J. Eq. 297, 96 A. 402, aff'd sub nom. La Monte v. Molt, 93 N.J. Eq. 229, 116 A. 269.

Directors of a trust company, who knew that the cashier loaned money, contrary to the bylaws, without advising the president, and that he repeatedly made improper entries with intent to conceal, a high misdemeanor under the statute, but nevertheless retained him against the warning of the banking commissioner, vested with supervision but not power of removal, are guilty of breach of duty, and liable for resulting loss, although they may have been good business men and have acted in good faith. Roseville Trust Co. v. Mott, 85 NJ. Eq. 297, 96 A. 402, aff'd sub nom. La Monte v. Mott, 93 N.J. Eq. 229, 116 A. 269.

[1304] Ashby v. Peters, 128 Neb. 338, 258 N.W. 639, 99 A.L.R. 843; Masonic Bldg. Corp. v. Carlsen, 128 Neb. 108, 258 N.W. 44.

[1305] Plyer v. Southern, 156 S.C. 416, 153 S.E. 277.

properly allocable to it, is gross negligence or at least bad faith, and a mere lack of prudence does not subject them to liability.[1306]

Officers and directors of trust companies occupy a position of trust with respect to their savings departments;[1307] they must exercise a high degree of good faith and diligence in dealing with deposits therein, and are derelict in their duties if they fail to direct the affairs of the companies themselves, or delegate their duties to others.[1308] Although a statute limiting loans to any one person by a trust company is mandatory and places restrictions on the power of directors, they are only prima facie responsible for losses resulting from violations thereof, and such responsibility may be rebutted by showing that the directors are without fault.[1309] The liability of directors of an insolvent trust company for acts resulting in loss is joint and several.[1310] And the liability of directors of a trust company for neglect of their duties and mismanagement of the company constitutes a "claim" belonging to the company under a statute authorizing the commissioner of banks, after taking possession of the property and business of a trust company, to collect all debts, claims and the like.[1311]

1306 Acampora v. Birkland, 220 F. Supp. 527.

Nonaffiliated directors of mutual fund company could not be held guilty of gross negligence so as to be personally liable to fund in failing to demand compliance to strict terms of contract with management company serving as investment adviser where policies involved except that leading to expenditure by fund for data processing equipment rental had been set for some years prior to their becoming board members and interpretations were buttressed by opinions of counsel and of independent auditor. Acampora v. Birkland, 220 F. Supp. 527.

1307 Bancroft Trust Co. v. Federal Nat'l Bank, 9 F. Supp. 350.

Directors of a company having a savings department are subject to same obligations towards savings as trustees of a savings bank. Cosmopolitan Trust Co. v. Mitchell, 242 Mass. 95, 136 N.E. 403.

1308 Bancroft Trust Co. v. Federal Nat'l Bank, 9 F. Supp. 350.

1309 Medford Trust Co. v. McKnight, 292 Mass. 1, 197 N.E. 649.

Directors of trust company who, as result of an honest nonnegligent mistake as to aggregate amount of loans to single borrower, approved various loans in violation of statute limiting loans to single borrower, held not liable for losses sustained by bank as result thereof. Medford Trust Co. v. McKnight, 292 Mass. 1, 197 N.E 649.

1310 LaMonte v. Lurich, 86 N.J. Eq. 26, 100 A. 1031, aff'd, 86 N.J. Eq. 251, 98 A. 1086.

1311 Cosmopolitan Trust Co. v. Mitchell, 242 Mass. 95, 136 N.E. 403 (Massachusetts statute).

The commissioner need not secure the permission of the court before suing the directors for neglect. Cosmopolitan Trust Co. v. Mitchell, 242 Mass. 95, 136 N.E. 403.

Facts which have been held to constitute[1312] or not constitute[1313] negligence of directors will be found in the footnote.

[1312] **Making bad loan.—**

Negligence of director of trust company was established, in the absence of evidence that, being present at meetings, he opposed making of bad loan. Cunningham v. Commissioner of Banks, 249 Mass. 401, 144 N.E. 447.

But directors were chargeable with negligence for losses caused by investment of trust funds in unsafe loan only as of time when investment was originally made, and were not required to anticipate subsequent default by borrower. Finley v. Exchange Trust Co., 183 Okla. 167, 80 P.2d 296, 117 A.L.R. 162.

Investments of trust funds.—

Directors of a trust company who were present and participated in approval of negligent investments of trust funds were presumed to have known facts rendering such investments unsafe, in absence of contrary showing. Finley v. Exchange Trust Co., 183 Okla. 167, 80 P.2d 296, 117 A.L.R. 162, wherein it was held that evidence was sufficient to hold directors individually liable for losses.

Failure to investigate title.—

Defendant, an officer of a company to which plaintiff had entrusted money to invest for her and look after the investment, having, when a trade for a mortgage was under consideration, prevented plaintiff from getting a lawyer to investigate its title and value, by objecting thereto and saying that the company would make an investigation, personally assumed the responsibility of employing adequate means therefor, so that having negligently failed to do so, and the mortgage traded for having proved fraudulent, defendant was liable for the loss, though under the working arrangement between defendant and the president of the company the duty of having investigation made devolved on the president. Goodnow v. Leeper (Mo.), 239 S.W. 135.

Examination of accounts.—

Where the examining committee of the board of trustees of a trust company, in attempting to comply with the statute, handled and counted the cash and assets, but did not investigate and report the value of securities carried on the books, and were also negligent in examining the accounts of depository banks, and in taking the treasurer's statement as to them, the trustees were liable for the resulting losses on the ground of negligence. Roseville Trust Co. v. Mott, 85 N.J. Eq. 297, 96 A. 402, aff'd sub nom. La Monte v. Mott, 93 N.J. Eq. 229, 116 A. 269.

[1313] **Failure to detect treasurer's manipulation.—**

In suit by commissioner of banking in behalf of an insolvent trust company against its directors for losses through their negligence, the examining committee of the board of directors insofar as falling to detect the treasurer's manipulation of the general ledger, held not guilty of culpable negligence, as honest effort to do their duty having been shown, and the thorough examination of an expert accountant not being required as to them. Roseville Trust Co. v. Mott, 85 N.J. Eq. 297, 96 A. 402, aff'd sub nom. La Monte v. Mott, 93 N.J. Eq. 229, 118 A. 269.

A director of an insolvent trust company whose only connection with the acts of an

(Text continued on page 353)

---

examining committee was a failure to report that certain securities were carried on the books at an excessive valuation is not liable as for negligence, where such fact was already known to the board of directors, and hence did not contribute to concealment of the treasurer's defalcations. Roseville Trust Co. v. Mott, 85 N.J. Eq. 297, 96 A. 402, aff'd sub nom. La Monte v. Mott, 93 N.J. Eq. 229, 116 A. 269.

Failure to purchase securities.—

Director of corporation which solicited handling and investment of money of others held not liable for losses sustained by failure to purchase promptly underlying securities to cover collateral trustee shares sold on installment plan, where director acted with reasonable promptness and vigor as soon as he received knowledge of sales on installment plan. Goodwin v. Simpson, 292 Mass. 148, 197 N.E. 628 (1935).

Director held not liable for money paid to salesman as commissions on installment sales of collateral trustee shares and for money paid to purchasers of collateral trustee shares on installment plan in lieu of dividends which would have been credited to them from underlying securities if underlying securities had been bought, where director acted with reasonable promptness and vigor as soon as he received knowledge of sales on installment plan. Goodwin v. Simpson, 292 Mass. 148, 197 N.E. 628 (1935).

Making loans.—

The executive committee of a trust company, acting as fiscal agent of a shipbuilding company and receiving subscriptions for its bonds, loaned money on the personal notes of parties financially responsible on the security of assignment, of right, under underwriting agreements, to bonds to be issued by the shipbuilding company, which agreements contained the provision that they were to be void unless the whole amount of bonds was underwritten, and such money was placed to the credit of the shipbuilding company with the trust company until the full amount should be raised. Such bonds then had a ready sale in the market. Held, that it could not be held to be an act of negligence upon the part of any director of the trust company to sanction the loan of money, under the circumstances. Kavanaugh v. Gould, 147 App. Div. 281, 131 N.Y.S. 1059.

The officers of a trust company invested a large sum in its own stocks. This did not appear on the books of the company or the reports to the executive committee formed from the board of directors, except so much charged to "advances." Nothing was in fact lost by such use of the trust company's money. There was also a further loan appearing on the books of $800,000 to one firm which was in excess of the amount that might lawfully be loaned to that firm, and there were other loans made inadequately secured. The trust company thereafter loaned the sum of $2,600,000 on the notes of the president of the company and another secured by the bonds of a shipbuilding company, of which the trust company was the financial agent, and the company in a short time became obligated to the amount of $4,100,000 on security of these bonds. The board of directors thereafter procured a syndicate to take these bonds from the company and pay the notes, so that no loss came to the trust company by reason of these unauthorized acts. At the time the trust company had loaned upwards of $5,000,000 at the par value of these bonds. Held, that the trust company could not well refuse thereafter to take these bonds as collateral for money loaned, and thus discredit them, inasmuch as it would have been impossible therefore to have formed a syndicate for the payment of the sum of $4,100,000, for which amount the president had unlawfully involved the trust company, so that loans thereafter made of smaller sums on the

Liabilities Incident to the Creation of an Executive Committee.—While directors of a trust company may delegate their work,[1314] they may not delegate their responsibility, and hence they are not excused from liability for losses suffered by their company because they commit their duties to an executive committee, relying upon it to examine loans and collateral.[1315] And if information comes to directors of an irregularity in the affairs of their company, they are bound to take steps to correct those irregularities, and to use every effort that a prudent business man would use in supervising his own affairs, with the right to rely on the vigilance of the executive committee to ascertain any irregularity in its management.[1316] Thus, the members of an executive committee of a trust company are bound to be on their guard to detect any irregularities or improvident acts on the part of the company's executive officers, and to scan critically the detailed reports which are made to them by such officers, and the diligence required of them is therefore greater and the rule of their liability more strict, than that of a director who is not a member of the committee.[1317] And where, under the bylaws of a trust company, it is the duty of its executive committee to require all loans

---

security of these shipbuilding bond, were not negligently authorized by the board of directors, and though the irregularities on the part of the president were sufficient to put the directors on guard against further irregularities on his part, and though they would be liable for losses arising from similar irregularities, they could not be held liable for the smaller loans made at a time when the bonds were not discredited and when the borrowers were men of acknowledged financial responsibility. Kavanaugh v. Gould, 147 App. Div. 281, 131 N.Y.S. 1059.

[1314] Coran v. Thorpe, 42 Del. Ch. 67, 203 A.2d 620 (1964).

That executive committee of board of directors of investment company made all decisions for purchase and sale of securities and thereafter reported them to board did not warrant finding that board had failed in its duty to exercise independent judgment ordinarily expected of corporate directors. Coran v. Thorpe, 42 Del. Ch. 67, 203 A.2d 620 (1964).

[1315] Kavanaugh v. Commonwealth Trust Co., 64 Misc. 303, 118 N.Y.S. 758, rev'd on other grounds sub nom. Kavanaugh v. Gould, 147 App. Div. 281, 131 N.Y.S. 1059. See Ashby v. Peters, 128 Neb. 338, 258 N.W. 639, 99 A.L.R. 843; Masonic Bldg. Corp. v. Carlsen, 128 Neb. 108, 258 N.W. 44.

Directors are not excused from liability because they commit some of their duties to executive committee or to directors of wholly owned subsidiary. Ashby v. Peters, 128 Neb. 338, 258 N.W. 639, 99 A.L.R. 843.

[1316] Kavanaugh v. Gould, 147 App. Div. 281, 131 N.Y.S. 1059.

While members of executive committee of trustee corporation are held to higher degree of responsibility than directors, directors, not members of executive committee must use same degree of care in attending to trustee's affairs as ordinary prudent person would use in own business. Masonic Bldg. Corp. v. Carlsen, 128 Neb. 108, 258 N.W. 44.

[1317] Kavanaugh v. Gould, 147 App. Div. 281, 181 N.Y.S. 1059.

and investments to be reported to it for approval, a failure of the committee to examine loans is not excused by the fact that the loans were not presented to the committee, it being its duty to require them to be presented.[1318]

Actions.[1319]—Because of the fiduciary relation between the directors of a trust company and its savings department, a suit in equity may be maintained to enforce the liability of directors for neglect and mismanagement, and the remedy at law is not exclusive.[1320] For other cases relating to a right of action, see the footnote.[1321]

[1318] Kavanaugh v Commonwealth Trust Co., 64 Misc. 303, 118 N.Y.S. 758, rev'd on other grounds sub nom. Kavanaugh v. Gould, 147 App. Div. 281, 131 N.Y.S. 1059.

[1319] As to actions generally, see § 18 of this chapter. As to actions to enforce shareholders' liability, see § 9 of this chapter.

[1320] Cosmopolitan Trust Co. v. Mitchell, 242 Mass. 95, 136 N.E. 403.

[1321] A suit is not premature where it is alleged that the company has lost a specific amount in bad loans as the result of negligence. Cosmopolitan Trust Co. v. Mitchell, 242 Mass. 95, 136 N.E. 403.

Assignment of right to sue.—

Bondholders' assignment to assignee of bonds for collection, together with all claims, choses in action, and rights possessed by assignors growing out of issuance of bonds, hold to have conferred upon assignee every right assignors had, including their right to sue officers of trustee corporation for damages for breach of trust. Wells v. Carlsen, 130 Neb. 773, 266 N.W. 618 (1936).

Subsequent action at law.—

That bondholders had first attempted to foreclose on mortgage held not to bar subsequent action at law by them against officers of trustee corporation to recover damages for breach of trust arising out of officers' conduct in allowing bonds to be sold based upon a leasehold but purporting to be based upon a mortgage upon the fee. Wells v. Carlsen, 130 Neb. 773, 266 N.W. 618 (1936).

Action held not objectionable as alleging negligence and fraud, where it was brought by bondholders against officers of trustee corporation to recover for their alleged fraudulent and negligent conduct in allowing bonds to be sold based upon a leasehold, but purporting to be upon mortgage upon the fee. Wells v. Carlsen, 130 Neb. 773, 266 N.W. 618 (1936).

Order of Securities Exchange Commission exempting sale by investment company of its common stock and notes of airlines from provisions of statute prohibiting securities transactions between investment companies and affiliated persons thereof unless transactions are fair and do not involve overreaching did not preclude stockholders of investment company from asserting violation of statute. Entel v. Allen, 270 F. Supp. 60 (S.D.N.Y. 1967).

Private right of action.—

Provision of Securities and Exchange Act relating to gross misconduct or gross abuse of trust in respect of any registered investment company gives rise to private right of action by

The stockholders of a trust company are not entitled to intervene and file a complaint charging misconduct of trustees in a creditor's suit for the appointment of a receiver.[1322] For other cases relating to parties and standing to sue, see the footnote.[1323]

A complaint containing confusingly irrelevant material is subject to dismissal.[1324] In a suit against the directors of a trust company for neglect and mismanagement, it is not necessary that the bill should state with precision the actual loss on each bad loan or investment, and where the bill contains adequate details and sufficient certainty in the statement of particular loans, it is not necessary that the specific connection of each defendant with each investment be particularized.[1325] For other cases relating to pleading, see the footnote.[1326]

---

which receiver of investment company may recover against company officers for alleged violations of securities laws. Securities & Exch. Comm'n v. Quing N. Wong, 42 F.R.D. 599 (D.P.R. 1967).

Special Securities and Exchange Commission action authorized by section relating to gross misconduct and abuse of trust by directors of investment companies and other, does not preempt civil remedy which may be enforced by victim in federal court. Brown v. Bullock, 194 F. Supp. 207 (S.D.N.Y. 1961), aff'd, 294 F.2d 415.

Stockholders' derivative action.—

Transaction which investment corporation entered into was approved by its board of directors in the exercise of honest, informed, reasonable business judgment under the circumstances and business and market conditions then prevailing and anticipated, and thus directors were not liable to stockholders who brought derivative action. Marco v. Bank of N.Y., 398 F.2d 628 (2d Cir. 1968).

The Small Business investment Company Act did not confer private right of action upon a corporation and its president who sought to have a loan agreement declared unenforceable as violative of the act.

Westland Capitol Corp. v. Lucht Eng'r, Inc., 308 N.W.2d 709 (Minn. 1981).

[1322] Austin v. Gerard, 61 F.2d 129.

[1323] **Suit by SEC.—**

Defendants, who were directors and officers and principal stockholders of service company, which managed and received fees as investment advisor to trust fund, were not amenable to suit by Securities and Exchange Commission under Investment Company Act, in absence of allegation of wrongdoing with respect to trust fund or its investors. Securities & Exchange Com. v. Insurance Sec. Inc., 146 F. Supp. 778, aff'd, 254 F.2d 642.

[1324] McCann v. Throckmorton, 232 App. Div. 216, 249 N.Y.S. 555.

[1325] Cosmopolitan Trust Co. v. Mitchell, 242 Mass. 95, 136 N.E. 403.

[1326] The precise extent of the responsibility of each of several directors sued is a matter of proof rather than pleading. Cosmopolitan Trust Co. v. Mitchell, 242 Mass. 95, 136 N.E. 403.

Other matters relating to actions are set out in the footnote.[1327]

Cause of action stated.—

Under statute prohibiting use of any manipulative or deceptive device or contrivance in connection with purchase or sale of any security, stockholders of investment company who alleged that director of investment company dominated both investment company and corporation which purchased stock and notes held by investment company and acted for his personal benefit had cause of action even though no deception was practiced on investment company and stockholders did not purchase or sell their stock or warrants in reliance on representations made in connection with sale. Entel v. Allen, 270 F. Supp. 60 (S.D.N.Y. 1967).

Complaint of mutual fund stockholders against officers and directors of fund alleging falsity of proxy statements which induced stockholders to forbear from terminating advisory and management contracts and that actions of officers and directors were violative of Investment Company Act of 1940, stated claim upon which relief could be granted. Brown v. Bullock, 194 F. Supp. 207 (S.D.N.Y. 1961), aff'd, 294 F.2d 415.

In action by superintendent of banks, as liquidator of trust company, against directors for accounting and judgment on ground of breach of fiduciary duties by directors, fourth amended petition was not subject to application to make definite and certain nor was it demurrable, where it specified principal transactions on which the several causes of action were predicated and set forth definitely the factual basis of the several complaints. Squire v. Guardian Trust Co. (Ohio C.P.), 84 N.E.2d 91.

Complaint, which alleged that plaintiff investor went to an investment counseling firm, that the firm recommended investment in a particular company based on unique information which it possessed, and that the firm either did not have such unique information or did not accurately pass it on to investor, stated a cause of action based upon breach of fiduciary duty. Schweiger v. Loewi & Co., 65 Wis. 2d 56, 221 N.W.2d 882 (1974).

[1327] **Service of process.—**

Where the same acts of former directors were alleged to constitute a violation of the Investment Company Act and also a violation of state law, the long-arm service of process provision of the Investment Company Act could be used to acquire personal jurisdiction over out-of-state director, with regard to nonfederal common-law claims. Townsend Corp. of America v. Davidson, 222 F. Supp. 1.

For purpose of determining motions by former directors of unregistered investment company to dismiss action by corporation seeking to hold directors individually liable for violation of section of Investment Company Act concerning transactions by investment companies on ground that venue was improperly laid in district and to quash service of process on ground that service was made outside the district private right of action may be implied under the act. Townsend Corp. of America v. Davidson, 222 F. Supp. 1.

Estoppel.—

That bondholders had first commenced a foreclosure action and prosecuted it to judgment held not to estop them, on theory bonds were merged in decree, from maintaining action against officers of trustee corporation to recover damages for alleged breach of trust, since action against officers was not based upon mortgage notes. Wells v. Carlsen, 130 Neb. 773, 266 N.W. 618 (1936).

(Text continued on page 359)

Bond required.—

Where stockholders of investment company alleging violation of statute prohibiting certain securities transactions between investment companies and affiliated persons thereof made no serious attempt for more than year and a half after they filed complaint to prosecute actions, and notices to take depositions upon oral examination were not served until after stockholders had received notice that actions would be called for review on dismissal calendar, stockholders were required to post original bond for costs pursuant to rule in amount of $500. Entel v. Allen, 270 F. Supp. 60 (S.D.N.Y. 1967).

Venue.—

Plaintiff in suit against investment company and its agent made for venue purpose prima facie case demonstrating right to prosecute cause against agent. Southwestern Inv. Co. v. Gibson (Tex. Civ. App.), 372 S.W.2d 754.

Liability enforceable in federal courts.—

Violation of Investment Company Act section making it unlawful for any principal underwriter to sell securities except pursuant to annually renewable written contract, subjects directors to liability which may be enforced in federal courts. Brown v. Bullock, 194 F. Supp. 207 (S.D.N.Y. 1961), aff'd, 294 F.2d 415.

Complaint by stockholders of mutual fund against directors of company showing totality of acts charged constituted gross misconduct and abuse of trust, charged statutory violations under Investment Company Act and stated claim cognizable in federal court. Brown v. Bullock, 194 F. Supp. 207 (S.D.N.Y. 1961), aff'd, 294 F.2d 415.

Burden of proof.—

Stockholder failed to sustain burden of showing lack of independence of board of directors of investment company as a whole with respect to purchase and sale of securities. Coran v. Thorpe, 42 Del. Ch. 67, 203 A.2d 620 (1964).

Burden of proving misconduct in suit against vice-president and director of corporation which solicited handling and investment money of others for losses sustained by failure to purchase promptly underlying securities to cover collateral trustee shares sold on installment plan was on plaintiff. Goodwin v. Simpson, 292 Mass. 148, 197 N.E. 628 (1935).

Admissibility of evidence.—

In bondholders' action against officers of trustee corporation for damages allegedly resulting from their breach of trust in allowing bonds to be sold based upon a leasehold but purporting to be based upon mortgage upon the fee, evidence of the insolvency of mortgagor at time of trial held properly admitted, since if mortgagor had been solvent bondholders would have been bound to mitigate their losses by first collecting from her. Wells v. Carlsen, 130 Neb. 773, 266 N.W. 618 (1936).

Witnesses.—

In action by assignee of bondholders, proof of misrepresentation and reliance thereon as to each particular bondholder was not necessary where scheme alleged and proved was that officers conspired to defraud a class of persons. And it was not necessary that all bondholders whom plaintiff represented be called as witnesses to prove breach of trust. Wells v. Carlsen, 130 Neb. 773, 266 N.W. 618 (1936).

(*Text continued on page 359*)

Evidence sufficient.—

Evidence held to establish that auction sale of collateral was fair, etc., so as to preclude recovery by trust company's stockholders and some directors for resulting loss. Litwin v. Allen, 25 N.Y.S.2d 667.

In an action against the officers of a trust company for the conversion of the proceeds Of a collection made by the corporation of which they were the principal officers, evidence held to sustain judgment for plaintiff. Sweet v. Montpelier Sav. Bank, etc., Co., 78 Kan. 47, 84 P. 542.

Evidence was sufficient to sustain a finding of legal malice with respect to wrongdoings committed by individual defendants and defendant investment company, in relation to plaintiffs. investments, so as to support award of punitive damages of $25,000 against defendants. McKeehan v. Wittels, 508 S.W.2d 277 (Mo. App. 1974).

Evidence insufficient.—

Evidence, in an action by stockholders of a trust company to charge directors for losses from negligent mismanagement, held insufficient to show the negligence alleged. Chambers v. Land Credit Trust Co., 92 Kan. 30, 139 P. 1178, *reh'g denied*, 92 Kan. 1032, 142 P. 248.

Evidence held not to how that officers and directors of loan company were guilty of gross negligence, or recreant in discharging their duties in loaning money to automobile dealers, with used automobiles as security, especially as no fraud, corruption, or profit on their part was pleaded, and in view of condition of prosperity at the time and past success of their business, but at most showed mere error of judgment on their part. Williams v. Fidelity Loan & Sav. Co., 142 Va. 43, 128 S.E 615, 45 A.L.R. 664.

Evidence held not to establish that directors profited at expense of trust company in buying and reselling stock, and hence were not liable for profits made on theory of "corporate opportunity." Litwin v. Allen, 25 N.Y.S.2d 667.

Evidence held not to warrant recovery by trust company's stockholders from company's officers and directors for loss resulting from participation in large loans. Litwin v. Allen, 25 N.Y.S.2d 667.

Evidence held not to establish improper influence upon directors and officers of trust company in arranging for sale of stock as ground for recovery of profits made by directors. Litwin v. Allen, 25 N.Y.S.2d 667.

Question for jury.—

In action far breach of trust against officers of trustee corporation, whether there were mere breaches of trust, whether defendants participated and aided in breaches, and whether plaintiff was damaged, held for jury. Wells v. Carlsen, 130 Neb. 773, 266 N.W. 618 (1936).

Finding that transactions complained of in stockholder's derivative action against directors of investment corporation were fully set forth and revealed in the corporation's records and that there was no evidence that any material information had been withheld or any fraud had been practiced was supported by record. Marco v. Bank of New York, 398 F.2d 628 (2d Cir. 1968).

Indemnification.—

When former corporate officers and directors defended themselves from alleged violations

Criminal Liability.[1328]—A trust company, by exercising some of the functions of a bank, does not lay its officers liable to prosecution for violation of banking laws.[1329]

A statute punishing a bank officer's embezzlement by receiving a deposit when his bank is insolvent was held to include officers of loan, trust, and safe

---

of the Investment Company Act, they were not parties to that action "by reason of being or having been a director or officer of the corporation" within meaning of statute providing that every corporation shall have power to indemnify former director or officer against all expenses incurred in connection with or arising out of any action to which the director or officer is a party by reason of being or having been a director or officer of the corporation. Tomash v. Midwest Technical Dev. Corp., 281 Minn. 21, 160 N.W.2d 273 (1968).

Counsel fees.—

In making an award for counsel fees and expenses in action to enjoin officers and trustees of investment trust to continue to act in such capacities and for appointment of receivers, district court should be allowed considerable latitude. Bailey v. McLellan, 159 F.2d 1014.

Attorneys who sought to defend trustees and officers of an investment trust against charges of abuse of trust and misconduct were not entitled to have their fees for such unsuccessful defense charged to the trust corpus. Bailey v. McLellan, 159 F.2d 1014.

Effect of consent decree.—

Under statute prohibiting any person who, by reason of misconduct, is enjoined from engaging in any conduct in connection with purchase or sale of security from serving in capacity of officer or director of any registered investment company, defendants who consented to entry of judgment enjoining them from certain acts and practices would be assumed to have been found guilty of misconduct, and subsequent conduct of defendants in acting as officers of investment company constituted violation of Investment Company Act. SEC v. Midland Basic, Inc., 283 F. Supp. 609 (D.S.D. 1968).

Securities and Exchange Commission is not required to litigate fully each and every action in order to establish such misconduct as will render applicable provisions of Investment Company Act of 1940 prohibiting any person enjoined by reason of misconduct from acting as officer or director of any registered investment company. Securities & Exch. Comm'n v. Midland Basic, Inc., 283 F. Supp. 609 (D.S.D. 1968).

Findings not erroneous.—

In an action in which defendants-common stock funds, which transferred plaintiffs' securities or their proceeds from liquidation to one plaintiffs son who had utilized a forged power of attorney, sought to avoid liability for the wrongful transfers, findings of the trial court that plaintiffs notified the defendants that their stock had been wrongfully taken within a reasonable time after they had notice of that fact were not clearly erroneous. First Nat'l Bank v. Hovey, 412 N.E.2d 889 (Mass. App. 1980).

[1328] See generally vol. 1, chapter 8, § 204 et seq.

[1329] Myers v. Heitman Trust Co., 289 Ill. App. 619, 7 N.E.2d 509; Dietrich v. Rothenberger, 25 Ky. L. Rptr. 338, 76 S.W. 271.

deposit companies.[1330] On the trial of an officer of a trust company for appropriating the company's funds by becoming indebted to it, guilty intent may be inferred from the fact of the debt.[1331] And an indictment alleging that the accused as director of a trust company permitted and procured the company to make an excessive loan to a firm of which he was a partner, is a plain statement of the act constituting the crime, and the indictment need not allege specifically in what manner he permitted the prohibited loan.[1332] Matters relating to the prosecution of an officer of a trust company for receiving gratuities or fees in connection with bank business,[1333] and making false reports as to the company's condition,[1334] appear in the footnote.

[1330] Walter v. State, 208 Ind. 231, 195 N.E. 268, 98 LLR. 607; Gillian v. State, 207 Ind. 661, 194 N.E. 360.

[1331] State v. Barnes, 108 Minn. 227, 122 N.W. 4.

[1332] People v. Knapp, 206 N.Y. 373, 99 N.E. 841, 19148 Ann. Cas. 248.

[1333] **Receiving fees.—**

Evidence that trust company officer demanded money as condition of continuance of furnishing credit to contractor by trust company, and that money thus demanded was paid, supported conviction for violation of statute prohibiting officers from receiving fees in connection with business of trust company. Commonwealth v. McKnight, 289 Mass. 530, 195 N.E. 499, petition for cert. dismissed, 296 U.S. 660, 56 S. Ct. 245, 80 L. Ed. 470, wherein evidence was held for jury. See also Commonwealth v. Ries, 337 Mass. 565, 150 N.E.2d 527.

Question whether fees received by officer and employee of trust company were received in connection with business of trust company and were in violation of statute prohibiting officer, from receiving fee in connection with certain business of trust company was for jury. Commonwealth v. Greenberg, 339 Mass. 557, 160 N.E.2d 181.

Instructions.—

In prosecution of vice-president, who was also lending officer, of trust company for, among other things, receiving gratuities in connection with bank business, trial court did not err in refusing instruction that there could be no conviction far receiving gratuities unless they were received in connection with business of trust company and not merely for arranging of a loan by one person to another. Commonwealth v. Ries, 337 Mass. 565, 150 N.E.2d 527.

In such prosecution denial of a request for instruction that it was immaterial that bar-rower and company bearing borrower's name were not separate legal entities if defendant accepted in good faith treatment by borrower of his personal account as separate from his business or company account, was not error. Commonwealth v. Ries, 337 Mass. 565, 150 N.E.2d 527.

In such prosecution, requested instructions that defendant could not be found guilty of receiving gratuities unless jury found one or more of functions performed by trust company constituted actual business of company, that if manner of collection of loans was a matter to which borrower was "indifferent" and for which he did not pay money they should not consider activities of collection department of trust company as its business in connection

III. FUNCTIONS AND DEALINGS.

a. General Considerations.

§ 13. Nature of Trust Company.

A bank is not a trust company, and a trust company unless so empowered, cannot do a banking business as incident to its major purpose.[1335] The primary and ordinary concept of a trust company is as a corporation to take and administer trusts.[1336] However, trust companies may be authorized to

---

with which defendant received fees from borrower, and that issuance of treasurer's checks of company could not be considered as trust company business in connection with which defendant received money, were properly denied. Commonwealth v. Ries, 337 Mass. 565, 150 N.E.2d 527.

In prosecution of vice-president, who was also lending officer of trust company, for receiving of gratuities in connection with bank business, transactions involving loans, mechanics of which were handled through trust company and which were collected by trust company, warranted charge that trust company's activities were business of company within contemplation of statute prohibiting officer of trust company from receiving any gift in connection with business of company and in instructing jury that sole question before them was whether vice-president had received gratuities from borrower. Commonwealth v. Ries, 337 Mass. 565, 150 N.E.2d 527.

Sufficiency of evidence.—

Evidence was sufficient to prove that vice-president received gratuities in connection with business of trust company. Commonwealth v. Ries, 337 Mass. 565, 150 N.E.2d 527.

[1334] In prosecution for making false report of condition of trust company, circumstantial evidence was admissible to prove knowledge of falsity or willfulness and intention to deceive. And uncontradicted evidence that report was false and that defendants signed and delivered it without examination and in entire disregard as to whether it was true or false was held to justify conviction. State v. Steneck, 118 N.J.L. 268, 192 A. 381, aff'd, 120 N.J.L. 188, 198 A. 848.

[1335] Loudoun Nat'l Bank v. Continental Trust Co., 164 Va. 536, 180 S.E. 548, 551, appeal dismissed, 297 U.S. 698, 56 S. Ct. 594, 80 L. Ed. 988.

The Massachusetts statutes make a distinction between trust companies and banks. Nash v. Brown, 165 Mass. 384, 43 N.E. 180.

Corporation organized under statutes governing trust companies had no power to engage in general banking, and could not obtain such power by amending its articles of incorporation, and its acts in both respects were ultra vires and void where it had not complied with statutes governing banking associations. Nelson v. Dakota Bankers Trust Co., 132 N.W.2d 903 (N.D. 1964).

[1336] People v. National Security Co., 189 App. Div. 38, 177 N.Y.S. 838, aff'd, 232 N.Y. 586, 134 N.E. 582; Loudoun Nat'l Bank v. Continental Trust Co., 164 Va. 536, 180 S.E. 548, appeal dismissed, 297 U.S. 698, 56 S. Ct. 594, 80 L. Ed. 988.

engage in banking functions,[1337] but the fact that a trust company is permitted to exercise some of the functions of a bank does not constitute it a "banking institution," just as the possession of certain trust privileges does not transform a banking corporation into a "trust company."[1338] However, it

---

[1337] **In general.—**

Loudoun Nat. Bank v. Continental Trust Co., 164 Va. 536, 180 S.E. 548, appeal dismissed, 297 U.S. 698, 56 S. Ct. 594, 80 L. Ed. 988; People v. National Sec. Co., 189 App. Div 38, 177 N.Y.S. 838, aff'd, 232 N.Y. 586, 134 N.E 582.

Trust companies are primarily commercial banks of deposit, and are owned by the stockholders and managed ultimately for profit. Petition of Allen, 242 Mass. 343, 136 N.E. 112.

In Georgia the act authorizing charters for trust companies with banking privileges is valid. Mulherin v. Kennedy, 120 Ga. 1080, 48 S.E. 437.

In Maryland a trust company is authorized to engage in the banking business. Union Trust Co. v. Harrisons' Nurseries, Inc., 180 Md. 651, 26 A.2d 812.

[1338] **In general.—**

People v. National Sec. Co., 189 App. Div. 38, 177 N.Y.S. 838, aff'd, 232 N.Y. 586, 134 N.E. 582; Loudoun Nat. Bank v. Continental Trust Co., 164 Va. 536, 180 S.E. 548, appeal dismissed, 297 U.S. 698, 56 S. Ct. 597, 80 L. Ed. 988

A trust company may be given powers incidental to a banking business, but the conferring of such powers for the purpose of facilitating its trust powers does not make it a bank or a banking institution. Hogg v. Armstrong, 112 W. Va. 142, 164 S.E. 496, 498.

An indorser on a note made "payable at any bank in Boston," is not held by its presentment to a loan and trust company, which is neither a national nor state bank, in the absence of evidence showing a well established custom to present such notes to trust companies for payment. Nash v. Brown, 165 Mass. 384, 43 N.E. 180.

In the District of Columbia, a trust company was held not a "national bank" within statute prohibiting issuance of attachment against national banking associations in actions in state court before final judgment. Loudoun Nat. Bank v. Continental Trust Co., 164 Va. 536, 180 S.E. 548, appeal dismissed, 297 U.S. 698, 56 S. Ct. 597, 80 L. Ed. 988.

In New York, trust companies are not in any proper sense of the word banking institutions. They are not banks, in the commercial sense of that word, and do not perform the functions of banks in carrying on the exchanges of commerce, although they receive money on deposit and invest it in loans, and so deal in money and securities for money. Mercantile Bank v. New York, 121 U.S. 138, 7 S. Ct. 826, 837, 30 L. Ed. 895.

Annuity, safe deposit, surety and trust companies, organized and regulated, pursuant to chapter of North Dakota statute governing such institutions, are banking institutions which do not possess all powers of banking associations, and were not, before 1968 amendment, empowered to conduct general banking business. Nelson v. Dakota Bankers Trust Co., 132 N.W.2d 903 (N.D. 1964).

Receiving deposits while insolvent.—

A trust company and its officers are not within the provisions of a statute which forbid

has been held that when full banking powers are given to a trust company it is thereby made a bank.[1339] And trust companies doing a general banking business may be classified by a legislature as banks for purposes of regulation.[1340] A mortgage company owed a statutory fiduciary obligation to all of its purchaser investors in handling both funds invested and payment collected from borrowers.[1341]

A trust company is also distinguished from a bank in that its deposits are strictly loans, not subject to check, and it may not issue its own notes for circulation nor buy and sell exchange in the ordinary course of its dealings.[1342] Outside the realm of banking a trust company's powers are much broader, extending into real estate transactions, trusteeships and the

---

officers of any banking institution from receiving deposits when the bank or banking institution is insolvent, though such company has and exercises some of the functions of a bank. State v. Reid, 125 Mo. 43, 28 S.W. 172.

Where a corporation is empowered to act as registrar and transfer agent of an-other corporation, the mere acting as registrar and transfer agent does not make the corporation a trust company, notwithstanding a statute granting such powers to trust and banking companies. People v. National Sec. Co., 189 App. Div. 38, 177 N.Y.S. 838, aff'd, 232 N.Y. 586, 134 N.E. 582.

Violation of banking laws.—

The exercise by a trust company of some of the functions of a bank does not make the company's officers liable to prosecution for violating the banking laws. Dietrich v. Rothenberger, 25 Ky. L. Rptr. 888, 75 S.W. 271; Myers v. Heitman Trust Co., 289 Ill. App. 619, 7 N.E.2d 509.

[1339] Sterling v. Tantum, 28 Del 409, 94 A. 176; Kansas v. Hayes, 62 F.2d 597.

Calling an institution a bank does not make it a bank in legal contemplation if it is not given the powers of a bank. And, conversely, calling an institution a trust company does not prevent its being a bank within the meaning of the law, if it possesses and exercises all the powers of a bank. Sterling v. Tantum, 28 Del. 409, 94 A. 176, quoted in Kansas v. Hayes, 62 F.2d 597.

Trust company having on deposit on demand, subject to check, moneys of city, county, and state, and moneys of savings and other banks, held under state laws and in fact "banking corporation." Kansas ex rel. Boynton v. Hayes, 82 F.2d 597.

It is common knowledge that trust companies under Kansas laws have long done large banking business by receiving public funds on deposit, and moneys of banks. Kansas v. Hayes, 62 F.2d 597.

[1340] In re Estate of Wellings, 192 Cal. 506, 221 P. 628.

[1341] In re Lemons & Associates, Inc., 67 Bankr. 198 (Bankr. D. Nev. 1986).

[1342] Myers v. Heitman Trust Co., 289 Ill. App. 619, 7 N.E.2d 509; Dietrich v. Rothenberger, 25 Ky. L. Rptr. 388, 75 S.W. 271.

conduct of property interests.[1343] The fact that a bank and a trust company are owned by the same stockholders and their affairs are conducted by the same board of directors and officers, does not destroy their separate corporate identities, create the relationship of principal and agent, or render one liable for the contracts and obligations of the other.[1344]

Departmental banks are single corporate entities, managed by a single board of directors and owned by shareholders participating in the combined profits and losses of the several departments, so that transactions between bank departments affecting a trust for which a bank is trustee create no immunity against self-dealing by the trustee as between the bank and the trust.[1345] And a bank having a trust department cannot act in the dual capacity of settler and trustee by creating a trust out of its own realty.[1346] A trust company with a savings department is a single entity, title to all properties is in that entity, and the directors are officers thereof.[1347] And a trust company, even in its savings department, is not a mutual institution.[1348] The ordinary rules of assignment, including those relating to notice, apply to an assignment of a note by the commercial department of a trust company to the savings department.[1349] A state statute prohibiting trust companies or similar corporations or national banks from advertising or circularizing the fact that they are authorized to act as executors does not amount to an invidious discrimination against banks and in favor of lawyers.[1350]

§ 14. Dealings in General.

Where an alleged contract under which a trust company agreed to act as trustee under a financial plan was terminable at will by either party without compensation to the other, the promoters of the plan could not recover expenses or damages on the trust company's refusal to perform the contract, and the company could not be held liable for breach on the theory that it had

---

[1343] Dietrich v. Rothenberger, 25 Ky. L Rptr. 838, 75 S.W. 271.

[1344] Farmers' Trust Co. v. Threlkeld, 257 Ky. 211, 77 S.W.2d 616.

[1345] In re Rees' Estate, 85 N.E.2d 563, 53 Ohio L. Abs. 385 (Ohio App.).

[1346] Gallagher v. Squire, 57 Ohio App. 222, 13 N.E.2d 373.

[1347] In re Prudential Trust Co., 244 Mass. 64, 138 N.E. 702.

Trust and commercial departments of company operating under one charter are merely component parts of single unit. Flack v. Hood, 204 N.C. 337, 168 S.E. 520.

[1348] In re Prudential Trust Co., 244 Mass. 64, 138 N.E. 702.

[1349] Cosmopolitan Trust Co. v. Leonard Watch Co., 249 Mass. 14, 143 N.E. 827.

[1350] New Hampshire Bankers Ass'n v. Nelson, 336 F. Supp. 1330 (D.N.H.), aff'd 460 F.2d 307 (1st Cir.), cert. denied, 409 U.S. 1001, 93 S. Ct. 320, 34 L. Ed 2d 262 (1972).

not terminated the contract but refused to recognize its existence.[1351] Similarly, where the president of an investment company orally stated that it would guarantee a payment, and that its directors by resolution had authorized him to so guarantee, the company was held not answerable therefor where it was not a party to the transaction, did not receive any consideration, and its officers did not sign the resolution or exercise the authority conferred.[1352] For other instances of dealings, see the footnote.[1353]

[1351] Chatham Plan v. Clinton Trust Co., 246 App. Div. 498, 286 N.Y.S. 179, appeal dismissed, 272 N.Y. 497, 4 N.E.2d 249.

[1352] Southern Glass Co. v. Consolidated Inv. Corp., 1 Cal. App. 2d 510, 36 P.2d 1077.

[1353] **In general.—**

In dealing with transactions between corporation acting as trustee and itself in capacity of bank, two capacities of corporation must be regarded as distinct and independent entities except that each must be charged with notice of other's acts. Corbett v. Hospelhorn, 172 Md. 257, 191 A. 691.

Where trust was attempted to be created by written declaration of combined bank and trust company, pursuant to which certificates of participation in first mortgage investments, held by company as trustee, were issued by it to itself and purchasers of interests in trust, it was held not valid as either express, constructive, or resulting trust. Arend v. Fulton, 58 Ohio App. 503, 5 N.E2d 792.

A trust company was more then a mere naked trustee where owner of realty executed bond mortgage to secure series A and series B notes all originally issued in favor of named corporation, and series A bonds were pledged by mortgage to trust company to secure indebtedness of original mortgagor to trust company and trust company was also named trusts; and the mortgage and series A bonds were thereafter sold by auctioneer to fourth party as nominee for benefit of trust company, Enochs v. Mississippi Tower Bldg., 210 Miss. 676, 50 So. 2d 551.

Statute forbidding banking institutions from guaranteeing evidences of indebtedness. held intended to protest an institution doing a banking business, and not a "trust company." Myers v. Heitman Trust Co., 280 Ill. App. 619, 7 N.E.2d 509.

Trust company held not relieved from liability to repurchase mortgage bonds which it had given its stockholder in exchange for stock when bonds were defaulted. Myers v. Heitman Trust Co., 289 Ill. App. 619, 7 N.E.2d 509.

A trust company which assented to deposit agreement among bank stockholders concerning stock of bank's newly organized affiliate securities corporation, received, certificates of stock in bank and affiliate, and acknowledged that it had received such certificates and held them pursuant to deposit agreement, became contractually bound to holders of transferable receipts issued by it, representing shares of such stock, to deal with certificates in manner described by deposit agreement. Commissioner of Banks v. Chase Securities Corp., 298 Mass. 285, 10 N.E.2d 472, appeal dismissed, 302 U.S. 660, 58 S. Ct. 476, 82 L. Ed. 510.

(Text continued on page 370)

Acting as agent, not trustee.—

The relationship between corporation and trust company, holding as corporation's transfer agent moneys deposited to redeem corporation's script certificate for stock dividends, was that of debtor and creditor, and trust company was not trustee for script holder, but agent to carry out corporation's offer to pay for unredeemed script, so that corporation could recover amount on deposit from trust company. Hupp Motor Car Corp. v. Guaranty Trust Co., 171 Misc. 21, 11 N.Y.S.2d 855.

A trust company which agreed to submit notes or bond. secured by mortgages or trust deeds to insurance company for purchase and to act as insurance company's agent in the collection and remittance of principal and interest on loans purchased as they became due was an "agent" rather than a "trustee" with respect to transactions subsequently negotiated. People ex rel. Barrett v. Cody Trust Co., 294 Ill. App. 342, 13 N.E.2d 829.

Where trust company became loan correspondent for any insurance company securing applications for loans in name of property owner which it submitted to insurance company accompanied by a description of the property and an appraisal, insurance company reserving exclusive right to determine what mortgages it would purchase, any duty of the trust company to furnish information not asked for would extend only to such information as it had reason to believe was unknown to the insurance company and was material, or had reason to believe that the insurance company would think to be material. Metropolitan Life Ins. Co. v. Union Trust Co., 268 App. Div. 474, 51 N.Y.S.2d 318 (1944), aff'd, 294 N.Y. 254, 62 N.E.2d 59.

Where trust company supplied insurance company with all information requested, and following the depression insurance company was required to take over several mortgaged properties and was compelled to pay taxes for improvements made prior to time of taking the mortgages, and insurance company was aware that such properties were in a newly developed locality, insurance company had no cause of action against trust company for fraudulent concealment or breach of duty. Metropolitan Life Ins. Co. v. Union Trust Co., 268 App. Div. 474, 51 N.Y.S.2d 318 (1944), aff'd, 294 N.Y. 254, 62 N.E.2d 59.

Acting as principal.—

Where investment bankers who had made several trades in bonds with customer, acting always as principals and never for customer's account, traded certificates costing $18,069.41 for customer's bonds which sold for $23, 800, there was no "fiduciary relation," "trustee relationship," or "agency" that would make bankers liable to account for profits. Metcalf v. Leedy, Wheeler & Co., 140 Fla. 149, 191 So. 890.

Where trust company sold securities to bank vice-president for which it received his personal check certified by bank, and trust company on receiving money from Federal Reserve Bank for use of bank delivered securities to vice-president personally, bank could not recover judgment against trust company on theory that bank's money was used to pay vice-president's personal obligation where thereafter bank was reimbursed by means of checks on vice-president's personal account, notwithstanding subsequent conversions of vice-president, as county treasurer, from county's general deposit with bank to cover diversion of money with which vice-president originally reimbursed bank. Hall v. Manufacturers Trust Co., 18 F. Supp. 173.

A trust company seeking to liquidate stock held as collateral for loan, which had a merely

(*Text continued on page 370*)

nominal market quotation and was of value primarily only as giving control of railroad, properly refused to attempt to dispose of such stock on the stock exchange where such attempt would necessitate making a market by buying as well as selling, in possible violation of Securities Exchange Act. Litwin v. Allen, 25 N.Y.S.2d 667.

Liability as custodian of securities safeguarding bondholders.—

Trust company, which was custodian of securities to safeguard bondholders against loss, was not liable to bondholder on default of company issuing bond, but liability of trust company, if any, must be based on alleged negligence resulting in loss of securities by allowing improper withdrawal. Union Deposit Co. v. Talbot, 101 Colo. 426, 73 P.2d 1389.

To entitle purchaser of guaranteed mortgage certificate to rescind on ground of misrepresentation, something more is required than mere offer to restore, and purchaser must actually tender certificate at time demand for return of purchase price is made or attempt to make tender. Fetzer v. Title Guarantee & Trust Co., 250 App. Div. 567, 294 N.Y.S. 922.

Purpose to make illegal loan not imputed.—

Where trust company purported to purchase stock in national bank from one who was controlling influence in both institutions, the purpose to make him an excessive loan with the stock as security cannot be imputed to such company by court in action against it by national bank's receiver to enforce stockholder's liability. Wellston Trust Co. v. Snyder, 87 F.2d 44.

A transaction whereby trust company purchased bonds at a price below the market, giving option to seller to repurchase for same price within six months, at which time if option was not exercised the trust company's wholly-owned subsidiary would take over the securities at the price paid, was a substitute for a loan and was not improper as a subterfuge for a loan wherein obligation to repay, which is the essential and most elementary requirement of a loan, was lacking. Litwin v. Allen, 25 N.Y.S.2d 667.

Such transaction would be given the construction placed upon it by all interested parties at the time of and after its consummation, regardless of who initiated the transaction and what form it was originally thought the transaction would take. Litwin v. Allen, 25 N.Y.S.2d 667.

Irregularity in meeting authorizing loan.—

When trust company received proceeds of Reconstruction Finance Corporation loan and gave promises to repay, an "indebtedness" existed whether or not resolution authorizing the loan was adopted at a regular meeting by a quorum of corporation directors, and neither trust company nor its stockholders could take advantage of any irregularity in such meeting. United States v. Freeman, 37 F. Supp. 720.

Loan company mortgagee as alter ego of bank obtaining mortgage.—

As respects whether minors were entitled to decree vacating decree which had authorized register to execute in minors' names a mortgage on minors' property to a loan company on ground that bank committed fraud in obtaining mortgage, the loan company as mortgagee was a mere alter ego of bank where loan company had same officials as bank and conducted its business in bank. Midgley v. Ralls, 234 Ala. 685, 176 So. 799.

Adviser's contract with investment company could not be construed as providing for exclusivity of services. Taussig v. Wellington Fund, Inc., 187 F. Supp. 179, aff'd, 313 F.2d 472.

(Text continued on page 370)

Designation of beneficiary in investment trust certificate.—

Where decedent's designation of beneficiary who would be entitled to his right and title in investment trust certificate in event of his death did not refer to beneficiary's heirs, assigns or estate and was revocable, and certificate could have been assigned, terminating beneficiary's interest, no right was vested in beneficiary but she received only contingent interest which failed when she died before decedent died, and decedent's estate, not beneficiary's estate, was owner of certificate. Johnson v. Corporate Leaders of America, Inc., 41 Misc. 2d 1030, 247 N.Y.S.2d 164.

Change of beneficiary of mutual funds.—

Provision in will bequeathing mutual funds to individual was ineffective to change beneficiary of mutual funds in company whose rules required that change of beneficiary be by written instrument delivered to company. In re Stein's Will, 42 Misc. 2d 787, 249 N.Y.S.2d 223 (Sur. Ct. 1964).

Limitation on investment company's contractual liability.—

Investment companies were not liable for breach of contracts, which provided for unlimited "in-and-out" privileges, nor were contracts specifically enforceable, where national securities association, of which companies were members, issued interpretation" limiting exercise of privileges under such contracts. Harwell v. Growth Programs, Inc., 315 F. Supp. 1184 (W.D. Tex. 1970).

Revocation of common-law rule as to trustee's holdings.—

Statute conferring upon trust companies the power to be appointed trustee under the same circumstances as those involving a legally qualified individual impliedly revoked commonlaw rule that trust companies cannot hold property in joint tenancy with the right of survivorship. Bank of Delaware v. Bancroft, 269 A.2d 254 (Del. Ch. 1970).

Express oral agreement with management consultant not shown.—

In action by management consultant against small business investment company to collect fees for management services rendered in connection with effort to rescue financially troubled manufacturing company, evidence including consultant's own testimony and evidence of prior practice between consultant and investment company failed to make case for jury on consultant's theory that there was express oral agreement on part of investment company to be directly and primarily responsible to consultant for his fees. Noonan v. Midland Capital Corp., 453 F.2d 459 (2d Cir. 1972).

Acceptance of offer to buy shares in investment fund.—

Investment fund's acceptance of plaintiff's offer to buy shares in the fund could be made by the fund by performance independently of the passing of the rights of the transferor to the plaintiff by delivery of the stock certificate to plaintiff. Kreis v. Mates Inv. Fund, Inc., 335 F. Supp. 1299 (E.D. Mo. 1971).

Where plaintiff mailed, from his residence in Missouri, a letter requesting to purchase shares in investment company, which was located in New York, and which was not registered pursuant to Missouri Securities Act, and the fund cashed plaintiff's Check which was enclosed with the letter and posted the sale to plaintiff on its books, neither the confirmation of the sale by the fund, nor the physical delivery of stock certificates to plaintiff

(Text continued on page 370)

had any effect on plaintiff's right to the shares. Kreis v. Mates Inv. Fund, Inc., 335 F. Supp. 1299 (E.D. Mo. 1971).

Anti-rebate provisions not violated.

—Registered mutual fund's use of its underwriter as a recipient of a give-up on understanding that underwriter's parent, the fund's investment advisor, would give the fund a credit against charges for investment advisory services would not be illegal as being contrary to anti-rebate provisions of exchange constitutions. Moses v. Burgin, 445 F.2d 369 (1st Cir.), rev'g 316 F. Supp. 31 (D. Mass.), cert. denied, 404 U.S. 994, 92 S. Ct. 532, 80 L. Ed. 2d 547 (1971).

Closing or termination fee.—

Where, in 1945 a mutual fund and the bank entered into a custodial agreement which contained a fee arrangement, including a closing or termination fee of one-twentieth of one percent of reasonable value of all securities held, authorization for a closing fee remained a valid part of contract between the parties and was not superseded or eliminated by 1955 letter agreement, which outlined new fee schedules for services by the bank, but which were silent as to termination arrangements as well as fees therefor. Crown Western Invs., Inc. v. Mercantile Nat'l Bank, 504 S.W.2d 785 (Tex. Civ. App. 1974).

Demand by bank of guaranty of corporation's indebtedness.—

Bank, which owned all of corporation's stock as trustee of voting trust, did not act unfairly in violation of federal banking regulations and did not engage in "unfair . . . acts or practices" in demanding and obtaining chief executive officer's guaranty of corporation's indebtedness to bank. First Nat'l Bank v. Slade, 399 N.E.2d 1047 (Mass. 1979).

Implied contractual relationship existed.—

Under Maryland law, implied contractual relationship existed between trust company and testatrix, for trust company to provide estate planning services for her in consideration of being named fiduciary under the will, which was broader than formal written agreement between parties for management of testatrix' investment trust company's visits to testatrix' house when summoned, company's estate planning activities, company's routine instruction of testatrix' attorney concerning testatrix' testamentary design, and company's assistance in the actual drafting of wills demonstrated existence of the relationship. Merrick v. Mercantile-Safe Deposit & Trust Co., 855 F.2d 1095 (4th Cir. 1988).

Under Maryland law, trust company's duty to named beneficiary in will, in exercising due care while performing estate planning services for testatrix, was not undermined by its inability to practice law, where company had already received legal advice that will provision later employed was ineffective as matter of law additional negligence of testatrix' attorney did not immunize trust company from liability where it had knowledge of the ineffectiveness of the will provision. Merrick v. Mercantile-Safe Deposit & Trust Co., 855 F.2d 1095 (4th Cir. 1988).

Negligent misrepresentations.—

Shareholders in investment company who voted against sale of company's assets could claim reliance on alleged negligent misrepresentations made by investment banking firm concerning fairness of sale, where majority of shareholders voted in favor of sale. Dowling v. Narragansett Capital Corp., 735 F. Supp. 1105 (D.R.I. 1990).

§ 15. Dealings with Trust Property.

In General.—The primary and ordinary concept of a trust company is as a corporation to take and administer trusts.[1354] And a foreign corporation organized to receive money for investment, which becomes the property of the corporation free of the certificate holders' control, is subject to regulation as doing a "trust business."[1355] Similarly, an investment company acting as an agent in securing a real estate loan holds any funds derived from the sale of the note and mortgage in its hands for negotiation, as a trust fund.[1356] And the manner in which a loan corporation must exercise its power to appoint a substitute trustee under a deed of trust is to be sought in the general law, the applicable statutes and the corporation's charter and bylaws.[1357] A trust

---

Whether circumstances imparted assertive quality to investment banking firm's opinion concerning value of investment company's stock sufficient to make reliance upon it justifiable was question of fact that could not be resolved by a motion to dismiss negligent misrepresentation claim against firm, where firm held itself out as expert in valuing stock and was perceived as having access to all information relevant to proper appraisal. Dowling v. Narragansett Capital Corp., 735 F. Supp. 1105 (D.R.I. 1990).

Investment banking firm's duty to exercise reasonable care in its assessment of adequacy of proposed purchase price for investment company's assets extended to company's shareholders, although firm was engaged by company to make assessment, where assessment was intended to guide shareholders in deciding whether to approve proposed sale of assets. Dowling v. Narragansett Capital Corp., 735 F. Supp. 1105 (D.R.I. 1990).

Trust company is not empowered to hold any stock of another bank. In re Bankers Trust Co., 636 N.Y.S.2d 741 (N.Y. App. Div. 1 Dep't 1995).

Statutory prohibition on trust company holding stock of another bank is limited to situations where bank invests in its own account, rather than as fiduciary. In re Bankers Trust Co., 636 N.Y.S.2d 741 (N.Y. App. Div. 1 Dep't 1995).

[1354] People v. National Security Co., 189 App. Div. 38, 177 N.Y.S. 838, aff'd, 232 N.Y. 586, 134 N.E. 582; Loudoun Nat. Bank v. Continental Trust Co., 164 Va. 536, 180 S.E. 548, appeal dismissed, 297 U.S. 698, 56 S. Ct. 597, 80 L. Ed. 988.

[1355] Hayden Plan Co. v. Wood, 97 Cal. App. 1, 275 P. 248.

[1356] Fidelity Nat. Bank v. Copeland, 138 Okla. 19, 280 P. 273.

[1357] Brown v. National Loan & Inv. Co., 139 S.W.2d 364 (Tex. Civ. App. 1940) (Texas corporation).

Where deed of trust held by loan corporation gave corporation power of sale in event of default in payment of obligation and power to appoint a substitute trustee if named trustee, who was corporation's president, refused to act, and corporation, when president refused to exercise power of sale upon default, purporting to act through its vice-president, such action being attested by secretary and executed with corporate seal, executed an instrument appointing a substitute trustee, and board of directors subsequently ratified the appointment, sale by substitute trustee to corporation was not void, as against judgment creditors of grantor in deed of trust claiming under judgments subsequent to execution and recording of

company's board of directors may delegate the general supervision of the management of trust estates to a committee whose action will be legal and binding without approval or further action of the board.[1358]

A trust company holding the funds of numerous beneficiaries may properly deposit such funds in a single trust account in another bank, if it keeps an accurate record of the contributions of the separate trusts.[1359] Where a trust company having charge of several trust funds belonging to separate estates and parties, uses a part thereof in its private business, and its cash balance on hand is made up of money belonging to all the funds commingled, for the purpose of ascertaining how much money of any particular fund it so used, only that fund's proportionate part of the cash on hand can be deducted from the cash balance due it.[1360] But where a fund was entrusted to a trust company for investment with the understanding that interest should be paid the owner monthly, but should be paid only out of interest collected from investment of the fund, the fund was a trust fund, and no implied agreement existed that the fund could be deposited in the company's general checking account.[1361] A bank exercising the powers of a trust company can receive money in trust and allow an agreed rate of interest thereon.[1362]

Where a trust agreement authorizes a trustee to sell its own securities to the trust estate or buy securities from the trust estate, the highest degree of

---

deed of trust. Brown v. National Loan & Inv. Co., 139 S.W.2d 364 (Tex. Civ. App. 1940).

[1358] Loud v. St. Louis Union Trust Co., 313 Mo. 552, 281 S.W. 744.

[1359] Finley v. Exchange Trust Co., 183 Okla. 167, 80 P.2d 296, 117 A.L.R. 162.

An arrangement whereby trust company deposited funds of several hundred trusts in single banking account, made loans in its own name, and subsequently sold particular loans to particular trust estates, sometimes issuing participation certificates to two or more trust estates, was not improper as constituting commingling of trust funds. Finley v. Exchange Trust Co., 183 Okla. 167, 80 P.2d 296, 117 A.L.R. 162.

[1360] St. Paul Trust Co. v. Kittson, 62 Minn. 408, 65 N.W. 74.

It is a well-recognized general rule that a trustee or fiduciary may not use trust property for his own benefit and if he does he is liable to a cestui que trust for profits made by him from the use of trust property. However, an exception to this general rule is recognized in the case of banks which under the decisional and statutory law of Pennsylvania are permitted to deposit trust funds as well as demand deposits in the commercial or savings department of their bank or in another bank, and while they may be liable for interest, they are not liable to the owner of such funds for profits made thereon by the bank. Stahl v. First Pennsylvania Banking & Trust Co., 411 Pa. 121, 191 A.2d 386, citing In re Moore's Estate, 211 Pa. 348, 60 A. 991.

[1361] Duncan v. Williamson, 18 Tenn. App. 153, 74 S.W.2d 215.

[1362] Conley v. Johnson, 101 Mont. 376, 54 P.2d 585.

care and skill required by law should be required of the trustee; where a trust company holds itself out as having a higher degree of skill than that possessed by an ordinary man, it should be held thereto whether or not it actually possesses such skill.[1363] And it is not improper to judge the advertisements and representations of an investment adviser by their impact on the segment of the public at which they are aimed.[1364]

[1363] **In general.—**

Finley v. Exchange Trust Co., 183 Okla. 167, 80 P.2d 296, 117 A.L.R. 162.

A corporation seeking business as a corporate fiduciary must maintain strict standards of a trustee. In re Longworth, 222 A.2d 561 (Me. 1966).

Trust company not negligent.—

Evidence held to authorize finding that trust company was not negligent in transferring mortgage loan held by it individually to trust estate, notwithstanding delinquencies occurring after transfer. Finley v. Exchange Trust Co., 183 Okla. 167, 80 P.2d 296, 117 A.L.R. 162.

But trust company was negligent in purchasing mortgage loans for trust estate where taxes on mortgaged property were delinquent for three years at time of purchase, and was liable to beneficiary of trust for resulting loss. Finley v. Exchange Trust Co., 183 Okla. 167, 80 P.2d 296, 117 A.L.R. 162.

[1364] **In general.—**

Marketlines, Inc. v. SEC, 384 F.2d 264, 5 A.L.R. Fed. 240 (2d Cir. 1967), cert. denied, 390 U.S. 947, 88 S. Ct. 1033, 19 L. Ed. 2d 1136 (1968).

See also §§ 2 and 11.1 of this chapter.

Newspapers as investment advisers.—

It is immaterial to determination whether a particular newspaper falls within exception to Investment Advisers Act for publishers of bona fide newspapers, news magazines or business or financial publications of general and regular circulation, whether usual newspapers are paid for using news items which they publish if they are not offered as investment advice; what matters is whether or not a specific publication is engaged in practices which the act is intended to regulate, such as offering of professional investment advice without revealing possibility of personal gain to publisher from what he reports or how he presents it. SEC v. Wall Street Transcript Corp., 422 F.2d 1371 (2d Cir. 1970), cert. denied, 398 U.S. 958, 90 S. Ct. 2170, 26 L. Ed. 2d 542.

Weekly publication, which was printed on newsprint in form of tabloid newspaper, which mainly reprinted reports assessing various security issues, which devoted nearly one-half of front page and part of second to index listing various companies by name and which was available by subscription or single copy, did not necessarily fall within exception to Investment Advisers Act of publisher of any bona fide newspaper, news magazine or business or financial publication of general and regular circulation. SEC v. Wall Street Transcript Corp., 422 F.2d 1371 (2d Cir. 1970), cert. denied, 398 U.S. 958, 90 S. Ct. 2170, 26 L. Ed. 2d 542.

Phrase "bona fide newspapers," in provision of Investment Advisers Act excluding publishers of bona fide newspapers from definition of investment advisers means those

For other cases dealing with problems arising as to handling of trust property, see the footnote.[1365]

---

publications which do not deviate from customary newspaper activities to such an extent that there is a likelihood that the wrongdoing which the act was designed to prevent has occurred; determination whether given publication comes within exclusion depends on nature of its practices rather than on purely formal indicia of a newspaper which it exhibits on its face or the size and nature of subscription list. SEC v. Wall Street Transcript Corp., 422 F.2d 1371 (2d Cir. 1970), cert. denied, 398 U.S. 958, 90 S. Ct. 2170, 26 L. Ed. 2d 542.

Fact that a publication includes financial information is not determinative of whether publication is a bona fide newspaper, news magazine or business or financial publication of general and regular circulation within exclusion of Investment Advisers Act. SEC v. Wall Street Transcript Corp., 422 F.2d 1371 (2d Cir. 1970), cert. denied, 398 U.S. 958, 90 S. Ct. 2170, 26 L. Ed. 2d 542.

Securities and Exchange Commission is agency best suited to decide in first instance whether publication falls within exception to Investment Advisers Act as a bona fide newspaper, news magazine or business or financial publication of general and regular circulation; it is not to be presumed that the Commission will not be fully aware of the importance of considerations of freedom of the press when it interprets and applies act's exclusions. SEC v. Wall Street Transcript Corp. 422 F.2d 1371 (2d Cir. 1970), cert. denied, 398 U.S. 958, 90 S. Ct. 2170, 28 L. Ed. 2d 542.

[1365] **Validity of contract to pay taxes.—**

A trust company, which had taken possession of mortgaged property under a first mortgage held by it in a mortgage pool, could not question the validity of its contract with the second mortgagee to pay back taxes on the ground that the courts supervising the liquidation of the mortgage pool had not approved the contract, as provided therein, since it was the company's duty to obtain such approval. Marian v. Peoples-Pittsburgh Trust Co., 149 Pa. Super, 653, 27 A.2d 549.

Improper assumption of inconsistent positions.—

A trust company acted improperly in striking a wife's name from a savings account held as an estate by the entirety after her commitment to an insane hospital, and subsequently assuming inconsistent positions as the wife's guardian and also as executor of her husband's will, under which the deposit was claimed as an asset of the estate. In re Gallagher's Estate, 352 Pa. 476, 43 A.2d 132.

"Entire bank" concept.—

One who hires a bank to act as trustee of estate does not intend that one individual will have power to make disbursements but, rather, believes and has a right to believe that the "entire bank" is working for him and providing the business judgment necessary to properly care for his life savings. Dunkley v. Peoples Bank & Trust Co., 728 F. Supp. 547 (W.D. Ark. 1989).

Bank was grossly negligent in allowing single individual to make disbursements from trust, and allowing disbursements which resulted in the use of family trust for benefit of surviving spouse at the expense of settler's child was a flagrant breach of bank's duty to the trust estate and the beneficiary. Dunkley v. Peoples Bank & Trust Co., 728 F. Supp. 547 (W.D. Ark. 1989).

Common Trust Funds.—In many states trust companies are authorized to invest their trust funds in common trust funds.[1366] For other cases dealing with common trust funds, see the footnote.[1367]

Bank did not violate its plans of operation by investing common trust funds in mutual funds.—

Bank, as trustee of common trust funds, did not violate its plans of operation, which defined bank's powers, by investing common trust funds in mutual funds, even though the plans of operation specifically limited investment to "equity type investments" in Fund A and to "fixed income investments" in Fund B, where there was no difference between such investments held as individual securities and the same investments held in mutual funds. In re OnBank & Trust Co., 649 N.Y.S.2d 592 (N.Y. App. Div. 4 Dep't 1996).

[1366] *Connecticut.*—Under statute authorizing any bank or trust company qualified in that state to act as fiduciary to establish a common trust fund, such bank or trust company must be one organized in accordance with Connecticut statutes relative to state banks and trust companies. In re Byles' Will, 125 N.Y.S.2d 871.

Missouri.—Only a bank acting as fiduciary or cofiduciary is eligible to invest trust funds in common trust fund maintained by bank. Leith v. Mercantile Trust Co. Nat'l Asso., 423 S.W.2d 75 (Mo. App. 1967).

New Hampshire.—Common trust fund plan, under which trusts were to be administered in conformity with laws of state and nation and federal reserve regulations, trust investment committee was to review investments, trustee was to act in good faith and to be governed by rule of prudence, and was to refrain from investing assets of testamentary trust contrary to provisions of will and investment in securities of any one corporation was not to exceed ten percent total value of common fund, was in accordance with Uniform Common Trust Fund Act and federal reserve regulations. Mechanicks Nat'l Bank v. D'Amours, 100 N.H. 461, 129 A.2d 859.

New York.—As to establishment, management and accounting for common trust funds established under the New York Common Trust Funds Law, see In re Bank, 189 Misc. 459, 67 N.Y.S.2d 444; In re Continental Bank & Trust Co., 189 Misc. 795, 67 N.Y.S.2d 806; In re Security Trust Co., 189 Misc. 748, 70 N.Y.S.2d 260, aff'd, 277 App. Div. 837, 97 N.Y.S.2d 922; In re Central Hanover Bank & Trust Co., 75 N.Y.S.2d 397; Mullane v. Central Hanover Bank, etc., Co., 339 U.S. 306, 70 S. Ct. 652, 94 L. Ed. 865; In re Lincoln Rochester Trust Co., 111 N.Y.S.2d 45.

Issuance by trustee of first discretionary common trust fund of participation units for United States Savings Bonds Series G at par was permissible under the statute. In re Chase Nat. Bank, 116 N.Y.S.2d 141.

Charge incurred for printing plan of operation could properly be imposed against principal of first discretionary common trust fund, over objections under that provision of the banking law prohibiting a trust company maintaining a common trust fund from making any charge against the fund for "management" thereof. In re Chase Nat. Bank, 116 N.Y.S.2d 141.

Reasonable disbursements incidental to administration of common trust fund are not charges for "management" within meaning of the statute. Nor is the disbursement by trustee for printing of reports of annual audit of common trust fund a charge for "management." In re Chase Nat. Bank, 206 Misc. 343, 132 N.Y.S.2d 592.

Investments for Customers.—Investment corporations must treat the capital investments of their stockholders as a trust fund, and use the highest good faith and conservative business diligence in its handling.[1368] A trust company holding itself out as especially skilled in the management of investments and which contracts to manage investments as an agent, is obligated to use that degree of care and skill which would ordinarily be

---

See also § 2 of this chapter.

[1367] **Fund is separate from trustee.—**

Where all the corpus of a trust was vested by bank in a discretionary common trust fund of the bank and the bank was a trustee of such fund and its purpose was the aggregating of multiple interests, the court was required to deal with such a fund as an entity separate from the trustee, and separate from the individual estates whose moneys were invested in participations in the fund. In re Stokes' Will, 24 Misc. 2d 872, 203 N.Y.S.2d 689.

Units of bank's common trust fund could not be assigned or transferred to party who claimed to be sole distributer or appointee of trust estate holding such units. Leith v. Mercantile Trust Co. Nat'l Ass'n, 423 S.W.2d 75 (Mo. App. 1967).

Investment in mutual funds by trustee of common trust fund does not constitute delegation of trustee's management duties in violation of banking law and its regulation, since trustee still maintains ultimate managerial control of investment by retaining paramount authority to buy, retain, or sell shares of mutual fund investment. In re OnBank & Trust Co., 637 N.Y.S.2d 647 (N.Y. Sur. 1996).

Charge against trust fund for management.—

Section of banking law prohibiting trustee of common trust fund from making any charge against fund for management thereof does not utilize any specialized or technical language or concepts that would mandate deference to unique expertise of banking department. In re OnBank & Trust Co., 637 N.Y.S.2d 647 (N.Y. Sur. 1996).

Banking law section, which prohibits trustee of common trust fund from making any charge against fund for management thereof, precludes trustee from subjecting common trust fund assets to mutual fund management fees, and banking department regulation must be read in conjunction with that section, no matter how department construes that regulation. In re OnBank & Trust Co., 637 N.Y.S.2d 647 (N.Y. Sur. 1996).

Banking law section prohibiting trustee of common trust fund from making any charge against fund for management thereof does not prohibit common trust funds from investing in mutual funds provided that any management fees charged by mutual funds be absorbed by trustee itself. In re OnBank & Trust Co., 637 N.Y.S.2d 647 (N.Y. Sur. 1996).

When banking law prohibited trustee of common trust fund from investing in mutual funds that charged fee for management of assets under their control, those management fees charged by mutual funds invested in by trustee, as well as any reduction of profit resulting therefrom, had to be reimbursed by trustee to common trust funds. In re Judicial Settlement of Fifth Accounting of OnBank & Trust Co., 637 N.Y.S.2d 647 (N.Y. Sur. 1996).

[1368] People v. Latta, 137 Misc. 208, 244 N.Y.S. 487.

exercised by one performing similar functions under like circumstances.[1369] And the same rule applies to an investment firm.[1370]

An investment banking corporation must disclose fully to an investor the facts concerning which he makes inquiry.[1371] Where an investment company

---

[1369] **In general.—**

Stephens v. Detroit Trust Co., 284 Mich. 149, 278 N.W. 799, holding that evidence established that trust company acted in good faith and with sufficient prudence and skill in making investments.

Acting as agent, not trustee.—

An agreement whereby widow appointed company as her "agent" to manage her property, providing that title and power of revocation should remain in widow, created relationship of "agency" rather than of "trust" especially in view of widow's subsequent active supervision of company's actions, and trust company was not liable as trustee for losses caused by failure to exercise high degree of care. Stephens v. Detroit Trust Co., 284 Mich. 149, 278 N.W. 799.

Effect of exculpatory clause.—

And provision in such agreement that company should be liable for loss "only in case of its bad faith or wilful default" was valid. Stephens v. Detroit Trust Co., 284 Web. 149, 278 N.W. 799.

Trust company held not liable.—

Evidence held not to establish that trust company was liable for losses caused by failure to sell widow's stock. Stephens v. Detroit Trust Co., 284 Mich. 149, 278 N.W. 799.

[1370] **In general.—**

O'Connor v. Burns, Potter & Co., 151 Neb 9, 36 N.W.2d 507.

No bad faith shown.—

Where, after defendant investment firm assumed duties of managing plaintiff's securities pursuant to agent agreement, defendant continued to invest in the same type of securities in which plaintiff, to knowledge of defendant, had previously invested, defendant was not chargeable with bed faith so as to be liable for losses sustained, in absence of instructions to the contrary. O'Connor v. Burns, Potter & Co., 151 Neb. 9, 36 N.W.2d 507.

Evidence did not establish that defendant investment firm, in managing plaintiff's securities pursuant to agency agreement, acted negligently or in bad faith so as to render defendant liable for losses. O'Connor v. Burns, Potter & Co., 151 Neb. 9, 36 N.W.2d 507.

[1371] Tone v. Halsey, Stuart & Co., 286 Ill. App. 169, 3 N.E.2d 142.

Corporation's statement that all statements contained in circular were official or based on information regarded by corporation as reliable, constituted representation that it knew that representations contained in circular were true. Tone v. Halsey, Stuart & Co., 286 Ill. App. 169, 3 N.E.2d 142.

Investment authority and activity must be clearly stated and the investing party must strictly conform to the specified investment powers. Bieze v. Coca, 54 Ill. App. 3d 7, 11 Ill. Dec. 652, 369 N.E2d 106 (1977), quoting Michie on Banks and Bank.

accepts money for investment, the investor has a right to rely on a fair performance of its obligation to invest or return the money, and the company cannot discharge itself from that obligation by showing that the investor accepted from a company officer a forged mortgage purporting to run directly from the borrower to him.[1372] And where investments in a particular loan made by a trust company as agent for its client are improvident and improper, a cause of action arises for its negligence in making such investment.[1373] A similar cause of action arises where a trust company which receives money to invest on first mortgage security invests it in worthless or depreciated securities.[1374] Contracts of investment security, debentures or certificates which cannot reasonably be expected to accumulate a reserve fund equal to the stipulated endowment values, within the stated period, without aid from lapses or appropriations from premiums on new business, are fraudulent, contrary to public policy and unlawful.[1375] Where a mortgage bond as delivered does not conform to the application for its purchase, the buyer is not bound, and where he is fraudulently induced to apply for the bond and make the initial payment, he can avoid the transaction in its entirety.[1376]

In the appended notes are set out decisions relating to bonds, mortgages and monetary certificates generally,[1377] agreements of repurchase or repay-

---

[1372] Ring v. Long Island Real Estate, etc., Inv. Co., 93 App. Div. 442, 87 N.Y.S. 682, aff'd sub nom. Ring v. Howell, 184 N.Y. 553, 76 N.E. 1107.

[1373] Wisconsin Trust Co. v. Cousins, 172 Wis. 486, 179 N.W. 801.

Receipt stating that trust company has on deposit with foreign correspondent sum on account of customer, receipt being payable at option of holder, either by check for foreign amount or by company at current buying rate of exchange, does not require deposit with foreign correspondent to credit of customer and there was no default until customer exercised option by demand on company for check or money; and there was no breach to carry on deposit in foreign country stated sum by failure to keep sufficient sum to meet all obligations of a similar nature than outstanding, where there was continuously a sum sufficient to pay order in controversy. Cosmopolitan Trust Co. v. Ciarla, 239 Mass. 32, 131 N.E. 337.

[1374] Woodard v. Citizens' Sav. & T. Co., 167 Wis. 435, 167 N.W. 1054.

[1375] State v. Interstate Sav. Inv. Co., 64 Ohio St. 283, 60 N.E. 220, 83 Am. St. R. 754, 52 L.R.A. 530.

[1376] Bankers' Mortg. Co. v. Rogers (Tex. Civ. App.), 61 S.W.2d 593.

[1377] **In general.—**

Erroneous description of property in mortgage certificate issued to investor, which stated that mortgage covered five instead of only two blocks, held to entitle investor to rescind contract and recover funds. Bohlken v. Title Guarantee & Trust Co., 158 Misc. 512, 286 N.Y.S. 836, rev'd on other grounds, 248 App. Div. 722, 290 N.Y.S. 129.

(Text continued on page 381)

"Participation certificates" in group mortgages are not true mortgage investments, the holders thereof being primarily creditors of the issuing company, for, although there is security for the debt, the security cannot be seized by the creditor, whereas in a true mortgage investment the mortgagee may seize the real property which secures the debt when a default occurs. In re Eagle's Estate, 169 Misc. 140, 7 N.Y.S.2d 173.

Savings bond providing for forfeiture if monthly payments ceased before expiration of first 18 months after issuance and such default continued for more than two years held valid and not so onerous as to sustain finding that seller was guilty of fraudulent intent in offering bond for sale to public and did not render seller liable for exemplary damages although buyer was entitled, because of seller's agent's fraud in inducing purchase, to recover payments made on bond. Bankers' Mortg. Co. v. Lane, 70 S.W.2d 264 (Tex. Civ. App. 1934).

Security for mortgage investment.—

Where trust company sold first mortgage participation certificate purporting to give holder part ownership in obligations described on back of certificate, and none was there described, certain church loan would be assumed to be the security in which holder of certificate had interest, since it was only obligation which company had in its participation account when certificate was issued and law assumed that trust company intended to act honestly. Croghan v. Savings Trust Co., 231 Mo. App. 1161, 85 S.W.2d 239.

Withdrawal of mortgage from trust as discharging obligation.—

Mortgage company's withdrawal of mortgage from trust for bondholders before default, as authorized by trust indenture, and assignment thereof to trustee individually as security for separate indebtedness, amounted to payment of mortgage debt, discharging obligation of both principal and surety on bond. Baltimore Trust Co. v. Metropolitan Cas. Ins. Co., 3 F. Supp. 404, aff'd, 68 F.2d 121.

Failure of customer to protest purchase.—

One who knew that trust company managing her property as agent had purchased certain stock and mortgage participation certificates in her behalf and made no protest could not later complain that purchases were not made upon her express direction, nor recover for resulting losses. Stephens v. Detroit Trust Co., 284 Mich. 149, 278 N.W. 799.

Surrender for cash before maturity.—

Buyer of savings bond issued by mortgage corporation held not entitled to surrender bonds for cash before maturity on terms provided for in statute regulating building and loan associations. Brollier v. Bankers' Mtg. Co., 137 Kan. 298, 20 P.2d 817.

Recovery on depreciated certificates.—

Subscriber, under provisions of thrift plan for payment of insurance premiums and purchase of mortgages or mortgage certificates, held not entitled to recover from trustee cash to amount of cash and face value of depreciated mortgage certificates invested, where pro rata share of cash on hand had not been allocated to subscriber, and in view of equal rights of other subscribers to pro rata distribution. Schwartz v. Harriman Nat. Bank, etc., Co., 150 Misc. 543, 270 N.Y.S. 888.

(*Text continued on page 381*)

Redeeming certificates for reduced amount.—

Persons redeeming certificates in management investment trust for reduced amount after directors had set up contingent reserve for taxes could not under indenture claim shares of reserve later paid back into general fund. Bacon v. Irving Investors' Management Co., 236 App. Div. 78, 258 N.Y.S. 150.

Sufficient declarations of trust.—

Record of trust company wherein was noted each trust's interest in mortgage purchased on behalf of all trusts, together with certificates issued by trustee and notices given to beneficiaries, constituted sufficient declarations of trust to protect adequately the interests of beneficiaries of all the trusts. In re Coulter's Estate, 121 N.Y.S.2d 531.

Placing mortgage in name of trust.—

Trust company on taking mortgage, carried in its own name, from mortgage pool and allotting it to particular trust should have taken title thereto as trustee by recorded instrument designating specific trust, and mere execution of declaration of trust on its books was insufficient compliance with Pennsylvania statute. In re Yost's Estate, 316 Pa. 463, 175 A. 383.

Failure of trust company to realize that mortgage allotted to specific trust could not be treated like mortgage in pool would not relieve it from consequences of failure to place mortgage in name of trust. In re Yost's Estate, 316 Pa. 468, 175 A. 383.

Beneficiary could require trust company's restoration with interest of trust fund expended for mortgage taken from mortgage pool and allotted to trust, where trustee took mortgage in its own name, and not as trustee of the estate; it is well settled that where a trustee invests trust money in property which he takes in his own name as an individual the beneficiary has the option to accept the investment or require the trustee to account for the money so invested, with interest. In re Yost's Estate, 316 Pa. 463, 175 A. 383 (1934).

Notice to beneficiaries of investment.—

Notice given by trust company to beneficiaries of various trusts of investment of principals of trust in one mortgage was not fatally defective because it did not state that trustee itself was selling the participation. In re Coulter's Estate, 121 N.Y.S.2d 531.

But it is also held that notice of investment of trust funds in mortgage participations required to be given to the cestuis must inform them of the self-dealing of the trustee and if such is omitted the notice is ineffective. And notice not informing the cestuis that participation was acquired from the trustee itself was insufficient for failure to comply with the statute. In re Schlussel's Trust, 117 N.Y.S.2d 48.

Where trust company's funds are advanced temporarily and solely for purpose of facilitating participation in mortgage held by company in its own right by a number of trusts in its charge, without persisting investment of company's funds in mortgage, there is not such self-dealing by company, as to require particular mention thereof in its notice to income beneficiaries of such temporary investment, but notice describing investment as in a mortgage participation and stating that company is payee of cost price is sufficient. In re Schlussel's Trust, 284 App. Div. 68, 130 N.Y.S.2d 566, modified, 284 App. Div. 876, 134 N.Y.S.2d 854.

Where mortgage had always been treated as a participation by the trust company, trustee

(*Text continued on page 381*)

---

was required to give statutory notice notwithstanding that the beneficial interest was transferred from another trust and not from the trustee individually. In re Schlussel's Trust, 117 N.Y.S.2d 48.

The statute makes no distinction between mortgages held by trust company individually and those held in a representative capacity, and it does not give unrestricted license to traffic in participations without notice to beneficiaries provided only that the notice has been given when the participation was first apportioned to an estate or fund. In re Schlussel's Trust, 117 N.Y.S.2d 48.

Permitted self-dealing.—

Investment of trust funds in mortgage participations held by the trustee is a form of "self-dealing" permitted only because of the statute, and where the statute is not complied with the statutory grace is lost and the case is a simple one of prohibited self-dealing by a fiduciary. In re Schlussel's Trust, 117 N.Y.S.2d 48.

Technical self-dealing.—

That trust company's self-dealing in mortgage participations in which trust funds were invested was only technical and not with a view to profit did not Justify relieving trustee of liability for losses sustained by investments in the participations with respect to principal losses thereon. In re Schlussel's Trust, 117 N.Y.S.2d 48.

When trustee surcharged for loss.—

Where interest of trust in a mortgage became a true participation when the mortgage was increased, giving a statutory notice of self-dealing by the trust company became obligatory, and where there was no evidence of any disclosure thereof trustee must be surcharged for loss sustained on the investment. In re Schlussel's Trust, 117 N.Y.S.2d 48.

Transactions not self-dealing.—

Where trust company invested funds of various trusts in part interests in mortgages by temporarily using its own money and then immediately allocating the interests in the mortgage to the various trusts, there was no such self-dealing as would require trustee to disclose its interests when making its account, in view of judicial determination that in such cases trustee actually has no interest in the mortgage. In re Coulter's Estate, 121 N.Y.S.2d 531.

Where subsidiary acquired interest in mortgage and on same day assigned it to parent trust company, which allocated it to trust accounts, and trust company as trustee purchased from itself as custodian for another a certain part of the mortgage, and no financial benefit accrued to trust company or subsidiary, there was no self-dealing, and decrees approving intermediate accounts were conclusive as to propriety of such investments. In re Coulter's Estate, 121 N.Y.S.2d 531.

Disaffirmance of self-dealing.—

In absence of notice to cestuis of self-dealing of the trustee in investment of trust funds in mortgage participations, investments therein became prohibited self-dealing which the cestuis might at their election disaffirm and such rule applied equally to participations which the trustee sold to the trust from other trusts which it was also administering. In re Schlussel's Trust, 117 N.Y.S.2d 48.

Exculpatory clauses of trust instrument were insufficient to relieve trust company from

ment,[1378] assignment of certificates and recordation of transfer,[1379] fraud,

---

liability to cestuis resulting from losses in mortgage participations because of self-dealing by the trustee. In re Schlussel's Trust, 117 N.Y.S.2d 48.

Release not giving immunity.—

Where trustee's investment of trust funds in mortgage participation paid for with trustee's funds and held in trustee's name constituted self-dealing though permitted by statute, release executed by cestuis could not give trustee immunity from liability unless there was a frank disclosure thereof. In re Schlussel's Trust, 117 N.Y.S.2d 48.

[1378] **Agreements to repurchase.—**

In action by purchaser of bonds against securities company for breach of contract whereby company allegedly agreed to repurchase bonds at any time at rate of 99 cents on dollar, plus accrued interest, sale and delivery of securities under terms of writing, which was allegedly a mere offer, constituted a contract. Edge v. Boardwalk Securities Corp., 115 N.J.L. 286, 179 A. 270.

Securities company could not escape liability for failure to repurchase bonds at certain price as agreed on ground that offer contemplated investment of $250,000 and that bonds purchased did not equal that sum, where, fairly and reasonably construed, proposal embraced offer to sell securities in any amount on terms indicated. Edge v. Boardwalk Securities Corp., 115 N.J.L. 286, 179 A. 270.

Language employed in alleged contract whereby securities company agreed to repurchase bonds at any time at certain price must be construed in light of subject-matter and surrounding circumstances. Edge v. Boardwalk Securities Corp., 115 N.J.L. 286, 179 A. 270.

Agreement to repay in cash amount deposited for investment entitled investor to repayment of money deposited in cash, and payment of judgment for breach of agreement subrogated company to investor's interest in investment. Osterling v. Commonwealth Trust Co., 320 Pa. 67, 181 A. 769.

Agreement held not affected by subsequent statute. Kefover v. Potter Title, etc., Co., 320 Pa. 51, 181 A. 771; Osterling v. Commonwealth Trust Co., 320 Pa. 67, 181 A. 769.

Agreement held not ultra vires guarantee of investment, and to entitle trustors to repayment of full amount invested rather than amount realized from investments. Kefovar v. Potter Title, etc., Co., 320 Pa. 51, 181 A. 771.

Trust company held not prohibited from performance of agreement by order appointing receiver for investment pool and prohibiting disbursements therefrom. Kefover v. Potter Title & Trust Co., 320 Pa. 51, 181 A. 771.

Deposit of bonds and cash under trust agreement guaranteeing repayment of "principal sum".—

Under trust agreement reciting deposit of "sundry moneys and securities, aggregating $3,870.79 of which $3,000 is represented by three $1,000 bonds bearing interest at 6¼ percent and $870.79 in cash," and providing that trust company guaranteed payment of "principal sum" within three months of demand and agreed to reinvest principal sum, and that trustee for compensation should take all income in excess of the 5 percent guaranteed to settlor, "principal sum" included aggregate of bonds and cash, and trustee was obligated on termination of trust to pay settlor entire corpus invested under the terms of the trust. In re

representations without authority and misrepresentation,[1380] interest,[1381] and the substitution of securities.[1382]

Cunningham's Estate, 328 Pa. 107, 195 A. 130.

Where settlor authorized trustee to deposit bonds with bondholders' committee on insolvency of the issuing company, authorization of deposit did not constitute an admission that the bonds might be returned to settlor instead of cash principal which they represented on termination of the trust. In re Cunningham's Estate, 328 Pa. 107, 195 A. 130.

[1379] **Assignment of investment certificates void for want of consideration.—**

Where agent, employed to dispose of certain patents owned by investment company which was in financially precarious condition organized a coal mining company having assets of doubtful value and sold to ruining company the patent, taking in exchange certain notes part of which was payable to agent who exchanged notes for investment company's bonds or full-paid certificates payable in future, investment company's certificates procured by agent were void for want of consideration. And assigns, of one of the certificates was not estopped from denying its validity in absence of showing that he was assured by officers of investment company that certificates were valid and would be paid. Clark v. Freeling, 196 Ark. 907, 120 S.W.2d 375.

Where investment company without consideration issued certificates which were regular in form and carried no notice of any infirmity, and there was no evidence to show that assignees who paid valuable consideration for them had notice, and it was shown that investment company's officers assured assignees of validity of certificates and that they would be paid, investment company, its receiver, and creditor, would not be heard to insist that certificates were void in the absence of showing of fraud or collusion, since assignee, of certificates were innocent holders for value. Clark v. Freeling, 196 Ark. 907, 120 S.W.2d 375.

Recordation of transfer on maker's books.—

Where monetary certificates entitled assignee to have transfer recorded on maker's books on performance of certain conditions, maker could not impose additional condition that transfer would only be recorded on assignee's oral agreement permitting maker to stamp certificates "not transferable." Such agreement would be void for want of consideration. And maker's refusal to record transfer unless assignee would so agree constituted election to call certificates in for liquidation according to maker's reserved privilege. Parkhurst v. Investors' Syndicate, 138 Kan. 7, 23 P.2d 589.

[1380] **Fraud inducing purchase.—**

Buyer of investment bond did not waive right to recover part payment for fraud inducing purchase by exchanging such bond for another which she was also fraudulently induced to purchase. Union Deposit Co. v. Moseley (Tex. Civ. App.), 75 S.W.2d 190.

Purchaser of first mortgage certificate held not entitled to recover back purchase price on ground of seller's fraud in concealing existence of judgment lien against property, where seller had guaranteed title and had power to wipe out lien by foreclosing its second mortgage. Levine v. Title Guarantee, etc., Co., 243 App. Div. 711, 277 N.Y.S. 93, aff'd, 268 N.Y. 595, 198 N.E. 421.

(Text continued on page 384)

Claim of fraud not affecting trust assets.—

Where contract certificates purchased from investment company required purchasers to make installment payment. to corporation which issued trust shares representing interest in a trust of common stock deposited with corporation by investment company, the assets held by corporation for purchasers were trust assets, and no purchasers by sustaining a claim for fraud against company or corporation could thereby obtain any interest in the trust asset. held for other purchasers, though particular trust assets were not earmarked for the benefit of any particular purchasers. Deckert v. Independence Shares Corp., 39 F. Supp. 592, rev'd on other grounds, Pennsylvania Co. for Insurance, etc. v. Deckert, 123 F.2d 979.

Representations without authority.—

A domestic trust company which is trustee under a mortgage securing corporate bonds, and is not interested in the company or the bonds, and receives no commission for their sale, has no authority to make representations to purchasers of the bonds as to their character, since it has no duties as trustee under the mortgage which would authorize it to make such representations. Davidge v. Guardian Trust Co., 203 N.Y. 331, 96 N.E. 751.

[1381] **Repayment with interest.—**

Where investment contract gave investor right to discontinue payments at any time and right to resume payments with complete preservation of rights except postponement of maturity of certificate, investor could not demand repayment with interest of what he had already paid, on theory of quasi contract, because certificate provided for no cash surrender value until payments had been made for 18-month period, where other party invited investor to resume payment. and tendered strict performance on its part. Aasland v. Investor's Syndicate, 192 Minn. 141, 255 N.W. 630.

A statute regarding the rate of interest on money held by a trust company acting as fiduciary is a special provision and does not apply to ordinary judgment. against the company. In re Baker's Estate, 161 Misc. 562, 293 N.Y.S. 538.

Statute making payment of interest by banking association at greater rate than authorized a misdemeanor applied to trust company of which defendant was officer and which was organized under provisions governing banking association. State v. Hart, 162 N.W.2d 499 (N.D. 1968).

Compensation of guarantee corporation for collecting interest on mortgage.—

A guarantee corporation issuing participation certificates under a mortgage guaranteed by it and guaranteeing the same rate of interest payable on the mortgage and providing for collection of the interest on the mortgage by it cannot under a regulation adopted by it deduct a part of the amount due the certificate holders as compensation for services in making the collections. In re Prudence Co., 96 F.2d 161.

The New York statute relative to the taking over by the superintendent of banks of mortgage guarantee corporations does not require or permit him to reimburse a guarantee corporation which has issued guaranteed participation certificates providing for no differential between the amounts payable under a mortgage and the amount payable to the certificate holders, for services in collecting interest on the mortgage, which, under its contract with the certificate holders, it was bound to perform without charge. In re Prudence Co., 96 F.2d 161.

Collections.—The owner of a draft sent to a trust company for collection as his agent retains control of the draft, and he may sue the collecting trust company for negligence.[1383]

On the other hand, trust company as collecting agent has such rights in and title to, the draft, as are necessary to enable it to make collection.[1384] Payment to a trust company from the drawee's deposit by his direction operates as payment against the owner.[1385] Upon the collection of a draft, the relation of agent and principal ceases and becomes that of debtor and creditor, and the proceeds may be mingled with a trust company's own money, notwithstanding a direction to remit.[1386] In such a case, where a

---

Where trustee undertook to pay interest on principal corpus semiannually, unless diverted at the request of the settlor, such interest on falling due became part of corpus or principal sum on which interest thereafter accrued, and trustee was bound to pay compound interest on additional income. In re Cunningham's Estate, 328 Pa. 107, 195 A. 130.

[1382] **No right to substitute.—**

Trust company which issued mortgage participation certificate stating that holder had interest in notes, bonds, or other obligations secured by first liens on real estate, and put up certain church loan as security for outstanding participation certificates, held to have no right to substitute other securities in place of church loan as against holder of certificate, whose interest in that loan was not thereby affected. Croghan v. Savings Trust Co., 231 Mo. App. 1161, 85 S.W.2d 239.

Holders of participation certificates acquired on faith of therein described security could not be compelled after payment and cancellation of security to accept in lieu thereof other security. Seaboard Trust Co. v. Shea, 118 N.J. Eq. 433, 180 A. 206.

Trust relationship created.—

Where owner delivered stock to president and treasurer of trust company to have stock sold and government bonds purchased with proceeds, but other investments ware purchased, trust, and not debtor and creditor, relationship arose between owner and trust company. Allison v. Ohio Sav., etc., Co., 51 Ohio App. 253, 200 N.E. 529.

Belated exercise of right of holder of certificate to ratify unauthorized substitution will he denied or curtailed as circumstances and equity require, so as not to prejudicially affect intervening rights of third parties. Seaboard Trust Co. v. Shea, 118 N.J. Eq. 433, 180 A. 206.

[1383] Hecker-Jones-Jewell Milling Co. v. Cosmopolitan Trust Co., 242 Mass. 181, 136 N.E. 333, 24 A.L.R. 1148; Central Trust Co. v. Hanover Trust Co., 242 Mass. 265, 136 N.E. 336.

[1384] Hecker-Jones-Jewell Milling Co. v. Cosmopolitan Trust Co., 242 Mass. 181, 136 N.E. 333, 24 A.L.R. 1148, citing Haskell v. Avery, 181 Mass. 106, 63 N.E. 15, 92 Am. St. R. 401.

[1385] Hecker-Jones-Jewell Milling Co. v. Cosmopolitan Trust Co., 242 Mass. 181, 136 N.E. 333, 24 A.L.R. 1148.

[1386] Hecker-Jones-Jewell Milling Co. v. Cosmopolitan Trust Co., 242 Mass. 181, 136

depositor deposits a small cash amount and checks in excess of the draft amount, and authorizes the charging of his account, the cash and checks are not impressed with a trust in favor of the drawer.[1387] And in a case where a trust company detached a bill of lading from a draft and attached it to a draft drawn by the drawee on third persons, and on receipt of a check placed the difference to the drawee's credit and sent a treasurer's check to the drawer of the first draft, it was held that the check so received was not impressed with a trust in favor of the drawer.[1388] A trust company, receiving bonds under an agreement to collect the coupons on certain conditions, is entitled to a commission on the amount collected.[1389] And where a trust company becomes an agent for the collection of checks deposited by a customer and drawn on other banks, it is an implied condition of the agency contract that the company will continue to do its ordinary business of banking according to the custom of refusing to allow a customer to draw on such checks until payment thereof by the drawee banks.[1390]

Depositary's Certification as to Securities.—A certification by a depositary that securities deposited by a company issuing mortgage certificates comply with an indenture, is unilateral on the part of the depositary, and when accepted by those who in reliance on it buy the mortgage certificates, becomes a binding contract.[1391] And depositary is liable to purchasers who

---

N.E. 333, 24 A.L.R. 1148; Central Trust Co. v. Hanover Trust Co., 242 Mass. 265, 136 N.E. 336.

[1387] Hecker-Jones-Jewell Milling Co. v. Cosmopolitan Trust Co., 242 Mass. 181, 136 N.E. 333, 24 A.L.R. 1148.

[1388] Central Trust Co. v. Hanover Trust Co., 242 Mass. 265, 136 N.E. 336.

[1389] Davis Trust Co. v. Smith, 226 F. 410.

[1390] Salem Elevator Works, Inc. v. Commissioner of Banks, 252 Mass. 366, 148 N.E. 220.

Where passbooks provide that checks are entered to the depositor's accounts subject to payment, and the trust company follows the custom of refusing to allow depositors to draw against checks until they are collected from drawee banks, facts held to show that, in depositing checks drawn on other banks by customers, relation between bank and customers was that of principal and agent, until checks were actually collected. Salem Elevator Works, Inc. v. Commissioner of Banks, 252 Mass. 366, 148 N.E. 220.

[1391] **In general.—**

Feldmeier v. Mortgage Secur., Inc., 34 Cal. App. 2d 201, 93 P.2d 593.

Effect of provision in indenture.—

Where depositary certified that it held securities required by indenture, though it did not, depositary was guilty of culpable negligence and actual fraud within meaning of statute, and breach of warranty, notwithstanding that indenture, which was incorporated by reference by

rely on its false certification for such damages as they may sustain.[1392] But a trust relation cannot arise in favor of a purchaser until the purchase is made where a certification precedes the purchase, and a certification that securities are sufficient is no guaranty of their legality, unless the certificate contains such a warranty in terms.[1393]

§ 16. Powers.

In General.—A trust company has only those powers that are conferred upon it by its charter and the statutes of its state, and is strictly limited to the exercise of such powers in such manner and by such agents as its charter and the law permit.[1394] And a statute may provide that acts done by a trust

---

the mortgage certificates, provided that the depositary could rely conclusively on affidavits of officers of company which issued the certificates, with reference to the securities, and was not responsible for passing on validity of the securities. Feldmeier v. Mortgage Secur., Inc., 34 Cal App. 2d 201, 93 P.2d 593.

And such provision would not authorize the depositary to state that securities were of a description and class authorized by the indenture, when they did, not even purport to he of that description and class. Feldmeier v. Mortgage Secur., Inc., 34 Cal. App. 2d 201, 93 P.2d 593.

Where indenture required company issuing mortgage certificates, to deposit notes secured by mortgages or trust deeds theretofore owned by it with the depositary, the deposit with depositary of note of company which issued the certificates did not conform to the requirements of the indenture, nor supply deficiency in earlier deposit, so as to relieve depositary's liability to holders of certificates. Feldmeier v. Mortgage Secur., Inc., 34 Cal. App. 2d 201, 93 P.2d 593.

[1392] **In general.—**

Feldmeier v. Mortgage Secur., Inc., 34 Cal. App. 2d 201, 93 P.2d 593.

The liability of the depositary is measured by statute providing that the measure of damages is the amount which will compensate an aggrieved party for all the detriment proximately caused by the breach or which, in the ordinary course of things, would be likely to result therefrom. Feldmeier v. Mortgage Secur., Inc., 34 Cal. App. 2d 201, 93 P.2d 593.

In suit by holders of certificates against depositary, trial court did not err in refusing to ascertain at the trial whether the certificate holders had been damaged, before the end of the process of realizing on the securities. Feldmeier v. Mortgage Securities, 34 Cal. App. 2d 201, 93 P.2d 593.

[1393] Feldmeier v. Mortgage Secur., Inc., 34 Cal. App. 2d 201, 98 P.2d 593.

[1394] **In general.—**

Perkins v. Fuquay, 106 Fla. 405, 148 So. 323; Ulmer v. Fulton, 129 Ohio St. 323, 195 N.E. 557; People ex rel. Barrett v. Cairo-Alexander County Bank, 363 Ill. 589, 2 N.E.2d 889; In re Trusteeship of First Minneapolis Trust Co., 202 Minn. 187, 277 N.W. 899.

As to trust company's ultra vires acts generally, see § 17 of this chapter.

Conveyance to Florida corporation as trustee, was not void on ground that it was not a

(Text continued on page 388)

---

trust company incorporated under the trust laws of Florida and that it was "ultra vires" for the corporation to hold title as trustee to land. Cleveland Mortg. & Inv. Co. v. Gage, 144 Fla. 758, 198 So. 677.

Illinois Trust Companies Act permits only corporations which have qualified thereunder to accept or execute trusts, be appointed assignees or trustees by deed, assignees, guardians, conservators, executors, administrators, or trustees under order of court. People ex rel. Barrett v. Cody Trust Co., 294 Ill. App. 342, 13 N.E.2d 829.

The Wisconsin statutes manifest intent to limit the powers of a trust company in handling a trust so that solvency of one trust would not be affected by any difficulties in connection with any other trust. United States v. Earling, 39 F. Supp. 864.

The enumeration of powers in the statute excludes all others and a trust company which is authorized to buy and sell government, state, municipal, and other bonds, and negotiable and nonnegotiable paper, stocks, and other investment securities, has no authority to purchase a controlling interest in the stock of another bank, for the purpose of operating and managing that bank. State v. Bankers' Trust Co., 157 Mo. App. 557, 138 S.W. 669.

The general powers to be exercised under a statute authorizing trust corporations to accept and execute trusts for married women in respect to their separate property, and "generally to have and exercise such powers as are usually had and exercised by trust companies," applied to trust for married women only. Crow v. Lincoln Trust Co., 144 Mo. 562, 46 S.W. 593.

Issuance of certificates of deposit.—

A Michigan trust company prior to 1937 and 1939 amendments had power to issue certificates of deposit in course of its business and as incident thereto. Union Guardian Trust Co. v. Emery, 292 Mich. 394, 290 N.W. 841.

Guaranty.—

Trust company authorized by statute and charter may become guarantor to same extent as individual and subject to general law of guaranty. And its guaranty of security issued by another corporation was not "ultra vires." Barnett v. Kennedy, 185 Okla. 409, 92 P.2d 963.

Sale, lease, or exchange of assets of state trust company could be made only to another corporation authorized to do business under laws of state and not to a national bank. In re Watkins' Estate, 113 Vt. 126, 30 A.2d 305.

Consolidation.—

Where nonresident trustee bank was consolidated with another nonresident bank, consolidated bank, unless otherwise disqualified, has same authority to serve as trustee as was possessed by bank which it absorbed. In re Trust Estate of Saulsbury, 43 Del Ch. 400, 233 A.2d 739 (1967).

Corporate trustee has power to accept quitclaim titles to land which is subject to a trust mortgage. Ziegler v. Simmons, 353 Mich. 432, 91 N.W.2d 819.

Statute authorizing trust companies to hold money on deposit in savings account for safekeeping, or in escrow or for investment, does not authorize trust companies to accept and pay out deposits on general checking accounts. Nelson v. Dakota Bankers Trust Co., 132 N.W.2d 903 (N.D. 1964).

company in contravention of the powers granted therein shall be void.[1395] Privileges specified in a general law cannot be added to or enlarged by a trust company's articles of incorporation, and in case of conflict between them, the general law will govern.[1396] But when a trust company is clothed with certain powers, it may also exercise whatever incidental powers may fairly be implied from those expressly conferred, and such powers as are reasonably necessary to enable it fully to exercise the granted powers according to common commercial and banking custom and usage.[1397] This

---

Practice of law.—

Congress has provided against practice of law by national bank while conducting its trust business where such practice by state banks or trust companies would be in contravention of state law. Green v. Huntington Nat'l Bank, 4 Ohio St. 2d 78, 212 N.E.2d 585 (1965).

Where testatrix sought advice of trustee bank in connection with her securities held by bank, she was entitled to legal advice independent of bank, and bank would have violated its duty as a fiduciary if trust officers had advised testatrix in matters of law in capacity of independent legal counsel. In re Longworth, 222 A.2d 561 (Me. 1966).

Stockholder's liability.—

A Wisconsin trust company bank cannot subject itself generally to a stockholder's liability. United States v. Earling, 39 F. Supp. 864.

[1395] New York State Loan, etc., Co. v. Helmer, 77 N.Y. 64.

Under a New York statute, notes issued by a loan and trust company are void, in the absence of an express charter power of issuance. New York State Loan, etc., Co. v. Helmer, 77 N.Y. 64.

Letter signed by charterers of steamship and trust company held not letter of credit, but one of guaranty in excess of trust company's authority to make, and hence steamship agents were not entitled to recover for dishonor of draft. Commercial Trust Co. v. American Trust Co., 256 Mass. 58, 152 N.E. 104.

[1396] Dunn v. O'Connor, 89 F.2d 820.

Hence, where statute under which bank and trust company was incorporated specified objects of incorporation and failed to authorize trust company to purchase stock in other corporations, purchase by trust company of block of stock in another bank was ultra vires and void notwithstanding provision in trust company's articles of incorporation purporting to authorize it to hold shares of stock in another corporation. Dunn v. O'Connor, 89 F.2d 820.

[1397] **In general.—**

Nowell v. Equitable Trust Co., 249 Mass. 585, 144 N.E. 749; Ulmer v. Fulton, 129 Ohio St. 323, 195 N.E. 557, 97 A.L.R. 1170.

Acting as insurance agent.—

A statute relating to powers of trust companies and providing that it might act as agent for the transaction of any business or the management of estates, held sufficiently comprehensive to include power to act as insurance agent. Saufley v. Botts, 209 Ky. 137, 272 S.W. 408; Saufley v. Lincoln Bank, etc., Co., 210 Ky. 346, 275 S.W. 802.

(Text continued on page 390)

Receipt of proceeds of municipal refunding bonds.—

Where bank acquired no authority to use proceeds of municipal refunding bonds except to apply them for prescribed purposes and was specifically enjoined not to commingle them with bank's own or other funds, the bank's authority to so receive the fund, and securities directed to be purchased with them was within powers possessed by the bank as a trust institution; when funds are so received with directions as to how and when they are to be disbursed, deposit is for a specific purpose, and they are trust funds and not subject to commingling or setoff by the bank. Rodin v. State ex rel. City of Cheyenne, 417 P.2d 180 (Wyo. 1966).

Taking transfer of note.—

A trust company empowered to receive deposits, to loan money, to purchase, invest in, and sell stocks, bills of exchange, bonds, and mortgages and other securities, and to invest moneys received by it in such securities as it may deem proper, is authorized to take a transfer of a note, and to recover thereon against the maker. Binghamton Trust Co. v. Clark, 32 App. Div. 151, 52 N.Y.S. 941, 28 N.Y. Civ. Proc. 1.

Trust company which sought to repurchase mortgage certificate sold by it at any time purchaser demanded repurchase could not defend action based on agreement on ground of ultra vires. Westchester Trust Co. v. Harrison, 249 App. Div. 828, 292 N.Y.S. 209 (1937), appeal dismissed. 274 N.Y. 588, 10 N.E2d 565.

Guaranteeing payment.—

Trust company held empowered to guarantee payment of principal and interest on bonds and mortgagee or participation certificates sold by company. Kelly v. Middlesex Title Guarantee, etc., Co., 116 N.J. Eq. 228, 172 A. 487; Kelly v. Middlesex Title Guarantee & Trust Co., 115 N.J. Eq. 369, 170 A. 892. See Osterling v. Commonwealth Trust Co., 320 Pa. 67, 181 A. 769; Smith v. Stricker, 123 Pa. Super. 181, 186 A. 369.

Trust company, engaged in general banking business, held authorized to guarantee payment of negotiable notes. Given v. Western, etc., Life Ins. Co., 115 W. Va. 727, 177 S.E. 777.

A statute which empowers a trust company to purchase, invest in and sell bonds impliedly sanctions its becoming guarantor with respect to such bonds. McCauley v. Ridgewood Trust Co., 81 N.J.L. 86, 79 A. 327; McFerson v. Kepner, 76 Colo. 523, 233 P. 148; Collings v. Guarantee Trust Co., 10 F. Supp. 462, aff'd, 78 F.2d 870, cert. denied, 295 U.S. 747, 55 S. Ct. 825, 79 L. Ed. 1692.

Assumption of obligation of purchaser.—

Where transaction of landowner with trust company whereby company undertook to furnish purchaser for certain property of landowner was within company's usual scope of business authorized by its charter, company's alleged contract of assumption of obligation of purchaser of such property being mere incident of company's agency in transacting the particular business, was not ultra vires. San Jacinto Trust Co. v. Goodwin (Tex. Civ. App.), 88 S.W.2d 525.

Executing note for benefit of company financed.—

A trust company organized under a statute authorizing such companies to act as agent or attorney in fact in the management of property, execute trusts, act as executor or guardian,

rule, however, has limits, and it has been said that every power not clearly granted must be regarded as withheld and prohibited.[1398] And a corporation

---

guaranty the fidelity of persons or corporations holding places of bust, loan money on collateral security, buy and sell securities, etc., has power to execute a note for the benefit of a railroad company which it was financing. First Nat. Bank v. Guardian Trust Co., 187 Mo. 494, 86 S.W. 109, 70 L.R.A. 79.

Pledge to secure deposits.—

Deposit of county funds in trust company and trust company's pledge of securities in return for deposit held valid, precluding recovery of securities by trust company's receiver, since trust company acted as "bank." Johnson v. Eddy, 138 Kan. 705, 27 P.2d 283.

Pledge to secure loan.—

A Massachusetts trust company has power to borrow money, and such power carries with it by necessary implication the right to secure the obligation by pledge of collateral. Salem Trust Co. v. Federal Nat. Bank, 11 F. Supp. 105, aff'd, 78 F.2d 407.

Pledge to indemnify indemnitor.—

Trust company had power to deposit government bonds with third party to counter indemnify indemnitor on trust company's bond given school district to procure deposit of school funds. National Surety Co. v. Franklin Trust Co., 313 Pa. 501, 170 A. 683, 95 A.L.R. 300.

Foreclosure of mortgage.—

Express power of investment company to collect principal and interest on secured note for buyer of certificate of ownership in first mortgage real estate bond held to imply power to foreclose on default of mortgagor without knowledge of buyer of certificate, though certificate also contained provision giving company option to foreclose or buy beck certificate upon request of buyer after default by mortgagor. Colorado Inv. & Realty Co. v. Newkirk, 95 Colo. 71, 32 P.2d 830.

Member of limited partnership.—

Where a trust company was organized as a private corporation under a statute which permitted a corporation to act as a trustee under any lawful express trust committed to it by contract or will and where its charter granted such power, the trust company as trustee of an express trust was legally qualified as a person to become a member of a limited partnership. Port Arthur Trust Co. v. Muldrow, 155 Tex. 612, 291 S.W.2d 312.

Taking over business of debtor.—

A trust company engaged, as authorized, in a general banking business, has every implied power that a bank would have, as to temporarily taking over the business of a debtor, to save the debt. Union Savings, etc., Co. v. Krumm, 88 Wash. 20, 152 P. 681.

Right to advertise services.—

Trust institution, qualified and authorized by law as legitimate business enterprise, has inherent right to advertise its trust services in appropriate ways. Frazee v. Citizens Fid. Bank & Trust Co., 393 S.W.2d 778 (Ky. 1964).

[1398] **In general.—**

People v. Cairo-Alexander County Bank, 363 Ill. 589, 2 N.E.2d 889.

not organized as a trust company cannot do a trust company business as incidental to the business for which it is chartered; in order to transact a trust business, it must comply with the law applicable to trust companies.[1399] Of course a statute authorizing trust companies to make contracts only authorizes contracts for proper corporate purposes.[1400]

Miscellaneous Powers.—It has been held that a trust company may be appointed as a special receiver,[1401] and the New York banking law

---

No new powers were given to trust companies generally by a provision that "every trust company incorporated by a special law shall possess the powers of trust companies incorporated under this chapter, and shall be subject to such provisions of this chapter as are not inconsistent with the special laws relating to such specially chartered company." Jenkins v. Neff, 186 U.S. 230, 22 S. Ct. 905, 46 L. Ed. 1140.

Acting in dual capacity of settlor and trustee.—

Combined bank and trust company held not authorized to act in dual capacity of settlor and trustee by creating trusts out of its own assets and selling participation certificates; such undertakings being opposed to public policy. Ulmer v. Fulton, 129 Ohio St. 323, 195 N.E. 557, 97 A.L.R. 1170.

Contract for operation of ship.—

A trust company as mortgagee of a ship had no power to enter into a contract with mortgagors for their mutual benefit for operation of ship, and to supply necessary capital for the undertaking. Flitner-Atwood Co. v. Fidelity Trust Co., 249 Mass. 333, 144 N.E. 218.

Suretyship.—

Ordinarily a loan company, organized to do a general brokerage business, to loan money, to negotiate bonds, etc., is not authorized to become a surety, as that act must generally be specifically authorized. Richeson v. National Bank of Mena, 96 Ark. 594, 132 S.W. 913.

Pledge of securities.—

It is held that a pledge by bank and trust companyof bonds deposited with state treasurer by trust department, to secure savings account and commercial account of depositor against loss, is beyond power of bank, precluding enforcement of lien in nature of pledge against proceeds of bonds. Leyvraz v. Johnson, 114 Fla. 396, 154 So. 159.

Trust company's pledge of securities to secure deposit of city moneys held ultra vires. And before trust company could repossess itself of such securities, it was required to return moneys received, and, in default of such return, city was entitled to credit amount received from sale of the securities against the deposit. Mount Vernon v. Mount Vernon Trust Co., 270 N.Y. 400, 1 N.E.2d 825.

1399 Marion Mtg. Co. v. State, 107 Fla. 472, 145 So. 222, holding that statutory powers granted to trust companies were limited to trust corporations.

1400 In re Bankers' Trust Co., 27 F.2d 912.

1401 Goff v. Goff, 54 W. Va. 364, 46 S.E. 177.

Where a trust company is appointed a special receiver in any case, the capital of the company together with any deposit required to be made with any officer of the state, whether

authorizes trust companies to be fiduciaries, but it was held that their appointments in surrogate's court must be made in accordance with the Surrogate's Court Act.[1402] And a combined bank and trust company has power to issue, secure with collateral, and sell bonds, but in the absence of fraud it cannot, as against the rights of bondholders and trustees, recover collateral given to secure such bonds.[1403] The rule that a bank may not pledge any of its assets as security for the deposits of some of its general depositors to the prejudice of its other depositors, is not applicable to transactions with an investment company which do not constitute a banking business.[1404] The illegal action of a trust company in accepting fidelity bonds from foreign insurance underwriters not operating under authority of the state insurance department as required by statute, could not be ratified by the stockholders of the trust company.[1405]

It is a general common law principle that banks cannot act as sureties.[1406] It is also provided by statute that a bank shall not lend its credit, bind itself as a surety to indemnify another, or otherwise become a guarantor.[1407]

As to plans for payment of unemployment benefits, see the footnote.[1408]

---

the deposit be a part of the capital or not, is to be taken and considered as the security required by law for the faithful performance of the duties of the trust company as receiver. Goff v. Goff, 54 W. Va. 364, 46 S.E. 177.

1402 In re Sorensen's Estate, 195 Misc. 742, 91 N.Y.S.2d 220.

1403 Wilson v. Louisville Trust Co., 242 Ky. 432, 46 S.W.2d 767.

1404 State ex rel. Rohn Shoe Mfg. Co. v. Industrial Com., 217 Wis. 138, 258 N.W. 449.

1405 Runcie v. Corn Exch. Bank Trust Co., 6 N.Y.S.2d 616, followed in Runcie v. Central Hanover Bank, etc., Co., 6 N.Y.S.2d 625.

1406 Douglas County v. Hamilton State Bank, 340 Ga. App. 801, 798 S.E.2d 509 (2017).

1407 Douglas County v. Hamilton State Bank, 340 Ga. App. 801, 798 S.E.2d 509 (2017). See O.C.G.A. § 7-1-290.

1408 Soliciting and receiving of payments by investment association and its issuance of income reserve contracts as part of employer's plan for payment of unemployment benefits held not doing of prohibited "banking business" by investment company. State ex rel. Rohn Shoe Mfg. Co. v. Industrial Com., 217 Wis. 138, 258 N.W. 449.

Investment of portion of employer's plan for payment of unemployment benefits under which investment company proposed to handle employment reserve fund held not invalid on theory investment company was undertaking trust in excess of its corporate authority, since in investing special fund as accumulated by employer's monthly deposits in special checking account at bank, investment company would be acting in fiduciary relation, but would not be engaging in business as trustee. State ex rel. Rohn Shoe Mfg. Co. v. Industrial Com., 217 Wis. 138, 258 N.W. 449.

Investment of portion of employer's plan for payment of unemployment benefits held not

Purchases and Sales.—The power of trust companies to purchase and sell property is generally a matter of statutory regulation; in determining such power the particular provisions of some of these statutes have been construed by the courts.[1409] And the following powers have been held to be conferred on trust companies by certain statutes: to buy all kinds of government, state, municipal and other bonds, negotiable and nonnegotiable papers, stocks and other investment securities, including bills of exchange;[1410] to deal in foreign exchange, and invest funds in foreign currency in carrying on a banking business by selling drafts on a depositary in a

---

invalid as against contention that investment company cannot pledge general assets for particular security of only employer's income reserve contract, since special beneficiaries were primarily entitled to special fund, and deposited securities purchased therewith, and claims of other contract holders or creditors of investment company were secondary under rule respecting special deposits. State ex rel. Rohn Shoe Mfg. Co. v. Industrial Com., 217 Wis. 138, 258 N.W. 449.

[1409] **In general.—**

Jenkins v. Neff, 186 U.S. 230, 22 S. Ct. 905, 46 L. Ed. 1140.

No power to purchase commercial paper was given trust companies by a New York statute authorizing trust companies to exercise the powers conferred on individual banks and bankers by another statute which provided that such banks and bankers may "take, receive, reserve, and charge on every loan or discount made, or upon any note, bill of exchange, or other evidence of debt, interest at the rate of 6 percent per annum; and such interest may be taken in advance." Jenkins v. Neff, 186 U.S. 230, 22 S. Ct. 905, 46 L. Ed. 1140.

Statutory limitation of the amount of bank stock which trust company may purchase or hold as collateral held inapplicable to ownership of stock in single national bank by trust company sued by such bank's receiver for amount of its liability as stockholder. Wellston Trust Co. v. Snyder, 87 F.2d 44.

Purchase of controlling interest in stock of bank.—

As the enumeration of powers in the statute excludes all others, a trust company which is authorized to buy and sell government, state, municipal, and other bonds, and negotiable and nonnegotiable paper, stocks, and other investment securities, has no authority to purchase a controlling interest in the stock of another bank, for the purpose of operating and managing that bank. State ex rel. Hadley v. Bankers' Trust Co., 157 Mo. App. 557, 138 S.W. 669.

Statute making it unlawful for any company to use its funds in purchase of stock in any other corporation held statement of general policy applicable to all District of Columbia corporations in absence of express statutory exception, and hence claim against insolvent bank and trust company for assessment on shares of stock in another bank purchased by trust company was properly rejected as invalid. Dunn v. O'Connor, 89 F.2d 820.

[1410] Crow v. Lincoln Trust Co., 144 Mo. 562, 46 S.W. 593.

Under such a statute a company has been held to have power to purchase stock of a Federal Reserve Bank. Hiatt v. United States, 4 F.2d 374, cert. denied, 268 U.S. 704, 45 S. Ct. 638, 69 L. Ed. 1167.

foreign country;[1411] to act as fiscal or transfer agent of any corporation, and in such capacity, to register certificates of stocks and bonds and purchase, invest in and sell stocks, bonds and other securities;[1412] and to purchase the stock of other banking institutions and increase its own capital stock to pay therefor if its capital is not thereby impaired.[1413] But it has been held that a trust company may not purchase its own stock,[1414] except to prevent a loss on a debt previously contracted in good faith.[1415]

Provisions of the Investment Company Act make it unlawful for an affiliated person of an investment company to purchase securities from such company without the Securities and Exchange Commission's approval,[1416]

[1411] Corsino v. Hanover Trust Co., 253 Mass. 5, 147 N.E. 868.

Where trust company sold lire under contract giving purchaser election to be paid in lire or in United States dollars, fact that trust company did not always have lire equivalent in amount to cover its outstanding obligations held not to make transaction illegal. Corsino v. Hanover Trust Co., 253 Mass. 5, 147 N.E. 868.

Massachusetts trust companies can make contracts, which are transactions in commercial department, for purchase and sale of money of foreign nations for future deliveries based on credit of buyer. Norling, etc., Co. v. Exchange Trust Co., 288 Mass. 444, 193 N.E. 1.

[1412] Kavanaugh v. Gould, 147 App. Div. 281, 131 N.Y.S. 1059, holding that under such a statute, as a corollary to its right to sell bonds, a trust company has a right to publish a prospectus descriptive of the bonds offered for sale.

[1413] Thom v. Baltimore Trust Co., 158 Md. 352, 148 A. 234. But see State v. Bankers' Trust Co., 157 Mo. App. 557, 138 S.W. 669.

[1414] Maryland Trust Co. v. National Mechanics' Bank, 102 Md. 608, 63 A. 70.

[1415] Barth v. Pock, 51 Mont. 418, 155 P. 282.

[1416] **In general.—**

SEC v. Sterling Precision Corp., 393 F.2d 214 (3d Cir. 1968). See also § 2 of this chapter.

What constitutes purchase.—

Redemption of security in substantial accordance with its terms is not "purchase" within Investment Company Act provision making it unlawful for affiliated person of registered investment company to knowingly purchase securities from such registered company without approval of Securities and Exchange Commission. Securities & Exch. Comm'n v. Sterling Precision Corp., 393 F.2d 214 (2d Cir. 1968).

Affiliated company's non-pro rate redemption of its debentures held by registered investment company was not such a deviation from debenture terms requiring pro rata redemption as to transform redemption into "purchase" within Investment Company Act provision making it unlawful for affiliated person of registered investment company to knowingly purchase from such registered company any security or other property without approval of SEC. Securities & Exch. Comm'n v. Sterling Precision Corp.,393 F.2d 214 (3d Cir. 1968).

Even if term "purchase" as used in Investment Company Act were read to cover a and prohibit an affiliated person from effecting any transaction in which such company is a participant.[1417] For other cases dealing with statutory

---

redemption, affiliated company's non-pro rata redemption of its debentures held by registered investment company did not require approval of SEC. Securities & Exch. Comm'n v. Sterling Precision Corp., 393 F.2d 214 (3d Cir. 1968).

[1417] **In general.—**

SEC v. Talley Industries, Inc., 399 F.2d 396 (2d Cir. 1968), cert. denied, 393 U.S. 1015, 89 S. Ct. 615, 21 L. Ed. 2d 560 (1969).

Word "transaction" used in statute making it unlawful for affiliated person of registered investment company to effect any transaction in which the registered company is a joint participant in contravention of rules and regulations of Securities Exchange Commission is not a technical term and any agreement by investment company and affiliate for each to buy stated amount of stock of third company and not to sell it without the other's consent would come within statute regardless of whether transaction was read to refer to each purchase or to entire course of dealing or both. Securities & Exch. Comm'n v. Talley Indus., 399 F.2d 396 (3d Cir. 1968), cert. denied, 393 U.S. 1015, 89 S. Ct. 615, 21 L. Ed. 2d 560 (1969).

Prohibition not limited to joint venture.—

Statute prohibiting affiliated person from effecting any transaction in which registered investment company is a joint participant in contravention of rules and regulations of SEC is not limited to typical joint venture in which each of the parties has a fractional share. SEC v. Talley Industries, Inc., 399 F.2d 396 (2d Cir. 1968), cert. denied, 393 U.S. 1015, 89 S. Ct. 615, 21 L. Ed. 2d 560 (1969).

Statute prohibiting affiliated person and registered investment company from effecting any transaction in which registered company is a joint participant in contravention of rule and regulations of SEC must be intended to reach situations not already covered by statute forbidding registered investment company, in contravention of Commission rules, to participate on a joint or a joint and several basis in any trading account in securities. Securities & Exch. Comm'n v. Talley Indus., 399 F.2d 396 (3d Cir. 1968), cert. denied, 393 U.S. 1015, 89 S. Ct. 615, 21 L. Ed. 2d 560 (1969).

Under statute prohibiting certain transactions in which registered investment company and affiliated person are joint participants, SEC may lawfully conclude that when affiliated person and registered investment company engage in plan to achieve together a substantial stock position in another company, they can have effected a transaction in which the registered company is a joint or joint and several participant with affiliate within meaning of statute even though there is no legally binding agreement between them. SEC v. Talley Industries, Inc., 399 F.2d 396 (2d Cir. 1968), cert. denied, 393 U.S. 1015, 89 S. Ct. 615, 21 L. Ed. 2d 560 (1969).

Suit by Securities and Exchange Commission charging that an affiliate of registered investment company had effected transaction in which investment company was a joint participant in violation of statute was a suit in equity whose essence lay in power of chancellor to do equity and mould each decree to necessities of case, and was not one for enforcement of order of Commission where weight must be given to agency's election of remedy. SEC v. Talley Industries, Inc., 399 F.2d 396 (3d Cir. 1968), cert. denied, 393 U.S. 1015, 89 S. Ct. 615, 21 L. Ed. 2d 560 (1969).

provisions regulating purchases and sales involving investment companies, see the footnote.[1418]

Industrial banks do not possess the power of commercial banks to discount generally or to buy and sell coin, bullion, and exchange.[1419]

§ 17. Ultra Vires Acts.

In General.—Whether a transaction of a trust company engaged in banking is ultra vires depends on the original good faith of its purpose in so acting.[1420] There is every reason to apply the rule of ultra vires to trust companies with some strictness, since the public interest that such a company not transcend its powers and embark in speculative or even

---

There was substantial evidence to support determination of SEC that dealings between registered investment company and corporation, which was an affiliated person by virtue of company's ownership of 9 percent of corporation's voting shares, to acquire shares of third corporation was the effecting of a transaction in which registered investment company was a joint or a joint and several participant with affiliated person within meaning of statute prohibiting such transactions which are in violation of rules of SEC. Securities & Exch. Comm'n v. Talley Industries, Inc., 399 F.2d 396 (3d Cir. 1968), cert. denied, 393 U.S. 1015, 89 S. Ct. 615, 21 L. Ed. 2d 560 (1969).

Court of appeals in reviewing order dismissing complaint by Securities and Exchange Commission charging violation of statute prohibiting certain transactions of affiliated persons and registered investment companies was not governed by statute making findings of SEC conclusive if supported by substantial evidence, but there was applicable the underlying principle that factual determination by agency responsible for execution of congressional policy invested with expertise should not be disturbed by court where there is substantial evidence to support determination. Securities & Exch. Comm'n v. Talley Indus., 399 F.2d 396 (3d Cir. 1968), cert. denied, 393 U.S. 1015, 89 S. Ct. 615, 21 L. Ed. 2d 560 (1969).

[1418] That related broker had made arrangement with new, related investment fund whereunder it would turn over to new fund its profits on brokerage transactions for fund did not require that broker make similar arrangement with older related fund. Kurach v. Weissman, 49 F.R.D. 304 (S.D.N.Y. 1970).

Small Business Investment Act.—

Fact that statute provides that a function of small business investment companies is to provide equity capital for small business concerns does not mean that the Small Business Investment Act does not prohibit purchases from individual stockholders, and activities of small business investment company violated the act where its purchases of shares from stockholders did not provide equity capital for two small business concerns, and the purchases were not a reasonably necessary part of the overall sound financing of each concern. ANA Small Business Invest., Inc. v. Small Business Administration, 391 F.2d 739 (9th Cir. 1968). See also § 2 of this chapter.

[1419] Modern Industrial Bank v. Graves, 260 App. Div. 349, 21 N.Y.S.2d 329, aff'd, 285 N.Y. 668, 34 N.E.2d 375.

[1420] Union Sav., etc., Co. v. Krumm, 88 Wash. 20, 152 P. 681.

legitimate business enterprises outside its lawful functions, is particularly strong.[1421] Thus, speculative undertakings by a trust company, subject to hazard and contingency of gain or loss, are ultra vires and a perversion of the powers conferred by its charter.[1422] And it was held that the fact trust

---

[1421] Nowell v. Equitable Trust Co., 249 Mass. 585, 144 N.E. 749.

[1422] **In general.—**

Perkins v. Fuquay, 106 Fla. 405, 143 So. 323.

Where trust company purchased block of railroad bonds at par, which was 5½ points below the market, giving seller an option to repurchase for the same price within six months, at which time if option was not exercised the trust company's wholly-owned subsidiary would take over the bonds at the price paid, such option agreement was "ultra vires" and unenforceable as creating an improper "contingent liability," even if the transaction were deemed an initial purchase by subsidiary financed by the trust company, constituting a short-term 5½ per cent investment by trust company. Litwin v. Allen, 25 N.Y.S.2d 667.

Trust company may not encourage purchase of securities in venture.—

State v. Barnes, 108 Minn. 230, 122 N.W. 11; State v. Barnes, 108 Minn. 527, 122 N.W. 12; Kavanaugh v. Gould, 147 App. Div. 281, 131 N.Y.S. 1059.

Trust company may not enter into contracts of guaranty for others.—

A trust company was organized under the New York statute by its vice-president, with the consent of its president, but without the knowledge of its directors, signed an instrument under seal, in the name of the company, guaranteeing to the owner of certain bonds and stocks of a certain corporation the sale thereof before a certain date at not less than a certain sum. The trust company at the time owned no bond or stock of such corporation, nor was it interested in the sale of its securities, otherwise than by the commission it might acquire. Held, that the contract was ultra vires. Gause v. Commonwealth Trust Co., 55 Misc. 110, 106 N.Y.S. 288, aff'd, 124 App. Div. 438, 108 N.Y.S. 1080, 196 N.Y. 134, 89 N.E. 476, 24 L.R.A. (n.s.) 967.

A guaranty by a loan and trust company, for a valuable consideration, of a promissory note given by one third party to another, and not negotiated by it, is ultra vires such a corporation organized under the Kansas statute for the purpose of transacting business of a loan and trust company and of buying and selling personal property, including commercial paper, with power to enter into "any obligation or contract essential to the transaction of its ordinary affairs," but forbidden to employ its property for any other purpose than to "accomplish the legitimate objects of its creation." Ward v. Joslin, 186 U.S. 142, 22 S. Ct. 807, 46 L. Ed. 1093.

Trust company's accommodation indorsement and guaranty of paper of banks for which it acted as financial agent held ultra vires and void under Georgia statute. In re Bankers' Trust Co., 27 F.2d 912.

Under the Massachusetts statute, a guaranty by a trust company of financial obligations incurred by an importer to another banker, issuing letter of credit for account of the importer, when security of bills of lading and other papers were assured to the other banker, but not to the trust company, was ultra vires. Nowell v. Equitable Trust Co., 249 Mass. 585, 144 N.E. 749.

company stockholders did not appear at a meeting and protest the proposed actions of their company did not estop them from challenging its ultra vires act of engaging in general banking.[1423] But a trust company may perform those acts which are customary,[1424] or which are incidental to its business as described in its charter.[1425] Although a bylaw of an investment company was seemingly violated, the company was not held to have acted ultra vires

---

Trust company may not act as promoter of corporation.—

A trust company organized under a statute, authorizing corporations to receive money in trust and to buy and sell all kinds of bonds and negotiable and nonnegotiable paper and stocks and other investment securities may not act as promoter of a corporation, and a contract so to do is ultra vires. Richard Hanlon Millinery Co. v. Mississippi Valley Trust Co., 251 Mo. 553, 158 S.W. 359.

Trust company may not purchase controlling interest in another corporation.—

Under statute authorizing trust companies to buy and sell government, state, municipal, and other bonds, and negotiable and nonnegotiable paper, stocks, and other investment securities, the purchase by a domestic trust company of the stock of a Kansas bank for the purpose of managing and operating such bank is not only ultra vires, but is against public policy, as creating a monopoly, and so is totally void. State ex rel. Hadley v. Bankers' Trust Co., 157 Mo. App. 557, 138 S.W. 669.

[1423] Nelson v. Dakota Bankers Trust Co., 132 N.W.2d 908 (N.D. 1964).

[1424] Gerold v. Cosmopolitan Trust Co., 245 Mass. 259, 139 N.E. 624.

Under the Massachusetts statute, a trust company has authority to contract for purchase of Austrian kronen. Agreed facts held to authorize inference that it was customary for trust companies to deal in foreign currency, and that contract to purchase such currency was not ultra vires. Gerold v. Cosmopolitan Trust Co., 245 Mass. 259, 139 N.E. 624.

[1425] **In general—**

Commercial Bank & Trust Co. v. Beach, 66 Colo. 226, 180 P. 982.

Statute prohibiting banks from purchasing stock of other corporations does not render ultra vires the purchase, for a customer, of stock in another corporation, by a bank and trust company; it being authorized by its articles of incorporation as a trust company to carry out the transaction. Commercial Bank, etc., Co. v. Beach, 66 Colo. 226, 180 P. 982.

Trust company, accepting trust and investing trust fund in certificates of interest in mortgages for beneficiary's benefit, as authorized by statute, cannot repudiate its agreement to repay principal to beneficiary in cash on termination of trust as ultra vires, in absence of statute prohibiting such agreement when made; contract not being divisible nor trust agreement a guaranty of mortgages. In re Roberts' Estate, 316 Pa. 545, 175 A. 869, 96 A.L.R. 450.

Under trust agreement guaranteeing payment of principal sum within three months of demand and payment of five percent interest on principal sum, use of the term "guarantee" imported primary obligation of the trustee, not a secondary one, as the word is customarily used, and trustee could not evade liability on ground that an undertaking of guarantee is ultra vires. In re Cunningham's Estate, 328 Pa. 107, 195 A. 130.

where it was not a party either directly or indirectly to the act in question.[1426] And one who enters into a legal contract with a trust company cannot repudiate it on the ground that the company has entered into another transaction which is ultra vires.[1427]

That a trust company was not authorized to hold incumbered realty did not afford the company a defense to its promise to indemnify the person purchasing the realty for it.[1428] But the guaranty of a trust company made as an inducement to effect sales of participating interests in mortgages, as part of a profit-making venture, was held beyond the company's power and against public policy, and no liability based upon the guaranty could be enforced against its receiver.[1429] And where a trust company's indorsement and guaranty of the paper of other banks for which it acted as financial agent was held ultra vires, the principle of estoppel could not be invoked to hold it liable to one acting in reliance thereon, especially where the claimant had knowledge of its lack of power.[1430]

Partly Executed Contracts.—There is a conflict in the decisions regarding ultra vires contracts which have been partly executed; the English doctrine is to the effect that no ultra vires contract can be enforced, but New York, and a growing number of other states, adopt a more liberal view and hold that the contracts of corporations, including trust companies, though ultra vires, will

---

Guaranteeing payment of bonds sold.—

Act of trust company authorized to sell bonds in making indorsement guaranteeing payment held not ultra vires under Georgia statute. In re Adair Realty, etc., Co., 35 F.2d 531.

[1426] Cosmopolitan Trust Co. v. Golub, 252 Mass. 574, 147 N.E. 847.

Where credit union issuing deposit book was not party directly or indirectly to a pledge of stock as security for loan from trust company subsequently taken over by commissioner of banks, loan was not illegal as in violation of a statute, prohibiting it from borrowing without permission of commissioner. Cosmopolitan Trust Co. v. Golub, 252 Mass. 574, 147 N.E 847 (1925).

[1427] Hiatt v. United States, 4 F.2d 374, cert, denied, 268 U.S. 704, 45 S. Ct. 638, 69 L. Ed. 1167.

The action of a trust company in becoming a member of the Federal Reserve System, though it might have been questioned by the stats of its incorporation, was not such an ultra vires act as made the transaction void, so that it can be questioned collaterally, and its affiliation was validated by a legislative act expressly extending the power to such companies. Hiatt v. United States, 4 F.2d 374, cert. denied, 268 U.S. 704, 45 S. Ct. 638, 69 L. Ed. 1167.

[1428] Williams v. Commercial Trust Co., 276 Mass. 508, 177 N.E. 588.

[1429] Reichert v. Metropolitan Trust Co., 262 Mich. 123, 247 N.W. 128.

[1430] In re Bankers' Trust Co., 27 F.2d 912.

nevertheless be enforced where either the person with whom the corporation has contracted or the corporation itself has received the full benefit thereof.[1431] Some courts, while holding that an ultra vires contract is wholly void, nevertheless allow recovery on a quantum meruit or implied contract basis.[1432] But an ultra vires contract of guaranty of a trust company will not

---

1431 **In general.—**

Gause v. Commonwealth Trust Co., 55 Misc. 110, 106 N.Y.S. 288, aff'd, 124 App. Div. 438, 108 N.Y.S. 1080, 196 N.Y. 134, 89 N.E. 476, 24 L.R.A. (n.s.) 967.

Contract to repurchase mortgage.—

Trust company selling mortgage, if retaining benefits, held estopped to urge agent exceeded authority or that contract through agent to repurchase mortgage was ultra vires. Hawkeye Securities Fire Ins. Co. v. Central Trust Co., 210 Iowa 284, 227 N.W. 637.

Guaranteeing payment of bond sold.—

If a contract of trust company, whereby, as an inducement to buy, it guaranteed payment of a negotiable bond which it sold, was ultra vires, defense of ultra vires, cannot be interposed, where money received as result of such contract was retained. McFerson v. Kepner, 76 Colo. 523, 233 P. 148.

Making secret profit as promoter of corporation.—

A corporation which receives money under an ultra vires contract may not excuse itself from liability under the contract by a plea of ultra vines, and a domestic trust company which acts as promoter of a corporation and makes a secret profit may not as a general rule rely on its ultra vires act. Richard Hanlon Millinery Co. v. Mississippi Valley Trust Co., 251 Mo. 553, 158 S.W. 359.

Performance not sufficient for recovery.—

Where a trust company guaranteed to plaintiff to sell certain stocks and bonds for him at a certain time at a fixed price, but there was no delivery to the company of such securities, there was no such performance by plaintiff as entitled him to recover on the ground that the contract of a corporation will be enforced, where the corporation has received the full benefit thereof, though it be ultra vires. Gause v. Commonwealth Trust Co., 55 Misc. 110, 106 N.Y.S. 288, aff'd, 124 App. Div. 438, 108 N.Y.S. 1080, 196 N.Y. 134, 89 N.E 476, 24 L.R.A. (n.s.) 967.

Illustrative case.—

Where trust company, to which realtor was indebted on security of his interest in subdivisions, refused to make another loan but agreed to purchase from plaintiff, to which realtor applied for loan, notes executed by realtor in case of default, company, which received proceeds of notes and placed them to realtor's credit on his open account, was liable to plaintiff on agreement, in absence of statute expressly prohibiting transaction, since it received an affirmative enrichment by transaction in form of greater security for realtors obligations. Briggs Commercial, etc., Co. v. Finley, 283 Mich. 1, 276 N.W. 877.

1432 In re Bankers' Trust Co., 27 F.2d 912; Nowell v. Equitable Trust Co., 249 Mass. 585, 144 N.E. 749.

An action to recover from a trust company by reason of execution of ultra vires contract

be enforced on the ground of equitable estoppel where the trust company has received no substantial benefit thereunder.[1433]

§ 18. Actions.

Parties.—The Securities Litigation Uniform Standards Act of 1998 (SLUSA) seeks to prevent state class actions alleging fraud from being used to frustrate the objectives of the Private Securities Litigation Reform Act of 1995. SLUSA bars private plaintiffs from bringing: (1) A covered class action (2) based on state law claims (3) alleging that defendant made a misrepresentation or omission or employed any manipulative or deceptive device (4) in connection with the purchase or sale of (5) a covered security.[1434] A covered security is one issued by an investment company registered under the Investment Company Act of 1940.[1435] A covered class action is one in which damages are sought on behalf of more than fifty persons or prospective class members.[1436] SLUSA operates wherever deceptive statements or conduct form the gravamen or essence of the claim. Because courts look to the substance of the allegations, plaintiffs cannot avoid preclusion through artful pleading that removes the covered words but leaves in the covered concepts. Were it otherwise, SLUSA enforcement would reduce to a formalistic search through the pages of the complaint for magic words—untrue statement, material omission, manipulative or deceptive device—and nothing more.[1437]

Pleading.—In a suit by a bank against a trust company for damages for the negligence of the company's agent who undertook to collect securities

---

based on equitable estoppel is not action on express ultra vires contract, but on implied contract to return or make compensation for property or money which defendant has no right to retain. Nowell v. Equitable Trust Co., 249 Mass. 585, 144 N.E. 749.

According to the federal rule, the court will only look to see if the disappointed panty is entitled to any relief outside of the contract, as by an action to recover what the repudiating party received by virtue of the repudiated contract Where the assets of the trust company do not appear to have been in any manner enriched there is no refund due by it. In re Bankers' Trust Co., 27 F.2d 912.

[1433] Nowell v. Equitable Trust Co., 249 Mass. 585, 144 N.E. 749.

[1434] Freeman Invs., L.P. v. Pac. Life Ins. Co., 704 F.3d 1110 (9th Cir. 2013). As to actions to enforce stockholders' liability, see § 8 of this chapter. As to actions to enforce liability of directors and officers, see § 12 of this chapter.

See 15 U.S.C.S. § 78bb(f)(1).

[1435] 15 U.S.C.S. § 77r(b)(2).

[1436] 15 U.S.C.S. § 78bb(f)(5)(B).

[1437] Freeman Invs., L.P. v. Pac. Life Ins. Co., 704 F.3d 1110 (9th Cir. 2013).

for the bank, a petition which alleges no facts showing damages on account of negligence is subject to demurrer; such petition is also demurrable for not showing that but for the negligence charged the bank could have collected the securities.[1438] The allegation of a complaint in an action to recover payments made under a profit-sharing savings bond, that the plaintiff performed all terms imposed upon him and made payments as provided, is an allegation of an ultimate fact which entitles him to show waiver or estoppel in respect to forfeiture for irregularity of payments, and he is not required to plead the facts constituting evidence of such estoppel.[1439] Where a contract made by an agent of a trust company is relied upon to bind the company, the identity of the agent and his authority to act for the company must be clearly set forth.[1440] And the contracts of a trust company are commonly presumed to be within its lawful power until the contrary appears; therefore, in a suit to enforce such a contract, the defense of ultra vires, if intended to be relied upon, must be set up in the answer.[1441] Where an investment company provided checking and stop payment services as an inducement for customers to continue doing business with the company, the company wrote checks drawn on its account pursuant to a loan to its customers, for which the company charged interest, and the company had established procedures for transmitting stop payment orders to the bank, the investment company was not acting as a "volunteer" on behalf of its customers and had a duty to comply with the standard of reasonable skill, care and diligence in connection with the customers' stop payment orders.[1442]

[1438] Farmers' Banking Co. v. Continental Trust Co., 35 Ga. App. 14, 132 S.E. 115.

A petition charging defendant trust company's agent's negligence in a certain sale was held bad as against demurrer, where allegations thereof showed that the agent was vested with discretion as to the time to sell, and that he in nowise breached such discretion. Farmers' Banking Co. v. Continental Trust Co., 35 Ga. App. 14, 132 S.E. 115.

[1439] Schoenberg v. Mutual Profit Realty Co., 94 Misc. 203, 158 N.Y.S. 264.

[1440] Germantown Trust Co. v. Emhardt, 321 Pa. 561, 184 A. 457.

In trust company's action on guaranty, affidavit of defense, alleging that guaranty was executed in reliance on contemporaneous parol contract, made by trust company's "real estate officers," that defendant would not be held thereon, was insufficient for failure to identify "real estate officers" who made alleged promise and to show their authority to act. Germantown Trust Co. v. Emhardt, 321 Pa. 561, 184 A. 457.

[1441] Nowell v. Equitable Trust Co., 249 Mass. 585, 144 N.E. 749.

[1442] Weiss v. Advest, Inc., 607 F. Supp. 803 (D.C. Pa. 1985).

In the appended notes will be found other decisions relating to complaints,[1443] and their sufficiency[1444] or insufficiency[1445] as stating a cause ofaction at law or in equity,[1446] and sufficiency of answers thereto.[1447]

[1443] **Allegations stricken.—**

In action to rescind sale of notes by defendant trust company on ground of fraud and deceit, complaint properly alleged reckless statements of fact made by defendant, but allegations as to illegality of defendant's acts could be struck out. Freeman v. Manufacturers Trust Co., 288 N.Y.S. 413.

Amendment—

In action upon written contract, under which investment company was to pay money to plaintiffs, and an ancillary contract between investment company and trust company whereby trust company was to pay money to plaintiffs, in case of default by investing company, out of investment company's funds in its possession, refusal to permit plaintiffs to amend complaint to include allegation that trust company had moneys in its possession which were payable toward plaintiffs' contract at time of plaintiffs' demand upon it held abuse of discretion. Slack v. Metropolitan Trust Co., 9 Cal App. 2d 87, 48 P.2d 755.

Timely filing.—

Where, soon after the date on which the directors of a trust company vote to merge it with a certain bank, a company stockholder instructs his counsel to institute suit, but at the request of the defendant's counsel suit is deferred pending a conference, such stockholder acts with reasonable diligence in filing a bill within a couple of days after the conference. Bonner v. Chapin Nat'l Bank, 251 Mass. 401, 146 N.E. 666 (1925).

Action not premature.—

Action by buyer of bonds for investment company's breach of contract to repay purchase price and interest held not premature, where prior to commencement of action two interest installments were defaulted, the seller failed to issue new bonds and expressly repudiated liability for interest or principal. Kressly v. District Bond Co., 138 Cal. App. 565, 32 P.2d 1112.

Action on $2,500 bond, dated August 8, 1927, was not prematurely brought on June 24, 1935, though bond was to be paid for in ten annual installments of $180 each, where holder made many advance payments, and where bond provided that, when advance payments with annual compound interest of 6 per cent amounted to $2, 600 before maturity, bond became payable, and that any payment in excess of $72 per year in advance should increase the cash surrender value and company's liability in amount equal to such payment and accumulated interest at rate of 6 per cent. Union Deposit Co. v. Talbot, 101 Colo. 426, 73 P.2d 1389.

[1444] In action by depositors and creditors of bank and trust company to establish liability of bank and of trust company and its officers and directors for deposits which were allegedly misappropriated, to impress trust on deposits, and for other appropriate relief, complaint stated cause of action in behalf of plaintiffs individually. Society Milion Athena, Inc. v. National Bank of Greece, 253 App. Div. 650, 3 N.Y.S.2d 677.

In action against trust company for alleged fraudulent acts whereby plaintiff lost money in real estate transaction, allegations that preliminary contract contained provision that, if realty should not be zoned for business purposes, plaintiff's money would be returned, but that final

(Text continued on page 406)

contract did not contain such provision, though trust company's agent, in whom plaintiff reposed confidence, stated that it did, and in reliance plaintiff signed contract and thereby lost money because realty was not zoned for business purposes, were sufficient to withstand demurrer. Fletcher Trust Co. v. Hauser, 105 Ind. App. 281, 11 N.E.2d 1012.

Chapter 11 trustee did not state negligent misrepresentation claim against investment banker under theory that banker issued "highly confident" letters that market would support transaction between debtor and another company and that banker allegedly made oral commitment to provide financing for transaction; letters were expressions of confidence that financing could be obtained under certain specified conditions, and did not constitute guarantees that deal could be financed regardless of any changes, and any oral assurances of financing were not accompanied by suggestion of terms on which such financing would be granted. In re Daisy Sys. Corp., 97 F.3d 1171 (9th Cir. 1996).

Banking Department regulation providing that a trust company administering common trust fund shall have the exclusive management thereof did not prohibit investment of common trust funds in mutual funds; such investments always remain subject to the "prudent man" rule expressly authorizing fiduciaries to invest in management type investment companies, and do not alter the trustee's fiduciary responsibilities. In re OnBank & Trust Co., 649 N.Y.S.2d 592 (N.Y. App. Cir. 4 Dept 1996).

Investment in mutual funds by trustee of common trust fund does not constitute improper delegation of its management authority; although mutual fund assumes responsibility of choosing individual investments, trustee maintains control by choosing mutual fund that is operated according to investment objectives consistent with those of underlying trust, and shares of the mutual fund can be redeemed almost immediately after request from shareholder, which also enables trustee to maintain close control over the investment. In re OnBank & Trust Co., 649 N.Y.S.2d 592 (N.Y. App. Div. 4 Dept 1996).

Fees charged by mutual fund to common trust funds would have to be absorbed by bank, as trustee for the common trust funds, rather than considered as merely part of the common trust funds' investment in the mutual fund, or an acquisition cost or expense related to maintenance of the assets; mutual fund's management fee was a charge to obtain benefit of investment expertise of manager or investment advisor of mutual fund, and as such, was barred by statute providing that common trust fund shall not be deemed separate trust fund on which commissions or other compensation is allowable, and that no trust company maintaining such a fund shall make any charge against such fund for the management thereof. In re OnBank & Trust Co., 649 N.Y.S.2d 592 (N.Y. App. Div. 4 Dept 1996).

1445 Allegation of purchaser, seeking to rescind contract of purchase of guaranteed mortgage certificate on ground of fraud, that prior to institution of action she made demand for purchase price and offered to restore certificate, held insufficient, in absence of allegation that purchaser actually tendered certificate at time demand was made or attempted to make tender. Fetzer v. Title Guarantee, etc., Co., 250 App. Div. 567, 294 N.Y.S. 922.

In action against trust company to recover purchase price of certificate on rescission of contract of purchase, complaint was defective for failure to allege a tender of certificate to defendant and that right to a return of purchase price was assigned by original purchaser or by his transferee to the plaintiff, where sale of certificate did not carry with it assignment of

(Text continued on page 406)

---

right to return of purchase price on rescission of purchase contract. Daniels v. Title Guarantee & Trust Co., 18 N.Y.S.2d 312.

Where no cause of action existed under California law against corporation for breach of its fiduciary duty, no cause of action was stated against trust company, which allegedly purchased stock without disclosing that it had material inside information about undisclosed contract, for aiding and abetting such a breach. State Teachers Retirement Bd. v. Fluor Corp., 566 F. Supp. 939 (D.C.N.Y. 1982).

1446 **Cause of action at law.—**

Complaint for rescission of investment purported]y made by defendant bank and trust company for plaintiff in participation in mortgage which was no longer in existence stated cause of action at law, though not in equity. Hirsh v. Central Hanover Bank, etc., Co., 251 App. Div. 24, 295 N.Y.S. 522.

No cause of action at law.—

Complaint of purchasers, in action against guaranty company as seller of guaranteed mortgage certificates, to recover purchase price paid therefor on ground of misrepresentations and illegality of guaranty, stated no cause of action at law, in absence of allegation that plaintiffs restored or offered to restore certificates and renewals. Voehl v. Title Guaranty & Trust Co., 155 Misc. 697, 278 N.Y.S. 984, aff'd, 242 App. Div. 762, 275 N.Y.S. 215, 266 N.Y. 682, 195 N.E. 371.

Where subscriber sought to recover cash and face value of mortgages and mortgage certificates turned over to trustee under thrift plan for payment of insurance premiums and purchase of mortgages or mortgage certificates, action at law held not proper remedy where it was impossible to determine value of trust estate and subscriber's pro rata share until value of property behind mortgages and mortgage certificates had been reduced to cash. Schwartz v. Harriman Nat. Bank, etc., Co., 150 Misc. 543, 270 N.Y.S. 888.

Cause of action in equity.—

The allegations of a bill that a banking institution and directors acted in collusion to divert the funds and property of a trust company, being admitted by demurrer, constitute fraud on the company and its stockholders, relief for which is in equity. Bonner v. Chapin Nat. Bank, 251 Mass. 401, 146 N.E. 666 (1925).

No cause of action in equity.—

Purchasers of guaranteed first mortgage certificates held not entitled to equitable relief; in action against guaranty company, as seller, to rescind on ground of defendant's misrepresentations and illegality of guaranty, since purchasers had adequate legal remedy. Voehl v. Title Guaranty & Trust Co., 155 Misc. 697, 278 N.Y.S. 984, aff'd, 242 App. Div. 762, 275 N.Y.S. 215, 266 N.Y. 662, 195 N.E. 371.

1447 That good faith and judgment were exercised by a trust company accepting fidelity bonds from foreign insurance underwriters not operating under authority of the New York insurance department as required by statute was no defense to stockholder's representative action against the trust company and its trustees based on the company's acceptance of such bonds. Nor was it a defense that stockholders predecessor in interest ratified acceptance of such bonds, or that stockholder had not exhausted all his means within the trust company to obtain the redress of his alleged grievances, or that he purchased stock for purpose of

Presumptions and Burden of Proof.—Cases relating to presumptions and inferences,[1448] and burden of proof[1449] are set out in the footnotes.

---

instituting action in behalf of competing insurance companies and had entered into conspiracy to coerce trust company to abandon such bonds. Robins v. Brooklyn Trust Co., 6 N.Y.S.2d 626.

See Runcie v. Corn Exchange Bank Trust Co., 6 N.Y.S.2d 616, followed in Runcie v. Central Hanover Bank, etc., Co., 6 N.Y.S.2d 625.

In such action allegations that it was to the advantage of the trust company to carry fidelity bonds with foreign underwriters that it had received value for which the premiums were paid, that directors accepted bonds in good faith under a mistake of law, and that trust company would have canceled bonds if the invalidity had been brought to its attention, were insufficient to state a defense. Runcie v. Empire Trust Co., 6 N.Y.S.2d 659. See Runcie v. Bankers Trust Co., 6 N.Y.S.2d 623.

[1448] In action for fraud and deceit, knowledge and intentional wrongdoing could be inferred in absence of proof to contrary from evidence that representations made by investment banking corporation to investor concerning financial conditions of companies whose securities investor was purchasing were untrue. Tone v. Halsey, etc., Co., 286 Ill. App. 169, 3 N.E.2d 142.

In stockholder's derivative action against diversified management investment company and individual officers and directors thereof, evidence of officer's past illegal conduct warranted inference that there was reasonable likelihood of future violations. Tanzer v. Huffines, 287 F. Supp. 273 (D. Del. 1968), aff'd, 408 F.2d 42 (3d Cir. 1969).

[1449] **Agency.—**

In action by partnership against trust company for alleged violation of duty of loyalty owed by agent to principal, burden of proving agency was upon plaintiffs. Mack v. American Security, etc., Co., 191 F.2d 775.

Type of relief.—

Holders of single investment mutual fund programs, seeking relief from refusal of sponsor to permit holders to move in and out of fund without payment of brokerage commissions as provided by contracts, would have burden of showing exact relief, if any, to which they were entitled, taking into consideration public interest to be protected by SEC and the NASD, which interpreted its rule, to forbid its members to be involved with unlimited manner in which the "in-and-out" privilege was being used. Harwell v. Growth Programs, Inc., 451 F.2d 240 (5th Cir. 1971).

Good faith.—

In action for fraud and deceit, evidence concerning falsity of representations made by investment banking corporation to investor concerning financial conditions of companies whose securities investor was purchasing held to make prima facie case which cast on corporation burden of introducing evidence that representations were made in good faith. Tone v. Halsey, etc., Co., 286 Ill. App. 169, 3 N.E.2d 142.

Existence of authority.—

In trespass to try title burden was upon defendant to negative existence of authority of plaintiff loan corporation to appoint substitute trustee, who sold property to plaintiff upon

Evidence.—In an action by a trust company on a promissory note, the testimony of an employee respecting entries on the books of the company tending to show that the note was transferred to its savings department and that certain items of interest had been paid, is admissible, defendant claiming that there was no transfer.[1450] And evidence that it was a recognized part of the business of banking as conducted in the place in question for banks and trust companies to buy, sell and deliver foreign exchange for immediate and future delivery, is properly admitted on the issue of the validity of such a contract.[1451] Other cases relating to the admissibility of evidence are set out in the appended note.[1452]

---

default. Brown v. National Loan, etc., Co., 139 S.W.2d 364 (Tex. Civ. App. 1940).

[1450] Cosmopolitan Trust Co. v. Leonard Watch Co., 249 Mass. 14, 143 N.E. 827.

[1451] Corsino v. Hanover Trust Co., 253 Mass. 5, 147 N.E. 868.

[1452] **Evidence held inadmissible.—**

In suit to recover payments made on savings bond and exemplary damages for fraud of defendant's agent, statements by president and local manager of defendant to plaintiff's attorney held inadmissible as evidence of fraud of agent, or that defendant authorized misrepresentations or acquiesced therein. Bankers' Mtg. Co. v. Baxter (Tex. Civ. App.), 66 S.W.2d 408.

In suit to recover payments made on savings bond and exemplary damages for fraud, statement of defendant's local manager regarding sales methods pursued by different agents held inadmissible, in absence of showing that defendant authorized or ratified such sales methods. Bankers' Mtg. Co. v. Baxter (Tex. Civ. App.), 66 S.W.2d 408.

In customer's action against investment bankers to compel accounting for profits on theory that fiduciary relationship existed in trade between customer and bankers, certified copies of rules of the Securities and Exchange Commission were inadmissible in evidence. Also, the N.R.A. code of fair competition for investment bankers was inapplicable. Metcalf v. Leedy, Wheeler & Co., 140 Fla. 149, 191 So. 690.

In action against industrial bank to recover twice amount of interest paid in automobile financing transaction, similar financing transactions should not be considered. Krim v. Morris Plan Industrial Bank, 173 Misc. 141, 17 N.Y.S.2d 472.

In suit to recover payments made on savings bond and exemplary damages for fraud, letter from defendant's general agent to its treasurer regarding advertising literature and referring to different sales of bonds, held inadmissible as immaterial. Bankers' Mtg. Co. v. Baxter (Tex. Civ. App.), 66 S.W.2d 408.

Evidence concerning the settlement of related state court will litigation was inadmissible in diversity suit by failed beneficiary alleging negligence by trust company which performed estate planning services for testatrix; while evidence was helpful in understanding total picture of events, it was not germane to issue of beneficiary's damages, and may have actually confused jury since beneficiary's children received a portion of the other suit's settlement. Merrick v. Mercantile-Safe Deposit & Trust Co., 855 F.2d 1095 (4th Cir. 1988).

Failed will beneficiary's deposition testimony was inadmissible in action against

In an action to recover monthly payments made by a plaintiff on a profit-sharing savings bond, evidence that the defendant accepted and retained deferred payments shows the defendant's waiver of regular and prompt payments.[1453] The issuance by a trust company of a draft on a bank in which it has insufficient funds is evidence of a fraud perpetrated on a payee bank.[1454] Where a plaintiff alleges that he was fraudulently induced by a trust company's officer to enter into a building operation, evidence that the officer was authorized to speak for the company and that he determined the general course of its business, sustains a finding of the company's responsibility for its officer's acts.[1455] See the footnote for other cases relating to the weight and sufficiency of evidence.[1456]

---

trust company for its negligent estate planning which denied beneficiary a bequest, as testimony, which demonstrated that beneficiary's interest was adverse to that of his children who recovered in settlement of related state court case, was irrelevant upon dismissal of his children as plaintiffs in federal court suit, and was not an admission that he benefited from state court settlement in favor of his children. Merrick v. Mercantile-Safe Deposit & Trust Co., 855 F.2d 1095 (4th Cir. 1988).

Evidence held admissible.—

In action for breach of trust against trustee corporation and officers thereof, evidence disclosing that for two years before and for two years subsequent to alleged breach of trust, trustee placed title to its land in names of certain employees and had them execute notes and mortgages, that trustee then took reconveyance of title from employees, assuming and agreeing to pay mortgage indebtedness held competent on question of intent. Masonic Bldg. Corp. v. Carlsen, 128 Neb. 108, 258 N.W. 44.

1453 Schoenberg v. Mutual Profit Realty Co., 94 Misc. 203, 158 N.Y.S. 264.

1454 Leach v. Central Trust Co., 203 Iowa 1060, 213 N.W. 777, 57 A.L.R. 1165.

1455 Miller v. Central Trust, etc., Co., 285 Pa. 472, 132 A. 579.

1456 Evidence held insufficient to fix liability for exemplary damages for fraudulent representations inducing purchase of investment bond. Union Deposit Co. v. Moseley (Tex. Civ. App.), 75 S.W.2d 190.

Evidence sustained finding of existence of contract whereby investment company, which had sold bonds, agreed to repay buyer in consideration of buyer's refraining from rescinding or instituting legal proceedings after default in interest payments. Kressly v. District Bond Co., 138 Cal. App. 565, 32 P.2d 1112.

In action by partnership against trust company for alleged violation of duty of loyalty owed by agent to principal, evidence supported finding that trust company had not consented, either expressly or by implication, to act as plaintiffs' agent. Mack v. American Security, etc., Co., 191 F.2d 775.

Evidence sustained finding that maker of note payable to trust company gave up right to have collateral sold to pay off note. Federal Nat. Bank v. O'Connell, 305 Mass. 559, 26 N.E.2d 539.

Evidence sustained finding that mortgage certificate holders relied on depositary's

(Text continued on page 410)

---

certification that securities deposited with it complied with indenture. Feldmeier v. Mortgage Securities, 34 Cal. App. 2d 201, 93 P.2d 593.

In action for alleged fraudulent acts of trust company whereby plaintiff lost money in real estate transaction, evidence sustained allegations that preliminary contract contained provision that, if realty should not be zoned for business purposes, plaintiff's money would be returned, but that final contract did not contain such provision, though trust company's agent, in whom plaintiff imposed confidence, stated that it did, and in reliance plaintiff signed contract and thereby lost money because realty was not zoned for business purposes. Fletcher Trust Co. v. Hauser, 105 Ind. App. 281, 11 N.E.2d 1012.

Evidence held to establish that customer was able businessman, and that defendant investment bankers were not guilty of overreaching and misrepresentation. Metcalf v. Leedy, Wheeler & Co., 140 Fla. 149, 191 So. 690.

Evidence held to establish that trust company kept sufficiently accurate accounts, in action against company to recover funds which company invested together with other funds. Finley v. Exchange Trust Co., 183 Okla. 167, 80 P.2d 296, 117 A.L.R. 162.

Evidence showing no conspiracy and that one complainant not defrauded.—

In suit against president of trust company and others for amount paid for mortgage participation certificates purchased in defaulted mortgage fraudulently placed in mortgage department by president, evidence held to show no conspiracy ab initio to defraud, and hence no liability on part of defendant who was involved in earlier transactions only. The evidence was further held to show that one complainant was not defrauded, and hence he was not entitled to relief. Pridmore v. Steneck, 122 N.J. Eq. 35, 191 A. 861.

Evidence establishing failure to file reports.—

Evidence in action by United States for determination that small business investment company licensed under Small Business Investment Act had violated Act and for recovery of unpaid balance of loan made to company by Small Business Administration established that company had failed to file audited financial report and program evaluation report required under Small Business Administration's regulations and that there had been no agreement with Administration's representatives dispensing with such obligation. United States v. Cape Fear Capital Corp., 286 F. Supp. 135 (M.D. Pa. 1968).

Evidence establishing collusion.—

In action by investors against principal stockholder of investment company and company to rescind purchase agreement, for an accounting, and for a determination that defendants were liable to investors money turned over for investment, evidence established collusion between defendants to obtain plaintiff's money which was to be lost to defendants through defalcation scheme. Milgrom v. Investment Management Co., 326 Mich. 401, 40 N.W.2d 201 (1950).

Testimony of company's agent.—

Where trust company alleged that payment to it was for extraordinary services, testimony of its agent that it was understood that no charges were to be made for collection of rents and for trip taken by company's employee in negotiating loan, precluded company from making claim for such items. Louisville Trust Co. v. Cummins, 288 Ky. 285, 156 S.W.2d 118.

Trial, Judgment and Recovery.—See the appended notes for decisions relating to instructions,[1457] questions for the jury,[1458] directing a verdict,[1459] and extent of recovery.[1460]

Evidence sufficient of tortious conduct.—

Evidence of conduct of bank and investment company once it had been informed of its error in liquidating client's account was sufficient to support finding that bank and investment company had engaged in tortious conduct of type warranting punitive damages, where bank and investment company failed to adequately respond to several inquiries of client's husband and attorney concerning disputed transaction. Bank of N.Y. v. Bright, 494 N.E.2d 970 (Ind. App. 1986).

Clear and convincing evidence required for either contract or tort theory.—

Client asserting claim against investment company and bank as result of improper liquidation of her account was required to establish, by clear and convincing evidence, that conduct exhibited elements of fraud, malice, gross negligence, or oppression, to recover punitive damages, regardless of whether she ultimately succeeded on theory of either breach of contract or tortious conversion. Bank of N.Y. v. Bright, 494 N.E.2d 970 (Ind. App. 1986).

No evidence customers acting as sureties.—

There was no evidence that customers of investment company were acting as sureties or implied sureties on their daughter's contracts to buy horses when they obtained checks drawn on company's bank account to be charged against loan in connection with customers' margin account so as to preclude determination that company's negligence in failing to stop payment on checks pursuant to customers' request was proximate cause of losses to customers. Weiss v. Advest, Inc., 607 F. Supp. 803 (D.C. Pa. 1985).

Negligence in failing to stop payment.—

There was sufficient evidence from which jury could find that investment company was negligent in failing to stop payment on checks drawn on company's bank account to be charged against loan in connection with customers' margin account and that negligence was proximate cause of customers' losses. Weiss v. Advest, Inc., 607 F. Supp. 803 (D.C. Pa. 1985).

Existence, effect and enforceability of investment company's customers' daughter's contracts to purchase horses, for which customers obtained checks drawn on investment company's bank account to be charged against loan in connection with customers' margin account, was not relevant in determining whether investment company breached duty of care owed to its customers when it failed to call bank and transmit customers' stop payment orders on checks. Weiss v. Advest, Inc., 607 F. Supp. 803 (D.C. Pa. 1985).

[1457] In an action for breach of contract whereby a securities company agreed to repurchase bonds "at any time," an instruction that the phrase "at any time" was not to be construed as importing a reasonable time was held error. Edge v. Boardwalk Securities Corp., 115 N.J.L. 286, 179 A. 270.

[1458] **The question of breach of trust,** and whether officers of trust company knowingly participated therein, held for jury. Masonic Bldg. Corp. v. Carlsen, 128 Neb. 108, 258 N.W. 44.

Time offer to repurchase bonds was to remain open held for jury. Edge v. Boardwalk

(Text continued on page 412)

Securities Corp., 115 N.J.L. 286, 179 A. 270.

Whether purchaser of bonds exercised repurchase option within reasonable time was for jury in purchaser's action against securities company for breach of contract to repurchase bonds "at any time" at certain rate. Edge v. Pancoast, 120 N.J.L. 216, 198 A. 825.

Whether treasurer of trust company was authorized to execute and sign contract of guaranty in name of company was held a question of fact for the jury. Nowell v. Equitable Trust Co., 249 Mass. 585, 144 N.E. 749.

Value.—

In action for breach of warranty in sale of debenture which plaintiff purchased for investment, question of what value would have been if debenture had been as represented held for jury. Doyle v. Union Bank & Trust Co., 102 Mont. 563, 59 P.2d 1171, 108 A.L.R. 1047.

In action for damages for breach of warranty in sale of debenture which plaintiff purchased for investment, evidence showing that at time of sale debenture had market value of price paid, subsequent appointment of receiver, default in payments of interest, and unexplained decline in assets and increase in liabilities of corporation held insufficient for jury as to actual value. of debenture at time of sale. Doyle v. Union Bank, etc., Co., 102 Mont. 563, 59 P.2d 1171, 108 A.L.R. 1047.

Miscellaneous questions.—

In an action by an insolvent trust company on a note transferred to the savings department, the following questions were held for the jury to decide: Whether the circumstances were such that the defendant was charged with notice of assignment, whether notice to both the commercial and savings department of the trust company to charge an account in the commercial department with a note assigned by the commercial department to the savings department constituted payment of the note, and whether the commercial department was authorized by the savings department to collect a note assigned to the savings department. Cosmopolitan Trust Co. v. Leonard Watch Co., 249 Mass. 14, 143 N.E. 827.

Unambiguous contract not for jury.—

Contract with investment service company for purchase of stock on installment plan held not ambiguous, so as to require court to submit interpretation of contract to jury, although containing provision, "Special Contract: No further installment payments required except periodic payment of interest," since such provision did not forgive installments on purchase price, but simply relieved purchaser from paying one-tenth of purchase price every 90 days, as contract elsewhere required. Simpson v. Securities Service Corp., 47 Ariz. 464, 56 P.2d 1044 (1936).

[1459] **Direction proper.—**

In an action on a note by a trust company, where the evidence is uncontradicted that the note in question had been transferred and assigned the trial judge is justified in directing a verdict to that effect. Cosmopolitan Trust Co. v. Leonard Watch Co., 249 Mass. 14, 143 N.E. 827.

Direction improper.—

Where record in action to recover purchase price of a mortgage certificate on ground of

Miscellaneous Matters.—In the appended notes will be found a number of decisions discussing matters relating to a right of action,[1461] conditions

---

alleged false representations failed to show as a matter of law that defendant trust company made any representation which was false in a material and substantial respect, directing judgment for plaintiff was error. Pedone v. Title Guarantee, etc., Co., 280 N.Y. 153, 19 N.E.2d 1000.

[1460] **Amount of investment recovered.—**

Where, in action for breach of trust against trustee corporation and officers thereof, beneficiary's evidence tended to establish that securities were worthless while defendants' evidence tended to disclose that securities were worth amount of investment, if usefulness or value of beneficiary's securities had been seriously affected and there had been breach of trust, beneficiary was entitled to recover whole amount of investment. Masonic Bldg. Corp. v. Carlsen, 128 Neb. 108, 258 N.W. 44.

Difference between purchase price and value.—

If investor purchased securities from investment banking corporation for investment in reliance on untrue representations as to financial condition of companies, and held them until companies failed without discovering falsity of representations, investor could recover in action for fraud and deceit the difference between amount he paid for securities and value of securities after failure of company. Tone v. Halsey, etc., Co., 286 Ill. App. 169, 3 N.E.2d 142.

Reasonable sum for services.—

Jury held authorized to find that trust company was entitled to a reasonable sum for services without making a finding upon each item of service alleged to have been performed. Louisville Trust Co. v. Cummins, 288 Ky. 285, 156 S.W.2d 118.

Interest.—

Where trust company had received proceeds of 8 per cent bonds held for plaintiff and had mingled proceeds with company's assets, in determining amount of money judgment which should be entered for plaintiff, plaintiff was entitled to 6 per cent interest per annum since date on which interest on bond was last collected by trust company and remitted to plaintiff. Hamilton v. Talbot, 141 Kan. 1, 39 P.2d 665.

Where plaintiff purchasing 5 percent bond from trust company had recovered judgment thereon against maker, and trust company collected full amount of judgment without interest from date of judgment, in determining amount of money judgment to which plaintiff was entitled against trust company, trust company held chargeable with full amount of judgment with straight interest at 6 percent per annum from date it collected money. Hamilton v. Talbot, 141 Kan. 1, 39 P.2d 665.

[1461] **No right of action for failure to conform to sound principles of operation.—**

The federal reserve regulation requiring national banks to conform to sound principles in operation of trust department did not create a right of action against bank for alleged failure to conform to sound principles and did not warrant fashioning a federal common law of sound trust principles. Blaney v. Florida Nat'l Bank, 357 F.2d 27 (5th Cir. 1966).

In action against trust company for amount deposited to redeem script certificates for plaintiff's stock dividends, court is not concerned with rights of holders of unredeemed script

precedent to actions,[1462] parties and standing to sue,[1463] service of process,[1464] venue,[1465] attorneys,[1466] and statute of limitations or laches.[1467]

---

to share equally with those who redeemed their script. Hupp Motor Car Corp. v. Guaranty Trust Co., 171 Misc. 21, 11 N.Y.S.2d 855.

[1462] **Tender of securities required.—**

Offer to return mortgage certificates held necessary before plaintiff could sue to recover sum paid for them. E.T.C. Corp. v. Title Guarantee, etc., Co., 271 N.Y. 124, 2 N.E.2d 284, 105 A.L.R. 999, holding that purchaser's letter stating it tendered back certificates and demanding return of purchase price was insufficient return.

Investor suing investment banking corporation for worthless securities sold him by corporation could not recover on ground of rescission where no evidence was offered supporting rescission and case was not tried on that theory, and securities were not tendered back to corporation but were made basis of claim in bankruptcy proceeding. Tone v. Halsey, etc., Co., 286 Ill. App. 169, 3 N.E.2d 142.

Pecuniary loss required.—

A pecuniary loss of lenders of money on forged bond and mortgage was essential to maintenance of action against trust company for negligence in failing to discover forgery and in taking acknowledgment to bond and mortgage and certifying that trust company's agent knew persons who executed such instruments. Where lenders did not rely on responsibility of any particular owner of mortgaged realty, and real owner subsequently ratified and accepted the original fraudulent transaction, lenders were not damaged, and hence had no cause of action against trust company, notwithstanding that lenders could rescind the transaction. Hermes v. Title Guarantee, etc., Co., 282 N.Y. 88, 24 N.E.2d 859.

Demand to bring action not required.—

A stockholder could maintain representative action against trust company and trustees thereof based on trust company's acceptance of fidelity bonds from foreign insurance underwriters not operating under authority of New York Insurance department as required by statute, without making any prior demand upon the trust company and the trustees that such an action be maintained. And the motives which prompted the stockholder to institute the action were immaterial. Runcie v. Empire Trust Co., 6 N.Y.S.2d 659; Runcie v. Corn Exch. Bank, etc., Co., 6 N.Y.S.2d 616.

Foreclosure of mortgage not required.—

That mortgage which secured bonds had not been foreclosed did not preclude bondholders from suing trust company on its guaranty of bonds. Collings v. Guarantee Trust Co., 10 F. Supp. 462, aff'd, 76 F.2d 870, cert. denied, 295 U.S. 747, 55 S. Ct. 825, 79 L. Ed. 1692.

Money damage not required.—

A stockholder, who seeks only that which Congress has provided for him as a matter of right under the Investment Company Act, need not show money damage to entitle him to sue, and it is enough if he shows that no one else will sue on his behalf. Breswick & Co. v. United States, 134 F. Supp. 132. See Alleghany Corp. v. Breswick & Co., 353 U.S. 151, 77 S. Ct. 763, 1 L. Ed. 2d 726.

[1463] **Nonjoinder.—**

Nonjoinder of trust company in suit against president thereof for amount paid for

(Text continued on page 416)

mortgage participation certificates purchased in defaulted mortgage fraudulently placed in mortgage department by president held not to preclude recovery against president where no objection was raised to nonjoinder until cause came on for final argument, despite allegations in bill of complaint that trust company was defunct and insolvent. Pridmore v. Steneck, 122 N.J. Eq. 35, 191 A. 861.

Improper parties.—

Shareholders who had not purchased interests in voting trust or its successor corporation were not proper parties to enforce Investment Company Act in connection with sale of voting trust interests, even if trust were deemed an investment company within Act, however, private remedy might be found to exist in favor of proper party. Greater Iowa Corp. v. McLendon, 378 F.2d 783 (8th Cir. 1067).

Representative capacity.—

An action to establish liability of bank and of trust company and its officers and directors for deposits which were allegedly misappropriated, to impress trust on deposits, and for other appropriate relief, could not be maintained by depositors and creditors in a representative capacity. Society Milion Athena, Inc. v. National Bank of Greece, 258 App. Div. 650, 8 N.Y.S.2d 677.

Standing to sue.—

Corporation whose stock had been purchased in open market by diversified open-end investment company lacked standing to sue investment company and others for alleged purchase of stock for control of issuing corporation, in-stead of investment, and engagement in joint enterprise or arrangement" between investment company and "an affiliated person" in violation of the Investment Company Act of 1940. General Time Corp. v. American Investors Fund, 283 F. Supp. 400 (S.D.N.Y.), aff'd, 403 F.2d 159 (2d Cir. 1968), cert. denied, 393 U.S. 1026, 89 S. Ct. 631, 21 L. Ed. 2d 570 (1969).

Standing to assert claims under Investment Company Act of 1940 extends to any person holding an ownership interest in a company subject to the Act. General Time Corp. v. American Investors Fund, Inc., 283 F. Supp. 400 (S.D.N.Y.), aff'd, 403 F.2d 159 (2d Cir. 1968), cent, denied, 393 U.S. 1026, 89 S. Ct. 631, 21 L. Ed. 2d 570 (1969).

Where individual members of an investors' association who had been injured by misconduct actionable under the securities laws were perfectly free to sue on their own behalf, and could sue individually or could attempt to represent a class, the investors association itself, which owned no stock in the corporation which had allegedly injured the individual members, did not have standing to bring the action on behalf of the individual members. Independent Investor Protective League v. Saunders, 64 F.RD. 564 (E.D. Pa. 1974).

Class action under Securities Litigation Uniform Standards Act.—

See Freeman Invs., L.P. v. Pac. Life Ins. Co., 704 F.3d 1110 (2013).

The American Bankers Association did not have associational standing to sue the government on a claim that a Federal Reserve Act amendment reducing the dividends to be paid on Federal Reserve Bank stock constituted a breach of contract. Each of the member banks described by the ABA owned a different amount of stock and thus would have suffered difference damages. The ABA itself had not suffered any loss, and it did not claim

(Text continued on page 416)

---

that any members had assigned to it the right to sue. American Bankers Association v. U.S., Fed. Banking L. Rep. (CCH) P 101-770 (Oct. 30, 2017).

1464 **Service on foreign corporation.—**

A foreign corporation which never engaged in business of making, issuing or guaranteeing investment contracts and never issued or offered any securities to public, was not an "investment corporation" within statute authorizing service of process on banking and insurance commissioner in action against any foreign investment corporation, so that service of summons and complaint in action against such corporation by leaving copies thereof in office of such commissioner was ineffectual and invalid. Daoud v. Kleven Inv. Co., 30 N.J. Super. 38, 103 A.2d 257.

Where citation was served on agent and manager of loan company operating under assumed name for a trust company, trust company was in court for all purposes, and judgment of court could not be successfully attacked by trust company for want of service and appearance. Employees Loan Co. v. Templeton (Tex. Civ. App.), 109 S.W.2d 774.

1465 The concept of "transacting business" under venue provisions of Investment Company Act of 1940, Securities Act of 1933, and Securities Exchange Act of 1934, requires less business activity than that necessary to sustain jurisdiction under a "doing business" or "minimum contacts" standard, and is intended to have a more flexible and broader meaning than the jurisdictional predicates. Zorn v. Anderson, 263 F. Supp. 745 (S.D.N.Y. 1966).

Where defendant's activities within district of suit would be sufficient to support jurisdiction of action based on violations of Investment Company Act of 1940, Securities Act of 1933, and Securities Exchange Act of 1934, the district also meets venue standards. Zorn v. Anderson, 263 F. Supp. 745 (S.D.N.Y. 1968).

Derivative nature of action based on violation of Investment Company Act of 1940, Securities Act of 1933, and Securities Exchange Act of 1934, would not cause venue based on defendant's transacting business within the district to fall. Zorn v. Anderson, 263 F. Supp. 745 (S.D.N.Y. 1966).

Venue under Investment Company Act of 1940 requires but one act of material importance to consummation of scheme within the forum district. Zorn v. Anderson, 263 F. Supp. 745 (S.D.N.Y. 1968).

Venue proper for one claim proper for all.—

Venue of action based on violations of Investment Company Act of 1940, Securities Act of 1933, and Securities Exchange Act of 1934, is proper for claim arising under all such Acts if there is proper venue under any one of such Acts. Zorn v. Anderson, 263 F. Supp. 745 (S.D.N.Y. 1968).

New York jurisdictional requisites not met.—

Despite its relationship with a trust company in New York, which was a correspondent but not an agent, a nonresident trust company, which transacted no business in New York, was not subject to New York jurisdiction, where the only activity of the nonresident trust company with respect to the underlying transactions in question was to perform services in Maine for its Maine depositor. Amigo Foods Corp. v. Marine Midland Bank-New York, 48 App. Div. 2d 628, 368 N.Y.S.2d 7 (1975).

b. Representation by Officers and Agents.

§ 19. In General.

The doctrine of respondeat superior applies to a trust company acting as a trustee, and the company is liable for any fraud or bad faith by its agents to whom the directors have entrusted the business, though the directors are not personally guilty of fraud or bad faith.[1468] And an investment company

---

[1466] **Appearance by attorney.—**

Banks acting as estate fiduciaries should appear in proceedings and hearings in probate court only by attorney. State Bar Ass'n v. Connecticut Bank & Trust Co., 131 A.2d 646, 20 Conn. Supp. 248.

The judgment in the above case was modified in State Bar Asso. v. Connecticut Bank & Trust Co., 145 Conn. 222, 140 A.2d 863, 69 A.L.R.2d 394, wherein it was held that the lower court erred in concluding as a matter of law that a bank's appearance and representation at probate court hearings by attorneys who were salaried employees could not and did not constitute the unlawful practice of law.

Fees.—

Under a custodial agreement between a mutual fund and the bank which provided that "should the custodian become involved in litigation in any manner whatsoever on account of this agreement" the mutual fund should pay to the custodian all reasonable attorneys' fees incurred by custodian, the mutual fund was obligated to pay the bank's attorneys' fees for any litigation on account of the agreement, including a suit between the parties. Crown Western Invs., Inc. v. Mercantile Nat'l Bank, 504 S.W.2d 785 (Tex. Civ. App. 1974).

[1467] Where company selling note to customer lulled her into a false sense of safety, the company when sued for rescission could not invoke the doctrine of laches nor urge that the customer should have disregarded her unreserved trust in the company and initiated other methods to discover the fraud. Farmers' Trust Co. v. Threlkeld, 257 Ky. 211, 77 S.W.2d 616

Buyers from investment corporation of bonds issued by building corporation, having stood by for over ten years while foreclosure proceedings were being litigated and receivers and trustees appointed for benefit of their bonds, without pursuing avenues of information available to them, could not, to justify their delay in suing investment corporation for fraudulent misrepresentations in sale of bonds, for breaches of trust and for accounting, set up ignorance of alleged misrepresentations to avoid effect of statute of limitations or laches. Litwin v. Halsey, etc., Co. 324 Ill. App. 525, 58 N.E.2d 737.

An investment corporation which purchased outright all bonds issued by building corporation under agreement obligating investment corporation to pay full agreed price for all bonds regardless of its ability to sell them was not a trustee or fiduciary of subsequent buyers from it who allegedly relied on prospectus containing false representations, hence, such subsequent purchasers could not avoid effect of bar of statute of limitations or their laches in asserting their alleged right to recover from investment corporation for such misrepresentations. Litwin v. Halsey, etc., Co., 324 Ill. App. 525, 58 N.E.2d 737.

[1468] **In general.—**

Minneapolis Trust Co. v. Menage, 73 Minn. 441, 76 N.W. 195.

has been held liable for misrepresentations by its sales man inducing the

---

Acts of officers administering trust.—

A corporate trustee must accept responsibility for acts of its officers done in course of administration of a trust. Kenny v. Citizens Nat. Trust, etc., Bank (Cal. App.), 269 P.2d 641.

An employee in trust department of trust company named as trustee in inter vivos trust agreement, who for some time before and alter execution of amendment to trust agreement had acted as agent of trust company in administration of trust, was acting in a fiduciary capacity toward settlor with reference to trust estate. Gibson v. Security Trust Co., 107 F. Supp. 766, aff'd, 201 F.2d 573. As to officers and agents generally, see §§ 9-12 of this chapter.

Person held agent.—

Where, incident to negotiations to install siding on defendants' house, person who was introduced as banker purported to authorize $350 loan to defendants, who were uneducated and nearly illiterate, and plaintiff trust company sent check to defendants for that amount without question, and signatures of defendants were obtained to note which was later assigned to trust company, person was agent of trust company, and latter was not an innocent purchaser for value. South Orange Trust Co. v. Conner, 228 S.C. 218, 89 S.E.2d 372.

Facts not affecting company's liability.—

That signers of note to trust company, obtained by fraud of its officers and used to take up earlier note given by one of such officers for money borrowed with which to purchase stock, were parties to trust agreement under which proceeds of the stock were to be applied on the note, held not to affect trust company's liability for its agents' fraud. Tremont Trust Co. v. Noyes, 246 Mass. 197, 141 N.E. 93.

Agent's contract binding on company.—

Contract by which defendant was to receive certain commissions on sale of real estate, signed by plaintiff on behalf of a trust company as its general manager, could not be construed as personal contract of plaintiff. Eads v. Murphy, 27 Ariz. 267, 232 P. 877.

Promise of agent to trust company's depositor that he would have her unmatured note payable to trust company paid off if she would refrain from withdrawing her account held binding contract between depositor and trust company. Lonergan v. Highland Trust Co., 287 Mass. 550, 192 N.E. 34.

Breach of trust.—

Where owner delivered stock to president and treasurer of trust company to have stock sold and government bonds purchased with proceeds and transactions were carried on trust company's ledger, trust company, and not president and treasurer individually became trustee, and was liable for breach of trust in purchasing other than government bonds. Allison v. Ohio Sav. & Trust Co., 51 Ohio App. 253, 200 N.E. 529.

Where officer of trust company steals trust fund held for investment and uses it for his own account and profit, charging losses against account and taking profits as his own, the owner may demand from the company an accounting in equity. Frier v. J. W. Sales Corp., 261 App. Div. 388, 25 N.Y.S.2d 576.

purchase of a bond.[1469] But one who deals with an agent of a loan, trust or investment company with knowledge of his agency is bound to ascertain the nature and extent of his authority, and the burden rests upon him to show that the agent had the required authority,[1470] unless the company is held

---

[1469] Hotaling v. A. B. Leach & Co., 126 Misc. 845, 214 N.Y.S. 452, aff'd, 221 App. Div. 756, 222 N.Y.S. 822, 247 N.Y. 84, 159 N.E. 870, 57 A.L.R. 1136.

[1470] **In general.—**

Interstate Securities Co. v. Third Nat. Bank, 231 Pa. 422, 80 A. 888.

Authority to make novation agreement.—

In action on note payable to trust company, payee. who interposed defense of release from liability through novation had burden of proving that chairman of trust company's board of directors had express authority from board or executive committee to make novation agreement, or that chairman had been allowed to exercise independent authority in similar matters on other occasions or that agreement had been brought to attention of board or committee and duly ratified. State v. Frasier, 133 Ohio St. 283, 13 N.E.2d 248.

Authority to accept note of third person in payment.—

In absence of special circumstances or a specific authorization, a person who was director, vice-president, treasurer, clerk of board of directors, and secretary of executive committee of trust company had no actual authority to accept note of third person in payment or extinguishment of a note payable to company. Whether such person had ostensible authority was a question of fact. Federal Nat. Bank v. O'Connell, 305 Mass. 559, 26 N.E.2d 539, holding that evidence showed such authority.

Where maker of note payable to trust company claimed that when he had proposed to sell pledged securities to obtain money to pay off note, third person interested in not having market hurt by selling of bonds had given trust company a note secured by same collateral in substitution of maker's note, maker to avail himself of principle of apparent authority on part of officer of trust company to accept such third person's note, was required to show that maker relied upon the manifestation of authority. Federal Nat. Bank v. O'Connell, 305 Mesa. 559, 26 N.E.2d 539.

Authority to guarantee sale.—

The right of a trust company to guarantee a sale of certain stock and bonds at a specified price within a certain time being questionable, the holder of the stock is put on inquiry as to the authority of an officer of the company to execute a guaranty of that nature on behalf of the company. Gause v. Commonwealth Trust Co., 55 Misc. 110, 106 N.Y.S. 288, aff'd, 124 App. Div. 438, 108 N.Y.S. 1080; 196 N.Y. 134, 89 N.E. 476, 24 L.R.A. (n.s.) 967.

Authority to dispense with approval of sale.—

Where vendees knew that a trust company was dealing with real estate in a representative capacity, provision of contract requiring approval of owner meant approval by trust committee or trust department of trust company. Gorman v. Mercantile-Commerce Bank & Trust Co., Co., 345 Mo. 1059, 137 S.W.2d 571, wherein evidence showed that vendees did not believe that trustee's agents had authority to make binding contract of sale without such approval.

estopped.[1471] And if an agent is without authority[1472] or acts merely in an

---

Fraud and deceit of agent of investment savings association held not to excuse holder of certificate in association from having read application for certificate providing that association should not be bound by representations made by agent in addition to or contrary to provisions thereof, in absence of showing that holder's eyesight was bad, or that she was prevented from reading contract by agent. Miller v. Quaker Sav. Ass'n, 53 Ga. App. 703, 186 S.E. 885 (1936).

Evidence admissible.—

In replevin by a trust company to recover bonds, it was proper to admit in evidence the written instructions to the agent showing that he had no authority for his act, where the fact of agency and defendant's knowledge thereof at the time of the transaction had already been shown. Interstate Sec. Co. v. Third Nat'l Bank, 231 Pa. 422, 80 A. 888.

Evidence inadmissible.—

Nor was there any error in excluding offered evidence that the agent, when acting under written instructions, had sometimes acted beyond their scope and in accord with his own discretion, and that his acts had been ratified by the company, in the absence of any offer to show an exercise of discretion extending to the binding of the company by a promise to pay the debt of a third person and a pledge of the company's securities therefor. Interstate Sec. Co. v. Third Nat'l Bank, 231 Pa. 422, 80 A. 888.

In action against mortgagee trust company to recover for supplies furnished ship, held court did not err in excluding evidence of vote of defendant's executive committee authorizing vice-president to act for defendant with reference to mortgage on ship and institute proceedings with reference to vessel, nor in excluding a report on the standing of mortgage liens; question in is-sue being authority of agent handling vessel to bind defendant. Flitner-Atwood Co. v. Fidelity Trust Co., 249 Mass. 333, 144 N.E. 218.

Evidence showing authority.—

In action by second mortgagee for breach of oral contract of trust company, as first mortgagee in possession, to pay taxes on mortgaged realty, evidence consisting of second mortgagee's undenied allegation that individual who negotiated contract for company was its duly authorized employee and agent, and of such individual's admission that he was in charge of servicing of delinquent mortgage. for company, sufficiently established such individual's authority. Marian v. Peoples-Pittsburgh Trust Co., 149 Pa. Super. 653, 27 A.2d 549.

Evidence not showing authority.—

Evidence did not establish that a trust company authorized an officer to sell or procure a purchaser for property which it had acquired at a sheriff's sale upon execution issued on an unpaid judgment against plaintiff by allegedly orally agreeing to confer upon plaintiff a right of redemption. Alter v. Logan Trust Co., 360 Pa. 491, 62 A.2d 25, 11 A.L.R.2d 1302.

[1471] Schoenberg v. Mutual Profit Realty Co., 94 Misc. 203, 158 N.Y.S. 264.

A mutual profit realty company, whose letter to a bondholder was signed by one as "assistant to the president," and the language of which showed that the writer had access to its files and the previous correspondence, could not urge that the letter was not authorized. Schoenberg v. Mutual Profit Realty Co., 94 Misc. 203, 158 N.Y.S. 264.

individual capacity,[1473] the company is not bound, unless such unauthorized acts are later ratified by the company.[1474] A trust company cannot be charged

---

[1472] **In general.—**

Morrison v. Tremont Trust Co., 252 Mass. 383, 147 N.E. 870.

Guaranty of payment—Authority of collection clerk to bind trust company by guaranty of payment of draft held not established. Morrison v. Tremont Trust Co., 252 Mass. 383, 147 N.E. 870.

Trust company held not liable for fraud or deceit in representing that draft would be paid, in absence of showing that telegram containing such representations was within authority of its agent. Morrison v. Tremont Trust Co., 252 Mass. 383, 147 N.E. 870.

[1473] **In general.—**

First Nat. Bank v. Bangor Trust Co., 297 Pa. 115, 146 A. 595.

Loan by officers as individuals.—

Trust company securing benefits of loan made by officers acting as individuals and officers of construction company was not liable for loan. First Nat'l Bank v. Bangor Trust Co., 297 Pa. 115, 146 A. 595.

Mortgage to pay individual debts.—

Mortgagee could not foreclose mortgage executed by trust company which was given to secure officers' individual debts where mortgagee knew that he was dealing with partnership composed of officers of company and accepted their note as individual obligation and when he received note and mortgage in suit knew that mortgaged property belonged to trust company, that no consideration moved to trust company for note and mortgage, and that they were executed by officers without authority from board of directors. Bordy v. Goodman-Buckley Trust Co., 131 Neb.342, 268 N.W. 286.

Mortgages could not foreclose mortgage executed by trust company to secure debt of partnership composed of officers, on theory that mortgagee's release of claim against partnership furnished adequate consideration for note and mortgage executed by trust company, where execution of note and mortgage was not authorized by board of directors, but was attempt by officer, to pay their individual obligation with assets of company. Bordy v. Goodman-Buckley Trust Co., 131 Neb. 342, 268 N.W. 286.

Handling trust funds.—

Where settlor sought an accounting of trust funds only from a trust company, a valid decree could not be rendered against its president and treasurer, who handled the funds as individuals. Allison v. Ohio Sav., etc., Co., 51 Ohio App. 253, 200 NE. 529.

[1474] **In general.—**

Litwin v. Allen, 25 N.Y.S.2d 667.

Accepting benefit, as ratification.—

A trust company, which held mortgaged realty under first mortgage after mortgagor's default, and which for three years accepted benefits of its employee's contract with second mortgagee requiring second mortgagee to make certain payments to company and requiring company to pay taxes, "ratified" contract and could not repudiate employee's authority to make it. Marian v. Peoples-Pittsburgh Trust Co., 149 Pa. Super. 653, 27 A.2d 549.

with notice of its agent's fraud, where its agent acts adversely to the company's interest.[1475] And it has been held that all of a trust company's compensation will not be disallowed under a building contract, where the wrongdoing in the inducement of the contract was by a single officer.[1476] A statute prohibiting a trust company officer from pledging the company's notes was held not coextensive with a statute prohibiting a bank officer from indorsing notes, and the latter statute was held not to prohibit a sale under an indorsement without recourse.[1477]

All acts by an investment company board not chosen in accordance with the Investment Company Act are not void, and the Securities and Exchange Commission acts properly in scrutinizing transactions of such a board taken during the sixty-day period within which the Act indicates that such board

---

A habitual exercise of power to appoint substitute trustees under deeds of trust by an officer of a loan corporation would justify exercise of such power without a resolution of corporation's board of directors. Brown v. National Loan & Inv. Co., 139 S.W.2d 364 (Tex. Civ. App. 1940).

Where loan corporation held deed of trust giving it power to appoint a substitute trustee in event of named trustee's failure to act, in event of default, authority could have been conferred, by a bylaw, on corporation's vice-president or president to exercise, in name of corporation, the power to appoint a substitute trustee when named trustee refused to exercise power of sale when default occurred. Brown v. National Loan, etc., Co., 139 S.W.2d 364 (Tex. Civ. App.1940).

Contract of employment by trust and savings bank of a bond salesman, though entered into by certain of its officers without authority, was made binding upon it by subsequent acquiescence of its board of directors, the contracting authority under its articles and bylaws, with knowledge of the facts. Bacon v. Bankers' Trust & Sav. Bank, 143 Minn. 318, 173 N.W. 719.

Negotiating bond purchase.—

The ratification of the acts of a trust company's officers in negotiating for the purchase of bonds giving the seller the option to repurchase was held essential in order to bind the company and its subsidiary, and in any case such ratification vitiated the possible later rescission of the transaction on the ground that it was not authorized by the directors. Litwin v. Allen, 25 N.Y.S.2d 667.

Ratification retroactive.—

Where trustee's board of directors by formal resolution ratified action taken by its trust officers in suing to foreclose a mortgage, the ratification related back to commencement of the suit, and it cannot be contended that suit was not authorized. Couch v. Central Bank & Trust Corp., 297 F. 213.

[1475] Appeal of Metropolitan Life Ins. Co., 310 Pa. 17, 164 A. 715.

[1476] Miller v. Central Trust, etc., Co., 285 Pa. 472, 132 A. 579.

[1477] Union Indemnity Co. v. Home Trust Co., 64 F.2d 906.

has power to secure a properly chosen board, and in not voiding transactions found to be reasonable and proper, including the obtaining of an exemption for the sale of stock and taking action pursuant to the exemption.[1478]

§ 20. President.

Those dealing with a trust company through its president are entitled to rely on his ostensible powers.[1479] And a trust company acting as trustee is liable for any fraudulent act of its president done in his official capacity.[1480] But for acts of a trust company president not in his official capacity, the trust company will not be liable,[1481] unless such acts are later ratified by the

---

1478 Nadler v. Securities & Exchange Com., 296 F.2d 63.

1479 **In general.—**

Six Little Tailors v. Old South Trust Co., 260 Mass. 41, 156 N.E. 681.

Indemnity agreement—

President of trust bank had authority to execute indemnity agreement. National Surety Co. v. Anacostia Finance Corp., 26 F.2d 985.

Agreement to renew insurance.—

Agreement of president of loan company, in taking mortgage, that company would renew insurance, held within apparent scope of president's authority. Kentucky Cash Credit Corp. v. Quisenberry, 232 Ky. 510, 23 S.W.2d 952.

Agreement to return deposit.—

Mortgagor could recover $5,000 which he deposited with mortgage company to secure release of mortgage assigned by him as collateral, under agreement with president that sum was returnable when $40,000 mortgage should be reduced to $35,000, when loan was so reduced, since president was authorized to make such agreement, absent evidence that bonds secured had previously been sold by mortgage company. First Trust Co. v. Shurtleff, 130 Neb. 476, 265 N.W. 543.

1480 Washington, etc., R. Co. v. Real Estate Trust Co., 177 F. 306, modified, 191 F. 566, cert denied, 223 U.S. 724, 32 S. Ct. 525, 56 L. Ed. 631.

Defendant trust company could not claim, as against the mortgagor, mortgage bonds which it held as trustee, and which its president, who was also an officer in the mortgagor company, fraudulently pledged to defendant, after the mortgage was satisfied, as collateral for fictitious loans. Reel Estate Trust Co. v. Washington, etc., R. Co., 191 F. 566, cert. denied, 223 U.S. 724, 32 S. Ct. 525, 56 L. Ed. 631.

1481 **In general.—**

Prudential Trust Co. v. Moore, 245 Mass. 311, 139 N.E. 645.

Misrepresentations by president to directors to induce execution of notes to company to replace assets illegally loaned by him, for which directors took personal notes of president, are not statements of officer of bank acting for it within official duties, and he has no authority to agree that company will not enforce such notes. Prudential Trust Co. v. Moore, 245 Mass. 311, 139 N.E. 645.

proper company officials.[1482] If unauthorized acts of a trust company's president are not illegal, they will not be void, but merely voidable at the

---

Recordation of plat.—

The president of a trust company to which land was entrusted to sell, not being so authorized by it, had no power to plat it and record the plat. Weber v. Aluminum Ore Co., 304 Ill. 273, 136 N.E. 685.

Acceptance of land as payment—

Bank president's statement that "they" would accept debtor's proposition to deed land in payment of debts to bank and loan company did not establish his agency for latter. Bruner v. Commerce Loan Co. (Tex. Civ. App.), 21 S.W.2d 26.

[1482] **In general.—**

National Surety Co. v. Anacostia Finance Corp., 26 F.2d 985.

Receiving benefits as ratification.—

Trust company's receipt and use of money solicited by president to enable resumption of business held ratification of his acts. Six Little Tailors v. Old South Trust Co., 260 Mass. 41, 156 N.E. 681.

Execution of indemnity bond.—

Directors of trust bank, having knowledge of payment of premium on surety bond and acquiescing therein, ratified execution thereof by president. National Surety Co. v. Anacostia Finance Corp., 26 F.2d 985.

Trustees of trust bank, on notice that president had executed indemnity bond, had duty of either rescinding action or permitting it to stand. National Surety Co. v. Anacostia Finance Corp., 26 F.2d 985.

Agreement by president of trust company for cancellation of indebtedness in consideration for conveyance of mortgaged property held not binding on company in absence of proof that he was authorized to make agreement, or that it had been ratified by the company. In re Bowen, 46 F. Supp. 631.

Purchase of stock.—

Trust company held to have ratified purchase of stock of another trust company by its president, and subject to statutory liability. Commissioner of Banks v. Tremont Trust Co., 259 Mass. 162, 156 N.E. 7.

Unauthorized contract not ratified.—

Where trust company furnished part of funds for construction of houses, taking first mortgages from borrowers as security, and agreed with third party, who furnished remainder of funds, to apply collections from sales of houses on amount advanced by third party, after trust company was repaid, trust company, by paying third party part of amount realized from sale of each of houses above proportionate share of loan of trust company, did not ratify unauthorized oral contract, if any, made by its president, that third party should loan funds directly to trust company and be repaid by trust company within one year. Blumberg v. Broad St Trust Co., 329 Pa. 471, 198 A. 27.

option of the party dealt with.[1483] The knowledge of a trust company president is ordinarily presumed to be that of the company.[1484] But knowledge of fraud of a trust company's president may or may not be imputed to the company,[1485] and a trust company president's knowledge acquired while he is acting in another capacity will not be imputed to the company.[1486]

§ 21. Vice-President.

The vice-president of a trust company, authorized to act in its president's absence, may accept on the company's behalf an agreement to receive a

---

[1483] Commissioner of Banks v. Tremont Trust Co., 259 Mass. 162, 156 N.E. 7.

[1484] Germania Safety Vault, etc., Co. v. Driskell, 66 S.W. 610, 23 Ky. L. Rptr. 2050.

A trust company, acting as administrator, deposited funds of the estate in an insolvent bank; the president of the trust company being president of the bank. Held, that his knowledge of the bank's condition was the knowledge of the trust company, in a controversy between it and the administer of the estate, though the rule might be otherwise in a controversy between the two corporations. Germania Safety Vault, etc., Co. v. Driskell, 66 S.W. 610, 23 Ky. L. Rptr. 2050 (1902).

[1485] **Knowledge not imputed.—**

Real Estate Trust Co. v. Washington, etc., Ry. Co., 191 F. 566, cert. denied, 223 U.S. 724, 32 S. Ct 525, 56 L. Ed. 631.

Knowledge of fraud of a trust company's president in depositing bonds of another as collateral under fictitious loans for his own benefit is not imputable to the company. Real Estate Trust Co. v. Washington, A. & Mt. V. R. Co., 191 F. 566, cert. denied, 223 U.S. 724, 32 S. Ct. 525, 56 L. Ed. 631.

Knowledge imputed.—

Where president and manager of loan company, who was also the president and manager of a trust company occupying the same offices, caused a mortgage not. to be transferred from the loan company to plaintiff at its face value in exchange for bonds, after part payment of note to loan company, and the loan company thereafter transferred such bonds to the trust company, the trust company was chargeable with notice of the fraud; the president's knowledge that note had been paid being imputed to the trust company. McFerson v. Bristol, 73 Colo. 214, 214 P. 395.

[1486] Tate v. Security Trust Co., 63 N.J. Eq. 559, 52 A. 313.

The president of a trust company, acting as attorney for other parties, negotiated the execution of a mortgage to his clients. The mortgage was subsequently assigned to the trust company, it not appearing who conducted this transaction on its behalf. Held, that the company was not chargeable with any knowledge its president may have had in regard to the purpose for which the mortgage was given. Tate v. Security Trust Co., 63 N.J. Eq. 559, 52 A. 313.

deposit and expend the same in acquiring named stocks.[1487] And a trust company vice-president whose particular duty is to solicit deposits, which, with the knowledge of the other officers, is done largely outside the banking offices, acts within the scope of his employment in procuring a deposit by an agreement that it will be made in the savings department.[1488] Also, a trust company vice-president was held apparently authorized to bind his company by selling notes endorsed in the company's name without recourse.[1489] The vice-president of a trust company acting as trustee for certain heirs is presumed to have authority to sign a petition and make a necessary affidavit in annexation proceedings affecting the township where the trust lands are situated.[1490] But in the absence of a showing of authority, it cannot be presumed as a matter of law that the vice-president of a domestic trust company, which is trustee under a mortgage securing corporate bonds, has authority to represent to a purchaser that the bonds are first-mortgage bonds, so as to make the company liable for such a representation.[1491]

§ 22. Treasurer.

In General.—Where a trust company receives a customer's bonds, sells them and holds the proceeds, it is estopped from setting up a want of authority of its treasurer to bind it by a certificate issued to the customer.[1492] And where a trust company's treasurer fails to turn over a guaranty note to its directors for discounting, but orders its teller to pay checks drawn by the beneficiary thereof, the directors can disaffirm the treasurer's act or, at their option, ratify it and hold the note as security for the amounts checked out.[1493] But where a trust company, in taking a note signed in blank by a first signer and filled in contrary to his instructions, and signed by others without knowledge thereof, was represented by its treasurer and vice-president, who knew of and participated in the fraud, the treasurer's knowledge was held imputable to the company, whether he acted as its officer or in collusion with the vice-president for whose benefit the note was used.[1494] And in such a

---

1487 Madison Trust Co. v. Carnegie Trust Co., 167 App. Div. 4, 152 N.Y.S. 517, aff'd, 215 N.Y. 475, 109 N.E. 580.

1488 Wasserman v. Cosmopolitan Trust Co., 252 Mass. 253, 147 N.E. 742.

1489 Union Indemnity Co. v. Home Trust Co., 64 F.2d 906.

1490 Appeal of Braddock Tp., 148 Pa. Super. 52, 24 A.2d 705.

1491 Davidge v. Guardian Trust Co., 203 N.Y. 331, 96 N.E. 751.

1492 Callendar v. Kelly, 190 Pa. 455, 42 A. 957.

1493 Mutual Bank v. Smith, 99 N.J.L. 13, 123 A. 98.

1494 Tremont Trust Co. v. Noyes, 246 Mass. 197, 141 N.E. 93, holding that the fact that

case, where one in charge of a company's savings department makes entries concerning a note's discount under its treasurer's direction, and its investment committee subsequently approves the note, the committee does not act in an independent executive capacity, so as to prevent an imputation of the treasurer's knowledge to the company,[1495]

Vice-President and Treasurer.—See the footnote.[1496]

Secretary and Treasurer.—Proof that the secretary and treasurer of a trust company is also its manager is sufficient to show that he has powers as great and extensive as a cashier of a bank.[1497] Acts performed by the secretary and treasurer of a loan company as agent for a borrower were held not imputable to the loan company.[1498]

§ 23. Other Officers.

Actuary.—Where an actuary of a trust company is held out to the public as competent to transfer securities belonging to the company in satisfaction of debts, such transfer by him, where there is no fraud or departure from established usage and the transaction is advantageous to the company, is binding upon the company.[1499]

Branch or Divisional Manager.—The powers of a branch manager of a trust company doing banking are not presumed to be limited to those of an

---

the signers of the note were members of its executive committee does not relieve the company of liability for the fraud of its agents.

1495 Tremont Trust Co. v. Noyes, 246 Mass. 197, 141 N.E. 93.

1496 Vice-president and treasurer of trust company had no implied authority to enter into oral agreement with plaintiff debtor whereby plaintiff would have right to redeem property, formerly owned by him and which was purchased by trust company at execution sale, upon assuming liability of first mortgage and paying trust company $30,000, where indebtedness of plaintiff to trust company was $57, 453.40. Alter v. Logan Trust Co., 360 Pa. 491, 62 A.2d 25, 11 A.L.R.2d 1302.

1497 State v. Scarlett, 91 N.J.L. 200, 102 A. 160, 2 A.L.R. 88.

1498 Baxter v. National Mortg. Loan Co., 128 Neb. 537, 259 N.W. 630.

1499 Creswell v. Lanahan, 101 U.S. 347, 25 L. Ed. 853 (1879).

The Freedman's Savings & Trust Company, through its agent, with the knowledge and consent of its trustees, borrowed money of A., and gave him therefor a note signed by its actuary, who afterwards transferred to A., in satisfaction thereof, certain securities belonging to the company. The actuary was held out to the public as competent to make such an exchange. There was no fraud or departure from established usage, and the transaction was advantageous to the institution. Held, that the commissioners appointed to wind up the affairs of the company were not entitled to a decree that A. surrender to them the securities. Creswell v. Lanahan, 101 U.S. 347, 25 L. Ed. 853 (1879).

ordinary cashier.[1500] But an investment company was held not liable for fraud in the sale of its capital stock by its divisional manager and agent whose agency only related to the sale of installment certificates.[1501]

Cashier or Bookkeeper.—Where a cashier and bookkeeper of a trust company assist in the hypothecation of certain shares of its stock to a bank as security for a loan made by the bank, and have full knowledge that such stock has been so pledged, such knowledge is the knowledge of the company, and the company cannot thereafter refuse to transfer the stock to the bank for nonpayment of the loan on the ground that it has a lien on the stock for an indebtedness to it created subsequent to the pledge.[1502] And where a bank and trust company, through its cashier, purchased corporate stock for a customer, taking his note for double the amount paid for the stock with the balance to be placed to his credit, the cashier fraudulently represented to the customer that the stock cost twice as much as it actually did, and the bank retained the benefit of the fraud, it was held liable therefor.[1503]

Chairman of Committees.—That a chairman of the executive and investment committees of a trust company had habitually exercised large powers without special delegation of authority for a number of years, constituted a holding out by the company that he was possessed of such authority, so that his ostensible powers became his real powers, and his exercise of such powers was held binding upon the company.[1504]

Director.—A director who is a member of the executive committee of a trust company, and as such practically dominates its policy, has sufficient

---

[1500] Union Sav., etc., Co. v. Krumm, 88 Wash. 20, 152 P. 681.

The question of apparent authority of the manager to take over a debtor's lumber business, and contract with one to haul logs was held for the jury. Union Sav., etc., Co. v. Krumm, 88 Wash. 20, 152 P. 681.

[1501] Culbreath v. Investors Syndicate, 203 S.C. 213, 26 S.E.2d 809, 147 A.L.R. 1144, so holding where stock sold was registered in divisional manager's name, company apparently had no interest therein or in proceeds of sale, and sale was against interest of company as preventing buyer's increased investment in installment certificates.

[1502] Birmingham Trust, etc., Co. v. Louisiana Nat. Bank, 99 Ala. 379, 13 So. 112, 20 L.R.A. 600.

And this is so, although such indebtedness was created after the cashier's death by officers having no knowledge of the loan by the bank. Birmingham Trust, etc., Co. v. Louisiana Nat. Bank, 99 Ala. 379, 13 So. 112, 20 L.R.A. 600.

[1503] Commercial Bank, etc., Co. v. Beach, 66 Colo. 226, 180 P. 982.

[1504] Lonergan v. Highland Trust Co., 287 Mass. 550, 192 N.E. 34.

authority to accept on its behalf an arrangement to act as trustee of a deposit to be used for acquiring stocks of other companies.[1505] But a director of a trust company who is the manager of its bond department has no authority by virtue of either position to bind the company by a promise to pay the debt of a third party to a bank, or to pledge the trust company's bonds to secure such payment.[1506]

Secretary.—A trust company secretary, having express authority to buy and sell securities, has no implied power in selling such securities to bind the company by a contract to repurchase on demand at "face value and accrued interest."[1507] Alleged false statements of a trust company secretary made in his individual capacity are inadmissible in an action against the company.[1508] And the fact that an investor, after having become acquainted with the secretary of an investment company through her dealings with the company, consults him with reference to certain independent legal matters, does not affect the liability of the company to her for funds invested by her through the secretary, and embezzled by him.[1509]

Teller.—Where a paying teller of a trust company exercising the functions of a banking company certifies a depositor's check, evidence that the teller was in the habit of making such certifications for the benefit of the payees of checks, and that all checks so certified were paid and taken up by the trust company, is sufficient to establish the agency of the teller in certifying such checks.[1510] Where a trust company which is a trustee under a mortgage securing bonds conducts the usual business of such an institution by separate departments of banking trusts, mortgages, and the like, knowledge of a teller in the banking department as to the mortgagor's default in the payment of interest coupons on bonds secured is imputable to the trust company as trustee.[1511]

1505 Madison Trust Co. v. Carnegie Trust Co., 167 App. Div. 4, 152 N.Y.S. 517, aff'd, 215 N.Y. 475, 109 N.E. 580.

1506 Interstate Securities Co. v. Third Nat. Bank, 231 Pa. 422, 80 A. 888.

1507 Eberlein v. Stockyards Mortg. & Trust Co., 164 Minn. 323, 204 N.W. 961.

1508 Pfeil v. Citizens Loan & Trust Co., Co., 89 Ind. App. 625, 167 N.E. 623.

1509 Ring v. Howell, 184 N.Y. 553, 76 N.E. 1107 Neb. 369, 246 N.W. 707.

Facts held insufficient to show that an investor dealt with the secretary of an investment company as an individual, and not in his official capacity as the company's representative. Ring v. Howell, 184 N.Y. 553, 76 N.E. 1107.

1510 Muth v. St. Louis Trust Co., 88 Mo. App. 596.

1511 Brown v. Fidelity Trust Co., 250 F. 321, cert. denied, 248 U.S. 564, 39 S. Ct. 9, 63 L. Ed. 423.

§ 24. Notice to or Knowledge of Officer or Agent.

In General.—Information acquired by a trust company's officer while acting for the company is imputable to it, regardless of where the information is received.[1512] Thus, notice to a trust company treasurer of a customer's claim to money in possession of the company is notice to the company.[1513] And a trust company actuary who is secretary of its board of directors and acts for its president, having special charge of its deposit and trust departments and its books, is an officer whose knowledge as to the insolvency of a depositor is imputable to the company.[1514] Where a contract for collection of premiums for an insurance company was executed by a bank's president, knowledge that the premiums collected, less commissions, were to be held as a trust until payment, was held imputed to the bank.[1515]

Knowledge Acquired Unofficially or Individually.—The knowledge of an officer of a trust company as to an assignment of a deposit would not be imputed to the company, where his connection with it did not relate to receiving deposits or crediting same,[1516] or where he acted as an individual for his own interest.[1517] Knowledge of a director of a bank, if any, concerning the advisability of an exchange of trust stock could not be imputed to the bank as trustee, in an action by the former beneficiaries against the former trustee for a breach of trust, where such director was not a trust officer of the bank and did not act in an advisory capacity or otherwise in the management of the trust department.[1518] And where a trust company's director, who is also president of another corporation, negotiates a loan with the company on behalf of a stockholder in the other corporation, the company is not chargeable with the director's knowledge as to an agreement pursuant to which the loan was procured.[1519] Similarly, when officers of an indorsee trust company who discount a note know of a dispute as to the amount of the note, the indorsee is charged with notice of the defense, but the mere fact that the directors of the payee are also directors of the trust

---

[1512] Federal Trust Co. v. Ireland, 124 Neb. 369, 246 N.W. 707. See also § 20 of this chapter.

[1513] Whitecotton v. Wilson, (Mo. App.) 197 S.W. 168.

[1514] Walsh v. Lowell Trust Co., 245 Mass. 445, 139 N.E. 789.

[1515] Maryland Casualty Co. v. Rottger, 99 Ind. 485, 194 N.E. 365.

[1516] Strudee v. Cuba Eastern R. Co., 196 F. 211.

[1517] First Nat. Bank v. Bangor Trust Co., 297 Pa. 115, 146 A. 595.

[1518] Clark v. American Nat'l Bank & Trust Co., 531 S.W.2d 563 (Tenn. Ct. App. 1974).

[1519] Haskell v. Columbus Sav. & T. Co., Co., 207 F. 322.

company does not show notice to the trust company.[1520] Where one of the larger stockholders of a debtor was a director of an indenture trustee, but that was the only official connection between them, it was held no presumption existed that he notified the indenture trustee of a payment of dividends by the debtor.[1521] For cases holding a trust company officer's knowledge or notice acquired while acting unofficially or individually imputable to his company, see the footnote.[1522]

Knowledge of Fraud.—If the agent of a trust company, in the course of the business in which he is employed, commits an independent fraud for his own benefit designedly against his principal, and it is essential to the carrying out of the fraud that he conceal the real facts from his principal, the presumption of constructive notice to the principal is destroyed, and the inference is instead that no communication was made.[1523]

Thus, a trust officer's knowledge of fraud inducing the execution of notes discounted through such officer's assistance by his trust company is not

---

1520 Title Guarantee, etc., Co. v. Pam, 232 N.Y. 441, 134 N.E. 525.

1521 In re Pittsburgh Terminal Warehouse, etc., Co., 69 F. Supp. 289.

1522 **Notice of trust.—**

Trust company, which held one of participating certificates issued by title company and was given new certificate when original mortgage was foreclosed and purchase-money mortgage taken on resale of premises, was chargeable with notice of trust, and could not benefit thereby at expense of another original certificate holder, where title company's president was director of trust company and its secretary had been director in trust company. In re Title & Mortg. Guar. Co., 246 App. Div. 146, 284 N.Y.S. 947, appeal dismissed, 270 N.Y. 645, 1 N.E.2d 872.

Knowledge of securities.—

In determining whether bank which was trustee under collateral trust indenture covering issue of holding company's debentures was grossly negligent, within meaning of indenture, in permitting substitution of particular securities as collateral, knowledge acquired by a vice-president of bank as director and representative of bank on governing boards of several corporations whose securities were accepted was to be attributed to bank, notwithstanding bank was large institution having some 40 or 50 vice-presidents, and that particular vice-president was not connected with trust department. Hazzard v. Chase Nat. Bank, 159 Misc. 57, 287 N.Y.S. 541, aff'd, 282 N.Y. 652, 26 N.E.2d 801.

1523 Camden Safe Deposit, etc., Co. v. Lord, 67 N.J. Eq. 489, 58 A. 607.

Where the president and cashier of a trust company embarked in a partnership undertaking with an executor, who executed a mortgage to the trust company on the property of the estate, the proceeds being used in the partnership venture, and not for the benefit of the estate, the knowledge of the president and cashier of the trust company of the fraudulent misapplication of the sum realized by the mortgage was not imputable to the trust company, and the mortgage was enforceable in its hand. Camden Safe Deposit, etc., Co. v. Lord, 67 N.J. Eq. 489, 58 A. 607.

imputable to the company so as to render its title defective.[1524] But where an officer of a trust company has no purpose to defraud the company, notice to him concerning the character of an accommodation note is notice to the company.[1525] And where a trust company officer alone acts in bad faith in discounting a note and misappropriating the proceeds, the company is bound by his knowledge of the fraud through which he obtained the note, notwithstanding a subsequent ratification by other officers ignorant of the nature of the transaction.[1526] For other cases relating to a trust company officer's knowledge of fraud as being imputed to his company, see the footnote.[1527]

Imputation of Knowledge to Third Party.—An officer of a trust company acted for it and not for the purchaser in the sale of a negotiable note payable to its order, and hence the purchaser was held not chargeable with the officer's knowledge that the company had agreed to hold the note only as

---

[1524] Egan v. Hemingway, 10 N.J. Misc. 466, 159 A. 703.

[1525] Jacobus v. Jamestown Mantel Co., 149 App. Div. 356, 134 N.Y.S. 418, aff'd, 211 N.Y. 154, 105 N.E. 210.

[1526] Tremont Trust Co. v. Noyes, 246 Mass. 197, 141 N.E. 93.

[1527] Knowledge of officer of escrow company as to fraud in escrow transactions held chargeable to trust company to which notes deposited in escrow were indorsed, of which escrow company officer was assistant trust officer. Honan v. National Thrift Corp., 14 Cal. App. 2d 458, 57 P.2d 967.

Trust company was liable to beneficiary of trust for loss caused by breach of trust by trustees who were officers of the trust company, and who purchased for trust estate securities from the trust company, since the company through knowledge of its officers who were the trustees participated in the breach of trust. Kinney v. Lindgren, 378 Ill. 415, 26 N.E.2d 471.

Mortgage banking firm's loan officer acted adversely to firm's interest in misrepresenting financial strength of loan applicants, and thus, his knowledge of misrepresentations could not be imputed to firm, and third party which joined officer as agent in defrauding firm could not avoid liability to firm. Anchor Equities, Ltd. v. Joya, 773 P.2d 1022 (Ariz. App. 1989).

Knowledge of results of investigation by mortgage banking firm's loan officer, as agent, into facts upon which false loan applications were based was not imputable to firm where investigation was performed by officer who submitted the applications and who was thus acting adversely to firm's interests. Anchor Equities, Ltd. v. Joya, 773 P.2d 1022 (Ariz. App. 1989).

Third party, who joined mortgage banking firm's loan officer in defrauding firm, could not avoid liability to firm on ground that he relied upon officer's apparent authority to perpetrate fraud; third party did not identify any conduct on firm's part that led him to believe that firm had given officer apparent authority to accept or submit fraudulent loan applications, and third party could not demonstrate that he reasonably relied upon officer's apparent authority when he submitted documents containing representations that third party knew were false. Anchor Equities v. Joya, 773 P.2d 1022 (Ariz. App. 1989).

collateral security for a pre-existing indebtedness, and was selling it in violation of an agreement with its makers.[1528]

§ 25. Dealings Through Mutual Agent.

An agent of an investment company which is itself an agent engaged in promoting sales of stock of a trust company is an agent of the trust company as well as the investment company.[1529] Under the rule that, where one of two innocent persons must suffer through the fraud of another, the loss must fall on him whose act or omission enabled the wrongdoer to commit the fraud, a railroad company cannot recover its mortgage bonds from a trust company, where the trustee of the bonds, who was both an officer of the railroad company and president of the trust company, fraudulently used the bonds for his own benefit as collateral for fictitious loans from the trust company, after other officers of the railroad company had negligently failed to see that the bonds, having been paid, were destroyed. In this transaction, the trustee-president acted for himself, and not as agent for the trust company, and the fault of the railroad company made the fraud on the trust company possible.[1530] But the trust company cannot claim, as against the railroad company, bonds which the trust company itself held as trustee, and which its president also fraudulently pledged; for the trust company, as trustee, was bound to keep the bonds safely for the railroad company, and it cannot change its relation as trustee custodian by any act of its own servant. In the custody of these bonds, and all his acts in relation thereto, the president acted as the agent of the trust company, and not as agent of the railroad.[1531]

Where a trust company's director, who is also president of another corporation, negotiates a loan with the company on behalf of a stockholder in the other corporation, the company is not chargeable with the director's knowledge as to an agreement pursuant to which the loan was procured.[1532] Similarly, a trust company, whose vice-president is also president of a railroad company and who procures the negotiation of an accommodation note borrowed to secure funds either for the railroad or for himself, is not

---

[1528] Le Brun v. Prosise, 197 Md. 466, 79 A.2d 543 (1951).

[1529] Crawford v. Davis (Tex. Civ. App.), 188 S.W. 436; Sweeney v. Davis (Tex. Civ. App.), 188 S.W. 438.

[1530] Real Estate Trust Co. v. Washington, etc., R. Co., 191 F. 566, cert. denied, 223 U.S. 724, 32 S. Ct. 525, 56 L. Ed. 631.

[1531] Real Estate Trust Co. v. Washington, etc., R. Co., 191 F. 566, cert. denied, 223 U.S. 724, 32 S. Ct. 525, 56 L. Ed. 631.

[1532] Haskill v. Columbus Bay, etc., Co., 207 F. 322.

chargeable with his knowledge thereof.[1533] And where officers of an indorsee trust company who discount a note know of a dispute as to the amount of the note, the mere fact that the directors of the payee are also directors of the trust company does not show notice to the trust company.[1534] An officer of a trust company who negotiated the sale of a negotiable note payable to the order of his company had an interest adverse to the purchaser's interest, and hence the purchaser was held not chargeable with knowledge acquired by the officer and not communicated to him, even if the officer acted as his agent in the transaction.[1535]

In view of debtor's submissions which alleged in essence that a financing company's refusal to timely consent to liquidation of certain collateral was effectively a refusal by a related trust company, and in view of various agreements indicating that the financing company might have been authorized to act as the trust company's agent in disposing of the collateral, debtor had sufficiently stated a claim against the trust company on the basis of the trust company's possible vicarious liability for the financing company's refusal to timely consent to liquidation.[1536]

c. Deposits.

§ 26. General Considerations.

Definitions.—The common understanding of "bank" under the Internal Revenue Code includes the following bare requisites: (1) The receipt of deposits from the general public, repayable to the depositors on demand or at a fixed time; (2) the use of deposit funds for secured loans and (3) the relationship of debtor and creditor between the bank and the depositor.[1537] For this purpose, it is erroneous to interpret "deposit" to include a

---

[1533] Jacobus v. Jamestown Mantel Co., 211 N.Y. 154, 105 N.E. 210.

Where the president of a trust company, who was also an officer and trustee for a railroad company, fraudulently used for his own benefit bonds which he held as trustee for the railroad company as collateral for fictitious loans from the trust company, knowledge of the fraud on the part of the president was not, under the circumstances, to be imputed to the trust company. Real Estate Trust Co. v. Washington, A. & Mt. V. R. Co., 191 F. 566, cert. denied, 223 U.S. 724, 32 S. Ct. 525, 56 L. Ed. 631.

[1534] Title Guarantee, etc., Co. v. Pam, 232 N.Y. 441, 134 N.E. 525.

[1535] LeBrun v. Prosise, 197 Md. 466, 79 A.2d 543 (1951).

[1536] Davidson Extrusion Corp. v. Manufacturers Hanover Trust Co., 533 N.Y.S.2d 733 (N.Y.A.D. 2 Dep't 1988).

[1537] Moneygram Int'l v. Comm'r, 664 Fed. Appx. 386 (5th Cir. 2016). See 26 U.S.C.S. § 581.

requirement that a bank hold its customers' funds for extended periods of time.[1538] The requirement in the federal tax statute that deposits be made from the general public is meant merely to differentiate between deposits received from sources in some way connected with the bank and those received from ordinary and unrelated customers of banking services.[1539]

Savings-and-loan institutions, also called "thrifts," collect customer deposits, which are maintained in interest-bearing savings accounts, and they originate and service mortgage loans funded by those deposits. Historically, thrifts were profitable because the interest they collected on outstanding loans exceeded the interest they paid out to customers.[1540]

Contractual Relation.—Trust companies may be authorized by statute to receive deposits.[1541] But the contract of a depositor and a trust company doing a banking business fixes the nature of the deposit; the contract need not be in any particular form and is governed by the mutual intention and understanding of the parties.[1542] By mutual consent, a trust company and a

---

[1538] Moneygram Int'l v. Comm'r, 664 Fed. Appx. 386 (5th Cir. 2016).

[1539] Moneygram Int'l v. Comm'r, 664 Fed. Appx. 386 (5th Cir. 2016).

[1540] WMI Holdings Corp. v. United States, 891 F.3d 1016 (2018).

[1541] **In general.**—

Denny v. Jefferson County, 272 Mo. 436, 199 S.W. 250.

Although trust company which was incorporated prior to enactment of banking code retained all powers which its charter provided, trust company was regulated under code provision which did not allow trust companies to accept general deposits. Albright Title & Trust Co. v. Banking Bd., 737 P.2d 925 (Okla. 1987).

Trust company incorporated by special law held to have right to receive deposits. Venner v. Farmers' Loan & Trust Co., 176 N.Y. 549, 68 N.E. 1125.

Savings investment department.—Trust company held authorized to establish a "savings investment department." Sindlinger v. Department of Financial Institutions, 210 Ind. 83, 199 N.E. 715, 105 A.L.R. 501.

Payment of interest.—

Trust companies may validly receive moneys on deposit as in case of ordinary banks where they pay even smallest rate of interest. Denny v. Jefferson County, 272 Mo. 436, 199 S.W. 250.

[1542] **In general.**—

Cooper v. Fidelity Trust Co., 134 Me. 40, 180 A. 794.

Statute directing trust companies to protect their savings deposits by segregating and holding assets of equal value as security for their payment was not statutory declaration or determination of what constituted savings deposits, and did not abrogate common-law rule that charter of deposit was determined by reference to agreement of trust company and depositor. Cooper v. Fidelity Trust Co., 134 Me. 40, 180 A. 794.

depositor can modify their contract of deposit, but the trust company cannot enlarge or abrogate the contract without the depositor's consent.[1543] But under a contract by a trust company to accumulate a stated sum and pay it to a depositor or his assigns on demand, the company had the right to end the relationship by payment of the amount deposited, with interest at the agreed rate up to the date of severance of the relationship.[1544] Such a contract is a negotiable instrument, although the words "payable to order or bearer" are omitted, and the surrender of the instrument by a depositor to a trust company operates as a discharge.[1545] And the fact that depositors make contracts which a company can only make in its capacity as a general banking institution, supposing that they are making deposits in its savings department, does not entitle the depositors to have them classified as such.[1546] The fact that the decedent "experimented" with "illegal" drugs did not raise the issue of his competency to execute a beneficiary designation form designating the beneficiaries of the investment account.[1547] The bald assertion that the decedent underwent psychiatric or psychological counseling, standing alone, did not raise the issue of his incapacity to execute the

---

Rules as set forth in passbook of trust company constituted the contract between company and depositors in savings investment department, but advertising matter distributed to customers as inducement to make deposits was to be considered along therewith to determine meaning and purpose of contract. Sindlinger v. Department of Financial Institutions, 210 Ind. 83, 199 N.E. 715, 105 A.L.R. 501.

[1543] Cooper v. Fidelity Trust Co., 134 Me. 40, 180 A. 794.

[1544] **In general.—**

Gerard v. Bank of New York & Trust Co., 265 N.Y. 336, 193 N.E. 165.

Letter not terminating agreement—

Statement in letter from trust company that company would pay amount of deposit or continue deposit pending adjudication of legal rights held not to terminate deposit agreement, as regards liability of trust company for interest accruing after statement was made. Gerard v. Bank of New York & Trust Co., 265 N.Y. 336, 193 N.E. 165.

[1545] Gerard v. Bank of New York & Trust Co., 265 N.Y. 336, 193 N.E. 165.

[1546] **In general.—**

Goldband v. Allen, 245 Mass. 143, 139 N.E. 834.

Contra in case of fraud.—

Depositors held entitled to have deposits classified in savings department, in view of false representations of bank's officers. Barkas v. Commissioner of Banks, 254 Mass. 451, 150 N.E. 178.

[1547] Poluliah v. Fidelity High Income Fund, 476 N.Y.S.2d 859 (N.Y.A.D. 1 Dep't 1934).

beneficiary designation form designating the beneficiaries of the investment account.[1548]

Nature of Deposit.—In some aspects, a trust company is a trustee of the depositors of its savings department,[1549] but in other aspects, the relation is

---

[1548] Poluliah v. Fidelity High Income Fund, 476 N.Y.S.2d 859 (N.Y.A.D. 1 Dep't 1984).

[1549] **In general.—**

Sindlinger v. Department of Financial Institutions, 210 Ind. 83, 199 N.E. 715, 105 A.L.R. 501.

Rule governing deposits in savings investment department of trust company, that investments securing deposits therein would be treated as special fund which, though owned by company, was set aside to determine order of payment of such savings investments, held not inconsistent with trustee and cestui que trust relationship between company and depositors, when construed with other provisions of contract between company and depositors. Sindlinger v. Department of Financial Institutions, 210 Ind. 83, 199 N.E. 715, 105 A.L.R. 501.

Fact that bank acted as trustee of money and property placed with it by trustor and that bank deposited moneys for safekeeping did not change trustor-trustee beneficiary relationship to creditor-debtor relationship. Leggroan v. Zion's Sav. Bank, etc., Co., 120 Utah 93, 232 P.2d 746.

That interest was to be paid depositors in savings investment department held not to change relationship between depositors and bank from that of cestui que trust and trustee to that of debtor and creditor, although it was factor to be considered in determining nature of relationship. Sindlinger v. Department of Financial Institutions, 210 Ind. 83, 199 N.E. 715, 105 A.L.R. 501.

Where investment certificates sold by bank and trust company provided that interest thereon should be paid only out of proceeds of management of specific investments, bank had no general obligation to pay interest, and holders did not thereby became general depositors or creditors of bank. Hack v. Christina, 213 Ind. 68, 11 N.E.2d 152.

Where investment certificates gave certificate holders no right to be paid out of trust company's general funds, but trust company in fact permitted holders to be paid out of general funds in many instances, any resulting prejudice to unpaid holders or to general depositors would not convert holders, as beneficiaries of trust arrangement, into general depositors, but should be adjusted between trust company and depositors and between trust company as trustee and holders. Hack v. Christina, 213 Ind. 68, 11 N.E.2d 152.

Right to deduct counterclaims.—

Under provision in investment certificate sold by bank and trust company giving company "right to deduct from any credit the amount of such counterclaims as it may have against the original owner," bank had no right to deduct all counterclaims that it could assert against general depositors, but could deduct, as against assignee of original owner, any counterclaim that it could have asserted against original owner. Hack v. Christina, 213 Ind. 68, 11 N.E.2d 152.

Trust company's method of bookkeeping could not reduce relationship between depositors in savings investment department and bank to that of debtor and creditor, if it were otherwise

that of debtor and creditor.[1550] It is also said that the relationship between an

---

established to be that of cestui que trust and trustee. Sindlinger v. Department of Financial Institutions, 210 Ind. 83, 199 N.E. 715, 105 A.L.R. 501.

Rule relating to power to change relation of trustee and cestui to that of debtor and creditor, by deposit, is applicable only to trust funds held for investment or distribution by bank chartered to do trust business, but is inapplicable to funds received by bank as agent in transaction which may be lawfully engaged in by bank which does not have a trust charter. Squire v. American Express Co., 131 Ohio St. 239, 2 N.E.2d 766.

Doctrine that trust and banking departments must be treated as separate and distinct entities cannot be invoked to impose trust on trust, or to convert trustee expressly appointed into constructive trustee. Newark Distributing Terminals Co. v. Hospelhorn, 172 Md. 279, 191 A. 701.

[1550] **In general.—**

Petitions of Allen, 241 Mass. 346, 136 N.E. 269.

Relation of depositor to trust company is ordinarily that of creditor, and amount of deposit constitutes debt of bank. Cooper v. Fidelity Trust Co., 132 Me. 260, 170 A. 726.

An administrator's deposit of funds belonging to an estate in a trust company, pursuant to an order requiring such deposit and prohibiting its withdrawal except on an order of court, is a general deposit only, ore-sting the relation of debtor and creditor. People by Webb v. California Safe Deposit & Trust Co., 168 Cal. 241, 141 P. 1181, 1915A A.L.R. 299.

The statute empowering a trust company to receive deposits in capacity of trustee, or under court order, or from depositaries, establishes the relation of creditor and debtor between depositor and trust company, and necessarily implies the incidental power of returning or paying the depositor in money or other agreed medium. State ex rel. Ervin v. Crookston Trust Co., 203 Minn. 512, 282 N.W. 138.

No duty to keep money separate.—

Trust company held under no duty to keep money on deposit in savings accounts separate from funds of other departments, since relationship of trust company and depositor was that of creditor and debtor, and no trust relationship existed. Statler v. United States Sav., etc., Co., 122 Pa. Super. 189, 186 A. 290, aff'd, 326 Pa. 247, 192 A. 250.

Payment of interest by trust company to its customer upon daily balance of funds he has placed in possession of company is strong indication that title to funds passed to company, and that relation between it and customer was that of debtor and creditor. Crancer v. Reichenbach, 130 Neb. 645, 266 N.W. 57.

Agreement for deposit of money as guaranty for performance of covenant against competition in contract for sale of business, describing and referring to trust company as depositary, and not trustee, and receipt signed by trust company in its general corporate capacity, authorized inference that deposit was made with trust company as a bank and not as a trustee, notwithstanding that transaction was actually handled by trust department since such circumstance was mere administrative detail, over which depositor had no control, and which did not affect relations created by written instrument. Dunlop Sand, etc., Corp. v. Hospelhorn, 172 Md. 279, 191 A. 701.

Phrase "deposited or lodged" in receipt issued by trust company acknowledging deposit

investment company and its depositors is one of trustee and beneficiary.[1551] But an investment company is entitled to keep the deposits of its several

---

of money was equivalent to "deposit," in view of reference to amount so deposited and allowance of interest "on such deposit" therein. Dunlop Sand, etc., Corp. v. Hospelhorn, 172 Md. 279, 191 A. 701.

Illustrative cases.—

Where New York trust company as trustee of a revocable trust which included a bank deposit placed such deposit in company's banking department, resulting relationship was that of debtor in banking department to creditor in the trust department. City Bank Farmers Trust Co. v. Pedrick, 69 F. Supp. 517, rev'd on other grounds, 168 F.2d 618, cert. denied, 335 U.S. 898, 89 S. Ct. 800, 98 L. Ed. 438.

Where bank trustee held undistributed income from a trust because of remittance restrictions and such income was held uninvested with appropriate entry showing deposits of such income, the relationship between the beneficiary and the bank was that of debtor-creditor and the deposit of undistributed income owed to the beneficiary was a bank deposit. City Bank Farmers Trust Co. v. United States, 174 F. Supp. 583.

Where depositor, while trust company was a going concern, deposited a check and the company delivered its official trust receipt, and a series of certified drafts aggregating the amount of the check to be delivered as soon as they were imprinted, the contract was one of general deposit and the relation of debtor and creditor was created, and as a general depositor the depositor was an unsecured general creditor of the trust company on subsequent insolvency. Janner v. Langdeau, 317 S.W.2d 787 (Tex. Civ. App.).

[1551] **In general.—**

Murry v. Hale, 203 F. Supp. 583. See also § 32 of this chapter.

Broad control over collateral.—

That investment company with which depositors deposited money for purchase of securities, which were largely loan collateral and were to pay specified amounts of interest to depositors, was to have broad control over and disposition of the collateral did not militate against existence of trust relationship between company and depositors. Murry v. Hale, 203 F. Supp. 583.

Effect of account authorizations.—

Provision of account authorizations signed by depositors in investment company, that company was not required to pay interest on balance in a depositor's account unless balance exceeded $500, did not negative existence of trust relationship rather than debtor-creditor relationship between company and depositors. Murry v. Hale, 203 F. Supp 583.

Failure to comply with account authorizations.—

Although investment company did not administer its program in a manner contemplated by account authorizations signed by depositors of money with such company, validity of original trusts created when deposits were made was not impeached and trust relationships were not terminated. Murry v. Hale, 203 F. Supp. 583.

Bankrupt investment company and depositors who had deposited money in such company had signed account authorizations permitting company to deal with their accounts in certain ways, and had received "trust receipts" indicating how much was deposited and what interest

depositors in a common trust account rather than establish a separate bank account for every depositor, provided the company keeps records of the amounts deposited by each depositor.[1552] And it has been held that the securities, investments and property of a savings departments of a trust company constitute a trust fund which must be kept strictly for the benefit of the depositors in that department until paid in full.[1553] A ward may assume that her money will be placed by her guardian trust company in its trust department, and therein kept in accordance with applicable statutes.[1554] But where the balance due under a contract is deposited with a trust company to pay over at a certain time, it is the agent of the depositor, and notice to it of an assignment of the fund is sufficient notice to the depositor.[1555] Money deposited as a savings deposit, and so accepted, constitutes such a deposit regardless of the disposition made of it by bank officials.[1556] And though the amount of deposits in savings departments are not limited by statute, such

---

rate would be paid on such amounts were not debtor and creditors, relationship was one of trust. Murry v. Hale, 203 F. Supp. 583.

Evidence established that depositors of money with investment company intended the deposits to be held by the company in trust pending the purchase of securities for the several accounts and that the securities, when acquired, should also be held in trust. Murry v. Hale, 203 F. Supp. 583.

[1552] Murry v. Hale, 203 F. Supp. 583.

[1553] Brogna v. Commissioner of Banks, 248 Mass. 241, 142 N.E. 746; Bancroft Trust Co. v. Federal Nat. Bank, 9 F. Supp. 350.

[1554] Morrison v. Lawrence Trust Co., 283 Mass. 236, 186 N.E. 54.

[1555] **In general.—**

Title Ins. & Trust Co. v. Williamson, Co., 18 Cal. App. 324, 123 P. 245.

Similar rule as to savings department.—

And notice to the savings department of a trust company to charge the amount of a note to an account in the commercial department is notice to the commercial department; the company being a single entity, with two departments, both of the same corporation. Cosmopolitan Trust Co. v. Leonard Watch Co., 249 Mass. 14, 143 N.E. 827.

[1556] Cronan v. Commissioner of Banks, 254 Mass. 444, 150 N.E. 193.

The mere ignorance of a trust company depositor of the contents of a certificate of deposit is insufficient to change its purport, if voluntarily accepted. Wasserman v. Cosmopolitan Trust Co., 252 Mass. 253, 147 N.E. 742.

And a deposit, though represented by a time certificate, is in fact a savings deposit, when procured by an agent of a trust company acting within the scope of his apparent authority, on an agreement that it would be treated as a savings deposit, and on representation that it had been placed in such department. Wasserman v. Cosmopolitan Trust Co., 252 Mass. 253, 147 N.E. 742.

deposits have the incidents of deposits in ordinary savings banks.[1557] But certificates of deposit in a trust company which bear interest and are payable on demand, on notice or at a fixed future time, and which do not define the character of the deposit, are commercial, not savings deposits.[1558] And a savings and loan association, not a commercial bank, trust company or corporation doing a trust business, cannot lawfully receive trust funds for safekeeping.[1559]

Withdrawal.—The requirement of notice of an intent to withdraw does not make a deposit invalid as a savings deposit.[1560] Thus, a deposit entered in a passbook, which provides for withdrawals only on presentation of the passbook is a savings deposit, and the depositor is not responsible for the company's failure to enter the deposit on the books of its savings department.[1561] And where presentation of a bank book evidencing a special interest account in a trust company is essential to the withdrawal of funds from the account, title to the deposit can be passed by delivery of the bank book.[1562] For other cases as to withdrawal of deposits, see the footnote.[1563]

1557 J. S. Lang Engineering Co. v. Commonwealth, 231 Mass. 367, 120 N.E. 843; Goldband v. Allen, 245 Mass. 143, 139 N.E. 834.

1558 Cooper v. Fidelity Trust Co., 134 Me. 40, 180 A. 794.

And holders of certificates could not share in assets segregated as security for savings deposits, notwithstanding listing of deposits as savings deposits by officials of trust company, or bank commissioner's directions based on erroneous interpretation of law that certificates were savings deposits or statute directing trust companies to protect their savings deposits by segregating and holding assets of equal value as security for their payment. Cooper v. Fidelity Trust Co., 134 Me. 40, 180 A. 794.

1559 In re Krueger's Estate, 173 Wash. 114, 21 P.2d 1030.

1560 Cronan v. Commissioner of Banks, 254 Mass. 444, 150 N.E. 193.

1561 Goldband v. Allen, 245 Mass. 143, 139 N.E. 834.

1562 In re Downey's Estate, 68 N.Y.S.2d 407.

1563 Deposit in savings investment association under contract providing for issuance of an investment annuity certificate and maturity thereof in designated number of years, and authorizing withdrawal of monthly payments with provision that initial payment should be payable when contract matured, held not to constitute deposit in ordinary savings bank, subject to withdrawal, and holder of certificate was not entitled to withdraw initial payment prior to maturity on ground of representation of association's agent that association was savings bank, in absence of showing of fraud or fiduciary relationship between parties. Miller v. Quaker Sav. Ass'n, 53 Ga. App. 703, 186 S.E. 885 (1936).

Statement of agent of investment savings association that holder of certificate would be entitled to withdraw money on demand, in contradiction of written provisions of certificate and application which provided that association was not bound by agent's representations not included therein, held not to relieve holder of certificate from binding effect of contract,

Claims to Deposits.—Under a New York statute, a bank or trust company is not required to recognize an adverse claim to a deposit held by it for the account of another, but it may or may not do so as it sees fit.[1564] The title to money or checks deposited with an insolvent mortgage and loan business operated by a partnership, does not because of fraud, pass to the firm, but can be recovered so long as identifiable.[1565]

§ 27. Incidental Powers and Rights.

Powers.—In the absence of statutory provisions, a trust company authorized to receive money on deposit has lawful authority to issue certificates of deposit therefor in the usual form.[1566] And if a trust company has the power to receive moneys on general deposit and pay them out on demand, it has the implied power to adopt such method as it may think best as to how money shall be paid out, whether that be upon check or otherwise, notwithstanding that a check, strictly speaking, must be drawn upon a bank or banker.[1567] It may be provided that a trust company is authorized to accept a deposit with which to acquire the stock of other concerns[1568] and it has been held that trust companies doing a banking business may certify checks.[1569] A state bank with the powers of a trust company can deposit money received as

---

or show fraud by association which would entitle her to recovery of initial payment before maturity of contract as provided therein. Miller v. Quaker Sav. Ass'n, 53 Ga. App. 703, 186 S.E. 885 (1936).

Where donor deposited $75,000 in cash with trust company which accepted "this money" with understanding that withdrawals might be made by donor and that trust might be terminated by either on 10 days' notice, the quoted words referred to the deposit and donor's legates was entitled to require the return of the full balance of the deposit in cash upon the giving of the agreed notice. Dickson v. Commonwealth Trust Co., 361 Pa. 612, 65 A.2d 408.

1564 Hozova v. Guaranty Trust Co., 66 N.Y.S.2d 875.

A bank or trust company may take advantage of its statutory option to refuse to recognize adverse claim to deposit of another than claimant as defense to claimant's actions for assigned portions of deposit, unless statute is fully complied with, but such option does not invalidate complaints and motions to dismiss them must be denied. Hozova v. Guaranty Trust Co., 66 N.Y.S.2d 875.

1565 Zimmerman v. United States, 171 F.2d 790, cert. denied, 337 U.S. 941, 69 S. Ct. 1513, 93 L. Ed. 1746.

1566 Bank of Saginaw v. Title & T. Co., 105 F. 491.

1567 State ex rel. Crow v. Lincoln Trust Co., 144 Mo. 562, 46 S.W. 593.

1568 Madison Trust Co. v. Carnegie Trust Co., 167 App. Div. 4, 152 N.Y.S. 517, aff'd, 215 N.Y. 475, 109 N.E. 580.

1569 State v. Scarlett, 91 NJ.L 200, 102 A. 160, 2 A.L.R. 83.

trustee in its commercial department, in which event it becomes a creditor.[1570] But under a statute empowering trust corporations to receive moneys and allow such interest thereon as may be agreed, such corporations have neither the express nor implied authority to receive money on general deposit, upon which no interest is allowed, to be paid out on demand.[1571]

Rights.—As a general rule, depositors in the savings department of a trust company have the same privileges as depositors in an ordinary savings bank.[1572] Where the ordinary relation of debtor and creditor exists between a trust company and its depositors and borrowers, the right of setoff applies precisely as it does between individuals.[1573] And where a check is deposited in a trust company with authority to collect it, the proceeds of the check when actually collected by the company or its agent, become the property of the company, which then becomes indebted to the depositor for the amount thereof.[1574] But where a check is received by a trust company specifically for collection, and it forwards same to its correspondent for collection, but it is not collected until after the trust company has failed, the correspondent is responsible to the depositor for the proceeds of the check, since in such case, the latter remains the owner thereof.[1575]

§ 28. Particular Statutory Provisions.

Provisions as to Savings Departments.—Statutory requirements that deposits in a trust company shall be special and placed in a separate

---

[1570] McDonald v. Fulton, 125 Ohio St. 507, 182 N.E. 504, 83 A.L.R. 1107.

[1571] State ex rel. Crow v. Lincoln Trust Co., 144 Mo. 562, 46 S.W. 593.

[1572] Dole v. Chattabriga, 82 N.H. 396, 134 A. 347.

[1573] Lawrence v. Lincoln County Trust Co., 123 Me. 273, 122 A. 765.

[1574] King v. Bowling Green Trust Co., 145 App. Div. 398, 129 N.Y.S. 977.

The payee of a check opened an account with C. Trust Company, and deposited currency, and the check endorsed in blank, without instructions as to the check, and received credit therefor. The check with other items was sent for "collection and credit" to B. Trust Company, and the check was collected and credited on the day of its receipt by B. Company. After the close of banking hours on that day, C. Company closed its doors, but B. Company did not learn of that fact until the following morning. There had been extensive dealings between the two companies and C. Company had a checking account with B. Company, and was accustomed to send to it bills for collection and credit. During the day, B. Company credited the check, it paid or certified drafts drawn against the checking account of C. Company, and at the close of business the checking account was overdrawn. Held, that the payee of the check could not recover from B. Company because the relation of C. Company to the payee had changed to that of debtor and creditor. King v. Bowling Green Trust Co., 145 App. Div. 398, 129 N.Y.S. 977.

[1575] King v. Bowling Green Trust Co., 145 App. Div. 398, 129 N.Y.S. 977.

department, that investments shall be made in accordance with the laws governing savings banks, and that deposits and investments shall not be mingled with other property, are mandatory.[1576] Under such a statute, in case of withdrawal or swapping of investments or other transactions, the equivalent must be restored to a trust company's savings department, and depositors in its commercial department are presumed to become customers with knowledge of the preferences established by law for the benefit of savings departments.[1577] And where money and securities of a savings department are transferred to a commercial department in exchange for securities not constituting lawful investments for savings deposits, the conflicting interests of the depositors are not to be worked out on the theory of tracing trust funds; in such a case, losses suffered by reason of the transfers to the commercial department must be made good out of the commercial department.[1578] A statute declaring the powers of trust companies and trust departments of savings banks was held not to authorize the transfer of trust funds held in a fiduciary capacity to the commercial side of an institution to be mingled with its own funds, or to authorize a loan of such trust funds to itself without security.[1579] Under a statute providing that all depositors in the savings department of a trust company shall be treated as a class and stand on the same footing, time deposits are permissible only in a commercial department, since special agreements as to the time of

---

[1576] **In general.—**

Petition of Allen, 240 Mass. 478, 134 N.E. 253. As to certificates of deposit under Investment Company Act, see § 2 of this chapter.

Statute was intended to be followed literally, and not to be extended by interpretation according to its presumed purpose, in view of fact that statute covered subject in minute detail. Medford Trust Co. v. McKnight, 292 Mass. 1, 197 N.E. 649.

And it cannot be enlarged by act or agreement of trust company officials, or by fiat of state banking department. Cooper v. Fidelity Trust Co., 134 Me. 40, 180 A. 794.

Statute held to have effected repeal, as respects savings deposits, of statute limiting liability of any one person to trust company. Medford Trust Co. v. McKnight, 292 Mass. 1, 197 N.E. 649.

The statute effected substitution of provisions governing investment of deposits in savings bank for provisions previously applicable to investment of savings deposits in a trust company and not merely to have added farther limitations thereto. Medford Trust Co. v. McKnight, 292 Mass. 1, 197 N.E. 649.

[1577] Petition of Allen, 240 Mass. 478, 134 N.E. 253.

[1578] Petition of Allen, 240 Mass. 478, 134 N.E. 253.

[1579] First Nat. Bank v. Commercial Bank, etc., Co., 163 Va. 162, 175 S.E. 775.

withdrawal and interest are not allowed in a savings department.[1580] And, under such a statute, the savings department of a trust company is prohibited from segregating deposits in excess of a certain amount while not segregating those of that sum and under.[1581] A statute permitting funds held in the trust department of a trust company awaiting investment or distribution to be deposited in its commercial department under certain conditions, does not manifest the intent that only funds held by a trust company as sole fiduciary can be so deposited.[1582]

Provisions as to Claims.—A statute requiring notice to a bank or trust company of adverse claims protects it, as stakeholder, against the hazard of

---

[1580] Goldband v. Allen, 245 Mass. 143, 139 N.E. 834.

[1581] Old Colony Trust Co. v. Corn, 220 Mass. 409, 107 N.E. 950.

[1582] New England Trust Co. v. Triggs, 334 Mass. 324, 135 N.E.2d 541, holding that the Massachusetts statute plainly was designed to qualify the rule declared in Morrison v. Lawrence Trust Co., 283 Mass. 236, 186 N.E. 54.

In proceeding to surcharge the account of trustees for premature sale of securities allegedly to benefit the trustee bank by deposit of proceeds in its commercial department pending distribution, there was no impropriety in depositing the funds with other trust funds awaiting investment or distribution in a single fiduciary account, where the separate interests of the several fiduciary accounts were noted at all times both in the deposit and in the securities which folly secured all of the funds. New England Trust Co. v. Triggs, 334 Mass. 324, 135 N.E.2d 541.

Funds which were held by a national bank in its fiduciary capacity as an executor of an estate pending the outcome of litigation to determine whether the bank would place the funds in a charitable trust or distribute them to the beneficiary were funds "awaiting investment" within the meaning of the Texas Banking Code provision which allows a state bank to use funds received in trust awaiting investment, provided that the bank sets aside in its trust department approved securities equal in face value to the amount of the fund, and within the meaning of a parallel United States Code provision, and the bank was authorized to invest funds in its own certificates of deposit pending final determination of their proper dispersal. Humane Soc'y v. Austin Nat'l Bank, 531 S.W.2d 574 (Tex. 1975), cert. denied, 425 U.S 976, 96 S. Ct. 2177, 48 L. Ed. 2d 800 (1976).

The phrase "awaiting investment" in the article of the Texas Banking Code which provides that funds received in trust by a state bank awaiting investment shall be carried in a separate account and shall not be used by the bank in conducting its business, unless the bank shall first set aside in the trust department United States bonds or other eligible security of a market value equivalent to the amount so used, means "awaiting investment or distribution, thus including funds received by the bank as executor." Humane Soc'y v. Austin Nat'l Bank, 531 S.W.2d 574 (Tex. 1975), cert. denied, 425 U.S. 976, 96 S. Ct. 2177, 48 L. Ed. 2d 800 (1976).

double liability.[1583] And a statute requiring a person claiming a deposit standing on the books of a trust company in the name of another, to either procure a restraining order or indemnify the trust company, is an indication of the state's solicitude for the solvency of banking institutions.[1584] Similarly, a statute providing for payment to a beneficiary on the death of a depositor making a deposit in trust therefor is intended only to protect trust companies.[1585] And the Ohio statute providing that when a deposit is made in any bank or trust company in the name of two or more persons, payable to either or the survivor, such deposit or any part thereof and any interest or dividend thereon, may be paid to either of such persons, whether the other is living or not, and the receipt or acquittance of the person paid is a sufficient release and discharge of the bank for any payment so made, was enacted for the protection of banks, and the right of any named in the account to the account, unless the contract and surrounding circumstances can be interpreted otherwise, must be established by evidence beyond or outside the terms of the contract.[1586]

Miscellaneous Provisions.—The fact that a statute forbids a trust company from maintaining a branch office and receiving deposits except at its own bank, does not make void the receipt of a deposit at a customer's office.[1587] An emergency banking act suspending withdrawal of deposits from, or assertion of claims against banks, was held applicable to funds paid a trust company as trustee for the purpose of paying mortgage interest coupons, where the funds were mingled with its general assets.[1588]

§ 29. Interest.

Under a statute which requires trust companies to allow interest upon general deposits, a trust company cannot contract to receive current deposits subject to check without allowing interest thereon.[1589] And trust companies must pay interest on a deposit to the credit of another in order to acquire the right to receive the same and pay it out on checks and drafts of the

---

1583 Bourgeois v. Chase Manhattan Bank, 139 F. Supp. 265 (New York statute). See also § 26 of this chapter.

1584 Lucas v. Central Missouri Trust Co., 349 Mo. 537, 162 S.W.2d 569.

1585 In re Gates, 107 N.J. Eq. 310, 152 A. 374 (1930).

1586 Jones v. Neu, 106 Ohio App. 161, 150 N.E.2d 858.

1587 State ex rel. American Surety Co. v. Haid, 325 Mo. 949, 30 S.W.2d 100.

1588 Ghingher v. Thomsen, 165 Md. 318, 168 A. 123.

1589 People v. California Safe Deposit, etc., Co., 22 Cal. App. 69, 133 P. 324. See also § 26 of this chapter.

depositor.[1590] A trust fund deposited in the savings department of a trust company for the purpose of drawing interest, and so received by the trust company, is entitled to the payment of interest.[1591] And a trust company which is a surety on the bond of a receiver cannot escape liability for payment of interest upon an open account kept by the receiver, merely because without the receiver's knowledge, it keeps the account in a ledger in which are kept indemnity deposits.[1592]

§ 30. Payment.

In General.—The certification of a check by a trust company has been held equivalent to payment; therefore, if a director of a trust company charged with overdrawing his account parts with a check which is certified, the situation as to him is as if the drawee had paid it.[1593] A certificate of deposit payable to one as special guardian of another is payable to the former personally, such words being merely descriptive.[1594] A trust company will be protected in paying a certificate of deposit though it has been assigned, if the company has no knowledge thereof, by a statute authorizing the transferee of a claim on demand to sue thereon subject to any defense existing against the transferor before notice of transfer, as payment is a complete defense.[1595] Where the treasurer of a trust company pays a check from the paying teller's drawer and instead of stamping it "paid" places it in a safe deposit box, such an act nevertheless constitutes payment.[1596] A trust company is required to pay out of an insolvent corporation's deposit, either to the corporation or its order, checks signed by the corporation's officers.[1597] But it is the duty of a trust company to know the state of a depositor's account, when paying checks shortly before its bankruptcy.[1598] And a trust company may be charged with notice by the form of a check against an estate's deposit account signed by two executors, that the executor presenting the check is not the sole executor, but the fact that the executors are also

---

[1590] Muth v. St. Louis Trust Co., 88 Mo. App. 596.

[1591] People by Webb v. California Safe Deposit & Trust Co., 22 Cal. App. 69, 133 P. 324.

[1592] People v. California Safe Deposit, etc., Co., 22 Cal. App. 69, 133 P. 324.

[1593] State v. Scarlett, 91 N.J.L. 200, 102 A. 160, 2 A.L.R. 83.

[1594] Walker v. State Trust Co., 40 App. Div. 55, 57 N.Y.S. 525.

[1595] Zander v. New York Sec. & Trust Co., 81 App. Div. 635, 81 N.Y.S. 1151, aff'd, 178 N.Y. 208, 70 N.E. 449, 102 Am. St. R. 442.

[1596] State v. Scarlett, 91 N.J.L. 200, 102 A.160, 2 A.L.R. 83.

[1597] Rogosin v. City Trust Co., 107 N.J. Eq. 79, 151 A. 834.

[1598] Cunningham v. Commissioner of Banks, 249 Mass. 401, 144 N.E. 447.

testamentary trustees does not render a trust company liable for paying a withdrawal check signed by only one of the executors as such.[1599] An investment firm was entitled to recover the excess amount the account holder was able to withdraw from his professional association account due to the firm's bookkeeping error.[1600] An account holder, who had requested liquidation of his account with the investment firm was not entitled to recover the full amount as shown in the account balance where such amount was the result of a bookkeeping error.[1601]

Production of Passbook.—Under passbook regulations, payments by a trust company in good faith and with due care to a person producing a passbook discharge the company.[1602] One making a trust deposit was held entitled to recover it without producing his passbook after revoking the trust, where the trust was for his wife's daughter and the wife and daughter had left the depositor, the wife refusing to give up the passbook.[1603]

Agreements as to Payment.—An agreement to keep a deposit in a trust company's commercial department does not show payment pro tanto, nor does an agreement by a borrower to keep on deposit in the commercial department a certain percentage of the amount of loans outstanding, to be applied in payment on default; such an agreement does not bind the company to look solely to the deposit for payment.[1604] And an agreement to look solely to a borrower's deposit in a trust company's commercial department for the payment of loans made from funds of its savings department is invalid.[1605]

§ 31. Segregated Assets.

A statute requiring a trust company receiving savings deposits to segregate assets at least equal to the amount of such deposits as security

---

1599 In re Hammer's Estate, 237 App. Div. 497, 261 N.Y.S. 478, aff'd, 261 N.Y. 677, 185 N.E. 789.

1600 Schimmel v. Merrill Lynch Pierce Fenner & Smith, Inc., 464 So. 2d 602 (Fla. App. 3 Dist. 1985).

1601 Schimmel v. Merrill Lynch Pierce Fenner & Smith, Inc., 464 So. 2d 602 (Fla. App. 3 Dist. 1985).

1602 Reynolds v. People's Trust & Guaranty Co., 9 N.J. Misc. 433, 154 A. 332, aff'd, 109 N.J.L. 170, 160 A. 637.

1603 McKeever v. Empire Trust Co., 270 N.Y.S. 494 (1934).

1604 Tremont Trust Co. v. Graham Furniture Co., 244 Mass. 134, 138 N.E. 330.

1605 Tremont Trust Co. v. Graham Furniture Co., 244 Mass. 134, 138 N.E. 330.

therefor should receive a liberal construction.[1606] A note so segregated under such a statute is segregated for its full face, and not for its face less deposits of its makers and indorsers as varying from time to time.[1607] A trust company's rule that it would maintain a "segregated" investment department in which it would receive and invest special deposits to be known as "savings investments," was held to mean that it would maintain a separate department for the purpose of receiving deposits to be invested, not that it would segregate such funds from all other funds of the bank, as respects the question whether by such deposits a trustee-beneficiary relation was established.[1608] Since a trust company, as the holder of a note segregated as security for savings deposits, is a trustee, a depositor has no right to set off deposits against the note, and the intention of a depositor to apply a certain deposit marked "Special" to the payment of his note so segregated, though made known to the company's treasurer, gives the depositor no right of setoff of such deposit against the note, where the deposit remains under his exclusive control and subject to withdrawal by him.[1609]

§ 32. Particular Deposits.

Fiduciary's Deposits.—A trust company may be justified in receiving a deposit to the credit of a decedent's estate, subject to the control of the executor making the deposit, though its officers know he is not the sole

---

[1606] **In general.—**

Lawrence v. Lincoln County Trust Co., 123 Me. 273, 122 A. 765.

Sufficient segregation.—

A trust company, having no investment book, so called, nevertheless has sufficiently segregated notes as required by statute, as security for savings deposits, by stamping on each page of its daily balance ledger, under heading "Assets," the words "Segregated for saving acc't" bracketed against the items of assets. Lawrence v. Lincoln County Trust Co., 123 Me. 273, 122 A. 765.

[1607] Lawrence v. Lincoln County Trust Co., 123 Me. 273, 122 A. 765.

[1608] Sindllnger v. Department of Financial Institutions (Ind. App.), 196 N.E. 717.

Five and one-half percent "savings investments" deposits established by trust company under rules providing for segregation of investment department's assets to determine order of payment, reserving right to demand statutory withdrawal notice, in which case deposits would be paid in order notices were received, providing for crediting of interest and empowering company to terminate agreement on notice, held to create debtor-creditor, not trustee-cestui que trust, relation between company and depositors. Sindlinger v. Department of Financial Institutions (Ind. App.), 196 N.E. 717.

[1609] Lawrence v. Lincoln County Trust Co., 123 Me. 273, 122 A. 765.

executor.[1610] Where testamentary trustees deposit a trust fund in their names as trustees with a trust company designated by the will, and receive a certificate of deposit in their names as trustees, the trust company is under no duty or obligation to inquire as to the terms of the trust and refuse to permit withdrawals not in strict compliance with its terms, in the absence of any knowledge or information as to the terms of the trust, any participation in the disposition of the trust moneys, or any advantage derived by it from the trustees' withdrawal of the deposit.[1611] But where a special guardian of an infant deposits the latter's money in a trust company which has notice that the owner is an infant, it is chargeable with notice of an order of court requiring the deposit to be made to the infant's credit, and is liable to the latter for payment to the guardian without special order of court.[1612] And money deposited under a will in the savings department of a trust company to be paid to a minor upon his reaching his majority, and accepted with knowledge of the terms of the will, is secured by the securities deposited with the state treasurer for the purpose of securing funds handled by the company as trustee.[1613] A trust company, receiving special deposits on interest to be paid to beneficiaries when they come of age, was held not entitled to a commission for holding and disbursing the deposits.[1614] A trust company has no right on an incompetent's death to deprive his conservator of the balance to the incompetent's credit, or to pay it to his executor who cannot sue the conservator until a settlement of his accounts.[1615] Where trustees deposited securities comprising the corpus of trusts with the depository trust company in a form under which all the trust deposits maintained by a fiduciary were merged into one account, the guardian ad litem of the beneficiary of one trust was entitled to verify the trust assets by reviewing the documents of transfer from the estate account to the merged account of the trustees and then with the company, thereby verifying that the estate securities were part of the assets deposited in the company, and the company must certify to the guardian ad litem that it had on hand securities

---

[1610] In re Hammer's Estate, 237 App. Div. 497, 261 N.Y.S. 478, aff'd, 261 N.Y. 677, 185 N.E. 789.

[1611] Clifford v. United States Trust Co., 203 App. Div. 160, 196 N.Y.S. 892.

[1612] Walker v. State Trust Co., 40 App. Div. 55, 57 N.Y.S. 525.

[1613] Walker v. State Trust Co., 40 App. Div. 55, 57 N.Y.S. 525.

[1614] Davis Trust Co v. Smith, 226 F. 410.

[1615] Day v. Old Colony Trust Co., 232 Mass. 207, 122 N.E. 189, 2 A.L.R. 1554.

in quantities either equal to or greater than quantities shown on the certificate submitted to it.[1616]

Special Deposits.—The contract under which money or property is deposited with an investment company determines whether the deposit is general or special, and, where a special purpose clearly appears, the fund is applicable first to the discharge of obligations to the special beneficiary for whom the fund is deposited, and claims of general creditors are secondary.[1617] But an agreement by a borrower to keep on deposit in a trust company's commercial department a certain percent of the amount of loans outstanding, to be applied in payment on default, does not show a special deposit creating a trust, and does not bind the company to look solely to the deposit for payment.[1618] Where a buyer places funds in a trust company for the payment of a draft, and the company promises the seller that the draft will be paid, the buyer cannot raise the contention that the seller cannot claim the money as a trust fund, where a second trust company assuming the first's obligations does not raise the question.[1619] Where it appeared that a mortgagor relied upon a trust company to apply funds deposited to his account to the payment of certain legal expenses incident to the title to property and reduction of a mortgage, and gave the company blank checks for such purpose, but other payments for a purpose of which the mortgagor had no knowledge were made, and the checks not returned to him, a bill in equity for an accounting was held authorized.[1620]

Deposits for Safekeeping.—Where a trust company receives bonds merely for safekeeping, it is bound to return them as is any bailee.[1621] And a trust

---

[1616] In re Will of Coe, 80 Misc. 2d 374, 363 N.Y.S.2d 265 (1975).

Depository trust company, holding many of the estate securities on deposit, should furnish a certificate certifying to the guardian ad litem that it has on hand certain securities and quantities which are either equal to or greater than the quantities shown on the certificates submitted to it by the custodian or fiduciary; that certificate will reflect the estate assets and, at least, provide the guardian ad litem with the knowledge that there is on hand at least the quantity of securities to cover what is supposed to be in the account. In re Estate of Rockefeller, 103 Misc. 2d 1041, 427 N.Y.S.2d 390 (1980).

[1617] State ex rel. Rohn Shoe Mfg. Co. v. Industrial Com., 217 Wis. 138, 258 N.W. 449. See also § 26 of this chapter.

[1618] Tremont Trust Co. v. C. H. Graham Furniture Co., 244 Mass. 134, 138 N.E. 330.

[1619] McClure Estate, Inc. v. Fidelity Trust Co., 243 Mass. 408, 137 N.E. 701.

[1620] Tharp v. St. Georges Trust Co., 27 Del. Ch. 216, 34 A.2d 253.

[1621] Crowder v. Story, 90 Ind. App. 598, 169 N.E. 470.

company receiving the stock of a corporation but realizing no dividends on it, is entitled to no commission simply for holding the stock.[1622]

Christmas Club and Thrift Account Deposits.—It has been held that Christmas Club deposits must be considered savings deposits.[1623] They do not, however, constitute a special fund to be distributed to Christmas Club depositors, but, on the insolvency of a trust company, they should be transferred to its savings department from its commercial department by the state official taking over the company for liquidation.[1624] The rules governing a trust company's thrift department have the same force as those governing savings banks.[1625] For other cases relating to thrift deposits, see the footnote.[1626]

[1622] Davis Trust Co. v. Smith, 226 F. 410.

[1623] In re Hanover Trust Co., 241 Mass. 273, 135 N.E. 166, 21 A.L.R. 1126.

[1624] Petition of Allen, 242 Mass 343, 136 N.E. 112.

[1625] McKeever v. Empire Trust Co., 270 N.Y.S. 494 (1934).

[1626] **Thrift deposits constitute a trust fund.—**

The charter of a trust company provided that all moneys deposited in its "thrift department" should be kept separate from other funds, should be invested in first real estate mortgages, and should be used only in fulfilling "thrift department" contracts, held, that a trust was created in favor of the certificate holders, and they alone were entitled to share in the fund on insolvency. Thayer v. National Real Estate Trust Co., 10 Del. Ch. 242, 97 A. 604.

Where the thrift fund is inadequate to pay all certificate holders in full, any moneys collected by the receiver from other sources should be treated as part of such fund because of the trust company's obligation to keep that fund intact. Thayer v. National Real Estate Trust Co., 10 Del. Ch. 242, 97 A. 604.

Who has right to participate in fund.—The action of a trust company and its records disclosing active certificates and certificates which had been terminated under a contract permitting the trust company to declare a forfeiture are the best evidence of the right of certificate holders to participate in the trust fund after the insolvency of such trust company. Thayer v. National Real Estate Trust Co., 10 Del. Ch. 242, 97 A. 604.

Under a provision of such contracts, deposits made by a certificate holder might be forfeited by a default in weekly payments continuing for five weeks. Held, that some affirmative action by the trust company was required to declare the default; otherwise delinquent certificate holders were entitled to share in the fund. Thayer v. National Real Estate Trust Co., 10 Del. Ch. 242, 97 A. 604.

Certificates which were improperly or irregularly rescinded prior to the lapse of the requisite time are entitled to share in such trust fund. Thayer v. National Real Estate Trust Co., 10 Del. Ch. 242, 97 A. 604.

And whenever the trust company failed to terminate a contract by declaring a default, the certificate remained in force and the holder thereof retained his interest in the fund, no matter

§ 33. Liability.

A trust company is bound to know the signature of its depositors, and its payment of a forged check over the counter or through a clearinghouse cannot be charged against a depositor if he is wholly free from any negligence contributing to the forgery.[1627] And the fact that checks for funds

---

how long the period of his delinquency. Thayer v. National Real Estate Trust Co., 10 Del. Ch. 242, 97 A. 604.

But where such trust company exercised its right to declare forfeiture. of moneys paid by delinquent certificate-holders, such action was final and precluded such certificate-holders from claiming any share of the thrift fund. Thayer v. National Real Estate Trust Co., 10 Del. Ch. 242, 97 A. 604.

Under a provision of such contracts, a certificate-holder even after default could be automatically reinstated in good standing by resuming payments within three months. Held, that all certificate-holders delinquent in payments for less than three months prior to the receivership were entitled to share in the fund. Thayer v. National Real Estate Trust Co., 10 Del. Ch. 242, 97 A. 604.

And where default had been declared and the defaulter's money forfeited, if the defaulter was thereafter reinstated, it was the duty of the trust company to restore to the thrift fund the money so forfeited. Thayer v. National Real Estate Trust Co., 10 Del. Ch. 242, 97 A. 604.

Priority.—

The holder of a "full-paid" certificate, while entitled to participate in the fund, has no right of priority over other certificate holders. Thayer v. National Real Estate Trust Co., 10 Del. Ch. 242, 97 A. 604.

Sums to be paid claimants.—

After paying the expenses of administration, to the amount of the fund should be added the aggregate sum of all moneys borrowed by certificate holders, and the total will be the fund for distribution to be divided among the claimants in proportion to the amount of each claim, and from the sum due each claimant should be deducted the amount of any loan made from the fund, together with interest thereon. Thayer v. National Real Estate Trust Co., 10 Del. Ch. 242, 97 A. 604.

Where certificate holders paid installments in advance of the last due date prior to receivership, the money so paid should be refunded to them before distributing the fund. Thayer v. National Real Estate Trust Co., 10 Del. Ch. 242, 97 A. 604.

In the case of certificate holders who borrowed money from the fund, held, that interest should be charged against them to date of the receivership. Thayer v. National Real Estate Trust Co., 10 Del. Ch. 242, 97 A. 604.

But where such certificate holders have made loans from the fund, the amount of their overpayments should be credited on such loans. Thayer v. National Real Estate Trust Co., 10 Del. Ch. 242, 97 A. 604.

1627 Grow v. Prudential Trust Co., 249 Mass. 325, 144 N.E. 93.

Payment made upon forged instrument is at peril of depositary. Rapp v. Manufacturers Trust Co., 15 Misc. 2d 332, 181 N.Y.S.2d 714.

received by a trust company on certain trusts are transferred to one of its directors does not alter the trust company's liability.[1628] And a depositary's payment of a depositor's check without the payee's endorsement or with an improper endorsement establishes a prima facie misappropriation of the depositor's funds, and the burden is then on the depositary to prove payment to the proper party.[1629]

Where a trust company, being instructed to deposit a certain amount to a customer's credit, drew a treasurer's check for that amount without authority and sent it to the customer at an address he had never communicated to the company, which resulted in the check being deposited to the account of a third party, it was held liable therefor.[1630] But under a stipulation not to hold a trust company liable on account of payment through "inadvertence or accident," it is exonerated from liability for the negligence of its bookkeeper in letting a check go through against a customer's account after payment is stopped.[1631] Unless the payee's endorsement is forged or unauthorized, a depositary is not liable to a drawer for an amount paid out on his check, even though a third party's endorsement precedes the payee's.[1632] And a trust company which had paid checks drawn by the treasurer of an association for

---

[1628] Madison Trust Co. v. Carnegie Trust Co., 167 App. Div. 4, 152 N.Y.S. 517, aff'd, 215 N.Y. 475, 109 N.E. 580.

[1629] **In general.—**

Rapp v. Manufacturers Trust Co., 15 Misc. 2d 332, 181 N.Y.S.2d 714.

Improper endorsement.—

A drawer of a check payable to "Holiday Pools, Inc." could recover from depositary which paid the check on an endorsement of "Holiday Pool Co., Inc." Rapp v. Manufacturers Trust Co., 15 Misc. 2d 332, 181 N.Y.S.2d 714.

No liability for payment to one of nonendorsing payees.—

Where a general contractor issued a check payable to the order of a masonry subcontract and a materialman who furnished materials to the subcontractor for work on a specified lot and the subcontractor paid the materialman in full by his own check for all materials on such job and deposited the general contractor's check in his account with the trust company without the endorsement of either payee, the trust company was not liable to the materialman, who had a claim against the subcontractor for materials furnished on other jobs, for the alleged conversion of the balance of the check. Star Block & Builders Supply Co. v. Cleveland Trust Co. (Ohio App.), 172 N.E.2d 623, appeal dismissed, 168 Ohio St. 336, 154 N.E.2d 442.

[1630] Sarafian v. Guaranty Trust Co., 209 App. Div. 686, 205 N.Y.S. 490.

[1631] Tremont Trust Co. v. Burack, 235 Mass. 398, 126 N.E. 782, 9 A.L.R. 1067.

[1632] Rapp v. Manufacturers Trust Co., 15 Misc. 2d 332, 181 N.Y.S.2d 714.

a considerable length of time, is justified in assuming that he is authorized to draw checks, and it is not liable for payment of a check drawn to cash and signed by the treasurer as such.[1633]

Where a depositor, claiming that the money in question was his own, but he wanted to keep this account separate from another account, opened an account with a trust company in his own name marked "Special," by depositing a trust check payable to his order as "trustee" signed in the name of another by the depositor as "attorney in fact," and the company made no investigation, and later the depositor made additional deposits of checks in this account, some of which were payable to him individually and some payable to him as executor, the company was held not liable for paying out the checks payable to the depositor individually, but was held liable for paying out the initial deposit and the checks payable to the depositor as executor because they were trust funds which the depositor had misappropriated; however, the acceptance of the deposit did not render the company liable for the depositor's conversion.[1634] But a trust company whose employee steals another trust company's money and uses it to make good his speculations, does not acquire good title as against the other trust company.[1635] And where a school district treasurer, who was also a trust company's bookkeeper, surreptitiously and unauthorizedly deposited school funds to the company's credit in a bank, and secretly withdrew and embezzled a part thereof, the company was held not liable where it had no knowledge of the deposit, its withdrawal or facts suggesting inquiry.[1636] But a trust company, having actual notice of an executor's unlawful deposit of an estate check in his personal account, is placed on inquiry as to the validity of subsequent transactions involving the estate's money.[1637]

Where a transfer of deposits from the savings to the commercial department of a trust company, in payment for notes transferred to the savings department, is illegal, the subsequent renewal of such notes is Illegal, and, since depositors in the savings department cannot be deprived

---

[1633] Madeiran Alliance Protective Ass'n v. Lowell Trust Co., 237 Mass. 89, 129 N.E. 440.

[1634] Whiting v. Hudson Trust Co., 234 N.Y. 394, 138 N.E. 33, 25 A.L.R. 1470.

[1635] Metropolitan Trust Co. v. Federal Trust Co., 232 Mass. 363, 122 N.E. 413.

[1636] American Surety Co. v. First Trust Co., 124 Neb. 874, 248 N.W. 697.

[1637] In re Hopkins' Estate, 161 Misc. 680, 293 N.Y.S. 786, holding that trust company became liable to estate for amount of check, not merely sum remaining after applying amount of executor's note for sum loaned by company to pay balance of purchase price of corporation stock above amount of such check thereto and balance of executor's account.

of funds by the mismanagement of officers in transferring deposits to the commercial department in exchange for notes not constituting proper savings department investments, the renewal of such notes does not extinguish the original indebtedness.[1638]

§ 34. Waiver and Estoppel.

A bank authorized to accept and execute trusts may be estopped to deny that it is a trust company.[1639] And vice versa, where a trust company has fully entered into the banking business, and keeps accounts of its depositors and pays checks against them as if it had been organized for that purpose, it cannot plead incapacity to certify checks on the ground that it is not chartered as a bank.[1640] Where the proper officer of a trust company certifies a check, the company is estopped to deny its liability to an innocent holder on the ground that the depositor's account is not good for that amount.[1641] A trust company whose letter induced a customer, after irregularities in payment of a profit-sharing savings bond, to make payments on the express understanding that they were to be withdrawn on a certain date, cannot repudiate its obligation to allow withdrawal at that time.[1642] But the acceptance of a certificate of deposit by a trust company's commercial department does not preclude its obtaining relief in a suit to fix the character

---

1638 Petition of Allen, 245 Mass. 448, 139 N.E. 800.

1639 People v. Citizens' Trust, etc., Bank, 272 Ill. App. 444.

When a bank is authorized by its charter to accept and execute trusts and accepts a deposit by an administrator on behalf of a minor which the bank knows is made by order of and is held subject to the order of the probate court under the Illinois statute, the bank accepts the deposit as a trust company and not as a bank, as a matter of law, and, notwithstanding it had not qualified under the act, it is estopped to deny that it is a trust company or that the deposit was accepted as a trust, and cannot in any way cause the deposit to become a general one and deprive the deposit of its character as a preferred claim upon the insolvency of the bank. People v. Citizens' Trust, etc., Bank, 272 Ill. App. 444.

1640 Muth v. St. Louis Trust Co., 88 Mo. App. 596.

1641 State v. Scarlett, 91 N.J.L. 200, 102 A. 160, 2 A.L.R. 83.

1642 Schoenberg v. Mutual Profit Realty Co., 94 Misc. 203, 158 N.Y.S. 264.

The holder of a profit-sharing savings bond, on the suggestion of the defendant issuing the bond, agreeing to continue his payment for a longer term to avail himself of a cash surrender privilege, show, a new agreement waiving the condition of regular and prompt payments. And under the provisions of such an instrument acceptance of the holder's payments, being a waiver of a condition upon which the forfeiture of a privilege was claimed to depend, requires no new or independent consideration. Schoenberg v. Mutual Profit Realty Co., 94 Misc. 203, 158 N.Y.S. 264.

of the deposit.[1643] And a loan association is not estopped from enforcing a written contract providing that a deposit is for a stock subscription, though the association's officer orally agreed to hold the deposit in trust.[1644]

§ 35. Actions.

Pleading.—A petition seeking recovery for interest upon deposits made by a receiver with a trust company states a cause of action upon an implied contract, where it alleges that the company was authorized to receive general deposits on which it was bound to pay interest, and that in reliance on such a holding out by the company, the receiver made deposits in an open current account.[1645] And a complaint alleging that a trust company which knew that certain accounts with a bank and itself in an estate's name belonged to a trust estate nevertheless credited proceeds to the personal account of a former trustee thereof, who deposited the estate's moneys to his own account with the trust company in payment of his personal indebtedness, states a cause of action against the trust company in favor of the estate.[1646] In an action against a trust company on a certificate of deposit, the company should not be allowed to answer alleging a fraud not perpetrated directly on the company but on a third party.[1647] A certificate of deposit for a commercial deposit in a trust company cannot be reformed to show a savings deposit on grounds of mistake in a proceeding by a conservator of the company for instructions as to whether the certificate holder must share in assets segregated as security for savings deposits, where the issue as to reformation is not raised or affirmatively pleaded.[1648]

Burden of Proof.—In a drawer's action against a depositary-drawee, the burden of proving that the payee's endorsement was forged is upon the plaintiff.[1649] And in an action against a trust company for alleged violation of the duty of loyalty owed by an agent to principal, the burden of proving agency is on the plaintiffs.[1650]

[1643] Cronan v. Commissioner of Banks, 254 Mass. 444, 150 N.E. 193.

[1644] In re Krueger's Estate, 173 Wash. 114, 21 P.2d 1030.

[1645] Stone v. St. Louis Union Trust Co., 183 Mo. App. 261, 166 S.W. 1091.

[1646] Pratt v. Commercial Trust Co., 105 Misc. 324, 174 N.Y.S. 88, aff'd, 188 App. Div. 881, 175 N.Y.S. 918.

[1647] Green v. Commercial Bank, etc., Co., 277 F. 527.

[1648] Cooper v. Fidelity Trust Co., 134 Me. 40, 180 A. 794.

[1649] Rapp v. Manufacturers Trust Co., 15 Misc. 2d 332, 181 N.Y.S.2d 714 (burden not sustained).

[1650] Mack v. American Sec. & Trust Co., 191 F.2d 775.

But in an action by a depositor to recover money withdrawn by forged check and improperly charged to him, the burden of proof is on the trust company to show that the depositor was guilty of such negligence as to preclude his recovery.[1651]

Presumptions and Inferences.—An auditor's finding that a trust company employee forged checks on a depositor's account in a large amount, was held to warrant an inference that charges by the company against such depositor's account were the forged checks though the checks themselves disappeared.[1652] And, where a school district treasurer, who was also a trust company's bookkeeper, made entries on the company's records showing that he had deposited school funds to the company's credit in a bank, and had withdrawn part thereof, it was held an inference that he acted for the company with its knowledge could be overcome by direct evidence to the contrary.[1653]

Evidence.—On the issue of liability of a trust company to one to whom it has issued a certificate of deposit, evidence as to dealings of the depositor with the company in relation to the deposit is admissible.[1654] For other cases dealing with admissibility[1655] and sufficiency[1656] of evidence, see the footnotes.

1651 Grow v. Prudential Trust Co., 249 Mass. 325, 144 N.E. 93.

1652 Grow v. Prudential Trust Co., 249 Mass. 325, 144 N.E. 93.

1653 American Surety Co. v. First Trust Co., 124 Neb. 874, 248 N.W. 697.

1654 Callendar v. Kelly, 190 Pa. 455, 42 A. 957.

On the issue as to the liability of a trust company to plaintiff on a certificate signed by the treasurer of the company, and reciting "Received of C. bonds as follows ($10,000): *** [Reciting the bonds]. This certificate bears interest at 6 per cent from date," it is competent to show a conversation between plaintiff and the treasurer, subsequent to the date of the certificate, in which plaintiff refused an offer by the treasurer, on behalf of the company, to take, as payment for the bonds, stock of the company, in which he said that they, or their equivalent in cash, with 6 per cent interest, would be returned to her any time she wished; also, a passbook issued to plaintiff on which she was credited with $150, which she testified was three months' interest on the certificate. Callendar v. Kelly, 190 Pa. 455, 42 A. 957.

1655 **Evidence of custom—**

In action by depositor against bank to recover amount which bank had paid out on forged withdrawal slip and presentation of passbook, evidence that it was custom of larger banks in city to allow tellers to pay out any amounts from savings accounts, when passbook is presented and there is nothing about signature on withdrawal slip to arouse suspicion, was admissible, though such custom could not alter bank's legal responsibility, since the evidence had bearing on question of ordinary care. Watts v. American Sec., etc., Co. (D.C. Mun. App.), 47 A.2d 100.

1656 Evidence held to support finding that an assignment, by which bonds deposited with a trust company were obtained from it, was forged, but not to show that the owner was in

Questions for Jury.—Whether a depositor was negligent in not discovering a forgery of checks by a trust company's bookkeeper sooner is a question of fact for the jury.[1657] And in a suit against a trust company for paying out money to a person fraudulently representing himself to be a depositor, it is for the jury to say whether or not the company questioned the person producing the passbook concerning his identification, and whether, in the exercise of ordinary care, it did all that it reasonably should have done to establish his identity before payment.[1658] For cases illustrating when a question is properly taken from the jury, see the footnote.[1659]

§ 36. Depositor's Right of Setoff.

In General.—The right to set off the amount of a deposit in a closed trust company against a depositor's liability to the company is wholly a creature of statute.[1660] And a depositor who owes a debt fully secured by mortgage to an insolvent trust company, has no right to have a creditor of the company

---

pari delicto so as to preclude his recovery from the company. Palmer v. Wells Fargo Bank & Union Trust Co., 213 Cal. 535, 2 P.2d 771.

In action by depositor against bank to recover amount which bank had paid out to depositor's stepson and stepson's friends on forged withdrawal slip and presentation of passbook providing that possession of the book shall be sufficient evidence of ownership thereof to authorize payment of money due thereon, evidence sustained finding that bank exercised reasonable care, though teller who paid out the money admitted that stepson and his friends appeared to be between 20 and 22 years old and signature card of depositor showed him to have been about 40 years old. Watts v. American Sec., etc., Co. (D.C. Mun. App.), 47 A.2d 100.

[1657] Grow v. Prudential Trust Co., 249 Mass. 325, 144 N.E. 93.

[1658] Wronski v. Franford Trust Co., 84 Pa. Super. 511.

[1659] **Directed verdict required.—**

In a suit by an assignee for the benefit of creditor. to recover money deposited by his assignor with the defendant trust company, it has been held that the undisputed evidence that the assignor had given the defendant certain notes, agreeing that, if his financial condition materially changed, they were to become due and payable at the option of the defendant, that they were endorsed by a party who subsequently failed, and that then the assignor agreed that, if he failed to secure another endorser, the notes should be charged off, which was then done because of such failure, thereby leaving a certain balance to his credit, requires a directed verdict for the assignee for that amount only, regardless of whether the assignor's financial condition had in reality changed, or whether he had made false representations to the defendant regarding the solvency of the endorser of the notes. Steiner v. Mutual Alliance Trust Co., 139 App. Div. 645, 124 N.Y.S. 184.

[1660] **In general.—**

Plymouth County Trust Co. v. Thornell, 291 Mass. 189, 197 N.E. 91. See also § 49 of this chapter. As to right of setoff of depositor in savings bank, see Chapter 16, § 28.

look to his deposit for setoff against the debt, rather than to the security given therefor.[1661] The doctrine of equitable setoff has no application to such cases;[1662] if it did apply, such a depositor would, in effect, be entitled to a greater share of the assets of an insolvent trust company than his nonborrowing fellow depositors.[1663]

Savings and Commercial Departments.—Although deposits in the savings department of a trust company have, in general, the incidents of deposits in a savings bank,[1664] a statute which allows a depositor in a savings bank to set off, at face value, his deposit against debts owed by him to the bank, does not apply to a depositor in the savings department of a trust company.[1665] Similarly, since a trust company's relation to a depositor in its savings department is that of trustee, while its relation to a depositor in its commercial department is that of common-law debtor, a depositor cannot set off his deposit against a debt due the company from the funds of the savings

---

Conditions precedent to right.—

Creditors' committee of steamship company in receivership seeking to compel insolvent trust company to allow setoff of amount of committee's deposit in trust company against dividend payable by steamship company held not entitled to assert right of setoff under statute where no action had been commenced against committee as contemplated by statute. Friedman v. Commissioner of Banks, 291 Mass. 108, 196 N.E. 264.

The New Jersey statute does not authorize a trust company to set off a corporation's deposit against its unmatured notes, where the corporation has not been adjudged insolvent. Rogosin v. City Trust Co., 107 N.J. Eq. 79, 151 A. 834.

1661 Prudential Realty Co. v. Allen, 241 Mass. 277, 135 N.E. 221, 25 A.L.R. 935.

But see Lippitt v. Thames Loan & Trust Co., Co., 88 Conn. 185, 90 A. 369, wherein it is held that a borrower from the commercial department of an insolvent trust company in the hands of a receiver may set off his deposit in the savings department against his loan from the commercial department, and the fact that he deposited with his savings deposit book two orders as collateral security at the time he procured the loan and is otherwise financially responsible does not prevent such setoff.—Editor's Note.

1662 Dole v. Chattabriga, 82 N.H. 396, 134 A. 347; Cosmopolitan Trust Co. v. Golub, 252 Mass. 574, 147 N.E. 847; Bachrach v. Commissioner of Banks, 239 Mass. 272, 131 N.E. 857; Cosmopolitan Trust Co. v. Suffolk Knitting Mills, 247 Mass. 530, 143 N.E. 138 (1924).

1663 Bachrach v. Commissioner of Banks, 239 Mass. 272, 131 N.E. 857; Prudential Realty Co. v. Allen, 241 Mass. 277, 135 N.E. 221, 25 A.L.R. 935; Dole v. Chattabriga, 82 N.H. 396, 134 A. 347.

1664 Bachrach v. Commissioner of Banks, 239 Mass. 272, 131 N.E. 857; Dole v. Chattabriga, 82 N.H. 396, 134 A. 347.

1665 Parent v. Rand, 88 N.H. 169, 185 A. 163; Bachrach v. Commissioner of Banks, 239 Mass. 272, 131 N.E. 857; Dole v. Chattabriga, 82 N.H. 396, 134 A. 347.

department.[1666] And in such a case it makes no difference that a depositor did not know from which department the money was borrowed,[1667] or that a note is an illegal investment for a savings department to make.[1668] An agreement by a trust company that it will set off a borrower's deposit in its commercial department against a debt owed its savings department is also of no effect.[1669] And since depositors in the commercial department of a trust company in the process of liquidation cannot set off claims for an amount due on a checking account against their liability to the savings department upon obligations held by it against them, they cannot indirectly do so by setting off executions.[1670] The savings department of a trust company, as assignee of a promissory note from its commercial department, takes subject to the maker's rights against the commercial department at the time of assignment; but a maker cannot offset a deposit made in the commercial department after the assignment, a claim for which did not become effective until the bank was closed, despite lack of notice of the assignment.[1671] Where a loss must fall on one of two innocent persons, either a commercial depositor whose note was assigned, or a savings department depositor who

---

[1666] Kelly v. Allen, 239 Mass. 298, 131 N.E. 855; Cosmopolitan Trust Co. v. Rosenbush, 239 Mass. 305, 131 N.E. 858, 16 A.L.R. 1484; Tremont Trust Co. v. Baker, 243 Mass. 530, 137 NE. 915; Dole v. Chattabriga, 82 N.H. 396, 134 A. 347.

If plaintiff's note is an asset of the savings department of a trust company, he does not have a right to apply his deposit in the commercial department as setoff as against bank commissioner taking possession of the trust company. Bieringer-Hanauer Co. v. Cosmopolitan Trust Co., 247 Mass. 73, 141 N.E. 566; Bailey v. Allen, 244 Mass. 499, 138 N.E. 915.

[1667] Kelly v. Allen, 239 Mass. 298, 131 N.E. 855.

Drawer of notes in savings department cannot set off deposit in commercial department though without knowledge notes were held by savings department. Tremont Trust Co. v. C. H. Graham Furniture Co., 244 Mass. 134, 138 N.E. 330; Bieringer-Hanauer Co. v. Cosmopolitan Trust Co., 247 Mass. 73, 141 N.E. 566.

[1668] Bieringer-Hanauer Co. v. Cosmopolitan Trust Co., 247 Mass. 73, 141 N.E. 566.

Where note for money loaned from general funds was placed with investments of savings department, corresponding amount being transferred to general funds, makers could not set off deposit in commercial department though note was not legal investment for savings department, savings department holding note as assignee with same authority and subject to same obligations as any commercial paper purchased without endorsement from holder not connected with commercial department. Cosmopolitan Trust Co. v. Rosenbush, 239 Mass. 305, 131 N.E. 858, 16 A.L.R. 1484.

[1669] Tremont Trust Co. v. Baker, 243 Mass. 530, 187 N.E. 915.

[1670] Cosmopolitan Trust Co. v. Suffolk Knitting Mills, 247 Mass. 530, 143 N.E. 138 (1924).

[1671] Cosmopolitan Trust Co. v. Leonard Watch Co., 249 Mass. 14, 143 N.E. 827.

will lose by depletion of the assets of that department if the commercial depositor's setoff against his note is allowed, it is the policy of the law that the loss must fall on the commercial depositor.[1672] On the other hand, there is no objection to a borrower from the commercial department of an insolvent trust company setting off his claim as a depositor against his debt.[1673]

When Right Determined.—In an action to recover on a note as an asset of an insolvent trust company, the rights of a defendant as plaintiff in setoff are determinable as of the date the commissioner of banks takes over the company for liquidation,[1674] or the date of filing of a notice of liquidation.[1675] But it was held a municipality could set off its deposit in an insolvent trust company against its indebtedness to the trust company on bonds not due on the date of its insolvency.[1676]

Consent and Mutuality.—Where a mortgage and bonds secured thereby were payable to a trust company or its successors and assigns, the mortgagors impliedly consented if consent was needed, to a sale of the bonds by the company which thereafter held the mortgage in trust for the bondholders, thus precluding the mortgagors from setting off deposits

---

1672 Cosmopolitan Trust Co. v. Leonard Watch Co., 249 Mass. 14, 143 N.E. 827.

1673 Lippitt v. Thames Loan, etc., Co., 88 Conn. 185, 90 A. 369; Parent v. Rand, 88 N.H. 169, 185 A. 163.

1674 Cosmopolitan Trust Co. v. Wasserman, 251 Mass. 514, 146 N.E. 772.

In determining right to set off deposit in closed trust company against depositors' liability as endorser on note, that trust companies were insolvent and that notes did not mature until after trust companies went into liquidation did not present a setoff, since deposits were due at that time and rights of parties were to be adjusted as of the date when commissioner took possession of the trust companies for purpose of liquidation. Commissioner of Banks v. Lee & Co., 291 Mass. 191, 197 N.E. 88.

Bill by creditors' committee of steamship company in receivership seeking to set off deposit in insolvent trust company against dividend payable to trust company held properly dismissed insofar as it sought a setoff of the entire deposit where committee did not show that on date when trust company closed they were under obligation to pay any particular sum to it. Friedman v. Commissioner of Banks, 291 Mass. 108, 196 N.E. 264.

1675 Fox v. Department of Financial Institutions, 212 Ind. 85, 7 NE.2d 39.

Deposit credits assigned to trust company's mortgagor about two years after company had gone into voluntary liquidation held not entitled to be set off under statute, since right of setoff is to be determined as of date of filing notice of liquidation, and when company went into voluntary liquidation, its assets became a trust fund for payment of its creditors and depositors pro rata so to permit set-off would be to allow a "preference." Fox v. Department of Financial Institutions, 212 Ind. 85, 7 N.E.2d 39.

1676 Neptune City v. Seacoast Trust Co., 116 N.J. Eq. 357, 173 A. 604.

against the mortgage after the company's insolvency.[1677] In order for there to be a right of setoff, mutuality must exist between the parties in question.[1678]

As to an endorser's right to set off his deposit against liability on a note, see the footnote.[1679]

[1677] Nicholas v. Gordon, 317 Pa. 469, 177 A. 791.

[1678] **In general.—**

Cosmopolitan Trust Co. v. Golub, 252 Mass 574, 147 N.E. 847.

Partnership asset and individual liability.—

Balance due partnership on checking account when insolvent trust company was taken over for liquidation cannot be set off against note of individual partner, notwithstanding partnership claim is signed to individual. Cosmopolitan Trust Co. v. Wasserman, 251 Mass. 514, 146 N.E. 772.

Personal asset and corporate liability.—

Endorser of note could not offset his personal deposit against liability of maker, a corporation in which he was principal stockholder. His direction to apply deposit would not entitle maker to be absolutely and unconditionally relieved. Commissioner could not be compelled to forego security given by maker of not. and accept deposit of endorser. Cosmopolitan Trust Co. v. S. Vorenberg Co., 245 Mass. 317, 139 N.E. 482.

Individual asset and joint liability.—

In action on note by closed trust company against husband and wife who were jointly and severally liable thereon, husband held not entitled to set off amount of deposit in trust company as against his liability on notes. Plymouth County Trust Co. v. Thornell, 291 Mass. 189, 197 N.E. 91.

[1679] In action against maker of note by closed trust company, endorser cannot appear and demand a set-off of his deposit against maker's liability even where endorser concedes his liability, since, if the holder looks to the maker for payment, endorser cannot secure preferred treatment over other general creditors of trust company by obtaining a set-off of his deposit against the liability of the maker. Commissioner of Banks v. Lee & Co., 291 Mass. 191, 197 N.E. 88.

Solvency of maker is determining factor against right of endorser to claim a set-off for amount of note against endorser's deposit in closed trust company when sued on note, since maker is primarily liable and endorser secondarily liable. Commissioner of Banks v. Lee & Co., 291 Mass. 191, 197 N.E. 88.

Depositor who was endorser on note of maker, who had become insolvent, held entitled to set off amount of notes against deposit in trust company when sued by commissioner on its liability as endorser. Commissioner of Banks v. T. C. Lee & Co., 291 Mass. 191, 197 N.E. 88.

Presumption of solvency of maker of note held not to prevail so as to defeat endorser's right of setoff of amount of note against deposit in closed trust company when endorser was sued by commissioner fl charge of trust company, where corporate maker of note had permitted itself to be sued on note several months overdue, as to which record disclosed no

Waiver and Estoppel.—See the footnote.[1680]

d. Loans, Discounts and Participation Certificates.

§ 37. In General.

Power to Lend and Discount.—Generally, the question of whether a trust company is empowered to lend money or discount commercial paper is determined by interpretation of its charter, or of the statute under which it is incorporated or by which it is governed.[1681] Under a statute authorizing trust companies to buy all kinds of negotiable and nonnegotiable paper, a trust company may acquire negotiable paper payable to an officer of the company and indorsed by him.[1682] But a trust company, incorporated under a general

---

possible ground of defense. Commissioner of Banks v. T. C. Lee & Co., 291 Mass. 191, 197 N.E. 88, holding that endorser was entitled to setoff, although there was no finding and no evidence as to the solvency and insolvency of the maker.

[1680] The issuance by the commissioner of banks of an assignable certificate of proof of a claim for a deposit in the commercial department "subject to rights of setoff to be hereafter determined," has been held not to waive the right or to estop the commissioner from applying dividends on the depositor's note held by savings department. Bailey v. Allen, 244 Mass. 449, 138 N.E. 915.

[1681] **In general.—**

Kieth v. Catchings, 64 Ga. 773.

Authority to lend money on land having been conferred on a trust company by its charter, a deed made to it conveys title, and a subsequent purchaser under an execution against the grantor acquires simply the right to redeem on payment of the debt. Kieth v. Catchings, 64 Ga. 773.

Authority to discount notes.—

Under a state banking law authorizing trust companies to receive deposits, and "to loan money on real or personal securities," to "purchase, invest in and sell stocks, bills of exchange, bonds and mortgages and other securities," and to invest the moneys received by it in trust "In the stocks or bonds of any state, or in such real or personal securities as it may deem proper," such a company may discount notes. Binghamton Trust Co. v. Auten, 68 Ark. 294, 57 S.W. 936, distinguishing New York State Loan, etc., Co. v. Helmer, 77 N.Y. 64. But see Jenkins v. Neff, 186 U.S. 230, 22 S. Ct. 905, 46 L. Ed. 1140, aff'g 163 N.Y. 320, 57 N.E. 408.

As to a statute signifying an intent to place state banks upon an equality with national banks, see Empire Trust Co. v. Coleman, 85 Misc. 312, 147 N.Y.S. 740, modified, 167 App. Div. 912, 151 N.Y.S. 1114; 222 N.Y 577, 118 N.E. 1057.

"Industrial banks" in New York do not possess the power of commercial banks to discount generally, but they are authorized to make industrial loans having an interest rate considerably in excess of 6 per cent. Modern Industrial Bank v. Graves, 260 App. Div. 349, 21 N.Y.S.2d 329, aff'd, 285 N.Y. 668, 34 N.E.2d 375.

[1682] Denny v. Jefferson County, 272 Mo. 436, 199 S.W. 250.

corporation act does not derive therefrom the power to lend money, lending money not being incidental to any of its corporate powers.[1683] And the question of which officer or officers of a trust company are authorized to make loans or discount commercial paper is generally determined by the bylaws of the company, which must be construed in the light of the statutes by which it is controlled and regulated.[1684] However, the fact that a transaction, from the point of view of a party receiving funds, meets substantially all requirements of a loan, does not make it a "loan" in law as affecting the propriety of a trust company's participation therein.[1685]

The definition of "bank" under the Internal Revenue Code provides that a substantial part of the taxpayer's business must consist of "making loans *and discounts*." The statute's use of the conjunctive "and" rather than the disjunctive "or" in this phrase indicates that "discounts" is a required element.[1686]

Contracts Concerning Loans Construed.—Where a trust company, as a pledgee of collateral, was charged by an agreement with the duty of giving the pledged collateral the same care it would if the collateral were in the company's own portfolio, it was required to exercise such care as prudent business men exercise in regard to their own property of a similar kind under similar circumstances.[1687] An agreement by a trust company discounting notes for a payee, that the proceeds should not be drawn against pending maturity of the notes, is valid without formal approval.[1688] And where a trust company arranged with a customer to discount his notes indorsed by another, the arrangement was held rescinded by the customer's subsequent

---

[1683] Mercantile Trust Co. v. Kastor, 273 Ill. 332, 112 N.E. 988.

[1684] Kavanaugh v. Commonwealth Trust Co., 64 Misc. 303, 118 N.Y.S. 758, rev'd on other grounds, 147 App. Div. 281, 131 N.Y.S. 1059.

There being a manifest distinction between making investments and making loans and discounts, a bylaw of a trust company providing that the executive committee may, in its discretion, authorize the president generally to make investments in such securities as are authorized by the charter of the company, and to dispose of such securities without previously consulting as to details with the committee, did not require all discounts of, and loans on, notes to be first submitted to the board or executive committee. Kavanaugh v. Commonwealth Trust Co., 64 Misc. 303, 118 N.Y.S. 758, rev'd on other grounds, 147 App. Div. 281, 131 N.Y.S. 1059.

[1685] Litwin v. Allen, 25 N.Y.S.2d 667.

[1686] Moneygram Int'l v. Comm'r, 664 Fed. Appx. 386 (5th Cir. 2016).

[1687] Montclair Trust Co. v. Star Co., 139 N.J. Eq. 211, 50 A.2d 481, modified, 141 N.J. Eq. 263, 265, 57 A.2d 7.

[1688] McCausland v. Roseville Trust Co., 84 N.J. Eq. 567, 94 A. 591.

giving of his check to the company and the company's repossession of the money credited on its books to the customer.[1689] Under an agreement between a trust company and its directors that loans made to it by them to reestablish its credit would only become payable when its surplus exceeded a certain sum, a director could not recover his loans from the company until its surplus exceeded that sum.[1690]

A payee is not required to resort to collateral before suing on a note authorizing the maker to apply a certificate on the note on the failure to perform certain conditions.[1691] Where a borrower takes out a so-called installment investment certificate under which weekly payments are to be made, and pledges it as security for a note, the bank deducts interest on the loan in advance, and the note by reason of nonpayment of installments becomes due, payments on the certificate must be deducted from the amount of the note due.[1692] But it also has been held that a loan by an investment company secured by a certificate issued by it entitles the company, after default in payment on the certificate, to judgment for the full amount of the note, although nearly all installments on the certificate have been paid, the maker not having the right to surrender the certificate in discharge of the note until all installments thereon have been paid.[1693] And it has been held that a statute empowering an investment company to impose a fine for each default in payment on a certificate assigned as collateral does not prevent a provision in a note that at the company's option it shall become due on such default from being operative.[1694] Similarly, a note given an investment company for a loan is not void because of a provision therein for payment of attorneys' fees in the event of default,[1695] and an installment investment certificate pledged to a loan company issuing it to secure a loan is a "security by way of assignment of chose in action or other evidence of Indebtedness."[1696] A borrower is entitled to cancellation of a chattel mortgage on his

---

[1689] Putman v. United States Trust Co., 223 Mass. 199, 111 N.E. 969.

[1690] Koster v. Lafayette Trust Co., 207 N.Y. 336, 100 N.E. 1117.

[1691] Morris Plan Co. v. Lillie, 265 Mass. 98, 163 N.E. 749.

[1692] Morris Plan Co. v. Osnato, 123 Misc. 428, 204 N.Y.S. 829.

[1693] Morris Plan Co. v. Cohen, 164 N.Y.S. 162.

[1694] Morris Plan Co. v. Currie, 161 N.Y.S. 292.

[1695] Morris Plan Co. v. White, 140 Misc. 775, 251 N.Y.S. 379.

[1696] People's Loan, etc., Co. v. Singer, 140 Misc. 383, 250 N.Y.S. 613.

repayment, according to contract, of the amount borrowed accompanied by a surrender of stock of the lender corporation.[1697]

A depositor in the commercial department of a trust company was held not released from liability as the maker of a note assigned by the commercial department to the savings department to the extent of damages caused by the failure of the savings department to present the note to the commercial department for payment before the company was closed, on the ground that the savings department was negligent.[1698] Where a director of a trust company allegedly deposited stock in the company in a spirit of generosity rather than as collateral, and he thereafter executed notes which established a lien on all securities left by him in the company's possession to the amount of his liability under the notes, the deposited stock became a part of the collateral for payment of the notes.[1699] And where a borrower agreed to keep a deposit in a trust company's commercial department to be applied in payment of notes on default, and the notes were either held originally by, or transferred to, the savings department, neither the insolvency of the commercial department nor the company's failure to exercise its right to apply the deposit, is indicative of a failure of consideration under the agreement.[1700]

A small-business concern did not have a private cause of action under the Small Business Act for lender's refusal to refund the unearned portion of prepaid interest following the early repayment of a loan.[1701]

Participation Mortgage Bonds and Certificates.—A trust company may issue participation mortgage bonds and certificates, and act as trustee for the holders thereof.[1702] Thus, under a statute relating to the investment of trust

---

[1697] Agricultural Credit Corp. v. Heim, 62 N.D. 344, 243 N.W. 809.

[1698] Cosmopolitan Trust Co. v. Leonard Watch Co., 249 Mass. 14, 143 N.E. 827.

[1699] Short v. Allegheny Trust Co., 330 Pa. 55, 198 A. 793.

[1700] Tremont Trust Co. v. Graham Furniture Co., 244 Mass. 134, 138 N.E. 330.

[1701] Aardwoolf Corp v. Nelson Capital Corp., 861 F.2d 46 (2d Cir. 1988).

[1702] **In general.—**

See In re Mutual Trust Co., 48 N.Y.S.2d 707; In re First Nat. Bank, etc., Co., 350 Pa. 125, 38 A.2d 15. See also 47 of this chapter.

Participation mortgage bonds.—

Where a trust company loaning money evidenced by note and secured by mortgage issued participation mortgage bonds, the trust company was trustee for holders of such bonds, notwithstanding for a time trust company owned part of bonds. Board of Comm'rs v. Cook, 141 Kan. 677, 42 P.2d 568.

funds by corporate trustees and other corporate fiduciaries, a transaction wherein a corporate trustee issued a participation certificate in a guaranteed mortgage owned by it, and assigned such certificate to itself as trustee, was held valid.[1703] And guaranteed mortgage certificates by which a guaranty company assigned to a plaintiff the equitable interest in a mortgage owned by the company incumbered the company's title to the mortgage with a lien, and hence the certificates were valuable, necessitating an offer to return them before the plaintiff could maintain a suit to recover the sum paid therefor.[1704]

Where trust company loaning money evidenced by note and mortgage issued participation bonds describing mortgage and certifying that holder of bonds had undivided interest in mortgage and debt secured thereby and interest thereon according to coupons attached, holder of bonds merely had pro rata interest in principal of and interest on mortgage debt when collected by trust company as trustee, and was not assignee of original mortgage to extent of his interest, especially in view of noncompliance with statute regarding assignment. Board of Comm'rs v. Cook, 141 Kan. 677, 42 P.2d 568.

Certificates.—

A bank and trust company had power to make loans on realty mortgages, to liquidate such mortgages by assignment or conveyance to investors, and hence to issue certificates pursuant to which bank held mortgages in trust as an investment fund for benefit of certificate holder. Hack v. Christina, 213 Ind. 68, 11 N.E.2d 152; Hack v. Jobes, 213 Ind. 90, 11 N.E.2d 161.

Holder of only part of participation bonds could not foreclose original mortgage unless trustee failed or refused to institute foreclosure proceeding, and unless all those united in interest by reason of being owner. of remainder of participation bonds were made parties plaintiff or defendant. Board of Comm'rs v. Cook, 141 Kan. 677, 42 P.2d 568.

Substitution of security.—

Trust company which issued mortgage participation certificate stating that holder had interest in notes, bonds, or other obligations secured by first liens on real estate, and put up certain church loan as security for outstanding participation certificates, held to have no right to substitute other securities in place of church loan as against holder of certificate, whose interest in that loan was not thereby affected. Croghan v. Savings Trust Co., 231 Mo. App. 1161, 85 S.W.2d 239.

Application of superintendent of banks for appointment of successor to take over assets which constituted security for liquidated trust company's bond and mortgage participation certificates would be treated as an application to resign, and successor might be appointed where trust company, as to such certificates, was a trustee and not an agent. In re Mutual Trust Co., 48 N.Y.S.2d 707.

[1703] In re Thomson's Estate, 135 Misc. 62, 237 N.Y.S. 622 (New York statute).

[1704] E.T.C. Corp. v. Title Guarantee & Trust Co., 271 N.Y. 124, 2 N.E.2d 284, 105 A.L.R. 999.

Letter by which purchaser of guaranteed mortgage certificates stated it tendered back certificates and demanded return of purchase price held insufficient return of certificates to permit purchaser to maintain suit to recover sum paid for them. E.T.C. Corp. v. Title

Financial Statements.—In the absence of a provision in a borrower's financial statement that the statement may be deemed to reflect the borrower's continued financial condition unless notification is given to the contrary, or of written or spoken words by the borrower from which such assurance may be inferred, the reasonable understanding is that a financial statement speaks as of its date, and that a borrower is charged only with the duty of not concealing material changes of which he has knowledge or is chargeable therewith.[1705]

Loans and Discounts in Violation of Statutes.—Loans above a certain amount by a trust company to its directors are generally prohibited by statute,[1706] but where consent to a loan of a certain amount to a director is required by statute, general consent is sufficient if otherwise in accordance with the statute.[1707] Where an act incorporating a safe-deposit and savings

---

Guarantee, etc., Co., 271 N.Y. 124, 2 N.E.2d 284, 105 A.L.R. 999.

[1705] **In general.—**

Monier v. Guaranty Trust Co., 82 F.2d 252, 104 A.L.R. 912 (1936), cert. denied, 298 U.S. 670, 56 S. Ct. 835, 80 L. Ed. 1393.

Borrower seeking credit does not impliedly warrant or represent that there has not occurred without his knowledge any detrimental change in conditions shown on his financial statement of prior date. Monier v. Guaranty Trust Co., 82 F.2d 252, 104 A.L.R. 912 (1936), cert. denied, 298 U.S. 670, 56 S. Ct. 835, 80 L. Ed. 1393.

Material falsity in the facts asserted in financial statement as existing on date of statement would be ground for rescinding loan made in reliance on statement, regardless of borrower's innocence in making false assertion. Monier v. Guaranty Trust Co., 82 F.2d 252, 104 A.L.R. 912 (1936), cert. denied, 298 U.S. 670, 56 S. Ct. 835, 80 L. Ed. 1393.

Claimed discrepancy of $28,000 in borrower's financial statement showing net worth of $463,000 held not to render statement substantially incorrect so as to authorize lender's rescission of loan. Monier v. Guaranty Trust Co., 82 F.2d 252, 104 A.L.R. 912 (1936), cert. denied, 298 U.S. 670, 56 S. Ct. 835, 80 L. Ed. 1393.

[1706] Wayne Title & Trust Co. v. Treat, 269 Pa. 303, 112 A. 679.

In a suit by a trust company on notes, affidavit of defense that the notes were signed without consideration as an accommodation for defendant's father and another who were respectively a director and president of plaintiff trust company at the time the notes were signed, and that the purpose of the signature was to violate the act of assembly which provides that no director of a trust company shall receive as a loan an amount greater than 10 percent of the capital stock actually paid in and surplus, held insufficient, and court properly made absolute plaintiff's rule for judgment Wayne Title & Trust Co. v. Treat, 269 Pa. 303, 112 A. 679.

[1707] Denny v. Jefferson County, 272 Mo. 436, 199 S.W. 250.

A loan by a trust company to a corporation, in which one of the trust company's directors was largely interested, there being no proof that such director as an individual was interested

institution does not authorize it to do a banking business, and the constitution and applicable statutes forbid such institution from carrying on such a business, heavy penalties being fixed for so doing, notes discounted by the company are void.[1708] Similarly, under an act prohibiting a corporation not expressly incorporated for banking purposes, from issuing evidences of debt upon loans, certificates issued by a trust company stating that the amount designated has been deposited in the company and they are payable in twenty years with interest, are void when given for a loan.[1709] But a statute providing that no trust company shall make any loan on the security of shares of its own capital stock, does not make void ab initio a promissory note given to a trust company for valid consideration, even though the trust company takes its own stock as collateral security for payment of the note.[1710] A statute limiting the liability of any one person to a trust company was held inapplicable to the investment of deposits of the savings department of a trust company.[1711] And though a trust company under its charter may invest only in such securities as are thereby authorized, if it has made an illegal loan, it may nevertheless enforce repayment thereof.[1712] Similarly, where a safe-deposit company is prohibited by statute from discounting

---

in the loan, did not violate a statute forbidding a loan to a director, directly or indirectly, without the consent of the majority of the directors. State v. Barnes, 108 Minn. 230, 122 N.W. 11.

[1708] In re Jaycox, F. Cas. No. 7287.

[1709] New York Life Ins. & Trust Co. v. Beebe, 7 N.Y. 364.

[1710] Steneck Trust Co. v. Minervini, 112 N.J.L. 530, 172 A. 71.

The validity of the federal and state statutes prohibiting certain banking institutions from making loans on the security of the shares of their own capital stock or becoming the purchaser of such shares could not be raised by one seeking recovery from trust company for the alleged unwarranted sale and purchase of its own stock owned by him and deposited with trust company as collateral for payment of his notes, but could be raised only by governmental authorities, where the stock had been sold and the proceeds applied to the payment of the debt. Short v. Allegheny Trust Co., 330 Pa. 55, 198 A. 793.

Where trust company held its own stock as collateral security for notes given in payment therefor until three months before receivership of company when stock, then worthless, was forwarded to stockholder without his request, and retained by him, stockholder could not escape liability on note on ground that trust company had violated statutory prohibition against corporation taking a lien on any part of its capital stock as security for loan or discount. Bell v. Aubel, 151 Pa. Super. 569, 30 A.2d 617.

[1711] Medford Trust Co. v. McKnight, 292 Mass. 1, 197 N.E. 649.

[1712] Davis Sewing Machine Co. v. Best (N.Y.), 30 Hun 638; Empire Trust Co. v. Coleman, 85 Misc. 312, 147 N.Y.S. 740, modified, 167 App. Div. 912, 151 N.Y.S. 1114; 222 N.Y. 577, 118 N.E. 1057.

notes or other commercial paper, and paper so discounted is declared to be void, such a company cannot enforce notes discounted by it, but may recover the money loaned, and where a mortgage is given to secure a note so discounted, it may be enforced.[1713] For other cases dealing with loans and discounts in contravention of statutory provisions, see the footnote.[1714]

Loans in Violation of Regulations.—Even if a loan by a small business investment company licensed under the Small Business Investment Act violated a regulation, it was held that this did not make the loan or guaranty contract unenforceable, where the regulation was essentially a delineation of authorized powers of small business investment companies and neither the

---

[1713] Pratt v. Short, 79 N.Y. 437, 35 Am. R. 531; Pratt v. Eaton, 79 N.Y. 449.

[1714] Mortgage and investment certificate contract held not illegal because of statute prohibiting "doing business" of selling contracts on which to predicate loan at some future date, regulating methods of "conducting business" by such concern and requiring permit from persons "engaging in the business" referred to, where transaction involved was only mortgage ever taken by lender on such plan. Wilson v. Federal Tax Co., 176 Okla. 90, 54 P.2d 363.

An escrow agreement between a trust company and borrower, pledging share of company's stock as security for loan, held not void, but merely voidable, since act prohibiting trust companies from making loans so secured can only be invoked by state or borrower to restrain or defeat enforcement of security and by latter only before execution of contract while security still subsists in company's hands. Richards v. Integrity Trust Co., 317 Pa. 513, 177 A. 28.

Statute providing that illegality no defense.—

Where stockholders of corporate debtor to procure loan for debtor from credit unions became shareholders in unions and debtor received money by checks payable to stockholders and deposited in debtor's bank account, chattel mortgagee executed by debtor to unions were valid, even though debtor as a corporation could not under state law belong to unions and thus could not borrow money from them, in view of statute providing that the illegality of a loan should be no defense in any action by a corporation to recover amount lent. In re Alpine Petroleum Corp., 41 F. Supp. 682.

Investment certificate of deposit of Morris Plan Bank held violative of statute forbidding a bank to issue or sell its certificates of deposit except for actual cash or its equivalent. Atlanta Coledrinx Co. v. Morris Plan Bank, 66 Ga. App. 854, 19 S.E.2d 205.

Title insurance.—

Mortgage company's business policy of refusing to accept title insurance policies issued by a particular title insurer in connection with home mortgage loans did not violate Rhode Island statute requiring that lending institutions allow prospective mortgagors to choose their own title attorney and providing that prospective mortgagor may permit lending institution to select its own attorney; by allowing borrowers to choose their own title attorney or by providing its own authorized closing attorney, mortgage company fell within the permissible second provision of statute. Mortgage Guarantee & Title Co. v. Commonwealth Mtg. Co., 730 F. Supp. 469 (D.R.I. 1990).

regulation nor the Act stated that loans in excess of such authority were void or unenforceable.[1715] There is a rebuttable presumption that a loan under the Small Business Investment Act is not repayable within a lesser period than that prescribed by the applicable regulation of the Small Business Administration.[1716] For other cases dealing with loans made by companies licensed under the Act, see the footnote.[1717]

[1715] Talco Capital Corp. v. Canaveral International Corp., 225 F. Supp. 1007, aff'd, 344 F.2d 962. As to regulations under Act generally, see § 1 of this chapter.

[1716] Hernstadt v. Programs for Television, Inc., 38 Misc. 2d 628, 232 N.Y.S.2d 683.

[1717] **Meaning of "single enterprise".—**

For purposes of Small Business Investment Act which limits aggregate amount of assistance a licensee may make to any single enterprise to 20 percent of licensee's combined capital and surplus unless approval of the Small Business Administration has been obtained, the term "single enterprise" may mean several business concerns if they are affiliated. United States v. Coleman Capital Corp., 295 F. Supp. 1016 (N.D. Ill. 1969).

Where one person was controlling stockholder and an executive officer of each of three corporations at time licensed investment company made loans to corporations, the corporations constituted a "single enterprise" for purposes of Small Business Investment Act which limits aggregate amount of assistance a licensee may make to any single enterprise to 20 percent of licensee's combined capital and surplus unless approval of Small Business Administration has been obtained. United States v. Coleman Capital Corp., 295 F. Supp. 1016 (N.D. Ill. 1969).

Violation found.—

Licensed investment company, which bought note evidencing personal loans made by its president and contributed cash proceeds as additional paid-in capital and surplus in order to obtain matching funds from Small Business Administration, violated Small Business Investment Act which specifies that loan made by license to small business concerns shall be used for sound financing, growth, modernization, and expansion of concerns. United States v. Coleman Capital Corp., 295 F. Supp. 1016 (N.D. Ill. 1069).

Violation not found.—

Stock purchase warrant, which was executed and delivered by plaintiff to defendant in connection with a transaction under the Small Business Investment Act wherein defendant advanced $23,000 to plaintiff, was an "equity security" given in connection with the transaction to provide equity capital, rather than security for a long-term loan to plaintiff and therefore was not within the prohibition of the Act that "such loan shall not provide any right in a licensee to acquire any stocks in the borrower, except through the medium of collateral security." Alliance Business Inv. Co. v. G—R Dev. Co., 447 P.2d 741 (Okla. 1968).

Estoppel inapplicable.—

Even if employees of Small Business Administration had knowledge that borrowing concern was connected with licensed investment company in manner violative of Small Business investment Act and regulations, and investment company was misled by nonaction on part of the administration for 18-month period, neither principles of estoppel nor any other equitable consideration entitled investment company to immunity from statutory and

Compensation for Handling Loans.—A loan company which exacts from a corporation making application for a loan an advance payment of attorney's fees and a commission, promising to refund them if the loan is not made through the loan company's fault, must return them on refusing the loan on the ground that the applicant is a corporation.[1718] See the footnote for other cases relating to compensation for handling loans.[1719]

Usury.—A loan is not rendered usurious merely because of an investment company's receiving fees and deducting interest in advance and taking as collateral an installment investment certificate, nor because of a clause in a note for the acceleration of maturity on the borrower's default.[1720]

---

regulatory prescriptions. United States v. Coleman Capital Corp., 295 F. Supp. 1016 (N.D. Ill. 1969).

[1718] Midland Sav., etc., Co. v. Foss Imp. Co., 34 Okla. 564, 126 P. 720.

[1719] **In general.—**

One handling loans for life insurance company held entitled to commissions he would have earned on loans, applications for which were turned over by company to its local office before completion thereof. Equitable Life Ins. Co. v. Crosley, 221 Iowa 1129, 265 N.W. 137.

No compensation for voluntary service.—

Evidence held to show that servicing of life insurance company's farm loans by investment company was voluntary service, rendered without expectation of payment therefor on part of either company, so that investment company was not entitled to compensation therefor. Equitable Life Ins. Co. v. Crosley, 221 Iowa 1129, 265 N.W. 137.

Nor could bank deduct an investigation fee from amount of interest charged where bank did not comply with conditions of statute authorizing lender to make a charge for investigation. Morris Plan Co. v. Hayes, 141 Misc. 239, 251 N.Y. 377.

Reimbursement for expenditures.—

One handling farm loans for life insurance company held entitled to allowance of amount paid by him after company terminated his agency for abstract bills, taxes on realty involved in company's mortgage foreclosure suits against him and fire insurance premiums. Equitable Life Ins. Co. v. Crosley, 221 Iowa 1129, 265 N.W. 137.

Fee for mortgage preparation.—

Where borrowers obtained a mortgage from the lender, the charging of a separate fee for the preparation of the standard mortgage form by the lender for the borrowers did not constitute the unauthorized practice of law under Michigan law. As the lender did not counsel or assist the borrowers in matters requiring legal discretion or profound legal knowledge, the lender did not engage in the practice of law and did not violate the statute. Dressel v. Ameribank, 468 Mich. 557, 664 N.W.2d 151 (2003). See Mich. Comp. Laws § 450.681.

[1720] **In general.—**

Morris Plan Co. v. Hayes, 141 Misc. 239, 251 N.Y.S. 377.

The sum of money actually loaned borrower by a bank operating a loan and investment

State usury laws govern the maximum rate of interest national banks can charge on loans, contracts made by national banks are governed and construed by state laws, and national banks' acquisition and transfer of property are based on state law. However, the states can exercise no control over national banks, nor in any wise affect their operation, except in so far as Congress may see proper to permit. Anything beyond this is an abuse, because it is the usurpation of power which a single state cannot give.[1721]

The Georgia Supreme Court believes that usury on a particular loan can only be determined by proper reference to the actual outstanding principal balance on that loan.[1722]

---

business under statutes relating to Morris Plan banks constitutes principal of debt, as respects whether loan is usurious. Citizens Industrial Bank v. Schmidt (Tex. Civ. App.), 112 S.W.2d 513.

Record sustained finding that transaction, by which Morris Plan Company loaned money for one year at 8 percent interest deducted in advance and took as security assignment of installment investment certificate contemporaneously issued to borrower which accumulated interest at 8 percent on each payment made thereon and when paid up could be surrendered in payment of debt or, if debt was otherwise paid, could be retained as investment, was not tainted with usury. Freed-Goodall Furniture Co. v. Morris Plan Co., 194 Okla. 556, 152 P.2d 902.

But bank could not assert that interest was not usurious under statute permitting lender to deduct interest in advance and make a charge for investigation where bank did not limit its interest rate to 6 percent as required by the statute. Morris Plan Co. v. Hayes, 141 Misc. 239, 251 N.Y.S. 377.

Bank could not assert that borrowers' simultaneous purchase of investment certificates, calling for monthly payments and deposited with bank as collateral security for leans, removed taint of usury, where borrowers were not informed that they were purchasing certificates and merely thought they were signing a receipt for the money loaned. Morris Plan Co. v. Hayes, 141 Misc. 239, 251 N.Y.S. 377.

A loan by a bank operating a loan and investment business under statutes relating to Morris Plan banks of $270, for use of which the borrowers paid $80 over a period of 10 month. in addition to liquidating the principal in monthly payment. of $80 each, was usurious as a matter of law, permitting recovery of statutory penalty of double amount of usury paid. Morris Plan Co. v. Hayes, 141 Misc. 239, 251 N.Y.S. 377.

1721 Watters v. Wachovia Bank, N.A., 127 S. Ct. 1559, 167 L. Ed. 2d 389 (U.S. 2007), superseded by statute as stated in Gordon v. Kohl's Dep't Stores, Inc., 172 F. Supp. 3d 840 (E.D. Pa. 2016) ("by the plain language of 12 U.S.C.S. § 25b, and in accordance with the Office of the Comptroller of the Currency's interpretation, the Dodd-Frank Act effectively overturned the subsidiary-preemption holding in Watters v. Wachovia Bank, N.A., 127 S. Ct. 1559, 167 L. Ed. 2d 389 (U.S. 2007)."). See 12 U.S.C.S. § 85.

1722 Southern Federal Sav. & Loan Asso. v. Lyle, 249 Ga. 284, 290 S.E.2d 455 (1982).

For other cases relating to usury involving savings and loan institutions, industrial banks, trust companies, etc., see the footnote.[1723]

[1723] **Constitutionality of statute or charter.—**

A statute authorizing theretofore usurious loans is a general law and not repugnant to the constitutional prohibition against special or local laws. Union Sav., etc., Trust Co. v. Dottenheim, 107 Ga. 606, 34 S.E. 217 (1899).

There is a dictum, however, in the case of Union Sav. Bank & Trust Co. v. Dottenheim, 107 Ga. 606, 34 S.E. 217 (1899), to the effect that such a special provision in a particular bank charter would be unconstitutional.—Editor's Note.

Industrial bank.—

Statute providing that the provisions of the usury laws shall not affect any loan made by any national bank or "any bank" or trust company duly incorporated under the laws of this state included an industrial bank organized under laws of state. Columbus Industrial Bank v. Miller, 125 Conn. 313, 6 A.2d 42 (1939).

Where makers of note for $739.88 received $695.45, the difference representing interest paid in advance, and parties orally agreed that makers were to pay face of note in 52 equal weekly payments, the first payment to be made one week from date of note, and payee was an industrial bank, the payee was entitled to charge interest in the manner and amount provided in the notes. Atlantic Industrial Bank v. Centonze, 130 Conn. 18, 31 A.2d 392.

Where holder of an allegedly usurious note was an industrial bank, maker was not entitled to surrender of note nor a declaration that the note was void, but his remedy was to collect back twice the amount of interest that he had paid. Rindge v. Morris Plan Industrial Bank, 17 N.Y.S.2d 471.

Where automobile dealer never drew so-called conditional sales contract signed by automobile buyer, saw it, or made price stipulated therein, but treated matter throughout as cash transaction, and sales price of automobile and dealers' invoice or bill of sale showed sale as having been made to two persons, transaction between buyer and industrial bank was in nature of "loan" and not "purchase of conditional sales agreement," as respects bank's liability for twice amount of interest paid, under Banking Law. Krim v. Morris Plan Industrial Bank, 173 Misc. 141, 17 N.Y.S.2d 472.

Installment certificate.—

The taking by an industrial loan and thrift company, operating under the Morris Plan, of an installment certificate, calling for payments on the certificate while the loan is maturing, does not render the loan usurious, in view of the fact that at maturity of the note the borrower may elect to pay the note and keep the certificate. Mesaba Loan Co. v. Sher, 203 Minn. 589, 282 N.W. 823.

An acceleration clause providing for acceleration of maturity on borrower's failure to make payment. under installment certificate, assigned as collateral to an industrial loan and thrift company operating under the Morris Plan, does not render the transaction usurious. Mesaba Loan Co. v. Sher, 203 Minn. 589, 282 N.W. 823.

Correction of unintentional error.—

Where trust company deducted additional sum as interest payment on loan when only a single sum was due, and error was corrected voluntarily and borrower was given due credit

Liability for Conversion of Proceeds of Loan.—See the footnote.[1724]

---

and mistake was unintentional, fact that resulting interest was in excess of 6 percent per annum through mistake gave borrower no right to an affirmative action nor a defense for usury. Ditmars v. Camden Trust Co., 10 N.J. Super. 306, 76 A.2d 280, modified, 10 N.J. 471, 92 A.2d 12, 35 A.L.R.2d 822.

The existence of generally recognized commercial custom of banks to compute interest on short term obligations on basis of 860 days per year instead of 365 and to compute interest every 90 days and deduct interest in advance, demonstrated that trust company did not intend to violate usury statute in so computing interest on borrower's loan, but if there was a violation, it was committed in error. Ditmars v. Camden Trust Co., 10 N.J. Super. 306, 76 A.2d 280, modified, 10 N.J. 471, 92 A.2d 12, 35 A.L.R.2d 822.

Evidence held not to support contention that unintentional error in deduction of interest had not been corrected. Ditmars v. Camden Trust Co., 10 N.J. Super. 306, 76 A.2d 280, modified, 10 N.J. 471, 92 A.2d 12, 35 A.L.R.2d 822.

What constitutes usury.—

Bank's increased expenses as to retirement of certain notes under circumstances of bank's own choice, and bank's added bookkeeping expense incident to loans were not expenses which could be added to lawful interest rate on notes without constituting usury, particularly where principal accounting was done by a warehouse company at which goods forming security for notes were stored, rather than by bank. Independent Foods v. Lucas County Sav. Bank, 70 N.E.2d 139 (Ohio App. 1946). Georgia Supreme Court adheres to the actual declining-principal balance method originally set out in Union Sav. Bank & Trust Co. v. Dottenheim, 107 Ga. 606, 34 S.E. 217 (1899), because the court believes that usury on a particular loan can only be determined by proper reference to the actual outstanding principal balance on that loan. Southern Federal Sav. & Loan Asso. v. Lyle, 249 Ga. 284, 290 S.E.2d 455 (1982).

Provision of New York banking law prescribing maximum rate of interest and authorizing recovery of penalty of twice amount of interest paid for charging usurious rate applies to savings banks as well as commercial banks. Lyons v. National Sav. Bank, 200 Misc. 652, 110 N.Y.S.2d 564, rev'd on other grounds, 280 App. Div. 339, 113 N.Y.S.2d 695.

[1724] **No liability for loan amount.—**

Where vendor and purchaser after agreeing to sale of realty, contacted manager of loan company and informed her that they desired to negotiate a loan on the realty, and manager who was also a notary public, prepared a credit deed, and vendor signed deed and left it in possession of manager, and manager without being authorized to do so by vendor, made out check to purchaser for balance due for realty, and purchaser endorsed and cashed check and converted funds to his own use, manager of loan company and owner of company, as principal of manager were not liable to vendor for amount of check, in absence of proof of promise by manager to protect vendor by collecting amount owing to vendor from purchaser. Nor was employee of loan company, who performed act. in connection with loan, liable to vendor, in absence of any independent knowledge or discretion on part of employee. Box v. May (La. App.), 50 So. 2d 692.

Liability for financing fee.—

Where vendor and purchaser after agreeing to sale of realty, contacted manager of loan

IV. INSOLVENCY AND RECEIVERS

§ 38. General Considerations.

Generally.—Legislatures have the power to provide the method by which the affairs of trust companies shall be wound up, and may designate the particular officer to institute proceedings therefor, the exercise of such power being dictated by sound public policy.[1725] Thus, where a statute provides an

---

company and informed her that they desired to negotiate a loan on the realty, and manager, who was also a notary public, pared a credit deed, and vendor signed and left it in possession of manager, and manager made out check to purchaser for balance due for realty less a certain sum representing a financing fee of 5 percent and purchaser endorsed and cashed check and converted funds to his own use, and there was no showing that vendor agreed to pay the financing fee, manager and owner of loan company were liable to vendor for amount of financing fee. Box v. May (La. App.), 50 So. 2d 692.

[1725] **In general.—**

Koch v. Missouri-Lincoln Trust Co. (Mo.), 181 S.W. 44. As to the reorganization of insolvent trust companies, see § 3 of this chapter.

Statute valid.—

The New Jersey statute authorizing the commissioner of banking to take possession of insolvent trust company's property without judicial warrant, is held not invalid. La Monte v. Lurich, 86 N.J. Eq. 26, 100 A. 1031, aff'd, 86 N.J. Eq. 251, 98 A. 1086.

Receiver.—

Under the Alabama statute the state superintendent of banks has exclusive authority to proceed against trust company, for the appointment of a receiver to liquidate its affairs. Montgomery Bank, etc., Co. v. State, 201 Ala. 447, 78 So. 825.

Under the District of Columbia statute, the comptroller of the currency may declare a trust company insolvent and appoint a receiver. Dunn v. O'Connor, 89 F.2d 820.

In Florida a receivership for a trust company is purely statutory. Therrell v. Rinaman 107 Fla. 110, 144 So. 327.

Conservator.—

In Maine the court is authorized to liquidate a hopelessly insolvent trust company through a conservator, instead of receiver or trustee, and conservatorship is governed by general rules applicable to receivers of trust and banking companies. Robinson v. Fidelity Trust Co., 140 Me. 302, 37 A.2d 273.

In order to have a conservator appointed under the Rhode Island statute for a frost company, it is not necessary that any action be taken by a court of equity under its general or statutory powers or that the company be adjudged insolvent or unable to meet its obligations as they mature, or that its dissolution be sought. Columbus Exch. Trust Co. v. Pennacchini, 68 R.I. 196, 27 A.2d 187.

Power of state examiner.—

An insolvent bank and trust company were subject to general Banking Laws by reason of the statute giving the state examiner, as to trust companies, all the power he has over banks,

exclusive procedure for liquidation of a trust company, and establishing a right to share in its assets, such procedure must be followed.[1726] But courts cannot read into such statutes any restriction on the powers of insolvent companies not existing at common law.[1727]

In certain states, a trust company may be liquidated by the commissioner of banking and insurance as its statutory agent, or by a receiver in insolvency proceedings.[1728] But a court's power to appoint a receiver should be

---

including the procedure involved in taking appeals. First Am. Bank & Trust Co. v. George, 239 N.W.2d 284 (N.D. 1976).

1726 **In general—**

Inland Properties Co. v. Union Properties (C.P.), 44 Ohio Op. 485, 98 N.E.2d 444.

Appointment of receiver.—

In bill by holder of trust company's mortgage participation certificates, holder's motion for a receiver or trustees of trust company would be denied where holder failed to allege that requirements under trust company act were observed. McDowell v. Mechanics' Trust Co., 13 N.J. Misc. 532, 179 A. 691.

If a statute provides an exclusive system for winding up the affairs of trust companies, a stockholder cannot take direct proceedings for the appointment of a receiver to wind up such a trust company but must apply through the prescribed channels for his appointment. Koch v. Missouri-Lincoln Trust Co. (Mo.), 181 S.W. 44.

That stockholders' petition seeking appointment of receiver of insolvent trust company set out fact. pertly existing prior to a certain statute present. no obstacle to exclusive application of that act, providing for appointment on proceedings by state bank commissioner. Koch v. Missouri-Lincoln Trust Co. (Mo.), 181 S.W. 44.

1727 Cosmopolitan Trust Co. v. Agoos Tanning Co., 245 Mass. 69, 139 N.E. 806.

1728 **In general—**

Prashker v. New Jersey Title Guarantee & Trust Co., 130 N.J. Eq. 391, 22 A.2d 259; Koch v. Morsemere Trust Co., 107 N.J. Eq. 516, 153 A. 498.

Trust company is deemed "closed" when it is possessed and its business is closed for the purpose of liquidation. Summit Trust Servs., Inc. v. Snyder, 936 P.2d 623 (Colo. App. 1997).

Winding up of insolvent trust company is confided to court of chancery, but commissioner of banking and insurance may liquidate company's affairs in case of corporate acts not of themselves amounting to insolvency. Koch v. Morsemere Trust Co., 107 N.J. Eq. 516, 153 A. 498.

Commissioner of banking and insurance may take possession of trust company's property and business only where company's assets will pay all depositors and creditor. Koch v. Morsemere Trust Co., 107 N.J. Eq. 516, 153 A. 498.

Statutory conditions jurisdictional.—

Statutory conditions under which court may appoint receiver for trust company are jurisdictional. Orshefsky v. Mechanics Trust Co., 120 N.J. Eq. 527, 187 A. 779.

Where officers, etc., had been removed from control over insolvent trust company's

exercised cautiously, and it should not take the affairs of a trust company from the possession of a commissioner and turn them over to a receiver or trustees unless the circumstances of the case and the ends of justice so require.[1729] It is also said that only in extreme cases may a state liquidator's general administration of a trust company be arrested or substituted by an equity receiver.[1730] And a statute authorizing a state banking official to close the doors of trust companies and take possession of their assets binds a trust company organized subsequent to its enactment to the same extent as if inserted in a special act of incorporation, but not to any greater extent.[1731]

It may be assumed that a trust company being liquidated by a state banking official is insolvent.[1732] "Insolvency," in its legal sense, exists whenever such an institution for any cause is unable to pay its debts in the ordinary course of business.[1733] But a court of equity has inherent power to

---

business and assets which had been taken over by state official, complainant. held not entitled to appointment of receiver for company, since there was nothing to which appointment could be ancillary. Orshefsky v. Mechanics Trust Co., 120 N.J. Eq. 527, 187 A. 779.

Small Business Administration.—

Small Business Administration (SBA) was entitled to permanent injunction and receivership of company which the SBA had licensed as small business investment company, with SBA continuing as receiver for purpose of liquidating the company and satisfying claims under court supervision; totality of circumstances were such that company's license should be forfeited and it should be dissolved. United States v. Vanguard Inv. Co., 694 F. Supp. 1219 (M.D.N.C. 1988).

[1729] Koch v. Morsemere Trust Co., 107 N.J. Eq. 516, 153 A. 498.

[1730] Amos v. Trust Co. of Florida, 54 F.2d 286, cert. denied, 285 U.S. 559, 52 S. Ct. 458, 76 L. Ed. 947; Smith v. Jones, 120 Fla. 237, 162 So. 496.

[1731] Cosmopolitan Trust Co. v. Mitchell, 242 Mass. 95, 136 N.E. 403.

[1732] Cunningham v. Commissioner of Banks, 249 Mass. 401, 144 N.E. 447.

[1733] Commonwealth v. Tradesmen's Trust Co., 237 Pa. 316, 85 A. 363.

As to grounds for declaration of insolvency under District of Columbia statute, see Dunn v. O'Connor, 89 F.2d 820.

Therefore, in a petition for a receiver to wind up the affairs of a company, a traverse to the averment of insolvency is ineffectual which admits that the institution has closed its doors. Commonwealth v. Tradesmen's Trust Co., 237 Pa. 316, 85 A. 363.

Small Business Administration established that corporation was capitally impaired in violation of regulation, that corporation did not give prompt written notice of impairment, and that corporation failed to cure, for purposes of determining whether SBA was entitled to preliminary injunction and temporary receivership; 1984 statement indicated that earnings deficit was 108.68 percent of private capital, 1985 statement also yielded impairment ratio in excess of 100 percent, and $400,000 of private capital figure was actually investment by a

appoint a receiver to liquidate a corporation or investment trust where fraud, mismanagement or abuse of trust is present, whether or not insolvency is also present.[1734] And where grounds other than insolvency for appointment of a receiver for an investment trust are present, a court's jurisdiction to liquidate the trust is not defeated by the supervening solvency of the trust.[1735] Under at least one state statute, a corporation commissioner's right to liquidate a delinquent loan company depends upon an impairment of the company's capital, or its violation of law and failure to comply with the

---

governmental entity. United States v. Vanguard Inv. Co., 667 F. Supp. 257 (M.D.N.C. 1987).

Small Business Administration established that corporation failed to make interest payments when due in violation of regulation, that corporation did not pay off remaining debt upon acceleration, and that corporation failed to meet financial reporting requirements, in addition to falling to give notice of and cure capital impairment, and thus, SBA would be appointed receiver and granted preliminary injunction. United States v. Vanguard Inv. Co., 667 F. Supp. 257 (M.D.N.C. 1987).

[1734] **In general.—**

Bailey v. Proctor, 160 F.2d 78.

Federal district court is vested with inherent equitable power to appoint trustee receiver upon prima facie showing of fraud mismanagement in operation of investment company. Securities & Exch. Comm'n v. Midland Basic, Inc., 283 F. Supp. 609 (D.S.D. 1968).

A district court had statutory power, in addition to inherent equitable power to appoint a trustee-receiver for a corporation found to have been an investment company, operating unregistered and in violation of the Investment Company Act, pursuant to a fraudulent scheme in violation of the fiduciary relationship running from corporate operators to unsuspecting stockholders. Securities & Exchange Comm. v. Keller Corp., 323 F.2d 397.

Consideration of appropriate remedy.—

When court of equity has exercised its jurisdiction to appoint receivers for investment company pursuant to complaint charging gross abuse of trust on part of trustees or officers, court, in determining what would be appropriate remedy to afford complete relief may consider fact that capital structure is not in conformity with standards and safeguards provided by Investment Company Act. Bailey v. Proctor, 160 F.2d 78.

Trial court did not abuse its discretion by appointing receiver pendente lite for diversified management investment company which failed to file annual report with Securities and Exchange Commission, sent stockholder misleading annual report and whose directors indicated almost flagrant disregard for affairs of company. Tanzer v. Huffines, 408 F.2d 42 (3rd Cir. 1969).

[1735] Bailey v. Proctor, 160 F.2d 78.

District court which appointed receivers for investment trust because of insolvency and abuse of trust by officers-trustees did not lose the power to order liquidation of trust because of intervening solvency of trust and removal of such officers-trustees and impossibility of their resuming control of trust. Bailey v. Proctor, 160 F.2d 78.

commissioner's orders relating thereto within the period allowed, not upon the solvency or insolvency of the company.[1736] And although such commissioner's general power of supervision of corporations organized under such statute is not inconsistent with a court's power of supervision over the voluntary dissolution of such a corporation where it is solvent and has fully complied with all provisions of the statute, a corporation so organized was held not entitled to proceed with the voluntary liquidation of its affairs under the supervision of a court while refusing to comply with the commissioner's order directing it to restore a deficiency of its capital.[1737]

The directors and stockholders of a trust company, being liable to stockholders and creditors for any damage accruing by reason of their negligence, are properly authorized to file a bill for the administration of the company's assets in equity to protect the rights of all concerned when it appears doubtful whether the company can successfully continue.[1738] And a provisional receivership of a trust company is authorized, even though its remaining assets are not in danger of further depletion, where its corporate dissolution can be forecast with reasonable certainty unless funds are provided for its debts and the safe and lawful resumption of its business.[1739] Moreover, a state banking official taking possession of an investment

---

[1736] In re Peoples Finance & Thrift Co., 61 Cal. App. 2d 11, 141 P.2d 742 (California Industrial Loan Act).

Corporation commissioner's order directing loan company to restore within 60 days the deficiency of its capital presently existing, stating approximate amount thereof, and directing a farther audit to determine exact amount was a sufficient compliance with Industrial Loan Act to authorize liquidation of the company by commissioner upon failure to comply with order, though farther audit disclosed a larger capital deficiency than stated in order. In re Peoples Finance, etc., Co., 61 Cal. App. 2d 11, 141 P.2d 742.

And company having made no effort to comply with commissioner's order could not complain because commissioner amended original order by fixing deficiency at an amount in excess of approximate amount stated in original order, and company under original order had only 13 days after such amendment to restore the deficiency. In re Peoples Finance, etc., Co., 61 Cal. App. 2d 11, 141 P.2d 742.

[1737] In re Peoples Finance, etc., Co., 61 Cal. App. 2d 11, 141 P.2d 742.

Hence, commencement of proceeding for voluntary dissolution under supervision of court did not deprive commissioner of jurisdiction to take charge of and liquidate corporation which failed to make good its capital impairment pursuant to commissioner's order, regardless of whether corporation was solvent in the sense of having sufficient assets to pay all creditors as distinguished from shareholders. In re Peoples Finance, etc., Co., 61 Cal. App. 2d 11, 141 P.2d 742.

[1738] Camden v. Virginia Safe Deposit, etc., Corp., 115 Va. 20, 78 S.E. 596.

[1739] Montgomery Bank, etc., Co. v. State, 201 Ala. 447, 78 So. 825.

company's assets was held not bound to defer an application for the appointment of a receiver for the statutory period to enable its officers, directors and stockholders to make good any deficit, in view of the directors' antecedent resolution consenting that the company be liquidated.[1740]

Where the Securities and Exchange Commission is entitled to an order enjoining a management investment company from violating provisions of the Investment Company Act regarding the redemption of shares, but the company has no functioning management so that there is no one to whom an injunction can effectively run, a permanent receiver will be appointed.[1741] And where the president and certain trustees of an investment trust have been guilty of gross abuse of trust, the Securities and Exchange Commission has authority under the Investment Company Act to ask for the appointment of receivers to take charge of the trust, and the appointment of receivers by a court is an appropriate exercise of its inherent equity power.[1742] Similarly, where a licensee under the Small Business Investment Act has engaged in violations of the Act or rules, regulations or orders issued pursuant to the Act, a court has the discretionary power under the Act to appoint a receiver and to grant injunctive relief.[1743]

[1740] Clark v. Mutual Loan, etc., Co., 88 F.2d 202.

[1741] Securities, etc., Comm. v. Fiscal Fund, 48 F. Supp. 712.

[1742] **In general.—**

Aldred Inv. Trust v. Securities, etc., Comm., 151 F.2d 254, cert. denied, 326 U.S. 795, 66 S. Ct. 486, 90 L. Ed. 483.

Provisions of act held inapplicable.—

Provisions of Investment Company Act of 1940 for appointing receiver were not applicable in action by SEC against directors of investment company and another corporation for alleged violations of Investment Company Act of 1940, Securities Act of 1938 and Securities Exchange Act of 1934. Securities & Exch. Comm'n v. Midland Basic, Inc., 283 F. Supp. 609 (D.S.D. 1968).

Illustrative case.—

Where long continued violations of Securities Exchange Act of 1934 and Investment Company Act of 1940 had been prima facie established, there had been no shareholders' meeting for 11 years, there had been two hasty attempts to dissolve corporations after Commission filed suit, corporations were not conducting any substantial business except for holding of securities and there was possibility that dissolution might release liabilities for past violations of Investment Company Act, appointment of receiver was not an abuse of discretion. Securities & Exch. Comm'n v. S & P Nat'l Corp., 360 F.2d 741 (2d Cir. 1966).

[1743] **In general.—**

First Louisiana Inv. Corp. v. United States, 351 F.2d 495 (5th Cir. 1965). See also § 1 of this chapter.

A trust company remains in existence as a corporate entity even though a state banking official has taken possession of its property and business.[1744] And a statute providing for the appointment of conservators for trust companies is not equivalent to an order of dissolution so as to terminate a company's contractual relations, and effect a cancellation of its lease of a bank building.[1745] But a state banking official's appointment of a receiver suspends the active rights of a trust company until revived by him or by a

---

Statutory provision jurisdictional.—

The statutory provision for receivership in a proceeding against a licensee for violation of the Small Business Investment Act is not only jurisdictional but affects the usual requirements for invoking an extraordinary remedy. First Louisiana Inv. Corp. v. United States, 351 F.2d 495 (6th Cir. 1965).

Discretionary matters.—

Appointment of a receiver and granting of a preliminary injunction in such a proceeding are, in no small measure, a discretionary matter. First Louisiana Inv. Corp. v. United States, 351 F.2d 495 (5th Cir. 1965).

The purpose of a federal receivership in connection with a small business investment corporation is to protect assets pending the Small Business Administration's recovery on its investment as well as to permit discovery of past abuses of program funds. United States v. Norwood Capital Corp., 273 F. Supp. 236 (D.8.C. 1967).

Illustrative cases.—

Failure of small business investment company to maintain at all times unimpaired capital or to adequately establish reserves for losses and uncollectables, its extension of financing in excess of 20 percent of its paid-in capital and surplus, its control of debtor companies through interlocking directorates, and its sale of stock held by it as investment in portfolio concern to its stockholder without Small Business Administration consent, constituted violations of Small Business Administration regulations sufficient to warrant issuance of injunction, appointment of receiver, entry of money judgment, and award for costs to United States. United States v. Boca Raton Capital Corp., 285 F. Supp. 504 (S.D. Fla. 1968).

Where district court held hearing and afforded investment corporation licensed under Small Business Investment Act and its president opportunity to submit evidence it was not error for court, in exercise of its discretion, to grant preliminary injunction and appoint a receiver pendente lite upon showing made by affidavit that certain funds had not been disbursed as required by the Act but rather had been diverted to benefit of president. First Louisiana Inv. Corp. v. United States, 351 F.2d 495(6th Cir. 1965).

[1744] Allen v. Cosmopolitan Trust Co., 247 Mass. 334, 142 N.E. 100; Cosmopolitan Trust Co. v. Suffolk Knitting Mills, 247 Mass. 680, 148 N.E. 138.

State official's seizure of trust company as unsound or insolvent institution supersedes power of officers, directors, and stockholders to carry on ordinary business, but such institution continues to exist as legal entity until final judicial confirmation of its liquidation, and may sue and be sued in its corporate name to dose up its business. Twyman v. Smith, 119 Fla. 365, 161 So. 427.

[1745] Cooper v. Casco Mercantile Trust Co., 134 Me. 372, 186 A. 885, 111 A.L.R. 548.

competent court's judgment.[1746] For example, a trust company, alter being taken over by a state banking official, cannot make an agreement extending the security of a mortgage held by it after payment of the mortgage.[1747] But a statute providing that the posting of a notice that a trust company is in the hands of a state banking official shall operate as a bar to "any proceedings" against the company or its assets, does not embrace a suit in rem which involves only a question of priority of liens between the insolvent company and another lien claimant.[1748]

[1746] **In general.—**

Power v. Amos, 94 Fla. 411, 114 So. 364 (1927); Schultz v. Imp. Co., 284 Web. 806, 279 N.W. 521.

Agency.—

Thus the agency of trust company for collection and remittance of interest on mortgage notes and bonds was terminated by insolvency. Andrew v. Metropolitan Life Ins. Co., 211 Iowa 282, 233 N.W. 473.

Trusteeship.—

Where a trust company named as trustee in a trust deed executed by a school district became insolvent and a receiver was put in control of its affairs, it was not competent to act as trustee. Tyronza Special School Dist. v. Speer, 94 F.2d 825.

Nevertheless, a trust company, trustee indeed of trust, may exercise power of sale and deliver deed, though insolvent and in hands of state liquidating agent. Mitchell v. Shuford, 200 N.C. 321, 158 SL 518.

Where insolvent bank or trust company acting as trustee is placed in hands of receiver, fiduciary positions held by it become vacant. In re Strasser's Estate, 220 Iowa 194, 262 N.W. 137.

Performance of contract.—

Trust company in receivership held not disabled from performing contract to convey bank building so as to defeat right to specific performance, where it still had legal title and could convey property and where it was to interest of company and of its creditors that it carry out contract. Louisville Trust Co. v. National Bank, 3 F. Supp. 909, rev'd on other grounds, 87 F.2d 97, cert. denied, 291 U.S. 665, 54 S. Ct. 440, 78 L. Ed. 1056.

[1747] In re Anthracite Trust Co., 154 Pa. Super. 553, 36 A.2d 727.

Where note to trust company recited that bond and mortgage given as collateral security for note also secured maker's other liabilities to company, but bond and mortgage were drawn for only amount of note, and insurer paid such amount to secretary of banking, as trust company's receiver, construction of mortgaged property, maker was entitled to return of note, bond, and mortgage, marked paid, and to satisfaction of mortgage. In re Anthracite Trust Co., 154 Pa. Super. 553, 36 A.2d 727.

[1748] Holt v. Crean, 342 Mo. 755, 117 S.W.2d 355.

The sale of realty covered by trust deed which secured note among assets of a trust company under special execution based on a tax bill for improvement. was not invalid as

Upon the sale of bonds deposited with a third party by a trust company to counter-indemnity the indemnitor of a depositor, the trust company when in the hands of a state banking official, was held entitled to the surplus remaining after the satisfaction of the indemnitor's claim to the exclusion of preexisting separate indemnitors.[1749] A trust company in liquidation was held not liable to a director for his donation to a fund advanced by directors to enable the company to write off a large loan, since the donation was supported by consideration and became an asset, not a debt, of the company.[1750] But an insolvent trust company's guaranty of bonds sold was held valid despite the failure of its corporate articles to specify the maximum indebtedness or liability that the company could incur, as required by statute.[1751] If the holder of a mortgage participation certificate guaranteed by a trust company taken over by a banking commissioner for liquidation, accepts a deed from the mortgagor releasing the obligation on the bond without the commissioner's consent, the company's liability under the guaranty is terminated in whole or in part, and the commissioner has a lien on the premises for the amount expended by him in the administration of the property involved.[1752]

A nonresident mortgagor, contracting a mortgage with a state banking institution as beneficiary and trustee, is presumed to have contracted with reference to the laws of that state, and the jurisdiction and authority of its examiner of banks and its courts over such institution in the event of its insolvency and liquidation.[1753]

---

violative of statute, notwithstanding that tax bill suit was prosecuted to judgment by default after such notice had been posted, since tax bill suit was a suit in rem. Holt v. Crean, 342 Mo. 755, 117 S.W.2d 355.

Such sale was not invalid under statute providing that no lien shall attach to property or assets of closed bank in hands of commissioner by reason of entry of judgment recovered against bank after commissioner baa taken possession, notwithstanding that judgment in tax bill suit was not entered until after commissioner had taken possession of trust company, where tax bill was issued before the commissioner took charge of the trust company, since lien of tax bill did not attach when tax bill suit went to judgment, but when the tax bill was issued. Holt v. Crean, 342 Mo. 755, 117 S.W.2d 355.

[1749] National Surety Co. v. Franklin Trust Co., 313 Pa. 501, 170 A. 683, 95 A.L.R. 300.

[1750] Leary v. Capitol Trust Co., 238 App. Div. 661, 265 N.Y.S. 856, aff'd, 263 N.Y. 640, 189 N.E. 735.

[1751] Dorman v. Bankers' Trust Co.'s Receiver, 259 Ky. 430, 82 S.W.2d 494.

[1752] Kelly v. Middlesex Title Guarantee, etc., Co., 116 N.J. Eq. 228, 172 A. 487.

[1753] **In general.—**

Enochs v. Mississippi Tower Bldg., 210 Miss. 676, 50 So. 2d 551 (Louisiana institution).

An administrative review process for claims against failed banks for which the Federal Deposit Insurance Corporation (FDIC) had been appointed as receiver was established by Congress in the Financial Institutions Reform, Recovery, and Enforcement Act of 1989 (FIRREA).[1754] As a receiver for failed lending entities, Congress anticipated that the FDIC would face numerous claims from various parties, and, as a result, established limits on judicial review of such claims.[1755] Under FIRREA, a court will lack jurisdiction as to any claim or action for payment from the assets of any depository institution for which the FDIC has been appointed receiver.[1756]

The Federal Housing Finance Agency (FHFA) was established by the Housing and Economic Recovery Act of 2008 (Recovery Act), which authorized the FHFA to undertake extraordinary economic measures to resuscitate the Federal National Mortgage Association (Fannie Mae) and the Federal Home Loan Mortgage Corporation (Freddie Mac). The Recovery Act authorized the Director of FHFA to appoint FHFA as either conservator

---

Mortgagor in Mississippi, when contracting mortgage with banking institution of Louisiana as beneficiary and trustee, is presumed to recognize and contract with reference to laws of and jurisdiction of its state bank examiner and court to provide for substitution of trustee to act in place and stead of insolvent banking institution in liquidation to collect assets for benefit of its creditors and stockholders. Enochs v. Mississippi Tower Bldg., 210 Miss. 676, 50 So. 2d 551.

Such mortgagor is presumed to recognize jurisdiction of Louisiana court to liquidate affairs of mortgagee, and to know that such jurisdiction and authority conferred by its laws will supersede any authority vested by mortgage in beneficiary and trustee in event of insolvency and liquidation. Enochs v. Mississippi Tower Bldg., 210 Miss. 676, 50 So. 2d 551.

Where Louisiana court in which liquidation of bank, nominated as trustee and beneficiary under bond mortgage, was being administered and in which situs of bonds and mortgage was located forbade trustee when insolvent to act in such capacity, trustee was required to obey and was incapacitated and unable to act under the mortgage. Enochs v. Mississippi Tower Bldg., 210 Miss. 676, 50 So. 2d 551.

Where Louisiana trust company was designated beneficiary and trustee under bond mortgage, and trust company thereafter became insolvent, and court, of perish in which liquidation was being administered and in which was located situs of bonds, prohibited trust company from acting as trustee under the mortgage, trustee could not thereafter act contrary to the mandate unless and until order was vacated. Enochs v. Mississippi Tower Bldg., 210 Miss. 676, 50 So. 2d 551.

[1754] Douglas County v. Hamilton State Bank, 340 Ga. App. 801, 798 S.E.2d 509 (2017).

[1755] Douglas County v. Hamilton State Bank, 340 Ga. App. 801, 798 S.E.2d 509 (2017).

[1756] Douglas County v. Hamilton State Bank, 340 Ga. App. 801, 798 S.E.2d 509 (2017).

or receiver for Fannie Mae and Freddie Mac for the purpose of reorganizing, rehabilitating, or winding up their affairs, and invests FHFA as conservator with broad authority and discretion over the operation of Fannie and Freddie.[1757]

The Recovery Act separately granted the Treasury Department temporary authority to purchase any obligations and other securities issued by Fannie and Freddie. That provision made it possible for Treasury to buy large amounts of Fannie and Freddie stock, and thereby infuse them with massive amounts of capital to ensure their continued liquidity and stability. Continuing Congress's concern for protecting the public interest, however, the Recovery Act conditioned such purchases on Treasury's specific determination that the terms of the purchase would protect the taxpayer, and to that end specifically authorized limitations on the payment of dividends. A sunset provision terminated Treasury's authority to purchase such securities after December 31, 2009. After that, Treasury was authorized only to hold, exercise any rights received in connection with, or sell, any obligations or securities purchased.[1758]

In 2008, concerned that a default by the Federal National Mortgage Association (Fannie Mae) and the Federal Home Loan Mortgage Corporation (Freddie Mac) would imperil the already fragile national economy, Congress enacted the Housing and Economic Recovery Act (Recovery Act), which established the Federal Housing Finance Agency (FHFA) and authorized it to undertake extraordinary economic measures to resuscitate the companies.[1759] The Recovery Act denominated Fannie and Freddie "regulated entities" subject to the direct supervision of the FHFA and the general regulatory authority of FHFA's director, who is charged with overseeing the prudential operations of Fannie Mae and Freddie Mac and ensuring that they operate in a safe and sound manner consistent with the public interest.[1760]

The Dodd-Frank Wall Street Reform and Consumer Protection Act[1761] was the first comprehensive effort to address the problems in the system that led—in sequence—to the subprime crisis, the housing crisis, and the

---

1757 Perry Capital LLC ex rel. Inv. Funds v. Mnuchin, 864 F.3d 591 (D.C. Cir. 2017).

1758 Perry Capital LLC ex rel. Inv. Funds v. Mnuchin, 864 F.3d 591 (D.C. Cir. 2017).

1759 Perry Capital LLC ex rel. Inv. Funds v. Mnuchin, 864 F.3d 591 (D.C. Cir. 2017).

1760 Perry Capital LLC ex rel. Inv. Funds v. Mnuchin, 864 F.3d 591 (D.C. Cir. 2017).

1761 12 U.S.C.S. § 25b.

financial crisisis.[1762] Nevertheless, according to one commentator, the extensive legislation contained in Dodd-Frank "deliberately did not deal with the biggest elephant (or perhaps elephants) in the room: Fannie Mae and Freddie Mac" and noted that "these government sponsored enterprises, behemoths of the secondary mortgage market" were in conservatorship and cost taxpayers over $ 130 billion, and yet, the current residential mortgage market was utterly dependent upon them for credit and liquidity.[1763]

§ 39. Rights, Powers, Duties and Liabilities of State Banking Officials.

State Banking Officials in General.—When a state banking official takes possession of the property and business of a trust company he becomes vested with title to and right of possession of, its property and assets, as liquidating agent primarily for the benefit of its creditors.[1764]

[1762] **Law Review.**—

Financial Reform Too Big To Fail? Emerging from the Financial Crisis with the Help of Increased Consumer Protection and Corporate Responsibility: Article: Laudable Goals and Unintended Consequences: The Role and Control of Fannie Mae and Freddie Mac, see 60 Am. U.L. Rev. 1489 (June 2011).

See also "Government Regulator Sues Wall Street Banks For Fraud in Subprime Mortgage Deals," https://www.huffingtonpost.com/2011/09/02/banks-sued-subprime-mortgage-deals_n_947349.html.

[1763] **Law Review.**—

"Financial Reform Too Big To Fail? Emerging from the Financial Crisis with the Help of Increased Consumer Protection and Corporate Responsibility: Article: Laudable Goals And Unintended Consequences: The Role and Control of Fannie Mae And Freddie Mac," see 60 Am. U.L. Rev. 1489 (June 2011).

[1764] **In general.**—

In re Citizens' Sav. & Trust Co., 171 Wis. 601, 177 N.W. 905.

In liquidation proceeding of trust company, commissioner of finance held trust company's assets for the benefit of depositors and other creditors. In re West St. Louis Trust Co., 347 Mo. 139, 146 S.W.2d 612.

Under Trust Company Act, liquidator shall be vested with full and exclusive power of control and may exercise any power thereof including right to reject any claim if he or she determines invalidity thereof and right to determine amount, if any, owing to each creditor, and priority class of its claim under the act. Summit Trust Servs. v. Snyder, 936 P.2d 628 (Colo. App. 1997).

Statute creating mortgage commission held to authorize commission to receive assets of insolvent trust companies held in course of administration by superintendent of banks notwithstanding error in section regarding manner in which superintendent of banks became possessed of property of insolvent companies or in directions as to filing notices. Hutchinson v. Nassau County Trust Co., 283 N.Y.S. 257.

Such an official may, therefore, bring an action for instructions essential to a correct distribution of a company's assets,[1765] but he may not petition a court for instructions in order to obtain approval of an action that he is required by statute to take on his own responsibility.[1766] And the discretion of such an officer in managing a company's affairs cannot be controlled or

---

In District of Columbia comptroller of currency has same power to take possession of trust company as to take possession of national bank, and he may take all necessary steps in liquidation of its affairs. Dunn v O'Connor, 89 F.2d 820.

Colorado.—Trust Company Act provides for broad delegation to liquidator of discretionary powers of the Colorado State Bank commissioner. Summit Trust Servs. v. Snyder, 936 P.2d 623 (Colo. App. 1997).

Conflict of laws rule.—

Mortgagor in Mississippi, when contracting mortgage with banking institution of Louisiana as beneficiary and trustee, is presumed to do so in recognition of authority conferred by statute on Louisiana state bank examiner to take possession of property and affairs of trustee in event of its insolvency and liquidation, and to take steps necessary to conserve its assets. Enochs v. Mississippi Tower Bldg., 210 Miss. 676, 50 So. 2d 551.

Assets not in custody of court.—

Assets of trust company in hands of commissioner of banks of Massachusetts are not in custody of state court. MacDonald v. Guy, 63 F.2d 334.

Res of void trust.—

Where trust company purportedly created trust out of its own assets by transferring real estate which it owned to itself as trustee and selling land trust certificates of equitable ownership to the public, and trust company thereafter became insolvent, the trust res, in event that the trust were declared void would finally rest in superintendent of banks as liquidator. Alburn v. Union Trust Co. (C.P.), 38 Ohio Op. 450, 80 N.E.2d 721, appeal dismissed, 150 Ohio St. 357, 82 N.E.2d 543, cert. denied, 336 U.S. 937, 69 S. Ct. 747, 93 L. Ed. 1096.

Notice to "persons" and "creditors" of bank taken possession of by banking commissioner was held to include state's claim for excise taxes from trust company in process of liquidation by banking commissioner. Commissioner of Banks v. Highland Trust Co., 283 Mass. 71, 186 N.E. 229.

Proceeds of stockholders' liability coming into possession of conservator of trust company being liquidated, although not assets of corporation in legal sense, together with proceeds of assets, make up fund for benefit of creditors. Cooper v. Fidelity Trust Co., 132 Me. 260, 170 A. 726.

Protection of possession of collateral.—

Even if trust agreement under which trust company delivered collateral as security for bonds issued by it made no provision for trust company's insolvency, trustees' possession of collateral would be protected. Wilson v. Louisville Trust Co., 242 Ky. 432, 46 S.W.2d 767.

[1765] In re Prudential Trust Co., 244 Mass. 64, 138 N.E. 702.

[1766] In re Cosmopolitan Trust Co., 240 Mass. 254, 133 N.E. 630.

overridden by a court unless manifestly abused.[1767] So where a trust company, in violation of statute, pledges securities of its savings department for the benefit of its commercial department, and a state banking official, after taking charge of the company, permits them to be sold, it is his duty to restore their equivalent in money to the savings department.[1768] While such an official is clothed with some of the powers of a receiver, he is not one,[1769] being more of an administrative than a judicial officer.[1770] And such official may take into his possession any trust property held by a trust company,[1771]

1767 **In general.—**

Bieringer-Hanauer Co. v. Cosmopolitan Trust Co., 247 Mass. 73, 141 N.E. 566.

Payment of debts.—

A court of chancery is without jurisdiction, in summary proceedings by creditor, to compel commissioner of banking in possession of trust company, to pay debts. United States v. Singac Trust Co., 112 N.J. Eq. 448, 164 A. 702.

Ratification of act.—

When the commissioner of banking had taken control of an insolvent trust company, it was for him to determine whether the interests of creditor and stockholders required ratification of the treasurer's previous act in honoring checks in reliance on a note held by him but not turned over to the directors, and by assigning the note he ratified the treasurer's act. Mutual Bank v. Smith, 99 N.J.L. 13, 123 A. 98.

1768 In re Cosmopolitan Trust Co., 240 Mass. 254, 133 N.E. 630.

1769 Commissioner of Banks v. Highland Trust Co., 283 Miss. 71, 186 N.E. 229; MacDonald v. Guy, 63 F.2d 334.

The state superintendent of banks taking possession of the assets and property of a trust company for purposes of liquidation, may sue and be sued in effect as a receiver. In re Carnegie Trust Co., 161 App. Div. 280, 146 N.Y.S. 809; Roseville Trust Co. v. Barney, 89 N.J.L. 550, 99 A. 343.

1770 Allen v. Prudential Trust Co., 242 Mass. 78, 136 N.E. 410; Cosmopolitan Trust Co. v. S. L. Agoos Tanning Co., 246 Mass. 69, 189 N.E. 306.

Commissioner of banks acts as public officer and not as receiver appointed by court. Commonwealth v. Allen, 240 Mass. 244, 133 N.E. 625; Framingham v. Allen, 240 Mass. 253, 133 N.E. 629; Allen v. Prudential Trust Co., 242 Mass. 78, 136 N.E. 410.

1771 **In general.—**

Power v. Amos, 94 Fla. 411, 114 So. 364 (1927), holding that Florida statute is not exclusive.

A statute is exclusive, however, which provides for a preliminary determination regarding trust funds in hands of secretary of banking. Cameron v. Carnegie Trust Co., 292 Pa. 114, 140 A. 768.

The commissioner of banking is not liable to file an account as guardian of a minor, where there is no record of any account in the books of the company or of any fund received or invested by it as guardian of the minor. Shaubach v. Morrison, 82 Pa. Super. 497.

but he is not authorized to administer trusts as the successor in trust of an insolvent company, since his duty is to wind up its affairs.[1772] However, if the trust beneficiaries fail to do so, he should apply for appointment of a new trustee.[1773]

[1772] **In general.—**

Sullivan v. Kuolt, 156 Wis. 72, 145 N.W. 210; State ex rel. Banister v. Cantley, 330 Mo. 943, 52 S.W.2d 397; State v. Cleveland Trust Co., 58 Ohio App. 16, 11 Ohio Op. 420, 15 N.E.2d 640.

A state officer who acts as receiver, or liquidating agent for an insolvent trust company, is not a trustee for, or representative of, bondholders secured by a trust indenture in which the company is named trustee, and is a mere custodian or conservator of the trust assets. Pouncey v. Fidelity Nat. Bank, etc., Co., 85 F.2d 486.

Where custody of corpus of trust and duty of accounting therefor is taken, by operation of law, from a trust company acting as executor of an estate, all the powers of the trust company as such trustee must cease and the trust company can no longer sue or be sued with reference to claims against the trust estate. State v. Cleveland Trust Co., 58 Ohio App. 16, 11 Ohio Op 420, 15 N.E.2d 640.

Power of sale.—

State bank examiner, as liquidating agent of trust company, could not exercise power of sale in trust deed, held by bank as trustee. Mitchell v. Shuford, 200 N.C. 321, 156 S.E. 513.

Allowance or rejection of claims.—

The superintendent of banks in possession of trust company acting as executor of estate could not allow or reject claims against estate, and, therefore, any statute of limitations relating either to the presentment of a claim to the executor or the bringing of suit against the executor on the claim was tolled and inoperative against the superintendent of banks. State v. Cleveland Trust Co., 58 Ohio App. 16, 11 Ohio Op. 420, 15 N.E.2d 640.

[1773] **In general.—**

Sullivan v. Kuolt, 156 Wis. 72, 145 N.W. 210.

In receivership proceeding against trust company, trustee under mortgage, court had jurisdiction to appoint successor trustee upon constructive notice to interested parties. Wallace v. Guaranty Trust Co., 259 Mich. 342, 243 N.W. 49.

No duty to account to successor.—

Upon insolvency of a banking and trust company and appointment of superintendent of banks as liquidator thereof, the fiduciary office of trustee of express trusts does not descend upon liquidator but becomes and remains vacant until a successor trustee is duly appointed and qualified. And the superintendent could not be compelled, by an action for an equitable accounting, to account to a successor trustee for acts of the company. National City Bank v. Guardian Trust Co., 137 Ohio St. 279, 18 Ohio Op. 42, 28 N.E.2d 763.

Error to appoint successor.—

Removal of liquidator-trustee of trust company, whose tenant held possession of valuable trust estate upon which mortgage given to trust company to secure bond issue had been foreclosed, and appointment of successor trustee and receiver, held error, in absence of

All claims against a trust company in liquidation should be established by and before the state banking official in possession of its property and business.[1774] He has the authority to determine the necessity of enforcing stockholders' statutory liability and to bring an action thereon,[1775] and as the representative of an insolvent company's creditors, he will protect available funds by setting up defenses to adverse claims.[1776] However, if such official is specifically authorized by statute to sue in the delinquent company's name, he has no legal capacity to sue in his own name for debts due the company.[1777]

It has been held that a state banking official taking possession of the property and assets of a trust company for liquidation cannot abandon burdensome contracts or assets.[1778] But it also has been held that an official taking such possession does not thereby accept a burdensome lease, and is merely liable for the rent accruing while he holds the premises in the transaction of his duties,[1779] a liability which he can terminate by assigning the lease and relinquishing possession of the property.[1780]

---

showing of fraud or mismanagement by liquidator trustee. Smith v. Jones, 120 Fla. 237, 162 So. 496.

1774 Cosmopolitan Trust Co. v. Suffolk Knitting Mills, 247 Mass. 530, 143 N.E. 138 (1924).

1775 Cosmopolitan Trust Co. v. Cohen, 244 Mass. 128, 138 N.E. 711.

Under the District of Columbia statute comptroller may make assessment. against trust company stockholders and enforce their personal liability. Dunn v. O'Connor, 89 F.2d 820.

1776 Appeal of Cameron, 91 Pa. Super. 495, rev'd on other grounds sub nom. Cameron v. Carnegie Trust Co., 292 Pa. 114, 140 A. 768; Perkins v. Fuquay, 106 Fla. 405, 143 So. 323.

1777 Van Tuyl v. New York Real Estate Security Co., 153 App. Div. 409, 138 N.Y.S. 541, aff'd, Carnegie Trust Co. v. New York Real Estate Security Co., 207 N.Y. 691, 101 N.E. 1096.

The commissioner of banking who had taken charge of trust company was entitled to maintain suit on notes held by trust company in name of trust company. Jefferson Trust Co. v. Ginsberg, 118 N.J.L. 496, 193 A. 794.

1778 Baldwin v. Commissioner of Banks, 283 Mass. 423, 186 N.E. 638, 89 A.L.R. 1212, wherein the rule was applied to render the savings department of a trust company owning stock in a national bank being liquidated liable to stockholder's assessment, notwithstanding trust company was in possession of commissioner of banks for purpose of liquidation.

1779 **In general.—**

Citizens Sav. & Trust Co. v. Rogers, 162 Wis. 216, 155 N.W. 155; In re Citizens' Sav., etc., Co., 171 Wis. 601, 177 N.W. 905.

It has been held that the rent stipulated in the lease is the proper measure of his liability,

In the appended note are set out cases illustrative of the extent of the miscellaneous powers and duties of state banking officials in this context.[1781]

---

and that no official act of his can defeat this obligation. In re Citizens' Sav., etc., Co., 171 Wis. 601, 177 N.W. 905.

See Towle v. Commissioner of Banks, 246 Mass. 161, 140 N.E. 747.

Renewal rate applicable.—

A mortgagee in possession of premises under clause giving him right to enter and collect rentals on default could recover for use and occupation of premises by secretary of banking as receiver for tenant at renewal rate provided in lease. Pennsylvania Co. for Ins. on Lives, etc. v. Harr, 320 Pa. 523, 183 A. 37.

Owner's notice of acceleration of whole rent for term after secretary of banking, as receiver, took over tenant trust company, would not estop owner from withdrawing notice and presenting claim against secretary for secretary's use and occupation of premises at renewal rate provided in lease, where secretary had not relied to his prejudice on notice. Pennsylvania Co. for Ins. on Lives, etc. v. Harr, 320 Pa. 523, 188 A. 37.

[1780] In re Citizens' Sav., etc., Co., 171 Wis. 601, 177 N.W. 905.

[1781] Temporary management of affairs of company.—When superintendent of banks took over trust company in liquidation, company was not finally divested of its property but the ordinary functions of its managers were suspended, and in the meanwhile the superintendent acted in their stead, merely managing temporarily the affairs of the company. Leal v. Westchester Trust Co., 279 N.Y. 25, 17 N.E.2d 673.

Completion of undertaking or continuation of employments.—

The superintendent of banks, as liquidator of trust company, is not obliged to terminate all activities immediately upon his appointment, close the bank and end all contract, or obligations, but may, in the exercise of good judgment, complete certain undertakings or continue certain employments to conserve the assets and bring about the best results for creditors. Leal v. Westchester Trust Co., 270 N.Y. 25, 17 N.E.2d 873.

Sale of assets.—

In liquidation proceeding it was the duty of the commissioner of finance and that of the circuit court to attempt to secure the highest price reasonably obtainable for the assets of trust company in possession of the commissioner to the end that the depositors and creditors might secure as large a percentage as possible on the claims. In re West St. Louis Trust Co., 347 Mo. 139, 146 S.W.2d 612.

Where court in liquidation of trust company authorized sale of lot by commissioner of finance for $1, 400 and before entering into binding contract commissioner received second offer of $2, 500, and sought new order to sell, court during term in which first order was entered, and after notice to first offerer and hearing, had jurisdiction to enter new order vacating first order and authorizing sale to second offerer on ground that mistake had been made in authorizing sale for $1, 400 when more could be obtained. In re West St. Louis Trust Co., 347 Mo. 139, 146 S.W.2d 612.

Exchange of collateral.—

Commissioner of banking and insurance had authority to surrender collateral held as security for loans by trust company and to receive in exchange other collateral, where

(*Text continued on page 495*)

---

exchange was to advantage of trust company and its creditors. Withers v. Mechanics Trust Co., 122 N.J. Eq. 413, 194 A. 148, 112 A.L.R. 471.

Buying at foreclosure sale.—

Banking commissioner taking over trust company which had guaranteed and sold mortgagee could at foreclosure sale bid in property for benefit of equitable owners and use in part payment amount due on decree. Kelly v. Middlesex Title Guarantee, etc., Co., 116 N.J. Eq. 228, 172 A. 487.

Where maker of note agreed to take title to mortgaged houses and complete them, in consideration of which mortgagee bank and trust company made loan and maker gave note for additional security for balance remaining due on loan to mortgagor with the mortgaged property as collateral, title to which was deeded to the mortgagee for that purpose, and the secretary of banking as receiver of mortgagee thereafter purchased mortgage at public sale, applying the proceeds to the reduction of the indebtedness of the maker of the note and subsequently sold the property deeded as collateral, the secretary of banking, as receiver, on selling mortgaged premises the equity in which was subject to mortgage he also held, was not required to apply the proceeds from the sale of mortgaged property in reduction of notemaker's indebtedness, but was entitled to apply the proceeds in liquidation of the mortgage owned by him in his own right. In re Olney Bank, etc., Co., 337 Pa. 357, 11 A.2d 150.

Taking conveyance of mortgaged premises.—

Banking commissioner taking over insolvent trust company which had guaranteed and sold mortgages could take conveyance of mortgaged premises from mortgagor, but, where conveyance was predicated on cancellation of bond and mortgage, commissioner should not accept conveyance without submitting matter to court, unless propriety of such arrangement unquestionably appeared. Kelly v. Middlesex Title Guarantee, etc., Co., 116 N.J. Eq. 228, 172 A. 487.

Resumption of business.—

Banking commissioner cannot burden the assets of trust company in his hands with obligations incurred for the purpose of resuming business Vigilante v. Old South Trust Co., 251 Mass. 385, 146 N.E. 670.

Duty of effectuating insurance.—

Banking commissioner taking over trust company had duty of effectuating insurance on premises covered by mortgages guaranteed by trust company, premium expense being payable in first instance out of general assets with commissioner being entitled to lien on income or principal of mortgage for reimbursement. Kelly v. Middlesex Title Guarantee, etc., Co., 116 N.J. Eq. 228, 172 A. 487.

Payment of taxes.—

Banking commissioner taking over insolvent trust company held not under duty to pay taxes against premises covered by mortgages guaranteed by trust company, but was under duty of notifying equitable owners in case of nonpayment of taxes. Kelly v. Middlesex Title Guarantee, etc., Co., 116 N.J. Eq. 228, 172 A. 487.

Where taxes, with interest and penalties, on properties owned, etc., by a trust company in liquidation approximated $703,505 payment by the banking commissioner under

(*Text continued on page 495*)

compromise with the city of $530,476 in foil settlement, was within his statutory authority to enter into compromises and settlements, and hence no action could be maintained against the commissioner by his successor based on a report by the governor charging misapplication of funds because some of the properties were allegedly not worth savings. In re New Jersey Title Guarantee & Trust Co., 136 N.J. Eq. 58, 40 A.2d 557.

Pooling income.—

Banking commissioner taking over insolvent trust company could pool in company's general assets income from bonds and mortgages wholly owned by company and income received from unassigned portion of partially assigned bonds and mortgages, but not income payable to assignees. Kelly v. Middlesex Title Guarantee, etc., Co., 116 N.J. Eq. 228, 172 A. 487.

Retention of interest collected on mortgages in pool.—

The secretary of banking, as receiver of closed trust company's mortgage pool, was not entitled to retain interest collected by him on some mortgages in pool which represented all the interest, advanced by trust company to holders of mortgage participation certificates, on other mortgages in default, but was bound to pay over amount collected to substituted trustee. In re Media-69th St. Trust Co., 329 Pa. 587, 197 A. 918, 115 A.L.R. 869.

The assertion of claims by secretary of banking, on his final accounting as receiver of closed trust company's trust mortgage pool after substituted trustee's appointment, for refund of interest collected by secretary on certain mortgages, unpaid interest on which trust company had advanced to holders of mortgage participation certificates, was premature. In re Media-69th St. Trust Co., 329 Pa. 587, 197 A. 918, 115 A.L.R. 869.

Possession of mortgage and bonds.—

Where trust company guaranteeing bonds and mortgages was entitled to retain one twelfth of interest as consideration, assignee held not entitled to possession of bonds and mortgages as against banking commissioner on trust company's insolvency. Kelly v. Middlesex Title Guarantee, etc., Co., 116 N.J. Eq. 228, 172 A. 487.

Release of liability.—

Where the superintendent of banks, on taking charge of a trust company, found certain securities which it held for petitioner, the superintendent had no right to exact, as a condition of delivering them, that petitioner execute a receipt releasing the trust company, such superintendent, and his deputy from liability for wrongful detention. In re Carnegie Trust Co., 162 App. Div. 76, 147 N.Y.S. 180.

Release of debtor's obligation.—

Secretary of banking as receiver of trust company would be required to procure court authority to release debtor's obligation to trust company on a bond secured by mortgage. Lancaster Trust Co. v. Engle, 337 Pa 176, 10 A.2d 381.

Release of interest.—

Banking commissioner taking over insolvent trust company which had guaranteed bonds and mortgages in consideration of right to retain one twelfth of interest could release right to interest in exchange for release of guaranty. Kelly v. Middlesex Title Guarantee, etc., Co., 116 N.J. Eq. 228, 172 A. 487.

Receivers in General.[1782]—A receiver appointed by a state banking official for a trust company takes title to the company's assets and affairs, and is charged with handling trust matters in the same manner as the original trustee.[1783] A receivership created under the Small Business Investment Act is governed by principles applicable to federal equitable receivers generally.[1784] A receiver takes over the assets of a trust company subject to all legal and equitable claims of others.[1785] However, a receiver of an insolvent trust company represents its stockholders and creditors; therefore, in such capacity he is authorized not only to collect its assets but to resist claims made by its alleged creditors.[1786] The receiver of a small business corporation is charged with responsibility for obtaining possession of assets of the corporation prior to its liquidation, and such responsibility includes bringing suit on any causes of action which the corporation has against its former directors, officers or majority shareholders.[1787] A court may authorize a receiver to foreclose a trust mortgage and preserve trust property during

---

[1782] As to receivers of banks, generally, see Chapter 6.

[1783] **In general.—**

Wasson Bond, etc., Co. v. Therrell, 113 Fla. 140, 151 So. 497.

Real property in another state.—

Receiver appointed by comptroller of currency for trust company incorporated in District of Columbia held not vested with title to real property of trust company in another state. Loudoun Nat'l Bank v. Continental Trust Co., 164 Va. 536, 180 S.E. 548, appeal dismissed, 297 U.S. 698, 56 S. Ct. 597, 80 L. Ed. 988.

[1784] United States v. Royal Bus. Funds Corp., 724 F.2d 12 (C.A.N.Y. 1983).

[1785] Terre Haute Trust Co. v. Scott, 94 Ind. App. 461, 181 N.E. 369; Rottger v. First-Merchants' Nat. Bank, 98 Ind. App. 139, 184 N.E. 267; Maryland Casualty Co. v. Rottger, 99 Ind. App. 485, 194 N.E. 365.

A solvent trust company's state court receiver, appointed at the instance of a creditor with an unliquidated claim, was not entitled to the proceeds of assets transferred to a national bank's receiver as a liquidating dividend in payment of the bank's stock in the company and allegedly converted, as a trust fund, until the establishment of the creditor's claim and the determination of whether the company was rendered insolvent by the distribution, and, if so, the receiver could recover only the amount which made the company insolvent and was needed to pay off unpaid creditors. Bancroft v. Taylor, 91 F.2d 579.

[1786] Dunn v. O'Connor, 89 F.2d 820.

Hence receiver of insolvent trust company was held to have right to contest claim of bank to money alleged to be due under contract whereby trust company undertook to turn over to bank its depositors and through that bank to liquidate its bills receivable. Dunn v. O'Connor, 89 F.2d 820.

[1787] Small Business Administration v. Segal, 383 F. Supp. 198 (D. Conn. 1974).

liquidation,[1788] and it may authorize to borrow money,[1789] but it has no jurisdiction to approve a change by a committee formed to protect holders of bonds issued by a company whereby a certain bank was designated a depository of the bonds.[1790] And the receiver of a savings and loan association was held bound to know that the association was not a commercial bank or trust company, and was unauthorized to receive trust funds for safekeeping for a depositor.[1791]

Conservators in General.—Under certain state statutes, a conservator appointed to liquidate a trust company is a ministerial officer of the courts, and subject to their direction and control.[1792] Such a conservator, in the absence of a statutory provision to the contrary, is governed by the general rules applicable to receivers of trust and banking companies.[1793] And a state banking official may authorize a conservator to borrow money and pledge a trust company's assets as security for the repayment thereof.[1794]

Upon appointment as conservator, the Federal Housing Finance Agency (FHFA), which is authorized by the Housing and Economic Recovery Act (Recovery Act) to undertake extraordinary economic measures to resuscitate (Fannie Mae) and the Federal Home Loan Mortgage Corporation (Freddie Mac), shall immediately succeed to all rights, titles, powers, and privileges of the regulated entity, and of any stockholder, officer, or director of such regulated entity with respect to the regulated entity and the assets of the regulated entity. In addition, the FHFA may take over the assets of and operate the regulated entity, and may preserve and conserve the assets and property of the regulated entity. The Recovery Act further invests the FHFA

[1788] Wallace v. Guaranty Trust Co., 259 Mich. 342, 243 N.W. 49.

[1789] Bassett v. Merchants' Trust Co., 115 Coax. 630, 161 A. 789, 82 A.L.R. 1223 (from Reconstruction Finance Corporation).

[1790] State ex rel. Landis v. Circuit Court of Eleventh Judicial Circuit, 106 Fla. 387, 143 So. 351.

[1791] In re Krueger's Estate, 173 Wash. 114, 21 P.2d 1030.

[1792] Cooper v. Fidelity Trust Co., 132 Me. 260, 170 A. 726 (Maine statute).

[1793] Robinson v. Fidelity Trust Co., 140 Me. 302, 37 A.2d 273; Cooper v. Fidelity Trust Co., 132 Me. 260, 170 A. 726.

[1794] In re Vervena, 54 R.I. 21, 169 A. 117.

State bank commissioner's order authorizing trust company's conservator to procure loan from Reconstruction Finance Corporation and transfer any assets in its savings or participation department as security therefor, authorized him to procure such loan for payment of dividends to saving, or participation depositors and pledge described securities, required by lender, as security. Petition of Vervena, 54 R.I. 21, 169 A. 117.

with expansive general powers, explaining that FHFA may, among other things, take such action as may be necessary to put the regulated entity in a sound and solvent condition and appropriate to carry on the business of the regulated entity and preserve and conserve its assets and property. FHFA's powers also include the discretion to transfer or sell any asset or liability of the regulated entity in default without any approval, assignment, or consent, and to disaffirm or repudiate certain contracts or leases. Consistent with Congress's mandate that FHFA's Director protect the public interest, the Recovery Act invested FHFA as conservator with the authority to exercise its statutory authority and any necessary "incidental powers" in the manner that the FHFA determines is in the best interests of the regulated entity or the Agency.[1795]

The Recovery Act sharply limits judicial review of FHFA's conservatorship activities, directing that no court may take any action to restrain or affect the exercise of powers or functions of the Agency as a conservator.[1796]

Liquidating Trustees.—See the footnote.[1797]

Deposit Required for Doing Business.—A superintendent of banks was held entitled to take possession of a fund required to be deposited for doing

---

[1795] Perry Capital LLC ex rel. Inv. Funds v. Mnuchin, 864 F.3d 591 (D.C. Cir. 2017).

[1796] Perry Capital LLC ex rel. Inv. Funds v. Mnuchin, 864 F.3d 591 (D.C. Cir. 2017).

[1797] **Payment of expenses.—**

Where liquidating trustees of insolvent trust companies were given power to compromise and take such other action and have such other powers as might in their judgment be necessary or proper for liquidating assets, with same power as if assets were owned by trustees in their own right, and controversy arose with heirs of trust companies' debtor, who had assigned large life policies to the trust companies, over payments of insurance, and payment of insured's hospital bill and burial expenses was expected to remove objection of heirs to payment of insurance proceeds to trustees, payment of those sums was within trustees' powers. United States Nat'l Bank v. Campbell, 354 Pa. 483, 47 A.2d 697.

Sale of bank building to trust company by trustee.—

See Behrman v. Egan, 17 N.J. Super. 598, 86 A.2d 606.

Renting property.—

Liquidator-trustee of trust company holding hotel property for benefit of bondholders during period of great depression in rents and real estate values, when property could not have been sold for price which would have been to interest of bondholders to accept, had duty of renting property to best possible advantage, since property had to be kept in repair and looked after, and some expenses had to be incurred by liquidator-trustee. Smith v. Jones, 120 Fla. 237, 162 So. 496.

business as a trust company, and to administer it with the other assets of a company.[1798]

Similarly, under one state statute, on the failure of any investment company required to deposit cash or securities with the state treasury, and the appointment of a receiver therefor, the receiver is required to use such deposit in liquidating the company's debts, but a court, after appointing the receiver, may not compel the comptroller to issue a warrant on the treasurer for the money and securities deposited before the adjudication of any debt against the company.[1799]

Estoppel.—Where for several years the president of a trust company executed on its behalf a guaranty of bonds sold and the company dissipated the sinking fund created for payment of the bonds, the banking commissioner was held estopped to deny the president's authority to execute the guaranty.[1800]

Attachment.—Where creditors of a foreign trust company which was in the hands of the banking commissioner of its home state, assigned their claims to a resident who attached assets of the trust company held by a domestic bank, the banking commissioner was accorded by comity the rights of an assignee under a voluntary assignment, and his rights were held superior to the attachment.[1801] But Virginia real estate owned by an insolvent trust company incorporated in the District of Columbia whose assets were being administered by a receiver, was held subject to attachment in a Virginia court by the trust company's Virginia creditors.[1802]

§ 40. Collection and Sale of Assets.

A receiver of an insolvent trust company is authorized to collect its assets and convert them into cash.[1803] And where a receiver has been appointed to

---

[1798] Huntington Nat. Bank v. Fulton, 49 Ohio App. 268, 1 Ohio Op. 71, 197 N.E. 204.

[1799] Ex parte Stephens, 100 Tex. 107, 94 S.W. 327 (Texas statute).

[1800] Dorman v. Bankers' Trust Co.'s Receiver, 259 Ky. 430, 82 S.W.2d 494.

[1801] Wulff v. Roseville Trust Co., 164 App. Div. 399, 149 N.Y.S. 683.

[1802] Loudoun Nat. Bank v. Continental Trust Co., 164 Va. 536, 180 S.E. 548, appeal dismissed, 297 U.S. 698, 56 S. Ct. 597, 80 L. Ed. 988.

[1803] Dunn v. O'Connor, 89 F.2d 820. As to expense of collecting assets, see § 50 of this chapter.

Reorganization trustee held authorized to dispose of securities deposited as security for collateral trust bonds issued by defunct trust company where trust agreement imposed duty of converting assets into cash, expert real estate man testified that price was fair and reasonable and that property would sell for less if sale was set aside and liquidation over

administer the estate of an insolvent loan company, it is his duty to collect securities deposited by the company with a trustee to secure its debentures.[1804] Similarly, assignees of an insolvent safe-deposit company have the power to sue for and recover assets of the company which it improperly disposed of.[1805] And receivers appointed by a state banking official for a trust company may sue for an amount erroneously allowed a debtor as an offset without awaiting the completion of liquidation.[1806]

Where a commissioner of banking in a foreign state sells the assets of an insolvent trust company to a corporation organized to take over its business, the purchasing corporation has the same right to recover assets of the insolvent trust company held by a domestic bank which had been attached by a domestic assignee of a trust company creditor as the commissioner would have.[1807] And where receivers for the property of a loan and investment association have been appointed in different states, and the receiver first appointed applies to a court in another state to have the funds there collected turned over to him for pro rata distribution among all members regardless of state lines, it is presumed that the court appointing him will apply the funds in that manner, and no pledge to that effect is required as a condition of turning the funds over to him.[1808] Transactions between a purchaser of notes and mortgages and an officer of a trust company which show an intention to sell and deliver such instruments, entitle such purchaser to principal and interest as against a claim of the company's receiver.[1809] A note is not paid by directing the application of an endorser's deposit and delivering the endorser's check on another bank for

long period would have entailed large expense without increasing net proceeds. Rubarts v. United States Trust Co., 257 Ky. 642, 78 S.W.2d 916.

Entire indebtedness on debentures was due and payable to Small Business Administration from licensed small business investment company, pursuant to federal regulation making entire indebtedness, of licenses issued to, held or guaranteed by SBA immediately due and payable to SBA whenever petition was filed in commencement of receivership, dissolution, or other similar creditor's rights proceeding. United States v. Vanguard Inv. Co., 694 F. Supp. 1219 (M.D.N.C. 1988).

1804 Girard Trust Co. v. McKinley-Lanning Loan, etc., Co., 135 F. 180 (Cir. Ct. E.D. Pa. 1905); Morrill v. American Reserve Bond Co., 151 F. 305.

1805 Pratt v. Short (N.Y.), 53 How. Prac. 506.

1806 Glidden v. Rines, 124 Me. 286, 128 A. 4.

1807 Wulff v. Roseville Trust Co., 164 App. Div. 399, 149 N.Y.S. 683.

1808 Smith v. Taggart, 87 F. 94.

1809 Crowder v. Sandusky, 91 Ind. App. 200, 170 N.E. 792.

the balance, in a state where there is a statute to the effect that a banking commissioner may accept only cash or its equivalent in payment therefor.[1810]

The Housing and Economic Recovery Act of 2008 (Recovery Act), which established the Federal Housing Finance Agency (FHFA) and authorized it to undertake extraordinary economic measures to resuscitate the Federal National Mortgage Association (Fannie Mae) and the Federal Home Loan Mortgage Corporation (Freddie Mac), including authorizing the director of the FHFA to appoint the FHFA as either conservator or receiver for Fannie and Freddie for the purpose of reorganizing, rehabilitating, or winding up their affairs,[1811] transfers some of the shareholders' rights to the FHFA during conservatorship and receivership and provides that others are retained by the shareholders during conservatorship but terminated during receivership. Specifically, the Act provides that as conservator or receiver, the FHFA shall by operation of law, immediately succeed to all rights, titles, powers, and privileges of the regulated entity, and of any stockholder with respect to the regulated entity and its assets.[1812] The Recovery Act further limits shareholders' rights during receivership by providing that the FHFA's appointment as receiver and consequent succession to the shareholders' rights terminates all rights and claims that the stockholders of the regulated entity may have against the assets or charter of the regulated entity or the FHFA except for their right to payment, resolution, or other satisfaction of their claims in the administrative claims process.[1813] The Recovery Act thereby transfers to the FHFA all claims a shareholder may bring derivatively on behalf of a company whilst claims a shareholder may lodge directly against the company are retained by the shareholder in conservatorship but terminated during receivership. The Act distinguishes between the transfer of rights with respect to the regulated entity and its assets in the succession clause and the termination of rights against the assets or charter of the regulated entity in the statute. Rights "with respect to" a company and its assets are only those an investor asserts derivatively on the company's behalf. Rights and claims "against the assets or charter of the regulated entity" are an investor's direct claims against and rights to the assets of the company once it is placed in receivership in order to be liquidated; that the

[1810] Cosmopolitan Trust Co. v. S. Vorenberg Co., 245 Mass. 317, 139 N.E. 482.

[1811] Perry Capital LLC ex rel. Inv. Funds v. Mnuchin, 864 F.3d 591 (D.C. Cir. 2017).

[1812] Perry Capital LLC ex rel. Inv. Funds v. Mnuchin, 864 F.3d 591 (D.C. Cir. 2017). See 12 U.S.C.S. § 4617(b)(2)(A)(i).

[1813] Perry Capital LLC ex rel. Inv. Funds v. Mnuchin, 864 F.3d 591 (D.C. Cir. 2017). See 12 U.S.C.S. § 4617(b)(2)(K)(i).

Recovery Act terminates such rights and claims in receivership indicates that shareholders' direct claims against and rights in the companies survive during conservatorship.[1814]

For other cases relating to the collection and sale of assets by receivers and similar officials, see the footnote.[1815]

§ 41. Distribution and Application of Assets, In General.

The equitable principle governing distribution of an insolvent's assets precludes an insolvent trust company from diverting to its own use a fund

---

[1814] Perry Capital LLC ex rel. Inv. Funds v. Mnuchin, 864 F.3d 591 (D.C. Cir. 2017).

[1815] **Resale of property.—**

Where intervener who made an oral contract with receivers of trust company for purchase of realty and entered in possession thereof, substantially failed to meet requirements of agreement, and committed waste, trial court did not abuse its discretion in dismissing intervener's petition praying for revocation of order authorizing receivers to resell realty and for cancellation of the deed issued in pursuance of such order. Application of Tobey, 141 Me. 296, 48 A.2d 776.

Proceeds of assigned insurance policies.—

Where bank, which controlled insolvent trust companies through direct or indirect stock ownership, supplied money through a subsidiary to make good impairments of insolvent trust companies, and insolvent trust companies assigned to subsidiary life policies held by them as security and executed instruments transferring policies with right to both parties to participate in insurance as their interests might appear, and without any promise to repay money advanced, instruments were "assignments," money supplied was not a "loan" and bank supplying money was not entitled to payment in full from proceeds of policies before liquidating trustees of insolvent trust companies received anything. United States Nat'l Bank v. Campbell, 354 Pa. 483, 47 A.2d 697.

The liquidating trustees were entitled to make prior charges against funds from policies on death of insured for sums paid as premiums on the policies both before and after assignments of the policies, and they were entitled to interest on premiums paid on the policies out of funds from the polities on death of insured. United States Nat. Bank v. Campbell, 354 Pa. 483, 47 A.2d 697.

The liquidating trustees were entitled to deduct from funds obtained on policies on death of insured, attorneys' fees paid by them in collecting the insurance. United States Nat'l Bank v. Campbell, 354 Pa. 483, 47 A.2d 697.

Construction of instruments.—

Where supplemental and collateral agreement between liquidators of trust company and purchaser of company's land were made part of order of district court authorizing execution of agreement, written instruments constituted part of same transaction and must all be construed together in determining intent and understanding of parties to deed. Singer v. Tatum, 251 Miss. 661, 171 So. 2d 134 (1965).

which it owes to creditors.[1816] Where state statutes regulate the final distribution of assets of insolvent trust companies, an insolvent trust company's assets must be distributed pursuant to such banking law.[1817] And the disposition of the assets of a trust company in accordance with a plan for reorganization filed in a liquidation action was held authorized by a statute relating to the powers and duties of a state superintendent of banks upon taking possession of a bank.[1818]

Proceeds from stockholders' liability on the stock of an insolvent trust company doing a banking business should be allocated in proportion to the allocation of capital stock between the company's trust and banking departments, and aside from statutory preference, such funds received by any department should be used in paying the general claims allowed in such department.[1819] But the assets of an insolvent trust company out of which statutory claims for items received for collection are payable do not include assets belonging to the trust or savings department of the insolvent,[1820] and all losses caused to the savings department by unlawful commingling of its assets with the general assets of a trust company must be made good out of the commercial department on the company's liquidation.[1821] Where a mutual investment and loan association, engaged in collecting money in small monthly installments from its members residing in various states and investing the same for their joint benefit, becomes insolvent, a contract is implied among its members that all its assets, after payment of debts due

---

[1816] In re Hatboro Trust Co.'s Case (Pa. C.P.), 57 Montg. 90.

Where a trust company sells participations in a mortgage pool and guarantees the payment of the principal and interest, and itself continues to own a part of the assets of the mortgage pool, and the assets constituting the pool have been definitely segregated and held as a separate trust apart from the general assets of the trust company, the trust company, upon its insolvency, does not have the right to participate with the certificate holders upon distribution of the assets, until certificate holders have been paid in full. In re Hatboro Trust Co.'s Case (Pa. C.P.), 57 Montg. 90.

[1817] Mann v. Bradford Sav. Bank & Trust Co., 71 Vt. 346, 45 A. 229.

The assets of an insolvent trust company which has been taken over by the superintendent of banks for liquidation must be distributed according to the state banking law. Alburn v. Union Trust Co. (C.P.), 38 Ohio Op. 450, 80 N.E.2d 721, appeal dismissed, 150 Ohio St. 357, 82 N.E.2d 543, cert. denied, 336 U.S. 937, 69 S. Ct. 747, 98 L. Ed. 1096.

[1818] Holmes v. Union Bank of Commerce, 79 Ohio App. 272, 73 N.E.2d 100, 35 Ohio Op. 22.

[1819] Reichert v. Fidelity Bank & Trust Co., 261 Mich. 107, 245 N.W. 808 (1932).

[1820] Reichert v. Fidelity Bank & Trust Co., 261 Mich. 107, 245 N.W. 808 (1932).

[1821] Baldwin v. Commissioner of Banks, 283 Mass. 423, 186 N.E. 638, 89 A.L.R. 1212.

nonmembers, shall be divided ratably among them according to their contributions to the common fund without reference to their place of residence.[1822] And directors who use their own funds to take over an investment disapproved by a state banking official, expecting to be paid from the profits, cannot be reimbursed from moneys otherwise applicable to the payment of depositors of a trust company in liquidation.[1823] But assignees of bonds guaranteed by a trust company which is taken over by a state banking official for liquidation, need not elect to retain their assigned interests and release their claim under the company's guaranty, or surrender such interests and file a claim under the guaranty.[1824]

A preference by an insolvent trust company was not unlawful at common law,[1825] nor are such preferences prohibited by the federal Bankruptcy Act.[1826] And a transfer of bonds by a trust company to secure a deposit of public funds was held not an illegal preference in contemplation of insolvency, where there was actual delivery of the bonds and neither party anticipated the trust company's insolvency.[1827]

§ 42. Filing, Presentment and Proof of Claims.

In General.—The time for filing and presenting claims varies with particular state statutes; accordingly, in one state it is held that a claimant

---

[1822] Smith v. Taggart, 87 F. 94.

[1823] Leary v. Capitol Trust Co., 238 App. Div. 661, 265 N.Y.S. 856, aff'd, 263 N.Y. 640, 189 N.E. 735.

[1824] Kelly v. Middlesex Title Guarantee, etc., Co., 116 N.J. Eq. 228, 172 A. 487.

[1825] Salem Trust Co. v. Federal Nat. Bank, 11 F. Supp. 105, aff'd, 78 F.2d 407.

Transaction whereby trust company, to cover its overdraft of commercial account with national bank, executed note and pledged collateral, held not tainted with fraud merely because it resulted in a preference. Salem Trust Co. v. Federal Nat. Bank, 11 F. Supp. 105, aff'd, 78 F.2d 407.

In suit to set aside trust company's transfer of notes, mortgages, and other securities, which allegedly resulted in preference, whether officers of transferee bank knew that trust company was insolvent held immaterial, and it was not error to fall to determine the fact. Salem Trust Co. v. Federal Nat. Bank, 78 F.2d 407.

[1826] Cosmopolitan Trust Co. v. Agoos Tanning Co., 245 Mass. 69, 139 N.E. 806.

The Bankruptcy Act does not prohibit insolvent trust companies from granting a preference to one creditor, since by express provision banking businesses are excluded from the operation of the Act. Cosmopolitan Trust Co. v. S. L. Agoos Tanning Co., 245 Mass. 69, 139 N.E. 806.

[1827] Cameron v. Allegheny County Home, 287 Pa. 326, 135 A. 133, holding that delivery of bonds within four months before insolvency did not crest, suspicion that parties contemplated insolvency.

against an insolvent trust company in the hands of the secretary of banking should present his claim when the secretary's account is before a court,[1828] while in another it is held that the date the commissioner of banks takes possession of the property and business of a trust company is the date for adjusting the rights of parties and fixing the amounts due general creditors.[1829] But in general, a failure to file a claim or bring suit within the statutory period bars recovery.[1830] Thus, a claim of preference against the assets of the commercial department of an insolvent trust company in liquidation, which

---

[1828] *Pennsylvania.*—Cameron v. Carnegie Trust Co., 292 Pa. 114, 140 A. 768.

Petition, filed before trust company's receiver rendered account of proceeds of indemnity bond, for preference in distribution of such proceeds, was premature. In re Royersford Trust Co., 318 Pa. 81, 178 A. 26.

Legal effect of bond, indemnifying trust company against loss of money or securities held thereby as trustee, being to indemnify it against loss caused by dishonesty of its officers who misappropriated trust funds, proceeds of bond were part of trust company's general assets, and trust beneficiaries, being merely general creditors, were required to file their exceptions to its receiver's account of such proceeds within 30 days after filing thereof. In re Royersford Trust Co., 318 Pa. 81, 178 A. 26.

Beneficiaries of trust funds, misappropriated by trustee, were not entitled to specification in notice of filing of account of proceeds of indemnity bond by trustee's receiver that trust funds were listed therein. In re Royersford Trust Co., 318 Pa. 81, 178 A. 26.

[1829] *Massachusetts.*—Cosmopolitan Trust Co. v. Suffolk Knitting Mills, 247 Mass. 530, 143 N.E. 138 (1924); Cunningham v. Commissioner of Banks, 249 Mass. 401, 144 N.E. 447.

Liability of trust company on contract for purchase of foreign currency was properly computed as difference between contract price and value at current rate of exchange on date commissioner took possession, and not on subsequent date when commissioner notified plaintiffs to cancel contract. Gerold v. Cosmopolitan Trust Co., 245 Mass. 259, 139 N.E. 624.

[1830] **In general.—**

Bowersock Mills, etc., Co. v. Citizens' Trust Co. (Mo. App.), 298 S.W. 1049; Zuroff v. Westchester Trust Co., 273 N.Y. 200, 7 N.E.2d 100, 109 A.L.R.1401.

Lack of knowledge does not extend period.—

Where claim against insolvent trust company for loss sustained by estate, of which trust company was a coexecutor, by retention of stock in trust company owned by decedent, was not filed within time fixed by superintendent of banks for presenting claims, such claim was barred by limitations, though beneficiary had no knowledge of claim until filing of final account after expiration of time fixed for filing claims and superintendent of banks as liquidator of trust company had custody of records and books of estate. Otis v. Union Trust Co. (Ohio Prob.), 87 N.E.2d 701, aff'd, sub nom. In re Stafford's Estate (Ohio App.), 69 N.E.2d 208.

Fraud does not extend period.—

Discovery of facts, such as fraud, which are basis of claim against insolvent trust company, after expiration of statutory time for filing claims against trust company, does not

was based on an alleged fraud upon settlors of inter vivos trusts, was held too late when made approximately nine years after the appointment of the claimant as substitute trustee of the securities or investment pool of the company.[1831]

Where a trust company at the time of its closing had on deposit in its name, awaiting investment, cash of a trust estate of which it was trustee, a

---

extend time for filing such claims. Zuroff v. Westchester Trust Co., 273 N.Y. 200, 7 N.E.2d 100, 109 A.L.R. 1401.

Action against insolvent trust company by buyer of notes under alleged fraudulent representation was barred by failure to file claim with commissioner of finance in charge of trust company within statutory period, though fraud was not discovered until later and though action was in equity and no money judgment was sought. Neathery v. Wells-Hine Trust Co., 229 Mo. App. 87, 75 S.W.2d 83.

In action against trust company and state superintendent of banks as liquidator thereof to rescind purchase of mortgage participation certificates because of fraud, complaint should have been dismissed, on ground that plaintiff did not previously file claim with liquidator pursuant to statute. Zuroff v. Westchester Trust Co., 284 N.Y.S. 468.

Recoupment inapplicable.—

General creditors of trust company in liquidation had adequate and complete remedy at law under State Banking Act and were not entitled to protection under the doctrine of recoupment after they had failed to make timely claim with superintendent of banks as provided by the Banking Act. Alburn v. Union Trust Co.(Ohio C.P.), 80 N.E.2d 721, appeal dismissed, 150 Ohio St. 357, 82 N.E.2d 543, cert. denied, 336 U.S. 937, 69 S. Ct. 747, 93 L. Ed. 1096.

Unjust enrichment inapplicable.—

Where trust company purportedly created trust out of its own assets by transferring real estate which it owned to itself as trustee and selling land trust certificates of equitable ownership to the public, but the trust company thereafter became insolvent and the trust property was conveyed by superintendent of banks to a successor trustee, certificate holders who had failed to pursue remedy at law as general creditors and sought to hay, trust declared void were not entitled to relief under doctrine of unjust enrichment. Alburn v. Union Trust Co. (Ohio C.P.), 80 N.E.2d 721, appeal dismissed, 150 Ohio St. 357, 82 N.E.2d 543, cert. denied, 336 U.S. 937, 69 S. Ct. 747, 93 L. Ed. 1096.

Illustrative case.—

Where trust company purportedly created trust out of its own assets by transferring real estate which it owned to itself as trustee and selling land trust certificates of equitable ownership to the public, and trust company thereafter became insolvent, certificate holders were forever barred, both in law and in equity, by their failure to comply with statutory provisions with respect to filing of claims, from asserting claims as general creditors of the trust company in liquidation. Alburn v. Union Trust Co. (Ohio C.P.), 80 N.E2d 721, appeal dismissed, 150 Ohio St. 357, 82 N.E.2d 543, cert. denied, 336 U.S. 937, 69 S. Ct. 747, 93 L. Ed. 1096.

[1831] Appeal of Washington Union Trust Co., 350 Pa. 363, 39 A.2d 137.

beneficiary seeking to release the cash was required to file a claim.[1832] And a commonwealth must file its claim for excise taxes due from a trust company in the process of liquidation by state banking officials.[1833] But when a trust company which is the duly appointed guardian of a minor is placed in the hands of a receiver, it is not necessary for the minor or anyone representing him to present to the receiver a claim against the trust company arising out of its conduct as guardian.[1834]

Notice to Present Claim.—Under a New York statute the superintendent of banks is not required to mail a notice to present a claim to a creditor whose name does not appear as a creditor on the books of a trust company, and notice by publication is sufficient.[1835] And the same is true of the statute in Ohio.[1836]

Proof of Claim.—Claims of creditors of an insolvent trust company may be proven before the state banking official or liquidator, or be established by a suit at law or in equity against the company itself.[1837] An administratrix of an alleged depositor in a trust company for which a conservator had been appointed in order to provide an opportunity for reorganization, was held entitled to file her claim as a creditor in equity court and prove it in accordance with existing law, and require payment to the same extent as other similar depositors.[1838]

A company which failed to object to a receiver's factual description of a transaction by which the company's money market account was pledged as

---

[1832] In re Howell's Will, 237 App. Div. 56, 280 N.Y.S. 510.

[1833] Commissioner of Banks v. Highland Trust Co., 283 Mass. 71, 186 N.E. 229.

[1834] In re Guardianship of Estate of Smart, 32 Haw. 943.

[1835] Zuroff v. Westchester Trust Co., 273 N.Y. 200, 7 N.E.2d 100, 109 A.L.R. 1401.

[1836] Inland Properties Co. v. Union Properties (Ohio App.), 88 N.E.2d 409, appeal dismissed, 150 Ohio St. 490, 83 N.E.2d 69.

Where names of plaintiffs, whose claims were based on alleged fact that they were depositors of trust company taken over for liquidation, did not appear as creditors on books of trust company, no notice by mail that plaintiffs should file claims was required to be given plaintiffs by statute. Inland Properties Co. v. Union Properties (Ohio App.), 88 N.E.2d 409, appeal dismissed, 150 Ohio St. 490, 83 N.E.2d 69.

[1837] Twyman v. Smith, 119 Fla. 365, 161 So. 427.

Small Business Administration's appropriate avenue of recovery from licensed small business investment company that was to be dissolved with respect to equity holdings and evidence was to make claim before receiver in order that priority could properly be assessed. United States v. Vanguard Inv. Co., 694 F. Supp. 1219 (M.D.N.C. 1988).

[1838] Mauro v. Vervena, 58 R.I. 24, 190 A. 796.

collateral for a commercial loan to a second entity would be deemed to have admitted receiver's description of the transaction, for the purposes of Small Business Administration's claim of violation of federal regulation, where the court had ordered the company to make specific, written objections to those portions of the receiver's report to which it objected and had stated that any portion of the report and recommendation to which specific, written objections were not made would be deemed admitted.[1839]

§ 43. Allowable Claims.

In General.—The question of what claims are allowable is usually governed by statute,[1840] and is wholly separate from any consideration of preference or priority.[1841] For example, installments of rent are not debts of a trust company so as to be provable until actually due.[1842] And until the amount of a lien of attachment by trustee process has been judicially determined, it is not a cognizable claim.[1843] A purchaser of a foreign order can recover from the trust company issuing it at the rate of exchange prevailing on the day the company breached its contract by stopping payment on it.[1844] And where, by special agreement with its bondholders, an investment company has set aside a reserve fund out of which to pay its bonds as they mature, on its dissolution the bondholders are entitled to have the fund applied to their claims only.[1845] A ruling of a state banking official allowing claims filed with him must be confined to such transactions as were originally presented to him, and cannot include matters of which he was not reasonably apprised by the filing of a claim.[1846] In the appended notes are

---

[1839] United States v. Vanguard Inv. Co., 694 F. Supp. 1219 (M.D.N.C. 1988).

[1840] New York Security, etc., Co. v. Lombard Inv. Co., 73 F. 537.

[1841] Fisher v. Davis, 278 Pa. 129, 122 A. 224.

[1842] Towle v. Commissioner of Banks, 246 Mass. 161, 140 N.E. 747.

Claims for rent not more than contingent when commissioner took possession could not be proved so as to share in dividends ordered to be paid on claims existing when commissioner took possession. Towle v. Commissioner of Banks, 246 Mass. 161, 140 N.E. 747.

[1843] Wogan v. Tremont Trust Co., 242 Mass. 505, 136 N.E. 394.

[1844] Beecher v. Cosmopolitan Trust Co., 239 Mass. 48, 131 N.E. 338.

[1845] Fell v. Securities Co., 11 Del. Ch. 101, 97 A. 610.

[1846] Gilbert v. Cousins, 172 Wis. 513, 179 N.W. 811; Sharpe v. Cousins, 172 Wis. 509, 179 N.W. 810.

No claim against the assets of an insolvent trust company in liquidation by the commissioner of banking having been filed with the commissioner it could not properly be interposed in the complaint in an action at law by claimant after the commissioner had rejected the claim. Wisconsin Trust Co. v. Cousins, 172 Wis. 511, 179 N.W. 811.

found other cases relating to claims for rent,[1847] claims for counsel fees,[1848] and miscellaneous matters relating to allowance of claims in general.[1849]

[1847] **Rent claim not allowable.—**

Claim for rent for period between time of receivership and rejection of lease, which was authorized by court, held not allowable where receiver did not occupy premises during such period. People v. Equitable Trust Co., 287 Ill. App. 619, 4 N.E.2d 802, aff'd, 366 Ill. 465, 9 N.E.2d 234.

Appointment of conservator for trust company held not to give lessor an allowable claim against the estate of trust company for future rent due under lease, where conservator by order of court declined to assume lease as obligation of the estate, lease contained no provision for cancellation and no covenant for penalty or damages in event of receivership, and no statute creating such liability existed. Cooper v. Casco Mercantile Trust Co., 134 Me. 372, 186 A. 885, 111 A.L.R. 548.

[1848] **Counsel fees claim not allowable.—**

Counsel fees for opposing the transfer of funds from the commercial department to the savings department of a trust company are not allowable in equity, since they are a claim arising out of a legal controversy. Rothstein v. Commissioner of Banks, 258 Mass. 196, 155 N.E. 7.

Counsel fees were not allowable out of proceeds of liquidation of assets of commercial department of insolvent trust company to attorney for depositors who did not create or preserve the fund for the benefit of all interested in the estate in liquidation. Appeal of Washington Union Trust Co., 350 Pa. 363, 39 A.2d 137.

Where industrial banker filed voluntary petition for appointment of receiver and liquidation of his assets for benefit of creditors, temporary receiver was appointed, payee of note executed by banker delivered to temporary receiver the collateral securing the note and filed intervention claiming that banker was indebted to payee on the note, permanent receiver was appointed, payee amended intervention to demand return of collateral, payee demanded attorney's fees under provision in note requiring banker to pay fees if note "be collected by or through an attorney" and receiver paid full amount due on note, the payee's debt was not "collected by or through an attorney" but on the contrary the payee and his attorney sought to prevent receiver from paying claim on note by demanding return of collateral, and consequently payee could not recover attorney's fees. Strickland v. Williams, 215 Ga. 175, 109 S.E.2d 761.

Where industrial banker filed voluntary petition for appointment of receiver and liquidation of his assets for benefit of creditors, court order appointing temporary receiver enjoined the filing of any proceedings of whatever kind against banker or his property or assets, payee of banker's not. delivered to receiver the collateral assigned by banker to payee, and payee filed intervention and demanded possession of collateral, the prohibition of the statute and the injunction in the order prevented payee from asserting claim for the attorney's fees provided in note, based on notice given 60 days subsequent to appointment of receiver. Strickland v. Williams, 215 Ga. 175, 109 S.E.2d 761.

[1849] To allow beneficiary of trust to rescind self-dealing transaction on part of bank as trustee in purchasing worthless securities for such trust, and to participate as a creditor in distribution and liquidation of assets of bank on equality with creditors of other departments

Secured Claims.—In some states secured depositors and creditors are allowed to prove only the balance of their claims above the value of their security,[1850] but in other jurisdictions a different rule prevails.[1851]

Tax Claims.—A state may file and prove its claim for excise taxes against a trust company although it did not accrue until after liquidation proceedings began.[1852] And a receiver of a lessee trust company which had assumed certain taxes was held liable for taxes levied prior to his receivership, even though the amount thereof was not ascertainable at the time of his appointment but became ascertainable during his receivership.[1853]

§ 44. Payment or Disallowance of Claims.

A person making a withdrawal from a savings account in a trust company and receiving a treasurer's check before its reorganization was held entitled to full and immediate payment thereof.[1854]

Disallowance of a claim is equivalent to a final adjudication of a claimant's rights.[1855]

---

of the same bank, is not "unjust enrichment." In re Binder's Estate, 137 Ohio St. 26, 27 N.E.2d 939, 129 A.L.R. 130.

No recovery in absence of fraud.—

Where contract authorizing transfer of assets of state bank for purpose of liquidation to a national bank and a trust company provided that mortgage notes should be transferred to trust company, but certain of such notes were first transferred to national bank and were then delivered to trust company for their face value, creditors of trust company, upon insolvency of both trust company and national bank, were not entitled to recover difference between actual value and face value of note, from national bank, in absence of any fraud in connection with transfer. South Bend State Bank v. Department of Financial Institutions, 213 Ind. 396, 11 N.E.2d 689.

[1850] Banks Comm'rs v. Security Trust Co., 70 N.H. 536, 49 A. 113.

[1851] See chapter 6, § 158.

[1852] Commissioner of Banks v. Highland Trust Co., 283 Mass. 71, 186 N.E. 229.

[1853] People v. Equitable Trust Co., 287 Ill. App. 619, 4 N.E.2d 802, aff'd, 366 Ill. 465, 9 N.E.2d 234.

[1854] Orifice v. Elizabeth Trust Co., 116 N.J.L. 110, 183 A. 192, holding that such person was not required to accept percentage of claim in preferred stock under reorganization act and reorganization plan adopted thereunder.

Such person was not a "depositor" as to withdrawn amount who would be subject to postponement in payment under direction of commissioner of banking and insurance made after delivery of check but before presentment. Orifice v. Elizabeth Trust Co., 116 N.J.L. 110, 183 A. 192.

[1855] Orban v. Union Guardian Trust Co., 281 Mich. 644, 275 N.W. 662.

§ 45. Preferences and Secured Claims.

In General.—A sound and reasonable classification of preferred claimants of an insolvent trust company will be permitted.[1856] But the right to preferential payments should not be implied or extended beyond the purview of a controlling statute.[1857] Creditors of an insolvent investment company

---

Mortgagor who claimed a credit on trust mortgage in an amount alleged to have been improperly paid out by trustee trust company to remedy defective construction in erection of building on mortgaged premises but who took possession of building, rented it, paid interest on bonds, reduced part of the principal, and failed to appeal from disallowance of their claim against trustee in receivership, were not entitled to credit as against successor trustee, since disallowance of the claim was equivalent to a final adjudication of their rights. Orban v. Union Guardian Trust Co., 281 Mich. 644, 275 N.W. 662.

Under Trust Company Act, liquidator shall be vested with full and exclusive power of control and may exercise any power thereof, including right to reject any claim if he or she determines invalidity thereof and right to determine amount, if any, owing to each creditor, and priority class of its claim under the act. Summit Trust Servs., Inc. v. Snyder, 936 P.2d 623 (Colo. App. 1997).

[1856] First State Trust, etc., Bank v. Therrell, 103 Fla. 1136, 138 So. 733 (1932). See also § 46 of this chapter. As to validity of preferences by insolvent trust company, see § 41 of this chapter. As to amount which secured creditors may prove, see § 43 of this chapter.

Amended plan of distribution and liquidation filed by receiver-liquidator for closed, state-chartered trust company, which distinguished between claims of those for whom trust company was first and only custodian of retirement accounts and claims of those whose accounts were initially with predecessor custodial bank, provided fair and reasonable distribution of assets and did not violate Trust Company Act. Summit Trust Servs., Inc. v. Snyder, 936 P.2d 623 (Colo. App. 1997).

[1857] **In general.—**

Central Trust Co. v. Hanover Trust Co., 242 Mass. 265, 136 N.E. 336.

As to general test to determine right to preferential payment, see First State Trust & Sav. Bank v. Therrell, 103 Fla. 1136, 138 So. 733.

Statute inapplicable to voluntary trusts.—Statute exempting trust companies from giving bonds respecting trusts to which appointed trustees by court and giving preference to debts owing by them in fiduciary capacities on dissolution or insolvency held inapplicable to voluntary trusts. Frederick Iron & Steel Co. v. Page, 165 Md. 212, 166 A. 738.

Mortgagor and individual testamentary trustee held not entitled to preference of claims against insolvent trust company as trustee under mortgage and will for money deposited to pay interest on bonds secured by mortgage and uninvested corpus of testamentary trust estate; such trusts being voluntary. Frederick Iron & Steel Co. v. Page, 165 Md. 212, 166 A 738.

Statute inapplicable to involuntary constructive trusts.—Statute providing that liabilities of trust company in fiduciary capacity shall be preferred to all other debts or liabilities held inapplicable to involuntary constructive trusts. Frederick County Comm'rs v. Page, 163 Md. 619, 164 A. 182.

must be paid in full before stockholders are entitled to distribute anything among themselves as dividends.[1858] A trust creditor is not entitled merely because he is such, to a preference over the general creditors of an insolvent trust company.[1859] And where in a suit to establish a constructive trust, a depositor shows no equity superior to that of other ordinary depositors who have suffered through unsound methods of a trust company, he is entitled to no priority over them.[1860] Similarly, where a company changes a fiduciary obligation to an ordinary debt, a depositor with knowledge cannot on the company's insolvency obtain a preference.[1861] But where a national bank's

---

Words "fiduciary capacities" in statute respecting liabilities preferred in distribution of assets of trust company refer to fiduciary capacities specified in statute. County Comm'rs of Frederick County v. Page, 163 Md. 619, 164 A. 182.

[1858] **In general.—**

Taylor v. Spurway, 72 F.2d 97; Taylor v. Commonwealth, 119 Ky. 731, 75 S.W. 244, 25 Ky. L. Rptr. 374.

Bylaws not authorizing funds to be distributed as dividend, against creditors.—

Where an investment company's bylaws provided that a surplus fund, consisting of 5 percent of the weekly collections or dues, should be used or invested as the directors might elect for the beet interest of the company, and an expense fund, consisting of 10 percent of the weekly collections and dues and transfer fees, should be used for current and such other expenses as the directors might direct, such bylaws did not authorize the directors of the corporation, while insolvent, to distribute dividends from such funds as against creditors of the corporation. Taylor v. Spurway, 72 F.2d 97.

[1859] **In general.—**

Butler v. Commonwealth Trust Co., 343 Pa. 143, 22 A.2d 718.

The beneficiary of a private trust will be given no preference over the general creditors of the company. Madison Trust Co. v. Carnegie Trust Co., 167 App. Div. 4, 152 N.Y.S. 517, aff'd, 215 N.Y. 475, 109 N.E. 580.

No trust relationship.—

That the depositor of funds in trust company acted in capacity of trustee for such funds did not create "trust" relationship so as to entitle depositor to preference upon company's insolvency, since fact that a trustee deposits trust funds does not make depositary a "trustee." Union Guardian Trust Co. v. Emery, 292 Mich. 394, 290 N.W. 841.

Claim for money received as guardian and placed in common fund, held not entitled to preference. Wainwright Trust Co. v. Dulin, 67 Ind. App. 476, 119 N.E. 387.

Clerk of court depositing money paid into court in commercial department of trust company never establishing trust department, and not taking security, had no right of preference. Campbell v. Allen, 241 Mass. 262, 135 N.E. 139.

[1860] Yesner v. Commissioner of Banks, 252 Mass. 358, 148 N.E. 224; Central Automobile Tire Co. v. Commissioner of Banks, 252 Mass. 363, 148 N.E. 226.

[1861] In re Receivership of Security Trust Co., 30 Hawaii 343.

receiver and the stockholders of a trust company controlled by the bank, received such company's assets, abstracted them and converted them to their own use, such assets were impressed with a trust ex maleficio, creating a lien in favor of the trust company's receiver as its creditors' representative.[1862]

Claims arising from transactions with the trust department of a state bank and trust company, also maintaining commercial and savings departments, are preferred on its insolvency.[1863] But under some statutes, preferred claims arising out of actual or constructive trust relationships incident to the trust department of an insolvent trust company can share only in the assets allocated to the trust department.[1864] And it has also been said that unpaid portions of trust or preferred claims should share pro rata with general claims in the assets of the respective departments of an insolvent trust company.[1865]

Where the proceeds of collateral are insufficient to pay obligations secured thereby, creditors whose claims are on a parity share pro rata in such proceeds,[1866] but this is not true where claims are not on a parity.[1867]

1862 Taylor v. Spurway, 72 F.2d 97.

1863 Cocke v. Hood, 205 N.C. 832, 170 S.E. 637.

1864 **In general.—**

Reichert v. Fidelity Bank & Trust Co., 261 Mich. 107, 245 N.W. 808 (1932).

Such claim could share in other assets of insolvent, in addition to those allocated to trust department, in case the banking department of the insolvent should have assets left after paying all claims against such department in full. Reichert v. Fidelity Bank & Trust Co., 261 Mich. 107, 245 N.W. 808 (1932).

In fixing amount of such claim, in particular department of insolvent trust company, there should be included all trusts ex maleficio and otherwise as to which fund cannot be traced. Reichert v. Fidelity Bank & Trust Co., 261 Mich. 107, 245 N.W. 808 (1932).

1865 Reichert v. Fidelity Bank & Trust Co., 261 Mich. 107, 245 N.W. 808 (1932).

1866 In re Phillippi, 329 Pa. 581, 198 A. 16; In re North City Trust Co., 327 Pa. 356, 194 A. 395.

The mere relationship of assignor and assignee of collateral dose not confer right of priority in favor of assignee in distribution of insufficient collateral, and if, on liquidation of security, proceeds are insufficient to satisfy secured claims in full, all claimants share in the fund pro rata. In re Phillippi, 329 Pa. 581, 198 A. 16.

1867 In re North City Trust Co., 327 Pa. 356, 194 A. 395.

Where insolvent trust company had pledged to Federal Reserve Bank certain notes secured by insurance trust, rule that creditors on parity share pro rats in collateral did not apply, since right of Reserve Bank to collateral of trust was superior to that of trust company, or of any one claiming through it. In re North City Trust Co., 327 Pa. 356, 194 A. 395.

That notes pledged by insolvent trust company to Federal Reserve Bank were not

As between Depositors and Creditors.—In the absence of legislation preferring depositors over other general creditors of a trust company, no such preference exists on its insolvency.[1868] But public policy is in no way contravened by the preferring of depositors.[1869] Statutes giving a preference to depositors on the insolvency of a bank of issue or of deposit and discount, do not include a trust company expressly denied the right to engage in banking.[1870]

And a statute giving a preference to depositors in a trust company does not apply to an assignment for the benefit of creditors executed prior to its enactment.[1871] But if a statute unqualifiedly provides that depositors are to be preferred to creditors, all deposits of an insolvent trust company, whether in its savings or commercial department, should be treated alike and paid after payment of the expenses of settling its receivership, irrespective of any charter provision entitling trust depositors to a preference.[1872] Where a trust company's savings depositors are given a preference, they can only share with its general creditors in its commercial assets for the balance of their claims after deducting the assets, properties and rights specially appropriated for their security.[1873]

Depositors of a trust company are entitled to preference on its liquidation over a claim of a receiver of an insolvent national bank for the trust

---

accompanied into hands of Reserve Bank by collateral consisting of insurance trust, was immaterial as respects right of Reserve Bank to claim priority as to collateral, which was insufficient to satisfy all obligations, over trust company, or any one claiming through it. In re North City Trust Co., 327 Pa. 356, 194 A. 395.

[1868] In re Prudential Trust Co.'s Assignment, 223 Pa. 409, 72 A. 798; Lippitt v. Thames Loan & Trust Co., Co., 88 Conn. 185, 90 A. 369.

Depositors in the savings department of trust company are entitled to share in distribution of general assets in same way and to same extent as company's other creditors. Parent v. Rand, 88 N.H. 169, 185 A. 163.

Depositors of trust company held not entitled to priority to general assets of company over liquidated claims of holders of title guaranties, guaranteed bonds and mortgages, or guaranteed participation certificate. Kelly v. Middlesex Title Guarantee, etc., Co., 116 N.J. Eq. 228.172 A. 487.

[1869] In re Cameron, 287 Pa. 560, 135 A. 295, 58 A.L.R. 554, aff'd, 276 U.S. 592, 48 S. Ct. 212, 72 L. Ed. 721.

[1870] In re Prudential Trust Co., 223 Pa. 409, 72 A. 798.

[1871] In re Prudential Trust Co., 223 Pa. 409, 72 A. 798.

[1872] Lippitt v. Thames Loan & Trust Co., 88 Conn. 185, 90 A. 369.

[1873] Petitions of Allen, 241 Mass. 346, 136 N.E. 269.

company's liability as a stockholder.[1874] A Pennsylvania statute governing the distribution of a trust company's assets on liquidation includes only time depositors in a favored class with persons having accounts subject to immediate check.[1875] A deposit with a trust company as escrow agent with a stipulation for interest after sixty days was held not a preferred claim on the company's insolvency, where the deposit remained with the company over sixty days.[1876] For other cases holding claimants to be depositors or

---

[1874] In re Cameron, 287 Pa. 560, 135 A. 295, 58 A.L.R. 554, aff'd, 276 U.S. 592, 48 S. Ct. 212, 72 L. Ed. 721.

[1875] **In general.—**

Appeal of Metropolitan Life Ins. Co., 310 Pa. 17, 164 A. 715, 86 A.L.R. 1301.

Interest and installments of principal due on mortgages, collected by trust company as agent for assignee of mortgagee, held not "deposit" so as to constitute preferred claim on trust company's insolvency. Appeal of Metropolitan Life Ins. Co., 310 Pa. 17, 164 A. 715, 86 A.L.R. 1301.

Stockbrokers who gave trust company cash and received treasurer's check therefor were "general creditors" and not "depositors," as respects their right to preference when trust company was taken over by secretary of banking. In re Northern Cent. Trust Co., 314 Pa. 189, 171 A. 597.

Stockbrokers who gave cash to trust company and received treasurer's check therefor could not claim preference on theory that company's officials must have known that company was insolvent and in commingling of funds became trustee ex maleficio, where secretary of banking could have taken over trust company on any of nine grounds and record did not show that insolvency was ground for taking over trust company. In re Northern Cent. Trust Co., 314 Pa. 189, 171 A. 597.

Stockbrokers who, on Friday and Saturday, gave trust company cash and received treasurer's check therefor, held not entitled to preference against assets of trust company which was taken over by secretary of banking on following Monday, where money did not become part of demand deposit account which stockbroker, maintained with bank. In re Northern Cent. Trust Co., 314 Pa. 189, 171 A. 597.

Holder of certified check.—

Statute providing that, in distribution of funds of trust company in course of liquidation, bona fide holders for value of certified checks on trust company shall be treated as "depositors," does not make holder of such check "depositor" in sense that he can that his own check or draft be honored and charged against fund, until he has presented certified check for deposit to his account. Franklin Trust Co. v. Philadelphia, 111 Pa. Super. 158, 169 A. 452.

Building and loan association paying liens against mortgaged premises with proceeds of loan through trust company held not entitled to preferred claim against assets of closed trust company as a "depositor" under circumstances. In re Gordon, 121 Pa. Super. 597, 184 A. 311.

[1876] J. G. Kuehnle Co. v. Fulton, 45 Ohio App. 386, 187 N.E. 81.

creditors,[1877] and dealing with a depositor's preference over stockholders and depositary priority,[1878] see the footnotes.

As between Depositors.—Special deposits in a trust company are entitled to preference on its insolvency,[1879] but general deposits are not so entitled.[1880]

[1877] **Creditor status.—**

Where a purchaser pays over purchase money to a trust company, which is to insure the title and make settlement with the seller, and the trust company delivers its own check, drawn on itself to the seller, for the balance due him, and the seller through some inadvertence delays in depositing the check for collection until after the trust company has gone into the hands of a receiver, the holder of the check is a general creditor of the trust company, and is not entitled to preference as a depositor, or as the cestui que trust of a trust fund. Commonwealth v. Tradesmen's Trust Co., 61 Pa. Super. 137.

Depositor status.—

Where a loan by the Reconstruction Finance Corporation to an insolvent trust company to pay dividends to savings depositors is not fully paid out of pledged assets, the remaining portion of a segregated fund would be subject to a first charge for repayment in full, and the Corporation would also have recourse to all rights which savings depositors would otherwise have in and to general assets. Bassett v. Merchants' Trust Co., 115 Conn. 530, 161 A. 789, 82 A.L.R. 1223.

[1878] **Depositor entitled to preference over stockholders.—**

Where surplus would remain after liquidating agent converted insolvent trust company's assets into cash and paid all liquidation expense and allowed claims of savings depositors in full, depositor, indebted to savings department, held entitled, in preference to stockholders' claim to surplus, to receive from liquidating agent so much of interest on loan as depositor would not have had to pay had deposit been set off against debt. Parent v. Rand, 88 N.H. 169, 185 A. 163.

Depositary priority not surviving consolidation.—

Where five corporations had united in series of consolidations to form trust company in which receivership funds were deposited, and charters of three contained no provision for depositary priority, and the other two charters provided for preference under conditions in some respects materially different, there was no right of priority for depositary which survived consolidation so as to give receivers preference. Storrs v. Ghinger, 166 Md. 572, 171 A. 849.

[1879] **In general.—**

Clime v. Union Trust Co., 99 Ind. App. 296, 189 N.E. 643.

Deposit held special.—

Evidence held to show that deposit in trust company in name of board of directors of proposed new bank was special deposit, for which such directors were entitled to preference against trust company's assets after its insolvency. In re Central Trust Co. (Mo. App.), 68 S.W.2d 919.

Contract to hold moneys in special fund.—

Moneys represented by treasurer's checks, deposited with trust company pursuant to

It may be provided by statute that the assets of the savings department of a

---

agreement between depositor and trust company, whereby such funds should not be considered as deposits and should be held in a special fund and not commingled with other funds of trust company, constituted a "special deposit," and hence depositor was entitled to a preference on trust company's insolvency, although such moneys were in fact commingled with general funds of trust company. In re Wellston Trust Co. (Mo. App.), 136 S.W.2d 430.

1880 **In general.—**

Dunlop Sand, etc., Corp. v. Hospelhorn, 172 Md. 279, 191 A. 701.

Presumption that deposits are general.—

Where there was either express authorization on part of trust company to mingle deposits, agreements to pay interest for use of funds, issuance of certificates of deposit, authority to use funds as banker, or deposits made without any conditions as to segregating of funds, and in other cases conditions of deposit referred to deposits as trust funds providing for separation of account and also authorized use of funds in depositor-creditor relationship, such deposits were not "trust funds" so as to entitle depositors to preference upon company's insolvency, in view of presumption that such deposits were "general," in absence of proof that they were special. Union Guardian Trust Co. v. Emery, 292 Mich. 394, 290 N.W. 841.

Agreement to repay on six months' written notice.—

Where plaintiff deposited money with trust company in trust and trust company agreed to repay the principal sum on six months' written notice, in action of assumpsit on the contract instituted after company was forced to liquidate its affairs, judgment awarding plaintiff a preference in the distribution of the company's assets was improper, since plaintiff was only a common "creditor." Fortna v. Commonwealth Trust Co., 341 Pa. 138, 19 A.2d 57.

Appellant's deposit to indemnify surety on appeal bond held general deposit creating relation of debtor and creditor, and not special deposit entitling depositor to preference upon trust company's suspension and giving of new bond, where company was expressly authorized to commingle deposit with general funds and was required to pay interest thereon, though company agreed to safely keep deposit as trustee. Cline v. Union Trust Co., 99 Ind. App. 296, 189 N.E. 643.

Where agreements with trust company provided for payment of interest or issuance of interest-bearing certificates of deposit by trust company to depositors, such deposits were "general" and hence depositors were not entitled to preference upon company's insolvency, and fact that deposits were referred to as trust funds or that it was expressly provided that trustee perform certain functions did not result in making deposits "trust funds." Union Guardian Trust Co. v. Emery, 292 Mich. 394, 290 N.W. 841.

Deposit with trust department under agreement that trust company would allow interest thereon is conclusively presumed to be "general deposit," in absence of manifestation of intent that deposit should not be general. Dunlop Sand, etc., Corp. v. Hospelhorn, 172 Md. 279, 191 A. 701.

Where bondholders' committee which sought to bid on property in foreclosure proceeding deposited money with trust company which was trustee under mortgage and receiver under foreclosure proceeding, and it was understood that fund not only could be deposited with trust company but also that it could be deposited under agreement under which interest would be paid, deposit by committee with trust company resulted only in depositor-creditor

trust company shall be impressed with a trust for the benefit of its savings depositors, and cannot be used to satisfy debts of the commercial department.[1881] Such a provision does not deprive a savings depositor of his right under a company's charter to a lien prior to creditors upon all assets of the company, or the right to share ratably in the funds in the hands of a receiver,[1882] the

---

relationship, and hence no right to preference resulted on company's insolvency. Union Guardian Trust Co. v. Emery, 292 Mich. 394, 290 N.W. 841.

That trust company depositary was authorized to act both as trustee and as bank would not affect conclusion that deposit, on which it agreed to pay interest, created relation of debtor and creditor, if deposit was made with company in general corporate capacity, and not as trustee. Dunlop Sand, etc., Corp. v. Hospelhorn, 172 Md. 279, 191 A. 701.

Where agreement permitted funds deposited to be mingled by trust company and used in its business, such deposits were "general" and relationship was one of debtor and creditor, and hence depositors were not entitled to preference upon company's insolvency. Union Guardian Trust Co. v. Emery, 292 Mich. 394, 290 N.W. 841.

Where directors voluntarily contributed to a special bond account for purpose of taking up depredation in regular bond account of trust company under agreement that money was to be returned to them when depredation of regular bond account was made up, and trust company was later closed for liquidation, the amounts so contributed were not "special deposits" entitling directors to preferred claims against assets of defunct trust company. Thomson v. Holt, 345 Mo. 296, 132 S.W.2d 974.

1881 **In general.—**

United States v. People's Trust Co., 17 F.2d 437, rev'd on other grounds, 23 F.2d 381.

Securities and assets in savings department constitute trust property for benefit of depositors in that department until they are paid in full, which cannot be depleted to benefit depositors under contracts which could only be made by commercial department. Goldband v. Allen, 245 Mass. 143, 139 N.E. 834.

Inapplicable to rejected claims.—

The commissioner must reserve in the savings department an amount for the payment of unclaimed deposits, wholly or partly, according as other depositors are paid, but he need reserve no money to meet rejected claims on which action has not been brought within time. In re Prudential Trust Co., 244 Mass 64, 138 N.E. 702.

1882 Lippitt v. Thames Loan & Trust Co., 88 Conn. 185, 90 A. 369.

Under a statute which provides that a trust company, transacting the business of a savings bank, shall conduct the business as a separate department and be amenable to the laws governing savings banks, where a trust company authorized to do a general banking and savings bank business fails, and its assets consist of securities held for the benefit of depositors in the savings department, securities deposited with trustees to secure the payment of debenture bonds, and unpledged assets, the relation between the different classes of claimants of the funds in the hands of the assignee and the trust company is that of debtor and creditor, and the depositor in the savings department as well as the holders of debenture bonds are entitled to share with the unsecured creditors in the distribution of the unpledged assets as to so much of their claims as are not satisfied out of the special funds created for

result then being that savings depositors become both creditors and trust beneficiaries.[1883] And depositors in commercial and savings departments of trust companies are presumed to have become such with knowledge of the preferences for the benefit of savings depositors.[1884] As regards rights on insolvency, negotiable notes transferred to a savings department in good faith for good consideration are regarded as deposited with trustees to protect the savings depositors.[1885] And moneys derived from the liability of trust company stockholders must be applied first to the payment of savings depositors, but money collected from directors for negligence or mismanagement becomes part of a company's general assets, in which savings depositors have no preferential right. And assets of a savings department remaining after payment of the savings deposits become part of the company's general assets.[1886] But where a trust company as trustee of a fund deposits such fund in its savings department under the authority of a statute requiring trust companies or banks receiving savings deposits to organize a separate department for such purpose, a claimant to such fund is not entitled to a preference over other depositors in the savings department on the company's insolvency, since all funds therein are trust funds.[1887]

Mortgage Participation Certificates.—The holders of guaranteed mortgage participation certificates of a trust company have a preferential right to the specific bond and mortgage to the extent of their interests assigned to them respectively, and to a general contingent claim against the company on its insolvency for the full amount due and to become due on such interests.[1888] But whether the holders of certificates of participation in a mortgage pool issued by a trust company are entitled to payment of the

---

their benefit. Bank Comm'rs v. Security Trust Co., 75 N.H. 107, 71 A. 377.

1883 In re Prudential Trust Co., 244 Mass. 64, 138 N.E. 702.

As respects priority on the insolvency of a trust company, savings investment deposits, established by the trust company under rules providing far segregation of investment department's assets and for repayment of depositor, only out of such separate assets, held "special deposit" for specific purposes and to create trustee-cestui que trust relationship between trust company and depositor. Sindlinger v. Department of Financial institutions, 210 Ind. 83, 199 N.E. 715, 105 A.L.R. 501.

1884 In re Prudential Trust Co., 244 Mass. 64, 138 N.E. 702.

1885 Dole v. Chattabriga, 82 N.H. 396, 134 A. 347.

1886 In re Prudential Trust Co., 244 Mass. 64, 138 N.E. 702.

1887 Tucker v. New Hampshire Trust Co., 69 N.H. 187, 44 A. 927; Bank Comm'rs v. Security Trust Co., 70 N.H. 536, 49 A. 113.

1888 **In general.—**

Kelly v Middlesex Title Guarantee, etc., Co., 116 N.J. Eq. 228, 172 A. 487, holding that

principal in full with interest after the insolvency of the company, before any payment is made to the holders of certificates issued by a receiver and representing a share of the company must depend upon the terms of the certificates.[1889] And where a trust company prior to its liquidation sold its

---

such holders were not entitled to preferential rights in any portions of bonds and mortgages remaining in ownership of trust company.

The holders of guaranteed first mortgage participation bonds issued by trust company, or trustees in their behalf, had the right to proceed against assets pledged for payment of bonds on trust company's default in payment of bonds. Tannenbaum v. Seacoast Trust Co. of Asbury Park, 16 N.J. Misc. 234, 198 A. 855, aff'd, 125 N.J. Eq. 360, 5 A.2d 778.

Holders of trust company's bond and mortgage participation certificates "payable" in 18 months were entitled, upon trust company's liquidation, to payment prior to payment of trust company on account of its retained interest in mortgages, or on account of certificates issued to itself. In re Mutual Trust Co., 48 N.Y.S.2d 707.

See also note 81 of this section.

Such holders could accept foreclosure sale to banking commissioner who had taken over trust company for liquidation as amount of their loss and be entitled to allowance of general claim for difference on waiving claim to further interest in mortgaged premises. Kelly v. Middlesex Title Guarantee, etc., Co., 116 N.J. Eq. 228, 172 A. 487.

Checks for interest—

Where trust company, shortly before being taken over by banking commissioner, sent out to holders of mortgages and mortgage participation certificates guaranteed by company checks for semiannual interest, holders of checks representing interest actually collected from mortgagors were entitled to prior and immediate payment, but holders of checks representing interest not collected from mortgagors were entitled to no preference except as against mortgaged premises. Kelly v. Middlesex Title Guarantee & Trust Co., 116 N.J. Eq. 228, 172 A. 487.

[1889] **In general.—**

In re First Nat'l Bank & Trust Co., 350 Pa. 125, 88 A.2d 15.

No priority allowed.—

Holders of mortgage certificates issued by trust company and its predecessor, reciting that first mortgages equal to principal amount had been sat aside to secure payment, held not entitled to priority over general depositors on trust company's liquidation, where trust company retained possession of mortgages and mortgage records indicated that they were its absolute property. Gretzinger v. Arehart (Ind. App.), 193 N.E. 714.

Upon insolvency of combined bank and trust company which had attempted to create trusts out of its own securities and had sold participation certificates therein to the public, holders of such certificates were placed in the position of general creditors only. Ulmer v. Fulton, 129 Ohio St. 323, 195 N.E. 557, 97 A.L.R. 1170.

Where trust company purportedly created trust out of its own assets by transferring real estate which it owned to itself as trustee and selling land trust certificates of equitable ownership to the public, and trust company thereafter became insolvent, certificate holders would be deemed general creditors of the trust company in liquidation. Alburn v. Union

assets to the Federal Deposit insurance Corporation for an amount equal to the company's deposit liabilities, and the Corporation acquired the company's bond and mortgage participation certificate which evidenced the company's retained interest, the Corporation was held to have acquired only the company's interest in the mortgages and the property securing the certificates issued to the public.[1890]

Claims of State and United States.—There is a conflict of authority as to whether a deposit of state funds is entitled to be preferred in the distribution of assets of an insolvent bank or trust company. In some jurisdictions it is held that in the absence of a constitutional or statutory provision, the state has no preferential right over general creditors, once in others it is held that the state, on account of its right under common law, has a preference over

---

Trust Co. (Ohio C.P.), 80 N.E.2d 721, appeal dismissed, 150 Ohio St. 357, 82 N.E.2d 543, cert. denied, 336 U.S. 937, 69 S. Ct. 747, 93 L. Ed. 1096.

Priority allowed.—

Under certificates of interests in mortgage pool set aside by trust company as separate trust, providing that trust company guaranteed payment without deductions for taxes, expenses, or losses incurred in management of pool, and providing for lower rate of interest than that realized by trust company on mortgages, where trust company sold certificates for only part of face value of mortgages and became insolvent, and mortgages were liquidated for less than their face value, certificate holders were entitled to full payment from proceeds of mortgages before receiver of trust company received any part of proceeds. In re Philippi, 329 Pa. 581, 198 A. 16.

Interest of company.—

Under terms of certificates of participation in mortgage pool issued by trust company, providing that trust company could issue to itself a certificate representing an interest in such pool but that such certificate should not be a claim against the pool until all other certificates were paid and retired, upon insolvency of trust company all prior certificates should be paid in full with interest before any payment is made on certificates representing interest of trust company. In re First Nat'l Bank & Trust Co., 350 Pa. 125, 38 A.2d 15.

Purchaser of certificates.—

In such case, that certificates issued by trust company to itself, and by receiver after insolvency, were purchased by other, did not create any equities in their favor as against holders of prior certificates. In re First Nat'l Bank & Trust Co., 850 Pa. 125, 88 A.2d 15.

1890 In re Mutual Trust Co., 48 N.Y.S.2d 707.

In such case, ordinary holders of the company's bond and mortgage participation certificates were not bound by certificates issued to the corporation and could establish that the relation between the trust company and the corporation was not that of debtor and creditor. In re Mutual Trust Co., 48 N.Y.S.2d 707.

other creditors and depositors.[1891] Thus, it has been held that the state is entitled to a preference upon liquidation of an insolvent trust company designated as a state depositary in which state funds are deposited,[1892] but such preference is subject to the claims of other creditors secured by specific liens.[1893] And a statute giving trust liabilities of an insolvent trust company preference over "other preferred debts," prefers them to the state's independently secured deposits.[1894] It also has been held that the state is not a preferred creditor with respect to excise taxes due from a trust company in the process of liquidation by a banking commissioner.[1895]

A claim of the United States for postal funds deposited with a trust company in liquidation was held entitled to preference.[1896] And a claim of the United States for income taxes due from an insolvent corporation which made real estate loans and sold mortgage notes with guaranty of payment, was held superior to a city's claim for personal property taxes.[1897] But the United States as a depositor in a trust company taken over by a state banking

---

[1891] **In general.—**

Commonwealth v. Allen, 240 Mass. 244, 133 N.E. 625.

For a further discussion of this subject, see chapter 6, §§ 170, 196.

No preferential right—

The commonwealth will not be entitled to a preferential payment of its deposit in a trust company, in the absence of a statute declaring such deposits to have priority over general deposits. Commonwealth v. Allen, 240 Mass. 244, 133 N.E. 625; Framingham v. Allen, 240 Mass. 253, 133 N.E. 629.

The funds of a state highway department deposited in insolvent trust company are not entitled to preference over deposits of other depositor, under theory of state's prerogative. Reichert v. Metropolitan Trust Co., 264 Mich. 182, 249 N.W. 625.

[1892] United States Fidelity, etc., Co. v. Carnegie Trust Co., 161 App. Div. 429, 146 N.Y.S. 804, aff'd, 213 N.Y. 629, 107 N.E. 1087; In re Carnegie Trust Co., 206 N.Y. 390, 99 N.E. 1096, 46 L.R.A. (n.s.) 260; Shippee v. Riverside Trust Co., 113 Conn. 661, 156 A. 43.

[1893] In re Carnegie Trust Co., 206 N.Y. 390, 99 N.E. 1096, 46 L.R.A. (n.s.) 260.

[1894] Public Indem. Co. v. Page, 161 Md. 239, 156 A. 791.

[1895] Commissioner of Banks v. Highland Trust Co., 283 Mass. 71, 186 N.E. 229.

[1896] United States v. People's Trust Co., 17 F.2d 437, rev'd on other grounds, 23 F.2d 381. See also chapter 6, §§ 171, 197.

[1897] Tropical Printing Co. v. Union Title Guarantee Co., 180 La. 702, 157 So. 684.

On insolvency of corporation, taxes due city held payable out of money remaining after payment of federal taxes and such costs as have preference over claim of United States and such costs as were necessary for collection of enough money to pay also taxes due city. Tropical Printing Co. v. Union Title Guarantee Co., 180 La. 702, 157 So. 534.

official, was held not entitled to a preferred claim in the absence of a showing of insolvency or other necessary specifications.[1898]

Particular Holdings in Regard to Preferences.—Drafts placed by a bank to a trust company's credit for a borrower have been held collected by the company on being credited by the bank, making the checks issued for the drafts preferred claims against the company on insolvency.[1899]

And a bank which sells a draft and receives in exchange a draft drawn by a trust company on a bank in which it has insufficient funds is entitled to a preferred claim for the amount thereof against the company's receiver.[1900] A trust company's general deposit account with another trust company is not entitled to priority on the latter's liquidation, even though consisting of funds held by the former in trust.[1901] Where one trust company places funds with another trust company on an express agreement that the latter purchase its stock therewith and hold it for the former, and it fails to perform, the former is not entitled to a preference over the latter's general creditors on its insolvency.[1902]

Where a trust company stockholder has no right to rescind his subscription after the company is taken over by a state banking official for liquidation, he cannot establish a debt or gain priority as to the funds in the official's hands.[1903] Money received by a trustee or receiver in bankruptcy and deposited subject to withdrawal by check with a trust company, a depositary designated by the state comptroller, although in constructive custody of a court, is not money paid into court within the meaning of the New York statutes, and the debt created thereby is not entitled to a preference in the event of bankruptcy, where such statutes refer to money

---

[1898] United States v. Singac Trust Co., 112 N.J. Eq. 448, 164 A. 702.

Where insolvency is necessary to entitle the sovereign to claim priority, the claim of United States against bank in liquidation by commissioner held not entitled to priority since insolvency within statute was not necessary to justify commissioner of banks taking possession of trust company, and no inference of insolvency can be inferred therefrom. United States v. Commissioner of Banks, 254 Mass. 173, 149 N.E. 883.

[1899] Kuniansky v. Mobley, 167 Ga. 852, 146 S.E. 898.

[1900] Leach v. Central Trust Co., 203 Iowa 1060, 213 N.W. 777, 57 A.L.R. 1165.

[1901] Appeal of North Philadelphia Trust Co., 315 Pa. 562, 173 A. 324.

Checks drawn to order of trust company, trustee, held deposited by it without restriction in its general banking account with bank. Newark Distributing Terminals Co. v. Hospelhorn, 172 Md. 291, 191 A. 707.

[1902] Madison Trust Co. v. Carnegie Trust Co., 215 N.Y. 475, 109 N.E. 580.

[1903] Bittenbender v. Cosmopolitan Trust Co., 253 Mass. 230, 148 N.E. 619.

paid or brought into the state courts, not into the federal bankruptcy court.[1904] The holders of checks issued by a trust company upon a bank in exchange for checks drawn upon the trust company by its depositors are not entitled to a preference granted by a statute to depositors in insolvent trust companies.[1905] And where a trust company retains a full commission, but has only partly performed a certain contract, the parties, after the company's insolvency, are entitled to a reduction in the commission charged, but may prove their claims only as general creditors.[1906] Where an insolvent transfers certain property to a trust company doing a general banking business in trust to convert same into cash and pay his creditors, and the company, after mingling the proceeds of such property in a general account, becomes insolvent, a claim of the insolvent's creditors to a preference over other creditors of the company as to such account is properly refused, even though the account never falls below the amount of such claim.[1907] And where a trust company deposits in a national bank for collection a certificate of deposit which it holds as a counter indemnity for liability on an executor's bond, and the bank credits the proceeds of the certificate to the company's account, thereafter the company reduces the account below the amount of the certificate, and on the insolvency of the company, the bank applies the whole balance as a setoff to its claim against the company, the executor cannot claim a preference over general creditors in the distribution of the assets of the insolvent company.[1908]

See the footnotes for additional instances of claims held preferred[1909] or not preferred,[1910] and cases relating to sufficiency of evidence.[1911]

[1904] Henkel v. Carnegie Trust Co., 213 N.Y. 185, 107 N.E. 346.

[1905] Commonwealth v. American Trust Co., 241 Pa. 153, 88 A. 430 (Pennsylvania statute).

[1906] Commonwealth v. Tradesmen's Trust Co., 250 Pa. 372, 95 A. 574.

[1907] Commonwealth ex rel. Bell v. Tradesmen's Trust Co., 250 Pa. 378, 95 A. 577 (1916).

[1908] Groff v. City Sav. Fund & Trust Co., 46 Pa. Super. 428.

[1909] Holders of "investment certificates" based on securities that had been segregated from bank's general assets, under which holders had no right to payment out of bank's general assets and had limited rights of withdrawal, were not general depositors but had equitable interest in trust fund created with segregated assets, irrespective of whether assets were originally acquired with bank's general funds or formally purchased from bank, and hence holders were not relegated to position of general creditors when bank became insolvent, but were entitled to full payment out of segregated assets. Hack v. Christina, 213 Ind. 68, 11 N.E.2d 152; Hack v. Jobes, 213 Ind. 90, 11 N.E.2d 161.

(Text continued on page 526)

Purchasers of thrift certificates.—

The failure of a corporation selling thrift certificates, entitling purchasers to bonds or annuities on payment of stipulated sums in installments, to continue as a going concern violated purchasers' contractual rights, and return of money received with legal interest, as on rescission after a breach going to the whole consideration, was thereupon required. Briney v. Mortimer, 92 F.2d 800.

Defaulting holders, who had right under contract to relieve themselves of delinquency by paying within two years, were entitled to return of money paid with legal interest, and if trust company's assets were insufficient to repay such sums, holders were entitled to participate therein on an equal pro rata basis with others having beneficial interests in trust. Briney v. Mortimer, 92 F.2d 800.

Where insolvent trust company, guaranteeing payment of bonds sold by it, had dissipated sinking fund for payment of bonds, some of which had been paid to trust company in full and the mortgages released, and other bonds had been paid only in part, holders of bonds sold by company were not entitled to priority over holders of other bonds of same series sold to others, but all holders of bonds sold by company were entitled to priority, as regards proceeds of mortgages securing bonds, over bonds owned by company. Dorman v. Bankers' Trust Co.'s Receiver, 259 Ky. 430, 82 S.W.2d 494.

Where claimant assigned mortgage through trust company and consideration was placed in company's miscellaneous account for express purpose of setting it aside for claimant, but company closed doors before payment was made, relationship was that of principal and agent and claimant was entitled to preference. Appeal of Reicheldifer, 115 Pa. Super. 454, 176 A. 52.

Costs and counsel fees, which commissioner of banking and insurance, in charge of liquidation of trust company, acting as administrator pendente lite, was directed to pay when commissioner was surcharged with sum embezzled by trust company's officers from funds of estate, could be made subject of preferred claim against assets of trust company in hands of commissioner. In re Tome River Trust Co. (N.J. Ch.), 192 A. 47.

[1910] **Purchase of draft.—**

Where the purchase of draft on foreign exchange by depositor from trust company was a commercial transaction and the trust company became insolvent before draft was paid, depositor could merely prove claim against commercial department of company and receive dividends therefor on same footing as other commercial creditors. Foley v. Commissioner of Banks, 292 Mass. 83, 197 N.E. 448.

Depositor withdrawing funds from savings department of trust company and purchasing draft on foreign bank, which was not paid because of trust company's insolvency, held to have only ordinary claim against general assets of trust company in liquidation, notwithstanding depositor was induced to purchase draft by officer who misrepresented value of draft beyond that imported by its terms. Foley v. Commissioner of Banks, 292 Mass. 83, 197 N.E. 448.

Payment in advance for foreign money.—

Where customer of trust company contracts for purchase of money of foreign nation and pays in advance therefor, such payment is not impressed with trust and is not held by trust

(Text continued on page 526)

company as trustee but as debtor, so that customer has only ordinary claim against general assets of trust company in liquidation. Norling, etc., Co. v. Exchange Trust Co., 288 Mass. 444, 193 N.E. 1.

Customer who deposited check in commercial department of trust company as security under contract for purchase of foreign money for future delivery had ordinary claim against general assets of trust company in liquidation, where trust company became owner of check when delivered and of its proceeds when collected. Norling & Bloom Co. v. Exchange Trust Co., 288 Mass. 444, 193 N.E. 1.

Proceeds of checks collected during bank holiday.—

Where the proceeds of checks deposited for collection in trust company before legal bank holiday were collected during holiday and placed to depositor's account, such proceeds became unconditional credits and depositor could not claim preferential trust on general assets of trust company to extent of proceeds after trust company closed. Ghingher v. Manufacturers' Finance Co., 168 Md. 560, 178 A. 600.

Judgment against trust company was not and is not a lien on the real estate transferred to the liquidating trustees or held by the trust company in trust for others. Fortna v. Commonwealth Trust Co. (Pa. C.P.), 50 Dauph. 211.

Holder, of "land trust certificates" created by an attempted trust agreement between bank and holders to create a trust out of bank's own realty were not entitled to preference over general creditors in liquidation proceedings against the bank Gallagher v. Squire, 57 Ohio App. 222, 13 N.E.2d 373.

"Volunteer" creating indemnity fund.—Where president of insolvent trust company deposited moneys and securities with secretary of banking to indemnify against loss by reason of overdrafts on trust estates or funds, he was a "volunteer" who could not invoke the principle of exoneration or subrogation to rights and securities of creditor, and beneficiaries of trust estates were entitled to be paid in full before anything could be returned to creator of indemnity fund. In re Bell, 344 Pa. 223, 25 A.2d 344.

Where depositor placed a check with a trust company which issued its official trust receipt and a series of certified drafts aggregating the amount of the check, depositor was not entitled to preference on insolvency of the trust company on the basis of a constructive trust based on alleged fraud. Janner v. Langdeau (Tex. Civ. App.), 317 S.W.2d 787.

Where depositor, while trust company was a going concern, deposited a check and the company delivered its official trust receipts and a series of certified drafts aggregating the amount of the check to be delivered as soon as they were imprinted, the contract was one of general deposit and the relation of debtor and creditor was created, and as a general depositor, the depositor was an unsecured general creditor of the trust company on subsequent insolvency. Janner v. Langdeau (Ten. Civ. App.), 317 S.W.2d 787.

Where insolvent trust company turned over state's deposit to new institution without knowledge that state had been reimbursed by surety companies, trustees of assets of company could recover such deposit on grounds that it was turned over by mistake and that sureties were not entitled to preference. This is true even though company officials were negligent in failing to discover whether payment had actually been made by surety companies. Smith v. Capital Bank, etc., Co., 325 Pa. 369, 191 A. 124.

§ 46. Property Held in Trust or Fiduciary Capacity.

In General.—Where money is paid to a bank or trust company for a specific purpose, it generally may be recovered as a trust deposit if not applied or if misapplied, there being a clear distinction in this regard between a general and special deposit.[1912] it should be noted that a trust

---

Where price of realty was received under escrow agreement authorizing trust company to use such fund in usual course of its business, and fund was deposited by trust company in banking department and commingled with general funds of such department, debtor and creditor relationship existed, and claim of party entitled to fund could not be accorded preference on liquidation of trust company. Squire v. Nally, 130 Ohio St. 582, 200 N.E. 840.

Where depositor's account was charged with cost of stock purchased for him through broker and amount credited to trust company's treasurer's account and treasurer's check was mailed to broker, but broker refused to deliver stock because of insolvency of trust company before payment of check, depositor held not entitled to preference under Bank Collection Act. Banks v. Commissioner of Banking and insurance, 118 N.J. Eq. 281, 178 A. 630.

Transfer of funds to treasurer's account was not such segregation of trust funds as entitled depositor to preference. Banks v. Commissioner of Banking and insurance, 118 N.J. Eq. 281, 178 A. 630.

Transfer of general deposit to trust account on order of bank president held ineffective as attempt to pledge assets of bank to secure and give priority to depositor, notwithstanding that pledge was made through auditor of public accounts, and hence depositor was not entitled to priority on ground that funds were secured by bank's deposit under provisions of Trust Companies Act. People v. Cairo-Alexander County Bank, 363 Ill. 589, 2 N.E.2d 889.

[1911] **Attempt to fraudulently obtain preference.—**

Evidence supported finding that alleged assignment by loan company was attempt to fraudulently obtain preferential position as preferred creditor. Cederlund v. Hub Loan Co., 88 N.J. Super. 238, 211 A.2d 809 (1965).

Payments not in fact preferential.—

Evidence supported finding that payments made by insolvent loan company and sought to be recovered by receiver were not in fact preferential. Cederlund v. Hub Loan Co., 88 N.J. Super. 238, 211 A.2d 809 (1965).

[1912] **In general.—**

Henson v. Lamb, 120 W. Va. 552, 199 S.E. 459. See also § 45 of this chapter.

Where trust company accepted, as a special deposit, money deposited for purpose of having it paid to insurance company to satisfy depositor's indebtedness to it and, by action of trust company's vice-president in writing ambiguous letter to depositor, caused him to believe that indebtedness had been satisfied, although trust company retained money until it became insolvent, deposit constituted a "trust ex maleficio." Henson v. Lamb, 120 W. Va. 552, 199 S.E. 459.

Money deposited with trust company, which was insurance company's collection agent, for purpose of having money paid to insurance company to satisfy depositor's debt to it was a "special deposit," and where it was not so paid, but was retained by trust company until

company's characterization of an account is not necessarily binding on its depositors.[1913] For example, a trust company's method of keeping a record of collected premiums required to be paid to an insurance company does not jeopardize the insurance company's right under an agreement requiring the trust company to hold collected premiums as a trust.[1914] No right of preference exists as to a fund collected by a trust company which the owner has directed held for him on open account; in such a situation the relation is merely that of debtor and creditor.[1915] And where at the time an investment company became insolvent, it held a fund as trustee, such fund was held not to pass by a receiver's sale of the company's assets, even though the sale was made under a court order providing that persons claiming an interest in the assets present their claims or be barred, and the trust beneficiary filed no claim.[1916]

Statutes and Court Rules.—State statute. may give preference to debts owed in a fiduciary capacity on the dissolution or insolvency of a trust company.[1917] And the failure of an insolvent trust company to comply with

---

company closed its doors, it came into hands of receiver of trust company charged with a trust in favor of depositor. Henson v. Lamb, 120 W. Va. 552, 199 S.E. 459.

Agent of depositor.—

As respect. whether funds deposited with trust company for purpose of having trust company pay depositor's indebtedness to third party were impressed with a trust, trust company was agent of depositor and not of third party, and hence payment to trust company was not payment to third party. Henson v. Lamb, 120 W. Va. 552, 199 S.E. 459.

1913 Lebaudy v. Carnegie Trust Co., 90 Misc. 490, 154 N.Y.S. 900.

1914 Maryland Casualty Co. v. Rottger, 99 Ind. App. 485, 194 N.E. 365.

1915 Lebaudy v. Carnegie Trust Co., 90 Misc. 490, 154 N.Y.S. 900.

1916 New York Security, etc., Co. v. Lombard Inv. Co., 75 F. 172.

1917 **In general.—**

Maryland.—Melville v. Central Trust Co., 165 Md. 597, 170 A. 175; Corbett v. Hospelhorn, 172 Md. 257, 191 A. 691, discussing statute and effect of amendment, Ghingher v. O'Connell, 165 Md. 267, 167 A. 184; Newark Distributing Terminals Co. v. Hospelhorn, 172 Md. 291, 191 A. 707.

Pennsylvania.—In re Risher's Will, 227 Win 104, 277 N.W. 160, 115 A.L.R. 790, holding that under the Pennsylvania statute relating to the liabilities of trust companies, cestuis que trust have a right of preference against all the assets of a trust company which receives an appointment to execute the trust, in case of any default by the trust company.

Statute does not apply to conventional trustees, only those appointed by court. Corbett v. Hospelhorn, 172 Md. 257, 191 A. 691, holding that court's assumption of jurisdiction to advise and direct trustee appointed in trust deed was not an "appointment" by court.

To constitute trust company a "depositary" within the statute respecting preferences,

a statute governing the handling of trust funds should not place a preferred claimant in the class of general creditors.[1918] But where a receiver deposits his estate's money with a trust company which is a surety on his bond, under an agreement that the money shall bear interest and be subject to check with

---

money deposited in trust company must have been paid into court as voluntary act or by order of judgment, and, when so paid, court must pas order that money be deposited with trust company. Melville v. Central Trust Co., 165 Md. 597, 170 A. 175.

The deposit should be of funds under the court's direct control, and not in the custody of a fiduciary appointed for the purpose. Storrs v. Ghinger, 166 Md. 572, 171 A. 849.

Money held by receivers and deposited in trust company was not in same situation as if it had been paid into court and deposited by court, so that receivers were not entitled to preferred claim on insolvency of trust company, though court directed deposit. Storrs v. Ghinger, 166 Md. 672, 171 A. 849.

Trust company did not receive as a depositary, within meaning of statute respecting preferences, funds deposited by receivers of corporation under direction of court Storrs v. Ghinger, 166 Md. 572, 171 A. 849.

Money which court may direct its proper fiscal official to deposit with trust company so as to give deposit a preference is that paid into court to avoid litigation, interest, and costs, to ascertain ownership or proper distribution, or to secure and preserve property pending litigation. Melville v. Central Trust Co., 165 Md. 597, 170 A. 175.

Deposit in bank subsequently becoming branch of trust company.—Where will directed executrix to deposit certain sum with pod banking institution, and orphans' court, on executrix' application, passed order that executrix deposit sum in national bank which later became branch of trust company which became insolvent, executrix held not entitled to preferred claim under statute giving preference to debts owed by trust companies in fiduciary capacity. Melville v. Central Trust Co., 165 Md. 597, 170 A. 175.

[1918] **In general.—**

First State Trust & Sav. Bank v. Therrell, 103 Fla. 1136, 138 So. 733.

No tracing requirement.—

And where a trust company, in violation of statute, did not invest half its capital stock in securities for the protection of fiduciary account, and failed to keep such assets separate from other assets, and kept no books showing trust business apart from banking business, the beneficiaries of fiduciary accounts nevertheless had a prior lien on the assets to the amount of one half the capital stock, without being required to trace or identify the fiduciary fund. Ohio Valley Bank, etc., Co. v. Pettit, 206 Ky. 818, 268 S.W. 535.

What shall be set aside is within court's discretion. Sauer's Trustee v. Dorman, 256 Ky. 569, 76 S.W.2d 625.

Where bank and trust company did not set aside 50 percent of capital stock for trust purposes and liquidating agent, upon bank's insolvency, applied for order approving proposed loan from Reconstruction Finance Corporation for purpose of distributing proceeds of loan among bank's creditors, order setting aside cash, which was less than 50 per cent of capital stock, and part of assets, as lien for trust estates, held not abuse of discretion. Sauer's Trustee v. Dorman, 256 Ky. 569, 76 S.W.2d 625.

the counter signature of the company, and such money is mingled with the general funds of the company which then becomes insolvent, the receiver cannot claim that he is entitled to have the whole balance of his account returned to him under a rule of court providing that corporations approved as sureties shall keep all moneys received by them from persona for whom they become sureties in a separate account.[1919] And a statute restricting the securities in which certain trust funds may be invested by trust companies does not prefer claims to such funds over other trust funds on insolvency.[1920]

Possession and Existence of Trust Res.—It has been held that a trust cannot be imposed on funds in the possession of a bank commissioner liquidating a trust company without proof that the funds came into his possession.[1921] And so one entitled to a certain trust fund had no right to preferential payment where such fund did not come into the possession of a commissioner but had been deposited by a trust company in another bank.[1922] A claimant who seeks a preference by reason of a trust is called upon to prove the existence of the trust, and in the absence of testimony on the point, there is no presumption that a trust exists.[1923] Proving that there was a trust at one time in particular property does not prove that such trust is impressed upon other property at a later time, without a showing that such other property is the proceeds of or substitute for the original.[1924]

[1919] Commonwealth ex rel. Pennsylvania Mut. Life Ins. Co. v. City Trust, etc., Co., 218 Pa. 50, 66 A. 995.

[1920] First State Trust & Sav. Bank v. Therrell, 103 Fla. 1136, 138 So. 733.

[1921] Sloane v. People's Trust Co., 83 N.H. 583, 145 A. 670.

[1922] Hecker-Jones-Jewell Milling Co. v. Cosmopolitan Trust Co., 242 Mass. 181, 136 N.E. 333, 24 A.L.R. 1148.

[1923] Bank Com'rs v. Security Trust Co., 70 N.H. 536, 49 A. 113.

Defendant trust company loaned money to a party, who gave a note secured by mortgage on certain land therefor, before such company's insolvency, which note and mortgage, assigned in blank, defendant sold and delivered to claimant, the assignment never being recorded. Subsequently defendant obtained the mortgagor's equity, and sold part of the land to other parties, releasing claimant's mortgage thereon without his authority or knowledge. Held, that no trust was created entitling claimant to a preference to other creditors in such company's assets. Bank Comm'rs v. Security Trust Co., 70 N.H. 536, 49 A. 113.

[1924] **In general.—**

Assigned Estate of Solicitors Loan & Trust Co., 3 Pa. Super. 244.

Where money received by a trust company as trustee is not kept distinct or in. vested in any specific way, but is mingled with the general mass of money on deposit, and used in the general banking business, and there is no means of tracing or ascertaining its identity in any form or species of property, the cestui que trust is not entitled to a preference over general

Bondholders.—The purchasers of bonds were held bound by the terms of a trust agreement which provided in effect that only bonds certified by the trustee were secured by trust funds, and the holders of uncertified bonds could not participate in the trust funds to the prejudice of holders of certified bonds.[1925] Bondholders of an investment company which maintained a reserve fund for payment of the bonds at maturity are entitled to preference in such reserve fund upon the company's dissolution and receivership, and are also entitled to participate for payment of the balance of their claims as

---

creditor, in a distribution of the funds in the hands of the assignees of such trust company. Assigned Estate of Solicitors Loan & Trust Co., 3 Pa. Super. 244.

Illustrative cases.—

Defendant trust company contracted to sell certain lend before insolvency, taking notes therefor, and agreeing to convey free of incumbrances on payment. Two of the notes were sold to claimants before maturity, and, on discovery that there was an outstanding mortgage on the land, claimants purchased same at time of the appointment of an assignee for defendant. The vendees stand ready to pay according to contract Held, that claimants were entitled to the entire balance due defendant on purchase price in payment of their notes as against other creditors of defendant, since their money is traceable to such interest. Bank Comm'rs v. Security Trust Co., 70 N.H. 536, 49 A. 113.

Defendant trust company sent claimants' certificates of deposit in payment of the proceeds of notes secured by the mortgage of land, collected by it without the claimants' authority, and then in claimants' possession, before insolvency, and also sent notes with the certificates to be held as collateral security, which certificates and collateral notes claimants retained. Held, that claimants were entitled to the benefit of such certificates and notes as against the assignee of such company in insolvency, since they ratified defendant's acts in making collections, and accepted the certificates and notes in payment Bank Comm'rs v. Security Trust Co., 70 N.H. 536, 49 A. 113.

Defendant trust company sold and delivered a certain note, payable to it on order, with interest according to attached coupons, and secured by mortgage on certain land, to claimant, before insolvency; the assignment being in blank and unrecorded. By the terms of the note, principal and accrued interest became due and payable on nonpayment of interest after a certain period, at the election of payees or assigns. Defendant guaranteed payment of principal and interest, and reserved the right to purchase the note at any time. The maker did not pay the coupons when due, but defendant advanced claimant sums represented by those due at a certain date, and took them up and held them. Claimant was never told of the maker's default at the time of sale defendant represented that certain liens on the land would be paid from money received from claimant, making the latter's mortgage a first lien. One of the liens was not paid, and defendant discharged claimant's mortgage, and gave a new mortgage to the holder of such lien for the amount due, without her knowledge or consent. Defendant subsequently acquired title to the equity in the land. Held, that claimant was not entitled to be paid the balance due on her note from defendant's assets in preference to unsecured creditors, since she took the risk of performance of the promise to pay prior to liens. Bank Comm'rs v. Security Trust Co., 70 N.H. 536, 49 A. 113.

[1925] Thede v. Colorado Nat'l Bank, 93 Cole. 26, 22 P.2d 1105.

general creditors in the company's assets.[1926] Similarly, where a trust company places a fund in trust as collateral security for the faithful performance of its guaranties, and at the time it is engaged only in guaranteeing and selling personal or corporate obligations, but afterwards it enters into the business of selling debenture bonds secured by other trust funds under other trust indentures, the trust fund first created is liable for the first class of obligations in preference to the claims of any other class.[1927] For other cases involving the rights of bondholders on insolvency, see the footnote.[1928]

Deposits in Banking or Commercial Department.—Where trust funds are deposited by a trust company as trustee in its banking department the trust beneficiaries are not entitled to priority,[1929] but if such deposit is the result of fraud and collusion, title does not pass to the banking department, and the property can be recaptured by the beneficiaries if it can be identified and

---

[1926] Fell v. Securities Co., 11 Del. Ch. 101, 97 A. 610.

[1927] American Loan & Trust Co. v. Northwestern Guaranty Loan Co., 166 Mass. 337, 44 N.E. 340.

[1928] **Trustee guilty of fraud.—**

In proceeding for liquidation of trust company which was trustee under trust deed securing bonds, bondholder was entitled to allowance of claim on bonds as claim against securities deposited with state auditor to secure trust creditors, on ground that trust company as trustee was guilty of fraud in using funds it received in trust capacity to pay bonds owned by company and its officers to exclusion of other bondholder, by representation that there was no possibility of bondholders collecting bonds. People v. Central Republic Trust Co., 300 Ill. App. 297, 20 N.E.2d 999.

[1929] **In general.—**

Newark Distributing Terminals Co. v. Hospelhorn, 172 Md. 291, 191 A. 707.

To entitle beneficiaries to trace, identify, and recapture funds, they must show that title to funds had not passed to banking department. Corbett v. Hospelhorn, 172 Md. 257, 191 A. 691.

Debtor-creditor relation created.—

Beneficiaries of trust funds deposited by trust company as trustee in its banking department without breach of trust held in general creditors" of banking department, and as such entitled neither to preference nor priority in distribution of assets of insolvent trust company, since deposit by trustees in banking department created relationship of debtor and creditor, and not that of trustee and cestui que trust. Corbett v. Hospelhorn, 172 Md. 257, 191 A. 691.

Deposit lawful.—

As respects right to preference, the deposit by trust company of fiduciaries' money in trust company's own beak, in a demand saving, deposit account drawing three percent interest, was lawful under statute. Stickle v. Guardian Trust Co., 133 Ohio St. 472, 14 N.E.2d 600.

traced.[1930] And a trust company, which could be inferred to have had knowledge that such a deposit was inconsistent with the degree of care and prudence imposed by a trust instrument, was held indebted to trust beneficiaries in a fiduciary capacity.[1931] And where a trust company guardian wrongfully placed its ward's money in its commercial department, mingling it with other funds, the ward was held entitled on the company's insolvency, to full reimbursement out of assets in the commercial department with any deficiency to be paid out of capital stock and stockholders' liability.[1932]

Illustrative Cases.—

Where trust company was appointed executor of an estate and deposited beneficiaries' money in its own bank sea savings amount, and thereafter became insolvent and was closed for liquidation by the superintendent of banks, and removed as executor by the probate court, administrator appointed to succeed trust company we. not entitled to preference to such claim, in absence of tracing deposit to particular fund. Stickle v. Guardian Trust Co., 138 Ohio St. 472, 14 N.E.2d 800.

The real issue was not between the administrator and the superintendent of banks as liquidator of the trust company, but between the equities of the administrator and the general depositors. Stickle v. Guardian Trust Co., 133 Ohio St. 472, 14 N.E.2d 600.

1930 **In general.—**

Newark Distributing Terminals Co. v. Hospelhorn, 172 Md. 291, 191 A. 707.

Knowledge of illegality required.—

Mere fact of such deposit did not make banking department trustee, notwithstanding that it knew of trust, unless deposit was to its knowledge unlawful. And in determining whether banking department was trustee ex maleficio, consideration would be given to fact that trustee and banking department were both integral parts of single corporate entity. Newark Distributing Terminals Co. v. Hospelhorn, 172 Md. 291, 191 A. 707.

Beneficiaries of trust funds held not entitled to priority on ground that banking department became trustee ex maleficio in retaining deposit with knowledge of impending insolvency, since, on deposit by trustee, relation of debtor and creditor was established between trustee and banking department and latter was under no duty to deplete assets by returning, of its own motion, funds in which all depositors had equal interest, but duty of safeguarding trust funds rested on trustee-depositor on whose order only deposit could be withdrawn. Corbett v. Hospelhorn, 172 Md. 257, 191 A. 691.

Such deposit held not fraudulent so as to entitle beneficiaries to preference where it failed to appear that officers of trust company were unreasonable in expecting to carry on business without interrupting payment of its obligations and to restore it to sound condition. Newark Distributing Terminals Co. v. Hospelhorn, 172 Md. 291, 191 A. 707.

1931 Newark Distributing Terminals Co. v. Hospelhorn, 172 Md. 291, 191 A. 707.

1932 Morrison v. Lawrence Trust Co., 283 Mass. 236, 186 N.E. 54, holding that such action by the company constituted gross breach of duty, authorizing ward to recover fell amount with interest.

Assignee or Successor of Company.—If there is property in the possession of an assignee of an insolvent trust company which was held in trust by the company, the trust beneficiaries are entitled to their interest in it notwithstanding the assignment.[1933] And it is immaterial what or how many changes were made by a trust company in the investment of trust property, or whether the changes were authorized or unauthorized, provided the identity of the property is preserved.[1934] The same principle applies and produces the same result if a trust company, instead of being trustee of a fund, held it as agent or in another fiduciary capacity.[1935] But according to some authorities, a

---

[1933] Bank Comm'rs v. Security Trust Co., 70 N.H. 536, 49 A. 113.

[1934] Bank Comm'rs v. Security Trust Co., 70 N.H. 536, 49 A. 113.

Where insolvent company which made real estate loans and sold mortgage notes with guaranty of payment deposited proceeds of notes in special trustee account, funds in such account did not lose identity as property of note holders and become mingled with funds of insolvent company because company borrowed and loaned part of funds and afterwards deposited other money to cover deficit. Tropical Printing Co. v. Union Title Guarantee Co., 180 La. 702, 157 So. 534.

Where a trust was created by money being left with a trust company whose assets were subsequently taken over by secretary of banking and the fund was always kept intact and could be identified, it was not necessary to the continued existence of trust and its enforcement against funds remaining in the secretary's hands that the money remain the same as that which was originally loft with company, the test being whether the fund could always be followed and distinguished. In re Bell, 147 Pa. Super. 471, 24 A.2d 101.

[1935] **In general.**—

Bank Comm'rs v. Security Trust Co., 70 N.H. 536, 49 A. 113.

Agency.—

Where agency of trust company to collect checks of depositors came to an end, when commissioner of banks took possession of its business and closed its doors, commissioner, in receiving proceeds of checks, if they could be traced into any particular fund, holds them for benefit of true owner. Salem Elevator Works, Inc. v. Commissioner of Banks, 252 Mass. 366, 148 N.E. 220.

Administrator.—

Where trust company, administrator, falls after commingling funds, beneficiaries may have preference over general depositors in cash on hand and securities. Glidden v. Gutelius, 96 Fla. 834, 120 So. 1.

Trustee under will.—

Trust company, acting as trustee under will, must continue, after closing and assumption of control by superintendent of banks, to pay income from estate's investments to life beneficiary. In re Nauman's Estate, 110 Pa. Super. 55, 167 A. 395.

Investment trust accounts.—

Claims based on personal investment trust accounts, which trust company agreed to hold

beneficial owner must trace his money or property into specific property in the possession of an assignee in order to be entitled to a preference over general creditors.[1936] if an owner does this, equity imposes a trust on such

---

in trust, keep invested, and collect and pay over income at stated intervals, less fees, held entitled to priority of payment on trust company's insolvency. In re Arcadia Trust Co., 240 App. Div. 166, 268 N.Y.S. 759.

Antecedent debt of trust company appointed executor of estate of its creditor is not a fiduciary obligation. Henry Waterhouse Trust Co. v. Vicars, 28 Hawaii 232.

[1936] **In general.—**

Bank Comm'rs v. Security Trust Co., 70 N.H. 536, 49 A. 113; Assigned Estate of Solicitors Loan & Trust Co., 3 Pa. Super. 244; Lebaudy v. Carnegie Trust Co., 90 Misc. 490, 154 N.Y.S. 900; In re Royersford Trust Co., 317 Pa. 490, 178 A. 288; In re Erie Trust Co., 326 Pa. 198, 191 A. 613.

Owner of a trust fund is entitled to claim only as a general creditor, where the funds have become so mingled with the insolvent trust company's funds as to lose their identity. Commonwealth v. Tradesmen's Trust Co., 250 Pa. 383, 95 A. 578.

Guardianship funds.—

In proceeding by successor guardian to establish preferred claim against insolvent trust company which had been original guardian, where trust relationship between parties was admitted, in order to be entitled to preference, it was incumbent on successor guardian to show that trust property, either in its original or substituted form, was in possession of receiver of the insolvent trust company. Knapp v. Northern Trust & Sav. Bank, 112 Ind. App. 656, 46 N.E.2d 278.

Hence, where funds of guardianship were invested in second mortgage bonds by trust company as guardian before trust company was placed in hands of receiver and pursuant to court order second mortgage bonds were delivered by trust company to its successor guardian and neither funds of guardianship nor property substituted therefor were in hands of receiver of original guardian, preferred claim could not be allowed against the insolvent original guardian. Knapp v. Northern Trust & Sav. Bank, 112 Ind. App. 656, 46 N.E.2d 278.

Where trust company transferred mortgage which it held as guardian of minor to itself and allotted to minor a participating interest in same mortgage and in another mortgage, and next day mortgagor paid trust company amount of mortgage by check on his bank account in trust company, minor held not entitled to priority on distribution of assets of trust company when it became insolvent, since payment was merely bookkeeping transaction involving no currency. In re Royersford Trust Co., 317 Pa. 490, 178 A. 288.

Money paid trust company by mistake.—

Payment of sum of money to trust company by mistake did not give creditor right to preference out of general assets of trust company when it became insolvent, where creditor did not trace money into some account or investment, the proceeds of which formed part of fund for distribution, even if payment of money by mistake made trust company constructive trustee. In re Bangor Trust Co., 317 Pa. 495, 178 A. 290.

Where checks were deposited with trust company for collection only, to enable depositor, on company's insolvency, to claim priority, it must be shown that money passed into definite

property or fund and implies that any withdrawal will not include it;

---

fund, distinguishable from general assets, it not being enough to show that it went into solvent estate and that proceeds remained unexpended somewhere in estate. Salem Elevator Works, Inc. v. Commissioner of Banks, 252 Mass. 366, 148 N.E. 220.

Trust company's unauthorized deposits of trust fund held not to justify ingrafting trust on general assets of trust company in process of liquidation, notwithstanding such deposits constituted misapplication of funds where deposits, which were not made in money and which did not augment assets of trust company, were not traceable into assets in hands of liquidating officer. Huntington Nat. Bank v. Fulton, 49 Ohio App. 268, 197 N.E. 204.

Wrongful investment of testamentary trust funds in mortgage participation certificates.—

The beneficiary of a testamentary trust who did not wish to limit her right to enforcement of a constructive trust of mortgage participation certificate in which trustee had wrongfully invested fund was relegated to asserting a claim for damages because of the deficiency in the trust fund resulting from the improper investment and for which the trustee would be liable to surcharge, far which she could enforce an equitable lien on the certificate, but claim was an unpreferred one against the general funds in the hands of the receiver. In re Stopp's Estate, 330 Pa. 493, 199 A. 493.

Such beneficiary was confined to an unpreferred claim against the assets of trust company, equal to difference between amount which orphans' court had decreed she was entitled to receive from trust company for having made improper investment, with interest to date of receivership, and amount that might be received by her from mortgage pool on liquidation of her interest therein as represented by participation certificate. In re Stopp's Estate, 330 Pa. 493, 199 A. 493.

Beneficiary was not presently entitled to cash payment from the secretary of banking as trustee of the mortgage pool, of amount which orphans' court had decreed she was entitled to receive from the trust company for having made an improper investment, but was limited to liquidation value of participation certificate after pool was finally liquidated. In re Stopp's Estate, 330 Pa. 493, 199 A. 493.

Embezzled funds.—

Surcharge, arising from embezzlement by trust company's officers of funds of estate for which trust company was appointed administrator pendant. lite, could not be made subject of preferential claim against assets in hands of commissioner of banking and insurance, in charge of liquidation of trust company, where charge of liquidation of trust company, where none of missing estate funds could be traced into hands of commissioner, and assets in commissioner's hands could not be identified with embezzled assets. In re Tome River Trust Co. (N.J. Ch.), 192 A. 47.

Building and loan association, paying liens on mortgaged premises with proceeds of loan through trust company, held not entitled to preferred claim against assets of closed trust company as a trust creditor, circumstances showing that there was no segregation of funds. In re Gordon, 121 Pa. Super. 597, 184 A. 311.

No trust established.—

In depositor's suit to establish constructive trust in its favor on property of trust company in hands of commissioner of banks, where there was no fund into which deposit could be

therefore, as long as there remains in the company's depositary an amount above the amount on which the trust is imposed, the trust beneficiaries are entitled to priority over general creditors.[1937] And even if a claimant's

---

traced, it having become part of general assets of company as distinguished from special property or particular fund, no trust was established in favor of plaintiff. Central Auto. Tire Co. v. Commissioner of Banks, 252 Mass. 363, 148 N.E. 226.

Where mortgages in which trust company invested funds placed in its hands to invest, as trustee, were later paid off and trust company reinvested proceeds in participating interests in another mortgage, cestui que trust held not entitled to priority on distribution of assets of trust company when it became insolvent, where cestui que trust did not trace funds further and mortgage in which funds were reinvested did not appear in account, so that there was nothing out of which cestui que trust could properly claim credit to. Royersford Trust Co., 317 Pa. 490, 178 A. 288.

Claims allowed preference because funds were deposited with insolvent trust company as trust funds which cannot be traced into tangible assets except by legal construction, and where cash on hand at time of closing is less than total amount of such claims, cannot share pro rata in cash on hand before general claims. Reichert v. Fidelity Bank & Trust Co., 261 Mich. 107, 245 N.W. 808 (1932).

[1937] **In general.—**

Cameron v. Carnegie Trust Co., 292 Pa. 114, 140 A. 768.

Where improperly converted assets of trust estate are traced into fund for distribution, preference is allowed on theory that such assets never have become part of those of trustee but at all times have remained, whether in original or substituted farm, the property of cestui que trust, and hence trustee's general creditors are not entitled to any share in their distribution; claim of trust beneficiary in such case being for reclamation of his own property. In re Erie Trust Co., 326 Pa. 198, 191 A. 613.

Claimant of converted funds is not entitled to priority against general creditor, unless there remains on deposit after conversion funds sufficient to pay his claim and claims of others similarly situated. Crowder v. Sandusky, 91 Ind. App. 200, 170 N.E. 792.

Insolvent trust company's deposits in other banks were required to be considered together with cash on hand and cub items at time of insolvency as constituting a single fund, sufficiently differentiated from company's general assets to meet requirements of law in regard to tracing of trust property. In re Erie Trust Co., 326 Pa. 198, 191 A. 613.

No tracing required.—

Beneficiaries of trust estate, part of which trust company as trustee misappropriated and for which misappropriation trust company was surcharged, held, upon trust company's insolvency, entitled to lowest level of cash and cash items and funds of company on deposit in other banks, reached between time when conversion occurred and when secretary of banking took possession of assets of company, notwithstanding beneficiaries did not trace money from their estate into any particular fund or bank deposit. In re Erie Trust Co., 326 Pa. 198, 191 A. 613.

Claimant had burden to show that at all times between deposit of funds and receiver's appointment, cub assets of trust company were equal to amount of funds claimed. Maryland

money is mixed with other money and deposited in a bank, loaned upon a promissory note or invested in other securities or property, which come into possession of an assignee, the claimant will have a charge upon the money, deposit, note, securities or property, and in that way may gain a preference over ordinary creditors.[1938]

Casualty Co. v. Rottger, 99 Ind. App. 485, 194 N.E. 365.

Illustrative cases.—

Owner, whose bond, left for safekeeping were converted by trust company's president, had preferred claim, where proceeds were commingled with trust company's funds, and there remained with company and receiver funds equaling value of bonds. Crowder v. Story, 90 Ind. App. 598, 169 N.E. 470. See also Webb v. O'Geary, 145 Va. 356, 133 S.E. 568.

Where lessee paid rent to trust company as trustee with check drawn on lessee's commercial account in trust company, and trust company gave cashier's checks to lessors, lessors were not entitled to preference over general creditor, on insolvency of trust company where purported trust had no corpus or res other than check given by lessee. Fulton v. Gardiner, 127 Ohio St. 77, 186 N.E. 724.

Club held not entitled to preferred claim against assets of insolvent trust company for funds which were deposited as trust funds, where on two occasions general funds of trust company were less than amount of club's deposits and club's funds could not be traced into tangible assets. intercollegiate Alumni Club v. Kirchner, 272 Web. 466, 262 N.W. 285.

[1938] **In general.—**

Bank Comm'rs v. Security Trust Co., 70 N.H. 536, 49 A. 113.

Right to enforce constructive trust or equitable lien.—

There a trustee by the wrongful disposition of trust property acquires other property, the beneficiary is entitled at his option either to enforce a constructive trust of the property so acquired or to enforce an equitable lien on it to so-cure his claim against the trustee for damages for breach of trust as long as the product of the trust property is held by the trustee and can be traced, but otherwise the claim of the beneficiary against the trustee for breach of trust is that of a general creditor. into In re Stopp's Estate, 330 Pa. 493, 199 A. 493.

Securities.—

Where trust company as fiduciary authorized to invest in securities commingles funds and invests them in lawful securities, cestuis que trust may have preference in securities. Glidden v. Gutelius, 96 Fla. 834, 120 So. 1.

Deposits.—

Where checks were deposited with trust company for collection, after it was taken over by commissioner of banking, depositor could follow proceeds wherever they could find them, in absence of superior right. Salem Elevator Works, Inc. v. Commissioner of Banks, 252 Mass. 366, 148 N.E. 220.

Deposit transmitted into securities.—

Investments made by trust company after time of conversion of cash from trust estate, from funds on deposit in other banks, held subject to claim of beneficiaries, since, if deposits were to be considered part offend into which trust res was sufficiently traced, any securities

One succeeding a trust company as administrator is not entitled to a preferred claim on its liquidation by reason of having deposited in its commercial department funds of an estate held temporarily.[1939] But where a trust company appointed trustee by a court became insolvent, the succeeding trustee was held to have a prior claim on its assets for the amount on deposit with it.[1940] Also, where a bank and trust company receives funds in trust for a special purpose, the succeeding trustee or owner of the funds is entitled to preference on the bank's insolvency,[1941] notwithstanding the trust department's account with the commercial department of the bank is overdrawn.[1942]

---

into which such deposits were transmitted were required to be regarded as merely substituted forms of trust property. In re Erie Trust Co., 326 Pa. 198, 191 A. 613.

Trust beneficiaries held entitled to preference over general creditors. In re Erie Trust Co., 326 Pa. 198, 191 A. 613.

[1939] McDonald v. Fulton, 125 Ohio St. 507, 182 N.E. 504, 83 A.L.R. 1107.

[1940] Ghingher v. O'Connell, 165 Md. 267, 167 A. 184.

[1941] **In general.—**

Smith v. Hood, 204 N.C. 343, 168 S.E. 526; Baltimore Trust Co. v. Hood, 204 N.C. 776, 168 S.E. 531; Baltimore Trust Co. v. Hood, 204 N.C. 777, 168 S.E. 531.

Owner of trust fund held entitled to preference on failure of bank, where bank and trust company as trustee under trust indenture received purchase price of bonds held as protection of bond issue but misappropriated it. First Nat'l Bank & Trust Co. v. Hood, 204 N.C. 351, 168 S.E. 628.

Trustee under will.—

Where trust company under instructions in will to hold trust estate separate and apart from other property or moneys of trust company deposited trust fund, in company's commercial and savings departments and subsequently was taken over by superintendent of banks for purposes of liquidation, successor trustee held entitled to claim lien on fund deposited with treasurer of state on parity with other similar liens, and on exhaustion of such fund deficiency constituted general claim against general assets of trust company on parity with unsecured claims against it. Huntington Nat. Bank v. Fulton, 49 Ohio App. 268, 197 N.E. 204.

Deposit for payment of interest.—

Person who deposited funds with insolvent bank and trust company as trustee to be held for payment of interest and principal upon note in hands of trustee for collection held entitled to preference. Flack v. Hood, 204 N.C. 337, 168 S.E. 520.

Where insolvent bank and trust company received, as trustee named in deed of trust, moneys for payment of interest on mortgage indebtedness, but failed to make such payment, succeeding trustee held entitled to preference to moneys so received by predecessor. Asheville Safe Deposit Co. v. Hood, 204 N.C. 346, 168 S.E. 524.

[1942] Smith v. Hood, 204 N.C. 343, 168 S.E. 526; Flack v. Hood, 204 N.C. 337, 168 S.E. 520.

Estoppel.—A trust company cannot assume in one capacity the obligation of a trustee, and also repudiate that relationship to the disadvantage of the beneficiary by depositing trust funds in its banking department and on insolvency estopping the beneficiary from tracing the funds into its vault.[1943] And other depositors of an insolvent trust company are not estopped, by the company's characterization of an account, from denying that the account was a trust account.[1944] in the absence of estoppels a creditor of an insolvent trust company does not waive his rights as a preferred creditor by filing his claim in the form of an ordinary debt.[1945] And a trustee which made advancements for which insolvent beneficiaries were liable, and for which it had a first lien on the trust property, was held not precluded from enforcing its lien because it accepted a note and collateral from some of the beneficiaries,[1946] For other cases dealing with estoppel in this context, see the footnote.[1947]

Miscellaneous Matters.—Instances of funds held constituting,[1948] or not constituting,[1949] trust funds giving a right to preference, and also cases

---

[1943] Maryland Cas. Co. v. Rottger, 99 Ind. App. 485, 194 N.E. 365.

[1944] Lebaudy v. Carnegie Trust Co., 90 Misc. 490, 154 N.Y.S. 900.

[1945] In re Receivership of Sec. Trust Co., 30 Haw. 848.

[1946] Bessel v. Department of Financial Institutions, 213 Ind. 446, 11 N.E.2d 683.

Under evidence that trustee made advancements for which insolvent beneficiaries were liable and for which trustee had first lien on trust property, that trustee accepted note of part of beneficiaries and collateral consisting of equities in heavily burdened property, under trust agreement reciting that trustee had demanded additional security, and under evidence that trustee mad, entry on its books by which overdraft on checking account of trust was balanced by note, liquidator of trustee was not precluded from enforcing first lien on trust property, as against contention that note and collateral were taken to create new indebtedness, to settle previous indebtedness, and to extinguish first lien on trust property. Bessel v. Department of Financial Institutions, 213 Ind. 446, 11 N.E.2d 683.

[1947] Where trust company receiver's account made no claim for reimbursement against trust estates by reason of an alleged advancement of interest, and executors of another claimed through the receiver subsequently making claim for alleged advancement, the receiver and the executors were "estopped" from making claim to fund as against holders of participating certificates. In re Bell, 344 Pa. 223, 25 A.2d 344.

[1948] Assets of estate received in capacity of executor constituted trust fund on trust company's insolvency, and executor cum testamento annexo had lien on assets set apart as security. Donnelly v. Slaughter, 114 N.J. Eq. 302, 168 A. 762, aff'd, 116 N.J. Eq. 542, 174 A. 507.

Agreement to hold insurance premiums in trust.—

Under agreement requiring trust company to remit collected premiums to insurance company, and to hold premiums collected, less commissions, as fiduciary trust until

(Text continued on page 543)

payment, trust held crested, which continued until trust company made payment in accordance with agreement. Maryland Casualty Co. v. Rottger, 99 Ind. App. 485, 194 N.E. 865.

Statement in contract that trust company could pay collected premiums in cash or by draft held not to negative trust and create relationship of debtor and creditor. Maryland Casualty Co. v. Rottger, 99 Ind. App. 485, 194 N.E. 365.

Premiums collected by trust company for insurance company held impressed with trust even if money was deposited with general funds of trust company. Maryland Cas. Co. v. Rottger, 99 Ind. App. 485, 194 N.E. 365.

Collections by trustee under bond issue.—

Where trust company as trustee under city street railway's bond issues agreed to collect rentals and to keep money separate from all other money of the company, and as trustee under a will and as guardian was required to keep segregated the funds collected, such funds constituted "trust funds" with right to preference upon company's insolvency. Union Guardian Trust Co. v. Emery, 292 Mich. 394, 290 N.W. 841.

Funds to pay bond coupons.—

Trust company accepting debtor's funds for sole purpose of paying coupons about to become due on bonds payable at trust company's office held funds as trustee or bailee, entitling debtor to preference on trust company's insolvency, though funds were commingled with company's general fund, banking law being inapplicable under circumstances. In re Arcadia Trust Co., 240 App. Div. 166, 288 N.Y.S. 759.

Substituted loan security.—

Where trust company had sold mortgage participation for which certain church loan was only security at that time, subsequently substituting different security in place of that loan, such loan security and its proceed, held impressed with trust in favor of holder of participation, entitling him to preferential claim against assets of company on its liquidation, since proceeds of that loan had augmented assets of company. Croghan v. Savings Trust Co., 231 Mo. App. 1161, 85 S.W.2d 239.

Where building and loan association entrusted proceeds of loan to trust company to pay liens and claim. on mortgaged premises by drawing check on association's account in trust company, proceeds of which were placed in account in commercial department, and checks were drawn by authorized agent of trust company, trust company was trustee for both borrowers and association, as respects right to preferred claim. In re Gordon, 121 Pa. Super. 597, 184 A. 311.

Where trust company gave treasurer's check for sum collected for holder of mortgage, and before check was paid commissioner took control of trust company because of insolvency and refused to honor check, assets collected by trust company were impressed under statute with a trust in favor of holder, and he was entitled to priority over general creditors. The company was acting as a bailee or trustee for holder as respects right to priority. McIlroy v. New Jersey Title Guarantee, etc., Co., 126 N.J. Eq. 462, 10 A.2d 469.

In such case, the treasurer's check was not "money" within statute providing that if collecting bank shall fall after having made collection, but without having remitted "money," assets of bank shall be impressed with a trust in favor of the owner of the amount collected.

(*Text continued on page 543*)

McIlroy v. New Jersey Title Guarantee & Trust Co., 126 N.J. Eq. 462, 10 A.2d 469.

[1949] **Deposit by executor.—**

Deposit in saving, and loan association in estate's name by executor signing stock subscription application card and taking passbook containing stock certificate for amount deposited held not trust fund entitling estate to preference on association's insolvency, though its officer orally agreed to hold deposit in trust. In re Krueger's Estate, 173 Wash. 114, 21 P.2d 1030.

Deposit by testamentary trustee.—

Where trust company took charge of bonds and coupons of testamentary trustee and made settlement semimonthly, meanwhile depositing such items into its own general funds, and being allowed to retain reserve to cover possible default. in payment of coupons, trust company held "debtor" and not "trustee" as regards testamentary trustee's right to preference on insolvency of trust company. Goodenough v. Union Guardian Trust Co., 275 Mich. 698, 267 N.W. 772.

Deposit, by minors.—

Statute providing that deposit in trust company in name of minor should be held for exclusive benefit of minor, should be paid to person in whose name deposit was made, and that receipt of minor should release trust company, held not to create trust relation between minor depositor and trust company, nor to give minor making deposit with trust company with other school children under system of savings instituted in public schools of city preferred claim to assets of trust company in liquidation. Phillips v. Savings Trust Co., 231 Mo. App. 1178, 85 S.W.2d 923.

Deposits of school children in city under savings deposit system, instituted as result of contract between board of education and organization known as Educational Thrift Service, Inc., made with trust company held not to create trust ex maleficio entitling school children to preferred claim to assets of trust company in liquidation where deposits were not made with depository designated by board, since money deposited was not' money of board, but belonged to school children. Phillips v. Savings Trust Co., 231 Mo. App. 1178, 85 S.W.2d 923.

Deposit for reimbursement.—

Provision in trust mortgage for deposit by mortgagor with bond underwriter of funds sufficient to reimburse bondholders for income tax paid on interest held not to create trust relationship between mortgagor and underwriter which would entitle mortgagor to preferred claim against underwriter's receiver for unexpended balance of deposit. People v. Straus & Co., 155 Misc. 610, 281 N.Y.S. 200.

Amount collected for taxes.—

Under agreement providing that from collections by trust company from properties there should be first paid all charges of trustee, all taxes and assessments, collection foes and expenses of administration, amount collected for taxes did not constitute a "bust fund" so as to entitle depositor to preference on company's insolvency, where primary obligation of paying taxes was upon vendees, and there was no stipulation for special deposit of such collections, and hence no "constructive trust" could be raised to give preferred states to such funds. Union Guardian Trust Co. v. Emery, 292 Mich. 394, 290 NW 841.

(Text continued on page 543)

Agreement precluding trust relation.—

Where agreement for deposit of fund, with trust company provided that deposits could be mingled or used with other funds, that interest would be paid by trust company, and that liability would be the ordinary general liability of debtor and creditor, no "trust" relation was created by the agreement so as to entitle depositors to preference upon company's insolvency. Union Guardian Trust Co. v. Emery, 292 Mich. 394, 290 N.W. 841.

Conversion by agent.—

That agent converted to his own use moneys trust company received in payment for bonds and mortgages did not constitute trust company trustee thereof so as to give assignee of mortgages preferred claim on trust company's insolvency. Appeal of Metropolitan Life Ins. Co., 310 Pa. 17, 164 A. 715, 86 A.L.R. 1301.

Fraud of agent.—

Trust company's agent's fraud, resulting in transference of second mortgages instead of first mortgages, did not, in absence of fraud of trust company, constitute it trustee of payments received from assignee. Appeal of Metropolitan Life Ins. Co., 310 Pa. 17, 164 A. 715, 86 A.L.R. 1301.

Deposits made with trust company which issued certificates of deposit could not be treated as a "trust" so as to entitle depositors to preference upon company's insolvency on theory that a depositor "trusts" a bank to pay his deposit on demand, or that any one who contracts with another "trusts" that such an agreement will be carried out, since while casually one may speak in such circumstances of a "trust" which is reposed, a "trust" in legal implication is susceptible of no such informality of language. Union Guardian Trust Co. v. Emery, 292 Mich. 394, 290 N.W. 841 (1940).

Duty of depositary to disburse properly according to agreement money deposited as guaranty of performance of contract for sale of business held insufficient to characterize relation between trust company depositary and persons entitled to receive deposit as that of trustee and cestui qua trust, notwithstanding that duties were fiduciary in a sense, and involved exercise of discretion. Dunlop Sand, etc., Corp. v. Hospelhorn, 172 Md. 279, 191 A. 701.

Where trust company was appointed as agent to distribute to bondholders funds from deposits with instructions to hold any funds not paid out subject to depositor's order, and company undertook such duties without compensation, and there was no segregation of deposit and no agreement that deposit was to be held in separate or trust fund, such deposit was not a "trust fund," and hence depositor was not entitled to preference upon company's insolvency. Union Guardian Trust Co. v. Emery, 292 Mich. 394, 290 N.W. 841 (1940).

That trust company was trustee under mortgage and receiver under foreclosure proceedings was immaterial on question of trust relationship between company and bondholder's committee which deposited money with the trust company. Union Guardian Trust Co. v. Emery, 292 Mich. 394, 290 N.W. 841 (1940).

Where director, voluntarily contributed to a special bond account for purpose of taking up depreciation in regular bond account of trust company under agreement that money was to be returned to them when depreciation was made up, the amounts so contributed did not constitute a "trust fund" for purpose specifically recited, entitling directors to preferred

relating to miscellaneous matters in connection with property alleged to be held in a trust or fiduciary capacity are set out in the footnote.[1950]

---

claims for such contributions, upon accomplishment of purpose being prevented by the taking over of the trust company for liquidation. The contract of deposit was not a "certificate of indebtedness" so as to authorize a statutory lien upon proceeds of regular bond account. Thomson v. Holt, 345 Mo. 296, 132 S.W.2d 974.

Evidence which showed bonds never reached their book value as of time contributions were made failed to show that purpose of contributions was accomplished, so as to entitle directors to their return. Thomson v. Holt, 345 Mo. 296, 132 S.W.2d 974.

[1950] **Statement held not fraudulent.—**

A statement by trust company's officers that company was obliged to have use of deposits for investment in order to pay interest was not a fraudulent representation on which to predicate "constructive trust" with consequent right of preference upon company's insolvency, because company was making no investments, where company by agreement was bound to pay interest whether funds were invested or not, and payment of interest out of its general funds and use of money to meet depositors' demands was not fraudulent if there was reasonable supposition that company was not hopelessly insolvent. Union Guardian Trust Co. v. Emery, 292 Mich. 394, 290 N.W. 841.

Commingling of funds.—

Funds impressed with a trust in hands of trust company with which they had been deposited did not lose their character as trust funds by being commingled with those of trust company, since trust once created cannot be destroyed by action of trustee, in absence of intervening right of a purchaser for value without notice. Henson v. Lamb, 120 W. Va. 552, 199 S.E. 459.

Allowances to trustee on accounting.—

Under trust fixing minimum price for sale of vacant lots by trustee at less than $45,000 and providing that lots might be withdrawn from trust on payment of 40 percent of list price, where lots, which produced no income, were sold in good faith for $84,000 in cash and realty worth $9,000, such realty declined in value because of depression, and deficit of $4,250.55 in its operation resulted, liquidator of trustee was entitled to allowance for deficit on accounting, whether or not trustee exceeded its powers under strict construction of trust. Bessel v. Department of Financial Institutions, 213 Ind. 446, 11 N.E.2d 683.

Under trust providing that purchasers of trust realty might make payments to agents of trustors, that trustors should be liable for collections by their agents, and that trustee should be responsible only for money coming into its hands, where purchasers, by mistake, made overpayments because of failure of agent of certain trustor to credit payments properly or deliver money to trustee, trustee repaid overpayments, and trustors were insolvent, liquidator of trustee was entitled to credit on accounting for amount of overpayments. Bessel v. Department of Financial Institutions, 213 Ind. 446, 11 N.E.2d 683.

Claimants of same rank to share pro rata.—

Where depositor had established trust ex maleficio against receiver of insolvent trust company, but record in equity suit did not disclose what other claims were outstanding, or what funds were available to meet them, it wee improper to provide unconditionally for payment of claim with interest from date of receivership, but decree should have provided

(Text continued on page 545)

---

that, if funds were insufficient, depositor would be required to share on pro rata basis with other claimants of same rank, and question of interest should have been deferred until final liquidation. Henson v. Lamb, 120 W. Va. 552, 199 S.E. 459.

Effect of security under statutory provision.—

Statutory provision that capital stock of trust company with liabilities of stockholders and fund deposited with treasurer of state shall be held as security for faithful discharge of duties undertaken by trust company held not intended to give claims against bank carrying on trust business, arising out of violation of its duties as fiduciary, preference over claims of other creditors insofar as capital stock of trust company with liabilities of stockholders thereunder is concerned. Huntington Nat'l Bank v. Fulton, 49 Ohio App. 268, 197 N.E. 204.

Profit made in purchase of collateral for trust estate.—

Beneficiary held entitled to recover as preferred claim from closed bank and trust company difference between face amount and actual market value of collateral purchased by it for trust estate, where bank and trust company received difference as profit. Lauerhass v. Hood, 205 N.C. 190, 170 S.E. 655.

Trust fund not subject to setoff.—

Where claimant's assignor left money with a trust company to be held in trust until released by an association and thereafter assignor assigned his right in the money to claimant, and company had notice of assignment, and association subsequently authorized payment of money to assignor or his nominee, and assignment was made before company attempted to set off a debt owing from assignor, the company did not hold the money as a "deposit" but as a "trust fund," and claimant, after the company was taken over by the secretary of banking, was entitled to the fund free from any claims of setoff by company. In re Bell, 147 Pa. Super. 471, 24 A.2d 101.

Where company sold mortgage notes with guaranty of payment, stipulations in notes and acts of mortgage, including provision that notes were payable solely at company's office, held to impose obligation on company to keep separate bank deposit for funds paid by note-makers to company as agent for note-holders. Tropical Printing Co. v. Union Title Guarantee Co., 180 La. 702, 157 So. 534.

In such a case funds paid in by note-makers and deposited in trustee account, whether deposited there directly when received or subsequently, and funds deposited with receivers by note-makers for payment to note-holders, held to belong to note-holders and payable to them without any deduction for costs of administration or for taxes assessed against corporation. Tropical Printing Co. v. Union Title Guarantee Co., 180 La. 702, 157 So. 534.

But money received from note-makers but deposited by company in its own bank account and never transferred to trustee account belonged to corporation rather than note-holders. Tropical Printing Co. v. Union Title Guarantee Co., 180 La. 702, 157 So. 534.

Ladies.—

In absence of showing that incompetent upon adjudication of restoration to sanity had any knowledge of impropriety of investments made by a trust company guardian or that his delay for considerable period after bonds purchased by guardian went into default before complaining of impropriety of investments constituted acquiescence in investments, incompetent held not guilty of such lashes in suing guardian as to deprive him of right to

§ 47. Money Received by Company Whose Insolvency Is Known to Its Officers.

A trust company which has received a note for collection is a trustee ex maleficio as to proceeds it receives after insolvency and mingles with its own funds. Therefore, an undenied allegation that an officer of a trust company knew of its insolvency when he accepted a certain note for collection necessitates the assumption that it was fraud for the company to receive the proceeds and mingle them with its general funds,[1951] and such proceeds may be traced into a loan which the company's receiver collects, and a preference be established thereby.[1952] Money procured by a trust company by false statements of one of its officers concerning its solvency, and In re turn for which a check on another bank is given, can be recovered from the assignees of the insolvent upon the check being dishonored.[1953] And to prove a claim for money received by a trust company with knowledge of its insolvency, it is not necessary for a plaintiff to trace proceeds belonging to him into a particular account existing when the company failed.[1954] But an averment that the officers of a trust company had knowledge of the company's insolvency was held insufficient to create a trust in favor of a depositor withdrawing funds to purchase a draft on a foreign bank at the instance of an officer of the company.[1955] And a distinction is drawn as respects whether the acceptance of deposits while in an insolvent condition raises a trust ex maleficio, between known irretrievable "insolvency" and mere "insolvency" accompanied by reasonable hopes, expectations and intentions of continuing business and repaying depositors; if officers of a trust company suppose that they can maintain its credit and surmount its difficulties, they are under no duty to disclose its affairs to its customers, and failure to so disclose cannot be held to be fraud.[1956]

---

preferred claim against guardian's receiver. Baxter v. Union Industrial Trust, etc., Bank, 273 Mich. 642, 263 N.W. 762.

[1951] Cameron v. Carnegie Trust Co., 292 Pa. 114, 140 A. 768.

[1952] Reserve Loan Life Ins. Co. v. Dulin, 82 Ind. App. 630, 135 N.E. 590.

[1953] Corn Exch. Nat. Bank v. Solicitors' Loan, etc., Co., 188 Pa. 330, 41 A. 536, 68 Am. St. R. 872.

[1954] Cameron v. Carnegie Trust Co., 292 Pa. 114, 140 A. 768.

[1955] Foley v. Commissioner of Banks, 292 Mass. 83, 197 N.E. 448.

[1956] Union Guardian Trust Co. v. Emery, 292 Mich. 394, 290 N.W. 841.

The acceptance of funds by trust company did not raise a "constructive bust" with consequent right of preference upon company's insolvency on ground that funds were accepted by company while in insolvent condition, where evidence failed to show that at

§ 48. Interest and Dividends

The appointment of receivers for a trust company and its assumption by the state obviates the necessity for any formal demand by depositors for the payment of their deposits so as to entitle them to interest.[1957] But a depositor is entitled to payment of interest after a trust company's dissolution only upon the balance which would have been due to him had he accepted several installments of principal at the time they were paid to creditors by the company's receivers.[1958] And as to creditors, where a trust company is declared insolvent and a receiver appointed, and its assets prove sufficient to pay all creditors in full, they are entitled to interest as against the company

---

time deposits were made official had no reasonable hope or expectation that their efforts to place company on a sound financial basis would prove successful, and that suspension of its business was inevitable. Union Guardian Trust Co. v. Emery, 292 Mich. 394, 290 N.W. 841.

[1957] People v. Merchants' Trust Co., 116 App. Div. 41, 101 N.Y.S. 255, aff'd, 187 N.Y. 293, 79 N.E. 1004.

Where act governing distribution of assets of insolvent trust company made no reference to interest upon deposits, common-law rule permitting preferred depositors to receive interest upon their deposits was applicable. And under such act assets of commercial department of trust company after payment of principal of deposits were applicable to payment of interest accruing on deposits after appointment of receiver. Appeal of Washington Union Trust Co., 350 Pa. 363, 39 A.2d 137.

But savings depositors are entitled only to amount of claims on date commissioner took possession without interest thereafter. In re Prudential Trust Co., 244 Mass. 64, 138 N.E. 702.

[1958] People v. Merchants' Trust Co., 116 App. Div. 41, 101 N.Y.S. 255, aff'd 187 N.Y. 293, 79 N.E. 1004.

and its stockholders.[1959] But no interest is allowed after the appointment of a receiver as between preferred and unpreferred creditors.[1960]

Holders of certificates of deposit issued by an insolvent trust company are entitled to the interest specified in their certificates, from the date of the last payment of interest up to and including the date on which a receiver is appointed, and thereafter at the legal rate upon the respective credit balances due to them up to the date of final payment of the principal.[1961] Similarly, trust company depositors having no interest contracts are entitled to interest at the legal rate upon the amount of their respective credit balances from the date of appointment of a receiver up to the date of final payment of the

---

[1959] **In general.—**

People v. Merchants' Trust Co., 116 App. Div. 41, 101 N.Y.S. 255, aff'd, 187 N.Y. 293, 79 N.E. 1004; People v. American Loan & Trust Co., 172 N.Y. 371, 65 N.E. 200.

But in Pennsylvania, where secretary of banking, in possession of a closed trust company as receiver, paid principal amounts of deposits and general creditors' claims in full, surplus was distributed to stockholders of company in preference to its use for payment of interest to depositors and general creditors, in view of the express provision in the Banking Code for payment of interest to depositors which is due prior to receivership. In re Guardian Bank, etc., Co., 330 Pa. 411, 199 A. 171.

Legislature by amending Banking Code so as to limit payment of interest on funds to interest accruing before receiver enters into possession impliedly recognized that interest was unrestricted theretofore. Appeal of Washington Union Trust Co., 350 Pa. 363, 39 A.2d 137.

Allowance held error.—

Allowance in judgment for plaintiff of interest on claim after affairs of trust company were placed in hands of state bank commissioner was error, where judgment merely established claim as unsecured claim and no showing was made of funds sufficient to pay all other common creditors interest on their claims after insolvency. Barnett v. Kennedy, 185 Okla. 409, 92 P.2d 963.

[1960] People v. American Loan, etc., Co., 172 N.Y. 371, 65 N.E. 200.

Payment of interest from the date of the appointment of the receiver to preferred creditors on their claims will not be allowed where such payment would exhaust the funds in the hand, of the receiver, and leave nothing for the unpreferred creditors.

People v. American Loan & Trust Co., 172 N.Y. 371, 65 N.E. 200.

A creditor of a trust company in process of liquidation cannot be permitted to increase his provable claim by the amount of interest due since the date when the commissioner of banks took possession of the trust company over general creditor, whose claims are ascertained as of that date. Cosmopolitan Trust Co. v. Suffolk Knitting Mills, 247 Mass. 530, 143 N.E. 138 (1924); Augello v. Hanover Trust Co., 253 Mass. 160, 148 N.E. 138; Cunningham v. Com'r of Banks, 249 Mass. 401, 144 N.E. 447.

[1961] People v. Merchants' Trust Co., 116 App. Div. 41, 101 N.Y.S. 255, aff'd, 187 N.Y. 293, 79 N.E. 1004.

principal.[1962] Interest on a loan by the Reconstruction Finance Corporation to an insolvent trust company to pay dividends to savings depositors should be paid out of the principal of segregated assets.[1963]

A claimant against a trust company in liquidation is entitled to interest on costs from the date a court directs payment of a dividend on his judgments.[1964] And a trust company creditor whose dividend is deferred by reason of an unsuccessful contest of his claim is entitled to interest on the dividend founded upon his judgments, notwithstanding he had been allowed interest in computing the amount of such judgments.[1965] But funds will not be reserved to pay deposits or other claims against a trust company which have been unproved within the time limits of a court decree.[1966] Where assets of a trust company's savings department were transferred to the commercial department in exchange for securities not constituting lawful investments for savings deposits or not approved by a committee, interest cannot be allowed in adjusting the conflicting rights of depositors.[1967]

Creditors of an insolvent trust company, holding securities for their indebtedness, were held entitled to dividends based only on the amount of indebtedness remaining unpaid after the sale of such securities, not on the full amount of the original debt.[1968] Depositors in a trust company's savings department not presenting claims within the time limit in their notice or prior to the authorization of dividends are entitled to the same dividends previously ordered paid to the other depositors.[1969] And a conservator of a trust company, having sound reason to believe that the liability of a stockholder would be difficult to collect, was held to have properly retained, as ordered, such stockholder's liquidating dividend; such liability was a

---

[1962] People v. Merchants' Trust Co., 116 App. Div. 41, 101 N.Y.S. 255, aff'd, 187 N.Y. 293, 79 N.E. 1004.

[1963] Bassett v. Merchants' Trust Co., 115 Conn. 530, 161 A. 789, 82 A.L.R. 1223.

[1964] In re Carnegie Trust Co., 161 App. Div. 280, 146 N.Y.S. 809.

[1965] In re Carnegie Trust Co., 161 App. Div. 280, 146 N.Y.S. 809.

[1966] In re Hanover Trust Co., 252 Mass. 348, 148 N.E. 130.

[1967] Petition of Allen, 240 Mass. 478, 134 N.E. 253.

[1968] In re United Security Trust Co., 321 Pa. 276, 184 A. 106.

[1969] Petitions of Allen, 241 Mass. 346, 136 N.E. 269.

proper setoff in equity against a dividend claim.[1970] See the footnote for other decisions relating to dividends in this context.[1971]

A party to a contract providing for the sole discretion of a board of directors to declare dividends violates the implied covenant of good faith and fair dealing if it acts arbitrarily or unreasonably, under Delaware law. Virginia law similarly provides where discretion is lodged in one of two

---

[1970] Cooper v. Fidelity Trust Co., 132 Me. 260, 170 A. 726.

[1971] **Recovery of dividend with interest.—**

Where commissioner of banks, after taking possession of trust company in which defendants' testator allegedly held stock, acted for benefit of company's creditors in withholding payment of dividend on deposit, which testator had in company's saving, department, in effort to hold defendants liable to creditors of trust company, and testator's estate was not subject to statutory liability, defendants could recover unpaid balance of dividend with interest at 6 per cent from date when dividend was paid to other creditor, of company. Director of Liquidations v. Wood, 306 Mass. 1, 26 N.E.2d 979.

Unclaimed dividend warrants.—

The act providing that unclaimed dividend warrants issued on the account of a defunct trust company should be canceled and money represented thereby should be paid to the trust company was inapplicable to warrants representing money in hands of comptroller which he received from a trust company which held them in capacity of trustee. Miller v. Lee, 149 Fla. 440, 6 So. 2d 4.

Surety entitled to dividend.—

Where negotiable certificate of deposit was transferred by payee as security for liability as surety on bond on which transferee was compelled to pay money, and payee was indebted to trust company, surety was entitled to any dividend on certificate up to amount paid out by him. National Surety Co. v. Allen, 243 Mass. 218, 137 N.E. 533.

Pledge of coupon-bearing certificates.—

Where a trust company created a mortgage pool issuing guaranteed coupon-bearing certificates, and certain holders thereof pledged them with the trust company as collateral for loans and subsequently a receiver took possession of trust company and a substituted trustee was appointed to liquidate the pool, and the pledgors were not in default, under the statute, the relationship of pledgor and pledges continued to exist between pledgers and trust company, and liquidation dividends belonged to the pledgors subject to the lien of the receiver of the trust company, and were not required to be turned over to the substituted trustee to be distributed among other certificate holders. In re Gordon 344 Pa. 262, 25 A.2d 304.

Court did not abuse its discretion in directing payment of 17½ per cent dividend on claims against reorganized trust company from money which general trustees and liquidating trustee thereof were authorized to borrow from bank for payment Of claims, though tracer claims in estimated amount less than money to be collected on stock assessment before payment of further dividends had not been established. O'Brien v. Hirschfeld, 285 Mich. 308, 281 N.W. 9.

parties to a contract such discretion must be exercised in good faith.[1972] A limit upon a board's discretion to withhold dividends stems from its fiduciary duties to shareholders, not from the terms of their stock certificates. Such fiduciary duties have no bearing upon whether contract terms imposed a duty to declare dividends. Therefore, the court rejected the claim by class plaintiffs that stock certificates guaranteed them a right to dividends, discretionary though they might be, and agreed with the the Federal Housing Finance Agency (FHFA) that the class plaintiffs had no enforceable right to dividends because the certificates accorded the companies complete discretion to declare or withhold dividends.[1973]

§ 49. Setoff.

A setoff cannot be allowed in distributing the assets of an insolvent trust company where its allowance will destroy the order or equality of distribution provided by statute.[1974] Thus, in an action by an insolvent trust company on a note, the defendant cannot counterclaim for more than the amount sued for and collect the difference until the rights of depositors are satisfied, where there exists a statute giving depositors and others preference.[1975] And trust company depositors seeking to set off an amount due them from checking and savings accounts are chargeable with knowledge that their statutory rights are similar to those of depositors in an ordinary savings bank.[1976]

Whatever right a state banking official has to set off a depositor's accounts with a trust company against the depositor's notes to the company, accrues

---

[1972] Perry Capital LLC ex rel. Inv. Funds v. Mnuchin, 864 F.3d 591 (D.C. Cir. 2017).

[1973] Perry Capital LLC ex rel. Inv. Funds v. Mnuchin, 864 F.3d 591 (D.C. Cir. 2017).

[1974] Lippitt v. Thames Loan & Trust Co., 88 Conn. 185, 90 A. 369.

A defendant may not have equitable set-off of claims which could not be set off at law against a claim of the trust company on a note, where to do so would be to give such depositor priority over other creditors entitled to share equally in any recovery from him. Cosmopolitan Trust Co. v. Wasserman, 251 Mass 514, 146 N.E. 772.

[1975] Fisher v. Davis, 278 Pa. 129, 122 A. 224.

[1976] Dole v. Chattabriga, 82 N.H. 396, 134 A. 347.

Under the Massachusetts statute, the depositor in the commercial department of a trust company held not entitled to maintain a cross action at law against the trust company, which was in the process of liquidation and in possession of the commissioner of banks, to recover the amount due on its checking account, where the trust company brought action to recover on a note, first discounted in its commercial department and paid at its face value with funds of that department. Cosmopolitan Trust Co. v. Suffolk Knitting Mills, 247 Mass. 530, 143 N.E. 138 (1924).

as of the date of the company's failure and appointment of a receiver for it.[1977] And a state banking official, occupying an insolvent trust company's business premises in performing his official duties, is entitled to set off a sum owing the insolvent by a bankrupt landlord is interest against the bankrupt's claim for rent. But he is not entitled to set off the insolvent's claim for money due from the landlord against a rent demand by the landlord after such landlord's adjudication in bankruptcy.[1978] A trust company in liquidation was held not entitled to counterclaim for payments made on a note of its directors who relieved the company of a disapproved investment.[1979] And a state banking official in charge of a trust company which as trustee under a will advanced interest payments to a life beneficiary before collections were made, could not set off against such prepayments interest collected since the company's closing, where the beneficiary permitted a setoff of such prepayments against her deposit.[1980]

A holder of a guaranteed mortgage participation certificate is not entitled to set off his claim under the guaranty against indebtedness owing by him to a trust company until the amount of his claim is definitely established.[1981] But where a bank and trust company unauthorizedly attempted to create trusts out of its own securities, consisting in whole or in part of mortgage obligations, the mortgagors on the insolvency of such company could set off their deposits against their indebtedness, regardless of whether their indebtedness was then due.[1982] A person indebted to a trust company on a note, and having a deposit to his credit therein, may set off the deposit against the amount due on the note upon suit thereon by a state banking official.[1983] Thus, where a trust company in which an administratrix had a deposit account passed into the hands of a receiver owning a claim against the intestate's estate, the administratrix was entitled to have the one set off

---

[1977] In re Gordon, 319 Pa. 367, 179 A. 592.

[1978] Citizens' Sav., etc., Co. v. Rogers, 162 Wis. 216, 155 N.W. 155.

[1979] Leary v. Capitol Trust Co., 238 App. Div. 661, 265 N.Y.S. 856, aff'd, 263 N.Y. 640, 189 N.E. 735.

[1980] In re Nauman's Estate, 110 Pa. Super. 55, 167 A. 395.

[1981] Kelly v. Middlesex Title Guarantee, etc, Co., 116 N.J. Eq. 228, 172 A. 487.

[1982] Ulmer v. Fulton, 129 Ohio St. 323, 195 N.E. 557, 97 A.L.R. 1170.

[1983] Roseville Trust Co. v. Barney, 89 N.J.L. 550, 99 A. 343.

Makers of notes payable to loan association held entitled to credit for payments on notes before association's insolvency and to tender balance due as full payment on notes. In re Trusteeship for Holders of Debentures, etc., 214 Iowa 884, 241 N.W. 308.

against the other.[1984] And in a suit on a note by an insolvent trust company under a statute allowing unliquidated damages arising from any contract to be set off whenever capable of liquidation by any known legal standard, a claim for bonds embezzled by the secretary-treasurer of the company is a proper setoff.[1985] A tenant under a lease with "trust company, agent" could set off his deposit in the trust company against rent to become due under the lease, where the unnamed principal was a building corporation which had been organized to take title to and hold the building for the company which owned all its stock.[1986] But in an action by an insolvent trust company, a defendant is not entitled to set off an amount paid for capital stock of the company when organized, because a certificate of increase of capital stock was not filed as required by statute.[1987] And a solvent trust company as the depository of an insolvent trust company's deposit representing a trust fund cannot set off such deposit against its deposit also representing a trust fund in the insolvent company.[1988]

Under a statute permitting mutual debts between plaintiffs and defendants to be set off, in an action by the receiver of an insolvent trust company against a partnership upon its negotiable note, one of the partners could not set off an individual debt due from the trust company unless the note was joint and several.[1989] And a state banking official was held not entitled to set off a depositor's insurance and agency accounts in an insolvent trust company against an amount due the company on the depositor's individual notes.[1990] Where an insolvent trust company held an amount which it had collected as agent of a correspondent bank, a sum due the company in its corporate capacity from the correspondent bank could not be set off against such amount held in trust[1991] Similarly, where, as between bondholders who

---

[1984] People by Webb v. California Safe Deposit & Trust Co., 168 Cal. 241, 141 P. 1181, 1915A L.R.A. 299.

And in such a case she was not limited to an action against the receiver or to the assertion of her claim in the insolvency proceedings. In re Bell, 168 Cal. 253, 141 P. 1179.

[1985] Fisher v. Davis, 278 Pa. 129, 122 A. 224.

[1986] In re Harr, 319 Pa. 89, 179 A. 238.

[1987] Cosmopolitan Trust Co. v. Wasserman, 251 Mass. 514, 146 N.E. 772.

[1988] Gordon v. Union Trust Co., 308 Pa. 493, 162 A. 293.

[1989] Lippitt v. Thames Loan, etc., Co., 88 Conn. 185, 90 A. 369.

[1990] In re Gordon, 319 Pa. 367, 179 A. 592, so holding though company's officials did not know of nature and character of such accounts, in absence of contention that they were misled.

[1991] Lippitt v. Thames Loan, etc., Co., 88 Conn. 185, 90 A. 369.

borrowed from a trust company and those who did not, there was a common venture as to a profit fund held in trust by the company for the payment of the bonds at maturity, the borrowing bondholders are not entitled to an equitable setoff in receivership proceedings.[1992]

For other cases dealing with the right of setoff in this context, see the footnote.[1993]

[1992] Fell v. Securities Co., 11 Del. Ch. 101, 97 A. 610.

[1993] **Trustees' certificates.—**

Where certificates issued to a trust company's creditors by trustees for such creditors had been purchased for five to fifteen cents on the dollar by unknown parties acting through other companies controlled by the trustees, and new certificates in smaller denominations had been issued, in lieu of the certificates so purchased, to persons indebted to the trustees, the new certificates were improperly set off against such persons' obligations to the trust estate, in the absence of circumstances, such as the obligors' insolvency, justifying acceptance of the certificates in satisfaction of claims. Behrman v. Egan, 17 N.J. Super. 598, 86 A.2d 606.

Agreement for setoff.—

Where owner of mortgaged land entered into contract for extension of mortgage and opened account with trust company falsely representing that it owned mortgage, owner was held entitled to enforce company's agreement that in case of insolvency any amount on deposit could be set off against amount due on mortgage, owner was held entitled to enforce agreement upon trust company's failure. Kisinger v. Pennsylvania Trust Co., 119 Pa. Super. 16, 180 A. 79, wherein finding of such agreement was held sustained by the evidence.

Plan for reorganization of trust company adopted under act relating to reorganization of banks and trust companies, whereby holders of guarantees released company from liability thereon, did not deprive either depositors or general creditors, including holders of guarantees, of right of setoff, but merely fixed amount of respective participation certificates to be received by depositors and other creditors in amount of such claims after allowance of any setoff to which they were respectively entitled under the law. Smith v. Stricker, 123 Pa. Super. 181, 186 A. 369.

Maker of note which was payable to trust company could offset amount of bonds which trust company had guaranteed and which were in default when plan for reorganization of trust company went into effect, notwithstanding that note had been transferred to liquidating trustees under reorganization plan, where trustees were voluntary assignees of note for purposes of liquidation and distribution only, and were not assignees for value. Smith v. Stricker, 123 Pa. Super. 181, 186 A. 369.

Setoff allowing undue preference.—

In suit by receiver of trust company, assets of which were abstracted and converted by certain stockholders and receiver of national bank controlling company, thereby defrauding company's creditors, to restore status quo, stockholder held not entitled to setoff for compensation allowed him by state court for services rendered to trust company prior to its receivership, since allowance of such setoff would allow stockholder undue preference over other creditors of company of like class. Taylor v. Spurway, 16 F. Supp. 566, rev'd on other grounds sub nom. Bancroft v. Taylor, 91 F.2d 579.

§ 50. Expenses of Administration and Compensation of Receivers and Their Attorneys.

General expenses of the liquidation of a trust company fall on its general assets.[1994] Assets of the savings department of a trust company, so far as needed to pay savings depositors, are not liable for general expenses, but incidental expenses necessary for particular conservation may be charged to the specific property concerned,[1995] and the same is true of securities deposited for the benefit of holders of debenture bonds issued by the company.[1996] And expenses of recovering for a trust company's savings department assets wrongfully appropriated by the commercial department, and enforcing stockholders' liabilities, must be paid from general funds.[1997]

1994 **In general.—**

Baldwin v. Commissioner of Banks, 283 Mass. 423, 168 N.E. 638, 89 A.L.R. 1212.

Allowance for acts done or expenses incurred in good faith by superintendent of banks in liquidation of trust company, in the interests of creditors or of the company, which result in loss, may be made out of the company's assets. Leal v. Westchester Trust Co., 279 N.Y. 25, 17 N.E.2d 673.

Costs of foreclosure.—

Banking commissioner taking over insolvent trust company could pay out of general assets expenses of foreclosing mortgages held by company as general assets, and in first instance pay out of general assets expenses of foreclosure of mortgages guaranteed, reimbursing general assets out of ultimately recovered proceeds of sale of mortgaged premises. Kelly v. Middlesex Title Guarantee & Trust Co., 116 NJ. Eq. 228, 172 A. 487.

Banking commissioner taking over trust company which had sold guaranteed mortgages and participation certificates would, ordinarily, in case of foreclosure sale, have prior right in proceeds of sale to extent of costs of foreclosure. Kelly v. Middlesex Title Guarantee, etc., Co., 116 N.J. Eq. 228, 172 A. 487.

As to lien on mortgaged premises for expenses of administration, see § 38 of this chapter.

1995 In re Prudential Trust Co., 244 Mass. 64, 138 N.E 702.

In a proceeding by the commissioner of banks for leave to transfer securities from the savings to the commercial department of a trust company, attorneys' fees for counsel representing the savings depositors are properly allowed out of the funds of the savings department. Petition of Allen, 240 Mass. 478, 134 N.E. 253.

Statutes held to require that savings department of trust company bear out of its own resources all expenses, losses, and depreciation of securities connected with its maintenance and management, before payment in full of deposits, and that trust company out of its general assets bear all other expenses, losses, and depredations, however caused. Baldwin v. Commissioner of Banks, 283 Mass. 423, 186 N.E. 638, 89 A.L.R. 1212.

1996 Bank Com'rs v. Security Trust Co., 75 N.H. 107, 71 A. 377.

1997 In re Prudential Trust Co., 244 Mass. 64, 138 N.E. 702.

For other cases relating to expenses of administration on a trust company's liquidation, see the footnote.[1998]

The amount of compensation to be allowed receivers of a trust or investment company and their counsel rests within the court's discretion.[1999] And permitting a receiver discharged on the reorganization of an insolvent

---

[1998] **Expenses apportioned between receiver and claimant.—**

In proceeding for liquidation of trust company, costs and expenses of hearing on claims which were allowed in part and disallowed in part were required to be apportioned equally between receiver and claimant. People ex rel. Barrett v. Central Republic Trust Co., 300 Ill. App. 297, 20 N.E.2d 999.

Claim for deposit to pay note-holders not taxed for costs.—

On insolvency of company which made real estate loans and sold mortgage notes with guaranty of payment, claim of individual for money deposited with company for payment to note-holders, claimant having obtained assignment from note-holders, should not be taxed for costs of administration since money belonged to claimant and not to insolvent corporation. Tropical Printing Co. v. Union Title Guarantee Co., 180 La. 702, 157 So. 534.

[1999] **In general.—**

People v. Knickerbocker Trust Co., 127 App. Div. 215, 217, 111 N.Y.S. 2, appeal dismissed, 193 N.Y. 649, 86 N.E. 1129.

District Court, appointing receiver for investment trust pursuant to complaint of Securities and Exchange Commission charging management of trust with gross abuse of trust, had sound discretion to allow compensation for legal services and for services of receivers. See Bailey v. Proctor, 160 F.2d 78 (1947), 166 F.2d 392 (1948).

Trustee's allowance.—

Trustee appointed for corporations operating as investment companies in violation of the Investment Company Act was entitled to an allowance of $100,000 based on his efforts and exertions in successfully selling approximately 480,000 shares of stock in a certain company at a net profit of approximately $2,000,000, in a race against time, due to falling value of the stock. Securities & Exch. Comm'n v. S & P Nat'l Corp., 267 F. Supp. 562 (S.D.N.Y. 1967).

Trustee's attorneys' award proper.—

Award of $50,000 plus stated disbursements was proper compensation for trustee's attorneys based on an allowance of approximately $48.00 an hour, under circumstances presented in action wherein a receiver and trustee were appointed for corporations operating their business as investment companies in violation of the Investment Company Act. SEC v. S & P. Nat'l Corp., 267 F. Supp. 562 (S.D.N.Y. 1967).

In derivative action brought by stockholder of management investment company on ground that individual defendants by virtue of their control of defendant corporation, which controlled plaintiff's company, had caused plaintiff's company substantial damage, allowance and imposition of costs and expenses of receivership pendente lite of plaintiff's company rested in sound discretion of court which could tax costs prior to final disposition of litigation, determine which of parties might be assessed and apportion costs among various parties. Tanzer v. Huffines, 315 F. Supp. 1140 (D. Del. 1970).

trust company to retain money as security for undetermined fees and expenses is proper.[2000] It is not necessary to institute a separate proceeding for allowance of compensation and expenses of temporary receivers of a company, the proper practice being to settle such claims in the proceeding by the receivers for the settlement of their accounts, and to direct payment thereof out of the company's assets before they are turned over to the persons otherwise entitled thereto.[2001] A state banking official as statutory receiver rendering services in a trust company's liquidation is not bound by a prior agreement of the company limiting or waiving his compensation.[2002] But the provisions of a banking act concerning payment of expenses of liquidation of closed banks would be considered in determining whether a statutory receiver was entitled to compensation for services rendered and expenses incurred in liquidation of a mortgage pool out of the income of the pool.[2003] And upon liquidation of a trust company issuing bond and

---

2000 Jennings v. Fidelity, etc., Trust Co., 240 Ky. 24, 41 S.W.2d 537.

2001 People v. Knickerbocker Trust Co., 127 App. Div. 215, 111 N.Y.S. 2, appeal dismissed, 193 N.Y. 649, 86 N.E. 1129.

2002 Philippi v. Beckman, 135 Pa. Super. 268, 5 A.2d 430 (1939).

An agreement, if any, between a trust company prior to its insolvency and participants in a mortgage pool which limited expenses or losses incurred in management of pool did not bind secretary of banking, subsequently appointed as statutory receiver, insofar as secretary's right to commissions for liquidating a mortgage pool was concerned. Philippi v. Beckman, 135 Pa. Super. 268, 5 A.2d 430 (1939).

A guaranty provision in participating trust certificates providing that a trust company guaranteed payment of principal and interest without deductions for expenses or losses incurred in management of a mortgage pool was applicable only when company was operating as a going concern and did not affect right of secretary of banking as statutory receiver to compensation for services in liquidating pool. Philippi v. Beckman, 135 Pa. Super. 268, 5 A.2d 430 (1939).

In collecting compensation for services in liquidation of a mortgage pool, secretary of banking, as statutory receiver of trust company, was not bound by provisions of agreement between trust company and participating mortgage certificate holders to the effect that commercial department of trust company should bear all losses or expenses incurred in management of mortgage pool. Philippi v. Beckman, 135 Pa. Super. 268, 5 A.2d 430 (1939).

2003 Philippi v. Beckman, 135 Pa. Super. 268, 5 A.2d 430 (1939).

Compensation of secretary of banking, as statutory receiver of a trust company, for services rendered and expenses incurred in liquidating a portion of a mortgage pool was payable out of income of pool, rather than by commercial department of company, notwithstanding that pool was set up by commercial department and that participating certificates issued to outside parties contained a guaranty of payment of principal and interest without provision for deduction for expenses or losses incurred in management of pool. Philippi v. Beckman, 135 Pa. Super. 268, 5 A.2d 430 (1939).

mortgage participation certificates which did not contemplate servicing charges or management fees, a state banking official was held entitled to reimbursement only for his necessary servicing and management.[2004] For other cases dealing with compensation of receivers on liquidation, see the footnote.[2005]

An attorney, accepting a court order allowing him compensation for ordinary services as attorney for a trust company's receivers, cannot claim additional compensation for disbursements, except in connection with extraordinary services subsequently rendered.[2006] For other cases relating to compensation of attorneys on liquidation, see the footnote.[2007]

§ 51. Actions.

Right of Action.—Under the usual liquidation statutes, a trust company remains in existence as a corporate entity even though a state banking official has taken possession of its property and business, and it is subject to

---

[2004] In re Mutual Trust Co., 48 N.Y.S.2d 707.

[2005] **Commission received for extending bonds.—**

In proceeding for liquidation of trust company which had been trustee under trust deed securing bonds, trust company would not be permitted to retain as against bondholders commission received for extending bonds by reason of which trust company was able to receive payment on bonds owned by itself and its officers after recommending extension by bondholders following serious default in payment of taxes. People v. Central Republic Trust Co., 300 Ill. App. 297, 20 N.E.2d 999.

[2006] **In general.—**

Reichert v. Metropolitan Trust Co., 266 Mich. 322, 253 N.W. 313, wherein evidence of extraordinary services was held to require increase of compensation.

Allowance of excessive fee to appraiser of assets of trust company in receivers' hands would not justify allowance of proportionately higher fee to receivers' attorney. Reichert v. Metropolitan Trust Co., 266 Mich. 322, 253 N.W. 313.

Attorney, not contesting court's order allowing fees for ordinary service, as attorney for trust company's receivers until after substitution of other attorneys over two months after entry of order, nor tendering his resignation, because of inadequacy of compensation granted, held bound by such order. Reichert v. Metropolitan Trust Co., 266 Mich. 322, 253 N.W. 313.

[2007] **Time of awarding attorney's fees.—**

An accrual against trust estate following appointment of a receiver and trustee for corporations operating their businesses as investment companies in violation of the Investment Company Act for services rendered by attorney, for corporate defendants would be deferred until conclusion of the case where it was not clear who controlled corporate defendants. SEC v. S & P. Nat'l Corp., 267 F. Supp. 562 (S.D.N.Y. 1967).

suits and actions in appropriate cases.[2008] Creditors of a trust company are entitled to have the true relationship concerning a depositor's account established by the course of dealing between the parties, and in conformity with the rule that equality is equity.[2009] But the fact that proceedings to collect a certain claim were by exceptions to distribution in liquidation of a trust company before judgment, rather than after, does not enlarge a creditor's right.[2010] And where a statute provides an exclusive method of procedure for liquidation of a trust company and establishing one's right to share in its assets, it must be followed.[2011] Thus, a transaction relied upon by a claimant against the assets of an insolvent trust company in the hands of a state banking official for liquidation, must be fully set forth by such claimant in a claim presented to and filed with the official before any other proceedings can be instituted by such claimant against the official, the assets in his hands, or securities pledged with the state treasurer by the company.[2012] And a purchaser of trust company assets is obligated to enforce a stockholders' liability before proceeding against directors guaranteeing the company's debt.[2013] A suit by debenture holders against an insolvent debenture company which has ceased to do business except to collect all

---

[2008] Cosmopolitan Trust Co. v. Suffolk Knitting Mills, 247 Mass. 530, 143 N.E. 138 (1924).

[2009] Lebaudy v. Carnegie Trust Co., 90 Misc. 490, 154 N.Y.S. 900.

[2010] In re Cameron, 287 Pa. 560, 135 A. 295, 58 A.L.R. 554, aff'd, 276 U.S. 592, 48 S. Ct. 212, 72 L. Ed. 721.

[2011] Inland Properties Co. v. Union Properties, 44 Ohio Op. 485, 98 N.E.2d 444 (Ohio C.P.), appeal dismissed, 150 Ohio St. 490, 83 N.E.2d 69.

In order for a claimant to establish his right to share in the asset, of a trust company which superintendent of banks has taken charge of for liquidation purposes, claimant must bring his action against superintendent of banks and defunct trust company in accordance with statute. Hence, an action to establish plaintiff as a depositor and creditor of defunct trust company and to obtain a share in distribution of that company's assets could not be maintained against corporation organized to assist superintendent of banks in liquidation of banks. Inland Properties Co. v. Union Properties, 44 Ohio Op. 485, 98 N.E.2d 444 (Ohio C.P.), appeal dismissed, 150 Ohio St. 490, 88 N.E.2d 69.

Evidence that depositor of trust company secured money with which to purchase foreign draft by withdrawal of savings deposit upon advice of company's officer held not to give depositor right of election to bring suit against commissioner of banks in charge of liquidating trust company, but depositor was required to follow course prescribed by liquidating statute as to proof of claims. Foley v. Commissioner of Banks, 292 Mass. 83, 197 N.E. 448.

[2012] Wisconsin Trust Co. v. Cousins, 172 Wis. 486, 179 N.W. 801.

[2013] Morse v. International Trust Co., 259 Mass. 295, 156 N.E. 443.

existing debentures, praying for the appointment of a receiver, a settlement of the affairs of the company, together with payment to the holders of the amounts paid by them less the amounts received from matured coupons, and a decree to prevent an officer of the company from obtaining possession of the guaranty fund of the company, may be maintained even though their debentures have not matured.[2014] But where the time of payment of a savings deposit with a trust company had been extended, when a depositor issued a writ to recover the deposit on the ground that notice of withdrawal had been given prior to the enactment of the statute authorizing the extension, the depositor could not recover the deposit since it was not payable when the writ was issued.[2015] And a decree by a court of equity fixing a time more than two years after a state banking official takes possession of a trust company as the time after which no new suit or action against him can be brought, has been held reasonable, valid and binding.[2016] For other cases relating to rights of action on insolvency of a trust company, see the footnote.[2017]

Parties and Standing to Sue.—Where an insolvent trust company's property is taken over by a state banking official the company is the party aggrieved, and its directors are in no position to object.[2018] In fact, when the receiver of a small business corporation is charged with the responsibility for obtaining assets of the corporation prior to its liquidation, such responsibility includes bringing suit on any causes of action which the corporation has

---

[2014] Christian v. Michigan Debenture Co., 134 Mich. 171, 96 N.W. 22.

[2015] Statler v. United States Sav., etc., Co., 122 Pa. Super. 189, 186 A. 290.

[2016] Suffolk Knitting Mills v. Cosmopolitan Trust Co., 252 Mass. 394, 147 N.E. 830.

[2017] **Adequacy of legal remedy.—**

Receiver of trust company, assets of which were abstracted and converted by certain stockholders and receiver of national bank controlling company, thereby defrauding latter's creditors, held entitled to equitable relief; money judgment at law not being complete adequate remedy. Taylor v Spurway, 72 F.2d 97.

Necessity for establishment of creditor's claim and determination of insolvency.—

A solvent trust company's state court receiver, appointed at instance of creditor with an unliquidated and unadjudicated claim, was not entitled to proceeds of assets transferred to national bank's receiver in payment of stock in company owned by bank and allegedly converted, as trust fund, until establishment of creditor's claim and determination of whether company was rendered insolvent by distribution, and, if so, receiver could recover only amount which made company insolvent and was needed to pay off unpaid creditors. Bancroft v. Taylor, 91 F.2d 579.

[2018] LaMonte v. Lurich, 86 N.J. Eq. 26, 100 A. 1031, aff'd, 86 N.J. Eq. 251, 98 A. 1086.

against its former directors, officers or majority shareholders.[2019] Under statutes authorizing a state banking official to sue in the name of a delinquent corporation for debts due such corporation, the official has no legal capacity to bring an action in his own name against a surety company on a bond and mortgage given to a delinquent trust company.[2020] Where a state banking official asks a court for an order to a trust company to show cause why he should not be allowed to transfer certain funds from one department of the company to another, the company is thereby given the right to appear and be heard.[2021] And where a statute authorizes receivers of a banking or trust company to enforce the double liability of shareholders for the benefit of creditors, a court decree assessing shareholders' liability and authorizing receivers to collect the same is not limited solely to shareholders at the time of receivership, but includes those who have died subsequent thereto and authorizes an action against their estates.[2022] An insolvent trust company's technical release of directors whose negligence caused its loss which contains a reservation of the right to sue non-parties thereto, does not discharge the latter, but is merely a covenant not to sue parties thereto.[2023]

A trust company is not a necessary party to a petition by a state banking official for instructions as to authority to transfer funds, the liability of stockholders not being affected,[2024] nor is it a proper party to a suit by its directors against a purchaser of its assets to effect the release of the directors as guarantors of its debt.[2025] Where an assignor assigns his entire claim to a deposit to another, he is not a necessary party to a suit to require a state banking official to issue a certificate of proof and pay a declared dividend.[2026] In a suit by a depositor in a closed bank and trust company to establish a lien in the nature of a pledge against the proceeds of securities deposited with the state treasurer, the latter was held a proper party.[2027] A supplemental bill is not necessary to make a liquidator of an insolvent trust company appointed

---

[2019] Small Business Administration v. Segal, 383 F. Supp. 198 (D. Conn. 1974).

[2020] Van Tuyl v. New York, etc., Security Co., 153 App. Div. 409, 138 N.Y.S. 541, aff'd, 207 N.Y. 691, 101 N.E. 1096.

[2021] In re Cosmopolitan Trust Co., 240 Mass. 254, 133 N.E. 630.

[2022] Johnson v. Libby, 111 Me. 204, 88 A. 647, 1916C Ann. Cas. 681.

[2023] LaMonte v. Lurich, 86 N.J. Eq. 26, 100 A. 1031, aff'd, 86 N.J. Eq. 251, 98 A. 1086.

[2024] In re Cosmopolitan Trust Co., 240 Mass. 254, 133 N.E. 630.

[2025] Morse v. International Trust Co., 259 Mass. 295, 156 N.E. 443.

[2026] Levenbaum v Hanover Trust Co., 253 Mass. 19, 148 N.E. 227.

[2027] Leyvraz v. Johnson, 114 Fla. 396, 154 So. 159.

under statute a party to a cause in which the trust company is interested.[2028] And where trust company creditors are represented in its receivership proceedings, their personal appearance is unnecessary.[2029] An action against a trust company in liquidation, for negligence in managing an apartment building, may be brought against the company or against the state superintendent of banks as liquidator, and the form or description of the defendant is immaterial.[2030] The receiver of an investment fund which was an unincorporated association under Colorado law, and thus had the capacity to sue, possessed standing to sue the fund's manager and others for dissipation of its assets in view of the grievous economic loss incurred by the fund from the operation of an alleged Ponzi scheme, which was fairly traceable to the challenged conduct of the defendants.[2031]

There is no private right of action for a bank's failure to report suspicious activity under the federal anti money laundering regulations. Therefore, claim against bank in case involving alleged Ponzi scheme for negligence with knowledge of fiduciary relationship was dismissed.[2032]

The Financial Institutions Reform, Recovery, and Enforcement Act of 1989 (FIRREA) is silent, and case law is largely unsettled, on whether FIRREA's exhaustion requirement must be satisfied before a party can bring an action against an entity that purchases assets and liabilities of a failed institution from the Federal Deposit Insurance Corporation (FDIC).[2033] Nothing in FIRREA carves out an exception for claims relating to the liabilities of a failed bank that have been assumed by a successor bank under a purchase and assumption agreement with the FDIC as receiver. Rather, the statutory subsection broadly covers, without any words of limitation or

---

[2028] Eureka Corp. v. Guardian Trust Co., 104 Fla. 117, 139 So. 198.

[2029] Jennings v. Fidelity, etc., Trust Co., 240 Ky. 24, 41 S.W.2d 537.

[2030] Leal v. Westchester Trust Co., 279 N.Y. 25, 17 N.E.2d 673.

An action by apartment owners for the negligence of a trust company in liquidation, in the management of the apartments resulting in damages to the building, would lie against the superintendent of banks in charge in his official capacity, as against the contention that the action must be against the superintendent personally. Leal v. Westchester Trust Co., 279 N.Y. 25, 17 N.E.2d 673.

[2031] Johnson v. Chilcott, 599 F. Supp. 224 (D.C. Colo. 1984).

[2032] Mansor v. JPMorgan Chase Bank, N.A., 183 F. Supp. 3d 250 (D. Mass. 2016). See 12 C.F.R. § 21.11, 31 C.F.R. § 1020.320.

[2033] Douglas County v. Hamilton State Bank, 340 Ga. App. 801, 798 S.E.2d 509 (2017).

restriction, any claim relating to any act or omission of a failed bank placed in receivership.[2034]

Intervention.—Where a trust company holding securities of a loan company in trust to secure its debentures, petitions a court in insolvency proceedings against the loan company asking for an order permitting it to collect or sell the securities in its hands, and making its costs and expenses a charge against the fund realized, debenture holders, who deny the company's right under the trust agreement to so charge costs and expenses, are entitled to intervene and contest such petition.[2035] And where a state banking official, having taken over a trust company, petitions a court for instructions as to his authority to transfer funds from the commercial to the savings department of the company, a depositor in the commercial department is entitled to intervene.[2036] But where a state banking official has taken a stand against any preference to the commonwealth and there is no adversary interest between him, the trust company and the general depositors, the latter are not entitled to intervene in the commonwealth's suit to compel payment of its claim as preferred.[2037] And in a state banking official's suit to foreclose a pledge securing a debt to an insolvent trust company, an intervention by creditors of certain corporations controlled by the debtors is demurrable.[2038] In proceedings to liquidate a savings and trust company, a depositor who had made deposits before the company came under the provisions of a certain statute, could not, by a petition in the nature of intervention, argue that an order requiring the state treasurer to pay to the state banking official money from funds belonging to the company and held under an earlier statute for the payment of claims, did not protect her rights.[2039] In an action against a trust company on a dishonored draft drawn by it, even though a state banking official has taken charge of the company, the plaintiff is entitled to judgment where the action is at law and the official does not intervene.[2040]

2034 Douglas County v. Hamilton State Bank, 340 Ga. App. 801, 798 S.E.2d 509 (2017).

2035 Girard Trust Co. v. McKinley-Lanning Loan, etc., Co., 135 F. 180 (Cir. Ct. E.D. Pa. 1905).

2036 In re Cosmopolitan Trust Co., 240 Mass. 254, 133 N.E 630.

2037 Commonwealth v. Allen, 240 Mass. 244, 133 N.E. 625; Framingham v. Allen, 240 Mass. 253, 133 N.E. 629.

2038 Paragould Land Co. v. Taylor, 178 Ark. 619, 11 S.W.2d 441.

2039 In re Liquidation of Citizens' Sav., etc., Co., 171 Wis. 198, 176 N.W. 870.

2040 American Express Co. v. Cosmopolitan Trust Co., 239 Mass. 249, 132 N.E. 26.

Jurisdiction.—A statute creating a state banking department, and providing for winding up corporations doing a banking business in state courts on suit by the state's attorney general in cases of a corporation's insolvency or in the public interest, does not impair a federal court's jurisdiction of a suit by nonresident creditors of a domestic trust company doing a banking business and unable to pay its debts as they mature, for liquidation of its assets and application of its assets to its debts by a receiver.[2041] But where, pending such a suit in federal court, a state attorney general obtains a decree dissolving a trust company and appointing a receiver which is not appealed, all purposes for which the federal court's jurisdiction was invoked having been served and on payment in full of all debts, the federal court cannot return the surplus then in the receiver's hands to the company or its stockholders, but must turn it over to the receiver appointed in the state court for distribution.[2042] In California, where an administrator has a claim for an unpaid deposit against a receiver of a trust company, and the receiver has a claim against the intestate for an unpaid loan, the superior court in insolvency proceedings has jurisdiction to determine the claims and enforce a set-off, since the court is one of general jurisdiction with power to apply legal and equitable principles in determining the question.[2043] And in Texas, a district court in which a trust company receivership suit is pending, has jurisdiction of claims of counties against the company and of the property securing the claims.[2044] A court's jurisdiction having attached to the general subject of liquidating a trust company's assets and distributing the proceeds, extends to every matter necessary to be dealt with in order to effect such purpose completely and finally, provided that any relief granted be germane to the subject matter and authorized by the pleadings.[2045] See the footnotes

---

[2041] Lyon v. McKeefrey, 171 F. 384, construing Pennsylvania statute.

[2042] Lyon v. McKeefrey, 171 F. 384.

[2043] People by Webb v. California Safe Deposit & Trust Co., 168 Cal. 241, 141 P. 1181, 1915A L.R.A. 299; In re Bell, 168 Cal. 253, 141 P. 1179.

[2044] Security Trust Co. v. Lipscomb County, 142 Tex. 572, 180 S.W.2d 151.

Jurisdiction of district court in trust company receivership suit to enter orders approving contracts whereby receiver delivered securities to counties for road bond deposits and counties released their claims for deposits was not dependent upon validity of contracts, since court had authority and was under duty to determine whether contracts were valid, and question went to merits and not to jurisdiction. Security Trust Co. v. Lipscomb County, 142 Tex. 572, 180 S.W.2d 151.

[2045] Robinson v. Hospelhorn, 169 Md. 117, 179 A. 515, 184 A. 903, 103 A.L.R. 740 (chancery court). See Taylor v. Spurway, 72 F.2d 97.

for other cases relating to equity jurisdiction[2046] and miscellaneous jurisdictional matters.[2047]

[2046] Court, having general equitable jurisdiction and jurisdiction in matter of claims against banks in process of liquidation, held to have jurisdiction of action by successor trustee to impress trust or declare lien on assets of original trustee which was a trust company in process of liquidation for items of trust estate owing by original trustee and ordered paid over to successor trustee. Huntington Nat. Bank v. Fulton, 49 Ohio App. 268, 197 N.E. 204.

Jurisdiction for accounting of assets.—

Bill of trust company's receiver held to present case within equity court's jurisdiction for accounting of company's assets, transferred to certain stockholders and receiver of national bank controlling company through another trust company, controlled by former company, and dummy corporation, even if assets received by such other trust company were liquidated for less than price ostensibly paid therefor. Taylor v. Spurway, 72 F.2d 97.

The court of chancery did not have jurisdiction, against consent of trust company and commissioner of banking and insurance, to determine in summary proceedings on petition and order to show cause questions raised by petition to recover from company and commissioner property wrongfully withdrawn from trust assets by company, where petition showed that property was not, at time of filing of original bill in proceedings wherein company and commissioner were defendants or at any time thereafter, in legal ownership or control of former or substituted trustees, and company and commissioner had never been trustees, notwithstanding that court, under original bill, had taken jurisdiction over trust estate and ordered commissioner and former trustees to convey trust property to a substituted trustee, since property sought to be recovered was not "in custodia legis." Tannenbaum v. Seacoast Trust Co., 128 N.J. Eq. 515, 17 A.2d 294.

[2047] **Intervening petition not dismissible for want of jurisdiction.—**

In suit to dissolve insolvent trust company, intervening petition of trust company's judgment creditor naming as additional parties defendant trust company's insurers under Lloyds' policies insuring trust company against loses, from payment of forged checks, and seeking satisfaction by insurers of judgment which arose out of payment of forged check, held not dismissible for want of jurisdiction over parties or of subject matter of petition. People v. Central Republic Trust Co., 290 Ill. App. 183, 8 N.E.2d 363 (1937).

Sufficiency of service or appearance to give jurisdiction.—

Service on deputy banking commissioner who was liquidating agent in charge of insolvent trust company held insufficient to bring trust company before court as a corporation for purpose of rendering personal judgment against company for which execution could issue in satisfaction of judgment. Louisville Joint Stock Land Bank v. Central Trust Co., 266 Ky. 122, 98 S.W.2d 287.

Where insolvent trust company and banking commissioner in charge of liquidation were joined as defendants in suit seeking personal judgment against trust company, and summons was served only on commissioner, action of commissioner's counsel, who did not purport to represent trust company as a corporation, in objecting to motion for receiver, held not appearance of trust company. Louisville Joint Stock Land Bank v. Central Trust Co., 266 Ky. 122, 98 S.W.2d 287.

In proceeding by executor and trustee under will of donor of power of appointment against

Pleading and Variance.—In the appended notes are set out cases relating to complaints,[2048] intervening petition,[2049] and variance.[2050]

---

corporate foreign trustee and individual trustee of donee of power of appointment, who was a nonresident, to account for appointed property, jurisdiction of individual trustee was acquired by personal service and citation within the state but jurisdiction of corporate trustee was not acquired by publication and personal service without state. In re Barrett's Estate, 132 N.Y.S.2d 755.

In proceeding to enjoin violations of Small Business Investment Act, federal district court may take exclusive jurisdiction of licensee and assets thereof, and has jurisdiction to appoint receiver to administer assets. United States v. Boca Raton Capital Corp., 285 F. Supp. 504 (S.D. Fla. 1968).

Courts lack jurisdiction as to claim or action for payment from assets of any depository institution for which FDIC is receiver.—

Douglas County v. Hamilton State Bank, 340 Ga. App. 801, 798 S.E.2d 509 (2017).

[2048] **Sufficient complaint.—**

Bill of trust company's receiver, suing receiver of national bank controlling company and others for injunction against declaration of dividends to national bank's depositors until trust company's assets, abstracted and converted by defendants, were returned to plaintiff, and other equitable relief; held to make case for setting aside entire transaction and restoring status quo ante. Taylor v. Spurway, 72 F.2d 97.

Insufficient complaints.—

In action by receiver of trust company upon fidelity bonds, plaintiff could not recover because complaint did not show that company sustained any loss. Albers v. Indemnity Ins. Co., 283 Ill. App. 260.

Complaint for rescission of sale of mortgage participation certificate, held insufficient for failure to allege that superintendent did not publish notice to file claim. Zuroff v. Westchester Trust Co., 273 N.Y. 200, 7 N.E.2d 100, 109 A.L.R. 1401.

Failure to allege presentation of claim.—

A complaint by owners of apartment building, who had appointed trust company their managing agent, against superintendent of banks in charge of such trust company in liquidation, alleging that nearly a year after the company went into liquidation, water pipes froze because of neglect and burst, causing damage, stated a good cause of action despite failure to allege presentation of claim to superintendent Leal v. Westchester Trust Co., 279 N.Y. 25, 17 N.E.2d 673.

Where plaintiffs whose claims were based on alleged fact that they were depositors of trust company taken over for liquidation, did not allege that they filed proofs of claims and that such claims had been rejected before actions were filed petitions did not state good causes of action. Inland Properties Co. v. Union Properties (Ohio App.), 88 N.E.2d 409, appeal dismissed, 150 Ohio St. 490, 83 N.E.2d 69.

Allegations as to value of securities.—

Allegations that receivership court's orders approving contracts of insolvent trust company's receiver with county commissioners' courts for compromise settlement of county's claims against company as county depository for road funds deposited therewith

Loan company was subject to subpoena where state Department of Revenue had the authority to enforce state tax laws against the loan company, which could not claim an exemption under statute because, although it was an operating subsidiary of a national bank, it was not a state or national bank. Therefore, the loan company was subject to the subpoena.[2051]

Defenses.—In a suit by receiver of an insolvent trust company to foreclose a mortgage given by a party in payment of his stock subscription, it is no defense that the company had no authority to receive anything but money in payment of its stock.[2052] And where an insolvent trust company sues its directors for losses resulting from their negligence, an answer that the company was being managed by a state banking official with legislative but without constitutional warrant, is irrelevant.[2053] In a suit by a state banking official having charge of the affairs of a trust company, as pledges of a deposit book issued by another company, a trial judge was not required to sustain the defense that the official had sold the deposit book and the debt represented by it, and had no enforceable interest, where such defense was supported only by a notice from an alleged purchaser to the company issuing

---

were unenforceable were not insufficient because of allegations that reasonable market value of securities transferred to county at height of depression were less than amount of deposits, in view of other allegations that values of securities were in fact less than amount of debts released. Security Trust Co. v. Lipscomb County, 142 Tex. 572, 180 S.W.2d 151.

Surplusage.—

In proceedings for permission to file claim against trust company being reorganized, allegations with reference to filing the claim as provided by statute relating to proceedings in insolvency would be disregarded as surplusage, where such allegations referred to proof of claim after permission to file had been obtained. Mauro v. Vervena, 58 R.I. 24, 190 A. 796.

2049 An intervening petition for allowance of claim in liquidation of a trust was of an equitable nature, and was not subject to the strict rule, of civil procedure requiring the pleading to disclose a single definite theory. New Albany Trust Co. v. Nadorff, 108 Ind. App. 229, 27 N.E.2d 116.

2050 Where intervening petition for allowance of claim in liquidation of trust company alleged that trust company executed written guarantee of bonds, and, in soliciting bondholder to reinvest proceeds of such bonds in other bonds of the same company, stated that the prior guaranty would be understood to apply to the new bonds, special finding, based on evidence introduced without objection, that bondholder was given the new bonds as renewal bonds, was not a "fatal variance" from petition. New Albany Trust Co. v. Nadorff, 108 Ind. App. 229, 227 N.E.2d 116.

2051 Miss. Dep't of Revenue v. Pikco Fin., Inc., 97 So. 3d 1203 (Miss. 2012). See Miss. Code Ann. § 27-21-3.

2052 Leavitt v. Pell (N.Y.), 27 Barb. 822.

2053 La Monte v. Lurich, 86 N.J. Eq. 26, 100 A. 1031, aff'd, 86 N.J. Eq. 251, 98 A. 1086.

the book.[2054] The fact that a trust company which sold a bank building obtained the appointment of a receiver for its property and conceded its insolvency, was held not a breach of the contract for sale of the building constituting a defense to the company's right to enforce the contract.[2055] For other cases relating to defenses arising in this context, see the footnote.[2056]

Burden of Proof—The burden of proving a statutory preference of trust beneficiaries against an insolvent trust company's assets to the prejudice of depositors is on the one claiming the preference.[2057] And a claimant asserting a claim for a loss on mortgages purchased from a trust company on the advice of its assistant vice-president, has the burden of proof on

---

[2054] Cosmopolitan Trust Co. v. Golub, 252 Mass. 574, 147 N.E. 847.

[2055] National Bank v. Louisville Trust Co., 67 F.2d 97, cert, denied, 291 U.S. 665, 54 S. Ct. 440, 78 L Ed. 1056.

[2056] **Laches.—**

A minority trust company stockholder filing petition January 13, 1933, and amended petition April 7, 1937, wherein he sought to hold a bank which liquidated assets of trust company liable for losses sustained by trust company, was barred by inches where contract by which bank undertook to liquidate assets of trust company was executed December 3, 1929. King v. Citizens, etc., Nat. Bank, 186 Ga. 336, 198 S.E. 70.

Where receiver of trust company which held unmatured, indorsed trade acceptances, applied part of indorser's deposit in company as advance payment of dividends in receiver's first account, indorser could not except thereto five years later after filing of receiver's fourth account. In re Parkway Trust Co., 134 Pa. Super. 316, 3 A.2d 930.

Liability of debtor to trust company, the business of which was discontinued in January, 1932, on bond given in 1927, was not extinguished by "laches" on part of secretary of banking and receiver of trust company or his successor which entered the bond of record as a judgment in May, 1938, upon learning of debtor's denial of liability thereon. Lancaster Trust Co. v. Engle, 337 Pa. 176, 10 A.2d 381.

Statute of limitations.—

Claim for accounting held not barred by six months' limitation statute. In re Prime, 249 App. Div. 28, 290 N.Y.S. 853.

Estoppel.—

In suit by a depositor to establish as preferred its claim against trust company in liquidation, the trust company or the commissioner of finance in charge of the liquidation thereof could not deny authority of trust company's treasurer to sign contract providing that funds received from depositor should not be considered as deposits, and should be held separate as a special fund and not commingled with other funds of trust company. In re Wellston Trust Co. (Mo. App.), 136 S.W.2d 430.

[2057] Frederick Iron, etc., Co. v. Page, 165 Md. 212, 166 A. 738.

allegations of fraud and deceit of the company.[2058] Under a statute requiring a trust company to invest one-half its capital stock in securities for the protection of fiduciary accounts, the burden is on the general creditors of an insolvent trust company which failed to keep its trust accounts as required by law, to clearly establish the identity of their funds to avoid the priority of beneficiaries' liens on assets for fiduciary funds.[2059] And in some states, a claimant asserting a preferred claim against an insolvent trust company has the burden of showing that at all times between the deposit of the funds sued for and a receiver's appointment, the company's cash assets were equal to the amount of the funds claimed.[2060] But a plea of ignorance of trust company officials as to the company's insolvency when it received a certain note for collection is an insufficient denial to place the burden of proof on a claimant.[2061] For cases dealing with the burden of proof in a suit for court approval of a trustees' account, see the footnote.[2062]

Sufficiency of Evidence.—Materially false statements in a prospectus of a debenture company with regard to investors and paid-in capital are sufficient evidence of fraud by the company and its officers in the sale of debentures.[2063] Where the evidence did not show that proceeds of checks deposited in a trust company for collection only were traceable to a particular fund, after the

---

[2058] People ex rel. Barrett v. Central Republic Trust Co., 300 Ill. App. 297, 20 N.E.2d 999.

[2059] Ohio Valley Bank, etc., Co. v. Pettit, 206 Ky. 818, 268 S.W. 535.

[2060] Maryland Casualty Co. v. Rottger, 99 Ind. App. 485, 194 N.E. 365 (Indiana law).

[2061] Cameron v. Carnegie Trust Co., 202 Pa. 114, 140 A. 768.

[2062] Burden was on trustees for trust company's creditors to justify their acceptance of certificates, issued by them to such creditors, as setoffs against note obligations and a mortgage obligation to trust estate; such setoffs being items of discharge. Behrman v. Egan, 17 N.J. Super. 598, 86 A.2d 606.

In suit by trustees for trust company's creditors and stockholders for court's approval of trustees' account, burden was not on beneficiaries to sustain validity of their criticism of trust administration, where they did not seek to show that there were more assets in trust estate than trustees acknowledged, but burden was on trustees to justify items of discharge for which they sought credit. Behrman v. Egan, 17 N.J. Super. 598, 86 A.2d 606.

Trustees for trust company's creditors and stockholders were bound to explain satisfactorily arbitrary reduction of $5,000 in purchase price of factory building, owned by realty company, entire capital stock of which was held by trustees, and sold by them to another realty company, controlled by same person who controlled third realty company to which trustees paid a commission, before approval of trustees' account by court. Behrman v. Egan, 17 N.J. Super. 598, 86 A.2d 606.

[2063] Christian v. Michigan Debenture Co., 134 Mich. 171, 96 N.W. 22.

company's insolvency, the depositors were held not entitled to priority.[2064] See the footnote for other cases relating to sufficiency of evidence[2065] and

---

[2064] Salem Elevator Works, Inc. v. Commissioner of Banks, 252 Mass. 366, 148 N.E. 220; Yesner v. Com'r of Banks, 252 Mass. 358, 148 N.E. 224.

[2065] **Right to preferences.—**

Testimony of corporation president and trust company official as to oral arrangement that cash, sent to trust company by corporation to release goods sold by latter from lien of trade acceptances drawn by it, should be held as separate fund for application on acceptances when due, held sufficient to sustain court's finding that corporation was entitled to preferences of its claim on liquidation of trust company to sum paid latter in anticipation of maturities of acceptances. Sears, etc., Corp. v. Squire, 132 Ohio St. 140, 5 N.E.2d 486 (1936).

Existence of trust relationship.—

Evidence justified decree dismissing claim against trust company in liquidation for loss on mortgages purchased from bank by claimant on advice of assistant vice-president on ground that no "fiduciary relationship" existed between claimant and company and that company had not been guilty of fraud and deceit in transaction. People ex rel. Barrett v. Central Republic Trust Co., 300 Ill. App. 297, 20 N.E.2d 999.

Propriety of distribution.—

In proceeding on accounting of liquidator of insolvent trustee, evidence established that trustee properly distributed trust receipts by making payment to officer of two corporate beneficiaries, after setting aside certain percentage for public improvement assessments, as required by trust. Bessel v Department of Financial Institutions, 213 Ind. 446, 11 N.E.2d 683.

Appointment of receiver.—

Evidence respecting management of corporation which was an investment company within meaning of federal statutes disclosed that in fairness to its stockholders the appointment of disinterested officer of court to administer corporation and to prosecute action against others was necessary and that a receiver should be appointed for that purpose. SEC v. Fifth Ave. Coach Lines, Inc., 289 F. Supp. 3 (S.D.N.Y. 1968).

Evidence in support of stockholder's motion warranted appointment of receiver pendante lite for diversified management investment company which failed to file annual report with Securities and Exchange Commission. sent stockholder a misleading annual report, and whose directors indicated an almost flagrant disregard for affairs of company. Tanzer v. Huffines, 287 F. Supp. 273 (D. Del. 1968), aff'd, 408 F.2d 42 (3d Cir. 1969).

Giving of notice.—

In action against receiver of trust company, corporate trustee of plaintiff's bonds, to recover for receiver's negligence in releasing mortgages securing bonds without bonds having been paid to trustee or receiver, where makers had precipitated bonds according to provision therefor, evidence held insufficient to show giving of notice by trustee to receiver of precipitation of the bonds, so as to render receiver liable. Executive Committee of Christian Education, etc. v. Fidelity, etc., Trust Co., 273 Ky. 715, 117 S.W.2d 958.

motions.[2066]

Findings.—A master's finding that there was no intention by a trust company's savings department or the makers of notes transferred thereto that a debt to the commercial department should be extinguished by the acceptance of renewal notes amounted to a finding that the original debt was not extinguished such finding could be based on facts and inferences including evidence regarding the course of business and the purpose of the transfers.[2067] A court in a trust company receivership case which approved contracts whereby counties received security for road bond deposits and released their claims for the deposits,[2068] necessarily determined that the contracts were valid, since such conclusion was essential to the decision made.[2069]

Judgments and Orders.—Orders of a receivership court barring all claims against an insolvent trust company after certain dates, did not bar a claim of a county against the company which had been approved by court order and on which only a partial payment had been made.[2070] But under certain state statutes, a decree of distribution entered on a final account in proceedings to liquidate a bank is conclusive on all persons, and a bank's claimants who fail to prove their claims in such proceedings are barred.[2071] For other cases relating to judgments and orders, see the footnote.[2072]

[2066] Motion of trustee-receiver of investment corporation for order authorizing him to call shareholders' meeting for election of directors was panted, but in view of uncertain status of large block of stock held by holding company subject to pledge to investment corporation and also subject to unapproved contract of sale to individual, such block would be sterilized, i.e., not permitted to vote at such shareholders' meeting. Securities & Exch. Comm'n v. Fifth Ave. Coach Lines, Inc., 308 F. Supp. 947 (S.D.N.Y. 1970).

[2067] Petition of Allen, 245 Mass. 448, 139 N.E. 800.

[2068] Security Trust Co. v. Lipscomb County, 142 Tex. 572, 180 S.W.2d 151.

Where county after receiving securities from insolvent trust company for unpaid county deposits had an unpaid balance and after receiver was appointed, court approved contract, whereby county accepted bond, having face value in excess of unpaid deposit, order released all the claims of county arising out of original deposit, even though securities delivered were not worth their face value. Security Trust Co. v. Lipscomb County, 142 Tex. 572, 180 S.W.2d 151.

[2069] Security Trust Co. v. Lipscomb County, 142 Tex. 572, 180 S.W.2d 151.

[2070] Security Trust Co. v. Lipscomb County, 142 Tex. 572, 180 S.W.2d 151.

[2071] No. No. 90 Bldg. & Loan Ass'n v. Allesandroni, 317 Pa. 30, 176 A. 235 (Pennsylvania statute).

Mortgagee which failed to prove mortgage in proceedings for liquidation of mortgagor trust company held precluded by decree of distribution in the liquidation proceedings,

(Text continued on page 572)

whereby surplus assets of trust company were distributed to its stockholders, from enforcing against stockholders deficiency judgment obtained at foreclosure sale subsequent to decree of distribution. No. No. 90 Bldg. & Loan Ass'n v. Allesandroni, 317 Pa. 30, 176 A. 235.

2072 Parties bound by judgment.—

Counties became parties to trust company receivership suit so as to be bound by judgment therein where counties entered into contracts with receiver and accepted bonds and warrants surrendered to counties pursuant to contracts whereby they released claims for road bond deposits as directed by the court's order. Security Trust Co. v. Lipscomb County, 142 Tex. 572, 180 S.W.2d 151.

Creditor not entitled to ignore insolvency and obtain personal judgment.—

Mortgagee bank which brought suit against mortgagors and insolvent trust company, which had assumed debt, and joined as defendant banking commissioner in charge of liquidation, but prayed judgment only against mortgagor. and trust company, held not entitled to ignore insolvency of trust company in such manner and obtain personal judgment against company for full amount of claim and thereby gain preference over other creditors. Louisville Joint Stock Land Bank v. Central Trust Co., 266 Ky. 122, 98 S.W.2d 287.

Decree ordering resale.—

In proceeding to liquidate trust company before court having jurisdiction of subject matter and all interested parties, the court had authority to order receiver appointed by it to resell farm owned by company on default of first purchaser. And the decree ordering resale was a conclusive judgment with same force and effect as any other final adjudication of court of competent jurisdiction. Tobey v. Poulin, 141 Me. 58, 38 A.2d 826, holding that court exercised sound discretion in ordering resale.

Order not adjudicating conflicting claims.—

Where court of chancery, under original bill in proceedings wherein trust company and commissioner of banking and insurance were defendants, took jurisdiction over trust estate and ordered commissioner and former trustees to convey trust property to a substituted trustee, and order did not adjudicate conflicting claims to ownership of trust property, such order could not be relied on as grounds for subsequent summary proceedings to recover from company and commissioner property wrongfully withdrawn from trust assets by company, especially where such property was not in court's custody. Tannenbaum v. Seacoast Trust Co., 128 N.J. Eq. 515, 17 A.2d 294.

Res judicata.—

Decree, dismissing suit by former depositors of insolvent trust company who had accepted cash or demand deposits in reorganized trust company, preferred stock thereof, and mortgage company's participation certificates in full satisfaction of amounts due them to enjoin payment of proceeds of subsequent sale of reorganized company's assets to reorganized company's stockholders, was not res judicata of certificate holders' right to surplus remaining after liquidation of reorganized company as against company's common stockholders. Temple v. Clinton Trust Co., 1 N.J. 219, 62 A.2d 690.

Decree, allowing account of mortgage company which issued participation certificates to depositors of insolvent trust company pursuant to plan of reorganization of trust company and approving substitution of other assets for some of those originally transferred to

Appeal and Review.—An order directing a trust company to turn over a mortgage certificate was reversed where the great weight of credible evidence established conclusively that it was delivered to the company as additional collateral security for a debt still unpaid.[2073] An appellate court erred in ordering immediate payment of a preferred claim on appeal from a decree allowing the claim, in view of the possible existence of other preferred claimants who might be prejudiced.[2074] For cases dealing with the right to appeal and grounds for appeal in this context, see the footnote.[2075]

---

mortgage company under reorganization, was not res judicata of certificate holders' right to surplus remaining after liquidation of reorganized trust company as against reorganized company's common stockholders. Temple v. Clinton Trust Co., 1 N.J. 219, 62 A.2d 690.

No right to reopen decree.—

A trust company's creditors and stockholders, as beneficiaries of trust created by contract between company and its directors, named as trustees, were not entitled to reopen chancery court's decree, approving trustees' transfer of bank building to company and assent to increase in company's capital, on ground that beneficiaries had no notice of trustees' action against representatives of holders of certificates issued by trustees to beneficiaries for such approval, and hence were not bound by decree, as questions presented for court's determination affected all certificate holders in common and could be disposed of adequately without joining all of them as parties. Behrman v. Egan, 17 N.J. Super. 598, 86 A.2d 606.

Decree not procured by fraud.—

Where proposed transfer of bank building to trust company by trustees for its creditors and stockholders was discussed with state banking commissioner, who did not disapprove thereof, company's directors, named as trustees, were repeatedly urged by banking department to increase company's capital, and transfer of building resulted in marked enhancement of value of company's stock, of which trust estate was majority holder, vice-chancellor's decree approving transfer, after considering all such matters in open court, was not improper as procured by fraud. Behrman v. Egan, 17 N.J. Super. 598, 86 A.2d 606.

[2073] Application of Golden, 258 App. Div. 798, 15 N.Y.S.2d 474.

[2074] Sears & Nichols Corp. v. Squire, 131 Ohio St. 140, 5 N.E.2d 486.

[2075] **Appeal too late.—**

Where holders of certificates, issued to trust company's creditors and stockholders by their trustees against company's assets and capital stock held by trustees, were notified of results of hearing, which led to chancery court's decree approving trustees' assent to increase in company's capital, within month thereafter, and none of them sought to intervene in chancery litigation or review court's action until three years later, their attack on decree in action then brought by trustees for approval of their account came too late, in absence of showing of fraud, even if they did not receive adequate notice of hearing. Behrman v. Egan, 17 N.J. Super. 598, 86 A.2d 606.

Short notice not ground for appeal.—A chancery decree, approving assent by trustees for trust company's creditors and stockholders to increase in company's capital, was not subject to attack by beneficiaries because they received only 14 days' notice of their preemptive right, respecting new stock issue, instead of 80 days' notice required by decree, in view of testimony that subscription lists were not closed and that no holders of certificates issued by trustees to beneficiaries were refused right to purchase stock. Behrman v. Egan, 17 N.J. Super. 598, 86 A.2d 606.

Discretion of supreme court.—

The supreme court exercised its discretion to decline an interlocutory review of an intermediate order making a partial determination as to priorities in the distribution of assets of a bank and trust company, which was in receivership, approving the use of a class action procedure on behalf of some claimants and determining that the findings of fact and conclusions of law made by the state banking board and affirmed by the supreme court in one of the decisions were binding on the receiver; not only was the order interlocutory but it was subject to modification and the record was very sketchy. First Am. Bank & Trust Co. v. Pfleger, 243 N.W.2d 165 (N.D. 1976).

CHAPTER XVIII.

CLEARINGHOUSES.

Synopsis

§ 1. **Nature and Status.**

§ 2. **Settlements and Transactions through Clearinghouse.**

§ 3. **Rights and Liabilities of Nonmembers.**

§ 4. **Security for Payment of Balances.**

§ 5. **Actions.**

§ 1. Nature and Status.

A clearinghouse is a voluntary association of banks facilitating the mutual interchange of business by affording a convenient method of obtaining daily settlements of balances between the banks forming the association, and also acting as a collecting agency for the member banks.[2076] It is an agent for

---

[2076] **In general.—**

Ellis v. Jones, 144 Ga. 120, 86 S.E. 317. See Rector v. City Deposit Bank Co., 200 U.S. 405, 26 S. Ct. 289, 50 L. Ed. 527.

It is common knowledge that a clearinghouse is what its name indicates; it is an association composed of a number of banks for convenient and expeditious handling of certain claims and credits against and in favor of members. Security Commercial & Sav. Bank v. Southern Trust & Commerce Bank, 74 Cal. App. 734, 241 P. 945.

"It is intended to afford a uniform and convenient method by which daily settlements of balances can be had between the banks entering into the association." Yardley v. Philler, 167 U.S. 344, 17 S. Ct. 835, 42 L. Ed. 192.

Definition.—

A clearinghouse is defined as: an ingenious device to simplify and facilitate the work of the banks in reaching an adjustment and payment of the daily balances due to and from each other, atone time and place, on each day. In practical operation it is a place where the representatives of all the member banks meet, and, under the supervision of a competent committee or officer selected by the associated banks, settle their accounts with each other, and make and receive payment of balances, and so "clear" the transactions of the day for which the settlement is made.

limited purposes,[2077] and a fiduciary representative of the member banks, with its duties involving the continuous exercise of skilled knowledge and cultivated judgment.[2078] Although occasion ally clearinghouses issue certificates which pass as currency,[2079] they are not mutual banks organized and

---

Andrew v. Farmers', etc., Sav. Bank, 215 Iowa 1336, 245 N.W. 226; Crane v. Fourth St. Nat'l Bank, 173 Pa. 566, 34 A. 296.

[2077] Rector v. City Deposit Bank Co., 200 U.S. 405, 26 S. Ct. 289, 50 L. Ed. 527.

It is the duty of such associations to clear or balance daily the claims of the respective banks, one against the other, resulting from the checks drawn upon and held by the different members. Assessments upon members are made solely for the purpose of paying rents, salaries, and similar expenditures. To effect the clearings each member of the association, on banking days, sends to the clearinghouse, at a specified hour, the checks held by it against the other banks. The checks sent by each member are considered as remaining the property of the member, the association being simply an agent for collection. Where a bank is entitled to a credit or payment corresponding to the excess which the sum of the checks presented by it exceed the sum of the checks against it, the clearinghouse pays that bank the difference by drawing its check upon one or more of the debtor banks; and each member constitutes the manager of the association its agent to draw a check or checks upon such member for any balance found to be due by that member. Rector v. City Deposit Bank Co., 200 U.S. 405, 26 S. Ct. 289, 50 L Ed. 527.

[2078] People's Sav. Bank v. First Nat. Bank, 102 Wash. 436, 173 P. 52.

[2079] **In general.—**

Crane v. Fourth St. Nat. Bank, 173 Pa. 566, 34 A. 296.

Certificate of deposit distinguished.—

A clearinghouse certificate in the form of an interest-bearing obligation or due bill, which is a legal equivalent of a promissory note, and, being payable on demand, bear, interest from its date, is essentially different from an ordinary certificate of deposit which merely certifies that a stated sum has been deposited and carries the implication that the money is held for safekeeping without interest. Hall v. First Nat. Bank (Tex. Civ. App.), 252 S.W. 828, modified, 254 S.W. 522.

Illustrative case.—

In addition to the function of affording a means for the daily clearing of balances, the clearinghouse association, by agreement among its members, issued, at periods when it was deemed best to do so, clearinghouse certificates. These certificates were delivered, under the discretion of the managers, when applied for by a member of the association, and were secured by the pledge of bills receivable or assets taken from the portfolio of the bank obtaining the certificates. These certificates were available as cash in settlements between the bank, and for other purposes; and the object of issuing them was, in times of panic or stringency, to create, to the extent of the certificates, solidarity of responsibility between the banks, as each bank was liable for a proportionate share of the certificates in case of default in their payment, thus fortifying the credit of one by the credit of all. Moreover, the certificates afforded a means by which a bank with good assets could use them in order to obtain certificates which were, for banking purposes, the equivalent of cash, when, from any

operated by the associate banks.[2080] This method of clearing checks through an established clearinghouse conveniently located to the adjacent territory has become an established custom of the banking business and a trade usage.[2081]

§ 2. Settlements and Transactions through Clearinghouse.

Rules Governing Generally.—Banks may associate themselves together and make rules for their own government, which as between the members of their association, supplement and may even supplant the law.[2082] However,

---

stringency or panic, the assets themselves, although entirely sound, could not be readily convertible into current money. Yardley v. Philler, 167 U.S. 344, 17 S. Ct. 835, 42 L. Ed. 192.

[2080] Crane v. Fourth St. Nat. Bank, 173 Pa. 566, 34 A. 296.

[2081] Lombard v. Anderson, 280 Ill. App. 283.

Where the practice of collecting checks through the clearinghouse prevailed only among banks making their exchanges through such house, but not among other banks, savings banks, or trust companies, or with respect to checks on private bankers, the practice was not a general custom. First Nat. Bank v. Fourth Nat. Bank, 89 N.Y. 412.

[2082] Security Commercial, etc., Bank v. Southern Trust, etc., Bank, 74 Cal. App. 734, 241 P. 945; Merchants Nat'l Bank v. Continental Nat'l Bank, 98 Cal. App. 523, 277 P. 354; Crocker-Woolworth Nat'l Bank v. Nevada Bank of San Francisco, 139 Cal. 564, 73 P. 456, 96 Am. St. Rep. 169, 63 L.R.A. 245. See First Nat'l Bank v. United States Nat'l Bank, 100 Ore. 264, 197 P. 647, 14 A.L.R. 479.

Dallas Clearinghouse Rules were not enforceable against payor bank, as rules could not be given certain and definite meaning or interpretation; thus, those rules could not vary terms of Uniform Commercial Code. Texas Am. Bank/Farmers Branch v. Abrams Centre Nat'l Bank, 780 S.W.2d 814 (Tex. App. 1989).

Dallas Clearinghouse Rules did not vary Uniform Commercial Code (UCC) section which provides that payor bank must return or send notice of dishonor or nonpayment on next banking day (i.e., that part of day on which bank is open to public for carrying on substantially all of its banking functions) following day on which it receives the relevant item; thus, where payor bank received bad check on Friday, but payee did not show that check was received during business hours, payer's return of check by 10:00 a.m. on Tuesday was timely. Texas Am. Bank/Farmers Branch v. Abrams Centre Nat'l Bank, 780 S.W.2d 814 (Tex. App. 1989).

Statute setting out duty of payer bank with regard to checks presented for payment did not apply to dispute between two banking institutions; duties of banks were controlled by rules of clearinghouse of which both banks were members. Bank One v. National City Bank, 66 Ohio App. 3d 91, 583 N.E.2d 439, jurisdictional motion overruled, 53 Ohio St. 3d 705, 558 N.E.2d 61 (1990).

Clearinghouse rules, which had force of agreement between member banks, shifted liability for failing to pay face value of underencoded check from drawee bank to processing bank which breached its agreement to verify and remove misencoded checks from

clearinghouse rules are not meant to have the effect of statutory law; while on a certain state of facts they might affect the outcome of a particular case, they are by no means the law. Such rules also differ in different places and are not binding on nonmembers.[2083] On the other hand, it has been held that a clearinghouse agreement may supersede a provision of the Uniform Commercial Code.[2084] "Settle," as defined by the Uniform Commercial Code, means to pay in cash, by clearinghouse settlement, in a charge or credit or by remittance, or otherwise as instructed. A settlement may be either final or provisional.[2085]

Presentment of a check drawn on a clearinghouse member bank and held by another member bank is sufficient when the check is presented through the clearinghouse in accordance with its rules.[2086] And the rule that "errors in exchanges shall be adjusted by the bank concerned," applies only to ascertaining that accounts are not overdrawn.[2087]

The regulations of clearinghouses generally provide that when checks which are not good are sent through the clearinghouse, the banks receiving them shall return them to the senders by or before a specified hour of the day on which they are received; under such a rule, payment of a check through the clearinghouse is provisional until the hour specified, but becomes

---

machinable items to be processed by drawee bank. Bank One v. National City Bank, 66 Ohio App. 3d 91, 583 N.E.2d 439, jurisdictional motion overruled, 53 Ohio St. 3d 705, 558 N.E.2d 61 (1990).

2083 Hamilton Nat'l Bank v. Swafford, 213 Tenn. 545, 376 S.W.2d 470.

2084 West Side Bank v. Marine Nat'l Exchange Bank, 37 Wis. 2d 661, 155 N.W.2d 587 (1968).

Clearinghouse agreement providing that unacceptable items are returnable through exchanges on second business day following date they are presented at exchange superseded provision of Uniform Commercial Code that item is finally paid when bank has completed process of posting. West Side Bank v. Marine Nat'l Exchange Bank, 37 Wis. 2d 661, 155 N.W.2d 587 (1968).

Modifications of provisions of Uniform Commercial Code by clearinghouse agreement expanding time in which entries might be reversed were within purpose of Code section permitting continued expansion of commercial practices through custom, usage and agreement of the parties. West Side Bank v. Marine Nat'l Exchange Bank, 37 Wis. 2d 661, 155 N.W.2d 587 (1968).

2085 Universal C.I.T. Credit Corp. v. Farmers Bank, 358 F. Supp. 317 (E.D. Mo. 1973). See U.C.C. § 4-104(a)(11).

2086 Geibe v. Chicago-Lake State Bank, 160 Minn. 89, 199 N.W. 514.

2087 Tradesmen's Nat. Bank v. Third Nat. Bank, 66 Pa. 435.

complete if the check is retained alter that hour.[2088] Such a rule is inapplicable to a check presented after the hour specified.[2089] And such a

---

[2088] **In general.—**

Merchants' Nat. Bank v. National Eagle Bank, 101 Mass. 281, 100 Am. Dec. 120.

Agreement must be clear.—

Banks, through clearinghouse rules to which they have subscribed, may foreclose their right to return a check after a certain time, but any agreement to do so must be clear. Thus it has been held that in the absence of clear and explicit provisions barring the right of a bank to return forged items after a given time that right is not lost Mechanics Nat'l Bank v. Worcester County Trust Co., 341 Mass. 465, 170 N.E.2d 476.

Time when checks regarded as paid.—

Checks cleared through the clearinghouse are not regarded as "paid" until time has passed under clearinghouse rules, during which drawee bank can return them to forwarding bank. Security-First Nat. Bank v. Bank of America Nat. Trust etc., Ass'n, 22 Cal. 2d 154, 137 P.2d 452; In re Smith, Lockhart & Co., 3 F.2d 444.

Payment of a check drawn on a bank which is a member of the association is not complete until the debtor bank has an opportunity to examine the items debited against it and has approved such debit by silence or affirmative acts. Columbia-Knickerbocker Trust Co. v. Miller, 156 A.D. 810, 142 N.Y.S. 440, aff'd, 215 N.Y. 191, 109 N.E. 179, 1917A Ann. Cas. 848.

When check has been paid and canceled by drawee bank and amount thereof has been charged to drawer's account and credit given to account of bank presenting check and drawee bank falls to return check to presenting bank within time allowed by clearinghouse rules, it is considered paid for all purposes. United States Fidelity, etc., Co. v. First Nat. Bank, 129 Neb. 102, 260 N.W. 798.

Sufficient notice that check "not good".—

A check is "not good" within clearinghouse rules, providing that checks returned as not good should be returned to the members from whom received before 3 o'clock of the same day, when the drawee bank refuses to pay it, and a memorandum on a check "assigned," together with notice of insolvency of the drawee, was a sufficient notice that the check was returned as "not good." Columbia-Knickerbocker Trust Co. v. Miller, 156 App. Div. 810, 142 N.Y.S. 440, aff'd, 215 N.Y. 191, 109 N.E. 179, 1917A Ann. Cas. 848.

Rule inapplicable to clearinghouse draft.—

Draft on clearinghouse association payable to creditor bank against debtor bank as result of setoff is not an unconditional obligation of such association subject to rules applying to negotiable instruments. Holbrook v. W. L. Moody & Co. (Tex. Civ. App.), 45 S.W.2d 685.

[2089] National City Bank v. Waggoner, 243 A.D. 305, 276 N.Y.S. 449, aff'd, 270 N.Y. 592, 1 N.E.2d 345.

Clearinghouse rule permitting bank discovering fraudulent character of deposit to return check thereon to member presenting it before 8 o'clock of day check went through clearinghouse was inapplicable to check presented after that hour to defendant bank, which had right as between it and drawee of check to maintain its position and refuse to redeem.

rule is not void as violating the duty of a collecting bank to the payee as well as the maker of a note to have the note ready for delivery on payment during the entire business day, and banks receiving and paying notes are bound by such a custom or agreement.[2090] In some jurisdictions it has been held that if a failure to return a check until after the hour specified under such a rule results from a mistake of fact, and the situation of the parties is not so changed thereby as to cause a loss to the bank to which the check is returned, the receiving bank may recover the amount of the check which it has paid.[2091] But in other jurisdictions it has been held that a receiving bank

---

National City Bank v. Waggoner, 243 App. Div. 305, 276 N.Y.S. 449, aff'd, 270 N.Y. 592, 1 N.E.2d 345.

2090 Atlas Nat'l Bank v. National Exch. Bank, 176 Mass. 300, 57 N.E. 605.

2091 **In general.—**

Atlas Nat. Bank v. National Exch. Bank, 176 Mass. 300, 57 N.E. 605; Merchants' Nat'l Bank v. National Bank of Commonwealth, 139 Mass. 513, 2 N.E. 89, disapproving Preston v. Canadian Bank, 23 F. 179; Citizens' Cent. Nat. Bank v. New Amsterdam Nat. Bank, 128 App. Div. 554, 112 N.Y.S. 973, aff'd, 198 N.Y. 520, 92 N.E. 1080.

No change in position of parties.—

A private banker had an arrangement with the F. Bank, whereby the F. Bank agreed to receive at the clearinghouse, and pay, checks upon him, subject to his approval, each day. A check drawn on the private banker by defendants, who had a balance with him to meet it, reached the clearinghouse the following morning, and was kept by the F. Bank beyond the usual time of day for making settlement with the banker, who that morning had absconded, being insolvent. Held, that the only risk the F. Bank took by retaining the check was that the bank which sent the check to the clearinghouse had by the delay changed its position so that the subsequent return worked an injury that would not have happened if the check had been returned within the time limited and as there was no change in this case, the F. Bank was entitled to recover. Madderom v. Heath, etc., Mfg. Co., 35 Ill. App. 588.

Where, under clearinghouse rules, a bank had the right to consider a check paid, and to treat it so in its dealings with others, unless the check should be returned by 1 o'clock, and there was a delay in it, return, occasioned by a mistake on the part of the messenger, the failure to present it before the time named did not work an absolute forfeiture as of a bad check, where there was no change of circumstances after the time when the bank had a right to treat the check as paid, and before it was returned, which subjected the bank to damage or loss. Merchants' Nat. Bank v. National Eagle Bank, 101 Mass. 281, 100 Am. Dec. 120.

That defendant bank, which, through the clearinghouse to which the parties belonged, had received payment of a check drawn on plaintiff bank, was not notified by plaintiff in the time provided by the clearinghouse rules that the check's certification by plaintiff's teller was forged and the check bad, does not relieve defendant of liability to refund; it having suffered no loss by the delay, having cashed the check by payment of currency before it was sent to the clearinghouse. National Bank v. Drovers', etc., Nat. Bank, 143 Md. 168, 122 A. 12, 30 A.L.R. 1019; Preston v. Canadian Bank of Commerce, 23 F. 179.

under such circumstances cannot recover the amount it paid.[2092] And where a bank receives a note as a debit item in its clearings, and treats the note as though it were a check, charges the maker with the amount thereof and does not return it within the time required under such a rule, and there is no mistake of fact, payment is absolute and the amount thereof cannot be recovered.[2093]

A clearinghouse rule requiring notice of nonpayment of items drawn on banks which are affiliated with members of the association, and have places of business located in a certain part of the city, to be given by telephone before 2:30 p.m. of the same day to member banks presenting items through the clearinghouse, was held valid and applicable even though a payee bank was not affiliated with the clearinghouse.[2094]

Illustrative case.—

Where teller of defendant bank negligently cashed check for more than $3,600 without making further inquiry, although he was not acquainted with the person who presented check, and although he called drawee and learned that there was no account standing in the name of the purported drawer, such check was cleared to drawee through clearinghouse, and it was discovered that check was forged, drawee was entitled to recover from defendant bank for money paid under mistake of fact, even though the check was not returned by next business day, and clearinghouse rules provided for return of items which had been received in check clearings of the same or the next preceding business day on each regular business day.

Mechanics Nat'l Bank v. Worcester County Trust Co., 341 Mass. 465, 170 N.E.2d 476.

[2092] National Bank of Commerce v. Mechanic's American Nat'l Bank, 148 Mo. App. 1, 127 S.W. 429; National Bank v. German-American Bank, 148 Mo. App. 21, 127 S.W. 434.

[2093] Atlas Nat'l Bank v. National Exch. Bank, 176 Mass. 300, 57 N.E. 605.

[2094] **In general.—**

Hallenbeck v. Leimert, 295 U.S. 116, 55 S. Ct. 687, 79 L. Ed. 1339.

Provision of Negotiable Instruments Law relating to giving of notice of dishonor held not to relate to time within which dishonored checks may be returned nor to tentative payments nor advice concerning an overdraft, and not to fix time within which notice of dishonor was required to be given payee bank, as indorser of checks, in order to fix liability of such indorser where drawee bank had already made irrevocable payment through clearinghouse. Hallenbeck v. Leimert, 295 U.S. 116, 55 S. Ct. 687, 79 L. Ed. 1339.

Illustrative case.—

Conduct of drawee bank in accepting delivery of checks from clearinghouse after settlement with clearinghouse in respect to such checks, and in failing to give notice of dishonor prior to 2:80 p. m. of that day in accordance with clearinghouse rules, constituted final, irrevocable payment of Checks, notwithstanding that payee bank was not a member of or affiliated with clearinghouse, and destroyed any right of drawee bank to reimbursement from payee bank. Hallenbeck v. Leimert, 295 U.S. 116, 55 S. Ct. 687, 79 L. Ed. 1339.

The rules made by members of a clearinghouse for their mutual convenience and protection may be waived by a bank which they aim to protect.[2095] But such a waiver cannot be withdrawn if damage to another party would result.[2096]

Payment through Clearinghouse.—Payment through a clearinghouse amounts merely to a system of set-offs and cancellations, whereby accounts are settled between member banks without the unnecessary transfer of actual funds.[2097] And a bank which is a member of a clearinghouse is presumed to know the usage and customs of banking transactions effected through that medium, including a knowledge of what constitutes payment.[2098] A contract by a bank to pay checks on another bank presented through a clearinghouse does not impose on such bank the same liability in regard to such checks as attaches to the drawee bank,[2099] since a drawee bank is the place of final

---

[2095] Corn Exch. Bank v. Fifth Nat. Bank, 123 Misc. 328, 205 N.Y.S. 777; In re Smith, Lockhart & Co., 3 F.2d 444.

Where a bank receiving a check on it through the clearinghouse returns it several days later to the bank from which it came, the latter bank, by refunding the money thereon, waives the rule of the clearinghouse requiring checks to be returned on the day they are received, and it cannot recover the money paid, though the first bank, on returning the check, stated that, if not paid, it would break off exchanges with the second bank. Stuyvesant Bank v. National Mechanics', etc., Ass'n, 7 Lans. (N.Y.) 197.

[2096] Corn Exch. Bank v. Fifth Nat'l Bank, 123 Misc. 328, 205 N.Y.S. 777.

On the day of bankruptcy but before the filing of the petition and without knowledge of its insolvency, the bank in which bankrupt was a depositor received checks given by it through the clearinghouse and charged the same to its account By the clearinghouse rules it had the right to return the checks at any time before 12 o'clock, and by custom the time limit might be waived and return permitted up to the time of closing of the exchange for the day. Learning of the bankrupt's embarrassment and fearing that it might not have sufficient funds of bankrupt because of uncollected checks deposited, the bank sought and received permission to return the checks and duly credited them to bankrupt's account; this was after 12 o'clock and after the filing of the petition. Later, finding that it had sufficient funds, the bank refunded the amount of the checks to the presenting banks. Held, that the waiver of the time limit by the presenting banks and acceptance of return of the checks put the parties in the same position as when the checks were first presented; that the bank was not legally bound to make the refund and was without right to do so from funds which then belonged to the bankrupt estate. In re Smith, Lockhart & Co., 3 F.2d 444.

[2097] Crocker-Woolworth Nat'l Bank v. Nevada Bank of San Francisco, 139 Cal. 564, 73 P. 456, 96 Am. St. R. 169, 63 L.R.A. 246.

[2098] Security Commercial, etc., Bank v. Southern Trust, etc., Bank, 74 Cal. App. 734, 241 P. 945.

[2099] Grant v. MacNutt, 12 Misc. 20, 33 N.Y.S. 62.

settlement of a check, where all prior mistakes, alterations or forgeries must be corrected or noted, and conclusively settled.[2100]

If both a bank collecting a check through a clearinghouse and the bank upon which it is drawn understand that the receiving of the check through the clearinghouse is not intended to constitute payment, it cannot be claimed by an indorser of the check that there has been payment.[2101] And a drawee bank's check given in settlement of a clearinghouse balance which includes overdrafts does not in itself constitute a final and irrevocable payment.[2102] Also, a clearinghouse transaction whereby checks are delivered to a representative of the bank upon which they are drawn, and the bank presenting them receives money or credit to cover their amount, does not in itself constitute payment of a check preventing the drawee bank from subsequently refusing its payment.[2103]

And a check which is presented at a clearinghouse and credited to the payee, but later on the same day is returned by the drawee, is held not to have been paid, though the payee in form repaid the amount to the drawee.[2104] Checks presented through a clearinghouse are not considered paid where the bank on which they are drawn refuses payment and returns them to the presenting bank,[2105] even though it erroneously states as a reason for refusing payment that they are not drawn on it.[2106] And in such a case, if a depositor dies before the checks are again presented, a direction to put the checks through again does not amount to actual payment, or an agreement to pay entitling the bank to make payment after the depositor's death, especially where it does not debit the depositor's account with their amount, but honors other checks leaving insufficient funds to meet the

---

[2100] United States Fidelity, etc., Co. v. First Nat. Bank, 129 Neb. 102, 260 N.W. 798.

[2101] Columbia-Knickerbocker Trust Co. v. Miller, 156 A.D. 810, 142 N.Y.S. 440, aff'd, 215 N.Y. 191, 109 N.E. 179, 1917A Ann. Cas. 348.

[2102] Hallenbeck v. Leimert, 72 F.2d 480, rev'd on other grounds, 295 U.S. 116, 55 S. Ct. 687, 79 L. Ed. 1339.

[2103] Sneider v. Bank of Italy, 184 Cal. 595, 194 P. 1021, 12 A.L.R. 993.

[2104] Eastman Kodak Co. v. National Park Bank, 231 F. 320, aff'd, 247 F. 1002.

[2105] Campbell v. Love, 168 Miss. 75, 150 So. 780.

Check returned to payee bank by drawee bank's correspondent bank after receiving notice of drawee bank's liquidation, held not paid when presented at clearinghouse, so that drawer could not recover amount thereof from correspondent bank. Campbell v. Love, 168 Miss. 75, 150 So. 780.

[2106] Sneider v. Bank of Italy, 184 Cal. 595, 194 P. 1021, 12 A.L.R. 993.

checks in question.[2107] The rule has been stated to be that payment may be shown by the intention to make it, evidenced by some unequivocal act, such as bookkeeping entries, or by the cancellation of a note or check and marking it paid.[2108] But where a check is presented through a clearinghouse and the drawee bank makes a note on a balance ledger account of a temporary debit for the check, that act alone does not amount to payment of the check or acceptance thereof so as to render the drawee bank liable to the payee.[2109] However, where a bank does not discover a forgery in time to return a check through the clearinghouse, the case must stand as if payment had been made directly at the bank.[2110]

Effect of Indorsements on Checks Passing through Clearinghouse.—It is competent for banks associated in a clearinghouse arrangement to make rules governing, as between themselves, the effect of indorsements of negotiable paper, and such rules supplant the law on the subject;[2111] and where a bank presents a check to a clearinghouse indorsed so that under the applicable rules it is not liable as a general indorser, such presentation does not render it liable as on a general indorsement.[2112] And member banks are bound by the significance accorded a clearinghouse stamp indorsement by their association.[2113] Thus, an indorsement by a clearinghouse stamp does

---

[2107] Sneider v. Bank of Italy, 184 Cal. 595, 194 P. 1021, 12 A.L.R. 993.

[2108] First Nat. Bank v. National Park Bank, 181 App. Div. 103, 168 N.Y.S. 422.

[2109] First Nat. Bank v. National Park Bank, 181 App. Div. 103, 168 N.Y.S. 422.

[2110] Metropolitan Trust Co. v. Federal Trust Co., 232 Mass. 363, 122 N.E. 413.

[2111] Crocker-Woolworth Nat'l Bank v. Nevada Bank of San Francisco, 139 Cal. 564, 73 P. 456, 96 Am. St. R. 169, 63 A.L.R. 245; Merchants Nat'l Bank v. Continental Nat'l Bank, 98 Cal. App. 523, 277 P. 354, citing First Nat. Bank v. United States Nat. Bank, 100 Ore. 264, 197 P. 547, 14 A.L.R. 479.

The constitution and rules of a clearinghouse provided that negotiable paper payable to a bank's order, deposited for clearance, should be indorsed by the original payee, but negotiable paper deposited for clearance by a member should bear its stamp, "For clearinghouse purposes only," and should guarantee validity and regularity of indorsements, and every bank should file with members a certified impression of its stamp. Held, that where a "raised" check payable to an individual was deposited by a bank stamped, "Pay through clearing-house," it conveyed no representations to the drawee that the depositor claimed to be the owner; and in an action by the drawee to recover from the other bank, it could show that it acted merely as collecting agent for the payee. Crocker-Woolworth Nat'l Bank v. Nevada Bank of San Francisco, 139 Cal. 564, 73 P. 456, 96 Am. St. ft 189, 83 L.R.A. 245.

[2112] Crocker-Woolworth Nat'l Bank v. Nevada Bank of San Francisco, 139 Cal. 564, 73 P. 456, 96 Am. St. R. 169, 68 L.R.A. 245.

[2113] Security Commercial, etc., Bank v. Southern Trust, etc., Bank, 74 Cal. App. 734, 241 P. 945; Merchants Nat'l Bank v. Continental Nat'l Bank, 98 Cal. App. 523, 277 P. 354.

not imply identification of the payee, nor does it indicate a purchase of the indorsed check.[2114] But it has been held that a clearinghouse rule that the clearinghouse indorsement shall not be construed to supply a "missing indorsement" does not apply to a forged indorsement, and in such a case, a collecting bank is liable to a drawee bank which pays a check bearing a forged indorsement.[2115] As between banks clearing through a clearinghouse which has a rule requiring the guaranty of prior indorsements, if a guaranty of prior indorsements contributes to or wholly causes the final payment of a check by a drawee, the drawee is entitled to relief against the guarantor where an indorsement is a forgery or unauthorized.[2116] An indorsement of payment made by a federal reserve bank on a check in accordance with a clearinghouse rule, was held not binding on the drawee bank which had not authorized payment or indorsement.[2117]

A bank receiving drafts for collection through a clearinghouse does not collect same as owner, but as agent for the owner, and is not responsible for the genuineness of indorsements.[2118] A bank on which a check is drawn indorsed in blank in the name of the payee, on taking it up in a clearinghouse, is presumed to have acted in good faith.[2119] Where a bank, a holder of a check, stamps upon it words intended as a transfer of it to another

---

[2114] Security Commercial, etc., Bank v. Southern Trust, etc., Bank, 74 Cal. App. 734, 241 P. 945.

[2115] Merchants Nat'l Bank v. Continental Nat'l Bank, 98 Cal. App. 523, 277 P. 354.

[2116] **In general.—**

Hibernia Nat'l Bank v. National Bank of Commerce, 16 So. 2d 352, 204 LA. 777.

Unauthorized indorsement.—

Where plaintiff bank made loan, evidenced by note, to state university, represented by its president, and issued a cashier's check payable to the university, defendant bank, accepting cashier's check for deposit upon president's indorsement and guaranteeing the indorsement, could not escape liability to plaintiff bank upon university repudiating president's authority in the entire transaction. Hibernia Nat. Bank v. National Bank of Commerce, 16 So.2d 352, 204 La. 777.

Burden of proof on guarantor bank.—

Where bank in honoring its cashier's check relied on defendant bank's guaranty of payee's indorsement which proved to be unauthorized, burden was on defendant bank when sued on its guaranty, and not upon the drawee bank, to show that defendant bank was authorized to collect amount of check drawn by the drawee bank to the order of payee. Hibernia Nat'l Bank v. National Bank of Commerce, 16 So. 2d 352, 204 LA. 777.

[2117] Grosner v. First Nat. Bank-Detroit, 5 F. Supp. 468.

[2118] Insurance Co. v. Fourth Nat. Bank, 14 F.2d 131.

[2119] Wedge Mines Co. v. Denver Nat'l Bank, 19 Colo. App. 182, 73 P. 873.

bank that has guaranteed its payment, and the latter bank receives it through a clearinghouse and pays it, the latter bank is entitled, the drawee being insolvent, to recover the amount thereof from the drawer.[2120] And a holder of a check on which payment has been received from a drawee bank must refund such payment to the drawee where the check bears a forged indorsement, if it also bears the genuine signature of the drawer, such recovery being permissible, both under common-law rules, and a clearinghouse rule attaching to a holder's indorsement a guaranty of previous indorsements.[2121] But the foregoing rule does not apply to signatures of drawers; therefore, indorsements placed by a holder of forged checks upon checks, when presented to the drawee bank for payment, do not constitute representations as to, or warranties of, the genuineness of a drawer's signature.[2122]

Effect of Insolvency.—The failure of a bank before settlement for the day with a clearinghouse association, but after surrendering demands against other banks and receiving credit on a settlement sheet, does not deprive the association of its right to collect such demands and apply the proceeds to settle debits against the bank in accordance with its rules.[2123] But an association has no lien giving it a right to appropriate to an indebtedness due it on a loan certificate account, against a receiver representing other creditors, a balance appearing in favor of the insolvent bank upon the last daily clearing made on the day of its failure, arising in reality after insolvency from withdrawals by banks presenting checks held against the insolvent.[2124] And a bank, which in payment of a clearinghouse check drawn

---

2120 Zinner v. National Bank, 54 Ill. App. 602.

Defendant drew a check on the banking house of H.S. & Co. and delivered it, after it was certified by the drawee, to the M. bank in payment of a note. Plaintiff, a member of the clearinghouse, had guaranteed to the M. bank payment of all certified checks drawn on H.S. & Co. which came into its hands. The M. bank stamped on the check, "Paid through the C. clearinghouse, June 3, 1893, to the M. bank"; and, through the clearing of that day, the check came into plaintiff's hands, and was paid. H.S. & Co. failed, and did not open their bank on June 3d. It was held that the stamp placed on the check by the M. bank was a transfer of the check to plaintiff, and entitled it to recover the amount thereof from the drawer. Zinner v. National Bank, 54 Ill. App. 602.

2121 First Nat. Bank v. United State. Nat. Bank, 100 Ore. 264, 197 P.547, 14 A.L.R. 479.

2122 First Nat. Bank v. United States Nat. Bank, 100 Ore. 264, 197 P. 547, 14 A.L.R. 479.

2123 Yardley v. Philler, 167 U.S. 344, 17 S. Ct. 835, 42 L. Ed. 192.

2124 Yardley v. Philler, 167 U.S. 344, 17 S. Ct 835, 42 L Ed. 192, holding that the appropriation of such balance by the association is a preference within the inhibition of a statute against preferences in the cases of insolvent banks.

in its favor on another member and held as a result of the day's clearings, receives the proceeds of checks presented by such other member for clearing on the day before it suspends payment, must account therefor to the bankrupt estate of such defaulting member, where the clearinghouse in the revision of the clearings made necessary by such suspension, eliminates and returns the checks debited against the defaulting member which were subsequently dishonored.[2125] A national bank which is the clearing bank in a clearinghouse association for a state bank on which its depositor has drawn checks in the ordinary course of business in good faith, may recognize and pay such checks drawn on the day the superintendent of banks takes possession of the state bank.[2126] And that a check was deposited ten minutes before the closing of an insolvent bank, and later was transferred to another bank in a clearing settlement made after banking hours, did not create an inference of fraud by the transferee bank in receiving the check where there was no evidence that it knew of the insolvency of the transferor bank at the time of clearing.[2127]

Mutual Credits Given by Banks on Settlement Made through Clearinghouse.—Mutual credits given on a settlement by two banks through a clearinghouse cannot, without notice given before the hour when banks usually pass checks to the credit of their depositors, be recalled by either one to the detriment of the other.[2128] Where a bank presents for clearance both checks which it owns and others which it holds for collection only, the amount due on the checks it owns should be applied first to the payment of checks drawn on it which are presented against it at the time of the same clearance.[2129] A balance shown by a clearinghouse certificate issued and accepted as evidencing a credit on the issuing bank's books against which the bolder of the certificate may draw, is a deposit within the protection of statutes relating to deposits, but if the parties' intention is that checks handled in the clearinghouse are to be offset against each other, and the

---

2125 Rector v. City Deposit Bank Co., 200 U.S. 405, 26 S. Ct. 289, 50 L. Ed. 527.

And this is no less true because the clearinghouse, under its rules, might have called on its other members to pay pro rata the amount of the checks drawn upon the defaulting member, and might have treated the credits in favor of the defaulting member as belonging proportionally to the contributing members, since, even under these rules, a check which was a result of the clearings of the previous day would not be entitled to participation. Rector v. City Deposit Bank Co., 200 U.S. 405, 26 S. Ct. 289, 50 L Ed. 527.

2126 People v. Bank, 70 Misc. 633, 127 N.Y.S. 908.

2127 League v. South Carolina Nat. Bank, 171 S.C. 265, 172 S.E. 121.

2128 Blaffer v. Louisiana Nat. Bank, 35 La. Ann. 251.

2129 Spokane Eastern Trust Co. v. United States Steel Products Co., 290 F. 884.

balance paid at once in cash or by a draft on another bank, the relation of depositor and depositee does not arise.[2130]

Reclamation of Checks Returned as Not Good.—A clearinghouse may provide that a bank charged by it with an amount of drafts or checks returned as not good can allow such charges to stand in the account of the clearinghouse, and seek reparations directly from the bank required to refund such amount under the rules of the clearinghouse.[2131] Where forged checks, payable to cash and unindorsed, are paid by a bank through a clearinghouse to another bank which has credited a depositor therefor, the paying bank cannot recover the amount of the checks since it is supposed to know the maker's signature if the payee in no way deceives it.[2132] And an owner of a check cannot make any claim for nonpayment against a clearinghouse agent of an indorsee upon its return by the drawee as not good.[2133]

Protection of Member Banks and Guarantee of Deposits.—Members of a clearinghouse association may be authorized to make necessary commitments to keep another member from failing in order to avoid loss to their own depositors and stockholders in a banking crisis; but each case of a guaranty of deposits of a member must be considered as it arises, and on its particular facts.[2134]

[2130] Hall v. First Nat. Bank (Tex. Civ. App.), 252 S.W. 828, modified, 254 S.W. 522.

[2131] Mt. Morris Bank v. Twenty-Third Ward Bank, 172 N.Y. 244, 64 N.E. 810.

[2132] Dedham Nat. Bank v. Everett Nat. Bank, 177 Mass. 392, 59 N.E. 62, 83 Am. St. R. 286 (1901).

Where forged checks, payable to cash, were deposited with defendant bank, and paid to it through the clearinghouse by plaintiff bank, the drawee, the fact that defendant had not required indorsement of the checks would not render it liable to refund the money received, on the ground that such fact led plaintiff to believe that the checks had been cashed for their apparent maker, since there was no custom for such requirement nor any duty of defendant to anticipate such result. Dedham Nat'l Bank v. Everett Nat'l Bank, 177 Mass. 392, 59 N.E. 62, 88 Am. St. R. 288.

[2133] Columbia-Knickerbocker Trust Co. v. Miller, 156 App. Div. 810, 142 N.Y.S. 440, aff'd, 215 N.Y. 191, 109 N.E. 179, 1917A Ann. Cas. 348.

[2134] **In general.**—

O'Connor v. Bankers Trust Co., 159 Misc. 920, 289 N.Y.S. 252 (1936), aff'd, 253 App. Div. 714, 1 N.Y.S.2d 641; 278 N.Y. 649, 16 N.E.2d 302.

Agreement upheld.—

Agreement to protect depositors of member bank held sufficiently definite, based on sufficient consideration, and not subject to defense of mutual mistake concerning actual condition of member bank. O'Connor v. Bankers Trust Co., 159 Misc. 920, 289 N.Y.S. 252 (1936), aff'd, 253 App. Div. 714, 1 N.Y.S. 2d 641; 278 N.Y. 649, 16 N.E.2d 302.

(Text continued on page 590)

Reasonable time was to be implied, where agreement to guarantee deposits of member bank did not specify exact time for performance. O'Connor v. Bankers Trust Co., 159 Misc. 920, 289 N.Y.S. 252 (1936), aff'd, 253 App. Div. 714, 1 N.Y.S. 2d 641; 278 N.Y. 649, 16 N.E.2d 802.

Apportionment of liability.—

Usage of clearinghouse association whenever concerted action was taken to apportion liability of member banks on basis of respective capital funds at time of making agreement held part of alleged agreement to protect depositors of member bank which was silent as to how liability would be apportioned among them. O'Connor v. Bankers Trust Co., 159 Misc. 920, 289 N.Y.S. 252 (1936), aff'd, 253 App. Div. 714, 1 N.Y.S.2d 641, 278 N.Y. 649, 16 N.E.2d 802.

Under such agreement, amount for which banks would be liable held susceptible of determination. O'Connor v. Bankers Trust Co., 159 Misc. 920, 289 N.Y.S. 252 (1936), aff'd, 253 App. Div. 714, 1 N.Y.S.2d 641; 278 N.Y. 649, 16 N.E.2d 302.

Member banks held without authority to confer on governing body of clearinghouse association general authority to bind members to guarantee deposits of another member, even if such power were limited to banking crises. O'Connor v. Bankers Trust Co., 159 Misc. 920, 289 N.Y.S. 252 (1936), aff'd, 253 App. Div. 714, 1 N.Y.S.2d 641, 278 N.Y. 649, 16 N.E.2d 302.

Clearinghouse committee held without authority to guarantee deposits of member. O'Connor v. Bankers Trust Co., 159 Misc. 920, 289 N.Y.S. 252 (1936), aff'd, 253 App. Div. 714, 1 N.Y.S.2d 641; 278 N.Y. 649, 16 N.E.2d 302.

Guarantee not implied.—

Where it was duty of clearinghouse committee to check up on financial operations of member bank, to order discontinuance of irregularities and to require change of management, taking of such steps held no basis for implying that deposits of such member bank were guaranteed. O'Connor v. Bankers Trust Co., 159 Misc. 920, 289 N.Y.S. 252 (1936), aff'd, 253 App. Div. 714, 1 N.Y.S.2d 641; 278 N.Y. 649, 16 N.E.2d 302.

Agreement by member banks to guarantee deposits of member held not implied from banks' knowledge of condition of such member, acquiescence in change of management, and its retention as member, even in light of advertisements calling attention to activities of association in behalf of member banks. O'Connor v. Bankers Trust Co., 159 Misc. 920, 289 N.Y.S. 252 (1936), aff'd, 253 App. Div. 714, 1 N.Y.S.2d 641; 278 N.Y. 649, 16 N.E.2d 802.

Effect of advertisements or past practices.—

Power to guarantee deposits held not conferred upon association or its governing body by advertisements which might be misleading, such as that association took steps to protect funds of depositors of member bank, nor by past practice. O'Connor v. Bankers Trust Co., 159 Misc. 920, 289 N.Y.S 252 (1936), aff'd, 253 App. Div. 714, 1 N.Y.S.2d 641; 278 N.Y. 649, 16 N.E.2d 302.

No estoppel to deny liability.—

Banks belonging to clearinghouse association not represented on committee, but whose officers were allegedly consulted as to guaranteeing deposits of member bank, held not estopped to deny liability on alleged contract of guaranty by committee acting on behalf of

Particular Actions.—If a bank is entitled to maintain an action to recover the amount of a check paid by mistake to another bank through a clearinghouse, the fact that the latter bank has credited the amount to the account of the customer depositing the check does not render the depositor, instead of such bank, liable to the action.[2135] It has been held not to be negligence for a clearinghouse agent to omit to send to the clearinghouse on Saturday a check on a bank which was closed on Friday, the agent having no knowledge or means of knowledge that the bank would resume payment on Saturday, the clearings having been made on Saturday before the bank opened.[2136] See the appended note for cases relating to other actions involving settlements and transactions through clearinghouses.[2137]

§ 3. Rights and Liabilities of Nonmembers.

Upon Whom Clearinghouse Rules Are Binding.—The rules of a clearinghouse association are adopted solely for the purpose of facilitating exchanges among its member banks.[2138] Thus, such rules do not affect the rights and liabilities of banks and persons who are not members of an

---

members. O'Connor v. Bankers Trust Co., 159 Misc. 920, 289 N.Y.S. 252 (1936), aff'd, 253 App. Div. 714, 1 N.Y.S.2d 641; 278 N.Y. 649, 16 N.E.2d 302.

[2135] Merchants' Nat'l Bank v. National Bank of Commonwealth, 139 Mass. 513, 2 N.E. 89.

[2136] Farmers', etc., Bank v. Third Nat. Bank, 165 Pa. 500, 30 A. 1008.

[2137] Where the holder in due course of no-fund check gave check to cover no-fund check to holder's agent bank, who made settlement with bank on which no-fund check was drawn after time when, under clearinghouse rules, agent bank would not have been required to do so, bank on which refund check was drawn held not liable to holder in due course on theory of money had and received, where neither bank was unjustly enriched by the settlement transaction. Liberty Nat'l Bank v. Vanderslice-Lynds Co., 338 Mo. 932, 95 S.W.2d 324 (1936).

Where a bank in one city, being indebted to a bank in another city for collections made, remits by its cashier's check on another bank in the latter city with which it has a sufficient deposit, which check is duly presented and paid through the clearinghouse, the transaction constitutes a complete appropriation of the fund to the creditor bank, and its ownership is not affected by its restoring the money to the bank paying the check on the same day, on the demand of the latter, made on learning of the suspension of the drawer, which return is required under such circumstances by the rules of the clearinghouse, of which both banks are members, but only for the purpose of protecting the paying bank, in case the payment should prove to have been unauthorized; nor will the fact that such bank, without right, pays the money to the receiver of the insolvent bank, prevent its recovery from the receiver by the payee of the check. National Union Bank v. Earle, 93 F. 330.

[2138] Manufacturers' Nat'l Bank v. Thompson, 129 Mass. 438, 87 Am. R. 878.

association or parties to its regulations.[2139] But while rules of a clearinghouse are not of their own force binding on nonmembers, such rules and the practices thereunder may have a bearing on the rights of third persons.[2140] For example, when by mutual consent, a bank that is not a member of a clearinghouse association is represented by a member bank, the outside bank becomes a party to, and is bound by, the clearinghouse association rules of which it has knowledge.[2141] Regular customers or depositors of banks, however, are not parties to the rules and regulations of a clearinghouse of

---

[2139] **In general.—**

National Exchange Bank v. Ginn & Co., 114 Md. 181, 78 A. 1026, 33 L.R.A. (n.s.) 968, 19140 Ann. Cas. 508; Manufacturers' Nat'l Bank v. Thompson, 129 Mass. 438, 87 Am. R. 378; Citizens' Cent. Nat. Bank v. New Amsterdam Nat. Bank, 109 N.Y.S. 872. See Hallenbeck v. Leimert, 72 F.2d 480, rev'd, 295 U.S. 116, 55 S. Ct. 687, 79 L. Ed. 1339. See also § 2 of this chapter.

Nonmembers of bank clearinghouse cannot claim benefit of clearinghouse rules. Liberty Nat'l Bank v. Vanderslice-Lynds Co., 338 Mo. 932, 95 S.W.2d 324.

Illustrative cases.—

The failure of a bank paying a check drawn by a depositor in favor of a third person, who forwards it through another bank for collection, to offer to return the check to the collecting bank and to demand repayment, within the time prescribed by the rules of the association, does not impair its right to recover the amount from the third person, providing its right to recover is otherwise perfect. National Exchange Bank v. Ginn & Co., 114 Md. 181, 78 A. 1026, 33 L.R.A. (n.s.) 968, 1914C Ann. Cas. 508.

An action by the holder against the drawee of a check for failure to observe a custom by which banks belonging to an association called the clearinghouse are bound to return checks presented through the clearinghouse, and which they have no funds to pay, upon the same day, or before banking hours of the next day, under penalty of being liable for the same, cannot be maintained where plaintiff is not a member of the association. Overman v. Hoboken City Bank, 30 N.J.L. 61.

A note was discounted by the B. Bank, and sent to the A. Bank, where payable, for collection, and there marked "Paid," by mistake, the discovery being made, later in the same morning, that the maker of the note had no funds in the bank, and at once the B. Bank and the indorsers were notified and the note duly protested. A contention took place between the banks as to whether, under the clearinghouse rules, the note not having been returned to the B. Bank before a certain hour of the day, it became the property of the A. Bank, but the dispute was settled by the payment of the amount of the note to the B. Bank, the payment being expressly made without waiver of any legal rights, and at the trial the B. Bank disclaimed title to the note. Upon a suit by the A. Bank against the indorsers, it was held that the note was not paid, and that defendants could not avail themselves of the clearinghouse rules. Manufacturers' Nat'l Bank v. Thompson, 129 Mass. 438, 87 Am. B. 376.

[2140] In re Smith, etc., Co., 8 F.2d 444; Hallenbeck v. Leimert, 295 U.S. 116, 55 S. Ct. 687, 79 L. Ed. 1339.

[2141] Geibe v. Chicago-Lake State Bank, 160 Minn. 89, 199 N.W. 514.

which their banks are members, and cannot, therefore, claim the benefit of them, nor be injuriously affected by them.[2142] A fortiori, the practices of banks belonging to a clearinghouse with respect to nonmembers thereof do not affect the rights of depositors in nonmember banks having no knowledge of such practices.[2143] And the rules of a clearinghouse as such do not govern the rights of nonmember drawers or payees of checks who do not contract with express reference to such rules.[2144]

Clearances Made by Nonmember through Member.—A bank which is a member of a clearinghouse association may only agree and arrange to clear for a nonmember bank in accordance with the conditions imposed by the constitution and rules of the association.[2145] Therefore, where a clearinghouse rule makes a member clearing for a nonmember "liable to the clearinghouse" for all checks, until delivery to each member of a written notice of the discontinuance of such agency, a member is liable to other members on checks on a nonmember for which it cleared which are in other members' hands at the time it gives them such notice of discontinuance, the clearinghouse's contract being for the use and benefit of its members.[2146] And where the rules of an association permit a member to clear for a nonmember, but require the nonmember's consent to be governed by its rules and regulations, such rules and regulations are a part of the contract between the nonmember and the member clearing for it, and the contract

---

[2142] Louisiana Ice Co. v. State Nat. Bank (La.), 1 McGloin 181; Merchants' Nat. Bank v. National Bank, 139 Mass. 513, 2 N.E. 89; Lowell Co-Op. Bank v. Sheridan, 284 Mass. 594, 188 N.E. 636, 91 A.L.R. 1176; Citizens' Cent. Nat. Bank v. New Amsterdam Nat. Bank, 109 N.Y.S. 872, citing Overman v. Hoboken City Bank, 30 N.J.L. 61.

[2143] Lowell Co-operative Bank v. Sheridan, 284 Mass. 594, 188 N.E. 636, 91 A.L.R. 1176.

[2144] Sneider v. Bank of Italy, 184 Cal. 595, 194 P. 1021, 12 A.L.R. 993; First Nat. Bank v. National Park Bank, 181 App. Div. 103, 168 N.Y.S. 422.

[2145] O'Brien v. Grant, 146 N.Y. 163, 40 N.E. 871, 28 L.R.A. 381.

[2146] Moore v. American Sav. Bank, etc., Co., 111 Wash. 148, 189 P. 1010.

In such a case, the member who paid other members' amount of checks on non-member in their hands at time it had notified them of discontinuance of clearing arrangements with nonmember is entitled to reimbursements out of securities deposited with it by nonmember, where such notice was given prior to time bank examiner took charge of nonmember for insolvency, though payment to other members was made subsequent thereto, notwithstanding a statute prohibiting a lien for payment advanced, a clearance made, or liability incurred after insolvency the lien having been created before insolvency. Moore v. American Sav. Bank, etc., Co., 111 Wash. 148, 189 P. 1010.

should be construed in the light of such rules.[2147] Where a nonmember agrees to pay an association a specified annual sum for the privilege of clearing through a member, and a contract is entered into between the two banks by which the member agrees to clear for the nonmember in consideration of a deposit of a certain sum of money and bills receivable, such arrangement constitutes a tripartite agreement upon ample consideration for the mutual benefit of the three parties, and the relation of principal and agent, which the contract between the banks creates, is merely a feature of the larger contractual relation existing between such parties.[2148] And a nonmember depositing securities for such purpose with a member clearing for it cannot avoid its contract by pleading that its deposit was ultra vires.[2149]

A clearinghouse member is entitled to protest fees in protesting checks paid by it, when such protest, though unnecessary, was made at the request of the state superintendent of banks;[2150] such member is also entitled to expenses incurred, including counsel fees in collecting bills receivable.[2151]

A rule of a clearinghouse that all checks and vouchers received by any member remain the property of the presenting member until actually paid, and should be returned to the clearinghouse by the receiving member on its failure to pay the balance due on demand, does not give a member the option of either paying or returning checks received by it on a nonmember for

---

[2147] Moore v. American Sav. Bank, etc., Co., 111 Wash. 148, 189 P. 1010.

Where such a contract was entered into by the New York clearinghouse association and two banks, one a member and the other not a member, it was held that a rule of the association, which provided that arrangements by a member to clear for an outside bank should not be discontinued without previous notice, and that the notice could not take effect until the completion of clearances on the day after receipt of the notice, was binding upon the parties to the contract, and that the member bank was required to pay checks on the nonmember presented to the clearinghouse on the day after notice of discontinuance was given, though it knew at the time that the other bank was insolvent. Such payments, therefore, were not within the prohibition of a statute against payments by an insolvent corporation made with intent to prefer creditors, and the money and securities held under the contract were applicable to the amount of the checks paid. O'Brien v. Grant, 146 N.Y. 163, 40 N.E. 871, 28 L.R.A. 381; Davenport v. National Bank, 194 N.Y. 568, 88 N.E. 1117.

[2148] O'Brien v. Grant, 146 N.Y. 163, 40 N.E. 871, 28 L.R.A. 361; Davenport v. National Bank, 194 N.Y. 568, 88 N.E. 1117.

[2149] Moore v. American Sav. Bank, etc., Co., 111 Wash. 148, 189 P. 1010.

[2150] Davenport v. National Bank, 194 N.Y. 568, 88 N.E. 1117.

[2151] Davenport v. National Bank of Commerce, 127 A.D. 391, 112 N.Y.S. 291, aff'd, 194 N.Y. 568, 88 N.E. 1117.

which it clears, such rule referring only to checks that are not good.[2152] And where a nonmember bank employs a member bank to present checks through a clearinghouse for it, the nonmember bank is bound by the member bank's refunding payment of a check returned later than the time allowed by clearinghouse rules even though the member bank so acted without authority.[2153] And where an owner of a draft not a member of a clearinghouse indorses it to a bank for collection, and it is sent by the bank to the clearinghouse in due course with other checks and drafts, and the bank is closed before the balance against it on the clearinghouse settlement is adjusted, and thereupon the drawee, a member of the clearinghouse, pays to the clearinghouse the amount of the draft, such payment, having been made to a stranger to the draft having no interest in the proceeds nor authority to act as agent for the owner, is no defense to an action by the owner against the drawee for the amount of the draft.[2154]

§ 4. Security for Payment of Balances.

A clearinghouse committee created by the agreement of several banks, which receives deposits from such banks of securities at a fixed ratio on their capital stock, and issues certificates therefor to be used in paying balances, becomes an owner for value of the securities.[2155] And such securities pledged by a clearinghouse member bank first for payment of its daily balances, and next as security for other indebtedness due to members of the association, will be held after payment of daily balances to meet a deficiency in other securities given by it to the clearinghouse committee to provide for payment of clearinghouse certificates issued to aid in maintaining its credit.[2156] Where the purpose of a deposit of security with a clearinghouse committee is to facilitate the legitimate business of banks, and the deposit involves no element of speculation and no business undertaking by or on behalf of the associated banks, it is not a violation of laws relating to national

---

[2152] Moore v. American Sav. Bank, etc., Co., 111 Wash. 148, 189 P. 1010.

[2153] Stuyvesant Bank v. National Mechanics', etc., Ass'n (N.Y.), 7 Lans. 197.

Any agency status between payor bank and related bank which received check for collection at clearinghouse because payor bank was not clearing member did not prevent related bank from being payor bank's transferor bank, for purposes of determining whether payor bank timely returned check or sent notice of dishonor. Pulaski Bank & Trust Co. v. Texas Am. Bank/Fort Worth, 759 SW.2d 723 (Tex. App. 1988).

[2154] Crane v. Fourth St. Nat'l Bank, 173 Pa. 566, 34 A. 296.

[2155] Philler v. Patterson, 168 Pa. 468, 32 A. 26, 47 Am. St. R. 896.

[2156] Philler v. Jewett, 166 Pa. 456, 31 A. 204.

banks.[2157] Where a bank has enjoyed and is enjoying the benefits of a transaction whereby it executed its notes to a clearinghouse association in return for clearinghouse certificates, and deposited collateral to secure same, and it has not offered to restore the certificates, neither it nor its creditors are entitled to rescission of the transaction and restoration of the collateral to its receiver, even if for any reason it or they would otherwise be entitled to so rescind.[2158] Upon the insolvency of a bank which is a member of a clearinghouse, the appropriation to be made of a sum realized from claims of the insolvent bank against other banks in possession of the clearinghouse on the day of insolvency is to be determined by the agreement of the parties interested, construed in the light of the constitution and rules of the clearinghouse, and the clearinghouse has no right to apply any part of such sum to its certificate loan account if such appropriation constitutes a preference prohibited by statute.[2159]

§ 5. Actions.

Since a clearinghouse association is the agent and fiduciary representative of the banks forming it, its dissolution will not be enjoined at the instance of a member thereof.[2160] A cause of action against a clearinghouse for giving a bank the false appearance of solvency, inducing the making of a deposit which was subsequently lost, does not belong to such bank on any conceivable theory, and hence the receiver of such bank could not represent it in an action against the clearinghouse and its officers.[2161] And where a bank acting as a clearinghouse between several contracting parties presents to one of such parties in one day two approximate balances in the nature of clearance statements, and owing to great financial excitement it is impossible to clear either statement, but the bank makes a large payment thereon as a favor, no action will lie against the bank as upon an account stated.[2162]

An action against a clearinghouse association on an alleged promise to protect depositors of a bank was held not premature because it was brought before the bank was liquidated, since such promise was not contingent on the

---

2157 Philler v. Patterson, 168 Pa. 468, 32 A. 26, 47 Am. St. R. 896.

2158 Booth v. Atlanta Clearing House Ass'n, 132 Ga. 100, 63 S.E. 907.

2159 Yardley v. Philler, 167 U.S. 344, 17 S. Ct. 835, 42 L. Ed. 192.

2160 People's Sav. Bank v. First Nat. Bank, 102 Wash. 436, 173 P. 52.

2161 Kimmich v. Potter, 112 F.2d 135, cert. denied, 311 U.S. 653, 61 S. Ct. 47, 85 L Ed. 418.

2162 National City Bank v. New York Gold Exch. Bank, 101 N.Y. 595, 5 N.E. 463.

failure of the depositors to collect from the bank, and liability accrued immediately on its default.[2163]

A clearinghouse association is properly sued in the name of a committee having the entire control of its business, funds and securities.[2164] And the banks composing a clearinghouse association are entitled to sue a collecting bank on its dishonored check although the bank is a partnership, and in such action the manager and cashier of the association are neither necessary nor proper parties.[2165]

In actions by and against a clearinghouse association, the usual rules of pleading are applicable.[2166]

In an action by a bank to recover from another bank an amount of checks paid by the former to the latter through a clearinghouse on the ground that the indorsements on the checks were fraudulent and unauthorized, the burden of establishing the fraudulent and unauthorized character of the indorsements is on the plaintiff.[2167] Where two banks deal with a clearinghouse through the agency of other banks which are members thereof, the rules of the clearinghouse are competent evidence in a suit by one of such banks to recover money paid through the clearinghouse on a note payable at it and held by the other, which had been certified by it by mistake.[2168] For other cases illustrating that the usual rules of evidence apply in actions by and against a clearinghouse association, see the footnote.[2169]

[2163] O'Connor v. Bankers Trust Co., 159 Misc. 920, 289 N.Y.S. 252 (1936), aff'd, 253 App. Div. 714, 1 N.Y.S.2d 641; 278 N.Y. 649, 16 N.E.2d 302.

[2164] Yardley v. Philler, 58 F. 746, rev'd on other grounds, 62 F. 645; 167 U.S. 344, 17 S. Ct. 835, 42 L. Ed. 192.

[2165] Ellis v. Jones, 144 Ga. 120, 86 S.E. 317.

[2166] Farmers', etc., Bank v. Third Nat. Bank, 165 Pa. 500, 30 A. 1008.

[2167] National Park Bank v. American Exch. Nat. Bank, 88 N.Y.S. 271.

[2168] Mt. Morris Bank v. Twenty-Third Ward Bank, 60 App. Div. 205, 70 N.Y.S. 78, aff'd, 172 N.Y. 244, 64 N.E. 810.

[2169] Evidence held insufficient to establish that officers of member banks authorized clearinghouse committee to guarantee deposits of one of member banks, or had notice of committee's assumption of such authority. O'Connor v. Bankers Trust Co., 159 Misc. 920, 289 N.Y.S. 252 (1936), aff'd, 253 App. Div. 714, 1 N.Y.S.2d 641; 278 N.Y. 649, 16 N.E.2d 302.

Evidence held insufficient to show that individual members of clearinghouse committee, who were not members when committee allegedly guaranteed deposits of member bank, warranted their authority to commit association or their respective banks to such an agreement. O'Connor v. Bankers Trust Co., 159 Misc. 920, 289 N.Y.S. 252 (1936), aff'd, 253

Where one bank sues to recover from another the amount of a check of one of its depositors paid by mistake through a clearinghouse, the recovery should be the difference between such amount and the sum on deposit to the drawer's credit.[2170]

App. Div. 714, 1 N.Y.S.2d 641; 278 N.Y. 649, 18 N.E.2d 302.

Evidence held to support finding that clearinghouse association draft was not presented within a reasonable time. Holbrook v. Moody & Co. (Tex. Civ. App.), 45 S.W.2d 685 (1931).

[2170] Merchants' Nat. Bank v. National Bank, 139 Mass. 513, 2 N.E. 89.

CHAPTER XIX.

TAXATION.

Synopsis

I. NATURE AND EXTENT OF POWER TO TAX BANKS.

§ 1. In General.

§ 1.5. Power of States.

§ 2. Power of United States.

§ 3. Power of Territories.

§ 4. Purposes of Taxation.

§ 5. Delegation of Power.

§ 6. Power to Cure Defects or Irregularities.

II. CONSTITUTIONAL REQUIREMENTS AND RESTRICTIONS.

§ 7. Constitutional Provisions as to Situs.

§ 8. General Laws, Equality and Uniformity In General.

§ 9. Classification of Subjects and Uniformity as to Same Subject.

§ 10. Double Taxation.

§ 11. Taxation According to Value.

§ 12. Miscellaneous Matters.

III. LIABILITY OF BANKS AND THEIR PROPERTY TO TAXATION.

a. Banks Other than National Banks.

§ 13. In General.

§ 14. Franchises and Privileges.

§ 15. Capital and Capital Stock.

§ 16. Shares of Stock in Hands of Stockholders.

§ 17. Dividends, Surplus and Undivided Profits.

§ 18. Deposits.

§ 19. Loans, Investments and Securities.

§ 20. Ownership or Possession of Property.

§ 21. Taxation on Circulation.

b. National Banks.

1. Federal Taxation.

§ 22. In General.

2. State Taxation.

(A). General Considerations

§ 23. In General.

§ 24. Real Property.

(B). National Bank Shares.

§ 25. In General.

§ 26. Prohibition of Discrimination Between National Bank Shares and Other Moneyed Capital.

§ 27. Validity of Statute Requiring Payment by Bank as Agent of Stockholders.

§ 28. Deposits.

§ 29. Dividends.

§ 30. Federal and Joint Stock Land Banks.

§ 31. Other Federal Banks and Agencies.

IV. EXEMPTIONS.

§ 32. In General.

§ 33. Irrevocability of Statutes Providing for Method of Taxation and Exemptions.

§ 34. Transferability of Charter Exemption.

§ 35. Waiver of or Estoppel to Claim Exemptions.

§ 36. Acquisition of Exempt Property to Evade Taxation.

V. PLACE OF TAXATION.

§ 37. Bank Property and Stocks.

§ 38. National Bank Shares.

VI. LEVY AND ASSESSMENT.

a. General Considerations.

§ 39. Proceedings for Assessment and Assessors.

b. Mode of Assessment.

§ 40. As Determined by Statute and Charter.

§ 41. Report or Statement by Bank.

§ 42. Proceedings for Discovery and Valuation of Property.

c. Valuation of Bank's Property and Income.

§ 43. In General.

§ 44. Valuation of Franchises and Privileges.

§ 45. Valuation of Capital or Capital Stock.

§ 46. Determination of Amount of Deposits.

§ 47. Valuation of Surplus and Undivided Profits.

d. Valuation of Shares.

§ 48. In General.

§ 49. Valuation of National Bank Shares.

§ 50. Valuation of Income and Deductions.

§ 51. Amendment or Alteration.

§ 52. Additional or Supplemental Assessment.

§ 53. Notice of Assessment.

§ 54. Assessment Rolls or Books.

§ 55. Equalization of Assessments.

e. Review, Correction, or Setting Aside of Assessment.

§ 56. In General.

§ 57. Grounds for Review.

§ 58. Right of Review.

§ 59. Creation and Organization of Boards of Review or Other Special Tribunals.

§ 60. Authority, Powers and Duties of Boards or Officers.

§ 61. Place and Time of Meeting of Boards.

§ 62. Notice to Interested Parties.

§ 63. Action to Set Aside Assessment or Abate Tax.

§ 64. Determination or Decision.

§ 65. Review of Decision of Board.

§ 66. Certiorari to Review Assessment.

§ 67. Mandamus to Correct Assessment

§ 68. Injunction to Restrain Assessment

VII. LIEN AND PRIORITY.

§ 69. Existence and Discharge of Lien.

§ 70. Transfer of Property.

VIII. PAYMENT AND REFUNDING OR RECOVERY OF TAX PAID.

a. Payment.

§ 71. In General.

§ 72. Method of Making Payment.

§ 73. Operation and Effect of Payment.

§ 74. Tender.

b. Refunding or Recovery of Taxes Paid.

§ 75. In General.

§ 76. Actions and Proceedings for Recovery of Taxes Paid.

IX. COLLECTION AND ENFORCEMENT.

a. Manner.

§ 77. In General.

§ 78. Summary Remedies.

§ 79. Action for Unpaid Taxes.

b. Remedies for Wrongful Enforcement.

1. Injunction.

§ 80. When Proper.

§ 81. Jurisdiction.

§ 82. Parties.

§ 83. Procedure.

§ 84. Scope of Inquiry.

§ 85. Extent of Relief Granted.
§ 86. Action for Damages.

X. FORFEITURES AND PENALTIES.

§ 87. Penalty for Nonpayment of Tax.
§ 88. Penalty for Failure to List Shares of Stock.
§ 89. Persons Liable for Penalties.
§ 90. Pleading In Penalty Action.

XI. LEGACY, INHERITANCE AND TRANSFER TAXES.

a. Statutory Provisions.

§ 91. In General.

b. Property Liable.

§ 92. In General.
§ 93. Particular Estates or Interests.
§ 94. Property of Nonresidents or Aliens.
§ 95. Situs of Property.
§ 96. Exemptions.
§ 97. Transfers Made in Contemplation of Death.
§ 98. Proceedings for Assessment.
§ 99. Review, Correction and Setting Aside Assessment.
§ 100. Refunding or Recovery of Taxes Paid.

I. NATURE AND EXTENT OF POWER TO TAX BANKS.

§ 1. In General.

Definitions and General Consideration.—All property is presumed to be subject to taxation.[2171]

The definition of "bank" in the Internal Revenue Code begins: "For purposes of sections 582 and 584, the term 'bank' means a bank or trust company incorporated and doing business under the laws of the United States (including laws relating to the District of Columbia) or of any

---

[2171] American Nat'l Bank & Trust Co. v. Department of Revenue, 183 Ill. Dec. 179, 611 N.E.2d 32 (Ill. App. 2 Dist. 1993).

State."[2172] The statute is not a model of statutory clarity. Its construction and circular use of the term bank are inherently ambiguous. However, the most consistent and harmonious reading of the definition of "bank" supports the conclusion that being a bank within the commonly understood meaning of that term is an independent requirement.[2173]

An interpretation under the Tax Code that "bank" must be given its common meaning, which is in essence the receipt of deposits and making of loans, is not purely duplicative of the statute's requirement that a substantial part of the taxpayer's business consists of receiving deposits and making loans and discounts because this later requirement adds an important modifier: "substantial part of the business." The statute thus qualifies these factors, requiring that a taxpayer seeking to take advantage of this tax benefit not only engage in the touchstone activities of a bank, but that these activities amount to a substantial part of its business.[2174]

Put another way, the term "bank" as used in the Tax Code imposes an independent element and should be given its common meaning. The common understanding of "bank" includes the following bare requisites: (1) The receipt of deposits from the general public, repayable to the depositors on demand or at a fixed time; (2) the use of deposit funds for secured loans and (3) the relationship of debtor and creditor between the bank and the depositor.[2175] For this purpose, it is erroneous to interpret "deposit" to include a requirement that a bank hold its customers' funds for extended periods of time.[2176] The requirement in the statute that deposits be made from the general public is meant merely to differentiate between deposits

---

[2172] See 26 U.S.C.S. § 581: "For purposes of sections 582 and 584 [26 U.S.C.S. §§ 582 and 584], the term "bank" means a bank or trust company incorporated and doing business under the laws of the United States (including laws relating to the District of Columbia) or of any State, a substantial part of the business of which consists of receiving deposits and making loans and discounts, or of exercising fiduciary powers similar to those permitted to national banks under authority of the Comptroller of the Currency, and which is subject by law to supervision and examination by State, or Federal authority having supervision over banking institutions. Such term also means a domestic building and loan association."

See also 26 U.S.C.S. § 582 as to bad debts, losses, and gains with respect to securities held by financial institutions; and 26 U.S.C.S. § 584 regarding common trust funds.

[2173] Moneygram Int'l v. Comm'r, 664 Fed. Appx. 386 (5th Cir. 2016).

[2174] Moneygram Int'l v. Comm'r, 664 Fed. Appx. 386 (5th Cir. 2016).

[2175] Moneygram Int'l v. Comm'r, 664 Fed. Appx. 386 (5th Cir. 2016).

[2176] Moneygram Int'l v. Comm'r, 664 Fed. Appx. 386 (5th Cir. 2016).

received from sources in some way connected with the bank and those received from ordinary and unrelated customers of banking services.[2177]

The term "basis" refers to a taxpayer's capital stake in property and is used to determine the gain or loss on the sale or exchange of property and the amount of depreciation allowances. The basis of an asset is typically its cost, also known as its cost basis.[2178]

A "debt cancellation contract" is defined as a loan term or contractual arrangement modifying loan terms under which a bank agrees to cancel all or part of a customer's obligation to repay an extension of credit from that bank upon the occurrence of a specified event.[2179]

The definitions for deferred revenue, prepaid income, and unearned income are: income received but not yet earned. "Unearned income" is defined as income received but not yet earned, such as rent received in advance or other advances from customers. Unearned income is usually classified as a current liability on a company's balance sheet, assuming that it will be credited to income within the normal accounting cycle.[2180]

The California Revenue and Taxation Code does not furnish a statutory definition of "financial corporations." The classification was adopted to avoid preferential tax treatment in favor of corporations in substantial competition with national banks. Under the governing test, the classification includes savings and loans as well as other kinds of moneyed corporations performing some of the functions of a national bank or dealing in money or financing in competition with activities of national banks.[2181]

Courts that have considered the meaning of "loans," as that term is used in the Internal Revenue Code provision defining "bank,"[2182] and its statutory

---

[2177] Moneygram Int'l v. Comm'r, 664 Fed. Appx. 386 (5th Cir. 2016).

[2178] WMI Holdings Corp. v. United States, 891 F.3d 1016 (5th Cir. 2018).

[2179] Gordon v. Kohl's Dep't Stores, Inc., 172 F. Supp. 3d 840 (E.D. Pa. 2016).

[2180] Fishbelt Feeds, Inc. v. Miss. Dep't of Revenue, 158 So. 3d 984 (Miss. 2014). See Miss. Code Ann. §§ 27-13-9, 27-13-11.

Because statutes require franchise tax to be calculated for the year preceding the date of the filing of the return, "deferred income" cannot represent a netted term, as expenses cannot be deducted retroactively. Fishbelt Feeds, Inc. v. Miss. Dep't of Revenue, 158 So. 3d 984 (Miss. 2014).

[2181] California Fed. Savings & Loan Assn. v. City of Los Angeles, 54 Cal. 3d 1, 812 P.2d 916 (1991).

[2182] 26 U.S.C.S. § 581.

predecessor,[2183] have defined this term as an agreement, either expressed or implied, whereby one person advances money to the other and the other agrees to repay it upon such terms as to time and rate of interest, or without interest, as the parties may agree. In another context, a loan of money is a contract by which one delivers a sum of money to another and the latter agrees to return at a future time a sum equivalent to that which he borrows. Notably, courts have repeatedly stated that interest is not required.[2184] In addition, the definition of "bank" under the Internal Revenue Code provides that a substantial part of the taxpayer's business must consist of "making loans *and discounts*." The statute's use of the conjunctive "and" rather than the disjunctive "or" in this phrase indicates that "discounts" is a required element.[2185]

When during the savings and loan crisis, the Federal Savings and Loan Insurance Corporation (FSLIC) lacked the funds to liquidate failing savings and loan associations, also called "thrifts," and, as thrift regulator and insurer of deposits, the FSLIC responded to the crisis by encouraging healthy thrifts to take over failing ones in what were called "supervisory mergers," thereby relieving the FSLIC of its deposit insurance liability for the insolvent thrifts, in exchange, it provided a package of non-cash incentives to acquiring thrifts, including "branching" rights.[2186] "Branching rights" permitted acquiring thrifts to open and operate branches in states other than their home states, which, prior to 1981, was generally prohibited. This prohibition was eliminated for thrifts entering into supervisory mergers across state lines.[2187]

"Regulatory accounting purposes" or "RAP" rights, by contrast, affected regulatory accounting treatment for business combinations. Formerly, regulations mandated, in part, that each thrift maintain a minimum capital of at least three percent of its liabilities, which presented an obstacle for healthy thrifts seeking to acquire failing ones because, by definition, failing thrifts' liabilities exceeded their assets. Regulators eliminated this obstacle by

---

2183 Former 26 U.S.C.S. § 104.

2184 Moneygram Int'l v. Comm'r, 664 Fed. Appx. 386 (5th Cir. 2016).

2185 Moneygram Int'l v. Comm'r, 664 Fed. Appx. 386 (5th Cir. 2016).

2186 WMI Holdings Corp. v. United States, 891 F.3d 1016 (2018).

Thrifts collect customer deposits, which are maintained in interest-bearing savings accounts, and they originate and service mortgage loans funded by those deposits. Historically, thrifts were profitable because the interest they collected on outstanding loans exceeded the interest they paid out to customers. WMI Holdings Corp. v. United States, 891 F.3d 1016 (2018).

2187 WMI Holdings Corp. v. United States, 891 F.3d 1016 (2018).

permitting acquiring thrifts to use generally accepted accounting principles (GAAP). In essence, GAAP allowed acquiring thrifts to treat failing thrifts' excess liabilities as an asset called "supervisory goodwill," which, in turn, could be counted toward the acquiring thrifts' minimum regulatory capital requirement and amortized over a forty-year period (later reduced to twenty-five years). The RAP rights provided by FSLIC guaranteed such treatment, regardless of future regulatory changes.[2188]

§ 1.5. Power of States.

In General.—With regard to the power of states to tax banks, the usual rule applies that the sovereignty of a state extends to everything which exists by its own authority, or is introduced by its permission,[2189] and where there is no exemption from taxation in a bank's charter, it may be taxed by a state without impairing any contract.[2190] A state so taxes by its own inherent

---

[2188] WMI Holdings Corp. v. United States, 891 F.3d 1016 (2018).

[2189] **In general.—**

Providence Bank v. Billings, 29 U.S. (4 Pet.) 514, 7 L. Ed. 939.

Statute taxing stock of foreign corporations doing business in state and employing capital in competition with banks, based on ratio of invested capital located in state, held not void as taxing property without local situs. National Sav., etc., Ass'n v. Gills, 35 F.2d 386, rev'd per stipulation, 282 U.S. 796, 51 S. Ct. 19, 75 L. Ed. 717; Oregon Mortg. Co. v. Gillis, 40 F.2d 944.

Interest income from obligations issued by Federal National Mortgage Association and Government National Mortgage Association was subject to state excise taxation. First Tenn. Bank v. Olsen, 736 S.W.2d 601 (Tenn. 1987).

Legislature possesses wide discretion in matters of taxation. Fidelity Bank v. Commonwealth Dep't of Revenue, 645 A.2d 452 (Pa. Commw. 1994).

Rules and regulations of State Department of Assessments and Taxation.—

Rules and regulations of the State Department of Assessments and Taxation are effective only insofar as they are reasonable and consistent with statutory scheme. State Dep't of Assessments & Taxation v. Loyola Fed. Sav. & Loan Ass'n, 79 Md. App. 481, 558 A.2d 428 (1989).

[2190] Providence Bank v. Billings, 29 U.S. (4 Pet.) 514, 7 L. Ed. 939; State Bank v. Knoop, 57 U.S. (18 How.) 369, 14 L. Ed. 977; Nathan v. Louisiana, 49 U.S. (8 How.) 73, 12 L. Ed. 992; Citizens' Sav. Bank v. Owensboro, 173 U.S. 636, 19 S. Ct. 530, 531, 43 L. Ed. 840; Farmers' & Traders' Bank v. Owensboro, 173 U.S. 663, 19 S. Ct. 875, 48 L. Ed. 850. See also McCulloch v. Maryland, 17 U.S. (4 Wheat.) 316, 4 L. Ed. 579; Osborn v. Bank, 22 U.S. (9 Wheat) 738, 6 L. Ed. 204; Portland Bank v. Apthorp, 12 Mass. 252.

Colorado's system of taxation of oil and gas interests was permissible under statute permitting taxation of real estate held by a federal land bank. Federal Land Bank v. Board of County Comm'rs, 788 F.2d 1440 (10th Cir. 1986).

taxing power, subject to the federal Constitution and valid federal laws.[2191] The deductions and credits against taxes otherwise due are matters of legislative grace and allowed only to the extent authorized by statute.[2192] It is a well-established doctrine, however, that state governments have no right to tax any of the constitutional means employed by the federal government to execute its constitutional powers.

Thus, the states have no power, by taxation or otherwise, to retard, impede, burden or in any manner control the operations of the constitutional laws enacted by Congress to carry into effect the powers vested in the

---

Even if de minimis exception existed to federal statute allowing inclusion of interest earned on federal government obligations in nondiscriminatory corporate franchise taxes, state's discriminatory taxation of such income in bank excise tax while exempting interest income earned on obligations of certain state agencies did not come within such exception economic incidence of discrimination reached into billions of dollars of increased federal expense. Cambridge State Bank v. Roemer, 457 N.W.2d 716 (Minn. 1990).

Congress has not occupied the entire field as to national banks. The National Bank Act, 12 U.S.C.S. § 1 et seq., leaves several areas to state regulation, so long as the state laws in those areas only incidentally affect the exercise of national bank powers. Congress speaks directly to the issue of taxation in 12 U.S.C.S. § 548 and former 12 C.F.R. § 7.4009, stating that national banks are subject to state taxation. Miss. Dep't of Revenue v. Pikco Fin., Inc., 97 So. 3d 1203, 2012 Miss. LEXIS 354 (Miss. 2012).

Former 12 C.F.R. § 7.4009, stating that national banks are subject to state taxation, was rescinded by the Dodd-Frank Act, but 12 U.S.C.S. § 548 is still in place, leaving national banks subject to state taxation. Miss. Dep't of Revenue v. Pikco Fin., Inc., 97 So. 3d 1203 (Miss. 2012).

[2191] Home Sav. Bank v. Des Moines, 205 U.S. 503, 27 S. Ct. 571, 51 L Ed. 901; Bank v. New York, 67 U.S. (2 Black) 620, 17 L. Ed. 451; Phelps v. Union Bank, etc., Co., 225 Ala. 238, 142 So. 552, aff'd, 288 U.S. 181, 53 S. Ct. 321, 77 L. Ed. 687; Elmhurst State Bank v. Stone, 346 Ill. 157, 178 N.E. 362.

Legislature's power in field of taxation is limited only by constitutional restriction. Hibernia Bank v. State Bd. of Equalization, 166 Cal. App. 3d 393, 212 Cal. Rptr. 556 (1985).

Former Tax Law § 1453(k-1) was statutorily coupled with the federal ordering rules set forth in 26 U.S.C.S. § 172, which specifically provided that the entire amount of a net operating loss (NOL) for any taxable year shall be carried to the earliest of the taxable years to which such loss may be carried (26 U.S.C.S. § 172(b)(2)). Thus, for banking corporation franchise tax purposes, application of this federal ordering rule was not a mere attempt by the Department of Taxation and Finance to achieve mechanical conformity with federal tax principles; it was statutorily required and, as such, said presumption served as the "starting point" for determining the amount of NOL that must be used to offset a taxpayer's entire net income. Matter of Toronto Dominion Holdings (U.S.A.), Inc. v Tax Appeals Trib. of The State of New York, 162 A.D.3d 1255; 77 N.Y.S.3d 800 (3d Dept. 2018).

[2192] Centerre Bank v. Director of Revenue, 744 S.W.2d 754 (Mo. 1988).

national government.[2193] One sovereign may not impose a discriminatory tax that adversely affects the activities of the other.[2194]

[2193] McCulloch v. Maryland, 17 U. S. (4 Wheat.) 316, 4 L. Ed. 579. See also Old Nat. Bank v. Berkeley County Court, 58 W. Va. 559, 52 S.E. 494, 8 L.R.A. (n.s.) 584, 6 Ann. Cas. 115; Owensboro Nat'l Bank v. Owensboro, 173 U.S. 664, 19 S. Ct. 537, 43 L. Ed. 850; In re Opinion of the Justices, 133 Me. 521, 177 A. 897; United States v. Lewis, 10 F. Supp. 471 (1935).

The test as to whether a tax laid on a federal instrumentality is constitutional, is whether it hinders or embarrasses the instrumentality in the performance of its governmental functions, and if it does, it is unconstitutional. Federal Land Bank v. Bismarck Lbr. Co., 70 N.D. 607, 297 N.W. 42.

Property owned by federal instrumentality is immune from real estate taxation unless waived. Federal Reserve Bank v. State, 313 N.W.2d 619 (Minn. 1981).

Areas, which were within Federal Reserve Bank's building and which were devoted to subtreasury functions, were not immune from real estate taxation. Federal Reserve Bank v. State, 313 N.W.2d 619 (Minn. 1981).

Local bank excise tax did not single out federal obligations or interest therefrom or in any other way treat them as special or direct objects of taxation but was "nonproperty" tax and corporate privilege tax and thus not discriminatory within meaning of federal exemption statute. Memphis Bank & Trust Co v. Garner, 624 S.W.2d 551 (Tenn. 1981).

Corporate franchise created by state can legitimately be taxed and such tax may be imposed without any deduction for federal securities or interest thereon. Memphis Bank & Trust Co. v. Garner, 624 S.W.2d 551 (Tenn. 1981).

Measure of bank excise tax by federal taxable income, including interest on federal obligations, was not prohibited under general federal exemptions statute or particular exemption statutes pertaining to certain types of obligations, nor by federal constitution. Memphis Bank & Trust Co. v. Garner, 624 S.W.2d 551 (Tenn. 1981).

Where economic but not legal incidence of tax falls on federal government, such tax generally does not violate constitutional immunity if it does not discriminate against holders of federal property or those with whom the federal government dealt. Memphis Bank & Trust Co. v. Garner, U.S. 103 S. Ct. 692, 74 L. Ed. 2d 562 (1983).

Generally, states are without power to tax federal instrumentality without consent of Congress. Sooner Fed. Sav. & Loan Ass'n v. Oklahoma Tax Comm'n, 662 P.2d 1366 (Okla. 1988).

A state cannot interpret and apply its own tax laws so as to nullify an exemption from local taxation created by an act of Congress and thus defeat the apparent intent of the Congress to provide a favorable market for federal securities; however, that intent is not defeated if the taxpayer has an adequate remedy against the illegal assessment. American Bank & Trust Co. v. Dallas County 679 S.W.2d 566 (Tex. App. 5 Dist. 1984).

Texas remedies are adequate for relief from any assessment of tax on securities held by bank that may be illegal because of the exemption provided by federal statute for federal government obligations; therefore Congress' intent in enacting the exemption is not defeated

(Text continued on page 611)

---

by the state taxing scheme. American Bank & Trust Co. v. Dallas County, 679 S.W.2d 566 (Tex. App. 5 Dist. 1984).

Tax exemption for government obligations that is required by constitution is not a total exclusion, but, instead, may be limited by charging obligations and their interest fair share of related expenses or burdens. First Nat'l Bank v. Bartow County Bd. of Tax Assessors, U.S., 105 S. Ct. 1516, 84 L. Ed. 3d 535 (1985).

Revenue statute providing for exemption from state or local taxation of obligations of United States, as amended in 1969, provided exemption no broader in scope than that which constitution requires for tax exemption for government obligations. First Nat'l Bank v. Bartow County Bd. of Tax Assessors, U.S., 105 S. Ct. 1516, 84 L. Ed. 2d 535 (1985).

State cannot tax federal instrumentality absent permissive federal legislation. Federal Land Bank v. Board of County Comm'rs, 788 F.2d 1440 (10th Cir. 1986).

Edge Act banks were not federal instrumentalities immune from state taxation, notwithstanding fact that Edge Act banks were chartered by the federal government and subject to strict federal regulation; Edge Act banks received financial assistance from federal government, and federal government did not rely on Edge Act banks to perform traditionally governmental acts, instead of relying upon banks' separate profit motivation which propelled banks towards mutually satisfactory end. Continental Bank International v. New York Dep't of Finance, 69 N.Y.2d 281, 513 N.Y.S.2d 964, 506 N.E.2d 525 (1987).

If judicial inquiry discloses that purpose of state legislation is to accomplish indirectly taxation of federal instrumentalities which cannot be taxed directly, tax must be stricken. First Union Nat'l Bank v. Florida Dep't of Revenue, 502 So. 2d 964 (Fla. App. 1987).

Judicial inquiry into nature of tax should focus on operation and practical effect of tax for purposes of determining whether state tax impermissibly bears upon income derived from federal instrumentalities. First Union Nat'l Bank v. Florida Dep't of Revenue, 502 So. 2d 964 (Fla. App. 1987).

Federal public debt statute is intended to invalidate all state and local taxes measured directly or indirectly by value of federal obligations or any interest thereon, except those exceptions specified in statute.

Pacific First Federal Sav. Bank v. Department of Revenue, 308 Or. 332, 779 P.2d 1033 (1989).

Only exceptions to statute invalidating state and local taxes on federal obligations are those specified in statute; there are no implied exceptions. Pacific First Federal Sav. Bank v. Department of Revenue, 308 Or. 332, 779 P.2d 1033 (1980).

State statute imposing license fee on bank was a nondiscriminatory, "nonproperty" tax in lieu of a franchise tax, within meaning of exception to federal statute exempting income from federal obligations from state taxation. National Bank v. State, Dep't of Revenue, 769 P.2d 990 (Alaska 1989).

Federal Home Loan Bank obligations held by bank were not exempt from state taxation under statute imposing license fee on bank. National Bank v. State, Dep't of Revenue, 769 P.2d 990 (Alaska 1989).

Fact that executive branch proposed legislation to allow state taxation practice, but encountered unreceptive Congress, is not evidence that practice interfered with nation's

National Banks.[2195]—In accordance with the doctrine set out above, a state is wholly without power to levy any tax, either direct or indirect, upon national banks, their property, assets or franchises, except when permitted to do so by Congress,[2196] and then only in conformity with such restrictions as

---

ability to speak with one voice, but is rather evidence that preeminent speaker decided to yield to others. Barclays Bank PLC v. Franchise Tax Bd., 512 U.S. 298, 114 S. Ct. 2268, 129 L. Ed. 3d 244 (1994).

[2194] Andover Sav. Bank v. Commissioner of Revenue, 387 Mass. 229, 439 N.E.2d 282 (1982).

[2195] See also §§ 24 to 26e of this chapter. As to other federal banks and governmental instrumentalities, see §§ 26½, 26½ of this chapter.

[2196] *United States.*—Security Sav. & Commercial Bank v. District of Columbia, 279 F. 185, 51 App. D.C. 316; Owensboro Nat'l Bank v. Owensboro, 1783U.S. 664, 19 S. Ct. 537, 43 L. Ed. 850; Davis v. Elmira Sav. Bank, 161 U.S. 275, 16 S. Ct. 502, 40 L. Ed. 700; McCulloch v. Maryland, 4 L. Ed. 579, 4 Wheat 316; Osborn v. Bank, 22 U.S. (9 Wheat.) 738, 6 L. Ed. 204; Brotherhood Co-Op. Nat. Bank v. Hurlburt, 26 F.2d 957; Bank of California v. Richardson, 248 U.S. 476, 39 S. Ct. 165, 63 L. Ed. 872; Des Moines Nat'l Bank v. Fairweather, 263 U.S. 103, 44 S. Ct. 23, 68 L. Ed. 191; First Nat. Bank of Guthrie Center v. Anderson, 269 U.S. 341, 46 S. Ct. 135, 70 L. Ed. 295; Swords v. Nutt, 11 F.2d 936; First Nat. Bank v. Hartford, 273 U.S. 548, 47 S. Ct. 462, 71 L. Ed. 767, 59 A.L.R. 1; Central Nat. Bank v. McFarland, 20 F.2d 416, aff'd, 26 F.2d 890, cert. denied, 278 U.S. 606, 49 S. Ct. 12, 73 L. Ed. 533; First Nat. Bank v. Beaman, 257 F. 729; Citizens' & Southern Nat'l Bank v. Atlanta, 46 F.2d 88, aff'd, 53 F.2d 557; Iowa-Des Moines Nat. Bank v. Bennett, 284 U.S. 239, 52 S. Ct. 133, 76 L. Ed. 265; United States v. Lewis, 10 F. Supp. 471 (1935); People v. Loughman, 100 F.2d 387; Federal Land Bank v. Board of County Comm'rs, 368 U.S. 148, 82 S. Ct. 282, 7 L. Ed. 3d 199.

Direct taxation of personal property by states against national banks has never been permitted. Mercantile Bank Nat'l Ass'n v. Berra, 796 S.W.2d 22 (Mo. 1990).

States are without power, unless authorized by Congress, to tax national banks. First Agricultural Nat'l Bank v. State Tax Comm'n, 392 U.S. 339, 88 S. Ct. 2173, 20 L. Ed. 3d 1188 (1968).

National banking institutions created and existing pursuant to federal statute were "instrumentalities of the United States" and were therefore immune from state and local taxes not within purview of federal statute dealing with state taxation of national bank shares. First Nat'l Bank v. Dickinson, 291 F. Supp. 855 (N.D. Fla. 1968), aff'd, 393 U.S. 409, 89 S. Ct. 685, 21 L. Ed. 3d 634 (1969). See 12 U.S.C.S. § 21.

The Constitution delegates to the United States the power to exempt national banking associations, their shares, and shareholders from taxation. Maricopa County v. Valley Nat'l Bank, 130 F.2d 356, aff'd, 318 U.S. 357, 63 S. Ct 587, 87 L. Ed. 834.

Texas bank shares tax statute violated section providing that tax is barred regard less of its form if federal obligations must be considered, either directly or indirectly, in computing tax where equity capital formula was usual and customary method employed in Texas to calculate tax. American Bank & Trust Co. v. Dallas County, U.S. , 103 S. Ct. 3369, 77 L. Ed. 3d 1072 (1983).

(Text continued on page 614)

Federal statute prohibiting states from imposing discriminatory taxes on national banks did not authorize Texas bank shares tax which was computed on basis of each bank's net assets without any deduction for value of the United States obligations held by bank so as to preclude determination that Texas tax violated statute prohibiting every form of taxation that would require either that federal obligations or interest thereon, or both, be considered, directly or indirectly, in computation of tax. American Bank & Trust Co. v. Dallas County, U.S. , 103 S. Ct. 3369, 77 L. Ed. 2d 1072 (1983).

Alabama.—Phelps v. Union Bank, etc., Co., 225 Ala. 238, 142 So. 552, aff'd, 288 U.S. 181, 53 S. Ct. 321, 77 L. Ed. 687; Ward v. First Nat. Bank, 225 Ala. 10, 142 So. 93 (1932); National Commercial Bank v. Mobile, 62 Ala. 284, 34 Am. Rep. 15.

California.—A state may tax a national bank only as permitted by the Bank of America. Nat'l Trust & Sav. Asso. v. State Board of Equalization, 26 Cal. Rptr. 348, 209 Cal. App. 2d 780; United States v. State Bd. of Equalization, 450 F. Supp. 1030 (N.D. Cal. 1978).

Colorado.—Bedford v. Colorado Nat. Bank, 104 Colo. 311, 91 P.2d 469; Colorado Nat'l Bank v. Bedford, 105 Colo. 373, 98 P.2d 1120, aff'd, 310 U.S. 41, 60 S. Ct. 800, 84 L. Ed. 1067.

Connecticut—First Nat. Bank, etc., Co. v. West Haven, 135 Conn. 191, 62 A.2d 671.

Georgia.—State Revenue Com. v. Hawkins, 48 Ga. App. 414, 172 S.E. 845; Goodwin v. Citizens, etc., Nat. Bank, 209 Ga. 908, 76 S.E.2d 620 (1953).

Idaho.—State v. Leonardson, 51 Idaho 646, 9 P.2d 1028.

Illinois.—People v. First Nat. Bank, 351 Ill. 435, 184 N.E. 645; National Bank of Hyde Park in Chicago v. Isaacs, 27 Ill. 2d 205, 188 N.E.2d 704.

Indiana.—Davis v. Sexton, 210 Ind. 138, 200 N.E. 233.

Iowa.—Iowa Nat. Bank v. Stewart, 232 N.W. 445, rev'd on other grounds, 284 U.S. 239, 52 S. Ct 138, 76 L. Ed. 265.

Kentucky.—Shelbyville v. Citizens Bank, 272 Ky. 559, 114 S.W.2d 719; Commonwealth v. Morrison, 2 A. K. Marsh. 75.

National Banks are "Instrumentalities of the United States" and hence not taxable by states without Congress' consent. Barnes v. Anderson Nat'l Bank, 293 Ky. 592, 169 S.W.2d 833, 145 L. Ed. 1066.

Maine.—Stetson v. Bangor, 56 Me. 274.

Maryland.—State Tax Com. v. Baltimore Nat'l Bank, 169 Md. 65, 180 A. 260, aff'd, 297 U.S. 209, 56 S. Ct. 417, 80 L. Ed. 586; State v. Buchanan, 5 Her. & J. 317, 9 Am. Dec. 534.

Massachusetts.—By virtue of the supremacy clause, state taxation of national banks is prohibited unless congressionally authorized. Andover Sav. Bank v. Commissioner of Revenue, 387 Mass. 229, 439 N.E.2d 282 (1982).

Michigan.—First Nat'l Bank v. St. Joseph, 46 Mich. 526, 9 N.W. 838.

Minnesota.—National banks are subject to no inherent power in the states to tax them. Such banks, their property, and shares of their capital stock are subject to state taxation only as Congress permits and a tax beyond that permission is void. Irvine v. Spaeth, 210 Minn. 489, 299 N.W. 204, appeal dismissed, 314 U.S. 575, 62 S. Ct 117, 86 L. Ed. 466.

(Text continued on page 614)

A federal instrumentality is immune from all state taxes, whether or not discriminatory, unless the state can show that Congress clearly and expressly has waived the immunity. County of St. Louis v. Federal Land Bank, 338 N.W.2d 741 (Minn. 1983).

Missouri.—National banks are instrumentalities of the federal government, and the states do not possess the sovereign power with respect to their taxation that exists with respect to citizens of the state generally, and only such taxes may be imposed by state against national banks as are contemplated by congressional enactment conferring such power. General American Life Ins. Co. v. Bates, 363 Mo. 143, 249 S.W.2d 458.

Montana.—Daly Bank & Trust Co. v. Board of Comm'rs, 33 Mont. 101, 81 P. 950.

State taxation of national banks is controlled by congressional authorization. Security Bank & Trust Co. v. Connors, 550 P.2d 1318 (Mont 1976).

New York.—Clark v. First Nat. Bank, 130 Misc. 352, 224 N.Y.S. 10; Bridgeport Sav. Bank v. Feitner, 191 N.Y. 88, 83 N.E. 592; People ex rel. Hanover Nat'l Bank v. Goldfogle, 234 N.Y. 345, 137 N.E. 611, cert. denied, 261 U.S. 620, 43 S. Ct. 432, 67 L. Ed. 830; Bank of Manhattan Co. v. Murphy, 267 App. Div. 458, 47 N.Y.S.2d 524, aff'd, 293 N.Y. 515, 58 N.E.2d 713; In re Bank of Manhattan Co., 293 N.Y. 515, 58 N.E.2d 713.

Congressional intention to deny state's power to tax Edge Act bank branches could not be inferred from language of statute authorizing nondiscriminatory taxation of Edge Act banks by home office state, which was at best ambiguous on that subject, or from surrounding debates, which indicated only an intent to subject Edge Act banks to state taxation. Continental Bank Int'l v. City of New York Dep't of Fin., 69 N.Y.2d 281, 513 N.Y.S.2d 954, 506 N.E.2d 525 (1987).

State may collect franchise tax on national banking associations or banks incorporated under laws of other jurisdictions, even though it does not possess the power to grant such corporations the license "to exist" in the state. Bankers Trust N.Y. Corp. v. Department of Fin., 79 N.Y.2d 457, 583 N.Y.S.2d 821, 593 N.E.2d 275 (1992).

Ohio.—Gray Knox Marble Co. v. Evatt, 31 Ohio Op. 467, 469, 16 Ohio Supp. 151.

Oklahoma.—Bonds issued by the Federal National Mortgage Association were not permanent public debts exempt from state taxation. In re First Fed. Sav. & Loan Ass'n, 743 P.2d 640 (Okla. 1987).

Interest on federal savings and loan associations' overnight/demand deposits placed in the Federal Home Loan Bank (FHLB) was subject to taxation by state; such deposits were not "obligations" of FHLB within statute exempting such obligations from all taxation. In re First Fed. Sav. & Loan Ass'n, 743 P.2d 640 (Okla. 1987).

Bonds issued by the Federal Home Loan Mortgage Corporation (FHLMC) and any interest thereon were exempt from state taxation, where state limited investment in FHLMC stock to five percent of savings and loan association assets. In re First Fed. Sav. & Loan Ass'n, 743 P.2d 640 (Okla. 1987).

Oregon.—First Nat'l Bank v. Marion County, 169 Ore. 595, 130 P.2d 9.

Pennsylvania.—Pittsburg v. First Nat'l Bank, 55 Pa. 45.

South Carolina.—Bulow v. Charleston (S.C.), 1 Nott. & McC. 527.

South Dakota.—Northwestern Nat'l Bank v. Gillis, 82 S.D. 457, 148 N.W.2d 293 (1967).

Congress may impose.[2197] Legislation enacted by Congress[2198] has long

---

Vermont.—State v. Clement Nat'l Bank, 84 Vt. 167, 78 A. 944, 1912D Ann. Cas. 22, aff'd, 231 U.S. 120, 34 S. Ct. 31, 58 L. Ed. 147.

Virginia.—Federal Land Bank v. Hubard, 163 Va. 860, 178 S.E. 16.

Washington.—Austin v. Seattle, 176 Wash. 654, 30 P.2d 646, 93 A.L.R. 208; Federal Land Bank v. Statelen, 191 Wash. 155, 70 P.2d 1053; Chase Nat. Bank v. Spokane County, 125 Wash. 1, 215 P. 374.

West Virginia.—BANK v. STATE, 58 W. Va. 559, 52 S.E. 494, 3 L.R.A. (n.s.) 584, 6 Ann. Cas. 115.

2197 First Nat. Bank v. Marion County, 169 Ore. 595, 130 P.2d 9; First Nat. Bank, etc., Co. v. West Haven, 135 Conn. 191, 62 A.2d 671.

Federal statute governing state taxation of national bank shares was intended to prescribe the only ways in which the states can tax national banks. First Agricultural Nat'l Bank v. State Tax Comm'n, 392 U.S. 339, 88 S. Ct. 2173, 20 L. Ed. 34 1138 (1968).

National banks and their shares are taxable by states only with consent of Congress and then only in accordance with such restrictions and in manner Congress has authorized. Marble Mortgage Co. v. Franchise Tax Bd., 241 Cal. App. 2d 26, 50 Cal. Rptr. 345 (1966).

A state may not tax national bank except as Congress consents, and then only in conformity with restrictions of that consent. Northwestern Nat'l Bank v. Gillis, 82 S.D. 457, 148 N.W.2d 293 (1967).

Congress did not, by enacting amendment to National Bank Act exempting from taxation by state all stocks, bonds, treasury notes and other obligations of the United States, intend to repeal the share tax authorization or the authority of the states to tax the shares of national banks in the hands of stockholders whose capital was wholly vested in stocks and bonds of the United States. Bartow County Bank v. Bartow County Bd. of Tax Assessors, 248 Ga. 703, 285 S.E.2d 920 (1982).

Bank Share Tax Act, insofar as it allows shares of stockholders of banks or banking associations, whether resident or nonresident owners, to be taxed at their fair market value on basis of net worth of bank without subtracting value of federal securities owned by bank, is not in contravention of federal statute exempting from state taxation all stocks, bonds, treasury notes, and other obligations of United States and is not in violation of the supremacy clause of the United States and Georgia Constitutions. Bartow County Bank v. Bartow County Bd. of Tax Assessors, 248 Ga. 703, 285 S.E.2d 920 (1982).

Interest income earned by federal savings and loan associations on the secondary reserve maintained by the Federal Home Loan Mortgage Corporation was subject to state corporate income tax. In re First Fed. Sav. & Loan Ass'n, 743 P.2d 640 (Okla. 1987).

2198 12 U.S.C.S. § 548.

Congress has not explicitly preempted state law as to taxation. The National Bank Act, 12 U.S.C.S. § 1 et seq., precludes state regulation of national banks in certain enumerated areas, but state taxation is not one of those areas. In fact, taxation is specifically exempted from the areas preempted by the National Bank Act. 12 U.S.C.S. § 548 provides: For the purposes of any tax law enacted under authority of the United States or any State, a national bank shall be treated as a bank organized and existing under the laws of the State or other jurisdiction

permitted state taxation of the shares of stock and the real property of national banks,[2199] but not the assessment of a state tax on the capital stock of a national bank where the tax is assessed against the banking corporation or association itself.[2200] The power of the states to tax national banks, on a nondiscriminatory basis, is greatly extended by amendment to the federal statute effective December 24, 1969, and a further amendment, effective

---

within which its principal office is located. Miss. Dep't of Revenue v. Pikco Fin., Inc., 97 So. 3d 1203, 2012 Miss. LEXIS 354 (Miss. 2012).

[2199] State ex rel. Hatfield v. Moreland, 152 Okla. 37, 3 P.2d 803; Land Title Bank, etc., Co. v. Ward, 20 F. Supp. 810, 1937 U.S. Dist. LEXIS 1474 (E.D. Pa. 1937). See also §§ 26a-26c of this chapter.

Federal statute authorizing state taxation of national banks is a grant of authority in prescribed form only, and is not merely a weapon of defense against such taxation. Gully v. First Nat. Bank, 81 F.2d 502, rev'd on other grounds, 299 U.S. 109, 57 S. Ct. 96, 81 L. Ed. 70.

Under such statute, only the tax against income of bank was a tax against bank; other forms of tax being upon shareholder.

Gully v. First Nat. Bank, 81 F.2d 502, rev'd on other grounds, 299 U.S. 109, 57 S. Ct. 96, 81 L. Ed. 70.

[2200] **In general.—**

People v. First Nat. Bank, 351 Ill. 435, 184 N.E. 645; School Dist. v. Lansing, 286 Mich. 244, 281 N.W. 883; Johnson v. Meagher County, 116 Mont. 565, 155 P.2d 750.

The assessment of state taxes against a national bank or its stockholders, if not in conformity with the act of Congress authorizing such taxation, is unauthorized and invalid. People v. First Nat. Bank, 351 Ill. 435, 184 N.E. 645.

A state had no authority to tax the capital stock, surplus, undivided profits, or other property of a national bank, since such a tax would be one against the corporation, which was not within the power of the state to levy. School Dist. v. Lansing, 286 Mich. 244, 281 N.W. 883.

Assessment must be to shareholders.—

The assessment of shares of national banks for ad valorem tax purposes was required to be to the shareholders and no other form of assessment was valid or enforceable. Flournoy v. First Nat. Bank, 3 So. 2d 244, 197 La. 1067.

Assessment against bank as agent of shareholders presumed.—

But where state under federal statute had elected to tax shares in national bank, assessment made directly against bank would be presumed to have been assessment against bank as agent of shareholders. Odland v Findley, 38 F. Supp. 563, rev'd on other grounds, 127 F.2d 948.

Statute sets outer limits.—

Federal statute governing state taxation of national bank shares marks outer limit within which states can tax national banks. First Agricultural Nat'l Bank v. State Tax Comm'n, 392 U.S. 339, 88 S. Ct. 2173, 20 L. Ed. 2d 1138 (1968).

January 1, 1972, rewrites the statute to read, in its entirety: "For the purpose of any tax law enacted under authority of the United States or any State, a national bank shall be treated as a bank organized and existing under the laws of the State or other jurisdiction within which its principal office is located."[2201] So while initially national banks were immune from state taxation, Section 548 of the National Bank Act was amended in 1969 to remove immunity from state taxation. The amended statute went into effect in 1972, and national banks are now treated the same as state banks for the purpose of state taxation. The amendment was meant to promote equality in state taxation of state banks vis-à-vis national banks, and banks vis-à-vis non-bank corporations.[2202] Section 548 is still in place, leaving national banks subject to state taxation.[2203] The reader's attention is directed to the

---

Tax held unauthorized.—

State tax assessed against national bank measured by value of shares of stock was not equivalent to tax on shareholders and therefore was unauthorized. People v. First Nat. Bank, 351 Ill. 435, 184 N.E. 645.

[2201] 12 U.S.C.S. § 548, as amended by Pub. L. 91-156, § 1(a), 83 State 434, effective December 24, 1969, and Pub. L. 91.156, § 2, 83 State 434, effective January 1, 1972.

See §§ 26a to 26e of this chapter.

The purpose of the 1969 permanent amendment of the federal statute concerning state taxation of national banks was to remove the immunity from state taxation previously granted national banks, thereby allowing states to treat, for tax purposes, such banks as state banks. Lake County Nat'l Bank v. Kosydar, 36 Ohio St. 2d 189, 65 Ohio Op. 2d 404, 305 N.E.2d 799 (1973).

In view of the 1969 temporary amendment to the National Bank Act authorizing the abolition of national banks' immunity from state taxation that the amendment was subject to the limitations and restrictions set forth in the then-existing act, the then-existing ban on a state's imposing more than one of four enumerated taxes on a national bank was continued until the effective date of the permanent amendment authorizing national banks to be treated as state banking organizations for state tax purposes; hence, it was impermissible to tax both shares of stock of a national bank in 1972 and also to impose a corporation license tax on such banks. Security Bank & Trust Co. v. Connors, 550 P.2d 1313 (Mont. 1976).

Under the federal statute preventing a state from imposing certain taxes on national banks prior to January 1, 1978 unless such imposition was authorized by "affirmative action" of the state legislature, the "affirmative action" requirement was designed to require the state, when imposing new taxes on national banks prior to January 1, 1978, to consider the impact of such taxes on the existing balance of taxation between national and state banks. Chase Manhattan Bank, N. A. v. Finance Administration of New York, 440 U.S. 447, 99 S. Ct. 1201, 59 L. Ed. 24 445 (1979).

[2202] Miss. Dep't of Revenue v. Pikco Fin., Inc., 97 So. 3d 1203 (Miss. 2012).

[2203] Miss. Dep't of Revenue v. Pikco Fin., Inc., 97 So. 3d 1203 (Miss. 2012).

Federal law does not preempt state law as to state taxation of national banks. Congress has

fact that some of the discussion of taxation of national banks in this chapter is based upon cases decided under the statute as it stood before these amendments.

No conflict necessarily arose between the act of Congress and a state law solely because the latter provided one method for taxation of state banks and other moneyed corporations, and another method for national banks,[2204] but if one method taxed elements of value which the other did not, it would be illegal.[2205] And it would be assumed that a federal statute limiting the taxation which might be imposed by a state with respect to national banks extended its protection to such banks as they pioneered new areas of finance.[2206] However, state taxation of a national bank at a rate approximately equivalent to that applied through all taxes on nonfinancial corporations was held valid and constitutional.[2207] The tax exemption granted by Congress to national banks is to be determined at least in part by nature of activities or services on which tax is imposed.[2208]

The Dodd-Frank Wall Street Reform and Consumer Protection Act radically changed the legal analysis governing preemption by the National

---

not explicitly preempted state law in this area, Congress has not occupied the entire field, and there is no conflict between federal and state law in this area. The National Bank Act does not preempt state taxation; in fact, it explicitly exempts it, leaving taxation to the states under 12 U.S.C.S. § 548 and 12 C.F.R. § 7.4009(c)(2). Section 7.4009 was rescinded by the Dodd-Frank Act, but 12 U.S.C.S. § 548 is still in place, leaving national banks subject to state taxation. Miss. Dep't of Revenue v. Pikco Fin., Inc., 97 So. 3d 1203 (Miss. 2012).

2204 San Francisco Nat. Bank v. Dodge, 197 U.S 70, 25 S. Ct. 384, 49 L. Ed. 669; National Bank v. Commonwealth, 76 U.S. (9 Wall.) 353, 19 L. Ed. 701.

2205 San Francisco Nat'l Bank v. Dodge, 197 U.S. 70, 25 S. Ct. 384, 49 L. Ed. 669.

So where in the one case, that of national banks, not only the value of all the tangible property, but also the value of all the intangible elements referred to is assessed and taxed, whilst in the other case, that of state banks and other moneyed corporations, their property is taxed, but the intangible elements of value which we have indicated are not assessed and taxed, the consequence being to give rise to the discrimination against national banks and in favor of state banks and other moneyed corporations forbidden by the act of Congress. San Francisco Nat. Bank v. Dodge, 197 U.S. 70, 25 S. Ct. 384, 49 L. Ed. 669.

2206 General Electric Credit Corp. v. Oregon State Tax Com., 231 Ore. 570, 373 P.2d 974.

2207 Franchise Tax Board v. Superior Court of Sacramento County, 36 Cal. 2d 538, 225 P.2d 905, citing Tradesmens Nat'l Bank v. Oklahoma Tax Com., 309 U.S. 560, 60 S. Ct. 688, 84 L. Ed. 947.

2208 Western States Bankcard Asso. v. San Francisco, 82 Cal. App. 3d 137, 133 Cal. Rptr. 36 (1976).

Bank Act (NBA).[2209] The NBA was revised by the Dodd-Frank Act, which went in effect July 21, 2011. The official title of the bill was: "A bill to promote the financial stability of the United States by improving accountability and transparency in the financial system, to end 'too big to fail,' to protect the American taxpayer by ending bailouts, to protect consumers from abusive financial services practices, and for other purposes." Dodd-Frank changed the financial regulatory structure, put regulation of the financial industry in the government's hands, and increased oversight of financial institutions.[2210]

The standard expressed in *Watters v. Wachovia Bank*, in which the United States Supreme Court held that a national bank's mortgage business, whether conducted by the bank itself or through the bank's operating subsidiary, is subject to the superintendence of the United States Office of the Comptroller of the Currency (OCC) and not to the licensing, reporting, and visitorial regimes of the several states in which the subsidiary operates,[2211] has been held not to apply in the aftermath of Dodd-Frank.[2212] Rather, courts are now directed to determine preemption by analyzing whether a state law is "irreconcilably in conflict" with the NBA.[2213] And the

---

[2209] Cline v. Bank of Am., N.A., 823 F. Supp. 2d 387 (S.D. W. Va. 2011). See 12 U.S.C.S. § 25b.

[2210] Miss. Dep't of Revenue v. Pikco Fin., Inc., 97 So. 3d 1203 (Miss. 2012).

[2211] See Watters v. Wachovia Bank, N.A., 127 S. Ct. 1559, 167 L. Ed. 2d 389 (U.S. 2007), superseded by statute as stated in Gordon v. Kohl's Dep't Stores, Inc., 172 F. Supp. 3d 840 (E.D. Pa. 2016) ("by the plain language of 12 U.S.C.S. § 25b, and in accordance with the Office of the Comptroller of the Currency's interpretation, the Dodd-Frank Act effectively overturned the subsidiary-preemption holding in Watters v. Wachovia Bank, N.A., 127 S. Ct. 1559, 167 L. Ed. 2d 389 (U.S. 2007).")

[2212] See Gordon v. Kohl's Dep't Stores, Inc., 172 F. Supp. 3d 840 (E.D. Pa. 2016); Miss. Dep't of Revenue v. Pikco Fin., Inc., 97 So. 3d 1203 (Miss. 2012).

Watters v. Wachovia Bank, N.A., 127 S. Ct. 1559, 167 L. Ed. 2d 389 (U.S. 2007), superseded by statute as stated in Gordon v. Kohl's Dep't Stores, Inc., 172 F. Supp. 3d 840 (E.D. Pa. 2016) ("by the plain language of 12 U.S.C.S. § 25b, and in accordance with the Office of the Comptroller of the Currency's interpretation, the Dodd-Frank Act effectively overturned the subsidiary-preemption holding in Watters v. Wachovia Bank, N.A., 127 S. Ct. 1559, 167 L. Ed. 2d 389 (U.S. 2007)."). See 12 U.S.C.S. § 85.

[2213] Meluzio v. Capital One Bank (USA), N.A., 469 B.R. 250 (N.D. W. Va. 2012); Pryor v. Bank of Am., N.A. (In re Pryor), 479 B.R. 694 (Bankr. E.D. NC 2012).

Conflict preemption analysis is focused on whether the targeted state statute is irreconcilably in conflict with the NBA. Stated another way, the inquiry distills to whether the state measure either: (1) Imposes an obligation on a national bank that is in direct conflict with federal law or (2) stands as an obstacle to the accomplishment and execution of the full

reservation of states' power to apply their laws of general applicability to national banks is reaffirmed by NBA's preemption provisions, which specify that laws governing the manner, content, or terms and conditions of any financial transaction or any account related thereto are not preempted as applied to national banks, unless: (1) The state law would have a discriminatory effect on national banks, in comparison with the effect of the law on a bank chartered by that state; (2) the state law would be preempted under the standard set forth in *Barnett Bank* or (3) the state law is preempted by a federal law other than the NBA.[2214] Dodd-Frank further clarified that the NBA does not occupy any field in any area of state law.[2215]

The area of regulation at issue in *Watters*—real estate lending—was a power exercised under federal law and specifically regulated by the National Bank Act (NBA). Taxation however is left to the states and is not regulated by the NBA and, as the United States Supreme Court in *Watters* recognized, the laws of the states in which national banks or their affiliates are located govern matters the NBA does not address.[2216] Therefore, a claim by an

---

purposes and objectives of Congress. Under the Dodd-Frank Act, the proper preemption test asks whether there is a significant conflict between the state and federal statutes—that is, the test for conflict preemption. Cline v. Bank of Am., N.A., 823 F. Supp. 2d 387 (S.D. W. Va. 2011).

[2214] Gordon v. Kohl's Dep't Stores, Inc., 172 F. Supp. 3d 840 (E.D. Pa. 2016). See 12 U.S.C.S. § 25b.

By codifying Barnett Bank, N.A. v. Nelson, 517 U.S. 25, 116 S. Ct. 1103, 134 L. Ed. 2d 237 (1996), the Dodd-Frank Act, 12 U.S.C.S. § 25b, directs courts to determine national bank preemption by analyzing whether a state statute is irreconcilably in conflict with the National Bank Act. Thus, courts must now determine whether the state measure either: (1) Imposes an obligation on a national bank that is in direct conflict with federal law or (2) stands as an obstacle to the accomplishment and execution of the full purposes and objectives of the United States Congress. Meluzio v. Capital One Bank (USA), N.A., 469 B.R. 250 (N.D. W. Va. 2012).

Because the Barnett Bank analysis is subsumed within Dodd–Frank, even assuming that Dodd–Frank's provisions did not apply, the preemption analysis essentially remained the same; in determining whether a statute is preempted by federal law, it is necessary to look first at Congress's intent in drafting the federal law. The congressional intent in enacting the NBA was to establish a national banking system that was free from intrusive state regulation. Sacco v. Bank of Am., N.A., 2012 U.S. Dist. LEXIS 178030 (D. N.C. 2012). See Barnett Bank, N.A. v. Nelson, 517 U.S. 25, 116 S. Ct. 1103, 134 L. Ed. 2d 237 (1996).

[2215] Gordon v. Kohl's Dep't Stores, Inc., 172 F. Supp. 3d 840 (E.D. Pa. 2016).

See 12 U.S.C.S. § 25b.

[2216] Miss. Dep't of Revenue v. Pikco Fin., Inc., 97 So. 3d 1203 (Miss. 2012).

Watters v. Wachovia Bank, N.A., 127 S. Ct. 1559, 167 L. Ed. 2d 389 (U.S. 2007),

operating subsidiary of a national banking association that the use of statutory subpoena power by the Mississippi Department of Revenue in administration of the finance company privilege tax was preempted by the NBA was rejected and the subsidiary was subject to the subpoena in conjunction with an audit regarding loan company's nonpayment of finance company privilege taxes. State law governs taxation, and under state law the subsidiary was not treated the same as its parent national bank and the federal statutory visitorial limitation was not applicable.[2217]

Nonresidents.—A state law providing that all persons doing business in the state as bankers, merchants or otherwise who are not residents of the state, should be assessed and taxed as if they were such residents, is valid.[2218] And shares of bank stock owned by nonresidents of a state may, by legislative enactment, be made taxable at the location of the bank of which they are representative.[2219] The stock of a national bank in one state which is held by a savings bank of another state is taxable in the former state, even though the savings bank's property is exempt under the laws of its own state.[2220] In the absence of a congressional action or the clearest constitutional mandate that the city's corporate taxation scheme was discriminatory, a branch office of an Edge Act bank having home office in another state was not immune from New York taxation.[2221]

Reclassification of Corporations.—The fact that a "Morris plan" company, incorporated under the California industrial loan law, was at one time subject only to taxation as a general corporation under that law, did not prevent the legislature from subsequently changing the rule and reclassifying

---

superseded by statute as stated in Gordon v. Kohl's Dep't Stores, Inc., 172 F. Supp. 3d 840 (E.D. Pa. 2016) ("by the plain language of 12 U.S.C.S. § 25b, and in accordance with the Office of the Comptroller of the Currency's interpretation, the Dodd-Frank Act effectively overturned the subsidiary-preemption holding in Watters v. Wachovia Bank, N.A., 127 S. Ct. 1559, 167 L. Ed. 2d 389 (U.S. 2007).")

2217 Miss. Dep't of Revenue v. Pikco Fin., Inc., 97 So. 3d 1203 (Miss. 2012).

2218 Duer v. Small, 7 Fed. Cas. (No. 4116) 1164, 4 Blatchf. 263, 17 How. Pr. 201; People v. Commissioner of Taxes (N.C.), 1 Thomp. & C. 630.

2219 Nashville v. Thomas, 45 Tenn. (5 Cold.) 600; Bedford v. Nashville, 54 Tenn. (7 Heisk.) 409, overruling Union Bank v. State, 17 Tenn. (9 Yerg.) 490. As to bank stock generally, see § 32 of this chapter.

2220 People v. Coleman, 63 Hun. 633, 18 N.Y.S. 675, 45 N.Y. St. R, 186, aff'd, People ex rel. Savings Bank of New London v. Coleman, 135 N.Y. 281, 81 N.E. 1022.

2221 Continental Bank Int'l v. City of New York Dep't of Fin., 69 N.Y.2d 281, 513 N.Y.S.2d 954, 506 N.E.2d 525 (1987).

corporations for purposes of taxation.[2222] And under a statute enabling state banks to become national banks, and requiring them to pay all taxes imposed upon them by state laws up to the date of their becoming national banks, a state bank is liable for taxes to the date of the official certificate of its compliance with the requirements of such statute.[2223]

Unemployment Compensation Taxes.—National banks may be taxed by a state or compelled to pay unemployment insurance contributions only as permitted by Congress and in conformity with the conditions annexed to such permission.[2224] In 1939, Congress granted to the states permission to require national banks, along with certain other "instrumentalities of the United States" previously exempt, to make contributions to an unemployment fund under a state unemployment compensation law.[2225] The term "instrumentality of the United States," within the meaning of provisions of state unemployment compensation acts exempting such an instrumentality from the provisions thereof was used to describe a government agency immune from state control.[2226] A federal joint stock land bank was not such an instrumentality,[2227] and a state corporation was not such an instrumentality merely because it was a member of a federal home loan bank.[2228] Similarly, it was held that a state bank was not an instrumentality of the federal government, exempt from taxes imposed by a state unemployment compensation act, because it was a member of the Federal Reserve System

---

[2222] Morris Plan Co. v. Johnson, 37 Cal. App. 2d 621, 100 P.2d 493 (1940).

The California Revenue and Taxation Code does not furnish a statutory definition of "financial corporations." The classification was adopted to avoid preferential tax treatment in favor of corporations in substantial competition with national banks. Under the governing test, the classification includes savings and loans as well as other kinds of moneyed corporations performing some of the functions of a national bank or dealing in money or financing in competition with activities of national banks. California Fed. Savings & Loan Assn. v. City of Los Angeles, 54 Cal. 3d 1, 812 P.2d 916 (1991).

[2223] Manufacturers', etc., Bank v. Commonwealth, 72 Pa. 70.

[2224] In re Bank of Manhattan Co., 293 N.Y. 515, 58 N.E.2d 713.

[2225] 26 U.S.C.S. § 3305. See Barnes v. Anderson Nat. Bank, 293 Ky. 592, 169 S.W.2d 833, 145 A.L.R. 1066; In re Bank of Manhattan, 293 N.Y. 515, 58 N.E.2d 713; First Nat'l Bank v. Bergan, 119 Mont. 1, 169 P.2d 233, 165 A.L.R. 1244.

[2226] Waterbury Sav. Bank v. 128 Conn. 78, 20 A.2d 455.

[2227] In re Liability, 263 App. Div. 1036, 33 N.Y.S.2d 434.

[2228] Capitol Bldg., etc., Ass'n v. Kansas Comm., 148 Kan. 446, 83 P.2d 106; Unemployment Compensation Comm. v. Jefferson Standard Life Ins. Co., 215 N.C. 479, 2 S.E.2d 584; Waterbury Sav. Bank v. Danaher, 128 Conn. 78, 20 A.2d 455.

and the Federal Deposit Insurance Corporation.[2229] And a federally chartered savings and loan association, a member of a federal home loan bank, was held to be an "instrumentality of the United States" within the meaning of such an act.[2230]

Income Taxes.—A state tax on a national bank's net income is valid against the bank itself, in view of the federal statute authorizing a state to tax national banks on their net income in lieu of taxes on shares of their stock or dividends thereon.[2231] It is said that such a tax is not on the corporate

---

[2229] Unemployment Compensation Com. v. Wachovia Bank & Trust Co., 215 N.C. 491, 2 S.E.2d 592; Fidelity-Philadelphia Trust Co. v. Hines, 337 Pa. 48, 10 A2d 553.

A state chartered mutual savings bank, though not exempt from contributions under the unemployment compensation act, was not liable for contributions during period it was designated as exempt under a regulation of the administrator of the act. Waterbury Sav. Bank v. Danaher, 128 Conn. 78, 20 A.2d 455.

[2230] Waterbury Sav. Bank v. Danaher, 128 Conn. 78, 20 A.2d 455.

[2231] **In general.—**

People v. Loughman, 100 F.2d 387, construing the New York statute and 12 U.S. C.A. § 548.

Income derived from tax-exempt securities.—

Oklahoma statute which imposes a tax on national banking associations according to or measured by net income, is not invalid as a levy on tax-exempt securities to the extent that net income therein referred to includes interest on federal securities which, prior to amendment, had been expressly excluded, in view of fact that change of policy was made pursuant to express authorization of federal statute. Tradesmens Nat'l Bank v. Oklahoma Tax Com., 309 U.S. 560, 60 S. Ct. 688, 84 L. Ed. 947, aff'g 185 Okla. 656, 95 P.2d 121.

A state statute levying a tax on national banks "according to, or measured by," the net income of such banks, is a valid and binding exercise of the state's taxing power, notwithstanding further provisions of the statute providing that such income should include the interest on obligations of the United States, or its possessions, or on securities issued under the authority of a congressional act, the income of which is tax free. First Nat'l Bank v. Oklahoma Tax Com., 185 Okla. 98, 90 P.2d 438. See Tradesmens Nat'l Bank v. Oklahoma Tax Com., 185 Okla. 656, 95 P.2d 121, aff'd, 309 U.S. 560, 60 S. Ct. 688, 84 L. Ed. 947.

A state tax on nonexistent income of national bank, with a minimum measured by dividends paid to stockholders, was not within permission given by federal statute. Commissioner of Corps. & Taxation v. Woburn Nat'l Bank, 815 Mass. 506, 58 N.E2d 654.

Election to be assessed on income.—

Where national bank which had no net income for tax year involved made election to come under state statute giving national bank annual election to be assessed on net income, the election created no contract binding on the commonwealth because of lack of consideration, so that later election filed after enactment of amendment providing minimum tax measured by dividends paid created valid contract binding both the commonwealth and

franchise, but is a special tax to be levied strictly in accordance with the federal statute.[2232] But it also has been held that a statute levying a tax on national banks "according to, or measured by," their net income, levies a franchise tax and not an income tax.[2233] A corporation license tax, which was based on the net income, was a tax on "net income" within the meaning of the then-existing provision of the National Bank Act governing state taxation of national banks.[2234] And a corporation, owned and organized by a national bank to take over its safe deposit business and not for the purpose of holding title to property, was denied exemption from a state income tax though the corporation turned over its entire income less expenses to the bank.[2235]

Sales Taxes.—Before the 1969 amendments to the federal statute governing state taxation of national banks, it was held that a national bank was immune from both use and sales taxes on purchases for its own use of tangible personal property.[2236] The federal statute as amended effective December 24, 1969, expressly authorizes the imposition of such taxes, on a nondiscriminatory basis.[2237] And a retailer is not entitled to refund of sales

---

the taxpayer. Commissioner of Corp., etc. v. Woburn Nat. Bank, 315 Mass. 505, 53 N.E.2d 554.

Federal Credit Union Act.—

Federal Credit Union Act prohibits only imposition of duty or burden on federal credit union of collecting or enforcing payment of state or local taxes assessed upon, and measured by, evaluation of personal property of the owners; statute has no apparent application to state's efforts to collect income taxes of conventional sort. Northeast Fed. Credit Union v. Neves, 837 F.2d 531 (1st Cir. 1988).

2232 Aberdeen Sav. & Loan Ass'n v. Chase, 157 Wash. 351, 289 P. 536, 71 A.L.R. 232.

2233 Tradesmens Nat'l Bank v. Oklahoma Tax Com., 185 Okla. 656, 95 P.2d 121, aff'd, 309 U.S. 560, 60 S. Ct. 688, 84 L. Ed. 947; Browning Co. v State Tax Comm., 107 Utah 457, 154 P.2d 993; Southern Pacific Co. v. McColgan, 68 Cal. App. 2d 48, 156 P.2d 81.

2234 Security Bank & Trust Co. v. Connors, 550 P.2d 1313 (Mont. 1976).

2235 In re First Nat. Safe Deposit Co., 351 Mo. 423, 173 S.W.2d 403.

2236 First Agricultural Nat'l Bank v. State Tax Comm'n, 392 U.S. 339, 88 S. Ct. 2173, 20 L. Ed. 24 1138 (1968).

2237 12 U.S.C.S. 548.

Had the legislature intended to exempt a savings and loan association from a use tax, it could and would have declared such intent in the act itself or specifically so provided in tax in lieu of other taxes" statute applicable to the savings and loan association, and in its failure to do so, the savings and loan association purchaser was not exempt from the use tax. Farm & Home Sav. Asso. v. Spradling, 538 S.W.2d 313 (Mo. 1976).

The fact that exemptions from the use tax are to be determined in light of the purpose of

taxes paid on account of sales to a state bank which is a member of the Federal Reserve System, on the ground that such bank is an instrumentality of the federal government.[2238] A section of the state constitution which required that all forms of taxation imposed on banks apply to all the banks located within the limits of the state did not expressly prohibit the imposition of the legal incidence of a tax on a nonbank entity, even though the economic burden of the tax fell on the state banks, unless the national banks were similarly burdened, either directly or indirectly.[2239] Thus, the imposition of a sales tax on retailers selling personal property to a state bank, resulting in the economic burden of a tax falling on the state bank, did not violate the section of the state constitution which required that any form of taxation apply to all banks located within limits of the state, even though the sales tax was not imposed on retailers selling personal property to national banks.[2240] Moreover, under California law, the legal incidence and economic burden of

---

the use tax and that the use tax was designed to complement the sales tax belies the construction of the law which would extend the exemption provisions of the "tax in lieu of other taxes" statute applicable to savings and loan association for a use tax but not to a sales tax. Farm & Home Sav. Asso. v. Spradling, 538 S.W.2d 313 (Mo. 1976).

In the enactment of a use tax, the legislature could not have intended to relieve purchases made by an association from the out of state merchants from a compensating use tax but to require that sales made by instate merchants to the association be subject to a sales tax and thereby give substantial competitive advantage to out-of-state merchants over resident merchants. Farm & Home Sav. Asso. v. Spradling, 538 S.W.2d 313 (Mo. 1976).

Sales tax is a tax upon gross receipts of the seller, not purchaser, and the fact that a duty is imposed upon the purchaser to pay an amount of tax to the seller does not alter the legal nature of the tax; consequently, the "exemption provisions of the tax in lieu of other taxes" statute applicable to savings and loan associations did not exempt a mutual savings and loan association from payment of the sales tax because it was a purchaser, not a seller. Farm & Home Sav. Ass'n v. Spradling, 538 S.W.2d 313 (Mo. 1976).

A purchaser, a mutual savings and loan association which was not exempt from sales tax, was not entitled to a two percent deduction for remitting same under the statute providing that from every remittance to the director of revenue made on or before the date when the same becomes due, the person required to remit the same shall be entitled to deduct and retain an amount equal to two percent thereof. Farm & Home Sav. Asso. v. Spradling, 538 S.W.2d 313 (Mo. 1978).

[2238] Western Lithograph Co. v. State Bd. of Equalization, 11 Cal. 2d 156, 78 P.2d 731, 117 A.L.R. 838.

[2239] Hibernia Bank v. State Bd. of Equalization, 166 Cal. App. 3d 393, 212 Cal. Rptr. 556 (1985).

[2240] Hibernia Bank v. State Bd. of Equalization, 166 Cal. App. 3d 393, 212 Cal. Rptr. 558 (1985).

the sales tax are two separate and distinct concepts.[2241] Furthermore, the legislative intent in imposing a sales tax was that the incidence of the tax be on the retailer, not upon the consumer.[2242]

Obligations of United States.—The borrowing and supremacy clauses of the United States Constitution do not prohibit the states from taxing personal property representing an interest in a federal instrumentality as long as the property interest is not taxed in a discriminatory manner when compared to similar investment property.[2243]

Retailer's Occupation Taxes.—The imposition of a retailer's occupation tax upon sellers on the basis of sales of office equipment and supplies to national banks does not offend the federal government's sovereign immunity or restrictions imposed by Congress as to taxation of national banks.[2244]

Recording Taxes.—National banks were formerly not subject to ad valorem recording taxes imposed by a state on long-term notes.[2245] And a tax on the consideration for a deed or the actual value of the property conveyed, which was required by a statute in addition to a regular fee for recording deeds was held a tax on grantees and unenforceable against a federal land bank as regards a deed of land acquired by mortgage foreclosure.[2246]

Franchise Taxes.—A national bank is obligated to pay state franchise taxes for its last year of business, even though it ceases to exist prior to the end of the year.[2247] "Franchise" tax imposed upon banks and savings and

---

2241 Hibernia Bank v. State Bd. of Equalization, 166 Cal. App. 3d 393, 212 Cal. Rptr. 556 (1985).

2242 Hibernia Bank v. State Bd. of Equalization, 166 Cal. App. 3d 393, 212 Cal. Rptr. 556 (1985).

2243 In re First Fed. Sav. & Loan Ass'n, 743 P.2d 640 (Okla. 1987).

2244 National Bank of Hyde Park in Chicago v. Isaacs, 27 Ill. 2d 205, 188 N.E.2d 704.

2245 Washington Loan & Banking Co. v. Golucke, 212 Ga. 98, 90 S.E.2d 575.

As to liability of national banks for taxes on the execution, delivery, or recordation of documents, see now 12 U.S.C.S. § 548, as amended effective December 24, 1969.

2246 Federal Land Bank v. Hubard, 163 Va. 860, 178 S.E. 16.

2247 Granite Nat'l Bank v. State Tax Comm'n, 30 Utah 2d 351, 517 P.2d 1310 (1974).

Where a state bank which was in existence for the same period of time as the national bank which was seeking refund of taxes, and whose net income was the same would pay, during its existence, substantially the same amount of franchise taxes as the national bank, the fact that the national bank's tax became payable at the end of the tax year while the state bank's tax became due and payable in advance at the beginning of the tax year was not so discriminatory as to violate federal statutes regulating state taxation of national banks.

loan associations based on adjusted federal income for a current tax year was indistinguishable from a Florida corporate income tax and, therefore, the tax was invalid to the extent it purported to include federal instrumentalities within its measure.[2248]

The state was not prohibited, by the doctrine of intergovernmental immunity, from including interest received on Federal Home Loan Banks consolidated bonds in calculating the bank's net income for purpose of nondiscriminatory franchise tax on financial institutions; the state was not taxing bonds or interest on them, but rather the privilege of doing business as a financial institution in corporate form in the state, with the tax measured by the net income which included interest on federal obligations.[2249]

Federal law does not preclude obligations of the United States from being included in the tax base for both a franchise tax and an excise tax, even when the corporation is subject to both taxes.[2250]

Excise Taxes.—The legislature's enactment of a single excise tax imposing tax substantially identical to that negated by a supreme court decision

---

Granite Nat'l Bank v. State Tax Comm'n, 30 Utah 2d 351, 517 P.2d 1310 (1974).

2248 First Union Nat'l Bank v. Florida Dep't of Revenue, 502 So. 2d 964 (Fla. App. 1987).

New York.—State may collect franchise tax on national banking associations or banks incorporated under laws of other jurisdictions, even though it does not possess the power to grant such corporations the license "to exist" in the state. Bankers Trust New York Corp. v. Department of Finance, 79 N.Y.2d 457, 583 N.Y.S.2d 821, 593 N.E.2d 275 (1992).

Presence of coexisting state franchise tax does not require conclusion that New York City's financial corporation tax is not a "franchise tax' within meaning of the federal public debt statute which exempts United States Government obligations and interest thereon from state or municipal taxation "except nondiscriminatory franchise or other nonproperty taxes in lieu thereof imposed on corporations"; number of acceptable forms of taxation can be imposed within nondiscriminatory franchise tax exemption, and statute does not limit the state to condition the exercise of corporate powers upon payment of only one tax. Bankers Trust N.Y. Corp. v. Department of Fin., 79 N.Y.2d 457, 583 N.Y.S.2d 821, 593 N.E.2d 275 (1992).

The New York City financial corporation tax, which is imposed on financial corporations for privilege of doing business in the city in a corporate or organized capacity, is a "franchise tax" within meaning of the federal public debt statute which exempts United States Government obligations and interest thereon from state or municipal taxation "except nondiscriminatory franchise or other nonproperty tax in lieu thereof imposed on corporations." Bankers Trust N.Y. Corp. v. Department of Fin., 79 N.Y.2d 457, 583 N.Y.S.2d 821, 593 N.E.2d 275 (1992).

2249 State Dep't of Assessments & Taxation v. Maryland Nat'l Bank, 310 Md. 664, 531 A.2d 294 (1987).

2250 First American Nat'l Bank v. Olsen, 751 S.W.24 417 (Tenn. 1987).

constituted violation of separation of powers, as it impaired inherent attribute of state supreme court's judgment.[2251]

Mortgage Taxes.[2252]

§ 2. Power of United States.

A bank incorporated and organized under the laws of a state with its principal place of business within the United States, is subject to the sovereign power of the United States, and is a proper object of taxation; its investments abroad are its property and part of its capital, and also taxable by the United States. Moreover, it is presumed that such investments are those that banks usually make in doing a banking business, and that their legal situs is at the home office of the bank.[2253] However, the United States may not tax the Instrumentalities which a state employs in the discharge of its essential governmental duties.[2254] On the other hand, such exemption from federal taxation does not extend to every instrumentality which a state may see fit to employ, but depends upon the nature of the particular undertaking.[2255]

[2251] First Nat'l Bank v. Commonwealth, 520 A.2d 895 (Pa. Commw. 1987).

[2252] In view of the federal statute providing that, for the purpose of any tax law enacted under authority of the United States or any state, a national bank shall be treated as a bank organized and existing under the laws of the state or other jurisdiction within which its principal office is located, states have no option but to treat national banks the same as state banks for tax purposes and, accordingly, the mortgage tax paid in Oklahoma by state banks must also be paid by national banks. First Nat'l Bank & Trust Co. v. Parham, 515 P.2d 1374 (Okla. 1973).

[2253] Nevada Bank v. Sedgwick, 104 U.S. 111, 26 L. Ed. 703.

Under Virginia law, penalties and interest were part of delinquent "taxes upon real estate" owned by Federal Reserve Bank property within meaning of statute which exempts Federal Reserve Banks from all taxation except taxes upon real estate given that there was no indication that Virginia rule was designed to discriminate against federal government. Federal Reserve Bank v. City of Richmond, 957 F.2d 134 (4th Civ. 1992).

[2254] Helvering v. Therrell, 303 U.S. 218, 58 S. Ct. 539, 82 L. Ed. 758.

Under rule exempting instrumentality of state government from federal taxation, there must be state ownership, and a showing of burden on the state by imposition and collection of the tax. First State Bank v. Thomas, 38 F. Supp. 849.

[2255] **In general.—**

Helvering v. Therrell, 303 U.S. 218, 58 S. Ct. 539, 82 L Ed. 758.

Under Social Security Act exempting an instrumentality of state, a private banking institution which carried on its own business under state charter for private profit and which handled business for city, state and county, but amount of which was rather small when compared to its entire business, was not an "instrumentality of the state" so as to be exempt

§ 3. Power of Territories.

The same power of taxation with respect to national banks exists in the territories as in the states.[2256] Thus, a territory or possession may not tax an instrumentality of its sovereign without the latter's consent.[2257] And a statute was necessary to permit territorial legislatures to tax national banks.[2258]

§ 4. Purposes of Taxation.

The validity of the taxation of banks, their property or shares of their stock for particular purposes, as for instance, for schools,[2259] or county or municipal purposes,[2260] is dependent upon the various state statutes. The

---

from social security tax, notwithstanding state statute declaring state banks to be instrumentalities of the state government since a "public purpose" does not mean "government function." First State Bank v. Thomas, 38 F. Supp. 849.

Where Social Security Act exempted instrumentality of state and state statute provided that state banking corporations should be deemed to be instrumentalities of the state government, court could go behind the definition of the state legislature in order to determine the real meaning of the word "instrumentality" as used in the federal act, and if the thing at which the federal act is directed is discovered, the levy will be sustained regardless of the name given it by the state if the tax is not burdensome to some state governmental function. First State Bank v. Thomas, 38 F. Supp. 849.

[2256] Talbott v. Silver Bow County, 139 U.S. 438, 11 S. Ct. 594, 35 L. Ed. 210, aff'g Board of Comm'rs v. Davis, 6 Mont. 306, 12 P. 688; People v. Moore, 1 Idaho 504.

Puerto Rico was held without statutory authority to tax national bank located within continental United States which conducted banking business through branches in Domenech v. National City Bank, 294 U.S. 199, 55 S. Ct. 366, 79 L. Ed. 857, aff'g National City Bank v. Domenech, 71 F.2d 13. And this applied to Philippine Islands. Posadas v. National City Bank, 296 U.S. 497, 56 S. Ct. 349, 80 L. Ed. 351.

[2257] District of Columbia Nat'l Bank v. District of Columbia, 348 F.2d 808 (D.C. Cir. 1965).

[2258] District of Columbia Nat'l Bank v. District of Columbia, 348 F.2d 808 (D.C. Cir. 1965).

Since the Guam territorial income tax, which generally mirrors the provisions of the federal tax code, was enacted by the United States Congress primarily to relieve the United States Treasury of the necessity of making direct appropriations, and since the Government of Guam is powerless to vary the terms of the federal income tax laws as applied to Guam except as permitted by Congress, the Guam territorial income tax is not a tax imposed by Guam for the purposes of a statute which allows a local government to tax the net income of a national bank but once, and thus the imposition on a national bank by the Government of Guam of a 4 percent net profit business privilege tax was not violative of that statute. Bank of America, Nat'l Trust & Sav. Ass'n v. Chaco, 539 F.2d 1226 (9th Cir. 1976).

[2259] Frend v. Deposit Bank, 19 Ky. L. Rptr. 825, 42 S.W. 102; Root v. Erdelmeyer, 37 Ind. 225; Evansville v. Bayard, 39 Ind. 450.

[2260] *Indiana.*—Craft v. Tuttle, 27 Ind. 332; Richmond v. Scott, 48 Ind. 568.

nature of a tax must be determined by its operation rather than its particular descriptive language.[2261] The nature of the tax is determined not by the character of the tax it displaces, but rather, by the manner in which it is imposed.[2262] Thus, it is the manner of operation which determines the nature of the tax, not the sanctions imposed for the failure to pay it.[2263]

§ 5. Delegation of Power.

The well-established rule that a state, in the distribution of the powers of government, may commit the power to levy certain taxes to one body and the power to levy others to another, applies to state taxation of banks, and a county or other municipal corporation may, in the exercise of power delegated by a state, tax the property of banks where the state itself would have had the power to levy such a tax.[2264]

§ 6. Power to Cure Defects or Irregularities.

With regard to state taxation of banks, the well-established doctrine applies that curative legislation is permissible in cases where the law imposes a tax upon property which, however, is overlooked by the assessor or otherwise omitted from assessment, or where some other faulty step is taken.[2265] It would seem, however, that a legislature cannot, under the guise

---

Iowa.—McGregor v. McGregor Branch, 12 Iowa 79.

Kentucky.—Louisville Trust Co. v. Louisville, 30 S.W. 991, 17 Ky. L. Rptr. 265.

Massachusetts.—Rich v. Packard Nat'l Bank, 138 Mass. 527.

New York.—Ontario Bank v. Bunnell, 10 Wend. 186.

Virginia.—Union Bank of Richmond v. Richmond, 94 Va. 318, 26 S.E. 821.

2261 Bank One Dayton, N.A. v. Limbach, 50 Ohio St. 3d 163, 553 N.E.2d 624 (1990).

2262 Centerre Bank v. Director of Revenue, 744 S.W.2d 754 (Mo. 1988).

2263 Centerre Bank v. Director of Revenue, 744 S.W.2d 754 (Mo. 1988).

2264 *United States.*—Citizens Nat'l Bank v. Kentucky, 199 U.S. 603, 26 S. Ct. 750, 50 L Ed. 329; Farmers' Bank v. Fox, 8 Fed. Cas. (No. 4658) 1031, 4 Cranch 330.

Alabama.—Baldwin v. City Council, 53 Ala. 437.

Georgia.—City Council of Augusta v. National Bank of Augusta, 47 Ga. 562.

Indiana.—De Pauw v. New Albany, 22 Ind. 204.

Kentucky.—Commonwealth v. Citizens' Nat. Bank, 117 Ky. 946, 80 S.W. 158, 25 Ky. L. Rptr. 2100, appeal dismissed, 199 U.S. 603, 26 S. Ct. 750, 50 L. Ed. 329.

Mississippi.—Huntley v. Bank of Winona, 69 Miss. 663, 13 So. 832.

North Carolina.—Bank of Greensboro' v. Commissioners of Greensboro', 74 N.C. 385.

South Carolina.—Bank v. Savannah, Dud. 130.

2265 First Nat. Bank v. Covington, 103 F. 523, appeal dismissed, 185 U.S. 270, 22 S. Ct.

of a curative statute, constitutionally enact a retroactive law imposing taxes for previous years upon the property of a bank which was not subject to taxation under any valid law during such years.[2266] But a state may collect such taxes to the extent that they would have been valid under a prior existing law.[2267]

II. CONSTITUTIONAL REQUIREMENTS AND RESTRICTIONS.

§ 7. Constitutional Provisions as to Situs.

It seems to be conceded that a tax cannot be assessed where there is no jurisdiction of either person or property.[2268] And while it is true, as a general rule at common law, that personal property has no situs of its own, but follows the person of its owner, the rule is merely one of convenience, and in the absence of a constitutional prohibition a legislature may change it.[2269] So where the Constitution does not prohibit it, a legislature may provide for taxing shares of national banks at the bank's location without regard to the residence of the owners of such shares.[2270] But a statute which provides that taxes are to be assessed by county authorities upon the shares of national banks in the county where the bank is located, without regard to the residence of the shareholder, is a violation of a state constitutional provision requiring the collection of uniform taxes on persons and property within the

---

645, 46 L. Ed. 906; 129 F. 792, aff'd, 198 U.S. 100, 25 S. Ct. 562, 49 L. Ed. 963.

It is within congressional power to authorize state's collection of taxes previously levied against national banks, though levy, when made, may have been invalid. McFarland v. Georgetown Nat. Bank, 208 Ky. 7, 270 S.W. 995.

2266 First Nat. Bank v. Covington, 103 F. 523, appeal dismissed, 185 U.S. 270, 22 S. Ct. 645, 46 L. Ed. 906; 129 F. 792, aff'd, 198 U.S. 100, 25 S. Ct. 562, 49 L Ed. 963.

2267 State v. First Nat'l Bank, 164 Minn. 235, 204 N.W. 874, aff'd, 273 U.S. 561, 47 S. Ct. 468, 71 L Ed. 774.

2268 First Nat. Bank v. Smith, 65 Ill. 44; Union Nat. Bank v. Chicago, 24 Fed. Cas. (No. 14, 374) 615, 3 Bias. 82.

2269 First Nat. Bank v. Smith, 65 Ill. 44.

2270 Schuylkill Trust Co. v. Pennsylvania, 302 U.S. 506, 58 S. Ct. 295, 82 L Ed. 392 (1938); First Nat. Bank v. Smith, 65 Ill. 44.

The Pennsylvania revenue statute taxing shares of stock in trust companies, construed by the state courts as applying to nonresident as well as resident shareholders, is valid. Schuylkill Trust Co. v. Pennsylvania, 302 U.S. 506, 58 S. Ct. 295, 82 L Ed. 392 (1938), aff'g Commonwealth v. Schuykill Trust Co., 327 Pa. 127, 193 A. 638.

jurisdiction of the body imposing same.[2271] On the other hand, a prohibition against deducting the value of real estate situated in a foreign state from the value of shares of stock of state banks and loan or investment companies does not violate the due process clause of the federal Constitution.[2272]

§ 8. General Laws, Equality and Uniformity In General.

General Consideration.—There is nothing in the federal Constitution which requires that state taxation be equal, uniform or just.[2273] With reference to state constitutions, there is generally a constitutional requirement that property be assessed under general laws and by uniform rules.[2274] But it is not necessary to the validity of a tax law that it operate upon all persons in a state alike. It is sufficient if it is general and uniform in its operation upon all persons similarly situated, and this is true whether individuals or corporations are affected.[2275] Thus, it would seem that tax laws must be general as distinguished from special.[2276] However, a law which provides a fixed and specific rule for the assessment of property of one class of corporations or individuals which is different from that applicable to all other classes, is not a special law within this prohibition.[2277]

[2271] Union Nat. Bank v. Chicago, 24 Fed. Cas. (No. 14, 874)615, 8 Bias. 82; Tresnon v. Board of Sup'rs, 120 Va. 203, 90 S.E. 615.

[2272] First Nat'l Bank v. Moon, 102 Kan. 334, 170 P. 33 (1918).

[2273] Commercial Trust Co. v. Hudson County Board, 86 N.J.L. 424, 92 A. 263, aff'd, 87 N.J.L. 179, 92 A. 799; Davidson v. New Orleans, 96 U.S. 97, 24 L Ed. 616; Memphis, etc., Co. v. Shelby, 109 U.S. 398, 3 S. Ct. 205, 27 L. Ed. 976; Home Ins. Co. v. New York, 134 U.S. 594, 10 S. Ct. 593, 33 L. Ed. 1025; Giozza v. Tiernan, 148 U.S. 657, 13 S. Ct. 721, 37 L. Ed. 599; State v. Clement Nat'l Bank, 84 Vt. 167, 78 A. 944, 1912D Ann. Cas. 22.

[2274] Mechanics' Nat. Bank v. Baker, 65 N.J.L. 113, 46 A. 586, aff'd 65 N.J.L. 549, 48 A. 582; Appeal of Banger, 109 Pa. 79; Hempstead County v. Hempstead County Bank, 73 Ark. 515, 84 S.W. 715; Union Nat. Bank v. Chi., 24 Fed. Cas. (No. 14, 374) 615, 3 Biss. 82; State ex rel. Campbell v. Brinkop, 238 Mo. 298, 143 S.W. 444.

Statute held not violative of constitutional prohibition against granting of special privileges or immunities even though inapplicable to national banks because in conflict with federal statute. Bankers Trust Co. v. Department of Treasury, 210 Ind. 530, 1 N.E.2d 935.

[2275] Primghar State Bank v. Rerick, 96 Iowa 238, 64 N.W. 801.

It is held that the legislature may enact statutes providing a different method for assessing banks from that for assessing other corporations and individuals. Stone v. General Elec. Contracts Corp., 193 Miss. 317, 7 So. 2d 811.

[2276] Primghar State Bank v. Rerick, 96 Iowa 238, 64 N.W. 801.

[2277] United States Exp. Co. v. Ellyson, 28 Iowa 370.

Therefore it has been held that an act which provided a specific rule for the assessment of express and telegraph companies operating and doing business within this state, different

And although the rule is that taxation of property should be by operation of a general law, where a particular kind of property is omitted from taxation for a given year, the legislature may pass a special law to cure the omission.[2278] The statute, which specifically excludes national banking corporations and shareholders who pay tax on their shares of stock under ad valorem laws, remains a viable statute on the question whether dividends from national bank stock are to be included in the definition of gross income, and its repeal could not be effected by implication.[2279] A tax operates retroactively only when the taxable event occurs prior to the date on which the tax becomes effective.[2280] The legislature is empowered to impose a reasonable excise on any franchise or privilege conferred by the Commonwealth, and the constitutional requirement that the excise be "reasonable" was not intended to give the judiciary the right to revise decisions of the legislature that might be thought unwise or inexpedient.[2281] The income-based portion of the excise tax levied on savings banks and cooperative banks satisfies the constitutional provisions authorizing the general court to impose reasonable excises on the privilege of transacting business as a corporation.[2282] It is not within the province of the court to invalidate the

---

from that applicable to the assessment of other property, was not a special law. United States Exp. Co. v. Ellyson, 28 Iowa 370.

And the same rule has been applied to the assessment of railway property. Central Iowa R. Co. v. Board, 67 Iowa 199, 25 N.W. 128; Chicago, etc., R. Co. v. Iowa, 94 U.S. 155, 24 L. Ed. 94. See also Missouri Val. & B. Co. v. Harrison Co., 74 Iowa 283, 37 N.W. 372.

We are of the opinion that the statute in question is general, not because it operates upon all persons within the state alike, but because it applies alike to all banking associations organized under the general incorporation laws of the state, known as state or commercial banks. Primghar State Bank v. Rerick, 96 Iowa 238, 64 N.W. 801.

[2278] McVeagh v. Chicago, 49 Ill. 318.

[2279] McNamara v. First Commerce Corp., 392 So. 2d 467 (La. App. 1980), cert. denied, 397 So. 2d 1361 (La. 1981).

[2280] First Fin. Group of N.H., Inc. v. State, 430 A.2d 162 (N.H. 1981).

The taxable event for the purposes of the business profits tax was the receipt of dividends by the parent corporation from the subsidiary bank, notwithstanding that such dividends were paid from earnings accumulated by the subsidiary prior to the passage of the statute governing the business profits tax; therefore, the business profits tax statute was not applied retroactively in disallowing deductions taken by the parent corporation for such dividends. First Fin. Group of N.H., Inc. v. State, 430 A.2d 162 (N.H. 1981).

[2281] Andover Sav. Bank v. Commissioner of Revenue, 387 Mass. 229, 439 N.E.2d 282 (1982).

[2282] Andover Sav. Bank v. Commissioner of Revenue, 387 Mass. 229, 489 N.E.2d 282 (1982).

excise tax on mutual banks merely because, due to recent economic changes, it has become unduly burdensome.[2283] That which is not within the statutory definition as to what constitutes a tax is excluded from the tax.[2284] Generally, the legislature is supreme in the area of taxation; therefore, constitutional restrictions on such legislative power must be strictly construed against limitation.[2285]

Courts will not declare taxation legislation unconstitutional unless it clearly, palpably and plainly violates the Constitution.[2286]

Equality and Uniformity of Taxation.—The rule that taxes must be uniform means that all individuals and all classes must be required to share the burdens of taxation uniformly with like individuals and like classes. It does not mean that taxes may be required of some which are not exacted of others, but that all persons subject to the same conditions must be uniformly taxed.[2287] Thus, it is not uniform to collect a double tax on property owned

---

[2283] Andover Sav. Bank v. Commissioner of Revenue, 387 Mass. 229, 489 N.E.2d 282 (1982).

[2284] American Sav. Bank v. State Tax Comm'n, 479 N.Y.S.2d 808 (N.Y.A.D. 3 Dep't 1984).

[2285] Hibernia Bank v. State Bd. of Equalization, 166 Cal. App. 3d 393, 212 Cal. Rptr. 556 (1985).

[2286] Fidelity Bank v. Commonwealth ex rel. Dep't of Revenue, 645 A.2d 452 (Pa. Commw. 1994).

The 1989 amendment, to bank share tax statute that were designed to recoup for Commonwealth revenue that it lost because of credits given banks for improperly paid bank shares taxes did not violate supremacy clause or separation of powers doctrine by effectively taxing same United States obligations that prior United States and Pennsylvania Supreme Court decisions declared Commonwealth could not tax; amendments did not abrogate bank's legal right to refund, but rather, gave refund in form of credit, which was specifically recognized in relevant statutes and case law. Fidelity Bank v. Commonwealth ex rel. Dep't of Revenue, 645 A.2d 452 (Pa. Commw. 1994).

The averaging provision of 72 P.S. § 7701.1(a) of the Shares Tax, 72 P.S. §§ 7701–7706, was not unconstitutional due to a lack of uniformity under Pa. Const. art. VIII, § 1 because the short-term disparity of result was warranted based on sufficiently distinguishable situations that warranted distinguishable results with respect to a merger or combination of two institutions that had both been previously taxed on their historic average values compared to a combination that introduced previously untaxable assets to the calculation. Leb. Valley Farmers Bank v. Commonwealth, 623 Pa. 455, 83 A.3d 107 (2013). (Article VII of the Tax Reform Code and all benefits associated with Article VII shall terminate on December 31, 2022, pursuant to 72 P.S. § 9979-C).

[2287] Primghar State Bank v. Rerick, 96 Iowa 238, 64 N.W. 801; Union Nat. Bank v. Chicago, 24 Fed. Cas. (No. 14, 374) 615, 3 Biss. 82.

by a bank or insurance company and a single tax on the same kind of

---

The tax on bank shares assessed by Dallas County did not constitute an unlawful discrimination against federal securities because it was levied on the difference between the actual cash values of each share and the proportionate amount per share at which the bank's real estate was assessed for taxation. Bank of Texas v. Childs, 615 S.W.2d 810 (Tex. Civ. App. 1981).

Bank excise tax which included interest income earned on obligations of federal government, but did not include interest income earned by banks on obligations of curtain state agencies, was discriminatory. Cambridge State Bank v. Roemer, 457 N.W.2d 716 (Minn. 1990).

California's worldwide combined reporting requirement for calculating corporate franchise tax for multinational enterprises did not violate commerce clause principles prohibiting discrimination against interstate commerce, requiring substantial nexus to taxing state, requiring fair apportionment, and requiring fair relation to services provided by state, even though compliance burdens allegedly would be prohibitive for foreign-owned enterprises; California allowed computations based on reasonable approximations, thus allowing foreign owner to avoid large compliance costs. Barclays Bank PLC v. Franchise Tax Bd., U.S. , 114 S. Ct. 2268, 129 L Ed. 2d 244 (1994).

California's reasonable approximations method of reducing burden of compliance with worldwide combined reporting method to determine corporate franchise tax for multinational enterprise did not violate due process; California's judiciary construed California law to curtail discretion of California tax officials, and rules governing international, multijurisdictional income allocation had inescapable imprecision given complexity of the subject matter. Barclays Bank PLC v. Franchise Tax Bd., U.S. , 114 S. Ct. 2268, 129 L Ed. 2d 244 (1994).

Fact that foreign multinational enterprise was exposed to risk of multiple taxation as result of California's worldwide combined reporting method for computing corporate franchise tax did not violate commerce clause; double taxation of foreign multinationals was not inevitable, alternative reasonably available to California would not eliminate risk of double taxation, and Congress held controlling rein. Barclays Bank PLC v. Franchise Tax Bd., US., 114 S. Ct. 2268, 129 L. Ed. 2d 244 (1994).

California's worldwide combined reporting requirement for calculation of corporate franchise tax did not prevent federal government from speaking with one voice in international trade and, therefore, did not violate commerce clause, even though executive branch actions, statements, and amicus filings sought to proscribe states' use of worldwide combined reporting; executive branch actions were merely predatory, and Congress refrained from exercising its authority to prohibit state-mandated worldwide combined reporting. Barclays Bank PLC v. Franchise Tax Bd., 512 U.S. 298, 114 S. Ct. 2268, 129 L. Ed. 2d 244 (1994).

Executive branch communications expressing federal policy, but lacking force of law, cannot render unconstitutional California's otherwise valid, congressionally condoned, use of worldwide combined reporting requirement for calculation of corporate franchise tax. Barclays Bank PLC v. Franchise Tax Bd., U.S., 114 S. Ct. 2268, 129 L Ed. 2d 244 (1994).

property held by an individual or manufacturing company,[2288] nor to reduce the tax rate on all intangibles in one class except bank stocks.[2289] But although equality and uniformity of taxation require that persons in one class be treated alike,[2290] absolute uniformity and equality of taxation in all cases and with respect to all kinds of property is not practical.[2291] And the uniformity of taxation requirement does not extend to different classes of businesses.[2292] Banking institutions are accorded privileges and rights not granted to other commercial corporations and they therefore may be classified separately by General Assembly for purposes of taxation and regulation.[2293] An act fixing the order and priority of claims against insolvent banks also does not violate a constitutional provision requiring uniform taxation.[2294]

Constitutional Restriction as a Limitation upon Legislature.—A constitutional requirement that taxation shall be uniform is a limitation upon the

---

2288 Campbell v. Brinkop, 238 Mo. 298, 143 S.W. 444.

2289 Omaha Nat. Bank v. Heintze, 159 Neb. 520, 67 N.W.2d 753.

Where legislature had classified all intangible property other than money and certain other intangibles in one class and where tax rate levied on all intangibles in this class had been reduced except that levied on bank stocks, statute which authorized levy of taxes upon bank stocks, insofar as it purported to levy tax which was in excess of tax levied on intangibles of same class, violated rule of uniformity required by state constitution and to that extent was unenforceable. Omaha Nat. Bank v. Heintze, 159 Neb. 520, 67 N.W.2d 753.

2290 Pullman State Bank v. Manring, 18 Wash. 250, 51 P. 464; Clark v. Maher, 34 Mont. 391, 87 P. 272; Appeal of Banger, 109 Pa. 79.

2291 Primghar State Bank v. Rerick, 96 Iowa 238, 64 N.W. 801.

If the ability of tax laws to stand successfully the test of equality of burden determines their validity, none of them can stand. Commonwealth v. Merchants' & Mfrs' Nat'l Bank, 168 Pa. 309, 31 A. 1065, aff'd, 167 U.S. 461, 17 S. Ct. 829, 42 L Ed. 236.

2292 In re National Bank 137 W. Va. 673, 73 S.E.2d 55.

Fact that certain reserves of life insurance companies are not taxed and certain deductions are allowed in arriving at actual value of intangible property of businesses such as building and loan associations small loan companies does not make tax against banks and industrial loan companies invalid as being discriminatory. In re National Bank, 137 W. Va. 673, 73 S.E.2d 655 (1952).

2293 Memphis Bank & Trust Co. v. Garner, 624 S.W.2d 551 (Tenn. 1981).

Local bank excise tax, which was in lieu of tax upon intangible personal property of banks and was successor to former tax upon shares of banking institutions, was not "discriminatory" on ground it was levied only upon banks. Memphis Bank & Trust Co. v. Garner, 624 S.W.2d 551 (Tenn. 1981).

2294 Baggett v. Mobley, 171 Ga. 268, 155 S.E. 334; Felton v. McArthur, 173 Ga. 465, 160 S.E. 419.

legislature in the exercise of its general power to levy taxes, not a restriction upon the people in the exercise of a power reserved to them by their constitution. So where the constitution of a state reserves to the people all legislative power as to banks and banking, that portion of the banking law of the state which regulates the taxation of capital stock of banks is not in violation of the constitutional requirement of uniformity.[2295]

Lack of Uniformity Due to Application of Law.—Where there is a lack of uniformity and equality in taxation which is due to the application of a law, it seems such law contravenes the constitutional requirement of uniformity and equality.[2296] So it has been held that where a tax statute prescribes a uniform method for taxing the stock of all incorporated banks, national as well as state, it must be construed in a suit involving a state bank as if the suit involved a national bank, in order to preserve the uniformity of taxation required by federal statute.[2297]

And several cases hold that where a state revenue statute applying both to state and national banks is invalid as to national banks, it is also void as to state banks.[2298] On the other hand, it has been held that such a statute does not violate the uniformity clauses of a state constitution or the Fourteenth Amendment as applied to state banks, merely because it may be invalid under the federal statute as applied to taxation of national banks by a

---

2295 State v. Hastings, 12 Wis. 47.

2296 Commonwealth v. Merchants', etc., Nat. Bank, 168 Pa. 309, 31 A. 1065, aff'd, 167 U.S. 461, 17 S. Ct. 829, 42 L. Ed. 236; Treasurer v. People's, etc., Bank, 47 Ohio St. 503, 25 N.E. 697, 10 L.B.A. 196.

2297 Security Sav. Bank v. Board of Review, 189 Iowa 463, 178 N.W. 562.

2298 State Bank of Omaha v. Endres, 109 Neb. 753, 192 N.W. 322; Ashland County Bank v. Butternut, 208 Wis. 90, 241 N.W. 638, 82 A.L.R. 865. See State v. Mady, 83 Mont. 418, 272 P. 691; Commercial State Bank v. Wilson, 53 S.D. 82, 220 N.W. 152; Voran v. Wright, 129 Kan. 1, 281 P. 938.

A statute providing for the taxation of bank stock on an ad valorem basis, being contrary to the federal statute relating to the taxation of national bank shares and void as to such banks, is void as to state banks. Ashland County Bank v. Butternut, 208 Wis. 90, 241 N.W. 638, 82 A.L.R. 865.

Where Nebraska statute was held invalid as to national banks because it conflicted with federal statute forbidding states to tax shares of a national bank at a greater rate than other moneyed capital, it was also held invalid as to state banks, because the latter would then be taxed at a higher rate than national banks, and therefore the taxation would conflict with that part of the state constitutional requiring taxes to be uniform as to class. State Bank of Omaha v. Endres, 109 Neb. 753, 192 N.W. 322.

state.[2299] And a law providing that shares of stock of banks in a particular locality shall be taxed without regard to the residence of the owner of the shares, being unconstitutional and void as to shareholders not residing in the district where a bank is located, is also void as to those who do reside there; otherwise, the tax would not be uniform.[2300]

Lack of Uniformity Due to Difference in Circumstances.—A law taxing banks which operates with practical uniformity at first may produce noticeable inequality as differences in location and management begin to develop. This inequality results from circumstances which a legislature could not foresee or provide against, and for that reason can-not be charged against the law; hence, particular banks cannot complain of a lack of equality of tax burden which results from circumstances, and is not produced by application of the law.[2301] When a United States Supreme Court decision effectively barred the state from taxing sales to national banks for a limited period, it was reasonable for the state to continue the application of its established method of taxing retailers selling to all other consumers, including state banks, and thus, continuing the imposition of the sales tax on retailers selling to state banks did not violate the equal protection clauses.[2302]

Lack of Uniformity Resulting from Misconduct of Officer.—Inequality or lack of uniformity in the assessment of property for taxation may result not only by applying different rates of assessment, but from misconduct of taxing officers by which property of one person or class of persons, or a particular class of property, is assessed at a valuation greater in proportion to its real or cash value than most other taxable property.[2303] In order to constitute "discrimination" in the practical administration of a tax law, it must appear that such discrimination is authoritative and intentional, and if a tax legally imposed is not discriminatory, it does not become discrimina-

---

[2299] Brophy v. Powell, 58 Ariz. 543, 121 P.2d 647. See also Bankers Trust Co. v. Department of Treasury, 210 Ind. 530, 1 N.E.2d 935.

State banks in the Missouri City of St. Joseph were subject to state tax on income from July 1, 1946, subject to credits for ad valorem tax on stock paid to city, although due to city tax, state tax was inoperative as to national banks in St. Joseph during 1946. First Nat. Bank v. Buchanan County, 356 Mo. 1204, 205 S.W.2d 726 (1947).

[2300] Union Nat. Bank v. Chicago, 24 Fed. Cas. (No. 14, 374) 615, 8 Bias. 82.

[2301] Commonwealth v. Merchants' & Mfrs' Nat'l Bank, 168 Pa. 309, 31 A. 1065, aff'd, 167 U.S. 461, 17 S. Ct. 829, 42 L Ed. 236.

[2302] Hibernia Bank v. State Bd. of Equalization, 166 Cal. App. 3d 393, 212 Cal. Rptr. 556 (1985).

[2303] First Nat. Bank v. Christensen, 39 Utah 568, 118 P. 778.

tory by the subsequent illegal acts of a ministerial officer or employee.[2304] Thus, bank stock was held taxable as against the contention that even if the applicable statutes were not discriminatory, the administrative practice of not assessing competitive capital was discriminatory.[2305]

§ 9. Classification of Subjects and Uniformity as to Same Subject.

In General.—Where a constitution provides generally that "all taxes shall be uniform upon the same class of subjects," property may be classified and different rates of taxation imposed thereon.[2306] Taxation is not a matter of exact science; hence, absolute equality and perfect uniformity are not required to satisfy the constitutional uniformity requirement. Scientific formulae, arithmetical deductions and mental contemplations, have small value in making assessments under our practical system of taxation. Some practical inequalities are obviously anticipated, and so long as the taxing scheme does not impose substantially unequal tax burdens, rough uniformity with a limited amount of variation is permitted. The Uniformity Clause requires only substantial uniformity, which means as nearly uniform as practicable in view of the instrumentalities with which and subjects upon which tax laws operate.[2307] For instance, shares of stock in banks and banking associations may be made a separate class for tax purposes.[2308] And a constitutional requirement of proportional contribution to the support of government is not intended to restrict a state to methods of taxation that operate equally upon all its inhabitants regardless of the variety and measure

---

[2304] Iowa Nat. Bank v. Stewart, 214 Iowa 1229, 232 N.W. 445.

[2305] State v. Leonardson, 51 Idaho 646, 9 P.2d 1028.

[2306] Savannah v. Weed, 84 Ga. 683, 11 S.E. 235, 8 L.R.A. 270.

Statutory amendment providing that bank shares tax will be based on average of value over six-year period, rather than on current values of taxable property, did not violate Uniformity Clause of Pennsylvania Constitution; use of averaging methodology discouraged bank from manipulating its holdings of federal obligations so as to artificially reduce its tax liability and minimize effect of random disturbances in value. Fidelity Bank v. Commonwealth Dep't of Revenue, 645 A.2d 452 (Pa. Commw. 1994).

For tax to be considered uniform, classification of taxpayers must be reasonable and tax itself must be applied with uniformity under similar kinds of businesses or property with substantial equality of tax burden on all members of class. Fidelity Bank v. Commonwealth ex rel. Dep't of Revenue, 645 A.2d 452 (Pa. Commw. 1994).

[2307] Leb. Valley Farmers Bank v. Commonwealth, 623 Pa. 455, 83 A.3d 107 (2013).

[2308] Bonaparte v. American-First Nat. Bank, 139 Okla. 189, 281 P. 958; Brophy v. Powell, 58 Ariz. 543, 121 P.2d 647.

of advantages derived from its protection and regulation.[2309] Such a constitutional provision does not forbid the classification of property for purposes of taxation,[2310] the true criterion being whether or not all property of the same class is taxed alike.[2311] Nor do such constitutional provisions require a uniform method of assessment, and a legislature, in prescribing methods for ascertaining the value of property to be taxed, may prescribe different regulations for different classes of property.[2312] Therefore, a tax on

---

[2309] State v. Clement Nat'l Bank, 84 Vt. 167, 78 A. 944, 1912D Ann. Cas. 22; In re Hickok's Estate, 78 Vt. 259, 62 A. 724, 6 Ann. Cas. 578.

[2310] **In general.—**

United States.—Sturges v. Carter, 114 U.S. 511, 5 S. Ct. 1014, 29 L. Ed. 240.

Illinois.—Hughes v. Cairo, 92 Ill. 339.

Louisiana—State v. Lathrop, 10 La. Ann. 398.

Michigan.—Youngblood v. Sexton, 32 Mich. 406, 20 Am. R. 654; Bacon v. Board of State Tax Comm'rs, 126 Mich. 22, 85 N.W. 307, 86 Am. St. R. 524, 80 L.R.A. 321; Graham v. St. Joseph, 67 Mich. 652, 35 N.W. 808.

New Jersey.—Mechanics' Nat. Bank v. Baker, 65 N.J.L. 113, 46 A. 586, aff'd, 65 N.J.L. 549, 48 A. 582; State Board of Assessors v. State, 48 N.J.L. 146, 4 A. 578, 8 A. 724.

Ohio.—Lee v. Sturges, 46 Ohio St. 153, 19 N.E. 560, 2 L.R.A. 556.

Intangible property.—

The provision of the constitution that all real property and tangible personal property in the state shall be taxed in proportion to its value must be interpreted as meaning that the legislature may tax intangible property or exempt it or tax certain classes of intangible property and exempt others. Bank of Texas v. Childs, 615 S.W.2d 810 (Tex. Civ. App. 1981).

[2311] Adams v. Bank, 78 Miss. 532, 29 So. 402.

The New York legislature has the power to select and classify industrial banks as to taxation, so long as all in the same class are treated alike, without infringing upon any constitutional right guaranteed by either the state or the federal constitution. Modern Industrial Bank v. Graves, 260 App. Div. 349, 21 N.Y.S.2d 329, aff'd, 285 N.Y. 668, 34 N.E.2d 375.

Bank tax credit statute requiring banks to pay 80 percent of bank shares tax before objecting to constitutionality of statute did not violate equal protection; because of strong state interest in financial stability, state could employ means to ensure timely payment prior to resolution of disputes over validity of tax, and, as distinct class, banks could be required to follow different procedures than other classes of taxpayers without violating equal protection. Fidelity Bank v. Commonwealth ex rel. Dep't of Revenue, 645 A.2d 452 (Pa. Commw. 1994).

[2312] Pacific Nat. Bank v. Pierce, 20 Wash. 675, 56 P. 936 (1899).

A revenue statute, construed as requiring consideration of par value of national bank's preferred stock as well as common stock in determining taxable value of shares of stock

national bank stock, though not applicable to state bank stock, has been held not unconstitutional for nonuniformity where a tax on state bank stock was otherwise provided.[2313] Moreover, if not restricted by constitutional provision, a legislature may impose a tax on one class of property, and completely exempt another class.[2314]

Banking institutions tax is not a property tax, but a substitute there-for, and thus does not run afoul of requirement of uniformity.[2315]

Tax Ad Valorem.—Where a state constitution provides that "all taxation shall be uniform upon the same class of subjects, and ad valorem on all property subject to be taxed," all real and personal property must be taxed according to its value.[2316] Thus, a constitution treats property as one subject

---

therein, is not unconstitutional as denying equal protection of laws to common stockholders of national bank, preferred stock of which was held by Reconstruction Finance Corporation and hence exempt from taxation, by denying them relief panted such stockholders of bank having no preferred stock issued to such Corporation, from burden of indirect double taxation. First Nat. Bank v. State Tax Comm., 43 N.M. 307, 92 P.2d 987, appeal dismissed, 308 U.S. 515, 60 S. Ct. 173, 84 L Ed. 439.

[2313] Montana Nat. Bank v. Yellowstone County, 78 Mont. 62, 252 P. 876.

[2314] Pacific Nat'l Bank v. Pierce County, 20 Wash. 675, 56 P. 936; Newport v. Mudgett, 18 Wash. 271, 51 P. 466; Pullman State Bank v. Manring, 18 Wash. 250, 51 P. 464.

[2315] Mercantile Bank v. Berra, 796 S.W.2d 22 (Mo. 1990).

[2316] **In general.—**

Savannah v. Weed, 84 Ga. 683, 11 S.E. 235, 8 L.R.A. 270. See § 12 of this chapter.

Taxpayer has burden of proof.—

In proceeding by bank, as taxpayer on appeal from assessment made on the bank's capital stock for ad valorem tax purposes, bank had burden of establishing that it had suffered a constitutional discrimination by having its property assessed upon basis of 100 per cent of its true and actual value. In re Kanawha Valley Bank, 144 W. Va. 346, 109 S.E.2d 649.

Assessment. held unconstitutional.—

Assessment of bank shares at 90 per cent of cash value, where other property was assessed at 75 per cent of cash value, held unconstitutional as unjust discrimination. Boonville Nat. Bank v. Schlotzhauer, 317 Mo. 1298, 298 S.W. 732, 55 A.L.R. 489.

For ad valorem tax purposes, assessment of shares of bank stock at 100 per cent of true and actual value, while other property in taxing unit was systematically assessed at lower percentage of its true and actual value, constituted a violation of tax limitation amendment of the constitution, and, therefore, bank was entitled to have its assessment reduced to comply with the constitution. In re Kanawha Valley Bank, 144 W. Va. 346, 109 S.E.2d 649, disapproving in part Charleston & S. Bridge Co. v. Kanawha County Court, 41 W. Va. 658, 24 S.E. 1002, appeal dismissed, 168 U.S. 704, 18 S. Ct. 941, 42 L. Ed. 1212; Christopher v. James, 122 W. Va. 665, 12 S.E.2d 813; In re Hancock County Federal Sav. & Loan Ass'n, 125 W. Va. 426, 25 S.E.2d 543; In re Charleston Fed. Sav. & Loan Ass'n, 126 W. Va. 506,

and prescribes a rule of uniformity as to it by requiring that all property subject to tax shall be taxed ad valorem.[2317]

Arbitrary Versus Reasonable Classification in General.—The question may arise as to whether a particular classification of property for purposes of taxation is an arbitrary classification violative of a prohibition in a state constitution forbidding such classification, or the federal Constitution which prohibits the passage of laws by the states which deny to any person within their jurisdiction equal protection of the laws.[2318] The federal Constitution thus requires that a classification of property for purposes of taxation be based on some distinction which bears a just relation to the purpose of the enactment,[2319] and that one class not be deprived of a privilege enjoyed by others under the same conditions.[2320] But the federal Constitution does not confine states to one system of taxation, and different systems require different methods to adjust them to the general purpose of the law in question.[2321] Therefore, diversity of taxation, both with respect to the amount imposed and the class selected for taxation or exemption, is not inconsistent with a perfect uniformity and equality of taxation in the proper sense of these terms.[2322]

---

30 S.E.2d 518, aff'd, 324 U.S. 182, 65 S. Ct. 624, 89 L. Ed. 857; Bankers Pocahontas Coal Co. v. County Court, 135 W. Va. 174, 62 S.E.2d 801; In re National Bank, 137 W. Va. 678, 78 S.E.2d 655; In re Tax Assessments Against Southern Land Co., 143 W. Va. 152, 100 S.E.2d 555.

[2317] Savannah v. Weed, 84 Ga. 683, 11 S.E. 236, 8 L.R.A. 270.

[2318] State v. Farmers & Mechanics Sav. Bank, 114 Minn. 95, 130 N.W. 445, rev'd on other grounds, 232 U.S. 516, 34 S. Ct. 354, 58 L. Ed 706.

[2319] Magoun v. Illinois, etc., Sav. Bank, 170 U.S. 283, 18 S. Ct. 594, 42 L. Ed. 1037; State v. Hoyt, 71 Vt. 59, 43 A. 973; State v. Clement Nat'l Bank, 84 Vt. 167, 78 A. 944, 1912D Ann. Cas. 22.

[2320] State v. Clement Nat'l Bank, 84 Vt. 167, 78 A. 944, 1912D Ann. Cas. 22; Soon Hing v. Crowley, 113 U.S. 703, 5 S. Ct. 730, 28 L. Ed. 1145.

[2321] State v. Clement Nat'l Bank, 84 Vt. 167, 78 A. 944, 1912D Ann. Cas. 22; Michigan Cent. R. Co. v. Powers, 201 U.S 245, 26 S. Ct. 459, 50 L. Ed. 744; Bell's G. R. Co. v. Pennsylvania, 134 U.S. 232, 10 S. Ct. 533, 33 L. Ed. 892.

Different systems, adjusted to the valuation of different kinds of property, may be adopted, and the method of collection may be varied to suit the necessities of the case. State v. Clement Nat'l Bank, 84 Vt. 167, 78 A. 944, 1912D Ann. Cas. 22; Tappan v. Merchants' Nat. Bank, 86 U.S. (19 Wall.) 490, 22 L. Ed. 189.

[2322] State v. Clement Nat'l Bank, 84 Vt. 167, 78 A. 944, 1912D Ann. Cas. 22; Pacific Exp. Co. v. Seibert, 142 U.S. 339, 12 S. Ct. 250, 35 L. Ed. 1035.

Equality of operation does not mean indiscriminate operation on persons merely as such, but on persons according to their relations. State v. Clement Nat'l Bank, 84 Vt. 167, 78 A.

There must be a reason for a classification, and the law demands a substantial distinction between the objects placed in a class and those excluded.[2323] Thus, where savings banks enjoy particular advantages under the law, a statute drawn with reference to such advantages may be justified under the constitution as a reasonable classification.[2324] Similarly, a tax on money competing with national banks with certain exceptions has been held valid,[2325] and depositors in national banks and taxpayers under the general law have been held not to be in the same class.[2326] And an act providing for the taxation of shares of national banks, state banks, banking associations and trust companies, is not unconstitutional as violating the requirement of uniformity for excluding private banks, as the latter have no shares and would therefore be classified on a different basis.[2327] Also, a statute levying a tax on the stock and real estate of banks was held not void because it taxed banks more heavily than loan companies, finance and securities companies

---

944, 1912D Ann. Cas. 22; Magoun v. Illinois Trust & Sav. Bank, 170 U.S. 283, 18 S. Ct. 594, 42 L. Ed. 1037.

[2323] State v. Farmers & Mechanics Sav. Bank, 114 Minn. 95, 130 N.W. 445, 861, rev'd on other grounds, 232 U.S. 516, 34 S. Ct. 354, 58 L. Ed. 706.

The very nature and functions of banking and money-loaning organizations are so different from those of ordinary individual, partnership and business corporations that they may be put in a separate class for taxation providing the effect of such classification does not violate the constitution. Brophy v. Powell, 58 Ariz. 543, 121 P.2d 647.

A state tax law that discriminates in favor of a certain class is not arbitrary if the discrimination is founded upon a reasonable distinction or difference in state policy. Bank of Texas v. Childs, 615 S.W.2d 810 (Tex. Civ. App. 1981).

If a state decides to give more favorable tax treatment to shareholders in a corporation that pays franchise taxes than to shareholders in corporations that do not pay such taxes, such a classification may not be regarded as arbitrary or unreasonable, and the constitutional principle of equality is not offended. Bank of Texas v. Childs, 615 S.W.2d 810 (Tex. Civ. App. 1981).

[2324] State v. Farmers & Mechanics Sav. Bank, 114 Minn. 95, 130 N.W. 445, 851, rev'd on other grounds, 232 U.S. 516, 34 S. Ct. 354, 58 L. Ed. 706.

[2325] People v. Goldfogle, 242 N.Y. 277, 151 N.E. 452.

Revenue statute taxing moneys and credits held not unconstitutional as conferring judicial discretion on taxing officer, though failing to prescribe definite rule for determining when capital competes with banking institutions. Bank of Miles City v. Custer County, 93 Mont. 291, 19 P.2d 885.

[2326] State v. Clement Nat'l Bank, 84 Vt. 167, 78 A. 944, 1912D Ann. Cas. 22.

[2327] Commercial Trust Co. v. Hudson County Board of Taxation, 86 N.J.L. 424, 92 A. 263, aff'd, 87 N.J.L. 179, 92 A. 799.

and the like,[2328] and a state statute taxing deposits in domestic banks at a lower rate than deposits in foreign banks, was held not violative of the constitution.[2329] And the classification of loan or investment companies with state and national banks for purposes of taxation does not infringe on a constitutional requirement that taxes be assessed and levied at a uniform and equal rate.[2330] On the same principle, stock in various classes of corporations may be differently assessed for taxes, in the discretion of the legislature.[2331] But a state law imposing a net income tax on banks and financial corporations but not on individuals, has been held unconstitutional.[2332] A tax scheme that levies against only one type of moneyed capital, bank stock, while not levying against any other moneyed capital in hands of individuals is illegal.[2333] The Tennessee statute imposing a tax on the net earnings of banks doing business in the state and defining net earnings as

---

2328 First Nat'l Bank v. Louisiana Tax Com., 289 U.S. 60, 53 S. Ct. 511, 77 L. Ed. 1030, 87 A.L.R. 840.

2329 Commonwealth v. Maden, 265 Ky. 684, 97 S.W.2d 561, 107 A.L.R. 1379; Madden's Ex'r v. Commonwealth, 277 Ky. 343, 126 S.W.2d 463.

The Kentucky statute taxing deposits in Kentucky banks at rate of 10 cents per $100, as compared with rate of 50 cents per $100 on deposit. in banks outside the state, did not deny "equal protection of the laws" or "due process of law," since the classification is reasonable and related to differences in difficulty and expense of tax collection.

Madden v. Commonwealth of Kentucky, 309 U.S. 83, 60 S. Ct 406, 84 L. Ed. 590, 125 A.L.R. 1383.

2330 First Nat'l Bank v. Moon, 102 Kan. 334, 170 P. 33 (1918).

2331 Mechanics' Nat'l Bank v. Baker, 65 N.J.L. 113, 46 A. 588, aff'd, 65 N.J.L. 549, 48 A. 582; Magnolia Bank v. Board of Sup'rs, 111 Miss. 857, 72 So. 697, 3 A.L.R. 1365, writ of error dismissed, 248 U.S. 546, 39 S. Ct. 135, 63 L. Ed. 414.

2332 Aberdeen Sav. & Loan Ass'n v. Chase, 157 Wash. 351, 289 P. 536, 71 A.L.R. 232; United Diversified Securities Corp. v. Chase, 157 Wash. 699, 289 P. 554, rehearing denied, 290 P. 897; Bank of Fairfield v. Spokane County, 173 Wash. 145, 22 P.2d 646.

2333 **In general.—**

Childs v. Reunion Bank, 587 S.W.2d 466 (Tex. Civ. App. 1979).

Since bank shares form a class of stock that, for tax purposes, may reasonably be distinguished from other in tangible property, including other shares of stack, statutes which form a basis for imposition of a tax on bank shares are not violative of equal protection because no shares of other corporations are so taxed. Bank of Texas v. Childs, 615 S.W.2d 810 (Tex. Civ. App. 1981).

There was no evidence that the tax on bank shares assessed by Dallas County was illegal on the ground that the bank shares in question were taxed at a greater rate than other moneyed capital in the hands of individuals. Bank of Texas v. Childs, 615 S.W.2d 810 (Tex. Civ. App. 1981).

including interest received on obligations of the United States and its instrumentalities and obligations of other states, but not interest earned on obligations of Tennessee and its political subdivisions, discriminates in favor of securities issued by Tennessee and its political subdivisions and against federal obligations and, therefore, the Tennessee bank tax impermissibly discriminates against the federal government and those with whom it deals.[2334]

Effect of Unjustified Classification.—Unjustified differences in the classification of property by a county assessor, without accompanying disparity in tax consequences, do not exceed the statutory authority of a state to tax the realty of a national bank to the same extent, according to its value, as other realty.[2335] But where bank vault doors and counterlines were classified as improvements to realty by a county assessor, and fixtures of other taxpayers generally were improperly classified as personalty, and special

---

[2334] Memphis Bank & Trust Co. v. Garner, 459 U.S. 392, 103 S. Ct. 692, 74 L. Ed. 2d 562 (1983).

[2335] Simms v. County of Los Angeles, 35 Cal. 2d 303, 217 P.2d 936, cert. denied, 340 U.S. 891, 71 S. Ct. 207, 95 L. Ed. 646.

Assessment of plaintiffs' bank vault doors and counterlines by county assessor as improvements to realty, and improper assessment of similar articles owned by others as personalty, did not violate equal protection clause of federal Constitution and provision of state constitution requiring all laws of a general nature to have uniform operations, where no attendant inequality of tax burdens resulted. Simms v. Los Angeles County, 35 Cal. 2d 303, 217 P.2d 936, cert. denied, 340 U.S. 891, 71 S. Ct. 207, 95 L. Ed. 646.

Fact that if plaintiffs' bank vault doors and counterlines had been improperly classified as personalty by county assessor, as assessor improperly assessed fixtures generally, plaintiffs would have been exempt from general city and county taxation under statutes and constitution, did not show that plaintiffs, by assessment of bank vault doors and counterlines as improvements to realty, were subjected to taxes not imposed upon others of the same class, or were otherwise prejudiced by the misclassification, so as to entitle plaintiffs to have assessment on bank vault doors and counterlines invalidated. Simms v. County of Los Angeles, 35 Cal. 2d 303, 217 P.2d 936, cert. denied, 340 U.S. 891, 71 S. Ct. 207, 95 L. Ed. 646.

Plaintiff's bank vault doors and counterlines were taxable in city, county and special assessment district in which they were located, and plaintiff was required to apply to board of equalization for relief before bringing action to recover taxes paid under protest, and vault doors and counterlines were not "tax exempt" so as to relieve plaintiff of necessity of applying to board of equalization for relief before bringing action, because similar property of others bad been systematically misclassified as personalty and therefore relieved of burden of special assessment district taxes, which circumstance would ordinarily require that plaintiff also be excused from paying such taxes. Security-First Nat. Bank v. Los Angeles County, 35 Cal. 2d 319, 217 P.2d 946, cert. denied, 340 U.S. 891, 71 S. Ct. 207, 95 L. Ed. 646.

district taxes were levied only upon realty, the special district taxes were held invalid as being discriminatory.[2336]

Excise Tax.—The legislature may not impose an excise tax which is based on false and unjust principles or which exacts assessments that are grossly oppressive or contrary to common right or which does not show a proper proportion between the benefits received and the sum paid for the enjoyment of them.[2337] The constitutionality of an excise tax must be judged in relation to the nature of the entity on which it is imposed.[2338]

Classification According to Use or Function.—The use to which property is put may form a legitimate basis for classification.[2339] For example, although the object for which trust companies are organized may resemble in some ways that for which banks exist, these objects are not identical, and their differences permit legislative discretion in classifying them separately.[2340] Cooperative banks' right to equal protection is not violated because mutual banks are taxed differently from state-chartered commercial banks; mutual banks and commercial banks are different in their organizational structure and purposes and have been subject to different methods of taxation over 150 years, and the legislature could reasonably conclude that those differences warrant different tax treatment.[2341]

[2336] Simms v. County of Los Angeles, 35 Cal. 2d 303, 217 P.2d 936, cert. denied, 340 U.S. 891, 71 S. Ct. 207, 95 L. Ed. 646.

When trial court concluded that, with respect to special assessment district charges, county taxing authorities discriminated against plaintiffs by singling out plaintiffs' banking fixtures for assessment as improvements to realty and thereby subjected plaintiffs to special district taxes which were not levied upon like property of others similarly situated, trial court should have ordered actions to recover taxes paid under protest resubmitted to board of equalization for determination of value of plaintiffs' buildings without the included fixtures, retaining jurisdiction of parties and subject matter until appropriate judgment could finally be rendered in conformity with rulings of board. Simms v. Los Angeles County, 35 Cal. 2d 303, 217 P.2d 936, cert. denied, 340 U.S. 891, 71 S. Ct. 207, 95 L. Ed. 646.

[2337] Andover Sav. Bank v. Commissioner of Revenue, 387 Mass. 229, 439 N.E.2d 288 (1982).

[2338] Andover Sav. Bank v. Commissioner of Revenue, 387 Mass. 229, 439 N.E.2d 282 (1982).

[2339] Mechanics' Nat. Bank v. Baker, 65 N.J.L. 113, 46 A. 586, aff'd, 65 N.J.L. 549, 48 A. 582; State Board of Assessors v. State, 48 N.J.L. 146, 4 A. 578, 8 A. 724.

[2340] Mechanics' Nat'l Bank v. Baker, 65 N.J.L. 118, 46 A. 586, aff'd, 65 N.J.L. 549, 48 A. 582.

[2341] Andover Sav. Bank v. Commissioner of Revenue, 387 Mass. 229, 439 N.E.2d 282 (1982).

Domestic and Foreign Corporations as Subjects of Different Classes.—It is competent for a legislature to place domestic and foreign corporations in different classes for purposes of taxation.[2342]

Shares of Residents and Nonresidents as Subjects of Different Classes.—A difference in the method of assessment of shares of resident stockholders and nonresident stockholders may be justified by a difference in conditions; for such purposes, shares of residents and nonresidents may be placed in separate classes, and the laws and rules applicable to each class be general and uniform.[2343]

State Banks and National Banks as Subjects of Different Classes in General.—The fact that national banks and banks organized under the laws of a state transact a similar kind of business does not mean that they must be taxed according to the same plan.[2344] Since national banks are organized and exist by virtue of acts of Congress, and are instruments of the federal government designed to aid it in the administration of a branch of public service,[2345] the states cannot exercise control over them, except with the consent of Congress, express or implied, and the power of the states to tax national banks is derived from.[2346] Thus, national banks and state banks are subject to limitations and regulations of power which have no application to

---

[2342] Bacon v. Board of State Tax Comm'rs, 126 Mich. 22, 85 N.W. 307, 86 Am. St. R. 524, 60 L.R.A. 321.

[2343] Mechanics' Nat'l Bank v. Baker, 65 N.J.L. 118, 46 A. 586, aff'd, 65 N.J.L. 549, 48 A. 582.

[2344] Primghar State Bank v. Rerick, 96 Iowa 238, 64 N.W. 801.

But where national banks and savings banks in the District of Columbia engaged in both savings account and commercial banking business, administrative classification for gross earnings tax purposes of state banks as savings banks and national banks as not savings banks was invalid as not in harmony with taxing statute. Hamilton Nat. Bank v. District of Columbia, 156 F.2d 843; 176 F.2d 624, cert. denied, 338 U.S 891, 70 S. Ct. 241, 242, 94 L. Ed. 547, 548.

[2345] Davis v. Elmira Sav. Bank, 161 U.S. 275, 16 S. Ct. 502, 40 L Ed. 700; Primghar State Bank v. Rerick, 96 Iowa 238, 64 N.W. 801. See Chapter 15, § 1.

[2346] Farmers', etc., Nat. Bank v. Dearing, 91 U.S. 29, 23 L. Ed. 196; First Nat. Bank v. Albia, 86 Iowa 28, 52 N.W. 334; Primghar State Bank v. Rerick, 96 Iowa 238, 64 N.W. 801.

The general purpose of the 1969 Amendment revising the national bank taxation statute to permit states to tax national banks as state banks effective January 1, 1973, was to promote equality in state taxation of banks vis-à-vis national banks and banks vis-a-vis nonbank corporations. United States v. State Bd. of Equalization, 639 F.2d 458 (9th Cir. 1980), cert. denied sub nom. Crocker Nat'l Bank v. State Bd. of Equalization, 451 U.S. 1028, 101 S. Ct. 3019, 69 L. Ed. 24 398 (1981).

each other, and each constitutes a class of corporations which may be properly subjected to a plan of taxation different from that applied to the other.[2347] And unlawful discrimination by a state in its taxation of national banking associations is not shown merely because a few corporations, out of a class of several thousand which ordinarily bear the same or a heavier tax burden, may sustain a lighter tax than that imposed on national banking associations.[2348]

However, it has been held that national bank shares and state bank shares belong to the same class of moneyed capital.[2349] But a statute taxing shares of state banks competing with exempt national banks was held not unconstitutional as denying state banks the equal protection of the laws.[2350] And taxation of national bank shares was held not discriminatory on the

---

[2347] Primghar State Bank v. Rerick, 96 Iowa 238, 64 N.W. 801.

State banks constitute another class with distinct powers and privileges and subject to different restrictions, and may properly be subjected to a plan of taxation applicable only to that and similar classes. Primghar State Bank v. Rerick, 96 Iowa 238, 64 N.W. 801; Commonwealth v. Covington Nat. Bank, 7 Ky. L. Rptr. 41.

The various restrictions on the permitted methods of taxation by a state on national banking associations located within its limits are designed to prohibit only those systems of state taxation which discriminate in practical operation against national banking associations or their shareholders as a class so that taxation of other moneyed capital in the state, or shares of state bank at a different rate, or assessment by a different method is not objectionable, in absence of discrimination. Tradesmens Nat'l Bank v. Oklahoma Tax Com., 309 U.S. 560, 60 S. Ct. 688, 84 L. Ed. 947.

The scheme of taxation adopted by Oklahoma for taxing national banking associations located within its limits does not discriminate against such associations. Tradesmens Nat'l Bank v. Oklahoma Tax Com., 309 U.S. 560, 60 S. Ct. 688, 84 L. Ed. 947.

Failure to tax state-chartered mutual banks and federal savings and loan associations alike, in that deposits portion of excise tax is not applied to the federal institutions, does not violate equal protection right of state-chartered mutual institutions. Andover Sav. Bank v. Commissioner of Revenue, 387 Mass. 229, 439 N.E.2d 282 (1982).

[2348] Tradesmens Nat'l Bank v. Oklahoma Tax Com., 309 U.S. 560, 60 S. Ct. 688, 84 L. Ed. 947.

Income from state and local obligations was lawfully included as a net income for mutual thrift institutions tax purposes in 1971, and thus the similar inclusion of income derived from a taxpayer's federal obligations did not have a discriminatory effect. First Fed. Sav. & Loan Ass'n v. Commonwealth, 360 A.2d 773 (Pa. Commw. 1976).

[2349] State Bank v. Board, 91 Ala. 217, 8 So. 852; State ex rel. Bank of Eagle v. Leonardson, 51 Idaho 648, 9 P.2d 1028.

[2350] Union Bank & Trust Co. v. Phelps, 288 U.S. 181, 53 S. Ct. 321, 77 L Ed. 687, 88 A.L.R. 1438.

The inclusion of both state and national bank shares in same class for taxation purposes

ground that no provision is made for the taxation of shares of other corporations when they have a value in excess of the property owned and assessed to such corporations.[2351] Similarly, a state tax on national bank stock is not objectionable as creating an unjust discrimination although the property, not the capital stock, of other corporations is taxed.[2352] And a statute taxing moneys and credits was held not discriminatory on the theory that shares of bank stock are assessed and taxed on the basis of their book value.[2353] Nor is a national bank discriminated- against because of an exemption of state and municipal bonds from taxation, nor because sums invested in notes, and the like secured by real estate mortgages by the bank's competitors are not taxed.[2354] Finally, the question of whether a state tax on shares of stock of a national bank constitutes an unlawful discrimination is a mixed question of law and fact, and in determining such question, loans made by bank stockholders and officers as individual investors may be considered.[2355]

Where a federal statute gives a state the power to require national banks to pay a certain tax, the right to tax state banks for a similar purpose is dependent, under the New York constitution,[2356] upon the exercise of the power as to national banks.[2357]

---

would not operate to invalidate statute taxing shares of state banks which was inapplicable to shares of national bank stock because of conflict with federal statute, since shares of national and state banks are not essentially the same kind of property for tax purposes, notwithstanding attempt by state to subject them to like treatment. Cherokee State Bank v. Wallace, 202 Minn. 582, 279 N.W. 410.

The statute which imposes tax on every bank in state is not unconstitutional as violative of provision of state constitution that taxes shall be uniform on the same class of subjects or of equal protection clause of federal Constitution, notwithstanding possible inapplicability of statute to shares of stock in national banks in view of federal statute limiting power of state to tax shares of stock in national banks. Cherokee State Bank v. Wallace, 202 Minn. 582, 279 N.W. 410.

2351 Merchants' Nat'l Bank v. Dawson County, 93 Mont 310, 19 P.2d 892.

2352 First Nat'l Bank v. Louisiana Tax Com., 175 La. 119, 143 So. 23.

2353 Bank of Miles City v. Custer County, 93 Mont 291, 19 P.2d 885.

2354 South Broadway Nat. Bank v. Denver, 51 F.2d 703.

2355 Ward v. First Nat. Bank, 225 Ala. 10, 142 So. 93 (1932).

2356 Bank of Manhattan Co. v. Murphy, 267 App. Div. 456, 47 N.Y.S.2d 524, aff'd sub nom. In re Bank of Manhattan Co., 293 N.Y. 515, 58 N.E.2d 713.

The constitutional provision that, where the state has "power to tax" a federal corporation, there shall be no discrimination in taxation between such corporations and other corporations, means the power to levy the specified tax in question, and cannot be read so as to make the nondiscriminatory provision applicable where the state has "any power to tax." Bank of

Uniformity of Rate.—A state cannot tax a national bank at a greater rate than competing capital[2358] in the same taxing district,[2359] and a statute forbidding such taxation adds nothing to the force of the constitution making

---

Manhattan Co. v. Murphy, 267 App. Div. 456, 47 N.Y.S.2d 524, aff'd sub nom. In re Bank of Manhattan Co., 293 N.Y. 515, 58 N.E.2d 713.

[2357] **In general.—**

In re Bank of Manhattan Co., 293 N.Y. 515, 58 N.E.2d 713.

A state law which imposes upon state banks or their shareholders as a class a higher tax than it imposes upon national banks or their shareholders as a class, where state would have power to impose a tax without discrimination upon national banks and their shareholders as a class is violative of constitutional prohibition against discrimination. In re Bank of Manhattan Co., 293 N.Y. 515, 58 N.E.2d 713.

The constitutional prohibition against discrimination in taxation between state and federal corporations engaged in substantially similar business as applied to banks is designed to prohibit only those systems of state taxation which discriminate in a practical operation in favor of a national banking association or its shareholders as a class and applies only within field where state has power to tax federal corporations which exercise substantially similar functions. In re Bank of Manhattan Co., 293 N.Y. 515, 58 N.E.2d 713.

Real estate and franchise taxes.—

When congressional consent is given for the assessment by the state of real property owned by a national bank and the state acts thereon, then only may a tax be levied upon the real property of state banks, and like nondiscriminatory action applies to franchise and unemployment payroll taxes. Bank of Manhattan Co. v. Murphy, 267 App. Div. 456, 47 N.Y.S.2d 524, aff'd sub nom. In re Bank of Manhattan Co., 293 N.Y. 515, 58 N.E.2d 713.

Contributions to unemployment insurance.—

Where Congress permitted state four forms of taxation upon national banking associations, state could not impose upon state banks any other form of taxation, however onerous, which it saw fit to impose except that state could compel state banks falling within general class of employers to contribute to unemployment insurance fund. In re Bank of Manhattan Co., 293 N.Y. 515, 58 N.E.2d 713.

Illustrative case.—

Where Congress on August 10, 1939, authorized state to require national banks to make contributions to unemployment insurance fund under state law, and state did not require levy of such tax against national banks until January 1, 1940, collection of unemployment contributions from state banks between August 10, 1939, and January 1, 1940, was unauthorized as an unconstitutional discrimination against state banks in favor of national banks. In re Bank of Manhattan Co., 293 N.Y. 515, 58 N.E.2d 713.

[2358] Iowa-Des Moines Nat. Bank v. Bennett, 284 U.S. 239, 52 S. Ct. 133, 76 L. Ed. 265, rev'g Iowa Nat. Bank v. Stewart, 214 Iowa 1229, 232 N.W. 445.

[2359] Hoenig v. Huntington Nat. Bank, 59 F.2d 479, rev'g Commercial Nat. Bank v. Franklin County, 45 F.2d 213, cert. denied, 287 U.S. 648, 53 S. Ct 93, 77 L Ed. 560.

taxes proportionate to property value.[2360] However, a difference in tax rate on gross earnings as between savings banks and national and all other incorporated banks may constitute a valid classification for tax purposes.[2361] Where a constitution provides that the property of private corporations, associations and individuals shall be taxed at the same rate, whenever the legislature levies a tax on a type of property, all property of that type must be taxed at the same rate whether it belongs to an individual, an association or a private corporation.[2362]

Allowing Deductions in Certain Instances.—Taxpayers more heavily taxed under a general law may be allowed a deduction denied to those who take advantage of the opportunities afforded by a special act.[2363] The allowance of a deduction for the value of United States bonds from the property of private banks in assessing their shares is proper.[2364] But acts providing that private banks were not permitted to deduct exempt securities and other liabilities as were others have been held not discriminatory.[2365] And an act authorizing the deduction of public building fund bonds owned by a bank from the assessed valuation of its shareholder's stock is not repugnant to a state constitutional provision requiring that all taxes be uniform as to the same class of subjects.[2366]

A statute requiring state banks and permitting national banks to pay a guaranty assessment on their surplus which is then exempt from taxation, does not discriminate against national banks.[2367] And that a national bank, in the taxing of its shares, was allowed a deduction of the full assessed value of its entirely paid for realty, while another national bank was only allowed

---

[2360] People v. Old Second Nat. Bank, 347 Ill. 640, 180 N.E. 408.

[2361] Hamilton Nat. Bank v. District of Columbia, 156 F.2d 843, cert. denied, 338 U.S. 891, 70 S. Ct. 241, 242, 94 L. Ed. 547, 548.

[2362] State Auditor v. Jackson County, 65 Ala. 142; Maguire v. Board, 71 Ala. 401.

[2363] State v. Clement Nat'l Bank, 84 Vt. 167, 78 A. 944, 1912D Ann. Cas. 22.

[2364] Head v. Board of Review, 170 Iowa 300, 152 N.W. 600.

[2365] Mannings Bank v. Armstrong, 204 Iowa 512, 211 N.W. 485.

That corporate capital invested in secured credits cannot be deducted from assessed value of shares, does not constitute illegal discrimination against shareholder despite the fact that secured credits in the hands of individuals are exempted from taxation. State ex rel. Bank of Eagle v. Leonardson, 51 Idaho 646, 9 P.2d 1028.

[2366] Board of Equalization v. Exchange Nat. Bank, 104 Okla. 93, 230 P. 728.

[2367] Capital Nat. Bank v. Jackson, 162 Miss. 658, 139 So. 163, cert. denied, 288 U.S. 550, 52 S. Ct. 504, 76 L. Ed. 1286.

a deduction for its equity in realty, showed no discrimination.[2368] But, a state law which provides that in determining the taxable value of stock of national banks only the assessed value of real property owned by such a bank shall be deducted from its other assets, is invalid because the National Banking Act provides that the full cash value of such real property must be deductible.[2369] And a statute imposing a tax on national bank stock, but denying an exemption for credits secured by a lien on realty on which a specific tax has been paid, is invalid as discriminatory.[2370]

Permitting Election.—In some cases a law furnishes two methods and rates for taxing the stock of national banks; this system has been attacked for want of uniformity and equality. However, a Pennsylvania law has been upheld on the ground that to induce banks to make their returns to the auditor general and to pay their taxes into the state treasury, the state could offer some inducement by relieving from local taxation such banks as might elect to pay a certain rate on their shares directly into the state treasury, and since all banks may enter this class, banks by not doing so are themselves responsible for the existence of the second class.[2371]

§ 10. Double Taxation.

In General.—Double taxation has been defined as the "requirement that one person or known subject of taxation shall directly contribute twice to the same burden while other subjects, belonging to the same class, are required to contribute but once."[2372] It may be said that the authorities almost uniformly state the principle that, unless forbidden by constitutional provisions, double taxation does not render a tax void.[2373] However, an intent to impose taxation which is double even from an economic standpoint, is not to be ascribed to a legislature in the absence of a clear unambiguous expression.[2374] In some cases state constitutions forbid double taxation,[2375]

2368 Citizens' & Southern Nat'l Bank v. Atlanta, 53 F.2d 557.

2369 Dennis v. First Nat. Bank, 55 Mont. 448, 178 P. 580.

2370 First Nat. Bank v. Detroit, 253 Mich. 89, 234 N.W. 151.

2371 Commonwealth v. Merchants' & Mfrs' Nat'l Bank, 168 Pa. 309, 31 A. 1065, aff'd, 167 U.S. 461, 17 S. Ct. 829, 42 L. Ed. 236.

2372 Second Ward Sav. Bank v. Milwaukee, 94 Wis. 587, 69 N.W. 359; Strader v. Manville, 33 Ind. 111.

2373 Pacific Nat. Bank v. Pierce, 20 Wash. 675, 56 P. 936 (1899); State v. Branin, 23 N.J.L. 484.

2374 East Livermore v. Livermore Falls Trust & Banking Co., 103 Me. 418, 69 A. 306, 15 A.L.R. (n.s.) 952, 13 Ann. Cas. 631; First Nat'l Bank v. Douglas County, 124 Wis. 15,

while in other states no such prohibition exists and double taxation may exist. Thus, it is held that the stock of incorporated banks may be taxed in the hands of stockholders, although a bank pays a tax on its capital, if authorized by a legislature, even though it is a second tax on the same property.[2376] Finally, it is said that double taxation may, in its operation, be unequal, oppressive and unjust, but if so, the remedy is not with the courts unless the constitution forbids it, and if it does not, the wisdom and justice of the legislature and its relations with its constituents furnish the only security against unjust and excessive taxation as well as against unwise legislation in general.[2377]

Construction of Statutes.—Tax statutes are to be construed strictly against the state, and they are especially to be so construed to avoid double taxation unless their language, interpreted according to recognized principles of statutory interpretation, fairly compels a contrary construction.[2378] Thus, the intent to levy a double tax must plainly appear; it will not be assumed.[2379] And an act declaring that a tax on bank shares is in lieu of all other taxes on such shares or on any personal property owned by banks, does not allow double taxation.[2380] For other cases construing tax statutes and involving double taxation of banks and their stockholders, see the footnote.[2381]

---

102 N.W. 315, 4 Ann. Cas. 84; Board of County Comm'rs v. Citizens Nat'l Bank, 23 Minn. 280.

All presumptions are against such imposition. Tennessee v. Whitworth, 117 U.S. 139, 6 S. Ct. 649, 29 L. Ed. 833.

2375 Cleveland Trust Co. v. Lander, 62 Ohio St. 268, 56 N.E. 1038, aff'd, 184 U.S. 111, 22 S. Ct. 394, 46 L. Ed. 458.

2376 Fish v. Branin, 23 N.J.L. 484.

2377 Fish v. Branin, 23 N.J.L. 484; Providence Bank v. Billings, 29 U.S. (4 Pet.) 514, 7 L. Ed. 939; McCulloch v. Maryland, 17 U.S. (4 Wheat) 316, 4 L. Ed. 579; Salem Iron Factory Co. v. Danvers, 10 Mass. 514; Smith v. Burley, 9 N.H. 423.

2378 East Livermore v. Livermore Falls Trust & Banking Co., 103 Me. 418, 69 A. 306, 15 L.R.A. (n.s.) 952, 13 Ann. Cas. 631.

2379 Pacific Nat'l Bank v. Pierce County, 20 Wash. 675, 56 P. 936.

2380 Commercial Trust Co. v. Hudson County Board, 87 N.J.L. 179, 92 A. 799.

2381 Where a license tax has been imposed upon a private banker to be measured exclusively "on the capital," such tax constitutes a charge on the capital itself, and an additional assessment on "capital otherwise taxed," is unlawful. Commonwealth v. Hutzler, 124 Va. 138, 97 S.E. 775.

No reasonable difference exists between banks and other corporations with respect to the purpose of a statute granting domestic corporation a deduction of the value of shares of stock owned by it in other Nebraska corporation in computing the value of share for intangible tax

What Constitutes Double Taxation Generally.—The general rule seems to be that the fact that property assessed for taxes in some way represents an indebtedness which is also due to or by another person does not relieve it from the burden of taxation.[2382] The dispositive inquiry in cases involving alleged double taxation is whether the two taxes are determined by separate and distinct factors.[2383]

It has been said that the capital stock of a bank and its shares of capital are distinct, and both may be taxed; so also a bank's franchise, surplus earnings and real estate are distinct from its capital stock and from each other, and a state may tax a bank under each of these headings without being guilty of imposing double taxation.[2384] On the other hand, it has been said that the capital, deposits, surplus and undivided profits of a bank have no existence except in the form of tangible property, money, rights and credits which have

---

purposes which justifies double tax effect on stockholders of a bank and not on stockholders of other business corporations. First Nat'l Bank & Trust Co. v. County of Lancaster, 177 Neb. 390, 128 N.W.2d 820 (1964).

Unintended double taxation.—

The purpose of the provision of the 1969 temporary amendment to the national bank taxation statute governing, among other things, automatic imposition of certain specific taxes if the state did not already impose a tax or an increased rate of tax in lieu thereof was to prevent unintended double taxation of national banks. United States v. State Bd. of Equalization, 639 F.2d 458 (9th Cir. 1980), cert denied sub nom. Crocker Nat'l Bank v. State Bd. of Equalization, 451 U.S. 1028, 101 S. Ct. 3019, 69 L. Ed. 2d 398 (1981).

The built-up rate of the California franchise tax on national banks was not imposed in lieu of the sales tax on sales of tangible personal property to national banks, for the purpose of 1969 temporary amendment to the national bank taxation statute, and, hence, in the bridge period covered by the amendment, December 24, 1969 to January 1, 1973, the automatic imposition of the sales tax could not possibly result in unintended double taxation of national banks, in violation of the amendment. United States v. State Bd. of Equalization, 639 F.2d 458 (9th Cir. 1980), cert. denied sub nom. Crocker Nat'l Bank v. State Bd. of Equalization, 451 U.S. 1028, 101 S. Ct. 3019, 69 L. Ed. 2d 398 (1981).

[2382] Gerard v. Duncan, 84 Miss. 731, 36 So. 1034, 66 L.R.A. 461; Campbell v. Brinkop, 238 Mo. 298, 143 S.W. 444.

[2383] First Fin. Group of N.H., Inc. v. State, 430 A.2d 162 (N.H. 1981).

Holding company which issued stock in order to finance acquisition of subsidiaries may not complain of double taxation when that stock is included is its franchise tax base; franchise tax statute taxes each corporate existence upon the par value of its outstanding shares and surplus. Boatmen's Bancshares, Inc. v. Director of Revenue, 757 S.W.2d 574 (Mo. 1988).

[2384] Franklin County Court v. Deposit Bank, 87 Ky. 370, 9 S.W. 212, 10 Ky. L. Rptr. 506. See Bradley v. People, 71 U.S. (4 Wall.) 459, 18 L Ed. 433; National Bank v. Commonwealth, 76 U.S. (9 Wall.) 353, 19 L. Ed. 701.

no existence except in the property of the bank, so that to tax both the former and the latter is to tax the same property twice and is unlawful[2385] It also has been held that to tax a bank itself on its capital stock at full face value when the stock is represented in whole or part by real estate taxed separately, amounts to double taxation to the extent that the capital is so represented.[2386] On the other hand, the taxation of bank stock in the name of its holders at actual market value is not objectionable as providing for double taxation, though the bank's capital is largely represented by real estate which is also taxable.[2387] And a prohibition against deducting from the value of shares of stock of state banks or loan and investment companies, the value of real estate situated in a foreign state, does not result in double taxation.[2388] A tax on realty owned by an insolvent bank does not constitute "double taxation" prohibited by a state constitution.[2389]

A bank's shares of stock are the legal property of its stockholders, and although the value of the shares is founded upon and dependent upon the value of the bank's property, they are nevertheless a kind of property separate and distinct in character and ownership from the capital or property of the bank.[2390] However, it has been said that to tax the shares of a corporation to its shareholders, and at the same time to tax the property of the corporation to the corporation itself, imposes in effect, if not in theory, a double tax burden on the shareholders.[2391] And there are decided cases

---

[2385] Murray v. Board of Comm'rs, 67 Colo. 14, 185 P. 262.

[2386] Hempstead County v. Hempstead County Bank, 73 Ark. 515, 84 S.W. 715; Frederick County Com'rs v. Farmers, etc., Nat. Bank, 48 Md. 117; State v. Harris, 286 Mo. 262, 227 S.W. 818.

[2387] Jefferson County Sav. Bank v. Hewitt, 112 Ala. 546, 20 So. 926; Illinois Nat'l Bank v. Kinsella, 201 Ill. 31, 66 N.E. 338.

It is well settled that the ownership of land by a corporation is entirely separate from the ownership of shareholders of stock in the corporation. The former is realty, the latter is personalty, under all circumstances. Jefferson County Sav. Bank v. Hewitt, 112 Ala. 546, 20 So. 926.

[2388] First Nat'l Bank v. Moon, 102 Kan. 334, 170 P. 33 (1918).

[2389] Folk v. Heckler, 210 Ind. 68, 1 N.E.2d 124.

[2390] Second Ward Sav. Bank v. Milwaukee 94 Wis. 587, 69 N.W. 359; State Bank v. Milwaukee, 18 Wis. 281; Van Allen v. Assessors, 70 U.S. (3 Wall.) 573, 18 L. Ed. 229; Porter v. Rockford, etc., R. Co., 76 Ill. 561; Bank v. Tennessee, 161 U.S. 134, 16 S. Ct. 456, 40 L Ed. 645, modified, 163 U.S. 416, 16 S. Ct. 1113, 41 L. Ed. 211.

[2391] East Livermore v. Livermore Falls Trust & Banking Co., 103 Me. 418, 69 A. 306, 15 L.R.A. (n.s.) 962, 18 Ann. Cas. 631, citing Tennessee v. Whitworth, 117 U.S. 139, 6 S. Ct. 649, 29 L. Ed. 833; Cheshire County Tel. Co. v. State, 63 N.H. 167; Salem Iron Factory

including banks within the doctrine that a tax upon the shares and also upon the assets of a corporation constitutes double taxation.[2392] Similarly, it has been said that to tax individual shareholders on the shares of a bank, and at the same time to tax the shares owned by the bank in other banks, imposes to that extent an extra burden on the shareholders.[2393] And shares of national bank stock owned by a trust company and taxed to the company cannot be taxed again to the company's stockholders.[2394] The imposition of a tax on

---

Co. v. Danvers, 10 Mass. 514; Stroh v. Detroit, 131 Mich. 109, 90 N.W. 1029.

[2392] **In general.—**

Kentucky.—In Commonwealth v. Bank, 118 Ky. 547, 81 S.W. 679, 26 Ky. L. Rptr. 407, the state sought to impose a tax on the notes, bonds, stocks, etc., owned by the bank, the shares of which were also taxed to the shareholders. The court held such a tax could not be imposed, and seemed to assume that it was double and destructive taxation, citing another Kentucky case, Louisville, etc., Mail Co. v. Barbour, 88 Ky. 73, 9 S.W. 516, 10 Ky. L. Rptr. 836, where such a tax was directly held to be double taxation.

Maine.—East Livermore v. Livermore Falls Trust & Banking Co., 103 Me. 418, 69 A. 306, 15 L.R.A. (n.s.) 952, 13 Ann. Cas. 631.

Maryland—

In Frederick County Com'rs v. Farmers', etc., Nat. Bank, 48 Md. 117, it was held that to tax the property of a bank and its capital stock at the same time would be double taxation. The result would be the same whether the capital stock was taxed in solido to the bank or in shares to the shareholders.

Pennsylvania.—In School Directors v. Carlisle Bank (Pa.), 8 Watts 289, the bank owned, by purchase for investment, stock of the United States Bank of Pennsylvania. The shares of its own stock were taxable to the holders. The school directors sought to tax the bank for the shares of the United States bank stock it owned. The court held that the bank could not be taxed for them, and this clearly upon the ground that it would be double taxation which the legislature could not have intended to impose.

Wisconsin.—In First Nat'l Bank v. Douglas County, 124 Wis. 15, 102 N.W. 315, 4 Ann. Cas. 34, the bank recovered back a tax levied upon its real estate, the court assuming that it constituted double taxation not allowed by the statutes of Wisconsin.

Government bond, held by bank.—

In Cleveland Trust Co. v. Lander, 62 Ohio St 266, 56 N.E. 1036, aff'd, 184 U.S. 111, 22 S. Ct. 394, 46 L. Ed. 456, the shares of the bank were taxable to the shareholders. The bank in behalf of the shareholders sought to hay, the government bonds held by the bank deducted in fining the taxable value of the shares. The court held that the shares were to be taxed at their value no matter what investments the bank made.

[2393] East Livermore v. Livermore Falls Trust & Banking Co., 103 Me. 418, 69 A. 306, 15 L.R.A. (n.s.) 952, 13 Ann. Cas. 631.

[2394] Schuylkill Trust Co. v. Pennsylvania, 296 U.S. 118, 56 S. Ct. 31, 80 L. Ed. 91; Commonwealth v. Schuykill Trust Co., 327 Pa. 127, 193 A. 638, aff'd, 302 U.S. 506, 58 S. Ct. 295, 82 L. Ed. 392; Commonwealth v. Union Trust Co., 345 Pa. 298, 27 A.2d 15 (1942).

the net income of national banks also precludes a state from levying an additional tax on shares of national bank stock on an ad valorem basis.[2395]

Curative Statutes as Imposing Double Taxation.—An act of a legislature which requires banks that have not paid a franchise tax under a prior act to be assessed on their stock for years subsequent to a certain date, is retroactive and invalid when applied to banks which paid the tax under the former act, since it imposes a double tax.[2396]

Prohibition Applies Only to Same State or Government.—The prohibition against double taxation applies only to taxation by the same state or government; the fact that property is taxable in a different form in another state does not render a domestic tax double taxation.[2397]

But taxation of the same property by different states is avoided by an act providing that an assessment shall render personal property taxable elsewhere immune from further taxation to the extent that its value has entered into such assessment.[2398]

Tax on Bank Deposits.—Deposits in a savings bank are not taxable to the bank and also to its depositors.[2399] Moreover, where depositors in a savings bank are taxable on their deposits, the bank is not liable to be taxed on national bank stock or city bonds in which it has invested moneys received on deposit.[2400] But the fact that mortgages held by a savings bank represent deposits, and its depositors are taxed, does not render taxation of the mortgages as real estate a double taxation within the prohibition of the constitution.[2401] And the purpose of a statute providing exemption from taxation of deposits belonging to any other financial institution is to prevent double taxation.[2402]

§ 11. Taxation According to Value.

In General.—The constitutions of the states generally provide that all property subject to taxation be taxed in proportion to its value; however,

---

2395 Board of Comm'rs v. State Board of Equalization, 155 Okla. 188, 8 P.2d 732.

2396 First Nat'l Bank v. Covington, 103 F. 523, appeal dismissed, 185 U.S. 270, 22 S. Ct. 645, 46 L Ed. 906; Covington v. First Nat. Bank, 198 U.S. 100, 25 S. Ct. 562, 49 L. Ed. 963.

2397 San Francisco v. Fry, 63 Cal. 470; Chesebrough v. San Francisco, 153 Cal. 559, 96 P. 288.

2398 People's Bank, etc., Co. v. Passaic County Board, 90 N.J.L. 171, 100 A. 155.

2399 Berry v. Windham, 59 N.H. 288, 47 Am. R. 202; Robinson v. Dover, 59 N.H. 521.

2400 Augusta Sav. Bank v. Augusta, 56 Me. 176.

2401 Common Council v. Board, 91 Mich. 78, 51 N.W. 787, 16 L.R.A. 59.

2402 Ohio Citizens Trust Co. v. Evatt, 146 Ohio St. 30, 63 N.E.2d 912.

perfect equality of taxation is impractical, and much must be left to legislatures as to methods of ascertaining and equalizing the value of property.[2403] But where a gross inequality provided by statute is clearly within the prohibition of the state's constitution, such statute will be declared inoperative.[2404] So where all property is required to be taxed in proportion to its value, property having a market value must be taxed at that value, and if bank stock is assessed at its full value while land is taxed at one half its value, there is a discrimination against holders of bank stock entitling them to enjoin collection of the tax.[2405] And it is not taxation in proportion to value if property owned by a bank or insurance company is taxed twice in different forms, while the same kind of property is taxed only once when held by an individual or manufacturing company.[2406]

Where a state board equalizes the assessment of a county by raising the applicable percentage to make it uniform with all property in different counties of the state, thereby raising the assessment of an individual taxpayer who has returned money in the bank for assessment at its full value, it is not a violation of a constitutional provision requiring all persons to pay a tax in

---

[2403] Blocklock v. Board (Mo.), 36 S.W. 1132; Ward v. Board of Equalization, 135 Mo. 309, 38 S.W. 648; HACKER v. HOWE, 72 Neb. 385, 101 N.W. 255; North Missouri R. Co. v. Maguire, 49 Mo. 490, 8 Am. R. 141, aff'd, 87 U.S. 46, 22 L. Ed. 287. See also § 10 of this chapter.

[2404] **In general.—**

Ward v. Board of Equalization, 135 Mo. 309, 36 S.W. 648; Blocklock v. Board (Mo.), 36 S.W. 1132.

Illustrative cases.—

Statute providing that certain bonds should be assessed for taxes at 10 per cent of market value is violative of constitution requiring property to be assessed at actual cash value. First Nat'l Bank v. Louisiana Tax Com., 175 La. 119, 143 So. 23.

Where bank having aggregate assets of approximately $12,000,000 paid to state bank commissioner, under 1935 statute, the same tax as did many other banks having aggregate assets of as much as $80,000,000, such tax, if it were assumed to be ad valorem tax on tangible property, did not conform to constitutional mandate that tangible property should be taxed in proportion to its value. Commercial Bank v. State, 121 Utah 576, 244 P.2d 364.

Where bank under 1935 statute paid charges to state bank commissioner in the amount of $3, 450 computed on the bank's aggregate assets of $11,828, 949.16 such charges, if treated as taxes on intangible property were not imposed in accordance with constitutional provision that tax on intangible property shall not exceed five mills on each dollar of taxation. Commercial Bank v. State, 121 Utah 576, 244 P.2d 364.

[2405] Porter v. Langley (Tex. Civ. App.), 155 S.W. 1042.

[2406] Campbell v. Brinkop, 238 Mo. 298, 143 S.W. 444.

proportion to the value of their property.[2407] A constitutional provision that all property subject to taxation shall be taxed according to its value is also complied with when the valuation of property is equalized with other property of the same kind in a county.[2408] And a state statute taxing the stock of foreign corporations using capital in competition with banks, based on the proportion of invested capital in the state, has been held not void as imposing a tax disproportionate to value.[2409] A state tax act which provides for taxation of bank stock does not violate a uniformity rule imposed by a constitution because it levies on the true value of property at a uniform rate in lieu of the variant rates prevailing in different taxing districts of the state, where such property has peculiarities which justify making it a class for assessment and taxation.[2410]

Method of Determining Value.—Under a constitution which provides for "a uniform and equal rate of assessment and taxation," and does not require a uniform method of valuation of property, but only "such regulations as shall secure a just valuation, for taxation of all property, both real and personal," the legislature must use its discretion as to the best method of securing a just valuation, and unless the method adopted is clearly inadequate to secure that result, it cannot be questioned.[2411]

§ 12. Miscellaneous Matters.

A statute providing that, in ascertaining the value of shares of a national bank for taxation, there shall be deducted the book value of all realty of the

---

[2407] HACKER v. HOWE, 72 Neb. 385, 101 N.W. 255.

Taxpayer failed to establish arbitrary or a systematic undervaluation of other properties compared to its bank property and failed to establish discriminatory assessment in violation of equal protection; taxpayer relied on preliminary appraisal of single property and did not introduce completed appraisals or evidence of actual market value of two special purpose properties. Empire State Bank v. Lyon County, 454 N.W.2d 616 (Minn. 1990).

[2408] Bank v. Hampton, 92 Ark. 492, 123 S.W. 753.

An increase in assessment of national bank stock as result of fiat increase by state tax commission in assessor's valuation of property in certain county, where valuation of bank property in other counties subject to same state levy was not increased by same rate of increase, was not unconstitutional under the constitution providing for a just valuation of all property for purpose of taxation. First Nat. Bank v. Patterson, 65 Colo. 166, 176 P. 498 (1917).

[2409] National Sav. & Loan Asso. v. Gillis, 35 F.2d 386, rev'd per stipulation, 282 U.S. 796, 51 S. Ct. 19, 75 L. Ed. 717.

[2410] Commercial Trust Co. v. Hudson County Board, 87 N.J.L. 179, 92 A. 799.

[2411] Whitney v. Ragsdale, 33 Ind. 107, 5 Am. R. 185.

bank which is assessed to the bank, does not violate a constitutional prohibition against the taxation of stock of a corporation when corporate property represented by such stock is within the state and has been taxed.[2412] And where a state constitution limits the rate of taxation in any one year, no tax having previously been imposed on national bank shares, an act imposing such a tax and declaring that it shall be operative during several preceding years as well as the current year, is in practical effect, levying within the current year a tax in excess of the rate prescribed by the constitution and is void.[2413]

The buyer's payment of the tax to the seller does not render the buyer's payment a tax paid to the state, so as to entitle the buyer to the tax credit.[2414]

A master-in-equity who issues a master's deed possesses no liability for payment of documentary stamp tax, and thus, there is no tax imposed on the judiciary in violation of the section of the South Carolina Constitution providing for separation of legislative, executive, and judicial powers of government.[2415]

III. LIABILITY OF BANKS AND THEIR PROPERTY TO TAXATION.

a. Banks Other than National Banks.

§ 13. In General.

Bank's Property Liable to State Taxation.—The property of a banking corporation is its franchise, capital invested, undivided surplus earnings and such other property, real or personal, as its charter authorizes it to have, and all of its property is liable to taxation as is the property of natural persons,[2416] unless it is otherwise provided in its charter,[2417] or is exempted

---

[2412] Miners Nat. Bank v. Silver Bow County (Mont.), 148 P.2d 538.

[2413] Maguire v. Board, 71 Ala. 401.

This question is distinguishable from what is known as escaped taxes. Such taxes have been properly levied and therefore the constitution does not prohibit the assessment and collection, which, it seems, may be provided for by retrospective legislation. Maguire v. Board, 71 Ala. 401.

[2414] Centerre Bank v. Director of Revenue, 744 S.W.2d 754 (Mo. 1988).

[2415] Loyola Fed. Sav. & Loan Men v. South Carolina Tax Comm'n, 417 S.E.2d 583 (S.C. 1992).

[2416] *United States.*—Gordon v. Appeal Tax Court, 44 U.S. (3 How.) 133, 11 L. Ed. 529; State Bank v. Knoop, 57 U.S. (16 How.) 369, 14 L. Ed. 977. See also, West River Bridge Co.

by statute,[2418] during the period of its existence as a bank and while transacting business as such.[2419] Some state statutes, however, providing for

---

v. Dix, 47 U.S. (6 How.) 507, 12 L. Ed. 535; McCulloch v. Maryland, 17 U.S. (4 Wheat.) 316, 4 L. Ed. 579; Weston v. Charleston, 27 U.S. (2 Pet.) 449, 7 L. Ed. 481; Philadelphia, etc., Steamship Co. v. Pennsylvania, 122 U.S. 326, 7 S. Ct. 1118, 30 L. Ed. 1200; Owensboro Nat'l Bank v. Owensboro, 173 U.S. 664, 19 S. Ct. 537, 43 L. Ed. 850; Farrington v. Tennessee, 95 U.S. 679, 24 L. Ed. 558; Bank of Hawaii v. Wilder, 8 F.2d 845, cert. denied, 270 U.S. 652, 46 S. Ct. 351, 70 L. Ed. 781.

California.—Main St. Sav. Bank & Trust Co. v. Hinton, 97 Cal. xvii, 32 P. 6.

Indiana.—See Lutz v. Arnold, 208 Ind. 480, 198 N.E. 840, 196 N.E. 702.

Louisiana.—In re New Orleans, etc., Banking Co., 4 La. Ann. 471.

Montana.—Daly Bank & Trust Co. v. Board of Comm'rs, 33 Mont. 101, 81 P. 950.

New York.—Bank v. Assessors (N.Y.), 25 Wend. 686; Van Nest v. Commissioners, 80 N.Y. 573.

Ohio.—Debolt v. Ohio Life Ins., etc., Co., 1 Ohio St 563, aff'd, 57 U.S. 416, 14 L. Ed. 997.

Pennsylvania.—Iron City Bank v. Pittsburgh, 37 Pa. 340.

South Carolina.—Dabney, etc., Co. v. Bank, 3 S.C. 124.

[2417] Dabney, etc., Co. v. Bank, 3 S. C. 124; Bank v. Commonwealth, 19 Pa. 144; Union, etc., Bank v. Memphis, 101 Tenn. 154, 46 S.W. 557; Farmers' Bank v. Henderson, 7 Ky. L. Rptr. 453.

[2418] **In general.—**

Farmers', etc., Nat. Bank v. Greene (Pa.), 1 Chest. Co. Rep. 129; Savings Bank v. Coleman, 135 N.Y. 231, 31 N.E. 1022.

Bank's nontaxable securities could not be taxed indirectly, by including value in assessed value of stock. Spokane & Eastern Trust Co. v. Spokane County, 153 Wash. 332, 280 P. 3.

The imposition of state sales tax on retailer of tangible personalty, sold to state bank, is not invalid as resulting in taxation of bank, contrary to state constitution and laws, as such tax is imposed only on retailer, not consumer. Western Lithograph Co. v. State Bd. of Equalization, 11 Cal. 2d 156, 78 P.2d 731, 117 A.L.R 838.

[2419] **In general.—**

Bank, becoming insolvent and being taken over by bank superintendent for liquidation, is no longer taxable as "bank." Federal Land Bank v. Yuma County, 42 Ariz. 45, 22 P.2d 405 (1933).

Illinois.—Ryan v. Gallatin, 14 Ill. 78.

Kentucky.—Bank v Commonwealth, 94 S.W. 620, 29 Ky. L. Rptr. 643, aff'd, 207 U.S. 258, 28 S. Ct. 82, 52 L. Ed. 197.

Maine.—Jones v. Winthrop Sav. Bank, 66 Me. 242.

New Hampshire.—Bartlett v. Carter, 59 N.H. 105.

New York—Oswego Bank v. Oswego Village (N.Y.), 12 Wend. 544; Metcalf v. Messenger (N.Y.), 46 Barb. 325; People v. Holland Trust Co., 139 App. Div. 353, 123 N.Y.S. 935.

the taxation of state and national banks and "other institutions of loan and discount," have been held to refer only to incorporated institutions,[2420] and not to apply to private unincorporated banks which are taxable under general law.[2421] Such statutes have, however, usually though not universally, been held to cover savings banks.[2422]

The definition of "bank" under the Internal Revenue Code[2423] provides that a substantial part of the taxpayer's business must consist of "making loans *and discounts*." The statute's use of the conjunctive "and" rather than the disjunctive "or" in this phrase indicates that "discounts" is a required element.[2424]

Who is Liable for Bank's Tax.—The assignees of a bank are bound, while the assets of such bank remain in their hands for administration, to discharge the taxes assessed upon it.[2425] Land owned by an insolvent bank in the hands of a statutory receiver was held taxable, as against the contention that tax was assessable only on the bank's shareholders' stock.[2426] And a conveyance tax statute was held applicable to a banking supervisor taking over an insolvent bank for liquidation.[2427] But a tax may be primarily against the

---

Vermont.—State v. Bradford Sav. Bank & Trust Co., 71 Vt. 234, 44 A. 349.

2420 Bowling Green v. Potter, 91 Ky. 66, 12 Ky. L. Rptr. 676, 14 S.W. 968, 10 L.R.A. 778; Commonwealth v. Fleming County Farmers' Bank, 39 S.W. 1041, 19 Ky. L. Rptr. 266; Collins v. First Industrial Bank, 85 Colo. 458, 276 P. 988.

2421 Bowling Green v. Potter, 91 Ky. 66, 12 Ky. L. Rptr. 678, 14 S.W. 968, 10 L.R.A. 778; State v German Sav. Bank, 103 Md. 196, 63 A. 481.

2422 Louisville Sav. Bank v. Commonwealth (Ky.), 14 B. Mon. 409; Los Angeles v. State Loan & Trust Co., 109 Cal. 396, 42 P. 149; Fidelity Sav. Bank v. State, 103 Md. 206, 63 A. 484.

2423 See 26 U.S.C.S. § 581: "For purposes of sections 582 and 584 [26 U.S.C.S. §§ 582 and 584], the term "bank" means a bank or trust company incorporated and doing business under the laws of the United States (including laws relating to the District of Columbia) or of any State, a substantial part of the business of which consists of receiving deposits and making loans and discounts, or of exercising fiduciary powers similar to those permitted to national banks under authority of the Comptroller of the Currency, and which is subject by law to supervision and examination by State, or Federal authority having supervision over banking institutions. Such term also means a domestic building and loan association."

See also 26 U.S.C.S. § 582 as to bad debts, losses, and gains with respect to securities held by financial institutions; and 26 U.S.C.S. § 584 regarding common trust funds.

2424 Moneygram Int'l v. Comm'r, 664 Fed. Appx. 386 (5th Cir. 2016).

2425 Ryan v. Gallatin, 14 Ill. 78.

2426 Federal Land Bank v. Yuma County, 42 Ariz. 45, 22 P.2d 405 (1933).

2427 Jenks v. State, 188 Wash. 472, 63 P.2d 369.

stockholders of a bank, and not against the bank as a corporation.[2428] And under a contract binding a transferee bank to pay such unknown claims against an insolvent bank as might be established during its period of receivership, the transferee was held not liable for taxes which could not have been duly established against the receiver.[2429]

Nature of Property Subject to Tax.—All the assets of a bank, including specie and balances in other banks must, if employed in any way whereby the bank obtains or reserves a percentage, premium, profit or consideration, be averaged for taxation; but specie unemployed, not on hand for sale and from which the bank derives no profit need not be returned to the assessor, and balances due from other banks, on which no interest, profit or consideration is reserved or received, also need not be so returned.[2430] And a bank holding stock of other corporations which it acquires in its business is assessable for taxes thereon, even though such corporations are located in the same state and their property is assessed and taxed therein.[2431] In some states, banks are taxable on their real estate, but are not taxable on their personal property, such personal property being deemed to be represented by shares of taxable capital stock, and there being nothing in the applicable statute to warrant double taxation.[2432] So also, in some states it is held that

---

[2428] Gibbons v. White, 47 Ariz. 180, 54 P.2d 555.

[2429] Gully v. First Nat. Bank, 81 F.2d 502, rev'd on other grounds, 299 U.S. 109, 57 S. Ct. 96, 81 L. Ed. 70.

Provision in contract that assignors of bank stock should be held harmless from statutory liability as shareholders, held not to impose liability upon transferee bank for back taxes of insolvent bank. Gully v. First Nat. Bank, 81 F.2d 502, rev'd on other grounds, 299 U.S. 109, 57 S. Ct. 96, 81 L. Ed. 70.

[2430] Stark County Bank v. McGregor, 6 Ohio St. 45; London, etc., Bank v. Block, 136 F. 138.

[2431] **In general.—**

Pacific Nat'l Bank v. Pierce County, 20 Wash. 675, 56 P. 936.

Right to state to tax resident corporation on bank credit in sister state is not affected by possibility that latter state may compel payment of second tax. Bridgeport Projectile Co. v. Bridgeport, 92 Conn. 316, 102 A. 644.

[2432] American Bank v. Mumford, 4 R.I. 478; Lenawee Co. Sav. Bank v. Adrian, 66 Mich. 273, 33 N.W. 304; Marshall v. State Bank of Marshall, 60 Tex. Civ. App. 508, 127 S.W. 1083; Ficklen v. New Orleans, 85 So. 330, 147 La. 567; People v. Toluca State Bank, 327 Ill. 638, 159 N.E. 240; Montana Nat. Bank v. Yellowstone County, 78 Mont. 62, 252 P. 876.

Ad valorem personal property tax, rather than leasehold excise tax, applied to improvements constructed on public lands by private party which had leased such lands from

the legislature, in imposing a tax on the property of an incorporated state bank, may tax either its property or its shares, but if they materially differ in value, the tax must be on the shares.[2433] And in still other states, any particular real or personal property to which a bank holds title, is not subject to taxation except indirectly as its value appears in the value of its capital stock.[2434] But under a statute requiring bank stock to be assessed in the names of its holders at actual market value, with the taxes to be paid by the bank, and further providing that nothing therein shall exempt any property subject to taxation under other laws, a bank's real estate is taxable, even though the market value of its stock is based on the value of its real estate.[2435] For cases dealing with the taxation of banking fixtures[2436] and income of banks in various states,[2437] see the footnotes.

---

governmental entity, where plain language of the lease agreement stated that improvements were to remain property of lessee during the term of the lease and would not become property of lessor until expiration or earlier termination of the lease. Washington Mut. Sav. Bank v State Dep't of Revenue, 893 P.2d 654 (Wash. App. 1995).

Improvements on land leased from government do not "become property of the lessor," within the meaning of leasehold excise tax statute, merely by virtue of fact that they must be surrendered to lessor at expiration or termination of the lease. Washington Mut. Sav. Bank v. State Dep't of Revenue, 893 P.2d 654 (Wash. App. 1995).

Where lease of public property plainly states that improvements are property of lessee during term of the lease, leasehold excise tax does not apply, and improvements should be taxed as leasee's personal property. Washington Mut. Sav. Bank v. State Dep't of Revenue, 893 P.2d 654 (Wash. App. 1995).

[2433] Cleveland Trust Co. v. Lander, 62 Ohio St. 266, 56 N.E. 1036, aff'd, 184 U.S. 111, 22 S. Ct. 394, 46 L. Ed. 456.

[2434] Valley Nat. Bank v. Apache County, 57 Ariz. 459, 114 P.2d 883.

[2435] Jefferson County Sav. Bank v. Hewitt, 112 Ala. 546, 20 So. 926.

[2436] Where advertising sign and night depository were so annexed to the realty as to become fixtures which constituted realty for the purpose of taxation, sign and night depository were assessable and taxable as real property. Ventura County v. Channel Islands State Bank, 251 Cal. App. 2d 240, 59 Cal. Rptr. 404 (1967).

Where bank had right under lease to remove sign and night depository from leased premises, items were affixed for purpose of banking trade and the removal could be effected without substantial injury to the premises and property was likely to remain installed until worn out or replaced or bank moved, the property, for tax purposes, belonged to the bank rather than the landowner. Ventura County v. Channel Islands State Bank, 251 Cal. App. 2d 240, 59 Cal. Rptr. 404 (1967).

Cross-references.—

As to difference in classification of fixtures of banks and other businesses, see § 10 of this chapter; as to state taxation of fixtures of national banks, see § 26a of this chapter.

[2437] *Alaska.*—Interest received by banks on state housing authority and Housing Finance

"Doing Business" Concept.—A state law granting reciprocal privileges to banking associations and corporations of other states does not change the law of taxation, but relates merely to the doing of business.[2438] For other cases relating to the concept of "doing business" as applied to the taxation of banks other than national banks, see the footnote.[2439]

Corporation bonds must be included within bank's "net income" under statute providing that the "license fee for each national bank and state bank, trust company and savings and loan association is seven percent of its net income" in order to avoid any unlawful discrimination against federal securities. National Bank v. State, Dep't of Revenue, 642 P.2d 811 (Alaska 1982).

Inclusion of interest received by banks on bonds issued by state housing authority and Housing Finance Corporation as "net income" within meaning of statute governing computation and imposition of business license fee or tax on banks, and defining "net income" as including "all other income" does not conflict with statute exempting interest income earned on state housing authority bonds from "taxes" or statute conferring certain tax exempt status on Housing Finance Corporation bonds, and therefore general specific rule of statutory construction was inapplicable and thus did not prevent inclusion of interest on the bonds within the term "net income." National Bank v. State, Dep't of Revenue, 642 P.2d 811 (Alaska 1982).

Indiana.—Income tax act held not to limit tax on banks and trust companies to earnings derived from lending of money or credit only. Bankers Trust Co. v. Department of Treasury, 210 Ind. 530, 1 N.E.2d 935.

Oklahoma.—Proceeds received by bank from life policies on the life of bank's president were not properly taxable as "income," within meaning of Oklahoma income tax law. Security Bank of Ponca City v. Oklahoma Tax Com., 185 Okla. 481, 94 P.2d 552.

As to classification under Oklahoma statute, see Board of County Comm'rs v. Remedial Finance Corp., 186 Okla. 648, 100 P.2d 240.

2438 Harvard Trust Co. v. Commissioner of Corps. & Taxation, 284 Mass. 225, 187 N.E. 596.

2439 **"Doing business" within state.—**

Corporation organized to hold, manage, and liquidate assets of state savings and loan association which were unacceptable for transfer to federal savings and loan association upon conversion to federal association and which managed part of assets consisting of real estate and business enterprises, the management of which necessitated aggressive activity not required by mere passive holding and liquidation, was "doing business" in state as a financial institution subject to state excise tax and exempt from all other state, county, and municipal taxes except upon realty. Alpha Corp. v. Multnomah County, 182 Ore. 671, 189 P.2d 988.

Under Kentucky statutes concerning property subject to local taxation and the taxation of shares of national banks, legislature intended such statutes to apply to all banks doing business in the state created under laws of state or under acts of Congress. Land v. Kentucky Joint Stock Land Bank, 279 Ky. 645, 131 S.W.2d 838.

Miscellaneous Matters.—For cases dealing with federal taxation of banks other than national banks,[2440] taxation of industrial loan companies,[2441] and recording taxes as applied to state banks,[2442] see the footnotes.

§ 14. Franchises and Privileges.

Definitions and General Consideration.—A bank franchise or privilege, as property, is according to its value, liable to taxation for the support of the government.[2443] Thus, a round sum or an annual charge, with or without

---

[2440] See Farrington v. Tennessee, 95 U.S. 679, 24 L Ed. 558. As to tax on circulation of banks other than national, see National Bank v. United States, 101 U.S. 1, 25 L. Ed. 979; Veazie Bank v. Fenno, 75 U.S. (8 Wall.) 533, 19 L Ed. 482; Hollister v. Zion's Coop. Mercantile Inst., 111 U.S. 62, 4 S. Ct. 263, 28 L. Ed. 352. As to tax imposed by Internal Revenue Act of June 30, 1864, upon bankers doing business as brokers, see United States v. Cutting, 70 U.S. (3 Wall.) 441, 18 L. Ed. 241; United States v. Flak, 70 U.S. (3 Wall.) 445, 18 L Ed. 243; Warren v. Shook, 91 U.S. 704, 23 L Ed. 421; Richmond v. Blake, 132 U.S. 592, 10 S. Ct. 204, 33 L Ed. 481.

[2441] Modern Industrial Bank v. Graves, 260 App. Div. 349, 21 N.Y.S.2d 329, aff'd, 285 N.Y. 668, 34 N.E.2d 375.

[2442] Recording tax not applicable to state banks.—The 1953 Georgia statute imposing tax on long-term notes did not repeal the 1952 statute declaring the policy of state to be that taxation between state and national banks should be equalized, and accordingly national banks not being subject to the ad valorem recording tax on long-term notes, state banks were likewise not subject to recording tax. Washington Loan & Banking Co. v. Golucke, 212 Ga. 98, 90 S.E.2d 575.

[2443] **In general.—**

United States.—London, etc., Bank v. Block, 117 F. 900, rev'd on other grounds, 136 F. 138.

Bank excise tax, which included interest income earned on obligations of federal government, was franchise tax, rather than income tax, within meaning of federal statute allowing interest on federal obligations to be included as measure of nondiscriminatory corporate franchise tax. Cambridge State Bank v. Roemer, 457 N.W.2d 716 (Minn. 1990).

Alabama.—State v. Elba Bank, etc., Co., 18 Ala. App. 253, 91 So. 917, cert. denied, 207 Ala. 711, 91 So. 922.

Colorado.—A bank which was currently taxed under the general corporate tax law and which sustained a net operating loss in 1970 was entitled to carry back that loss to prior tax years, years when the bank was taxed under the so-called franchise tax law that had been repealed. Golden State Bank v. Dolan, 543 P.2d 1307 (Colo. App. 1975).

Delaware.—The Delaware bank franchise tax under Del. Code Ann. tit. 5, § 1101 has a two-fold structural apportionment mechanism: (1) A bank domiciled in Delaware would not be taxed on income attributable to United States Office of Thrift Supervision (OTS) authorized out-of-state branches or subsidiaries, to the extent that other states tax that portion of the income and (2) a bank not domiciled in Delaware would be taxed only on the income attributable to a Delaware branch or subsidiary. Under the 2006 amendment, a bank may

(Text continued on page 668)

---

choose to be taxed under the § 1101 method or under an alternative method established in Del. Code Ann. tit. 5, § 1101A. The alternative franchise tax is the sum of two components: (1) A tax on the entire net income that is apportioned to the state of Delaware and (2) a location benefit tax reflecting the value of utilizing Delaware's banking laws and bank system. The three factors used for apportionment are: (1) Property; (2) payroll and (3) receipts. Lehman Bros. Bank, FSB v. State Bank Comm'r, 937 A.2d 95, 2007 Del. LEXIS 496 (Del. 2007).

Department of the Treasury is removing chapter V of title 12, Code of Federal Regulations (CFR), which contains regulations of the former Office of Thrift Supervision (OTS). The OTS, a Bureau of the Department of the Treasury, was abolished effective October 19, 2011, and its rulemaking authority and operative rules were transferred to other agencies pursuant to the Dodd-Frank Wall Street Reform and Consumer Protection Act. Because those agencies have issued regulations that supersede chapter V, chapter V is no longer necessary. 82 FR 47083, 47084.

Florida.—Nonproperty excise tax on privilege of operating bank or savings association within the state was a nondiscriminatory franchise tax with exception to prohibition of state taxation of United States obligations where tax inclusion of all interest earned on federal, state and local debt obligations in the tax base for purpose of measuring the tax. Department of Revenue v. First Union Nat'l Bank, 513 So. 2d 114 (Fla. 1987).

Indiana.—Financial institutions tax, described as franchise tax measured by taxpayer's adjusted gross income or apportioned income for privilege of exercising its franchise or corporate privilege of transacting business of financial institution in state, was not direct tax on federal and municipal bond., but rather was excise tax on exercise of corporate privilege of operating as financial institution in state. Indiana Dep't of State Revenue v. Fort Wayne Nat'l Corp., 649 N.E.2d 109 (Ind. 1995).

Kentucky.—Providence Banking Co. v. Webster, 108 Ky. 527, 57 S.W. 14, 22 Ky. L. Rptr. 214; Middlesboro v. Coal, etc., Bank, 108 Ky. 680, 57 S.W. 497, 22 Ky. L. Rptr. 380.

Maine.—Jones v. Winthrop Sav. Bank, 66 Me. 242.

The state tax on trust and banking companies is not a "property tax," but "excise tax" on such companies' right to exercise privileges of their franchises, and is not laid on companies' property, deposits or business, but on value of their "franchises," that is, their capacity to transact business and enjoy privileges granted by their charter, and hence is lawful. Robinson v. Fidelity Trust Co., 140 Me. 302, 37 A.2d 273.

Maryland.—Baltimore v. Baltimore & O. R. Co. (Md.), 6 Gill. 288, 48 Am. Dec. 531.

Massachusetts.—Even though subject to state bank excise tax, interest paid by bank to generate income was subject to federal reduction of deduction for interest paid to generate income "exempt from taxes," and reduction of deduction had to be applied for purpose of calculating bank's state excise tax. Boston Safe Deposit & Trust Co. v. Commissioner of Revenue, 406 Mass. 195, 547 N.E.2d 909 (1989).

Missouri.—Bank tax imposed "for privilege of exercising its corporate franchise within the state according to and measured by its net income for the preceding year" was nondiscriminatory franchise tax which fell outside prohibition against taxing federal obligations or interests thereon. Centerre Bank v. Director of Revenue, 744 S.W.2d 754 (Mo. 1988).

(Text continued on page 668)

New York.—Newburgh Sav. Bank v. Peck, 22 Misc. 477, 50 N.Y.S. 820, aff'd, 32 App. Div. 624, 52 N.YS. 259; 157 N.Y. 51, 51 N.E. 412.

Legislature is permitted to impose franchise tax on privilege of doing business in state as corporate entity, regardless of whether entity shows net profit. Savings Bank v. New York State Tax Comm'n, 485 N.Y.S.2d 903 (N.Y.A.D. 4 Dep't 1985).

A former tax law imposed a franchise tax on banking corporations for the privilege of exercising a franchise or doing business in New York (former Tax Law § 1451(a)). Computation of the franchise tax was based upon either a percentage of a banking corporation's entire net income (ENI), its taxable assets, its alternative entire net income or a fixed dollar amount, whichever base resulted in imposition of the highest tax. For purposes of computing ENI, a banking corporation was allowed a deduction for its net operating losses (NOLs), which, with the exception of four statutory exceptions, were presumably the same as the federal NOL deduction allowed under 26 U.S.C.S. § 172. Matter of Toronto Dominion Holdings (U.S.A.), Inc. v Tax Appeals Trib. of The State of New York, 162 A.D.3d 1255; 77 N.Y.S.3d 800 (3d Dept. 2018).

Ohio.—Ohio corporate franchise tax is a true franchise tax for purposes of federal law barring taxation of obligations of United States government except in a nondiscriminatory franchise tax. Bank One Dayton, N.A. v. Limbach, 50 Ohio St. 3d 163, 553 N.E.2d 624 (1990).

Assets which are excluded in calculating franchise tax, such as stock and debts of public utility and insurance companies which are 80 percent owned by the corporate taxpayer, land devoted exclusively to agricultural use, pollution and energy conversion facilities, and property located in enterprise zones are not comparable to obligations of the federal government, so that inclusion of those obligations in the calculation does not render the franchise tax discriminatory with respect to the federal obligations and thus unlawful. Bank One Dayton v. Limbach, 50 Ohio St. 3d 163, 553 N.E.2d 624 (1990).

Fact that corporations other than financial institutions are charged lower rate on their franchise tax does not discriminate against federal obligations which are included in calculation of the tax of financial institutions in violation of the intergovernmental tax immunity doctrine. Bank One Dayton v. Limbach, 50 Ohio St. 3d 163, 553 N.E.2d 624 (1990).

Oregon.—Unlike state corporation income tax, state excise tax is tax on corporations that do business within state and is measured by net income as statutorily defined. Pacific First Fed. Sav. Bank v. Department of Revenue, 308 Or. 332, 779 P.2d 1033 (1989).

State excise tax assessed annually on corporations for privilege of carrying on or doing business in state is "franchise tax," and thus within exception to federal statute invalidating state and local taxes on federal obligations, even though tax is largely measured by corporation's net income. Pacific First Federal Sav. Bank v. Department of Revenue, 308 Or. 332, 779 P.2d 1033 (1989).

Corporation that carries on business within state must pay minimum state excise tax even though it does not generate net income. Pacific First Fed. Sav. Bank v. Department of Revenue, 308 Or. 332, 779 P.2d 1033 (1989).

Even if federal public debt statute except. only one state franchise tax from its prohibition

reference to a bank's capital stock, may be imposed by a legislature for a banking franchise.

Franchise tax is computed on the basis of the previous accounting period closing immediately prior to the accrual date, to be known as the measuring date.[2444] Therefore, the value of a corporation's "deferred income" for a given year is not affected by expenses incurred during any future accounting period.[2445] To determine the amount of capital that is to be included in the franchise-tax base under the statute, the book value of the accounts as regularly employed in conducting the affairs of the corporation shall be accepted as prima facie correct.[2446]

Payment of such a sum or charge constitutes a contract and is a limitation upon the power of the legislature imposing it, and upon succeeding

---

on state or local taxation of federal obligations, state corporation excise tax could be applied to interest earned on federal obligations, where second state franchise tax was based on amount of capital stock authorized in corporation's articles of incorporation, rather than on interest earned on federal obligations. Pacific First Federal Sav. Bank v. Department of Revenue, 308 Or. 332, 779 P.2d 1033 (1989).

South Carolina.—Dabney, etc., Co. v. Bank, 3 S.C. 124.

Tennessee.—State v. Lincoln Sav. Bank, 82 Tenn. 42; Union, etc., Bank v. Memphis, 101 Tenn. 154, 46 S.W. 557.

Utah.—The tax imposed by statute requiring banks or corporations annually to pay the state for privilege of exercising its corporate franchise, or doing business in state, based upon its net income allocated to the state, is not a "property tax" nor an "organization tax," but a "tax on the privilege of exercising the corporate franchise." American Inv. Corp. v. State Tax Comm'n, 101 Utah 189, 120 P.2d 331.

Vermont.—State v. Clement Nat'l Bank, 84 Vt. 167, 78 A. 944, 191W Ann. Cas. 22.

Industrial bank was subject to tax under statute providing for franchise tax on corporation based on net income rather than to lesser tax prescribed by statute imposing tax on banks and companies doing a banking business. Morris Plan Industrial Bank v. Graves, 23 N.Y.S.2d 312 (1940).

Trust company not exercising privilege of functioning as bank held not taxable as bank. Union Trust Co. v. Spokane County, 145 Wash. 193, 259 P. 9.

Right of state to tax resident corporations on bank credit. in sister state does not rest wholly on fiction that movables follow owner, but also on protection which state affords to corporate privileges and business. Bridgeport Projectile Co. v. Bridgeport, 92 Conn. 316, 102 A. 644.

[2444] Fishbelt Feeds, Inc. v. Miss. Dep't of Revenue, 158 So. 3d 984 (Miss. 2014). See Miss. Code Ann. § 27-13-17(1). [Repealed effective January 1, 2028].

[2445] Fishbelt Feeds, Inc. v. Miss. Dep't of Revenue, 158 So. 3d 984 (Miss. 2014).

[2446] Fishbelt Feeds, Inc. v. Miss. Dep't of Revenue, 158 So. 3d 984 (Miss. 2014).

legislatures, to impose any further tax upon the franchise.[2447] Statutes which provide for the taxation of the "privileges and franchises" of savings banks manifestly have no application to foreign savings banks,[2448] nor would a statute taxing banking corporations which do business in a state apply to a foreign corporation which does not do business in the state, and only has certain bonds and notes on deposit therein.[2449]

A bank and a bank holding company were not a "unitary business" for state privilege tax purposes; the bank and the holding company were subject to different types of taxes, different tax rates, and different measures of income.[2450] The interest paid by a bank holding company on a debt incurred in purchasing bank stock could not be allowed as a deduction from the bank's privilege tax.[2451]

Insolvent or Restricted Banks.—A bank which is voluntarily or otherwise restricted, but allowed to remain in the hands and under the management of its officers, and otherwise to exercise and enjoy its charter rights and

---

[2447] Gordon v. Appeal Tax Court, 44 U.S. (3 How.) 133, 11 L. Ed. 529; Provident Inst. v. Massachusetts, 73 U.S. (6 Wall.) 611, 18 L. Ed. 907; Society for Sav. v. Coite, 73 U.S. (6 Wall.) 594, 18 L Ed. 897, 904; Provident Inst. for Savings v. Commonwealth, 259 Mass. 124, 156 N.E. 36.

Annual franchise tax imposed on domestic corporations, based on net income which included income earned on stocks and obligations of the United States, did not violate supremacy or borrowing clauses of Federal Constitution, where corporation was not subject to franchise tax, regardless of amount of income, if it was dissolved, ceased operation, or withdrew from state during tax year. Savings League of Wisconsin, Ltd. v. Wisconsin Dep't of Revenue, 141 Wis. 2d 918, 416 N.W.2d 650 (1987).

Legislative purpose in enacting annual franchise tax on domestic corporations allegedly to reach and tax otherwise nontaxable federal income was irrelevant to constitutionality of tax so long as tax operated in constitutional way. Savings League of Wis., Ltd. v Wisconsin Dep't of Revenue, 141 Wis. 2d 918, 416 N.W.2d 650 (1987).

The annual franchise tax imposed on domestic corporations and measured by income was constitutional in that it measured tax on corporate franchise by entire net income, without any discrimination between exempt income and nonexempt income. Savings League of Wisconsin, Ltd. v. Wisconsin Dep't of Revenue, 141 Wis. 2d 918, 416 N.W.2d 650 (1987).

[2448] People ex rel. Savings Bank of New London v. Coleman, 136 N.Y. 231, 31 N.E. 1022.

[2449] United States Trust Co. v. Commonwealth, 245 Mass. 75, 139 N.E. 794.

[2450] First Nat'l Bank v. Kansas Dep't of Revenue, 13 Kan. App. 2d 706, 779 P.2d 457 (1989).

[2451] First Nat'l Bank v. Kansas Dep't of Revenue, 13 Kan. App. 2d 706, 779 P.2d 457 (1989).

privileges, is liable for a tax assessed on its franchise.[2452] But if a bank is placed in a receiver's hands, ousted from its properties and facilities, and deprived of its right or privilege to exercise its "franchise," neither the bank nor its receiver is liable for a corporate franchise tax assessed thereafter, as such rule also prevails where a bank is taken over by a state banking official without court proceedings.[2453] However, a bank may be "doing business," so as to be subject to a franchise tax, even after a conservator has been appointed, as against the contention that there is no difference between a conservator and a liquidator.[2454]

Merged or Converted Banks.—A New York statute providing that in the event of the merger of a state banking institution into a national bank, the resulting taxpayer shall be liable for the unpaid tax on the entire previous year's net income of the institution merged, means that for the purpose of such taxation, a "merger" is deemed to result when one such institution acquires substantially all the assets of another.[2455] For cases involving other

---

[2452] Robinson v. Fidelity Trust Co., 140 Me. 302, 37 A.2d 273, citing Commonwealth v. Barnstable Sav. Bank, 126 Mass. 526; Shippee v. Riverside Trust Co., 113 Conn. 661, 156 A. 43.

[2453] **In general.—**

Robinson v. Fidelity Trust Co., 140 Me. 302, 37 A.2d 273.

The appointment of conservator to liquidate insolvent trust company did not work dissolution thereof, but suspended company's functions and authority over its property and effects and deprived it of right and power to exercise privilege of doing business under franchise so that state excise tax subsequently assessed against company was invalid. Robinson v. Fidelity Trust Co., 140 Me. 302, 37 A.2d 273.

Effect of failure to file statutory certificate.—

Where bank ceased to do business and filed a certificate of election to dissolve and banking permit was canceled, its decision to wind up became irrevocable on distribution of assets to shareholders, and for practical purposes bank was "dissolved" and its dissolution was "effective" within statute relieving bank from liability for subsequent franchise taxes, notwithstanding failure to file statutory certificate of dissolution. Bank of Alameda County v. McColgan, 69 Cal. App. 2d 464, 159 P.2d 31.

[2454] People v. Richardson, 37 Cal. App. 2d 275, 99 P.2d 366.

That bank engaged in several normal banking activities while under conservator authorized finding that it was "doing business." People v. Richardson, 37 Cal. App. 2d 275, 99 P.2d 366.

[2455] Manufacturers Trust Co. v. Bates, 277 App. Div. 917, 98 N.Y.S.2d 535.

Evidence supported finding that transaction between petitioner, a state banking institution, and a national bank resulted in a merger which rendered petitioner, as resulting taxpayer, liable for corporate franchise tax based upon income earned by the national bank for the previous year. Manufacturers Trust Co. v. Bates, 277 App. Div. 917, 98 N.Y.S.2d 535.

state tax statutes as applied to the merger or conversion of a state bank into a national bank, see the footnote.[2456]

[2456] Under statutes, the 1965 bank tax liability of state bank which converted into national bank on December 24, 1964, was measured at rate of seven percent of net income from period December 25, 1964, to December 31, 1964, and not at rate of seven percent of its total net income for 1964. Mercantile Trust Co. Nat'l Ass'n v. Missouri State Tax Comm'n, 446 S.W.2d 751 (Mo. 1969).

The statutory scheme set forth in Article VII of the Tax Reform Code, 72 P.S. §§ 7701–7706, produces a tax advantage to a Pennsylvania institution which has merged with an out-of-state bank, while the surviving entity of the merger of two institutions has no such advantage, unless it has merged with an institution fewer than six years old. Leb. Valley Farmers Bank v. Commonwealth, 27 A.3d 288 (Pa. Commw. Ct. 2011), rev'd, Leb. Valley Farmers Bank v. Commonwealth, 623 Pa. 455, 83 A.3d 107 (2013) (holding that out-of-state bank is not an "institution" for purposes of the shares tax, and thus, is not subject to the tax).

(Article VII of the Tax Reform Code and all benefits associated with Article VII shall terminate on December 31, 2022, pursuant to 72 P.S. § 9979-C).

Once the averaging methodology of Article VII of the Tax Reform Code, 72 P.S. § 7701.1(a), is severed in limited circumstances, the institution resulting from merger/acquisition of an out-of-state bank must be treated as a new institution for purposes of calculating the taxable amount of shares. Accordingly, for purposes of the merger year, the taxable amount of shares shall be calculated pursuant to 72 P.S. § 7701.1(b) with no divisor or a divisor of one. The following tax year, the taxable amount of shares can be calculated using a divisor of two and so forth going forward, thereby following § 7701.1(a) and determining the taxable amount of shares based upon a historical average share value. Precluding use of a six year average share value in only certain circumstances will cure the Uniformity Clause, Pa. Const. art. VIII, § 1, violation without impairing the intended statutory purpose, as such procedure will yield a fair approximation of full share value for all institutions. In the case of merger of two institutions, one of which is fewer than six years old, the surviving institution can simply be treated as if it were the age of the younger merged partner. Leb. Valley Farmers Bank v. Commonwealth, 27 A.3d 288 (Pa. Commw. Ct. 2011), rev'd, Leb. Valley Farmers Bank v. Commonwealth, 623 Pa. 455, 83 A.3d 107 (2013) (holding that out-of-state bank is not an "institution" for purposes of the shares tax, and thus, is not subject to the tax).

(Article VII of the Tax Reform Code and all benefits associated with Article VII shall terminate on December 31, 2022, pursuant to 72 P.S. § 9979-C).

The averaging provision of 72 P.S. § 7701.1(a) of the Pennsylvania Shares Tax was not unconstitutional due to a lack of uniformity under Pa. Const. art. VIII, § 1 because the short-term disparity of result was warranted based on sufficiently distinguishable situations that warranted distinguishable results with respect to a merger or combination of two institutions that had both been previously taxed on their historic average values compared to a combination that introduced previously untaxable assets to the calculation. Leb. Valley Farmers Bank v. Commonwealth, 623 Pa. 455, 83 A.3d 107 (2013).

(Article VII of the Tax Reform Code and all benefits associated with Article VII shall terminate on December 31, 2022, pursuant to 72 P.S. § 9979-C).

Special Statutory Taxes.—A statute which provides for a special privilege tax measured by the gross profits or income of investment companies levies a privilege tax, and gross receipts are used solely to measure the tax, but the tax is not on gross receipts or profits.[2457] And a contract between a foreign parent corporation and its subsidiary investment corporation, wherein the parent is designated as an independent contractor while acting on behalf of the subsidiary does not preclude a state from showing that the parent is acting as the agent of the subsidiary in carrying on an investment business in the state, as respects whether the corporations are subject to the special privilege tax assessed against investment companies.[2458] The United States was held a "resident" of a state within a statute imposing a corporation license fee at a percentage of the total net income received by a corporation from all sources within the state, including interest on bonds, notes or other interest-bearing obligations of residents, and thus a bank corporation's net income on United States government bonds was from sources within the state and was held subject to tax.[2459] And the classification "financial corporation" in the California Bank and Corporation Franchise Tax Act was intended to comply with the federal statute prohibiting discrimination in taxation between national banks and other financial corporations, and refers to corporations dealing in "other moneyed capital" as that term is used in the federal statute.[2460]

[2457] Investors Syndicate of America, Inc. Vallen, 198 Tenn. 288, 279 S.W.2d 497.

[2458] Investors Syndicate of America, Inc. Vallen, 198 Tenn. 288, 279 S.W.2d 497.

[2459] Montana Bank v. Casey, 135 Mont. 104, 337 P.2d 935.

[2460] **In general.—**

Marble Mortg. Co. v. Franchise Tax Board, 241 Cal. App. 2d 26, 50 Cal. Rptr. 345 (1966). See 12 U.S.C.S. § 548.

As to corporations dealing in "other moneyed capital" within the meaning of the federal statute, see § 26c(2) of this chapter. In ascertaining whether company is "financial corporation," question to be considered is whether or not activities of corporations involved dealing in money or financing in competition with those activities of national banks, and competition with national banks may exist even though terms and conditions of business transactions are not identical. Marble Mortg. Co. v. Franchise Tax Board, 241 Cal. App. 2d 26, 50 Cal. Rptr. 345 (1966).

In determination whether corporation is "financial corporation" taxable at bank rate rather than at general corporation rate, focus is on competition among financial business for investment capital, and danger sought to be averted is that such capital might abandon national banks for other financial enterprises if latter were made relatively more profitable by preferential tax treatment; but ultimate attention is directed by relevant federal law to question of whether "other moneyed capital" employed in competition with business of national banks receives favored tax treatment, for it is primarily that capital which is

§ 15. Capital and Capital Stock.

Capital.—Banking capital attached to a banking franchise is property, owned by persons, corporate or natural, on which they are liable to be taxed as in the case of all other property, for support of the government,[2461] unless specifically exempted.[2462] The capital of a bank and the shares into which its capital stock is divided and held by individual shareholders are separate property, as respects the taxation of bank.[2463] Banking capital was formerly taxed by the federal government, but the law has been repealed.[2464] The public securities of the United States, whether held by corporations or individuals, are exempt from taxation by the states for any purpose; such immunity from state taxation not only exempt such securities from taxes levied directly on the holder of same, but even where such securities form a part of the capital stock of a bank, the rule is well established that a state cannot tax such capital stock without deducting such portion thereof as is made up of such public securities.[2465] The burden of proving the existence

---

attracted to or dissuaded from investment in national banks by relative profitability of other financial enterprises available for investment. Marble Mortgage Co. v. Franchise Tax Bd., 241 Cal. App. 2d 26, 50 Cal. Rptr. 345 (1966).

[2461] *United States.*—Gordon v. Appeal Tax Court, 44 U.S. (3 How.) 133, 11 L. Ed. 529; Canal, etc., Co. v. New Orleans, 99 U.S. 97, 25 L. Ed. 409.

Iowa.—Davenport Nat. Bank v. Board, 64 Iowa 140, 19 N.W. 889; Iowa State Sav. Bank v. Burlington, 98 Iowa 737, 61 N.W. 851.

Louisiana.—New Orleans v. People's Bank, 27 La. Ann. 646; New Orleans v. New Orleans Canal, etc., Co., 29 La. Ann. 851, aff'd, 99 U.S. 97, 25 L. Ed. 409.

New York.—Bank v. Assessors 25 Wend. 686, modified, 2 Hill 353; PEOPLE ex rel. BANK OF WATERTOWN, 1 Hill 616; BOARD OF SUPERVISORS OF NIAGARA v. PEOPLE ex rel. MCMASTER & HARVEY, 7 Hill 504; People ex rel. Van Nest v. Commissioners of Taxes & Assessments, 80 N.Y. 578; Metcalf v. Messenger, 46 Barb. 325.

Texas.—City Bank v. Bogel, 51 Tex. 355.

Wisconsin.—First Nat. Bank v. Douglas, 124 Wis. 15, 102 N.W. 315.

[2462] New Orleans v. People's Bank, 27 La. Ann. 646; New Orleans v. Citizens' Bank, 167 U.S. 371, 17 S. Ct. 905, 42 L. Ed. 202; New Orleans v. New Orleans Canal, etc., Co., 29 La. Ann. 851; Union, etc., Bank v. Memphis, 111 F. 561, rev'd, 189 U.S. 71, 23 S. Ct. 604, 47 L. Ed. 712; Bank v. Oxford, 70 Miss. 504, 12 So. 203; Trustees v. Deposit Bank, 75 Ky. (12 Bush) 538; Cleveland, etc., Coal v. O'Brien, 8 Ohio App. 247, aff'd, 98 Ohio St. 14, 120 N.E. 214.

[2463] First State Bank v. State Tax Comm., 40 N.M. 319, 59 P.2d 667.

[2464] Selden v. Equitable Trust Co., 94 U.S. 419, 24 L Ed. 249, distinguished in Richmond v. Blake, 132 U.S. 592, 10 S. Ct. 204, 33 L Ed. 481; Nevada Bank v. Sedgwick, 104 U.S. 111, 26 L Ed. 703.

[2465] *United States.*—Home Sav. Bank v. Des Moines, 205 U.S. 503, 27 S. Ct. 571, 51 L.

(Text continued on page 675)

Ed. 901. See New York v. Commissioners, 67 U.S. (2 Black) 620, 17 L. Ed. 451, 25 How. Pr. 9; Gordon v. Appeal Tax Court, 44 U.S. (3 How.) 133, 11 L. Ed. 529.

But see People v. Commissioners, 18 How. Pr. 245; Bank Tax Case, 69 U.S. (2 Wall.) 200, 17 L. Ed. 793; Provident Ins. v. Massachusetts, 73 U.S. (6 Wall.) 611, 18 L. Ed. 907; National Bank v. Commonwealth, 76 U.S. (9 Wall.) 353, 19 L Ed. 701; Palmer v. McMahon, 133 U.S. 660, 10 S. Ct. 324, 33 L. Ed. 772.

Florida.—Lewis State Bank v. Bridges, 115 Fla. 784, 156 So. 144.

Illinois.—Chicago v. Lunt, 52 Ill. 414.

Indiana.—Whitney v. Madison, 23 Ind. 331.

Iowa.—Ottumwa Sav. Bank v. Ottumwa, 95 Iowa 176, 63 N.W. 672; German-American Sav. Bank v. Burlington, 118 Iowa 84, 91 N.W. 829.

Missouri.—State v. Rogers, 79 Mo. 283.

Montana.—Statute taxing moneys and credits and moneyed capital held not invalid as taxing shares of state banking corporations solely because of their ownership of United States securities in violation of federal statute. if the sole or principle purpose of the statute is to tax indirectly securities of United States or income therefrom, it is invalid. Bank of Miles City v. Custer County, 93 Mont. 291, 19 P.2d 885.

New Jersey.—Newark City Bank v. Assessor of Fourth Ward, 30 N.J.L. 13.

Texas.—Provision that federal government obligations are exempt from taxation under state or local authority is not applicable to state tax on securities held by a bank, in absence of any computation based on the amount of such federal obligations or the interest on them. American Bank & Trust Co. v. Dallas County, 679 S.W.2d 566 (Tex. App. 5 Dist. 1984).

Federal statute providing that federal government obligations are exempt from taxation under state or local authority does not require a specific deduction for the proportionate value of the federal obligations held by bank in valuing the shares of bank stock for taxation so long as the method of assessment does not directly or indirectly involve any computation which takes federal obligations into account mathematically as a factor in determining the value. American Bank & Trust Co. v. Dallas County, 679 S.W.2d 566 (Tex. App. 5 Dist. 1984).

Method of assessment of bank shares, for purposes of state on tax securities held by the bank, by the "equity capital formula" which took into consideration value of bank's assets in computing the taxable value, was illegal to extent that it considered the value of government obligations held by bank along with bank's other assets in computing the tax. American Bank & Trust Co. v. Dallas County, 679 S.W.2d 566 (Tex. App. 5 Dist. 1984).

Tax assessor's formula for determining property taxes to be assessed on banks violated federal law in that it took into account, at least indirectly, federal obligations that constituted part of banks' assets, where assessor computed tax by determining total amount of capital assets of each bank and subtracting from that figure only bank's liabilities and assessed value of real estate owned by bank. Charles Schreiner Bank v. Kerrville Independent School Dist., 683 S.W.2d 468 (Tex. App. 4 Dist. 1984).

In enacting statute which exempts federal obligations from taxation under state or municipal or local authority, Congress intended to invalidate all taxes measured directly or indirectly by value of federal obligations, except those specified in that statute. Charles

of such investment is, however, on the bank.[2466] But as to state securities, it has been held that a tax on shares of bank stock is not a tax on the property of the bank, and hence shareholders are not entitled to deduct from the value of such shares the amount of capital stock of the bank which is invested in public building bonds and guaranty fund warrants.[2467]

Ordinarily, a corporation may only deduct its capital losses from its capital gains. The Internal Revenue Code, however, provides an exception for banks, which are permitted to deduct capital losses against ordinary income.[2468]

Capital Stock.—The capital stock of a bank is the money paid, authorized or required to be paid in as the basis of the business of the bank, and the means of conducting its operations, and such capital stock is subject to taxation as is other property,[2469] where there is no express exemption

---

Schreiner Bank v. Kerrville Indep. School Dist., 683 S.W.2d 466 (Tenn. App. 4 Dist., 1984).

[2466] Canal, etc., Co. v. New Orleans, 99 U.S. 97, 25 L Ed. 409.

[2467] Board of Equalization v. First State Bank, 77 Okla. 291, 188 P. 116.

Tax held charge against bank shareholders' stock, not bank's capital or assets. Federal Land Bank v. Yuma County, 42 Ariz. 45, 22 P.2d 405 (1933).

[2468] Moneygram Int'l v. Comm'r, 664 Fed. Appx. 386 (5th Cir. 2016).

[2469] **In general.—**

United States.—Farrington v. Tennessee, 95 U.S. 679, 24 L. Ed. 558; Owensboro Nat'l Bank v. Owensboro, 173 U.S. 664, 19 S. Ct. 537, 43 L. Ed. 850; Tennessee v. Whitworth, 117 U.S. 129, 6 S. Ct. 645, 29 L. Ed. 830; Providence Bank v. Billings, 29 U.S. (4 Pet.) 514, 7 L. Ed. 939; New York ex rel. Bank of Commerce v. Commissioners of Taxes, 67 U.S. (2 Black) 620, 17 L. Ed. 451, 25 How. Pr. 9; Nathan v. Louisiana, 49 U.S. (8 How.) 73, 12 L. Ed. 992; Ohio Life Ins., etc., Co. v. Debolt, 57 U.S. (16 How.) 416, 14 L. Ed. 997; National Bank v. Commonwealth, 76 U.S. (9 Wall.) 353, 19 L. Ed. 701; Bailey v. Clark, 88 U.S. (21 Wall.) 284, 22 L. Ed. 651.

Indiana.—State v. State Bank (Ind.), 6 Blackf. 349; State Bank v. Brackenridge (Ind.), 7 Blackf. 395.

Iowa.—Iowa State Sav. Bank v. Burlington, 98 Iowa 737, 61 N.W. 851.

Kansas.—First Nat'l Bank v. Moon, 102 Kan. 334, 170 P. 33 (1918).

Kentucky.—Louisville Sav. Bank v. Commonwealth (Ky.), 14 B. Mon. 409; Commonwealth v. Bank (Ky.), 9 B. Mon. 1; Shelby County Trust Co. v. Shelbyville, 91 Ky. 578, 16 S.W. 460, 13 Ky. L. Rptr. 150.

Louisiana.—State v. Citizens' Bank of Louisiana, 52 La. Ann. 1086, 27 So. 709, rev'd, Citizens' Bank v. Parker, 192 U.S. 73, 24 S. Ct. 181, 48 L. Ed. 346.

Maine.—State v. Waldo Bank, 20 Me. 470.

Mississippi.—District Attorney v. Simmons, 70 Miss. 485, 12 So. 477.

Montana.—Montana Nat. Bank v. Yellowstone County, 78 Mont. 62, 252 P. 876.

therefor.[2470] And where a bank allows the assets of an insolvent bank to be transferred to it in consideration of its assuming liabilities, it is liable for the

---

New Jersey.—Gordon v. New Brunswick Bank, 6 N.J.L. 100.

New York.—People v. Commissioners, 40 Barb. 334, rev'd, 26 N.Y. 163, 69 U.S. 200, 17 L. Ed. 793; People v. Olmsted, 45 Barb. 644.

Oklahoma.—Board of Equalization v. First State Bank, 77 Okla. 291, 188 P. 115.

Pennsylvania.—Iron City Bank v. Pittsburgh, 37 Pa. 340.

Tennessee.—State v. Nashville Sav. Bank, 84 Tenn. 111.

Virginia.—State Bank of Virginia v. Richmond, 79 Va. 113; Sussex County v. Jarratt, 129 Va. 672, 106 S.E. 384, 387.

Wisconsin.—State Bank v. Milwaukee, 18 Wis. 281; First Nat'l Bank v. Douglas County, 124 Wis. 15, 102 N.W. 315.

Matter of local concern.—

The assessment and taxation of shares of stock in a bank is a matter of local concern. Cook v. Citizens State Bank (Ky.), 304 S.W.2d 931.

Taxing personalty.—

Taxing shares of bank stock was in effect taxing bank's personalty. Home State Bank v. Whatcom County, 169 Wash. 486, 14 P.2d 21.

Insolvent bank.—

Where bank, after having all its capital stock assessed in its name, became insolvent, commissioner of banking in charge thereof could not avoid tax on ground individual stockholders had no property from which he might be reimbursed. Bergen County v. Englewood Title Guarantee, etc., Co., 14 N.J. Misc. 320, 184 A. 630.

Credit association loaning only to dairymen who were members of cooperative creamery, but who loaned on chattel mortgages, held engaged in business in competition with banks, and hence its capital stock was taxable. Intermountain Agric. Credit Ass'n v. Payette County, 54 Idaho 307, 31 P.2d 267.

[2470] **In general.—**

Georgia.—Cherokee Ins., etc., Co. v. Justices, 28 Ga. 121.

Indiana.—Connersville v. Bank, 16 Ind. 105.

Kentucky.—Lincoln County Court v. National Bank, 10 Ky. Op. 561, 8 Ky. L. Rptr. 139.

Montana.—State v. Mady, 83 Mont. 418, 272 P. 691.

New Hampshire.—Somersworth Sav. Bank v. Somersworth, 68 N.H. 402, 44 A. 534.

New York—National Bank v. Elmira, 53 N.Y. 49.

Pennsylvania.—In re McMullin's Estate, 272 Pa. 284, 116 A. 232.

Virginia.—West v. Newport News, 104 Va. 21, 51 S.E. 206.

"Capital" within statute providing that shares of bank's preferred stock and capital represented thereby shall not be assessed or taxed refers to the money contributed by the purchasers of preferred shares and reflected in bank's capital structure. National Bank v. Division of Tax Appeals, 2 N.J. 570, 67 A.2d 458, rev'g 1 N.J. Super. 286, 64 A.2d 240,

payment of the insolvent's capital stock taxes.[2471] A statute taxing the net income of banks has been held to repeal laws taxing shares of bank stock.[2472]

The Pennsylvania Shares Tax is imposed on the average taxable amount of a banking institution's shares of capital stock. Calculation of the tax is based on the book value of the bank's net assets (adjusted to deduct value attributable to United States obligations).[2473] The shares tax is not based on current assets, but on the average assets of the institution over the prior six years. The averaging provision is not an adjunct section applicable or inapplicable depending on the corporate history of the institution. To hold it applicable some of the time but not others is not appropriate, for it is the express statutory methodology of calculating the tax for every taxable institution. The "non-uniform" treatment arises from the combination provision, which treats the joinder of previously taxable institutions in such a manner as to prevent the dissipation of historically taxable assets. The averaging provision clearly applies to all institutions and does not speak at all to combinations. The combination provision in turn is silent on the methodology applicable to a combination of an institution and a non-institution; in that situation, it simply does not apply.[2474]

The Pennsylvania Shares Tax is only applicable post-merger if there is an "institution" to tax. When the merger or combination adds previously untaxed assets to the institution's value, the averaging calculation used by the Commonwealth treats the assets as previously non-existent. The assets, however, are new to the reach of Pennsylvania's tax. While these assets may have existed pre-merger, they were not subject to tax pre-merger. The Commonwealth thus benefits from such a merger, as the addition of taxable assets enriches the public coffers. Because the averaging provision is the method of calculating tax, the additional assets will not be immediately reflected dollar-for-dollar in the average taxable assets of the post-merger

---

aff'g National Bank v. Middlesex County Board of Taxation, 26 N.J. Misc. 249, 59 A.2d 270.

[2471] State ex rel. Wyatt v. Cantley, 325 Mo. 67, 26 S.W.2d 978; State v. Citizens' State Bank, 274 Mo. 60, 202 S.W. 382.

[2472] Board of Comm'rs v. State Board of Equalization, 155 Okla. 183, 8 P.2d 732.

[2473] Leb. Valley Farmers Bank v. Commonwealth, 623 Pa. 455, 83 A.3d 107 (2013). See 72 P.S. § 7701.1. (Article VII of the Tax Reform Code and all benefits associated with Article VII shall terminate on December 31, 2022, pursuant to 72 P.S. § 9979-C).

[2474] Leb. Valley Farmers Bank v. Commonwealth, 623 Pa. 455, 83 A.3d 107 (2013). See 72 P.S. § 7701.1(a). (Article VII of the Tax Reform Code and all benefits associated with Article VII shall terminate on December 31, 2022, pursuant to 72 P.S. § 9979-C).

institution. What is significant, however, is that the adding of assets to the reach of Pennsylvania's tax law is a tangibly different scenario than merging two previously taxed institutions. This in turn justifies the short-term disparity of result, for the situations are sufficiently distinguishable to warrant distinguishable results. The merger or combination of two institutions, both previously taxed on their historic average values, is a different scenario than a combination that introduces previously untaxable assets to the calculation. There is no unconstitutional disparity of treatment in this legislative scheme.[2475]

To prevent corporate maneuvering from creating a loss of revenue under the shares tax, when two institutions merge, the "combination provision" of the shares tax provides, in part, that the combination of two or more institutions into one shall be treated as if the constituent institutions had been a single institution in existence prior to as well as after the combination and the book values and deductions for United States obligations from the Reports of Condition of the constituent institutions shall be combined.[2476]

§ 16. Shares of Stock in Hands of Stockholders.

In General.—It is well established that shares of bank stock fall within the definition of property, and as such, may be taxed in the hands of shareholders.[2477] And an exemption from taxation of the capital of a banking

---

[2475] Leb. Valley Farmers Bank v. Commonwealth, 623 Pa. 455, 83 A.3d 107 (2013). See 72 P.S. §§ 7701-7706. (Article VII of the Tax Reform Code and all benefits associated with Article VII shall terminate on December 31, 2022, pursuant to 72 P.S. § 9979-C).

[2476] Leb. Valley Farmers Bank v. Commonwealth, 623 Pa. 455, 83 A.3d 107 (2013). See 72 P.S. § 7701.1. (Article VII of the Tax Reform Code and all benefits associated with Article VII shall terminate on December 31, 2022, pursuant to 72 P.S. § 9979-C).

[2477] **In general.—**

United States.—New Orleans v. Citizens' Bank, 167 U.S. 371, 17 S. Ct. 905, 42 L. Ed. 202; Bank v. Tennessee, 161 U.S. 134, 16 S. Ct. 456, 40 L. Ed. 645, modified, 163 U.S. 416, 16 S. Ct. 1113, 41 L. Ed. 211; Owensboro Nat'l Bank v. Owensboro, 173 U.S. 664, 19 S. Ct. 537, 43 L. Ed. 850; Home Sav. Bank v. Des Moines, 205 U.S. 503, 27 S. Ct. 571, 51 L. Ed. 901; Brown v. French, 80 F. 166; People's Sav. Bank v. Layman, 134 F. 635; Exchange Nat'l Bank v. Miller, 19 F. 372; Tennessee v. Whitworth, 117 U.S. 129, 6 S. Ct 645, 29 L. Ed. 830.

Alabama.—A bank stockholder is liable for ad valorem tax assessed against his bank stock, where subsequent to assessment bank failed without paying tax. And this applies where stock is owned by domestic life insurance company. Pratt v. State, 25 Ala. App. 258, 145 So. 163, cert. denied, 226 Ala. 14, 145 So. 165.

Arkansas.—Gates v. Bank of Commerce, etc., Co., 185 Ark. 502, 47 S.W.2d 806.

Connecticut.—Shippee v. Riverside Trust Co., 113 Conn. 661, 156 A. 43.

(Text continued on page 681)

Illinois.—Statutes relating to taxation of bank stock deal exclusively with bank stock and every type of bank within state is embraced thereby, the one intent being to assess and tax stockholders on shares of stock owned by them. People ex rel. Palmer v. National Life Ins. Co., 367 Ill. 35, 10 N.E.2d 398.

Indiana.—State v. State Bank (Ind.), 6 Blackf. 349.

Iowa.—Henkle v. Keota, 68 Iowa 334, 27 N.W. 250.

Massachusetts.—Revere v. Boston, 123 Mass. 375.

Missouri.—State v. Shryack, 179 Mo. 424, 78 S.W. 808.

Montana.—Daly Bank & Trust Co. v. Board of Comm'rs, 33 Mont. 101, 81 P. 950.

New Hampshire.—Tucker v. Aiken, 7 N.H. 113.

New Jersey.—Clinton Trust Co. v. State Board of Tax Appeals, 125 N.J.L. 275, 15 A.2d 605; Stratton v. Collins, 43 N.J.L. 562; Mechanics' Bank v. Thomas, 26 N.J.L. 181.

New Mexico.—Statutory provision that stockholders of every bank shall be assessed and taxed for value of their shares refers to all stockholders of banks and all shares of bank stock to extent of state's power or authority to tax such shares. First Nat. Bank v. State Tax Comm., 43 N.M. 307, 92 P.2d 987, appeal dismissed, 308 U.S. 515, 60 S. Ct. 173, 84 L. Ed. 439.

Ohio.—CLEVELAND TRUST CO. v. LANDER, 19 Ohio C.C. 271, 10 Ohio C. Dec. 452, aff'd, 62 Ohio St. 266, 56 N.E. 1036; 184 U.S. 111, 22 S. Ct. 394, 46 L. Ed. 456.

Pennsylvania.—Alleghany v. Shoenberger (Pa.) 1 Grant Can. 35.

Tax imposed by statute, purporting on its face to levy a tax on the property of the stockholders in a trust company, represented by the shares he owns, is a tax on the shares as such and not on the assets of the company. Schuylkill Trust Co. v. Pennsylvania, 302 U.S. 506, 58 S. Ct. 295, 82 L. Ed. 392 (1938).

Tennessee.—Union Bank v. State, 17 Tenn. 490.

Texas.—Harrison v. Vines, 46 Tex. 15.

Virginia.—Stockholders of Bank of Abingdon v. Washington County, 88 Va. 293, 13 S.E. 407; Union Bank of Richmond v. Richmond, 94 Va. 316, 26 S.E. 821.

Bank stockholder is entitled to protection of constitution, as respects right of state to tax his stock. First State Bank v. State Tax Comm., 40 N.M. 319, 59 P.2d 667.

Shares of bank stock are "intangibles," as respects taxation. First State Bank v. State Tax Comm'n, 40 N.M. 319, 59 P.2d 667.

The shares of a bank which discontinued business on May 29, 1931 were subject to assessment for that year on the basis of their value as of April 1, and as agent for its stockholders the bank was obligated for payment of the tax thereon when levied. Crosby v. First Nat'l Bank, 102 Colo. 43, 76 P.2d 734.

Amendment of statute relating to taxation of personal property used in business did not repeal statutes relating to taxation of bank stocks, but repealed only those parts which were inconsistent to extent of any inconsistency sections relating to bank stock remained in force and automatically applied to bank stock owned by domestic life insurance companies whenever such stock was excepted from operation of statute relating to business personal

(Text continued on page 681)

---

property. People ex rel. Palmer v. National Life Ins. Co., 367 Ill. 35, 10 N.E.2d 398.

Determination of tax.—

In determining tax on shares of trust company, formula, in which numerator consisted of capital paid in, surplus and undivided profit. determined by book values, less book value of investments for which fall deduction was made, and denominator consisted of book values of permanent investments, less book value of investments for which full deduction had been made, and multiplicand was book value of shares and securities which were to be apportioned, with result thus obtained increased or diminished by amount of appreciation or depreciation in shares and securities apportioned, was proper. Commonwealth v. Schuykill Trust Co., 327 Pa. 127, 193 A. 638, aff'd, 302 U.S. 506, 58 S. Ct. 295, 82 L. Ed. 392.

A trust company was not entitled to complain that in determining tax on shares state apportioned value of nontaxable securities between capital stock account and other assets in view of right of commonwealth to deduct entire value of nontaxable securities from capital stock account on proof by trust company that securities had been purchased out of such account or refuse to allow any deduction if trust company failed to establish that securities had been purchased out of capital stock account. Commonwealth v. Schuykill Trust Co., 327 Pa. 127, 193 A. 638, aff'd, 302 U.S. 506, 58 S. Ct. 295, 82 L. Ed. 392.

In determining tax on shares of a trust company, where some of the permanent investments of the company were in securities which were exempt in determining the tax base, and it could not be established whether such securities were purchased with the trust company's net assets or with deposits, the court in fixing the tax base properly applied the "apportionment formula" which ascertains the ratio which the net asset, bear to the total permanent investments and applies that ratio to the exempt securities. Commonwealth v. Union Trust Co., 345 Pa. 298, 27 A.2d 15 (1942).

Nondiscriminatory statute.—

Pennsylvania statute taxing shares of stock in trust companies, as construed by the state courts, as requiring federal securities, other than national bank shares, to be treated in the same manner as tax-exempt stock of state corporations in calculating the tax base, is not discriminatory. Schuylkill Trust Co. v. Pennsylvania, 302 U.S. 506, 58 S. Ct. 295, 82 L. Ed. 392 (1938), aff'g 327 Pa. 127, 193 A. 638.

See also Commonwealth v. Union Trust Co., 345 Pa. 298, 27 A.2d 15 (1942).

Statute does not discriminate against other federal securities, because of the fact that the shareholders of a trust company whose investments consist of national bank stock will pay no tax while these holding shares in a trust company which owns only other federal securities will not be entitled to a similar total exemption unless it can be shown that the securities were purchased from capital, surplus, and undivided profits. Schuylkill Trust Co. v. Pennsylvania, 302 U.S. 506, 58 S. Ct. 295, 82 L. Ed. 392 (1938).

The inability of a state to measure a tax on shares in trust companies by certain assets exempted by federal law does not preclude it from reckoning in the tax base all those it can reach. Schuylkill Trust Co. v. Pennsylvania, 302 U.S. 506, 58 S. Ct. 295, 82 L. Ed. 392 (1938).

Discriminatory statute.—

Statute authorizing tax on shares of capital stock of trust company, measure of which tax corporation does not, of necessity, exempt shareholders on their shares of bank stock,[2478] and such shares are taxable without reference to the securities on which their value is based.[2479] Hence, the fact that part of a bank's assets making up the value of its shares consists of nontaxable United States bonds does not entitle the bank to a deduction for such bonds.[2480] Bank share tax, insofar as it allowed shares of stockholders of banks or banking associations to be taxed at their fair market value on the basis of the net worth of the bank, without subtracting the value of federal securities owned by the bank, violated the federal statute exempting all federal

---

was to be determined by exclusion of securities already taxed or exempted from tax pursuant to state statutes, held invalid as discriminating against national bank shares owned by trust company which had already paid tax upon such shares, and as in effect imposing double taxation. Schuylkill Trust Co. v. Pennsylvania, 296 U.S. 113, 56 S. Ct. 31, 80 L. Ed. 91.

Such statute was also held invalid as discriminating against government securities and other securities entitled to tax exemption because issued by federal instrumentalities. Schuylkill Trust Co. v. Pennsylvania, 296 U.S. 113, 56 S. Ct. 31, 80 L. Ed. 91.

In taxing shares in domestic corporation which owns national bank shares, federal securities, tax exempt or already taxed shares, state must tax all shares or omit the national bank stock and federal securities, lest securities exempt by federal statute be discriminated against. Fidelity, etc., Fire Corp. v. Laser, 172 Md. 652, 193 A. 164.

2478 New Orleans v. Citizens' Bank, 167 U.S. 371, 17 S. Ct. 905, 42 L. Ed. 202; Owensboro Nat. Bank v. Owensboro, 173 U.S. 664, 19 S. Ct. 537, 43 L. Ed. 850; Bank v. Tennessee, 161 U.S. 134, 16 S. Ct. 456, 40 L. Ed. 645, modified, 163 U.S. 416, 16 S. Ct. 1113, 41 L. Ed. 211.

2479 Montana Nat. Bank v. Yellowstone County, 78 Mont. 62, 252 P. 876.

States may not levy taxes on United States securities, but may tax shares of stock in banks and other corporations whose assets consist wholly or partly of such securities as property of owners of such shares. Peter Kiewit Sons' Co. v. Douglas County, 161 Neb. 93, 72 N.W.2d 415.

2480 People's Sav. Bank v. Layman, 134 F. 635; Home Sav. Bank v. Des Moines, 205 U.S. 503, 27 S. Ct. 571, 51 L. Ed. 901; German-American Sav. Bank v. Burlington, 118 Iowa 84, 91 N.W. 829; National State Bank v. Burlington, 119 Iowa 696, 94 N.W. 234; First Nat. Bank v. Independence, 123 Iowa 482, 99 N.W. 142; People's Sav. Bank v. Des Moines (Iowa), 101 N.W. 887; CLEVELAND TRUST CO. v. LANDER, 19 Ohio C.C.R. 271, 10 Ohio Cir. Dec. 452, aff'd, 62 Ohio St. 266, 56 N.E. 1036; 184 U.S. 111, 22 S. Ct. 394, 46 L. Ed. 456. But see § 17 of this chapter.

A state, in taxing the property in the share, of a trust company, need not make any exemption or concession on account of the value therein reflected from the company's ownership of obligations of the government or its instrumentalities other than national bank stock. Schuylkill Trust Co. v. Pennsylvania, 302 U.S. 506, 58 S. Ct. 295, 82 L. Ed. 392 (1938), aff'g 327 Pa. 127, 193 A. 638.

See Tradesmens Bank, etc., Co. v. Cumberland County Board of Taxation, 20 N.J. Misc. 107, 25 A.2d 20.

obligations from state taxation.[2481] Bank share tax was computed by reducing bank's net worth by the percentage of the bank's assets held in the form of federal securities so as to remove from the tax base so much of its net worth as was represented by the federal securities, subtracting the total deductions from the net worth, leaving the taxable share value, and dividing the taxable share value by the number of offsetting shares.[2482] The capital stock of a banking corporation and the shares into which such stock is divided and held by individual shareholders being separate property,[2483] such capital stock and the shares of stock in the hands of shareholders may both be taxed without constituting double taxation.[2484] And a statute providing for the assessment of shares of bank stock does not permit "double taxation" of a bank's property, where under the statute the property of the bank itself is not directly subject to taxation.[2485] But in some jurisdictions, shares of stock in a bank whose property is required by law to be returned for taxation, are not taxable in the hands of shareholders.[2486] So also, the statutes of some states enable banks to exempt their shareholders from all other taxation by collecting a certain percentage upon the par value of all

---

[2481] Bartow County Bank v. Bartow County Bd. of Tax Assessors, 312 S.E.2d 102 (Ga. 1984).

[2482] Bartow County Bank v. Bartow County Bd. of Tax Assessors, 312 S.E.2d 102 (Ga. 1984).

Bank share tax had to be calculated by proportionate method of deduction, that is, determining extent to which federal obligations were represented in bank's assets, and then deducting exempt federal obligations to extent that they were represented in net worth, by which share tax is measured, since allowing deduction from bank's net worth of percentage of assets attributable to federal obligations fully insulates federal obligations from tax without insulating bank's taxable assets at the same time. Bartow County Bank v. Bartow County Bd. of Tax Assessors, 312 S.E.2d 102 (Ga. 1984).

[2483] Citizens', etc., Nat. Bank v. Atlanta, 53 F.2d 557; Bank of Commerce v. Tennessee, 161 U.S. 134, 16 S. Ct. 456, 40 L. Ed. 645, modified, 163 U.S. 416, 16 S. Ct 1113, 41 L Ed. 211.

See Owensboro Nat'l Bank v. Owensboro, 173 U.S. 664, 19 S. Ct. 537, 43 L. Ed. 850.

[2484] Bank of Commerce v. Tennessee, 161 U.S. 134, 16 S. Ct. 456, 40 L. Ed. 645, modified, 163 U.S. 416, 16 S. Ct. 1113, 41 L. Ed. 211. See also Owensboro Nat'l Bank v. Owensboro, 173 U.S. 664, 19 S. Ct. 537, 43 L. Ed. 850; Farrington v. Tennessee, 95 U.S. 679, 24 L. Ed. 558; Van Allen v. Assessors, 70 U.S. (8 Wall.) 573, 18 L. Ed. 229; People v. Commissioners, 71 U.S. (4 Wall.) 244, 18 L. Ed. 344; Union Bank v. Richmond, 94 Va. 316, 26 S.E. 821; People ex rel. Englis v. Feitner, 30 Misc. 215, 63 N.Y.S. 464.

[2485] Brophy v. Powell, 58 Ariz. 543, 121 P.2d 647.

[2486] Atlanta v. Bankers' Financing Co., 130 Ga. 534, 61 S.E. 122; Gillespie v. Gaston, 67 Tex. 599, 4 S.W. 248; Daly Bank & Trust Co. v. Board of Comm'rs, 33 Mont. 101, 81 P. 950; Western Inv. Banking Co. v. Murray, 6 Ariz. 215, 56 P. 728.

their shares and paying same into the state treasury.[2487] The Georgia statute imposing a property tax on the fair market value of the shares of bank stockholders, as construed by the Georgia supreme court, to allow the bank to deduct from net worth not the full value of the United States obligations it held but, rather, only a percentage of the fair obligations attributable to the assets, did not violate the revenue statute providing for an exemption from state or local taxation of obligations of the United States.[2488]

Statutes Requiring Payment of Tax by Bank.—It is clearly within the power of a state legislature to provide, as is done in a number of jurisdictions, that taxes assessed on shares of bank stock shall or may be paid by the banks,[2489] that they may recover from the owners of such shares the

---

[2487] Appeal of Truby, 96 Pa. 52.

[2488] First Nat'l Bank v. Bartow County Bd. of Tax Assessors, U.S., 105 S. Ct. 1516, 84 L Ed. 2d 535 (1985).

[2489] *United States.*—Citizens' Bank v. Board, 54 F. 73, rev'd on other grounds, 167 U.S. 371, 17 S. Ct. 905, 42 L Ed. 202; Brown v. French, 80 F. 166; Central Nat'l Bank v. United States, 137 U.S. 355, 11 S. Ct. 126, 34 L. Ed. 703; Stapylton v. Thaggard, 91 F. 93; Boston v. Beal, 51 F. 306, aff'd, 55 F. 26.

Florida.—Statute providing that stockholder shall not be taxed for stock, provided it is returned for taxation by corporation and taxes are paid by corporation, or corporate property is assessed where located and taxes are then paid on such property, held not mandatory, but to permit a bank, in its discretion, to return and pay taxes on its stocks in hands of its stockholders, as their agent, and to relieve stockholder in such event from paying the taxes. Lewis State Bank v. Bridges, 115 Fla. 784, 156 So. 144 (1934).

Where bank makes proper return of bank stock for assessment purposes, assessment could be made against bank as agent of stockholder; but where bank made no return of bank stock and did not pay tax, assessment could have been made against stockholder directly. Lewis State Bank v. Bridges, 115 Fla. 784, 156 So. 144.

City could not assess bank's stock directly against bank where bank failed to return it for taxation. Lewis State Bank v. Bridges, 115 Fla. 784, 156 So. 144.

Iowa.—State Exch. Bank v. Parkersburg, 112 Iowa 104, 83 N.W. 793.

Kansas.—Lyman v. First Nat. Bank, 6 Kan. App. 74, 49 P. 639, rev'd, 59 Kan. 410, 53 P. 125.

Kentucky.—Hager v. Citizens' Nat'l Bank, 127 Ky. 192, 105 S.W. 403, 32 Ky. L. Rptr. 95.

Michigan.—Muskegon v. Lange, 104 Mich. 19, 62 N.W. 158.

Missouri.—State v. Shryack, 179 Mo. 424, 78 S.W. 808; State v. First Nat. Bank, 180 Mo. 717, 79 S.W. 943; Stanberry v. Jordan, 145 Mo. 371, 46 S.W. 1093; Mahan v. Merchants' Bank, 160 Mo. 640, 61 S.W. 676; St. Louis Mut. Life Ins. Co. v. Charles, 47 Mo. 462.

Nebraska.—State ex rel. Breckenridge v. Fleming, 70 Neb. 523, 97 N.W. 1063.

New Mexico.—Tax on bank stock assessed against shareholder notwithstanding paid by

amounts so paid or deduct same from dividends accruing on such shares,[2490] and that such amounts are a lien on such shares which must be paid before a transfer thereof can be made.[2491] And a statute incorporating such provisions set up ample machinery for collection of the tax.[2492] Further, under a statute requiring banks to pay taxes assessed on their stock, and entitling them to deduct such taxes from dividends or to en force a statutory lien against the stock therefor, no resolution of a bank's board of directors is necessary to entitle it to pay taxes assessed on its stocks and deduct same

---

bank out of annual earnings. First State Bank v. State Tax Comm'n, 40 N.M. 319, 59 P.2d 667.

New York—National Copper Bank v. Wells, 58 Misc. 252, 110 N.Y.S. 829; Schaeffler v. Barker, 33 N.Y.S. 1042, 87 Hun. 194, aff'd, 148 N.Y. 731, 42 N.E. 725; Aetna Ins. Co. v. New York, 7 App. Div. 145, 40 N.Y.S. 120, aff'd, 153 N.Y. 331, 47 N.E. 593.

Ohio.—CLEVELAND TRUST CO. v. LANDER, 19 Ohio C.C.R. 271, 10 Ohio C. Dec. 452, aff'd, 62 Ohio St. 268, 56 N.E. 1036; 184 U.S. 111, 22 S. Ct. 394, 46 L. Ed. 456.

Tennessee.—Sloan v. Columbia, 144 Tenn. 197, 232 S.W. 663.

Virginia.—Union Bank v. Richmond, 94 Va. 316, 26 S.E. 821.

Washington.—Jefferson v. First Nat. Bank, 38 Wash. 255, 80 P. 449.

[2490] **In general.—**

State v. Shryack, 179 Mo. 424, 78 S.W. 808; Citizens' Bank v. Board, 54 F. 73, rev'd on other grounds, 167 U.S. 371, 17 S. Ct. 905, 42 L. Ed. 202; Klauss v. Citizens' Nat. Bank, 46 Ind. App. 683, 93 N.E. 558; Gracy v. Catron, 118 Mo. 280, 24 S.W. 439.

Under the Illinois statute bank stockholders, and not state bank, are primarily liable for tax on capital stock of bank. People v. Oak Park Trust, etc., Bank, 351 Ill. 334, 184 N.E. 643; People v. First Nat. Bank, 351 Ill. 435, 184 N.E. 645.

And the bank is not liable for taxes assessed on shares of its stockholders, in absence of failure to withhold taxes from dividends. People v. Amalgamated Trust, etc., Bank, 350 Ill. 549, 183 N.E. 601.

Under a statute assessing shares of stock and making it the duty of every bank and its managing officers to retain so much of any dividends belonging to stockholders as shall be necessary to pay taxes levied upon the shares, the liability is that of the stockholders and not the bank, and the bank is not primarily liable. Chicago Title, etc., Co. v. Central Trust Co., 312 Ill. 396, 144 N.E. 165.

[2491] **In general.—**

State v. Shryack, 179 Mo. 424, 78 S.W. 808; Schaffler v. Barker, 87 Hun. 194, 33 N.Y.S. 1042, aff'd, 148 N.Y. 731, 42 N.E. 725; Shainwald v. First Nat'l Bank, 18 Idaho 290, 109 P. 257.

The bank's lien may be foreclosed in the same manner as any other lien on property of like manner, even if the stock is owned by nonresident. Brophy v. Powell, 58 Ariz. 543, 121 P.2d 647.

[2492] Brophy v. Powell, 58 Ariz. 543, 121 P.2d 647.

from dividends.[2493] Where a statute constitutes a bank the agent of its shareholder for the purpose of tax payment, the reasonable implication is that in all matters regarding the tax, the bank stands in the shoes of its principal and has the authority to pay with or without protest, and bind its principal by such action.[2494] A state statute requiring banks to pay taxes assessed against their stockholders on their shares, and giving them a lien thereon for the amount advanced, is based on the theory that banks hold assets of their stockholders from which they can protect themselves; thus, payment of such taxes cannot be enforced against the receiver of an insolvent national bank, nor against its assets in his hands.[2495] So also, it has been held that a bank cannot be compelled to use its assets to pay a tax on certain shares of its stock where it cannot reimburse itself against its stockholder as provided by law.[2496] But in at least one jurisdiction, it has been held that under an act taxing banks on their shares of stock, such tax was payable out of the common funds of the banks.[2497] And where a state statute taxing bank stock requires banks to pay such taxes out of dividends on their stock, and a federal statute taxes all dividends declared by such banks, banks must return for taxation the part of such dividends paid for state taxes, and are taxable on the entire amount of such dividends.[2498]

Payment for Liquidated Bank.—A bank, the president and secretary of which acknowledged the receipt of assets of a liquidated bank and the assumption of its liabilities in communications to a state bank commissioner, was held estopped to deny its liability for payment of a tax levied on capital stock owned by stockholders of the liquidated bank prior to its dissolution.[2499]

[2493] Kennedy v. Citizens' Nat. Bank, 128 Iowa 561, 104 N.W. 1021.

[2494] Brophy v. Powell, 58 Ariz. 543, 121 P.2d 647.

[2495] Stapylton v. Thaggard, 91 F. 93; Boston v. Beal, 55 F. 26.

Statute permitting bank or loan and trust company to have stock assessed against it does not contemplate assessment against corporation's stock or assets. Ward County v. Baird, 55 ND. 670, 215 N.W. 163.

[2496] St. Johns Nat'l Bank v. Bingham Tp., 113 Mich. 203, 71 N.W. 588; Redhead v. Iowa Nat. Bank, 127 Iowa 572, 103 N.W. 796; Hershire v. First Nat. Bank, 35 Iowa 272; Farmers', etc., Nat. Bank v. Hoffmann, 93 Iowa 119, 61 N.W. 418.

[2497] Attorney General v. Bank, 21 N.C. 216; 40 N.C. 71.

[2498] Central Nat. Bank v. United States, 137 U.S. 355, 11 S. Ct. 126, 34 L. Ed. 703.

[2499] Crosby v. First Nat'l Bank, 102 Colo. 48, 76 P.2d 734.

Liability of liquidating bank was not dependent on issues relating to whether tax lien had attached to stock of liquidated bank in absence of attempt to enforce a lien for the tax on the specific property assessed. Crosby v. First Nat'l Bank, 102 Colo. 43, 76 P.2d 734.

§ 17. Dividends, Surplus and Undivided Profits.

Dividends.—A state may impose a tax on dividends declared by a bank,[2500] within the limits set by the charter of such bank.[2501] Where depositors in a savings bank did not receive a fixed rate of interest, but received a share of the net profits of the bank, such share was held a "dividend" within the meaning of the Internal Revenue Act of 1864, not "interest," and taxable thereunder.[2502] But until a dividend is declared out of a bank's surplus, its shareholders have no title to it the right and title thereto is in the bank.[2503] Where a bank had no earnings out of which dividends could be declared on its stock, and none were declared, a receiver of an insolvent bank was held not chargeable with taxes assessed against its shareholders.[2504]

Surplus and Undivided Profits.—It seems to be well established that surplus and undivided profits of a bank are subject to taxation.[2505] And a

---

When one by his voluntary act or by operation of law assumes or has imposed upon him a liability to pay a tax such as that on bank shares, he cannot escape the obligation on the theory that when the assumption was made or the duty imposed the amount of the tax not been ascertained. Crosby v. First Nat'l Bank, 102 Colo. 43, 76 P.2d 734.

2500 **In general.—**

State v. Commercial Bank, 7 Ohio 125; State v. Franklin Bank, 10 Ohio 91; State v. Farmers' Bank, 11 Ohio 94; Allegheny v. Shoenberger (Pa.), 1 Grant Cas. 35; In re Pennsylvania Bank Assignees' Account, 39 Pa. 103; State v. Tax Collector, 18 S.C. 654.

Property tax.—

A tax on dividends derived from corporate stock levied as on money in bank is a property tax. Waterman v. Lebanon, 78 N.H. 23, 96 A. 657.

Dividends disbursed by federal home loan bank to its stockholders were income to such federally chartered savings and loan associations and subject to taxation under State Income Tax Code. Sooner Fed. Sav. & Loan Ass'n v. Oklahoma Tax Comm'n, 662 P.2d 1366 (Okla. 1988).

2501 State v. Commercial Bank, 7 Ohio 125; Commonwealth v. Easton Bank, 10 Pa. 442.

2502 Cary v. Savings Union, 89 U.S. (22 Wall.) 38, 22 L. Ed. 779.

2503 State v. Bank, 95 Tenn. 221, 31 S.W. 993, modified, 161 U.S. 134, 16 S. Ct. 456, 40 L. Ed. 645; 163 U.S. 416, 16 S. Ct. 1113, 41 L. Ed. 211; Grenada Bank v. Adams, 87 Miss. 669, 40 So. 4; Pollard v. First Nat. Bank, 47 Kan. 406, 28 P. 202.

2504 State v. State Trust & Sav. Bank, 31 N.M. 282, 245 P. 253.

2505 **In general.—**

Iowa.—Iowa State Sav. Bank v. Burlington, 98 Iowa 737, 61 N.W. 851.

Kansas.—Pollard v. First Nat'l Bank, 47 Kan. 406, 28 P. 202; First Nat'l Bank v. Moon, 102 Kan. 334, 170 P. 33 (1918).

bank is liable for such a tax imposed upon it,[2506] provided it has been legally assessed.[2507] Moreover, surplus and undivided profits of a bank are not exempt from taxation under a charter exempting its capital stock from taxation.[2508] However, where the surplus of a bank, under its charter and the laws of its state, is held to belong to its depositors,[2509] or is a guaranty fund which the bank Is by statute required to keep and which cannot be used for dividends,[2510] it is exempt from taxation. And the only portion of the surplus capital of a bank subject to taxation is that not invested in taxpaying property or property exempt from taxation.[2511] But a corporation's money, as part of

---

Minnesota.—State v. Farmers', etc., Sav. Bank, 114 Minn. 95, 130 N.W. 445, rev'd on other grounds, 232 U.S. 516, 34 S. Ct. 354, 58 L. Ed. 706.

New Hampshire.—First Nat'l Bank v. Peterborough, 56 N.H. 38, 32 Am. R. 416; First Nat. Bank v. Concord, 59 N.H. 75; Petition of Union Five Cents Sav. Bank, 68 N.H. 384, 36 A. 17.

New Jersey.—State v. Utter, 34 N.J.L. 489.

New York.—People ex rel. Savings Bank of New London v. Coleman, 135 N.Y. 231, 31 N.E. 1022.

Tennessee.—State use of Memphis v. Bank of Commerce, 95 Tenn. 221, 31 S.W. 993, modified, 161 U.S. 134, 16 S. Ct. 456, 40 L. Ed. 645; 163 U.S. 416, 16 S. Ct. 1113, 41 L. Ed. 211.

Wisconsin.—State Bank v. Milwaukee, 18 Wis. 281.

Definition of undivided profits.—

For purpose of taxation the "undivided profits" of a state bank are profits not set aside as surplus or distributed in dividends. First Nat'l Bank v. Moon, 102 Kan. 334, 170 P. 33 (1918).

2506 State use of Memphis v. Bank of Commerce, 95 Tenn. 221, 31 S.W. 993, modified, 161 U.S. 134, 16 S. Ct. 456, 40 L. Ed. 645; 163 U.S. 416, 16 S. Ct. 1113, 41 L. Ed. 211; State v. President, Directors & Co. of Bank of Smyrna, 7 Del. (2 Houst.) 99, 73 Am. Dec. 699.

2507 State v. Bank, 95 Tenn. 221, 31 S.W. 993, modified, 161 U.S. 134, 16 S. Ct. 456, 40 L. Ed. 645; 163 U.S. 416, 16 S. Ct. 1113, 41 L. Ed. 211; State ex rel. Jacobs v. Assessor, 37 La. Ann. 850.

2508 State use of Memphis v. Bank of Commerce, 95 Tenn. 221, 31 S.W. 993, modified, 161 U.S. 134, 16 S. Ct. 456, 40 L. Ed. 645; 163 U.S. 416, 16 S. Ct. 1113, 41 L. Ed. 211.

2509 Groton Sav. Bank v. Barker, 154 N.Y. 122, 47 N.E. 1103; Newburgh Sav. Bank v. Peck, 22 Misc. 477, 50 N.Y.S. 820, aff'd, 32 App. Div. 624, 52 N.Y.S. 259, and 157 N.Y. 51, 51 N.E. 412; People v. Beers (N.Y.), 67 Row. P. 219; State v. Tunis, 23 N.J.L. 548; Mechanics' Sav. Bank v. Granger, 17 R.I. 77, 20 A. 202.

2510 Laconia Sav. Bank v. Laconia, 67 N.H. 324, 38 A. 384.

2511 Mechanicks' Nat'l Bank v. Concord, 68 N.H. 607, 44 A. 704; Beard v. People's Sav. Bank, 53 Ind. App. 186, 101 N.E. 325.

its moneyed capital, surplus and profits actually invested in its business, is not exempt from assessment merely because it is in a bank in another state.[2512]

§ 18. Deposits.

Former Federal Tax.—The United States formerly imposed a tax of one twenty-fourth of one percent per month on deposits made with any person or corporation engaged in banking, but the statute provided for such tax was repealed in 1883.[2513]

State Tax.—With regard to a state's taxation of deposits in banks, decisions vary in different jurisdictions. Thus, according to some authorities, moneys deposited in a bank by its customers become the property of the bank and are taxable as such,[2514] while according to others, bank deposits

---

[2512] In re Assessment of Chickasha Cotton Oil Co., 80 Okla. 101, 194 P. 215; In re Assessment of Chickasha Milling Co., 80 Okla. 102, 194 P. 217.

[2513] **In general.—**

Savings Bank v. Archbold, 104 U.S. 708, 26 L. Ed. 901; Bank for Sav. v. Collector, 70 U.S. (8 Wall.) 495, 18 L. Ed. 207; Oulton v. Savings Inst., 84 U.S. (17 Wall.) 109, 21 L. Ed. 618 (construction of statute).

State funds on deposit were taxable.—

Manhattan Co. v. Blake, 148 U.S. 412, 13 S. Ct. 640, 37 L. Ed. 504.

Deposits in savings banks.—

Savings Bank v. Archbold, 104 U.S. 708, 26 L. Ed. 901; Bank for Sav. v. Collector, 70 U.S. (8 Wall.) 495, 18 L. Ed. 207; Oulton v. Savings Inst., 84 U.S. (17 Wall.) 109, 21 L. Ed. 618.

Entry in depositor's passbook.—

Oulton v. Savings Inst., 84 U.S. (17 Wall.) 109, 21 L. Ed. 618.

Regulation limiting right to withdraw.—

Oulton v. Savings Inst., 84 U.S. (17 Wall.) 109, 21 L. Ed. 618.

[2514] **In general.—**

United States.—Spring Valley Water Co. v. City and County of San Francisco, 225 F. 728, aff'd 246 U.S. 391, 38 S. Ct. 356, 62 L. Ed. 790.

California.—Los Angeles v. State Loan, etc., Co., 109 Cal. 396, 42 P. 149. But see Yuba v. Adams & Co., 7 Cal. 35.

Massachusetts.—Commonwealth v. People's, etc., Sav. Bank, 87 Mass. (5 Allen) 428; Commonwealth by Board of Comm'rs v. Barnstable Sav. Bank, 126 Mass. 526; J. S. Lang Engineering Co. v. Commonwealth, 231 Mass. 367, 120 N.E. 843.

Missouri.—State v. Gehner, 320 Mo. 901, 9 S.W.2d 621, 59 A.L.R. 1041; State ex rel. Missouri State Life Ins. Co. v. Gehner, 320 Mo. 691, 8 S.W.2d 1068.

are taxable to depositors, not to banks.[2515] In some jurisdictions, a state tax

---

Nevada.—State v. Carson City Sav. Bank, 17 Nev. 146, 30 P. 703.

New Hampshire.—In re Union Five Cents Sav. Bank, 68 N.H. 384, 36 A. 17; Wyatt v. State Bd. of Equalization, 74 N.H. 552, 70 A. 387. But see In re Perry, 16 N.H. 44.

New Jersey.—Bridgewater v. Amerman, 37 N.J.L. 408.

Ohio.—The Ohio statutes make the financial institution the collector of the tax on deposits. So the tax is assessed in the name of the depositee and provision made for passing it on to the depositor. Thus it is the credit which is taxed and the creditor, that is, the depositor, is required ultimately to bear the burden. Merchants, etc., Fed. Sav., etc., Ass'n v. Evatt, 138 Ohio St. 457, 35 N.E.2d 831, 135 A.L.R. 1474.

Texas.—Under the statutes relating to taxation of cash, money on deposit in banks is subject to taxation, and fact that ordinary bank deposit creates relationship of debtor and creditor between bank and owner does not alter fact that for tax purposes, deposit is property and is taxable as such. Whelan v. State, 155 Tax. 14, 282 S.W.2d 878.

Vermont.—Montpelier Sav. Bank v. Montpelier Sav. Bank & Trust Co. v. Montpelier, 73 Vt. 364, 50 A. 1117; State v. Clement Nat'l Bank, 84 Vt. 187, 78 A. 944, 1912D Ann. Cas. 22; State v. Franklin County Sav. Bank & Trust Co., 74 Vt. 246, 52 A. 1069.

Bank deposits are "chosen in action" and "intangible property" for purposes of taxation. Hence, state ad valorem property tax on New York deposits of Delaware corporation whose tax sites was in Missouri held not void on ground there was no statute specifically providing for such taxes. Smith v. Ajax Pipe Line Co., 87 F.2d 567, cert. denied, 300 U.S. 677, 57 S. Ct. 670, 81 L. Ed. 882.

The tax is an "ad valorem property tax" on bank deposits as separate items of property, and as such cannot be considered as parts of manufacturing plants where goods are made and sold. People v. McGraw Elec. Co., 375 Ill. 241, 30 N.E.2d 903.

Bank in hand of receivers.—

Commonwealth by Commissioner of Sav. Banks v. Lancaster Sav. Bank, 123 Mass. 493; City Nat. Bank v. Baker Co., 180 Mass. 40, 61 N.E. 223.

A savings bank in the possession of a bank commissioner, held not liable to the tax imposed on deposits. Greenfield Sav. Bank v. Commonwealth, 211 Mass. 207, 97 N.E. 927.

A closed bank or loan association in charge of superintendent as liquidator is a "financial institution" within statute regarding taxation of deposits. Ohio Citizens Trust Co. v. Evatt, 146 Ohio St. 30, 63 N.E.2d 912.

[2515] **In general.—**

Colorado.—Murray v. Board of Comm'rs, 67 Colo. 14, 185 P. 262.

Connecticut—Savings Bank v. New London, 20 Conn. 111.

Indiana.—Beard v. People's Sav. Bank, 53 Ind. App. 185, 101 N.E. 325.

Iowa.—Branch v. Marengo, 43 Iowa 600.

Kansas.—Mitchell v. Comm'rs of Leavenworth Co., 9 Kan. 344.

Kentucky.—Commonwealth v. Bank, 118 Ky. 547, 81 S.W. 679, 26 Ky. L. Rptr. 407; Deposit Bank v. Daviess County, 102 Ky. 174, 39 S.W. 1030, 44 L.R.A. 825, aff'd, 173 U.S.

on a state bank of a percentage of the amount of its deposits is held to be a franchise tax, not a tax on property, and valid as such.[2516] And it has been held that a savings institution, having a portion of its deposits invested in federal securities declared by Congress to be exempt from taxation under state authority, is liable to tax on account of such deposits.[2517] But a tax assessed against the savings department of a bank, based on the amount of

---

663, 19 S. Ct. 875, 43 L. Ed. 850; Commonwealth v. Wathen, 126 Ky. 573, 104 S.W. 364, 31 Ky. L. Rptr. 980; Commonwealth v. Alford, 187 Ky. 106, 218 S.W. 721.

Nebraska.—Critchfield v. Nance County, 77 Neb. 807, 110 N.W. 538.

Ohio.—Exchange Bank of Columbus v. Hines, 3 Ohio St. 1. But see Ellis v. Linck, 2 Ohio St xlii.

Pennsylvania.—Tax on interest-bearing deposits in incorporated bank is imposed against depositor for county purposes rather than against bank for state purposes. In re Schuetz' Estate, 114 Pa. Super. 602; 174 A. 832, holding that repeal of tax did not prevent collection of tax accrued before repeal.

Texas.—Campbell v. Wiggins, 2 Tex. Civ. App. 1, 20 S.W. 730, aff'd, 85 Tex. 424, 21 S.W. 599; Campbell v. Riviere (Tex. Civ. App.), 22 S.W. 998; Victory v. State (Tex. Civ. App.), 134 S.W.2d 477, aff'd, 138 Tex. 285, 158 S.W.2d 760.

Under statute segregating bonds, notes and other evidences of indebtedness from deposits with any bank or firm doing banking business for taxation purposes, first class is made up of securities to which maxim noscitur a sociis applies, while second class deals with money held on demand. Commonwealth v. Stringfellow, 173 Va. 284, 4 S.E.2d 357.

Bank accounts of corporation kept in bank outside of state of corporation's domicile are taxable in state of domicile unless shown to be within exception to general rule that intangible personal property has situs of domicile of owner for tax purposes. Peter Kiewit Sons', Inc. v. Douglas County, 172 Neb. 710, 111 N.W.2d 734.

Sites of bank accounts, which were located in banks outside of Nebraska but belonged to corporation domiciled in Nebraska, was Nebraska for purposes of taxation, where all deposits and withdrawals were controlled by principal office of corporation in Nebraska. Peter Kiewit Sons', Inc. v. County of Douglas, 172 Neb. 710, 111 N.W.2d 734.

[2516] Provident Institution v. Massachusetts, 73 U.S. (6 Wall.) 611, 18 L. Ed. 907; Society for Sav. v. Coite, 73 U.S. (6 Wall.) 594, 18 L. Ed. 897; State v. Clement Nat'l Bank, 84 Vt. 167, 78 A. 944, 1912D Ann. Cas. 22.

State tax imposed on savings deposits in bank and trust company is a franchise tax, not property tax. Shippee v. Commercial Trust Co., 115 Conn. 313, 161 A. 781; Shippee v. Riverside Trust Co., 113 Conn. 661, 156 A. 43.

[2517] Provident Inst. v. Massachusetts, 73 U.S. (6 Wall.) 611, 18 L. Ed. 907. See also Bank v. Collector, 70 U.S. (3 Wall.) 495, 18 L. Ed. 207; Society for Sav. v. Coite, 73 U.S. (8 Wall.) 594, 18 L. Ed. 897, 914; Hamilton Co. v. Massachusetts, 73 U.S. (6 Wall.) 632, 18 L. Ed. 904; Snyder v. Bettman, 190 U.S. 249, 23 S. Ct. 803, 47 L. Ed. 1035.

Although a savings bank has invested a portion of its funds in United States securities, the tax imposed in Massachusetts may be assessed upon the whole average amount of its deposits, as therein provided, and may be collected in full. Commonwealth v. Provident Inst.

deposits in such department on the day Subsequent to the appointment of a temporary receiver taking possession of the bank's assets and administering its affairs, is invalid.[2518]

What Constitutes Deposit.—A "deposit," as used in a state statute imposing taxes thereon, includes not only general deposits but special deposits and deposits for specific purposes,[2519] and the term is intended to

---

for Sav., 94 Mass. (12 Allen) 312, aff'd, Provident Inst. v. Massachusetts, 73 U.S. (6 Wall.) 611, 18 L. Ed. 907.

[2518] Bassett v. Merchants' Trust Co., 115 Conn. 364, 161 A. 785.

[2519] **In general.—**

Second Federal Sav. & Loan Ass'n v. Evatt, 141 Ohio St. 616, 49 N.E.2d 756.

A savings deposit on hand for more than six months was held "money on deposit' so as to be subject to ad valorem tax. Hamilton Nat. Bank v. Chattanooga, 165 Tenn. 283, 54 S.W.2d 943.

Savings deposits invested in ground rents.—

State v. Central Sav. Bank, 67 Md. 290, 10 A. 290.

Certificates of deposit in banks in South Dakota and Minnesota are money subject to taxation. Knudtson v. Citizens' Nat. Bank, etc., Co., 62 S.D. 71, 251 N.W. 810.

A credit balance with a stock exchange broker being practically the same as a credit balance with a bank was taxable under statute imposing tax on deposits with any bank or firm doing banking business. Commonwealth v. Stringfellow, 173 Va. 284, 4 S.E.2d 357.

Contractor's interest with retained government lien held taxable.—

Where, to provide contractor with funds to perform contract, United States advanced payments not to exceed amount specified, and contractor was to deposit fluids in special bank account, and if United States terminated contract, contractor was required to repay remaining balance, and United States retained lien upon balance to secure repayment of advances, and withdrawals were subject to approval of contracting officer, title to funds was in contractor rather than in United States for purposes of ad valorem taxes by state subdivisions, and contractor's interest had taxable value. Timm Aircraft Corp. v. Byram, 34 Cal. 2d 632, 213 P.2d 715.

Loan transaction taxable.—

Where note is executed and delivered to a bank to obtain a loan and bank enters note on its books as an asset and sets up thereon in a counter entry a liability in amount of note but not in name of borrower with understanding that amount borrowed shall be paid out to third persons to accomplish purpose for which the loan was made, the liability so set up constitutes a taxable deposit even though loan is subject to cancellation on happening of a condition subsequent.

First Cent. Trust Co. v. Evatt, 145 Ohio St. 160, 60 N.E.2d 926.

Obligations created by certifying checks not deposits.—

Amounts set side by banks on the designated November tax day to redeem and satisfy banks' obligations created by certifying checks were not "deposits" within taxation statute,

be understood as it is in ordinary conversation and business transactions.[2520] And it has been held under such a statute that general deposits in out-of-state banks, withdrawable as such by a depositor domiciled in the state, and deposited but not segregated and designated by such depositor: (1) As taxes collected for federal and state governments; (2) as taxes on corporate dividends payable to aliens under provisions of the Internal Revenue Code; (3) as funds for payment of dividends to holders of record of preferred and common shares of the depositor declared as of a previous date but payable on a subsequent date and (4) as royalties due to owners of oil leases, are taxable by the state as deposits of such depositor.[2521]

The definition of "bank" in the Internal Revenue Code refers to deposits in the banking context, and for this purpose, "deposits" should have a narrower definition than its broadest possible meaning. The term "deposit" always has had a meaning of its own, peculiar to the banking business, and one that the courts should recognize and deal with according to commercial usage and understanding. The essential elements of a deposit include the following: (1) A deposit must involve the placement of funds with another for safekeeping and (2) those funds must be subject to the control of the depositor such that they are repayable on demand or at a fixed time.[2522] One of the chief functions of a bank is the receipt of deposits from the general public, repayable to the depositors on demand or at a fixed time. The term "deposit" signifies the act of placing money in the "custody" of a bank, to be withdrawn at the will of the depositor.[2523] It is an error to interpret "deposit" for purposes of defining a "bank" under the Code to include a requirement that a bank hold its customers' funds for extended periods of time.[2524]

---

and, therefore banks were not required to include such amounts in their report of taxable deposits or required to pay a tax thereon. First Nat. Bank v. Peck, 162 Ohio St. 64, 120 N.E.2d 725.

[2520] First Nat. Bank v. Peck, 162 Ohio St. 64, 120 N.E.2d 725.

[2521] Pure Oil Co. v. Peck, 162 Ohio St. 375, 123 N.E.2d 428, appeal dismissed, 349 U.S. 925, 75 S. Ct. 770, 99 L. Ed. 1257.

[2522] Moneygram Int'l v. Comm'r, 664 Fed. Appx. 386 (5th Cir. 2016).

[2523] Moneygram Int'l v. Comm'r, 664 Fed. Appx. 386 (5th Cir. 2016).

[2524] Moneygram Int'l v. Comm'r, 664 Fed. Appx. 386 (5th Cir. 2016).

§ 19. Loans, Investments and Securities.

As a general rule, banks may properly be taxed on notes, mortgages, stocks, and other securities or evidences of indebtedness held by them,[2525] and in some states such taxation is expressly required by the constitution.[2526]

[2525] *Florida.*—Mortgage recordings were subject to documentary stamp tax; legislature specifically added word "mortgages" into class of documents subject to documentary stamp tax and statute specifically recognizing mortgagee as class of instruments which could be conditioned or defeasible existed at time legislature added "mortgages" into class. Barnett Bank v. State Dep't of Revenue, 571 So. 2d 527 (Fla. App. 1990).

Promise to pay contained in credit agreement was part of face of recorded mortgages so that mortgages were subject to documentary stamp tax, and taxable amount was properly calculated based on maximum loan amounts mortgage document itself, as evidence of indebtedness, was being taxed so that recording of mortgage document triggered imposition of documentary stamp tax. Barnett Bank v. State Dep't of Revenue, 571 So. 2d 527 (Fla. App. 1990).

Illinois.—Bank v. Hamilton, 21 Ill. 53.

Iowa.—Farmers' Loan, etc., Co. v Newton, 97 Iowa 502, 66 N.W. 784.

Maryland—State v. Baltimore, 105 Md. 1, 65 A. 369, 11 Ann. Cas. 716.

State income tax was due on payments made to taxpayer by investment trust for short-term United States government securities, representing amounts received from third parties with respect to particular government securities in excess of amount paid to parties for same securities in repurchase ("repo") transactions; although each transaction was structured as a purchase of securities by trust followed by a sale, federal obligations were security for what was, in economic effect, a loan by trust to a third-party seller-borrower. Comptroller of Treas. v. First United Bank & Trust, 320 Md. 352, 578 A.2d 192 (1990).

Massachusetts.—United States Trust Co. v. Commonwealth, 245 Mass. 75, 139 N.E. 794.

Mississippi.—Bank v. State, 12 S. & M. 456.

New York.—International Banking Corp. v. Raymond, 117 App. Div. 62, 102 N.Y.S. 85, aff'd, 188 N.Y. 551, 80 N.E. 1117.

Oregon.—Pennick v. American Nat'l Bank, 126 Ore. 615, 268 P. 1012.

Pennsylvania.—Philadelphia Sav. Fund Soc. v. Yard, 9 Pa. 359; Pennsylvania Co. for Ins. v. Board of Revision, 139 Pa. 612, 21 A. 163; Commonwealth v. McKean County, 200 Pa. 383, 49 A. 982; Hunter's Appeal (Pa.), 10 A. 429; Appeals of Loughlin (Pa.), 10 A. 832; Commonwealth v. Clairton Steel Co., 229 Pa. 246, 78 A. 131.

As to possession of loan proceeds and the like, see § 22 of this chapter.

New York.—

The annual general assessment imposed by the Banking Department on mortgage banks does not constitute an unconstitutional tax. Matter of Homestead Funding Corp. v. State of N.Y. Banking Dept., 95 A.D.3d 1410, 944 N.Y.S.2d 649 (N.Y. App. Div. 3d Dep't 2012). See N.Y. Const. art. XVI, § 1.

[2526] Robinson v. Ward, 18 Ohio St. 293.

In some jurisdictions savings banks are expressly exempt from taxation on certain of their investments;[2527] as, for instance, bank stock in which such savings banks have invested money received on deposit,[2528] certain investments in real estate,[2529] loans secured by mortgages on real estate and the like.[2530] But the fact that loans made by a bank are secured by property which is exempt from taxation does not render such loans also exempt.[2531] Under a statute declaring that a real estate mortgage is deemed an interest in land for purposes of taxation, and that bank shares shall be assessed only after deducting the value of real estate taxed to a bank, mortgages held by a bank must be taxed to it and deducted from the value of its shares, even though the mortgagors agree to pay the taxes.[2532] The provision of the Income Tax Act requiring the addition of federal tax-exempt interest payments to a corporation's base income does not require amortized bond premiums from the interest payments on state or municipal bonds to be included by taxpayers in computing their base income.[2533]

The common meaning of "bank" for purposes of the Internal Revenue Code includes secured loans. For instance, a dictionary definition of bank in the commercial context includes the making loans of money on collateral security. And it is well established that the relationship between a bank and its depositors is similar to that of debtor and creditor. Normally, funds deposited with a bank are general deposits which create a debtor-creditor

---

[2527] Rutland Sav. Bank v. Rutland, 52 Vt. 463; People's Sav. Bank v. Monongahela River, etc., Coke Co., 29 Pa. Super. 153.

Inclusion of corporation's income from municipal housing authority bonds and Housing Finance Agency bonds in calculating corporation's entire net income for purpose of imposing franchise tax was not illegal indirect tax, even though income derived from such bond was free from taxation by state. Anchor Sav. Bank, F.S.B. v. Chu, 498 N.Y.S.2d 898 (N.Y. App. Div. 3 Dep't 1988).

[2528] Worcester County Ins. v. Worcester, 64 Mass. (10 Cash.) 128; Providence Inst. v. Gardiner, 4 R.I. 484; Somersworth Sav. Bank v. Somersworth, 68 N.H. 402, 44 A. 534.

[2529] Rockingham, etc., Sav. Bank v. Portsmouth, 52 N.H. 17; In re Suffolk Sav. Bank, 149 Mass. 1, 20 N.E. 331.

[2530] State v. Amoskeag Sav. Bank, 71 N.H. 535, 53 A. 739.

[2531] Savings & Loan Soc. v. San Francisco, 131 Cal. 358, 63 P. 666.

[2532] Latham v. Board, 91 Mich. 509, 52 N.W. 15; Augusti v. Citizens Bank, 46 La. Ann. 529, 15 So. 74.

[2533] Moline Nat'l Bank v. Department of Revenue, 111 Ill. App. 3d 1088, 67 Ill. Dec. 680, 444 N.E.2d 1164 (1983).

relationship between the bank and its depositor.[2534] Courts that have considered the meaning of "loans" as that term is used in the Code definition of "bank" have defined this term as an agreement, either expressed or implied, whereby one person advances money to the other and the other agrees to repay it upon such terms as to time and rate of interest, or without interest, as the parties may agree. In another context, a loan of money is a contract by which one delivers a sum of money to another and the latter agrees to return at a future time a sum equivalent to that which he borrows. Notably, courts have repeatedly stated that interest is not required.[2535]

The central inquiry for determining if a transaction is a bona fide loan for tax purposes is whether it is the intention of the parties that the money advanced be repaid. This is a factual question. The U.S. Court of Appeals for the Fifth Circuit has endorsed a non-exhaustive seven-factor test to determine whether the parties to a transaction intended it to be a loan. Under this test, courts look to: (1) Whether the promise to repay is evidenced by a note or other instrument; (2) whether interest was charged; (3) whether a fixed schedule for repayments was established; (4) whether collateral was given to secure payment; (5) whether repayments were made; (6) whether the borrower had a reasonable prospect of repaying the loan and whether the lender had sufficient funds to advance the loan and (7) whether the parties conducted themselves as if the transaction were a loan.[2536]

The section in the Internal Revenue Code defining "bank" provides that a substantial part of the taxpayer's business must consist of making "loans and discounts."[2537] The statute's use of the conjunctive "and" rather than the disjunctive "or" in this phrase indicates that discounts is a required element. The conjunctive use of the word "and" indicates that each aspect must be satisfied.[2538]

The annual franchise tax imposed on domestic corporations and measured by corporate income did not discriminate between exempt and nonexempt

---

[2534] Moneygram Int'l v. Comm'r, 664 Fed. Appx. 386 (5th Cir. 2016). See 26 U.S.C.S. § 581.

[2535] Moneygram Int'l v. Comm'r, 664 Fed. Appx. 386 (5th Cir. 2016).

[2536] Moneygram Int'l v. Comm'r, 664 Fed. Appx. 386 (5th Cir. 2016).

[2537] 26 U.S.C.S. § 581.

[2538] Moneygram Int'l v. Comm'r, 664 Fed. Appx. 386 (5th Cir. 2016).

income and, therefore, could be imposed on income earned on federal obligations.[2539]

A document, though entitled "First Supplemental Indenture of Mortgage and Deed of Trust," was not subject to documentary tax, where the document was merely an agreement whereby the parent corporation agreed to guarantee payment in the event a newly acquired subsidiary defaulted on existing first mortgage bonds and where the agreement did not release the subsidiary from liability on the bonds not merely provided additional security.[2540]

§ 20. Ownership or Possession of Property.

An equitable holder of real property, rather than a holder of bare legal title, is subject to taxation.[2541] It seems that a bank may properly be taxed on property held by it in trust in the same manner that other trustees are taxed,[2542] but not on property pledged to it as collateral security for a debt.[2543] And a statute providing for assessment of the average value of moneys and credits in the possession of a corporation making loans, has no application when loans are made in the name of a corporation by private persons, but the corporation never possesses or controls any of the moneys.[2544] On the other hand, moneys, credits and evidences of indebtedness, employed and invested within a state by a foreign banking corporation doing business therein, are not exempt from taxation under a law exempting moneys of a nonresident under the control or in the possession of his agent in the state when transmitted to such agent for investment or otherwise, where they are not in the hands of an agent, but in the corporation's own

---

[2539] Savings League of Wis., Ltd. v. Wisconsin Dep't of Revenue, 141 Wis. 2d 918, 416 N.W.2d 650 (1987).

[2540] Department of Revenue v. Sun Bank, 556 So. 2d 1154 (Fla. App. 1990).

[2541] First Union Nat'l Bank v. Ford, 636 So. 2d 523 (Fla. App. 1993).

[2542] In re Philadelphia Sav. Fund Soc., 4 Clark 155, 7 Pa. L.J. 186; Downes v. State, 22 Tex. Ct. App. 393, 3 S.W. 242.

County, rather than bank, was "equitable owner" of property used for county offices, for purposes of exemption from ad valorem taxation, where county engaged in financing arrangement whereby individual investors purchased certificates of participation to raise funds for county government offices, title to land was held by bank as trustee for individual investors until they were fully reimbursed by county, bank was paid one-time fee for acting as trustee, and county had sole obligation to maintain property, to provide insurance, and to pay all taxes. First Union Nat'l Bank v. Ford, 636 So. 2d 523 (Fla. App. 1993).

[2543] Waltham Bank v. Waltham, 51 Mass. (10 Met.) 334.

[2544] Farmers' Loan, etc., Co. v. Newton, 97 Iowa 502, 66 N.W. 784.

hands, and where they are not sent to the corporation for collection, but belong to it, and are needed and used in its business.[2545] The owner of real property on January 1 in any year is liable for the taxes of that year.[2546]

The liability of an insolvent bank, as mortgagor, for taxes on land where its bank building is located is not shifted to the mortgagee because he takes possession of the premises after default on the mortgage and collects the rents and profits.[2547] And money, notes and credits in the hands of assignees or liquidators of insolvent state banks have been held subject to taxation.[2548] But the fact that a bank customarily paid a tax on its shares does not authorize assessment of a tax against the bank after it is insolvent, the shares being its stockholders' property.[2549] Where a bank decided to protect its investment and avoid a foreclosure by purchasing a food store so that it could be operated without interruption as a going business, and store owners sold their equity in satisfaction of the debt and quit the business, the bank as buyer became their successor and liable for sales taxes owed by them, and the fact that the bank's objective was to be a short term owner and in turn to sell going business to a third party did not alter its successor status under successor liability statute.[2550] Tax upon real property is charge upon real

---

[2545] International Banking Corp. v. Raymond, 117 App. Div. 62, 102 N.Y.S. 85, aff'd, 188 N.Y. 551, 80 N.E. 1117.

[2546] First Nat'l Bank v. Mid-Central Food Sales, Inc., 129 Ill. App. 3d 1002, 85 Ill. Dec. 4, 473 N.E.2d 372 (1984).

Party in control of and benefitting from property is party responsible for real estate taxes. La Grange State Bank v. Glen Ellyn, 227 Ill. App. 3d 308, 591 N.E.2d 480, 169 Ill. Dec. 307 (1992).

[2547] Hood v. McGill, 206 N.C. 83, 173 S.E. 20.

[2548] Gerard v. Duncan, 84 Miss. 731, 36 So. 1034, 68 L.R.A. 461; Ryan v. Gallatin, 14 Ill. 78; State v. Bank, 50 La. Ann. 696, 23 So. 464; Tharpe v. Gormley, 48 Ga. App. 731, 173 S.E. 212, rev'd on another point, 184 Ga. 605, 192 S.E. 211; Jenks v. State, 188 Wash. 472, 63 P.2d 369.

[2549] People v. Toluca State Bank, 327 Ill. 638, 159 N.E. 240.

[2550] **In general.—**

Bank of Commerce v. Woods, 585 S.W.2d 577 (Tenn. 1970).

Contention of bank, suing to recover sales taxes paid under protest, that successor liability statute imposed liability upon transferee only if it failed to withhold sufficient amount of purchase money to cover the amount of unpaid taxes, and that because it did not provide any money to defaulting debtors-food store owners in connection with its purchase of store, it was not required to withhold amount of unpaid taxes, provided no basis for relief; because such statute broadly imposed duty on successor of taxpayer who sold out or quit his business, and use of words "purchase money" could not be construed as limitation on such

estate, not personal obligation of any person.[2551] Neither common-law rules governing the relationship between the owner of land and the lessee nor intention of the parties as expressed in their contract concerning whether a structure is to be treated as real or personal property is controlling in the field of taxation.[2552] Colorado could classify oil and gas interests as realty for the purposes of taxing such interests held by the federal land bank.[2553] Furthermore, under Colorado law, when oil or mineral rights have been severed from the surface estate and are owned by persons other than the owners of the surface rights, two separate and distinct freehold estates exist and are subject to property taxation.[2554] Thus, where a federal land bank had reserved all or some of the mineral interests beneath certain lands, entitling it to receive the revenues in the form of lease bonuses, rentals, and leasing and production royalties, under Colorado law, those mineral interests were "real property" and subject to Colorado's ad valorem taxes within the waiver provision of the Farm Credit Act which exempts federal land banks from all state, municipal and local taxation, except for taxes upon real estate

---

duty. Bank of Commerce v. Woods, 585 S.W.2d 577 (Tenn. 1979).

Evidence that bank liable for sales taxes.—

In a suit brought by a bank to recover sales taxes paid under protest, in which issue was whether the bank, which was transferred secured property by defaulting debtors-food store owners, and which operated store as a going business for a short time and then sold it to a third party was successor of, and liable for sales taxes owed by, owners-debtors, within the purview of the successor liability statute, bank's contention that it actually was foreclosing on its secured interest rather than purchasing assets of the store, despite execution of purchase and sale agreement, was not supported by the evidence, because it was obvious from deposition of bank president that it was the intention of the parties that foreclosure be avoided. Bank of Commerce v. Woods, 585 S.W.2d 577 (Tenn. 1979).

Bank assumed risk taxes not paid.—

It would have been a simple procedure for a bank to require a certificate from the Department of Revenue that defaulting debtors-food store owners had paid sales taxes due state in connection with its purchase of store assets, and it would have been one more factor to weigh in bank's decision whether to foreclose on its security interest or continue business, and when the bank decided to purchase the store instead of foreclosing on loan, it took the risk that it would be liable for unpaid sales taxes, because public interest in efficient collectibility of state revenue could not be jeopardized on account of private business decisions. Bank of Commerce v. Woods, 585 S.W.2d 577 (Tenn. 1979).

[2551] Merv E. Hilpipre Auction Co. v. Solon State Bank, 343 N.W.2d 452 (Iowa 1984).

[2552] Pacific Metal Co. v. Northwestern Bank, 667 P.2d 958 (Mont. 1983).

[2553] Federal Land Bank v. Board of County Comm'rs, 788 F.2d 1440 (10th Cir. 1986).

[2554] Federal Land Bank v. Board of County Comm'rs, 788 F.2d 1440 (10th Cir. 1986).

according to value.[2555] Moreover, a tax on royalty interest is not a tax on oil and gas severed from realty, but is, by its very terms, a tax upon rights reserved in mineral interest holders as the lessors and owners of the deed.[2556] However, the exclusion of the selling price of oil and gas delivered to the United States government in the valuation of oil and gas interests under Colorado law did not render the federal land bank exempt from the taxation of its mineral interests under Colorado's ad valorem tax statute.[2557]

Components of a bank's computer system can be classified and taxed as real property when found by the trial court to be fixtures in a special purpose building designed primarily to accommodate computers, as opposed to a general purpose building, thus, taxation of computer components as real property was appropriate where the building design included extensive major structural improvements specifically constructed to accommodate computers, including a special air conditioning system with a dedicated chiller and unusual cross-over chilled water piping installation, uninterruptible power supply, halon gas fire suppression and security system.[2558]

Property belonging to state is presumed to be immune from taxation unless there is clear manifestation of intent to tax it.[2559]

§ 21. Taxation on Circulation.

Express provision has been made by Congress for taxation of the circulation of both state and national banks.[2560] The purpose of taxing

---

[2555] Federal Land Bank v. Board of County Comm'rs, 788 F.2d 1440 (10th Cir. 1986).

[2556] Federal Land Bank v. Board of County Comm'rs, 607 F. Supp. 1137 (D.C. Colo. 1985).

[2557] Federal Land Bank v. Board of County Comm'rs, 607 F. Supp. 1137 (D.C. Colo. 1985).

[2558] Crocker Nat'l Bank v. City & County of San Francisco, 204 Cal. App. 3d 1185, 251 Cal. Rptr. 704.

[2559] First Union Nat'l Bank v. Ford, 636 So. 2d 523 (Fla. App. 1998).

[2560] Veazie Bank v. Fenno, 75 U.S. (8 Wall.) 533, 19 L. Ed. 482. As to tax on national bank circulation, see 12 U.S.C.S. § 541.

The tax of 10 percent which state banks are required to pay on the amount of notes of any person, or of any state bank, etc., "used for circulation and paid out by them" (former 26 U.S C.S. § 4881), applied to amounts paid out by the state bank in its own previously issued notes, as well as to payments in notes of persons or other state banks. Deposit Sav. Ass'n v. Mayer, 7 Fed. Cas. 504 (No. 8818), 1876 U.S. App. LEXIS 1693 (1876); Deposit Sav. Ass'n v. Marks, 7 Fed. Cas. 503 (No. 8812), 3 Woods 553.

The provision "that every person, firm, association, other than national bank associations, and every corporation, state bank, or state banking association, shall pay a tax of 10 per cent

circulating notes of a national bank is not revenue, but to reimburse the treasury for expenses incurred in printing the notes and all other expenses; the purpose of the tax on state banks is revenue, coupled with the policy of ultimately compelling retirement of state bank notes.[2561] The statutory provision that whenever the outstanding circulation of any bank does not exceed five percent of its capital, "said circulation shall be free from taxation," does not extend to national banks; it is intended only as an inducement to state banks to convert into national banks, by exempting from taxation all their circulating medium below five percent of their capital issued under state organization.[2562] And the word "issued," as used in the act placing a tax of one twelfth of one percent a month on the "average amount of circulation issued by any bank," means not only making notes, but also includes putting them into circulation.[2563]

b. National Banks.

1. Federal Taxation.

§ 22. In General.

National banks are subject to a duty of one half of one percent each half year, upon the average amount of their notes in circulation.[2564]

---

on the amount of their own notes used for circulation and paid out by them" (former 26 U.S.C.S § 4881), must be construed as limited in its effect to notes payable in money; otherwise all sorts of negotiable paper, such as "grain receipts," fare tickets, and the like, might be subject to the same taxation. In re Aldrich, 16 F. 369 (N.D. N.Y. 1883); United States v. Wilson, 106 U.S. 620, 2 S. Ct. 85, 27 L. Ed. 310. See also Hollister v. Zion's Coop. Mercantile Inst., 111 U.S. 62, 4 S. Ct. 263, 28 L. Ed. 352; Philadelphia, etc., R. Co. v. Pollock, 19 F. 401. See now 12 U.S.C.S. § 541.

[2561] Merchants' Nat. Bank v. United States, 42 Ct. CL 6, aff'd, 214 U.S. 33, 29 S. Ct. 593, 53 L Ed. 899.

[2562] 26 U.S.C.S. § 4883(a); Merchants' Nat. Bank v. United States, 42 Ct. CL 6, aff'd, 214 U.S. 33, 29 S. Ct. 593, 53 L. Ed. 899.

[2563] Former 26 U.S.C.S. § 4881(aX1); Deposit Sav. Ass'n v. Mayer, 7 Fed. Cas. 504 (No. 3818), 1876 U.S. App. LEXIS 1693 (1876).

[2564] 12 U.S.C.S. § 541; First Nat'l Bank v. Province, 20 Mont. 374, 51 P. 821; Van Allen v. Assessors, 70 U.S. (8 Wall.) 573, 18 L. Ed. 229.

2. State Taxation.

(A). General Considerations

§ 23. In General.

Effect of Federal Statute.—As has already been seen, in the absence of congressional action, a state cannot tax any property of a national bank, and even then such property can only be so taxed to the extent that Congress has granted permission to do so.[2565] The federal statute setting forth methods by

---

[2565] **In general.—**

People v. First Nat. Bank, 351 Ill. 435, 184 N.E. 645; People v. Loughman, 100 F.2d 387; Bedford v. Colorado Nat. Bank, 104 Colo. 311, 91 P.2d 469; School Dist. v. Lansing, 286 Mich. 244, 281 N.W. 883; Clark v. First Nat'l Bank, 130 Misc. 352, 224 N.Y.S. 10; Daly Bank, etc., Co. v. Board, 33 Mont. 101, 81 P. 950; Stetson v. Bangor, 56 Me. 274; First Nat'l Bank v. Bergan, 119 Mont. 1, 169 P.2d 233, 165 A.L.R. 1244; First Nat'l Bank & Trust Co. v. West Haven, 135 Conn. 191, 62 A.2d 671; Goodwin v. Citizens & Southern Nat'l Bank, 209 Ga. 908 (1953), 76 S.E.2d 620, 655; In re National Bank, 137 W. Va. 673, 73 S.E.2d 665; First Nat'l Bank v. State, 262 Ala. 155, 77 So. 2d 653; Security-First Nat'l Bank v. Franchise Tax Board, 55 Cal. 2d 407, 11 Cal. Rptr. 289, 359 P.2d 625, appeal dismissed, 368 U.S. 3, 82 S. Ct. 15, 7 L. Ed. 2d 16. See § 1 of this chapter.

National bank cannot be taxed by state governments or political subdivisions upon their property or shares except as Congress may grant that right by express permission and mere silence of Congress in such aspect in itself constitutes a ban. Odland v. Findley, 38 F. Supp. 563, 20 Ohio Op. 530, 1941 U.S. Dist. LEXIS 3269 (1941), rev'd on other grounds, State ex rel. Henneford v. Yelle, 12 Wn.2d 434, 121 P.2d 948, 1942 Wash. LEXIS 401 (1942).

National banks are not merely private businesses but rather are agencies of the United States created by it to promote its fiscal policies and financed by private capital and such banks and their shares are taxable by the states only with the consent of Congress and then only in accordance with such restrictions as Congress may place. Morris & Essex Inv. Co. v. Director of Division of Taxation, 33 N.J. 24, 161 A.2d 491.

Property held as security.—

The rule that property of a national bank cannot be taxed by a state except as expressly authorized by Congress does not apply to personal property which the bank holds merely as security. Chase Nat'l Bank v. Spokane County, 125 Wash. 1, 215 P. 374.

Dividends.—

Congress in enacting statute relating to taxation of national banking association by states did not intend to extend implied restrictions of the statute to a tax on dividends paid by holding company to taxpayer out of dividends received by the holding company from national banks. Irvine v. Spaeth, 210 Minn. 489, 299 N.W. 204, appeal dismissed, 314 U.S. 575, 62 S. Ct. 117, 86 L. Ed. 466.

Statute permitting national bank to elect taxation method must be construed in light of preexisting law, remedy, and object to be accomplished. McMorrow v. National Shawmut Bank, 259 Mass. 14, 156 N.E. 48.

which a state may tax national banks was designed to allow the states considerable freedom in working out equitable tax systems.[2566] And the various restrictions placed by the federal statute on the permitted methods of taxation were designed to prohibit only those systems of state taxation which discriminate in practical operation against national banks or their shareholders as a class.[2567] Thus, in exercise of the permission granted by Congress to tax national banks, a state is not obliged to apply the same system of taxation to them as it uses in taxation of other property, provided no injustice, inequality or discrimination is inflicted on them,[2568] nor does the federal statute even require a state to adopt the same scheme for taxing all banks, state or national.[2569] However, the limitations of the federal statute cannot be avoided by administrative interpretation nor by action of a state legislature.[2570]

A national bank may be made agent of state to collect valid tax imposed on third person with whom bank deals. Northwestern Nat'l Bank v. Gillis, 82 S.D. 457, 148 N.W.2d 293 (1967).

Personal property tax on assets held in trust.—

The collection of a personal property tax from assets held by national banks in trust for others did not violate a federal statute prohibiting states from levying the intangible personal property tax against national banking associations in that the personal property tax was levied against banks as trustees, and not against national banking associations as such. Hanley v. Kusper, 61 Ill. 2d 452, 337 N.E.2d 1 (1975).

2566 Security-First Nat'l Bank v. Franchise Tax Board, 55 Cal. 2d 407, 11 Cal. Rptr. 289, 359 P.2d 625, appeal dismissed, 368 U.S. 3, 82 S. Ct. 15, 7 L. Ed. 2d 16.

California's "in lieu" tax scheme was designed not to promote the banking business but primarily to make possible state taxation of national banks. Western States Bankcard Assn. v. San Francisco, 19 Cal. 3d 208, 137 Cal. Rptr. 183, 561 P.2d 273 (1977).

2567 Irvine v. Spaeth, 210 Minn. 489, 299 N.W. 204, appeal dismissed, 314 U.S. 575, 62 S. Ct. 117, 86 L Ed. 466; Security-First Nat. Bank v. Franchise Tax Board, 55 Cal. 2d 407, 11 Cal. Rptr. 289, 359 P.2d 625, appeal dismissed, 368 U.S. 3, 82 S. Ct. 15, 7 L. Ed. 2d 16; Tradesmens Nat'l Bank v. Oklahoma Tax Com., 309 U.S. 560, 60 S. Ct. 688, 84 L. Ed. 947; Michigan Nat'l Bank v. Michigan, 365 U.S. 467, 81 S. Ct. 659, 5 L. Ed. 2d 710.

2568 First Nat'l Bank v. Oklahoma Tax Com., 185 Okla. 98, 90 P.2d 438; Tradesmens Nat'l Bank v. Oklahoma Tax Com., 185 Okla. 656, 95 P.2d 121, aff'd, 309 U.S. 560, 60 S. Ct 688, 84 L. Ed. 947.

Tax rate parity between national and state banking institutions is a prerequisite for any tax upon national banks. Western States Bankcard Assn. v. San Francisco, 19 Cal. 3d 208, 137 Cal. Rptr. 183, 561 P.2d 278 (1977).

2569 Citizens', etc., Nat. Bank v. Atlanta, 53 F2d 557. See Tradesmens Nat'l Bank v. Oklahoma Tax Com., 309 U.S. 560, 60 S. Ct. 688, 84 L Ed. 947.

2570 First Nat. Bank v. State, 262 Ala. 155, 77 So.2d 653.

Specific Provisions of Federal Statute Prior to 1969 Amendments.—The federal statute prior to its 1969 amendment permitted the states to tax only the shares of stock or net income of a national bank, as well as its real property.[2571] The statute not only furnished the authority of the states to tax,

---

State cannot, by any definition of income, alter terms of federal statute allowing states to tax national banks. First Nat. Bank v. State, 262 Ala. 155, 77 So2d 653.

Former Tax Law § 1453(k-1) was statutorily coupled with the federal ordering rules set forth in 26 U.S.C.S. § 172, which specifically provided that the entire amount of a net operating loss (NOL) for any taxable year shall be carried to the earliest of the taxable years to which such loss may be carried (26 U.S.C.S. § 172(b)(2)). Thus, for banking corporation franchise tax purposes, application of this federal ordering rule was not a mere attempt by the Department of Taxation and Finance to achieve mechanical conformity with federal tax principles; it was statutorily required and, as such, said presumption served as the "starting point" for determining the amount of NOL that must be used to offset a taxpayer's entire net income. Matter of Toronto Dominion Holdings (U.S.A.), Inc. v Tax Appeals Trib. of The State of New York, 162 A.D.3d 125, 577 N.Y.S.3d 800 (3d Dept. 2018).

In an instance where claiming a New York net operating loss (NOL) deduction results in a banking corporation having a negative entire net income (ENI) for a given year, the taxpayer only has to claim that portion of its available New York NOL deduction necessary to reduce its ENI to zero. This is based on the federal rule that NOL deductions are limited to the amount necessary to bring a taxpayer's taxable income to zero (26 U.S.C.S. § 172(b)(2)(B)), which, by application thereof, effectively serves to rebut the presumption that a taxpayer's New York NOL must be the same as its federal NOL. Matter of Toronto Dominion Holdings (U.S.A.), Inc. v Tax Appeals Trib. of The State of New York, 162 A.D.3d 1255; 77 N.Y.S.3d 800 (3d Dept. 2018).

2571 **In general.—**

State ex rel. Hatfield v. Moreland, 152 Okla. 37, 3 P.2d 803; Land Title Bank, etc., Co. v. Ward, 20 F. Supp. 810, 1937 U.S. Dist. LEXIS 1474 (E.D. Pa. 1937); Gully v. First Nat. Bank, 81 F.2d 502, rev'd on other grounds, 299 U.S. 109, 57 S. Ct. 96, 81 L. Ed. 70. As to income tax, see § 1 of this chapter. As to tax on real property, see § 26b of this chapter. As to tax on stock, see § 26c of this chapter.

Statutory provision.—

The legislature of each State may determine and direct, subject to the provisions of this section, the manner and place of taxing all the shares of national banking associations located within its limits. The several States may: (1) Tax said shares; or (2) include dividends derived therefrom in the taxable income of an owner or holder thereof; or (3) tax such associations on their net income or (4) tax according to or measured by their net income, provided the following conditions are complied with:

1. (a) The imposition by any State of any one of the above four forms of taxation shall be in lieu of the others, except as hereinafter provided in subdivision (c) of this clause.

(b) In the case of a tax on said shares the tax imposed shall not be at a greater rate than is assessed upon other moneyed capital in the hands of individual citizens of such State coming into competition with the business of national banks: Provided, that bonds, notes or other

(Text continued on page 705)

evidences of indebtedness in the hands of individual citizens not employed or engaged in the banking or investment business and representing merely personal investments not made in competition with such business, shall not be deemed moneyed capital within the meaning of this section.

(c) In case of a tax on or according to or measured by the net income of an association, the taxing State may, except in case of a tax on net income, include the entire net income received from all sources, but the rate shall not be higher than the rate assessed upon other financial corporations nor higher than the highest of the rates assessed by the taxing State upon mercantile, manufacturing, and business corporations doing business within its limits: Provided, however, that a State which imposes a tax on or according to or measured by the net income of, or a franchise or excise tax on, financial, mercantile, manufacturing, and business corporations organized under its own laws or laws of other states and also imposes a tax upon the income of individuals, may include in such individual income dividends from national banking association located within the State on condition that it also includes dividends from domestic corporations and may likewise include dividends from national banking associations located without the State on condition that it also includes dividends from foreign corporations, but at no higher rate than is imposed on dividends from such other corporations.

(d) In case the dividends derived from the said shares are taxed, the tax shall not be at a greater rate than is assessed upon the net income from other moneyed capital.

2. The shares of any national banking association owned by nonresident of any State, shall be taxed by the taxing district or by the State where the association is located and not elsewhere; and such association shall make return of such shares and pay the tax thereon as agent of such nonresident shareholders.

3. Nothing herein shall be construed to exempt the real property of associations from taxation in any State or any subdivision thereof; to the same extent, according to its value, as other real property is taxed. 12 U.S.C.S. § 548, prior to 1989 amendments.

Effect of two state statutes applicable to national banks.—

Where a state statute taxing shares of national bank, was the only legally effective law relating to their taxation prior to an act of Congress authorizing taxing of incomes from such stock but permitting only one of such methods of taxation to be operative, such state statute remained as the only permissible method of taxing national banks thereafter, notwithstanding that the state income tax act taxed incomes without exempting national banks. Buder v. First Nat. Bank, 16 F.2d 990.

State electing to tax shares of stockholders of national banks is without authority to levy tax en national branch banks measured by value of capital employed in their operation. Goodwin v. Citizens, etc., Nat. Bank, 209 Ga. 908, 76 S.E.2d 620 (1953).

Statute taxing branch national banks on capital employed therein could not be construed as intended to tax only shares of stockholders. Goodwin v. Citizens, etc., Nat. Bank, 209 Ga. 908, 76 S.E.2d 620 (1953).

Income tax.—

In determining whether state tax on national banks according to or measured by net income violates limitation set by federal statute, consideration must be given to state tax

but also prescribed the limitations on their power,[2572] and any tax in excess of the power granted was held void.[2573] Thus, it was held a state could not collect a sales tax on rentals received by a national bank from the tenants of an office building owned by the bank.[2574] The federal statute also excluded from state taxation all personal property owned by a national bank.[2575] And

structure as a whole, and not merely to taxes of kind imposed on banks. Security-First Nat'l Bank v. Franchise Tax Board, 55 Cal. 2d 407, 11 Cal. Rptr. 289, 359 P.2d 625, appeal dismissed, 368 U.S. 3, 82 S. Ct. 15, 7 L. Ed. 2d 16.

[2572] Tarrant v. Bessemer Nat. Bank, 7 Ala. App. 285, 61 So. 47; Clark v. First Nat. Bank, 130 Misc. 352, 224 N.Y.S. 10.

The statute imposing a state tax on income of banks was inoperative as to national banks in the Missouri City of St. Joseph during the tax year 1946, since the stock of such banks was subject to ad valorem tax levied by city for 1948 and power of state to tax national banks is expressly limited to one of the four methods authorized by statute. First Nat. Bank v. Buchanan County, 356 Mo. 1204, 205 S.W.2d 726 (1947).

[2573] Owensboro Nat. Bank v. Owensboro, 173 U.S. 664, 19 S. Ct. 537, 43 L. Ed. 850; O'Neil v. Valley Nat. Bank, 58 Ariz. 539, 121 P.2d 646.

[2574] O'Neil v. Valley Nat. Bank, 58 Ariz. 539, 121 P.2d 646.

[2575] **In general.—**

Daly Bank, etc., Co. v. Board, 33 Mont. 101, 81 P. 950; First Nat'l Bank v. Province, 20 Mont. 374, 51 P. 821; State v. First Nat. Bank, 4 Nev. 348; San Francisco v. Crocker-Woolworth Nat. Bank, 92 F. 273; First Nat. Bank v. San Francisco, 129 Cal. 96, 61 P. 778; National Bank of Arizona v. Long, 6 Ariz. 311, 57 P. 639; Middletown Nat. Bank v. Middletown, 74 Conn. 449, 51 A. 138; Rosenblatt v. Johnston, 104 U.S. 462, 26 L. Ed. 832. See also People v. Weaver, 100 U.S. 539, 25 L. Ed. 706; Covington City Nat. Bank v. Covington, 21 F. 484; First Nat. Bank v. Kreig, 21 Nev. 404, 32 P. 641; Clark v. First Nat'l Bank, 130 Misc. 352, 224 N.Y.S. 10; Roberts v. American Nat. Bank, 97 Fla. 411, 121 So. 554; State Tax Comm'n v. Shattuck, 44 Ariz. 379, 38 P.2d 631; Bank of California v. King County, 16 F. Supp. 976; Security-First Nat'l Bank v. Franchise Tax Board, 55 Cal. 2d 407, 11 Cal. Rptr. 289, 359 P.2d 625, appeal dismissed, 368 U.S. 3, 82 S. Ct. 15, 7 L. Ed. 2d 16; United States Nat'l Bank v. County of Los Angeles, 234 Cal. App. 2d 195, 44 Cal. Rptr. 286 (1965).

Statute prescribing four methods by which state may tax national banks exempts personal property of national bank from direct assessment and taxation by state regardless of amount or kind of business in which national banking association may engage. First Nat'l Bank & Trust Co. v. McDonald, 289 F. Supp. 493 (W.D. Okla. 1968).

Personal property of national banks could not be directly assessed to them by a town for purposes of taxation. First Nat. Bank, etc., Co. v. West Haven, 135 Conn. 191, 62 A.2d 671.

State tax collector's assessment against national bank on value of its personalty, rather than against shareholders or their shares of stock, held invalid. Gully v. First Nat. Bank, 81 F.2d 502, rev'd on other grounds, 299 U.S. 109, 57 S. Ct. 96, 81 L Ed. 70.

That state tax collector's assessment against national bank on value of its personalty was based upon bank's voluntary return and that bank had acquiesced in such assessment until

a state could not tax a national bank upon its capital or capital stock as distinguished from its shares in the hands of shareholders.[2576] Under a

---

after its failure, held not to estop receiver from raising illegality of tax, since after insolvency personalty could not be taxed in receiver's hands. Gully v. First Nat. Bank, 81 F.2d 502, rev'd on other grounds, 299 U.S. 109, 57 S. Ct. 96, 81 L. Ed. 70.

Prior to 1969 change in federal law lessening restrictions on state taxation of national banks, state sales tax could not be imposed on sale. of tangible personal property to national banks. Hibernia Bank v. State Bd. of Equalization, 166 Cal. App. 3d 393, 212 Cal. Rptr. 556 (1985).

Personal property held by the bank merely as security was subject to state personal property tax. Chase Nat. Bank v. Spokane County, 125 Wash. 1, 215 P. 374.

Banking fixtures and equipment.—

Since Congress has not consented to the taxation by states of personalty of national banks, banking fixtures and equipment of national bank, if taxable at all by the state as the property of the bank, could be taxed only as realty. First Nat. Bank v. Marion County, 169 Ore. 595, 130 P.2d 9.

Vault door and frame owned and installed by national bank in leased building and permanently annexed to realty of lessor were "real property" and subject to taxation, notwithstanding that bank was a short term lessee. Trabue Pittman Corp. v. County of Los Angeles, 29 Cal. 2d 385, 175 P.2d 512. For prior opinions, see 161 P.2d 10, 168 P.2d 156.

Equipment consisting of tellers' cages, wickets, counters, partitions, coupon booths, and other items having characteristics of normal trade fixtures installed by national bank in leased building were taxable as improvements to realty rather than as personalty notwithstanding that as between bank and lessor such items might also have been trade fixtures. Trabue Pittman Corp. v. Los Angeles County, 29 Cal. 2d 385, 175 P.2d 512. For prior opinions, see 161 P.2d 10, 168 P.2d 156.

Where all improvements installed by lessee national bank in leased building were assessable as improvements to realty rather than personalty, the entire building including all improvements was properly assessed to lessor notwithstanding lease reserved bank's right to remove all improvements placed on premises. Trabue Pittman Corp. v. County of Los Angeles, 29 Cal. 2d 385, 175 P.2d 512. For prior opinions, see 161 P.2d 10, 168 P.2d 158.

As to difference in classification of fixtures of banks and other businesses, see § 10 of this chapter, as to state taxation of fixtures of banks generally, see § 15 of this chapter.

The California Bank and Corporation Franchise Tax Act does not tax personalty of national banks in violation of federal statute. Security-First Nat'l Bank v. Franchise Tax Board, 55 Cal. 2d 407, 11 Cal. Rptr. 289, 359 P.2d 625, appeal dismissed, 368 U.S. 3, 82 S. Ct. 15, 7 L. Ed. 2d 16; United States Nat'l Bank v. Los Angeles County, 234 Cal. App. 2d 195, 44 Cal. Rptr. 286 (1965).

[2576] **In general.—**

State v. Security Nat'l Bank, 139 Minn. 162, 165 N.W. 1067.

The assessment of a state tax on the capital stock of a national bank, made against the banking corporation or association itself, is unauthorized and void. People v. First Nat'l Bank, 351 Ill. 435, 184 N.E. 645; School Dist. v. Lansing, 286 Mich. 244, 281 N.W. 883.

former provision of the statute, state franchise taxes also could not be imposed,[2577] but a pre-1969 amendment authorizing a tax by a state on national banks according to, or measured by, their entire net income received from all sources, subject only to certain restrictions as to rates, authorized a franchise tax measured by net income including interest on tax-exempt federal securities.[2578]

State tax assessed against national bank measured by value of shares of stock is not equivalent to tax on shareholders and therefore is unauthorized. People v. First Nat'l Bank, 351 Ill. 435, 184 N.E. 646.

The assessment of shares of national banks for ad valorem tax purposes must be to the shareholders and no other form of assessment is valid or enforceable. Flournoy v. First Nat. Bank, 3 So.2d 244, 197 La. 1067.

Capital stock, surplus and undivided profits of national bank cannot be assessed *eo nomine* either against bank or against shareholders. Roberts v. American Nat'l Bank, 97 Fla. 411, 121 So. 554.

Capital invested in government securities.—

A state may not lay a tax upon the moneyed capital of a national bank invested in government securities. National Bank v. Commonwealth (U. S.), 9 Wall. 353, 19 L. Ed. 701; BANK v. STATE, 58 W. Va. 559, 52 S.E. 494, 3 L.R.A. (n.s.) 584, 6 Ann. Cas. 115; Sumter v. National Bank, 62 Ala. 464, 34 Am. R. 30; Salt Lake City Nat. Bank v. Golding, 2 Utah 1; Merchants' Nat. Bank v. United States, 101 U.S. 1, 25 L. Ed. 979; Beard v. People's Sav. Bank, 53 Ind. App. 185, 101 N.E. 325.

Assessment against bank presumed to be as agent.—

But where state under federal statute had elected to tax shares in national bank, assessment made directly against bank would be presumed to have been assessment against bank as agent of shareholders. Odland v. Findley, 38 F. Supp. 563, 20 Ohio Op. 530, 1941 U.S. Dist. LEXIS 3269, rev'd on other grounds, State ex rel. Henneford v. Yelle, 127 F.2d 948, 1942 Wash. LEXIS 401 12 Wn.2d 434 (1942).

[2577] Third Nat'l Bank v. Stone, 174 U.S. 432, 19 S. Ct. 759, 43 L Ed. 1035; Owensboro Nat. Bank v. Owensboro, 173 U.S. 664, 19 S. Ct. 537, 43 L. Ed. 850; Louisville v. Third Nat'l Bank, 174 U.S. 435, 19 S. Ct. 874, 43 L. Ed. 1037; Louisville v. Citizens' Nat'l Bank, 174 U.S. 436, 19 S. Ct. 874, 43 L Ed. 1037; First Nat. Bank v. Louisville, 174 U.S. 438, 19 S. Ct. 876, 43 L. Ed. 1038; Graves v. County First Nat'l Bank, 108 Ky. 194, 56 S.W. 16, 21 Ky. L. Rptr. 1656; George Schuster & Co. v. Louisville, 124 Ky. 189, 89 S.W. 689, 28 Ky. L. Rptr. 588; State v. Clement Nat'l Bank, 84 Vt. 167, 78 A. 944, 1912D Ann. Cas. 22, aff'd, 231 U.S. 120, 34 S. Ct. 31, 58 L. Ed. 147.

A tax on deposits in savings banks and trust companies is invalid in the case of national bank because it amounts to a franchise tax. State v. Clement Nat'l Bank, 84 Vt. 167, 78 A. 944, 1912D Ann. Cas. 22, aff'd, 231 U.S. 120, 34 S. Ct. 31, 58 L. Ed. 147.

[2578] **In general.—**

Tradesmens Nat'l Bank v. Oklahoma Tax Com., 309 U.S. 560, 60 S. Ct. 688, 84 L. Ed. 947.

Specific Provisions of Federal Statute after 1969 Amendments.—Effective December 24, 1989, the federal statute was amended to allow states and their political subdivisions to impose any tax (other than a tax on intangibles) which is imposed generally on a nondiscriminatory basis throughout their jurisdiction on a national bank having its principal office therein in the same manner and to the same extent as such tax is imposed on state banks. These provisions were in addition to the other methods of taxation authorized by the statute prior to the 1969 amendments.[2579] Further, as to national banks not having their principal offices in a state, the amendments authorized a state to impose certain sales and use, real property, stamp, tangible personal property, license, excise, and similar taxes, provided such taxes are imposed generally throughout such state's jurisdiction on a nondiscriminatory basis.[2580] Finally, after January 1, 1972, the entire federal statute on this subject simply states: "For the purpose of any tax law enacted under authority of the United States or any State, a national bank shall be treated as a bank organized and existing under the laws of the State or other jurisdiction within which its

---

Congress may authorize a state to impose a tax on the franchise of a national banking association, and any immunity attaching to franchise under statute which, prior to amendment, provided alternatives whereby a state might impose a tax on national banking associations, could be withdrawn by Congress and franchise subjected to state taxing power. Tradesmens Nat'l Bank v. Oklahoma Tax Com., 309 U.S. 560, 60 S. Ct. 688, 84 L. Ed. 947.

The tax imposed by statute requiring banks or corporations annually to pay the state for privilege of exercising its corporate franchise, or doing business in the state, based upon its net income allocated to state, is not an "income tax" but is a tax on the privilege of exercising the corporate franchise, or on privilege of doing business in the state. J. M. & M. S. Browning Co. v. State Tax Comm'n, 107 Utah 457, 154 P.2d 998.

As to franchise tax in event of merger of state banking institution into national bank, see § 16 of this chapter.

In lieu of personalty tax.—

The excess franchise tax imposed on national banks by statute is in lieu of any tax on personal property. United States Nat'l Bank v. County of Los Angeles, 234 Cal. App. 2d 195, 44 Cal. Rptr. 286 (1965).

The prohibition of the state from interfering with instrumentalities of the national government does not condemn a state tax which is neither a property tax on tax exempt government securities nor a direct income tax on income derived from them, but a franchise tax measured by net income. Southern Pacific Co. v. McColgan, 68 Cal. App. 2d 48, 156 P.2d 81.

[2579] Former 12 U.S.C.S. § 548(5)(a).

[2580] Former 12 U.S.C.S. § 548(5)(b).

principal office is located."[2581] Section 548 of the National Bank Act is still in place, leaving national banks subject to state taxation.[2582]

As a result of Congress's sweeping reform of federal financial regulatory oversight in the Dodd-Frank Wall Street Reform and Consumer Protection Act,[2583] however, the legal analysis governing preemption by the National Bank Act (NBA) changed radically.[2584] The Dodd-Frank Act directs courts to determine preemption by analyzing whether a state law is "irreconcilably in conflict" with the NBA.[2585] The reservation of states' power to apply their laws of general applicability to national banks is reaffirmed by the NBA's preemption provisions which specify that laws governing the manner, content, or terms and conditions of any financial transaction or any account related thereto are not preempted as applied to national banks unless: (1) The state law would have a discriminatory effect on national banks, in comparison with the effect of the law on a bank chartered by that state; (2) the state law would be preempted under the standard set forth in *Barnett Bank* or (3) the state law is preempted by a federal law other than the NBA.[2586]

[2581] Pub. L. 91-156, § 2, 83 Stat. 434.

[2582] Miss. Dep't of Revenue v. Pikco Fin., Inc., 97 So. 3d 1203 (Miss. 2012).

Federal law does not preempt state law as to state taxation of national banks. Congress has not explicitly preempted state law in this area, Congress has not occupied the entire field, and there is no conflict between federal and state law in this area. The National Bank Act does not preempt state taxation; in fact, it explicitly exempts it, leaving taxation to the states under 12 U.S.C.S. § 548 and 12 C.F.R. § 7.4009(c)(2). Section 7.4009 was rescinded by the Dodd-Frank Act, but 12 U.S.C.S. § 548 is still in place, leaving national banks subject to state taxation. Miss. Dep't of Revenue v. Pikco Fin., Inc., 97 So. 3d 1203 (Miss. 2012).

[2583] 12 U.S.C.S. § 25b.

[2584] Cline v. Bank of Am., N.A., 823 F. Supp. 2d 387 (S.D. W. Va. 2011).

[2585] Meluzio v. Capital One Bank (USA), N.A., 469 B.R. 250 (N.D. W. Va. 2012); Pryor v. Bank of Am., N.A. (In re Pryor), 479 B.R. 694 (Bankr. E.D. NC 2012).

Conflict preemption analysis is focused on whether the targeted state statute is irreconcilably in conflict with the NBA. Stated another way, the inquiry distills to whether the state measure either: (1) Imposes an obligation on a national bank that is in direct conflict with federal law or (2) stands as an obstacle to the accomplishment and execution of the full purposes and objectives of Congress. Under the Dodd-Frank Act, the proper preemption test asks whether there is a significant conflict between the state and federal statutes—that is, the test for conflict preemption. Cline v. Bank of Am., N.A., 823 F. Supp. 2d 387 (S.D. W. Va. 2011).

[2586] Gordon v. Kohl's Dep't Stores, Inc., 172 F. Supp. 3d 840 (E.D. Pa. 2016). See 12 U.S.C.S. § 25b.

By codifying Barnett Bank, N.A. v. Nelson, 517 U.S. 25, 116 S. Ct. 1103, 134 L. Ed. 2d 237 (1996), the Dodd-Frank Act, 12 U.S.C.S. § 25b, directs courts to determine national

Dodd-Frank further clarified that the NBA does not occupy any field in any area of state law.[2587]

The Office of Thrift Supervision (OTS) was abolished effective October 19, 2011, following the enactment of the Dodd-Frank Act, and its rulemaking authority and operative rules were transferred to other agencies.[2588] The Office of the Comptroller of the Currency (OCC) revised its own regulations to mirror the preemption framework present in the Dodd-Frank Act.[2589]

Statutory Terms.—The term "financial corporations," as used in the federal statute forbidding a state to impose a higher tax on national banks than on other financial corporations, designates and includes moneyed corporations performing some of the functions of a national bank, and means corporations dealing in money as distinguished from other commodities.[2590]

---

bank preemption by analyzing whether a state statute is irreconcilably in conflict with the National Bank Act. Thus, courts must now determine whether the state measure either: (1) Imposes an obligation on a national bank that is in direct conflict with federal law or (2) stands as an obstacle to the accomplishment and execution of the full purposes and objectives of the United States Congress. Meluzio v. Capital One Bank (USA), N.A., 469 B.R. 250 (N.D. W. Va. 2012).

Because the Barnett Bank analysis is subsumed within Dodd–Frank, even assuming that Dodd–Frank's provisions did not apply, the preemption analysis essentially remained the same; in determining whether a statute is preempted by federal law, it is necessary to look first at Congress's intent in drafting the federal law. The congressional intent in enacting the NBA was to establish a national banking system that was free from intrusive state regulation. Sacco v. Bank of Am., N.A., 2012 U.S. Dist. LEXIS 178030 (D. N.C. 2012). See Barnett Bank, N.A. v. Nelson, 517 U.S. 25, 116 S. Ct. 1103, 134 L. Ed. 2d 237 (1996).

[2587] Gordon v. Kohl's Dep't Stores, Inc., 172 F. Supp. 3d 840 (E.D. Pa. 2016). See 12 U.S.C.S. § 25b.

[2588] 82 FR 47083, 47084.

Department of the Treasury is removing chapter V of title 12, Code of Federal Regulations (CFR), which contains regulations of the former Office of Thrift Supervision (OTS). The OTS, a Bureau of the Department of the Treasury, was abolished effective October 19, 2011, and its rulemaking authority and operative rules were transferred to other agencies pursuant to the Dodd-Frank Wall Street Reform and Consumer Protection Act. Because those agencies have issued regulations that supersede chapter V, chapter V is no longer necessary. 82 FR 47083, 47084.

[2589] Pryor v. Bank of Am., N.A. (In re Pryor), 479 B.R. 694 (E.D. Bankr. NC 2012). See 12 U.S.C.S. § 25b (effective July 21, 2011).

[2590] **In general.—**

Morris Plan Co. v. Johnson, 37 Cal. App. 2d 621, 100 P.2d 493 (1940).

A Morris Plan Company, which was incorporated under the industrial loan law and which was in substantial competition with national banks in the locality, was a "financial

And the classification "financial corporations" in the California Bank and Corporation Franchise Tax Act was made for the purpose of complying with the federal statute, and the term is used in the same sense as in the federal statute.[2591] A corporation does not come within the term "financial corporations" unless it is in substantial competition with the business of national banks.[2592] The difference between "mercantile, manufacturing, and business corporations" and "financial corporations" within the meaning of the federal

---

corporation" within the meaning of the federal statute. Morris Plan Co. v. Johnson, 37 Cal. App. 2d 621, 100 P.2d 493 (1940).

Life insurance company is a "financial corporation" in competition with national banks, within scope of congressional act authorizing states to tax national banks. Grange Mut. Life Co. v. State Tax Comm., 76 Idaho 303, 283 P.2d 187.

[2591] **In general.—**

Crown Finance Corp. v. McColgan, 23 Cal. 2d 280, 144 P.2d 331.

Determination as to inclusion in class.—

Financial corporations being placed in special class without definition by federal statute prohibiting tax discrimination between national banks and financial corporations, other portions of such statute, prohibiting greater tax on national bank shares than on moneyed capital competing with national banks' business, should control in determining whether corporation is "financial corporation" within state. Bank and Corporation Franchise Tax Act. Crown Finance Corp. v. McColgan, 23 Cal. 2d 280, 144 P.2d 331.

The facts that national banks, unlike other corporations transacting business of purchasing conditional sales contracts from retail dealers, look only to dealers' credit, insist on recourse to dealers, and require reserves, are not controlling in determining whether such other corporations compete with national banks and hence are "financial corporations" subject to franchise taxes at rate levied on such banks. Crown Finance Corp. v. McColgan, 23 Cal. 2d 280, 144 P.2d 331.

The California Revenue and Taxation Code does not furnish a statutory definition of "financial corporations." The classification was adopted to avoid preferential tax t reatment in favor of corporations in substantial competition with national banks. Under the governing test, the classification includes savings and loans as well as other kinds of moneyed corporations performing some of the functions of a national bank or dealing in money or financing in competition with activities of national banks. California Fed. Savings & Loan Assn. v. City of Los Angeles, 54 Cal. 3d 1, 812 P.2d 916 (1991).

No violation of federal statute.—

California Bank and Corporation Franchise Tax Act does not impose on national banks tax rate higher than permitted by federal statute and does not tax personalty of national banks in violation of federal statute. Security-First Nat'l Bank v. Franchise Tax Board, 55 Cal. 2d 407, 11 Cal. Rptr. 289, 359 P.2d 625, appeal dismissed, 368 U.S. 3, 82 S. Ct. 15, 7 L. Ed. 2d 16.

[2592] Crown Finance Corp. v. McColgan, 23 Cal. 2d 280, 144 P.2d 331.

Competition may exist between national banks and corporations dealing in moneyed capital, so as to render such corporations subject, as "financial corporations," to state

statute, is that financial corporations deal In moneyed capital.[2593] Language of the statute providing that "net income" upon which a franchise tax was to be computed was "taxable income as properly computed for federal income tax purposes" plainly dictated that the starting point for computation of net income for franchise tax purposes was the taxable income figure reported on the federal income tax return, and accordingly, the interest deduction allowed on a national bank's federal income tax return, on which the bank was allowed to deduct for a period of ten years, commencing with 1969 taxable year, the percentage of interest previously reported as income should have been allowed in the computation of state franchise tax imposed by the statute enacted in 1970.[2594] Dividends and interest paid to members of federal savings and loan associations are not "operating expenses" within the statute providing for deduction of operating expenses to determine net operating income on which the excise is computed.[2595] Levy of retail sales tax by comptroller of the treasury on rental payments under electronic equipment leases entered into by a national bank was not permitted under temporary federal statute providing that no sales or use tax shall be imposed upon purchases, sales, and use of tangible personal property which is subject matter of written contract of purchase entered into by national bank, where under state law term "contractor purchase" included lease of tangible personal property and there was nothing to suggest that Congress intended the temporary federal statute to differentiate between sales and rentals in the application of state sales and use taxes.[2596]

---

franchise taxation at rate levied on national banks, though such competition does not extend to all aspects of national banks' business. Crown Finance Corp. v. McColgan, 23 Cal. 2d 280, 144 P.2d 331.

Evidence showed that plaintiffs were substantially competing with national banks in business of dealing in moneyed capital and purchasing conditional sales contracts from retail dialers at discounts and hence were "financial corporations" subject to franchise taxes at same rates. Crown Finance Corp. v. McColgan, 23 Cal. 2d 280, 144 P.2d 331.

[2593] Crown Finance Corp. v. McColgan, 23 Cal. 2d 280, 144 P.2d 331.

[2594] First Nat'l Bank v. Bair, 252 N.W.2d 723 (Iowa 1977).

[2595] First Federal Sav. & Loan Asso. v. State Tax Com., 363 N.E.2d 474 (Mass. 1977).

There was no basis for assuming that the legislature intended to import accounting practice into statutory language imposing an excise on savings and cooperative banks and federal savings and loan associations, and thus to permit accounting principles to be the guide to the meaning of the words "operating expenses" therein. First Federal Sav. & Loan Asso. v. State Tax Com., 363 N.E.2d 474 (Mass. 1977).

[2596] Comptroller of Treasury v. Maryland Nat'l Bank, 408 A.2d 758 (Md. App. 1979), quoting Michie on Banks and Banking.

Determination of Validity of Tax.—The propriety of the imposition of a state tax on an activity or service performed by a national bank should be determined on the basis of whether the activity or service is reasonably related or incidental to the accomplishment of its bank functions.[2597]

And a state income or franchise tax on national banks is valid so long as the resulting burden does not exceed the burden to which state banks and mercantile, business, manufacturing and financial corporations are subject.[2598] But in determining the discriminatory character of a state tax imposed upon national banking associations as compared with state savings and loan

---

Statute providing that no sales or use tax shall be imposed upon the purchases, sales and use of tangible personal property which is subject matter of written contract of purchase entered into by national bank was designed to avoid imposition of unexpected sale. and use taxes on a national bank on all purchases, sales and use of tangible personal property by a national bank where a written contract covering such transaction was entered into prior to September 1, 1969. Comptroller of Treas. v Maryland Nat'l Bank, 408 A.2d 753 (Md. App. 1979), quoting Michie on Banks and Banking.

[2597] First Nat'l Bank v. Commissioner of Revenue, 80 N.M. 699, 460 P.2d 64, cert. denied, 80 N.M. 707, 460 P.2d 72 (1969), appeal dismissed, 397 U.S. 661, 90 S. Ct. 1407, 25 L. Ed. 2d 643 (1970).

Services of maintenance and process of other banks' accounts were not reasonably necessary or incident to business or functions of national banking association hence state was not precluded by federal law from levying pass receipts tax on association's receipts collected for such services; and, in any event, association could pass tax on to banks for which it performed services and therefore was not the real taxpayer. First Nat'l Bank v. Commissioner of Revenue, 80 N.M. 699, 460 P.2d 64, cert. denied, 80 N.M. 707, 460 P.2d 72 (1989), appeal dismissed, 397 U.S. 661, 90 S. Ct. 1407, 25 L. Ed. 2d 643 (1970).

Where Krugerrands are transferred as medium of exchange, coins remain intangible personal property, not subject to tax, but where they are transferred as investment commodity, they become tangible personal property within meaning of General Sales Tax Act. Michigan Nat'l Bank v. Department of Treas., 339 N.W.2d 515 (Mich. App. 1988).

Provision in General Sales Tax Act permitting Department of Treasury to regard certain persons as agents for purposes of act did not impose liability on bank for sales tax as agent for coin dealer, but merely restated law that principal, or dealer, can be held liable, tax-wise, for acts of its agent, and did not impose liability upon agent for acts of his principal. Michigan Nat'l Bank v. Department of Treas., 339 N.W.2d 515 (Mich. App. 1983).

[2598] Security-First Nat'l Bank v. Franchise Tax Board, 55 Cal. 2d 407, 11 Cal. Rptr. 289, 359 P.2d 625, appeal dismissed, 368 U.S. 3, 82 S. Ct. 15, 7 L. Ed. 2d 16.

Intention of Congress in authorizing states to tax national banks was to prevent discrimination against national banks by imposition upon them of heavier burden of taxation than that applied to other corporations, particularly "financial corporations" in competition with them. Grange Mut. Life Co. v. State Tax Comm'n, 76 Idaho 308, 283 P.2d 187.

associations, the court will look to the effect of the tax, not its rate.[2599] At one time it was held that a state could not impose a tax on a president of a national bank doing business in the state, on the grounds that such president is an officer prescribed by Congress, through whom, in part, the business of the bank must be carried on, and a tax on such president would be a burden on a federal agency.[2600] It also was held that the appointment of a conservator for a national bank under the Bank Conservation Act did not destroy its corporate entity so as to absolve it from taxation where it was subsequently reorganized and continued to function under its original charter.[2601]

Merger.—Where a newly formed banking corporation acquired all capital assets of another banking corporation by merger, the surviving banking association was liable for a financial institution excise tax for the succeeding year even though it had done no business during the year of reorganization, and the tax would be measured by the net income of the acquired banking association during the year of reorganization.[2602]

Lease or Sale.—Transactions whereby a bank bought and leased back customers' equipment in order to increase its lending limit to its customers were in reality financing arrangements and not leases involving transfer of title which would be subject to sales tax where customers retained all indicia of ownership before and after the transactions.[2603]

§ 24. Real Property.

A state and its political subdivisions have the power to tax real property of national banks with other real property in the state.[2604] This power has

---

2599 Michigan Nat'l Bank v. Michigan, 365 U.S. 467, 81 S. Ct. 659, 5 L. Ed. 2d 710.

2600 Linton v. Childs, 105 Ga. 567, 32 S.E. 617; Provident Inst. v. Massachusetts, 73 U.S. (6 Wall.) 611, 18 L. Ed. 907.

2601 Freeborn County v. First Nat. Bank, 199 Minn. 29, 270 N.W. 908.

2602 Birmingham Trust Nat'l Bank v. State, 292 Ala. 335, 294 So. 2d 153 (1974).

2603 Bullock v. Citizens Nat'l Bank, 663 S.W.2d 923 (Tex. App. 8 Dist. 1984).

2604 **In general.—**

United States.—12 U.S.C.S. § 548(3); (prior to January 1, 1972); Stephens v. Reed, 121 F.2d 696; Land Title Bank, etc., Co. v. Ward, 20 F. Supp. 810, 1937 U.S. Dist. LEXIS 1474 (E.D. Pa. 1937), citing People v. Weaver, 100 U.S. 539, 25 L. Ed. 705 (1879).

California.—United States Nat'l Bank v. County of Los Angeles, 234 Cal. App. 2d 196, 44 Cal. Rptr. 286 (1965).

Florida.—Roberts v. American Nat'l Bank, 97 Fla. 411, 121 So. 554.

Montana.—Miners Nat. Bank v. Silver Bow County, 148 P.2d 538.

never been abridged by Congress; on the contrary, it has always been protected and preserved.[2605]

Local property tax falls on land itself, not on landowner's equity in land.[2606]

Oklahoma.—State v. Moreland, 152 Okla. 37, 3 P.2d 803.

"According to its value" as used in statute retaining in the states and their subdivisions the power to tax real property of a national bank to the same extent, according to its value as other real property is taxed, does not limit the manner of collection of state taxes but merely limits the tax which a state might levy to an ad valorem tax levied upon the same basis as all real estate similarly situated in the taxing district. Land Title Bank & Trust Co. v. Ward, 20 F. Supp. 810, 1937 U.S. Dist. LEXIS 1474 (E.D. Pa. 1937).

The trade fixtures and equipment of national bank, all, or practically all, of which could be removed from leased premises without any substantial injury to building, could not be taxed to the national bank as "realty." First Nat. Bank v. Marion County, 169 Ore. 595, 130 P.2d 9. See also § 26a of this chapter.

Bank's night depository equipment, drive-up window equipment, vault doors and remote transaction units, which were physically integrated with bank's land and buildings and adapted to the use of the realty, were fixtures and subject to taxation as real property. Michigan Nat'l Bank v. City of Lansing, 96 Mich. App. 551, 293 N.W.2d 626 (1980).

For tax classification purposes, test for determining whether an item is a fixture is whether a reasonable person would consider the item to be a permanent part of the property, taking into account annexation, adaptation, and other objective manifestations of permanence. Crocker Nat'l Bank v. City & County, 49 Cal. 3d 881, 264 Cal. Rptr. 139, 782 P.2d 278 (1989).

Electronic data processing equipment were not fixtures for tax purposes as most of the equipment was: (1) General purpose "off the-shelf" equipment; (2) not physically attached to the building other than through standardized quick-disconnect plugs inserted into a power source ; (3) readily movable without damage to itself or the building and (4) not designed or modified for the building, which was not modified for its equipment. Crocker National Bank v. City and County of San Francisco, 49 Cal. 3d 881, 264 Cal. Rptr. 139, 782 P.2d 278 (1989).

2605 Land Title Bank& Trust Co. v. Ward, 20 F. Supp. 810, 1937 U.S. Dist. LEXIS 1474 (E.D. Pa. 1937).

Thus in section 41 of the Act of June 3, 1864, 13 State 112, which provided for the incorporation of national banks, is found the following proviso: "Provided, also, That nothing in this act shall exempt the real estate of associations from either state, county or municipal taxes to the same extent, according to its value, as other real estate is taxed." This proviso has been retained in substantially the same form ever since. Land Title Bank, etc., Co. v. Ward, 20 F. Supp. 810, 1937 U.S. Dist. LEXIS 1474 (E.D. Pa. 1937).

2606 First NH Bank v. Town of Windham, 639 A.2d 1089 (N.H. 1994).

(B). National Bank Shares.

§ 25. In General.

Taxation of Shares Authorized by Federal Statute.—A national bank is an instrumentality of the federal government, and a state and its subdivisions are without power by virtue of any state law to levy a tax upon shares of its stock,"[2607] which are taxable only as Congress permits.[2608]

[2607] Gully v. First Nat. Bank, 81 F.2d 502, rev'd on other grounds, 299 U.S. 109, 57 S. Ct. 96, 81 L. Ed. 70; Cherokee State Bank v. Wallace, 202 Minn. 582, 279 N.W. 410.

National banking institutions created and existing pursuant to federal statute were "instrumentalities of the United States" and were therefore immune from state and local taxes not within purview of federal statute dealing with state taxation of national bank shares. First Nat'l Bank v. Dickinson, 291 F. Supp. 855 (N.D. Fla. 1968), aff'd, 393 U.S. 409, 89 S. Ct. 685, 21 L. Ed. 2d 634 (1969).

National banks are not merely private businesses but rather are agencies of the United States created by it to promote its fiscal policies and financed by private capital, and such banks and their shares are taxable by the states only with the consent of Congress and then only in accordance with such restrictions as Congress may place. Morris & Essex Inv. Co. v. Director of Division of Taxation, 33 N.J. 24, 161 A.2d 491.

[2608] **In general.—**

Johnson v. Meagher County, 116 Mont. 565, 155 P.2d 750.

Stock in national banks may be taxed only by consent of Congress. State Tax Com. v. Baltimore Nat'l Bank, 174 Md. 403, 199 A. 119; Irvine v. Spaeth, 210 Minn. 489, 299 N.W. 204, appeal dismissed, 314 U.S. 575, 62 S. Ct. 117, 86 L. Ed. 466; Maricopa County v. Valley Nat. Bank, 130 F.2d 356, aff'd, 318 U.S. 357, 63 S. Ct. 587, 87 L. Ed. 834.

The federal statutes concerning state taxation of shares in national banking associations furnish the exclusive authority governing state taxation as to national banks. Bedford v. Colorado Nat'l Bank, 104 Colo. 311, 91 P.2d 469.

Federal statute governing state taxation of national bank shares was intended to prescribe the only ways in which the states can tax national banks. First Agricultural Nat'l Bank v. State Tax Comm'n, 392 U.S. 339, 88 S. Ct. 2173, 20 L. Ed. 2d 1138 (1968).

Statute marks outer limits.—

Federal statute governing state taxation of national bank shares marks outer limit within which states can tax national banks. First Agricultural Nat'l Bank v. State Tax Comm'n, 392 U.S. 339, 88 S. Ct. 2173, 20 L. Ed. 2d 1138 (1968).

Congressional silence constitutes ban.—

National banks cannot be taxed upon their shares except as Congress may grant that right by express permission, and mere silence of Congress in such respect in itself constitutes a ban. Odland v. Findley, 38 F. Supp. 563, 20 Ohio Op. 530, 1941 U.S. Dist. LEXIS 3269, rev'd on other grounds, State ex rel. Henneford v. Yelle, 127 F.2d 948, 1942 Wash. LEXIS 401 12 Wn.2d 434 (1942).

However, such shares in the hands of individual shareholders have, by express enactment of Congress,[2609] been placed within the reach of the taxing power of states.[2610] But such shares cannot be assessed for ad

---

[2609] See 12 U.S.C.S. § 548 (prior to January 1, 1972). See also § 26a of this chapter.

[2610] **In general.—**

United States.—Van Allen v. Assessors, 70 U.S. (3 Wall.) 573, 18 L. Ed. 229; People v. Commissioners, 71 U.S. (4 Wall.) 244, 18 L. Ed. 344; Tappan v. Merchants' Nat. Bank, 86 U.S. (19 Wall.) 490, 22 L. Ed. 189; Bank of Redemption v. Boston, 125 U.S. 60, 8 S. Ct. 772, 31 L. Ed. 689; Van Slyke v. Wisconsin, 154 U.S. 581, 14 S. Ct 1168, 20 L. Ed. 240; Aberdeen Bank v. Chehalis, 166 U.S. 440, 17 S. Ct. 629, 41 L. Ed. 1069; Citizens' Nat. Bank v. Kentucky, 217 U.S. 443, 30 S. Ct. 532, 54 L. Ed. 832 (1970); First Nat. Bank v. Farwell, 7 F. 518, 10 Biss. 270; Exchange Nat'l Bank v. Miller, 19 F. 372; Whitney Nat. Bank v. Parker, 41 F. 402; Hager v. American Nat. Bank, 159 F. 396; Hager v. Louisville Nat. Banking Co., 159 F. 402; Buder v. First Nat. Bank, 16 F.2d 990, cert. denied, 274 U.S. 743, 47 S. Ct. 588, 71 L. Ed. 1321; First Nat. Bank v. Covington, 129 F. 792, aff'd, 198 U.S. 100, 25 S. Ct. 562, 49 L. Ed. 963; Boise City Nat. Bank v. Ada County, 37 F.2d 947; First Nat. Bank v. Adams, 258 U.S. 362, 42 S. Ct. 323, 66 L. Ed. 661.

Taxation, against stockholder, of stock in national bank, held not to constitute taxation of bank's property. Citizens', etc., Nat. Bank v. Atlanta, 46 F.2d 88, aff'd, 58 F.M 557.

Alabama.—Sumter v. National Bank, 62 Ala. 464, 34 Am. R. 30.

Arizona.—Consolidated Nat. Bank v. Pima, 5 Ariz. 142, 48 P. 291.

Arkansas.—First Nat. Bank v. Board, 92 Ark. 335, 122 S.W. 988.

California.—McHenry v. Downer, 116 Cal. 20, 47 P. 779, 45 L.R.A. 737; Crocker v. Scott, 149 Cal. 575, 87 P. 102; First Nat. Bank v. San Francisco, 129 Cal. 96, 61 P. 778; Bank of California Nat. Ass'n v. Roberts, 173 Cal. 398, 160 P.225, rev'd on other grounds, 248 U.S. 497, 39 S. Ct. 171, 63 L. Ed. 381; Bank of California Nat. Ass'n v. Richardson, 175 Cal. 813, 165 P. 152, rev'd on other grounds, 248 U.S. 476, 39 S. Ct. 165, 63 L. Ed. 372.

Florida.—Roberts v. American Nat. Bank, 97 Fla. 411, 121 So. 554.

Idaho.—People v. Moore, 1 Idaho 504.

Illinois.—People v. Bradley, 39 Ill. 130, rev'd on other grounds, 71 U.S. (4 Wall.) 459, 18 L. Ed. 433; People v. First Nat'l Bank, 351 Ill. 435, 184 N.E. 645.

Indiana.—Wright v. Stilz, 27 Ind. 338; Whitney v. Ragsdale, 33 Ind. 107, 5 Am. R. 185; Stilts v. Tutewiler, Wils. 507.

Iowa.—Morseman v. Younkin, 27 Iowa 350.

Kentucky.—Scobee v. Bean, 109 Ky. 528, 59 S.W. 860, 22 Ky. L. Rptr. 1076; Commonwealth v. Citizens' Nat'l Bank, 117 Ky. 946, 80 S.W. 158, 25 Ky. L. Rptr. 2100, appeal dismissed, Citizens Nat'l Bank v. Kentucky, 199 U.S. 603, 26 S. Ct. 750, 50 L. Ed. 329; Commonwealth v. Jackson, 61 S.W. 700, 22 Ky. L. Rptr. 1788; Citizens' Nat. Bank v. Commonwealth, 118 Ky. 51, 80 S.W. 479, 81 S.W. 686, 25 Ky. L. Rptr. 2254; Farmers' Nat. Bank v. Commonwealth, 80 S.W. 1198.

Louisiana.—Statute taxing bank shares makes no distinction between national and state banks. Flournoy v. First Nat'l Bank, 197 La. 1067, 3 So. 2d 244.

valorem taxation at a rate greater than other moneyed capital in the hands of

---

Maine.—Abbott v. Bangor, 54 Me. 540; In re Opinion of the Justices, 133 Me. 521, 177 A. 897.

Massachusetts.—Austin v. Board of Alderman, 96 Mass. (14 Allen) 359, aff'd, 74 U.S. (7 Wall.) 694, 19 L. Ed. 224; Flint v. Board of Aldermen, 99 Mass. 141, 96 Am. Dec. 718.

Michigan.—National Bank. v. Detroit, 277 Mich. 571, 269 N.W. 602; Manufacturers Nat'l Bank v. Detroit, 285 Mich. 278, 280 N.W. 760; First Nat. Bank v. St. Joseph, 46 Mich. 526, 9 N.W. 838; Davis v. Kalamazoo, 1 Mich. N.P. 16.

Minnesota.—Smith v. Webb, 11 Minn. 500, 11 Gilf. 378; State v. First Nat'l Bank, 164 Minn. 235, 204 N.W. 874, aff'd, 273 U.S. 561, 47 S. Ct. 468, 71 L. Ed. 774.

Missouri.—Lionberger v. Rowse, 43 Mo. 67; First Nat. Bank v. Meredith, 44 Mo. 500; Curtis v. Ward, 58 Mo. 295; Clapp v. Ward, 58 Mo. 296.

Montana.—Statute held valid. Merchants' Nat'l Bank v. Dawson County, 93 Mont. 310, 19 P.2d 892.

New Jersey.—Fox v. Haight, 31 N.J.L. 399; Jewell v. Hart, 31 N.J.L. 434; State v. Smith, 55 N.J.L. 110, 25 A. 277; Mechanics' Nat'l Bank v. Baker, 65 N.J.L. 113, 46 A. 586, aff'd, 65 N.J.L. 549, 48 A. 582.

New Mexico.—Statute requiring assessment of bank stockholders for taxes on value of their shares in bank's name as their agent is not invalid in respect to national bank as taxing it in manner not permitted by federal statutes, as taxes are against stockholders, not bank. First Nat'l Bank v. State Tax Comm'n, 43 N.M. 307, 92 P.2d 987, appeal dismissed, 308 U.S. 515, 60 S. Ct. 173, 84 L. Ed. 439.

New York.—Utica v. Churchill, 33 N.Y. 161, rev'd on other grounds, 70 U.S. (3 Wall.) 573, 18 L. Ed. 229; First Nat'l Bank v. Fancher, 48 N.Y. 524; Utica v. Churchill, 43 Barb. 650.

North Carolina.—Kyle v. Fayetteville, 75 N.C. 445.

Ohio.—PARKER v. SIEBERN, 3 Ohio Dec. Rep. 441; Frazer v. Siebern, 16 Ohio St. 614.

Pennsylvania.—Mintzer v. Montgomery, 54 Pa. 139; Pittsburgh v. First Nat. Bank, 65 Pa. 45; Strong v. O'Donnell, 32 Leg. Int. 283; Gorley v. Bowlby, 8 Pa. County Ct. 17.

South Carolina.—Charleston v. People's Nat. Bank, 5 S.C. 103, 22 Am. R. 1.

Texas.—Harrison v. Vines, 46 Tex. 15; Adair v. Robinson, 6 Tex. Civ. App. 275, 26 S.W. 734; First Nat. Bank v. Lampasas, 33 Tex. Civ. App. 530, 78 S.W. 42 (1903).

Utah.—Salt Lake City Nat. Bank v. Golding, 2 Utah 1; First Nat. Bank v. Christensen, 39 Utah 568, 118 P. 778.

Washington.—Bakery. King, 17 Wash. 622, 50 P. 481; Pacific Nat'l Bank v. Pierce County, 20 Wash. 675, 56 P. 936.

West Virginia.—BANK v. STATE, 58 W. Va. 559, 52 S.E. 494, 3 L.R.A. (n.s.) 584, 6 Ann. Cas. 115; In re National Bank, 137 W. Va. 673, 73 S.E.2d 655 (1952).

Wisconsin.—Bagnall v. State, 25 Wis. 112.

Federal statute extends to territorial governments, and sets the limits of their exercise of the power. Domenech v. National City Bank, 294 U.S. 199, 55 S. Ct. 368, 79 L. Ed. 857.

(Text continued on page 722)

Inapplicable to District of Columbia.—

The statute relating to state taxation of national bank shares was addressed to state legislatures and was inapplicable to gross earnings tax to which banks in District of Columbia were subject, although statute was relevant as indication of congressional policy. Hamilton Nat. Bank v. District of Columbia, 156 F.2d 843.

Right rests upon exception.—

The state's right to tax shares of national banks rests upon exception by which the states are empowered to tax such shares. Price Flavoring Extract Co. v. Lindheimer, 368 Ill. 450, 14 N.E.2d 476.

Congress did not intend by the amendment to the federal exemption statute to withdraw in any respect its consent to state taxation of national or state bank share. Bank of Texas v. Childs, 615 S.W.2d 810 (Tex. Civ. App. 1981).

State taxation of state bank shares as well as of national bank shares falls within the original exception to the exemption provided by federal statute. Bank of Texas v. Childs, 615 S.W.2d 810 (Tex. Civ. App. 1981).

The federal exemption statute both before and after amendment must be construed as a specific statute with respect to state taxation of bank shares and, therefore, as prevailing as against a more general exemption of federal securities provided by the consent statute. Bank of Texas v. Childs, 615 S.W.2d 810 (Tex. Civ. App. 1981).

The 1969 revision of the federal exemption statute was not intended to withdraw the consent of Congress to state taxation of bank shares to the extent of federal securities held by the banks. Bank of Texas v. Childs, 615 S.W.2d 810 (Tex. Civ. App. 1981).

Since it is apparent that when Congress enacted the federal exemption statute, it was focusing on the particular question of the taxation of bank shares, and that when it amended the consent statute, it was focusing on the general exemptions of federal securities, including both principal and interest, from state and local taxation, and since no clear intention was manifested by the amendment to extend the exemption to bank shares to the extent of the bank's holding of federal securities, the apparent intention was to leave unimpaired the consent to such taxation. Bank of Texas v. Childs, 615 S.W.2d 810 (Tex. Civ. App. 1981).

The plan conceived by Dallas County for imposing a tax on bank shares was not invalid because of its failure to deduct the federal securities held by the bank from its net assets in determining value of its shares. Bank of Texas v. Childs, 615 S.W.2d 810 (Tex. Civ. App. 1981).

Federal statute is a grant of authority in prescribed form only, and is not merely a weapon of defense against such taxation. Gully v. First Nat. Bank, 81 F.2d 502, rev'd on other grounds, 299 U.S. 109, 57 S. Ct. 96, 81 L. Ed. 70.

The federal statute is merely a "waiver" of immunity against reassessment of taxes, enabling legislature to tax through authority delegated by state constitution, but not to exempt from taxation. Flournoy v. First Nat. Bank, 3 So. 2d 244, 197 La. 1067.

Statute must conform with conditions of federal permission.—

People's Nat'l Bank & Trust Co. v. Westchester County, 261 N.Y. 342, 185 N.E. 405; United States v. Lewis, 10 F. Supp. 471, 1935 U.S. Dist. LEXIS 1715 (1935); Cherokee

(Text continued on page 722)

State Bank v. Wallace, 202 Minn. 582, 279 N.W. 410.

Consent to taxation may be withdrawn.—

Congress by consenting to taxation of share, of stock of national bank by states confers a "privilege" for which nothing is given by the state or received by the United States, which privilege is a mere "bounty" or "gratuity," and hence can be withdrawn by Congress at any time. Maricopa County v. Valley Nat. Bank, 130 F.2d 356, aff'd, 318 U.S. 357, 63 S. Ct 587, 87 L. Ed. 834

The tax authorized is against the holders of shares, and is measured by the value thereof and not by the assets of the bank, without deduction of its liabilities. State v. First Nat. Bank, 273 U.S. 561, 47 S. Ct. 468, 71 L. Ed. 774.

The tax imposed by statute on shares of banking institutions based on fair market value of shares is imposed upon the stockholders, not on the bank. Owensboro Nat'l Bank v. Department of Revenue, 394 S.W.2d 461 (Ky. 1965).

The tax levied by the state must be a tax upon shareholders and not upon the assets of the bank notwithstanding the bank pays the tax as agent of shareholders. Odland v. Findley, 38 F. Supp. 563, 20 Ohio Op. 530, 1941 U.S. Dist. LEXIS 3269 (1941), rev'd on other grounds, State ex rel. Henneford v. Yelle, 127 F.2d 948, 1942 Wash. LEXIS 401, 12 Wn.2d 434 (1942).

The tax is imposed against the stockholders only the bank being their agent with the right of reimbursement. Board of Supervisors v. State Nat. Bank, 300 Ky. 620, 189 S.W.2d 942.

The tax has exclusive relation to distinct value of shares, and such shares are taxable without regard to capital or value or character of property owned by bank. Board of Supervisors v. State Nat. Bank, 300 Ky. 620, 189 S.W.2d 942.

Preferred stock of national banks is within purview of statute requiring assessment and taxation of bank stockholders on value of their shares, though such banks were not authorized to issue preferred stock when statute was enacted. First Nat. Bank v. State Tax Comm., 43 N.M. 307, 92 P.2d 987, appeal dismissed, 308 U.S. 515, 60 S. Ct. 173, 84 L. Ed. 439.

Shares owned by agency of federal government, such as Reconstruction Finance Corporation, was held subject to state taxation in Baltimore Nat'l Bank v. State Tax Com., 297 U.S. 209, 56 S. Ct. 417, 80 L. Ed. 586. See United States v. Lewis, 10 F. Supp. 471, 1935 U.S. Dist. LEXIS 1715 (1935).

But subsequent federal act providing that, notwithstanding any privilege or consent previously granted, shares of preferred stock of national bank acquired by Reconstruction Finance Corporation should not be subject to any taxation by any state or local taxing authority, prevented state taxation of national bank's preferred stock owned by Reconstruction Finance Corporation, and bank could not be required to pay tax in respect of such stock. State Tax Com. v. Baltimore Nat'l Bank, 174 Md. 403, 199 A. 119.

The federal statute, as applied to taxes which became a lien on the shares prior to effective date of the statute, is not unconstitutional as depriving the state and its political subdivisions of their property without "due process of law" or as taking away stat's "reserved powers." Maricopa County v. Valley Nat'l Bank, 130 F.2d 356, aff'd, 318 U.S. 357, 63 S. Ct. 587, 87 L. Ed. 834.

(Text continued on page 722)

The federal act does not violate the Tenth Amendment, since the authority by which end stock was previously taxed did not stem from "powers reserved to the states," nor the Fifth Amendment, even though the enforcement of tax liens impressed on stock before effective date of the act is prevented. Maricopa County v. Valley Nat'l Bank, 318 U.S. 357, 63 S. Ct. 587, 87 L. Ed. 834.

Where situs of national bank stock owned by nonresidents is in the state where the association is located, such stock is assessable for taxation by such state to the same extent as taxes are imposed by the state. First Trust Joint Stock Land Bank v. Dallas (Tex. Civ. App.), 167 S.W.2d 783.

Bank's practice to pay tax without charging it back to owners of stock held not to render owners of stock any the less liable for the tax as respects application of the statute to stock of the Reconstruction Finance Corporation, since requirement of stat its that bank collect the tax merely provides a convenient method of collection. United States v. Lewis, 10 F. Supp. 471, 1935 U.S. Dist. LEXIS 1715 (1935).

Relationship to other types of taxation.—

The federal statute permitting state taxation of national bank shares does not prohibit the state from imposing a franchise tax on holding companies on basis of net income from dividends on stock held. Oliver Continuous Filter Co. v. McColgan, 48 Cal. App. 2d 800, 120 P.2d 682.

Statute imposing tax on income from any source, unless expressly exempted thereby or not taxable under state or federal constitution, did not change state's method of taxing shares of national banks' stock by substituting tax on dividends thereon for ad valorem tax on such shares. Johnson v. Meagher County, 116 Mont. 565, 155 P.2d 750.

National banks were relieved from former ad valorem tax on shares by the act taxing dividends received from shares of state and national banks in same manner as taxable dividends of corporations. Little Rock v. Arkansas Corp. Com., 209 Ark. 18, 189 S.W.2d 382.

State exceeding statutory power.—

Statute taxing branch national banks on capital employed therein could not be construed as intended to tax only shares of stockholders. Goodwin v. Citizens, etc., Nat. Bank, 209 Ga. 908, 76 S.E.2d 620 (1953).

Where the state of Ohio assessed tax on national bank shares against bank and when the tax was not paid certified delinquent tax to recorder in same form that tax had been carried plus a ten percent penalty, there was no authority in either state or federal law to shift liability from shareholders to property of bank, and the 10 percent penalty was not an assessment of "penalty" under Ohio statute authorizing assessment of penalty of $100 per day for delay of bank in collecting and paying tax on shares. Odland v. Findley, 38 F. Supp. 563, 20 Ohio Op. 530, 1941 U.S. Dist. LEXIS 3269 (1941), rev'd on other grounds, State ex rel. Henneford v. Yelle, 127 F.2d 948, 1942 Wash. LEXIS 401, 12 Wn.2d 434 (1942).

Figures shown on bank's books controlling.—

The Department of Revenue is not permitted to take the depreciated or appreciated value of a bond portfolio, and apply those figures against an amount of an undivided profit as shown on the books of the bank, and adjust the surplus figure as shown on books of the bank

citizens of a state.[2611] Such a tax is not invalid, however, because of a provision that the assessor shall make his valuation of such shares from a bank's statement of its capital, surplus and undivided profits.[2612]

Extent of State's Power to Tax Shares.—With the exception of the conditions expressed in the federal statute, the power of states to impose a tax upon shares of stock of national banks in the hands of stockholders is

---

to arrive at the bank's assessed value; in determining what proportion of the value of stock assessed to the stockholders is to be classified within the seven percent classification and what proportion is to be classified within the 30 percent classification for the purposes of taxation, the department is required by the statute to use only those figures shown on the books of the bank. First Nat'l Bank v. Department of Revenue, 541 P.2d 1219 (Mont. 1975).

Application of partial-year prorated tax assessment.—

Where a bank had been continuously engaged in the banking business for many years, a statute imposing a partial-year prorated tax assessment on a taxpayer who engages in business after the first day of January in any year did not apply to a bank which in May of the tax year purchased a truck wash and related equipment and entered into a five-year lease, although the bank bad not previously been required to pay a tax on tangible personalty used in the business due to an exemption of financial institutions from the payment of such tax and in May for the first time engaged in the nonexempt business of holding personalty for leasing. First Nat'l Bank v. Kosydar, 45 Ohio St. 2d 101, 341 N.E.2d 579, 74 Ohio Op. 2d 206 (1976).

Ratio.—

Numerator and denominator of apportionment factor of taxpayer for years 1973, 1974 and 1975 properly should include amount of taxpayer's interest income for such years from United States government obligations, even though such interest income was exempt from the state income tax. Continental Ill. Nat'l Bank & Trust Co. v. Lenckos, 115 Ill. App. 3d 538, 71 Ill. Dec. 156, 450 N.E.2d 844 (1983).

2611 **In general.—**

American Nat. Bank v. Andrews, 140 Okla. 266, 283 P. 253; In re Assessment of First Nat'l Bank, 58 Okla. 508, 160 P. 469, 1917B L.R.A. 294; Bonaparte v. American-First Nat. Bank, 139 Okla. 189, 281 P. 958; Price Flavoring Extract Co. v. Lindheimer, 368 Ill. 450, 14 N.E.2d 476.

Moneyed capital defined.—

Interest bearing demands against persons or corporations, and money loaned or invested in securities, including personal investment of surplus funds, are deemed "moneyed capital" employed in competition with national banks, as the term is used in the federal statute, relative to taxation of national banks' shares by state. State v. First Nat'l Bank, 164 Minn. 235, 204 N.W. 874, aff'd, 273 U.S. 561, 47 S. Ct. 468, 71 L. Ed. 774.

2612 Hannan v. First Nat. Bank, 269 F. 527, appeal dismissed, 266 U.S. 638, 45 S. Ct. 9, 69 L. Ed. 482; Des Moines Nat'l Bank v. Fairweather, 263 U.S. 103, 44 S. Ct. 28, 68 L. Ed. 191.

unrestricted.[2613] The stock of a state bank owned by a national bank, but not taxable to it, is to be considered an asset of the national bank in determining the value of its stock taxable to stockholders.[2614] But, a tax may be imposed on national bank shares, even though the capital of the bank is invested in United States securities[2615] or nontaxable bonds.[2616]

[2613] **In general.—**

United States.—Des Moines Nat. Bank v. Fairweather, 263 US. 103, 44 S. Ct. 23, 68 L. Ed. 191; Hager v. Am. Nat. Bank, 169 F. 396; Hager v. Louisville Nat. Banking Co., 159 F. 402.

Idaho.—People v. Moore, 1 Idaho 504.

Kentucky.—Richardson v. State Nat'l Bank, 135 Ky. 772, 123 S.W. 294.

Maine.—Stetson v. Bangor, 56 Me. 274.

Montana.—First Nat'l Bank v. Dawson County, 66 Mont. 321, 213 P. 1097.

New Jersey.—State v. Mayor & Common Council of Newark, 39 N.J.L. 380, rev'd on other grounds, 40 N.J.L. 558.

Pennsylvania.—Commonwealth v. Girard Nat. Bank, 6 Phila. 431.

Texas.—Dean v. Kopperl, 1 Tex. App. Civ. Cas. (White & W.) 409.

Test of validity of tax.—

Whether state law violates federal law authorizing taxation of national bank shares as personal property of owner depends on whether tax otherwise affects bank. Clark v. First Nat'l Bank, 130 Misc. 352, 224 N.Y.S. 10.

United States statute, providing for inclusion of shares of national bank in personal property of owner, subject to tax does not invalidate state laws making bank agent of stockholders to collect tax. Clark v. First Nat'l Bank, 130 Misc. 352, 224 N.Y.S. 10.

[2614] Bank of California v. Richardson, 248 U.S. 476, 39 S. Ct. 165, 63 L. Ed. 372.

[2615] **United States**—Van Allen v. Assessors, 70 U.S. (3 Wall.) 573, 18 L. Ed. 229; People v. Commissioners, 71 U.S. (4 Wall.) 244, 18 L. Ed. 344; Bradley v. People, 71 U.S. (4 Wall.) 459, 18 L. Ed. 433; Provident Inst. v. Massachusetts, 73 U.S. (6 Wall.) 611, 18 L. Ed. 907; National Bank v. Commonwealth, 76 U.S. (9 Wall.) 358, 19 L. Ed. 701; Lionberger v. Rouse, 76 U.S. (9 Wall.) 468, 19 L. Ed. 721; Evansville Bank v. Britton, 105 U.S. 322, 26 L. Ed. 1053; Cleveland Trust Co. v. Lander, 184 U.S. 111, 22 S. Ct. 394, 46 L. Ed. 456; Home Sav. Bank v. Des Moines, 205 U.S. 503, 27 S. Ct. 571, 51 L. Ed. 901. See Palmer v. McMahon, 133 U.S. 660, 10 S. Ct. 324, 38 L. Ed. 772; Merchants' & Mfrs' Bank v. Pennsylvania, 167 U.S. 461, 17 S. Ct. 829, 42 L. Ed. 238; Snyder v. Bettman, 190 U.S. 249, 23 S. Ct. 803, 47 L. Ed. 1035; First Nat. Bank v. Farwell, 7 F. 518; Mercantile Bank v. New York, 121 U.S. 138, 7 S. Ct. 826, 30 L. Ed. 895; Aberdeen Bank v. Chehalis County, 166 U.S. 440, 17 S. Ct. 629, 41 L. Ed. 1069; Exchange Nat. Bank v. Miller, 19 F. 372; Hager v. Am. Nat. Bank, 159 F. 396; Hager V. Louisville Nat. Banking Co., 159 F. 402; Owensboro Nat'l Bank v. Owensboro, 173 U.S. 664, 19 S. Ct. 537, 43 L. Ed. 850.

Alabama.—McIver v. Robinson, 53 Ala. 456.

Exceptions to the principle that a state may not encroach upon the borrowing power of the United States government by taxing federal obligations exist where Congress has consented to the state's imposition of a tax upon stockholders' interests in a national bank, measured by corporate asset values, without making any deduction for federal obligations owned by the banks.[2617] Trial court in tax refund case erred in finding that bond premiums should be amortized and excluded in computing amount of interest income from state and municipal bonds.[2618] Bank shares tax

---

Illinois.—People v. Bradley, 39 Ill. 130, rev'd on other grounds, 71 U.S. (4 Wall.) 459, 18 L. Ed. 433.

Indiana.—A tax upon the shares of a bank is not a tax upon the property or capital of the bank. Wright v. Stilz, 27 Ind. 338.

Iowa.—First Nat. Bank v. Anderson, 196 Iowa 587, 192 N.W. 6, rev'd on other grounds, 269 U.S. 341, 46 S. Ct. 135, 70 L. Ed 295; Farmers', etc., Sav. Bank v. Neighbour, 195 Iowa 394, 192 N.W. 159.

Montana.—Montana Nat. Bank v. Yellowstone County, 78 Mont. 62, 252 P. 876.

State could not impose a tax upon stockholders' interests in a national bank, measured by corporate asset values, without making a deduction for federal obligations owned by the bank. First Sec. Bank v. Montana Dep't of Revenue, 580 P.2d 913 (Mont. 1978).

Nebraska.—Such a tax is not a tax upon the bank, and the fact that the value of United States obligations is considered in ascertaining the value of shares does not render the tax unlawful. State v. First Nat'l Bank, 103 Neb. 280, 171 N.W. 912.

New Jersey.—State v. Haight, 31 N.J.L. 399; Jewel' v. Hart, 31 N.J.L. 434.

New York.—People v. Assessors, 44 Barb. 148, 29 How. Pr. 371.

Ohio.—Frazer v. Siebern, 16 Ohio St. 614.

Texas.—Harrison v. Vines, 46 Tex. 15; Adair v. Robinson, 6 Tex. Civ. App. 275, 25 S.W. 734.

2616 First Nat'l Bank v. Board of Equilization, 92 Ark. 335, 122 S.W. 988.

The provision of Federal Farm Loan Act, that first mortgages executed to federal land banks shall be deemed instrumentalities of the government, and shall be exempt from federal, state, municipal, and local taxation, is valid, and must prevail over any inconsistent laws of a state. Federal Land Bank v. Crosland, 261 U.S. 374, 48 S. Ct. 385, 67 L. Ed. 703, 29 A.L.R. 1.

Imposition of bank shares tax on national bank did not violate state statute exempting all state and municipal obligations from taxation where bank shares tax was imposed on capital owned and employed by bank in its banking operations, which capital was property interest separate from state and municipal obligations themselves. Dale Nat'l Bank v. Commonwealth, 465 A.2d 965 (Pa. 1983).

2617 Montana Bankers Ass'n v. Montana Dep't of Revenue, 580 P.2d 909 (Mont. 1978).

2618 Continental Ill. Nat'l Bank & Trust Co. v. Lenckos, 115 Ill. App. 3d 538, 71 Ill. Dec. 156, 450 N.E.2d 844 (1983).

imposed on a national bank violated the federal statute exempting obligations of the United States from taxation by or under state authority where the tax was computed on the basis of equity capital and where equity capital was determined in part by the bank's ownership of United States obligations.[2619] Characterizing a tax on bank shares as a tax for privilege of doing business did not cure a violation of the federal statute exempting United States obligations from taxation by or under state authority where imposing a tax on the bank for the privilege of doing business would not effect a change in the means of calculating its bank shares tax by eliminating a determination of the tax in part by the bank's ownership of United States obligations.[2620] And national bank stock may be assessed for purposes of taxation at an amount above its par value, if such a valuation is used by state law in assessing other moneyed capital for taxes;[2621] it may also be separated from the person of its owner, and given a situs of its own for purposes of taxation.[2622] And if bank stock is taxed on its fair cash value, it is appropriate to determine such value on actual sales of the stock, coupled with consideration of other elements entering into the fair cash value of such shares.[2623] The manner in which such taxes shall be assessed and collected, and the place where they shall be imposed upon resident stockholders, are left to the discretion of the legislature of the state where each bank is located.[2624] Thus, under a state statute providing that the "equalization," collection, penalties and laws relating to other personal property in a taxing district shall apply to bank stock, the value of such stock need not be "equalized" with other personal property in a county in view of explicit statutory language levying a tax on bank stock at its fair cash value.[2625] And a state may tax national bank stock under a different system from other

---

[2619] Dale Nat'l Bank v. Commonwealth, 465 A.2d 965 (Pa. 1983).

[2620] Dale Nat'l Bank v. Commonwealth, 465 A.2d 965 (Pa. 1983).

[2621] State v. Mayor & Common Council of Newark, 39 N.J.L. 380; Hepburn v. School Directors, 90 U.S. (28 Wall.) 480, 23 L. Ed. 112.

[2622] Tappan v. Merchants' Nat. Bank, 86 U.S. (19 Wall.) 490, 22 L. Ed. 189; Kyle v. Fayetteville, 75 N.C. 445; Abbott v. Bangor, 54 Me. 540.

[2623] Owensboro Nat'l Bank v. Department of Revenue, 394 S.W.2d 461 (Ky. 1965).

The fair cash value of bank stock for the purpose of an ad valorem tax is not controlled by the mere addition of the value of bank's assets, whether they be the 100 percent cash value of tangible property, or various other assets, including good will, etc. Owensboro Nat'l Bank v. Department of Revenue, 394 S.W.2d 461 (Ky. 1965).

[2624] State v. Mayor & Common Council of Newark, 39 N.J.L. 380, rev'd on other grounds, 40 N.J.L. 558; Bagnall v. State, 25 Wis. 112.

[2625] Owensboro Nat'l Bank v. Department of Revenue, 394 S.W.2d 461 (Ky. 1966).

property, provided no inequality arises.[2626] For cases dealing with methods of valuation of national bank stock for tax purposes, other than those discussed in the text, see the footnote.[2627]

Shares Owned by Another National Bank.—The obvious intention of the federal statute is to permit a state in which a national bank is located to tax, subject to the limitations prescribed, all shares of its capital stock without regard to their ownership; the proper inference therefore is that the law permits the taxation of national banks owning shares of capital stock of another national bank on the same basis as all other shares.[2628] But the federal statute does not allow stock of one national bank owned by another such bank, and so taxed to it, to be considered as an asset of the owner bank for purposes of taxing its stockholders on their shares.[2629]

Shares Owned by Savings Bank or Other Corporation.—Stock of national banks in one state, which is held by a savings bank of another state, is taxable in the first state though the savings bank's property is exempt under the laws of its own state.[2630] And a state's determination of the amount of franchise tax to be levied on a corporation, by treating its shares of national

---

[2626] Montana Nat. Bank v. Yellowstone County, 78 Mont. 62, 252 P. 876.

[2627] A statute providing that each share in a bank is to be taxed only for the difference between its actual cash value and the proportionate amount per share at which its real estate is assessed, is susceptible of but one construction and is expressed in plain and unambiguous language. Abilene v. Meek, 311 S.W.2d 654 (Tex. Civ. App. 1958).

Under such a statute, in determining value of real estate city was required to accept its own assessed value thereof and not value as shown by bank statement which reflected indebtedness against real estate. Abilene v. Meek, 311 S.W.2d 654 (Tex. Civ. App. 1958).

The Edge Act, as amended, does not prohibit the state of Texas from assessing ad valorem taxes on shares of stock owned by nonresident shareholders of an Edge Act bank doing business in Texas. Houston v. Morgan Guaranty International Bank, 666 S.W.2d 524 (Tex. App. 1 Dist. 1983).

[2628] Bank of Redemption v. Boston, 125 U.S. 60, 8 S. Ct. 772, 31 L. Ed. 689; Bank of California v. Richardson, 248 U.S. 476, 39 S. Ct. 165, 63 L. Ed. 372; First Nat'l Bank v. Durr, 246 F. 163, aff'd sub nom. First Nat. Bank v. Beaman, 257 F. 729.

A statute exempting finance corporation's capital surplus and income from taxation does not extend exemption applicable to federal agencies generally so as to withdraw from state taxation stock which one national bank may hold in another. State Tax Com. v. Baltimore Nat'l Bank, 169 Md. 65, 180 A. 260.

[2629] Bank of California v. Richardson, 248 U.S. 476, 39 S. Ct 165, 63 L. Ed. 372.

[2630] People ex rel. Sav. Banl v. Xoleman, 18 N.Y.S. 675, 63 Hun 633, 45 N.Y. St. Rep. 136, aff'd, 135 N.Y. 231, 31 N.E. 1022.

bank stock as securities which if owned by a natural person residing in the state would be liable to taxation, is permissible.[2631]

§ 26. Prohibition of Discrimination Between National Bank Shares and Other Moneyed Capital.

In General.—The power to tax national bank shares is given to a state subject to the express restriction that such shares shall not be taxed at a greater rate than is assessed on other moneyed capital of individual citizens of the state coming into competition with national banks.[2632] Thus, a state

---

[2631] A. J. Tower Co. v. Commonwealth, 223 Mass. 371, 111 N.E. 966.

[2632] **In general.—**

United States.—12 U.S.C.S. § 548; Van Allen v. Assessors, 70 U.S. (3 Wall.) 573, 18 L. Ed. 229; People v. Commissioners, 71 U.S. (4 Wall.) 244, 18 L. Ed. 344; Bradley v. People, 71 U.S. (4 Wall.) 459, 18 L. Ed. 433; Lionberger v. Rouse, 76 U.S. (9 Wall.) 468, 19 L. Ed. 721; Hepburn v. School Directors, 90 U.S. (23 Wall.) 480, 23 L. Ed. 112; Adams v. Nashville, 95 U.S. 19, 24 L. Ed. 369; People v. Weaver, 100 U.S. 539, 25 L. Ed. 705; Pelton v. National Bank, 101 U.S. 148, 25 L. Ed. 901; Albany County v. Stanley, 105 U.S. 305, 26 L. Ed. 1044; Evansville Bank v. Britton, 105 U.S. 322, 26 L. Ed. 1053; Boyer v. Boyer, 113 U.S. 689, 5 S. Ct. 706, 28 L. Ed. 1089; Mercantile Nat. Bank v. New York, 121 U.S. 138, 7 S. Ct 826, 30 L. Ed. 895; National Newark Banking Co. v. Newark, 121 U.S. 163, 7 S. Ct. 839, 30 L. Ed. 904; Stanley v. Supervisors of Albany, 121 U.S. 535, 7 S. Ct. 1234, 30 L. Ed. 1000; Williams v. Albany, 122 U.S. 154, 7 S. Ct. 1244, 30 L. Ed. 1088; Davenport Bank v. Davenport Board of Equalization, 123 U.S. 83, 8 S. Ct. 73, 31 L. Ed. 94; Bank of Redemption v. Boston, 125 U.S. 60, 8 S. Ct. 772, 31 L. Ed. 689; Whitbeck v. Mercantile Nat. Bank, 127 U.S. 193, 8 S. Ct. 1121, 32 L. Ed. 118; Palmer v. McMahon, 133 U.S. 660, 10 S. Ct. 324, 33 L. Ed. 772; Talbott v. Silver Bow, 139 U.S. 438, 11 S. Ct. 594, 35 L. Ed. 210; First Nat. Bank v. Ayers, 160 U.S. 660, 16 S. Ct. 412, 40 L. Ed. 573; Aberdeen Bank v. Chehalis County, 166 U.S. 440, 17 S. Ct. 629, 41 L. Ed. 1069; Merchants' & Mfrs' Bank v. Pennsylvania, 167 U.S. 461, 17 S. Ct. 829, 42 L. Ed. 238; First Nat. Bank v. Chapman, 173 U.S. 205, 19 S. Ct. 407, 43 L. Ed. 669; San Francisco Nat. Bank v. Dodge, 197 U.S. 70, 25 S. Ct. 384, 49 L. Ed. 669; Albany City Nat. Bank v. Maher, 6 F. 417; First Nat. Bank v. Waters, 7 F. 152; First Nat. Bank v. Farwell, 7 F. 518; Evansville Nat'l Bank v. Britton, 8 F. 867, 10 Biss. 503, aff'd, 105 U.S. 322, 26 L. Ed. 1053; Supervisors v. Stanley, 12 F. 82; Stanley v. Albany, 15 F. 483, aff'd, 121 U.S. 535, 7 S. Ct 1234, 30 L. Ed. 1000; Exchange Nat. Bank v. Miller, 19 F. 372; First Nat'l Bank v. Lucas County, 25 F. 749, appeal dismissed, 131 U.S. 450, 9 S. Ct. 804, 33 L. Ed. 201; Mercantile Nat. Bank v. New York, 28 F. 776, aff'd, 121 U.S. 138, 7 S. Ct. 826, 30 L. Ed. 895; Richards v. Rock Rapids, 31 F. 505; First Nat'l Bank v. Richmond, 39 F. 309, appeal dismissed, 149 U.S. 769, 13 S. Ct. 1044, 37 L. Ed. 959; Whitney Nat. Bank v. Parker, 41 F. 402; First Nat. Bank v. Herbert, 44 F. 158; Puget Sound Nat. Bank v. King, 57 F. 433; Mercantile Nat. Bank v. Shields, 59 F. 952; National Bank v. Baltimore, 92 F. 239; National Bank v. Baltimore, 100 F. 24; First Nat. Bank v. Covington, 103 F. 523, appeal dismissed, 185 U.S. 270, 22 S. Ct 645, 46 L. Ed. 906; People's Nat'l Bank v. Marye, 107 F. 570, modified, 191 U.S. 272, 24 S. Ct. 68, 48 L. Ed. 180; Nevada Nat'l Bank v. Dodge, 119 F. 57; Covington v. First Nat. Bank, 198 U.S. 100,

(Text continued on page 730)

---

25 S. Ct. 562, 49 L. Ed. 963; City Nat. Bank v. Paducah, 5 F. Cas. 755 (No. 2743); First Nat Bank v. Douglas County, 9 F. Cas. 84 (No. 4799); Nelson v. First Nat. Bank, 42 F.2d 30; Boise City Nat. Bank v. Ada County, 37 F.2d 947; Toy Nat. Bank v. Nelson, 38 F.2d 261, cert. denied, 299 U.S. 546, 57 S. Ct. 9, 81 L. Ed. 402; Public Nat. Bank v. Keating, 38 F.2d 279, aff'd, 47 F.2d 561; 284 U.S. 587, 52 S. Ct. 137, 76 L. Ed. 507; Hannan v. First Nat. Bank, 269 F. 527, appeal dismissed, 266 U.S. 638, 45 S. Ct. 9, 69 L. Ed. 482; Eddy v. First Nat. Bank, 275 F. 550, appeal dismissed, 260 U.S. 752, 43 S. Ct 10, 67 L. Ed. 496; Minnehaha Nat. Bank v. Anderson, 2 F.2d 897, aff'd, sub nom. Alexander v. Mare, 5 F.2d 964; Munn v. Des Moines Nat. Bank, 18 F.2d 269; Central Nat. Bank v. McFarland, 20 F.2d 416, aff'd, 26 F.2d 890, cert. denied, 278 U.S. 606, 49 S. Ct. 12, 73 L. Ed. 533; Brotherhood Co-op. Nat'l Bank v. Hurlburt, 21 F.2d 86; First Nat. Bank v. Anderson, 269 U.S. 341, 46 S. Ct. 135, 70 L. Ed. 295; Brotherhood Co-Op. Nat. Bank v. Hurlburt, 26 F.2d 957; Georgetown Nat. Bank v. McFarland, 273 U.S. 568, 47 S. Ct. 467, 71 L. Ed. 779; Minnesota v. First Nat'l Bank, 273 U.S. 561, 47 S. Ct. 468, 71 L. Ed. 774; Montana Nat'l Bank v. Yellowstone County of Montana, 276 U.S. 499, 48 S. Ct. 331, 72 L. Ed. 673; Amoskeag Sav. Bank v. Purdy, 231 U.S. 373, 34 S. Ct. 114, 58 L. Ed. 274.

Alabama.—National Commercial Bank v. Mayor, Aldermen & Common Council of Mobile, 62 Ala. 284, 84 Am. R. 16; Pollard v. State, 65 Ala. 628; Maguire v. Board, 71 Ala. 401; Tarrant v. Bessemer Nat. Bank, 7 Ala. App. 285, 61 So. 47.

Arizona.—Consolidated Nat. Bank v. Pima, 5 Ariz. 142, 48 P. 291.

California.—Miller v. Heilbron, 58 Cal. 133; McHenry v. Downer, 116 Cal. 20, 47 P. 779, 45 L.R.A. 737.

Florida.—Roberts v. American Nat'l Bank, 97 Fla. 411, 121 So. 554.

Illinois.—Illinois Nat'l Bank v. Kinsella, 201 Ill. 31, 66 N.E. 338.

Indiana.—Wright v. Stilz, 27 Ind. 338; Wasson v. First Nat. Bank, 107 Ind. 206, 8 N.E. 97; First Nat. Bank v. Turner, 154 Ind. 456, 57 N.E. 110.

Iowa.—Hubbard v. Board of Supervisors, 23 Iowa 130; National State Bank v. Burlington, 119 Iowa 696, 94 N.W. 234; First Nat'l Bank v. Estherville, 150 Iowa 95, 129 N.W. 476; Des Moines Nat'l Bank v. Des Moines, 153 Iowa 336, 133 N.W. 767; Iowa Nat. Bank v. Stewart, 232 N.W. 445; Des Moines Nat. Bank v. Fairweather, 191 Iowa 1240, 184 N.W. 313, aff'd, 263 U.S. 103, 44 S. Ct. 23, 68 L. Ed. 191; First Nat. Bank v. Burke, 201 Iowa 994, 196 N.W. 287; Citizens' Nat'l Bank v. Johnston, 199 Iowa 460, 202 N.W. 382; Poweshiek County Sav. Bank v. Johnston, 199 Iowa 555, 202 N.W. 384; Montezuma Sav. Bank v. Board of Review, 202 N.W. 386; Jasper County Sav. Bank v. Board of Review, 202 N.W. 887; Head v. Board of Review, 170 Iowa 300, 152 N.W. 600; Welfare Loan Soc. v. Des Moines, 205 Iowa 1400, 219 N.W. 534; Universal Loan Corp. v. Board of Review, 205 Iowa 1391, 219 N.W. 536.

Kansas.—First Nat. Bank v. Fisher, 45 Kan. 726, 26 P. 482; Voran v. Wright, 129 Kan. 601, 284 P. 807.

Kentucky.—Commonwealth v. First Nat. Bank, 67 Ky. (4 Bush.) 98, 96 Am. Dec. 285, aff'd, 76 U.S. 353, 19 L. Ed. 701; Deposit Bank of Owensboro v. Daviess County, 102 Ky. 174, 39 S.W. 1030, 19 Ky. L. Rptr. 248, 44 L.R.A. 825, aff'd sub nom. Citizens' Sav. Bank v. Owensboro, 173 U.S. 636, 19 S. Ct. 530, 43 L. Ed. 840; Scobee v. Bean, 109 Ky. 526, 59 S.W. 860, 22 Ky. L. Rptr. 1076 Marion Nat. Bank v. Burton, 121 Ky. 876, 90 S.W. 944, 28

(*Text continued on page 730*)

Ky. L. Rptr. 864, 10 L.R.A. (n.s.) 947; Schuster & Co. v. Louisville, 124 Ky. 189, 89 S.W. 689, 28 Ky. L. Rptr. 588; Commonwealth v. Covington Nat'l Bank, 7 Ky. L. Rptr. 41; Richmond v. Madison Nat'l Bank & Trust Co., 215 Ky. 262, 284 S.W. 1089.

Maine.—Stetson v. Bangor, 56 Me. 274.

Massachusetts—Providence Inst. v. Boston, 101 Mass. 575, 3 Am. R. 407; A. J. Tower Co. v. Commonwealth, 223 Mass. 371, 111 N.E. 966; Central Nat. Bank v. Lynn, 259 Mass. 1, 156 N.E. 42, cert. denied, 280 U.S. 516, 50 S. Ct. 65, 74 L. Ed. 587.

Michigan.—First Nat'l Bank v. St. Joseph, 46 Mich. 526, 9 N.W. 838.

Minnesota.—Limitation on the power of the state to tax shares in national banks does not limit or deprive state of its constitutional power to tax corporations of its own creation. Cherokee State Bank v. Wallace, 202 Minn. 582, 279 N.W. 410.

Missouri.—Lionberger v. Rowse, 43 Mo. 67 aff'd sub nom. Lionberger v. Rouse, 76 U.S. (9 Wall.) 468, 19 L. Ed. 721.

Montana.—Board of Comm'rs v. Davis, 6 Mont. 306, 12 P. 688; First Nat'l Bank v. Dawson County, 66 Mont. 321, 213 P. 1097; Montana Nat'l Bank v. Yellowstone County, 82 Mont. 380, 267 P. 304; Commercial Nat'l Bank v. Custer County, 76 Mont. 45, 245 P. 259; State ex rel. Conrad Banking Corp. v. Mady, 83 Mont. 418, 272 P. 691.

Nebraska.—Bressler v. Wayne County, 32 Neb. 834, 49 N.W. 787, 13 L.R.A. 614; State Bank v. Endres, 109 Neb. 753, 192 N.W. 322; Central Nat. Bank v. Sutherland, 113 Neb. 126, 202 N.W. 428.

New Jersey.—State v. Boyd, 32 N.J.L. 273; Stratton v. Collins, 43 N.J.L. 562; Mechanics' Nat. Bank v. Baker, 65 N.J.L. 113, 46 A. 586, aff'd, 65 N.J.L. 549, 48 A. 582; Commercial Trust Co. v. Hudson County Board of Taxation, 86 N.J.L. 424, 92 A. 263, aff'd, 87 N.J.L. 179, 92 A. 799.

New Mexico.—First Nat'l Bank v. McBride, 20 N.M. 381, 149 P. 353.

New York.—Gallatin Nat. Bank v. Commissioners, 67 N.Y. 516, aff'd, 94 U.S. 415, 24 L. Ed. 164; Williams v. Weaver, 75 N.Y. 30, aff'd, 100 U.S. 547, 25 L. Ed. 708; Jenkins v. Neff, 163 N.Y. 320, 57 N.E. 408, aff'd, 186 U.S. 230, 22 S. Ct 905, 46 L. Ed. 1140; Jenkins v. Neff, 29 Misc. 59, 60 N.Y.S. 582, aff'd, 47 App. Div. 394, 62 N.Y.S. 321; 163 N.Y. 320, 57 N.E. 408; 186 U.S. 230, 22 S. Ct. 905, 46 L. Ed. 1140; In re Petition of McMahon, 11 Daly 214, aff'd, 102 N.Y. 176, 6 N.E. 400; 133 U.S. 660, 10 S. Ct. 324, 33 L. Ed. 772; People v. Coleman, 44 Hun. 47; People v. Assessors, 44 Barb. 148, 29 How. Pr. 871; People v. Goldfogle, 234 N.Y. 345, 137 N.E. 611, cert. denied, 261 U.S. 620, 43 S. Ct. 432, 67 L. Ed. 830; People v. Breder, 129 Misc. 787, 223 N.Y.S. 579.

North Carolina.—McAden v. Commissioners of Mecklenburg County, 97 N.C. 355, 2 S.E. 670.

Ohio.—Frazer v. Siebern, 16 Ohio St. 614; Chapman v. First Nat. Bank, 56 Ohio St. 310, 47 N.E. 54, aff'd, 173 U.S. 205, 19 S. Ct. 407, 43 L. Ed. 669; Cleveland Trust Co. v. Lander, 62 Ohio St. 266, 56 N.E. 1036, aff'd, 184 U.S. 111, 22 S. Ct. 394, 46 L. Ed. 456; First Nat'l Bank v. Chapman, 9 Ohio C.C. 79, 4 Ohio Cir. Dec. 252, rev'd on other grounds, 56 Ohio St. 310, 47 N.E. 54; 173 U.S. 205, 19 S. Ct. 407, 43 L. Ed. 669.

Oklahoma.—Comanche County v. American Nat. Bank, 122 Okla. 34, 252 P. 408; Bonaparte v. American-First Nat. Bank, 139 Okla. 189, 281 P. 958.

statute Imposing a tax on national bank shares is violative of the federal statute if it discriminates in favor of moneyed capital invested in actual and

---

Oregon.—Ankeny v. Blakley, 44 Ore. 78, 74 P. 485.

Pennsylvania.—Everett's Appeal, 71 Pa. 217; Gorgas's Appeal, 79 Pa. 149; Boyer's Appeal, 103 Pa. 387, rev'd on other grounds, 113 U.S. 689, 5 S. Ct. 706, 28 L. Ed. 1089; Pleish v. Hartranft, 1 Leg. Gas. R. 46; Markoe v. Hartranft, 15 Am. L. Rag. 487.

Tennessee.—McLaughlin v. Chadwell, 54 Tenn. 389; First Nat. Bank v. Sevier County, 161 Tenn. 676, 30 S.W.2d 243.

Texas.—Engelke v. Schlender, 75 Tex. 559, 12 S.W. 999; Primm v. Fort, 23 Tex. Civ. App. 605, 57 S.W. 86.

Utah.—Commercial Nat'l Bank v. Chambers, 21 Utah 324, 61 P. 560, 56 L.R.A. 346, aff'd, 182 U.S. 556, 21 S. Ct. 863, 45 L. Ed. 1227.

Vermont.—State v. Clement Nat'l Bank, 84 Vt. 187, 78 A. 944, 1912D Ann. Cas. 22, aff'd, Clement Nat'l Bank v. Vermont, 231 U.S. 120, 34 S. Ct. 31, 58 L. Ed. 147.

Virginia.—Burrows v. Smith, 95 Va. 694, 29 S.E. 674; Richmond v. Merchants Nat'l Bank, 124 Va. 522, 98 S.E. 643, rev'd on other grounds, Merchants' Nat'l Bank v. Richmond, 256 U.S. 635, 41 S. Ct. 619, 65 L. Ed. 1135.

Washington.—First Nat. Bank v. Chehalis, 6 Wash. 64, 32 P. 1051; Washington Nat. Bank v. King, 9 Wash. 607, 38 P. 219; Newport v. Mudgett, 18 Wash. 271, 51 P. 466; Pacific Nat. Bank v. Pierce, 20 Wash. 675, 56 P. 936 (1899); National Bank of Commerce v. King County, 153 Wash. 351, 280 P. 16.

West Virginia.—The state having adopted congressionally approved method of taxing shares of national banks in the hands of shareholders is limited to that one method and may not tax such shares at a rate pester than the rate imposed upon other moneyed capital in competition with the business of national banks. In re National Bank, 137 W. Va. 673, 73 S.E.2d 655 (1952).

Wisconsin.—First Nat. Bank v. Hartford, 187 Wis. 290, 203 N.W. 721, rev'd on other grounds, 273 U.S. 548, 47 S. Ct. 462, 71 L. Ed. 767; Van Slyke v. State, 23 Wis. 655.

"Rate of taxation".—

For comparative purposes, "rate of taxation" within intendment of federal statute limiting state tax upon shares of stock in national banks, is the proportion the tax assessed bears to the base taxed as determined by valuations, deductions, exemptions and like factors and not the amount of millage statutorily prescribed. Commonwealth v. Mellon Nat'l Bank & Trust Co., 374 Pa. 519, 98 A.2d 168, cert. denied, 346 U.S. 875, 74 S. Ct. 127, 98 L. Ed. 383.

Discrimination resulting from Supreme Court decision.—

Imposition of state tax on capital stock of national bank for 1934 at a greater effect the rate than that paid by trust companies constituted violation of federal statute, even though such discrimination resulted from United States Supreme Court decision that federal securities owned by trust company must be deducted in computing capital stock in trust company subject to state tax under tax statute allowing trust companies to deduct investments in shares of corporations liable to pay state capital stock tax or specifically relieved therefrom by law. Commonwealth v. Mellon Nat. Bank, etc., Co., 374 Pa. 519, 98 A.2d 168, cert. denied, 346 U.S. 875, 74 S. Ct. 127, 98 L. Ed. 383.

substantial competition with capital invested in national bank stock.[2633] And

---

Parent holding companies.—

Under prior state laws on the subject, including a statute the clear meaning of which was to the effect that by taxing state banks the same as national banks no income tax would be imposed on state banks because prior state law specifically and federal law prohibited the same, dividends from national bank stock do not constitute taxable income to a parent holding company of a bank for state income tax purposes, even after Congress removed the previous obstacle to such taxation. McNamara v. First Commerce Corp., 392 So. 2d 467 (La. App. 1980), cert. denied, 397 So. 2d 1361 (La. 1981).

[2633] **In general.—**

Citizens', etc., Nat. Bank v. Atlanta, 53 F.2d 557; Boise City Nat. Bank v. Ada County, 48 F.2d 222; Knowles v. First Nat. Bank, 58 F.2d 232; Public Nat'l Bank v. Keating, 47 F.2d 561, 81 A.L.R. 497, aff'd, 284 U.S. 587, 52 S. Ct. 137, 76 L. Ed. 507; Hoenig v. Huntington Nat. Bank, 59 F.2d 479, cert. denied, 287 U.S. 648, 53 S. Ct. 93, 77 L. Ed. 560; Ward v. First Nat. Bank, 225 Ala. 10, 142 So. 93 (1932); First Nat'l Bank v. Louisiana Tax Com., 175 La. 119, 143 So. 28; Bancorporation v. Korzen, 64 Ill. 2d 200, 355 N.E.2d 31 (1976).

Competition contemplated by statute governing state taxation of shares of national bank need not necessarily be with all phases of bank's business. Boise City Nat. Bank v. Ada County, 48 F.2d 222.

"Competition" within statute prohibiting discriminatory taxation against national bank share, is limited to employment of moneyed capital substantially as in loan and investment features of banking, and does not apply to competition for deposits. Hoenig v. Huntington Nat. Bank, 59 F.2d 479, cert. denied, 287 U.S. 648, 53 S. Ct. 93, 77 L. Ed. 560, rev'g Commercial Nat. Bank v. Franklin County, 45 F.2d 213.

"Competition" within federal statute providing that national bank shares shall not be taxed at greater rate than moneyed capital coming into "competition" with the business of national banks, does not mean that there should be a competition as to all phases of the business of national banks but implies the performance of some banking functions performed by a national bank, and statute is violated whenever capital, substantial in amount when compared with the capitalization of national banks, is employed, either in a business or by private investors, in the same sort of transactions as those in which national banks engage, and in the same locality in which they do business. Morris Plan Co. v. Johnson, 37 Cal. App. 2d 621, 100 P.2d 493 (1940).

Use of funds not so minimal as not to constitute substantial competition.—

Corporation which was engaged in dealing in first deeds of trust on realty that were initially acquired in corporation's name through use of funds supplied to it by banks and thereafter assigned to institutional investor, could not avoid taxation at bank rate rather than general corporation rate on theory that because its capitalization was at $115,000 its use of funds was so minimal that it could not be considered to be in substantial competition with national banks and that it used only funds borrowed from banks to finance its acquisition of mortgage loans, where record disclosed that such was not the case. Marble Mortgage Co. v. Franchise Tax Ed., 241 Cal. App. 2d 26, 50 Cal. Rptr. 345 (1966).

A Morris Plan Company, incorporated under industrial loan law, held in "substantial competition with national banks," within meaning of federal statute. Morris Plan Co. v.

whether a state tax on shares of stock in a national bank violates the federal

---

Johnson, 37 Cal. App. 2d 621, 100 P.2d 493 (1940).

Building and loan associations are not in competition with national banks so as to invalidate local taxes on bank stock on ground of discrimination in favor of building and loan associations. Hoenig v. Huntington Nat. Bank, 59 F.2d 479, rev'g Commercial Nat. Bank v. Franklin County, 45 F.2d 213, cert. denied, 287 U.S. 648, 53 S. Ct. 93, 77 L. Ed. 560.

Savings and loan associations operate in a narrow, restricted field, and are markedly different in character, purpose and organization from national banks, and are not in substantial competition with national banks within contemplation of federal statute conferring upon state power to tax national banks provided that tax imposed shall not be at a greater rate than is assessed by other moneyed capital in hands of individual citizens of such state coming into competition with business of national banks. Michigan Nat. Bank v. State, 358 Mich. 611, 101 N.W.2d 245, aff'd, 365 U.S. 467, 81 S. Ct. 659, 5 L. Ed. 2d 710.

Finance and mortgage companies held not in "competition with national bank" so as to invalidate local taxes on national bank shares on ground of discrimination. Hoenig v. Huntington Nat. Bank, 59 F.2d 479, cert. denied, 287 U.S. 648, 53 S. Ct. 93, 77 L. Ed. 560, rev'g Commercial Nat'l Bank v. Treasurer of Franklin County, 45 F.2d 213; First Nat'l Bank v. Louisiana Tax Com., 175 La. 119, 143 So. 23.

And small loan companies making loans, as a rule, secured by chattel mortgages, are not in competition with national banks. First Nat'l Bank v. Louisiana Tax Com., 175 La. 119, 143 So. 23.

Sale of mortgages acquired by way of loan or discount with view to reinvesting is activity in competition with national banks. Marble Mortgage Co. v. Franchise Tax Bd., 241 Cal. App. 2d 26, 50 Cal. Rptr. 345 (1966).

Corporation engaged in purchase and assignment of first deeds of trust could not avoid taxation at bank rate rather than general corporation rate on theory that "service fees" received for servicing loans of institutional assignees was not same type of income as interest earned by national banks on first deeds of trust where one segment of interest received by banks constituted compensation for performance of functions similar to those performed by corporation; i.e., acquisition of mortgage including necessary appraisals and collection of payments on loan. Marble Mortg. Co. v. Franchise Tax Board, 241 Cal. App. 2d 26, 50 Cal. Rptr. 345 (1966).

Corporations engaged in dealing in first deeds of trust on realty initially acquired in corporation', name through use of funds supplied to it by banks that were thereafter assigned to institutional investors could not avoid taxation at bank rate rather than general corporation rate on theory that loans were made only to support its servicing business, where major share of gross income came from activities prior to assignment and where service charge was in fact share of interest exactly like that retained by national bank for servicing loans. Marble Mortg. Co. v. Franchise Tax Board, 241 Cal. App. 2d 26, 50 Cal. Rptr. 345 (1966). Where acquisition of deeds of trust by corporation engaged in purchase and assignment of such deeds of trust reduced investment opportunities available to banks and income received by corporation as result of making loans on first deeds of trust was of same type as income earned by banks in dealing with mortgagee, corporation was in substantial competition with national banks and taxable at bank rate rather than general corporation rate. Marble Mortg.

statute depends upon the overall result produced, regardless of the motive of the taxing authority, not upon a hostile or unfriendly intent of such authority.[2634]

Purpose of Provision.—The purpose of the federal statute relating to taxing moneyed capital competing with national banks is to subject such moneyed capital to the same taxation as is imposed on national bank shares,[2635] and to protect capital invested in national banks from unfriendly discrimination by the states in exercising their taxing power.[2636] The language of the statute must be read in light of this policy.[2637] Thus, if state

---

Co. v. Franchise Tax Board, 241 Cal. App. 2d 26, 50 Cal. Rptr. 345 (1966).

Fact that state had power to equalize taxation between bank and competing capital by compelling payment of unpaid of amounts theretofore assessed was not material as respected validity of tax. Iowa-Des Moines Nat'l Bank v. Bennett, 284 U.S. 239, 52 S. Ct. 133, 76 L. Ed. 265, rev'g Iowa Nat. Bank v. Stewart, 214 Iowa 1229, 232 N.W. 445.

[2634] Commonwealth v. Mellon Nat. Bank, etc., Co., 374 Pa. 519, 98 A.2d 168, cert. denied, 346 U.S. 875, 74 S. Ct. 127, 98 L. Ed. 383.

[2635] People v. Goldfogle, 242 N.Y. 277, 151 N.E. 452; Merchants' & Mfrs' Bank v. Pennsylvania, 167 U.S. 461, 17 S. Ct. 829, 42 L. Ed. 236; National Bank v. Commonwealth, 76 U.S. (9 Wall.) 353, 19 L. Ed. 701; Lionberger v. Rouse, 76 U.S. (9 Wall.) 468, 19 L. Ed. 721; Boyer v. Boyer, 113 U.S. 689, 5 S. Ct. 706, 28 L. Ed. 1089; Mercantile Nat. Bank v. New York, 121 U.S. 138, 7 S. Ct. 826, 30 L. Ed. 895; Davenport Bank v. Davenport Board of Equalization, 123 U.S. 83, 8 S. Ct. 73, 31 L. Ed. 94; First Nat. Bank v. Ayers 160 U.S. 660, 16 S. Ct. 412, 40 L. Ed. 573; Aberdeen Bank v. Chehalis, 166 U.S. 440, 17 S. Ct. 629, 41 L. Ed. 1069. See also First Nat'l Bank v. Chapman, 173 U.S. 205, 19 S. Ct. 407, 43 L. Ed. 669; Jenkins v. Neff, 186 U.S. 230, 22 S. Ct. 905, 46 L. Ed. 1140; Stanley v. Supervisors of Albany, 121 U.S. 535, 7 S. Ct. 1234, 30 L. Ed. 1000; People v. Commissioners, 71 U.S. (4 Wall.) 244, 18 L. Ed. 344; Albany City Nat. Bank v. Maher, 6 F. 417.

[2636] Bedford v. Colorado Nat'l Bank, 104 Colo. 311, 91 P.2d 469.

The purpose of federal restriction on state taxation of national banks is to render it impossible for state to create and foster an unequal competition with national banks by favoring shareholders in state banks or individuals interested in private banking or engaged in operations and investments normally common to banking business. First Nat'l Bank v. Anderson, 269 U.S. 341, 46 S. Ct. 135, 70 L. Ed. 295; H. A. S. Loan Service, Inc. v. McColgan, 21 Cal. 2d 518, 133 P.2d 391, 145 A.L.R. 349; Crown Finance Corp. v. McColgan, 23 Cal. 2d 280, 144 P.2d 331.

Restrictive language in the Illinois statute, relating to the taxation of bank share. and requiring that the taxation of such shares shall not be at a greater rate than that assessed against any other moneyed capital in the hands of an individual citizen, must be given the same meaning ascribed to federal statute using that language with respect to the taxation of national bank shares; that is, neither national nor state bank shares may be placed at a tax disadvantage. Bancorporation v. Korzen, 64 Ill. 2d 200, 355 N.E.2d 31 (1976).

[2637] Mercantile Bank v. New York, 121 U.S. 138, 7 S. Ct. 826, 30 L. Ed. 895; Merchants', etc., Nat. Bank v. Pennsylvania, 167 U.S. 461, 17 S. Ct. 829, 42 L. Ed. 236.

and national banks are treated equally, and the latter are not assessed at a greater rate than the former, national bank shareholders have not been Illegally assessed, unless there is a clear discrimination in favor of moneyed capital other than that employed in either state or national banks.[2638] However, the statutory provision was not intended to prohibit the exemption of particular kinds of property.[2639] A tax on the capital of a bank is not the

---

In determining whether a corporation was taxable as financial corporation under State Bank and Corporation Franchise Tax Act, the court was required to look to intent of federal statute prohibiting tax discrimination against national banks. H. A. S. Loan Service, Inc. v. McColgan, 21 Cal. 2d 518, 133 P.2d 391, 145 A.L.R. 349.

[2638] **In general.—**

First Nat'l Bank v. Chapman, 173 U.S. 205, 19 S. Ct. 407, 43 L. Ed. 669; Merchants', etc., Nat. Bank v. Pennsylvania, 167 U.S. 461, 17 S. Ct. 829, 42 L. Ed. 236; Lionberger v. Rouse, 76 US. (9 Wall.) 468, 19 L. Ed. 721.

Contract not to tax state banks above a certain amount—

Where a state, having disabled itself with a contract with the only two banks of issue in the state from collecting a tax above a certain amount from them, and having other banks not of issue possessed of greater capital than those of issue, laid a tax on all shares of stock in banks and incorporated companies generally, held, that the fact that the state could not collect a tax beyond a certain amount in the two banks of issue, which it had at that time was no bar to the collection of the tax on the shares of the national banks for a greater amount. Lionberger v. Rouse, 76 U.S. (9 Wall.) 468 19 L. Ed. 721.

Failure to tax state banks.—

Under the National Banking Act of 1884, 13 State 111, in the case of Van Allen v. Assessors, 70 U.S. (3 Wall.) 573, 18 L. Ed. 229, the taxing law of New York, which was in question, was held to be invalid, because it levied no taxes upon shares in state banks at all, the tax being assessed upon the capital of the banks after deducting that portion which was invested in securities of the United States and it was held that this tax on the capital was not a tax on the shares of the stockholders equivalent to that on the shares of national banks. Mercantile Bank v. New York, 121 U.S. 138, 7 S. Ct. 826, 30 L. Ed. 895. See also People v. Commissioners of Taxes & Assessments, 94 U.S. 415, 24 L. Ed. 164; People v. Commissioners, 71 U.S. (4 Wall.) 244, 18 L. Ed. 344; Bradley v. People, 71 U.S. (4 Wall.) 459, 18 L. Ed. 433.

[2639] Adams v. Nashville, 95 U.S. 19, 24 L. Ed. 369; Hepburn v. School Directors, 90 U.S. (23 Wall.) 480, 23 L. Ed. 112; Mercantile Bank v. New York, 121 U.S. 138, 7 S. Ct. 826, 30 L. Ed. 895; Richards v. Rock Rapids, 31 F. 505; National Newark Banking Co. v. Newark, 121 U.S 163, 7 S. Ct. 839, 30 L. Ed. 904.

Under federal statute conferring upon state power to tax national bank shares provided that tax imposed is not at a greater rate than is assessed upon other moneyed capital in hands of individual citizens of state coming into competition with business of national banks, general rule of partial exemption under the statute applies to savings and loan associations. Michigan Nat'l Bank v. State, 358 Mich. 611, 101 N.W.2d 245, aff'd, 365 U.S. 467, 81 S. Ct. 659, 5 L. Ed. 2d 710.

same thing as a tax upon the shares which compose the capital,[2640] and where a state imposes a tax upon the capital of state banks, shares in the hands of shareholders being exempt from tax, it cannot impose a tax on national bank shares.[2641]

Provision Construed and Applied.—The statutory provision does not require perfect equality between state and national banks,[2642] but only that the system of taxation in a state shall not work a discrimination favorable to its own citizens and corporations, and unfavorable to holders of shares in national banks.[2643] Thus, the statute does not require states, in taxing their own corporations, "to conform to the system of taxing the national banks

---

[2640] Bradley v. People, 71 U.S. (4 Wall.) 459, 18 L. Ed. 433.

[2641] Bradley v. People, 71 U.S. (4 Wall.) 459, 18 L. Ed. 433; Van Allen v. Assessors, 70 U.S. (3 Wall.) 573, 18 L. Ed. 229.

[2642] Davenport Bank v. Davenport Board of Equalization, 123 U.S. 83, 8 S. Ct. 73, 31 L. Ed. 94.

That the language does not mean entire equality is evident from the fact that, if the capital of national banks were taxed at a much lower rate than other moneyed capital in the state, the banks would have no right to complain, and the law in that respect would not violate the provision, of the act of Congress for the protection of national banks. Davenport Bank v. Davenport Board of Equalization, 123 U.S. 83, 8 S. Ct. 73, 31 L. Ed. 94.

[2643] **In general.—**

Davenport Bank v. Davenport Board of Equalization, 123 U.S. 83, 8 S. Ct. 73, 31 L. Ed. 94; Bank of Redemption v. Boston, 125 U.S. 60, 8 S. Ct. 772, 31 L. Ed. 689; First Nat. Bank v. Chapman, 173 U.S. 205, 19 S. Ct. 407, 43 L. Ed. 669; Williams v. Albany, 122 U.S. 154, 7 S. Ct. 1244, 30 L. Ed. 1088. See also Stanley v. Supervisors of Albany, 121 U.S. 535, 7 S. Ct. 1234, 30 L. Ed. 1000; Supervisors v. Stanley, 105 U.S. 305, 26 L. Ed. 1044.

Question of fact.—

Ascertainment of the existence of competition and inequality in taxation of national bank shares, as compared with moneyed capital competing with national banks, as respects validity of state taxing statutes, involves questions of fact.

People's Nat'l Bank & Trust Co. v. Westchester County, 261 N.Y. 342, 185 N.E. 405, aff'g 237 App. Div. 827, 260 N.Y.S. 996.

Whether state statute imposing tax on stock of every bank and mortgage loan company in state, organized under laws of state or of the United States, permits discriminatory rate of taxation in favor of moneyed capital and capital investment, within state as represented by credits or intangibles and against moneys invested in shares of national banks, is question of fact and of law, since discrimination must be shown to exist in fact Cherokee State Bank v. Wallace, 202 Minn. 582, 279 N.W. 410.

There must be unwarranted discrimination and this must be made to appear from proof, to render tax on national bank shares invalid as discriminatory. First Nat. Bank v. Jackson County, 227 Ala. 448, 150 So. 690.

upon the shares of their stock in the hands of their owners"; if there is no unfavorable discrimination against national bank stockholders, the states' method of assessing and collecting taxes is not controlled by act of Congress.[2644] And the fact that a special system of taxation of national banks may not be as favorable as the general system of taxation in an isolated case, does not render such system unlawful as discriminating against national banks, so long as there is no intentional discrimination or inequality in its effect upon their stockholders.[2645] However, the restriction of the federal statute applies to the actual incidents and practical burden of the tax imposed.[2646] And even where no discrimination arises on the face of a state tax statute, nevertheless, if it appears that a system created by the state in its practical execution produces an actual and material discrimination against national banks, it is the duty of the courts to hold such statute to be in conflict with the federal statute, and therefore void.[2647] But if neither the necessary

---

Purpose of California statute.—

The manifest purpose of legislature in establishing classification of financial corporations which were made subject to bank and corporation franchise tax was to avoid tax discrimination against national banks, denounced by federal statute. H. A. S. Loan Service, Inc. v. McColgan, 21 Cal. 2d 518, 133 P.2d 391, 145 A.L.R. 349.

[2644] Davenport Bank v. Davenport Board of Equalization, 123 U.S. 83, 8 S. Ct. 73, 31 L. Ed. 94; San Francisco Nat. Bank v. Dodge, 197 U.S. 70, 25 S. Ct 384, 49 L. Ed. 669; First Nat. Bank v. Chapman, 173 U.S. 205, 19 S. Ct. 407, 43 L. Ed. 669; Palmer v. McMahon, 133 U.S. 660, 10 S. Ct. 324, 33 L. Ed. 772; Mercantile Bank v. New York, 121 U.S. 138, 7 S. Ct. 826, 30 L. Ed. 895; Crocker v. Scott, 149 Cal. 575, 87 P. 102; First Nat. Bank v. Board, 92 Ark. 335, 122 S.W. 988; Bank of Redemption v. Boston, 125 U.S. 60, 8 S. Ct. 772, 31 L. Ed. 689; Richards v. Rock Rapids, 31 F. 505; Newark Banking Co. v. Newark, 121 U.S. 163, 7 S. Ct. 839, 30 L. Ed. 904.

[2645] Bridgeport Sav. Bank v. Feitner, 191 N.Y. 88, 83 N.E. 592; State v. Clement Nat. Bank, 84 Vt. 167, 78 A 944, 1912D Ann. Can 22.

[2646] Michigan Nat'l Bank v. State, 358 Mich. 611, 101 N.W.2d 245, aff'd, 365 U.S. 467, 81 S. Ct. 659, 5 L. Ed. 2d 710.

[2647] **In general.—**

Davenport Bank v. Davenport Board of Equalization, 123 U.S. 83, 8 S. Ct. 73, 31 L. Ed. 94; San Francisco Nat'l Bank v. Dodge, 197 U.S. 70, 25 S. Ct. 384, 49 L. Ed. 669; Supervisors v. Stanley, 105 U.S. 305, 26 L. Ed. 1044; Stanley v. Albany, 121 U.S. 535, 7 S. Ct. 1234, 30 L. Ed. 1000. See also Hills v. Exchange Bank, 105 U.S. 319, 26 L. Ed. 1052; Evansville Bank v. Britton, 105 U.S. 322, 26 L. Ed. 1053; Pelton v. Commercial Nat. Bank, 101 U.S. 143, 25 L. Ed. 901; Cummings v. National Bank, 101 U.S. 153, 25 L. Ed. 903; Boyer v. Boyer, 113 U.S. 689, 5 S. Ct. 706, 28 L. Ed. 1089; Whitbeck v. Mercantile Nat. Bank, 127 U.S. 193, 8 S. Ct 1121, 32 L Ed. 118; Wright v. Stilz, 27 Ind. 338; Covington v. First Nat. Bank, 198 U.S. 100, 25 S. Ct. 562, 49 L. Ed. 963; City Nat. Bank v. Paducah, 5 F. Cas. 755 (No. 2, 743).

and usual nor probable effect of a state system of assessment is to discriminate against national banks, no evidence is given that the legislature intended to make such a discrimination, and there is no proof that such system works an actual and material discrimination, the Supreme Court will not hold the statute unconstitutional.[2648]

State's tax structure as a whole must be considered.—

In determining whether Bank and Corporation Franchise Tax Act discriminates against national banks as prohibited by federal statutes, court must consider state's tax structure as a whole and ascertain therefrom whether tax burden is greater on national banks than on state banks or mercantile, business, manufacturing, and financial corporations. H. A. S. Loan Service, Inc. v. McColgan, 21 Cal. 2d 518, 133 P.2d 391, 145 A.L.R. 349.

[2648] **In general.—**

Davenport Nat. Bank v. Davenport Board, 123 U.S. 83, 8 S. Ct. 73, 31 L. Ed. 94; National Bank v. Kimball, 103 U.S. 732, 26 L. Ed. 469; First Nat'l Bank v. Chapman, 173 U.S. 205, 19 S. Ct. 407, 43 L. Ed. 669; San Francisco Nat. Bank v. Dodge, 197 U.S. 70, 25 S. Ct. 384, 49 L. Ed. 669; Mercantile Nat. Bank v. New York, 121 U.S. 138, 7 S. Ct. 826, 30 L. Ed. 895; Stanley v. Albany, 121 U.S. 535, 7 S. Ct. 1234, 30 L. Ed. 1000; Williams v. Albany, 122 U.S. 154, 7 S. Ct. 1244, 30 L. Ed. 1088; First Nat. Bank v. Farwell, 7 F. 518, 10 Biss. 270; National State Bank v. Burlington, 119 Iowa 696, 94 N.W. 234; Jenkins v. Neff, 186 U.S. 230, 22 S. Ct. 905, 46 L. Ed. 1140. See also Newark Banking Co. v. Newark, 121 U.S. 163, 7 S. Ct. 839, 30 L. Ed. 904.

Tax at different rate or assessed by different method.—

It is not a valid objection to a state tax on national bank shares that other moneyed capital in state is taxed at a different rate or assessed by a different method unless it appears that difference in treatment results in fact in a discrimination unfavorable to holders of shares of national banks. Michigan Nat. Bank v. State of Michigan, 365 U.S. 467, 81 S. Ct. 659, 5 L. Ed. 2d 710.

The taxation of other moneyed capital in the state, or shares of state bank at a different rate, or assessment by a different method is not objectionable, in absence of discrimination. Tradesmens Nat'l Bank v. Oklahoma Tax Com., 309 U.S. 560, 60 S. Ct. 688, 84 L. Ed. 947.

Michigan statute taxing national association shares at different rates taking into account the additional moneyed capital controlled by the national bank shares did not place a greater burden on national bank shares than on other moneyed capital and did not discriminate against national banks or their shareholders as a class. Michigan Nat'l Bank v. Michigan, 365 U.S. 467, 81 S. Ct. 659, 5 L. Ed. 2d 710.

Since there was no tax disadvantage either to national or state bank shares with respect to the imposition of personal property taxes on shares of bank stock held by corporations in the proscribed sense under the Illinois statute respecting taxation of bank shares at no greater rate than assessed upon other moneyed capital in hands of individual citizens, in that individual investors were free from personal property tax upon all bank shares and other moneyed capital while corporate investors were taxed upon both, imposition of personal property tax on the corporate owners of bank stock was not proscribed. Bancorporation v. Korzen, 64 Ill. 2d 200, 355 N.E.2d 31 (1976).

The term "moneyed capital," as employed in the federal statute respecting state taxation of shares in national banks means capital employed in the business of making loans on collateral, discounting negotiable paper and dealing in securities in order to make a profit.[2649] The term does not include capital which does not compete with the business of national banks, and it

---

Intangible tax law.—

There is no presumption that intangible tax law imposes a greater rate upon state and national banks than is assessed upon other moneyed capital in hands of individual citizens of state coming into competition with business of national banks. Michigan Nat. Bank v. State, 358 Mich. 611, 101 N.W.2d 245, aff'd, 365 U.S. 467, 81 S. Ct. 659, 5 L. Ed. 2d 710.

Intangible tax statute taxing state and national banks at a different rate or assessing such banks by a different method than method employed to tax savings and loan associations did not violate federal statute conferring upon state power to tax national bank shares providing tax did not impose a greater rate than was assessed upon other moneyed capital in hands of individual citizens of state coming into competition with business of national banks, when there was practical equality of total tax imposed upon savings and loan associations and upon national banks and any difference could be justified as partial exemptions. Michigan Nat'l Bank v. State, 358 Mich. 611, 101 N.W.2d 245, aff'd, 365 U.S. 467, 81 S. Ct. 659, 5 L. Ed. 2d 710.

Existence in county of other moneyed capital taxed as moneys and credits.—

That there was in county in which plaintiff bank was located other invested moneyed capital in hands of individual citizens which was taxed as moneys and credits was insufficient on which to predicate determination as matter of law that tax imposed against shares of stock in national banks was at a higher rate than moneyed capital coming into competition therewith in violation of federal statute. Cherokee State Bank v. Wallace, 202 Minn. 582, 279 N.W. 410 (1938).

The law authorizing a state tax on national bank shares at a rate not greater than that assessed on other moneyed capital is violated by different tax on capital substantial in amount when compared with capitalization of national banks which is employed either in a business or by private investors in same sort of transactions as those in which national banks engage and in same locality in which they do business. Cherokee State Bank v. Wallace, 202 Minn. 582, 279 N.W. 410 (1938).

Invalid method of levying.—

Taxes assessed against national bank shares at greater rate than assessed against moneyed capital of individual citizens engaged in same or similar business held not per as invalid only method of levying being invalid. First Nat. Bank v. Jackson County, 227 Ala. 448, 150 So. 690.

[2649] **In general.—**

Crown Finance Corp. v. McColgan (Cal. App.), 135 P.2d 694, rev'd on other grounds, 23 Cal. 2d 280, 144 P.2d 331.

Definitions.—

"Moneyed capital" is difference between the credits and debts. Davis v. Sexton, 210 Ind. 138, 200 N.E. 233.

must be satisfactorily shown by proof that moneyed capital claimed to be given an unjust advantage does so compete.[2650] However, the statutory prohibition is not directed solely against capital invested in state banks or

---

The significance of this expression has been defined by this court in the case of Mercantile Nat. Bank v. New York, 121 U.S. 138, 7 S. Ct. 826, 30 L. Ed. 895, cited in Palmer v. McMahon, 133 U.S. 660, 10 S. Ct. 324, 33 L. Ed. 772, as follows: The term "moneyed capital," as used in Rev. State § 5219, respecting state taxation of shares in national banks, embraces capital employed in national banks, and capital employed by individuals when the object of their business is the making of profit by the use of their moneyed capital as money. Talbott v. Silver Bow County, 139 U.S. 438, 11 S. Ct. 594, 35 L. Ed. 210. See also People v. Commissioners, 71 U.S. (4 Wall.) 244, 18 L. Ed. 344.

The words "moneyed capital" do not embrace any moneyed capital in the sense just defined, except that in the hands of individual citizens. This excludes moneyed capital in the hands of corporations, although the business of some corporations may be such as to make the shares therein belonging to individuals moneyed capital in their hands, as in the case of banks. A railroad company, a mining company, an insurance company, or any other Corporation of that description, may have a large part of its capital invested in securities payable in money, and so may be the owners of moneyed capital; but the shares of stock in such companies held by individuals are not moneyed capital. Mercantile Bank v. New York, 121 U.S. 138, 7 S. Ct. 826, 30 L. Ed. 895.

The words "other moneyed capital," as used in the statute providing that the shares in national banks shall not be assessed at a greater rate than other moneyed capital in the hands of individual citizens, do not mean all the capital, the value of which is measured in terms of money, nor all forms of investment in which the interest of the owner is expressed in money, nor shares of stock represented by certificates showing that the owner is entitled to an interest expressed in money value in the entire property of the corporation, nor real or personal property, such as ordinary chattels or commodities, nor investments in manufacturing and industrial enterprises; but dose include shares of stock or other interests owned by individuals in enterprise. in which the capital employed in carrying on the business is money, and the object of the business is the making of a profit by the use of money. First Nat. Bank v. Christensen, 39 Utah 568, 118 P. 778.

The limitation applies solely to a parallel with the individual or corporation whoa. capital in money is used with a view to compensation for the use of the money. Talbott v. Silver Bow County, 139 U.S. 438, 11 S. Ct. 594, 35 L. Ed. 210.

[2650] **In general.—**

First Nat'l Bank v. Chapman, 173 U.S. 205, 19 S. Ct. 407, 43 L. Ed. 669; Talbott v. Silver Bow County, 139 U.S. 438, 11 S. Ct. 594, 35 L. Ed. 210; Commercial Nat. Bank v. Chambers, 182 U.S. 556, 21 S. Ct. 863, 45 L. Ed. 1227; Jenkins v. Neff, 186 U.S. 230, 22 S. Ct. 905, 46 L. Ed. 1140; Aberdeen Bank v. Chehalis, 166 U.S. 440, 17 S. Ct. 629, 41 L. Ed. 1069; Exchange Nat. Bank v. Miller, 19 F. 372; Merchants' Nat'l Bank v. Dawson County, 93 Mont. 310, 19 P.2d 892.

National banks seeking to establish invalidity of state law taxing bank stock and property must prove that during tax year moneys of national banks were in fact employed in substantial amount in business carried on during year by less heavily taxed nonbanking

competing capital employed in private banking, but also applies wherever capital substantial in amount when compared with the capitalization of national banks, is employed in the same kind of transactions as those engaged in by national banks in the same locality in which they do business.[2651] On the other hand, stock held in insurance companies and other business, trading, manufacturing and miscellaneous corporations, whose business and operations are unlike those of banking institutions, is not moneyed capital in the statutory sense.[2652] In the footnotes are additional

---

concerns. First Nat'l Bank v. Louisiana Tax Com., 289 U.S. 60, 53 S. Ct. 511, 77 L. Ed. 1030, 87 A.L.R. 840.

To constitute a violation of federal law, it must appear as a matter of fact that amount of capital employed in business or by private investors is substantial and comes into competition with business of national banks and that tax imposed on such competing capital is at a lower rate than that applied to shares of national banks with which there is competition. Cherokee State Bank v. Wallace, 202 Minn. 582, 279 N.W. 410.

A conflict between a state statute, taxing national bank shares, and federal statute, permitting state taxation of such shares at a rate no greater than imposed upon other moneyed capital in hands of individual citizens of the state coming in competition with national banks, may not be established by showing merely that other moneyed capital is employed in business in which national banks are authorized to engage, without showing actual substantial competition. In re National Bank, 137 W. Va. 673, 73 S.E.2d 655 (1952).

And where capital is not so employed as to come into general and substantial competition with business of national banks, it is within discretion of state to tax it at a different rate from that levied on capital of such banks. Crown Finance Corp. v. McColgan (Cal. App.), 135 P.2d 694.

[2651] Crown Finance Corp. v. McColgan (Cal. App.), 135 P.2d 694, rev'd on other grounds, 23 Cal. 2d 280, 144 P.2d 331.

The act of Congress which protects national banks from injurious discrimination does not limit the standard of comparison to the "moneyed capital" invested in the "incorporated banks" of a state, but extends to all "moneyed capital in the hands of individual citizens of the state." To equalize the shares of national banks as to part only of that moneyed capital, is not to equalize them as to the whole, which is necessary to comply with the statute. First Nat'l Bank v. Lucas County, 25 F. 749, appeal dismissed, 131 U.S. 450, 9 S. Ct. 804, 33 L. Ed. 201.

[2652] First Nat. Bank v. Chapman, 173 U.S. 205, 19 S. Ct. 407, 43 L. Ed. 669; Aberdeen Bank v. Chehalis County, 166 U.S. 440, 17 S. Ct. 629, 41 L. Ed. 1069; Bank of Commerce v. Seattle, 166 U.S. 463, 17 S. Ct. 996, 41 L. Ed. 1079 Mercantile Bank v. New York, 121 U.S. 138, 7 S. Ct. 826, 30 L. Ed. 895; First Nat'l Bank v. Ayers, 160 U.S. 660, 16 S. Ct. 412, 40 L. Ed. 573; Talbott v. Silver Bow, 139 U.S. 438, 11 S. Ct. 594, 35 L. Ed 210; Hepburn v. School Directors, 90 U.S. (23 Wall.) 480, 23 L. Ed. 112; Davenport Bank v. Davenport Board of Equalization, 123 U.S. 83, 8 S. Ct. 73, 31 L. Ed. 94; Bank of Redemption v. Boston, 125 U.S. 60, 8 S. Ct. 772, 31 L. Ed. 689; Evansville Bank v. Britton, 105 U.S. 322, 26 L. Ed. 1053.

cases holding that certain moneyed capital competes,[2653] or does not

---

The investment. and assets of insurance companies, and interest of individuals therein, are not "moneyed capital coming into competition with national banks" as respects taxation of national bank shares. Merchants' Nat. Bank v. Dawson County, 93 Mont. 310, 19 P.2d 892.

[2653] **In general.—**

Title Guarantee Loan & Trust Co. v. State, 228 Ala. 636, 155 So. 305.

Money invested in firm carrying on general banking business held taxable as moneyed capital competing with business of national banks. People ex rel. Pratt v. Goldfogle, 242 N.Y. 277, 151 N.E. 452.

Money' invested in firm doing private banking, commission, and investment business, including receiving deposits subject to check and bills of exchange, discounting of commercial paper, loans on personal security with deposit of collateral security, and dealing in foreign exchange, was competing with national banks, and was subject to taxation as such. People ex rel. Pratt v. Goldfogle, 213 App. Div. 706, 211 N.Y.S. 110, aff'd, 242 N.Y. 277, 151 N.E. 452.

Money employed in making farm loans on real estate mortgages held taxable as money competing with national banks. People v. Goldfogle, 242 N.Y. 277, 151 N.E. 452.

Corporation engaged in loaning money on first mortgages and selling loans to public and guaranteeing payment thereof held taxable as employing "moneyed capital in competition with national banks." People v. Burke, 253 N.Y. 93, 170 N.E. 505.

Corporation lending money repayable in installments on investment certificates held taxable as employing "moneyed capital in competition with national banks." People ex rel. Title & Mortg. Guarantee Co. v. Burke, 253 N.Y. 93, 170 N.E. 505.

Loan service corporation, negotiating small loans for borrowers through a finance company, was in active competition with national banks, so as to require service corporation to be classified as a "financial corporation" subject to state franchise tax, in view of federal law prohibiting state tax discrimination against national banks. H. A. S. Loan Service, Inc. v. McColgan, 21 Cal. 2d 518, 133 P.2d 391, 145 A.L.R. 349.

Shares of stock purchased as temporary investment by one engaged in business competing with national banks held taxable as moneyed capital competing with national banks. People v. Goldfogle, 242 N.Y. 277, 151 N.E. 452.

Capital deposited in national bank as cash reserve by person competing with national banks does not cease to be employed in competition with such banks, within statute taxing moneyed capital competing with national banks. People v. Goldfogle, 242 N.Y. 277, 151 N.E 452.

Fees held charges for lending "moneyed capital" rather than service charges.—

Fees for making and servicing construction loans, "point" charges for making federally insured loans and other preassignment earnings of corporation engaged in purchase and assignment of first deeds of trust were charges for lending "moneyed capital" rather than for rendering service to institutional assignees. Marble Mortgage Co. v. Franchise Tax Ed., 241 Cal. App. 2d 26, 50 Cal. Rptr. 345 (1966).

compete,[2654] with national banks.

[2654] **In general.—**

Annuities, bonds, notes, royalties, accounts, money loaned on conditional sales contracts, money on deposit, checks, drafts, and shares in building and loan associations are not "moneyed capital" coming in competition with the capital of national banks. Davis v. Sexton, 210 Ind. 138, 200 N.E. 233.

Capital invested in savings bank is not "moneyed capital in competition with national banks." Merchants' Nat'l Bank v. Dawson County, 93 Mont. 310, 19 P.2d 892.

Money invested in stock brokerage firm, which loaned customers difference between purchase price of stock and amount paid on price, or on margin, for which it charged interest, was not subject to tax on moneyed capital competing with national banks, where brokers, in order to effect such loans, borrowed all or as much as they could from banks. People ex rel. Broderick v. Goldfogle, 213 App. Div. 677, 211 N.Y.S. 85, aff'd, 242 N.Y. 540, 152 N.E. 418; People v. Goldfogle, 213 App. Div. 715, 211 N.Y.S. 119, aff'd, 242 N.Y. 541, 152 N.E 418.

Money invested in stock brokerage firm doing "odd lot" and "specialist" business, buying and selling stocks on its own account, and carrying only a few accounts for personal accommodation of firm members. and their relatives, held not in competition with national banks and not taxable, "odd lot" business consisting in buying or selling any amount of stock from one share to 99, and equalizing broker's position by purchasing or selling in 100-share lots, and "specialist" being floor broker, specializing in limited group of stocks. People v. Goldfogle, 213 App. Div. 702, 211 N.Y.S. 107, aff'd, 242 N.Y. 542, 152 N.E. 419.

Money invested in seats in New York Cotton Exchange and Chicago Board of Trade and in stock brokerage firm engaged in buying and selling stock, bonds, and commodities solely for customers, principally on margin and remainder for cash, its profits being from commissions, and which financed customers' purchases with its own funds and with additional money borrowed from banks, trust companies, and other brokers, held not in competition with national banks, and was not subject to taxation notwithstanding it charged interest on customers' debit balances as incident to buying and selling securities. People v. Goldfogle, 213 App. Div. 713, 211 N.Y.S. 117, aff'd, 242 N.Y. 546, 152 N.E. 420; People v. Goldfogle, 242 N.Y. 277, 151 N.E. 452.

Individuals' merely personal investments not made in competition with banking or investment business, are not deemed "moneyed capital" within statute prohibiting state taxation of national banks' stock at higher rates than moneyed capital employed in competition with such banks. Toy Nat. Bank v. Smith, 8 F. Supp. 638, rev'd on other grounds sub nom. Hammerstrom v. Toy Nat'l Bank, 81 F.2d 628, cert. denied. 299 U.S. 546, 57 S. Ct. 9, 81 L. Ed. 402.

Capital of building and loan association is not "employed capital" in competition with national banks. Merchants' Nat. Bank v. Dawson County, 93 Mont. 310, 19 P.2d 892.

Finance and investment companies were not engaged in business which was in competition with business of national banks, and hence tax on national bank shares was not illegal on ground that bank shares were taxed at greater rate than competing moneyed capital in substantial amount in hands of individual citizens invested in shares of financing and investment companies. Davis v. Sexton, 210 Ind. 138, 200 N.E. 233.

Discrimination in Manner of Assessment.—Any system of assessment of taxes which exacts from an owner of national bank shares a larger sum in proportion to their actual value than it does from the owner of other moneyed capital valued in like manner, taxes such shares at a greater rate within the meaning of the federal statute.[2655] This rule refers to the entire process of assessment, whether the discrimination be by valuation or by rate of assessment on such valuation.[2656] Presumptively, the nominal or par value of bank shares is their true value, any profits normally going in dividends to

---

investment company, buying and selling complete issues of corporate bonds secured by realty mortgages, having powers defined by statute and not having power to receive deposits or to issue it own debenture bonds or notes secured by deeds or deeds of trust, held not in competition with national banks, and not subject to taxation on that score. People v. Goldfogle, 213 App. Div. 710, 211 N.Y.S. 114, aff'd, 242 N.Y. 543, 152 N.E. 419.

Livestock commission houses, making cattle and feeder loans with aid of national banks discounting their papers, held not in competition with such banks, as required to entitle latter to recover taxes paid on their stock assessed at higher rate than moneyed capital invested by others such loans. Toy Nat. Bank v. Smith, 8 Supp. 638, rev'd on other grounds sub nom. Hammerstrom v. Toy Nat'l Bank, 81 F.2d 628, cert. denied, 299 U.S. 546, 57 S. Ct. 9, 81 L. Ed. 402.

Small loan companies, making character or salary loans, and finance and securities companies, loaning money on notes for prices of automobiles, radios, etc., held not in competition with national banks, as required to entitle latter to recover taxes on their stock assessed at higher rate then moneyed capital loaned by others. Toy Nat'l Bank v. Smith, 8 F. Supp. 638, rev'd on other grounds sub nom. Hammerstrom v. Toy Nat'l Bank, 81 F.2d 628, cert. denied 299 U.S. 546, 57 S. Ct. 9, 81 L. Ed. 402.

Textile factor, which stored and sold principals goods, guaranteed purchaser's credit, and made advances to principal against consignments or accounts assigned to it, on which advances it charged interest, held not subject to statute, taxing money competing with national banks; distinction between "advances" and loans" being that loans are repayable at maturity, while advances are not repaid by party receiving them, but are covered by proceeds of consigned goods. People v. Goldfogle, 213 App. Div. 719, 211 N.Y.S. 122.

2655 **In general.**—

Pelton v. Commercial Nat. Bank, 101 U.S. 143, 25 L. Ed. 901; People v. Weaver, 100 U.S. 539, 25 L. Ed. 705; Hager v. Citizens' Nat'l Bank, 127 Ky. 192, 105 S.W. 403, 32 Ky. L. Rptr. 95, appeal dismissed, 212 U.S. 585, 29 S. Ct. 681, 53 L. Ed. 661.

Where no discrimination in rate of assessment was shown, tax on cash value of national bank shares held not illegal. Davis v. Sexton, 210 Ind. 138, 200 N.E. 233.

2656 People v. Weaver, 100 U.S. 539, 25 L. Ed. 705; Stanley v. Supervisors of Albany, 121 U.S. 535, 7 S. Ct. 1234, 30 L. Ed. 1000; Whitbeck v. Mercantile Nat'l Bank, 127 U.S. 193, 8 S. Ct. 1121, 32 L. Ed. 118; Boyer v. Boyer, 113 U.S. 689, 5 S. Ct. 706, 28 L. Ed. 1089, Pelton v. National Bank, 101 U.S. 148, 25 L. Ed. 901; Cummings v. National Bank, 101 U.S. 158, 25 L. Ed. 903; Supervisors v. Stanley, 105 U.S. 305, 26 L. Ed. 1044; Evansville Bank v. Britton, 105 U.S. 322, 26 L. Ed. 1053. See also Hills v. Exchange Bank,

the stockholders, and this method of valuation as applied to all banks, national and state, comes as close as is practical, considering the nature of the property, to securing uniformity and equality of taxation, and cannot be considered as discriminating against either kind of bank.[2657] But valuation may be made at the actual value of such shares, even if over par, if the rate of taxation is the same,[2658] and may include the added value arising from bank franchises, although there is no such added value for unincorporated banks subject to taxation.[2659] However, individual instances of omission or undervaluation are insufficient to invalidate an entire assessment.[2660] And a state statute curing irregularities in the assessment of national bank shares for certain years was held not in conflict with the act of Congress respecting the taxation of such shares.[2661]

Discrimination in Deduction of Indebtedness.—The taxation of national bank shares under a state statute which does not allow a shareholder to deduct the amount of his bona fide indebtedness from their assessed value as may be done in other investments of moneyed capital, is a discrimination forbidden by the federal statute.[2662] But where an owner of what is termed

---

105 U.S. 319, 26 L. Ed. 1052; Mercantile Nat. Bank v. New York, 121 U.S. 138, 7 S. Ct. 826, 30 L. Ed. 895.

Nor is it any less an unlawful discrimination that the national bank shares are in fact assessed below "their true value in money." First Nat'l Bank v. Lucas County, 25 F. 749, appeal dismissed, 131 U.S. 450, 9 S. Ct. 804, 33 L. Ed. 201.

[2657] Stanley v. Supervisors of Albany, 121 U.S. 535, 7 S. Ct. 1234, 30 L. Ed. 1000; Supervisors v. Stanley, 105 U.S. 305, 26 L. Ed. 1044. See also Williams v. Supervisors of Albany, 122 U.S. 164, 7 S. Ct. 1244, 30 L. Ed. 1088.

[2658] Hepburn v. School Directors, 90 U.S. (28 Wall.) 480, 23 L. Ed. 112; Mercantile Bank v. New York, 121 U.S. 138, 7 S. Ct. 826, 30 L. Ed. 895. See also People v. Commissioners, 94 U.S. 415, 24 L. Ed. 164; Palmer v. McMahon, 133 U.S. 660, 10 S. Ct. 324, 33 L. Ed. 772.

[2659] First Nat'l Bank v. Chapman, 173 U.S. 205, 19 S. Ct. 407, 43 L. Ed. 669.

[2660] Supervisors v. Stanley, 105 U.S. 305, 26 L. Ed. 1044; Stanley v. Supervisors of Albany, 121 U.S. 535, 7 S. Ct. 1234, 30 L. Ed. 1000. See San Francisco Nat. Bank v. Dodge, 197 U.S. 70, 25 S. Ct 384, 49 L. Ed. 669, where an agreed statement of facts that the assessment was illustrative of others, was held to prevent this rule from applying. See also Hills v. Exchange Bank, 105 U.S. 319, 26 L. Ed. 1052; Evansville Bank v. Britton, 105 U.S. 322, 26 L. Ed. 1053; Palmer v. McMahon, 133 U.S. 660, 10 S. Ct. 324, 33 L. Ed. 772; People's Nat'l Bank v. Marye, 191 U.S. 272, 24 S. Ct. 68, 48 L. Ed. 180; National Bank v. Kimball, 103 U.S. 732, 26 L. Ed. 469.

[2661] Williams v. Albany, 122 U.S. 154, 7 S. Ct. 1244, 30 L. Ed. 1088.

[2662] Evansville Bank v. Britton, 105 U.S. 322, 26 L. Ed. 1053; Merchants' Nat'l Bank v. Richmond, 256 U.S. 635, 41 S. Ct. 619, 65 L. Ed. 1135. See People v. Weaver, 100 U.S.

"credits" in a state statute is permitted to deduct certain classes of debts from those credits, with taxes to be assessed on the remainder, while a national bank shareholder is not permitted to deduct his debts from the value of his shares as assessed for taxation, there is not a per se illegal discrimination against the latter, it not appearing what proportion of such credits is "moneyed capital."[2663] And debts incurred in the actual conduct of a business, incorporated or unincorporated, may be deducted under a law providing therefor, in ascertaining the proper valuation of such business, without there being a discrimination against national bank shares although no such deduction is provided as to them.[2664] Moreover, there is no reason why a statute which does not provide for such deduction should not remain the law as to state banks or banking associations or private bankers, nor is it void as to a shareholder in a national bank who owes no debts which he could deduct from the assessed value of his shares, as the denial of this right does not affect him; he pays the same amount of tax that he would if the law gave him the deduction. Even in cases where such indebtedness does exist and ought to be deducted, an assessment is voidable, not void, and a shareholder must show the assessing officer what his debts are, and take the necessary steps to secure a correction,[2665] unless it is clear that such steps would be unavailing because of the fixed purpose of the assessor to allow no

---

539, 25 L. Ed. 705; Supervisors v. Stanley, 105 U.S. 305, 26 L. Ed. 1044; Hills v. Exchange Bank, 105 U.S. 319, 26 L. Ed. 1052; Whitbeck v. Mercantile Nat. Bank, 127 U.S. 193, 8 S. Ct. 1121, 32 L. Ed. 118; First Nat'l Bank v. Chapman, 173 U.S. 205, 19 S. Ct. 407, 43 L. Ed. 669; Newark Banking Co. v. Newark, 121 U.S. 163, 7 S. Ct. 839, 30 L. Ed. 904; Stanley V. Albany, 121 U.S. 535, 7 S. Ct 1234, 30 L. Ed. 1000; City Nat. Bank v. Paducah, 5 F. Cas. 755 (No. 2743), 2 Flip. 61; Pollard v. State, 65 Ala. 628; Boyer v. Boyer, 113 U.S. 689, 5 S. Ct. 706, 28 L. Ed. 1089; Palmer v. McMahon, 133 U.S. 660, 10 S. Ct. 324, 33 L. Ed. 772; Cummings v. National Bank, 101 U.S. 153, 25 L. Ed. 903; Mercantile Bank v. New York, 121 U.S. 138, 7 S. Ct. 826, 30 L. Ed. 895.

Tax on cash value of national bank shares held not illegal where bona fide indebtedness was deducted in arriving at value. Davis v. Sexton, 210 Ind. 138, 200 N.E. 233.

[2663] First Nat. Bank v. Chapman, 173 U.S. 205, 19 S. Ct. 407, 43 L. Ed. 669, distinguishing Whitbeck v. Mercantile Nat. Bank, 127 U.S. 193, 8 S. Ct. 1121, 32 L. Ed. 118. See Commercial Nat. Bank v. Chambers, 182 U.S. 556, 21 S. Ct. 863, 45 L. Ed. 1227. But see Boyer v. Boyer, 113 U.S. 689, 5 S. Ct. 706, 28 L. Ed. 1089.

[2664] First Nat'l Bank v. Chapman, 173 U.S. 205, 19 S. Ct. 407, 43 L. Ed. 669; Bridgeport Sav. Bank v. Feitner, 191 N.Y. 88, 83 N.E. 592.

[2665] Supervisors v. Stanley, 105 U.S. 305, 26 L. Ed. 1044; Stanley v. Supervisors of Albany, 121 U.S. 535, 7 S. Ct. 1234, 30 L. Ed. 1000. See also Hills v. Exchange Bank, 105 U.S. 319, 26 L. Ed 1052; Evansville Bank v. Britton, 105 U.S. 322, 26 L. Ed. 1053; Palmer v. McMahon, 133 U.S. 660, 10 S. Ct. 324, 33 L. Ed. 772; People v. Weaver, 100 U.S. 539, 25 L. Ed. 705.

such deductions,[2666] or where the law makes no provision for such deductions.[2667] And a judgment that a tax was illegally assessed because the deduction of bona fide debts of shareholders of a national bank from the valuation of their shares was not made, as the law allowed in the taxation of "credits" in the hands of individuals, and an illegal discrimination was thereby made against a national bank, is not conclusive proof of the existence of discrimination as to assessments of such stock for other years.[2668]

Discrimination in Deduction of Real Estate Outside of State.—The refusal to allow a deduction of the value of real estate in other states owned by a national bank from the value of its shares of stock, where such a deduction is not authorized by state law in valuing shares of stock of other corporations, does not constitute an illegal discrimination against such banks or deny them the equal protection of the laws.[2669]

Necessity for Affirmative Showing of Discrimination.—Where there is no means of ascertaining whether there is unfavorable tax discrimination against shareholders of national banks and in favor of other moneyed capital in the hands of individual citizens, and there is nothing upon the face of a state's statute which shows such discrimination, it would seem that a case has not been made out for the intervention of the courts. Discrimination must be affirmatively shown, as there is a presumption against it.[2670] And such

---

2666 Hills v. Exchange Bank, 105 U.S. 319, 26 L. Ed. 1052.

2667 Whitbeck v. Mercantile Nat. Bank, 127 U.S. 193, 8 S. Ct. 1121, 32 L. Ed. 118.

Under the decision in Hills v. Exchange Bank, 105 U.S. 319, 26 L. Ed. 1052, the bank was entitled to relief by injunction against the collection of the illegal tax on the bank shares, and the fact that they did not make a demand for the deduction of their indebtedness from the assessed value of the shares of their bank stock before the entire process of the appraisement and equalization of the value of said shares for taxation had been completed, and the tax duplicate for said year had been delivered in accordance with law to the treasurer of said county for the collection of said taxes, did not defeat their right to have it made by this bill in chancery, for the reason that the court expressly finds that "the laws of Ohio make no provisions for the deduction of the bona fide indebtedness of any shareholder from the shares of his stock and provide no means by which said deduction can be secured." Whitbeck v. Mercantile Nat. Bank, 127 U.S. 193, 8 S. Ct. 1121, 32 L. Ed. 118.

2668 Lander v. Mercantile Bank, 186 U.S. 458, 22 S. Ct. 908, 46 L. Ed. 1247. See also First Nat'l Bank v. Chapman, 173 U.S. 205, 19 S. Ct. 407, 43 L. Ed. 669.

2669 Commercial Nat. Bank v. Chambers, 182 U.S. 556, 21 S. Ct. 863, 45 L. Ed. 1227.

2670 People's Nat'l Bank & Trust Co. v. Westchester County, 261 N.Y. 342, 185 N.E. 405, aff'g 237 App. Div. 827, 260 N.Y.S. 996; First Nat'l Bank v. Chapman, 173 U.S. 205, 19 S. Ct. 407, 43 L. Ed. 669, distinguishing Whitbeck v. Mercantile Nat. Bank, 127 U.S. 193,

illegal discrimination must at least be definitely and clearly charged for any relief to be based thereon.[2671]

§ 27. Validity of Statute Requiring Payment by Bank as Agent of Stockholders.

The statutory appointment of national banks to pay a state tax as agent of their stockholders Is not inconsistent with federal law pertaining to national banks.[2672] And such a bank may be required to pay a tax out of its corporate funds, be authorized to deduct the amount paid for each stockholder from his

---

8 S. Ct. 1121, 32 L. Ed. 118. See also Mercantile Bank v. New York, 121 U.S. 138, 7 S. Ct. 826, 30 L. Ed. 895; Jenkins v. Neff, 186 U.S. 280, 22 S. Ct. 905, 46 L. Ed. 1140; Supervisors v. Stanley, 105 U.S. 305, 26 L. Ed. 1044; Davenport Bank v. Davenport Board of Equalization, 123 U.S. 83, 8 S. Ct. 73, 31 L. Ed. 94.

[2671] Aberdeen Bank v. Chehalis, 166 U.S. 440, 17 S. Ct. 629, 41 L. Ed. 1069; Bank v. Seattle, 166 U.S. 463, 17 S. Ct. 996, 41 L. Ed. 1079; National Bank v. Kimball, 103 U.S. 732, 26 L. Ed. 469.

[2672] *United States.*—National Bank v. Allen, 223 F. 472, cert. denied, 239 U.S. 642, 36 S. Ct. 163, 60 L. Ed. 482; Newark Banking Co. v. Newark, 121 U.S. 163, 7 S. Ct. 839, 30 L. Ed. 904; Van Slyke v. Wisconsin, 154 U.S. 581, 14 S. Ct. 1168, 20 L. Ed. 240; Aberdeen Bank v. Chehalis, 166 U.S. 440, 17 S. Ct. 629, 41 L. Ed. 1069; Citizens Nat'l Bank v. Kentucky, 199 U.S. 603, 26 S. Ct. 750, 50 L. Ed. 329; National Bank v. Commonwealth, 76 U.S. (9 Wall.) 353, 19 L. Ed 701; Bell's G. R. Co. v. Pennsylvania, 134 U.S. 232, 10 S. Ct. 533, 33 L. Ed. 892; Lionberger v. Rouse, 76 U.S. (9 Wall.) 468, 19 L. Ed. 721; First Nat Bank v. Douglas County, 9 F. Cas. 84 (No. 4, 799), 3 Dill. 330; Merchants' & Mfrs' Bank v. Pennsylvania, 167 U.S. 461, 17 S. Ct. 829, 42 L. Ed. 236; Charleston Nat. Bank v. Melton, 171 F. 743; Findley v. Odland, 127 F.2d 948.

Alabama.—National Commercial Bank v. Mayor, Aldermen & Common Council of Mobile, 62 Ala. 284, 34 Am. R. 15; Sumter v. National Bank, 62 Ala. 464, 34 Am. R. 30.

Indiana.—Whitney v. Ragsdale, 33 Ind. 107, 5 Am. B. 185.

Iowa.—Head v. Board of Review, 170 Iowa 300, 152 N.W. 600.

Kentucky.—Commonwealth v. First Nat. Bank, 67 Ky. (4 Bush) 98, 96 Am. Dec. 285, aff'd, 76 U.S. (9 Wall.) 353, 19 L. Ed. 701.

Michigan.—State may make bank its agent to collect taxes from bank's individual stockholders on the shares. School Dist. v. Lansing, 286 Mich. 244, 281 N.W. 883.

Ohio.—Statute making taxes assessed on shares of stock in a bank a lien on shares until paid, and imposing on bank and banking association duty to collect taxes due on shares, as in effect prior to January 1, 1931, imposed tax on shares of stock and not upon the property of the bank, hence did not violate statute prescribing manner of taxation of national banks. Union Sav. Bank v. Pancoast, 142 Ohio St. 6, 50 N.E.2d 157, aff'd sub nom. Second Nat. Bank v. Findley, 320 U.S. 714, 64 S. Ct. 260, 88 L. Ed. 420.

Washington.—Baker v. King County, 17 Wash. 622, 50 P. 481.

dividends,[2673] or have the option of paying a different and larger tax on the par value of its shares or the regular rate on their actual value.[2674] The liability of national banks for a state tax on their stock which they fail to collect as required by state statute may or may not be discharged by their insolvency after such liability has fully matured.[2675]

§ 28. Deposits.

It has been held that there is nothing in the relationship of a national bank to the federal government that protects its depositors from taxation, and no congressional authority is needed to enable a state to tax national bank deposits to depositors.[2676] And a statute providing for assessment of

---

[2673] National Bank of Commerce v. Allen, 223 F. 472, cert. denied, 239 U.S. 642, 36 S. Ct. 163, 60 L. Ed. 482; Head v. Board of Review, 170 Iowa 300, 152 N.W. 600; Farrington v. Tennessee, 95 U.S. 679, 24 L. Ed. 558; National Bank v. Commonwealth, 76 U.S. (9 Wall.) 353, 19 L. Ed. 701; Central Nat'l Bank v. United States, 137 U.S. 355, 11 S. Ct. 126, 34 L. Ed. 703; Merchants', etc., Nat. Bank v. Pennsylvania, 167 U.S. 461, 17 S. Ct 829, 42 L. Ed. 236; Whitney Nat. Bank v Parker, 41 F. 402; Mechanics' Nat'l Bank v. Baker, 65 N.J.L. 113, 46 A. 586, aff'd, 65 N.J.L. 549, 48 A. 582; Aberdeen Bank v. Chehalis County, 166 U.S. 440, 17 S. Ct. 629, 41 L. Ed. 1069; Citizens Nat'l Bank v. Kentucky, 217 U.S. 443, 30 S. Ct. 532, 54 L. Ed. 832 (1970); Baker v. King County, 17 Wash. 622, 50 P. 481.

[2674] Merchants', etc., Nat. Bank v. Pennsylvania. 167 U.S. 461, 17 S. Ct. 829, 42 L. Ed. 236; Waite v. Dowley, 94 U.S. 527, 24 L. Ed. 181.

[2675] Findley v. Odland, 127 F.2d 948 (liability not discharged).

That a tax lawfully imposed on shares of stock of a national bank could, under Mississippi statute, be required to be paid by such bank as agent for shareholders, held not to render receiver of national bank liable for state, county, and municipal taxes, even if tax were properly assessed against shares, since insolvency ended any statutory agency to pay. Gully v. First Nat. Bank, 81 F.2d 502, rev'd on other grounds, 299 U.S. 109, 57 S. Ct. 96, 81 L. Ed. 70.

[2676] **In general.—**

State v. Clement Nat'l Bank, 84 Vt. 167, 78 A. 944, 1912D Ann. Cas. 22.

Election to pay as agent.—

It is sometimes provided that if a national bank so elects it may pay to the state taxes on deposits, and that it shall be lawful for such bank to deduct the taxes so paid from the interest or deposits then or thereafter held by it belonging to the person from whom the tax is due. State v. Clement Nat'l Bank, 84 Vt. 167, 78 A. 944, 1912D Ann. Cas. 22.

County funds not taxable deposit.—

General unsegregated bank deposit in name of "Clerk of Courts, ... County" which was broken down on books of clerk and contained money held by clerk to be paid to litigants pending outcome of litigation was a deposit belonging in its entirety to county and was not a taxable deposit. First Nat. Bank v. Bowers, 104 Ohio App. 495, 150 N.E.2d 459.

interest-bearing national bank deposits to a depositor at their face value is not invalid for failure to provide for official valuation, nor can an owner of an interest-bearing national bank deposit object to assessment of his deposit at its full value because of the possibility the bank may prove insolvent.[2677] But escrow funds on deposit in a national bank and used in the bank's general business were held not assessable to the bank for property tax purposes as "solvent credits" owned, claimed, possessed or controlled by it.[2678]

§ 29. Dividends.

A state taxing national bank shares and exempting national banks from payment of income taxes could not include dividends from such shares in the taxable income of a shareholder.[2679]

§ 30. Federal and Joint Stock Land Banks.

A federal land bank is an instrumentality of the national government, and it is constitutionally endowed with the same immunity from state taxation as the national government would have enjoyed if it had engaged in such banking activity directly.[2680] The statute governing waiver of immunity from

---

Application of deposits portion of excise tax to state-chartered mutual thrift institutions but not to federal savings and loan associations is not contrary to legislative intent and does not constitute an unconstitutional usurpation of legislative function. Andover Sav. Bank v. Commissioner of Revenue, 387 Mass. 229, 439 N.E.2d 282 (1982).

[2677] State v. Clement Nat'l Bank, 84 Vt. 167, 78 A. 944, 1912D Ann. Cas. 22.

[2678] Bank of America Nat. Trust, etc., Ass'n v. Board of Sup'rs, 93 Cal. App. 2d 75, 208 P.2d 772.

[2679] State Revenue Com. v. Hawkins, 48 Ga. App. 414, 172 S.E. 845.

[2680] **In general.—**

Federal Land Bank v. De Rochford, 69 N.D. 382, 287 N.W. 522.

See West Co. v. Johnson, 20 Cal. App. 2d 95, 66 P.2d 1211, appeal dismissed, 302 U.S. 638, 58 S. Ct 45, 82 L. Ed. 497.

Subject only to real estate tax.—

Federal land bank as an agency and instrumentality of federal government was exempt from payment of taxes except on real estate, and failure of county to impose ad valorem taxes on bank's promissory notes secured by deed of trust liens on real estate and its deposits in banks of state could not be considered in passing on question of discrimination or substantial injury to bank by reason of taxing system which imposed ad valorem taxes on bank's severed mineral interests. Federal Land Bank v. State (Tex. Civ. App.), 314 S.W.2d 621, rev'd on other grounds, 160 Tax. 282, 329 S.W.2d 847.

Personal property tax.—

A federal land bank is a constitutionally created federal instrumentality, immunized from

taxes on real estate held by a Federal Land Bank limits the tax which a state may levy on a Federal Land Bank's real estate to an ad valorem tax for which the real estate is assessed and the tax rate is applied on the same basis to the assessed value of all real estate similarly situated in the taxing district.[2681] Federal statute governing waiver of immunity from taxes on real estate held by a Federal Land Bank precluded the imposition of a severed mineral interest tax, which was not an ad valorem tax, on Federal Land Bank's severed mineral interests.[2682]

Shares of stock of a joint stock land bank organized under the federal Farm Loan Act are subject to state and county taxation unless exempted by state or federal law[2683] and Congress could make joint stock land bank

---

personal property taxes on activities in furtherance of its lending functions. Federal Land Bank v. Board of County Comm'rs, 368 U.S. 146, 82 S. Ct. 282, 7 L. Ed. 2d 199.

Federal lend bank's interest in retained mineral estate, although held for more than five years and past time when loss on defaulted mortgage was recouped, was exempt from Kansas personal property tax. Federal Land Bank v. Board of County Comm'rs, 368 U.S. 146, 82 S. Ct. 282, 7 L. Ed. 2d 199.

A federal land bank acted in furtherance of its governmental function in retaining mineral interest when it disposed of land acquired by mortgage foreclosure, and such interest was exempt from taxation. Federal Land Bank v. Board of County Comm'rs, 368 U.S. 146, 82 S. Ct. 282, 7 L. Ed. 2d 199.

Motor vehicle privilege tax.—

A federal land bank is exempt from payment of state privilege tax on motor vehicles operated by the bank within the state for purpose of carrying on its business. Roberts v. Federal Land Bank, 189 Miss. 898, 196 So. 763.

2681 St. Louis County v. Federal Land Bank, 338 N.W.2d 741 (Minn. 1983).

2682 St. Louis County v. Federal Land Bank, 338 N.W.2d 741 (Minn. 1983).

Tax imposed on severed mineral interests is not an ad valorem tax, in that it never varies according to the location or quality of the mineral interest, and by its own terms is inapplicable to mineral interests whose value has been determined. County of St. Louis v. Federal Land Bank, 338 N.W.2d 741 (Minn. 1983).

2683 **In general.—**

Land v. Kentucky Joint Stock Land Bank, 279 Ky. 645, 131 S.W.2d 838.

Such shares of stock are not exempted from taxation under constitution of Kentucky or act of Congress. Land v. Kentucky Joint Stock Land Bank, 279 Ky. 645, 131 S.W.2d 838.

A joint stock land bank organized under federal Farm Loan Act was a "national bank" within state statute concerning taxation of shares of national banks, and hence shares of stock of such bank were subject to state and county assessments, especially in view of provisions of federal Farm Loan Act empowering the taxing authorities to assess and tax shares of a joint stock land bank in same manner as shares in national banking associations. Land v. Kentucky Joint Stock Land Bank, 279 Ky. 645, 131 S.W.2d 838.

bonds exempt from state taxation as instrumentalities of the United States, without at the same time making the United States liable on such bonds.[2684]

Mortgages held by federal land banks are exempt from a mortgage registration fee.[2685]

§ 31. Other Federal Banks and Agencies.

Federal Reserve Bank.—A mortgage to a federal reserve bank securing a loan made for industrial purposes is exempt from state tax since such bank is an operating agency of the federal government.[2686]

Federal intermediate credit banks and banks of cooperatives are "governmental instrumentalities" as respects imposition of taxes by a state, even though the major portion of business transacted by them is essentially with private individuals.[2687]

Federal savings and loan associations are instrumentalities of the federal government, and their assets, franchise and property cannot be taxed except

---

Personal property tax.—

The federal statutes authorizing states to tax stock of national banking associations within the state, which were incorporated by reference into statute authorizing taxation of shareholders of joint stock land banks did not manifest an intent that joint stock land bank stock should escape taxation by the domiciliary state, but, under the statutes, such stock may be included in the valuation of the personal property of such owner. First Trust Joint Stock Land Bank v. Dallas (Tex. Civ. App.), 167 S.W.2d 783.

Where situs of stock of a joint stock land bank located in Texas is determined to be in Texas, such stock owned by nonresidents and residents is taxable to the same extent as other personal property is taxed in Texas, where Texas has assessed an ad valorem tax on all personal property within the state. First Trust Joint Stock Land Bank v. Dallas (Tex. Civ. App.), 167 S.W.2d 783.

[2684] Bankers Farm Mortg. Co. v. United States, 69 F. Supp. 197, cert. denied, 331 U.S. 831, 67 S. Ct. 1510, 91 L. Ed. 1846.

[2685] Federal Land Bank v. Thompson, 12 Kan. App. 2d 561, 751 P.2d 679 (1988).

[2686] Federal Reserve Bank v. Register of Deeds, 288 Mich. 120, 284 N.W. 667.

[2687] **In general.—**

West Co. v. Johnson, 20 Cal. App. 2d 95, 66 P.2d 1211, appeal dismissed, 302 U.S. 638, 58 S. Ct. 45, 82 L. Ed. 497.

Note not exempt from stamp tax.—

A note mailed to "Columbia Bank for Cooperatives of Columbia, S.C.", which was an instrumentality of the United States organized under Farm Credit Act, was not exempt from Florida documentary stamp tax under federal Constitution or Farm Credit Act. Plymouth Citrus Growers Ass'n v. Lee, 157 Fla. 893, 27 So. 2d 415.

to the extent permitted by Congress.[2688] And the difference between such

---

[2688] **In general.—**

Merchants & Mechanics Federal Sav. & Loan Ass'n v. Evatt, 138 Ohio St. 457, 35 N.E.2d 831; State v. Minnesota Federal Sav., etc., Ass'n, 218 Minn. 229, 15 N.W.2d 568 (1944).

Federal home loan banks are "federal instrumentalities," entitled to certain tax immunities. Association of Data Processing Serv. Organizations, Inc. v. Federal Home Loan Bank Bd., 568 F.2d 478 (6th Cir. 1977).

Deposits not taxable.—

There is no federal statute which permits the state to tax deposits in a federal savings and loan association. Merchants, etc., Fed. Sav., etc., Ass'n v. Evatt, 138 Ohio St. 457, 35 N.E.2d 831.

Loans by home loan bank to association not taxable.—

Provisions of Home Owners' Loan Act barring discriminatory state taxation of federal savings and loan associations left unimpaired exemption from state taxation conferred in Federal Home Loan Bank Act for loans by such a bank to such an association. Laurens Federal Sav. & Loan Ass'n v. South Carolina Tax Com., 365 U.S. 517, 81 S. Ct. 719, 5 L Ed. 2d 749, rev'g 236 S.C. 2, 112 S.E.2d 716.

Documentary stamp taxes.—

Statute exempting advances by federal home loan banks from state taxation barred state from requiring federal savings and loan association therein to pay documentary stamp taxes on promissory notes executed by association in favor of federal home loan bank to cover loans from bank to association. Laurens Federal Sav. & Loan Ass'n v. South Carolina Tax Com., 365 U.S. 517, 81 S. Ct. 719, 5 L Ed. 2d 749, rev'g 236 S.C. 2, 112 S.E.2d 716.

Franchise taxes.—

Federal savings and loan association was not free from state franchise taxes became it did not held a franchise from the state. First Federal Sav., etc., Ass'n v. Johnson, 49 Cal. App. 2d 465, 122 P.2d 84.

In view of state statute authorizing the taxing of all banks, including national banking associations, located within the state, and all financial, mercantile, manufacturing and business corporations, levy of franchise taxes against a federal savings and loan association was not void because the state failed to take advantage of the authorization conferred by the Federal Savings and Loan Association Act to tax such association's franchise and income by thereafter enacting a statute to that effect, since the association was a "financial corporation" within the statute. First Federal Sav., etc., Ass'n v. Johnson, 49 Cal. App. 2d 465, 122 P.2d 84.

Franchise tax based on income.—

In view of provision of federal statute that no state taxing authority shall impose any tax on a federal savings and loan association greater than that imposed by such authority on other similar local mutual or cooperative thrift and home-financing institutions, the state may impose on a federal savings and loan association, franchise tax computed on basis of annual net income derived from investments of both local funds and federal funds, where the tax is not greater than that levied on a similar state institution. First Federal Sav., etc., Ass'n v. Johnson, 49 Cal. App. 2d 465 122 P.2d 84.

associations and state credit unions constitutes a reasonable ground for distinguishing between them for tax purposes, so that a statute imposing income taxes on such associations is valid, even though credit unions are specifically exempted from such taxes.[2689] But a statute allowing state building and loan associations credit against their net taxable income for interest and dividends paid to their members was held void as discriminating against federal building and loan associations; however, such statute may be upheld by eliminating the unconstitutional discriminatory provision so that a regulation of the state tax commission allowing federal associations the same credit allowed to state associations, is valid.[2690] The Federal Home Loan Bank Act does not prohibit a state from taxing dividends received by a savings and loan association from stock it owns in a Federal Home Loan Bank.[2691] The exemption from state taxation for principal or interest of "[a]ll notes, bonds, debentures, or other such other obligations issued by" the Federal Savings and Loan Insurance Corporation does not apply to repayment of contributions made to the FSLIC secondary reserve, since the obligation to pay such contributions is not "issued" by the FSLIC.[2692] The refund of contributions made to the Federal Savings and Loan Insurance

---

Association may assume tax liability.—

Where federal savings and loan association made a loan secured by a construction mortgage and, after receiving back the check for the proceeds of the loan from the borrower properly endorsed by him, placed the amount thereat to the credit of a "due borrowers account for which a so-called breakdown was kept showing the various with the amounts paid or payable to each borrower, the credits in the due-borrowers exeunt are "general deposits fee a specific purpose," and taxable as such, and though the association is an "instrumentality of federal government" it could assume liability of the borrower. Merchants & Mechanics Federal Sav. & Loan Ass'n v. Evatt, 138 Ohio St. 457, 35 N.E. 2d 831, 135 A.L.R. 1474.

[2689] State v. Minnesota Federal Sav. etc., Ass'n 218 Wan. 229, 15 N.W.2d 568, construing 12 U.S.C.S. § 1464.

State credit unions are not "other similar local mutual or cooperative thrift and home financial institutions," exemption of which from state income taxes violates federal statute prohibiting state from imposing higher taxes on federal savings and loan associations than on other such similar institutions. State v. Minnesota Federal Sav., etc., Ass'n 218 Minn. 229, 15 N.W.2d 568 (1944).

[2690] State v. Minnesota Federal Sav. & Loan Ass'n, 218 Minn. 229, 15 N.W.2d 568 (1944).

[2691] Bell Fed. Sav. & Loan Ass'n v. Dep't of Revenue, 111 Ill. App. 3d 890, 67 Ill. Dec. 562, 444 N.E.2d 798 (1982).

[2692] Bell Fed. Sav. & Loan Ass'n v. Dep't of Revenue, 111 Ill. App. 3d 890, 67 Ill. Dec. 562, 444 N.E.2d 798 (1982).

Corporation secondary reserve are exempt from state taxation only when they constitute "capital, reserves, surplus, and Income" of the FSLIC, and are not tax exempt when title to such funds passes to a savings and loan association as a refund of the association's pro rata share of such reserve.[2693]

IV. EXEMPTIONS.

§ 32. In General.

Federal Exemptions.—Bonds and securities exempted from taxation by the federal government cannot be taxed directly or indirectly by the states.[2694] Interest earned on government national mortgage association certificates was neither constitutionally immune from state taxation nor did

---

[2693] Bell Fed. Sav. & Loan Ass'n v. Department of Revenue, 111 Ill. App. 3d 890, 67 Ill. Dec. 562, 444 N.E.2d 798 (1982).

[2694] Iowa Loan, etc., Co. v. Fairweather, 252 F. 605; East Helena State Bank v. Rodgers, 73 Mont. 210, 236 P. 1090; Federal Land Bank v. Crosland, 261 U.S. 374, 43 S. Ct. 385, 67 L. Ed. 703, 29 A.L.R. 1.

The federal statute exempting Puerto Rican bonds from federal or state taxation includes by implication the same exception contained in federal statute exempting obligations of the United States from taxation, that such obligations are exempt "except as otherwise provided by law"; therefore, interest received by a bank on Puerto Rican bonds held by the bank was includable in its taxable net income for the purposes of the computation of the bank excise tax, under the subdivision of the statute providing that the state statutory exemption from taxation for obligations of the United States and its possessions is not applicable to corporations taxable under the excise tax statute. Rochester Bank & Trust Co. v. Commissioner of Revenue, 305 N.W.2d 776 (Minn. 1981).

Section providing that, except as otherwise provided by law, all stocks, bonds, treasury notes and other obligations of the United States shall be exempt from taxation by or under state or municipal or local authority applied to income in form of interest earned by bank on various federal obligations, primarily notes and bills of the United States Treasury and obligating of federal credit banks. Memphis Bank & Trust Co. v. Garner, U.S., 103 S. Ct. 692, 74 L. Ed. 2d 562 (1983).

Exemption of all stocks, bonds, treasury notes and other obligation. of United States from every form of taxation that would require that either the obligations or the interest thereon, or both, be considered, directly or indirectly, in computation of tax, bars all such taxes, regardless of their form. American Bank & Trust Co. v. Dallas County, U.S., 103 S. Ct. 3369, 77 L. Ed. 2d. 1072 (1983).

When Congress amended statute provided that all stocks, bonds, treasury notes and other obligations of the United States shall be exempt from taxation by or under state or municipal or local authority to add sentence stating that exemption extends to every form of taxation that would require that either obligations or interest thereon, or both, be considered, directly or indirectly in computation of tax, Congress intended to sweep away formal distinctions and to invalidate all taxes measured directly or indirectly by the value of federal obligations, except

it constitute other obligations of United States that it was not exempt from state taxation under federal statute.[2695]

State Exemptions Generally.—The people of a state may confer upon their legislature the power to exempt banks and other corporations taxation either wholly or partially, and by general legislation or contracts embodied in charters. Therefore, whether a state legislature has the power to exempt a corporation from taxation depend upon the powers which have been vested in or withheld from such legislature by its state's constitution, and there is nothing in the United States Constitution forbidding state legislatures from making such exemptions.[2696]

---

those taxes specified in amendment. American Bank & Trust Co. v. Dallas County, U.S., 103 S. Ct. 3369, 77 L. Ed. 2d 1072 (1983).

Corporate excise taxes imposed on banks and attributable to inclusion in banks' net earnings of interest earned on obligations of the United States unconstitutionally discriminated against federal obligations where the "net earning" did not include interest on Tennessee and local obligations. Midland Bank & Trust Co. v. Olsen, 717 S.W.2d 580 (Pa. 1986).

[2695] Farmers & Traders State Bank v. Johnson, 76 Ill. Dec. 565, 458 N.E.2d 1365 (Ill. App. 4 Dist. 1984).

Interest earned on federal national mortgage association certificates was not constitutionally exempt from state taxation nor did it constitute other obligations of the United States so that it was not statutorily exempt from state taxation, in that certificates did not carry a binding promise by the United States to pay specified sums at specified times, they did not have congressional authorization pledging full faith and credit of the United States in support of promise to pay, and certificates were not used to secure credit for government, but to attract private capital so that government credit would not be necessary. Farmers & Traders State Bank v. Johnson, 76 Ill. Dec. 565, 121 Ill. App. 3d 43, 458 N.E.2d 1365 (Ill. App. 4 Dist. 1984).

[2696] **In general.—**

Piqua State Bank v. Knoop, 57 U.S. (18 How.) 369, 14 L. Ed. 977; Ohio Life Ins. & Trust Co. v. Debolt, 57 U.S. (16 How.) 416, 14 L. Ed. 997, citing Providence Bank v. Billings, 29 U.S. (4 Pet) 514, 7 L. Ed. 939; New Orleans v. Bank of Lafayette, 27 La. Ann. 376.

The Pennsylvania Shares Tax, as set forth in Article VII of the Tax Reform Code, 72 P.S. §§ 7701–7706, is imposed only upon institutions, which are defined to include, inter alia, every bank operating as such and having capital stock which is incorporated under any law of the Commonwealth of Pennsylvania, under the law of the United States or under the law of any other jurisdiction and is located within the Commonwealth, pursuant to 72 P.S. § 7701.5. Thus, an out-of-state bank without any contacts with the Commonwealth is not an institution for purposes of the shares tax. Under the plain language of the statute, the combination provision applies only where two institutions, for example, two Pennsylvania banks, have merged. Leb. Valley Farmers Bank v. Commonwealth, 27 A.3d 288 (Pa. Commw. Ct. 2011), rev'd on other grounds, 623 Pa. 455, 83 A.3d 107 (2013). (Article VII of the Tax Reform Code and all benefits associated with Article VII shall terminate on

Such an exemption does not violate the requirements of the Constitution or federal statutes as to equality and uniformity of taxation.[2697] Tax exemptions are not to be inferred lightly, nor will exemptions be applied unless they are already granted by statute.[2698] For example, such an exemption does not violate the provisions of the National Banking Act because such act was not intended to curtail the power of states as to taxation, or prohibit the exemption of particular kinds of property, but to protect corporations formed under its authority from unfriendly discrimination by states in the exercise of their taxing power.[2699]

December 31, 2022, pursuant to 72 P.S. § 9979-C).

Federal statute does not grant exemption power.—

The federal statute permitting states to tax shares of national banks does not enable legislature to exempt from taxation. Flournoy v. First Nat'l Bank, 197 La. 1067, 3 So. 2d 244.

Unauthorized exemption from taxation may not be upheld on the ground that statute granting the exemption is a wise and wholesome exercise of the police power for conservative and sound banking practice and stable public policy. Hibernia Nat'l Bank v. Louisiana Tax Com., 195 La. 43, 196 So. 15.

Substitute tax.—

Constitutional provision permitting the General Assembly to substitute another form of taxation for the tax on bank shares is an exemption from taxation on property in addition to those exemptions specifically enumerated in a constitutional provision setting forth permissible exemptions from taxation on property. Mercantile Bank Nat'l Ass'n v. Berra, 796 S.W.2d 22 (Mo. 1990).

Statute imposing banking institutions tax as a substitute for all taxes on tangible and intangible personal property of banking institutions is a proper exercise of legislative authority granted by constitutional provision allowing the General Assembly to substitute another form of taxation for the tax on bank shares. Mercantile Bank Nat'l Ass'n v. Berra, 796 S.W.2d 22 (Mo. 1990).

[2697] New Orleans v. People's Bank of New Orleans, 32 La. Ann. 82; New Orleans v. Commercial Bank, 10 La. Ann. 735; Carolina Nat. Bank v. Spigner, 106 S.C. 185, 90 S.E. 748; Stillman v. Lynch, 56 Utah 540, 192 P. 272, 12 A.L.R. 552; Bemis Bro. Bag Co. v. Louisiana Tax Com., 158 La. 1, 103 So. 337.

The statutory rule that the rate of taxation on shares in national banks should be no greater than on moneyed capital of individuals, does not limit power of legislature to exempt state bonds from taxation. Smith v. Kansas City Title, etc., Co., 255 U.S. 180, 41 S. Ct. 243, 65 L. Ed. 577; In re Walters Nat. Bank, 100 Okla. 155, 228 P. 953; Board of Equalization v. Exchange Nat. Bank, 104 Okla. 93, 230 P. 728; In re First State Bank, 68 Okla. 88, 171 P. 864.

[2698] In re Protest of First Federal Sav. & Loan Asso., 743 P.2d 640 (Okla. 1987).

[2699] **In general.—**

Adams v. Nashville, 95 U.S. 19, 24 L. Ed. 369, citing People v. Commissioners, 71 U.S.

Where the amount of an exemption in comparatively small, and not large enough to make a material difference in the rate assessed upon national bank shares, it is not obnoxious to the prohibition of discrimination against national bank shares in state taxation; exact equality is unnecessary.[2700] But such exemptions should be founded upon just reason, and not operate as an

---

(4 Wall.) 244, 18 L. Ed. 344; Hepburn v. School Directors, 90 U.S. (23 Wall.) 480, 23 L. Ed. 112; Davenport Nat. Bank v. Davenport Board, 123 U.S. 83, 8 S. Ct. 73, 31 L. Ed. 94; Mercantile Bank v. New York, 121 U.S. 138, 7 S. Ct. 826, 30 L. Ed. 895; Boyer v. Boyer, 113 U.S. 689, 5 S. Ct. 706, 28 L. Ed. 1089; Talbott v. Silver Bow County, 139 U.S. 438, 11 S. Ct. 594, 35 L. Ed. 210, where an exemption of the stock of corporations whose entire capital was invested in assessable property in the territory was held not an illegal discrimination.

Exemption of deposits in savings banks, or of moneys belonging to charitable institutions, allowed for reasons of public policy and not as an unfriendly discrimination against investments in national bank shares, should not be regarded as forbidden by 12 U.S.C.S. § 548. Aberdeen Bank v. Chehalis County, 166 U.S. 440, 17 S. Ct. 629, 41 L. Ed. 1069; First Nat. Bank v. Chapman, 173 U.S. 205, 19 S. Ct. 407, 43 L. Ed. 669; Mercantile Bank v. New York, 121 U.S. 138, 7 S. Ct. 826, 30 L. Ed. 895; Jenkins v. Neff, 186 U.S. 230, 22 S. Ct. 905, 46 L. Ed. 1140; Davenport Bank v. Davenport Board of Equalization, 123 U.S. 83, 8 S. Ct. 73, 31 L. Ed. 94; Bank v. Boston, 125 U.S. 60, 8 S. Ct. 772, 31 L. Ed. 689.

State or municipal securities undoubtedly represent moneyed capital, but as from their nature they are not ordinarily the subjects of taxation, they are not within the reason of the rule established by Congress for the taxation of national bank shares. Mercantile Bank v. New York, 121 U.S. 138, 7 S. Ct. 826, 30 L. Ed. 895. See also Adams v. Nashville, 95 U.S. 19, 24 L. Ed. 369; Boyer v. Boyer, 113 U.S. 689, 5 S. Ct. 706, 28 L. Ed. 1089.

No illegal discrimination.—

Exemptions of the shares of capital stock held by individuals in all private corporations of the state, "except banking institutions, and except those which by virtue of any contract in their charters or other contracts with this state are expressly exempted from taxation, and except mutual life insurance companies specially taxed," and of the deposits in saving, banks, create no illegal discrimination. Newark Banking Co. v. Newark, 121 U.S. 163, 7 S. Ct. 839, 30 L Ed. 904.

[2700] Mercantile Bank v. New York, 121 U.S. 138, 7 S. Ct. 826, 30 L. Ed. 895; Newark Banking Co. v. Newark, 121 U.S. 163, 7 S. Ct. 839, 30 L. Ed. 904; Davenport Bank v. Davenport Board of Equalization, 123 U.S. 83, 8 S. Ct. 73, 31 L. Ed. 94; Bank of Redemption v. Boston, 125 U.S. 60, 8 S. Ct. 772, 31 L. Ed. 689. See also Lionberger v. Rouse, 76 U.S. (9 Wall.) 468, 19 L. Ed. 721; Boyer v. Boyer, 113 U.S. 689, 5 S. Ct. 706, 28 L. Ed. 1089. In Hepburn v. School Directors, 90 US. (23 Wall.) 480, 23 L. Ed. 112, it was held that the exemption from taxation by the statute of "all mortgages, judgments, recognizances, and moneys owing upon articles of agreement for the sale of real estate" did not make the shares in national banks unequal and invalid. This was decided in the negative on two grounds: (1) That the exemption was founded upon the just reason of preventing a double burden by the taxation both of property and of the debts secured upon it and (2) because it was partial only, net operating as a discrimination against investments in national bank shares. Mercantile Bank v. New York, 121 U.S. 138, 7 S. Ct. 826, 30 L. Ed. 895.

unfriendly discrimination against investments in national bank shares.[2701] Substantial equality must be preserved, and it is sometimes difficult to determine when this rule has been infringed.[2702] A state tax that imposes a greater burden on holders of federal property than on holders of similar state property impermissibly discriminates against federal obligations.[2703] The Tennessee statute imposing a tax on the net earnings of banks doing business in the state and defining net earnings as including interest received on obligations of the United States and its instrumentalities and obligations, of other states, but not interest earned on obligations of Tennessee and its political subdivisions, discriminates in favor of securities issued by Tennessee and its political subdivisions and against federal obligations and, therefore, the Tennessee bank tax impermissibly discriminates against the federal government and those with whom it deals.[2704] And exemptions in favor of other moneyed capital may be so substantial in amount as to take the case out of the operation of the rule that it is not absolute equality that is contemplated by the federal statute, but as substantial equality is attainable, and required by the law of the land in respect of state taxation of national bank shares, when inequality is so palpable as to show that the discrimination against capital invested in such shares is serious, the courts have no alternative but to intervene.[2705]

The statute which imposes an excise tax on a corporation and which includes obligations of the state in the tax base does not conflict with the statute exempting state obligations from taxation.[2706]

Specific State Exemptions.—In many, if not all, of the states, the legislatures have seen fit to exempt certain banks or classes of banks from

---

[2701] Home Owners' Loan Corp. v. Barone, 164 Misc. 187, 298 N.Y.S. 531.

The right to make exemptions such as panted by statute exempting Home Owners' Loan Corporation and certain federal banks from payment of mortgage recording tax is generally vested in the legislature, and such exemptions are upheld by the courts unless they lack a reasonable ha. sis and are clearly arbitrary and unreasonable. Home Owners' Loan Corp. v. Barone, 164 Misc. 187, 298 N.Y.S. 531, holding valid statute exempting Home Owners' Loan Corporation and certain federal banks from payment of a mortgage recording tax.

[2702] Mercantile Nat. Bank v. New York, 121 U.S. 138, 7 S. Ct 826, 30 L Ed. 895; Boyer v. Boyer, 113 U.S. 689, 5 S. Ct 706, 28 L. Ed. 1089.

[2703] Memphis Bank & Trust Co. v. Garner, U.S., 103 S. Ct. 692, 74 L. Ed. 2d 562 (1983).

[2704] Memphis Bank & Trust Co. v. Garner, U.S., 103 S. Ct. 692, 74 L. Ed. 2d 562 (1983).

[2705] Boyer v. Boyer, 113 U.S. 689, 5 S. Ct. 706, 28 L. Ed. 1089. See also Mercantile Bank v. New York, 121 U.S. 138, 7 S. Ct. 826, 30 L. Ed. 895.

[2706] First Am. Nat'l Bank v. Olsen, 751 S.W.2d 417 (Tenn. 1987).

taxation, either in whole or in part,[2707] or to provide for their exemption in certain respects; for instance, with regard to their real estate[2708] or so much of it as may be employed in their business,[2709] their capital or capital stock,[2710] or the property in which their capital may be invested.[2711] And savings banks are frequently favored by states in exemptions from taxation, either in whole or in part, on their deposits[2712] or investments.[2713] Amendment temporarily increasing tax rate for thrift institutions did not violate

---

[2707] President & Directors of Bank v. Edwards, 27 N.C. 516; Bank of Cape Fear v. Deming, 29 N.C. 55; State Bank v. Charleston (S.C.), 8 Rich. L. 842.

[2708] Dyer v. Branch Bank, 14 Ala. 622.

[2709] De Soto Bank v. Memphis, 65 Tenn. 415, 32 Am. R. 530; Bank of Commerce v. McGowan, 74 Tenn. 703, aff'd sub nom. Bank v. Tennessee, 104 U.S. 493, 26 L. Ed. 810; New Haven v. City Bank of New Haven, 31 Conn. 106.

[2710] People ex rel. Savings Bank of New London v. Coleman, 135 N.Y. 231, 31 N.E. 1022; State ex rel. Citizens' Bank of Louisiana v. Board of Assessors, 48 La. Ann. 35, 18 So. 753; In re New Orleans Improv. & Banking Co., 4 La. Ann. 471; New Orleans v. Commercial Bank of New Orleans (La.), 5 Rob. 151; Penrose v. Chaffraix, 106 La. 250, 30 So. 718; State v. Butler, 81 Tenn. (18 Lea) 400; Peiper v. Lancaster (Pa.), 10 Lanc. Bar. 131; Bank of Commerce v. Tennessee, 161 U.S. 134, 16 S. Ct. 546, 40 L. Ed. 645, modified, 163 U.S. 416, 16 S. Ct. 1113, 41 L. Ed. 211; Shelby v. Union, etc., Bank, 161 U.S. 149, 16 S. Ct. 558, 40 L. Ed. 650.

County Personal Property Tax Act excludes from taxation bank or trust company stock which is liable to or relieved from state capital stock franchise tax. Chester County v. Herdeg, 539 A.2d 486 (Pa. Commw. 1988).

[2711] Bank of Commerce v. Tennessee, 161 U.S. 134, 16 S. Ct. 456, 40 L. Ed. 645, modified, 163 U.S. 416, 16 S. Ct. 1113, 41 L. Ed. 211. As to exemption of stock and real estate, see Municipality Number One v. Louisiana State Bank, 5 La. Ann. 394; New Haven v. City Bank, 31 Conn. 106; Lackawanna v. First Nat. Bank, 94 Pa. 221.

[2712] Heermance v. Dederick, 35 App. Div. 29, 54 N.Y.S. 519, aff'd, 158 N.Y. 414, 53 N.E. 163; Savings Bank v. Archbold, 104 U.S. 708, 26 L. Ed. 901; People ex rel. Savings Bank of New London v. Coleman, 135 N.Y. 231, 31 N.E. 1022.

[2713] Bourguignon Bldg. Ass'n v. Commonwealth, 98 Pa. 54

Savings language stating that tax exemptions for certain state and local debt obligations should not be applicable to any tax imposed on interest, income or profits on debt obligations owed by corporations was sufficiently broad to encompass taxes imposed on privilege of operating bank or savings and loan in Florida. Department of Revenue v. First Union Nat'l Bank, 513 So. 2d 114 (Fla. 1987).

Mutual Thrift Institution Tax Act imposes direct tax on net income and not on privilege of conducting business; accordingly, interest on tax-exempt commonwealth obligations held for investment by mutual thrift institution need not be included in that institution's net income and is not taxable under the Act. First Fed. Sav. & Loan Ass'n v. Commonwealth, 528 Aid 942 (Pa. 1987).

statute exempting certain thrift institution income from tax base.[2714] Also, in many jurisdictions, banks are exempted from general taxation upon payment of an annual tax of a certain percent,[2715] or the performance of certain other conditions.[2716] A taxpayer may amortize the premium he pays for a state or municipal bond, and the amortized premium may be excluded from his calculation of base income for state income tax purposes.[2717]

Construction of Exemption Statutes.—Under an act authorizing the taxation of stock of corporations in the hands of stockholders, and exempting from taxation so much of the property of corporations as is represented by stock taxed in the hands of stockholders, the real estate of a bank is exempt from taxation as it belongs to its stockholders, and is represented by stock in their hands.[2718] And where a bank does not pay its taxes as provided by a statute imposing a tax measured by its entire assets in lieu of all other taxes, the taxation of such bank is governed by a statute providing that the paid in capital of banks shall be taxed at its market value, since such statute remains operative if the other statute is not complied with.[2719] It also has been held that where a bank is a public corporation, chartered for the benefit of a state, exemption of the property of such bank

---

[2714] First Trust Sav. Bank v. Commonwealth, 688 Aid 1000 (Pa. Commw. 1991).

[2715] *United States.*—National Bank v. Chester County, 14 F. 239.

Delaware.—State v. President, Directors & Co. of Bank of Smyrna, 7 Del. 99, 73 Am. Dec. 699.

Illinois.—State Bank of Illinois v. People, 5 Ill. (4 Scam.) 303.

Indiana.—State Bank v. Madison, 3 Ind. 43.

Kentucky.—Farmers Bank of Kentuckey v. Commonwealth, 69 Ky. (6 Bush) 127; Commonwealth v. Fleming County Farmers' Bank, 39 S.W. 1041, 19 Ky. L. Rptr. 266; Bolling Green v. Barclay, etc., Co., 12 Ky. L. Rptr. 190, 228.

Mississippi.—Bank v. Oxford, 70 Miss. 504, 12 So. 203.

Pennsylvania.—Lackawanna v. First Nat. Bank, 94 Pa. 221; Wilkes-Barre, etc., Sav. Bank v. Wilkes-Barre, 148 Pa. 601, 24 A. 111; Commonwealth v. Clairton Steel Co., 222 Pa. 293, 71 A. 99.

Tennessee.—State use of Memphis v. Union & Planters' Bank, 91 Tenn. (7 Pick.) 546, 19 S.W. 758.

But see State v. Hernando Ins. Co., 97 Tenn. 85, 36 S.W. 721.

[2716] Gordon v. Appeal Tax Court, 44 U.S. (8 How.) 133, 11 L. Ed. 529.

[2717] Moline Nat'l Bank v. Department of Revenue, 111 ill. App. 3d 1086, 67 Ill. Dec. 680, 444 N.E.2d 1164 (1983).

[2718] Belvidere Bank v. Tunis, 23 N.J.L. 546.

[2719] Bank v. Oxford, 70 Miss. 504, 12 So. 203.

from taxation is necessarily implied, even though not provided for in its charter.[2720]

Tax exemptions are not granted by implication.[2721] Furthermore, grants of immunity from taxation are in derogation of the sovereign power of the state and are strictly construed.[2722] The general laws which impose taxes are construed strictly against the taxing authority and in favor of the taxpayer, but statutes which grant tax exemptions are construed against the taxpayer and in favor of the taxing authority.[2723] The party claiming a tax exemption has the burden of proving that the exemption applies.[2724] Since taxation is the rule and exemption is the exception, and since exemptions from taxation are not favored, the general rule is that a grant of exemption from taxation is never presumed. On the contrary, in all cases having doubt as to legislative intention, the presumption is in favor of the taxing power, and the burden is on claimant to prove or establish clearly his or her right to exemption, bringing himself or herself clearly within terms of such conditions that

---

[2720] Nashville v. Bank of Tennessee, 31 Tenn. 269.

[2721] American Bank & Trust Co. v. Dallas County, 679 S.W.2d 566 (Tax. App. 5 Dist. 1984).

[2722] American Bank & Trust Co. v. Dallas County, 679 S.W.2d 566 (Tex. App. 5 Dist. 1984).

Statutes granting tax exemptions are construed strictly in favor of taxation. American Nat'l Bank & Trust Co. v. Department of Revenue, 183 Ill. Dec. 179, 611 N.E.2d 32 (Ill. App. 2 Dist. 1993).

[2723] First Sec. Bank v. State, Dept of Transp., 735 P.2d 1044 (Idaho App. 1986).

Taxpayer failed to show that its renewal note merely extended or continued identical contractual obligations of original four promissory notes, and thus, taxpayer failed to carry its burden of showing that it was entitled to exemption from documentary stamp tax liability upon renewal. American Nat'l Bank v. Department of Revenue, 593 So. 2d 1173 (Fla. App. 1992).

Taxpayer has burden to establish its entitlement to protection of statute providing exemption from documentary stamp tax for renewal notes when renewal note only extends or continues identical contractual obligations of original promissory note and evidences part or all of original indebtedness evidenced thereby. American Nat'l Bank v. Department of Revenue, 593 So.2d 1173 (Fla. App. 1992).

Burden is on taxpayer to demonstrate entitlement to exemption claimed. South Boston Sav. Bank v. Commissioner, 418 Mass. 695, 640 N.E.2d 462 (1994).

[2724] American Nat'l Bank & Trust Co. v. Department of Revenue, 183 Ill. Dec. 179, 611 N.E.2d 32 (Ill. App. 2 Dist. 1993).

Employer seeking relief from charges bears burden of proving it lies within relieving provisions of Unemployment Compensation Law or relief will be denied. First Nat'l Bank v. Unemployment Camp. Bd. of Review, 619 A.2d 801 (Pa. Commw. 1992).

statute may impose.[2725] Other cases dealing with the construction of local exemption statutes will be found in the footnote.[2726]

[2725] Fishbelt Feeds, Inc. v. Miss. Dep't of Revenue, 158 So. 3d 984 (Miss. 2014).

[2726] **In general.—**

United States.—Buder v. First Nat. Bank, 16 F.2d 990, cert. denied, 274 U.S. 743, 47 S. Ct. 588, 71 L. Ed. 1321.

Georgia.—Baggett v. Mobley, 171 Ga. 268, 155 S.E. 334.

The statute prohibiting taxation of any state chartered or federal savings and loan association on its "franchise," etc., uses quoted word in the general sense as being synonymous with license" and "occupation." Griffin v. First Federal Sav., etc., Ass'n, 80 Ga. App. 217, 55 S.E.2d 771.

Neither federal savings and loan associations incorporated under laws of the United States and having their principal offices or places of business in Georgia nor building and loan associations incorporated under laws of Georgia are subject to tax on long-term notes imposed by Intangible Property Tax Act of 1953. Atlanta Federal Sav. & Loan Asso. v. Simmons, 224 Ga. 483, 162 S.E.2d 342 (1968), overruling Fulton County Federal Sav. & Loan Ass'n v. Simmons, 210 Ga. 621, 82 S.E.2d 16 (1954).

Construction of Intangible Property Tax Act so that savings and loan associations and building and loan associations were not subject to tax on long-term note, was not a constitutionally prohibited exemption from taxation as this was merely limitation on method of ad valorem taxation. Atlanta Fed. Sav. & Loan Ass'n v. Simmons, 224 Ga. 483, 162 S.E.2d 342 (1968).

Hawaii.—In re Bank of Hawaii's Taxes, 28 Hawaii 197.

Illinois.—Trial court's judgment which purported to grant tax exemption for property used for religious purposes was appropriately treated as reversal of Department of Revenue's ruling, rather than as outright grant of tax exemption which would have been beyond trial court's authority to give under the Administrative Review Act, where trial court had acted within its authority but had used the wrong language in its judgment American Nat'l Bank & Trust Co. v. Department of Revenue, 183 Ill. Dec. 179, 611 N.E.2d 32 (Ill. App. 2 Dist. 1993).

Louisiana.—The legislature may not fix basis for valuation of shares of bank stock for assessment purpose. that will result in total or partial exemption of value of the stock from taxation. Hibernia Nat'l Bank v. Louisiana Tax Com., 195 La. 43, 196 So. 15.

Whether an exemption be called a deduction or an allowance is not determinative of whether it is unauthorized, for if it is, in fact, an exemption, or is equivalent thereto, then the act granting it violates the constitutional provision against exemptions not enumerated therein. Hibernia Nat'l Bank v. Louisiana Tax Com., 195 La. 43, 196 So. 15.

Statute providing that value of bank shares shall be fixed annually for assessment purposes and shall not exceed the par value of the shares plus any amount in which the combined declared surplus, undivided profits, and contingent reserve may exceed the per value of the common capital thereof purports in effect to grant an exemption and is unconstitutional to that extent. Hibernia Nat'l Bank v. Louisiana Tax Com., 195 La. 43, 196 So. 15.

Montana.—Bank of Miles City v. Custer County, 93 Mont. 291, 19 P.2d 885.

(Text continued on page 766)

Nebraska.—Advance payments made to building and loan associations for purpose of defraying taxes and insurance upon property mortgaged as security for loans are the property of the associations and exempt from intangible tax. First Fed. Bar. & Loan Ass'n v. Board of Equalization, 182 Neb. 25, 152 N.W.2d 8 (1967).

New York.—People ex rel. Hanover Nat'l Bank v. Goldfogle, 234 N.Y. 345, 137 N.E. 611, cert. denied, 261 U.S. 620, 43 S. Ct. 432, 67 L. Ed. 830.

Ohio.—The purpose of statute providing exemption from taxation of deposits belonging to any other financial institution was to prevent double taxation. Ohio Citizens Trust Co. v. Evatt, 146 Ohio St. 30, 63 N.E.2d 912.

Deposits in Ohio bank by Ohio corporation which had its principal office in Ohio but which operated its plant in Tennessee, which deposits were withdrawable only by certain officers having offices in Ohio, although constituting deposits used in business in a foreign state, did not "arise out of business transacted outside of Ohio" within meaning of code section excepting from taxation property of residents of Ohio used in and arising out of business transacted outside the state. First Nat'l Bank v. Evatt, 16 Ohio Supp. 130, 32 Ohio Op. 277.

Shares of stock in Ohio financial institutions owned by foreign or domestic insurance companies, or by resident or nonresident dealers in intangibles, are not subject to the intangible personal property tax. National City Bank v. Porterfield, 15 Ohio St. 2d 235, 239 N.E.2d 61 (1968), overruling National City Bank v. Bowers, 172 Ohio St. 378, 176 N.E.2d 227 (1961).

Oklahoma.—Wenner v. Mothersead, 129 Okla. 273, 264 P. 816; In re First State Bank, 68 Okla. 88, 171 P. 864; Zusman v. First State Bank, 178 Okla. 330, 63 P.2d 760.

The term "Morris Plan companies" as used in the Intangible Income Tax Code is used in its generic sense, and the exemption from payment of intangible taxes as provided for in the statute should be allowed not only to Morris Plan companies, but such exemption should be allowed uniformly on all those operating identical business such as an industrial finance corporation where both companies accepted money from the public for "investment certificates" and both were within the class of finance businesses commonly called industrial banks and neither carried on a phase of finance business which was not also conducted by the other. County Board of Equalization v. Muskogee Industrial Finance Corp., 357 P.2d 224. See Morris Plan Co. v. Johnson, 37 Cal. App. 2d 621, 100 P.2d 493 (1940).

Bank holding company could not reduce stat. income tax through separate deduction of federal net operating lasses over and above federal net operating loss deduction reflected on federal return for corresponding tax year; such losses could only be reflected through determination of taxable income, which was tied to federal definition of that term. Utica Bankshares Corp. v. Oklahoma Tax Comm'n, 892 P.2d 979 (Okla. 1994).

Taxpayer which was intrastate entity could claim, for state income tax purpose., fall amount of federal net operating loss (NOL) deduction allowed for federal tax purposes, as statute limiting amount of NOL which could be included in state tax calculation applied only to interstate entities. Utica Bankshares Corp. v. Oklahoma Tax Comm'n, 892 P.2d 979 (Okla. 1994).

Statute governing inclusion of federal net operating loss (NOL) deduction for state tax

(Text continued on page 766)

---

purposes, function of which was to limit amount of carryback losses at state level to that portion of federal NOL attributable to activities carried on in state, did not operate to reduce federal NOL deduction allowed in state tax calculation where all of taxpayer's federal losses were derived from state activities or sources and difference between federal NOL and state loss for respective tax year was due to differences in taxable income. Utica Bankshares Corp. v. Oklahoma Tax Comm'n, 892 P.2d 979 (Okla. 1994).

Pennsylvania.—Bellevue Realty Sav., etc., Co. v. Monongahela River Consol. Coal, etc., Co., 68 Pa. Super. 149.

Under the Pennsylvania statute taxing shares of stock, shares of trust company in. vested in stock of corporations which are relieved from the payment of a capital stock tax held not taxable. Commonwealth v. Provident Trust Co., 319 Pa. 385, 180 A. 16 (1935).

South Carolina.—National Union Bank v. Neil, 106 S.C. 173, 90 S.E. 744; Carolina Nat. Bank v. Spigner, 106 S.C. 185, 90 S.E. 748.

Building and loan associations.

—Legislature could exempt from taxation stock of building and loan associations not competing with banks. State v. Leonardson, 51 Idaho 646, 9 P.2d 1028; Ryan v. Tax Com. of Kansas, 132 Kan. 1, 294 P. 938.

Statute, exempting from taxation capital, property, and shares of building and loan associations, industrial loan corporations, etc., competing with banks accepting deposits and doing general commercial business, held not unconstitutional. Union Bank & Trust Co. v. Phelps, 288 U.S. 181, 53 S. Ct. 321, 77 L. Ed. 687, 83 A.L.R. 1438. See Bank of Fairfield v. Spokane County, 173 Wash. 145, 22 P.2d 646.

Homestead associations are regarded as quasi-public institutions, entitled to special favors in way of tax exemptions. First Nat'l Bank v. Louisiana Tax Com., 175 La. 119, 143 So. 23.

Exemption of state banks from income tax and exclusion of dividends on their stock from taxpayers' pass income are Justifiable classifications, and not discriminatory. Reynolds Metal Co. v. Martin, 269 Ky. 378, 107 S.W.2d 251, appeal dismissed, 302 U.S. 646, 58 S. Ct. 146, 82 L. Ed. 502.

Exemption of credit unions from franchise tax on banks.—

Distinctions between credit unions and federal savings and loan associations and cooperative banks, including distinctions in size of operation, statutory restrictions and provisions, lending policy, ratio of real estate and unsecured loans to total assets and compensation of officers, permitted reasonable classification of credit unions as exempt from franchise tax on banks. Manchester Federal Savings & Loan Ass'n v. State Tax Comm., 105 N.H. 17, 191 A.2d 529.

Credit union held not a "nonprofit organization".—

Credit union which distributes its income to its members in form of dividends, however beneficial to its members as to loans and encouragement of savings, does not come within concept of a "nonprofit organization" so as to give its tax-exempt status. Central Credit Union v. Comptroller of Treasury, 243 Md. 175, 220 A.2d 568 (1966).

Bank vault doors were held "real property" within meaning of tax exemption statute, although listed by bank as personal property. San Diego Trust, etc., Bank v. San Diego

(Text continued on page 766)

County, 16 Cal. 2d 142, 105 P.2d 94, 133 A.L.R. 416, cert. denied, 312 U.S. 679, 61 S. Ct. 449, 85 L. Ed. 1118.

"Moneyed capital" and equipment—

The tangible personal property of a title guarantee loan and trust company, such as office furniture, equipment and abstract books, was not exempt from ad valorem taxation under statute exempting from such taxation all "moneyed capital" employed in a business, the privilege of engaging in which is thereby taxed. Title Guarantee Loan, etc., Co. v. Hamilton, 238 Ala. 602, 193 So. 107.

Surplus" of bank exempted from taxation means excess in aggregate value of all assets over sum of all liabilities, including capital stock. Board of Sup'rs v. Jefferson County Bank, 171 Miss. 50, 156 So. 599.

Surplus of bank exempted from taxation is real, and not mere book surplus; and book surplus of bank, which was completely wiped out by its losses, was not tax exempt. Board of Sup'rs v. Jefferson County Bank, 171 Miss. 50, 156 So. 599.

Interest-bearing bank accounts.—

If bank account can be identified as an entity, it differs from other accounts, and may be taken out of class without creating unlawful exemption as respects validity of act exempting from taxation interest-bearing bank accounts. In re Donnelly's Estate, 113 P. Super, 274, 173 A. 876.

As respects validity of act exempting from taxation interest-bearing bank accounts, maintenance of banking system by encouraging depositors to open and keep nontaxable Interest-bearing accounts is public policy of state which identifies bank account as separate and distinct entity. In re Donnelly's Estate, 113 Pa. Super. 274, 173 A. 876.

Act exempting from local taxation interest-bearing bank accounts held constitutional, where such accounts were distinguishable by benefit which they afforded to banking system from all trade and professional and individually beneficial accounts bearing interest. In re Donnelly's Estate, 113 Pa. Super. 274, 173 A. 876.

Interest received by banks.—

Where private corporation agreed to advance money to state highway commission, but money was advanced by banks, and corporation executed its notes to lending banks and assigned to trustee its interest in contracts with state highway commission, and with city, which agreed to pay interest on loan, to secure note., state's and city's obligations were thereby appropriated to lending banks, and interest banks received was exempt from income tax. Norfolk Nat. Bank v. Commissioner of Internal Revenue, 66 F.2d 48.

Secured credits competing with capital invested in bank stock are not exempted, under statutes. State ex rel. Bank of Eagle v. Leonardson, 51 Idaho 646, 9 P.2d 1028.

Debts due by banks or others for loans not secured by mortgage on property located within state are not exempt from taxation as "credits" under present or prior constitution. New Orleans Securities Co. v. New Orleans, 139 So. 635, 173 La. 1097.

Mortgages owned by casual investors.—

Statute taxing moneys and credits and moneyed capital held not invalid because subjecting to taxation mortgages owned by banks and their competitors while exempting mortgages

§ 33. Irrevocability of Statutes Providing for Method of Taxation and Exemptions.

A state statute incorporating certain banks and providing for a specific method of taxing such banks, creates a contract between the state and the banks, limiting the state's power to tax them to the method so provided,[2727] and it has been held that this contract cannot be impaired by a subsequent

---

owned by casual investors. Bank of Miles City v. Custer County, 93 Mont. 291, 19 P.2d 885.

Statute authorizing bank to deduct awn at which its real estate is returned for taxation from market value of bank shares, in returning shares for taxation, held not violative of constitutional provisions regarding exemptions. Moultrie v. Moultrie Banking Co., 177 Ga. 714, 171 S.E.131.

Act fixing priority of claims against insolvent banks is not in violation of constitutional prevision invalidating laws exempting property from taxation. Felton v. McArthur, 173 Ga. 465, 160 S.E. 419.

Exemption of value of real estate acquired by foreclosure.—

In calculating the vain. of bank shares for taxation, the bank was entitled to deduct from the market value of its shares the value at which real estate, acquired by the bank through foreclosure and not used for bank premises, was returned for ad valorem taxation, and the statute permitting such deduction was not a constitutionally impermissible exemption of property from taxation. Richmond County Bd. of Tax Assessors v. Georgia R.R. Bank & Trust Co., 242 Ga. 23, 247 S.E.2d 761 (1978).

"Capital".—

Word "capital" as used in act providing that "no tax shall be assessed upon capital of banks or banking associations . . ." refers to capital assets and exempts national banks from ad valorem taxes levied on their personal property. Citizens & Southern Nat'l Bank v. Fulton County, 245 Ga. 441, 265 S.E.2d 559 (1980).

Nonresident and resident beneficiaries.—

Trust administered by North Carolina trustee, with both resident and nonresident beneficiaries, was not entirely exempt from taxation on intangible personal property when trustee had decision to distribute all income to nonresident beneficiaries unless all income was actually distributed to nonresident beneficiaries. NCNB Nat'l Bank v. Powers, 347 S.E.2d 77 (N.C. App. 1986).

Trust administered by North Carolina trustee was exempt from intangible personal property taxation in accordance with ratio of nonresident beneficiaries to total beneficiaries. NCNB Nat'l Bank v. Powers, 347 S.E.2d.77 (N.C. App. 1986).

[2727] *United States.*—Georgia R., etc., Co. v. Wright, 132 F. 912, modified, 216 U.S. 420, 30 S. Ct. 242, 54 L. Ed. 544; Louisville v. Bank, 174 U.S. 439, 19 S. Ct. 753, 43 L Ed. 1039.

Louisiana.—Municipality No.1 v. Louisiana State Bank, 5 La. Ann. 394.

Ohio.—Commercial Bank v. Bowman, 1 Handy 246, 12 Ohio Dec. Reprint 125.

South Carolina.—State v. Charleston, 5 Rich. L. 561.

Tennessee.—State use of Memphis v. Union & Planters' Bank, 91 Tenn. 546, 19 S.W. 758.

state constitution statutory enactment.[2728] Thus, a provision that a bank shall pay a certain portion of its dividends to the state in lieu of all taxes is clearly a contract that neither its property nor its valuable franchise shall be taxed at any time thereafter.[2729]

§ 34. Transferability of Charter Exemption.

Immunity from taxation granted to a banking corporation by its charter is personal, and cannot be transferred by sale of the charter without the state's consent.[2730] And the granting to a corporation, in the act chartering it, of all "powers, rights, reservations, restrictions, and liabilities," of another corporation does not confer upon it immunity from taxation which the other corporation enjoyed under a provision in its charter for a special tax.[2731] Similarly, even though a state statute authorizes any company having the power to receive moneys in trust to do a general banking business without forfeiting any right, privilege or immunity granted in its original charter, an insurance company incorporated before the enactment of such statute and authorized by its charter to receive moneys in trust, loses, upon undertaking a banking business, the immunity from general taxation given by its charter, since it then, in effect, becomes a new company, and is, as such, subject to a constitutional provision requiring all property to be taxed.[2732] But such an exemption may not be lost by the consolidation of an exempt bank with a trust company.[2733]

§ 35. Waiver of or Estoppel to Claim Exemptions.

A bank may waive its right to exemption from taxation, either expressly,[2734] or by implication, as where a bank winds up its affairs as a state

---

[2728] Dodge v. Woolsey, 59 U.S. (18 How.) 331, 15 L Ed. 401. See State Bank v. Knoop, 57 U.S. (16 How.) 369, 14 L. Ed. 977, citing Mechanics', etc., Bank v. Debolt, 59 U.S. (18 How.) 380, 15 L Ed. 458; Mechanics', etc., Bank v. Thomas, 59 U.S. (18 How.) 384, 15 L Ed. 460; Jefferson Branch Bank v. Skelly, 66 U.S. (1 Black) 436, 17 L. Ed. 173.

[2729] Jefferson Branch Bank v. Skelly, 66 U.S. (1 Black) 436, 17 L. Ed. 173; Franklin Branch Bank v. Ohio, 66 U.S. (1 Black) 474, 17 L. Ed. 180; State v. State Bank (Ind.), 7 Blackf. 393.

[2730] State v. Mercantile Bank, 95 Tenn. 212, 31 S. W. 989, aff'd, 161 U.S. 161, 198, 200, 16 S. Ct. 461, 476, 40 L. Ed. 656, 669, 670.

[2731] State use of Memphis v. Mercantile Bank, 95 Tenn. 212, 31 S.W. 989, aff'd, 161 U.S. 161, 198, 200, 16 S. Ct. 461, 476, 40 L. Ed. 656, 669, 670.

[2732] Memphis City Bank v. Tennessee, 161 U.S. 186, 16 S. Ct. 468, 40 L. Ed. 664.

[2733] Jewett City Sav. Bank v. Board of Equalization, 116 Conn. 172, 164 A. 643.

[2734] Deposit Bank of Owensboro v. Daviess County, 102 Ky. 174, 39 S.W. 1030, 19 Ky. L. Rptr. 248, 44 L.R.A. 825.

corporation and organizes as a national bank under the national banking law.[2735] But it is also held that change of a state bank to a national bank is a mere transition, not the creation of a new bank with new stockholders so as to change the identity of its shares and thereby lose their exemption from taxation.[2736] And the fact that assessors, in valuing shares of national bank stock which were assessed to the owner thereof, erroneously omitted a part of its capital stock which was used to purchase real estate, does not preclude the bank itself from asserting exemption of its real estate from taxation.[2737]

§ 36. Acquisition of Exempt Property to Evade Taxation.

Where the facts tend to show that a bank's purchase of United States bonds was for the purpose of evading taxation—the bonds being purchased immediately before, and sold immediately after, the date as of which the bank's property was listed for taxation, and never being taken into its possession, but left on special deposit in a distant bank—the transaction may be regarded as fraudulent, and the bank assessed with the amount invested in such bonds.[2738] But where a bank owned practically all the stock in a realty company which it had incorporated, and had controlled for many years, and such company owned a large amount of tax-exempt securities, it was held not to constitute fraud for the purpose of escaping taxation on the values represented by such securities.[2739]

V. PLACE OF TAXATION.

§ 37. Bank Property and Stocks.

In General.—The real estate of a bank, including its banking house, is subject to taxation where such real estate is located.[2740] On the other hand,

---

[2735] Lionberger v. Rowse, 43 Mo. 67, aff'd sub nom. Lionberger v. Rouse, 76 U.S. 468, 19 L. Ed. 721.

[2736] **In general.—**

Jewett City Sav. Bank v. Board of Equalization, 116 Conn. 172, 164 A. 643.

Change of national bank back to state bank held mere transition and did not cause shares of state bank to lose their identity and right to exemption from taxation. Jewett City Sav. Bank v. Board of Equalization, 116 Conn. 172, 164 A. 643.

[2737] First Nat'l Bank v. Douglas County, 124 Wis. 15, 102 N.W. 315.

[2738] In re Peoples Bank, 203111.300, 87 N.E. 777; Jones v. Seward, 10 Neb. 154, 4 N.W. 946; Dixon v. Ha]stead, 23 Neb. 697, 37 N.W. 621.

[2739] State v. Buder, 308 Mo. 237, 271 S.W. 508, 39 A.L.R. 1199.

[2740] President, Directors, etc. of Tremont Bank v. Boston, 55 Mass. (1 Cush.) 142; Nashua Sav. Bank v. Nashua, 46 N.H. 389; Orange Nat. Bank v. Williams, 58 N.J.L. 45, 32

the general rule is that property of an intangible nature, such as credits, bills receivable, bank deposits, bonds, promissory notes, mortgage loans, judgments and corporate stock, has no situs of its own for purposes of taxation, and is therefore assessable only at its owner's domicile, regardless of the actual location of the evidence of such debt or security, although the actual situs of certain classes of tangible personal property, as well as intangible property having similar characteristics, such as money, state and municipal bonds, circulating bank notes and shares of stock in private corporations, may have a situs for taxation where they are permanently kept which is separate and apart from the owner's domicile.[2741] Thus, it has been held that notes executed by corporate officers outside of the state where their corporation was located, and mailed to the payee bank also outside of the state, were not taxable in the state, but that notes executed by a corporation within the state and mailed to the payee bank outside of the state had a taxable situs within the state.[2742] And notes held for collection by a bank in a state other than the domicile of their owner do not acquire a business situs in such state so as to subject them to taxation therein, as against the domicile state.[2743]

A. 745; Loften v. Citizens' Nat. Bank, 86 Ind. 341.

The realty should be assessed at place where situated, whether bank is solvent or insolvent. Folk v. Heckler, 210 Ind. 68, 1 N.E.2d 124.

[2741] **In general.—**

Great Southern Life Ins. Co. v. Austin, 112 Tex. 1, 243 S.W. 778 (1922).

A domestic corporation is liable to taxation at its place of residence on bank credits in another state. Bridgeport Projectile Co. v. Bridgeport, 92 Conn. 316, 102 A. 644.

Insurance company's cash in banks outside state and credits due from outside agents held taxable in state of its principal office. State v. Gehner (Mo.), 8 S.W.2d 1068.

Vehicles.—

The fact that the principal place of business of a national bank was in another state did not give the state the right to tax auto trucks in the state belonging to such bank, where the trucks were acquired in a transaction at the bank's principal place of business. Chase Nat'l Bank v. Spokane County, 125 Wash. 1, 215 P. 374.

[2742] Graniteville Mfg. Co. v. Query, 44 F.2d 64, aff'd, 283 U.S. 376, 51 S. Ct. 515, 75 L. Ed. 1126.

A note mailed to bank in another state and payable there was not exempt from Florida documentary stamp tax on ground that note was not a completed transaction in Florida where note was made in Florida, loan was used in Florida, and loan was in all essential factors a Florida transaction. Plymouth Citrus Growers Ass'n v. Lee, 157 Fla. 893, 27 So. 2d 415.

[2743] Hinckley v. San Diego County, 49 Cal. App. 668, 194 P. 77.

Where will of resident of California was probated in another state, and the estate was

Statutory Provisions.—Under a statute providing that the property of corporations and firms shall be listed for taxation by their principal accounting officer or an agent or partner thereof, a listing of the property of a banking firm by its cashier and principal accounting officer in the county of his residence is proper, though another partner resides in a different county.[2744] And under a statute providing that the personalty, moneys and credits connected with or growing out of all business transacted directly or indirectly by or through servants, employees or agents of any bank having an officer or agency for the transaction of business in more than one assessment district, shall be taxable in the assessment district where said business is done, notes taken by a branch bank in the ordinary course of business and held as a part of its assets, are taxable in the district where such branch bank is located, though they have been transferred and credited by its parent institution to another branch bank.[2745] For other cases involving specific statutory provisions as to the place of taxation of bank property and stocks, see the footnote.[2746]

---

being administered therein, and where beneficiaries named in will were not residents of California, notes held by bank in such other state for collection at time of testator's death were not taxable in California, pending administration of the estate, since ownership of notes was not vested in a resident of the state at such time. Hinckley v. San Diego County, 49 Cal. App. 668, 194 P. 77.

[2744] Swallow v. Thomas, 15 Kan. 66.

[2745] Farmers' Loan, etc., Co. v. Fonda, 114 Iowa 728, 87 N.W. 724.

[2746] *Delaware.*—Bank was domiciled in Delaware for franchise tax purposes where, although the statute did not define "principal office" and "headquarters," it did define a similar term—"located"; under the statute, a savings institution is "located" in the state in which the amount of aggregate deposits of all its offices in that state is greatest. The bank had only one office where its deposit operations were conducted, and that office was located in Delaware. Furthermore, the court noted a recent amendment to the Delaware bank franchise law that defines, for the first time, the term "headquarters." Under the new provision, the "headquarters" of a national banking association are located in the state of the bank's home office as designated in its charter. Although that amendment is effective for tax years post-2006 (and, thus, not applicable to the case), the definition is instructive and fully supported the holding by the Commissioner and the superior court that the bank was domiciled in Delaware for franchise tax purposes. Lehman Bros. Bank, FSB v. State Bank Comm'r, 937 A.2d 95 (Del. 2007). See 5 Del. C. § 831(8).

Georgia.—A nonresident, nonprofit cooperative bank which, although it did not regularly solicit loans in Georgia, did do some solicitation in Georgia and, on numerous occasions, sent to Georgia officers and agents and which furnished information to potential debtor in Georgia about its loan policies had sufficient connection with Georgia to be subjected to personal intangible property tax on long-term notes which it held and which were secured by real estate located in Georgia. Columbia Bank for Coops. v. Blackmon, 232 Ga. 344, 206 S.E.2d 424 (1974).

Shares of Bank Stock.—In the absence of a statutory provision to the contrary, shares of bank stock are taxed at the owner's domicile.[2747] State legislatures may, however, provide for taxation of shares of bank stock at a

---

Massachusetts.—Under the Massachusetts statute it is provided that all personal estate shall be assessed to the owner in the city of which he is a resident, except that all goods, wares, merchandise, and other stock in trade in cities other than where the owner resides shall be taxed in those places where the owner hires or occupies manufactories, stores, shop., or wharves. Under such statute it has been held that where one resides in one city and carries en the business of a banker and broker at an office in another city, the capital used in the business is taxable at the place of his residence. Prince v. Boston, 193 Mass. 545, 79 N.E. 741.

Texas.—When applied to taxation, common-law rule of "mobilia sequuntur personam," i.e., movables follow the person, merely means that situs of personal property for purposes of taxation is the domicile of the owner unless there is a statute to the contrary, property is tangible and has acquired an actual situs of its own in state or place other than where owner is domiciled, or, in cases of intangible property, it has acquired a business situs in a state other than the one where the owner is domiciled. Houston v. Morgan Guaranty International Bank, 666 S.W.2d 524 (Tex. App. 1 Dist 1983).

[2747] **In general.—**

Connecticut.—Hartford Fire Ins. Co. v. Hartford, 3 Conn. 15; Savings Bank v. New London, 20 Conn. 111.

Indiana.—Madison v. Whitney, 21 Ind. 261.

Massachusetts.—Goldsbury v. Warwick, 112 Mass. 384.

Michigan.—Howell v. Cassopolis, 35 Mich. 471.

Pennsylvania.—Strong v. O'Donnell, 31 Leg. Int. 289, 10 Phila. 575.

Statute held to have established situs of shares of domestic trust company in the state for purposes of taxation. Commonwealth v. Provident Trust Co., 319 Pa. 385, 180 A. 16 (1935).

Tennessee.—Nashville v. Thomas, 45 Tenn. 600.

Texas.—Stock of a banking corporation, being a species of "personal property," is taxable in the state where the place of business or domicile of the corporation is located. First Trust Joint Stock Land Bank v. Dallas (Tax. Civ. App.), 167 S.W.2d 783.

West Virginia.—Watson v. Fairmont, 38 W. Va. 183, 18 S.E. 467.

Determination by assessor as to place of taxation.—

Van Wagenen v. Board of Supervisors, 74 Iowa 716, 39 N.W. 105.

Illustrative cases.—

Bank stock of deceased held taxable to administrator in place of latter's residence. Kent v. Exeter, 68 N.H. 469, 44 A. 607.

Where a Kentucky resident owned much intangible personal property, consisting of corporate stocks, and the certificates were deposited in New York banks, the property had its legal situs in Kentucky, and such situs continued even after the death of the owner until the appointment of an administrator. Fidelity & Columbia Trust Co. v. Louisville, 245 U.S. 54, 38 S. Ct. 40, 62 L. Ed. 145, 1918C L.R.A. 124.

place other than the owner's domicile, and in some jurisdictions a bank's domicile is the situs for taxation of such stock.[2748]

Deposits.—The situs for taxation of bank deposits depends on whether such deposits are considered as the property of, and taxable to, a bank or its

---

[2748] **In general.—**

London v. Hope, 80 S.W. 817, 26 Ky. L. Rptr. 112; Bedford v. Nashville, 54 Tenn. 409; McLaughlin v. Chadwell, 54 Tenn. 389; State v. Lewis, 118 Wis. 432, 95 N.W. 388. And see South Nashville St B. Co. v. Morrow, 87 Tenn. 406, 11 S.W. 348, 2 L.R.A. 853; Bank of Bramwell v. County Court, 36 W. Va. 341, 15 S.E. 78; Nashua Sav. Bank v. Nashua, 46 N.H. 389; School Dist. v. Lansing, 286 Mich. 244, 281 N.W. 883; Brophy v. Powell, 58 Ariz. 543, 121 P.2d 647.

The property right represented by shares of stock in domestic trust company is within the taxing jurisdiction of the state of the corporation's domicile, though the ownership of the stock may also be a taxable subject in another state. Schuylkill Trust Co. v. Pennsylvania, 302 U.S. 506, 58 S. Ct. 295, 82 L. Ed. 392 (1938).

Amendatory statute making bank stock subject to taxation in county wherein bank has an office to carry on "its business" has the same meaning, as respects place of taxation, as amended statute making bank stock subject to taxation in county wherein bank has an office to carry on a "banking business," and hence bank stock is not taxable in county other than county where principal office of bank is located unless bank does a "banking business" in such other county. State Tax Comm. v. Yavapai County Sav. Bank, 52 Ariz. 374, 81 P.2d 86.

Bank which receives and pays out no deposits in a given county is not carrying on a "banking business" therein. State Tax Comm. v. Yavapai County Sav. Bank, 52 Ariz. 374, 81 P.2d 86.

Nor is bank which maintained office in county other than county wherein its principal office was located merely for purpose of making collections on loans, contracts of sale and leases, superintending its property, obtained through loans, and advertising it for sale, and not for purpose of receiving and paying out deposits, engaged in "banking business" in such other county. State Tax Comm. v. Yavapai County Sav. Bank, 52 Ariz. 374, 81 P.2d 86.

Joint-stock land bank as agent.—

State of Texas was authorized to collect from joint-stock land bank domiciled within state, as agent for nonresident shareholders, ad valorem taxes on stock owned by such shareholders. First Trust Joint Stock Land Bank v. Dallas (Tax. Civ. App.), 167 S.W.2d 783.

Illustrative case.—

Where stock owned by Delaware corporation owning controlling interest in stock of banks located in several states had acquired business situs in Minnesota for purposes of state taxation, fact that two other states, pursuant to federal statute, had adopted scheme of taxing stock of both state and national banks doing business therein held not to render taxation in Minnesota of stock of banks located in such states unconstitutional. First Bank Stock Corp. v. Minnesota, 301 U.S. 234, 57 S. Ct. 677, 81 L. Ed. 1061, 113 A.L.R. 228.

depositor;[2749] when taxable to a depositor, such deposits should be taxed at his domicile.[2750] And for taxation purposes, money is transitory property; its mere presence on deposit in a bank does not necessarily render it subject to taxation there.[2751] Accordingly, it has been said that bank deposits may be taxed at the domicile of the owner, or where they have acquired a business situs, or where they are actually kept, although the latter rule does not preclude their taxation in the state of the depositor's domicile.[2752]

[2749] National State Bank v. Pierce, 17 F. Cas. 1238 (No. 10,052).

[2750] **In general.—**

Connecticut.—Bridgeport Projectile Co. v. Bridgeport, 92 Conn. 316, 102 A. 644.

Georgia.—Fulton County v. Wright, 146 Ga. 447, 91 S.E. 487.

Kentucky.—Ewald v. Louisville, 168 Ky. 71, 181 S.W. 1095, modified, 171 Ky. 509, 188 S.W. 652, and aff'd sub nom. Fidelity & Columbia Trust Co. v. Louisville, 245 U.S. 54, 38 S. Ct. 40, 62 L. Ed. 145, 1918C L.R.A. 124; Harting v. Lexington, 43 S.W. 415, 19 Ky. L. Rptr. 1829.

Missouri.—State v. Gehner, 320 Mo. 901, 9 S.W.2d 621, 59 A.L.R. 1041; State v. Gehner, 8 S.W.2d 1066.

New Hampshire.—Waterman v. Lebanon, 78 N.H. 23, 95 A. 657.

Ohio.—Cleveland, etc., Coal Co. v. O'Brien, 8 Ohio App. 247, aff'd, 98 Ohio St. 14, 120 N.E. 214.

Oregon.—Pennick v. American Nat. Bank, 126 Ore. 615, 268 P. 1012.

Tennessee.—Grundy County v. Tennessee, etc., R. Co., 94 Tenn. 295, 29 S.W. 116.

Corporate depositor.—

Statute providing that bank deposits shall be assessed for taxation in township, city, town, or school district where owner of such deposits resides applies to corporations, and "domicile" of domestic corporation within meaning of statute is at place of its domicile as provided in its charter. State v. Stephenson-Browne Lbr. Co., 180 Okla. 619, 71 P.2d 991.

[2751] Tampa v. Palmer, 89 Fla. 514, 105 So. 115.

Missouri held proper tax situs for New York bank deposits of Delaware corporation doing an interstate oil pipeline business across Missouri, where corporation's officials, only general office, business books, and records were located in Missouri, at office from which all active operations were conducted except making of contract. for transportation of oil and collection and deposit of money therefor. Smith v. Ajax Pipe Line Co., 87 F.2d 567, cert. denied, 300 U.S. 677, 57 S. Ct. 670, 81 L. Ed. 882.

[2752] **In general.—**

Great Southern Life Ins. Co. v. Austin, 112 Tex. 1, 243 S.W. 778.

Generally an ordinary bank deposit has a situs for purpose of taxation at the domicile of the owner. Roach v. First Sav., etc., Ass'n (Tax. Civ. App.), 203 S.W.2d 1006.

Taxable in state of depositor's domicile only.—

Bank deposits, for purposes of ad valorem-taxation, have situs at domicile of depositor

(Text continued on page 775)

---

only. Baldwin v. Missouri, 281 U.S. 586, 50 S. Ct. 436, 74 L. Ed. 1056, 72 A.L.R. 1303.

A bank deposit is a credit which has no situs for taxation purpose, except at the domicile of the depositor. State ex rel. American Cent. Ins. Co. v. Gehner, 320 Mo. 901, 9 S.W.2d 621, 59 A.L.R. 1041.

Taxable in state of depositor's domicile and elsewhere.—

Deposits in bank in Missouri, owned by resident of Kentucky, held taxable at the owner's domicile, even though also taxable in Missouri, and whether tax was on the property or on the person. Fidelity & Columbia Trust Co. v. Louisville, 245 U.S. 54, 38 S. Ct. 40, 62 L. Ed. 145, 1918C L.R.A. 124.

Taxable in commercial domicile.—

A bank balance is an intangible asset with taxable situs in the state in which corporation owning it has its commercial domicile. In re New York, O. & W. R. Co., 161 F.2d 518.

Illinois bank accounts of Indiana ship company having a commercial domicile in Michigan where corporation's overall business was transacted, were properly included in computation of corporation's privilege fee in Michigan. Chicago, Duluth & Georgian Bay Transit Co. v. Michigan Corp. & Sec. Com., 319 Mich. 14, 29 N.W.2d 303.

Exemption from taxation in state of domicile.—

Where parts of funds in bank accounts of Ohio corporation in foreign states in excess of minimum balances were used by corporation in its business in Ohio, the minimum balances were not "used in business in such other state" within meaning of statute so as to be exempt from taxation in Ohio. Kroger Grocery, etc., Co. v. Evatt, 149 Ohio St 448, 79 N.E.2d 228.

For a bank deposit of one domiciled within the state to have a tax situs outside the state, there must be a compliance with all conditions contained in code section giving such deposits a situs outside the state under certain circumstances. Kroger Grocery, etc., Co. v. Evatt, 149 Ohio St 448, 79 N.E.2d 228.

Where Ohio chain store corporation having its principal office and doing business in Ohio maintained for use of retail stores outside Ohio bank accounts in the same localities as the stores, and maintained, by company policy, minimum balances in the accounts, and withdrew such balances only when the stores were closed, such minimum balances were not "withdrawable in course of business" outside Ohio within meaning of statute, and therefore had a tax situs in Ohio. Kroeger Grocery, etc., Co. v. Evatt, 149 Ohio St. 448, 79 N.E.2d 228.

Taxable in state of business situs.—

Where a nonresident establishes a business in the state and manages it by resident agents, money in bank and debts due it, accumulated from the business, are taxable under the Kentucky statute declaring all personal property situated in the state subject to taxation. Commonwealth v. Dun & Co., 126 Ky. 108, 102 S.W. 859.

A Delaware corporation's funds which consisted of accumulated reserves coming from corporation's three divisions, one of which was in Illinois, and which were held subject to needs and demands for additional capital of the three divisions, and which were deposited in bank, acquired situs in Illinois, and were under jurisdiction of the taxing authorities at office of corporation in Cook County. People v. McGraw Elec. Co., 375 Ill. 241, 30 N.E.2d 903.

§ 38. National Bank Shares.

Shares of stock in national banks are personal property, and though they are a species of personal property which, in one sense, is intangible and incorporeal, the law which created them can separate them from their owner's person for the purposes of taxation, and give them a situs of their own,[2753] and this has been done by Congress declaring such shares of stock owned by nonresidents of a state to be taxable where the particular bank is

---

Moneys collected as interest and principal of notes, mortgages, and other securities kept within the state for use or reinvestment, though the owner is domiciled in another state, and the moneys are deposited in a bank to his credit, are subject to taxation under the Louisiana statute providing for taxation of credits arising from business done in the state, at the business domicile of a nonresident owner, his agent, or representative. New Orleans v. Stempel, 175 U.S. 309, 20 S. Ct. 110, 44 L. Ed. 174.

A foreign corporation had an agent in New Orleans, where it received and where it sold fruit, and received the price for the same. Part of the proceeds were withheld in the hands of the agents for purposes incidental to the prosecution of its business, and part deposited to the credit of the company, subject to the check of its local agent also for the prosecution of its business here, and for such other purposes as the company might direct it to be applied to. The company transacted business in New Orleans precisely as did resident businessmen and firms. It was held that an assessment of the cash in bank of said corporation was proper. Bluefields Banana Co. v. Board of Assessors, 49 La. Ann. 43, 21 So. 627.

Where taxpayer was a Delaware corporation, but its real estate was in Ohio, and its bank deposits were received and disbursed in Ohio alone, its Cleveland bank deposits did not have a foreign situs and were subject to a franchise tax in Ohio. Corner Co. v. Bowers, 164 Ohio St. 429, 131 N.E.2d 581.

Bank account of trustee domiciled in another county, which was used to purchase notes evidencing loans on personal property made through branch office of investment company in county where bank account was maintained, and notes thus sold and delivered to trustee in county of his domicile were subject to taxation in such county and not in county where bank account was maintained and loans were made and collected. County Assessor of Garfield County v. Greer, 195 Okla. 540, 159 P.2d 737.

Illustrative cases.—

Money of an Ohio corporation on deposit in a bank located in another state, is, under the Ohio statute, taxable in Ohio. Cleveland, etc., Coal Co. v. O'Brien, 98 Ohio St 14, 120 N.E 214.

Deposits of Ohio corporation in Ohio bank, which were not withdrawable by any officer or agent of corporation outside the state, had a taxable situs in Ohio. First Nat. Bank v. Evatt, 16 Ohio Supp. 130, 32 Ohio Op. 277.

[2753] Tappan v. Merchants' Nat'l Bank, 86 U.S. (19 Wall.) 490, 22 L. Ed. 189.

located and nowhere else.[2754] Such provision does not violate the constitutional rule requiring uniformity of taxation.[2755]

[2754] **In general.—**

United States.—12 U.S.C.S. § 548 prior to amendment effective January 1, 1972; Supervisors v. Stanley, 105 U.S. 305, 26 L. Ed. 1044; Bristol v. Washington, 177 U.S. 133, 20 S. Ct. 585, 44 L. Ed. 701; First Nat'l Bank v. Covington, 103 F. 523, appeal dismissed, 185 U.S. 270, 22 S. Ct. 645, 46 Ed. 906; Austin v. Aldermen, 74 U.S. (7 Wall.) 694, 19 L. Ed. 224; Tappan v. Merchants' Nat'l Bank, 86 U.S. (19 Wall.) 490, 22 L. Ed. 189; Citizens', etc., Nat. Bank v. Atlanta, 46 F.2d 88.

Alabama.—McIver v. Robinson, 53 Ala. 456

Illinois.—First Nat. Bank v. Smith, 65 Ill. 44.

Maine.—Packard v. Lewiston, 55 Me. 456.

Michigan.—Howell v. Cassopolis, 35 Mich. 471.

New Jersey.—State v. Haight, 31 N.J.L. 399; State v. Hart, 31 N.J.L. 434; State v. Cook, 32 N.J.L. 347; De Baun v. Smith, 55 N.J.L. 110, 25 A. 277.

The shares of capital stock of a national bank owned by a nonresident must be assessed for taxes in the taxing district where the bank is located. Crossley v. East Orange, 62 N.J.L. 583, 41 A. 712.

[2755] Tappan v. Merchants' Nat. Bank, 86 U.S. (19 Well.) 490, 22 L. Ed. 189.

New York.—People v. Commissioners, 35 N.Y. 423, aff'd, 71 U.S. (4 Wall.) 244, 18 L. Ed. 344; Utica v. Churchill, 43 Barb. 550.

North Carolina.—Kyle v. Fayetteville, 75 N.C. 449; Buie v. Fayetteville, 79 N.C. 267.

Pennsylvania.—Bucks v. Ely, 6 Phila. 414.

Tennessee.—Nashville v. Thomas, 45 Tenn. 600.

Vermont.—Clapp v. Burlington, 42 Vt. 579, 1 Am. R. 355.

Statutory provision.—

"The shares of any national banking association owned by nonresidents of any State, shall be taxed by the taxing district or by the State where the association is located and not elsewhere . . . ." 12 U.S.C.S. § 548, subsec. 2, prior to amendment effective January 1, 1972.

Purpose of statute.—

The purpose of the federal statute authorizing taxation of the shares of any national banking association owned by nonresidents of any state by the taxing district in which the association is located was to preclude discrimination against such stock, and subject to compliance with such objective and other specific restrictions, to leave to the states the manner and place of taxing such shares. Passaic v. Clifton, 23 NJ. Super. 333, 93 A.2d 17, aff'd, 12 N.J. 466, 97 A.2d 437.

"Located" refers to territorial limits of taxing authority.—

The word "located" within the federal statute authorizing taxation of the shares of any national banking association owned by nonresidents of any state by the taxing district in which the association is located refers to the territorial limits of the authority which levies

(Text continued on page 778)

---

the tax, and, hence, whether the bank was located in one of two cities in the same county was immaterial, if the tax were a county tax. Passaic v. Clifton, 23 N.J. Super. 333, 93 A.2d 17, aff'd, 12 N.J. 466, 97 A.2d 437.

"Visitorial Power."—

"Visitorial power" under the National Bank Act, 12 U.S.C.S. § 1 et seq., refers to a sovereign's supervisory powers over corporations. Any inquiry into the operation of a bank is not automatically a visitorial power that is prohibited under 12 U.S.C.S. § 484. The exclusively federal power to visit national banks is not the power to oust all state regulation of those entities. The Office of Comptroller of Currency has no objections to state officials examining records of national banks for the purpose of ascertaining payment of applicable taxes. Miss. Dep't of Revenue v. Pikco Fin., Inc., 97 So. 3d 1203, 2012 Miss. LEXIS 354 (Miss. 2012).

Predecessor statutory provisions.—

The act of Congress of 1868, giving a legislative construction to the words "place where the bank is located and not elsewhere," as used in § 41 of the Act of 1864, as to which the decisions had not been in harmony, permitted the state to determine and direct the manner and place of taxing resident shareholder., but provided expressly that nonresidents should be taxed only in the city or ton where the bank was located. Newark Banking Co. v. Newark, 121 U.S. 163, 7 S. Ct. 839, 30 L. Ed. 904; First Nat. Bank v. Covington, 103 F. 523, appeal dismissed, 185 U.S. 270, 22 S. Ct. 645, 46 L Ed. 906; Tappan v. Merchants' Nat. Bank, 86 U.S. (19 Wall.) 490, 22 L. Ed. 189; Howell v. Cassopolis, 35 Mich. 471; First Nat. Bank v. Province, 20 Mont. 374, 51 P. 821; Crossley v. East Orange, 62 N.J.L. 583, 41 A. 712; Kyle v. Fayetteville, 75 N.C. 449; Strong v. O'Donnell, 81 Leg. Int. 269, 10 Phila. 575; National Bank of Arizona v. Long, 6 Ariz. 311, 57 P. 639.

The word "place," as used in the proviso in Act Cong. June 3, 1864, c. 106, § 41, permitting state taxation of shares in national banks, refers to the location of the bank, and not to the state authority under which the tax is to be assessed; and shares held by a citizen are taxable in the town where the bank is located, and not where he resides. Packard v. Lewiston, 55 Me. 456.

With regard to a state tax, the word "place" meant state, and, with regard to a county and township or city tax, it meant those localities, respectively. State v. Haight, 31 N.J.L. 399.

Shares of nonresident stockholders in national banks are taxable at the place where the bank is located. Farmers' Nat. Bank v. Cook, 32 N.J.L. 347.

Stockholders in a national or state bank, the capital of which is invested wholly or in part in bonds or securities of the United States, are subject to taxation under state authority at the place where such bank is located, and not elsewhere, upon the value of their respective shares of the capital of such bank, and nonresident stockholders are liable to such taxation in the same manner and to the same extent as resident stockholders. People ex rel. Kennedy v. Commissioners of Taxes, 35 N.Y. 423, aff'd, 71 U.S. 244, 18 L. Ed. 344. See Utica v. Churchill, 33 N.Y. 161; Van Allen v. Assessors, 70 U.S. 573, 18 L. Ed. 229.

Act of May 20, 1864, empowering the authorities of Fayetteville to impose the same tax on nonresidents, pursuing their ordinary vocations in the town, as upon the residents, authorizes a tax upon the shares in a national bank located in the town, and held by one who conducts his ordinary business therein, but whose residence is in the county, outside the

VI. LEVY AND ASSESSMENT.

a. General Considerations.

§ 39. Proceedings for Assessment and Assessors.

Assessment proceedings are governed by the respective state statutes as interpreted by the state courts.[2756] The "assessment of tax" consists merely

---

corporate limits. Moore v. Mayor & Comm'rs of Fayetteville, 80 N.C. 154, 30 Am. R. 75.

A state law, assessing for taxation shares of national bank at any other than the place where the banks are located, is void. Nashville v. Thomas, 45 Tenn. 600.

[2756] *United States.*—Washington Water Power Co. v. Shoshone County, 270 F. 377.

Alabama.—Ceylon Co. v. Hawkins, 206 Ala. 246, 89 So. 754.

Iowa.—First Nat'l Bank v. Hayes, 186 Iowa 892, 171 N.W. 715; Mannings Bank v. Armstrong, 204 Iowa 512, 211 N.W. 485.

Louisiana.—Fact that guidelines used by assessors to determine ad valorem taxes reflected a value as of January 1, 1979, rather than the January 1, 1980, value required by statute did not operate to invalidate the assessment made in respect to the taxpayer's machinery and equipment as long as it did not exceed the value which would have been reached had the tables been properly updated and as long as all similarly situated taxpayers were treated alike. Dow Chem. Co. v. Pitre, 468 So. 2d 747 (La. App. 1985).

Maine.—Robinson v. Fidelity Trust Co., 140 Me. 302, 37 A.2d 273.

Massachusetts.—Lang Engineering Co. v. Commonwealth, 231 Mass. 367, 120 N.E. 843.

Ohio.—Statute providing that tax commission shall fix day as of which taxable deposits in financial institutions shall be listed and assessed, applies only to deposits and has no application to assessments of surplus or reserves and undivided profits of financial institutions. First Federal Sav., etc., Ass'n Evatt, 143 Ohio St. 243, 28 Ohio Op. 150, 54 N.E.2d 795.

Where capital of incorporated financial institution was divided into shares all of which were withdrawable, the withdrawable shares were properly included in the "deposits" and were properly excluded from the "capital" account, in making assessment under statute providing manner of assessing both capital and deposits in financial institutions. First Federal Sav., etc., Ass'n v. Evatt, 143 Ohio St. 243, 28 Ohio Op. 150, 54 N.E.2d 795.

Oklahoma.—Taxable income of a federal savings and loan association for 1975 as adjusted in 1976 was to be achieved by starting with what was reported to the federal government, a loss, as required by the state statutes, and adding dividends paid to depositors as required by the state statutes and judicial decision and then deducting tax-exempt interest received by the association from federal obligations as authorized by the state statutes, and, after amending federal returns to carry back 1975 federal loss so as to offset income reported to the Internal Revenue Service in 1972 and 1973, the association could properly file amended state returns for 1972 and 1973 conforming to the lesser amount reported in the amended federal return despite contention that the association was thereby carrying back the same federal loss and deducting it a second time against 1972 and 1973 state income and was thereby benefitting twice from the single loss. Continental Fed. Sav. & Loan Ass'n v.

of the ascertainment of the amount due.[2757] Thus, a state board of tax commissioners or similar body, being a creature of a legislature, can exercise only the powers conferred by statute in the manner prescribed therein.[2758] Where a statute gives a board of county commissioners power to supervise the official conduct of all county officers and see that they faithfully perform their duties, such board has jurisdiction to direct an assessor to comply with the law as to methods of assessment of bank stock and other property, and the board's right to so direct is not limited to the period when it acts as a board of equalization.[2759] And if a bank is solvent on the designated tax day, its shares are assessable as of that date even though it later becomes insolvent.[2760]

It is the duty of an assessor to determine the actual cash value of both the real estate and shares of stock of a bank, and his conclusions are not controlled by their book value as shown by the bank's records or by a statement of its assets and liabilities furnished him by bank officers, such being intended merely to aid him.[2761] But in the absence of other evidence as to the market value of shares of national bank capital stock, an assessor's conclusions as entered upon the assessment roll are presumed to declare the full actual cash value thereof and are binding upon shareholders and the courts.[2762] The law presumes the assessor has properly performed his duty

---

Oklahoma Tax Comm'n, 601 P.2d 743 (Okla. App. 1979).

Utah.—McCornick & Co. v. Bassett, 49 Utah 444, 164 P. 852.

Virginia.—Sussex County v. Jarratt, 129 Va. 672, 106 S.E. 384, rehearing denied, 106 S.E. 627.

2757 F.W. Woolworth Co. v. State Dep't of Revenue, 699 P.2d 1 (Colo. App. 1984).

2758 F.W. Woolworth Co. v. State Dep't of Revenue, 699 P.2d 1 (Colo. App. 1984).

2759 Stillman v. Lynch, 56 Utah 540, 192 P. 272, 12 A.L.R. 552.

2760 Buder v. First Nat. Bank, 16 F.2d 990, cert. denied, 274 U.S. 743, 47 S. Ct. 588, 71 L. Ed. 1321.

2761 Citizens' Nat'l Bank v. Baker County Board of Equalization, 109 Ore. 669, 222 P. 341.

Where advertising sign and night depository were so annexed to the realty as to become fixtures which constituted realty for the purpose of taxation, sign and night depository were assessable and taxable as real property. County of Ventura v. Channel Islands State Bank, 251 Cal. App. 2d 240, 59 Cal. Rptr. 404 (1967).

Fact that advertising sign and night depository of bank were classifiable as realty did not require that improvements be assessed to the lessor-owner of the land. County of Ventura v. Channel Islands State Bank, 251 Cal. App. 2d 240, 59 Cal. Rptr. 404 (1967).

2762 Bank of Carthage v. Thomas, 330 Mo. 19, 48 S.W.2d 930; Citizens' Nat'l Bank v. Baker County Board of Equalization, 109 Ore. 669, 222 P. 341.

and has assessed all properties fairly and on an equal basis.[2763] It would be clearly improper, if not blatantly illegal, for a board of equalization to base its assessments on the needs of the governmental agency involved, since the monetary needs of the governmental agency are irrelevant in the process of determining proper assessments.[2764] Determinations concerning the value of the property subject to taxation cannot be considered the "tax plan" since such determinations have nothing to do with determining the method by which the required revenue is to be raised.[2765] Thus, a tax "plan" which requires the taxation of exempt property is blatantly illegal and fundamentally and indefensibly wrong.[2766] Where one governmental entity "levies taxes by or for" another entity, the entity for whom taxes are levied must have the taxing power, the levying officers exercise that power as ex officio officers of that entity, and the taxes collected are those of the "levied for" entity.[2767]

b. Mode of Assessment.

§ 40. As Determined by Statute and Charter.

In General.—Since states have the power to tax banks and their property, it follows that they may by statute prescribe the manner in which such taxes shall be assessed.[2768] When a mode of assessment has been fixed by statute or incorporated in a bank's charter, it is conclusive on the state until

---

The burden is on the proposed taxpayer to show that part of the moneyed capital employed in competing with national banks has been so segregated to other purposes that it should not be taxed. People v. Goldfogle, 242 N.Y. 277, 151 N.E. 452; People v. Goldfogle, 123 Misc. 399, 205 N.Y.S. 870, aff'd, 213 App. Div. 677, 211 N.Y.S. 85, aff'd, 242 N.Y. 540, 152 N.E. 418.

[2763] Bank of Am. v. County of Fresno, 127 Cal. App. 3d 295, 179 Cal. Rptr. 497(1981).

[2764] Charles Schreiner Bank v. Kerrville Independent School Dist., 683 S.W.2d 466 (Tex. App. 4 Dist. 1984).

[2765] Charles Schreiner Bank v. Kerrville Indep. School Dist., 683 S.W.2d 466 (Tex. App. 4 Dist. 1984).

[2766] Charles Schreiner Bank v. Kerrville Indep. School Dist., 683 SW.2d 466 (Tex. App. 4 Dist. 1984).

[2767] Bell Community Redevelopment Agency v. Woosley, 214 Cal. Rptr. 788 (Cal. App. 2 Dist. 1985).

[2768] Hager v. Citizens' Nat'l Bank, 127 Ky. 192, 32 Ky. L Rptr. 95, 105 S.W. 403, 914, error dismissed, 212 U.S. 585, 29 S. Ct. 681, 53 L. Ed. 661; Westminster v. Westminster Sav. Bank, 92 Md. 62, 48 A. 34; Bridgeport Sav. Bank v. Feitner, 191 N.Y. 88, 83 N.E. 592; State v. Clement Nat'l Bank, 84 Vt. 167, 78 A. 944, 1912D Ann. Cas. 22. See also § 34 of this chapter. Although legislature may not exempt property from taxation in violation of constitution, it may establish reasonable methods for assessing taxes. Cherry River Nat'l

repealed.[2769] But the power of taxation being an incident to sovereignty and an extraordinary right, it must be exercised pursuant to authority given, so that an assessment of bank stock against a bank in the manner prescribed by a repealed law and inconsistent with existing law, was held invalid and unenforceable.[2770] Where, however, a tax has been legally assessed and is due, the repeal of the act under which the assessment was made does not affect such assessment.[2771]

Validity of Statutes Providing for Retrospective Assessment.—A state may provide for the retrospective assessment of a bank's property for taxation purposes.[2772]

Bank v. Lorenson, 406 S.E.2d 714 (W. Va. 1991).

Purposes of savings bank statute, governing permissible uses of bank's funds, and excise tax statute which exempts pass-through certificates, are not identical, and purposes have never been explicitly connected by the legislature despite numerous amendments. South Boston Sav. Bank v. Commissioner of Revenue, 418 Mass. 695, 640 N.E.2d 462 (1994).

[2769] *Iowa.*—Mannings Bank v. Armstrong, 204 Iowa 512, 211 N.W. 485.

Kentucky.—Johnson v. Commonwealth, 37 Ky. (7 Dana) 338.

Louisiana.—New Orleans v. Southern Bank, 11 La. Ann. 41.

New York.—Gallatin Nat. Bank v. Commissioners, 67 N.Y. 516, aff'd sub nom. People v. Commissioners of Taxes & Assessments, 94 U.S. 415, 24 L Ed. 164.

Ohio.—Commercial Bank v. Bowman, 1 Handy 246, 12 Ohio Dec. Reprint 125.

Pennsylvania.—Commonwealth v. Easton Bank, 10 Pa. 442.

Tennessee.—Union & Planters' Bank v. Memphis, 107 Tenn. 66, 64 S.W. 13.

Washington.—Bank of Fairfield v. Spokane County, 173 Wash. 145, 22 P.2d 646, followed, Spokane & Eastern Trust Co. v. Spokane County, 173 Wash. 699, 22 P.2d 656, holding that in taxing banks for a certain year they were entitled to credit for amount already paid for taxes for that year.

[2770] Klauss v. Citizens' Nat. Bank, 46 Ind. App. 683, 93 N.E. 558.

[2771] State v. Waterville Sav. Bank, 68 Me. 515; Appeal Tax Court v. Western Maryland R. Co., 50 Md. 274; Debolt v. Ohio Life Ins., etc., Co., 1 Ohio St. 563, aff'd, 57 U.S. 416, 14 L. Ed. 997.

[2772] Richardson v. State Nat'l Bank, 135 Ky. 772, 123 S.W. 294, error dismissed, 225 U.S. 696, 32 S. Ct. 838, 56 L. Ed. 1262; Dodge v. Nevada Nat. Bank, 109 F. 726.

There was no due process violation in retroactivity of 1989 amendments to Tax Reform Code, under which value of bank shares was averaged over six-year period, which average was taxed as current shares, where: (1) Amendments were intended to recoup expected shortfall in that year's bank shares taxes, which was legitimate legislative concern; (2) values of shares in preceding five years was part of calculation only to determine reliable reflection of value of shares to be taxed in current year; (3) purpose of determining reliable value of property subject to tax was legitimate and the averaging method was rational means to that

Construction of Remedial Statutes.—Remedial statutes enacted for the purpose of curing defects in prior laws, and placing all banking institutions in the state upon exactly the same footing for taxation, must be liberally construed to effectuate such purpose.[2773] And where it is apparent that the intent of a statute relating to the taxation of banks or shares of stock therein is to substitute a new liability for the old as of a certain date, and relieve a bank or its stockholders from all liability after such date under any other law, such statute is self-executing and operates to take such property from the roll and void any assessment made in violation thereof.[2774]

Bank in Liquidation.—When a bank is placed in liquidation and taken over by a superintendent of banks, he acts in the capacity of statutory receiver and trustee of the bank's assets, and land owned by the bank should be assessed to him.[2775]

Miscellaneous Statutory Provisions.—For other cases relating to statutes determining the mode of assessment of banks and their property for taxation purposes, see the footnote.[2776]

---

purpose. Fidelity Bank v. Commonwealth ex rel. Dep't of Revenue, 645 A.2d 452 (Pa. Commw. 1994).

2773 Hager v. Citizens' Nat'l Bank, 127 Ky. 192, 105 SW. 403, 32 Ky. L. Rptr. 95, error dismissed, 212 U.S. 585, 29 S. Ct. 681, 53 L. Ed. 661; Minnehaha Nat. Bank v. Anderson, 2 F.2d 897; Hughes v. City Trust & Sav. Co., 151 La. 313, 91 So. 747.

2774 First Nat. Bank v. Binghamton, 72 App. Div. 854, 76 N.Y.S. 526.

2775 Quinn v. Hannon, 262 Ala. 630, 80 So. 2d 239.

2776 *Alabama.*—Ad valorem tax on bank shares could not be diminished by amount of excise tax levied and assessed by state tax commission under the statutes. Union Bank & Trust Co. v. Phelps, 228 Ala. 236, 153 So. 644.

Arizona.—Where bank is going concern, statutory tax method, under which assessor may consider bank's surplus, reserve fund, undivided profits, par and market value of stock, and other trustworthy information, is exclusive, but cannot be used for insolvent bank. Federal Land Bank v. Yuma County, 42 Ariz. 45, 22 P.2d 405 (1933).

Under the statutes, banks are not assessed directly upon actual value of their assets, tangible and intangible. Gibbons v. White, 47 Ariz. 180, 54 P.2d 555.

Indiana.—Bank realty cannot be taxed as part of personal assets of bank under the statutes, whether bank is solvent or insolvent. Folk v. Heckler, 210 Ind. 68, 1 N.E.2d 124.

Michigan.—Under a statute providing that the aggregate value of bank stock may be assessed in one lump sum to the bank, if it shall request such assessment, the assessor must assess the owners of the shares directly, in the absence of such request. School Dist. v. Lansing, 286 Mich. 244, 281 N.W. 883.

A letter written by bank president to assessor authorizing assessment of all bank stock to president "et al." indicated that bank desired to be assessed in one lump sum. School Dist. v. Lansing, 286 Mich. 244, 281 N.W. 883.

§ 41. Report or Statement by Bank.

In General.—Under state statutes, banks or certain classes thereof may be required to make, and file with an assessor or other specified official, a written or sworn statement of their capital,[2777] property,[2778] legal investments In real estate,[2779] assets and deposits,[2780] undivided profits and

---

The purpose of the statute is to render assessment and collection of taxes more expedient and convenient for all parties concerned, and to simplify collection of tax from nonresident shareholders, and it contemplates that the shares shall be assessed and not the capital stock of the bank itself and that the tax shall be assessed in solido against bank as agent for its shareholders, to be paid by bank and collected by it from stockholders, either by deduction from dividends of the amount so paid or by a charge to expenses. School Dist. v. Lansing, 286 Mich. 244, 281 N.W. 883.

Oklahoma.—Banks are classified for purpose of net income tax laid under the statute. Board of Comm'rs v. State Board of Equalization, 155 Okla. 183, 8 P.2d 732.

Under the statute, an income taxpayer is not assessed on that portion of his income received as interest on certain specified tax-exempt governmental securities. Oklahoma Tax. Comm., First Nat. Bank, etc., Co., 178 Okla. 260, 62 P.2d 1220.

State tax commission in determining amount of bank's income tax held without authority to strike that percentage of bank's claimed deduction for business operating expenses which equal percentage of total income received as interest upon tax-exempt securities on which bank was not required to pay tax. Oklahoma Tax Comm. v. First Nat. Bank, etc., Co., 178 Okla. 260, 62 P.2d 1220.

[2777] Bank of Bramwell v. County Court, 36 W. Va. 341, 15 S.E. 78; Board of Comm'rs v. Topeka Equipment Co., 26 Kan. 363.

[2778] Seward v. Cattle, 14 Neb. 144, 15 N.W. 337; Daly Bank & Trust Co. v. Board of Comm'rs, 33 Mont. 101, 81 P. 950; Oregon & Washington Mortg. Sav. Bank v. Catlin, 15 Ore. 342, 15 P. 462; Stanberry v. Jordan, 145 Mo. 371, 46 S.W. 1093.

Bank, in filing its financial institution return of taxable property for the year 1964, properly excluded from the book value of its taxable shares the value of shares held by foreign insurance companies, domestic insurance companies and all dealers in intangibles. National City Bank v. Porterfield, 44 Ohio Op. 2d 202, 15 Ohio St. 2d 235, 239 N.E.2d 61 (1968).

[2779] Paul v. McGraw, 3 Wash. 296, 28 P. 532.

[2780] State v. Sterling, 20 Md. 502.

The Ohio statute requiring deposits in financial institutions to be returned for taxation except those of the state or other "subdivision" thereof does not include a state agency such as a metropolitan housing authority organized under state law, and hence deposits of rents collected from tenant in a low-rent housing project owned and operated by such authority, and the moneys loaned or contributed by the federal government in furtherance of such project are taxable deposits. First Cent. Trust Co. v. Evatt, 145 Ohio St. 160, 30 Ohio Op 347, 60 N.E.2d 926.

Moneys and funds collected by superintendent of banks in precise of liquidation of closed

surplus or reserve fund,[2781] and the names and addresses of their stockholders,[2782] the amount of stock held by each,[2783] the par value of their shares

---

bank or moneys and funds collected by superintendent of building and loan associations in process of liquidation of closed loan association and deposited by either of them in open financial institution constitute deposits of "any other financial institution" within statute regarding taxation of deposits and are not required to be returned as taxable deposits by such open financial institution. Ohio Citizens Trust Co. v. Evatt, 146 Ohio St. 30, 63 N.E.2d 912, 31 Ohio Op. 521.

The fact that defense corporation did not draw checks against deposits in taxpayer bank until items purchased and invoices therefor were approved by the federal government, or that deposits were made by defense corporation for specific purpose of paying therefrom the expenses incurred by it in operating its shell-loading plant, or that deposits were moneys advanced to the defense corporation for such purpose by the federal government did not make deposits nonwithdrawable or destroy the ordinary relationship between a depositor and the bank so as to relieve bank of obligation of returning such deposits for purpose of taxation. First Nat. Bank v. Evatt, 32 Ohio Op. 277, 16 Ohio Supp. 130.

2781 Paul v. McGraw, 3 Wash. 296, 28 P. 532.

2782 *Indiana.*—Whitney v. Ragsdale, 83 led. 107, 5 Am. R. 185; Strader v. Manville, 33 Ind. 111.

Iowa.—Farmers', etc., Nat. Bank v. Hoffman. 93 Iowa 119, 61 N.W. 418.

Kentucky.—Hager v. Citizens' Nat'l Bank, 127 Ky. 192, 105 S.W. 403, 32 Ky. L. Rptr. 95, error dismissed, 212 U.S. 585, 29 S. Ct. 681, 53 L. Ed. 661.

Massachusetts.—National Bank of Commerce v. New Bedford, 155 Mass. 313, 29 N.E. 532 (1892).

Missouri.—St Louis Bldg., etc., Ass'n v. Lightner, 47 Mo. 393; Gracy v. Catron, 118 Mo. 280, 24 S.W. 439.

Washington.—Ladd v. Gilson, 26 Wash. 79, 66 P. 126.

2783 *United States.*—First Nat'l Bank v. Hughes, 6 F. 737, appeal dismissed, 106 U.S. 523, 1 S. Ct. 489, 27 L. Ed. 268.

Arizona.—Western, etc., Banking Co., v. Murray, 6 Ariz. 215, 56 P. 728.

Iowa.—Farmers', etc., Nat. Bank v. Hoffman, 93 Iowa 119, 61 N.W. 418.

Massachusetts.—National Bank v. New Bedford, 155 Mass. 313, 29 NL 532.

Michigan.—Crittenden v. Mt. Clemens, 86 Mich. 220, 49 N.W. 144.

Missouri.—St. Louis Bldg., etc., Ass'n, Lightner, 47 Mo. 393; Gracy v. Catron, 118 Mo. 280, 24 S.W. 439; State v. Merchants' Bank, 160 Mo. 640, 61 S.W. 676.

Failure of bank president, in delivering a list of shares of stock in his bank to county assessor, for taxes, to place opposite the name of each owner the value of same, and tax due thereon, did not vitiate the assessment in view of the statute, such omissions being irregularities to be disregarded. State v. People's Bank, 263 S.W. 205 (Mo. 1924).

Nebraska.—First Nat. Bank v. Webster County, 77 Neb. 815, 113 N.W. 190.

Washington.—Paul v. McGraw, 3 Wash. 296, 28 P. 532.

and the amount paid up.[2784] Bank officers making an assessment list act as agents of the stockholders, both in listing stock for taxation and in paying the taxes levied against said stock.[2785] But a trust company acting for a nonresident treasurer of a corporation in paying interest and remitting coupons to him for cancellation, has been held not required to assess and deduct a tax imposed by statute.[2786] A statute requiring receivers to list property in their hands for taxation includes bank receivers,[2787] and a statute imposing the duty of filing a tax return on a bank's president or cashier does not relieve an insolvent bank's receiver of such duty.[2788]

A national bank, which was subject to state privilege tax, could not file a consolidated state income tax return with its holding company, which was a corporation not subject to the privilege tax but, rather, to the corporate tax.[2789]

Failure to Make Report or Statement.—In some states there is an express provision for listing and assessing property and adding to the taxable valuation thereof a certain percentage as a penalty in case of refusal to furnish a verified statement required or list property for taxation.[2790] For cases relating to the effect of a failure to file an ownership statement with respect to a bank's taxable property, see the footnote.[2791]

[2784] Paul v. McGraw, 3 Wash. 296, 28 P. 532.

[2785] Brown v. Hennessey State Bank, 78 Okla. 141, 189 P. 355; In re Durant Nat'l Bank, 107 Okla. 65, 230 P. 712; Hamilton v. International Bank, 114 Okla. 28, 242 P. 858; Hamilton v. Exchange Nat'l Bank, 114 Okla. 30, 242 P. 860.

[2786] Commonwealth v. Barrett Mfg. Co., 246 Pa. 301, 92 A. 302; Sowers v. First Nat'l Bank, 89 Okla. 160, 213 P. 876.

[2787] Federal Land Bank v. Yuma County, 42 Ariz. 45, 22 P.2d 405 (1933).

[2788] Hazen v. Hardee, 78 F.2d 230.

Although national bank was insolvent and comptroller had levied 100 percent assessment on stock, receiver held obligated to file tax return, since, under statute, tax on earnings was payable from any fund remaining after payment of depositors, even though fund resulted from stock assessment. Hazen v. Hardee, 78 F.2d 230.

[2789] First Nat'l Bank v. Kansas Dep't of Revenue, 18 Kan. App. 24 706, 779 P.2d 457 (1989).

Fact that bank and bank holding company filed consolidated federal income tax return did not mean that they should file consolidated state tax return. First Nat'l Bank v. Kansas Dep't of Revenue, 13 Kan. App. 2d 706, 779 P.2d 457 (1989).

[2790] Farmers' Loan, etc., Co. v. Fonda, 114 Iowa 728, 87 N.W. 724.

[2791] Where, on date of assessment, bank owned, claimed, possessed and controlled night depository and advertising sign located on building upon land belonging to a person other than the bank and neither owner of land nor bank filed with the county assessor written

Conclusiveness of Statement.—It seems that a bank's statement or return of property as required by statute, while prima facie correct, is not absolutely conclusive either on the state or the bank.[2792] Thus, where a statute provides that a bank shall furnish an assessor a statement showing the "amount of capital stock, surplus, and undivided earnings," and that the assessor shall fix the stock's value on the basis of such items, the assessor must accept these items as they appear upon the bank's books, and has no power to make deductions for "slow, doubtful and bad paper," it being the duty of the bank, if it believes it is entitled to a deduction, to enter such deduction on its books.[2793] But under a statute requiring an assessor to assess property "at its full cash value," where a bank returns its property at a certain value, and claims an unauthorized reduction of one third of its alleged value, a return of the whole amount by the assessor is not an increase of the assessment.[2794]

---

statement attesting to their ownership and sign and depository constituted real property, sign and depository were properly assessed to bank. Ventura County v. Channel Islands State Bank, 251 Cal. App. 2d 240, 59 Cal. Rptr. 404 (1967).

County assessor, in his discretion, could assess on the unsecured roll the advertising sign and night depository attached to leasehold realty, but owned by lessee bank, where neither bank nor owner of land elected to avail themselves of right to file written statement attesting to separate ownership. Ventura County v. Channel Islands State Bank, 251 Cal. App. 2d 240, 59 Cal. Rptr. 404 (1967).

[2792] In re First Trust Co., 93 Neb. 795, 142 N.W. 542; Northwestern Bank of Ireton v. Van Roekel, 202 Iowa 237, 207 N.W. 345; Champaign County Bank v. Smith, 7 Ohio St. 42; First Nat'l Bank v. City Council of Estherville, 136 Iowa 203, 112 N.W. 829; Brown v. French, 80 F. 166; Wilmington v. Ricaud, 90 F. 214; Hempstead County v. Bank of Hope, 74 Ark. 37, 84 S.W. 1030.

Banks furnishing an assessor information to make assessments, do not thereby acquiesce and become estopped from questioning the validity of the taxes levied on them. Brotherhood Co-Op. Nat. Bank v. Hurlburt, 26 F.2d 957.

Where a bank and trust company's stock was wrongfully assessed under an act, which was unconstitutional, and was repealed, the bank is not estopped to contest validity of the tax because it furnished the assessor with the information on which the assessment was made, in view of the statutory penalty for failure to give such information. Union Bank & Trust Co. v. Moore, 62 Mont. 132, 204 P. 361.

[2793] Avoca State Bank v. Burke, 193 Iowa 1055, 188 N.W. 675.

Under a statute prescribing the mode of assessing bank stock, the assessor has no powers except to compute the assessment in the manner prescribed from the statement furnished by the bank. Security Sav. Bank v. Board of Review, 189 Iowa 463, 178 N.W. 562.

[2794] First Nat. Bank v. Bailey, 16 Mont. 135, 40 P. 175.

§ 42. Proceedings for Discovery and Valuation of Property.

Under a state statute providing that for the purpose of correctly listing property for taxation, an assessor may inspect the books of corporations, it has been held that he cannot examine the account of any depositor in a bank, regardless of whether or not such depositor must pay taxes in the state.[2795] Under a statute providing that prior to an equalization hearing the applicant may cause an exchange of information and that parties may not introduce evidence on matters not so exchanged, it is not the rule that unless the taxpayer who initiates the exchange gives the assessor all the information in the taxpayer's possession directly relating to evidence sought to be introduced at the hearing that the statute bars introduction of any testimony on the subject.[2796]

The provision of the Property Tax Code requiring that the appraisal review board give notice to the property owner of the appraised value of his land was not unconstitutional as denying lienholder due process.[2797]

2795 Applegate v. State, 158 Ind. 119, 63 N.E. 16.

2796 Bank of Am. v. County of Fresno, 127 Cal. App. 3d 295, 179 Cal. Rptr. 497(1981).

Use of statute providing for exchange of information before an equalization hearing triggers a mutual exchange of information and either party may obtain from the other information stating the basis of the party's opinion of value and disclosure includes, if pertinent, income or replacement costs in addition to comparable sales. Bank of Am. v. County of Fresno, 127 Cal. App. 3d 295, 179 Cal. Rptr. 497 (1981).

Statute providing for exchange of information prior to an equalization hearing is to be given a reasonable and common sense interpretation and if the exchange of information provides reasonable notice to the opposition concerning the subject matter to be presented at the hearing through the testimony of witnesses and evidence, the statute has been complied with and purpose of the exchange of information has been satisfied. Bank of Am. v. County of Fresno, 127 Cal. App. 3d 295, 179 Cal. Rptr. 497 (1981).

Statute providing for exchange of information prior to an equalization hearing does not require that details of the evidence to be introduced be exchanged. Bank of Am. v. County of Fresno, 127 Cal. App. 3d 295, 179 Cal. Rptr. 497 (1981).

Where assessor was advised that at equalization hearing taxpayer would offer evidence as to poor water and soil conditions of the property the assessor had no basis for objecting to proffered testimony detailing such conditions. Bank of Am. v. County of Fresno, 127 Cal. App. 3d 295, 179 Cal. Rptr. 497 (1981).

Although assessor was not expressly notified that taxpayers witnesses at equalization hearing would testify to vine and grape quality, since assessor was notified that there would be testimony on the subject of "crop yields," it was error to exclude testimony on quality of the vineyard and grapes. Bank of Am. v. County of Fresno, 127 Cal. App. 3d 295, 179 Cal. Rptr. 497 (1981).

2797 First Nat'l Bank v. Huffman Indep. School Dist., 770 S.W.2d 571 (Tex. App. 1989).

In matters of taxation, the requirement of due process is satisfied if the assessed party is given an opportunity to be heard before some assessment board at some stage of proceedings.[2798]

c. Valuation of Bank's Property and Income.

§ 43. In General.

General Consideration.—As a general rule, the property and assets of a bank are to be taxed just as the property of natural persons is taxed,[2799] i.e., at its actual and true value.[2800] Thus, in ascertaining the value of a bank's assets for taxation, securities owned by the bank will be taken at their actual value when it exceeds their face value.[2801] But a bank cannot value its assets at one figure for purposes of carrying on business, and then seek a reduction

---

[2798] First Nat'l Bank v. Huffman Indep. School That., 770 S.W.2d 571 (Tex. App. 1989).

[2799] Griffin v. Heard, 78 Tex. 607, 14 S.W. 892 (1890).

Under a state statute providing for the assessment and taxation of bank stockholders upon the value of their shares, but at no greater rate than that assessed upon any other moneyed capital in the hands of individual citizens, where a constitutional amendment had prohibited the taxation of moneyed capital in the hands of individual citizens, any tax on bank shares would be in excess of the rate on moneyed capital in the hands of individual citizens, and therefore is invalid. Bancorporation v. Korzen, 29 Ill. App. 3d 526, 331 N.E.2d 159 (1975).

[2800] Ankeny v. Blakley, 44 Ore. 78, 74 P. 485; Bank v. Miller, 177 N.Y. 461, 69 N.E. 1103.

Banks' bare financial statements, which contained lists of resources including property not subject to taxation, were insufficient descriptions of property on which persons could make demand that the assessor and the county clerk meet with such persons for the purpose of determining the value of the banks' property and fixing a fee pursuant to a statute permitting a taxpayer to collect an award for reporting personal property which has not been assessed. Rottinghaus v. Holder, 550 S.W.2d 462 (Ark. 1977).

While actual and reproduction cost are some evidence of value, constitutional standard, which requires that property tax assessments reflect "true cash value" and standard of General Property Tax Act, which defines that term to mean "the usual soiling price" of property, are market-based. First Fed. Sav. & Loan Ass'n v. City of Flint, 415 Mich. 702, 329 N.W.2d 755 (1982).

For taxation purposes, market value is price which willing buyer would pay willing seller under normal economic conditions. Home Fed. Sav. Bank v. Larimer County Bd. of Equalization, 857 P.2d 562 (Colo. App. 1998).

Market value approach to value mandates that tax appraiser determine probable sales price for property by considering what other properties comparable to subject property actually sold for in marketplace at or about date for which value is sought for subject property. Home Fed. Sav. Bank v. Larimer County Bd. of Equalization, 857 P.2d 562 (Colo. App. 1993).

[2801] Groton Sav. Bank v. Barker, 19 App. Div. 64, 45 N.Y.S. 811, rev'd on other grounds, 154 N.Y. 122, 47 N.E. 1103.

of taxes by substituting figures which, if submitted elsewhere, would result in the loss of its franchise.[2802] Tax-exempt interest income on obligations of the United States could not be taken into consideration in apportioning the taxpayer bank's taxable income under a formula utilized to determine the portion of the financial institution's multi-state business income which could be taxed by Illinois.[2803]

Tangible personal property owned by a bank may not be separately taxed in addition to a tax on the bank's shares of stock even if, under applicable constitutional principles, the legislature could decide to tax banks twice by taxing both their shares and their property where the legislature has not chosen to do so.[2804]

Valuation of Real and Personal Property.—Under an ordinance directing a tax "on all personal property, money, and credits, including all capital stock," the personal property of a bank is to be ascertained by adding to its paid-up capital, stockholders' demand notes for unpaid stock which bear interest and are held by the bank.[2805] Final sentence of statute governing

---

Promise to pay contained in credit agreement was part of the face of recorded mortgages so that mortgages were subject to documentary stamp tax and taxable amount was properly calculated based on maximum loan amount; mortgage document itself as evidence of indebtedness, was being taxed so that recording of mortgage document triggered imposition of documentary stamp tax. Barnett Bank of South Florida v. State, Dep't of Revenue, 571 So. 2d 527 (Fla. App. 1990).

2802 Second Nat'l Bank & Trust Co. v. State Board of Tax Appeals, 114 N.J.L. 573, 178 A. 96.

2803 Continental Ill. Nat'l Bank & Trust Co. v. Lenckos, 102 Ill. 2d 210, 80 Ill. Dec. 81, 464 N.E.2d 1064 (1984).

2804 Cherry River Nat'l Bank v. Lorenson, 406 S.E.2d 714 (W. Va. 1991).

2805 State Bank of Virginia v. Richmond, 79 Va. 113.

County assessor was entitled to place all of bank's personal property on unsecured list, and bank was not entitled to refund of property taxes paid while on incorrect roll, even though bank owned more than $200 worth of real estate in county, such that all personal property would not ordinarily be placed on "unsecured" roll, where assessor demanded list of property from bank and received applicable Department of Revenue forms from bank, on which bank failed to indicate that it owned any real estate in county; assessor had right to rely upon bank's representations. First Interstate Bank v. State Dep't of Revenue, 871 P.2d 1178 (Ariz. Tax 1994).

Fact that statute limiting listing of personal property on unsecured tax roll allows assessor to switch property from unsecured to secured tax rolls and vice versa, under certain circumstances does not authorize county assessor to place personal property on whatever list it deems appropriate; rather, statute simply recognizes that changes may be necessary and are allowable and make. clear that some misplacement will be tolerated for limited period. First

intangible property tax, which does not base the tax on the annual yield of the intangible property, but bases it instead only on the taxable portion thereof which by definition applies a fraction which will vary from association to association and excludes from the intangible property income of the association income or yield derived from obligations of the United States, violated constitutional provision stating that tax on intangible personal property is to be based only on the annual yield.[2806] And real estate owned by a national banking association must not be assessed at a higher percentage than other real estate of the same class and character situated in the county and municipality where the tax is sought to be levied.[2807] While rental income from agricultural preserves under Williamson Act is to be capitalized for assessment purposes, nonliving improvements are to be assessed at fair market value.[2808] In utilizing capitalization of income method to value agricultural preserve land under Williamson Act, the expenses which are deductible in arriving at net income are any ordinary and necessary charges for production and maintenance with exclusion of depletion, debt retirement, interest on funds and taxes.[2809] Under Maryland law, where movable personalty is involved, where income must be earned, or a transfer must occur before a sales or use tax can apply, recordation of the particular tax is a precondition for the generation of a lien.[2810] Colorado's assessment method which valued a producing mineral interest by the past year's production did not create a severance or excise tax on minerals for the purposes of taxing such interests held by the federal land bank.[2811] Furthermore, Colorado's method of assessing mineral interests which valued producing mineral interests by the past year's production was not unlawfully unrelated to "value" as required by the statute permitting taxation of a federal land bank.[2812] Moreover, Colorado, by placing a token one dollar per acre minimum valuation for nonproducing mineral interests, did not violate the federal statute permitting taxation of real estate held by

---

Interstate Bank v. State Dep't of Revenue, 871 P.2d 1178 (Ariz. Tax 1994).

[2806] Jefferson Sav. & Loan Ass'n v. Goldberg, 626 S.W.2d 640 (Mo. 1982).

[2807] 12 U.S.C.S. § 548, prior to amendment effective January 1, 1972; First Nat. Bank v. Albright, 13 N.M. 514, 86 P. 548, aff'd, 208 U.S. 548, 28 S. Ct. 349, 52 L. Ed. 614.

[2808] Bank of America v. County of Fresno, 127 Cal. App. 3d 295, 179 Cal. Rptr. 497(1981).

[2809] Bank of Am. v. County of Fresno, 127 Cal. App. 3d 295, 179 Cal. Rptr. 497(1981).

[2810] Maryland Nat'l Bank v. Mayor of Balt., 723 F.2d 1138 (CA. Md. 1983).

[2811] Federal Land Bank v. Board of County Comm'rs, 788 F.2d 1440 (10th Cir. 1986).

[2812] Federal Land Bank v Board of County Comm'rs, 788 F.2d 1440 (10th Cir. 1986).

federal land bank.[2813] Thus, as long as the interest held by the federal land bank is characterized fairly as real estate, the taxation is reasonably connected to the value, and all such interest owners are treated alike, the system is sufficient under the federal statute permitting taxation of real estate held by the bank.[2814] The assessment of producing leaseholds based upon the selling price of the oil and gas produced from the mineral interest as set out in Colorado's Constitution and statutes is taxation "according to value" within the provision of the Farm Credit Act which waives the federal land bank's immunity from nondiscriminatory state and local taxation.[2815] Additionally, under Colorado law, the flat per acre valuation of mineral interest was to be used only when a better or more ready assessment of actual value was not possible; thus, the requirement of the Farm Credit Act that real estate taxes be imposed according to the value on the mineral interest of the federal instrumentalities did not preclude the application of Colorado's tax to a federal land bank which held nonproducing royalty interest.[2816] Valuation of real property for tax purposes is speculative and arbitrary if based upon a happening of uncertain event rather than upon what the property would fairly and reasonably bring at a present fair sale.[2817] In order to qualify for assessment as farmland, real property must have been used as a farm for two years preceding the tax year in question.[2818] In determining whether property is entitled to a farmland classification for tax assessment purposes, the focus is on the present use of the property.[2819]

[2813] Federal Land Bank v. Board of County Comm'rs, 788 F.2d 1440 (10th Cir. 1986).

[2814] Federal Land Bank v. Board of County Comm'rs, 788 F.2d 1440 (10th Cir. 1986).

[2815] Federal Land Bank v. Board of County Comm'rs, 607 F. Supp. 1137 (D.C. Colo. 1985).

[2816] Federal Land Bank v. Board of County Comm'rs, 607 F. Supp. 1137 (D.C. Colo. 1985).

[2817] Du Page Bank & Trust Co. v. Property Tax Appeal Bd., 104 Ill. Dec. 590, 151 Ill. App. 3d 624, 502 N.E.2d 1250 (1986).

[2818] DuPage Bank & Trust Co. v. Property Tax Appeal Bd., 151 Ill. App. 3d 624, 104 Ill. Dec. 590, 502 N.E.2d 1250 (1986).

[2819] DuPage Bank & Trust Co. v. Property Tax Appeal Bd., 151 Ill. App. 3d 624, 104 Ill. Dec. 590, 502 N.E.2d 1250 (1986).

Trial court erred in applying farmland classification to property, and in reducing assessed valuation for tax purposes on that basis, in the absence of any evidence to establish that subject property was farmed prior to 1981, the tax year in question, and then allowed to lie fallow as farming practice. DuPage Bank & Trust Co. v. Property Tax Appeal Bd., 151 Ill. App. 3d 624, 104 Ill. Dec. 590, 502 N.E.2d 1250 (1986).

Taxpayer failed to establish that assessment of his property was improper under doctrine

Taxpayer's lots in fully developed subdivision containing roads and utilities were to be individually assessed to ascertain true cash value of properties for ad valorem taxation, notwithstanding fact that properties, if assessed together, would have had lower market value.[2820]

Cost to hold lots in a fully developed subdivision, containing roads and utilities, could not be deducted from the market value for the purposes of determining the true cash valuation for ad valorem taxation.[2821]

Valuation of Bank Building.—In computing the value of a federal land bank building for taxation, an assessor must give due weight to the following factors: prior assessments, the book value thereof as reflected in the bank's public statements, the particular use to which it is devoted, the original and reproduction cost thereof less depreciation and values of comparable buildings, as well as the capitalization of the estimated income from the building.[2822] But an assessor's valuation of a bank building at an amount appreciably less than previously agreed on by him and the bank through the

---

of constructive fraud, by comparing assessed valuation of property with that of property classified as farmland or open space, in view of the fact that specially classified property was not comparable with other real property because manner in which its value was determined for tax purposes was different. DuPage Bank & Trust Co. v. Property Tax Appeal Bd., 151 Ill. App. 3d 624, 104 Ill. Dec. 590, 502 N.E.2d 1250 (1986).

Evidence that fair market value of subject property on date of assessment was $2.7 million and that its assessed valuation was $476,060, or approximately 17 percent, which was countywide assessment median, failed to establish that valuation of property was fraudulently excessive. Du Page Bank & Trust Co. v. Property Tax Appeal Bd., 104 Ill. Dec. 590, 151 Ill. App. 3d 624, 502 N.E.2d 1250 (1086).

2820 First Interstate Bank, N.A. v. Department of Revenue, 306 Or. 450, 760 P.2d 880 (1988).

Developer's discount method of appraisal, under which market price of properties is reduced by rate of return based on expected profit, taking into account expected time necessary to sell lots, was not permissible method of valuing taxpayer's lots in fully developed subdivision for purposes of ad valorem taxation; discount method of valuation resulted in determination of properties' value to current owner or their value as investment, which was not market value. Only by valuing property at its highest and best use could true cash value of property be determined. First Interstate Bank, N.A. v. Department of Revenue, 306 Or. 450, 760 P.2d 880 (1988).

2821 First Interstate Bank v. Department of Revenue, 306 Or. 450, 760 P.2d 880 (1988).

2822 **In general.—**

State v. Federal Reserve Bank, 25 F. Supp. 14.

Any of three methods for determining a "true cash value" of assessed property, i.e., market value as determined by comparable selling prices, reproduction cost less depreciation, and capitalization of income, may be used so long as it is reasonably related to

years that it was on the tax rolls, was held not arbitrary or discriminatory.[2823] Under certain state statutes, the rule for valuation of a bank building for purposes of taxation is the full value which could ordinarily be obtained at a private sale.[2824] "Special purpose property," for tax valuation purposes, is

---

fair market valuation and is accurate. First Fed. Sav. & Loan Ass'n v. City of Flint, 104 Mich. App. 609, 305 N.W.2d 553 (1981).

Original cost properly considered but not controlling.—

Original cost of construction is properly to be considered on the question of the valuation for tax purposes, but it is not controlling. Bostian v. Franklin State Bank, 167 N.J. Super. 564, 401 A.2d 549 (1979).

Whether chattels should be treated as realty.—

In a proceeding for the assessment of the real property tax on bank premises, the relevant test as to whether chattels should be treated as realty was whether the removal of the chattels would do irreparable or serious physical injury or damage to the freehold. Bostian v. Franklin State Bank, 167 N.J. Super. 564, 401 A.2d 549 (1979).

Allowance for economic obsolescence.—

Bank's cross appeal from an assessment of real property taxes on bank premises, based on a supposed refusal of the judge of taxation to allow for the economic obsolescence of the premises, was without merit where allowance for obsolescence was factored into the assessor's computations which were accepted by judge of taxation. Bostian v. Franklin State Bank, 167 N.J. Super. 564, 401 A.2d 549 (1979).

Allowance for functional obsolescence.—

Where the record in a proceeding for the assessment of real property taxes on bank premises revealed abundant evidence of overimprovements and features uniquely designed for the special purpose of the home office bank building and which might well not be recoverable as part of the fair market price, remand was necessary to permit the making of findings and conclusions relative to the issue of the functional obsolescence so that the correctness of the decision by the state division of tax appeals to allow nothing for functional obsolescence could be reviewed. Bostian v. Franklin State Bank, 167 N.J. Super. 564, 401 A.2d 549 (1979).

[2823] State v. Federal Reserve Bank, 25 F. Supp. 14.

[2824] State v. Board of Review, 237 Wis. 306, 296 NW 614.

Although, in respect to statutory provisions imposing a tax on the shares of stockholders of banks or banking associations, a company owned a bank building in Augusta which was at one time fully paid for, the company had thereafter borrowed funds, conveying a mortgage on the building as collateral, and therefore the company would not be allowed to deduct the full value of the building rather than just the equity value from the value of its shares. Properly construed, the statute means that the full value of realty may be deducted only when the realty is fully paid for on January 1 of the particular tax year; otherwise, only the equity value may be deducted. Georgia R.R. Bank & Trust Co. v. Richmond County Bd. of Tax Assessors, 142 Ga. App. 417, 236 S.E.2d 95 (1977).

The tax tribunal did not make an error of law or adopt a wrong principle in holding that the cost approach provided the best indication of the value of a building owned by the

property that is treated in market as adapted to or designed and built for a special purpose; a special purpose property becomes such either by its use for unique functions or by distinctive, specially designed structural details.[2825] In light of fact that market value of special purpose property cannot readily be determined by existence of financial market, other methods of valuation of such property for tax purposes must be resorted to, such as reproduction cost.[2826] The value of a building occupied by a savings and loan association did not include the amounts expended for physical improvements that the hearing officer found were made to enhance the bank's "image" or "business," without regard to whether the expenditures added to the "cash" or "usual selling price" of the property.[2827] Expenditures that merely

---

taxpayer, a savings and loan association. First Fed. Sav. & Loan Ass'n v. City of Flint, 104 Mich. App. 609, 305 N.W.2d 553 (1981).

The tax tribunal did not make an error of law or adopt a wrong principle in holding that the assessing municipality was not required to assess the value of taxpayer's building by determining the price which could be obtained on the open market where the building was especially suited for use as a bank building, was not obsolete, and was being used far the particular use for which the building was designed and altered. First Federal Sav. & Loan Asso. v. Flint, 104 Mich. App. 609, 305 N.W.2d 553 (1981).

Constitution and General Property Tax Act do not authorize tax on value of lumber or marble incorporated into building, but on market value of completed structure and land. First Fed. Sav. & Loan Ass'n v. City of Flint, 415 Mich. 702, 329 N.W.2d 755 (1982).

[2825] Federal Reserve Bank v. State, 313 N.W.2d 619 (Mich. 1981).

Building which was specifically designed to meet needs of Federal Reserve Bank and which contained such features as a three-story vault, heliport and firing range, was a "special purpose building" for tax valuation purposes, though it was asserted that most of building could be converted to general office specs and related facilities without substantial modification. Federal Reserve Bank v. State, 313 N.W.2d 619 (Minn. 1981).

Bank could be appraised under cost approach as special purpose building, even if bank was not special purpose in every respect; structure, character, and design of building for use as bank dominated. Empire State Bank v. Lyon County, 454 N.W.2d 616 (Mich. 1990).

Taxpayer failed to establish that its bank in agricultural town was functionally obsolete and that taxpayer was entitled to additional discount in fair market value, even if bank was overbuilt for current economic circumstances; bank still adequately performed function as bank and county did provide discount for economic obsolescence because designated portions of bank were not currently in use. Empire State Bank v. Lyon County, 454 N.W.2d 616 (Minn. 1990).

[2826] Federal Reserve Bank v. State, 313 N.W.2d 619 (Minn. 1981).

In light of fact that Federal Reserve Bank building was a special purpose building, assessor's exclusive reliance on reproduction cost approach in valuing building for real estate purposes was not error. Federal Reserve Bank v. State, 313 N.W.2d 619 (Minn. 1981).

[2827] First Federal Sav. & Loan Ass'n v. Flint, 415 Mich. 702, 329 N.W.2d 755 (1982).

enhance the image or business of the owner do not increase the value for property tax purposes; the only expenditures that do are those that add to the cash value or selling price of the property.[2828]

Deduction of Debts.—In some jurisdictions, statutes authorizing the deduction of bona fide debts from the credits of any person required to list his property for taxation are held inapplicable to banks,[2829] while in others such statutes are held to apply thereto.[2830] But under a statute providing for the taxation of credits, and for the deduction of liabilities not exempt from taxation, bills payable to banks and not taxable to them cannot be so deducted.[2831] In an action for recovery of a tax on moneys in a bank paid under protest, and illegal because debts had not been deducted, an assessment could not be justified on the grounds that the value of the taxpayer's other property had been reduced by the assessor in an amount in excess of the moneys in the bank.[2832] And a statute providing that shares of stockholders in banks shall be deducted where they are taxed in another city or county, is not repealed by implication by an act providing for the payment by banks of taxes assessed against their stockholders.[2833]

Deduction of Losses.—The loss carryover provision of the corporate excise tax is intended to permit the carryover of actual economic losses, and all taxable income is included in determining whether such an actual loss exists for excise tax purposes, including taxable income from state and federal obligations.[2834]

Ordinarily, a corporation may only deduct its capital losses from its capital gains. The Internal Revenue Code, however, provides an exception for banks, which are permitted to deduct capital losses against ordinary

---

[2828] First Fed. Sav. & Loan Ass'n v. City of Flint, 415 Mich. 702, 329 N.W.2d 755 (1982).

[2829] Board of Comm'rs v. Fidelity Sav. Ass'n, 31 Colo. 47, 71 P. 376; Ellis v. Linck, 3 Ohio St. 66; Hewitt v. Traders' Bank, 18 Wash. 326, 51 P. 468; Schoonover v. Petcina, 126 Iowa 261, 100 N.W. 490. See also § 39d of this chapter.

[2830] Daly Bank, etc., Co. v. Board, 33 Mont. 101, 81 P. 950; Clark v. Maher, 34 Mont. 391, 87 P. 272.

[2831] Mortgage, etc., Co. v. New Orleans, 97 So. 44, 153 La. 1073.

[2832] United States Radio Corp. v. Wayne County, 192 Mich. 449, 158 N.W. 1030.

[2833] Treason v. Board of Sup'rs, 120 Va. 203, 90 S.E. 615.

[2834] First Am. Nat'l Bank v. Olsen, 751 S.W.2d 417 (Tenn. 1987).

income.[2835] But where corporation was not a "bank" as it is defined under the Code, it could not offset its capital losses against ordinary income.[2836]

Deduction of Deposits.—In those jurisdictions where bank deposits are taxable to the bank as its property rather than to the depositors, it is generally held that banks, in ascertaining their property for taxation, are not entitled to deduct deposits held by them from their gross assets, moneys and credits.[2837] In the case of savings banks, however, it is held in some jurisdictions that for the purpose of ascertaining the amount of property of a savings bank for taxation, the amount of its deposits is deducted from its gross assets.[2838] And under a statute providing that private bankers shall list for taxation their money on hand, in transit and in the hands of others subject to draft, except treasury notes, and their bills receivable and other credits, and that from this total deduct their amount of "money on deposit," it has been held that private bankers are entitled to deduct the full amount due their depositors, though part of the money deposited may be treasury notes, "money on deposit" meaning general deposits, not special deposits held by a bank as a bailee.[2839]

Deduction or Consideration of Taxes Paid.—At least one state statute directs the deduction of certain taxes paid by savings banks on their real

---

[2835] Moneygram Int'l v. Comm'r, 664 Fed. Appx. 386 (5th Cir. 2016). See 26 U.S.C.S. § 581.

[2836] Moneygram Int'l v. Comm'r, 664 Fed. Appx. 386 (5th Cir. 2016). See 26 U.S.C.S. § 582.

[2837] Security, etc., Trust Co. v. Hinton, 97 Cal. 214, 32 P. 3; Bank v. Oxford, 70 Miss. 504, 12 So. 203; Ellis v. Linck, 3 Ohio St. 66; Bank of Metropolis v. Weber, 41 F. 413; Suffolk Sav. Bank v. Commonwealth, 151 Mass. 103, 23 N.E. 728.

Savings bank's investments in pass-through certificates were "loans secured by the mortgage of real estate," within plain and ordinary meaning of express words of statute providing that savings bank could deduct the amount of the unpaid balances of such loans from average amount of deposits or savings accounts and share capital in calculating excise tax owed, as bank acquired pro rata share of various such loans, where funds expended by bank in acquiring pass-through certificated replaced funds of original mortgage lender, certificates evidenced bank's possession of undivided beneficial interest in pool of loans secured by mortgages, and bank was entitled to receive payments of principal and interest collected by servicing entity from individual mortgagors, and was entitled to receive benefit of any prepayments of principal. South Boston Sav. Bank v. Commissioner, 418 Mass. 695, 640 N.E2d 462 (1994).

[2838] Bridgeport Sav. Bank v. Barker, 154 N.Y. 128, 47 N.E. 973; Groton Sav. Bank v. Barker, 19 App. Div. 64, 45 N.Y.S. 811, rev'd on other grounds, 154 N.Y. 122, 47 N.E. 1103.

[2839] Griffin v. Heard, 78 Tex. 607, 14 S.W. 892 (1890).

estate.[2840] And it has been held that a franchise tax commissioner in setting the bank tax rate of national banks properly included in his computations personal property taxes paid by cooperatives.[2841]

Nature of Taxable Activity.—Where no agreement between the consumer and the out-of-state dealer existed, nor did the consumer know of the existence or identity of out-of-state dealer or did dealer know of existence or identity of consumer, and the dealer charged the bank for Krugerrands and delivered them to the bank and the bank in turn charged the consumer and was paid by the consumer, whereupon it delivered coins to the consumer, there was a sale of coins by the out-of-state coin dealer to the bank and resale at retail by the bank to the consumer for consideration, the latter transfer of ownership being a taxable event upon which the bank was obligated to pay sales tax, despite the contention that the bank was only a conduit between consumer and the coin dealer in light of its maintaining no inventory of coins.[2842]

§ 44. Valuation of Franchises and Privileges.

A franchise tax imposed upon savings banks in proportion to their average deposits is for the privilege of continuing their business as corporations, and the amount thereof may be fixed on such basis as the state legislature may prescribe.[2843] Cases construing various state franchise tax statutes will be found in the footnote.[2844]

[2840] Savings Bank v. Wilcox, 117 Conn. 188, 167 A. 709; Savings Bank of Rockville v. Wilcox, 117 Conn. 196, 167 A. 713.

Savings bank, in making tax return in 1982, held not entitled to deduct back taxes paid on lands acquired through mortgage foreclosures and assessed against farmer owners in years preceding year 1930. Savings Bank v. Wilcox, 117 Conn. 188, 167 A. 709.

[2841] Security-First Nat'l Bank v. Franchise Tax Board, 55 Cal. 2d 407, 11 Cal. Rptr. 289, 359 P.2d 625, appeal dismissed and cert. denied, 368 U.S. 3, 82 S. Ct. 15, 7 L. Ed. 2d 16.

Amount of personal property taxes of nonfinancial corporations to be considered by franchise tax commissioner in setting bank tax rate of national banks is amount required to be paid by nonfinancial corporations rather than amount which assessors properly should have required nonfinancial corporations to pay. Security-First Nat'l Bank v. Franchise Tax Board, 55 Cal. 2d 407, 11 Cal. Rptr. 289, 359 P.2d 625, appeal dismissed and cert. denied, 368 U.S. 3, 82 S. Ct. 15, 7 L. Ed. 2d 16.

[2842] Michigan Nail Bank v. Department of Tress., 339 N.W.2d 515 (Mich. App. 1983).

[2843] State v. Franklin County Sav. Bank & Trust Co., 74 Vt. 246, 52 A. 1069; Westminster v. Westminster Sav. Bank, 92 Md. 62, 48 A. 34; Bank v. Miller, 84 App. Div. 168, 82 N.Y.S. 621, modified, 177 N.Y. 461, 69 N.E. 1103.

[2844] *Iowa.*—Literal interpretation of taxation statutes so as to allow a national bank to use, in its computation of the state franchise tax imposed by a statute enacted in 1970, the interest

(Text continued on page 800)

---

deduction allowed on its federal income tax return pursuant to the Internal Revenue Service agreement authorizing the bank to deduct from its taxable income for a period often years, commencing with 1969 taxable year, 10 percent of the interest previously reported as income, did not result in absurd, impractical or unreasonable consequences, notwithstanding contentions that such interpretation was absurd because it was affected by events which occurred prior to the first taxable year in which the state franchise tax was in existence, thus making the statute retroactive, that it ignored the concept of the taxable year and that it allowed the taxpayer to escape the tax by using the IRS agreement which was intended only to avoid double tax. First Nat'l Bank v. Bair, 252 N.W.2d 723 (Iowa 1977).

Louisiana.—Short-term liabilities are not "borrowed capital," within meaning of statute providing for deduction from franchise tax base of holding corporation of amount of its investments and advances to its subsidiary banking corporation, but only to extent that they exceed difference between holding corporation's total assets on the one hand and capital stock, surplus, undivided profits, and borrowed capital on the other. McNamara v. First Commerce Corp., 442 So. 2d 1266 (La. App. 4 Cir. 1988).

Maryland.—Savings and loan association could not report a negative taxable income on its state franchise tax form, to the extent that this would permit it to claim a double benefit for its net operating losses by claiming losses in both the taxable and carryover years. State Dep't of Assmts. & Taxation v. Loyola Fed. Sav. & Loan Ass'n, 79 Md. App. 481, 558 A.2d 428 (1989).

Massachusetts.—Attleboro Trust Co. v. Commissioner of Corps. & Taxation, 257 Mass. 43, 153 N.E. 333; Tower Co. v. Commonwealth, 223 Mass. 371, 111 N.E. 966; Boston R. Holding Co. v. Commonwealth, 215 Mass. 493, 102 N.E. 650, 1914D Ann. Cas. 621; United States Trust Co. v. Commonwealth, 245 Mass. 75, 139 N.E. 794.

The excise imposed by a Massachusetts statute on savings and cooperative banks and federal savings and loan associations is a franchise tax" and not a tax on gross receipts and is a type of tax authorized by federal statute, though measured in part by income, and even if it be considered a tax on income, the excise, which is directed against net operating income rather than gross income, is authorized; payments of interest or dividends need not be deducted for the purpose of arriving at a tax on income or a franchise tax authorized by Congress. First Federal Sav. & Loan Asso. v. State Tax Com., 363 N.E.2d 474 (Mass. 1977).

Missouri.—For franchise tax, tax base of corporation doing business solely in state should never be less than par value of corporation's outstanding shares of stock. Boatmen's Bancshares, Inc. v. Director of Revenue, 757 S.W.2d 574 (Mo. 1988).

For franchise tax, "surplus" is defined as the excess of assets employed in the business over the par value of outstanding capital stock. Boatmen's Bancshares, Inc. v. Director of Revenue, 757 S.W.2d 574 (Mo. 1988).

New York.—Under statute dealing with computation, by domestic banking corporation, of the "alternative minimum tax base," to be used in determining franchise tax liability, computation of amount of interest deemed to have been paid to depositors called for computation of simple interest, credited annually, and not compound interest. American Sav. Bank v. State Tax Comm'n, 469 N.Y.S.2d 299 (N.Y. Sup. Ct. 1983).

Under statute dealing with computation, by domestic banking corporation, of "alternative minimum tax base," principal to which ceiling rate of 8.5 percent was to be applied was to

(Text continued on page 800)

---

consist solely of amount of deposits furnished by depositor during year, without regard to actual interest payment, computed and accrued by bank, and such principal excluded interest payments actually earned and subsequently forfeited because of premature withdrawal. American Sav. Bank v. State Tax Comm'n, 469 N.Y.S.2d 299 (N.Y. Sup. Ct. 1983).

Oklahoma.—The reserve for bad debt method of accounting was not prohibited by the tax statute and was available to national banks in computing franchise tax. Oklahoma Tax Com. v. Liberty Nat'l Bank & Trust Co. (Okla.), 289 P.2d 388.

Pennsylvania.—Notwithstanding provisions of statute making interest from certain obligations tax exempt, franchise or excise taxes may be measured by property, including obligations of United States and Commonwealth, or income therefrom, which could not, of itself, be amenable to direct property tax. Philadelphia Sav. Fund Soc'y v. Commonwealth, 467 A.2d 420 (Pa. Commw. 1983).

Notwithstanding provisions of statute making interest from certain obligations tax exempt, franchise or excise taxes may be measured by property, including obligations of United States and Commonwealth, or income therefrom, which could not, of itself, be amenable to direct property tax. Philadelphia Sav. Fund Soc'y v. Commonwealth, 487 A.2d 420 (Pa. Commw. 1983). For purpose of determining whether certain governmental obligations are exempt from all taxation except inheritance and estate taxes, property tax on income is distinguished from franchise tax on privilege of doing business in Commonwealth in that in case of franchise tax, it is not interest per so that is being taxed, but privilege of doing business, and measure of that tax is net income or earnings of taxable entity from all sources. Philadelphia Sav. Fund Soc'y v. Commonwealth, 467 A.2d 420 (Pa. Commw. 1983).

South Dakota.—The statute imposing a tax on a bank or finance corporation's privilege of doing business within the state establishes a scheme of apportionment of net income which applies indifferently to foreign and domestic corporations, and was intended to relate the excise tax to the actual value of the privilege granted, and thus exact something in the nature of a quid pro quo. Northwest Finance Co. v. Nord, 70 S.D. 549, 19 N.W.2d 578 (1945).

Under the statute, income from operation of business in another state and from intangibles which have acquired a business situs in that state is excluded from the privilege tax base, whereas income of domestic financial corporation, engaged in business wholly within the state, from intangibles located elsewhere but not having a business situs outside of state, follows residence of recipient. Northwest Finance Co. v. Nord, 70 S.D. 549, 19 N.W.2d 578 (1945).

Income of branch operated as a separate and distinct business in North Dakota was subject to provision that persons engaged in business within and without the state should be taxed only on such income as is derived from business transacted within the state, rather than provision that income derived from land contracts, mortgages, stocks, bonds, and securities, or from the sale of similar intangible personalty should follow residence of recipient, and hence should not be included. Northwest Finance Co. v. Nord, 70 S.D. 549, 19 N.W.2d 578 (1945).

Tennessee.—Federal law does not include obligations of the United States being included in the tax base for both a franchise tax and an excise tax, even when corporation is subject to both taxes. First Am. Nat'l Bank v. Olsen, 751 S.W.2d 417 (Tenn. 1987).

Texas.—State comptroller of public accounts correctly ruled that, under the location of the

§ 45. Valuation of Capital or Capital Stock.

While the precise method of valuing capital or capital stock of banks for taxation purposes varies in different states, the usual method is to assess same at its actual value,[2845] after deducting therefrom the value of their exempt property[2846] or property otherwise taxed.[2847]

---

payer rule, the interest and dividends derived from national banks located in Texas were includable in the corporate payee's Texas gross receipts for the purpose of assessing the franchise tax since to hold otherwise would mean that the Texas legislature intended to continue the unequal treatment between the recipients of income from state banks and the recipients of income from national banks, and the legislature merely intended to preserve the status quo in reference to the taxation of banks, both national and state, until it chose to impose additional taxation at a later time. Bullock v. National Bancshares Corp., 584 S.W.2d 268 (Tex. 1979).

Washington.—Savings and loan association, which had its home office in Washington but which did business at offices in both Washington and Oregon, which was required by federal regulation to keep a percentage of its deposits in liquid funds, including short-term investments, and which invested such funds exclusively at its home office, was entitled to apportion the income earned on such investments between the states of Washington and Oregon for the purpose of the business occupation tax. Oregon branches "contributed" to performance of the service, i.e., short-term investment, by supplying approximately one-half the funds employed. Pacific First Federal Sav. & Loan Asso. v. State, 92 Wash. 2d 402, 598 P.2d 387 (1979).

Delaware.—

The measure of the franchise tax depends importantly on whether the banking organization is domiciled in Delaware. Under Del. Code Ann. tit. 5, § 1101(a), a federal savings bank with its principal office in Delaware is taxed on all its taxable income. But, under line 4(b) of its return, a bank may deduct from its reported income the portion that was earned from activities conducted outside Delaware by branches or subsidiaries subject to income taxation under the laws of another state, a line 4(b) deduction. Under Del. Code Ann. tit. 5, § 1101(b), a federal savings bank not headquartered in Delaware is subject to a more limited bank franchise tax, imposed only on the income of the bank's Delaware branches or subsidiaries, if any. The Delaware bank franchise tax statute does not define the terms principal office or headquartered. Under § 1101(a)(1)(b)(2), a Delaware bank with out-of-state branches and subsidiaries may reduce its taxable income by that portion of the net operating income before taxes, verifiable by documentary evidence which is derived from business activities carried on outside Delaware and subject to income taxation under the laws of another state. Lehman Bros. Bank, FSB v. State Bank Comm'r, 937 A.2d 95, 2007 Del. LEXIS 496 (Del. 2007).

2845 *Colorado.*—Board of Comm'rs v. Murray, 71 Colo. 522, 208 P. 472.

Georgia.—Daniel v. Bank of Clayton County, 154 Ga. 282, 114 S.E. 210.

Idaho.—Weiser Nat'l Bank v. Washington County, 30 Idaho 332, 164 P. 1014.

Iowa.—Citizens' State Bank v. Burke, 188 N.W. 677.

Mississippi.—Bank of Commerce v. Adams County, 130 Miss. 37, 93 So. 442;

(Text continued on page 803)

Merchants', etc., Bank v. Kosciusko, 149 Miss. 835, 116 So. 88.

A bank's "capital stock and surplus" for taxation is difference between aggregate true value of realty and total true value of assets, including land and personalty. Board of Sup'rs v. Riverside Bank, 158 Miss. 653, 131 So. 80; National Bank v. Board of Sup'rs, 159 Miss. 62, 132 So. 95.

Nebraska.—Peters Trust Co. v. Douglas County, 113 Neb. 596, 203 N.W. 1001; In re First Trust Co., 93 Neb. 795, 142 N.W. 542; Nemaha County Bank v. County Board, 103 Neb. 53, 170 N.W. 500; In re Citizens State Bank, 110 Neb. 704, 194 N.W. 796; In re Assessment of State Bank, 95 Neb. 665, 146 N.W. 1046.

New Hampshire.—Word "annually" in statute governing tax assessment of banks based on capital stock owned by banks is used to require the Board of Tax and Land Appeals to annualize such assessments; thus, tax assessments on banks established only a few months before such assessments should have been prorated to reflect only that portion of the year during which banks were in operation, and since they were not, banks were entitled to tax abatement. In re Village Bank & Trust Co., 471 A.2d 1187 (N.H. 1984).

New Jersey.—People's Bank, etc., Co. v. Passaic County Board, 90 N.J.L. 171, 100 A. 155.

Ohio.—Milford Nat. Bank v. Searles, 9 Ohio App. 76.

Pennsylvania.—Commonwealth v. Semet-Solvay Co., 262 Pa. 234, 105 A. 92.

Either "accrual basis" or "cash basis" accounting is valid for purposes of measuring the actual value of the subject bank's stock in order to determine the shares tax liability, but the responsibility rests with the department of revenue to make such valuation, a task in which it is accorded substantial discretion. First Nat'l Bank v. Commonwealth, 396 A.2d 909 (Pa. Commw. Ct. 1979).

For purposes of a bank shares tax, the test of actual value is what is a reasonable sum which will reflect the material worth of the assets. So long as the determination of the actual value of the asset at a given date is based on the facts and reasonable indicia of material worth, the action of the department of revenue will not be disturbed. First Nat'l Bank v. Commonwealth, 396 A.2d 909 (Pa. Commw. Ct. 1979).

For the purposes of a bankshares tax, the taxing authority may not arbitrarily assign values to the bank's assets contrary to that supplied by the bank in its shares tax return. First Nat'l Bank v. Commonwealth, 396 A.2d 909 (Pa. Commw. Ct. 1979).

On a claim by a bank for a refund of part of the share, tax on the basis of a reduction of reported value of the shares for the "Reserve for Declared but Unpaid Dividends" and the "Reserve for Taxes," the board of finance and revenue and the department of revenue properly denied an attempt by the bank to mix concepts peculiar to cash basis and accrual accounting principles on its bank's shares tax return. First Nat'l Bank v. Commonwealth, 396 A.2d 909 (Pa. Commw. Ct. 1979).

Utah.—Tax Commission finding of 25 percent expense ratio in determination of fair value of commercial office building under income approach to value method was not supported by substantial evidence. First Nat'l Bank v. County Bd. of Equalization, 799 P.2d 1163 (Utah 1990).

Wisconsin.—State v. Leuch, 155 Wis. 500, 144 N.W. 1122.

(Text continued on page 803)

Pennsylvania.—The Pennsylvania Shares Tax, as set forth in Article VII of the Tax Reform Code, 72 P.S. §§ 7701–7706, is imposed on the taxable amount of a banking institution's shares of capital stock. Although intended to tax current value, in order to mitigate the effect of year to year fluctuations, the statute mandates in 72 P.S. § 7701.1(a), that the taxable amount of shares is based upon an average share value, which is determined using the current year share value and the share values for the preceding five years. Leb. Valley Farmers Bank v. Commonwealth, 27 A.3d 288 (Pa. Commw. Ct. 2011), rev'd, 623 Pa. 455, 83 A.3d 107 (2013).

(Pursuant to 72 P.S. § 9979-C, Article VII shall terminate on December 31, 2022.)

The averaging provision of 72 P.S. § 7701.1(a) of the Shares Tax was not unconstitutional due to a lack of uniformity under Pa. Const. art. VIII, § 1 because the short-term disparity of result was warranted based on sufficiently distinguishable situations that warranted distinguishable results with respect to a merger or combination of two institutions that had both been previously taxed on their historic average values compared to a combination that introduced previously untaxable assets to the calculation. Leb. Valley Farmers Bank v. Commonwealth, 623 Pa. 455, 83 A.3d 107 (2013). (Pursuant to 72 P.S. § 9979-C, Article VII shall terminate on December 31, 2022.)

2846 *Idaho.*—Washington County v. First Nat. Bank, 35 Idaho 438, 206 P. 1054.

Indiana.—Sims v. Fletcher Sav., etc., Co., 194 Ind. 93, 142 N.E. 121.

Iowa.—Campbell v. Centerville, 69 Iowa 439, 29 N.W. 596; Lamont Sav. Bank v. Luther, 200 Iowa 180, 204 N.W. 430.

Louisiana.—First Nat'l Bank v. Board of Reviewers, 41 La. Ann. 181, 5 So. 408.

Maryland.—Hess v. Westminster Sav. Bank, 134 Md. 125, 106 A. 263.

Massachusetts.—Lexington Sav. Bank v. Commonwealth, 252 Mass. 180, 147 N.E. 569.

Michigan.—A national bank's purchase of shares of safe deposit company for purpose of having safe deposit business operated adjacent to its banking offices was an investment of capital, surplus, and undivided profit, and amount thereof should have been deducted in assessing capital stock tax. Manufacturers Nat. Bank v. Detroit, 292 Mich. 31, 289 N.W. 318.

Where it could have been determined from national bank's records with reasonable certainty that bank's investment in tax-free government securities represented an investment of capital, surplus, and undivided profits, board of assessors erroneously made capital stock tax assessment upon proportion rule theory. Manufacturers Nat. Bank v. Detroit, 292 Mich. 31, 289 N.W. 318.

Minnesota.—In re Farmers' State Bank, 160 Minn. 320, 200 N.W. 89.

Mississippi.—Bank of Tupelo v. Board of Sup'rs, 155 Miss. 436, 124 So. 482.

Missouri.—State v. Gehner, 319 Mo. 1048, 5 S.W.2d 40.

Nebraska.—In re First Nat. Bank, 103 Neb. 280, 171 N.W. 912; In re Assessment of State Bank, 95 Neb. 665, 146 N.W. 1046; Seward v. Cattle, 14 Neb. 144, 15 N.W. 337.

2847 *Idaho.*—First Nat'l Bank v. Board of Comm'rs, 40 Idaho 391, 232 P. 905.

New Jersey.—Camden v. Camden Safe Deposit & Trust Co., 84 N.J.L. 37, 85 A. 1026.

The "shares tax" in Pennsylvania is set forth in the Pennsylvania Tax Reform Code; it is imposed on the average taxable amount of a banking institution's shares of capital stock. Calculation of the tax is based on the book value of the bank's net assets (adjusted to deduct value attributable to

---

New York.—Savings Bank v. Coleman, 135 N.Y. 231, 31 N.E. 1022.

Texas.—Traditional concept of "market value" is irrelevant in determining value of bank shares for tax purposes since market value of bank's assets would necessarily be based on consideration of government obligations held by bank, with result that tax computation based on such market value would necessarily run afoul of federal statute which prohibits state or municipal or local authorities from taxing federal obligations. Charles Schreiner Bank v. Kerrville Indep. School Dist., 683 S.W.2d 466 (Tax. App. 4. Dist. 1984).

Washington.—Scandinavian-American Bank v. Pierce County, 85 Wash. 348, 148 P. 18.

Indiana.—State Bank v. Brackenridge, 7 Blackf. 395.

Iowa.—First Nat. Bank v. Albia, 86 Iowa 28, 52 N.W. 334; Campbell v. Centerville, 69 Iowa 439, 29 N.W. 596.

Louisiana.—First Nat'l Bank v. Board of Reviewers, 41 La. Ann. 181, 5 So. 408.

Nebraska.—In re First Trust Co., 93 Neb. 795, 142 N.W. 542; In re Citizens State Bank, 110 Neb. 704, 194 N.W. 796.

New Jersey.—Myers v. Campbell, 64 N.J.L. 186, 44 A. 863.

The provision of Bank Stock Tax Act for deduction of assessed valuation of real estate owned by bank having been designed to prevent double taxation of real estate, assessed value of that real estate which was not computed originally in computation of value of taxable shares is not deductible. Bank of Passaic & Trust Co. v. Passaic County, 25 N.J. Misc. 470, 55 A.2d 455 (1947).

An equitable title will satisfy the requirement of ownership of real estate, assessed value of which bank desire, deducted in computing value of bank stock for tax purposes. Bank of Passaic & Trust Co. v. Passaic County, 25 N.J. Misc. 470, 55 A.2d 455 (1947).

Where bank contracted for purchase of real estate in December but did not pay purchase price until February, when title passed, and did not carry property on its books as its real estate of January 1, real estate did not represent investment of part of capital, surplus and undivided profits of bank as of January 1, so as to have been necessarily included in computation of value of shares for bank stock. And assessed valuation of such real estate could not be deducted in such computation, notwithstanding that bank had an equitable title. Bank of Passaic & Trust Co. v. Passaic County, 25 N.J. Misc. 470, 55 A.2d 455 (1947).

New York.—People ex rel. Tradesmen's Nat'l Bank v. Commissioners of Taxes & Assessments, 69 N.Y. 91; Jenkins v. Neff 163 N.Y. 320, 57 N.E. 408, aff'd, 186 U.S. 230, 22 S. Ct. 905, 46 L Ed. 1140; Savings Bank v. Coleman, 135 N.Y. 231, 31 N.E. 1022.

Texas.—"Equity capital formula," that is, computing tax by determining total amount of capital assets and subtracting from that figure the liabilities and assessed value of real estate owned, is usual and customary method used in state to arrive at value of shares of bank stock for property tax purposes. Charles Schreiner Bank v. Kerrville Independent School Dist., 683 S.W.2d 466 (Tex. App. 4 Dist. 1984).

United States obligations).[2848] The Pennsylvania shares tax is imposed only upon "institutions," which is defined to include every bank operating as such and having capital stock which is incorporated under any law of this Commonwealth, under the law of the United States or under the law of any other jurisdiction and is located within this Commonwealth. Thus, an out-of-state bank is not an "institution" for purposes of the shares tax, and thus, is not subject to the tax.[2849]

§ 46. Determination of Amount of Deposits.

A taxpayer's money on deposit in a bank subject to withdrawal on demand is not a "credit," and for taxation purposes, the taxpayer's debts may not be deducted therefrom.[2850] And funds of a receiver of an insolvent private bank deposited subject to the receiver's order in other banks, have been held assessable under a state statute, such funds being "money on hand," not "funds in the hands of other banks, bankers, brokers, or others subject to draft," to be listed under such statute as credits.[2851] Negotiable demand notes are not assessable ad valorem under a statute taxing "money on hand or on deposit."[2852]

§ 47. Valuation of Surplus and Undivided Profits.

The total of a bank's undivided profits, surplus and accumulations which it reports to a tax assessor should be the actual total of such items, not that carried on its books in case the latter is fictitious.[2853] And a bank is not entitled to withhold from assessment a part of its undivided profits as a reserve to make good possible losses from bad debts which it may never incur.[2854] But it has been held that under a statute requiring savings banks to

---

[2848] Leb. Valley Farmers Bank v. Commonwealth, 623 Pa. 455, 83 A.3d 107 (2013). (Pursuant to 72 P.S. § 9979-C, Article VII of the Pennsylvania Tax Reform Code shall terminate on December 31, 2022.)

[2849] Leb. Valley Farmers Bank v. Commonwealth, 623 Pa. 455, 83 A.3d 107 (2013). See 72 P.S. § 7701.5. (Pursuant to 72 P.S. § 9979-C, Article VII of the Pennsylvania Tax Reform Code shall terminate on December 31, 2022.)

[2850] HAGERTY v. McNEILL, 7 Ohio C.C. 388, 4 Ohio C. Dec. 647, rev'd on other grounds, 51 Ohio St. 255, 37 N.E. 526; White v. Lincoln, 79 Neb. 153, 112 N.W. 369; Gray v. Street Comm'rs of Boston, 138 Mass. 414.

As to deduction of debts generally, see § 89a of this chapter.

[2851] Bond v. Moore, 300 Ill. 32, 132 N.E. 777.

[2852] Hedges v. Shipp, 166 Tuna. 451, 62 S.W.2d 49.

[2853] Bank of Commerce v. Adams County, 130 Miss. 37, 93 So. 442.

[2854] Bank of Arizona v. Howe, 293 F. 600.

pay a certain annual tax on the par value of their surplus and undivided earnings, bonds and securities in which such surplus is invested must be appraised at their market value whenever such value is less than their par value.[2855] And a state, in taxing as credits the surplus of a savings bank, must omit from the computation of its assets, bonds issued by territorial municipalities which are exempt from taxation.[2856]

d. Valuation of Shares.

§ 48. In General.

General Consideration.—It is the general rule that shares of bank stock should be assessed at their full and true market value,[2857] and that it is

---

[2855] Bank v. Miller, 177 N.Y. 461, 69 N.E. 1103; State v. Clement Nat'l Bank, 84 Vt. 167, 78 A. 944, 1912D Ann. Cas. 22; Smith v. Stephens, 173 Ind. 564, 91 N.E. 167, 30 L.R.A. (n.s.) 704.

[2856] Farmers & Mechanics Sav. Bank v. Minnesota, 232 U.S. 516, 34 S. Ct. 354, 58 L. Ed. 706.

[2857] **In general.—**

United States.—People's Nat'l Bank v. Marye, 107 F. 570, modified, 191 U.S. 272, 24 S. Ct. 68, 48 L. Ed. 180.

Arizona.—Gibbons v. White, 47 Ariz. 180, 54 P.2d 555, holding that true cash value depends primarily upon earning power of stock and difference between assets and liabilities of bank.

Maryland.—Schley v. Montgomery County Comm'rs, 106 Md. 407, 67 A. 250.

Mississippi.—Bank of Oxford v. Lafayette County, 79 Miss. 152, 29 So. 825 (1901).

Missouri.—State ex rel. Gracy v. Catron, 118 Mo. 280, 24 S.W. 439; St. Louis Bldg. & Sav. Asso. v. Lightner, 47 Mo. 393.

Montana.—Montana Nat'l Bank v. Yellowstone County, 78 Mont. 62, 252 P. 876.

New Jersey.—Stratton v. Collins, 43 N.J.L. 562; Newark v. Tunis, 81 N.J.L. 45, 78 A. 1066, aff'd, 82 N.J.L. 461, 81 A. 722.

New York.—People v. Assessors, 2 Hun 583

North Carolina.—Pullen v. Corporation Com., 152 N.C. 548, 68 S.E. 155.

Ohio.—Cleveland Trust Co. v. Lander, 62 Ohio St. 266, 56 N.E. 1036, aff'd, 184 U.S. 111, 22 S. Ct. 394, 46 L. Ed. 456.

Oregon.—Ankeny v. Blakley, 44 Ore. 78, 74 P. 485.

Washington.—Bank of Fairfield v. Spokane County, 173 Wash. 145, 22 P.2d 646.

Assessor not to adopt only one method.—Under the West Virginia statute bank shares are to be assessed "at their true and actual value" to be ascertained according to the best information obtainable. And the assessor is not required or authorized to adopt a single arbitrary method, even though in the majority of cases such method proves more accurate than any other single method. In re National Bank, 137 W. Va. 673, 73 S.E.2d 655 (1952).

erroneous to assess them at their par value when their actual or market value

---

Selling price is not the sole criterion of true value of bank stock for purposes of taxation. Second Nat. Bank, etc., Co. v. State Board, 114 N.J.L. 573, 178 A. 96.

Averaging methodology.—

The averaging methodology set forth in Article VII of the Tax Reform Code, 72 P.S. §§ 7701–7706, is intended to provide a more reliable reflection of the value of shares to be taxed in the current year; it discourages a bank from manipulating its holdings of federal obligations so as to artificially reduce its tax liability and minimizes the effect of random disturbances in value. However, the averaging method produces a reliable and, over time, accurate reflection of share values only in the first merger scenario described above, or for an institution which has not been involved in a merger. On the other hand, the averaging methodology required by 72 P.S. § 7701.1(a) to calculate the taxable amount of shares results in an arbitrary reduced value which does not provide a reliable or accurate reflection of the share value sought to be taxed. Consequently, to the extent that the averaging provision set forth in § 7701.1(a) renders an artificially low tax base for only certain taxpayers, it frustrates the purpose of using a historical average share value, is unconstitutional and cannot be employed. That conclusion, however, does not mandate that the averaging provision be completely stricken from the Tax Code. Nor must the averaging requirement be stricken in every instance of merger. Public policy favors severability. Leb. Valley Farmers Bank v. Commonwealth, 27 A.3d 288 (Pa. Commw. Ct. 2011), rev'd, 623 Pa. 455, 83 A.3d 107 (2013). (Article VII of the Tax Reform Code and all benefits associated with Article VII shall terminate on December 31, 2022, pursuant to 72 P.S. § 9979-C).

The averaging methodology required by Article VII of the Tax Reform Code, 72 P.S. § 7701.1(a), can be severed or limited when the taxable amount of shares results from the merger of an institution with a non-institution or an institution that has been in existence for fewer than six years without rendering the remainder of the Shares Tax incapable of execution. Precluding application of § 7701.1(a) in those limited circumstances furthers the intent of the statutory scheme, which is to impose the tax on an amount which is a reliable reflection of an institution's share value, while allowing the benefits of six-year averaging to continue in the in-state merger or non-merger situations. That the Shares Tax remains capable of execution without the averaging provision is evident by the fact that prior to 1990, the taxable amount of shares was calculated based upon the data from a single year. Section 7701.1(b) provides the manner in which each year's taxable amount of shares shall be determined. Leb. Valley Farmers Bank v. Commonwealth, 27 A.3d 288 (Pa. Commw. Ct. 2011), 623 Pa. 455, 83 A.3d 107 (2013).

(Article VII of the Tax Reform Code and all benefits associated with Article VII shall terminate on December 31, 2022, pursuant to 72 P.S. § 9979-C).

To the extent the Commonwealth Court of Pennsylvania's decision in First Union National Bank v. Commonwealth, 867 A.2d 711 (Pa. Commw. Ct. 2005), sanctions use of the six-year averaging methodology to calculate taxable amount of shares following a merger of an institution with an out-of-state bank or an institution fewer than six years old, it is overruled. Leb. Valley Farmers Bank v. Commonwealth, 27 A.3d 288 (Pa. Commw. Ct. 2011), rev'd, 623 Pa. 455, 83 A.3d 107 (2013).

(Article VII of the Tax Reform Code and all benefits associated with Article VII shall terminate on December 31, 2022, pursuant to 72 P.S. § 9979-C).

(Text continued on page 808)

Statute makes market value sale criterion.—

Under Tennessee statute requiring that shares of bank stock be assessed for taxes at not less than "actual cash value" thereof, computed by considering market value and, if none, actual value of shares or any other evidence of value thereof, market value of bank stock, shown to have such value, should be the test in making assessment, without considering other elements. Knoxville v. Hamilton Nat'l Bank, 179 Tenn. 332, 165 S.W.2d 937.

Book value not sole criterion.—

Under the Pennsylvania statute which imposes tax on "actual value' of capital shares of banks, "actual value" includes unrecognized appreciation in value of shares, and is not limited to the book value at which bank, in accordance with sound accounting principles, valued shares. Commonwealth v. Butler County Nat. Bank, 376 Pa. 66, 101 A.2d 699.

In determining tax assessment against shares of banks and industrial loan associations, all pertinent methods or evidence obtainable must be considered and neither the sale, price method nor the book vain. method is to be used exclusively. In re National Bank, 137 W. Va. 673, 73 S.E.2d 655 (1952).

Use of book value upheld.—

Where nothing in statute required fiscal officers of commonwealth to accept values prevailing in market for VA and FHA mortgages unless so doing contributed to more accurate determination of actual value of bank's shares, and bank's actual experience with these mortgages did not justify any such conclusion, commonwealth's procedures for taxing VA and FHA mortgage loans at book value contributed to a more accurate determination of actual value of bank's shares and should be sustained. Commonwealth v. Mellon Nat'l Bank & Trust Co., 420 Pa. 393, 217 A.2d 391 (1966).

Where commonwealth's procedures for taxing VA and FHA mortgage loans at book value contributed to more accurate determination of actual value of bank's shares, commonwealth was also correct in adding bank sums consisting of discounts on mortgages purchased from other lenders, since only in this way would their face value be reflected in computation of tax. Commonwealth v. Mellon Nat'l Bank & Trust Co., 420 Pa. 393, 217 A.2d 391 (1986).

Stock assessed at full par value held assessed at greater than actual value. Freeborn County v. First Nat. Bank, 199 Minn. 29, 270 N.W. 908.

Assessment at higher percentage of value than other property in taxing unit.—

A bank whose shares of stock are assessed at one hundred percent of true and actual value, while other property in the taxing unit is systematically assessed at a lower percentage of its true and actual value, is entitled to have its assessment reduced to comply with the provisions of the West Virginia constitution requiring uniformity of taxation. Re Stock Kanawha Valley Bank, 144 W. Va. 346, 109 S.E.2d 649.

Effect of bank's statement on valuation.—

Under statute, value of shares of bank stock for taxation purposes must be deduced by state tax commission from facts submitted to it by officers of bank. First State Bank v. State Tax Comm'n, 40 N.M. 319, 59 P.2d 667.

Tax board is not bound by bank's statement, but must, from all the evidence, determine

is in excess of such par value.[2858] The ultimate basis of valuation for taxing stock issued by banks is their corporate assets,[2859] and in determining the value of their shares, each and every item of property of a bank and its value must be considered.[2860] Thus, the fact that mortgages owned by a bank are

---

true value of bank stock for purposes of taxation. Second Nat. Bank, etc., Co. v. State Board, 114 N.J.L. 573, 178 A. 96.

Impairment of bank's capital could not be considered by state tax commission in determining value of shares of bank stock for tax purposes, notwithstanding that impairment was found by bank examiner before date of return. First State Bank v. State Tax Comm'n, 40 N.M. 319, 59 P.2d 667.

Statute providing mathematical rule for determining value of shares of bank stock for tax purposes cannot be deviated from by state tax commission. First State Bank v. State Tax Comm., 40 N.M. 319, 59 P.2d 667.

Statute providing for limitation in valuing bank shares for taxation held unconstitutional when applied to stock of national or state banks. Flournoy v. First Nat. Bank, 3 So. 2d 244, 197 La. 1067.

Where tax was imposed on unrecognized appreciation in value of capital shares, under statute which imposes tax on actual value of capital shares in banks, bank could not deduct from taxable value the amount of federal income tax which would have been due on appreciation if it had been recognized by sale. Commonwealth v. Butler County Nat. Bank, 376 Pa. 66, 101 A.2d 699.

Cases decided under statute imposing tax on capital shares of corporations doing trust business are pertinent to questions, concerning valuation of stock, arising under statute trapping tax on capital shares of bank, since method of valuation is the same in both statutes. Commonwealth v. Butler County Nat'l Bank, 376 Pa. 66, 101 A.2d 699.

Action of board in fixing value not disturbed absent arbitrary action.—

In assessing bank shares tax, so long as determination of actual value of an asset at a given date is based on facts and reasonable indicia of material worth, action of department of revenue will not be disturbed in making its determination, however, department cannot arbitrarily assign values to a bank's assets which are different than those supplied by the bank in its shares tax return. Citizens Nat'l Bank & Trust Co. v. Commonwealth, 437 A.2d 1327 (Pa. Commw. 1981).

2858 People v. Assessors (N.Y.), 2 Hun 583; Alexander v. Thomas, 70 Miss. 517, 12 So. 708; West v. Newport News, 104 Va. 21, 51 S.E. 206.

2859 Citizens' Bank of Galena v. Tax Com. of Kansas, 132 Kan. 5, 294 P. 940.

2860 Brophy v. Powell, 58 Ariz. 543, 121 P.2d 647.

Statute providing for assessment of shares is not unconstitutional on ground that it grants an exemption from taxation to property owned by bank, notwithstanding its value only appears indirectly as one of the component elements of the value of the shares of stock in the hands of the stockholders. Brophy v. Powell, 58 Ariz. 543, 121 P.2d 647.

In determination of amount of bank's bank shares tax, department of revenue properly determined bank's capital value by including as undivided profits amount contained in bank's reserve for losses on loans and allowing bank a credit of an amount based upon

considered in computing the value of the bank's shares for taxation does not establish that a tax is levied on the mortgages as such.[2861] Shares of bank stock may be rated for taxation at more than would be produced by dividing the bank's capital and surplus among all its shares, the bank's business and franchises being entitled to consideration in fixing the real worth of such shares.[2862]

But a fund reported by a state banking official as remaining in his hands after the assets of an insolvent bank, supplemented by voluntary contributions from its stockholders, had been applied to its debts, is not taxable as the value of the shares of its stock.[2863]

Consideration of United States Bonds.—United States bonds owned by a bank are property which tends to enhance the value of its capital stock, and are properly considered in determining the assessable value of its shares; this is the rule where a tax is assessed against a bank's individual shareholders.[2864]

---

yearly average of bank's actual loan losses for the five-year period immediately preceding the tax year. Citizens Nat'l Bank & Trust Co. v. Commonwealth, 437 A.2d 1327 (Pa. Commw. 1981).

Amendment in 1972 to bank tax statute, precluding credit for tax paid on "tangible personal property . . . held for lease or rental" was not intended to change treatment of real estate in same statute; phrase "held for lease or rental" does not modify "real estate" in the amended statute, and, thus, bank is not entitled to credit against the bank tax for tax paid on any real estate. Citizens Bank & Trust Co. v. Director of Revenue, 639 S.W.2d 833 (Mo. 1982).

Although bank had right to protest taxing of stock by filing notice with appraisal review board, bank did not preserve its right to contest ownership of stock by filing a protest with tax assessor collector; filing of that notice did not preserve bank's right to challenge ownership of stock. First Bank v. Harris County, 804 S.W.2d 588 (Tex. App. 1991).

[2861] Bank of Miles City v. Custer County, 93 Mont. 291, 19 P.2d 885.

[2862] State v. Collins, 43 N.J.L. 562.

"Book value" of corporate stock, that is, value based on tangible assets and liabilities, is an improper measure of value for tax purposes, because it disregards elements of good will, dividend earning power, and other intangible features that ordinarily tend to give the stock a selling value in excess of pure book value. Board of Sup'rs v. State Nat'l Bank, 300 Ky. 620, 189 S.W.2d 942.

[2863] People v. Bank of Shasta County, 172 Cal. 507, 157 P. 606.

[2864] Security Sav. Bank v. Carroll, 128 Iowa 230, 103 N.W. 379; National State Bank v. Burlington, 119 Iowa 696, 94 N.W. 234; First Nat. Bank v. Independence, 123 Iowa 482, 99 N.W. 142; St. Louis Bldg., etc., Ass'n v. Lightner, 47 Mo. 393; National Union Bank v. Neil, 106 S.C. 173, 90 S.E. 744.

Tax may be levied upon shareholders of state or national banks though tax is measured by corporate assets which include federal obligations and though payment of tax by corporation

But if a tax is assessed against a bank, although nominally on its shares, such bonds may not be included in assessing the value of the shares for taxation.[2865] And where United States bonds owned by a bank are not considered in determining the assessable value of its shares, the omission cannot be afterwards remedied by assessing them to the bank as omitted property.[2866]

Deductions in General.—A bank in valuing stock for assessment purposes may make deductions as authorized by statute.[2867] Settlement of a tax on the

---

as collecting agent is required. Society for Sav. v. Bowers, 349 U.S. 143, 75 S. Ct. 607, 99 L. Ed. 950.

2865 Home Sav. Bank v. Des Moines, 205 U.S. 503, 27 S. Ct. 571, 51 L. Ed. 901, rev'g Peoples Sav. Bank v. Des Moines (Iowa), 101 N.W. 867.

Where state property tax on book value of capital employed by banks or property representing such capital at aggregate amount of capital, surplus or reserve fund and undivided profits, was in terms imposed on "shares of shareholders," and taxing statute contained no provision giving to bank a right to recover tax from depositors or giving the state a right to collect tax from depositors if bank could not pay it, and no common-law right of bank to reimbursement from shareholders was demonstrated to court, tax was against bank and not shareholders and obligations of federal government could not be included in measure of tax. Society for Savings v. Bowers, 349 U.S. 143, 75 S. Ct. 607, 99 L Ed. 950.

Georgia statute imposing property tax on fair market value of shares of bank stockholders, as construed by Georgia supreme court, to allow bank to deduct from net worth not full value of United States obligations it held but, rather, only percentage of fair obligations attributable to assets, did not violate revenue statute providing for exemption from state or local taxation of obligations of United States. First Nat'l Bank v. Bartow County Bd. of Tax Assessors, U.S., 105 S. Ct. 1516, 84 L Ed. 2d 535 (1985).

2866 Security Sav. Bank v. Carroll, 128 Iowa 230, 103 N.W. 379.

2867 **In general.—**

Hibernia Nat'l Bank v. Louisiana Tax Com., 195 La. 43, 196 So. 15.

Deduction for preferred stock.—

Under statutes assessing tax upon shares of common stock of bank, where bank, as part of reorganization plan, issued preferred stock having par value of $25, redeemable at double its par value, bank property, before levying of tax on common stock, was entitled to deduction for preferred stock only on basis of such stock having par value of $25, in absence of any showing that, under terms of the reorganization, preferred stock must be redeemed or that a reserve must be set up and maintained inviolate to meet redemption requirements. Clinton Trust Co. v. State Board of Tax Appeals, 125 N.J.L. 275, 15 A.2d 605.

The purpose of the legislature in inserting the words "retirable value" in the taxing statute which provides for ascertaining the value of each share of bank's common stock by deducting from capital, surplus and undivided profits the assessed value of real property and the aggregate par or "retirable value" of outstanding preferred stock was to give a surer approach to the intrinsic value of the common stock and to cause the assessing body to use

shares of a domestic trust company must be made according to equitable principles, and the formula used for determining the portion of the company's permanent investments that was purchased out of capital, surplus and undivided profits should be as scientifically correct as possible and applied consistently.[2868] A bank which did not suffer actual loss in its bond account and which did not actively trade or sell its bonds acted improperly in creating a reserve for possible bond losses and segregating such amount from the undivided profits and was not entitled to deduct bond loss reserve in ascertaining the value of its shares for taxation purposes.[2869] Interest and dividend payments made to depositors by savings banks and cooperative

---

whichever preferred stock value would more accurately measure the common stock value. National Bank v. Division of Tax Appeals, 2 N.J. 570, 67 A.2d 458, rev'g 1 N.J. Super. 286, 64 A.2d 240, aff'g National Bank v. Middlesex County Board of Taxation, 26 N.J. Misc. 249, 59 A.2d 270.

Under statute providing in part that the value of bank's common stock shall be ascertained by adding capital, surplus and undivided profits, and by deducting therefrom an amount equal to the aggregate par or retirable value of preferred stock, where the retirable value of preferred stock was double its par value, the retirable rather than the par value should have been deducted. National Bank v. Division of Tax Appeals, 2 N.J. 570, 67 Aid 458, rev'g 1 N.J. Super. 286, 64 A.2d 240, aff'g National Bank v. Middlesex County Board of Taxation, 26 NJ. Misc. 249, 59 A.2d 270.

Deduction for real property.—

Agreement between lessor of land and lessee bank that building which bank was to erect on premises was to be real property of bank for duration of lease entitled bank to have building assessed to it as its real property and bank was entitled to deduct assessed valuation of new structure from assessed valuation of capital stock. State v. Pioneer Citizens Bank, 456 P.2d 422 (Nev. 1969).

2868 Commonwealth v. Provident Trust Co., 319 Pa. 385, 180 A. 16 (1935).

In determining amount of tax on shares of domestic trust company, the denominator of the fraction to determine the proportionate deduction for securities not shown to have been purchased out of capital, surplus or undivided profits is the book value of permanent investments. Commonwealth v. Provident Trust Co., 319 Pa. 385, 180 A. 16 (1935).

In determining the amount of tax on shares of domestic trust company the multiplicand of the fraction to determine the proportionate deduction for securities not shown to have been purchased out of capital, surplus or undivided profits is the book value of the shares to be apportioned. Commonwealth v. Provident Trust Co., 319 Pa. 385, 180 A. 16 (1935).

In determining tax on shares of capital stock of trust company, market value of stock owned by company in other corporations should not be deducted from capital stock, surplus, and undivided profits, where there was no proof that stock so owned was purchased out of paid-in capital stock, surplus, and undivided profit. Commonwealth v. Schuylkill Trust Co., 315 Pa. 429, 173 A. 309, rev'd on other grounds, 296 U.S. 113, 56 S. Ct. 31, 80 L. Ed. 91 (1938).

2869 Montana Nat'l Bank v. State Dep't of Revenue, 539 P.2d 722 (Mont 1975).

banks are analogous to corporate dividends and, thus, are not deductible as "operating expenses" in computing the income-based portion of the excise tax.[2870] Payments made to holders of certificates of deposits are not deductible as "operating expenses" in computing the excise tax liability of savings banks or cooperative banks.[2871]

Deduction of Stockholders' Debts.—In some jurisdictions it is held that the debts of an individual bank shareholder may not be deducted from the value of his shares of stock,[2872] but in others it has been held that in listing property for taxation, a stockholder of a state bank is entitled to have his share of capital stock included in the total of his credits from which his debts may be deducted.[2873]

Deduction of Property Exempt or Otherwise Taxed.—A state, in taxing the shares of a bank or trust company, need not make any exemption or concession on account of the value reflected therein because of the company's ownership of obligations of the government or its instrumentalities,[2874] other than national bank stock.[2875] Thus, the fact that a part or all

---

Propriety of a deduction for a reserve account for possible bond loss in ascertaining the value of shares of a bank for taxation purposes does not rest solely on the sufficiency or insufficiency of supporting data upon which the reserve account is based; such a deduction is disallowed by the general principle that a liability does not accrue as long as it remains contingent. Montana Nat'l Bank v. Department of Revenue, 539 P.2d 722 (Mont. 1975).

[2870] Andover Sav. Bank v. Commissioner of Revenue, 387 Mass. 229, 439 N.E.2d 282 (1982).

[2871] Andover Sav. Bank v. Commissioner of Revenue, 387 Mass. 229, 439 N.E.2d 282 (1982).

[2872] Commercial Nat'l Bank v. Chambers, 21 Utah 324, 61 P. 560, 56 L.R.A. 846, aff'd, 182 U.S. 556, 21 S. Ct. 863, 45 L. Ed. 1227; Morril v. Bentley, 150 Iowa 677, 130 N.W. 734; Williams v. Weaver, 75 N.Y. 30, aff'd, 100 U.S. 547, 25 L. Ed. 708; People ex rel. Cagger v. Dolan, 36 N.Y. 59; Creighton Nat'l Bank v. Knox County, 108 Neb. 610, 188 N.W. 301.

[2873] Bramel v. Manring, 18 Wash. 421, 51 P. 1050; Bridgeport Sav. Bank v. Barker, 17 Misc. 180, 40 N.Y.S. 1001, aff'd, 154 N.Y. 128, 47 N.E. 973.

[2874] Schuylkill Trust Co. v. Pennsylvania, 302 U.S. 506, 58 S. Ct. 295, 82 L. Ed. 392 (1938), aff'g 327 Pa. 127, 193 A. 638.

In determining tax on shares of a trust company, federal securities owned by the company may be included in the base or measure of the tax to the company's shareholders in regard to such securities, the only requirement being that they not be discriminated against but be given the same exemption accorded non-federal securities. Commonwealth v. Union Trust Co., 345 Pa. 298, 27 A.2d 15 (1942).

States may not levy taxes on United States securities, but may tax shares of stock in banks and other corporations whose assets consist wholly or partly of such securities as property of

of the capital of a national bank is invested in United States bonds, or securities which are exempt from taxation, does not entitle a shareholder to any deduction from assessment on the full value of his shares.[2876]

In ascertaining the true value of bank stock for taxation purposes under the laws of some states, where assessors ascertain the value of such stock from the total value of the bank's property, they must include the value of the bank's real estate and tax-exempt securities, and cannot deduct such value in making their assessment.[2877] In other jurisdictions, however, in making an

---

owners of such shares, and in valuing shares for taxation, value of such securities held by corporation need not be deducted. Peter Kiewit Sons' Co. v. Douglas County, 161 Neb. 93, 72 N.W.2d 415.

[2875] Schuylkill Trust Co. v. Pennsylvania, 302 U.S. 506, 58 S. Ct. 295, 82 L. Ed. 392 (1938), aff'g 327 Pa. 127, 193 A. 638.

In determining tax on share, of a trust company, the court properly deducted national bank stock. Commonwealth v. Union Trust Co., 345 Pa. 298, 27 A.2d 15 (1942).

In determining the amount of tax on share, of domestic trust company, value of shares of federal reserve bank owned by company must be disregarded, since Congress has prohibited any state taxation of such shares. Commonwealth v. Provident Trust Co., 319 Pa. 385, 180 A. 16 (1935).

[2876] Hannan v. First Nat. Bank, 269 F. 527, appeal dismissed, 266 U.S. 638, 45 S. Ct. 9, 69 L. Ed. 482.

Though Ohio has power to tax the depositors' intangible interests of ownership in an incorporated mutual savings bank, and to use net worth of such bank as measure of value without excluding federal securities from assets of corporation, in computation of such net worth, Ohio did not properly exercise such power unless statute which in effect was tax on bank rather than tax on depositors' interests. Broadview Sav. & Loan Co. v. Peck, 165 Ohio St. 82, 133 N.E.2d 366, appeal dismissed, 352 U.S. 801, 77 S. Ct. 20, 1 L. Ed. 2d 37.

[2877] *Massachusetts.*—Old Colony Trust Co. v. Commonwealth, 220 Mass. 409, 107 N.E. 950.

Nebraska.—An assessor is required to assess the stock of a bank at its real value, and where a bank owns real estate of a greater value than that at which it is carried on the bank books, the excess should be considered in fixing the value of the stock. First Nat'l Bank v. Webster County, 77 Neb. 815, 113 N.W. 190.

New Jersey.—In computing the tax value of shares of bank stock under New Jersey statute no deduction is allowable for tax exempt securities, since tax on shares would not constitute tax on securities. Tradesmens Bank, etc., Co. v. Cumberland County Board of Taxation, 20 N.J. Misc. 107, 25 A.2d 20. See Mechanics' Nat. Bank v. Baker, 65 N.J.L. 113, 46 A. 586, aff'd, 65 N.J.L. 549, 48 A. 582. It was formerly held otherwise. Lippincott v. Lippincott, 75 N.J.L. 795, 69 A. 502.

New York.—In re First Nat. Bank, 182 N.Y. 460, 75 N.E 306.

Oklahoma.—In re Assessment of First Nat. Bank, 93 Okla. 233, 220 P. 909, 57 A.L.R. 890.

assessment against the holders of state or national bank stock, an assessor is required to deduct from the total valuation of such stock, not only the assessed valuation of a bank's real property, but also the total value of all nontaxable securities held by the bank.[2878] And non-taxable shares of a

---

Banks should be assessed and taxed on the value of their shares of stock, and a tax on the shares of stock is not a tax on the property of the corporation, and therefore shareholders are not entitled to have a deduction from the value of the shares of the amount of capital stock of the company which is invested in public building bonds and guaranty fund warrants. Brown v. Hennessey State Bank, 78 Okla. 141, 189 P. 355.

South Carolina.—A state legislature, in passing acts taxing bank stock in the hands of shareholders, is presumed to have known that, in fixing the value of stock for purposes of taxation to shareholders, no deduction can be made on account of securities of the corporation exempt from taxation. National Union Bank v. Neil, 106 S.C. 173, 90 S.E. 744.

West Virginia.—The value of non-taxable securities owned by national banks and industrial loan companies represents part of the value of the shares of stock, and should not be deducted from the assets of such banks or companies in determining the assessment value of such shares. In re National Bank, 137 W. Va. 673, 73 S.E.2d 655 (1952).

2878 *Connecticut.*—Appeal of Barrett, 73 Conn. 288, 47 A. 243.

Georgia.—Statute authorizing bank to deduct sum at which bank's real estate is returned for taxation from market value of bank shares, in returning shares for taxation, held valid. Moultrie v. Moultrie Banking Co., 177 Ga. 714, 171 S.E. 131.

In respect to statutory provisions imposing a tax on the shares of stockholders of banks or banking associations, the value of a stockholder's lands located outside the state of Georgia may not be deducted from the value of the banking shares. Georgia Railroad Bank & Trust Co. v. Richmond County Board of Tax Assessors, 142 Ga. App. 417, 236 S.E.2d 95 (1977).

Bank share tax was computed by reducing bank's net worth by percentage of bank's assets held in form of federal securities so as to remove from tax base so much of its net worth as was represented by federal securities, subtracting total deductions from net worth, leaving taxable share value, and dividing taxable share value by number of offsetting shares. Bartow County Bank v. Bartow County Bd. of Tax Assessors, 312 S.E.2d 102 (Ga. 1984).

Idaho.—Independent Sch. Dist. v. Lemhi County, 43 Idaho 285, 251 P. 619; Solomon v. Board of Com'rs, 43 Idaho 291, 251 P. 620.

Indiana.—Smith v. Stephens, 173 Ind. 564, 91 N.E. 167, 30 L.R.A. (n.s.) 704.

Iowa.—Security Sav. Bank v. Carroll, 128 Iowa 230, 103 N.W. 379.

Kansas.—First Nat'l Bank v. Moon, 102 Kan. 334, 170 P. 33 (1918); Citizens' Bank of Galena v. Tax Com. of Kansas, 132 Kan. 5, 294 P. 940.

The deduction of real estate of state banks necessary for convenient transaction of business, including furniture and fixtures to be made from value of stock in hands of stockholders, may not exceed value of realty which banks may hold for that purpose. First Nat'l Bank v. Moon, 102 Kan. 334, 170 P. 33 (1918).

Michigan.—Tax-exempt securities held to represent capital, surplus, and undivided profits, so that their value was deductible in assessing taxes on shares, where they were

(Text continued on page 816)

---

purchased when bank had no deposits and its only funds were those paid for capital stock, and investment was condition precedent to right do business. National Bank v. Detroit, 272 Mich. 610, 262 N.W. 422.

Deduction in assessment of bank shares allowable for tax-exempt securities representing investment of capital, surplus, and undivided profits could not be allocated entirely to common stock, where preferred stock was owned by nontaxable entity, though actual payment for such securities was made out of funds derived from sale of common stock. National Bank v. Detroit, 272 Mich. 610, 262 N.W. 422.

Statement to assessor, by bank suing to recover overpayment of taxes on shares, held to show deduction claimed on account of tax-exempt securities representing investment of capital, surplus, and undivided profits, though statement did not show source of funds with which investment was made, where it claimed exemption for entire amount and at subsequent bearings bank fully and completely disclosed such source. National Bank v. Detroit, 272 Mich. 610, 262 N.W. 422.

Statute providing for deduction of tax-exempt capital investment securities in assessing common stock held constitutional. National Bank of Detroit v. Detroit, 277 Mich. 571, 269 N.W. 602.

Under such statute proper method to fix deduction for stock of undeterminable source, in assessing tax, was to apply ratio of monthly average of total capital during calendar year to sum of monthly averages of total capital and deposits to monthly average of tax-exempt securities during same period. National Bank v. Detroit, 277 Mich. 571, 269 N.W. 602.

Missouri.—State v. Buder, 295 Mo. 63, 242 S.W. 979.

Montana.—A bank which owned real estate and was liable for taxes on it was entitled to deduct the real estate from the value of its shares for the purpose of determining the tax on the shares, even though the bank mistakenly omitted such item on its statement to tax authorities. Montana Nat'l Bank v. State Dep't of Revenue, 539 P.2d 722 (Mont. 1975).

New Jersey.—Statute providing that assessed value of "real property of bank" should be deducted in determining value of bank's stock for tax purposes did not permit deduction of assessed value of realty owned by another corporation, all capital stock of which was owned by bank. Hackensack Trust Co. v. Hackensack, 116 N.J.L. 343, 184 A. 408.

Words "real property of such bank," in statute meant "real property owned by such bank"; "of" being used in its possessive sense. Hackensack Trust Co. v. Hackensack, 116 N.J.L. 343, 184 A. 408.

New Mexico.—Realty owned by bank is part of bank's capital stock, as respects taxation of bank stock. First State Bank v. State Tax Comm'n, 40 N.M. 319, 59 P.2d 667.

Holder of bank stock has only statutory right and not constitutional right to have value of realty which goes to make up true value of stock deducted from capital structure in determining value of stock for taxation purposes. First State Bank v. State Tax Comm., 40 N.M. 319, 59 P.2d 667.

North Carolina.—Pullen v. Corporation Com., 152 N.C. 548, 68 S.E. 155.

Virginia.—Commonwealth v. Virginia Bank & Trust Co., 110 Va. 552, 66 S.E. 853.

Washington.—Bank of Fairfield v. Spokane County, 173 Wash. 145, 22 P.2d 646.

corporation holding tax-exempt securities are not rendered taxable because they are held by another corporation engaged in banking.[2879]

Shares of stock of a national bank which are owned by a trust company, having once been taxed to the company, cannot again be made the base or measure of a tax on the company's shareholders.[2880] The geographical limit on mortgage loans which qualify for deduction from taxable deposits in computing the excise tax levied on mutual banks does not impermissibly discriminate against interstate commerce.[2881]

Valuation by Assessor on Failure or Refusal of Owner to Do So.—Under a law requiring shares of banking associations to be rated for taxation, the valuation thereof may be made by an assessor if the owner fails or refuses to place a taxable value on such property.[2882] And the jurisdiction of tax officials to assess a tax on bank stock is not affected by the existence of outside facts bearing on the proper measure of a deduction which were never called to their attention.[2883]

Sufficiency of Assessment.—A gross assessment of shares of stock of a bank at seventy-five percent of the value of its aggregate capital stock is not subject to the objection that the value of each share is not specified where such value is ascertainable by simple computation by an auditor.[2884]

§ 49. Valuation of National Bank Shares.

In General.—It is a well-established rule that shares of stock of national banks should be assessed at their actual, not their par value.[2885]

West Virginia.—Dillon v. Graybeal, 60 W. Va. 357, 55 S.E. 398.

Wisconsin.—Second Ward Sav. Bank v. Leuch, 155 Wis. 493, 144 N.W. 1119.

2879 State ex rel. Orr v. Buder, 308 Mo. 237, 271 S.W. 508, 39 A.L.R. 1199.

2880 Schuylkill Trust Co. v. Pennsylvania, 296 U.S. 113, 56 S. Ct. 31, 80 L. Ed. 91, rev'g 315 Pa. 429, 173 A. 309.

2881 Andover Sav. Bank v. Commissioner, 387 Mass. 229, 439 N.E.2d 282 (1982).

2882 Dean v. Kopperl, 1 Tax. App. Civ. Cas. (White & W.) 409; Security Sav. Bank v. Carroll, 131 Iowa 605, 109 N.W. 212.

2883 Citizens' Sav. Bank v. New York, 166 N.Y. 594, 59 N.E. 1120; Stanley v. Albany, 121 U.S. 535, 7 S. Ct. 1234, 30 L. Ed. 1000.

2884 Citizens' Nat. Bank v. Klauss, 47 Ind. App. 50, 93 N.E. 681.

2885 *United States.*—People v. Commissioners, 94 U.S. 415, 24 L Ed. 164; Exchange Nat'l Bank v. Miller, 19 F. 372; St. Louis Nat. Bank v. Papin, 21 F. Cas. 203 (No. 12, 239), 4 Dill. 29.

But there is an early decision to the effect that national bank shares cannot be included in the valuation for taxation by or under state authority at more than the par value thereof, and

And the excess of assets over liabilities of a national bank on a particular date is of no importance in determining the fair cash value of its shares for purposes of taxation if there is sufficient evidence of the amount of which the shares could have been sold on that date.[2886] As previously discussed, the

---

that the taxation of such shares above the par value is not merely an irregularity, but renders the whole tax inoperative and void. Union Nat. Bank v. Chicago, 24 F. Cas. 615 (No. 14, 374), 8 Bias. 82.

Kansas.—Shares of in national banks, state banks, and loan or investment corporations in the hands of stockholders are to be assessed at their true value, which may or may not coincide with their book value. First Nat'l Bank v. Moon,102 Kan. 334, 170 P. 33 (1918).

Massachusetts.—

National Bank of Commerce v. New Bedford, 155 Mass. 313, 29 N.E. 532 (1892); National Bank of Commerce v. New Bedford, 175 Mass. 257, 56 N.E. 288.

Nebraska.—First Nat. Bank v. Webster County, 77 Neb. 815, 113 N.W. 190.

New Jersey.—Newark v. Tunis, 82 N.J.L. 461, 81 A. 722.

New York.—People ex rel. Gallatin Nat'l Bank v. Commissioners of Taxes & Assessments, 67 N.Y. 561; People v. Commissioners, 8 Hun 536, aff'd, 67 N.Y. 516; 94 U.S. 415, 24 L. Ed. 164.

Ohio.—Under statute relating to the taxation of financial institutions, as in effect prior to January 1, 1931, all the shares of the shareholders in an incorporated bank or banking association located in Ohio, incorporated or organized under the laws of Ohio or United States, are required to be listed for taxation at their true value in money. Union Sav. Bank v. Pancoast, 142 Ohio St. 6, 50 N.E.2d 157, aff'd sub nom. Second Nat. Bank v. Findley, 320 U.S. 714, 64 S. Ct. 260, 88 L Ed. 420.

Oregon.—Ankeny v. Blakley, 44 Ore. 78, 74 P. 485; Citizens' Nat. Bank v. Baker County Board of Equalization, 109 Ore. 669, 222 P. 341.

Pennsylvania.—Appeal of Everitt, 71 Pa. 216.

Utah.—Continental Nat. Bank v. Naylor, 54 Utah 49, 179 P. 67.

West Virginia.—The assessor is required to adopt a method or methods of arriving at the real and actual value of bank shares from the best information obtainable and is not required or authorized to adopt a single arbitrary method, even though in the majority of the cases such method proves more accurate than any other single method. In re National Bank, 137 W. Va. 673, 73 S.E.2d 655 (1952).

In assessing shares of stock of federal savings and loan associations and national banks the assessor is directed to find the assessment values by using the best information obtainable. In re National Bank, 137 W. Va. 673, 73 S.E.2d 655 (1952).

In determining tax assessments against shares of national banks, all pertinent methods of evidence obtainable must be considered and neither the sales price method nor the book value method is to be used exclusively. In re National Bank, 137 W. Va. 673, 73 S.E.2d 655 (1952).

[2886] **In general.—**

National Bank of Commerce v. New Bedford, 175 Mass. 257, 56 N.E. 288.

provisions of the National Banking Act prohibit the taxation of national bank shares at a greater rate than is assessed on other moneyed capital in the hands of individual citizens of a state.[2887] However, in estimating the value of shares of stock of national banks for purposes of taxation, the value of United States bonds owned by such banks may be considered.[2888] and the rule is the same for shares of stock of industrial corporations held by national banks.[2889] For cases involving the construction of local statutes taxing national bank shares, see the footnote.[2890]

In determining fair cash values of national bank stock for tax purposes, the question is what would stock have sold for on day of assessment in ordinary course of trade. Board of Supervisors v. State Nat. Bank, 300 Ky. 620, 189 S.W.2d 942. But see Citizens Fid. Bank & Trust Co. v. Reeves (Ky.), 259 S.W.2d 432.

In absence of a market for national bank stock, the estimate of fair market value for tax purposes must be upon theories deducible from the various elements that enter into its value. Board of Sup'rs v. State Nat'l Bank, 300 Ky. 620, 189 S.W.2d 942.

In absence of substantial evidence as to value of actual market price of national bank stock for purpose of taxation, neither balance sheet nor earnings of the business enterprise can be ignored in considering value of the stock. Board of Supervisors v. State Nat. Bank, 300 Ky. 620, 189 S.W.2d 942.

[2887] See § 26c(2) of this chapter.

[2888] National State Bank v. Burlington, 119 Iowa 696, 94 N.W. 234; People v. Commissioners (N.Y.), 8 Hun 538, aff'd, 67 N.Y. 516, 94 U.S. 415, 24 L. Ed. 164.

[2889] Brown v. First Nat. Bank, 175 S.W. 1122 (Tex. Civ. App.).

[2890] *United States.*—Buder v. First Nat. Bank, 16 F.2d 990, cert. denied, 274 U.S. 743, 47 S. Ct. 588, 71 L. Ed. 1321; Minnehaha Nat. Bank v. Anderson, 2 F.2d 897.

Alabama.—Tarrant v. Bessemer Nat. Bank, 7 Ala. App. 285, 61 So. 47.

California.—California adopted the in lieu tax on net income and made it applicable to all banks located within state because tax-rate parity between national and state banking institutions was prerequisite for any tax upon national bank. Hibernia Bank v. State Bd. of Equalization, 166 Cal. App. 3d 393, 212 Cal. Rptr. 556 (1985).

Iowa.—First Nat. Bank v. Hayes, 186 Iowa 892, 171 N.W. 715.

Mississippi.—Miller v. Citizens' Nat'l Bank, 144 Miss. 533, 110 So. 439; Adams v. First Nat. Bank, 116 Miss. 450, 77 So. 195.

Montana.—First Nat'l Bank v. Dawson County, 66 Mont. 321, 213 P. 1097.

Where national bank set up on its books and in its statement, as an asset, the full face value of notes including unearned and uncollected interest, taxing authorities, in ascertaining value of shares of bank, properly considered notes at their face amounts as an asset and as part of bank's loans and discounts. Miners Nat'l Bank v. Silver Bow County, 116 Mont. 31, 148 P.2d 538.

New Mexico.—In determining taxable value of national bank stock, par value of preferred stock as well as common stock may be considered, though preferred stock is owned by

(Text continued on page 820)

Reconstruction Finance Corporation and hence non-taxable. First Nat. Bank v. State Tax Comm., 43 N.M. 307, 92 P.2d 987, appeal dismissed, 308 U.S. 515, 60 S. Ct. 173, 84 L. Ed. 439.

New York.—People v. Cantor, 111 Misc. 420, 183 N.Y.S. 443, aff'd, 231 N.Y. 514, 132 N.E. 869.

Oregon.—Citizens' Nat'l Bank v. Baker County Board of Equalization, 109 Ore. 669, 222 P. 341.

Pennsylvania.—Commonwealth fiscal officers are not bound by the taxpayer's own valuations in computing liability for bank shares taxing, but the commonwealth may not arbitrarily assign values without regard to facts, nor may it assign value without sufficient data on which to base its conclusion. First Nat'l Bank & Trust Co v. Commonwealth Bd. of Fin. & Revenue, 11 Pa. Commw. 175, 312 A.2d 848 (1978).

The policy of the department of revenue and auditor general of accepting, as an accounting basis for purposes of the bank shares tax, either cash or accrual accounting, so long as it was the accounting method utilized in reports to shareholders and for internal purposes, would be unlawful, unless the taxing authorities reserved the right to question the report of actual cash value of shares, regardless of the method of accounting employed. First Nat'l Bank & Trust Co. v. Commonwealth Board of Finance & Revenue, 11 Pa. Commw. 175, 312 A.2d 848 (1978).

Tennessee.—As a bank excise tax is to be calculated in the same manner as a general corporate excise tax and is really nothing more than an additional excise tax payable to local governments, the first year of business for the purpose of new bank credit is that year, or part of the year, in which the new bank begins doing business and at the end of which it has first closing. Commerce Union Bank v. State Bd. of Equalization, 615 S.W.2d 151 (Tenn. 1981).

Under the section of the bank tax statute governing new bank credit, for taxpayers beginning business in the third calendar year prior to the effective date of the statute and closing their books on December 31 of that year, the tax based upon earnings of the year immediately preceding the effective date of the statute would have been entitled to 60 percent credit, similarly, for the taxpayer beginning business in the fourth calendar year preceding the effective date of the statute, a credit of 40 percent should have been allowed for the tax based upon earnings of the year prior to the effective date of the statute. Commerce Union Bank v. State Bd. of Equalization, 615 S.W.2d 151 (Tenn. 1981).

Texas.—A bank was not entitled to deduct the value of an office tower in arriving at the amount of ad valorem taxes owed on bank stock where the value of the office tower was not included and considered in arriving at the value of the stock. Midland v. Midland Nat'l Bank, 607 S.W.2d 303 (Tex. Civ. App. 1980).

Virginia.—The stock value envisioned for purposes of the tax assessed against shareholders of a bank based on the value of their stock is not market value but the value of the proprietorship or equity of the stockholders. Virginia Nat'l Bank v. Commonwealth, 214 Va. 719, 204 S.E.2d 426 (1974).

"Capital notes" issued by a bank to increase its capital funds for the use in its business, which were unsecured and subordinate to deposits and certain other liabilities of the bank, did not constitute capital of the bank so as to increase the value of its capital stock for purposes of the tax assessed against stockholders on their shares of stock in the bank, since

Deduction of Stockholders' Debts.—With regard to the right of holders of national bank shares to deduct their bona fide debts from the assessed value of their shares, the rule differs in the various jurisdictions. In some states it is held that a taxpayer is entitled to such a deduction,[2891] and only the excess of the value of such shares over the amount of their owner's interest-bearing indebtedness is subject to taxation;[2892] while in others, owners of shares in national banking associations are not entitled to deduct their bona fide indebtedness from the assessed valuation of their stock,[2893] unless, as has been held in some jurisdictions, the owner has no other credits from which a deduction of his bona tide debts may be made.[2894]

Deduction of Property Exempt or Otherwise Taxed.—The allowance of a deduction for property exempt or otherwise taxed in assessing shares of national bank stock depends upon particular statutes in the various jurisdictions.[2895]

---

the notes constituted nothing more than evidences of the bank's indebtedness to outside creditors, though under certain federal regulations they might be considered capital for some purposes, such as computing lending limits and the amounts that might be invested in certain transactions. Virginia Nat'l Bank v. Commonwealth, 214 Va. 719, 204 S.E.2d 426 (1974).

Wisconsin.—Krembs v. Merrill, 183 Wis. 241, 197 N.W. 818.

2891 First Nat. Bank v. Washington County, 17 Idaho 306, 105 P. 1053; Whitbeck v. Mercantile Nat. Bank, 127 U.S. 193, 8 S. Ct. 1121, 32 L. Ed. 118; Mercantile Nat. Bank v. Shields, 59 F. 952; Supervisors v. Stanley, 12 F. 82; First Nat'l Bank v. City Council of Albia, 86 Iowa 28, 52 N.W. 334; Ruggles v. Fond du Lac, 53 Wis. 436, 10 N.W. 565.

2892 Stanley v. Supervisors of Albany, 121 U.S. 535, 7 S. Ct. 1234, 30 L. Ed. 1000; Richards v. Rock Rapids, 31 F. 505; Peavey v. Greenfield, 64 N.H. 284, 9 A. 722; McAden v. Commissioners of Mecklenburg County, 97 N.C. 355, 2 S.E. 670; Farmington v. Downing, 67 N.H. 441, 30 A. 345; Weston v. Manchester, 62 N.H. 574.

2893 *Indiana.*—First Nat. Bank v. Turner, 154 Ind. 456, 57 N.E. 110.

Kansas.—Dutton v. Citizens' Nat'l Bank, 53 Kan. 440, 36 P. 719.

Ohio.—Chapman v. First Nat'l Bank, 56 Ohio St. 310, 47 N.E. 54; Niles v. Shaw, 50 Ohio St. 370, 34 N.E. 162; State Nat. Bank v. Shields, 1 Ohio Dec. 609, 31 Wkly. L. Bull. 303, 321.

Texas.—Primm v. Fort, 23 Tex. Civ. App. 605, 57 S.W. 86.

Utah.—Commercial Nat. Bank v. Chambers, 21 Utah 324, 61 P. 560, 56 L.R.A. 346, aff'd, 182 U.S. 556, 21 S. Ct. 863, 45 L. Ed. 1227.

Virginia.—Burrows v. Smith, 95 Va. 694, 29 S.E. 674.

West Virginia.—West Virginia Nat. Bank v. Dunkle, 65W. Va. 210, 64 S.E. 531.

2894 Indianapolis v. Vajen, 111 Ind. 240, 12 N.E. 311; Wasson v. First Nat. Bank, 107 Ind. 206, 8 N.E. 97.

2895 United States.—Hannan v. First Nat'l Bank, 269 F. 527, appeal dismissed, 266 U.S. 638, 45 S. Ct. 9, 69 L Ed. 482; People's Nat. Bank v. Marye, 107 F. 570, modified, 191 U.S.

(*Text continued on page 822*)

272, 24 S. Ct. 68, 48 L. Ed. 180; Charleston Nat. Bank v. Melton, 171 F. 743; Nevada Nat. Bank v. Dodge, 119 F. 57.

Idaho.—First Nat. Bank v. Washington County, 17 Idaho 306, 105 P. 1053.

Iowa.—Des Moines Nat. Bank v. Fairweather, 191 Iowa 1240, 184 N.W. 313, aff'd, 263 U.S. 103, 44 S. Ct. 23, 68 L. Ed. 191.

Kansas.—First Nat'l Bank v. Moon, 102 Kan. 334, 170 P. 33 (1918).

Michigan.—Stockholder of national bank is entitled, in fixing assessed value of shares, to deduction of credits secured by lien on realty on which specific tax had been paid. First Nat. Bank v. Detroit, 253 Mich. 89, 234 N.W. 151; Equitable, etc., Trust Co. v. Detroit, 253 Mich. 97, 234 N.W. 154; First Nat'l Bank v. Board of State Tax Comm'rs, 253 Mich. 98, 234 N.W. 154.

Deduction of federal reserve bank stock in its entirety held proper in assessing national bank's common stock. National Bank v. Detroit, 277 Mich. 571, 269 N.W. 602.

Minnesota.—State v. First Nat'l Bank, 164 Minn. 235, 204 N.W. 874, 273 U.S. 561, 47 S. Ct. 468, 71 L. Ed. 774.

Montana.—In ascertaining value of shares of national bank for taxation, amount of deduction for realty was amount at which bank examiners permitted bank to carry realty on books as an asset in connection with transaction of banking business, rather than amount at which realty was assessed for taxation purposes. Miners Nat'l Bank v. Silver Bow County, 116 Mont. 31, 148 P.2d 538.

In ascertaining value of shares of national bank for taxation, bank was not entitled to deduction for reserve for losses on bonds, where such item, as listed in bank's statement to assessor, did not cover all bonds, and hence ignored appreciation of part of bonds, and question of whether entire bond account showed gain notwithstanding losses on some items. Miners Nat'l Bank v. Silver Bow County, 116 Mont. 31, 148 P.2d 538.

Nebraska.—In re First Nat. Bank, 103 Neb. 280, 171 N.W. 912.

New Hampshire.—Strafford Nat. Bank v. Dover, 58 N.H. 316.

New Jersey.—Newark v. Tunis, 81 N.J.L. 45, 78 A. 1066, aff'd, 82 N.J.L. 461, 81 A. 722.

New York.—People ex rel. Sav. Banl v. Xoleman, 18 N.Y.S. 675, 63 Hun. 633, aff'd, 135 N.Y. 231, 31 N.E. 1022.

Oklahoma.—In re Assessment of First Nat'l Bank, 58 Okla. 508, 160 P. 469, 1917B L.R.A. 294; Board of Equalization v. People's Nat. Bank, 79 Okla. 312, 193 P. 622; In re Tradesmen's State Bank, 82 Okla. 74, 198 P. 479; Longcor v. Central State Bank, 85 Okla. 108, 204 P. 1099; In re Walters Nat. Bank, 100 Okla. 155, 228 P. 953; Board of Equalization v. Exchange Nat. Bank, 104 Okla. 93, 230 P. 728.

South Carolina.—National Union Bank v. Neil, 106 S.C. 173, 90 S.E. 744.

Texas.—Brown v. First Nat. Bank, 175 S.W. 1122 (Tex. Civ. App. 1915).

Utah.—Continental Nat. Bank v. Naylor, 54 Utah 49, 179 P. 67.

West Virginia.—The value of nontaxable securities owned by national banks represents part of the value of shares of stock of the bank, and should not be deducted from the assets of such banks in determining the assessment value of such shares. In re National Bank, 137 W. Va. 673, 73 S.E.2d 655 (1952).

§ 50. Valuation of Income and Deductions.

The particular income tax statute in question controls the determination of income tax deductions.[2896] Thus, it was held that under a tax law allowing a credit for interest paid on indebtedness in computing net income forming the basis of the tax, a savings and loan association was entitled to credit on account of dividends paid to its member.[2897] On the other hand, it has been held that interest paid by a national bank to its depositors on their savings

---

[2896] *Alabama.*—In determining tax deductions when ascertaining net income for payment of excise tax for privilege of conducting a financial institution, the presumption exists that taxes specifically excepted as not deductible are the only taxes not to be deducted. Title Guarantee Loan, etc., Co. v. State, 228 Ala. 636, 155 So. 305.

Ad valorem taxes on personal property, corporate franchise tax, and corporate permit fee paid by company, held not deductible when ascertaining company's excise tax for privilege of conducting business employing moneyed capital coming into competition with business of national banks. Title Guarantee Loan, etc., Co. v. State, 228 Ala. 636, 155 So. 305.

California.—Where bank's losses resulting from default in bonds held by it occurred before 1938, and the facts were known to an executive officer of the bank, such losses could not be deducted from income for 1933 as basis for computing franchise tax, notwithstanding that bonds were written down during 1933 on direction of superintendent of banks. People v. Richardson, 37 Cal. App. 2d 275, 99 P.2d 366.

New York.—A trust company, transferring shares of its stock to trustees far issuance and sale to officers and designated employees of company in payment of extra compensation, pursuant to profit-sharing plan, was not entitled to deduct difference between amount received for such shares and fair market value thereof from its taxable income. People ex rel. New York Trust Co. v. Graves, 265 App. Div. 94, 37 N.Y.S.2d 900, 290 N.Y. 785, 50 N.E.2d 108.

Former Tax Law § 1453(k-1) was statutorily coupled with the federal ordering rules set forth in 26 U.S.C.S. § 172, which specifically provided that the entire amount of a net operating loss (NOL) for any taxable year shall be carried to the earliest of the taxable years to which such loss may be carried (26 U.S.C.S. § 172(b)(2)). Thus, for banking corporation franchise tax purposes, application of this federal ordering rule was not a mere attempt by the Department of Taxation and Finance to achieve mechanical conformity with federal tax principles; it was statutorily required and, as such, said presumption served as the "starting point" for determining the amount of NOL that must be used to offset a taxpayer's entire net income. Matter of Toronto Dominion Holdings (U.S.A.), Inc. v Tax Appeals Trib. of The State of New York, 162 A.D.3d 1255; 77 N.Y.S.3d 800 (3d Dept. 2018).

Nothing in the language of former Tax Law § 1453(k-1) provides a banking corporation with the option to deduct none of its available New York net operating loss carryover deduction in subsequent years where it posts a positive entire net income, solely because its franchise tax liability for that year is calculated using an alternative tax base (former Tax Law § 1453(k-1)). Matter of Toronto Dominion Holdings (U.S.A.), Inc. v Tax Appeals Trib. of The State of New York, 162 A.D.3d 1255; 77 N.Y.S.3d 800 (3d Dept. 2018).

[2897] Aberdeen Sav. & Loan Ass'n v. Chase, 157 Wash. 351, 289 P. 536, 290 P. 697, 71 A.L.R. 232.

accounts is not deductible in computing its gross earnings within a statute imposing a tax on the gross earnings of such banks.[2898] But the tax on national banks under the California Bank and Corporation Franchise Tax Act is measured by their net income rather than gross income.[2899] Interest from obligations which are generally tax exempt could be included in the measurement of tax due from a thrift institution subject to the provisions of the Mutual Thrift Institutions Tax Act.[2900] A franchise tax imposed upon a national bank was "income tax" to be added back to the federal taxable income, which had exempted it, as net earnings to be taxed by the state; "income taxes" means taxes based upon income, including franchise taxes.[2901] A thrift's branching and regulatory accounting purposes (RAP) rights are considered intangible assets for tax purposes, and, as such, are generally subject to abandonment loss deductions and amortization deductions under the Internal Revenue Code.[2902]

A Michigan bank and trust company properly utilized a state statute dealing with allocation and apportionment of income, in conjunction with another state statute formerly dealing with the taxable income of a financial organization, in computing its taxable income, where the bank's income was attributable to activities in Michigan and London, England.[2903] Additionally, a Michigan bank and trust company, in computing its taxable income for its Michigan financial institutions tax returns, could not utilize a state statute dealing solely with the taxable income of a taxpayer whose income-producing activities are confined solely to Michigan, where the bank's income was attributable to activities in Michigan and London, England.[2904] A state statute imposing a 9.7 percent income tax on financial institutions was applicable to a Michigan bank and trust company which, in addition to being a financial organization under the state statute, was also a "financial

---

[2898] Hamilton Nat. Bank v. District of Columbia, 156 F.2d 843.

[2899] Security-First Nat. Bank v. Franchise Tax Board, 55 Cal. 2d 407, 11 Cal. Rptr. 289, 359 P.2d 625, appeal dismissed, 368 U.S. 3, 82 S. Ct. 15, 7 L. Ed. 2d 16.

[2900] Philadelphia Sav. Fund Soc'y v. Commonwealth, 467 A.2d 420 (Pa. Commw. 1988).

[2901] Maryland Nat'l Bank v. State Dep't of Assmts. & Taxation, 57 Md. App. 269, 469 A.2d 907 (1984).

[2902] WMI Holdings Corp. v. United States, 891 F.3d 1016 (2018). See 26 U.S.C.S. §§ 165, 167(a).

[2903] Detroit Bank & Trust Co. v. Department of Treasury, 377 N.W.2d 425 (Mich. App. 1985).

[2904] Detroit Bank & Trust Co. v. Department of Treasury, 377 N.W.2d 425 (Mich. App. 1985).

institution" as defined in the state statute.[2905] Thus, a Michigan bank and trust company, properly deducted, in determining its Michigan taxable income, its distributive share of losses sustained from participating in a Utah-administered partnership trust for leveraged-lease transactions, where the bank did not derive any fees, commissions, or other compensation for financial services rendered in Utah, the bank's activities of considering, studying, and arranging participation in a transaction took place in Michigan, participation in the transaction was part of the bank's regular banking business, and the bank had obtained a letter ruling from the IRS indicating that the tax consequences of its participation in the partnership trusts would be favorable for federal income tax purposes.[2906] A Michigan bank and trust company properly utilized a state statute dealing with the allocation and apportionment of income, in conjunction with a former state statute dealing with the taxable income of a financial organization, in computing its taxable income, where the bank's income was attributable to activities in Michigan and London, England.[2907] Similarly, a Michigan bank and trust company, in computing its taxable income for its Michigan financial institutions tax returns, could not utilize a state statute dealing solely with the taxable income of a taxpayer whose income-producing activities are confined solely to Michigan, where the bank's income was attributable to activities in Michigan and London, England.[2908] The former state statute setting forth only the rule for the attribution of taxable income of a financial organization, rather than another statute providing the usual method for apportioning business income and excepting the income of a financial organization from its provisions, was the applicable provision to determine the proper attribution of taxable income of a Michigan bank and trust company, where the participation by the bank with the other financial institutions in a leveraged-lease transaction was undertaken in the normal, regular course of the bank's banking business.[2909] Pursuant to the state statute governing the computation of the alternative minimum tax, the alternative minimum tax

---

[2905] Detroit Bank & Trust Co. v. Department of Treasury, 377 N.W.2d 425 (Mich. App. 1985).

[2906] Detroit Bank & Trust Co. v. Department of Treasury, 377 N.W.2d 425 (Mich. App. 1985).

[2907] Detroit Bank & Trust Co. v. Department of Treasury, 377 N.W.2d 425 (Mich. App. 1985).

[2908] Detroit Bank & Trust Co. v. Department of Treasury, 377 N.W.2d 425 (Mich. App. 1985).

[2909] Detroit Bank & Trust Co. v. Department of Treasury, 377 N.W.2d 425 (Mich. App. 1985).

base should be computed by applying the statutory 3.5 percent rate to the account balance using the taxpayer bank's compounding and crediting practices, without consideration of interest forfeited to depositors due to early withdrawal.[2910] The Department of Revenue could assess taxes against a savings and loan under the provisions of the Mutual Thrift Institutions Tax Act, based upon the interest income received by the savings and loan from its holdings of various obligations issued by the Commonwealth, its agencies, or political subdivisions.[2911]

Deductions are allowed only when plainly authorized.[2912]

§ 51. Amendment or Alteration.

Whether a tax assessment is subject to amendment or alteration depends on the particular statutes in the various jurisdictions.[2913]

[2910] American Sav. Bank v. State Tax Com., 65 N.Y.2d 824, 482 N.E.2d 916, 493 N.Y.S.2d 120 (1985).

[2911] First Fed. Sav. & Loan Ass'n v. Commonwealth, 498 A.2d 455 (Pa. Commw. 1985).

[2912] State Dep't of Assmts. & Taxation v. Loyola Fed. Sav. & Loan Ass'n, 79 Md. App. 481, 558 A.2d 428 (1989).

[2913] *Florida.*—Clerical error that occurred when $260,000, rather than $775,000, was entered in computer of property appraiser's office as assessed value of property was correctible by back assessment of ad valorem taxes. Robbins v. First Nat'l Bank, 651 So. 2d 184 (Fla. App. 1995).

Failure of property appraiser to obtain prior approval of Property Appraisal Adjustment Board for back assessment of ad valorem taxes, to correct clerical error, was not fatal, given fact that taxpayer was, in any event, afforded proper due process hearing before Board after back assessment was made. Robbins v. First Nat'l Bank, 651 So. 2d 184 (Fla. App. 1995).

Illinois.—Once tax rules have been certified to Court of Appeals, assessor can no longer change assessments. First Nat'l Bank & Trust Co. v. Rosewell, 93 Ill. 2d 388, 67 Ill. Dec. 87, 444 N.E.2d 126 (1982).

Iowa.—Under statute providing that capital stock of savings banks is to be assessed to the bank on the basis of the actual value of the stock, and showing that it is not contemplated that any further assessment shall be made for money and credits, and statute providing that the treasurer shall make assessments when property subject to taxation has been, from any cause, not listed and assessed, the county treasurer has no authority to add to the assessment of a savings bank a certain sum as "money and credits" intended to represent the difference between the assessment of capital stock as made by the assessor and the par value of the capital stock. German Sav. Bank v. Trowbridge, 124 Iowa 514, 100 N.W. 333.

Kansas.—Under statute limiting the amount a bank may invest in a building to one-third of its capital and surplus, and the taxation statute, requiring the assessor in fixing the amount on which stockholders shall pay taxes, to deduct from the gross value of all the shares the assessed value of a bank building to the extent of one-third of the capital and surplus, an amendment of the banking act by which the proportion referred to is changed from one-third

§ 52. Additional or Supplemental Assessment.

Provision is usually made by statute in the various states for an additional or supplemental assessment of bank property or shares of bank stock which have been omitted from taxation, and the manner in which such additional or supplemental assessment shall be made is also prescribed.[2914] However,

---

to one-half, no change being made in the taxation law, does not increase the amount of deduction to be made by the assessor. Topeka State Bank v. Tax Com. of Kansas, 114 Kan. 267, 217 P. 304.

Ohio.—The statutes relating to the duties of the county auditor when any person makes a false tax return or statement of his personalty, subject to taxation, or the assessor has omitted or made an erroneous return, and authorizing him to correct such return, and to charge such person on the duplicate with the proper amount of taxes, apply only to persons required to make returns of their property for taxation; and the stock of a shareholder in a bank being returnable by the cashier, though the indebtedness of a stockholder has been erroneously deducted from the value of his shares by the county auditor, such deduction cannot be placed on the duplicate as an omission, and the taxes collected thereon. State v. Akins, 63 Ohio St. 182, 57 N.E. 1094; Lander v. Mercantile Nat. Bank, 118 F. 785.

Corporate taxpayer would be permitted to amend its personal property tax returns so as to change the type of returns filed from independent to consolidated returns. First Banc Group, Inc. v. Lindley, 22 Ohio Op. 3d 297, 68 Ohio St. 2d 81, 428 N.E.2d 427 (1981).

Oklahoma.—National bank stock assessed to shareholders, after amount invested in nontaxable securities has been erroneously deducted, cannot be reassessed as "property not listed and assessed," within statute, where no legal steps are taken to review assessment through board of county commissioners and appeal to courts. Hamilton v. International Bank, 114 Okla. 28, 242 P. 858 (1924); Hamilton v. Exchange Nat. Bank, 114 Okla. 30, 242 P. 860.

Washington.—Under statute providing for deduction of bank's realty from assessment against stockholders, and in view of section relating to bank's holding of realty, bank seeking to have its assessment reduced must allege and prove status of realty entitling it to deduction. Scandinavian American Bank v. Pierce County, 93 Wash. 671, 161 P. 469.

2914 *Indiana.*—Daily v. Washington Nat'l Bank, 163 Ind. 476, 72 N.E. 260.

Under an act requiring the taxation of capital stock in national banks, an assessment of such stocks which has been omitted by the county auditor when he delivered the tax duplicate to the treasurer should be inserted by the latter, but, if correct assessments be made by the auditor after such delivery and are acted upon by the treasurer, it is sufficient. Strader v. Manville, 33 Ind. 111.

Iowa—Judy v. National Stats Bank, 133 Iowa 252, 110 N.W. 605.

Where an assessor in assessing the stock of a national bank exempted therefrom the amount of the bonds of United States and all municipal corporations, owned by the bank, the county authorities have no right to assess the stock of omitted property on the theory that the bonds were not exempt from taxation. Judy v. National State Bank, 133 Iowa 252, 110 N.W. 605.

Kentucky.—Commonwealth v. Citizens' Nat. Bank, 117 Ky. 946, 80 S.W. 158, 25 Ky. L. Rptr. 2100, appeal dismissed, 199 U.S. 603, 26 S. Ct. 750, 50 L. Ed. 329; London v. Hope, 80 S.W. 817, 26 Ky. L. Rptr. 112; Commonwealth v. Riley, 115 Ky. 140, 72 S.W. 809, 24

to sustain the validity of a supplemental assessment, it must appear that the items of property assessed were not assessed in the original assessment, and were omitted by mistake.[2915] And in determining what was assessed in an original assessment, a court is bound by the assessment itself which cannot be modified or limited by other evidence.[2916] Therefore, if assessors have once assessed an item of property, that assessment cannot be revised by supplemental assessment.[2917] Thus, it has been held that an assessment of back taxes on the surplus of a bank on which taxes have been previously levied and paid, is unauthorized even though such surplus was taxed at an undervaluation.[2918] And it has been held that a taxing official cannot assess shares of bank stock for taxes for prior years, where there has been no levy

---

Ky. L. Rptr. 2005; Commonwealth v. Mt. Sterling Nat. Bank, 99 S.W. 958, 30 Ky. L. Rptr. 954.

Louisiana.—Where valuation of national bank's stock for tax purposes was limited as required by statute which was subsequently held unconstitutional, the original assessment was void with respect to a "separable portion," and hence statute requiring further assessment of property which has been "erroneously assessed" or "improperly assessed" or "omitted" was applicable and authorized supplementary assessment. And bank could not void collection on equitable grounds. Flournoy v. First Nat. Bank, 3 So. 2d 244, 197 La. 1067.

Missouri.—The director of revenue had no claim against bank in connection with the 1981 bank tax due unless the director determined that an additional amount was due and mailed notice thereof to the bank and unless the bank thereafter filed a timely petition for review with the Administrative Hearing Commission and the Commission. decided the case or unduly delayed. Commercial Bank v. James, 658 S.W.2d 17 (Mo. 1983).

2915 **In general.—**

Sweetsir v. Chandler, 98 Me. 145, 56 A. 584.

A supplemental assessment may be laid on property omitted by mistake in the original assessment, even though it may result in raising more money than was voted to be raised. Sweetsir v. Chandler, 98 Me. 145, 56 A. 584.

Generally, items or species of property of any character of corporations assessed on their moneyed capital surplus, etc., not reported together with their value, to assessor, may be assessed as omitted property. In re Durant Nat. Bank, 107 Okla. 65, 230 P. 712.

A supplemental assessment is a part of the original assessment, and an amendment of it. Sweetsir v. Chandler, 98 Me. 145, 56 A. 584.

And it must be made to the same person as the original assessment was properly made to. Sweetsir v. Chandler, 98 Me. 145, 56 A. 584.

2916 Sweetsir v. Chandler, 98 Me. 145, 56 A. 584.

2917 Sweetsir v. Chandler, 98 Me. 145, 56 A. 584.

2918 Bank of Oxford v. Lafayette County, 79 Miss. 152, 29 So. 825 (1901); Langhout v. First Nat. Bank, 191 Iowa 957, 183 N.W. 506; In re Durant Nat. Bank, 107 Okla. 65, 230 P. 712.

on such shares during the prior years.[2919] Moreover, assessors cannot cure an error in the amount of an assessment of money at interest by securing a revaluation through a supplemental assessment, even though their error arose from their ignorance of the specific securities in which the money at interest was invested.[2920]

§ 53. Notice of Assessment.

It seems that stockholders of a national bank are required to take notice of their state law providing for the assessment and taxation of their shares, and the general law creating a board of equalization and fixing the time and place where they may appear to apply for a reduction of their assessments[2921] and a notice required to be given to a bank of the assessment of the shares of its stockholders is sufficient notice to the stockholders under such statutory provisions.[2922] But it has been held that a tax assessed against bank shares without notice and opportunity to be heard, is not merely irregular, but void.[2923] Compliance with the notice provision of the statute governing an increase in the assessed valuation of real property for purposes of taxation is mandatory, and failure by an assessor to give requisite notice of an increase in assessed valuation renders any increase in valuation and any tax computed thereon void.[2924]

§ 54. Assessment Rolls or Books.

Nature and Necessity.—In assessing bank property or bank shares for taxation, an assessment roll or book prepared in the manner prescribed for the assessment of property generally is essential, and such bank property or shares are not assessed, though in a verified list, until recorded in an assessment roll as required by statute.[2925] The list made by an assessor, not the list returned by an individual taxpayer, constitutes the assessment roll.[2926] And an auditor's duty to transcribe assessments into tax books and

---

2919 Sussex County v. Jarratt, 129 Va. 672, 106 S.E. 384, rehearing denied, 106 S.E. 627.

2920 Sweetsir v. Chandler, 98 Me. 145, 56 A. 584.

2921 Nevada Nat'l Bank v. Dodge, 119 F. 57; Merchants', etc., Bank v. Pennsylvania, 167 U.S. 461, 17 S. Ct. 829, 42 L. Ed. 236; People ex rel. Chamberlain v. Smith, 2 N.Y.S. 460, 50 Hun 39.

2922 Nevada Nat'l Bank v. Dodge, 119 F. 57.

2923 Second Nat'l Bank v. New York, 213 N.Y. 457, 107 N.E. 1039.

2924 United Mo. Bank v. March, 650 S.W.2d 678 (Mo. App. 1983).

2925 Oregon & W. M. Sav. Bank v. Jordan, 16 Ore. 113, 17 P. 621; Iowa Nat'l Bank v. Stewart (Iowa), 232 N.W. 445.

2926 Vicksburg Bank v. Adams, 74 Miss. 179, 21 So. 401.

make the necessary computations and extensions is ministerial; he is without power to change classifications and assessments of property.[2927]

Requisites and Sufficiency.—Where the property or shares of a bank are sought to be taxed, the assessment rolls and books must meet the requirements of the applicable statute in the respective jurisdiction.[2928] And an assessment roll must designate the owner or person to whom property is sought to be assessed,[2929] and give a description of the property on which the assessment is made.[2930] An assessment of bank stock need not, however, show on the face of the assessment list that the stock is not exempt from taxation.[2931]

Once county assessors request lists of taxpayer's real and personal property, taxpayer must correctly list its property, and assessors are entitled to rely on list furnished by taxpayer and to tax property accordingly. First Interstate Bank v. State Dep't of Revenue, 871 P.2d 1178 (Ariz. Tax 1994).

[2927] Iowa Nat. Bank v. Stewart (Iowa), 232 N.W. 445, followed, Home Sav. Bank v. Stewart, 232 N.W. 471.

[2928] Ludeman v. Cerro Gordo County, 204 Iowa 1100, 216 N.W. 712; Peterke v. Turner (Iowa), 195 N.W. 203; First Nat. Bank v. Burke, 201 Iowa 994, 196 N.W. 287; Main Street Bank v. Richmond, 122 Va. 574, 95 S.E. 386; Langhout v. First Nat. Bank, 191 Iowa 957, 183 N.W. 506; Citizens' Bank v. Baker County Board of Equalization, 109 Ore. 669, 222 P. 341; State v. Cantley, 325 Mo. 67, 26 S.W.2d 976.

The omission of the city clerk to extend upon the assessment roll the amount to be paid by each holder of bank shares, until alter such roll has been delivered to the city treasurer, does not render the taxation of such shares void. First Nat. Bank v. Waters, 7 F. 152; Citizens' Nat'l Bank v. Klauss, 47 Ind. App. 50, 93 N.E. 681.

Assessment entered in column entitled "all other personal property required to be listed" could not be deemed assessment of credits, bank stock, or money in bank which were required to be listed in separate columns. People v. Pullman Car, etc., Corp 355 Ill. 438, 189 N.E. 278.

[2929] *United States.*—Albany City Nat. Bank v. Maher, 6 F. 417; First Nat. Bank v. Hungate, 62 F. 548.

California.—Title Guaranty & Trust Co. v. County of Los Angeles, 3 Cal. App. 619, 86 P. 844; Commercial Nat. Bank v. Schlitz, 6 Cal. App. 174, 91 P. 750.

Illinois.—People v. Hibernian Banking Ass'n, 245 Ill. 522, 92 N.E. 305.

Indiana.—Small v. Lawrenceburgh, 128 Ind. 231, 27 N.E. 500.

Iowa.—Watkins v. Couch, 142 Iowa 164, 120 N.W. 485.

Louisiana.—Castles v. New Orleans, 46 La. Ann. 542, 15 So. 199.

[2930] Savings & Loan Soc. v. San Francisco, 131 Cal. 356, 63 P. 665; State ex rel. Batz v. Lewis, 118 Wis. 432, 95 N.W. 388; Judy v. National State Bank, 133 Iowa 252, 110 N.W. 605.

[2931] Monroe v. New Canaan, 43 Conn. 309.

Applying the foregoing rules, it has been held that a tax on the stock of a national bank assessed in the name of the bank is a valid tax, and is binding as such upon the stockholders.[2932] And where money was deposited in a bank pending suit pursuant to an order of court, an assessment thereof was held not vitiated because it was assessed to the bank as receiver, or because of misdescription and commingling by the taxing officers.[2933] An assessment of national bank stock was held not invalid because the words "as agent" were omitted therefrom.[2934] Similarly, a bank tax on "money on hand, at interest or on deposit," will not be abated because of an assessor's omission of the statutory words, "surplus capital."[2935] Where a national bank furnished to an assessor a verified statement of its capital, surplus and undivided profits, and a complete list of its shareholders, giving their addresses and the number of shares held by each, which was in effect the same as the assessment rolls prescribed by statute though not in the precise form of such rolls, the fact that the assessor did not enter in the blank space in the statement provided therefor the number of shares of each shareholder, and the taxable value thereof, because of a belief that an act authorizing deduction of a bank's investments in government tax-free securities was valid and left nothing to tax, did not establish a failure by the assessor to assess such shares.[2936] Where personal property held by bank stockholders who resided in the town where their bank was situated, was valued and taxed to them in the same "duplicate" as the assessment and valuation of the bank stock although carried on a separate line, it was held that there was a sufficient compliance with a statutory requirement for including the valuation of such stock in that of personal property.[2937] So, also, such a requirement has been held to be substantially complied with where, in making up an assessment roll, assessors place the valuation of bank shares in a separate item in the column in which personal property is placed.[2938] And the entry of assessments for national bank shares upon a list or book separate from other assessments of personal property of individuals does not

---

[2932] State v. Security Nat. Bank, 143 Minn. 408, 173 N.W. 885.

[2933] Spring Valley Water Co. v. San Francisco, 225 F. 728, aff'd, 246 U.S. 391, 38 S. Ct. 356, 62 L. Ed. 790.

[2934] Atlantic Nat'l Bank v. Simpson, 136 Fla. 809, 188 So. 636.

[2935] First Nat. Bank v. Concord, 59 N.H. 75.

[2936] First Nat. Bank v. Anderson, 196 Iowa 587, 192 N.W. 6, rev'd on other grounds, 269 U.S. 341, 46 S. Ct. 135, 70 L. Ed. 295.

[2937] State v. Cook, 32 N.J.L. 347.

[2938] Williams v. Weaver, 75 N.Y. 30, aff'd, 100 U.S. 547, 25 L Ed. 708.

render them void.[2939] Where a national bank did not return the shares of its nonresident stockholders as required by statute, an assessor was authorized to assess the shares according to his information and best judgment, and the bank could not complain that the assessment did not show the names or number of such stockholders, the number of shares assessed, and the like.[2940] But an assessment specifying the name and location of a bank, the amount assessed, the amount levied, and the total levy for a county and district, without specifying the names of stockholders, the number of shares of stock held by each stockholder, the value of such stock, and the amount of taxes due, as required by statute for the assessment of bank stock, has been held not an assessment of such stock, but rather an assessment of the bank's capital stock.[2941]

Unsecured Rolls.—See the footnote.[2942]

§ 55. Equalization of Assessments.

In General.—Statutes in the various jurisdictions provide for equalization boards,[2943] and govern matters relating to the equalization of assessments.[2944]

2939 McMahon v. Palmer, 102 N.Y. 176, 6 N.E. 400, 55 Am. it 796, aff'd, 133 U.S. 660, 10 S. Ct. 324, 33 L. Ed. 772.

2940 Atlantic Nat'l Bank v. Simpson, 136 Fla. 809, 188 So. 636.

2941 Sussex County v. Jarratt, 129 Va. 672, 106 S.E. 384.

2942 Where advertising sign and night depository were assessed to bank which was not the assessed of the building or of the land upon which they were located and taxes thereon were not a lien on real property, sufficient in opinion of assessor to secure payment of the taxes, sign and night depository were properly assessed to bank on the unsecured roll. Ventura County v. Channel Islands State Bank, 251 Cal. App. 2d 240, 59 Cal. Rptr. 404 (1967).

2943 Bank of America Nat'l Trust & Sav. Asso. v. Mundo, 37 Cal. 2d 1, 229 P.2d 345. The equalization of assessments among the different counties of a state is to be made by the state board of equalization. Territory v. First Nat. Bank, 10 N.M. 283, 65 P. 172; HACKER v. HOWE, 72 Neb. 385, 101 N.W. 255.

Under some statutes county commissioners or supervisors constitute boards of equalization for their counties, whose duty it is to equalize the valuation of the taxable property under such rules as may be prescribed by law. Weiser Nat'l Bank v. Jeffreys, 14 Idaho 659, 95 P. 23; Cassett v. Sherwood, 42 Iowa 623; People ex rel. Geneva v. Board of Sup'rs, 50 Misc. 63, 100 N.Y.S. 330, aff'd, 114 App. Div. 915, 100 N.Y.S. 1136, rev'd on other grounds, 188 N.Y. 1, 80 N.E. 381; Borough v. Board, 70 N.J.L. 196, 56 A. 124; Campbell v. Minnehaha Nat. Bank, 11 S.D. 133, 76 N.W. 10.

2944 **In general.—**

Weiser Nat. Bank v. Jeffreys, 14 Idaho 659, 95 P. 23.

The method of equalizing the valuation of taxable property in the several counties in a state, provided for by statute, applies to the taxable property in a county, and not to property

The jurisdiction of boards of equalization being special, any acts which are not authorized by express terms of the applicable statute are without validity.[2945] Thus, such a board is not authorized to treat bank stocks as composing a class distinct from other stocks, even where only bank stocks are assessed in a county.[2946] And a board cannot consider a previous reduction in the assessment of stock of one bank in fixing the total valuation and assessment of bank stock in a county, since it is limited to classes and has no power to equalize the value of a specific person's property or different pieces of property.[2947] But a state board of equalization acts judicially, and an assessor's valuation of bank stock is not binding on the board.[2948] And a state board's valuation of bank stock in excess of its actual value will not be interfered with, absent gross excessiveness or discrimination.[2949] Under a statute requiring such a board, whenever it is satisfied that a valuation has not been made with reasonable uniformity by different county assessors, to equalize such assessments throughout the state, the board has power to

---

over which the taxing power has no jurisdiction. Weiser Nat. Bank v. Jeffreys, 14 Idaho 659, 95 P. 23.

Statement to state comptroller.—

Under a New York statute It was held that a statement of state board of equalization to state comptroller of assessed valuations of property properly included assessed valuations of bank stock. New York v. Schoeneck, 93 Misc. 645, 158 N.Y.S. 595, aff'd, 174 App. Div. 901, 159 N.Y.S. 1105, aff'd, 219 N.Y. 646, 114 N.E. 1062.

Shareholder held not deprived of opportunity for equalization.—

The fact that statutes providing for the assessment of shares of stock in a bank make it the duty of the assessors to collect the tax immediately from the bank when they make assessment where the shareholder has not sufficient real estate within the county to pay the tax, does not deprive the shareholder of an opportunity for equalization of the tax imposed upon the shareholders, since the bank is the agent of the shareholder both for the purpose of the payment of the tax and for the purpose of making protest if it so desires or is so instructed by the shareholders. Brophy v. Powell, 58 Ariz. 543, 121 P.2d 647.

2945 **In general.—**

Campbell v. Minnehaha Nat. Bank, 11 S.D. 133, 76 N.W. 10.

Reduction of assessment.—

A county equalization board was held without authority to reduce an assessment on bank stock to equalize it with the assessment of other property, where the state board fixed the true value of the stock at amount originally assessed. Bank of Tupelo v. Board of Sup'rs, 155 Miss. 436, 124 So. 482.

2946 Coler v. Sterling, 11 S.D. 140, 76 N.W. 12.

2947 State ex rel. Gardner v. Harris, 286 Mo. 262, 227 S.W. 818.

2948 Bank of Carthage v. Thomas, 330 Mo. 19, 48 S.W.2d 930.

2949 Bank of Carthage v. Thomas, 330 Mo. 19, 48 S.W.2d 930.

equalize the valuation fixed for capital stock of banks where the tax rolls show that the valuation was not reasonably uniform, whether or not an appeal has been taken by a taxpayer.[2950]

Estoppel.—The unconditional tender of county and state taxes on bank stock as rendered for taxation by a bank's cashier has been held to estop a bank stockholder from asserting error or arbitrary action by an equalization board in increasing the stock's valuation for tax purposes.[2951]

e. Review, Correction, or Setting Aside of Assessment.

§ 56. In General.

It may be stated as a general rule that where assessments on property of a bank or shares of bank stock are irregular, excessive or unequal, the remedy provided by statute therefor is exclusive.[2952] Property tax assessments can be held to be constructively fraudulent if shown to be based upon an assessor's lack of knowledge or if so obviously excessive as to require

---

[2950] Territory v. First Nat. Bank, 10 N.M. 283, 65 P. 172.

[2951] Doneghy v. State (Ten. Civ. App.), 240 S.W.2d 331.

[2952] *United States.*—National Rockland Bank v. Boston, 296 F. 743, rev'd on other grounds sub nom. Fourth AU. Nat'l Bank v. City of Boston, 300 F. 29; People's Sav. Bank v. Layman, 134 F. 635; State Railroad Tax Cases, 92 U.S. 575, 23 L. Ed. 663.

California.—Merrill v. Gorham, 6 Cal. 41.

Connecticut.—Waterbury Sav. Bank v. Lawler, 46 Conn. 243; Seeley v. Westport, 47 Conn. 294, 36 Am. R. 70.

Illinois.—Ottawa Glass Co. v. McCaleb, 81 m. 556; Porter v. Rockford, etc., R. Co., 76 Ill. 561.

Indiana.—Senour v. Matchett, 140 Ind. 636, 40 N.E. 122.

Iowa.—Iowa Nat. Bank v. Stewart (Iowa), 232 N.W. 445; Macklot v. Davenport, 17 Iowa 379.

Missouri.—State ex rel. Gracy v. Bank of Neosho, 120 Mo. 161, 25 S.W. 372.

The statutory scheme for determination and collection of the state bank tax, including provisions for administrative and judicial review, is orderly, comprehensive and specific, indicating legislative intent that its provisions are mandatory and exclusive. Commercial Bank v. James, 658 S.W.2d 17 (Mo. 1983).

Nebraska.—State v. American State Bank, 114 Neb. 740, 209 N.W. 621.

New York.—Mayor v. Meserole, 26 Wend. 132.

Oregon.—Oregon, etc., Sav. Bank v. Jordan, 16 Ore. 113, 17 P. 621.

Pennsylvania.—Stewart v. Maple, 70 Pa. 221; Hughes v. Kline, 30 Pa. 227.

such a construction.[2953] Thus, where a bank has returned in its list of property for taxation its capital stock as property owned, possessed or controlled by it, if it desires to object to being thus assessed, it must go before a board of equalization for a correction.[2954] And where an assessor makes an unauthorized assessment of shares of bank stock to a bank, and the bank does not ask a board of equalization to correct such erroneous assessment, it cannot enjoin the collection of the taxes imposed thereunder, in the absence of a valid excuse for its failure to apply to such board.[2955] Similarly, under a statute providing that the amount of a franchise tax shall be final if no protest is flied within sixty days, such an amount is not subject to question by a bank where no protest has been filed, irrespective of whether true estoppel exists against it.[2956] Finally, taxpayers complaining to a board of review may make informal objections to their assessments, but they should make all objections which they have at such time.[2957] Courts will liberally construe a statutory right to appeal a tax matter so as to permit a case to be considered on its merits.[2958] The board of equalization is not concerned with the amount of money to be raised; its sole concern is to insure that assessments are proper and truly reflect "market value."[2959] Valuation of real property for tax purposes is speculative and arbitrary if based upon the happening of a uncertain event rather than upon what the property would fairly and reasonably bring at a present fair sale.[2960] Fraud must be established by clear and convincing evidence, but deliberate misconduct by a tax assessor need not be shown.[2961] In view of the fact that

---

[2953] In re Application of County Collector of Pike County, 133 Ill. App. 3d 142, 88 Ill. Dec. 311, 478 N.E.2d 626 (1985).

[2954] First Nat'l Bank v. Bailey, 15 Mont. 301, 39 P. 83.

[2955] Meyer v. Rosenblatt, 78 Mo. 495; Oteri v. Parker, 42 La. Ann. 374, 7 So. 570; Board of Comm'rs v. Searight Cattle Co., 3 Wyo. 777, 31 P. 268; Meade v. Haines, 81 Mich. 261, 45 N.W. 836; First Nat. Bank v. Bailey, 15 Mont 301, 39 P. 83.

[2956] People v. Richardson, 37 Cal. App. 2d 275, 99 P.2d 366; as to estoppel or waiver, see § 48 of this chapter.

[2957] Iowa Nat. Bank v. Stewart (Iowa), 232 N.W. 445.

[2958] City Nat'l Bank & Trust Co. v. Property Tax Appeal Bd., 73 Ill. Dec. 555, 454 N.E.2d 652 (Ill. 1983).

[2959] Charles Schreiner Bank v. Kerrville Independent School Dist., 683 S.W.2d 466 (Tex. App. 4 Dist. 1984).

[2960] Du Page Bank & Trust Co. v. Property Tax Appeal Bd., 104 Ill. Dec. 590, 151 Ill. App. 3d 624, 502 N.E.2d 1250 (1986).

[2961] Du Page Bank & Trust Co. v. Property Tax Appeal Bd., 104 Ill. Dec. 590, 151 Ill. App. 3d 624, 502 N.E.2d 1250 (1986).

the township assessor based his valuation of the subject property on sales of comparably zoned property also having road frontage, and the taxpayer did not offer any contrary evidence of fair market value, the assessor's valuation was not speculative, and was based upon valid factors existing at the time of assessment.[2962]

§ 57. Grounds for Review.

An error in the valuation of shares of bank stock is grounds for the review of an assessment.[2963] And when the assets of a savings bank have been reduced in value below the amount due to depositors, a petition may be maintained for abatement of taxes to such extent.[2964]

§ 58. Right of Review.

Persons Entitled to Seek Review.—As to assessments of bank property or shares of bank stock, the general rule applies that an appeal to the proper board or other tribunal may be made by anyone aggrieved by an assessment,[2965] having an Interest in the property assessed.[2966] And under a statute

---

[2962] DuPage Bank & Trust Co. v. Property Tax Appeal Bd., 151 Ill. App. 3d 624, 104 Ill. Dec. 590, 502 N.E.2d 1250 (1986).

[2963] People v. Assessors (N.Y.), 2 Hun 583; Appeal of Everitt, 71 Pa. 216.

[2964] In re Wolfeborough Sav. Bank, 69 N.H. 84, 39 A. 522.

[2965] Apgar v. Hayward, 110 N.Y. 225, 18 N.E. 85.

Where bank stock was assessed at 50 percent of value, while other property was valued at not exceeding 44 percent of value, bank could contest tax directly in courts. Yakima Valley Bank, etc., Co. v. Yakima County, 149 Wash. 552, 271 P. 820.

[2966] People v. Wall St. Bank (N.Y.), 89 Hun 625; People ex rel. First Nat'l Bank v. Button, 17 N.Y.S. 315, 63 Hun 624.

Assignee of note secured by deed of trust had standing to contest validity of back taxes to extent necessary for determination of whether those taxes constitute breach of covenant against incumbrances. Inland Real Estate Corp. v. Oak Park Trust & Sav. Bank, 127 Ill. App. 3d 535, 82 Ill. Dec. 670, 469 N.E.2d 204 (1983).

Property owner after foreclosure had right to use administrative procedures of Tax Code. Bank of Am. Nat'l Trust & Sav. Ass'n v. Dallas Cent. Appraisal Dist., 765 S.W.2d 451 (Tex. App. 1988).

Taxpayer which owned bank on office tower on tax-exempt land whose air rights were leased from city had standing to appeal from decision of county board of revision, notwithstanding that city was listed as owner of parcel on tax bill, where taxpayer's name and address also appeared on tax bill under mailing address designation; moreover, statute does not confer standing for appeal to court of common pleas only on record owner of underlying real estate. First Nat'l Bank Ctr. Assoc. v. Hamilton Cty. Bd. of Revision, 70 Ohio App. 3d 46, 590 N.E.2d 387 (1990), jurisdictional motion overruled, 58 Ohio St. 3d 703, 569 N.E.2d 511 (1991).

providing that banks shall pay taxes assessed to their stockholders on their stock, and may recover from each stockholder his proportion of such taxes, on an assessment against a bank's stockholders, the bank itself is a party in interest, and has a right to appear before a board of review to complain of the assessment,[2967] and may also appeal from the board's decision.[2968] Similarly, under a statute providing that no person shall question the valuation of personal property assessed against him, unless in person or by agent he presents his objections before a board of review and discloses all personalty liable to assessment, a bank can appear by its officers and object to an assessment of bank stock.[2969] Where a city has a direct interest in the amount and validity of a state and county tax levied on its taxpayers, and is unjustly affected by the illegal action of a county board, it is entitled to sue to correct same.[2970] And a law providing that any bank which claims that taxes assessed upon it are inequitable may apply for an abatement thereof, may be applied to a cause of action which accrues before the enactment thereof, as such act merely changes the mode of judicial procedure for enforcement of a right without affecting the right itself.[2971]

A taxpayer bank's contention that it was improperly taxed as owner of stock should have been timely raised in protest filed under the tax code, and the failure to exhaust administrative remedies precluded it from seeking a judicial appeal.[2972]

Estoppel or Waiver.[2973]—With regard to assessments against banks or on shares of bank stock, the usual rule applies that prior statements by an owner

---

[2967] **In general.—**

First Nat. Bank v. Independence, 123 Iowa 482, 99 N.W. 142; National Bank of Commerce v. New Bedford, 155 Mass. 313, 29 N.E. 532 (1892).

Contra.—

Application to correct assessment on bank stock must be made by stockholders, as taxpayer, since bank, not being liable for tax, except out of funds of stockholders, is not party in interest.Leesburg v. Loudoun Nat'l Bank, 141 Va. 244, 126 S.E. 196.

[2968] First Nat'l Bank v. Independence, 123 Iowa 482, 99 N.W. 142.

[2969] Second Ward Sav. Bank v. Leuch, 155 Wis. 493, 144 N.W. 1119.

[2970] People v. Supervisors, 16 Barb. 607; Colonial Life Assur. Co. v. Board of Supervisors, 24 Barb. 166; People ex rel. Geneva v. Board of Sup'rs, 50 Misc. 63, 100 N.Y.S. 330, aff'd, 114 App. Div. 915, 100 N.Y.S. 1136, rev'd on other grounds, 188 N.Y. 1, 80 N.E. 381.

[2971] In re Wolfeborough Sav. Bank, 69 N.H. 84, 39 A. 522.

[2972] Harris County Appraisal Dist. v. Texas Nat'l Bank, 775 S.W.2d 66 (Tex. App. 1989).

[2973] See also § 46 of this chapter.

as to the assessable nature of his property will not estop him to question the legality of assessments made against his property.[2974] And a failure to file a statement of taxable property with an assessor or board of review does not preclude a claim that the board erred in not granting the relief requested.[2975] Moreover, a bank is not estopped to deny liability for a tax levied on its capital stock as the bank's personal property by reason of the fact that for several years it has paid such tax.[2976] The fact that a bank, after due protest, paid in full a tax assessed on its shares of stock in the hands of shareholders is no ground for objecting to the bank's claim for an abatement of tax, where such payment is by statute made an express condition of the granting of an abatement.[2977] And where stock which a bank owns in another corporation or itself is not subject to taxation for school purposes, the bank does not waive its objection to the assessment of a school tax by ignoring it and omitting to appeal therefrom in the manner prescribed by statute.[2978] Similarly, where an assessor states to the officers of a national bank, when it presents its list of stock to him for taxation, that such stock will be assessed at a certain value, but he assesses it at a higher value and the bank is given

---

[2974] **In general.—**

Mahkonsa Invest Co. v. Fort Dodge, 125 Iowa 148, 100 N.W. 517.

Contra—

Bank held estopped, in action for taxes, to question statement to assessor listing worthless paper as bill receivable. State v. Citizens' Bank, 171 Minn. 29, 213 N.W. 45.

[2975] Bank of Tustin v. Burdell Tp., 184 Mich. 131, 150 N.W. 367.

Under a statute requiring the assessor to deduct from the aggregate amount of capital stock, surplus and undivided profits, the amount of investments in real estate, and base his assessment upon the remainder, the failure of a bank to furnish the assessor a verified statement of its property within the time required is no sufficient reason for the refusal of the board of equalization to equalize such assessment, thus penalizing the bank by a double tax on its real estate. Leesburg v. Loudoun Nat. Bank, 141 Va. 244, 126 S.E. 196.

Question as to whether state taxing authority's "unitary business" method of apportioning income to multi-national company's in-state operations unconstitutionally interfered with power of executive branch of federal government to conduct foreign affairs was sufficiently preserved for judicial review, notwithstanding company's alleged failure to raise question in administrative proceeding before the California Franchise Tax Board; it would have been a futile exercise to raise this constitutional issue, involving sensitive matters of international relations, before Board. Barclays Bank International Ltd. v. Franchise Tax Bd., 275 Cal. Rptr. 626 (Cal. App. 3 Dist. 1990), rehearing denied.

[2976] Farmers', etc., Bank v. Hoffman, 93 Iowa 119, 61 N.W. 418.

[2977] National Bank of Commerce v. New Bedford, 155 Mass. 313, 29 N.E. 532 (1892); Spokane & Eastern Trust Co. v. Spokane County, 153 Wash. 332, 280 P. 3.

[2978] School Directors v. Carlisle Bank (Pa.), 8 Watts 289.

no notice thereof, it may maintain an action for relief against such valuation, though it does not go before a board of equalization and ask for a reduction, since the assessor's act is a fraud on the bank.[2979] Where the supervisors of a county improperly assess shares of bank stock in a certain city other than in the manner provided by statute, whereby the tax of said city is increased, the city is not deprived of its right to have its shares reduced to the proper amount, though the tax rolls have been distributed among the various town collectors and it is impossible to divide the deficiency created by such illegal tax among the towns which should have been charged with it originally.[2980]

Where the officers of a bank furnish an assessor with the names of its shareholders, together with the amount of stock held by each, and make no objection on the ground of irregularity of the assessment, are themselves a party to it, and the claims of the assessor are substantially correct, such officers cannot argue that his error in assessing shares to the bank instead of its stockholder rendered the assessment void and the collector a trespasser.[2981] And a tax assessor cannot be presumed to have personal knowledge of the private affairs of persons assessed unless they choose to furnish it, such as the amount of debts owing by a holder of bank stock subject to taxation, and if a taxpayer takes no steps to have a tax altered, he will be assumed to admit its correctness.[2982] A taxpayer who fails to appeal from a board of assessment in the matter of taxation of bank stock is held precluded from subsequently questioning his assessment.[2983]

§ 59. Creation and Organization of Boards of Review or Other Special Tribunals.

The power to review, correct or set aside assessments is vested by statutes of various states in boards of equalization or other special tribunals.[2984] And an objection that a member of a board of equalization is not a freeholder as required by statute, cannot be made in an action by a bank to recover taxes paid.[2985]

[2979] Citizens' Nat'l Bank v. Columbia County, 23 Wash. 441, 63 P. 209.

[2980] Geneva v. Board, 100 N.Y.S. 330, aff'd, 100 N.Y.S. 1136.

[2981] St. Louis Bldg. & Sav. Asso. v. Lightner, 47 Mo. 393.

[2982] First Nat. Bank v. St. Joseph, 46 Mich. 526, 9 N.W. 838.

[2983] Rockingham v. Hood, 204 N.C. 618, 169 S.E. 191.

[2984] Oregon, etc., Sav. Bank v. Jordan, 16 Ore. 113, 17 P. 621; State ex rel. Gracy v. Bank of Neosho, 120 Mo. 161, 25 S.W. 372; Sioux Falls Sav. Bank v. Minnehaha County, 29 S.D. 146, 135 N.W. 689, 1914D Ann. Cue. 910; Iowa Nat. Bank v. Stewart (Iowa), 232 N.W. 445.

[2985] State Nat'l Bank v. Memphis, 116 Tenn. 641, 94 S.W. 606, 7 L.R.A. (n.s.) 663.

§ 60. Authority, Powers and Duties of Boards or Officers.

In General.—It is the duty of boards of equalization or review to equalize assessments,[2986] and in so doing, they have the power and jurisdiction to make either additions or reductions to assessments of bank property of stock by an assessor.[2987] Thus, where an inequality exists in the assessment of property within a county, an owner of property discriminated against is entitled to a correction of his assessment, although such relief necessitates the reduction of the valuation of his property below its true cash value.[2988] Such boards have the power to correct errors and omissions in the assessment rolls in the state or county in which they act[2989] when proceedings are brought within the proper time.[2990] Thus, with respect to assessments of bank property or shares, as in the case of assessments of

---

[2986] State Nat'l Bank v. Memphis, 116 Tenn. 641, 94 S.W. 606, 7 L.R.A. (n.s.) 663; Ankeny v. Blakley, 44 Ore. 78, 74 P. 485.

Whether assessments alleged to be discriminatory as to bank's personalty were made as the bank charges and whether they resulted in unequal taxation were the issues before state board of equalization and it was within the power of the board to correct the alleged discriminatory assessment. Bank of America Nat'l Trust & Sav. Asso. v. Mundo, 37 Cal. 2d 1, 229 P.2d 345.

[2987] Ward v. Board of Equalization, 135 Mo. 309, 36 S.W. 648; Blocklock v. Board (Mo.), 36 S.W. 1132; Oregon & W. M. Sav. Bank v. Jordan, 16 Ore. 113, 17 P. 621; Mannings Bank v. Armstrong, 204 Iowa 512, 211 N.W. 485; Elliott v. Rhoads, 203 Iowa 218, 212 N.W. 468; Beveridge v. Beer, 595.1). 563, 241 N.W. 727, 84 A.L.R. 189.

Finance company's creation of large savings deposit, which was left in bank but short time, held ineffective attempt to evade taxation, and assessment was properly increased. Whiting Finance Co. v. Hopkins, 199 Cal. 428, 249 P. 853 (1926).

[2988] First Nat. Bank v. Board, 36 Colo. 265, 84 P. 1111.

[2989] Union, etc., Nat. Bank v. Board, 65 Neb. 408, 91 N.W. 286, rev'd, 65 Neb. 410, 92 N.W. 1022.

If, by reason of error or misapprehension, tax on deposits in savings departments of trust companies due in year before from corporation petitioning for abatement of corporate franchise tax was incorrectly assessed, error could be corrected in assessing tax for following year. J. S. Lang Engineering Co. v. Commonwealth, 231 Mass. 367, 120 N.E. 843.

[2990] Union Stock Yards Nat'l Bank v. Board of County Comm'rs, 65 Neb. 408, 91 N.W. 286, rev'd, 65 Neb. 410, 92 N.W. 1022, in which It was held that the board had power to make such corrections within a certain period from the time the taxes would, if legally assessed, have become delinquent.

Where the statute, provided for an appeal within 30 days after mailing notice of assessments, board of tax appeals had no jurisdiction to hear and consider a "petition on appeal" not filed until 16 months after mailing certificate of assessments. Leimbach v. Evatt, 141 Ohio St. 191, 25 Ohio Op. 279, 46 N.E.2d 859.

Where trustees of bank in liquidation failed to take timely appeal from preliminary assessment on bank assets, the assessment became final and board of tax appeals had no

property of natural persons or other corporations, a board of equalization has power to correct an assessment: (1) When tax-exempt property has been assessed;[2991] (2) where property has been assessed to a party who does not own it;[2992] (3) or where there has been a double assessment;[2993] and (4) sometimes even where the person assessed has taken no appeal to the board.[2994]

The Tax Commission cannot be heard to contest validity of its own rules, made under apparent statutory authority, and promulgated to public for their governance in Commission matters.[2995]

Where no appeal is taken from an assessment of a bank's stock, a commissioner of revenue is not authorized to strike out an assessment of value of "corporate excess," though the bank subsequently failed.[2996] And a revenue commissioner was held without power to direct a municipal tax accountant to strike from the records a valuation in excess of the assessed value of property of a state bank which closed after a stock tax was levied.[2997] But, where, pursuant to an informal understanding, the correction

---

authority to grant refunds or exercise further jurisdiction, and its refusal to treat belated appeal as an application for final assessment certificate was neither unreasonable nor unlawful. Leimbach v. Evatt, 141 Ohio St. 191, 46 N.E.2d 859, 25 Ohio Op. 279.

[2991] First Nat'l Bank v. Bailey, 15 Mont. 301, 39 P. 83.

[2992] First Nat'l Bank v. Bailey, 15 Mont. 301, 39 P. 83; Ankeny v. Blakley, 44 Ore. 78, 74 P. 485.

[2993] First Nat'l Bank v. Bailey, 15 Mont. 301, 39 P. 83.

Assessment on land owned by bank, with no allowance therefor on assessment of capital stock, involves excessive assessment on capital stock within jurisdiction of county board of equalization, and not double taxation. Mossy Creek Bank v. Jefferson County, 153 Tenn. 332, 284 S.W. 64.

[2994] State Nat. Bank v. Memphis, 116 Tenn. 641, 94 S.W. 606, 7 L.R.A. (n.s.) 663.

[2995] Hibernia Nat'l Bank v. Louisiana Tax Comm'n, 652 So. 2d 662 (La. App. 1995).

Tax Commission was estopped to contend that its own written instructions to property taxpayers that 30-day appeal period ran from date of its transmittal letter, which was consistent both with basic due process notice requirements and administrative procedure, was invalid. Hibernia Nat'l Bank v. Louisiana Tax Comm'n, 652 So. 2d 662 (La. App. 1995).

[2996] Chowan County v. Commission of Banks, 202 N.C. 672, 163 S.E. 808.

Under the North Carolina statute neither the state board of assessment nor the commissioner of the revenue has original jurisdiction to hear indiscriminate complaints of individual taxpayers concerning overvaluation, where no appeal was taken. Caldwell County v. Doughton, 195 N.C. 62, 141 S.E. 289; Chowan County v. Commissioner of Banks, 202 N.C. 672, 163 S.E. 808.

[2997] Rockingham v. Hood, 204 N.C. 618, 169 S.E. 191.

of an erroneous assessment of shares of bank stock was postponed until the bank could pay the taxes as then assessed and avoid a penalty, a taxing official was not, by such payment, deprived of the power to correct the assessment.[2998]

Complaint or Statement.—As to assessment of banks, the usual rule applies that to authorize a board of equalization to increase an assessment, a complaint must be made, and testimony taken upon same, which supports such increase; otherwise, a board has no such power.[2999] And where a statute requires it, the filing of a verified statement showing the name of each shareholder of a bank is a condition precedent to maintaining an action for the abatement of a tax.[3000]

Procedure in General.—See the footnote.[3001]

Evidence.—Effect of presumption that assessor has properly performed his duty and fairly assessed all property is to impose on the applicant the burden of proving that the property has not been correctly assessed.[3002] As to admissibility of evidence in certain cases, see the footnote.[3003]

[2998] Lamont Sav. Bank v. Luther, 200 Iowa 180, 204 N.W. 430.

[2999] Dixon County v. Halstead, 23 Neb. 697, 37 N.W. 621.

[3000] Central Nat. Bank v. Lynn, 259 Mass. 1, 156 N.E. 42.

[3001] **Application for rehearing.—**

Timeliness of application for rehearing of decision of Tax Commission in property tax matter was governed by Tax Commission rule permitting rehearing request to be made before appeal has been filed or Commission's decision has become final, which was promulgated under Commission's statutory grant of rulemaking power over its hearings, rather than by general 10-day rule established under the Administrative Procedure Act. Hibernia Nat'l Bank v. Louisiana Tax Comm'n, 652 So. 2d 662 (La. App. 1995).

Exchange of witness lists.—

Board of Assessment Appeals (BAA) rule requiring parties to exchange witness lists 10 days prior to hearing had legitimate relationship to express statutory provisions and objectives, where, since BAA's procedures did not allow discovery, witness list and exhibit were only means by which party could gain knowledge of those who would testify and subject matter of their testimony in order properly to prepare for cross-examination of witnesses and presentation of rebuttal witnesses and exhibits. Am. Sav. Bank v. Boulder County Bd. of Comm'rs, 888 P.2d 360 (Colo. App. 1994).

[3002] Bank of America v. County of Fresno, 127 Cal. App. 3d 295, 179 Cal. Rptr. 497(1981).

The law presumes that property tax assessments are correct, and board of equalization decisions which adopt the assessor's position are protected by the substantial evidence rule. Bank of Am. v. County of Fresno, 127 Cal. App. 3d 295, 179 Cal. Rptr. 497 (1981).

Prima facie case of overassessment of restricted open space land under the capitalization

Assessment of Omitted Property.—In some jurisdictions boards of equalization or review, in making corrections, may place on an assessment roll, property of a bank or shares of bank stock which have been omitted by an assessor.[3004] Accordingly, it has been held that unassessed property in the

---

of income method requires taxpayer to offer independent proof of the capitalized income value of the land, as statutorily defined, and this requires evidence of projected annual income and expenses from the property together with the capitalization rate to be used in determining value and if taxpayer wishes to adopt the capitalization rate used by the assessor he should be able to do so by stipulation or by offering the assessor's records. Bank of Am. v. County of Fresno, 127 Cal. App. 3d 295, 179 Cal. Rptr. 497 (1981).

To establish a prima facie case of overassessment of restricted open space land, specifically, a vineyard, it was incumbent on taxpayer, relying on capitalization of income method, to present some evidence of projected future income expenses and not just evidence of past losses. Bank of Am. v. County of Fresno, 127 Cal. App. 3d 295, 179 Cal. Rptr. 497 (1981).

3003 A rule which is restricted to fair market value ad valorem assessments should not apply to a capitalization income situation and, hence, at equalization hearing, taxpayer should have been allowed to present evidence concerning crop year production and sales revenue to corroborate witness' testimony and evidence was not excludable on relevancy grounds, in that it applied to a date more than 90 days after the lien date. Bank of Am. v. County of Fresno, 127 Cal. App. 3d 295, 179 Cal. Rptr. 497 (1981).

If taxpayer attempted to utilize assessor's opinion of rental value of bare unimproved land to establish a ratio of value between living and nonliving improvements, such evidence was properly excluded at equalization hearing as assessor's opinion of rental value of other land was not in evidence in that assessor had not yet commenced his case-in-chief. Bank of Am. v. County of Fresno, 127 Cal. App. 3d 295, 179 Cal. Rptr. 497 (1981).

Where preequalization hearing stipulation of $75 per acre rental value of bare unimproved land was vacated, taxpayer did not indicate that purpose for use of such figure was to derive a capitalization rate but, rather, to show that 88 percent of rental value of land with nonliving improvements was attributable to land and 12 percent to improvements, with consideration also had of values related two different, unrelated parcels, assessor's objection was properly sustained on ground of improper foundation, relevancy and use of impermissible method of valuing restricted open space land, i.e., agricultural preserve. Bank of America v. County of Fresno, 127 Cal. App. 3d 295, 179 Cal. Rptr. 497 (1981).

3004 Oregon, etc., Sav. Bank v. Jordan, 16 Ore. 113, 17 P. 621; Bank of Oxford v. Lafayette County, 79 Miss. 152, 29 So. 825 (1901); Richardson v. State Nat'l Bank, 135 Ky. 772, 123 S.W. 294, 1189.

Where certain banks returned for assessment the amount of capital stock, surplus, and undivided profits, from which they deducted large amounts for alleged uncollectible credits, omitting to state the number and amount of shares of capital stock paid in, an assessment on such statements did not preclude the state revenue agent from assessing their capital stock, surplus, and undivided profits as omitted property. Adams v. People's Bank, 108 Miss. 346, 66 So. 407.

Where taxpayer, owning jewelry, notes, and bank deposits, was assessed for personalty on

hands of a receiver of a private bank may be properly assessed by a board of review, it being the receiver's duty to list taxable property even though he is not actually the owner thereof.[3005] Under some statutes, where a proper tax return has been made of national bank stock, and the stockholders have been allowed to deduct their indebtedness therefrom as in the case of other moneyed capital, a county auditor in a subsequent year has no power to place the amount of such deductions in the duplicate list as an omission, and collect taxes thereon notwithstanding such deductions were not authorized by law.[3006]

§ 61. Place and Time of Meeting of Boards.

The time, place and duration of meetings of boards of equalization or review are usually fixed by statute, and if at the time a valuation of a bank's capital stock is increased by such a board, the board is not legally in session, its acts are void;[3007] and in such a case, a court of equity may properly exercise its preventive jurisdiction by injunction to protect parties threatened with injury.[3008] A legislature may, however, constitutionally legalize special meetings of a state board which are not authorized by the statute creating the board.[3009]

§ 62. Notice to Interested Parties.

As a general rule, it is essential that a taxpayer who may be affected by the action of a board of equalization or review with regard to his assessment, receives due notice of the proposed action of the board; such rule is as applicable to assessment of bank property or bank stock as it is to assessments of other property, at least where an increase in valuation is proposed.[3010] And a tax against a bank on its stock, based on an assessment

---

valuation of household goods only, subsequent assessment for jewelry, etc., as omitted property made by county board of taxation was proper, and it was not bound to take proceedings as in case of undervalued property. Fidelity Trust Co. v. Essex County Board, 90 N.J.L. 51, 100 A. 334.

[3005] Bond v. Moore, 300 Ill. 32, 132 N.E. 777.

[3006] Mercantile Nat. Bank v. Lander, 109 F. 21, aff'd, 118 F. 785 (Ohio statutes). See Farmers', etc., Bank v. Board, 97 Cal. 318, 32 P. 312.

[3007] Yocum v. First Nat. Bank (Ind.), 38 N.E. 599.

[3008] Yocum v. First Nat'l Bank (Ind.), 38 N.E. 599. As to injunctions to restrain assessments generally, see § 58 of this chapter.

[3009] First Nat. Bank v. Isaacs, 161 Ind. 278, 68 N.E. 288.

[3010] **In general.—**

United States.—Lander v. Mercantile Bank, 186 U.S. 458, 22 S. Ct. 908, 46 L. Ed. 1247.

increased by a board without notice to the bank, is invalid to the extent of such increase.[3011] It had been held, however, that such notice is not necessary for the assessment of omitted property,[3012] or where capital stock of a bank has been previously assessed to the wrong party.[3013]

§ 63. Action to Set Aside Assessment or Abate Tax.

In General.—The requirement that a national bank file a verified statement of the names of its shareholders as a condition precedent to bringing an abatement suit cannot be waived by assessors.[3014] The filing of

---

California.—Farmers', etc., Bank v. Board, 97 Cal. 318, 32 P. 312; Security Sav. Bank & Trust Co. v. Board of Sup'rs, 99 Cal. 19, 34 P. 437.

New York.—Bridgeport Sav. Bank v. Feitner, 191 N.Y. 88, 83 N.E. 592.

Ohio.—EUCLID AVE. SAV. & BANKING CO. v. HUBBARD, 12 Ohio C. Dec. 279, 22 Ohio C.C.R. 20.

Oregon.—Ankeny v. Blakley, 44 Ore. 78, 74 P. 485; Oregon & W. M. Sav. Bank v. Jordan, 16 Ore. 113, 17 P. 621.

Washington.—Ladd v. Gilson, 26 Wash. 79, 66 P. 126.

Evidence held to show that proceedings resulting In Increased valuation of bank stock for tax purposes were duly had as to notice and appearance. Doneghy v. State (Tax. Civ. App.), 240 S.W.2d 331.

Notice to tax authorities.—

Director of consolidated tax collection for several taxing entities did not have right to notice and opportunity to be heard to protest appraisal review board's change in appraised value of single taxpayer's property. Carr v. Bell Sav. & Loan Ass'n, 786 S.W.2d 761 (Tex. App. 1990).

Timely notice of appeal, mistakenly filed with appraisal district, but actually received by appraisal review board satisfied jurisdictional requirements for protesting appraisal value of the property. Harris County Appraisal Dist. v. Texas Nat'l Bank, 775 S.W.2d 66 (Tex. App. 1989).

Failure of taxpayer appealing from decision of county board of revision to name as party to appeal board of education which filed countercomplaint before board of revision did not amount to jurisdictional defect. First Nat'l Bank Ctr. Assoc. v. Hamilton Cty. Bd. of Revision, 70 Ohio App. 3d 46, 590 N.E.2d 387, jurisdictional motion overruled, 58 Ohio St. 3d 703, 569 N.E.2d 511 (1991).

[3011] McFarland v. Georgetown Nat. Bank, 208 Ky. 7, 270 S.W. 995, aff'd, 273 U.S. 568, 47 S. Ct. 467, 71 L. Ed. 779.

[3012] Oregon & W. M. Sav. Bank v. Jordan, 16 Ore. 113, 17 P. 621; Ladd v. Gilson, 26 Wash. 79, 66 P. 126.

[3013] Ankeny v. Blakley, 44 Ore. 78, 74 P. 485.

[3014] Central Nat. Bank v. Lynn, 259 Mass. 1, 156 W.E. 42; 266 Mass. 145, 164 N.E. 927, cert. denied, 280 U.S. 516, 50 S. Ct. 65, 74 L. Ed. 587.

a suit challenging a decision to tax certain property before the governing body set the tax rate was sufficient to satisfy the time requirements so as to escape the burden of proving substantial injury, since it is only in the determination of the tax rate that the governing body truly relies on the assessment roles.[3015] A "tax plan" cannot be put into operation before the tax rate has been established and the taxpayer knows what his tax liability will be under the "plan" so that the taxpayer cannot be penalized for failing to file suit after the rules have been certified but before the tax rate has been established.[3016] In a proceeding by a bank for reduction of taxes on the ground that its stock, surplus and undivided profits were assessed at a higher valuation than other property, it is not necessary for the bank to prove directly that all other property was undervalued for purposes of assessment; it is sufficient if it proves a reasonable number of representative cases from which such conclusion can be drawn.[3017] And in such a case, the fact that undervaluation of property by tax officials is intentional and systematic will be inferred from their acts.[3018] But the failure to prove that national bank stock is taxed at a greater rate than competing capital is fatal in an application to correct an assessment on such ground, it being insufficient merely to allege that the tax is illegal and exceeds certain other local taxes.[3019] And a national bank seeking to establish the invalidity of a state law taxing bank stock and property must prove that during the tax year moneys of the bank were employed in a substantial amount in the same business carried on during the year by less heavily taxed nonbanking concerns.[3020] Where, in a suit by a national bank to require a state board to deduct the value of its federal securities from an assessment, the bank does not claim that its shares were fixed at too high a valuation, nor show that it has attempted to obtain a reduction of the assessment or that any prejudicial error was committed in valuing the shares, except in failing to deduct the value of the securities, it is immaterial what information the board used in making the assessment.[3021] Where a state statute gave national banks the

---

[3015] Charles Schreiner Bank v. Kerrville Indep. School Dist., 683 S.W.2d 466 (Tex. App. 4 Dist. 1984).

[3016] Charles Schreiner Bank v. Kerrville Indep. School Dist., 683 S.W.2d 466 (Tex. App. 4 Dist. 1984).

[3017] Washington County v. First Nat'l Bank, 35 Idaho 438, 206 P. 1054.

[3018] Washington County v. First Nat'l Bank, 35 Idaho 438, 206 P. 1054.

[3019] Leesburg v. Loudoun Nat. Bank, 141 Va. 244, 126 S.E. 196.

[3020] Clark v. Herkimer County, 8 N.Y.S.2d 675.

[3021] Hagar v. Citizens' Nat'l Bank, 127 Ky. 192, 105 S.W. 403, 32 Ky. L. Rptr. 95,

option of paying a tax not within the congressional permission in lieu of a tax lawfully assessable, and a national bank elected to pay such tax, and consequently the public authorities made no attempt to impose the tax lawfully assessable, it was held to be in effect a compromise which could not be set aside, except on a ground destroying its validity as a contract.[3022] And where an assessment of national bank stock has been made in the wrong district, a court may, in an action by the aggrieved party to set aside the assessment, direct that an assessment be made in the proper district.[3023]

Where a taxing plan is "fully unlawful and fundamentally wrong" because it results in the taxing of exempt property, there is no justification for judicial blindness and tolerance disguised as rules relating to the burden of proof; absent justification for rules shielding the taxing agencies which impose illegal taxes, the requirement that taxpayers show substantial injury should not be extended to cases of taxation of exempt property.[3024] If a taxpayer shows that his property was actually assessed a substantially higher percentage of its market value than the percentage used for other property, relief will be limited to the amount or the extent of the excess.[3025]

Persons Entitled to Sue.—Under a statute permitting the enforcement of taxes on bank stock by levy and sale, and authorizing banks to pay taxes on their stock, a bank has sufficient interest to sue to compel the deduction of the value of bank buildings and land on which they are situated from the gross amount of taxes assessed against its stock.[3026] And where a statute authorizes a trustee of an express trust to bring suit in his own name without joining the beneficiary, a national bank may bring suit for relief against an excessive tax on its stock without joining the stockholders, since a trust is imposed on the bank for payment of such tax.[3027]

Tax Code's failure to authorize a hearing for the owner after foreclosure to protest appraisal of the property deprived the owner of property without due process where: (1) The owner first received notice of the appraised value

---

appeal dismissed, 212 U.S. 585, 29 S. Ct. 681, 53 L. Ed. 661.

3022 Commissioner of Corp., etc. v. Woburn Nat. Bank (Mass.), 53 N.E.2d 554.

3023 Crossley v. East Orange, 62 N.J.L. 583, 41 A. 712.

3024 Charles Schreiner Bank v. Kerrville Indep. School Dist., 683 S.W.2d 466 (Tex. App. 4 Dist. 1984).

3025 Charles Schreiner Bank v. Kerrville Independent School Dist., 683 S.W.2d 466 (Tex. App. 4 Dist. 1984).

3026 Second Ward Sav. Bank v. Leuch, 155 Wis. 493, 144 N.W. 1119.

3027 Citizens' Nat'l Bank v. Columbia County, 23 Wash. 441, 63 P. 209.

when it received tax statements approximately three months after the appraisal records were submitted to the review board; (2) the owner's subsequent, written notice to challenge the appraisal was untimely and (3) since the board approved the appraisal records on the date that they were submitted, the owner was precluded from filing any late notice of protest.[3028]

Evidence.—Substantial evidence supported the trial court's finding that the assessor failed to give the requisite notice of an increase in the assessed valuation of real property, and, thus, the increase in valuation from $134,400 to $434,000 and the taxes computed thereon were void.[3029] The evidence sustained valuation of a bank's property for tax purposes at $839,790, notwithstanding testimony of the bank's experts placing the value at $422,000 or $390,000.[3030] Burden of proving deduction in civil tax case was properly placed upon taxpayer, which was afforded advance notice of authorities and documents on which Department of Revenue relied at hearing and was allowed to present evidence and arguments.[3031]

§ 64. Determination or Decision.

In General.—Under a statute providing that bank stock shall be entered for taxation in the names of the respective holders thereof, the fact that a board of review's resolution provides for assessment of the "capital stock" of a bank partnership, while the assessment as entered describes the property as "capital," is immaterial.[3032]

Conclusiveness of Decision.—The action of statutory boards upon applications for the review, correction or setting aside of assessments, if within their jurisdiction, is conclusive except as otherwise provided by law,[3033] and

---

[3028] Bank of Am. Nat'l Trust & Sav. Ass'n v. Dallas Cent. Appraisal Dist., 765 S.W.2d 451 (Tex. App. 1988).

[3029] United Mo. Bank v. March, 650 S.W.2d 678 (Mo. App. 1988).

[3030] First Nat'l Bank & Trust v. Otoe County, 233 Neb. 412, 445 N.W.2d 880 (1989).

[3031] Farmers & Traders State Bank v. Johnson, 76 Ill. Dec. 565, 458 N.E.2d 1365 (Ill. App. 4 Dist. 1984).

[3032] State v. Lewis, 118 Wis. 432, 95 N.W. 388.

[3033] State v. Bank, 120 Mo. 161, 25 S.W. 372. See also Ladd v. Gilson, 26 Wash. 79, 66 P. 126.

Where a city council, sitting as a board of review, after due notice and hearing, fixed the actual value of shares of bank stock and the taxable value, as returned by the assessor from statements furnished by the banks which showed no improper deductions, and the values as so fixed were duly certified to the auditor, spread upon his records, the tax levied thereon, and the books made up and turned over to the treasurer, held, that an attempted correction thereafter by the auditor, in which he assumed to increase the actual and taxable values of

in the absence of fraud.[3034] And such a decision cannot be attacked except on direct appeal by a party in interest to a court provided by statute.[3035] Thus, if no appeal is taken the decision of a statutory board becomes final.[3036] But it has been held that a decision of a board of review on objections made to an assessment of bank stock certificates from which no appeal is taken does not constitute an adjudication against taxing officials, so as to preclude a county auditor from correcting the assessment in the hands of a treasurer after discovering the board's decision to be erroneous.[3037]

Such questions as when hearing is closed, and whether and when it may be reopened, reconsidered, or reheard, are within statutory grant to Tax Commission of rule-making power over hearings.[3038]

§ 65. Review of Decision of Board.

Appeal from County to State Board.—In some jurisdictions, express provision is made for appeal from the action of a county board of review to a state board of tax commissioners, and under such a provision a bank is entitled to appeal from the action of the county board in fixing its assessments.[3039] It has been held, however, that under such a provision, no

---

such shares because of supposed omission of the board of review to include, in computing such values, the full value of certain United States bonds shown by the statements to be owned by the banks, was not an authorized correction of a clerical error or computation, but rather a new assessment, unauthorized and illegal. First Nat. Bank v. Weber, 196 Iowa 1155, 192 N.W. 890.

Denial to county Board of Commissioners (BOC) of right to call witness which it had inadvertently omitted from its witness list in taxpayer's action for refund on real property taxes was abuse of discretion, where taxpayer's attorney had implicit knowledge of BOC's witness and of subject matter of witness' testimony, and where, by barring witness from testifying, Board of Assessment Appeals received no evidence from BOC. 1st Am. Sav. Bank v. Boulder County Bd. of Comm'rs, 888 P.2d 360 (Colo. App. 1994).

[3034] Pingree Nat'l Bank v. Weber County, 54 Utah 599, 183 P. 334.

[3035] Wray v. Cleveland Stats Bank, 134 Miss. 41, 98 So. 442. See also § 56 et seq. of this chapter.

[3036] In re Omitted Assessment against Stockholders of Commercial Nat. Bank, 125 Okla. 257, 257 P. 380.

[3037] First Nat. Bank v. Burke, 201 Iowa 994, 196 N.W. 287.

[3038] Hibernia Nat'l Bank v. Louisiana Tax Comm'n, 652 So. 2d 662 (La. App. 1995).

[3039] **In general.—**

First Nat. Bank v. Isaacs, 161 Ind. 278, 68 N.E. 288; People ex rel. Preble v. Priest, 90 App. Div. 520, 85 N.Y.S. 481, aff'd, 180 N.Y. 532, 72 N.E. 1149.

Authority of county auditor as to record.—Under a statute providing that on receiving notice of an appeal from an action of the county board of review fixing a bank's assessment,

appeal will lie to correct an error of a county board in not including in the aggregate assessment the value of bank stock, mandamus being the proper remedy to correct such an error.[3040]

Review by Courts.—In a number of jurisdictions, express provision is made by statute for appeals from orders of boards of equalization or review to a court of law.[3041] And such statutes may provide for trial de novo of all

---

the county auditor shall make out a written statement showing the substance of the complaint made, if any, and the action of the board thereon, which shall be transmitted to the state auditor, to be laid before the state board of tax commissioners, the county auditor has no authority to include in the record a certificate explanatory of the action of the county board, and stating that it had overlooked certain real estate. First Nat. Bank v. Isaacs, 161 Ind. 278, 68 N.E. 288.

Conclusiveness of state board's valuations.—

Under a statute providing that the state board of tax commissioners shall, on appeal from an assessment, assess the property in controversy, and the state auditor shall certify to the county auditor the changes made, and the amounts assessed by the state board shall be by the county auditor extended on the tax duplicates in lieu of the amounts fixed by the township or county officers, the county auditor has no power to revise or change the valuations made by the state board. First Nat. Bank v. Isaacs, 161 Ind. 278, 68 N.E. 288.

[3040] People ex rel. Preble v. Priest, 90 App. Div. 520, 85 N.Y.S. 481, aff'd, 180 N.Y. 532, 72 N.E. 1149.

[3041] First Nat. Bank v. Independence, 123 Iowa 482, 99 N.W. 142; German-American Sav. Bank v. Burlington, 118 Iowa 84, 91 N.W. 829; Greensburg Deposit Bank v. Commonwealth, 230 Ky. 798, 20 S.W.2d 979; State v. Harris, 286 Mo. 262, 227 S.W. 818.

Petition to review decision of Property Tax Appeal Board denying reductions in assessments of corporate taxpayer's real estate in county was timely filed within 85-day period fixed by statute and was not subject to being dismissed, notwithstanding failure to issue summonses within that period, where failure was not due to fault of taxpayer, but was due to an error entirely within office of circuit court. City Nat'l Bank & Trust Co. v. Property Tax Appeal Bd., 73 Ill. Dec. 555, 454 N.E.2d 652 (Ill. 1983).

Reviewing court is not bound by conclusions of law of the Department of Revenue or the trial court. Farmers & Traders State Bank v. Johnson, 76 Ill. Dec. 565, 458 N.E.2d 1365 (Ill. App. 4 Dist. 1984).

City and school district, which both introduced copy of delinquent tax record, certified by property taxing authority to be true and correct, with amount stated thereon to be unpaid, were entitled to judgment against foreign Edge Act corporation doing business in Texas for unpaid ad valorem taxes on shares of such corporation, since corporation failed to rebut such evidence forming city's and school district's prima facie case. Houston v. Morgan Guaranty International Bank, 666 S.W.2d 524 (Tex. App. 1 Dist. 1983).

Only district court had jurisdiction to review decision of tax administrator assessing franchise tax on bank and finding that bank had been deficient In payment. Old Colony Bank v. Clark, 517 A.2d 249 (R.I. 1986).

Bank was precluded from seeking judicial relief for taxation of its stock where bank did

questions arising before the board.[3042] On appeal, the burden of proving a

---

not exhaust its administrative remedies under the tax code. First Bank v. Harris County, 804 S.W.2d 588 (Tex. App. 1991).

Petition for review of decision of Tax Commission had to be filed within 30 days of Commission's decision disposing of application for rehearing, either under judicial review statute specifically addressing Commission decisions or, if that statute did not provide 30 days to sue for judicial review after decision denying rehearing, under Administrative Procedure Act (APA) residual delay provisions. Hibernia Nat'l Bank v. Louisiana Tax Comm'n, 652 So. 2d 662 (La. App. 1995).

In addition to the general constitutional right to open access to courts for redress of injury, property taxpayers have specific constitutional right to judicial review of assessor's assessments, after review by parish governing authority and then by tax commission. Hibernia Nat'l Bank v. Louisiana Tax Comm'n, 652 So. 2d 662 (La. App. 1995).

Because property taxpayers' right to judicial review of assessment is constitutional, restrictions on its exercise must be narrowly construed. Hibernia Nat'l Bank v. Louisiana Tax Comm'n, 652 So. 2d 662 (La. App. 1995).

[3042] **In general.—**

Iowa Nat. Bank v. Stewart (Iowa), 232 N.W. 445.

Appeal from action by county board of equalization is an equity action tried de novo in the district court. First Nat'l Bank & Trust v. Otoe County, 233 Neb. 412, 445 N.W.2d 880 (1989).

On appeal to the supreme court, equity case involving action by county board of equalization is a trial of factual questions de novo on the record, requiring the supreme court to reach a conclusion independent of the findings of the trial court when credible evidence conflicts, the supreme court may give weight to the fact that the trial judge observed the witnesses and accepted one version of the facts over another. First Nat'l Bank & Trust v. Otoe County, 233 Neb. 412, 445 N.W.2d 880 (1989).

Necessity for raising objections before board.—

Plaintiffs were required in their complaints to the board of review to make all objections to the proposed assessment which they then had, though the objections might be made very informally; however informally made, if called to the attention of the board of review, objections would be reviewed on appeal in the district court and would there be triable de novo. Iowa Nat'l Bank v. Stewart (Iowa), 232 N.W. 445.

Case tried on stipulation.—

Case on appeal from assessment of capital stock of bank could not be remanded for ascertainment of unauthorized payment of dividends disclosed by evidence which should be added to value of capital stock, where case was tried under written agreement on sole question of exemption of book surplus from taxation. Board of Sup'rs v. Jefferson County Bank, 171 Miss. 50, 156 So. 599.

Necessity of raising objections before board.—

Petition wherein bank alleged that it was improper for the director of revenue to take the position that the license tax ordinance enacted by city was invalid and to deny the bank a credit against the state bank tax for the sums paid to the city under the ordinance failed to

wrongful assessment is upon the party alleging it.[3043] The holding below

---

contain statutorily required facts showing two or more persons having claims against bank and, hence, failed to state a claim upon which interpleader could be granted since, while it might be inferred that the director had determined that an additional amount of state bank tax was due from the bank for the year in question, there was no basis for an inference that the required notice had been mailed or the prescribed administrative remedies pursued. Commercial Bank v. James, 658 S.W.2d 17 (Mo. 1988).

Notice.—

Notice which bank filed with tax assessor and collector contesting taxation of stock because federal obligations were considered in computing tax did not preserve bank's right to challenge owner ship of stock. First Bank v. Harris County 804 S.W.2d 588 (Tex. App. 1991).

Notice of protest to paying tax on bank stock, which bank did not file until almost a year after it had paid taxes, was untimely and did not preserve bank's right to challenge ownership of stock. First Bank v. Harris County, 804 S.W.2d 588 (Tex. App. 1991).

Substantial evidence test.—

Appellate court applying substantial evidence test on review of Tax Commission action must consider both evidence that supports factual findings and evidence that detracts from findings. First Nat'l Bank v. County Bd. of Equalization, 799 P.2d 1163 (Utah 1990).

[3043] Comanche County v. American Nat'l Bank, 122 Okla. 34, 252 P. 408.

Burden was on city to establish money in hands of bank did not truly represent sum available for taxation by reason of fraud whereby moneys were converted into non-taxable securities. Board of Comm'rs v. State Board of Taxes & Assessments, 107 N.J.L. 35, 151 A. 364, aff'd, 108 N.J.L. 195, 156 A. 377.

In determining amount of tax on shares of domestic trust company, burden was on company to show that the shares of stocks of other corporations which company claimed were not taxable were purchased out of capital, surplus and undivided profits. The company may sustain burden by showing that the investment was inherently a part of the capital stock structure, or that it was earmarked and set up as made out of the capital account. Commonwealth v. Provident Trust Co., 319 Pa. 385, 180 A. 16 (1935).

Taxpayer, as party challenging assessment, has burden to show that correct appraisal depended on adoption of its preferred method of valuation. First Interstate Bank, N.A. v. Department of Revenue, 306 Or. 450, 760 P.2d 880 (1988).

When county board of equalization has determined the value of property, uniformly and impartially assessed through a formula in substantial compliance with statutes governing taxation, taxpayer seeking reversal of board's action must show more than a difference of opinion concerning the assessed value of the taxpayer's real estate. First Nat'l Bank & Trust v. Otoe County, 233 Neb. 412, 445 N.W.2d 880 (1989).

In taxpayer's appeal from action of county board of equalization, taxpayer has the burden to prove by clear and convincing evidence that the action of the county board of equalization, in fixing or determining the value of the real estate, is unauthorized by or contrary to constitutional or statutory provisions governing taxation. First Nat'l Bank & Trust v. Otoe County, 233 Neb. 412, 445 N.W.2d 880 (1989).

will not be disturbed absent a showing of arbitrary assignment of value or abuse of discretion.[3044]

The Court of Special Appeals reviews factual determinations of the tax court under a "substantial evidence" standard and may not substitute its judgment for that of the tax court.[3045] However, the Court of Special Appeals can substitute its judgment for that of the tax court in matters of law.[3046]

[3044] **No systematic or arbitrary undervaluation of property shown.—**

In proceeding in which Federal Reserve Bank challenged real estate tax assessment against its building, evidence supported tax courts finding that there bad not been any intentional, arbitrary or systematic undervaluation of other property such that bank was denied equal protection. Federal Reserve Bank v. State, 313 N.W.2d 619 (Minn. 1981).

Arbitrary assignment of values not shown.—

In assessing bank shares tax, so long as determination of actual value of an asset at a given date is based on facts and reasonable indicia of material worth, action of department of revenue will not be disturbed; in making its determination, however, department cannot arbitrarily assign values to a bank's assets which are different than those supplied by the bank in its shares. Citizens Nat'l Bank & Trust Co. v. Commonwealth, 437 A.2d 1327 (Pa. Commw. 1981).

Allowing intervention not an abuse of discretion.—

Trial court did not abuse its discretion in allowing the state revenue commissioner to intervene in appeal, by the county board of tax assessors from determinations of the board of equalization in favor of banks on issue respecting constitutionality of the bank share tax act. Bartow County Bank v. Bartow County Bd. of Tax Assessors, 248 Ga. 703, 285 S.E.2d 920 (1982).

Insufficient evidence to show service of process on tax authorities.—

Evidence was insufficient to support lower court's determination that personal service of process was made upon tax authorities to allow challenge of taxpayer's assessment, despite testimony which supported court's determination, where credibility of such witness was so undermined by seemingly irreconcilable inconsistencies that lower court's findings were not supportable by fair interpretation of evidence. Chemical Bank v. Davis, 520 N.Y.S.2d 44 (N.Y. App. Div. 2 Dep't 1987).

Evidence insufficient to support determination.—

Evidence was insufficient to support any determination that lots in fully developed subdivision had no immediate market value, so as to require that property be valued at amount of money that would justly compensate owner for loss of property, where there was no evidence as to normal length of time necessary for sale of subdivision lots or amount necessary to justly compensate taxpayer. First Interstate Bank v. Department of Revenue, 306 Or. 450, 760 P.2d 880 (1988).

[3045] State Dep't of Assmts. & Taxation v. Loyola Fed. Sav. & Loan Ass'n, 79 Md. App. 481, 558 A.2d 428 (1989).

[3046] State Dep't of Assmts & Taxation v. Loyola Fed. Sav. & Loan Ass'n, 79 Md. App. 481, 558 A.2d 428 (1989).

A court of appeals reviews a decision of the U.S. Tax Court in the same manner as decisions of the district courts. The court of appeals therefore examines a summary judgment decision de novo as it does other summary judgment decisions. Questions of statutory interpretation are issues of law and are reviewed without deference to the tax court.[3047]

§ 66. Certiorari to Review Assessment.

In some jurisdictions, it is expressly provided by statute that a writ of certiorari to review an assessment may be allowed on petition of any person claiming to be aggrieved thereby,[3048] provided application for the writ is made within the prescribed time.[3049] Under such a statute, a national bank may maintain certiorari in its own name to set aside an assessment upon shares of its stockholders, where the bank is made agent for collection of

---

When administrative agency decision construing revenue laws involves only questions of law, reviewing court exercises an independent review. Boatmen's Bancshares, Inc. v. Director of Revenue, 757 S.W.2d 574 (Mo. 1988).

Question of whether savings and loan association could report a negative taxable income on its state franchise tax form was question of law, which Court of Special Appeals reviewed de novo. State Dep't of Assmts. & Taxation v. Loyola Fed. Sav. & Loan Ass'n, 79 Md. App. 481, 558 A.2d 428 (1989).

3047 Moneygram Int'l v. Comm'r, 664 Fed. Appx. 386 (5th Cir. 2016).

3048 **In general.—**

American Exch. Nat. Bank v. Purdy, 196 N.Y. 270, 89 N.E. 838; Mercantile Nat. Bank v. New York, 27 Misc. 32, 57 N.Y.S. 254; Bank v. Miller, 84 App. Div. 168, 82 N.Y.S. 621; State ex rel. Batz v. Lewis, 118 Wis. 432, 95 N.W. 388.

Defective joint petition.—

Though parties similarly situated may join in a single proceeding for reduction of a tax assessment, a petition by a single bank stockholder, purporting to be on behalf of himself and other stockholder, for certiorari to review the decision of the tax commissioners in refusing to reduce the assessment of the stock of such bank, which failed to show any authority in such stockholder, or in any other signer of the petition, to represent the other stockholders, and which also failed to show that the application to the commissioners has been made properly and in due time by all purported petitioners, or someone duly authorized by them, was fatally defective as a joint petition. Kohler v. Feitner, 71 App. Div. 572, 76 N.Y.S. 245.

3049 American Exch. Nat. Bank v. Purdy, 196 N.Y. 270, 89 N.E. 838.

It is customary for courts in certiorari to review an assessment for taxes, to apply the limitations of civil actions. People ex rel. Importers' & Traders' Nat'l Bank v. Purdy, 167 App. Div. 50, 152 N.Y.S. 275.

A remedy even for jurisdictional defects in the assessment of a tax may be barred by a statutory limitation. People v. Purdy, 154 App. Div. 529, 139 N.Y.S. 180, aff'd, 207 N.Y. 758, 101 N.E. 455.

taxes and a penalty is imposed for its failure to pay same to the receiver of taxes.[3050] So, also, it has been held that an owner of shares of bank stock listed by the bank in a previous owner's name and assessed in such name, may proceed under a statute allowing a writ of certiorari to review an assessment at the instance of an aggrieved party.[3051] A writ of certiorari will also lie upon the relation of a savings bank to review an assessment of its real property claimed to be excessive.[3052] The burden of proving that a state's system of taxation so discriminates against national banks as to place on them a burden of taxation greater than is imposed on other moneyed capital, is on the party seeking review of an assessment by certiorari, and the proceeding must be dismissed if he fails to sustain it.[3053]

§ 67. Mandamus to Correct Assessment

Mandamus will lie to correct an assessment of a bank's property or shares of its stock where the correction does not involve the performance of judicial functions, but only the performance of a ministerial duty,[3054] for instance, where a board of supervisors makes a mathematical error in distributing a tax imposed on bank stock.[3055] Taxing authorities should not be allowed to escape an injunction or mandamus attack on their taxing schemes by lulling taxpayers into a false sense of security.[3056]

§ 68. Injunction to Restrain Assessment

Where there is a disregard of constitutional requirements and restrictions as to the manner of assessing banks, their property or stock, a court of equity

---

[3050] Mercantile Nat'l Bank v. New York, 27 Misc. 32, 57 N.Y.S. 254; aff'd, 50 App. Div. 628, 63 N.Y.S. 1111; 172 N.Y. 35, 64 N.E. 756; American Exch. Nat. Bank v. Purdy, 196 N.Y. 270, 89 N.E. 838.

[3051] People ex rel. Schaeffler v. Barker, 33 N.Y.S. 1042, 87 Hun 194, aff'd, 148 N.Y. 731, 42 N.E. 725.

[3052] People ex rel. Bank for Sav. v. Miller, 84 App. Div. 168, 82 N.Y.S. 621, modified, 177 N.Y. 461, 69 N.E. 1103.

[3053] People ex rel. Hanover Nat'l Bank v. Goldfogle, 118 Misc. 79, 193 N.Y.S. 601, aff'd, 202 App. Div. 712, 195 N.Y.S. 753, rev'd on other grounds, 234 N.Y. 345, 137 N.E. 611, cert. denied, 261 U.S. 620, 43 S. Ct. 432, 67 L. Ed. 830.

[3054] People ex rel. Lawyer v. Board of Sup'rs, 39 Misc. 162, 79 N.Y.S. 145; Geneva v. Board, 114 App. Div. 915, 100 N.Y.S. 1136, rev'd on other grounds, 188 N.Y. 1, 80 N.E. 381; People v. Board (N.Y.), 46 Barb. 588.

[3055] People ex rel. Lawyer v. Board of Sup'rs, 39 Misc. 162, 79 N.Y.S. 145.

[3056] Charles Schreiner Bank v. Kerrville Independent School Dist., 683 S.W.2d 466 (Tex. App. 4 Dist. 1984).

has the power and duty to interfere by injunctive process.[3057] And where inequality arises from the misconduct of an officer, banks whose shares of stock are assessed at a higher rate or valuation than the general mass of property may invoke the aid of a court to compel the officer to reduce the excessive assessment.[3058] The taxing authorities should not be allowed to escape an injunction or mandamus attack on their taxing schemes by lulling taxpayers into a false sense of security.[3059] The banks were justified in relying on the promise by the board of equalization that they would be notified when the decision as to their protest had been reached, and in withholding the filing of the suit for an injunction until they were notified of that decision.[3060] But it has been held that an injunction to restrain a county assessor and collector from making any new and additional assessment of a bank's capital stock and property is improperly issued; until an assessment is made and a tax levied, no one is injured and it cannot be determined whether or not the assessment is proper.[3061] Tax liability does not rise to lien status unless expressly provided for by statute.[3062]

[3057] Appeal of Banger, 109 Pa. 79; Bates v. Parker, 227 Ill. 120, 81 N.E. 334.

Parties.—

For purposes of determining whether the Tax Injunction Act bars federal instrumentality from challenging state tax law without joinder of the United States, principled, rather than formalistic approach requires inquiry into nature of the federal instrumentality and its claim where instrumentality exists primarily to perform governmental functions, it is superfluous to require the United States to be joined as a party. Federal Land Bank v. Board of County Comm'rs, 582 F. Supp. 1507 (D.C. Colo. 1984).

Federal land bank, as instrumentality of the federal government, acting as agent of the United States government and performing services for it, was not required by the Tax Injunction Act to join the United States as a party in action challenging Colorado taxation on the bank's oil and gas royalty interests. Federal Land Bank v. Board of County Comm'rs, 582 F. Supp. 1507 (D.C. Colo. 1984).

[3058] Lively v. Missouri, etc., R. Co., 102 Tex. 545, 120 S.W. 852; Raymond v. Chicago Union Tract. Co., 207 U.S. 20, 28 S. Ct. 7, 52 L. Ed. 78; Taylor v. Louisville & N. R. Co., 88 F. 350, cert denied, 172 U.S. 647, 19 S. Ct. 887, 43 L. Ed. 1182; First Nat'l Bank v. Christensen, 39 Utah 568, 118 P. 778.

[3059] Charles Schreiner Bank v. Kerrville Indep. School Dist., 683 S.W.2d 466 (Tenn. App. 4 Dist.1984).

[3060] Charles Schreiner Bank v. Kerrville Indep. School Dist., 683 S.W.2d 466 (Tex. App. 4 Dist. 1984).

[3061] First Nat. Bank v. Albright, 13 N.M. 514, 86 P. 548, aff'd, 208 U.S. 548, 28 S. Ct. 349, 52 L. Ed. 614.

[3062] Heritage Bank for Sav. v. Doran, 399 Mass. 855, 507 N.E.2d 690 (1987).

VII. LIEN AND PRIORITY.

§ 69. Existence and Discharge of Lien.

Where a state statute provides that all personal taxes shall become a lien on personal property on a certain date of each year, and shall take precedence over any sale, assignment, chattel mortgage, levy or other lien on such personal property executed or made after said date, except where such property is sold in the regular course of trade, such statute applies to shares of bank stock as it does to other personalty.[3063] Taxes are a first lien on real property from and including the first of January in the year the taxes are levied.[3064] But if a statute providing for a bank's payment of taxes assessed

---

[3063] St Johns Nat. Bank v. Bingham, 113 Mich. 203, 71 N.W. 588.

Under the Georgia statute, a bank stockholder's statutory liability is not entitled to preference over a claim for taxes In the distribution of the proceeds of his property. Whitehurst v. Gormley, 48 Ga. App. 121, 172 S.E. 78.

The department of revenue, which became a lien creditor of the debtor before the bank perfected its security interest in two vehicles of the debtor, took priority. Sun First Nat'l Bank v. Miller, 397 So. 2d 943 (Fla. App. 1981).

Lien which the state, by demand and notice and thereafter issuance of a tax warrant, obtained for certain taxes, including franchise taxes, on real and personal property of creditor was not subject to subsequently docketed judgment In favor of creditor for amount of surplus monies from mortgage foreclosure sale, and tax lien, being in existence prior in time to judgment, was to be given priority over that judgment regardless of whether there was any further notice by state to third parties as of date for filing a franchise tax return. Key Bank v.5 K's Bldg. Corp., 463 N.Y.S.2d 992 (N.Y. Sup. 1983).

County had valid real estate tax lien, for purposes of satisfying outstanding tax obligations of manufacturer on manufacturer's industrial equipment subsequently sold at auction, even though property was erroneously listed, as of date lien attached, on assessor's records and on county auditors tax list as being owned by party to whom manufacturer had sold land on which property was located. Merv E. Hilpipre Auction Co. v. Solon State Bank, 343 N.W.2d 452 (Iowa 1984).

Where manufacturing equipment subject to real estate tax was sold by taxpayer before real estate taxes for the tax year were actually levied, county had no claim to sale proceeds for payment of the taxes subsequently levied. Merv E. Hilpipre Auction Co. v. Solon State Bank, 343 N.W.2d 452 (Iowa 1984).

Term "that property" in statute giving tax lien to secure payment of all taxes for the year on"that property" does not refer to each individual item of property but, rather, gives a floating lien which attaches to all inventory items; tax lien attaches to all inventory property as a whole and the unit as it exists at the time of seizure for payment of delinquent taxes is subject to sale to enforce payment of the tax lien. City of Dallas v. Cornerstone Bank, 879 S.W.2d 264 (Tex. App. 1994).

[3064] First Nat'l Bank v. Mid-Central Food Sales, Inc., 129 Ill. App. 3d 1002, 85 Ill. Dec. 4, 473 N.E.2d 372 (1984).

to its shareholders does not create a lien on its property, no such lien exists;[3065] in such case, a lien for nonpayment of taxes can only be enforced against the property of the shareholders.[3066] Whereas assessment merely enters property subject to taxes and its taxable valuation on the tax rolls, levy creates an obligation, and therefore no lien arises until tax is actually levied.[3067] Tax upon real property is a charge upon real estate, not a personal obligation of any person.[3068] Real estate taxes become liens on assessed real estate against all persons except the state and are first liens superior to all other encumbrances.[3069]

County's mobile home tax lien had priority over lien of creditor who had financed purchase of mobile home. First Fed. Sav. Bank v. Trolinger, 441 N.W.2d 215 (S.D. 1989).

[3065] Yakima Valley Bank & Trust Co. v. Yakima County, 149 Wash. 552, 271 P. 820; Union Sav. Bank v. Pancoast, 142 Ohio St. 6, 50 N.E.2d 157, aff'd sub nom. Second Nat. Bank v. Findley, 320 U.S. 714, 64 S. Ct. 260, 88 L. Ed. 420.

Under statute making taxes assessed on shares of stock in a bank a lien on shares until paid, and imposing on bank duty to collect taxes due thereon, placing of levy of taxes on tax duplicate against bank instead of respective owners of shares of stock did not constitute a lien on real estate of bank. Union Sav. Bank v. Pancoast, 142 Ohio St. 6, 50 N.E.2d 157, aff'd sub nom, Second Nat'l Bank v. Findley, 320 U.S. 714, 64 S. Ct. 260, 88 L. Ed. 420.

[3066] Ward County v. Baird, 55 N.D. 670, 215 N.W. 163.

[3067] Merv E. Hilpipre Auction Co. v. Solon State Bank, 343 N.W.2d 452 (Iowa 1984).

[3068] Merv E. Hilpipre Auction Co. v. Solon State Bank, 343 N.W.2d 452 (Iowa 1984).

No judicial intervention is necessary for town to realize wealth from land subject to automatic lien that arises by force of law to secure payment of annual property taxes. First NH Bank v. Town of Windham, 639 A.2d 1089 (N.H. 1994).

[3069] In general.—Merv E. Hilpipre Auction Co. v. Solon State Bank, 343 N.W.2d 452 (Iowa 1984).

Trial court did not err when it implicitly applied equitable "anti-merger doctrine" to keep first mortgage alive and superior to county's personal property tax liens after earlier foreclosure proceeding in which county was not joined and mortgagee purchased mortgaged property at sheriff's sale, in absence of proof that mortgagee's failure to join county in earlier foreclosure was attended by some inequitable conduct. First Federal Sav. & Loan Ass'n v. Nath, 839 P.2d 1336 (Okla. 1992).

Legislature has power to create statutory liens and to establish the priorities thereof, including the power to grant priority or superiority to tax liens over bona fide conveyances of encumbrances. Liberty Nat'l Bank & Trust Co. v. Vanderkraats, 899 S.W.2D 511 (Ky. App. 1995).

Ad valorem taxes assessed after duly recorded mortgage do not become liens until assessed but are given priority over mortgagees. Liberty Nat'l Bank & Trust Co. v. Vanderkraats, 899 S.W.2d 511 (Ky. App. 1995).

Tax lien statute that speaks in terms of lien being valid or invalid against bona fide mortgagee created priorities; that is, lien attaches immediately to all property, but until notice

Even though a bank's perfected security interest in manufacturing equipment subject to real property tax antedated the county's tax lien, the county's lien was superior to the bank's security interest.[3070] County could assert a claim against the proceeds of the sale of manufacturing equipment subject to a real estate tax in order to recover back taxes owed by the manufacturing company, even though the statutory scheme for collection of real estate taxes was limited to in rem proceeding and provided no means to transfer a lien from the property to the sale proceeds, where: (1) The manufacturer did not have funds to clear the property of liens before the sale; (2) the manufacturer guaranteed the title on the property sold at auction; (3) under the auction agreement the auctioneer was authorized to sell the property without restrictions on title with the right to withhold money to clear any outstanding liens and (4) good title could not be passed without satisfying the county's superior tax lien.[3071]

Bank, as prior lienholder on manufacturing equipment, rather than the sale purchaser, had no standing to complain, in a challenge to the county's priority to proceeds of the sale, of the inconsistency in title to the property on the county tax records.[3072] Lien for property taxes on property con-

---

thereof is filed, bona fide purchaser is given priority and after notice is filed the Revenue Cabinet of the Commonwealth of Kentucky has priority. Liberty Nat'l Bank & Trust Co. v. Vanderkraats, 899 S.W.2d 511 (Ky. App. 1996).

Tax lien statute gave Kentucky priority for tax liens ahead of mortgagee, even though part of the tax liability was assessed after the mortgage was recorded; recording of tax lien before mortgage put mortgagee on notice of all prior and future assessments against the taxpayers. Liberty Nat'l Bank & Trust Co. v. Vanderkraats, 899 S.W.2d 511 (Ky. App. 1996).

Superiority of federal lien over state.—

Deed of trust lien acquired by Federal Deposit Insurance Corporation (FDIC) when it became bank's receiver was property of FDIC and, therefore, local taxing authorities could not foreclose on lien for real property taxes on property subject to FDIC's lien without FDIC's consent. State v. Bankerd, 838 S.W.2d 639 (Tex. App. 1992).

Federal statute allowing state court judgment to discharge lien held by United States did not require application of state law to determine whether foreclosure of tax lien extinguished preexisting deed of trust lien held by Federal Deposit Insurance Corporation (FDIC); Federal Deposit Insurance Act required FDIC's consent to foreclosure before lien held by FDIC could be extinguished. State v. Bankerd, 838 S.W.2d 639 (Tex. App. 1992).

Local taxing authorities cannot take action to collect unpaid taxes assessed against property which would have effect of reducing or destroying value of federally held purchase money mortgage lien. State v. Bankerd, 838 S.W.2d 639 (Tex. App. 1992).

3070 Merv E. Hilpipre Auction Co. v. Solon State Bank, 343 N.W.2d 452 (Iowa 1984).

3071 Merv E. Hilpipre Auction Co. v. Solon State Bank, 343 N.W.2d 452 (Iowa 1984).

3072 Merv E. Hilpipre Auction Co. v. Solon State Bank, 343 N.W.2d 452 (Iowa 1984).

demned and acquired by the State Department of Transportation in December 1982 attached on the first Monday in January in 1988, since the condemnation proceeding created a grantor-grantee relationship.[3073] Sales tax liens are governed by 'first in time, first in line' principle.[3074] Furthermore, sales taxes do not become a lien against real or personal property until a tax warrant is recorded and they become a lien on the property of the delinquent taxpayer in the same manner as a recorded judgment.[3075]

Moreover, sales taxes are not within the statute which gives priority status to unpaid ad valorem taxes by making such taxes a first lien on assessed property.[3076] Thus, the Department of Revenue's sales tax warrant was not entitled to priority over a bank's perfected security interest which was recorded prior to the recordation of the tax warrant.[3077] The priority afforded sales and use tax claims by the statute granting such claims priority in the case of an assignment for the benefit of creditors applies only in relation to other claims against the fiduciary estate and did not determine the priority of tax claims over antecedent perfected security interests.[3078] Thus, a state tax claim is accorded priority over an antecedent lien, including a perfected security interest, only when the applicable statute clearly so provides.[3079]

3073 Norwest Bank (N.A.)-Duluth v. Goodyear Tire & Rubber Co., 346 N.W.2d 377 (Minn. App. 1984).

3074 American Bank of Merritt Island v. Con's Cycle Center, Inc., 466 So. 2d 255 (Fla. App. 5 Dist. 1985).

3075 American Bank of Merritt Island v. Con's Cycle Center, Inc., 466 So. 2d 255 (Fla. App. 5 Dist. 1985).

3076 American Bank of Merritt Island v. Con's Cycle Center, Inc., 466 So. 2d 255 (Fla. App. 6 Dist. i985).

3077 American Bank of Merritt Island v. Con's Cycle Center, Inc., 466 So. 2d 255 (Fla. App. 6 Dist. 1985).

3078 Farmers & Merchants Nat'l Bank v. Schlossberg, 306 Md. 48, 507 A.2d 172 (1986).

3079 Farmers & Merchants Nat'l Bank v. Schlossberg, 306 Md. 48, 507 A.2d 172 (1986).

State's tax lien for unpaid sales and use taxes was a "statutory lien" within meaning of provision of Uniform Commercial Code that secured transactions article does not apply to statutory liens; however, in determining relative priority to be accorded the tax, the lien law as it existed prior to enactment of Title 9 applied and, hence, previously perfected security interest or chattel mortgage had priority over state's tax lien, notwithstanding that subsequently recorded tax lien had status of a judgment lien. Farmers & Merchants Nat'l Bank v. Schlossberg, 306 Md. 48, 507 A.2d 172 (1986).

City's personal property tax lien was superior to security interest of taxpayer's lender, even though security agreement was perfected before assessment of taxes. Michigan Nat'l Bank v. City of Auburn Hills, 193 Mich. App. 109, 483 N.W.2d 436 (1992).

Mortgagees discharging a tax lien by payment are not volunteers, and generally are entitled to be subrogated to a state's lien for reimbursement.[3080] Under one state statute, a bank paying taxes on mortgaged land at the mortgagor's request was held subrogated to a tax lien for the amount paid, with interest at the legal rate from the date of a judgment foreclosing the lien.[3081] Due to nature of purchase money security interest taken by bank upon loan of entire purchase price of automobile, debtor never had Interest in automobile other than equitable interest and thus never had interest to which previously filed tax lien could attach.[3082] It was appropriate to refer to Article 9 of the Uniform Commercial Code in construing statute governing priority of tax liens over renewals of existing contract liens.[3083] Statute governing priority of state tax liens over renewals of existing contract liens should be construed to allow, insofar as possible, existing security agreement to establish priority of advance to be made at later date.[3084] Even though the commonwealth made demand on corporate

---

[3080] **In general.—**

Quarry Sav. Bank, etc., Co. v. First Nat. Bank, 185 Ark. 433, 47 S.W.2d 802.

But a junior mortgagee who paid taxes or furnished money therefor, taking tax receipt in its name as agent for mortgagors, could not be subrogated to state's lien as against senior mortgagee not notified of junior mortgagee's actions. Corning Bank, etc., Co. v. Federal Land Bank, 186 Ark. 165, 52 S.W.2d 975.

[3081] Citizens Sav. Bank, etc., Co. v. Spencer, 105 S.W.2d 678 (Tex. Civ. App. 1937); Citizens Sav. Bank, etc., Co. v. Spencer, 105 S.W.2d 680 (Tex. Civ. App. 1937).

Evidence held to show that bank was subrogated to tax lien. Citizens Sav. Bank, etc., Co. v. Spencer, 105 S.W.2d 678 (Tex. Civ. App. 1937).

Money judgment in favor of defendant bank against plaintiffs in suit to foreclose trust deeds for taxes paid by such bank at codefendant's request held erroneous, in absence of evidence of express or implied contract by plaintiffs, who were lienholders, not owners of land, to repay bank tax money advanced thereby. Citizens Sav. Bank, etc., Co. v. Spencer, 105 S.W.2d 678 (Tex. Civ. App. 1937).

[3082] Commerce Union Bank v. Possum Holler, Inc., 620 S.W.2d 487 (Tenn. 1981).

Purchase money security interest in collateral takes priority over state tax lien arising under former statute concerning lien of taxes collectible by commissioner of revenue, since only interest "belonging to the debtor" in such case is of equitable nature. Commerce Union Bank v. Possum Holler, Inc., 620 S.W.2d 487 (Tenn. 1981).

[3083] Commerce Union Bank v. Possum Holler, Inc., 620 S.W.2d 487 (Tenn. 1981).

See now T.C.A., § 47-9-101 et seq.

[3084] Commerce Union Bank v. Possum Holler, Inc., 620 S.W.2d 487 (Tenn. 1981).

Fact that bank filed new "Note and Security Agreement" and obtained additional collateral each time loans were consolidated, although tending to support position of commissioner of revenue that such actions constituted renewals of contract liens inferior to previously filed

officers to pay corporations' taxes, the commonwealth did not have a lien against the corporate officers, where no separate personal assessments were made against the corporate officers, and no assessments were deemed to have been made against them.[3085]

A judgment obtained by a municipality for the nonpayment of earned income and net profits taxes was not a 'municipal claim' and was not entitled to priority over a prior recorded mortgage under the statute which provided that municipal claims which were timely imposed or assessed against real estate should be fully paid before any other claims; taxes were not imposed or assessed against real estate, and, until judgment was obtained, real estate was unaffected by unpaid earned income and net profits taxes.[3086]

Department of Treasury would be entitled to levy on entire amount in bank account held jointly by delinquent taxpayer and innocent third party, and bank would be required to pay over entire amount, notwithstanding fact that creditors of one depositor cannot reach entire account and notwithstanding limitation on Department's levy power, which re quires it to proceed upon warrant in all respects and in same manner as prescribed by law in respect to executions issued against property upon judgments.[3087]

§ 70. Transfer of Property.

A purchaser of bank property at a judicial sale takes the property subject to a tax lien for the year in which the sale is made.[3088] And no one can be an innocent purchaser of land as against a lien held by a state for taxes due.[3089] It has also been held that taxes levied on property received by a

---

tax lien, did not alone outweigh fact that debtor remained continuously indebted to bank and progressively increased amount of total indebtedness as time passed so as to allow characterization of consolidation transactions as existing liens created by contract prior to filing of tax lien. Commerce Union Bank v. Possum Holler, inc., 620 S.W.2d 487 (Tenn. 1981).

Where both original loan and subsequent loans were used by debtor in its business as would naturally be contemplated by debtor and bank, bank was entitled to rely on future advance clause contained in original security agreement so as to characterize security interests arising from subsequent loans as existing liens created by contract prior to filing of tax lien. Commerce Union Bank v. Possum Holler, Inc., 620 S.W.2d 487 (Tenn. 1981).

3085 Heritage Bank for Sav. v. Doran, 399 Mass. 855, 507 N.E.2d 690 (1987).

3086 Horizon Fin. v. Furrick, 541 A.2d 42 (Pa. Commw. 1988).

3087 Department of Treas. v. Comerica Bank, 201 Mich. App. 318, 506 N.W.2d 283 (1993).

3088 Pennick v. American Nat. Bank, 126 Ore. 615, 268 P. 1012.

3089 Texas Bank, etc., Co. v. Bankers' Life Co., 43 S.W.2d 631 (Tex. Civ. App.).

bank as security are a lien thereon.[3090] But where one in whose name bank stock has been taxed sells or mortgages it for full value before personal taxes become a lien thereon under a state statute, it is held that the taxes cannot be collected from the purchaser or mortgagee.[3091] A purchaser of real property cannot avoid the consequences of a property tax lien on the purchased realty where the lien represents taxes accrued before the date of sale.[3092] Under Maryland law, the state has retained the right to require the first application of proceeds from the sale of property to taxes due and payable by the time of distribution, a right that is immediately perfected, if not enforceable until the sale actually occurs, at the very moment an interest in the real estate arises.[3093]

State's tax lien against taxpayer's property was created by operation of law under statute governing delinquent taxes as soon as tax remained unpaid after last day for filing the tax return and payment, and although lien would have been ineffective as against any bona fide purchaser or encumbrancer who obtained interest in taxpayer's property before the lien was recorded, as against taxpayer, statute imposed no recording requirement, and thus state could collect entire amount of tax lien from proceeds of mortgage foreclosure sale of taxpayer's property, even though only a portion of such amount was recorded as a lien prior to the notice of lis pendens. Heritage Sav. & Loan Ass'n v. Schaller, 438 A.2d 849 (Conn. 1981).

[3090] Pennick v. American Nat. Bank, 126 Ore. 615, 268 P. 1012.

"Documentary stamp tax" is excise tax on promise to pay, and tax is measured by amount financed; tax is on document itself and not on transaction contemplated by document, and thus liability to pay tax, as well as amount of tax, must be solely determined by form and face of instrument and not by proof of extrinsic facts. Department of Revenue v. Citizens Nat'l Bank, 618 So. 2d 252 (Fla. App. 1992).

Borrower's agreement with lender to obtain future advance as provided for in original loan documents was not a "renewal" of original loan obligation triggering liability for documentary stamp tax on full amount of outstanding loan; although transaction enlarged extent of borrower's indebtedness to bank, and payments on existing note were modified and merged with payments on future advance portion of debts, original loan obligations were not altered or replaced, and purpose of loan transaction was not to extend time for payment of original loans. Department of Revenue v. Citizens Nat'l Bank, 618 So. 2d 252 (Fla. App. 1992).

[3091] St. Johns Nat'l Bank v. Bingham Tp., 113 Mich. 203, 71 N.W. 588.

A suit to enjoin the collection of such tax of one who purchased the bank shares after taxation, because the purchase was before the tax became a lien on them, is not necessary, this being a matter which can be interposed as a defense in the action by the taxing authority to recover the tax. St. Johns Nat. Bank v. Bingham, 113 Mich. 203, 71 N.W. 588.

[3092] Maryland Nat'l Bank v. Baltimore, 723 F.2d 1138 (CA. Md. 1988).

[3093] Maryland Nat'l Bank v. Mayor of Bait., 723 F.2d 1138 (CA. Md. 1983).

VIII. PAYMENT AND REFUNDING OR RECOVERY OF TAX PAID.

a. Payment.

§ 71. In General.

Banks Duty to Pay Taxes on Stock.—A state's power to require a bank to pay taxes levied on shares of bank stock in the hands of its stockholders is recognized.[3094] And under a statute requiring banks to return and pay taxes on their share of stock at full market value, a tax is imposed on the shares as the property of the stockholders, and payment by a bank is merely a convenient method of agency for collecting the tax; therefore, a bank has a right to reimbursement from its stockholders for their tax liability.[3095] It has been held that a proceeding by a state against a liquidator of an insolvent bank to collect taxes assessed against its shareholders cannot be maintained, where it is not alleged or proven that the liquidator has, or the bank had, any assets of such shareholders.[3096] However, the duty of a bank to pay capital stock taxes if it has sufficient assets, creates a personal liability.[3097]

[3094] Rockingham v. Hood, 204 N.C. 618, 169 S.E. 191; State v. Barnesville Nat'l Bank, 134 Minn. 315, 159 N.W. 754. See also §§ 18, 26c(3) of this chapter.

Although it is customary for banks to be billed for a personal property tax on shares of their stock and for them to pay the tax on behalf of their stockholders, the primary liability for the tax is on the stockholders and not on the bank. Bank & Trust Co. v. Cullerton, 25 Ill. App. 3d 721, 324 N.E.2d 29 (1975).

[3095] **In general.—**

In re Feliciana Bank, etc., Co., 78 So. 169, 143 La. 46; Daniel v. Bank of Clayton County, 154 Ga. 282, 114 S.E. 210; State v. Citizens' State Bank, 274 Mo. 60, 202 S.W. 382.

The bank's duty is to pay taxes out of shareholders' funds or property in its possession. Flournoy v. First Nat'l Bank, 197 La. 1067, 3 So. 2d 244.

[3096] **In general.—**

In re Feliciana Bank & Trust Co., 143 La. 46, 78 So. 169.

Claim of state tax collector against national bank for taxes imposed on shares of its stock, even if enforceable against bank would not survive its insolvency nor be enforceable against its receiver, since assets of bank could not be taken from its creditors and paid to tax collector for benefit of stockholders. Gully v. First Nat. Bank, 183 Miss. 385, 184 So. 615.

Contra.—

Liquidator held liable for taxes on shares of stock levied before bank was closed. Rockingham v. Hood, 204 N.C. 618, 169 S.E. 191.

Bank commissioner held not liable to apply assets of insolvent bank to payment of taxes on bank stock. Taylor v. Hale, 186 Ark. 873, 56 S.W.2d 428, 87 A.L.R. 1016.

The process for ensuring compliance by foreign-based corporate groups with California's worldwide combined reporting method of allocating income did not violate the due process clause; the discretion vested in the franchise tax board to accept reasonable approximations and to make materiality and advance determination decisions was subject to reasonably adequate standards to guide enforcement.[3098]

Payment of Indebtedness Tax on Loans.—Bank which paid indebtedness tax on three of five loans to debtor and which actually overpaid such tax since two of such loans were in part consolidations of prior loans upon which bank had already paid tax made good-faith effort to comply with indebtedness tax statute.[3099]

A mortgagee bank's payment of delinquent taxes on debtors' property did not deny the mortgagors' due process right to a hearing before the board of county commissioners to defend the use of public office money certificates to pay the taxes on the property because the bank's action simply shifted the controversy from the county commissioner's office to the courts.[3100]

Time of Payment.—A tax on shares of bank capital stock "accrues" when it is due and payable, notwithstanding that the taxpayer has until a later date

---

Liquidator not estopped to deny liability.—

Taxes assessed against common capital stock of bank, pursuant to statute, do not constitute a "debt" of the bank, nor are the "assets" of the bank in liquidation liable for the payment thereof, where the bank has not by resolution assumed the taxes in accordance with statute. And in such case, the fact that bank had uniformly for a number of years, until it was closed, paid the taxes would not "estop" its liquidator to deny liability for payment. Reilly v. Margate Trust Co., 127 N.J. Eq. 343, 13 A.2d 210.

Liability of stockholders.—

Where national bank had all its stock assessed against bank instead of against individual shareholders, under statute providing therefor, and receiver was appointed for bank upon insolvency, and bank had no assets with which to pay tax, individual stockholders thereupon became legally obligated to pay their proportionate amounts of the tax. School Dist. v. Lansing, 286 Mich. 244, 281 N.W. 883.

[3097] State v. Cantley, 325 Mo. 67, 26 S.W.2d 976.

[3098] Barclays Bank Int'l Ltd. v. Franchise Tax Bd., 10 Cal. App. 4th 1742, 14 Cal. Rptr. 537 (1992).

[3099] Commerce Union Bank v. Possum Holler, Inc., 620 S.W.2d 487 (Tenn. 1981).

[3100] Federal Land Bank v. Parsons, 777 P.2d 1218 (Idaho App. 1989).

to pay it.[3101] Property taxes are not due and payable until the lien against the property attaches.[3102]

Interest.—A bank for whom a conservator had been appointed was held properly charged with interest on its unpaid franchise tax, notwithstanding that its affairs were in the custody of the law.[3103] But where a state bank which was a member of the federal reserve system, with reasonable cause and in good faith, sought an interpretation of a statute to determine whether it was an "instrumentality of the United States" exempt from making contribution to an unemployment compensation fund, it was held entitled to relief from an interest charge above the rate of six percent.[3104]

Payment by Transferee or Merged Bank.—Where a new bank took over an old insolvent bank's assets and liabilities, the new bank could rely on the terms of a creditor's agreement under which its liability extended only to those claims established against the old bank during its receivership, and was held not liable for taxes of the old bank not so established.[3105] A seller's failure to affix required stamps to bank shares sold to a buyer who subsequently receives in exchange therefor shares in a merged bank, does not preclude an action by a receiver of the merged bank to recover an assessment against the buyer as a shareholder.[3106]

3101 Union Bank & Trust Co. v. Phelps, 228 Ala. 236, 153 So. 644.

3102 Norwest Bank (N.A.)-Duluth v. Goodyear Tire & Rubber Co., 346 N.W.2d 377 (Minn. App. 1984).

Since a lien for property taxes on property acquired and condemned by State Department of Transportation in December 1982 did not attach until January 1983, property taxes on condemned property did not become payable until January 1983, so that the bank, which paid property taxes prior to due date on behalf of trust which owned the condemned property, could not seek reimbursement from lessee for the property taxes paid but not owed. Norwest Bank (N.A.)-Duluth v. Goodyear Tire & Rubber Co., 346 N.W.2d 377 (Minn. App. 1984).

3103 People v. Richardson, 37 Cal. App. 2d 275, 99 P.2d 366.

3104 Fidelity-Philadelphia Trust Co. v. Hines, 337 Pa. 48, 10 A.2d 553.

3105 Gully v. First Nat. Bank, 183 Miss. 385, 184 So. 615.

A provision in the contract of the old bank's stockholders, under which they had assigned their stock for the benefit of the new bank, that they should be held harmless from statutory liability as stockholder, did not justify a direct suit by the state tax collector against the new bank for the old bank's back taxes even if they were included in the agreement, before the stockholders' liability was established, since the agreement constituted an "indemnity" contract. Gully v. First Nat'l Bank, 183 Miss. 385, 184 So. 615.

3106 Rogers v. Ballenberg, 68 F.2d 730.

Personal Property Taxes.—The buyers' payment of personal property taxes after they purchased the inventory of a bankrupt furniture business which had been assigned to the bank was involuntary, and thus they were entitled to reimbursement from the bank for the delinquent property taxes paid by them.[3107]

Under the Federal Credit Union Act, a state may include the holdings of any federal credit union in evaluating the personal property of owners thereof for tax purposes, but it may not impose upon the credit union any duty of collecting or enforcing payment of such taxes.[3108]

Real Property Taxes.—The owner of land is obligated to pay all real estate taxes and can shift the tax liability to lessee only if there is clear agreement to that effect.[3109]

Payment at Bank.—Payment of taxes to a bank which is designated as a county depository and authorized by the county treasurer to receive taxes, has been held a sufficient payment thereof.[3110] And where provision is made for payment of taxes to a bank, it depends on the particular statute whether the bank is considered the agent of the taxpayer or the taxing authority.[3111] Where a bank is considered the agent of the taxpayer, one paying taxes at the bank instead of to the tax officer must stand the loss if the bank fails before the tax officer receives the money.[3112] But where a bank is the agent of the taxing authority, taxpayers paying taxes to the bank and receiving tax receipts delivered to the bank by the county treasurer to be given taxpayers on the payment of taxes, are held to have paid taxes to the treasurer, and cannot be required to repay taxes on the bank's insolvency.[3113] And where a county treasurer deposited county funds in a bank, and used the bank as a

---

[3107] Palmer v. First Nat'l Bank, 692 P.2d 386 (Kan. App. 1984).

[3108] Northeast Fed. Credit Union v. Neves, 664 F. Supp. 640 (D.N.H 1987).

[3109] Ceres Terms., Inc., v. Chicago City Bank & Trust Co., 259 Ill. App. 3d 836, 635 N.E.2d 485 (1994).

[3110] Saunder v. Best, 127 Kan. 135, 272 P. 173.

[3111] Ward County v. Baird, 55 N.D. 670, 215 N.W. 163; Scheafer v. McFarland, 49 S.D. 605, 207 N.W. 982.

[3112] Scheafer v. McFarland, 49 S.D. 605, 207 N.W. 982.

Depositing money in bank in name of county treasurer did not make it public money. Scheafer v. McFarland, 49 S.D. 605, 207 N.W. 982.

[3113] Ward County v. Baird, 55 N.D. 670, 215 N.W. 163.

County treasurer must have money for taxes paid to him in cash before delivering tax receipts to taxpayer or bank receiving payment. Ward County v. Baird, 55 N.D. 670, 215 N.W. 163.

medium for the collection of taxes by placing tax receipts in its hands, and permitting it to collect the taxes and credit them to the county's deposit account, the delivery to the bank of a receipt for the taxes assessed against the bank, and the credit of such amount to such deposit account, constituted, as between the county and the treasurer, a collection of the tax due from the bank.[3114] But in a suit to prevent a county treasurer from cancelling tax receipts issued for checks which were not paid, evidence that the treasurer tendered the checks to a bank after closing hours, that a deposit slip and the checks were put in a certain place for the next day's business, that the bank was insolvent and did not reopen, that the deposit was not entered nor the checks charged against the accounts of the makers, and that the bank receiver returned them to the county treasurer, was held erroneously excluded.[3115]

§ 72. Method of Making Payment.

A tax act providing for different methods of taxation of bank stock if payment was made before certain dates, was held to intend to provide separate ways of satisfying tax liability, either of which could be taken advantage of.[3116]

§ 73. Operation and Effect of Payment.

In General.—Where a tax on the franchise of a national bank similar to that imposed on state banks is void, a bank which paid such tax for a certain year should nevertheless list its property for that year, and be credited with the amount it paid on the tax.[3117] Where a bank pays taxes assessed on its stock as required by statute, its claim for reimbursement against the holders thereof is an asset of the bank which it is entitled to collect.[3118]

Credit established for taxes paid to the state is available only to the person or entity bearing the legal incidence of the tax.[3119]

[3114] Brown v. Sheldon State Bank, 139 Iowa 83, 117 N.W. 289. See also § 64 of this chapter.

[3115] Beloit Bldg. Co. v. Staley, 118 Kan. 141, 234 P. 57.

[3116] Commonwealth v. Central Nat. Bank, 293 Pa. 404, 143 A. 105.

[3117] Citizens' Nat. Bank v. Commonwealth, 118 Ky. 51, 80 S.W. 479, 81 S.W. 686; Farmers' Nat. Bank v. Commonwealth (Ky.), 80 S.W. 1193.

[3118] Kennedy v. Citizens' Nat. Bank, 128 Iowa 561, 104 N.W. 1021; Shainwald v. First Nat. Bank, 18 Idaho 290, 109 P. 257.

See also §§ 18, 26c(3), 62 of this chapter.

[3119] Centerre Bank v. Director of Revenue, 744 S.W.2d 754 (Mo. 1988).

Sales taxes paid by a bank on the purchases of tangible personal property were not taxes paid to the state, and hence, could not be taken as a credit against a bank tax.[3120] However, use taxes paid by a bank on the purchases of tangible personal property were taxes paid to the state, and thus, could be taken as credit against a bank tax.[3121]

A subsidiary bank, which was a member of an affiliated group of banks for federal income tax purposes, was entitled to deduct as ordinary and necessary business expenses, payments to the parent company equal to the subsidiary bank's federal income tax liability as if it had filed a separate federal income tax return instead of filing a consolidated return.[3122]

Tax Receipts or Certificates.—Where a state treasurer received by mistake from a bank, less than the amount of tax due on its capital stock, his receipt "in full" for such tax does not bar the state from recovering the true amount.[3123]

Where a bank depositary of county funds pursuant to custom gave the county treasurer a deposit slip for the amount of taxes due by a depositor in return for a receipt for taxes, and where on failure of the bank, the county treasurer's indemnitor was required, in indemnifying the treasurer for deposits lost, to include in such payment the amount of such taxes, the indemnitor could not recover against the depositor on the theory that it was subrogated to the right of the treasurer to enforce the tax claim, since the indemnitor's payment to the treasurer was to reimburse him for the loss of deposits, and was not a payment of taxes, the tax claim against the depositor belonging to the bank's receiver.[3124]

§ 74. Tender.

In the case of an assessment of taxes on the shares of a bank in the hands of shareholders, the usual rule applies that the owner of taxable property seeking to enjoin the collection of an alleged excessive tax must first pay or tender so much of the tax as is justly due.[3125] Where, however, an original assessment is void, and has not been validated, there is no necessity for a

---

[3120] Centerre Bank v. Director of Revenue, 744 S.W.2d 754 (Mo. 1988).

[3121] Centerre Bank v. Director of Revenue, 744 S.W.2d 754 (Mo. 1988).

[3122] Centerre Bank v. Director of Revenue, 744 S.W.2d 754 (Mo. 1988).

[3123] Centerre Bank v. Director of Revenue, 744 S.W.2d 754 (Mo. 1988).

[3124] National Surety Co. v. Canon Block Inv. Co., 68 Colo. 171, 187 P. 522.

[3125] National Bank v. Kimball, 103 U.S. 732, 26 L. Ed. 469; Cummings v. Merchants' Nat. Bank, 101 U.S. 153, 25 L Ed. 903.

tender by shareholders of such sum as might equitably be due on account of their taxes.[3126] For a tender of taxes due from a bank or upon bank stock to be valid, it must be made so that the party refusing it is in the wrong.[3127] And the tender by a bank of a portion of a tax, on condition that it be received in full satisfaction of its whole tax, does not relieve the bank from nonpayment penalties on the whole amount.[3128]

b. Refunding or Recovery of Taxes Paid.

§ 75. In General.

General Consideration.—In the case of banks, as of natural persons and other corporations, It seems that payment of a tax without legal duress of person or property is considered voluntary and cannot be recovered.[3129] But

---

[3126] Albany City Bank v. Maher, 9 F. 884.

[3127] State v. Carson City Sav. Bank, 17 Nev. 146, 30 P. 703.

[3128] State v. Carson City Sav. Bank, 17 Nev. 146, 30 P. 703.

[3129] **In general.—**

Bank v. Chalfant, 52 Cal. 170; Wills v. Austin, 53 Cal. 152; Merrill v. Austin, 53 Cal. 379; Security Nat. Bank v. Young, 55 F.2d 616, cert. denied, 286 U.S. 551, 52 S. Ct. 502, 76 L. Ed. 1287; Gates v. Bank of Commerce, etc., Co., 185 Ark. 502, 47 S.W.2d 806; Crescent City Bldg., etc., Ass'n v. New Orleans, 141 So. 412, 19 La. App. 613; First Nat'l Bank v. Beaverhead County, 88 Mont. 577, 294 P. 956; State ex rel. Hatfield v. Moreland, 152 Okla. 37, 3 P.2d 803; Commonwealth v. Safe Deposit, etc., Co., 155 Va. 458, 155 S.E. 897.

Generally, one who pays tax voluntarily cannot enforce claim for its recovery. San Antonio Indep. School Dist. v. National Bank of Commerce, 626 S.W.2d 794 (Tex. App. 1981).

Payment of taxes, with knowledge of all facts, is not rendered involuntary by fact that it was paid in mistaken belief that statute or ordinance under which it was levied was valid. First Bank v. Conrad, 350 N.W.2d 580 (N.D. 1984).

In absence of statute to contrary, person who has paid license fee or tax which is illegal or in excess of sum which might lawfully be exacted cannot recover amount paid if payment was made voluntarily with full knowledge of facts, although it was made in good faith, through mistake or in ignorance of law, unless recovery is permitted by agreement entered into at time payment was made. First Bank v. Conrad, 350 N.W.2d 580 (N.D. 1984).

Any action by holder of deed of trust against county assessor based on alleged invalid imposition of back taxes was barred by voluntary-payment doctrine where purchasers' managing agent paid back taxes, interest and penalties for subject years without protest, notwithstanding contention that assignee was not suing for refund but damages to it and his interest in the property caused by the assessor. Inland Real Estate Corp. v. Oak Park Trust & Sav. Bank, 127 Ill. App. 3d 535, 82 Ill. Dec. 670, 469 N.E.2d 204 (1983).

Taxes voluntarily, though erroneously, paid cannot be recovered unless recovery is authorized by statute. Inland Real Estate Corp. v. Oak Park Trust & Sav. Bank, 127 Ill. App.

(*Text continued on page 871*)

3d 535, 82 Ill. Dec. 870, 469 N.E.2d 204 (1983).

Under "volunteer rule," one who pays a tax voluntarily, that is, without compulsion or duress, has no valid claim for repayment; this is so because every man is supposed to know the law, and if he voluntarily makes a payment which is not compelled to be made by him under the law, he cannot afterward assign ignorance of the law as a reason why he should be furnished with legal remedies to recover it. Palmer v. First Nat'l Bank, 692 P.2d 386 (Kan. App. 1984).

Tax voluntarily paid cannot be recovered, even though it was illegal. Texas Nat'l Bank v. Harris County, 765 S.W.2d 823 (Tex. App. 1988).

In the absence of statutory authority, taxes which are paid voluntarily, although erroneously and under an unconstitutional statute, cannot be refunded. Community Fed. Sav. & Loan Ass'n v. Director of Revenue, 752 S.W.2d 794 (Mo. 1988).

Person who voluntarily pays an illegal tax has no claim for repayment. City of Laredo v. South Tea. Nat'l Bank, 775 S.W.2d 729 (Tex. App. 1989).

Public policy reason for voluntary payment doctrine is to prevent the taxing entity from using funds paid by taxpayer in a given budget year and subsequently being required to refund those amounts. City of Laredo v. South Tex. Nat'l Bank, 775 S.W.2d 729 (Tex. App. 1989).

Bank failed to raise fact issue about its affirmative defense of fraud in bank's action to recover illegal taxes paid to county; thus, bank failed to show fraud as necessary to be entitled to recover taxes which had been voluntarily paid. First Bank v. Harris County, 804 S.W.2d 588 (Tenn. App. 1991).

State was not required to refund to taxpayer bank's taxes paid on income from federal government exemptions which was illegally imposed because corresponding income on state obligations was exempted from franchise taxation; severance of the exemption from the rest of the tax statute was sufficient relief. Cambridge State Bank v. James, 480 N.W.2d 647 (Minn. 1992). Effect of payment without protest—Tax on national bank's capital stock, knowingly listed as personal property instead of moneys and credits and paid without protest, held not recoverable as "erroneously paid." Montana Nat'l Bank v. Yellowstone County of Montana, 276 U.S. 499, 48 S. Ct. 331, 72 L. Ed. 673.

Where bank paid without protest half of city taxes on shares based on allegedly incorrect valuation, and subsequently paid second half under protest, recovery was limited to overpayment of taxes paid under protest. National Bank v. Detroit, 272 Mich. 610, 262 N.W. 422.

Failure to deduct deduction allowed was held not a "mistake of fact" but a negligent omission and bank could not recover tax paid. Savings Bank of Rockville v. Wilcox, 117 Conn. 196, 167 A. 713;

Involuntary payment—National bank's payment of tax on shares of bank's stock-made lien on stock, held "involuntary payment" as to stockholders, and action could be maintained in stockholders' behalf to recover payment. People ex rel. First Nat'l Bank v. Schadt, 237 App. Div. 233, 261 N.Y.S. 849.

Trust company, voluntarily agreeing to settlement of claim for city tax on stock of national bank, of which such company was successor, without authorization by its

a bank paying under protest to avoid an impending tax warrant may sue to recover an illegal exaction.[3130] Payment of taxes by bank which did not fall in category of payment made with full knowledge of all facts, as bank was

---

shareholders, cannot recover amount of payment as made in shareholders' behalf without authorization of settlement by them. Manufacturers' & Traders' Trust Co. v. Buffalo, 266 N.Y. 319, 194 N.E. 841.

Duress.—

Where one makes a tax payment which is the obligation of another and such has been made under duress, a valid claim for repayment exists. Palmer v. First Nat'l Bank, 692 P.2d 386 (Kan. App. 1984).

Property tax was not paid under duress, so as to permit refund suit under exception to rule that taxes voluntarily paid cannot be recovered, where payment was made to avoid statutory penalties and interest and avoid black mark on taxpayer bank's annual certified audit, which would affect its ability to procure a blanket bond, the claimed adverse effects were unrelated to the scope of the taxing statute, and the statute itself did not result in "business compulsion" in sense that nonpayment would deprive taxpayer of right to do business. Texas Nat'l Bank v. Harris County, 765 S.W.2d 823 (Tex. App. 1988).

Ad valorem property tax on stock mistakenly paid by bank could not be recovered, under "duress" or "fraud" exceptions to voluntary payment rule; bank would not have been subjected to any onerous burden for nonpayment, such as would have potentially deprived it of the right to do business. First Bank v. Deer Park Indep. School Dist., 770 S.W.2d 849 (Tex. App. 1989).

Absent showing that taxation statute has onerous summary penalties and burdens in statute itself, fact that party pays tax required by law which is later declared unconstitutional does not, as matter of law, mean payment was made under implied duress. First Bank v. Harris County, 804 S.W.2d 588 (Tenn. App. 1991).

Potential penalties under tax code for bank's failure to pay assessed tax on stock did not include loss of right to do business in state; thus, payment of tax by bank was not made under implied duress as necessary for bank to be entitled to exemption from voluntary payment rule precluding bank's recovery of illegal tax. Although tax lien would have jeopardized bank's standing with governmental authorities regulating bank, penalties could have been avoided by protesting tax. First Bank v. Harris County, 804 S.W.2d 588 (Tex. App. 1991).

3130 Bank of Holyrood v. Kottmann, 132 Kan. 593, 296 P. 357 (1931).

Showing national bank at time of tax payment gave notice that suit would be instituted for its recovery, served protest in writing, and received receipt expressly recognizing payment under protest, established payment under protest. Ward v. First Nat. Bank, 225 Ala. 10, 142 So. 93 (1932).

Issuance of tax warrant, service by the sheriff and the corresponding threat of seizure and sale of one's property is sufficient duress or compulsion to make payment of excessive property taxes owed by another, be considered "involuntary," for purposes of right to reimbursement. Palmer v. First Nat'l Bank, 692 P.2d 386 (Kan. App. 1984).

Payment of taxes to avoid harsh penalties is not voluntary payment of taxes precluding refund. Community Fed. Sav. & Loan Ass'n v. Director of Revenue, 752 S.W.2d 794 (Mo.

unaware that it was paying taxes on valuation different from what it rendered, was not a "voluntary payment" within rule denying recovery for taxes paid voluntarily and with compulsion.[3131] In no case can a state be compelled to refund a tax voluntarily paid upon a claim of technical illegality in an assessment, provided the property on which the tax is paid is legally taxable.[3132] But a tax which discriminates against national banks in favor of other moneyed capital is an unlawful tax which if paid, may be recovered.[3133] Where assessors have jurisdiction of a person or corporation subject to taxation, and have a description of the amount and value of the property belonging thereto, but commit an error in determining what portion of the property is liable to taxation, the error is a judicial one and may be reviewed on certiorari, but an action will not lie to recover money paid on

---

1988). See also Bank of Holyrood v. Kottmann, 132 Kan. 593, 296 P. 357 (1931) (bank was not precluded from exercising its privilege of paying illegal taxes under protest and then maintaining an action to recover them at a later date).

Showing national bank at time of tax payment gave notice that suit would be instituted for its recovery, served protest in writing, and received receipt expressly recognizing payment under protest, established payment under protest. Ward v. First Nat. Bank, 225 Ala. 10, 142 So. 93 (1932).

[3131] San Antonio Indep. School Dist. v. National Bank of Commerce, 626 S.W.2d 794 (Tex. App. 1981).

Taxpayer was entitled to refund for overpayment of property taxes in previous tax year when both county and revenue department concurred that classification had been erroneous; taxpayer did not waive right to obtain refund by failing to seek relief in each tax year involved because taxpayer was not then aware that classification was erroneous. Arizona Telco Fed. Credit Union v. Arizona Dep't of Revenue, 764 P.2d 20 (Ariz. App. 1988).

"Error," within meaning of statute providing that taxpayer may obtain abatement or refund if assessment is "erroneous" or there has -been some clerical "error," did not encompass error made by taxpayer in failing to ensure that its recorded deed properly described land conveyed taxpayer was not entitled to relief from tax assessed against it as record owner of property, notwithstanding that it had intended to convey land in question and that beneficial ownership of land rested with purchaser and purchaser's assignees. Citibank v. Board of Assmt. Appeals, 826 P.2d 871 (Colo. App. 1992).

[3132] People ex rel. Bull v. Miner, 46 Ill. 374; First Nat'l Bank v. Sanders County, 85 Mont. 450, 279 P. 247; Columbia v. Peurifoy, 148 S.C. 349, 146 S.E. 93; Second Nat. Bank v. New York, 160 App. Div. 491, 145 N.Y.S. 800, modified, 213 N.Y. 457, 107 N.E. 1039; Krembs v. Merrill, 183 Wis. 241, 197 N.W. 818

[3133] Commercial State Bank v. Wilson, 53 S.D. 82, 220 N.W. 152; Toy Nat. Bank v. Nelson, 38 F.2d 261, cert. denied, 299 U.S. 546, 57 S. Ct. 9, 81 L. Ed. 402; First Nat'l Bank v. Eddy, 47 S.D. 233, 197 N.W. 290; First Nat. Bank v. Hartford, 187 Wis. 290, 203 N.W. 721, rev'd, 273 U.S. 548, 47 S. Ct. 462, 71 L. Ed. 767, 59 A.L.R. 1; Commercial Nat'l Bank v. Board of Sup'rs, 168 Iowa 501, 150 N.W. 704, 1916C Ann. Cas. 227; Krembs v. Merrill, 183 Wis. 241, 197 N.W. 818; National Bank v. King County, 153 Wash. 351, 280 P. 16.

such erroneous assessment.[3134] And where trustees of a bank in liquidation fail to take a timely appeal from a preliminary assessment on the bank's assets, a board of tax appeals has no authority to grant refunds.[3135] Relief was available to a bank, claiming a credit against a state bank tax for amounts pursuant to a license tax ordinance enacted by city, by paying the license tax and taking whatever steps were necessary to preserve its right to a refund, filing a bank tax return with the director of revenue and claiming as a credit the amount paid to city, awaiting a determination by the director that additional tax was due, appealing the determination to the Administrative Hearing Commission, and obtaining judicial review of any adverse commission decision.[3136]

Proof of substantial injury is not required for the refund of illegally assessed taxes In cases involving the taxation of exempt property.[3137] The voluntary payment doctrine did not preclude the refund of ad valorem taxes on bank shares which had been paid into the registry of the court pursuant to an agreement of the parties and a court order.[3138]

A bank was entitled to apply immediately for a refund of excess bank tax, and was not required first to carry any excess bank tax credit against gross income tax forward or backward to other tax years before applying for excess credit.[3139]

Taxes on Shares, Shareholders and Capital Stock.—When a receiver of a bank pays taxes assessed against it, believing that such taxes are properly assessed against the bank instead of its stockholders, he is bound by such act whether it Is correct or not, as it is money paid under mistake of law and cannot be recovered.[3140] On the other hand, a cashier of a national bank may

---

[3134] Genessee Valley Nat. Bank v. Livingston (N.Y.), 52 Barb. 223.

Commonwealth violated neither United States Constitution nor state law by giving credit, rather than cash refunds, to banks who paid improper single excise taxes; credits were "meaningful backward-looking relief," required under Federal Constitution, as they provided exact monetary amount (plus interest) to eradicate unfair aspect of prior tax but were applied to present or future assessed taxes rather than handed out in cash form, and use of credits is specifically authorized by state law. Fidelity Bank, N.A. v. Commonwealth by & Through Department of Revenue, 645 A.2d 452 (Pa. Commw. 1994).

[3135] Leimbach v. Evatt, 141 Ohio St. 191, 46 N.E.2d 859.

[3136] Commercial Bank of St. Louis County v. James, 658 S.W.2d 17 (Mo. 1988).

[3137] City of Laredo v. South Tax. Nat'l Bank, 775 S.W.2d 729 (Tex. App. 1989).

[3138] City of Laredo v. South Tax. Nat'l Bank, 775 S.W.2d 729 (Tex. App. 1989).

[3139] Indiana Dep't of State Revenue v. Horizon Bancorp, 644 N.E.2d 870 (Ind. 1994).

[3140] Bristol v. Morganton, 125 N.C. 365, 34 S.E. 512.

act as agent of the bank in listing its property for taxation, but he has no authority to list its capital stock for assessment against it, and the cashier's mistake in so listing capital stock will not estop the bank from recovering taxes paid under protest on such void assessment.[3141] And where a bank pays taxes on its capital stock under an apparently valid but actually void assessment, it may recover such payment as made under duress.[3142]

Money erroneously paid by a trust company for taxes on its shares, thereafter refunded to the company, is the property of its individual stockholders, not the company,[3143] and the stockholders, by signing an agreement authorizing the trust company to sue to recover such taxes, have not waived their right to the refund.[3144]

Application of Credits.—Bank's credits for bank taxes paid in the current year were to be applied against the bank's current year gross income tax liability before applying credits for bank taxes paid in a prior year.[3145]

Statutory Provisions.—In a national bank's action to recover taxes paid, a state supreme court's repudiation of a construction of the statute under which an unlawful assessment was made, does not defeat the bank's recovery.[3146] Property tax payments made under an allegedly unconstitutional statute could not be recovered under another statute, which applied only in cases where the tax was correctly assessed but the taxpayer erred in paying it.[3147] The meaning of a statute for refunding excessive bank taxes must be ascertained in the light of general legislative and judicial knowledge, and it cannot be presumed that such a statute was intended to favor banks delinquent In payment as against banks not so delinquent.[3148] And a bank is not prevented from prosecuting an action to recover taxes paid on its reserved profits under protest, by a statute which provides that whoever

---

[3141] Weiser Nat'l Bank v. Jeffreys, 14 Idaho 659, 95 P. 23.

[3142] Second Nat'l Bank v. New York, 213 N.Y. 457, 107 N.E. 1039; Ashland County Bank v. Butternut, 208 Wis. 90, 241 N.W. 638, 82 A.L.R. 865.

[3143] Richmond Trust Co. v. Christian, 150 Va. 244, 142 S.E. 528.

[3144] Richmond Trust Co. v. Christian, 150 Va. 244, 142 S.E. 528.

[3145] Indiana Dep't of State Revenue v. Horizon Bancorp, 644 N.E.2d 870 (Ind. 1994).

[3146] Montana Nat'l Bank v. Yellowstone County of Montana, 276 U.S. 499, 48 S. Ct. 331, 72 L. Ed. 673.

[3147] Texas Nat'l Bank v. Harris County, 765 S.W.2d 823 (Ten. App. 1988).

[3148] Central Trust Co. v. Howard, 275 Mass. 153, 175 N.E. 461.

Statute held to require that assessed taxes be paid before bank may bring itself within offer to refund certain taxes. Central Trust Co. v. Howard, 275 Mass. 153, 175 N.E. 461.

neglects to make return of his ratable property shall have no remedy if overtaxed, since the tax is not an overtax, but a void tax.[3149] But a bank, by filing a waiver under a refunding statute, was held not exonerated from payment of taxes assessed before passage of the statute.[3150] For other cases involving statutory provisions with respect to the recovery of taxes paid, see the footnote.[3151]

Interest on Refunds.—Where a statute authorizing a tax refund contains no provision for interest, taxpayers who voluntarily pay the tax before challenging its validity are not entitled to interest on the refund.[3152] But where a statute curing an imperfect assessment of bank stock is not an ordinary curative statute legalizing an assessment as of the date it was originally made, but only makes an assessment legal as of the time steps are taken under the statute, interest on the taxes paid may be recovered from the

---

[3149] Mechanics' Sav. Bank v. Granger, 17 R.I. 77, 20 A. 202.

[3150] Central Trust Co. v. Howard, 275 Mass. 153, 175 N.E. 461.

[3151] Taxpayer was not entitled to adjustment of income tax return of previous year because of loss sustained on stock of a bank, assets of which were in process of liquidation and not finally distributed, in view of statutory provision that losses upon liquidation of corporation should be recognized only in the year in which corporation made its final distribution. Marshall v. Wisconsin Tax Com., 222 Wis. 221, 267 N.W. 913.

In action by taxpayer for refund on income tax of previous year because of alleged loss on stock of bank, assets of which were in process of liquidation, but not distributed, fact that bank was a national bank did not prevent application of state statute providing that losses upon liquidation should be recognized only in the year corporation made final distribution. Marshall v. Wisconsin Tax Com., 222 Wis. 221, 267 N.W. 913.

Mistake of law.—

Property tax payments made under allegedly unconstitutional statute could not be recovered on basis of mistake of fact, within exception to rule that taxes voluntarily paid cannot be recovered, as mistake, if any, was one of law. Texas Nat'l Bank v. Harris County, 765 S.W.2d 823 (Tex. App. 1988).

Statute authorizing taxpayer to apply for refund of taxes erroneously paid applied only in assets where there had been calculation error or the like, and not where tax payment had been made pursuant to mistake of law. First Bank v. Deer Park Indep. School Dist., 770 S.W.2d 849 (Tex. App. 1989).

Definitions.—

Terms "overpayment" and "erroneous" as used in statute authorizing refunds, of overpayments or erroneous payments of taxes include the term "illegal" and include taxes which are paid under an unconstitutional statute. Community Fed. Sav. & Loan Ass'n v. Director of Revenue, 752 S.W.2d 794 (Mo. 1988).

[3152] Commonwealth v. Safe Deposit & Trust Co., 155 Va. 458, 155 S.E. 897.

time of payment to the time of validation of the assessment.[3153] Taxpayer who paid, under protest, a recording tax on the mortgage of a national banking association, which tax subsequently was determined to be levied unconstitutionally, was entitled to interest on the refund of such tax paid by the tax commission more than eight years after the tax was illegally collected.[3154]

A statute authorizing a taxpayer to contest ad valorem taxes by seeking judicial review and authorizing refund to include interest at rate of two percent per annum was not repealed by a later statute enacted as part of a statutory scheme governing sales taxes, which fixed interest at rate of fifteen percent.[3155]

Refund Anticipation Loans.—A refund anticipation loan (or "RAL") is a loan that is made to a taxpayer at or about the time of filing his or her income tax return and that is expected to be repaid to the lender directly from the proceeds of the borrower's anticipated tax refund. Generally, the borrower receives cash or a check in the amount of the refund, minus the bank's loan fees and a fee charged by an independent entity that prepares the loan application.[3156]

§ 76. Actions and Proceedings for Recovery of Taxes Paid.

Conditions Precedent.—In order for taxes paid by a bank or on bank stock to be recovered In an action, all statutory requirements imposing conditions precedent must be complied with; for instance, making an application to the proper tribunal for relief,[3157] and demanding a refund.[3158]

[3153] People ex rel. American Exchange Nat'l Bank v. Purdy, 199 N.Y. 51, 92 N.E. 232; People ex rel. Merchants' Nat'l Bank v. Purdy, 143 App. Div. 277, 128 N.Y.S. 119, aff'd, 202 N.Y. 599, 95 N.E. 814.

[3154] CC&F Buffalo Development Co. v. Tully, 103 Misc. 2d 1060, 427 N.Y.S.2d 392 (1980).

Fact that recording tax on the mortgage of a national banking association, which tax taxpayer paid under protest, subsequently was determined to be levied unconstitutionally as opposed to being wholly void or unconstitutional per se did not render such tax levy an "erroneous collection" so as to render taxpayer ineligible for interest on amount of tax refunded. CC&F Buffalo Development Co. v. Tully, 103 Misc. 2d 1060, 427 N.Y.S.2d 392 (1980).

[3155] First Nat'l Bank of Commerce v. New Orleans, 555 So. 32d 1345 (La. 1990).

[3156] Pac. Capital Bank, N.A. v. Connecticut, 542 F.3d 341 (2nd Cir. 2008) (superseded by statute as stated in Gordon v. Kohl's Dep't Stores, Inc., 172 F. Supp. 3d 840 (E.D. Pa. 2016).).

[3157] *United States.*—Toy Nat'l Bank v. Nelson, 38 F.2d 261; National Rockland Bank v.

(Text continued on page 878)

Boston, 296 F. 743, rev'd on other grounds sub nom. Fourth Atl. Nat'l Bank v. City of Boston, 300 F. 29.

Alabama.—A complaint in action brought under statute relating to actions against county for refund of money paid as taxes assessed against capital stock of national bank, held demurrable for failure to allege that claim had been presented to court of county commissioners, and disallowed or reduced. National Bank v. Marshall County, 229 Ala. 369, 157 So. 444.

California.—Where bank did not make timely application to the board of equalization for relief from assessments complained of, it could not maintain an action for recovery of taxes paid. Bank of America Nat'l Trust & Sav. Asso. v. Mundo, 37 Cal. 2d 1, 229 P.2d 345.

Colorado.—Union Nat'l Bank v. Board of Comm'rs, 75 Colo. 298, 225 P. 851.

Kentucky.—Grayson County Nat. Bank v. Leitchfield, 114 S.W. 289.

Michigan.—Bank of Tustin v. Burdell Tp., 184 Mich. 131, 150 N.W. 367.

New York.—Citizens' Sav. Bank v. New York, 166 N.Y. 594, 59 N.E. 1120; Second Nat'l Bank v. New York, 213 N.Y. 457, 107 N.E. 1039.

Oklahoma—Bretz v. El Reno State Bank, 71 Okla. 283, 177 P. 362; American Nat. Bank v. Andrews, 140 Okla. 266, 283 P. 253.

Taxpayer was not entitled to recover for allegedly unconstitutional taxes or fees if he ignored protest procedures in statute setting forth procedure for challenging allegedly unconstitutional fee or tax. Owner-Operator Indep. Drivers Ass'n v. Anthony, 879 P.2d 845 (Okla. App. 1994).

Oregon.—Allen v. Bilyeu, 100 Ore. 576, 198 P. 208.

Tennessee.—Mossy Creek Bank v. Jefferson County, 153 Tenn. 332, 284 S.W. 64.

Washington.—Spokane & Eastern Trust Co. v. Spokane County, 153 Wash. 702, 280 P. 354.

3158 Bristol v. Morganton, 125 N.C. 365, 34 S.E. 512.

Where purpose of bank in seeking to recover taxes paid under protest on ground that the assessors intentionally discriminated against it in favor of other property owners was to obtain a review of the decision of the board of equalization, an application to the board for correction of the alleged discriminatory assessment was a prerequisite to the maintenance of the action. Bank of America Nat'l Trust & Sav. Asso. v. Mundo, 37 Cal. 2d 1, 229 P.2d 345.

Taxpayer's failure to follow statutory procedures for protesting property valuation and recovery of property taxes paid under allegedly unconstitutional statute precluded such recovery. Texas Nat'l Bank v. Harris County, 765 S.W.2d 823 (Tex. App. 1988).

Taxpayer sufficiently complied with county claim statute prior to bringing suit to recover alleged overpayment by filing petition with county assessor challenging valuation of property, though proper party to receive notice was county treasurer; county, rather than particular office or agency, was real party in interest, and notice to assessor gave county ample opportunity to investigate and determine whether to pay requested refund. Arizona Telco Fed. Credit Union v. Arizona Dep't of Revenue, 764 P.2d 20 (Ariz. App. 1988).

If person who claims tax or any part thereof to be invalid for any reason other than the valuation of the property has paid the same to the treasurer or other proper authority in all

The state is free to provide for refunds only to taxpayers who paid under protest.[3159] But where taxes wrongfully assessed are involuntarily paid under duress and coercion, a taxpayer's right to recover such taxes cannot be defeated by a failure to comply with such statutory conditions.[3160]

Generally, all adequate administrative remedies for recovering a tax illegally collected must be exhausted before resort is made to the courts.[3161] But a bank need not apply to a board of equalization before suing to recover a tax on stock where state court decisions make such application futile.[3162]

Accrual of Action.—A bank's action for a tax refund accrued at the time of the city's written denials of a timely claim for a refund, rather than at the time the United States Supreme Court approved a proportional method of computing tax exemption for federal securities from the Georgia Bank

---

respects as though the tax was legal and valid, he or she may within 30 days demand return of the tax in writing from the county treasurer and may sue after 90 days. First Nat'l Bank v. Heiden, 241 Neb. 893, 491 N.W.2d 699 (1992).

[3159] Owner-Operator Indep. Drivers Ass'n v. Anthony, 879 P.2d 845 (Okla. App. 1994).

[3160] Security Nat. Bank v. Young, 55 F.2d 616, 84 A.L.R. 100, cert. denied, 286 U.S. 551, 52 S. Ct. 502, 76 L. Ed. 1287.

Bank failed to raise fact issue about its affirmative defense of mutual mistake of fact as necessary to be entitled to exception from voluntary payment rule prohibiting recovery of illegal tax; bank did not raise fact issue as to whether county made mistake when it issued invoice for tax. First Bank v. Harris County, 804 S.W.2d 588 (Tex. App. 1991).

Bank failed to produce evidence to raise issue of fact of express duress as affirmative defense, and thus bank was not exempt from voluntary payment rule prohibiting recovery of illegal tax. First Bank v. Harris County, 804 S.W.2d 588 (Tex. App. 1991).

Bank's allegations of affirmative defense of duress in its pleadings seeking refund of taxes paid to county did not raise fact issues about its defenses; thus, county was not required to disprove banks affirmative defenses as matter of law. First Bank v. Harris County, 804 S.W.2d 588 (Tex. App. 1991).

[3161] First Nat'l Bank v. Harrison County, 57 F.2d 56, cert. denied, 287 U.S. 611, 53 S. Ct. 13, 77 L. Ed. 531; Hammerstrom v. Toy Nat. Bank, 81 F.2d 628, cert. denied, 299 U.S. 546, 57 S. Ct. 9, 81 L. Ed. 402.

In suit for tax refund based on assessor's alleged improper discrimination by classifying bank stock, an allegation that there was not sufficient time to ascertain facts and procure evidence thereof to present to the board of tax review was held an insufficient excuse for not pursuing the administrative remedy before resorting to judicial relief. Crawford County Trust, etc., Bank v. Crawford County, 66 F.2d 971, cert. denied, 291 U.S. 664, 54 S. Ct. 439, 78 L Ed. 1055.

[3162] Montana Nat'l Bank v. Yellowstone County of Montana, 276 U.S. 499, 48 S. Ct. 331, 72 L. Ed. 673.

Shares Tax Act, which merely affirmed the formula previously articulated by the Georgia Supreme Court.[3163]

Pleading.—Courts are without jurisdiction to consider grounds not set forth in tax refund claim.[3164]

Standing to Sue.—It seems that where a bank has paid taxes on shares of its stock, an action to recover such payment may be maintained either in the bank's name without joining stockholders,[3165] or by a stockholder,[3166] unless a statute specifically provides in whose name suit shall be brought.[3167] But it has been held in an action by a national bank to recover taxes paid by it on its real estate, its capital stock having been assessed without any deduction therefor, that the wrong, if any, was done to the stockholders in

---

[3163] Gwinnett Fed. Sav. & Loan Ass'n v. City of Buford, 185 Ga. App. 200, 363 S.E.2d 597 (1987), cert. denied.

Correspondence from city attorney in response to bank's claims for tax refund following United States Supreme Court's finding that Georgia Banks Shares Act violated federal law did not create issue of fact as to whether city had agreed in writing to extend period of limitation for filing an action for refund, as city flatly denied taxpayer's claim for refund in both letters. Gwinnett Federal Sav. & Loan Asso. v. Buford, 185 Ga. App. 200, 363 S.E.2d 597 (1987), cert. denied.

[3164] Barclays Bank Int'l Ltd. v. Franchise Tax Bd., 10 Cal. App. 4th 1742, 14 Cal. Rptr. 2d 537 (1992).

Taxpayers' commerce clause and due process clause arguments set forth in their consolidated protests, which were transformed by law into claims for refund, were sufficient to encompass "compliance burden"issues. Barclays Bank Int'l Ltd. v. Franchise Tax Bd., 10 Cal. App. 4th 1742, 14 Cal. Rptr. 2d 537 (1992).

[3165] In general.—State Nat. Bank v. Memphis, 116 Tenn. 641, 94 S.W. 606, 7 L.R.A. (n.s.) 663; First Nat. Bank v. Achenbach, 110 Okla. 246, 237 P. 574; Security Nat'l Bank v. Young, 55 F.2d 616, 64 A.L.R. 100, cert. denied, Security Nat. Bank v. Young, 286 U.S. 551, 52 S. Ct. 502, 76 L. Ed. 1287; Ward v. First Nat. Bank, 225 Ala. 10, 142 So. 93 (1932).

National banks, paying the tax assessed upon shares of stock therein as agent of their shareholders, have an implied right of action, if necessary, to recover the amount so paid. Tower Co. v. Commonwealth, 223 Mass. 371, 111 N.E. 966.

National bank suing to recover taxes paid by it on capital stock held "real party in interest." Boise City Nat. Bank v. Ada County, 37 F.2d 947; McFarland v. Central Nat. Bank, 26 F.2d 890, cert. denied, 278 U.S. 606, 49 S. Ct. 12, 73 L. Ed. 533.

Bank held entitled to sue for overpayment of taxes on shares assessable to owners, where bank is liable for payment of taxes with right to obtain repayment from stockholders. National Bank v. Detroit, 272 Mich. 610, 262 N.W. 422.

[3166] Guaranty Trust Co. v. New York, 108 App. Div. 192, 95 N.Y.S. 770; Aetna Ins. Co. v. New York, 7 App. Div. 145, 40 N.Y.S. 120, aff'd, 153 N.Y. 331, 47 N.E. 593.

[3167] Fiman v. Hughes County, 55 S.D. 204, 225 N.W. 711.

overvaluing their stock, not to the bank in assessing its real estate to it, and therefore the bank could not recover.[3168] A liquidator or receiver of an insolvent bank may maintain an action on the bank's tax refund claims.[3169] And under a statute providing that any person against whom any tax is levied or who may be required to pay a tax, and who pays it under protest, may commence an action for its recovery, a national bank which paid a tax on its capital stock assessed to it has the right to maintain such an action on either statutory ground.[3170]

For purposes of statute allowing suit for refund of property taxes, "person" is any number of persons and any copartnership, association, joint stock company, corporation, or other entity that may be the owner of property.[3171]

As to other matters relating to standing to sue, see the footnote.[3172]

Miscellaneous Matters.—For cases relating to miscellaneous matters pertaining to actions and proceedings for recovery of taxes paid, see the footnote.[3173]

[3168] Board v. First Nat. Bank, 25 Ind. App. 94, 57 N.E. 728.

[3169] Crawford County Trust & Sav. Bank v. Crawford County, 66 F.2d 971, cert. denied, 291 U.S. 664, 54 S. Ct 439, 78 L Ed. 1055.

Receiver of national bank was entitled to bring action to recover bank's payment of state taxes on bank stock. Clark v. Herkimer County, 8 N.Y.S.2d 675.

[3170] First Nat. Bank v. Eddy, 47 S.D. 297, 198 N.W. 554.

[3171] First Nat'l Bank v. Heiden, 241 Neb. 893, 491 N.W.2d 699 (1992).

[3172] Judgment creditor which had obtained ownership of property but then conveyed it to another under agreement whereby it agreed to hold the grantee harmless for the payment of any taxes which accrued did not thereafter have standing to sue for return of taxes which it paid on behalf of the grantee. First Nat'l Bank v. Heiden, 241 Neb. 893, 491 N.W.2d 699 (1992).

[3173] In general.—Appeal from state board of equalization was not exclusive remedy, and bank could maintain action to recover taxes paid, where it did not object to amount of "assessment" made by board, but objected to "apportionment" of assessment among counties in which bank did business. Valley Nat. Bank v. Apache County, 57 Ariz. 459, 114 P.2d 883.

Determination of true value of shares.—Under statute providing for assessment of shares of stock in bank, if shareholder-taxpayer, acting either directly or through his agent, the bank, is dissatisfied with valuation fixed on his shares, he may pay the tax under protest and, in an action to recover tax illegally collected, obtain determination of true value of the shares. Brophy v. Powell, 58 Ariz. 543, 121 P.2d 647.

Burden of proof.—Burden was on national banks, suing for taxes paid on shares of their stock, assessed at higher rate than moneyed capital used by others In making loans secured by mortgages on realty, to show that petitioners were not only authorized to make such loans,

(Text continued on page 882)

---

but actively engaged In loaning substantial amounts on such security, to establish unjust discrimination against them. Toy Nat. Bank v. Smith, 8 F. Supp. 638, rev'd on other grounds, Hammerstrom v. Toy Nat. Bank, 81 F.2d 628, cert. denied, 299 U.S. 546, 57 S. Ct 9, 81 L. Ed. 402.

In an action by the receiver of a national bank to recover the payment of taxes on stock on the ground that the assessments were void because based on a greater rate than assessments against individual citizens in competition with the business of the bank, the receiver had the burden to establish the cause of action notwithstanding defendant offered no testimony. Clark v. Herkimer County, 8 N.Y.S.2d 675 (1938).

Receiver was required to show inequality of rate and competition, and thereby present for determination such questions of fact, wherein evidence was held to establish right of receiver to recover. Clark v. Herkimer County, 8 N.Y.S.2d 675 (1938).

Money judgment.—Bank shareholders claiming an illegal tax was collected are not entitled, under the Iowa statute, to a money judgment in the alternative. First Nat. Bank v. Harrison County, 57 F.2d 56, cert. denied, 287 U.S. 611, 53 S. Ct. 13, 77 L. Ed. 531.

Evidence.—Where notices of valuation of personalty and real property did not indicate that total tax liability of taxpayer bank was to be increased over value rendered by bank's comptroller, tax bill in form of six separate statements did not indicate valuation of properties listed and city and school district used different assessment ratios and rates, there was sufficient evidence to support jury's finding that comptroller did not or should not have known that taxes were to be computed on larger figures rather than on smaller. San Antonio Indep. School Dist. v. National Bank of Commerce, 626 S.W.2d 794 (Tex. App. 1981).

In action for reimbursement of state sales and federal withholding taxes paid by liquor stores' manager from lender which held secured interest in the inventory and equipment of store as collateral for loan to purchase stores, evidence was sufficient to support jury verdict in favor of manager. First Bank v. Dollar, 159 Ga. App. 815, 285 S.E.2d 203 (1981).

Issue deemed preserved for review.—Where issue was not raised in tax refund proceeding in department of revenue because issue was secondary to other questions in case that had already been ruled against taxpayer, but issue was raised for first time in summary judgment proceedings in superior court, issue was preserved for review by Court of Appeals. Continental Bank v. Arizona Dep't of Revenue, 131 Ariz. 6, 638 P.2d 228 (1981).

Equal protection issue not barred.—Although claim for sales tax refund did not raise any equal protection issue, plaintiffs seeking refund were not barred from raising equal protection issue before trial court and court of appeal, since claims for refund were filed before United States Supreme

Court's decision which gave rise to plaintiffs' equal protection claims. Hibernia Bank v. State Bd. of Equalization, 166 Cal. App. 3d 393, 212 Cal. Rptr. 556 (1985).

Jurisdiction.—Trial court had subject matter jurisdiction over taxpayer's claim for relief from overpayment of property taxes where both county and department concurred that overpayment had been made. Arizona Telco Fed. Credit Union v. Arizona Dep't of Revenue, 764 P.2d 20 (Ariz. App. 1988).

Tax tribunal had jurisdiction to interpret tax penalty provision pertaining to redemption of real property sold at tax sale and to order refund of the penalty even though tax sale was

IX. COLLECTION AND ENFORCEMENT.

a. Manner.

§ 77. In General.

The manner in which assessed taxes are to be collected is controlled by the statutes of the particular taxing district.[3174] The power of a state to

---

conducted pursuant to order of the circuit court; penalty necessarily was related to actual delinquent taxes, interest, and special assessment fees which had to be paid in order to redeem the property. Standard Fed. Sav. Bank v. Genesee County, 208 Mich. App. 569, 528 N.W.2d 793 (1995).

Limitations.—Savings and loan association lost its right of appeal from denial of request for tax refunds paid by institutions which it acquired where it failed to take an appeal within 30 days of the decision against it, despite its contention that decisions were not final until the last of the decisions against the various associations which it had acquired. Community Fed. Sav. & Loan Ass'n v. Director of Revenue, 752 S.W.2d 794 (Mo. 1988).

Accrual of claim.—Bank's claim for refund of excess bank tax paid, beyond what could be credited against gross income tax liability, accrued on due date for filing income tax return, rather than at conclusion of period during which excess credit could be carried forward. Indiana Dep't of State Revenue v. Horizon Bancorp, 644 N.E.2d 870 (Ind. 1994).

Laches.—Doctrine of laches could not be applied to deny delinquent taxpayer's right to redeem property sold at tax sale, where it was tax sale purchaser who interposed arguments of standing and incorporation, which protracted foreclosure litigation and where taxpayer simply requested that court defer its entry of foreclosure of civil right of redemption for reasonable amount of time in order that taxpayer could assemble funds necessary to redeem. LaValley v. Rock Point Aero Sport Club, 104 Md. App. 123, 655 A.2d 60 (1995).

Notice requirement.—Redemption period for real property, which had state equalized value of over $1,000 and which had been levied upon for delinquent taxes, did not expire until owner of significant property interest was notified of hearing before Department of Treasury; accordingly, property owner which never received such notice was not required to pay postexpiration penalty in order to redeem property. Standard Fed. Sav. Bank v. Genessee County, 208 Mich. App. 569, 528 N.W.2d 793 (1995).

Phrase "following the expiration of the redemption periods provided," as used in tax penalty statute providing for imposition of 50 percent penalty after redemption period expires with regard to property sold at tax sale, referred to standard redemption period provided by another tax statute which sets date certain as extended by subdivision of penalty statute providing extension pending notification of property owner of hearing before Department of Treasury; to hold otherwise would render subdivision providing extension without meaning or function. Standard Fed. Sav. Bank v. Genesee County, 208 Mich. App. 569, 528 N.W.2d 793 (1995).

[3174] *Arizona.*—Pinal County v. Hammons, 30 Ariz. 36, 243 P. 919.

Georgia.—McWhorter v. Chattooga County, 154 Ga. 289, 114 S.E. 203.

Iowa.—Where specific remedy is provided for tax collection, such remedy must be

compel payment of a tax does not end until payment is made,[3175] and a state is not prejudiced in its right to collect a tax by failing to furnish information as promised in answer to a bank's inquiry about the right to pay taxes on a certain basis.[3176] Where taxes are voluntarily paid without any suggestion of invalidity, it is the duty of a collecting officer to collect the taxes.[3177] Since Congress has given the states the right to tax national bank shares, states have the right to prescribe reasonable regulations for the collection of such tax.[3178] The county's failure to file a tax claim against the estate of the bankrupt furniture business did not foreclose other avenues of recovery.[3179] The county's notice of tax foreclosure which misnamed the property owner was sufficient to apprise the mortgagee of the pending tax sale, where the notice described the property by location, dimensions and tax map number.[3180]

---

followed statutory remedy is exclusive. Merv E. Hilpipre Auction Co. v. Solon State Bank, 343 N.W.2d 452 (Iowa 1984).

Maine.—Weld v. Bangor, 59 Me. 416.

Mississippi.

Missouri.—Robertson v. Harrison County, 127 Miss. 281, 90 So. 8; State ex rel. Wyatt v. Cantley, 325 Mo. 67, 26 S.W.2d 976.

North Dakota.—Baird v. Burke County, 53 N.D. 140, 205 N.W. 17.

South Dakota.—Scheafer v. McFarland, 49 S.D. 605, 207 N.W. 982.

[3175] Iowa Nat. Bank v. Stewart (Iowa), 232 N.W. 445.

State Department of Assessments and Taxation had authority to assess franchise tax deficiencies for years prior to year it first began to administer franchise tax, as long as assessments were made within limitations period. State Dep't of Assmts. & Taxation v. Loyola Fed. Sav. & Loan Ass'n, 79 Md. App. 481, 558 A.2d 428 (1989).

[3176] Commonwealth v. Central Nat'l Bank, 293 Pa. 404, 143 A. 105.

[3177] Commonwealth v. Safe Deposit & Trust Co., 155 Va. 458, 155 S.E. 897.

[3178] National Rockland Bank v. Boston, 296 F. 743, rev'd on other grounds sub nom. Fourth Atl. Nat'l Bank v. City of Boston, 300 F. 29; McFarland v. Georgetown Nat. Bank, 208 Ky. 7, 270 S.W. 995.

[3179] Palmer v. First Nat'l Bank, 692 P.2d 386 (Kan. App. 1984).

[3180] Key Bank of Cent. New York v. County of Broome, 116 A.D.2d 90, 500 N.Y.S.2d 434 (N.Y. App. Div. 3 Dep't 1986).

Mortgagee was not denied its due process rights when auditor failed to send to mortgagee any notice regarding tax sale or issuance of tax deed; auditor acted in conformity with requirements of notice statute, and mortgagee had right under statute to be notified of tax delinquency and tax sale by annually requesting such notice on form provided by county auditor's office and agreeing to pay small fee to cover mailing if such notice were sent, but mortgagee had made no such request. Miller Reeder Co. v. Farmers State Bank, 588 N.E.2d 506 (Ind. 1992).

Under the Federal Credit Union Act, a state may include the holdings of any federal credit union in evaluating the personal property of the owners thereof for tax purposes, but it may not impose upon the credit union any duty of collecting or enforcing the payment of such taxes.[3181]

The Federal Credit Union Act granted a federally chartered credit union an exemption from any attempt at levy or collection of tax delinquency against the accounts of the credit union members by Maine taxing authorities.[3182]

For purposes of tax sale of real property, it is not what land is really worth, but what it would bring, that should guide taxing authority in estimating how much property should be sold.[3183]

§ 78. Summary Remedies.

In some states provision is made for the collection of taxes on shares of bank stock in a summary manner, as by a rule that stockholders produce their shares for sale for payment of taxes claimed to be due thereon,[3184] or by issuance of execution.[3185] But whatever summary method is provided for,

---

[3181] Northeast Fed. Credit Union v. Neves, 664 F. Supp. 640 (D.N.H. 1987).

[3182] Northeast Federal Credit Union v. Neves, 664 F. Supp. 640 (D.N.E 1987).

[3183] South Carolina Fed. Sav. Bank v. Atlantic Land Title Co., 442 S.E.2d 630 (S.C. App. 1994).

There are no fixed guidelines as to what constitutes excessive levy in tax sale of real property. South Carolina Fed. Sav. Bank v. Atlantic Land Title Co., 442 S.E.2d 630 (S.C. App. 1994).

Tax sale of real property does not necessarily exact excessive levy because it brings considerably more than tax debt or because it brings inadequate price. South Carolina Fed. Sav. Bank v. Atlantic Land Title Co., 442 S.E.2d 630 (S.C. App. 1994).

County treasurer had no duty to partition property before tax sale, and treasurer did not exact excessive levy in tax sale, despite possibility that sale price for entire unpartitioned tract might have been low, where evidence suggested that partitioned portion of property would not have brought sufficient price to satisfy tax debt. South Carolina Fed. Sav. Bank v. Atlantic Land Title Co., 442 S.E.2d 630 (S.C. App. 1994).

[3184] Parker v. Shareholders of Citizens' Bank, 49 La. Ann. 105, 21 So. 232.

Where a bank is not made a party to a rule against the stockholders to surrender their shares to be sold for taxes due thereon, neither service on the cashier of a copy of the rule, nor of a notice by the collector to surrender shares liable for taxes, is legal service on the bank. Parker v. Shareholders, 49 La. Ann. 105, 21 So. 232.

In New York, express provision is made for the enforcement of the payment of taxes on shares of bank stock owned by nonresidents by a lien on and sale of the stock. New York v. McLean, 170 N.Y. 374, 63 N.E. 380; McLean v. Myers, 11 N.Y.S. 635, 58 N.Y. Super. Ct. 337, rev'd, 134 N.Y. 480, 32 N.E. 63.

[3185] Burke v. Speer, 59 Ga. 353.

the mandate of the statutes of the particular jurisdiction must be followed.[3186]

Where stock was properly returned by a bank to the tax receiver, the stockholder being liable to pay the tax, the collector could issue executions therefor. Burke v. Speer, 59 Ga. 353.

[3186] *United States.*—McFarland v. Central Nat. Bank, 26 F.2d 890, cert. denied, 278 U.S. 606, 49 S. Ct. 12, 73 L. Ed. 533.

Alabama.—State v. Jefferson County Bank, 200 Ala. 287, 76 So. 53.

Georgia.—Citizens & Southern Bank v. State, 151 Ga. 696, 108 S.E. 161.

Indiana—Mortgagee was entitled to personal service or actual notice by mail of tax sale of mortgaged property, where mortgagee's address was readily identifiable from records. Miller Reeder Co. v. Farmers State Bank, 545 N.E.2d 593 (Ind. App. 1989).

County auditor's failure to send notice of tax sale to taxpayer's mortgagee violated mortgagee's due process rights. Miller Reeder Co. v. Farmers State Bank, 545 N.E.2d 593 (Ind. App. 1989).

Evidence supported conclusion that actual notice often sale was sent by certified mail to mortgagee bank where: (1) Certified mall return receipt copies reflected signatures of bank employees on mailings addressed to bank; (2) auditor testified that the only possible enclosure would have been newspaper advertisement of forthcoming tax sale and (3) employer bank would have knowledge of its employees imputed. Indiana Federal Sav. & Loan Ass'n v. Breitinger, 551 N.E.2d 1172 (Ind. App 1990).

Notice of tax sale mailed to mortgages bank was adequate, although '"notice" consisted of page of newspaper containing listing of properties for sale at upcoming tax sale listed alphabetically by names of delinquent taxpayer owners and mortgagee bank claimed it should have been mailed notice containing only information pertinent to its interest in particular mortgaged property. Indiana Fed. Sav. & Loan Ass'n v. Breitinger, 551 N.E.2d 1172 (Ind. App. 1990).

Mortgagee bank could not complain that it did not receive notice of tax sale in form prescribed by statutes when mortgagee had to request such notice to be entitled to form notice, but had made no such request; mortgagee bank received actual notice of forthcoming tax sale, and its own decision not to request form notice precluded mortgagee bank from receiving form notice. Indiana Fed. Sav. & Loan Ass'n v. Breitinger, 551 N.E.2d 1172 (Ind. App. 1990).

Minnesota.—State v. Citizens' State Bank, 171 Minn. 29, 213 N.W. 45.

Missouri.—Statute requiring any person purchasing property at a delinquent land tax auction to conduct title search and give notice to all parties claiming interest in the property does not contain express language or necessary or unavoidable implication that it should have retroactive application and can only be applied prospectively. Great S. Sav. & Loan Ass'n v. Payne, 771 S.W.2d 940 (Mo. App. 1989).

Nebraska.—State v. American State Bank, 114 Neb. 740, 209 N.W. 621.

New York.—New York v. McLean, 170 N.Y. 374, 63 N.E. 380.

County did not have power to make tax sale subject to already extinguished mortgage; statutory scheme allowed only for survival of public claims for taxes, liens or other encumbrances. Central Federal Sav. F.S.B. v. Laurels Sullivan County Estates Corp., 145 A.D.2d 1, 537 N.Y.S.2d 642 (1989).

Thus, where a state statute provides for taxation of shares of national banks, and that taxes against such shares shall be levied against their holder in the personal property list, the state legislature has the power to provide that the taxes "shall be paid by the bank," and in collecting such taxes a collector may make distress of the bank's property.[3187] But a statute declaring that a bank shall pay the taxes of its stockholders assessed on its stock, but that if a bank does not pay such taxes, the individual stockholders shall be liable therefor, does not authorize a levy of tax warrants against the property of a bank to compel the payment of taxes due from delinquent stockholders.[3188] The assessment that flows from corporate tax return would be against the corporation, not against corporate officers.[3189] The liability of corporate officers for failure to pay withholding taxes to the commonwealth could not be deemed to arise from information required to be shown on the face of corporate tax returns, as corporate officers were not taxpayers required to file a return.[3190]

North Dakota.—Ward County v. Baird, 55 N.D. 670, 215 N.W. 163.

Oklahoma.—Gourd v. Guaranty Nat. Bank, 90 Okla. 298, 217 P. 358; Stuckey v. Jones, 121 Okla. 290, 249 P. 918.

Pennsylvania—State supreme court's determination that prior notice requirements of Tax Sale Act were constitutionally infirm did not require Common Pleas Court to set aside tax sale as remedy to mortgagee, which had not received notice of sale. First Pennsylvania Bank, N.A. v. Lancaster County Tax Claim Bureau, 521 A.2d 114 (Pa. Commw. 1967).

[3187] First Nat Bank v. Douglas County, 9 F. Cas. 84 (No. 4799), 3 Dill. 330.

[3188] First Nat'l Bank v. Lyman, 59 Kan. 410, 53 P. 125; Gourd v. Guaranty Nat. Bank, 90 Okla. 298, 217 P. 358.

Assessments of national bank stock should be made against the shareholders personally. And the collector has no right to collect the tax by selling the property of the bank, or the shares or other property of the shareholders, except that of the delinquent ones. First Nat. Bank v. Meredith, 44 Mo. 500.

Where a warrant attached to an assessment against a stockholder in a bank for the amount of his stock directs the collector to collect from the persons named, and to levy the same on their goods and chattels, the collector is not authorized to levy upon and collect the same out of the property of the bank, although the bank holds funds with which the tax should have been paid. The contract between the bank and its stockholders cannot thus be enforced. First Nat. Bank v. Fancher, 48 N.Y. 524.

[3189] Heritage Bank for Sav. v. Doran, 399 Mass. 855, 507 N.E.2d 690 (1987).

[3190] Heritage Bank for Sav. v. Doran, 399 Mass. 855, 507 N.E.2d 690 (1987).

Any prior existing lien becomes void upon issuance of tax deed, and reconveyance of title from tax title holder to party with pretax-sale interest does not affect validity of tax deed.[3191]

§ 79. Action for Unpaid Taxes.

Right of Action.—In the absence of statute, it seems to be the general rule that an action will not lie to recover unpaid taxes, and this rule is applicable to taxes levied on banks or bank stock.[3192] In a number of jurisdictions, however, such actions are expressly authorized.[3193] Since such actions are statutory, they cannot be maintained unless the respective statute has been substantially complied with.[3194] Property taxes are not a personal obligation but rather a lien against the property.[3195] Since tax on real estate is not personal obligation or debt of any person, proceedings for collection of taxes is one in rem.[3196]

[3191] Lincoln Park Fed. Sav. & Loan Ass'n v. DRG, Inc., 175 Ill. App. 3d 176, 124 Ill. Dec. 790, 529 N.E.2d 771 (1988).

Purchasers of property from tax deed owners had title superior to that of pretax-sale mortgagee, under doctrine of equitable conversion, even if tax deed owner was no longer owner of property at time it sold it and purchasers had not paid entire purchase price under contract, where office of recorder of deeds showed that tax deed owner owned property in fee simple at time it was sold to purchaser. Lincoln Park Federal Sav. & Loan Ass'n v. DRG, Inc., 175 Ill. App. 3d 176, 124 Ill. Dec. 790, 529 N.E.2d 771 (1988).

[3192] Judy v. National State Bank, 133 Iowa 252, 110 N.W. 605; Shearer v. Citizens' Bank, 129 Iowa 564, 105 N.W. 1025; Board of Comm'rs v. First Nat'l Bank, 48 Kan. 561, 30 P. 22.

No ordinary action is available to county for collection of real estate taxes, and no statutory provision is made for collection of such taxes except through enforcement of lien. Merv E. Hilpipre Auction Co. v. Solon State Bank, 343 N.W.2d 452 (Iowa 1984).

Among limited defects which render tax sales absolutely null, and therefore incurable by prescription, are prior payment of taxes. Commercial Nat'l Bank v. Dance, 661 So. 2d 551 (La. App. 1995).

[3193] Judy v. National State Bank, 133 Iowa 252, 110 N.W. 605; Shearer v. Citizens' Bank, 129 Iowa 564, 105 N.W. 1025; Board of Comm'rs v. First Nat'l Bank, 48 Kan. 561, 30 P. 22; McLean v. Myers, 134 N.Y. 480, 32 N.E. 63; People v. Old Second Nat. Bank, 347 Ill. 640, 180 N.E. 408.

[3194] Judy v. National State Bank, 133 Iowa 252, 110 N.W. 605.

[3195] Norwest Bank (N.A.)-Duluth v. Goodyear Tire & Rubber Co., 346 N.W.2d 377 (Minn. App. 1984).

[3196] Merv E. Hilpipre Auction Co. v. Solon State Bank, 343 N.W.2d 452 (Iowa 1984).

A bank's right to dispute the payment of a tax bill is not cut off by the fact that it does not appeal from a county board of appeals where no appeal lies from the action of such board in any case.[3197]

Pleading and Defenses.—A declaration in an action against a bank to recover taxes need not state the various statutes or steps under which the taxes were assessed, or the statutory conditions or reservations with respect thereto.[3198] In such an action, a claim that bonds held by a bank are exempt should be set up in the answer instead of the rejoinder, since it is a defense to the cause of action.[3199] It is a good defense to a tax assessment made against a bank that at the time the assessment was made, the law required a bank's property to be assessed against its stockholders, and a collector cannot recover in a suit against a bank for such taxes.[3200] But taxpayers cannot absolve themselves from liability for payment of legally imposed taxes by setting up an auditor's illegal act in changing a classification and assessment.[3201] And a suit to compel payment of a tax cannot be defended on the ground that national bank stock on which the tax was levied was not taxable because it was pledged as security, the remedy being by appeal from the assessment.[3202]

Statute of Limitation.—As to the time when a right of action for unpaid taxes against property or shares of a bank accrues, and the time within which such an action must be brought, no definite rule can be stated; these matters depend upon the statutory provisions in the various states.[3203]

Process.—Whether "legal process" has been used to seize property within the meaning of the tax lien statute is determined by defining the term in its ordinary and commonly accepted meaning; such process includes proceedings begun by writ, warrant, summons, order or mandate, or those which invoke the aid of judicial process or decree.[3204]

[3197] State ex rel. Mahan v. Merchants' Bank of Jefferson City, 160 Mo. 640, 61 S.W. 676.

[3198] People v. Old Second Nat'l Bank, 347 Ill. 640, 180 N.E 408.

[3199] Citizens' Nat. Bank v. Commonwealth, 82 Ky. L. Rptr. 1116, 108 S.W. 281.

[3200] State ex rel. Mahan v. Merchants' Bank of Jefferson City, 160 Mo. 640, 61 S.W. 676.

[3201] Iowa Nat. Bank v. Stewart (Iowa), 232 N.W. 445.

[3202] Farmington v. Downing, 67 N.H. 441, 30 A. 345.

[3203] Commonwealth v. Commonwealth Bank, 39 Mass. (22 Pick.) 176; Citizens' Nat. Bank v. Commonwealth, 118 Ky. 51, 80 S.W. 479, 81 SW. 686.

[3204] Palmer v. First Nat'l Bank, 692 P.2d 386 (Kan. App. 1984).

Mortgagee was not denied its due process rights when auditor failed to send to mortgagee any notice regarding tax sale or issuance of tax deed; auditor acted in conformity with

Notice.—Due process provisions of state constitution require that known mortgagee receive actual notice of tax deed, of mortgagee's right to redeem, and of consequences of not doing so; tax deed extinguishes mortgagee's valuable equity interests.[3205]

Parties.—A statute requiring actions to be brought in the name of the real party in interest has been held to apply to proceedings to enforce the collection of taxes against banks or bank shares.[3206] Thus, under a statute providing that when a tax is assessed upon shares of capital stock of a bank, a treasurer shall demand payment from the bank's cashier, and thereupon it shall be the cashier's duty to pay same, an action to collect a tax assessed against a bank stockholder upon a cashier's refusal to pay cannot be brought against the cashier, it being the bank's duty to pay such tax.[3207] And a receiver of a bank stands in the shoes of his bank for the purpose of paying taxes owed by it, and is the only person against whom proceedings may be instituted by a state to collect such taxes.[3208] An amendment adding parties to a suit for unpaid taxes is properly refused where not germane to the original suit.[3209]

Evidence and Burden of Proof.—In actions to enforce the collection of taxes against banks or on shares of their stock, the usual rules relating to evidence and burdens of proof in civil actions generally seem to apply.[3210]

---

requirements of notice statute, and mortgagee had right under statute to be notified of tax delinquency and tax sale by annually requesting such notice on form provided by county auditor's office and agreeing to pay small fee to cover mailing if such notice were sent, but mortgagee had made no such request. Miller Reeder Co. v. Farmers State Bank, 588 N.E.2d 506 (Ind. 1992).

[3205] First NH Bank v. Town of Windham, 639 A.2d 1089 (N.H. 1994).

[3206] State ex rel. Hill v. Wabash R. Co., 169 Mo. 563, 70 S.W. 132; Hill v. Atchison, etc., B. Co., 169 Mo. 578, 70 S.W. 1118.

[3207] Muskegon v. Lange, 104 Mich. 19, 62 N.W. 158; Commonwealth v. Commonwealth Bank, 39 Mass. (22 Pick.) 176.

[3208] People ex rel. Nelson v. Bank of Rushville, 271 Ill. App. 130 (1933).

[3209] Gully v. First Nat. Bank, 81 F.2d 502, rev'd on other grounds, 299 U.S. 109, 57 S. Ct. 96, 81 L Ed. 70.

Refusal to permit state tax collector to amend complaint in suit against bank for taxes assessed against insolvent national bank, liabilities of which transferee bank had allegedly assumed, to add as parties defendant insolvent bank and trustees under a creditors' agreement, held not error, since amendment was not germane to original suit. Gully v. First Nat. Bank, 81 F.2d 502, rev'd on other grounds, 299 U.S. 109, 57 S. Ct. 96, 81 L Ed. 70.

[3210] **In general.—**

State v. Merchants' Bank, 160 Mo. 640, 61 S.W. 676.

Costs.—A legislature may require that all costs incident to the collection of a tax be paid by the owner of assessed property or from the proceeds of the sale of such property.[3211]

b. Remedies for Wrongful Enforcement.

1. Injunction.

§ 80. When Proper.

In General.—With regard to the propriety of an injunction as a remedy for wrongful enforcement of a tax against banks or shares of bank stock, the

---

Evidence subject to subpoena.—

Under fiscal code section that information gained by administrative department as result of returns, investigations, etc., under statutes imposing taxes shall be confidential except for official purposes, use in court of tax of share reports of all banks and trust companies filed with department of revenue, to prove that tax on national banks' shares constituted greater burden than similar tax on those of state banks, and was therefore illegal, was for "official purposes," and such evidence could be subpoenaed under discretionary control of trial judge. Commonwealth v. Mellon Nat'l Bank & Trust Co., 360 Pa. 103, 61 A.2d 430.

Evidence held sufficient.—

In suit to recover taxes, interest and penalties due county and state on bank stock under valuation as set by equalization board, the record was sufficient to show the delinquent taxes and that they were unpaid, particularly in view of unconditional tender of taxes on stock as rendered for taxation by taxpayer. And evidence was held to support finding that board in arriving at taxable value of bank stock had not refused to receive evidence tendered by taxpayer. Doneghy v. State, 240 S.W.2d 331 (Tex Civ. App.).

Evidence that cashier with permission of stockholder rendered for taxation stock in bank as well as property of the bank, that equalization board gave notice to bank to show cause why the rendition made by it should not be raised for county and state tax purposes and that cashier appeared before board on behalf of bank and stockholders and made a sworn statement in writing to board with regard to the rendition showed that the proceedings resulting in increased valuation of bank stock for tax purposes were duly had as to rendition, notice and appearance. Doneghy v. State, 240 S.W.2d 331 (Tex Civ. App.).

Burden of proof.—

In a suit against the superintendent of banks to recover deficiency in franchise tax paid by him as liquidator of particular bank, he had burden of proving that certain debts became "uncompensated losses" or "recoverable in part only" during particular year, within terms of statute specifying allowable deductions from income by which tax was measured, as respects both the fact of loss and the time of loss. People v. Richardson, 37 Cal. App. 2d 275, 99 P.2d 366.

Tax sales are presumed valid, and party attacking sale has burden of proving its alleged invalidity. Commercial Nat'l Bank v. Dance, 661 So. 2d 551 (La. App. 1995).

[3211] First Trust, etc., Bank v. West Lake Inv. Co., 105 Fla. 590, 141 So. 894.

usual rule applies that it is only where a tax is void or voidable that a court of equity will interfere to prevent its collection.[3212] The remedy for all other wrongs and errors in an assessment or levy such as mere irregularities or defects must be sought from the taxing officers, or by appeal in the manner provided by statute.[3213] Thus, an injunction is proper to restrain the collection of an illegal tax[3214] where there is no adequate legal remedy[3215]

[3212] Carpenter v. Jones County, 130 Iowa 494, 107 N.W. 435; Bank of Arizona v. Howe, 293 F. 600.

Independent grounds for equitable jurisdiction in cases involving real estate taxes exist only when unauthorized tax is levied or an exempt property is taxed, and, in all other situations, equity will assume jurisdiction only when no adequate legal remedy is available. First Nat'l Bank & Trust Co. v. Rosewell, 93 Ill. 2d 388, 67 Ill. Dec. 87, 444 N.E.2d 126 (1982).

[3213] Carpenter v. Jones County, 130 Iowa 494, 107 N.W. 435; First Nat'l Bank v. Bailey, 15 Mont. 301, 39 P. 83; Albuquerque Nat. Bank v. Per,., 5 N.M. 664, 25 P. 776, aff'd, 147 U.S. 87, 13 S. Ct. 194, 37 L. Ed. 91; St. Louis Nat. Bank v. Papin, 21 F. Cas. 203 (No. 12, 289), 4 Dill. 29; Albany City Nat. Bank v. Maher, 6 F. 417.

That a tax on the land owned by insolvent bank was assessed to bank rather than bank superintendent as *ex-officio* receiver, held mere irregularity, not warranting equitable interference. Federal Land Bank v. Turn. County, 42 Ariz. 45, 22 P.2d 405 (1933).

Error in assessing shares of bank stock, by deducting from aggregate of capital, surplus, and undivided profits, the assessed value of real estate instead of its book value, did not make assessment void, and, where bank did not appear before board of review and make complaint, it thereby waived such error, and could not have injunctive relief. Lamont Sav. Bank v. Luther, 200 Iowa 180, 204 N.W. 430.

Independent grounds for equitable jurisdiction in cases involving real estate taxes exist only when unauthorized tax is levied or an exempt property is taxed, and, in all other situations, equity will assume jurisdiction only when no adequate legal remedy is available. First Nat'l Bank & Trust Co. v. Rosewell, 93 Ill. 2d 388, 67 Ill. Dec. 87, 444 N.E.2d 126 (1982).

[3214] Citizens' Nat. Bank v. Murrow (Iowa), 188 N.W. 769; Hills v. National Albany Exch. Bank, 12 F. 92; Osborn v. Bank, 22 U.S. (9 Wheat.) 738, 6 L. Ed. 204; Bank of California v. King County, 16 F. Supp. 976.

National bank's request for assessment of stock direct to bank did not estop it from suing to enjoin collection of unlawful tax. Brotherhood Co-Op. Nat. Bank v. Hurlburt, 26 F.2d 957.

[3215] People's Nat. Bank v. Marye, 107 F. 570, modified, 191 U.S. 272, 24 S. Ct. 68, 48 L Ed. 180; National Bank of Unionville v. Staats, 155 Mo. 55, 55 S.W. 626; Mercantile Nat'l Bank v. New York, 27 Misc. 32, 57 N.Y.S. 254, aff'd, 50 App. Div. 628, 63 N.Y.S. 1111, 172 N.Y. 35, 64 N.E. 756; Robinson v. Wilmington, 65 F. 856; Hagenbuch v. Howard, 34 Mich. 1; Mechanics' & Traders' Branch of State Bank v. Debolt, 1 Ohio St. 591; Chemical Bank v. New York (N.Y.), 12 How. Pr. 476; Stone v. Farmers' Bank, 174 U.S. 409, 19 S. Ct. 880, 43 L. Ed. 1027; Charleston Nat. Bank v. Melton, 171 F. 743; Woolsey v. Dodge, 30 F. Cas. 606 (No. 18,082), aff'd, 59 U.S. 331, 15 L. Ed. 401; Pelton v. Commercial Nat. Bank, 101

and the threatened injury is great or irreparable;[3216] in case of excessive or unequal assessments or valuations;[3217] where property not subject to tax is

---

U.S. 143, 25 L. Ed. 901; Cummings v. National Bank, 101 U.S. 153, 25 L. Ed. 903; Covington City Nat. Bank v. Covington, 21 F. 484; Hills v. Exchange Bank, 105 U.S. 319, 26 L. Ed. 1052; Gadsden v. American Nat'l Bank, 225 Ala. 490, 144 So. 93; First Nat. Bank v. Gildart, 64 F.2d 873, cert. denied, 290 U.S. 631, 54 S. Ct. 50, 78 L. Ed. 549.

[3216] People's Nat'l Bank v. Marye, 107 F. 570, modified, 191 U.S. 272, 24 S. Ct. 68, 48 L. Ed. 180; First Nat. Bank v. Meredith, 44 Mo. 500; National Loan, etc., Bank v. Jones, 103 S.C. 80, 87 S.E. 482.

Where a void tax, if paid, could be recovered back, held, that there was an adequate remedy at law, and that no irreparable injury authorizing an injunction was threatened. Merchants' State Bank v. McHenry County, 31 N.D. 108, 153 N.W. 386.

Injunction to prevent collection of additional real estate taxes on commercial property was properly granted where the $8 million assessment for 1978 was excessive and constructively fraudulent, in that it would have been unjust to require owner of property to lose over $200,000 in interest by borrowing money in order to pursue its legal remedy of paying the taxes under protest and then challenging collector's application for judgment in court. First Nat'l Bank & Trust Co. v. Rosewell, 101 Ill. App. 3d 459, 57 Ill. Dec. 13, 428 N.E.2d 563 (1981).

[3217] **In general.—**

National Bank v. Kimball, 103 U.S. 732, 26 L. Ed. 469; First Nat'l Bank v. Holmes, 246 Ill. 362, 92 N.E. 893; Citizens' Nat'l Bank v. Board of Comm'rs, 83 Kan. 376, 111 P. 496; Parker v. Raleigh Sav. Bank, 152 N.C. 253, 67 S.E. 492; Langley v. Smith, 59 Ten. Civ. App. 584, 126 S.W. 660; Pelton v. Commercial Nat. Bank, 101 U.S. 143, 25 L. Ed. 901; Cummings v. Merchants' Nat. Bank, 101 U.S. 153, 25 L. Ed. 903; First Nat'l Bank v. Lucas County, 25 F. 749, appeal dismissed, 131 U.S. 450, 9 S. Ct. 804, 33 L. Ed. 201; First Nat. Bank v. Hungate, 62 F. 548.

Facts held not to show excessive assessment or discrimination.—

Carpenter v. Jones County, 130 Iowa 494, 107 N.W. 435; Adams v. Beman, 10 Kan. 37; Mercantile Nat'l Bank v. Mayor, etc., of New York, 172 N.Y. 35, 64 N.E. 756; Ankeny v. Blakley, 44 Ore. 78, 74 P. 485; First Nat. Bank v. Holmes, 246 Ill. 362, 92 N.E. 893; Rosenburg v. Weekes, 67 Tex. 578, 4 S.W. 899; Albuquerque Nat. Bank v. Perea, 147 U.S. 87, 13 S. Ct. 194, 37 L. Ed. 91; Exchange Nat. Bank v. Miller, 19 F. 372.

Payment-under-protest-tax-objection remedy provided in revenue statute is adequate legal remedy to overtaxation; therefore, taxpayers' equitable action seeking injunction against collection of further taxes was improper. First Nat'l Bank & Trust Co. v. Rosewell, 93 Ill. 2d 388, 67 Ill. Dec. 87, 444 N.E.2d 126 (1982).

Failure to provide interest upon refunded tax payments does not render payment-under-protest remedy an inadequate means of challenging tax assessment. First Nat'l Bank & Trust Co. v. Rosewell, 93 Ill. 2d 388, 67 Ill. Dec. 87, 444 N.E.2d 126 (1982).

Payment-under-protest-tax-objection remedy provided in revenue statute was not an inadequate means of protesting tax assessment on ground that taxpayer's principal asset, property being taxed, did not generate sufficient income to pay taxes under protest, or that taxpayer would have to borrow at high interest rates money with which to pay tax. First

assessed;[3218] to avoid a multiplicity of suits,[3219] or to prevent a cloud on title.[3220] An injunction is also the appropriate remedy where there is a tax on national bank shares in excess of that on other moneyed capital in competition therewith,[3221] or if an erroneous valuation is made systematically and intentionally with respect to one or more classes of property with the intention of imposing upon that class an undue burden of taxation.[3222] And in a suit to enjoin collection of a tax assessed to high proportionately, good faith and lack of specific intent to injure by the taxing authorities is immaterial.[3223]

Injunctions to prevent collection of real estate taxes are generally allowed only when the property is exempt from taxes, when the tax is unauthorized

---

Nat'l Bank & Trust Co. v. Rosewell, 93 Ill. 2d 388, 67 Ill. Dec. 87, 444 N.E.2d 126 (1982).

[3218] Lenawee Co. Sav. Bank v. Adrian, 66 Mich. 273, 33 N.W. 304.

An injunction will lie against the collection of a tax levied on exempt securities. Miami Trust, etc., Bank v. Botts, 61 Okla. 154, 160 P. 727.

Illinois courts grant equitable relief by way of injunction against collection of property taxes only when the tax is unauthorized by law or when the tax is levied on exempt properties, on the basis that the state statutory refund procedure is an adequate legal remedy. Rosewell v. La Salle Nat'l Bank, 450 U.S. 503, 101 S. Ct. 1221, 67 L. Ed. 2d 464, cert. denied, 451 U.S. 1011, 101 S. Ct. 2349, 68 L. Ed. 2d 864 (1981).

[3219] National Albany Exch. Bank v. Hills, 5 F. 248, rev'd on other grounds, 105 U.S. 319, 26 L. Ed. 1052; Albany City Nat. Bank v. Maher, 6 F. 417; Merchants' State Bank v. McHenry County, 31 N.D. 108, 153 N.W. 386.

Bank failing to file list of stockholders and number of shares held by each as required by statute became liable for payment of tax, and, having right to recover from county taxes not legally laid, is not entitled to injunction against collection of taxes on ground that multiplicity of suits may be avoided. First Nat. Bank v. Patterson, 65 Colo. 166, 176 P. 498 (1917).

[3220] MacOmb v. Lake County, 9 S.D. 466, 70 N.W. 652.

[3221] **In general.**

—Roberts v. American Nat. Bank, 97 Fla. 411, 121 So. 554.

Banks held not estopped to maintain suit to enjoin collecting taxes in excess of that on other moneyed capital because of having loaned money to competitors. Munn v. Des Moines Nat. Bank, 18 F.2d 269.

[3222] Lacy v. McCafferty, 215 F. 352 (8th Cir. 1914).

The application by taxing authorities of the same illegal and discriminatory method of assessment of the property of a bank for a second year evidences an intentional and systematic violation of the constitutional rights of the bank, which entities it to relief by injunction. Bank of Arizona v. Howe, 293 F. 600 (D. Ariz. 1923); Roberts v. American Nat. Bank, 94 Fla. 427, 115 So. 261.

[3223] Brown v. First Nat. Bank, 175 S.W. 1122 (Tex. Civ. App.).

by law or void, or when the tax, or assessment upon which the tax is based, is fraudulent or constructively fraudulent and remedy at law is inadequate.[3224]

Conditions Precedent.—As has been discussed, there must be special circumstances which bring a case within a recognized ground of equity jurisdiction, and render injunctive relief necessary to the adequate protection of a complainant's rights.[3225] Accordingly, it is held that discriminatory taxation will not be enjoined, though willful and intentional, where a complaining taxpayer has an adequate legal or statutory remedy which he has not exhausted without success.[3226] But it has also been held that a national bank is entitled to an injunction to restrain the collection of a discriminatory tax against its shares, notwithstanding its alleged failure to seek a hearing before a board of review.[3227] Similarly, a national bank has been held not required to apply for a refund as a condition precedent to restraining the collection of excessive capital stock taxes.[3228] Application for injunctive relief must also be made promptly.[3229] The illegality of a tax assessment is not sufficient to entitle the taxpayer to injunctive relief without proof that a lower tax would be due under a proper assessment.[3230] Thus, when a suit is brought to collect a tax, the fact that the taxing authorities have arbitrarily disregarded the true and legal basis of arriving at the assessed valuation does not, of itself, entitle a litigating taxpayer to relief, as the taxpayer must establish the actual market value of his property in order to show that the arbitrary or unlawful plan or scheme of arriving at the assessed valuation resulted in substantial injury to him.[3231]

[3224] First Nat'l Bank & Trust Co. v. Rosewell, 101 Ill. App. 3d 459, 57 Ill. Dec. 13, 428 N.E.2d 563 (1981).

[3225] People's Nat. Bank v. Marye, 107 F. 570, modified, 191 U.S. 272, 24 S. Ct. 68, 48 L. Ed. 180.

[3226] First Nat'l Bank v. McBride, 20 N.M. 381, 149 P. 353.

A national bank could not enjoin the collection of a tax under a state law at the time the assessments were not final but in process of settlement in a state court in a proceeding essentially administrative in character. First Nat'l Bank v. Gildart, 64 F.2d 873, cert. denied, 290 U.S. 631, 54 S. Ct 50, 78 L. Ed. 549.

[3227] Knowles v. First Nat'l Bank, 58 F.2d 232.

[3228] State v. Cantley, 325 Mo. 67, 26 S.W.2d 976.

[3229] First Nat. Bank v. Patterson, 65 Colo. 166, 176 P. 498 (1917); Munn v. Des Moines Nat. Bank, 18 F.2d 269.

[3230] American Bank & Trust Co. v. Dallas County, 679 S.W.2d 566 (Tex. App. 5 Dist. 1984).

[3231] American Bank & Trust Co. v. Dallas County, 679 S.W.2d 566 (Tex. App. 5 Dist. 1984).

§ 81. Jurisdiction.

A national bank may maintain suit in federal court to enforce its right given by state statute to enjoin the collection of taxes levied on an illegal assessment[3232] without seeking relief from county and state authorities.[3233]

§ 82. Parties.

In General.—In accordance with the general rule as to parties in equitable proceedings, only those interested who may be injuriously affected by the collection of a tax on banks or shares of stock therein are entitled to sue for an injunction to restrain such collection.[3234] But discriminatory taxation may be enjoined when willful and intentional, though accomplished by undervaluation of property of taxpayers other than the complainant.[3235]

Right of Banks to Sue.—According to a number of decisions, where a bank is required by law to pay taxes assessed on its shares and reimburse itself from its shareholders, it may sue to enjoin the collection of taxes illegally assessed, as it stands in a trust relationship and such suit will prevent a multiplicity of actions.[3236] Where, however, shares of stock of a bank are by statute assessable against and payable by their owners, it seems that a bank cannot, in its own name and for itself sue to restrain the collection of a tax on such shares.[3237] And a national bank which fails to return the shares of its nonresident stockholders as required by federal statute cannot enjoin the collection of taxes assessed against it as agent for such stockholders on the ground that it could not be reimbursed because

---

[3232] Mercantile Nat. Bank v. Hubbard, 105 F. 809, rev'd on other grounds sub nom. Lander v. Mercantile Bank, 186 U.S. 458, 22 S. Ct. 908, 46 L. Ed. 1247.

[3233] Brotherhood Co-Op. Nat. Bank v. Hurlburt, 21 F.2d 85.

[3234] Evansville Nat. Bank v. Britton, 8 F. 867, aff'd, 105 U.S. 322, 26 L. Ed. 1053.

[3235] First Nat'l Bank v. McBride, 20 N.M. 381, 149 P. 353.

[3236] Whitney Nat. Bank v. Parker, 41 F. 402; Evansville Nat. Bank v. Britton, 8 F. 867, aff'd, 105 U.S. 322, 26 L. Ed. 1053; Jones v. Rushville Nat'l Bank, 138 Ind. 87, 37 N.E. 338; Charleston Nat'l Bank v. Melton, 171 F. 743; People's Nat. Bank v. Marye, 107 F. 570, modified, 191 U.S. 272, 24 S. Ct. 68, 48 L. Ed. 180; Roberts v. American Nat'l Bank, 97 Fla. 411, 121 So. 554; Hannan v. First Nat'l Bank, 269 F. 527, appeal dismissed 266 U.S. 638, 45 S. Ct. 9, 69 L. Ed. 482.

[3237] Northwestern Loan, etc., Co. v. Muggli, 7 S.D. 527, 64 N.W. 1122; Northwestern Loan & Banking Co. v. Muggli, 8 S.D. 160, 65 N.W. 442. And see First Nat. Bank v. Meredith, 44 Mo. 500; People's Nat. Bank v. Marye, 107 F. 570, modified, 191 U.S. 272, 24 S. Ct. 68, 48 L. Ed. 180; Waseca Co. Bank v. McKenna, 32 Minn. 468, 21 N.W. 556; Cleveland Trust Co. v. Lander, 10 Ohio C. Dec. 462, 19 Ohio C.C.E. 271, aff'd, 62 Ohio St. 266, 56 N.E. 1036; 184 U.S. 111, 22 S. Ct. 394, 46 L. Ed. 456.

many shares had been transferred to persons other than their owners at the time of assessment, since a bank cannot complain of what is occasioned by its own wrong.[3238] Two banks against whose stock the same illegal taxes have been separately assessed, cannot join in a suit to enjoin the collection thereof.[3239]

Right of Shareholder to Sue.—A shareholder may bring suit to enjoin the collection of a state tax on the shares of a national bank on the ground of the illegal assessment of such shares arising from the failure to deduct from their valuation debts owed by the bank's shareholders.[3240]

Who May Sue for Consolidated or Insolvent Banks.—Where the consolidation of a state and a national bank was authorized by state law, the consolidation was held effective for purposes of enjoining the state from collecting taxes accruing after the consolidation on personal property allegedly owned by the state bank.[3241] A receiver of an insolvent national bank occupies a fiduciary relationship to the bank's creditors, and may sue in equity to enjoin the collection of taxes illegally assessed against the bank's stock.[3242] But an assignee for the benefit of creditors is not entitled to sue to enjoin the collection of a tax because of the action of the assignors of bank stock in falsely stating the value of bank property for purposes of taxation, there being no fraud by the taxing officers.[3243]

§ 83. Procedure.

Pleading.—As to a bank's application for an injunction to restrain the collection of a tax, the usual rules as to pleading in equitable proceedings apply, and an applicant must, in its pleading, show that it is entitled to the relief demanded.[3244] Thus, a bill to restrain the collection of a state tax upon the shares of a national bank is bad on demurrer where it does not appear that there is any statutory discrimination or that such shares, under any rule established by assessing officers, are treated higher in proportion to their

---

[3238] Atlantic Nat'l Bank v. Simpson, 136 Fla. 809, 188 So. 636.

[3239] Jones v. Rushville Nat'l Bank, 138 Ind. 87, 37 N.E. 338.

[3240] Hills v. Nat. Albany Exch. Bank, 12 F. 93.

[3241] Seattle-First Nat'l Bank v. Spokane County, 196 Wash. 419, 83 P.2d 359.

[3242] Brown v. French, 80 F. 166.

[3243] New Albany Trust Co. v. Taylor, 82 Ind. App. 1, 144 N.E. 855.

[3244] First Nat. Bank v. Greger, 157 Ind. 479, 62 N.E. 21; Winfield Bank v. Nipp, 47 Kan. 744, 28 P. 1015; Bank of Santa Fe v. Buster, 50 Kan. 356, 31 P. 1094.

actual value than other moneyed capital.[3245] And a national bank's mere allegation that illegal state taxes have been assessed states no ground for injunctive relief in federal court in the absence of a positive averment that the time for a hearing before a state board of review and appeal to a state court have expired.[3246] Even though suit for injunction seeking to command tax collector to desist from assessing or collecting ad valorem taxes on stock of bank was not filed until tax plan had already been put into effect, tax collector's plea in bar was properly denied where taxpayers were diligent in bringing suit.[3247]

Burden of Proof.—A national bank seeking to prevent the collection of a tax levied upon its shareholders on the ground that other moneyed capital is taxed at a lower rate has the burden of showing that such other capital is invested in competition with it.[3248] And a complainant shareholder has the same burden.[3249] The shareholders in a state banking corporation, who sought injunctive relief from tax assessments on securities held by the bank, had the burden to show that their property has been assessed at a higher figure than a proper assessment based on market value unless there was a proper deduction for the federal securities held by the bank; the contention that the exact injury is shown mathematically by subtracting the proportionate value of the bank's federal obligations from assessed value through the use of the "equity capital formula" of computing assessed value which took into account federal obligation held by the banks was not sufficient.[3250]

[3245] **Insufficient complaints.—**

National Bank v. Kimball, 103 U.S. 732, 26 L. Ed. 469; Wagoner v. Loomis, 37 Ohio St. 571; Charleston Nat'l Bank v. Melton, 171 F. 743; First Nat'l Bank v. Anderson, 196 Iowa 587, 192 N.W. 6, rev'd on other grounds, 269 U.S. 341, 46 S. Ct. 135, 70 L. Ed. 295; Richmond v. Madison Nat. Bank, etc., Co., 215 Ky. 262, 284 S.W. 1089; Public Nat'l Bank v. Keating, 38 F.2d 279, aff'd, 284 U.S. 587, 52 S. Ct. 137, 76 L. Ed. 507.

Sufficient complaints.—

Brotherhood Co-op. Nat'l Bank v. Hurlburt, 21 F.2d 85; Roberts v. American Nat'l Bank, 94 Fla. 427, 115 So. 261; Toy Nat. Bank v. Nelson, 38 F.2d 261; First Nat'l Bank v. Anderson, 269 U.S. 341, 46 S. Ct. 135, 70 L. Ed. 295.

[3246] Albertville Nat. Bank v. Marshall County, 71 F.2d 848.

[3247] Childs v. Reunion Bank, 587 S.W.2d 466 (Tex. Civ. App. 1979).

[3248] Continental Nat. Bank v. Naylor, 54 Utah 49, 179 P. 67; First Nat. Bank v. Anderson, 196 Iowa 587, 192 N.W. 6, rev'd on other grounds, 269 U.S. 341, 46 S. Ct. 135, 70 L Ed. 295.

[3249] Davis v. Sexton, 210 Ind. 138, 200 N.E. 233.

[3250] American Bank & Trust Co. v. Dallas County, 679 S.W.2d 566 (Tex. App. 5 Dist. 1984).

Evidence.—The general rules as to sufficiency[3251] and insufficiency[3252] of evidence apply in proceedings to restrain the collection of taxes levied against banks.

§ 84. Scope of Inquiry.

Where a national bank, agreeing that a tax is proper, pays the tax under an agreement reserving a particular contention, the only substantial controversy, as regards an application for an injunction, involves the contention so reserved.[3253] But where it is shown that an affidavit and demand for deduction of shareholders' debts from the valuation of their national bank shares for taxation would have been unavailing, the shareholders may be

---

[3251] Minnehaha Nat. Bank v. Anderson, 2 F.2d 897.

In an action to invalidate taxes levied, evidence showed bank stock was valued as whole without reference to what was exempt. Bank of Fairfield v. Spokane County, 173 Wash. 145, 22 P.2d 646.

Owner of commercial property met its burden of proving that the $8 million assessment on the property for 1978 was excessive and constructively fraudulent where assessor admitted that under applicable standards proper assessment was between $8.4 million and $4.3 million, and county board of appeals had no known reason for affirming the $8 million assessment, in that county board was bound to apply the same general standards used by assessor.

First Nat'l Bank & Trust Co. v. Rosewell, 101 Ill. App. 3d 459, 57 Ill. Dec. 13, 428 N.E.2d 563 (1981).

[3252] McFarland v. Georgetown Nat. Bank, 208 Ky. 7, 270 S.W. 995, aff'd, 273 U.S. 568, 47 S. Ct. 467, 71 L. Ed. 779; Continental Nat. Bank v. Naylor, 54 Utah 49, 179 P. 67.

Shareholders in state banking corporation failed to show substantial injury by illegal ad valorem assessment on their shares such as would justify injunctive relief from the illegal assessment, where: (1) The assessment was illegal due to the formula used in computing the assessed value which took into account the federal obligations held by the bank; (2) shareholders made no attempt to prove market value of their stock or what a proper valuation would be after an appropriate deduction for federal securities held by the bank and (3) taxable value of the shares would have been equal to or greater than the assessments under attack if assessors had based their assessment on the true market value rather than book value and made a proportionate deduction for the value of the federal securities. American Bank & Trust Co. v. Dallas County, 679 S.W.2d 566 (Tex. App. 8 Dist. 1984).

Although taxpayers suing for injunctive relief before official certification of the tax rolls may not have the burden to show precise dollar amount of the increased tax burden placed on them by an illegal assessment, they must nonetheless show substantial injury in order to be entitled to injunctive relief; if their claim is that their property is assessed at a higher percentage of its market value than other property, they must show the actual market value of their property because otherwise they have failed to show that their assessments were excessive. American Bank & Trust Co. v. Dallas County, 679 S.W.2d 566 (Tex. App. 5 Dist. 1984).

[3253] Citizens' & Southern Nat'l Bank v. Atlanta, 53 F.2d 557.

permitted to show in an action by the bank brought on their behalf, the deductions to which they are entitled, and the collection of the amount of such deductions will be enjoined.[3254] Where a statute provided that no injunction shall be granted by any court or judge to restrain the collection of taxes except where the tax is illegal or unauthorized by law, the action of a board of equalization in determining the assessed valuation of bank stock after a hearing is final, and not reviewable in an action by the bank to restrain collection of a tax which is not illegally based on such assessment.[3255] In view of the judicial review afforded a taxpayer in the tax-objection remedy to over-assessment of property taxes, the issuance of a writ of certiorari in a taxpayer's action seeking to enjoin the collection of real estate taxes upon trust property and seeking damages against individuals who are members of a county board of tax appeals was erroneous.[3256]

§ 85. Extent of Relief Granted.

Where national bank shares are taxed beyond the limit established by Congress, an injunction will be granted only as to such excess.[3257] Similarly, upon a bill in equity to enjoin the collection of a tax upon shares in a national bank because the tax is greater than that imposed on state banks, a court may grant an injunction only upon the condition that the complainants or their bank pay a tax equal to that which might have been lawfully assessed if the bank were a state bank.[3258] And where a bank intentionally returns a valuation of its property at three fourths of its true value, and by connivance with a county board of equalization secures a similar valuation of all other property, but a state board of equalization corrects the valuation as to the bank's property only, equity will not relieve the bank from its predicament even though other taxpayers may have profited by the transaction.[3259] Trial judge did not err in assessing costs against tax collector in suit seeking

---

[3254] Hills v. Exchange Bank, 105 U.S. 319, 26 L. Ed. 1052.

[3255] Continental Nat. Bank v. Naylor, 54 Utah 49, 179 P. 67.

[3256] First Nat'l Bank & Trust Co. v. Rosewell, 93 Ill. 2d 388, 67 Ill. Dec. 87, 444 N.E.2d 126 (1982).

[3257] Whitney Nat. Bank v. Parker, 41 F. 402.

[3258] Frazer v. Siebern, 16 Ohio St. 614.

In suit to enjoin assessment or collection of ad valorem taxes on stock of bank, record did not support contention that injunction should not be granted because taxpayers failed to do equity in that they did not voluntarily render their personal property for taxing purposes. Childs v. Reunion Bank, 587 S.W.2d 466 (Tex. Civ. App. 1979).

[3259] Chickasha Nat'l Bank v. Cloud, 40 Okla. 623, 139 P. 1134.

permanent injunction commanding tax collector to desist from assessing or collecting ad valorem taxes on stock of bank.[3260]

§ 86. Action for Damages.

A sheriff who wrongfully seizes bank property to satisfy a tax levy against a bank stockholder on his stock is liable to the bank for actual damages, the fact that the bank could have treated the conversion of its property as a payment on behalf of the stockholder being no defense.[3261]

X. FORFEITURES AND PENALTIES.

§ 87. Penalty for Nonpayment of Tax.

Under its police power, a state may prescribe and enforce reasonable penalties for nonpayment of taxes,[3262] and taxpayers who show no legal excuse for not paying their taxes are liable for such penalties notwithstanding the pendency of an appeal.[3263] Where a bank is liable for the entire amount of taxes levied against it, its tender of a portion of the amount on the condition that it be received in full satisfaction of its liability, does not relieve it from penalties for nonpayment on the whole amount.[3264] But where a bank tenders taxes legally due before the time fixed by statute for the accrual of penalties for nonpayment, it is not liable for penalties in an action to recover an amount exceeding that legally due for which it is not liable.[3265] The purpose of the statute providing for judicial redemption of land sold at a tax sale is to preserve the right of redemption, without a limit of time, if the landowner seeking to redeem has retained possession.[3266] In order to obtain relief under the statute, plaintiff must have possession of the land, plaintiff must be a member of the class of those allowed under the statute to redeem, there must be a claim to the land by defendant under a tax title or proceeding, and there must be no action pending to enforce or teat

---

3260 Childs v. Reunion Bank, 587 S.W.2d 466 (Tex. Civ. App. 1979).

3261 First Nat. Bank v. Lyman, 59 Kan. 410, 53 P. 125.

3262 First Trust, etc., Bank v. West Lake Inv. Co., 105 Fla. 590, 141 So. 894.

3263 Iowa Nat. Bank v. Stewart (Iowa), 232 N.W. 445.

3264 State v. Carson City Sav. Bank, 17 Nev. 146, 30 P. 703.

Such penalties may be avoided by paying the entire tax under protest, and then bringing an action to recover the portion alleged to be illegal. State v. Carson City Sav. Bank, 17 Nev. 146, 30 P. 703.

3265 First Nat. Bank v. Lampasas, 33 Tex. Civ. App. 530, 78 S.W. 42 (1903).

3266 Stallworth v. First Nat'l Bank, 432 So. 2d 1222 (Ala. 1983).

defendant's claim.[3267] For purposes of the statute, if the landowner seeking to redeem has retained possession, the character of the possession need not be actual and peaceable, but may be constructive and scrambling and, where there is no real occupancy of the land, constructive possession follows the title of the original owner and can only be cut off by adverse possession of the tax purchaser.[3268] In order for the "short statute of limitations" for tax deed cases to bar judicial redemption under the statute, the tax purchaser must prove continuous adverse possession for three years after he is entitled to demand the tax deed.[3269] The evidence was sufficient to establish that the property owner and after his death the trustee under the owner's will had either actual, scrambling, or constructive possession of the subject property, so as to permit the trustee to seek statutory judicial redemption of the property, which defendant claimed under a tax deed.[3270] The trial court's judgment that the tax sale was defective and void, the tax purchaser had no right, title or interest in the subject property and that the bank was entitled to judicial redemption pursuant to statute was not clearly erroneous.[3271]

§ 88. Penalty for Failure to List Shares of Stock.

Where officers of a bank fail to list its shares of stock for taxation as required by statute,[3272] a penalty is usually imposed.[3273]

§ 89. Persons Liable for Penalties.

A bank president usually is not liable in his private capacity for a penalty imposed on his bank for nonpayment of taxes.[3274]

[3267] Stallworth v. First Nat'l Bank, 432 So. 2d 1222 (Ala. 1983).

[3268] Stallworth v. First Nat'l Bank, 432 So. 2d 1222 (Ala. 1983); Rioprop Holdings, LLC v. Compass Bank, 2018 Ala. Civ. App. LEXIS 7 (2018).

[3269] Stallworth v. First Nat'l Bank, 432 So. 2d 1222 (Ala. 1983); Rioprop Holdings, LLC v. Compass Bank, 2018 Ala. Civ. App. LEXIS 7 (2018).

[3270] Stallworth v. First Nat'l Bank, 432 So. 2d 1222 (Ala. 1983).

[3271] Stallworth v. First Nat'l Bank, 432 So. 2d 1222 (Ala. 1983).

[3272] See § 37 of this chapter.

[3273] Newman v. Wait, 46 Vt. 689; Commonwealth v. Citizens' Nat. Bank, 117 Ky. 946, 80 S.W. 158, appeal dismissed, Citizens Nat'l Bank v. Kentucky, 199 U.S. 603, 26 S. Ct. 750, 50 L. Ed. 329.

[3274] Judson v. State (Ala.), Minor 150.

§ 90. Pleading In Penalty Action.

In a summary proceeding against a bank president for a penalty for his bank's default, the bank must be described by its corporate name.[3275]

XI. LEGACY, INHERITANCE AND TRANSFER TAXES.

a. Statutory Provisions.

§ 91. In General.

In General.—An inheritance tax is a tax upon the privilege of receiving property, and case decisions place the financial onus of payment upon the beneficiaries under the will, absent testamentary direction.[3276]

Constitutionality.—It is held that it is unconstitutional for a state to impose an inheritance tax on a bank deposit in the state belonging to a nonresident decedent domiciled in another state, where the documentary evidence of the deposit is also in the latter state.[3277] But it was formerly held that a state could constitutionally impose a transfer or inheritance tax on a local bank deposit standing to the credit of a nonresident decedent.[3278] And it has been held that a transfer tax on a resident decedent's bank deposits in another state is unconstitutional insofar as it allows no deduction for transfer taxes paid in the state of residence.[3279] It is also held that shares of corporate

---

[3275] Judeon v. State (Ala.), Minor 150.

[3276] Merchants & Planters Bank v. Myers, 644 S.W.2d 683 (Tenn. Ct. App. 1982).

Former West Virginia inheritance tax is ultimately responsibility of recipient of specific property, unless testator or testatrix clearly and specifically expresses otherwise in will. First Nat'l Bank v. McGill, 377 S.E.2d 464 (W. Va. 1988).

Clause in will which contains general direction to personal representative to pay debts, expenses and taxes, or similar "stock" language, is not sufficient by itself to shift liability for former West Virginia inheritance tax from specific devisees or legatees to residuary estate. First Nat'l Bank v. McGill, 377 S.E.2d 464 (W. Va. 1988).

[3277] Guaranty Trust Co. v. State, 36 Ohio App. 45, 172 N.E. 674. See also § 84 of this chapter.

This holding is in accord with the presently approved doctrine of the Supreme Court that no state may tax anything not within her jurisdiction without violating the Fourteenth Amendment. Farmers' Loan, etc., Co. v. Minnesota, 280 U.S. 204, 50 S. Ct. 98, 74 L. Ed. 371, 65 A.L.R. 1000.

[3278] Blackstone v. Miller, 188 U.S. 189, 23 S. Ct. 277, 47 L. Ed. 439, overruled, Farmers' Loan, etc., Co. v. Minnesota, 280 U.S. 204, 50 S. Ct. 98, 74 L. Ed. 371, 65 A.L.R. 1000.

[3279] In re Scott's Estate, 129 Misc. 625, 222 N.Y.S. 515.

stock can be constitutionally subjected to an inheritance tax by only one state.[3280]

Violation of Provisions.—A trust company which transfers a deposit it holds as executor of a decedent's estate from its general fund to a separate account in compliance with a state trust act, does not violate a state inheritance tax law.[3281]

Retroactive Operation.—Where the rights of parties under a joint deposit bank account are fixed at the time of deposit and before an act amending a then existing statute is passed, such amendment cannot be given retroactive effect.[3282] But it has been held that a survivor's acquired interest in a joint bank account is subject to succession taxes, though the account was created before passage of the statute imposing the tax, where the joint owner dies subsequent to the statute's effective date.[3283]

b. Property Liable.

§ 92. In General.

A deposit in a savings bank in the name of a depositor, for or in trust for, a named third person, is subject to transfer tax.[3284] And bank deposits, notes and government bonds have been held to create a debtor-creditor relation-

---

[3280] First Nat'l Bank v. Maine, 284 U.S. 312, 52 S. Ct 174, 76 L. Ed. 313, 77 A.L.R. 1401, rev'g 130 Me. 123, 154 A. 103. See also § 84 of this chapter.

[3281] Ryon v. Guarantee Trust Co., 117 N.J. Eq. 502, 176 A. 575.

[3282] In re Maguire's Estate, 99 Misc. 466, 165 N.Y.S. 1067.

[3283] Tax Com. of Ohio v. Hutchison, 120 Ohio St. 361, 166 N.E. 352 (Ohio statute).

[3284] In re Palm's Estate, 148 N.Y.S. 1044.

Under the California statute, savings and loan accounts, voluntarily established and opened, gratuitously and without consideration, by one depositing his funds therein in his own name as trustee for his adult son, to whom trustee's will left his entire estate, were subject to inheritance tax on his death, as a transfer intended to take effect at death, where accounts were intended as gift to son, trustee had absolute control of investment of trust funds, and son never had physical possession or custody thereof. Estate of Goldfader, 131 Cal. App. 2d 533, 280 P.2d 799.

North Carolina estate taxes attributable to including value of qualified terminable interest property (QTTP) trust assets in decedent's estate were payable from assets of QTIP trust decedent's will directed executor to recover any such taxes from the trust and explicitly provided that taxes levied against her estate should not be charged against share of anyone taking under her will. Branch Banking & Trust Co. v. Staples, 461 S.E.2d 921 (N.C. App. 1995).

Apportionment of North Carolina estate tax is controlled by method prescribed in decedent's will. Branch Banking & Trust Co. v. Staples, 461 S.E.2d 921 (N.C. App. 1995).

ship as respects inheritance tax liability.[3285] Certain United States treasury bonds, known as "Flower Bonds," which were redeemable and in fact redeemed at par or face value to discharge federal estate tax liability, were properly includable for state inheritance tax purposes at their value on the open market.[3286]

State inheritance taxes are not taxes on property for purposes of the constitutional article protecting a homestead from the forced sale for payment of all debts except taxes due thereon.[3287]

§ 93. Particular Estates or Interests.

Joint Tenancies.—It is generally held under state statutes that on the death of a joint tenant in a bank deposit, the survivor's right of succession is taxable.[3288] However, the surviving joint tenant, being possessed of one half

---

3285 State v. Baldwin's Estate, 323 Mo. 207, 19 S.W.2d 732.

3286 Third Nat'l Bank v. Olsen, 637 S.W.2d 453 (Tenn. 1982).

3287 Cornerstone Bank v. Randle, 869 S.W.2d 580 (Tex. App. 1998).

Although testator's surviving spouse's interest in homestead property that was separate property of testator was subject to inheritance tax, surviving spouse never acquired the property subject to inheritance taxation and, thus, was not personally liable for inheritance tax; homestead interest was not an interest intended to take effect in possession or enjoyment after death but, like a joint tenancy with right of survivorship, vested before the property became subject to inheritance tax. Cornerstone Bank, N.A. v. Randle, 869 S.W.2d 580 (Tex. App. 1993).

Assignee of state could not seek reimbursement for payment of inheritance taxes originally owing to state on testator's homestead property that was occupied by surviving spouse by foreclosing upon surviving spouse's possessory homestead interest where surviving spouse was not personally liable for inheritance tax such that no lien could attach to his possessory homestead right. Cornerstone Bank v. Randle, 869 S.W.2d 580 (Tex. App. 1998).

3288 **In general.—**

In re Horler's Estate, 180 App. Div. 608, 168 N.Y.S. 221; Tax Com. of Ohio v. Hutchison, 120 Ohio St. 361, 166 N.E. 352; Marble v. Treasurer & Receiver Gen., 245 Mass. 504, 139 N.E. 442.

Survivor's tax liability is fixed at time of death.—

A surviving depositor's inheritance tax liability with respect to joint and survivorship accounts was fixed at time of death of decedent and no waiver, change of title, transfers, or agreements by the survivor thereafter could affect tax. In re Estate of Williams (Ohio Prob.), 138 N.E.2d 189.

Illustrative case.—

Where decedent was a joint owner with her sister of certain bank deposits, to which they had equally contributed, and of certain bonds and mortgages and a mortgage certificate, in the acquisition or purchase of which they had each contributed equally, the surviving sister's

of the deposit at all times, is usually only liable for transfer tax on one half of its amount.[3289] On the other hand, some states hold that only the donative portion or amount of an account which is not contributed by the one succeeding thereto, is taxable as a succession.[3290] Thus, although bank accounts stand in the joint names of decedent and another, payable to either, if it satisfactorily appears that all moneys deposited were the sole property of the survivor, such accounts are not subject to transfer tax.[3291] And under at least one state statute it has been held that on the death of a joint tenant, the interest acquired by the survivor in a joint bank account was not subject to inheritance tax, since no "transfer" of property was involved, the property merely remaining with the survivor.[3292]

Surviving Spouse's Interests.—In some states, a joint deposit account of husband and wife, payable to the survivor and subject to withdrawal in its entirety by either, is subject to inheritance tax on the death of the husband, except to the extent of the excess of the wife's contributions over her

---

claim in her schedules that the deposits, mortgages, and certificate, were not taxable because they did not come to her through decedent's will, devising all her property to such surviving sister, but that she succeeded to them by right of survivorship, was erroneous. In re Weissbach's Estate, 111 Misc. 501, 183 N.Y.S. 771.

3289 In re Reardon's Estate, 182 N.Y.S. 218; In re Teller's Estate, 178 App. Div. 450, 165 N.Y.S. 517, appeal dismissed, 223 N.Y. 565, 119 N.E. 1081; In re Weissbach's Estate, 111 Misc. 501, 183 N.Y.S. 771; In re Thompson's Estate, 85 Misc. 291, 147 N.Y.S. 157, 12 Mills 35.

The New York statute, however, has been held to provide that upon the death of a joint tenant, the whole amount of the joint tenancy is liable for a transfer tax just as if it were property passing by will. In re Reynolds' Estate, 120 Misc. 424, 199 N.Y.S. 494; In re Dolbeer's Estate, 226 N.Y. 623, 123 N.E. 381.

3290 In re Combs' Estate, 90 N.E.2d 440 (Ohio App.).

3291 In re Van Deusen's Estate, 118 Misc. 212, 193 N.Y.S. 762.

And savings bank deposits which were payable to a decedent or his sister who had furnished the money, or to the survivor, were held not subject to transfer tax as a part of decedent's estate, where there was never any purpose on his part to acquire title thereto. In re Buchanan's Estate, 100 Misc. 628, 166 N.Y.S. 947, aff'd, 184 App. Div. 237, 171 N.Y.S. 708.

3292 In re Lowry's Estate, 314 Pa. 518, 171 A. 878.

But under a subsequent amendment of the Pennsylvania statute, it has been held that where deceased placed certain stocks and bank accounts in the names of himself, his wife and daughter as joint tenants with the right of survivorship, and not as tenants in common, was seized of an undivided one-third interest, and deceased's interest was subject to inheritance tax. In re Kleinschmidt's Estate, 362 Pa. 353, 67 A.2d 117.

withdrawals.[3293] And under at least one state statute, where money deposited in a bank in the joint names of spouses originally belonged to the surviving husband and never belonged to the deceased wife, no inheritance tax is due on its transfer to the husband.[3294] Where land is conveyed to a husband and wife as tenants by the entirety, it has been held not subject to transfer tax upon the death of the husband, title passing to the wife by virtue of her estate.[3295]

Miscellaneous Interests.—A deposit in a bank creating a tentative trust is not subject to transfer tax where the trust is revoked by the death of the beneficiary during the lifetime of the trustee.[3296] Since payment to an attorney for his client is the equivalent of payment to the client, a bank deposit payable to a decedent as attorney for another is not chargeable with transfer tax.[3297]

§ 94. Property of Nonresidents or Aliens.

Bank Deposits.—Before the days of inheritance taxes, it was well settled that the situs of intangible property was at all times the domicile of its owner.[3298] Thus, when several states sought to levy inheritance taxes against various elements of value of a decedent's estate, it was held that a state had

---

[3293] Holman v. Mays, 154 Ore. 241, 59 P.2d 392 (Oregon statute).

Where fluctuation in joint banking account was caused by large deposits made by husband and checks issued against account in large amounts presumably for investment purposes by husband from his earnings and profits in his business, and wife made small deposits from her earnings but used most of her earnings for home and family expenses, substantially entire balance in checking account was contributed by husband, and was taxable as a succession together with amount of note and government bond, purchased from funds in joint checking account. In re Combs' Estate, 90 N.E.2d 440 (Ohio App.).

Where decedent died possessed of joint and survivorship deposits with his widow, the widow upon death of decedent had an immediate right of ownership and possession and enjoyment of entire proceeds of accounts and because of her succession to account as sole owner, such survivorship accounts were subject to inheritance tax. In re Estate of Williams, 138 N.E.2d 189 (Ohio Prob.).

[3294] In re Hanson, 125 Mont. 174, 232 P.2d 342 (Montana statute).

The distinction in the statute between property held in the joint names of two or more persons and property deposited in the joint names in banks or other institutions is a valid distinction in view of the general commercial understanding relating thereto. Petition of Hanson, 125 Mont. 174, 232 P.2d 342.

[3295] In re Thompson's Estate, 85 Misc. 291, 147 N.Y.S. 157, 12 Mills 35.

[3296] In re Thompson's Estate, 85 Misc. 291, 147 N.Y.S. 157, 12 Mills 35.

[3297] In re Buchanan's Estate, 184 App. Div. 237, 171 N.Y.S. 708.

[3298] In re Lloyd's Estate, 185 Wash. 61, 52 P.2d 1269 (1921).

the right to levy such taxes on a bank deposit standing to the credit of a person domiciled in another state.[3299] Such holdings led to an irreconcilable conflict between the states in exercising their powers with reference to inheritance taxes imposed upon a single estate, and it became recognized that the practice of permitting different states to tax the same testamentary transfer on different and perhaps inconsistent principles disturbed good relations and produced discontent among the states.[3300] To solve the problem, the Supreme Court of the United States laid down the general rule that the situs of intangibles for inheritance tax purposes is the domicile of their owner.[3301] And this rule now controls as to bank deposit so that transfers of ownership thereof are taxable only in the state of a decedent's domicile.[3302] But it has been held that deposits in banking institutions

---

[3299] Hoyt v. Keegan, 183 Iowa 592, 167 N.W. 521; In re Scott's Estate, 129 Misc. 625, 222 N.Y.S. 515.

In Blackstone v. Miller, 188 U.S. 189, 23 S. Ct. 277, 47 L. Ed. 439, it was held that a deposit in a New York trust company to the credit of Blackstone, who died domiciled in Illinois, was subject to a transfer tax imposed by New York, notwithstanding the fact that the whole succession, including the deposit, had been similarly taxed in Illinois. That decision was overruled by Farmers Loan & Trust Co. v. Minnesota, 280 U.S. 204, 50 S. Ct. 98, 74 L. Ed. 371, 65 A.L.R. 1000 (1930).

An inheritance tax statute, providing for a tax on all personal property "physically" in the state, was construed to include a bank account of a nonresident decedent, the case holding that "physically" is not the equivalent of "corporeally." Succession of Page, 89 So. 876, 149 La. 623 (1921).

[3300] In re Lloyd's Estate, 185 Wash. 61, 52 P.2d 1269 (1921).

[3301] Farmers Loan & Trust Co. v. Minnesota, 280 U.S. 204, 50 S. Ct. 98, 74 L. Ed. 371, 65 A.L.R. 1000 (1930). See also § 80 of this chapter.

[3302] *United States.*—In Baldwin v. Missouri, 281 U.S. 586, 50 S. Ct. 436, 74 L. Ed. 1056, 72 A.L.R. 1303, the court decided that credits for cash deposited In Missouri banks, United States coupon bonds, and certain promissory notes, largely secured by liens on Missouri lands and given by Missouri citizens, and all physically within the state of Missouri, were not subject to transfer tax in Missouri, the owner having died testate and domiciled in Illinois.

Louisiana.—Money on deposit in Louisiana belonging to the succession of one who was domiciled, resided, and died in another state, and whose estate was inherited by nonresident heirs and legatees by the laws of that state, is not subject to the inheritance tax levied by the inheritance tax law of Louisiana. Succession of Harrow, 140 La. 570, 73 So. 683, 1917D L.R.A. 281.

Maine.—State by Robinson v. First Nat'l Bank, 130 Me. 123, 154 A. 103, rev'd on other grounds, 284 U.S. 312, 52 S. Ct. 174, 76 L. Ed. 313, 77 A.L.R. 1401.

New Jersey.—Hasbrouck v. Martin, 120 N.J. Eq. 96, 183 A. 735.

Ohio.—Guaranty Trust Co. v. State, 36 Ohio App. 45, 172 N.E. 674.

outside of a state are subject to state inheritance tax, if title thereto passes through executors, or the property during administration comes within the state's jurisdiction.[3303]

The foregoing general rule has been held applicable where deposits are made by a United States decedent in banks in foreign countries.[3304] However, the rule that for inheritance tax purposes the situs of intangibles is their owner's domicile, was held inapplicable to bank deposits by a decedent domiciled in Canada, since in such case the reason for the rule did not exist.[3305]

Bank Stock.—Shares of corporate stock may be subjected to death transfer tax only in the state of their owner's domicile.[3306] Thus, under a state statute imposing an inheritance tax on property of every kind owned by any decedent domiciled within the state at the time of his death even though the property is situated outside the state, stocks of national banks owned by a decedent domiciled in the state but not kept therein are subject to inheritance tax, notwithstanding the federal statute providing that the shares of any national bank owned by nonresidents shall be taxed in the city and town where the bank is located, not elsewhere, such statute referring only to the imposition of general or annual taxes upon property levied in the lifetime of the owner.[3307] And where a nonresident decedent only had a right to an accounting as to stock in a state bank held by a trustee under his father's will, a subsequent transfer thereof to his executor was held not subject to transfer

---

Oregon.—In re Klose's Estate, 147 Ore. 512, 34 P.2d 636.

Washington.—In re Lloyd's Estate, 185 Wash. 61, 52 P.2d 1269 (1921).

3303 Williams v. State, 81 N.H. 341, 125 A. 661, 39 A.L.R. 490.

3304 In re Klose's Estate, 147 Ore. 512, 34 P.2d 636.

Domiciliary state held situs, for inheritance tax purposes, of deposit in German bank as against contention that under German law deposit could not be withdrawn from Germany; withdrawal therefrom being unnecessary since amount exceeding deposit was required to pay legatees in Germany. In re Klose's Estate, 147 Ore. 512, 34 P.2d 636.

3305 In re Lloyd's Estate, 185 Wash. 61, 52 P.2d 1269 (1921), holding that state may levy inheritance tax on bank deposits in state made by decedent whose domicile was in Canada and whose sole heir was resident of Wales.

3306 First Nat'l Bank v. Maine, 284 U.S. 312, 52 S. Ct. 174, 76 L. Ed. 313, 77 A.L.R. 1401, rev'g 130 Me. 123, 154 A. 103, wherein it was held that a state may impose a succession tax when the exercise of an essential privilege incident to the transfer of title to property depends on the state law. See also § 80 of this chapter.

3307 In re Sherwood's Estate, 122 Wash. 648, 211 P. 734; State ex rel. Graff v. Probate Court of St. Louis County, 128 Minn. 371, 150 N.W. 1094, 1916A L.R.A. 901.

tax.[3308] Under an agreement between nonresident executors and legatees, whereby the executors held the assets of an estate, a nonresident legatee's right thereto was held a mere chose in action and not taxable, though stock in a bank located in the state was among the assets; and in such a case, the distribution of such stock by the foreign executors after the death of the nonresident legatee would not render it taxable as part of the legatee's estate.[3309]

Miscellaneous Property.—Where a nonresident was a member of a resident banking partnership, and made advances to the partnership which were used in its business, on his death the balance due thereon was held subject to transfer tax under a statute imposing such tax on the transfer by will or intestacy of capital invested in business in the state by a nonresident doing business therein as a principal or partner.[3310] And, where a decedent, a nonresident engaged in selling theater tickets, deposited stocks and bonds in a bank as collateral for a loan which was used in his business, such securities were properly considered invested capital.[3311] Where real estate mortgages belonging to a nonresident had been kept for many years in one state, and just prior to their owner's death were delivered by an agent to the owner in another state who redelivered them to the agent, and the agent deposited them in a bank in still another state to avoid payment of a collateral inheritance tax levied by the first-mentioned state on the owner's death, such removal was ineffective for such purpose.[3312]

§ 95. Situs of Property.

Generally, as has been discussed, a domiciliary state has the exclusive right to impose an inheritance tax on "intangible personalty" such as a bank account.[3313] The following items have also been held taxable by a state: (1) A savings account in a foreign bank when its owner was domiciled in the state;[3314] (2) a promissory note owned by a resident though held by a foreign

---

[3308] In re Phelps' Estate, 100 Misc. 87, 165 N.Y.S. 75, aff'd, 181 App. Div. 82, 168 N.Y.S. 536.

[3309] In re Phelps' Estate, 181 App. Div. 82, 168 N.Y.S. 536.

[3310] In re Henry's Estate, 237 N.Y. 204, 142 N.E. 586.

[3311] In re Tyson's Estate, 113 Misc. 306, 184 N.Y.S. 398, aff'd, 201 App. Div. 840, 192 N.Y.S. 955.

[3312] In re Adams' Estate, 167 Iowa 382, 149 N.W. 531, 1915C L.R.A. 95.

[3313] In re Klose's Estate, 147 Ore. 512, 34 P.2d 636. See § 84 of this chapter.

[3314] Appeal of Silberman, 105 Conn. 192, 134 A. 778, aff'd in part and rev'd in part sub nom. Blodgett v. Silberman, 277 U.S. 1, 48 S. Ct. 410, 72 L. Ed. 749.

bank[3315] and (3) bank stocks, cash, jewelry and securities situated in another jurisdiction and owned by a decedent domiciled within the state.[3316]

§ 96. Exemptions.

It has been held that an exemption from transfer tax does not apply to separate transfers by a wife of mortgages and bank accounts to her husband, there being but one transfer occurring on the wife's death.[3317] And it has been held that where savings bank deposits in the names of a husband and wife are payable to either or the survivor, the beneficial interest therein passing to the wife on the husband's death and the property received by her under her husband's will should be added together in determining both the death tax thereon and the applicable exemption.[3318] For cases involving various exemptions under particular state statutes, see the footnote.[3319]

[3315] People v. Forman, 322 Ill. 223, 153 N.E. 376.

[3316] In re Sherwood's Estate, 122 Wash. 648, 211 P. 734.

It has been held that stock in a Missouri national bank owned by a Virginia decedent is subject to Virginia inheritance taxes as are funds derived from sale thereof, notwithstanding the state of Missouri imposed and collected inheritance taxes. Cornett's Ex'rs v. Commonwealth, 127 Va. 640, 105 S.E. 230, relying on the case of Blackstone v. Miller, 188 U.S. 189, 23 S. Ct. 277, 47 L Ed. 439, overruled, Farmers Loan & Trust Co. v. Minnesota, 280 U.S. 204, 50 S. Ct. 98, 74 L. Ed. 371, 65 A.L.R. 1000 (1930).

[3317] In re Horler's Estate, 180 App. Div. 608, 168 N.Y.S. 221.

[3318] Marble v. Treasurer & Receiver Gen., 245 Mass. 504, 139 N.E. 442.

[3319] *Arkansas.*—IRS decision, that federal estate tax marital deduction did not apply to trust assets held for benefit of surviving spouse because second codicil did not provide for surviving spouse to receive trust income at least annually, was not determinative of construction of deceased spouse's will and codicils or assessment of Arkansas state death taxes. Pledger v. Worthen Bank & Trust Co., 319 Ark. 155, 889 S.W.2d 732 (1994).

Deceased spouse's will and two codicils were correctly interpreted to provide for payment of estate assets into testamentary trust for benefit of surviving spouse and quarterly annual distribution of trust income, together with principal distributions needed for surviving spouse's care and maintenance, notwithstanding determination by IRS that trust did not require annual distributions of income, as required to qualify for federal estate marital deduction. Pledger v. Worthen Bank & Trust Co., 319 Ark. 155, 889 S.W.2d 732 (1994).

Property held in trust for benefit of surviving spouse qualified for state marital deduction and was exempt from Arkansas death taxes, notwithstanding IRS determination that trust instrument did not require at least annual distributions of income, as needed to qualify for federal estate tax marital deduction. Pledger v. Worthen Bank & Trust Co., 319 Ark. 155, 889 S.W.2d 732 (1994).

Ohio.—The statute exempts from the estate tax a succession to or for the use of an institution for purposes only of public charity carried on in whole or in a substantial part within the state. In re Oglebay's Estate, 162 Ohio St. 1, 120 N.E.2d 437.

§ 97. Transfers Made in Contemplation of Death.

Whether or not a transfer is made in contemplation of death and for the purpose of evading an inheritance tax depends on the intent of the parties. But since such intent is difficult to ascertain, statutes have been passed in many jurisdictions imposing controlling conditions such as a time limit on transfers; these statutes have been interpreted by the courts.[3320]

§ 98. Proceedings for Assessment.

Where there is an ancillary administration in a state, the courts of that state have jurisdiction to determine the liability of shares of stock in a local bank

---

Where bank by resolution created a foundation, which was not a legal entity, had no governing board was not incorporated, held no assets and had no members, but functioned solely to designate the charitable beneficiaries of trusts and decedent's trust agreement named bank as trustee, the bank was an "institution" within the statute. In re Oglebay's Estate, 162 Ohio St. 1, 120 N.E.2d 437.

Oklahoma.—Cash, loans on stock certificate securities, and accounts receivable of a building and loan association are not exempt from taxation under the statute. Home Bldg., etc., Ass'n v. State, 156 Okla. 89, 9 P.2d 731.

[3320] People v. Continental Illinois Bank & Trust Co., 344 Ill. 123, 176 N.E. 305, 75 A.L.R. 538; Worcester County Nat'l Bank v. Commissioner of Corps. & Tax., 275 Mass. 216, 175 N.E. 726; Plainfield Trust Co. v. McCutcheon, 108 N.J.L. 201, 154 A. 629; In re Kiernan's Estate, 134 Misc. 868, 237 N.Y.S. 290, aff'd, 227 App. Div. 782, 237 N.Y.S. 811; In re Gurnsey's Estate, 177 Cal. 211, 170 P. 402; McDougald v. Boyd, 172 Cal. 753, 159 P. 168; In re Bender's Estate, 182 N.Y.S. 217; In re Durfee's Estate, 79 Misc. 655, 140 N.Y.S. 594, 10 Mills 173; In re Von Bernuth's Estate, 143 N.Y.S. 672, In re Halligan's Estate, 82 Misc. 30, 143 N.Y.S. 676, 11 Mills 34; In re Reed's Estate, 89 Misc. 632, 154 N.Y.S. 247, 14 Mills 56; In re Wille's Estate, 111 Misc. 61, 182 N.Y.S. 366; In re Klein's Estate, 92 Misc. 318, 156 N.Y.S. 585, 15 Mills 297; In re Rudolph, 92 Misc. 347, 156 N.Y.S. 825, 15 Mills 323; In re Brennan, 92 Misc. 423, 157 N.Y.S. 141; In re Dalsimer's Estate, 148 N.Y.S. 914; In re Seaich's Estate, 136 Misc. 201, 240 N.Y.S. 524; In re Henderson's Estate, 198 N.Y.S. 799; In re Reynold's Estate, 168 N.Y.S. 803.

Trust created by opening of bank accounts in New York by testatrix domiciled in New Jersey, for her brother and cousin, which were never revoked by testatrix, held taxable under New Jersey estate transfer tax statute whether trusts were irrevocable or revocable and whether trusts took effect prior to death of testatrix or were given effect at time of their creation but in contemplation of death of testatrix. Hasbrouck v. Martin, 120 N.J. Eq. 96, 183 A. 735.

Where savings accounts were created more than three years before decedent's death, and were payable to decedent or his niece or survivor thereof, niece had possession of passbooks part of time prior to decedent's death, and decedent did not, by subsequent words or acts restrict niece's rights arising by inference from manner of the deposits, a right of property was created by decedent donor and the accounts were not subject to inheritance tax. In re Renz' Estate, 338 Mich. 347, 61 N.W.2d 148.

and money on deposit therein to a collateral inheritance tax.[3321] As to the inquiry which the law allows a taxing official to make to determine whether the estate of a nonresident decedent is subject to taxation, the official should be given latitude.[3322]

And in a proceeding to fix transfer tax on the estate of a decedent which included a joint interest in certain bank deposits, it was held that an appraiser, in lieu of other evidence, might consider an affidavit showing that decedent and her sister, the devisee of all decedent's property, inherited their money and other property from their parents and a brother, and that each contributed one half to the deposits.[3323] But where a legatee claimed a testator's bank account in a foreign country as compensation for services, and enjoined the bank from paying it to the executor, an amount which the legatee with the executor's permission withdrew pursuant to a judicial order of compromise providing that money so withdrawn should not be deemed part of his legacy, was held properly excluded in computing the domiciliary state's inheritance tax.[3324] The principle of equitable apportionment is favored in Missouri over the "burden on the residue"' rule when there is no clearly expressed intention of the grantor or testatrix as to the burden of paying death taxes.[3325] The general rule is that an executor is entitled to credit his accounts for expenses necessarily and properly included in good faith, in transacting with reasonable care and diligence the business of the estate, upon proof of particular items of expense claimed.[3326] Moreover, "interest" is simply the cost of using money, and there should be no differentiation for purposes of deductibility by the executor of the estate as to administrative expense whether interest is paid on taxes or on money

---

[3321] In re Culver's Estate, 159 Iowa 679, 140 N.W. 878.

[3322] In re Green, 184 App. Div. 376, 171 N.Y.S. 494, rev'g,In re Green's Estate, 102 Misc. 45, 168 N.Y.S. 364, wherein it was held that until a nonresident is shown to be doing business in the state, evidence as to what banks his money is deposited in, the amount thereof, or kind of notes money was invested in, is properly excluded as immaterial, in an appraisal for purposes of the transfer tax.

[3323] In re Weissbach's Estate, 111 Misc. 501, 183 N.Y.S. 771.

[3324] In re Klose's Estate, 147 Ore. 512, 34 P.2d 636.

[3325] Boatmen's Union Nat'l Bank v. Welton, 640 S.W.2d 497 (Mo. App. 1982).

Estate and gift taxes were properly spread proportionately among distributees where deceased's will only directed that taxes be paid promptly and did not direct that taxes be paid from estate's residue. Wright v. Union Nat'l Bank, 307 Ark. 301, 819 S.W.2d 698 (1991).

Intent to shift burden of estate and gift taxation must clearly appear in will. Wright v. Union Nat'l Bank, 307 Ark. 301, 819 S.W.2d 698 (1991).

[3326] Cleveland Bank & Trust Co. v. Olsen, 682 S.W.2d 200 (Tenn. 1984).

borrowed to pay taxes.[3327] Furthermore, interest on money borrowed by the executor from a private lender to pay federal estate taxes is deductible as an administrative expense.[3328] Similarly, interest paid by an executor on state inheritance tax, federal estate tax, and certain debts incurred by the decedent prior to death were deductible as administrative expenses for the purposes of the inheritance and estate tax.[3329]

The Department of Revenue was entitled to extended time for filing an independent action against an estate where the Department did not file an independent action against the estate within the required thirty-day period in reliance on the representations of the personal representative and the attorney that the claim would be paid without litigation.[3330]

§ 99. Review, Correction and Setting Aside Assessment.

It has been held that where it is conceded on an appeal from an order assessing a transfer tax that an administrator's affidavit inadvertently misstated the market value of bank stock of an estate, and thus tax was assessed on an improper valuation, the error may be corrected though two years have elapsed since the making of such order.[3331]

§ 100. Refunding or Recovery of Taxes Paid.

Payment of transfer tax on a nonresident decedent's stock in a domestic corporation is a "voluntary payment," not recoverable by subsequent suit.[3332] Similarly, a statute providing for the refunding of inheritance taxes wrongfully collected is inapplicable to a suit to recover a tax where the taxpayer and the state are both parties and a judgment for the tax is paid without objection.[3333]

[3327] Cleveland Bank & Trust Co. v. Olsen, 682 S.W.2d 200 (Tenn. 1984).

[3328] Cleveland Bank & Trust Co. v. Olsen, 682 S.W.2d 200 (Tenn. 1984).

[3329] Cleveland Bank & Trust Co. v. Olsen, 682 S.W.2d 200 (Tenn. 1984).

[3330] Department of Revenue v. Florida Nat'l Bank, 516 So. 2d 1147 (Fla. App. 1987).

[3331] In re Boyle, 92 Misc. 143, 153 N.Y.S. 173 (1915).

[3332] Gates v. Bank of Commerce & Trust Co., 185 Ark. 502, 47 S.W.2d 806 (1931).

[3333] Gates v. Bank of Commerce & Trust Co., 185 Ark. 502, 47 S.W.2d 806 (1931).